Fiction Index
for Readers 10 to 16

Subject Access to Over 8200 Books
(1960–1990)

by
Vicki Anderson

McFarland & Company, Inc., Publishers
Jefferson, North Carolina, and London

British Library Cataloguing-in-Publication data are available

Library of Congress Cataloguing-in-Publication Data

Anderson, Vicki, 1928–
    Fiction index for readers 10 to 16 : subject access to over 8200
books (1960–1990) / by Vicki Anderson.
      p.   cm.
    Includes bibliographical references and index.
    ISBN 0-89950-703-4 (lib. bdg. : 50# alk. paper) ∞
    1. Young adult fiction – Stories, plots, etc. – Indexes.
2. Children's stories – Stories, plots, etc. – Indexes.   3. Young
adult fiction – Bibliography.   4. Children's stories – Bibliography.
I. Title.
Z1037.A52   1992
[PN1009.A1]
016.80883′0835 – dc20   91-50954
                                          CIP

Manufactured in the United States of America

McFarland & Company, Inc., Publishers
 Box 611, Jefferson, North Carolina 28640

TABLE OF CONTENTS

177952

INTRODUCTION

The purpose of this reference book is to help the library staff identify fiction books by specific subjects. As a working librarian for 25 years I found that young adult readers ask for very specific books. "I want a book about an 11 year old." "I want a book about cults." "My teacher wants me to read a book about the elderly ... about migrant workers ... about courage."

As librarians we are not bibliotherapists, but we do find occasion to suggest a specific book to certain readers. The loss of a friend through a family move, death or a misunderstanding, as well as many other personal problems, can be eased by the right book.

As an aid to these requests and needs plus the many other reader's guidance services rendered, this index should be a valuable tool. It includes about 8200 different titles arranged under more than 200 specific subject headings. The bibliography section was not compiled from *Books in Print* or publisher's catalogs. The books were read and approved by librarians who have them in their collections. These books are mostly hardbound editions. Paperbacks are included when they are reissues of an earlier clothbound book or are of significant value to a library collection.

The range of reading levels is quite broad. Titles that can be read by a young person reading a bit below grade level and titles that can be read by the ones reading at adult level are included. The emphasis is on the reader between the ages of 10 and 16. Because the reading ability of this short age range is quite broad, I did not specify grade levels. There are books of easy readability, ones that attract the reluctant reader and ones that challenge the competent reader. Nor did I star those of literary excellence. (I did identify the Newbery winners.) This list is based on books of interest and popularity—those books that were most widely circulated.

As in any list of books, some may raise questions about those titles that have not been included, and about those that were. I included all appropriate books I could find for the selected age group and time frame. The copyright dates for the selected books range from 1960 to 1990 (there are a few from 1991). The Newbery winners, the "classics" and some basic library collection books are included regardless of date. Some of the books may be out of print but this index is not intended as a buyer's guide. It is intended to identify, organize and make broader use of the books on the shelves.

The Annotated Bibliography is arranged alphabetically by author with full bibliographic information. There is a short description for each book. These annotations were gleaned from the book itself, reviews, jackets, catalog cards, reader input and any other source I could find.

The selection of subject headings was based on experience, repeated requests and ease of location. Many fiction books have multiple subjects and there is no way of anticipating every user's opinion about the major or minor subjects of a book. I chose to list the titles under the headings I found most appropriate. Undoubtedly others might have placed some of these titles in different subject areas. This is my best attempt to categorize where they would be most useful and most easily located.

The Subject Index, which is the heart of the book, lists each work alphabetically by author, under one to four subjects. From the point of view of both the library user and the librarian, a too-long list is as frustrating as no list at all. So I tried to keep the individual lists short. If the number of titles became too long I assigned subheadings or divided the list into logical subdivisions. This detailed special feature is what should help any user find the specific book wanted. The Subject Index has *see* and *see also* notations as a further aid to the user. The following additional explanations are worth noting about the Subject Index.

American History is subdivided into *Colonial Period; Frontier and Pioneer Life;* and *West, American.*

American History is also found under *Revolutionary War; Civil War, American; World War I;* and *World War II.*

Animals can be found under *Animals, Wild; Animals, Tame; Cats; Dogs; Horses, Trained; Horses, Wild;* and *Pets.* Under the *Animals, Wild* and *Animals, Tame* headings, the specific animal is given in parentheses after each title as an aid to the user. No designation means there are several kinds of animals involved in that book.

In addition to book lists for *Baseball; Basketball;* and *Football,* there is a *Sports* heading. After each book title under this heading, the specific sport is given in parentheses.

Birds are divided into *Wild* and *Tame.*

Both *Boys* and *Girls* stories are subdivided into age groups: *Pre-Teen; Teen;* and *Mature.*

In the section *Classics,* one will find the generally accepted pieces of literature that have stood the test of time. These are older works that are still widely read.

Books listed under *Countries Other Than United States* are individually identified as to which country. One country specified at the end of several book titles by the same author means that all the preceding titles relate to that one country.

There is a heading for *Crimes* but there is also a section for *Delinquency; Kidnapping; Smuggling;* and *Stealing.*

Elderly is a separate category, different from *Grandparents.*

Family stories are also put into several different, more specific, categories: *Family Problems; Fathers; Mothers;* and *Grandparents.*

Fantasy, because it is a subject about which many children's books have been written, is subdivided into seven subsections: *Animals; Dolls; Good Versus Evil; Places; Spells; Wishes;* and *Words.*

Friendship is a general subject heading. There is also, more specifically, two other categories: *Friendship among Boys* and *Friendship among Girls.*

Handicapped includes various types of handicaps but *Blindness; Deafness;* and *Mentally Handicapped* are listed separately.

Historical Fiction has four sections: *B.C.; Ancient; Medieval;* and *Modern.*

Illness is further identified as to what kind: cancer; epilepsy, etc.

Immigrants are identified by nationality.

Minorities are found under *Asians; African Americans; Latinos;* and *Native Americans.*

Mystery is a long list and so two additional categories, *Mystery/Kidnapping* and *Mystery/Stealing,* were added. In all three categories the emphasis is on the mystery not on the specific crime, therefore these books are not listed under a crime-related topic.

Science Fiction ("*Sci Fi*" for space reasons) encompasses a great many themes (and a great number of titles). The solution was to separate, as much as was possible, the main thrust of the story. These will be found under subheadings *Earth; Future; Moon; Planets; Space Travel; Time Travel; Underseas* and *Universe.*

Siblings are found under *Brothers; Sisters; and Brothers and Sisters.*

War includes all wars other than *Revolutionary War; Civil War, American; World War I;* and *World War II,* which have separate headings.

In *Working World* is a wide range of books about summer- and part-time jobs, child labor, management and labor problems, school and court assignments, etc.

Also to be noted are the sections that are not really subjects but are books often requested by readers: *Fairy Tales; Legends; Humorous; Suspense;* and *Values,* as well as the previously mentioned *Classics* and *Historical Fiction.*

There are three separate lists at the end of the subject index that will be useful: Books with fewer than 100 pages, books with more than 300 pages, and books that are translated into English from foreign language publications.

I found as I compiled this book that fiction subject indexing is a never ending proposition — and rightly. There are many new books being written on subjects not previously covered. Years ago a list like this would not include *Child Abuse, Gays, Anorexia,* etc. And I'm sure lists for future collections will include subjects not listed here.

This fiction index will have several uses in the library. It should allow any user to locate and easily identify books wanted on specific subjects (since this book encompasses many books in a typical fiction collection, a title index has been included to enable the reader to quickly access the bibliographic information and annotation. This book can be used to evaluate a collection in terms of balance. A particular list may show that there is a shortage of titles in a subject area.

Individual subject lists can be used as a promotional device. You can present a list in an attractive booklet format to hand to those readers that are interested only in one area, like mystery or romance. As new books come in the list can be updated. The subject lists can be used to make promotional displays in the library using specific books. For instance, romance in February, automobiles in May, baseball in the spring and football in the fall.

This list is not definitive but it is as complete and as accurate as I could make it. It should be expanded and refined as new books and new subjects come to the fore. But hopefully it is a start to answer the request: "I want a book about...."

Vicki Anderson, fall 1991

SUBJECT INDEX

Acting

Allan, Mabel. *On Stage, Flory.*
Anderson, Mary. *You Can't Get There from Here.*
Auch, Mary Jane. *Glass Slippers Give You Blisters.*
Ball, Zachary. *Tent Show.*
Bowers, Gwendolyn. *At the Sign of the Globe.*
Campbell, Harper. *Looking for Hamlet: A Haunting at Deeping Lake.*
Chambers, John. *Footlight Summer.*
Cone, Molly. *Big Squeeze.*
Crane, Caroline. *Lights Down the River.*
Cross, Gillian. *Dark Behind the Curtain.*
Cunningham, Julia. *Silent Voice.*
Daneman, Meredith. *Francie and the Boys.*
Dickinson, Peter. *Seventh Raven.*
Ende, Michael. *Ophelia's Shadow Theatre.*
Fecher, Constance. *Leopard Dagger.*
Fiedler, Jean. *Yardstick for Jessica; Year the World Was Out of Step with Jancy Fried.*
Garfield, Leon. *Sound of Coaches.*
Gormley, Beatrice. *More Fifth Grade Magic.*
Grace, Fran. *Very Private Performance.*
Greene, Constance. *Star Shine.*
Hayes, Sheila. *No Autographs Please.*
Hewett, Hilda. *Harriet and the Cherry Pie.*
Holmes, Barbara. *Charlotte Shakespeare and Annie the Great.*
Hughes, Dean. *Nutty the Movie Star.*
Johnston, Norma. *Glory in the Flower.*
Kingman, Lee. *Break a Leg, Betsy Maybe.*
Krensky, Stephen. *Wilder Plot.*
Lattimore, Eleanor. *Little Tumbler.*
Levinson, Nancy. *Ruthie Greene Show.*
McCaughrean, Geraldine. *Little Lower Than the Angels.*
Martin, Ann. *Stage Fright.*
Matthews, Ann. *Starring Punky Brewster.*
Miklowitz, Gloria. *Love Story, Take Three.*
Miles, Betty. *Secret Life of the Underwear Champ.*
Miller, Alice. *Make Way for Peggy O'Brien.*
Morganroth, Barbara. *In Real Life, I'm Just Kate.*
Murphy, Barbara. *Ace Hits Rock Bottom.*
Myers, Walter. *Crystal.*
Newman, Robert. *Case of the Murdered Players.*
O'Daniel, Janet. *Part for Addie.*
Oppenheimer, Joan. *Working on It.*

Paperny, Myra. *Wooden People.*
Park, Barbara. *Almost Starring Skinnybones.*
Paterson, Katherine. *Master Puppeteer.*
Pevsner, Stella. *Break a Leg.*
Randall, Janet. *Girl from Boothill.*
Reading, J.P. *Bouquets for Brimbal.*
Roos, Stephen. *And the Winner Is...*
Service, Pamela. *When the Night Wind Howls.*
Shyer, Marlene. *Adorable Sunday.*
Singer, Marilyn. *Course of True Love Never Did Run Smooth.*
Swallow, Pamela. *Leave It to Christy.*
Sweeney, Joyce. *Right Behind the Rain.*
Tchudi, Stephen. *Burg-O-Rama Man.*
Terris, Susan. *Stage Brat.*
Tolan, Stephanie. *Liberation of Tansy Warner.*
Ure, Jean. *What If They Saw Me Now?*
Voigt, Cynthia. *Come a Stranger.*
Walden, Amelia. *My World's the Stage; When Love Speaks.*
Wersba, Barbara. *Dream Watcher.*
White, Dori. *Sarah and Katie.*
Williams, Barbara. *Tell the Truth, Marly Dee.*

Adoption

See also: Foster Homes; Orphans

Arthur, Ruth. *Requiem for a Princess.*
Auch, Mary Jane. *Pick of the Litter.*
Bawden, Nina. *Finding.*
Carter, Mary. *Tell Me My Name.*
Caudill, Rebecca. *Somebody Go and Bang a Drum.*
Delton, Judy. *Angel's Mother's Wedding.*
Derby, Pat. *Visiting Miss Pierce.*
Faulkner, Nancy. *Stage for Rom.*
Fenisong, Ruth. *Boy Wanted.*
First, Julia. *I, Rebekah, Take You, the Laurences.*
Green, Phyllis. *Grandmother Orphan.*
Hale, Arlene. *Nothing but a Stranger.*
Howard, Ellen. *Her Own Song.*
Johnston, Norma. *To Jess, with Love and Memories.*
Jones, Diana. *Archer's Goon; Cart and Cwidder.*
Klein, Norma. *What It's All About.*
Lifton, Betty. *I'm Still Me.*
Lowry, Lois. *Find a Stranger, Say Goodbye.*
Lyons, Dorothy. *Pedigree Unknown.*

1

McDonald, Joyce. *Mail-Order Kid.*
Miles, Miska. *Aaron's Door.*
Mills, Claudia. *Boardwalk with Hotel.*
Myers, Walter. *Me, Mop and the Moondance.*
Nixon, Joan. *Place to Belong.*
Read, Efreida. *Brothers by Choice.*
Silman, Roberta. *Somebody Else's Child.*
Swetman, Evelyn. *Yes, My Darling Daughter.*

Adventure

See also: Courage; Pirates; Sea and Ships; Spies; Survival; Wilderness

Adams, Andy. *Trail Drive.*
Adrian, Mary. *Fireball Mystery.*
Agle, Nan. *Makon and the Dauphin.*
Aiken, Joan. *Bridle the Wind; Go Saddle the Sea; Nightbirds on Nantucket; Stolen Lake; Teeth of the Gale; Whispering Mountain.*
Alcock, Vivien. *Travelers by Night.*
Alexander, Lloyd. *Beggar Queen; Drackenberg Adventure; El Dorado Adventure; Illyrian Adventure; Jedera Adventure; Marvelous Misadventures of Sebastian.*
Allan, Mabel. *Night Wind.*
Almedingen, E.M. *Young Mark.*
Amerman, Lockhart. *Cape Cod Casket; Guns in the Heather.*
Anderson, Margaret. *Hairy Beast in the Woods; In the Circle of Time; In the Keep of Time; Journey of the Shadow Bairns.*
Andrews, J.S. *Cargo for a King.*
Angell, Judie. *One-Way to Ansonia.*
Annixter, Jane. *Wagon Scout.*
Armstrong, Richard. *Big Sea.*
Arnold, Oren. *Mystery of Superstition Mountain.*
Asimov, Janet. *Package in Hyperspace.*
Avery, Lynn. *Cappy and the River.*
Avi. *Emily Upham's Revenge; Man from the Sky; Shadrach's Crossing.*
Bacon, Katharine. *Pip and Emma.*
Barber, Antonia. *Affair of the Rockerbye Baby.*
Bawden, Nina. *White Horse Gang.*
Beatty, John. *At the Seven Stars.*
Beatty, Patricia. *Bad Bell of San Salvador; How Many Miles to Sundown?; Jonathan Down Under; Long Way to Whiskey Creek; Red Rock Over the River.*
Bell, Gertrude. *Posse of Two.*
Benchley, Nathaniel. *Beyond the Mists.*
Benezra, Barbara. *Nuggets in My Pocket.*
Bennett, Jay. *Killing Tree.*
Bentley, Phyllis. *Adventures of Tom Leigh.*
Berna, Paul. *Knights of King Midas; Mule on the Expressway; Mystery of Saint Salgue.*
Bess, Clayton. *Tracks.*
Bethancourt, T.E. *Tune in Yesterday.*
Blackwood, Gary. *Dying Sun.*
Blum, Robert. *Girl from Emeraline Island.*

Bodelson, Anders. *Operation Cobra.*
Bodker, Cecil. *Silas and Ben Godik; Silas and the Runaway Coach.*
Bond, Ann. *Saturdays in the City.*
Bond, Nancy. *Country of Broken Stone.*
Bonham, Frank. *Honor Bound.*
Bonzon, Paul. *Orphans of Simitra.*
Booky, Albert. *Son of Manitou.*
Borchard, R. *Donkeys for Rogador.*
Boston, Lucy. *Guardians of the House; River of Green Knowe.*
Bosworth, J.A. *White Water, Still Water.*
Bowen, Betty. *For Love of a Donkey.*
Bradley, Marion. *Hunters of the Red Moon.*
Brady, Esther. *Toad on Capitol Hill.*
Branscum, Robbie. *Adventures of Johnny May; Murder of Hound Dog Bates.*
Brauman, Franz. *Milik and Amina.*
Brick, John. *Yankees on the Run.*
Brink, Carol. *Andy Buckram's Tin Men.*
Brittain, Bill. *Who Knew There'd Be Ghosts?*
Brooks, Jerome. *Big Dipper Marathon.*
Brown, Fern. *Baby-Sitter on Horseback.*
Brown, Roy. *Battle of Saint Street; Day of the Pigeons; White Sparrow.*
Bulla, Clyde. *Down the Mississippi; Marco Moonlight; Viking Adventure.*
Bunyan, John. *Pilgrim's Progress.*
Burchard, Peter. *Rat Hell.*
Butters, Dorothy. *Ten Leagues to Boston Town.*
Butterworth, Oliver. *Narrow Passage.*
Byars, Betsy. *Trouble River.*
Carlsen, Ruth. *Monty and the Tree House.*
Carlson, Natalie. *Sailor's Choice.*
Carse, Robert. *Winter of the Whale.*
Catherall, Arthur. *Arctic Sealer; Camel Caravan; Death of an Oil Rig; Kidnapped by Accident; Lone Seal Pup; Lost Off the Grand Bank; Prisoner in the Snow; Sicilian Mystery; Strange Intruder; Yugoslav Mystery.*
Chamberlain, Elinor. *Mystery of the Jungle Airstrip.*
Chauncy, Nan. *High and Haunted Island.*
Cheatham, K. Follis. *Bring Home the Ghost.*
Cheney, Cora. *Case of the Iceland Dogs; Mystery of the Disappearing Cars; Treasure of Lin Li-Ti.*
Cherryh, C.J. *Angel with the Sword.*
Chetwin, Grace. *Riddle and the Rune.*
Chittun, Ida. *Hermit Boy.*
Christgau, Alice. *Laugh Peddler.*
Christian, Mary. *Dead Man in Catfish Bay; Mystery of the Double, Double Cross; Phantom of the Operetta.*
Christopher, Matt. *Return of the Headless Horseman.*
Clark, Joan. *Wild Man in the Woods.*
Clark, Mavis. *Sky Is Free.*
Clarke, Tom. *Big Road.*
Clements, Bruce. *Prison Window, Jerusalem Blue.*
Cleven, Catherine. *Pirate Dog.*

Hilts, Len. *Timmy O'Dowd and the Big Ditch.*
Hobson, Polly. *Mystery House.*
Hodges, Margaret. *Avenger.*
Holmvik, Oyvind. *Crack of Doom.*
Honig, Donald. *Journal of One Davey Wyatt.*
Hope, Anthony. *Prisoner of Zenda.*
Houston, James. *Akavak: An Eskimo Journey; Frozen Fire; River Runners.*
Howard, Elizabeth. *Mystery of the Metro.*
Howard, Moses. *Ostrich Chase.*
Hoyt, Helen. *Aloha, Susan.*
Hutchins, Pat. *Curse of the Egyptian Mummy.*
Innis, Pauline. *Hurricane Fighters.*
Jacobs, Helen. *Secret of the Strawberry Place.*
Jennings, Gary. *Rope in the Jungle.*
Johnson, Dorothy. *Farewell to Troy.*
Johnston, Norma. *Strangers Dark and Gold.*
Jones, Diana. *Drowned Ammet; Eight Days of Luke.*
Jones, Terry. *Saga of Eric the Viking.*
Jonsson, Runer. *Viki Viking.*
Kastner, Erich. *Little Man; Little Man and the Big Thief; 35th of May.*
Keele, Lugman. *Java Jack.*
Kelly, Jeffery. *Tramp Steamer and the Silver Bullet.*
Kirchgessner, Maria. *High Challenge.*
Klaveness, Jan. *Ghost Island.*
Knott, Bill. *Dwarf on Black Mountain.*
Knudson, Poul. *Challenge.*
Kotzwinkle, William. *Trouble in Bugland.*
Krantz, Hazel. *Secret Raft.*
Kruss, James. *My Great-Grandfather, the Heroes and I.*
Lambert, Charles. *Copper Nail.*
Lane, Carolyn. *Ghost Island.*
Le Carre, John. *Little Drummer Girl.*
Leighton, Margaret. *Voyage to Coromandel.*
Levin, Betty. *Brother Moose; Hawk High; Put on My Crown.*
Levitin, Sonia. *Journey to America; Return.*
Levy, Elizabeth. *Shadow Nose.*
Levy, Mimi. *Caravan from Timbuktu.*
Lilius, Irmelin. *Gold Crown Lane; Goldmaker's House; Horse of the Night.*
Lindgren, Astrid. *Karlsson-on-the-Roof; Ronia, the Robber's Daughter.*
Line, David. *Soldier and Me.*
Lovett, Margaret. *Great and Terrible Quest; Jonathan.*
Lukeman, Tim. *Witchwood.*
McGiffin, Lee. *High Whistle Charlie.*
McGraw, Eloise. *Mara Daughter of the Nile.*
McHargue, Georgess. *Talking Table Mystery.*
McKillip, Patricia. *Fool's Run.*
McLean, Allan. *Sound of Trumpets.*
McLean, Susan. *Pennies for the Piper.*
McNeill, Janet. *Other People.*
Maddox, Bill. *Rags and Patches.*
Madlee, Dorothy. *Miss Lindlow's Leopard.*
Mahy, Margaret. *Tricksters.*
Mantle, Winifred. *Chateau Holiday; Penderel*

Puzzle; Question of the Painted Cave.
Marshall, Catherine. *Julie.*
Matthews, Greg. *Further Adventures of Huckleberry Finn.*
Mayne, William. *Glass Ball.*
Melnikoff, Pamela. *Star and the Sword.*
Milton, Hilary. *Emergency! 10-33 on Channel 11.*
Moe, Barbara. *Ghost Wore Knickers.*
Moeri, Louisa. *Downwind.*
Monjo, F.N. *Prisoners of the Scrambling Dragon; Willie Jasper's Golden Eagle.*
Moore, Emily. *Just My Luck.*
Moore, Ruth. *Wilderness Journey.*
Mooser, Stephen. *Hitchhiking Vampire.*
Morgan, Mary. *Rainbow for Susan.*
Morpurgo, Michael. *Twist of Gold.*
Morrison, Lucile. *Mystery of Shadow Walk.*
Mowat, Farley. *Curse of the Viking Grave.*
Murphy, Shirley. *Sand Ponies.*
Murray, Marguerite. *Odin's Eye.*
Namioka, Lensey. *Samurai and Long-Nosed Devils.*
Nicole, Christopher. *Operation Manhunt; Operation Neptune.*
Nixon, Joan. *High Trail to Danger.*
Nolan, Lucy. *Secret at Summerhaven.*
Norton, Andre. *Green Dragon; No Night Without Stars.*
O'Dell, Scott. *Amethyst Ring; Black Star, Bright Dawn; Captive; King's Fifth.*
Ogilvie, Elisabeth. *Becky's Island.*
Olesky, Walter. *Bug Scanner and the Computer Mystery.*
Oliver, Stephen. *Glitter, the Gooder and the Ghost.*
Ormondroyd, Edward. *Castaways on Long Ago.*
Otis, James. *Toby Tyler, Ten Weeks with a Circus.*
Ottley, Reginald. *Bates Family.*
Paige, Harry. *Johnny Stands.*
Palmer, Myron. *Egyptian Necklace; Treachery in Crete.*
Parker, Richard. *Perversity of Pipers; Private Beach.*
Patchett, Mary. *Ajax and the Haunted Mountain.*
Paulsen, Gary. *Dogsong.*
Pedersen, Elsa. *Dangerous Flight.*
Pendergraft, Patricia. *Brush Mountain.*
Peyton, K.M. *Plan for Birdmarsh.*
Picard, Barbara. *Lost John: A Young Outlaw in the Forest of Arden.*
Pinkwater, Daniel. *Borgel; Yobgorgle, Mystery Monster of Lake Ontario.*
Pirsig, Robert. *Zen and the Art of Motorcycle Maintenance.*
Place, Marian. *Nobody Meets Bigfoot.*
Polland, Madeleine. *Born to Be Proud.*
Price, Willard. *Amazon Adventure; Diving Adventure; Elephant Adventure; Gorilla Adventure; Lion Adventure; Safari Adventure; South Sea Adventure; Volcano Adventure; Whale Adventure.*

Pryor, Bonnie. *Seth of the Lion People.*
Pyle, Howard. *Merry Adventures of Robin Hood.*
Rabinowitz, Ann. *Knight on Horseback.*
Ransome, Arthur. *Swallows and Amazons.*
Rendell, Ruth. *Talking to Strange Men.*
Rice, Eve. *Remarkable Return of Winston Potts Crisply.*
Riddell, Ruth. *Haunted Journey.*
Riding, Julia. *Space Traders Unlimited.*
Ritchie, Rita. *Night Coach to Paris; Pirates of Samarkand.*
Roberts, Glenys. *Richard Knight's Treasure.*
Roberts, Willo. *Caroline.*
Robinson, Richard. *Captain Sintar.*
Rockwood, Joyce. *Groundhog's Horse.*
Rogers, Raboo. *Rainbow Factor.*
Roper, Pamela. *Guardian Angel.*
Rugh, Belle. *Crystal Mountain.*
Ruthin, Margaret. *Katrina of the Lonely Isles.*
Rylant, Cynthia. *Fine White Dust.*
St. George, Judith. *In the Shadow of the Bear.*
Salassi, Otto. *And Nobody Knew They Were There.*
Sankey, Alice. *Hit the Bike Trail.*
Sant, Kathryn. *Desert Chase.*
Schaff, Louise. *Skald of the Vikings.*
Schealer, John. *Zip-Zip Goes to Venus.*
Schellie, Don. *Kidnapping Mr. Tubbs.*
Scott, Dustin. *Return of Mojave Joe.*
Scott, J.M. *Michael Anonymous.*
Sefton, Catherine. *In a Blue Velvet Dress.*
Service, Pamela. *Reluctant God.*
Shore, Laura. *Sacred Moon Tree.*
Shub, Elizabeth. *Cutlass in the Snow.*
Shura, Mary. *Run Away Home.*
Shyer, Marlene. *Grandpa Ritz and the Luscious Lovelies.*
Simons, Roger. *Dolphin Sailed North.*
Singer, Marilyn. *Leroy Is Missing.*
Slepian, Janice. *Alfred Summer.*
Smaridge, Norah. *Mystery at Greystone Hall; Secret of the Brownstone House.*
Smith, Alison. *Trap of Gold.*
Smith, George. *Bayou Boy.*
Smith, T.H. *Cry to the Night Wind.*
Smith, Wanda. *Ash Brooks, Super Ranger.*
Southall, Ivan. *Golden Goose; King of the Sticks.*
Spillane, Mickey. *Day the Sea Rolled Back.*
Spinelli, Jerry. *Dump Days.*
Stapp, Arthur. *Too Steep for Baseball.*
Steele, William. *Year of the Bloody Sevens.*
Stein, Conrad. *Me and Dirty Arnie.*
Stephan, Hanna. *Quest.*
Stephens, Peter. *Towapper, Puritan Renegade.*
Stevenson, Drew. *Case of the Horrible Swamp Monster; Case of the Visiting Vampire; Case of the Wandering Werewolf.*
Stevenson, Robert Louis. *Kidnapped.*
Stevenson, William. *Bushbabies.*
Stewart, A.C. *Elizabeth's Tower.*
Stoutenberg, Adrien. *Where to Now, Blue?*

Stuart, Morna. *Marassa and Midnight.*
Swarthout, Glendon. *Bless the Beasts and the Children.*
Talbot, Charlene. *Great Rat Island Adventure.*
Tavo, Gus. *Trail to Lone Canyon.*
Taylor, Theodore. *Odyssey of Ben O'Neal; Teetoncey; Walking Up a Rainbow.*
Thiele, Colin. *Hammerhead Light; Shadow on the Hills.*
Thomas, Jane. *Courage at Indian Deep.*
Thruelsen, Richard. *Voyage of the Vagabond.*
Todd, Leonard. *Best Kept Secret of the War.*
Townsend, John. *Top of the World.*
Traylor, Sarah. *Red Wind.*
Treece, Henry. *Burning of Njal; Man with a Sword; Road to Miklagard; Splintered Sword; Swords from the North; Viking's Sunset.*
Turner, Gerry. *Silver Dollar Hoard of Aristotle Gaskin.*
Turner, Phillip. *Grange at High Force; Sea Peril; War on the Darnel.*
Twain, Mark. *Adventures of Huckleberry Finn.*
Ulyatt, Kenneth. *Longhorn Trail.*
Unnerstad, Edith. *Peep-Larssons Go Sailing.*
Van Iterson, Siny. *Spirits of Chocamata.*
Van Stockum, Hilda. *Winged Watchman.*
Van Woerkuna, Dorothy. *Pearl in the Egg.*
Verne, Jules. *Around the World in Eighty Days.*
Verney, John. *February's Road; Friday's Tunnel.*
Wales, Robert. *Harry.*
Walker, Diana. *Dragon Hill.*
Wallace, Barbara. *Peppermints in the Parlor.*
Wallace, Bill. *Trapped in Death Cave.*
Walsh, Jill P. *Gaffer Samson's Luck; Torch.*
Walters, Hugh. *Blue Aura; Terror by Satellite.*
Warner, Gertrude. *Surprise Island.*
Watson, Simon. *No Man's Land.*
Weaver, Harriett. *Beloved Was Bahamas: A Steer to Remember.*
Weir, Rosemary. *Mystery of the Black Sheep.*
Welch, Ronald. *Bowmen of Crecy; Hawk; Nicholas Carey; Tank Commander.*
Wellman, Manly. *Mystery of the Lost Valley; River Pirates.*
Wibberley, Leonard. *John Treegate's Musket; Peter Treegate's War.*
Wier, Ester. *Gift of the Mountains.*
Willard, Barbara. *Eight for a Secret; Gardener's Grandchildren.*
Willard, Nancy. *Firebrat.*
Williams, Barbara. *Mitzi and Frederick the Great.*
Williams, Jay. *Danny Dunn and the Swamp Monster; Danny Dunn on a Desert Island; Danny Dunn on the Ocean Floor.*
Windsor, Patricia. *Something's Waiting for You, Baker D.*
Winn, Janet. *Home in Flames.*
Winterfeld, Henry. *Castaways in Lilliput.*
Wismer, Donald. *Starluck.*
Wood, William. *Billyboy.*
Wormser, Richard. *Kidnapped Circus.*

Wrightson, Patricia. *Balyet.*
Wuorio, Eva-Lis. *Detour to Danger; October Treasure; Venture at Midsummer.*
Yolen, Jane. *Boy Who Spoke Chimp.*
York, Carol. *Takers and Returners.*
Yvart, Jacques. *Rising of the Wind Adventures Along the Beaufort Scale.*
Zaring, Jane. *Sharks in the North Woods.*

Africa

Abrahams, Robert. *Bonus of Redonda.*
Barnes, Gregory. *Wind of Change.*
Bess, Clayton. *Story for a Black Night.*
Bulla, Clyde. *Sherman, D.R.*
Catherall, Arthur. *Camel Caravan.*
Christopher, John. *Dom and Va.*
Fleming, Elizabeth. *Takula Tree.*
Gordon, Sherba. *Waiting for the Rain.*
Guillot, Rene. *Fofana; Riders of the Wind.*
Jones, Betty. *King Solomon's Mine.*
Jones, Toeckey. *Go Well, Stay Well.*
Naidoo, Beverly. *Journey to Jo'Burg.*
Price, Willard. *African Adventure.*
Schatz, Letta. *Taiwo and Her Twin.*
Sherman, D.R. *Lion's Paw.*
Stevenson, William. *Bushbabies.*
Van Stockum, Hilda. *Mago's Flute.*
Venable, Alan. *Hurry the Crossing.*
Wellman, Alice. *Tatu and the Honey Bird; Wilderness Has Ears.*

African Americans

Armstrong, William. *Sounder; Sour Land.*
Ball, Dorothy. *Don't Drive Up a Dirt Road.*
Barrett, William. *Lilies of the Field.*
Blinn, William. *Brian's Song.*
Blume, Judy. *Iggie's House.*
Bonham, Frank. *Nitty-Gritty.*
Bontemps, Arna. *Lonesome Boy.*
Bowes, Elmer. *Trials of David Clark.*
Brooks, Bruce. *Moves Makes the Man.*
Brown, Claude. *Children of Ham.*
Burchard, Peter. *Bimby.*
Butterworth, W.E. *Leroy and the Old Man.*
Carlson, Natalie. *Marchers for the Dream.*
Childress, Alice. *Rainbow Jordan.*
Christopher, Matt. *No Arm in Left Field.*
Cohen, Barbara. *Thank You, Jackie Robinson.*
Coles, Robert. *Dead End School.*
Collier, James. *War Comes to Willy Freeman; Who Is Carrie?*
Coolidge, Olivia. *Come by Here.*
Delton, Judy. *Kitty in the Summer.*
Engel, Beth. *Big Words.*
Erwin, Betty. *Behind the Magic Line.*
Fast, Howard. *Freedom Road.*

Fitzhugh, Louise. *Nobody's Family Is Going to Change.*
Fox, Paula. *How Many Miles to Babylon?*
Graham, Lorenz. *North Town; Return to South Town.*
Guy, Rosa. *Disappearance; Edith Jackson; Ruby.*
Hamilton, Virginia. *Little Love; Magical Adventures of Pretty Pearl; Sweet Whispers, Brother Rush; Zeely.*
Hansen, Joyce. *Out from This Place; Which Way to Freedom?*
Herlicky, Dirlie. *Ludie's Song.*
Hunt, Irene. *William.*
Hunter, Kristin. *Lou in the Limelight; Soul Brother and Sister Lou.*
Hurmance, Belinda. *Tancy.*
Irwin, Hadley. *I Be Somebody.*
Jackson, Jesse. *Sickest Don't Always Die the Quickest; Tessie.*
Jordan, June. *His Own Where.*
Kelley, S. *Summer Growing Thing.*
Kimbrough, Richard. *Cross-Country Courage.*
Krementz, Jill. *Sweet Pea.*
Kristof, Jane. *Steal Away Home.*
Lipsyte, Robert. *Contender.*
Mackinnon, Bernie. *Meantime.*
Mebane, Mary. *Mary.*
Micklish, Rita. *Sugar Bee.*
Morrison, Toni. *Bluest Eye.*
Morse, Evangeline. *Brown Rabbit: Her Story.*
Myers, Walter. *Fast Sam, Cool Clyde and Stuff; Motown and Didi; Young Landlords.*
Neigoff, Mike. *Free Throw.*
Nelson, Theresa. *Devil Storm.*
Parks, Peter. *Learning Tree.*
Petry, Ann. *Tituba of Salem Village.*
Quigley, Martin. *Original Colored House of David.*
Rinaldi, Ann. *Wolf by the Ears.*
Sebestyen, Ouida. *On Fire; Words by Heart.*
Siegal, Beatrice. *Basket Maker and the Spinner.*
Stevens, Shane. *Rat Pack.*
Stolz, Mary. *Wonderful, Terrible Time.*
Tate, Eleanora. *Secret of Gumbo Grove; Thank You, Dr. Martin Luther King, Jr.*
Taylor, Mildred. *Let the Circle Be Unbroken; Roll of Thunder, Hear My Cry.*
Thomas, Joyce. *Marked by Fire.*
Wagner, Jane. *J.T.*
Walker, Mary. *Maggot; To Catch a Zombi.*
Walter, Mildred. *Have a Happy...; Lillie of Watts: A Birthday Discovery; Lillie of Watts Takes a Giant Step.*
Wilkinson, Brenda. *Ludell; Ludell and Willie; Ludell's New York Time.*
Williams, Edward. *Not Like Niggers.*
Wilson, Johnniece. *Oh, Brother.*

Airplanes

Blish, James. *Vanished Jet.*
Butterworth, W.E. *Helicopter Pilot.*
Conn, Martha. *Crazy to Fly.*
Dank, Milton. *Khaki Wings; Red Flight Two.*
Domke, Todd. *Grounded.*
Forsythe, Frederick. *Shepherd.*
Gay, Kathlyn. *Girl Pilot.*
George, Jean. *Hold Zero.*
Halacy, D.S. *Sky Trap.*
Hallstead, William. *Ev Kris, Aviation Detective.*
Hamley, Dennis. *Landings.*
Hay, Daddy. *Hit the Silk.*
Mark, Jan. *Thunder and Lightnings.*
Milton, Hilary. *Blind Flight; Mayday! Mayday!*
Peyton, Karen. *Edge of a Cloud.*
Richard, Adrienne. *Wings.*
Tomerlin, John. *Fledgling; Sky Clowns.*
White, Robb. *Survivor.*

Alaska

Bell, Margaret. *To Peril Strait.*
Calvert, Patricia. *Hour of the Wolf.*
Catherall, Arthur. *Lone Seal Pup.*
George, Jean. *Water Sky.*
Irwin, Hadley. *I Be Somebody.*
Morey, Walt. *Deep Trouble; Scrub Dog of Alaska.*
Nicol, Clive. *White Shaman.*
Paulsen, Gary. *Dogsong.*
Pinkerton, Katherine. *Second Meeting.*
Rogers, Fred. *Secret Moose.*
Taylor, Theodore. *Children's War.*

Alcohol Abuse

Allman, Paul. *No Pain, No Gain.*
Angier, Bradford. *Ask for Love and They Give You Rice Pudding.*
Arrick, Fran. *Nice Girl from Good Home.*
Bates, Betty. *Picking Up the Pieces.*
Bell, William. *Crabbe's Journey.*
Branscum, Robbie. *Cheater and Flitter Dick.*
Brookins, Dana. *Alone in Wolf Hollow.*
Bunting, Eve. *Sudden Silence.*
Carlson, Dale. *Wild Heart.*
Cavallaro, Ann. *Blimp.*
Corcoran, Barbara. *All the Summer Voices; Horse Named Sky; Person in the Potting Shed.*
Crutcher, Chris. *Crazy Horse Electric Game.*
Culin, Charlotte. *Cages of Glass, Flowers of Time.*
D'Ambrosio, Richard. *No Language but a Cry.*
Deaver, Julie. *Say Goodnight, Gracie.*

De Clements, Barthe. *No Place for Me.*
Dexter, Patricia. *Emancipation of Joe Tepper.*
Dixon, Paige. *Walk My Way.*
Donovan, John. *I'll Get There. It Better Be Worth the Trip.*
Dorman, N.B. *Laughter in the Background.*
Due, Linnea. *High and Outside.*
Dunnahoo, Terry. *Who Needs Espie Sanchez?*
Forman, James. *Pumpkin Shell.*
Fosburgh, Liza. *Cruise Control.*
Fox, Paula. *Moonlight Man.*
Froehlich, Margaret. *Reasons to Stay.*
Geller, Mark. *Raymond.*
Gottschalk, Elin. *In Search of Coffee Mountains.*
Greenberg, Jan. *Exercises of the Heart.*
Greene, Bette. *Them That Glitter/Them That Don't.*
Greene, Sheppard. *Boy Who Drank Too Much.*
Guy, Rosa. *New Guy Around the Block.*
Haddad, Carolyn. *Last Ride.*
Halvorson, Marilyn. *Cowboys Don't Cry.*
Hanes, Mari. *Wild Child.*
Harrah, Michael. *First Offender.*
Holland, Isabelle. *Jennie Kiss'd Me.*
Hoppe, Joanne. *April Spell.*
Kenny, Kevin. *Sometimes My Mom Drinks Too Much.*
Kropp, Paul. *Wilted.*
Lawrence, Louise. *Dram Road.*
Lee, Mildred. *People Therein.*
Malmgren, Dallin. *Whole Nine Yards.*
Mathis, Sharon. *Listen for the Fig Tree.*
Mazer, Harry. *War on Villa Street.*
Mazer, Norma. *When We First Met.*
Morrison, Toni. *Bluest Eye.*
Murphy, Shirley. *Sand Ponies.*
Myers, Walter. *It Ain't All for Nothin'.*
Neville, Emily. *Garden of Broken Glass.*
Newton, Suzanne. *I Will Call It Georgie's Blues.*
Orr, Rebecca. *Gunner's Run.*
Osborne, Mary. *Last One Home.*
Paulsen, Gary. *Crossing.*
Randall, Florence. *All the Sky Together.*
Roos, Stephen. *You'll Miss Me When I'm Gone.*
Rylant, Cynthia. *Blue-Eyed Daisy.*
Samuels, Gertrude. *Yours, Brett.*
Schulte, Elaine. *Whither the Wind Bloweth.*
Scoppettone, Sandra. *Late Great Me.*
Seabrooke, Brenda. *Home Is Where They Take You In.*
Smith, Marya. *Winter Broker.*
Snyder, Anne. *First Step; My Name Is Davy, I'm an Alcoholic.*
Springer, Nancy. *Not on a White Horse.*
Stolz, Mary. *Edge of Next Year.*
Sweeney, Joyce. *Center Line.*
Talbert, Marc. *Dead Birds Singing.*
Tapp, Kathy. *Smoke from the Chimney.*
Taylor, William. *Paradise Lane.*
Voigt, Cynthia. *Izzy, Willy-Nilly.*
Warwick, Delores. *Learn to Say Goodbye.*
Windsor, Patricia. *Diving for Roses.*

Wolkoff, Judie. *Where the Elf King Sings.*
Wright, Betty. *Secret Window.*
Zindel, Paul. *Pardon Me, You're Stepping on My Eyeball!*

American Frontier

See: Frontier and Pioneer Life

Animals, Tame

See also: Cats; Dogs; Horses, Trained; Pets

Bawden, Nina. *Peppermint Pig.*
Bradbury, Bianca. *Dogs and More Dogs.*
Brenner, Barbara. *Hemi: A Mule.*
Burnford, Sheila. *Incredible Journey.*
Carris, Joan. *Pets, Vets and Marty Howard.*
Caufield, Don. *Never Steal a Magic Cat.*
Corbett, Scott. *Case of the Gone Goose.*
Corbett, W.J. *Pentecost, The Chosen One; Song of Pentecost.* (Mice)
De Jong, Meindert. *Along Came a Dog.*
De Roo, Anne. *Cinnamon and Nutmeg.*
Gardner, Dic. *Danny and the Great Ape Komba.*
Glaser, Dianne. *Case of the Missing Six.*
Godden, Rumer. *Operation Sippacik.* (Donkey)
Greenwald, Sheila. *Mat Pit and the Tunnel Tenants.*
Holland, Isabelle. *Alan and the Animal Kingdom.*
Honeycutt, Natalie. *Best Laid Plans of Jonah Twist.*
Hurwitz, Johanna. *Much Ado About Aldo.*
Johnston, Louisa. *Monkey in the Family.*
Jones, Rebecca. *Germy Blew It Again.* (Gerbil)
Keane, John. *Sherlock Bones, Tracer of Missing Pets.*
King-Smith, Dick. *Babe: The Gallant Pig; Fox Busters; Pigs Might Fly; Queen's Nose.*
Kingman, Lee. *Year of the Raccoon.*
Kjelgaard, Jim. *Tigre (Jaguars).*
Levitin, Sonia. *Reigning Cats and Dogs.*
Lofting, Hugh. *Voyage of Dr. Dolittle.*
Morgan, Alison. *All Kinds of Prickles.* (Goat)
North, Sterling. *Rascal.* (Raccoon)
Norton, Andre. *Catseye.*
O'Brien, Robert. *Mrs. Frisby and the Rats of NIMH.*
Pevsner, Stella. *Me, My Goat and My Sister's Wedding.*
Phipson, Joan. *Birkin.* (Calf)
Schweitzer, Byrd. *Amigo.* (Prairie Dog)
Smith, Eunice. *Jennifer Is Eleven.* (Calf)
Sponsel, Heinz. *Keeper of the Wild Bulls.*
Wayne, Jennifer. *Sprout.* (Rabbit)
Weaver, Harriett. *Beloved Was Bahamas: A Steer to Remember.*
Whitmore, Arvella. *You're a Real Hero, Amanda.*
Willard, Barbara. *Three and One to Carry.*

Williams, Barbara. *Mitzi and the Elephants.*
Wood, Phyllis. *Five Color Buick and a Blue-Eyed Cat.*

Animals, Wild

Aaron, Chester. *American Ghost.* (Mountain Lion)
Adams, Richard. *Watership Down.* (Rabbits)
Alcock, Vivien. *Travelers by Night.* (Elephant)
Anderson, Margaret. *Hairy Beast in the Woods.*
Annixter, Jane. *Horns of Plenty; Last Monster.*
Arkin, Alan. *Lemming Condition.*
Baker, Betty. *Dupper.* (Prairie Dog)
Bawden, Nina. *Henry.* (Squirrel)
Beebe, B.F. *Coyote, Come Home; Run, Light Buck, Run.*
Bell, Clare. *Clan Ground; Ratha's Creatures.* (Cats)
Benchley, Nathaniel. *Kilroy and the Gull.*
Biesterveld, Betty. *Run, Reddy, Run.* (Fox)
Borchard, R. *Donkeys for Rogador.*
Bornstein, Ruth. *Little Gorilla.*
Boston, Lucy. *Stranger at Green Knowe.* (Gorilla)
Buchwald, Art. *Bollo Caper.* (Leopard)
Bulla, Clyde. *Beast of Lor.* (Elephant)
Byars, Betsy. *Midnight Fox.*
Call, Hughie. *Peter's Moose.*
Canning, Victor. *Runaways.* (Cheetah)
Caras, Roger. *Mara Simba, African Lion.*
Carner, C. *Tawny.* (Deer)
Carrick, Carol. *Elephant in the Dark.*
Carroll, Jeffrey. *Climbing to the Sun.* (Mountain Goat)
Carson, John. *Mystery of the Missing Monkey.*
Catherall, Arthur. *Big Tusker; Camel Caravan; Lapland Outlaw* (Deer); *Man-Eater.* (Leopard)
Chadwick, Lonnie. *Don't Shoot.* (Bears)
Clark, Ann. *Secret of the Andies.* (Llama)
Cline, Linda. *Weakfoot.* (Panther)
Corcoran, Barbara. *Sasha, My Friend.* (Wolf)
Cunningham, Julia. *Macaroon.* (Raccoon)
Dana, Barbara. *Zucchini.* (Ferret)
Dann, Colin. *Animals of Farthing Wood; Ram of Sweetriver.*
Davis, Verne. *Devil Cat Screamed* (Cougar); *Orphan of the Tundra.* (Musk Ox)
De Felice, Cynthia. *Weasel.*
Denzel, Justin. *Snowfoot.* (Fawn)
Derleth, August. *Beast in Holger's Woods.*
De Trevino, Elizabeth. *Nacar, White Deer.*
Dillon, Eilis. *Family of Foxes.*
Dinneen, Betty. *Luck of Leopards.*
Dixon, Paige. *Silver Wolf; Summer of the White Goat.*
Donovan, John. *Family* (Ape); *Wild in the World.* (Wolf)
Du Bois, William. *Gentleman Bear.*
Eckert, Allan. *Incident at Hawk's Hill.* (Badger)
Edmonds, Walter. *Beaver Valley; Wolf Hunt.*

Ellis, Mel. *Flight of the White Wolf.*
Feil, Hila. *Windmill Summer.* (Raccoon)
Fisher, Aileen. *Summer of Little Rain.* (Beaver)
Fisher, Clay. *Valley of the Bear.*
Foote, Timothy. *Great Ringtail Garbage Caper.*
Forsman, Bettie. *From Lupita's Hill.*
Foster, Elizabeth. *Long Hungry Night.* (Wolf)
Fox, Paula. *One-Eyed Cat.*
George, Jean. *Coyote in Manhattan; Julie of the Wolves; My Side of the Mountain.*
Gipson, Fred. *Curly and the Wild Boar.*
Gould, Lilian. *Jeremy and the Gorillas.*
Griffiths, G.D. *Mattie, the Story of a Hedgehog.*
Guillot, Rene. *Grishka and the Bear; Grishka and the Wolves; Little Dog Lost; Mokokambo, Lost Tail* (Bear Cub); *Sama.* (Elephant)
Hallard, Peter. *Kalu and the Wild Boar.*
Hamilton, Carol. *Dawn Seekers.* (Kangaroo Rat)
Hancock, Niel. *Dragon Winter.* (Otter)
Harmon, Lyn. *Flight to Jewell Island.* (Wolf)
Hart, Dorothy. *Animal Orphans.* (Panther)
Healey, Larry. *Claw of the Bear.*
Houston, James. *Wolf Run.*
Jacques, Brian. *Mossflower.*
Johnson, Burdetta. *Little Red.* (Javelina)
Johnson, James. *Pepper, A Puerto Rican Mongoose; Ringtail.* (Raccoon)
Keith, Harold. *Susy's Scoundrel.* (Coyote)
Kendall, Lace. *Rain Boat.*
Key, Alexander. *Preposterous Adventures of Swimmer.* (Otter)
Kipling, Rudyard. *Jungle Book.*
Kjelgaard, James. *Coyote Song; Haunt Fox; Hidden Trail* (Elk); *Nose for Trouble.*
Ladd, Elizabeth. *Fox Named Rufus.*
Landsman, Sandy. *Castaways on Chimp Island.*
Lauritzen, Jonreed. *Glitter-Eyed Wouser.* (Sheep)
Lawson, Robert. *Rabbit Hill; Tough Winter.*
Le Vert, John. *Flight of the Cassowary.*
Levin, Betty. *Ice Bear.*
Lippincott, Joseph. *Coyote, the Wonder Wolf.*
McGowen, Tom. *Odyssey from River Bend.*
Madlee, Dorothy. *Miss Lindlow's Leopard.*
Mannix, Daniel. *Outcasts.* (Skunk)
Mayerson, Evelyn. *Coydog.* (Coyotes)
Mian, Mary. *Nip and Tuck War.*
Miles, Miska. *Wharf Rat.*
Millstead, Thomas. *Cave of Moving Shadows.*
Montgomery, John. *Foxy; My Friend Foxy.*
Morey, Walt. *Gentle Ben* (Bear); *Gloomy Gus* (Bear); *Kavik the Wolf Dog; Sandy and the Rock Star.* (Cougar)
Morpurgo, Michael. *Little Foxes; Mr. Nobody's Eyes.* (Monkey)
Namovicz, Gene. *To Talk in Time.* (Fox)
North, Sterling. *Wolfling.*
Ottley, Reginald. *Bates Family.* (Sheep)
Patchett, Mary. *Ajax and the Haunted Mountain; End of the Outlaws.* (Cat)
Peake, Katy. *Indian Heart of Carrie Hodges.*
Price, Willard. *African Adventure; Amazon Adventure; Elephant Adventure; Gorilla Adventure; Lion Adventure; Safari Adventure.*
Quimby, Myrtle. *Cougar.*
Rawlings, Marjorie. *Yearling.* (Deer)
Rogers, Fred. *Secret Moose.*
Roth, Arthur. *Iceberg Hermit.*
Roy, Ron. *Chimpanzee Kid.*
Salten, Felix. *Bambi.* (Deer)
Sargent, Pamela. *Alien Child.*
Savage, Deborah. *Rumor of Otters.*
Scott, Dustin. *Mojave Joe; Return of Mojave Joe.* (Coyote)
Scott, Jane. *Cross Fox.*
Sherman, D.R. *Lion's Paw.*
Sherwan, Earl. *Mask, the Door Country Coon.*
Shura, Mary. *Mister Wolf and Me; Run Away Home* (Goat); *Tale of Middle Length.*
Snyder, Zilpha. *Fabulous Creature.* (Deer)
Steele, William. *Magic Amulet.*
Stern, Cecily. *Different Kind of Gold.*
Stevenson, James. *Here Comes Herb's Hurricane.*
Stevenson, William. *Bushbabies.* (Monkey)
Thiam, Djibi. *My Sister, the Panther.*
Thiele, Colin. *Fight Against Albatross Two.*
Thomas, Kathleen. *Goats Are Better Than Worms.*
Thompson, Eileen. *Golden Coyote.*
Thompson, Jean. *Brother of the Wolves.*
Turnbull, Ann. *Wolf King.*
Uhl, Marion. *Spiral Horn.*
Van Stockum, Hilda. *Mago's Flute.* (Goat)
Voight, Virginia. *Girl from Johnnycake Hill.* (Bears)
Wallace, Bill. *Ferret in the Bedroom, Lizards in the Fridge; Red Dog; Shadow on the Snow.*
Warren, Billy. *Black Lobo.* (Wolf)
Weaver, Harriett. *Frosty: A Raccoon to Remember.*
Wellman, Alice. *Wilderness Has Ears.* (Leopard)
Wier, Ester. *Long Year.* (Wolf)
Wilson, Willie. *Up Mountain One Time.* (Mongoose)
Yolen, Jane. *Children of the Wolf.*
Zistal, Era. *Dangerous Year.* (Skunk)

Anorexia

Hautzig, Deborah. *Second Star to the Right.*
Josephs, Rebecca. *Early Disorders.*
Levenkron, Steven. *Best Little Girl in the World.*
Ruckman, Ivy. *Hunger Scream.*
Snyder, Anne. *Goodbye, Paper Doll.*
Willey, Margaret. *Bigger Book of Lydia.*

Arts and Artists

Bulla, Clyde. *Benito.*
Byars, Betsy. *Cartoonist.*
Curry, Jane. *Lotus Cup.*

Asians

Asthma

See: Illness

Automobiles

Ballet

Allan, Mabel. *Ballet Family; Dancing Garlands: Ballet Family Again.*
Asher, Sandy. *Just Like Jenny.*
Baron, Nancy. *Tuesday's Child.*
Corcoran, Barbara. *Child of the Morning.*
Crayder, Dorothy. *Joker and the Swan.*
Dean, Karen. *Stay on Your Toes, Maggie Adams.*
Estoril, Jean. *We Danced in Bloomsbury Square.*
Farrar, Susan. *Samantha on Stage.*
Giff, Patricia. *Poopsie Pomerantz, Pick Up Your Feet.*
Hlibok, Bruce. *Silent Dancer.*
Hooks, William. *Doug Meets the Nutcracker.*
Johnson, Annabel. *Peculiar Magic.*
Landis, James. *Sister Impossible.*
Levenkron, Steven. *Best Little Girl in the World.*
McNeil, Florence. *Miss P and Me.*
Malcom, Johanna. *Terrible Tryouts.*
Rabinowich, Ellen. *Underneath I'm Different.*
Robinson, Nancy. *Ballet Magic.*
Ryan, Mary. *Dance a Step Closer; I'd Rather Be Dancing.*
Simon, Marcia. *Special Gift.*
Smith, Doris. *Karate Dancer.*
Streatfeild, Noel. *Ballet Shoes.*
Ure, Jean. *Most Important Thing.*
Walker, Mary. *Maggot.*
Weir, Joan. *Career Girl.*
Williams-Garcia, Rita. *Blue Tights.*
Zindel, Bonnie. *Star for the Latecomer.*

Baseball

Adler, David. *Jeffrey's Ghost and the Leftover Baseball Team.*
Archibald, Joe. *Right Field Runt.*
Baron, Nancy. *Tuesday's Child.*
Bishop, Curtis. *Little League Double Play; Little League Heroes; Little League, Little Brother; Little League Stepson; Little League Victory.*
Boswell, Thomas. *How Life Imitates the World Series.*
Bowen, Robert. *Hot Corner Blues; Lightning Southpaw.*
Carol, Bill. *Lefty's Long Throw.*
Cebulash, Mel. *Ruth Marini, Dodger Ace.*
Christopher, Matt. *Baseball Flyhawk; Catcher with a Glass Arm; Dog That Pitched a No-Hitter; Fox Steals Home; Hit-Away Kid; Kid Who Only Hit Homers; Look Who's Playing First Base; Mystery Coach; No Arm in Left Field; Shortstop from Tokyo; Spy on Third Base; Too Hot to Handle; Wild Pitch; Year Mom Won the Pennant.*
Cohen, Barbara. *Thank You, Jackie Robinson.*
Cole, Stephen. *Pitcher and I.*

Corbett, Scott. *Baseball Bargain; Baseball Trick; Homerun Trick.*
Cox, William. *Wild Pitch.*
Creighton, Don. *Little League Old Timers.*
De Clements, Barthe. *Sixth Grade Can Really Kill You.*
Dygard, Thomas. *Rookie Arrives.*
Elish, Dan. *Jason and the Baseball Bear.*
Eller, Scott. *Short Season.*
Ethridge, Kenneth. *Viola, Furgy, Bobbi and Me.*
Fisher, Leonard. *Noonan: A Novel About Baseball, ESP and Time Warps.*
Friendlich, Dick. *Backstop Ace; Sweet Swing.*
Gault, William. *Stubborn Sam; Trouble at Second.*
Gelman, Steve. *Baseball Bonus Kid.*
Giff, Patricia. *Left-Handed Shortstop.*
Glenn, Mel. *Squeeze Play: A Baseball Story.*
Green, Anne. *Valley Cup.*
Harmon, A.W. *Base Hit.*
Harris, Robbie. *Rosie's Double Dare.*
Hayes, William. *Hold That Computer.*
Heavilin, Jay. *Fast Ball Pitcher.*
Heuman, William. *Horace Higby and the Scientific Pitch.*
Higdon, Hal. *Horse That Played Center Field; Last Series.*
Honig, Donald. *Johnny Lee.*
Hurwitz, Johanna. *Baseball Fever.*
Jackson, C. Paul. *Bud Baker, College Pitcher; High School Backstop; Little Major Leaguer; Rookie Catcher with the Atlanta Braves; Tom Mosley — Midget Leaguer; World Series Rookie.*
Kalb, Jonah. *Goof That Won the Pennant.*
Kaufman, Stephen. *Does Anyone Know the Way to Thirteen?*
Kelly, Jeffrey. *Basement Baseball Club.*
Kidd, Ronand. *Who Is Felix the Great.*
Klass, David. *Different Season.*
Knudson, R.R. *Zanboomer.*
Konigsburg, E.L. *About the B'nai Bagels.*
Lee, Robert. *Iron Arm of Michael Glenn.*
Lewis, Marjorie. *Wrongway Applebaum.*
Lord, Bette. *In the Year of the Boar and Jackie Robinson.*
McCormick, Wilfred. *Big Ninth; Incomplete Pitcher; Last Putout; No Place for Heroes; Tall at the Plate; Three-Toed Pitch.*
MacKellar, William. *Mound Menace.*
Marek, Magot. *Matt's Crusade.*
Maule, Tex. *Last Out.*
Park, Barbara. *Skinnybones.*
Parkinson, Ethelyn. *Good Old Archibald.*
Philbrook, Clem. *Ollie's Team and the Baseball Computer; Ollie's Team and the Million Dollar Mistake; Ollie's Team and the 200 Pound Problem; Ollie's Team Plays Biddy Baseball.*
Quigley, Martin. *Original Colored House of David.*
Scholefield, Edmond. *Tiger Rookie.*
Scholz, Jackson. *Center Field Jinx.*
Slote, Alfred. *Hang Tough, Paul Mather; Jake;*

Matt Gargan's Boy; Rabbit Ears; Tony and Me; Trading Game.
Smith, Carole. *Hit and Run Connection.*
Smith, Robert. *Bobby Baseball.*
Taves, Isabella. *Not Bad for a Girl.*
Tolle, Jean. *Great Pete Penney.*
Tunis, John. *Keystone Kids; Kid Comes Back; Kid from Tomkinville; Rookie of the Year.*
Walden, Amelia. *Stay to Win.*
Young, I.S. *Carson at Second.*
Zirpoli, Jane. *Roots in the Outfield.*

Basketball

Archibald, Joe. *Backcourt Commando.*
Bach, Alice. *Waiting for Johnny Miracle.*
Bates, Betty. *Picking Up the Pieces.*
Bishop, Curtis. *Fast Break; Rebound.*
Boatright, Lori. *Out of Bounds.*
Brooks, Bruce. *Moves Make the Man.*
Carris, Joan. *Rusty Timmons' First Million.*
Carson, John. *Coach Nobody Liked.*
Christopher, Matt. *Johnny Long Legs; Long Shot for Paul; Red-Hot Hightops.*
Cox, William. *Home Court Is Where You Find It; Unbeatable Five.*
Davis, Russell. *Some Town You Brought Me To.*
Dixon, Paige. *Pimm's Cup for Everybody.*
Dygard, Thomas. *Tournament Upstart.*
Gault, William. *Showboat in the Back Court.*
Geibel, James. *Blond Brother.*
Heuman, William. *Backcourt Man; Powerhouse Five; Wonder Five.*
Hoobler, Thomas. *Revenge of Ho-Tai.*
Hughes, Dean. *Nutty Can't Miss.*
Jackson, Alison. *My Brother, the Star.*
Jackson, C. Paul. *Bud Plays Senior High Basketball; Stepladder Steve Plays Basketball.*
Jackson, O.B. *Southpaw in the Mighty Mite League.*
Keith, Harold. *Brief Garland.*
Knudson, R.R. *Zanbanger.*
McCormick, Wilfred. *One Bounce Too Many.*
Myers, Walter. *Hoops.*
Neigoff, Mike. *Free Throw.*
Parkinson, Ethelyn. *Merry Mad Bachelors.*
Peck, Robert. *Basket Case; Soup's Hoop.*
Philbrook, Clem. *Ollie's Team and the Alley Cats; Ollie's Team and the Basketball Computer.*
Savitz, Harriet. *On the Move.*
Walton, Todd. *Inside Moves.*
Young, Isador. *Two-Minute Dribble.*

Birds, Tame

Aiken, Joan. *Arabel and Mortimer; Arabel's Raven; Mortimer Says Nothing; Mortimer's Cross.*
Anderson, Mary. *Matilda Investigates.*

Arthur, Robert. *Mystery of the Stuttering Parrot.*
Bothwell, Jean. *Parsonage Parrot.*
Brandel, Marc. *Mystery of the Two-Toed Pigeon.*
Brown, Roy. *Day of the Pigeons.*
Campbell, R.W. *Where the Pigeons Go to Die.*
Cunningham, Julia. *Viollet.*
Cusack, Isabel. *Mr. Wheatfield's Loft.*
Fry, Rosalie. *Fly Home, Columbina.*
George, Jean. *Cry of the Crow; Summer of the Falcon.*
Hinchman, Jane. *Talent for Trouble.*
Jamison, Cecilia. *Lady Jane.*
King-Smith, Dick. *Harry's Mad.*
Ladd, Elizabeth. *Trouble on Heron's Neck.*
Lofting, Hugh. *Dr. Dolittle and the Green Canary; Dr. Dolittle's Caravan.*
Mowat, Farley. *Owls in the Family.*
Mukerji, Dhan. *Gay-Neck.*
Wild, Elizabeth. *Along Came a Blackbird.*
Woolf, Virginia. *Widow and the Parrot.*
Wrightson, Patricia. *Night Out-Side.*

Birds, Wild

Bach, Richard. *Jonathan Livingston Seagull.*
Bancroft, Griffing. *Snowy: The Story of an Egret.*
Barford, Carol. *Let Me Hear the Music.*
Baylor, Byrd. *Hawk, I'm Your Brother.*
Bickman, Jack. *Baker's Hawk.*
Bowen, John. *Squeak: A Love Story.*
Bulla, Clyde. *White Bird.*
Bunting, Eve. *One More Flight.*
Byars, Betsy. *House of Wings.*
Callen, Larry. *Sorrow's Song.*
Canning, Victor. *Flight of the Grey Goose.*
Carlson, Natalie. *Evangeline, Pigeon of Paris.*
Colum, Padraic. *White Sparrow.*
Deleon, Eric. *Pitch and Hasty Check It Out.*
Fall, Thomas. *My Bird Is Romeo.*
Gage, Wilson. *Wild Goose.*
George, Jean. *Gull Number 737; Who Really Killed Cock Robin?*
Jewett, Sarah. *White Heron, A Story of Maine.*
Jones, Adrienne. *Hawks of Chelney.*
Knudson, R.R. *Rinehart Shouts.*
Langton, Jane. *Fledgling.*
Lasky, Kathryn. *Home Free.*
Levin, Betty. *Hawk High.*
Lipp, Frederick. *Some Lose Their Way.*
Mayne, William. *Antar and the Eagles.*
Milton, Joyce. *Save the Loonies.*
Murphy, Robert. *Wild Geese Calling.*
Murphy, Shirley. *Flight of the Fox.*
Paige, Harry. *Johnny Stands.*
Parkinson, Ethelyn. *Rupert Piper and the Dear, Dear Birds.*
Phipson, Joan. *Fly Into Danger.*
Robertson, Keith. *In Search of a Sandhill Crane.*
Savage, Deborah. *Flight of the Albatross.*
Schroder, Amund. *Bird That Got Left Behind.*

Snyder, Zilpha. *And Condors Danced.*
Thiele, Colin. *Storm Boy.*
Tolan, Stephanie. *Time to Fly Free.*
Wallace, Luke. *Blue Wings.*
White, E.B. *Trumpet of the Swan.*
Williams, Ursula. *Earl's Falconer.*

Blacks

See: African Americans

Blindness

Allan, Mabel. *Flash Children; View Beyond My Father.*
Anderson, Paul. *Boy and the Blind Storyteller.*
Bawden, Nina. *Witch's Daughter.*
Butler, Beverly. *Gift of Gold; Light a Single Candle; Maggie by My Side.*
Canty, Mary. *Green Gate.*
Christian, Mary. *Mystery at Camp Triumph.*
Christopher, Matt. *Stranded.*
Clewes, Dorothy. *Guide Dog.*
Cookson, Catherine. *Go Tell It to Mrs. Golightly.*
Dickinson, Peter. *Annerton Pit.*
Eyerly, Jeannette. *Seeing Summer.*
Fine, Anne. *Summer House Loon.*
First, Julia. *Absolute, Ultimate End.*
Fleischman, Paul. *Finzel the Farsighted.*
Garfield, James. *Follow My Leader.*
Griffiths, Helen. *Wild Horse of Santander.*
Holland, Isabelle. *Unfrightened Dark.*
Johnson, Emily. *Spring and the Shadow Man.*
Kennedy, Richard. *Dark Princess.*
Kent, Deborah. *Belonging.*
Little, Jean. *From Anna; Listen for the Singing.*
Mathis, Sharon. *Listen for the Fig Tree.*
Micklish, Rita. *Sugar Bee.*
Milton, Hilary. *Blind Flight.*
Neufeld, John. *Touching.*
Phipson, Joan. *Watcher in the Garden.*
Sommerfelt, Aimee. *Road to Agra.*
Ter Haar, Jaap. *World of Ben Lighthart.*
Thompson, Estelle. *Hunter in the Dark.*
Ure, Jean. *See You Thursday.*
Whitney, Phyllis. *Secret of the Emerald Star.*
Witheridge, Elizabeth. *Dead End Bluff.*
Wolf, Bernard. *Connie's New Eyes.*

Boats

Adkins, Jan. *Workboats.*
Berna, Paul. *Secret of the Missing Boat.*
Bond, Nancy. *Voyage Begun.*
Bradbury, Bianca. *Loner.*
Catherall, Arthur. *Night of the Black Frost.*
Ervin, Janet. *Last Trip of the Luno.*

Feldman, Alan. *Lucy Mastermind.*
Fry, Rosalie. *Riddle of the Figurehead.*
Gibbs, Alonzo. *One More Day.*
Graham, Robin. *Dove.*
Havrevold, Finn. *Undertow.*
Heuman, William. *Horace Higby, Coxswain of the Crew.*
Hilts, Len. *Timmy O'Dowd and the Big Ditch.*
Jones, Adrienne. *Sail, Calypso.*
Kingman, Lee. *Luck of the Miss L.*
Knudson, R.R. *Rinehart Shouts.*
Krantz, Hazel. *Secret Raft.*
Ladd, Elizabeth. *Marty Runs Away to Sea.*
Leonard, Constance. *Marina Mystery.*
Lindgren, Astrid. *Seacrow Island.*
Macken, Walter. *Island of the Great Yellow Ox.*
Mattson, Olle. *Mickel Seafarer.*
Mayne, William. *Pig in the Middle.*
Melcher, Marguerite. *Catch of the Season.*
Mowat, Farley. *Black Joke.*
Ogan, Margaret. *Choicy.*
Paulsen, Gary. *Voyage of the Frog.*
Peyton, K.M. *Plan for Birdmarsh.*
Peyton, Karen. *Sea Fever.*
Randall, Florence. *All the Sky Together.*
Simons, Roger. *Dolphin Sailed North.*
Stolz, Mary. *Lands End.*
Stoutenberg, Adrien. *Where to Now, Blue?*
Thruelsen, Richard. *Voyage of the Vagabond.*
Townsend, John. *Tom Tiddler's Ground.*
Trease, Geoffrey. *No Boats on Bannermere.*
Unnerstad, Edith. *Peep-Larssons Go Sailing.*
Venable, Alan. *Hurry the Crossing.*
Walsh, Jill P. *Huffler.*
Wartski, Maureen. *My Name Is Nobody.*
Willard, Barbara. *Eight for a Secret.*
Wortman, Elmo. *Almost Too Late.*

Boys

See: Boys, Mature; Boys, Pre-Teen; Boys, Teen

Boys, Mature

Aiken, Joan. *Teeth of the Gale.*
Ashley, Bernard. *Dodgem.*
Avery, Gillian. *Call of the Valley.*
Avi. *Place Called Ugly.*
Bennett, Paul. *Follow the River.*
Bethancourt, T.E. *Where the Deer and the Cantaloupe Play.*
Bonham, Barbara. *Challenge of the Prairie.*
Borland, Hal. *When the Legends Die.*
Brancato, Robin. *Uneasy Money.*
Butterworth, W.E. *Return to Racing.*
Dank, Milton. *Game's End.*
Dexter, Patricia. *Emancipation of Joe Tepper.*
Dixon, Paige. *May I Cross Your Golden River.*
Fritz, Jean. *I, Adam.*

Grant, Cynthia. *Hard Love.*
Grice, Frederick. *Out of the Mines.*
Hallstead, William. *Ev Kris, Aviation Detective.*
Hamner, Earl. *You Can't Get There from Here.*
Hegarty, Reginald. *Rope's End.*
Higgins, Colin. *Harold and Maud.*
Hildick, Florence. *Jim Starling and the Colonel.*
Hillinger, Brad. *Wings Are Gone.*
Hinton, S.E. *Taming the Star Runner.*
Howard, Elizabeth. *Mystery of the Metro.*
Johnson, Annabel. *Memory of Dragons.*
Johnston, Norma. *Timewarp Summer.*
Kerr, M.E. *I'll Love You When You're More Like Me.*
Lee, Mildred. *Fog.*
Lee, Robert. *Day It Rained Forever.*
Line, David. *Soldier and Me.*
Lipsyte, Robert. *Summerboy.*
McCormick, Wilfred. *Eagle Scout.*
Madison, Arnold. *Think Wild.*
Maguire, Gregory. *Lights on the Lake.*
Mazer, Harry. *Hey, Kid! Does She Love Me?; I Love You, Stupid.*
Meltzer, M. *Underground Man.*
Menuis, Opal. *No Escape.*
Mowat, Farley. *Black Joke.*
Ney, John. *Ox and the Prime-Time Kid; Ox Under Pressure.*
Parker, Richard. *Quarter Boy.*
Pedersen, Elsa. *Fisherman's Choice.*
Poole, Victoria. *Thursday's Child.*
Rees, David. *Risks.*
Richard, Adrienne. *Pistol.*
Richardson, Grace. *Douglas.*
Richardson, Judith. *David's Landing.*
Riter, Dorris. *Edge of Violence.*
Roos, Stephen. *You'll Miss Me When I'm Gone.*
Roth, David. *Best of Friends.*
Say, Allen. *Ink-Keeper's Apprentice.*
Schleier, Curt. *You'd Better Not Tell.*
Scott, J.M. *Michael Anonymous.*
Smith, George. *Bayou Boy.*
Sutcliff, Rosemary. *Knight's Fee.*
Terry, Douglas. *Last Texas Hero.*
Turner, Kermit. *Rebel Powers.*
Warnlof, Anna. *Upstairs.*
Welch, Ronald. *Mohawk Valley.*
Wersba, Barbara. *Carnival in My Mind.*
Zindel, Paul. *Amazing and Death-Defying Diary of Eugene Dingman.*

Boys, Pre-Teen

Bell, Thelma. *Two Worlds of Davy Blount.*
Blume, Judy. *Superfudge.*
Bradbury, Bianca. *Boy on the Run; Three Keys.*
Byars, Betsy. *Cracker Jackson; Eighteenth Emergency; Midnight Fox.*
Carlson, Dale. *Charlie the Hero.*
Carrick, Carol. *Elephant in the Dark.*

Cleary, Beverly. *Henry and Beezus; Henry and Ribsy; Henry and the Clubhouse; Henry and the Paper Route; Henry Huggins.*
Clifford, Eth. *Harvey's Horrible Snake Disaster; Harvey's Marvelous Monkey Mystery.*
Collier, James. *Teddy Bear Habit.*
Cunningham, Julia. *Onion Journey.*
Dahl, Roald. *James and the Giant Peach.*
Danziger, Paula. *Make Like a Tree and Leave.*
Delton, Judy. *Only Jody.*
Dickens, Charles. *Oliver Twist.*
Fleischman, Sid. *Ghost on Saturday Night.*
Foltz, Mary Jane. *Nicolau's Prize.*
Frascino, Edward. *Eddie Spaghetti; Eddie Spaghetti on the Home Front.*
Garfield, James. *Follow My Leader.*
Garthwaite, Marion. *Mario.*
Giff, Patricia. *Winter Worm Business.*
Gilson, Jamie. *Double Dog Dare; Hello, My Name Is Scrambled Eggs.*
Gipson, Fred. *Little Arliss.*
Gonzalez, Gloria. *Gaucho.*
Greene, Constance. *Ears of Louis; Unmaking of Rabbit.*
Gripe, Maria. *Elvis and His Friends; Elvis and His Secret.*
Grund, Josef. *You Have a Friend, Pietro.*
Heide, Florence. *Time's Up.*
Hildick, E.W. *Doughnut Dropout.*
Hughes, Dean. *Honestly, Myron; Nutty and the Case of the Mastermind Thief; Nutty for President.*
Hurwitz, Johanna. *Aldo Applesauce.*
Kaufman, Stephen. *Does Anyone Know the Way to Thirteen?*
Kirk, Ruth. *David, Young Child of the Quileutes.*
Klein, Norma. *Blue Trees, Red Sky; Robbie and the Leap Year Blues.*
Krensky, Stephen. *Wilder Plot.*
Krumgold, Joseph. *And Now Miguel.*
Lindgren, Astrid. *Emil and Piggy Beast; Emil's Pranks.*
Little, Jean. *Different Dragons.*
MacLachlan, Patricia. *Arthur, for the Very First Time.*
Mannix, Daniel. *Outcasts.*
Mazer, Harry. *Guy Lenny.*
Morgan, Alison. *All Kinds of Prickles; Paul's Kite.*
Naylor, Phyllis. *One of the Third Grade Thonkers.*
Oz, Amos. *Soumchi.*
Pierce, Meredith. *Woman Who Loved Reindeer.*
Rockwell, Thomas. *Hey, Lover Boy.*
Rodgers, Mary. *Summer Switch.*
Shura, Mary. *Jefferson.*
Slepian, Jan. *Getting on With It.*
Slote, Alfred. *Friends Like That.*
Southall, Ivan. *Long Night Watch.*
Sussman, Susan. *Casey the Nomad.*
Swenson, Judy. *Learning My Way: I'm a Winner.*
Swinnerton, A.R. *Rocky the Cat.*

Tate, Joan. *Luke's Garden; and Gramp.*
Townsend, John. *Rob's Place.*
Weik, Mary. *Jazz Man.*

Boys, Teen

Abrahams, Robert. *Bonus of Redonda.*
Adler, Carole. *Roadside Valentine.*
Aleksin, Anatoli. *Late Born Child.*
Ames, Mildred. *Philo Potts, or the Helping Hand Strikes Again.*
Anckarsvard, Karin. *Doctor's Boy; Robber Ghost.*
Angier, Bradford. *Ask for Love and They Give You Rice Pudding.*
Asher, Sandy. *Everything Is Not Enough.*
Avi. *Romeo and Juliet — Together (and Alive) at Last.*
Babbitt, Natalie. *Herbert Rowbarge.*
Baker, Elizabeth. *This Stranger, My Son.*
Ball, John. *Judo Boy.*
Barnwell, Robinson. *Head into the Wind.*
Barrett, Anne. *Midway.*
Bauer, Marion. *On My Honor.*
Beatty, Patricia. *Jonathan Down Under.*
Bell, W. Bruce. *Little Dab of Color.*
Berry, B.J. *Just Don't Bug Me.*
Bethancourt, T. E. *Dog Days of Arthur Cane.*
Blue, Rose. *Me and Einstein.*
Blume, Judy. *Then Again, Maybe I Won't.*
Bograd, Larry. *Bad Apple; Bernice Entertaining; Better Angel.*
Bonham, Frank. *Cool Cat; Durango Street; Hey, Big Spender; Mystery of the Fat Cat; Nitty-Gritty; Viva Chicano.*
Bredes, Don. *Hard Feelings.*
Bridgers, Sue Ellen. *Permanent Connections.*
Brinley, Bertrand. *New Adventures of the Mad Scientists' Club.*
Brooks, Jerome. *Make Me a Hero.*
Brown, Roy. *Escape the River; White Sparrow.*
Buchan, Stuart. *Guys Like Us.*
Bulla, Clyde. *Marco Moonlight.*
Bunting, Eve. *Is Anybody There?*
Burch, Robert. *D. J.'s Worst Enemy.*
Butler, William. *Butterfly Revolution.*
Byars, Betsy. *Bingo Brown and the Language of Love; Burning Questions of Bingo; T.V. Kid.*
Callen, Larry. *Deadly Mandrake; Muskrat War; Pinch; Sorrow's Song.*
Campbell, R.W. *Where the Pigeons Go to Die.*
Campion, Wardi. *Casa Means Home.*
Carter, Alden. *Wart, Son of Toad.*
Cheatham, K. Follis. *Best Way Out.*
Childress, Alice. *Hero Ain't Nothin' but a Sandwich.*
Chukovskii, Kornei. *Silver Crest.*
Church, Richard. *Down River; Five Boys in a Cave.*
Clifford, Eth. *I Never Wanted to Be Famous.*
Cohen, Barbara. *Benny; Born to Dance Sambe.*

Collier, James. *Rich and Famous.*
Conford, Ellen. *Revenge of the Incredible Dr. Rancid and His Youthful Assistant, Jeffrey.*
Cookson, Catherine. *Nipper.*
Corbin, William. *Prettiest Gargoyle.*
Danziger, Paula. *Everyone Else's Parents Said Yes.*
Davies, Andrew. *Conrad's War.*
Derby, Pat. *Visiting Miss Pierce.*
Dillon, Eilis. *Coriander; Family of Foxes; Fort of Gold.*
Dixon, Paige. *Promises to Keep.*
Domke, Todd. *Grounded.*
Donovan, John. *I'll Get There. It Better Be Worth the Trip.*
Draper, Cena. *Rim of the Ridge.*
Duncan, Lois. *They Never Came Home.*
Dunlop, Eileen. *Fox Farm.*
Dygard, Thomas. *Halfback Tough.*
Eige, Lillian. *Cady.*
Fiddler, Katheryn. *Haki the Shetland Pony.*
Fife, Dale. *Who's in Charge of Lincoln?*
Filson, Brent. *Puma.*
Fisher, Laura. *Never Try Nathaniel.*
Fisher, Lois. *Wretched Robert.*
Fitzgerald, John. *Great Brain; Great Brain at the Academy; Great Brain Does It Again; Great Brain Reforms; Me and My Little Brain; More Adventures of the Great Brain; Return of the Great Brain.*
Fleming, Alice. *Welcome to Grossville.*
Fosburgh, Liza. *Summer Lion.*
Fox, Paula. *Blowfish Live in the Sea.*
Frick, C.H. *Comeback Guy.*
Fritzhand, James. *Life Is a Lonely Place.*
Galgut, Damon. *Sinless Season.*
Gathje, Curtis. *Disco Kid.*
Geller, Mark. *My Life in the Seventh Grade.*
Gilbert, Nan. *Dog for Joey.*
Golding, William. *Lord of the Flies.*
Gould, Lilian. *Jeremy and the Gorillas.*
Graber, Richard. *Little Breathing Room; Pay Your Respects.*
Graham, Lorenz. *North Town.*
Grant, Cynthia. *Summer Home.*
Gray, Elizabeth. *I Will Adventure.*
Gray, Genevieve. *Sore Loser.*
Green, Phyllis. *Empty Seat.*
Greene, Constance. *Double and Dare O'Toole; Getting Nowhere; Love Letters of J. Timothy Owen.*
Greenwald, Sheila. *Mat Pit and the Tunnel Tenants.*
Griffiths, Helen. *Journal of a Teenage Genius.*
Guy, Rosa. *Ups and Downs of Carl Davis III.*
Halacy, Daniel. *Secret of the Cove.*
Hall, Lynn. *Sticks and Stones.*
Hamilton, Virginia. *Planet of Junior Brown.*
Havis, Allan. *Albert the Astronomer.*
Haynes, Betsy. *Shadow of Jeremy Pimm.*
Heck, B. Holland. *Cactus Kevin.*
Heide, Florence. *Banana Twist.*

Henkes, Kevin. *Return to Sender.*
Herman, Charlotte. *Difference of Ari Stein.*
Hicks, Clifford. *Alvin Fernald, Foreign Trader; Alvin Fernald, Master of a Thousand Disguises; Alvin Fernald, Mayor for a Day; Alvin Fernald, Superweasel; Alvin Fernald, T.V. Anchorman; Alvin's Secret Code; Alvin's Swap Shop; Marvelous Inventions of Alvin Fernald; Peter Potts; Pop and Peter Potts; Wacky World of Alvin Fernald.*
Hill, Marjorie. *Secret of Avalon.*
Hinton, S.E. *Outsiders; Rumble Fish; That Was Then, This Is Now.*
Hoff, Syd. *Irving and Me.*
Honeycutt, Natalie. *All New Jonah Twist.*
Hopper, Nancy. *Ape Ears and Beaky; Hang On, Harvey.*
Hughes, Dean. *Family Pose.*
Hurwitz, Johanna. *Yellow Blue Jay.*
Hutchins, Pat. *Curse of the Egyptian Mummy.*
Ish-Kishor, Sulamith. *Our Eddie.*
Janeczko, Paul. *Bridges to Cross.*
Jeffries, Roderic. *Trapped.*
Kemp, Gene. *Charlie Lewis Plays for Time; Gowie Corby Plays Chicken.*
Kerr, M.E. *Son of Someone Famous.*
Kidd, Ronald. *Dunker.*
Klein, Norma. *Snapshots.*
Korman, Gordon. *Semester in the Life of a Garbage Bag.*
Krensky, Stephen. *Wilder Summer.*
Kropp, Paul. *Wilted.*
Krumgold, Joseph. *Henry 3.*
Larimer, Tamela. *Buck.*
Lee, Benjamin. *It Can't Be Helped.*
Lee, Mildred. *Skating Rink.*
Levine, Betty. *Great Burgerland Disaster.*
Levitin, Sonia. *Mark of Conte.*
Lindquist, Willis. *Burma Boy.*
Lipsyte, Robert. *Summer Rules.*
Lord, Athena. *Luck of Z.A.P. and Zoe.*
Love, Dandra. *Dive for the Sun.*
McCloskey, Robert. *Centerburg Tales; Homer Price.*
McGraw, Eloise. *Hideaway.*
MacKellar, William. *Secret of the Dark Tower; Secret of the Sacred Stone.*
McMahan, Ian. *Fox's Lair; Lake Fear.*
McNamara, John. *Revenge of the Nerd.*
Maddock, Reginald. *Pit.*
Madison, Arnold. *Danger Beats the Drum.*
Major, Kevin. *Dear Bruce Springsteen; Far from Shore; Thirty-Six Exposures.*
Mann, Peggy. *There Are Two Kinds of Terrible.*
Mannix, Daniel. *Healer.*
Mark, Jan. *Under the Autumn Garden.*
Marney, Dean. *Just Good Friends.*
Mauser, Patricia. *Bundle of Sticks.*
Mayerson, Evelyn. *Coydog.*
Miles, Betty. *Sink Or Swim.*
Milton, Hilary. *November's Wheel.*
Moeri, Louise. *Save Queen of Sheba.*

Morey, Walt. *Gentle Ben; Gloomy Gus; Runaway Stallion.*
Morton, Jane. *I Am Rubber, You Are Glue.*
Muehl, Lois. *Hidden Year of Devlin Bates.*
Murphy, Barbara. *Ace Hits the Big Time; No Place to Run.*
Naylor, Phyllis. *Beetles, Lightly Toasted; Eddie, Incorporated.*
Neville, Emily. *It's Like This, Cat.*
Ney, John. *Ox Goes North; Ox, the Story of the Kid at the Top.*
Norris, Gunilla. *Standing in the Magic.*
North, Sterling. *Wolfling.*
Norton, Andre. *Seven Spells to Sunday.*
Offit, Sidney. *Adventures of Homer Fink; Boy Who Made a Million; What Kind of a Guy Do You Think I Am?*
Ogan, Margaret. *Choicy.*
Okimoto, Jean. *Jason's Women.*
Parini, Jay. *Patch Boys.*
Park, Barbara. *Maxie, Rosie and Earl—Partners in Crime.*
Parkinson, Ethelyn. *Good Old Archibald.*
Patchett, Mary. *Brumby, the Wild White Stallion; Warrimood.*
Paterson, Katherine. *Park's Quest.*
Paulsen, Gary. *Popcorn Days and Buttermilk Nights.*
Peck, Robert. *Arly; Soup; Soup and Me; Soup for President; Soup in the Saddle; Soup on Fire; Soup on Ice; Soup on Wheels; Soup's Drum; Soup's Goat; Soup's Hoop; Soup's Uncle.*
Petersen, P.J. *Good-Bye to Good Ol' Charlie.*
Peyton, Karen. *Pattern of Roses; Pennington's Last Term.*
Phipson, Joan. *Birkin.*
Pitts, Paul. *Racing the Sun.*
Place, Marian. *Juan's Eighteen Wheeler Summer.*
Platt, Kin. *Ape Inside Me; Doomsday Gang.*
Potok, Chaim. *Chosen.*
Potter, Marian. *Mark Makes His Move.*
Prince, Alison. *How's Business.*
Provost, Gary. *Good If It Goes.*
Rawls, Wilson. *Where the Red Fern Grows.*
Richard, Adrienne. *Accomplice.*
Robertson, Mary. *Tarantula and the Red Chugger.*
Robinson, Barbara. *Across from Indian Shore.*
Robinson, Jean. *Strange but Wonderful Cosmic Awareness of Duffy Moon.*
Rodgers, Raboo. *Island of Peril.*
Roos, Stephen. *Confessions of a Wayward Preppie.*
Rosenblatt, Arthur. *Smarty.*
Ruckman, Ivy. *What's an Average Kid Like Me Doing Way Up Here?*
Sachar, Louis. *There's a Boy in the Girls' Bathroom.*
Salinger, J.D. *Catcher in the Rye.*
Savitz, Harriet. *Fly, Wheels, Fly.*
Schneider, Benjamin. *Winter Patriot.*
Schwartz, Joel. *Upchuck Summer.*

Brothers

See also: Brothers and Sisters

Brothers and Sisters

See also: Brothers; Sisters

Bullies

Honeycutt, Natalie. *All New Jonah Twist.*
Hopper, Nancy. *Hang On, Harvey.*
Jones, Diana. *Witch Week.*
Karl, Jean. *Beloved Benjamin Is Waiting.*
Kaufman, Stephen. *Does Anyone Know the Way to Thirteen?*
Keeton, Elizabeth. *Esmeralda.*
King, Stephen. *Carrie.*
Krumgold, Joseph. *Henry 3.*
Lipp, Frederick. *Some Lose Their Way.*
Lipsyte, Robert. *One Fat Summer.*
Lorenzo, Carol. *Heart of Snowbird.*
Mauser, Patricia. *Bundle of Sticks.*
Mazer, Harry. *War on Villa Street.*
Miles, Miska. *Gertrude's Pocket.*
Neville, Emily. *Seventeenth-Street Gang.*
Paulsen, Gary. *Dancing Carl.*
Perl, Lila. *Marleen, Horror Queen.*
Provost, Gary. *Popcorn.*
Roberts, Willo. *Magic Book.*
Robinson, Nancy. *Wendy and the Bullies.*
Sacher, Louis. *There's a Boy in the Girls' Bathroom.*
Sachs, Marilyn. *Veronica Ganz.*
Shura, Mary. *Chester; Polly Panic.*
Singer, Marilyn. *Clue in Code.*
Sivers, Brenda. *Snailman.*
Steiner, Barbara. *Oliver Dibbs and the Dinosaur Cause.*
Stolz, Mary. *Bully on Barkham Street; Dog on Barkham Street; Explorer of Barkham Street.*
Tannen, Mary. *Huntley, Nutley and the Missing Link.*
Tate, Joan. *Luke's Garden; and Gramp.*
Taylor, William. *Paradise Lane.*
Terris, Susan. *On Fire.*
Townsend, John. *Pirate's Island.*
Townsend, Susan. *Secret Diary of Adrian Mole Aged 13¾.*
Van Leeuwen, Jean. *Benjy and the Power of Zingies.*
Wellman, Manly. *River Pirates.*
Wells, Rosemary. *Through the Hidden Door.*

Buried Treasure

See: Treasure Trove

Camps and Camping

Anderson, Mary. *You Can't Get There from Here.*
Angell, Judie. *In Summertime It's Tuffy.*
Bell, William. *Crabbe's Journey.*
Blair, Cynthia. *Strawberry Summer.*
Busselle, Rebecca. *Bathing Ugly.*
Chambers, Aidan. *Seal Secret.*
Christian, Mary. *Mystery at Camp Triumph.*

Cole, Brock. *Goats.*
Conford, Ellen. *Hail, Hail, Camp Timberwood.*
Corbett, Scott. *Pippa Passes.*
Corcoran, Barbara. *August, Die She Must; Mystery on Ice; You're Allegro Dead.*
Danziger, Paula. *There's a Bat in Bunk Five.*
Derleth, August. *Ghost of Black Hawk Island.*
De Roo, Anne. *Scrub Fire.*
Duncan, Lois. *They Never Came Home.*
Dygard, Thomas. *Wilderness Peril.*
French, Michael. *Us Against Them.*
Gauch, Patricia. *Night Talks.*
George, Jean. *Hook a Fish, Catch a Mountain.*
Gilson, Jamie. *Four B Goes Wild.*
Hildick, E.W. *Ghost Squad and the Ghoul of Grunberg.*
Hodges, Margaret. *Freewheeling of Joshua Cobb; Hatching of Joshua Cobb.*
Hotchner, A.E. *Looking for Miracles.*
Howe, James. *Nighty-Nightmare.*
Johnson, Annabel. *Grizzly.*
Jones, Ron. *Acorn People.*
Kastner, Erich. *Lisa and Lottie.*
Kherdian, David. *Beyond Two Rivers; It Started with Old Man Bean.*
Klein, Robin. *Hating Alison Ashley.*
Lasky, Kathryn. *Jem's Island.*
Levy, Elizabeth. *Come Out Smiling.*
Lipsyte, Robert. *Summer Rules.*
McDonnell, Christine. *Just for the Summer.*
Manes, Stephen. *Slim Down Camp.*
Martin, Ann. *Bummer Summer.*
Miles, Betty. *Sink or Swim.*
Moe, Barbara. *Ghost Wore Knickers.*
Ney, John. *Ox Goes North.*
O'Connor, Jane. *Yours 'Till Niagara Falls.*
Park, Barbara. *Buddies.*
Pascal, Francine. *Love and Betrayal and Hold the Mayo.*
Petersen, P.J. *Going for the Big One.*
Roos, Stephen. *My Horrible Secret.*
Ruckman, Ivy. *No Way Out.*
Sachs, Marilyn. *Laura's Luck.*
Sankey, Alice. *Hit the Bike Trail.*
Schwartz, Joel. *Upchuck Summer; Upchuck Summer Revenge.*
Schwartz, Sheila. *Growing Up Guilty.*
Smith, Robert. *Jelly Belly.*
Stolz, Mary. *Wonderful, Terrible Time.*
Stren, Patti. *I Was a Fifteen-Year-Old Blimp.*
Swarthout, Glendon. *Bless the Beasts and the Children.*
Williams, Ursula. *Castle Merlin.*
Zaring, Jane. *Sharks in the North Woods.*

Cancer

See: Illness

Careers

See: Working World

Cats

Adler, Carole. *Cat That Was Left Behind.*
Alexander, Lloyd. *Cat Who Wished to Be a Man; Time Cat: The Remarkable Journeys of Jason and Gareth.*
Anderson, Mary. *F.T.C. and Company; F.T.C. Superstar.*
Angell, Judie. *Home Is to Share and Share and Share.*
Bacon, Peggy. *Ghost of Opalina.*
Baker, Margaret. *Porterhouse Major.*
Berger, Frederica. *Nuisance.*
Berna, Paul. *Clue of the Black Cat.*
Bolton, Carole. *Good-Bye Year.*
Butler, Beverly. *Ghost Cat.*
Calhoun, Mary. *Witch of Hissing Hill.*
Caufield, Don. *Never Steal a Magic Cat.*
Chambers, John. *Fritz's Winter.*
Christian, Mary. *Maltese Feline.*
Cleary, Beverly. *Socks.*
Coatsworth, Elizabeth. *Cat Who Went to Heaven.*
Coblentz, Catherine. *Blue Cat of Castletown.*
Corbett, Scott. *Turnabout Trick.*
Corcoran, Barbara. *Which Witch Is Which?*
Curry, Jane. *Parsley, Sage, Rosemary and Time.*
De Weese, Gene. *Calvin Nullifer; Dandelion Caper.*
Estes, Eleanor. *Pinky Pye.*
Feagles, Anita. *Twenty-Seven Cats Next Door.*
Fisher, Lois. *Puffy P. Pushycat, Problem Solver.*
Fosburgh, Liza. *Bella Arabelle.*
Fry, Rosalie. *Matelot, Little Sailor of Brittany.*
Gates, Doris. *Cat and Mrs. Cary.*
Goldberger, Judith. *Looking Glass Factor.*
Graeber, Charlotte. *Mustard.*
Gray, Nicholas. *Grimbold's Other World.*
Greaves, Margaret. *Cat's Magic.*
Griffiths, G.D. *Abandoned.*
Griffiths, Helen. *Mysterious Appearance of Agnes; Russian Blue.*
Haas, Dorothy. *Poppy and the Outdoors Cat.*
Hahn, Mary. *Doll in the Garden; A Ghost Story.*
Heide, Florence. *Mystery of the Silver Tag.*
Hildick, E.W. *Case of the Condemned Cat; Cat Called Amnesia; Manhattan Is Missing.*
Howe, James. *Bunnicula; Celery Stalks at Midnight.*
Hurwitz, Johanna. *Hurricane Elaine.*
King, Stephen. *Pet Sematary.*
King-Smith, Dick. *Martin's Mice; Mouse Boucher.*
Kurtz, Katherine. *Legacy of Lehr.*

Lattimore, Eleanor. *Felicia.*
Lawson, Robert. *Captain Kidd's Cat.*
Lisle, Janet. *Dancing Cats of Applesap.*
Little, Mary. *Old Cat and the Kitten.*
McHargue, Georgess. *See You Later, Crocodile.*
McHugh, Elisabet. *Beethoven's Cat; Wiggie Wins the West.*
McIntyre, Vonda. *Barbary.*
Majors, G. *Who Would Want to Kill Hallie Pankey's Cat?*
Michaels, Barbara. *Here I Stay.*
Nash, Mary. *Mrs. Coverlet's Detectives.*
Neville, Emily. *It's Like This, Cat.*
Nixon, Joan. *Gift.*
Norton, Andre. *Star Ka'at; Star Ka'at and the Plant People; Star Ka'at's World; Star Ka'at and the Winged Warriors; Uncharted Stars; Year of the Unicorn; Zero Stone.*
Orgel, Doris. *Whiskers Once and Always.*
Parsons, Elizabeth. *Upside-Down Cat.*
Patchett, Mary. *End of the Outlaws.*
Roberts, Willo. *More Minder Curses.*
Robinson, Nancy. *Just Plain Cat.*
Roos, Kelly. *Incredible Cat Caper.*
Ruckman, Ivy. *Melba the Brain.*
Sachs, Elizabeth-Ann. *Shyster.*
Senn, Steve. *Born of Flame; Spacebread.*
Shura, Mary. *Mary's Marvelous Mouse; Search for Grissi.*
Singer, Marilyn. *Where There's a Will, There's a Wag.*
Sleigh, Barbara. *Carbonel, King of the Cats; Kingdom of Carbonel.*
Smith, Alison. *Help! There's a Cat Washing in Here.*
Steele, Mary. *Life (and Death) of Sarah Elizabeth Harwood.*
Stolz, Mary. *Cat in the Mirror; Cat Walk.*
Swinnerton, A.R. *Rocky the Cat.*
Taylor, Theodore. *Sniper.*
Townsend, J. David. *Cats Stand Accused.*
Tuttle, Lisa. *Catwitch.*
Veglahn, Nancy. *Follow the Golden Goose.*
Wagner, Jane. *J.T.*
Wallace, Bill. *Snot Stew.*
Walter, Mildred. *Lillie of Watts; A Birthday Discovery.*
Weber, Judith. *Lights, Camera, Cats.*
Williams, Tad. *Tailchaser's Song.*
Williams, Ursula. *Island Mackenzie.*
Woolley, Catherine. *Ginnie and the Mystery Cat.*
Wright, Betty. *My New Mom and Me.*
York, Carol. *Dead Man's Cat.*

Child Abuse

Asher, Sandy. *Things Are Seldom What They Seem.*
Avi. *Sometimes I Think I Hear My Name.*
Baehr, Patricia. *Falling Scales.*

Bates, Betty. *It Must've Been the Fish Sticks.*
Branscum, Robbie. *Girl; To the Tune of a Hickory Stick.*
Bulla, Clyde. *Benito.*
Burch, Jennings. *They Cage the Animals at Night.*
Byars, Betsy. *Pinballs.*
Childress, Alice. *Rainbow Jordan.*
Cole, Barbara. *Don't Tell a Soul.*
Conrad, Pam. *Holding Me Here.*
Corcoran, Barbara. *Winds of Time.*
Cross, Gillian. *On the Edge.*
Crutcher, Chris. *Chinese Handcuffs.*
Culin, Charlotte. *Cages of Glass, Flowers of Time.*
Cunningham, Julia. *Burnish Me Bright; Come to the Edge.*
D'Ambrosio, Richard. *No Language But a Cry.*
Davies, Peter. *Fly Away Paul.*
Dixon, Paige. *Walk My Way.*
Dorman, N.B. *Laughter in the Background.*
Fairfax-Lucy, Brian. *Children of the House.*
Geller, Mark. *Raymond.*
Grant, Cynthia. *Kumquat May, I'll Always Love You.*
Hall, Lynn. *Boy in the Off-White Hat.*
Hermes, Patricia. *Solitary Secret.*
Holland, Barbara. *Creepy-Mouse Coming to Get You.*
Howard, Ellen. *Gilly Flower.*
Hunt, Irene. *Lottery Rose.*
Irwin, Hadley. *Abby, My Love.*
Jacoby, Alice. *My Mother's Boyfriend and Me.*
Johnson, Annabel. *Memory of Dragons.*
Jones, Diana. *Eight Days of Luke.*
Klass, Sheila. *To See My Mother Dance.*
Klein, Norma. *Bizou; Snapshots.*
Lunn, Janet. *Root Cellar.*
McCracken, Mary. *Lovey: A Very Special Child.*
MacDonald, Shelagh. *No End to Yesterday.*
MacPherson, Margaret. *Rough Road.*
Magorian, Michelle. *Good Night, Mr. Tom.*
Mathieson, Theodore. *Island in the Sand.*
Mazer, Norma. *Silver.*
Miklowitz, Gloria. *Secrets Not Meant to Be Kept.*
Moeri, Louise. *Girl Who Lived on the Ferris Wheel.*
Morrison, Toni. *Bluest Eye.*
Nathanson, Laura. *Trouble with Wednesday.*
O'Hanlon, Jacklyn. *Fair Game.*
Orr, Rebecca. *Gunner's Run.*
Pendergraft, Patricia. *Hear the Wind Blow; Miracle at Clement's Pond.*
Petersen, P.J. *Going for the Big One.*
Reeves, Bruce. *Street Smarts.*
Roberts, Willo. *Don't Hurt Laurie; Megan's Island.*
Sachs, Marilyn. *December Tale; Bear's House.*
Schlee, Ann. *Ask Me No Questions.*
Schneider, Jennifer. *Daybreak Man.*
Simons, Wendy. *Harper's Mother.*
Smith, Doris. *Tough Chauncey.*

Smith, Marya. *Winter Broker.*
Snyder, Zilpha. *And Condors Danced.*
Strang, Celia. *This Child Is Mine.*
Sturgeon, Theodore. *Dreaming Jewels.*
Sutcliff, Rosemary. *Witch's Brat.*
Swan, Helen. *Dear Elizabeth: Diary of an Adolescent Victim of.*
Sweeney, Joyce. *Center Line.*
Talbert, Marc. *Paper Knife.*
Tapp, Kathy. *Sacred Circle of the Hula Hoop.*
Taylor, William. *Paradise Lane.*
Thrasher, Crystal. *End of a Dark Road.*
Walker, Diana. *Hundred Thousand Dollar Farm.*
Woolverton, Linda. *Running Before the Wind.*
Zindel, Paul. *To Take a Dare.*

Circus

Alcock, Vivien. *Travelers by Night.*
Alcott, Louisa May. *Under the Lilacs.*
Alexander, Lloyd. *Marvelous Misadventures of Sebastian.*
Ashley, Bernard. *Dodgem.*
Bacon, Martha. *In the Company of Clowns.*
Beatty, Patricia. *How Many Miles to Sundown?*
Bradley, Michel. *Norwood Tor.*
Brooks, Walter. *Freddy and the Men from Mars.*
Chekov, Anton. *Kashtanka.*
Cunningham, Julia. *Far in the Day.*
Du Bois, William. *Alligator Case.*
Kastner, Erich. *Little Man; Little Man and the Big Thief.*
Lofting, Hugh. *Dr. Dolittle's Caravan; Dr. Dolittle's Circus.*
Malot, Hector. *Foundling.*
Norton, Andre. *Green Dragon.*
Otis, James. *Toby Tyler; or Ten Weeks with a Circus.*
Perl, Lila. *Tybee Trimble's Hard Times.*
Rounds, Glen. *Day the Circus Came to Lone Tree.*
Spence, Eleanor. *Green Laurel.*
Sturgeon, Theodore. *Dreaming Jewels.*
Wismer, Donald. *Starluck.*
Wormser, Richard. *Kidnapped Circus.*

Civil War, American

Allan, Mabel. *Johnny Reb.*
Beatty, Patricia. *Charley Skedaddle; Turn Homeward, Hannalee.*
Bell, Bertrude. *Posse of Two.*
Bonham, Frank. *Honor Bound.*
Brick, John. *Yankees on the Run.*
Burchard, Peter. *Jed; North by Night; Rat Hell.*
Clapp, Patricia. *Tamarack Tree.*
Climo, Shirley. *Month of Seven Days.*
Dick, Trella. *Island on the Border.*

Hall, Anna. *Cyrus Holt and the Civil War.*
Hansen, Joyce. *Which Way to Freedom?*
Harris, Christie. *Confessions of a Toe-Hanger.*
Haugaard, Erik. *Orphans of the Wind.*
Hickman, Janet. *Zoar Blue.*
Hunt, Irene. *Across Five Aprils.*
Kassem, Lou. *Listen for Rachel.*
Keith, Harold. *Rifles for Watie.*
Lawson, John. *Spring Rider.*
McGiffin, Lee. *Coat for Private Patrick; Horse Hunters.*
Meader, Stephen. *Muddy Road to Glory; Phantom of the Blockade.*
Moore, S.E. *Secret Island.*
Norton, Andre. *Rebel Spurs.*
Shore, Laura. *Sacred Moon Tree.*
Sneve, Virginia. *Betrayed.*
Taylor, Florence. *Gold Dust and Bullets.*
Wellman, Manly. *Ghost Battalion; Ride, Rebels!*
Wisler, G. Clifton. *Thunder on the Tennessee.*
Yep, Laurence. *Mark Twain Murders.*

Classics

Alcott, Louisa May. *Eight Cousins; Jo's Boys and How They Turned Out; Little Men; Little Women; Old Fashioned Girl; Rose in Bloom.*
Brontë, Charlotte. *Jane Eyre.*
Brontë, Emily. *Wuthering Heights.*
Bunyan, John. *Pilgrim's Progress.*
Carroll, Lewis. *Alice's Adventures in Wonderland; Through the Looking Glass.*
Cather, Willa. *My Antonia.*
Cervantes, Miguel. *Don Quixote de la Mancha.*
Coolidge, Susan. *What Katy Did.*
Cooper, James. *Last of the Mohicans.*
Defoe, Daniel. *Robinson Crusoe.*
Dickens, Charles. *David Copperfield; Great Expectations; Oliver Twist.*
Dodge, Mary. *Hans Brinker.*
Dumas, Alexandre. *Three Musketeers.*
Du Maurier, Daphne. *Rebecca.*
Eliot, George. *Silas Marner.*
Grahame, Kenneth. *Wind in the Willows.*
Hale, Edward E. *Man Without a Country.*
Hugo, Victor. *Hunchback of Notre Dame.*
Huxley, Aldous. *Brave New World.*
Irving, Washington. *Legend of Sleepy Hollow; Rip Van Winkle.*
Jackson, Helen. *Ramona.*
Kipling, Rudyard. *Captains Courageous.*
Knight, Eric. *Lassie Come Home.*
London, Jack. *Call of the Wild.*
Milne, A.A. *House at Pooh Corner; Winnie the Pooh.*
Montgomery, Lucy. *Anne of Green Gables.*
Nesbit, Edith. *Story of the Treasure Seekers.*
O. Henry. *Gift of the Magi.*
Orwell, George. *Animal Farm; Nineteen Eighty-Four.*

Poe, Edgar Allan. *Fall of the House of Usher.*
Pyle, Howard. *Men of Iron; Merry Adventures of Robin Hood; Otto of the Silver Hand.*
Rawlings, Marjorie. *Yearling.*
Ruskin, John. *King of the Golden River.*
Salinger, J.D. *Catcher in the Rye.*
Shelley, Mary. *Frankenstein.*
Steinbeck, John. *Of Mice and Men.*
Stevenson, Robert. *Kidnapped; Strange Case of Dr. Jekyll and Mr. Hyde; Treasure Island.*
Swift, Jonathan. *Gulliver's Travels.*
Tolkien, J.R.R. *Hobbit.*
Twain, Mark. *Adventures of Huckleberry Finn; Prince and the Pauper; Adventures of Tom Sawyer.*
Verne, Jules. *Around the World in Eighty Days; Twenty Thousand Leagues Under the Sea.*
White, E.B. *Charlotte's Web.*
Wyss, Johann. *Swiss Family Robinson.*

Cloning

Ames, Mildred. *Anna to the Infinite Power.*
Cooper, Margaret. *Code Name: Clone; Solution: Escape.*
MacGregor, Ellen. *Miss Pickerell Takes the Bull by the Horns.*
Slote, Alfred. *Clone Catcher.*
Vinge, Joan. *Snow Queen.*

College

Archibald, Joe. *Crazy Legs McBain; Powerback.*
Arundel, Honor. *Terrible Temptation.*
Bolton, Carole. *Never Jam Today.*
Bonnell, Dorothy. *Why Did You Go to College, Linda Warren?*
Bowen, Robert. *Hot Corner Blues.*
Bowers, John. *November . . . December.*
Bunting, Eve. *Will You Be My POSSLQ.*
Butler, Beverly. *Gift of Gold; Light a Single Candle.*
Dahl, Borghild. *This Precious Year.*
Dailey, Virginia. *Keys to Lawrence House.*
Du Jardin, Rosamond. *Double Feature; Real Thing; Showboat Summer.*
Dygard, Thomas. *Quarterback Walk-On.*
Etter, Les. *Morning Glory Quarterback.*
Francis, Helen. *Big Swat.*
Gault, William. *Little Big Foot.*
Girion, Barbara. *In the Middle of a Rainbow.*
Goffstein, M.B. *Underside of the Leaf.*
Hager, Alice. *Love's Golden Circle.*
Hagon, Priscilla. *Mystery at the Villa Blanca.*
Hawes, Evelyn. *Madras-Type Jacket.*
Heyman, Anita. *Final Grades.*
Jackson, C. Paul. *Bud Baker, College Pitcher; Rose Bowl Pro.*

Colonial America

Computers

Contemporary Issues

See also: Drug Abuse; Ecology; Poverty; Women's Rights; Racial Interaction

Aldiss, Brian. *Year Before Yesterday.*
Archer, Jeffrey. *Shall We Tell the President?*
Bograd, Larry. *Kolokol Papers; Los Alamos Light.*
Bonham, Frank. *Chief.*
Boutis, Victoria. *Looking Out.*
Bryan, C.D. *Friendly Fire.*
Bunting, Eve. *Mother, How Could You; Surrogate Sister.*
Burton, Hester. *Time of Trial.*
Catherall, Arthur. *Yugoslav Mystery.*
Conford, Ellen. *Genie with the Light Blue Hair.*
Corcoran, Barbara. *Strike.*
Cormier, Robert. *I Am the Cheese.*
Dizenzo, Patricia. *Why Me?*
Dunne, Mary. *Reach Out, Ricardo.*
Eyerly, Jeannette. *Radigan Cares.*
Facklam, Margery. *Trouble with Mothers.*
Feagles, Anita. *Twenty-Seven Cats Next Door.*
Gold, Sharlya. *Time to Take Sides.*
Hentoff, Nat. *Day They Came to Arrest the Book; In the Country of Ourselves.*
Johnson, Annabel. *Last Knife.*
Kalb, Jonah. *Kids' Candidate.*
Kerr, Helen. *Grave Allegra.*
Kerr, M.E. *What I Really Think of You.*
Kingman, Lee. *Peter Pan Bag.*
Knott, Bill. *Dwarf on Black Mountain.*
Koertge, Ron. *Where the Kissing Never Stops.*
Lang, Othmar. *If You Are Silenced, I Will Speak for You.*
McCarty, Rega. *Lorna Evan: Social Worker.*
Marek, Magot. *Matt's Crusade.*
Miles, Betty. *Maudie and Me and the Dirty Book.*
Molarsky, Osmond. *Montalvo Bay.*
Muehl, Lois. *Worst Room in the School.*
Mulford, Philippa. *If It's Not Funny, Why Am I Laughing?*
Myers, Walter. *Nicholas Factor.*
Orwell, George. *Animal Farm.*
Pfeffer, Susan. *Matter of Principal.*
Pinkwater, Jill. *Buffalo Brenda.*
Rockwood, Joyce. *Enoch's Place.*
Sacks, Margaret. *Beyond Safe Boundaries.*
Smith, Dennis. *Final Fire.*
Smith, Doris. *Moonshadow of Cherry Mountain; Return to Bitter Creek.*
Tolan, Stephanie. *Great Skinner Strike.*
Townsend, John. *Kate and the Revolution.*
Young, Bob. *One Small Voice.*

Countries Other Than United States

Almedinger, E.M. *Crimson Oak.* (Russia)
Baer, Edith. *Frost in the Night.* (Germany)
Beatty, Patricia. *Bad Bell of San Salvador.*
Bloch, Marie. *Bern, Son of Mikula.* (Kiev)
Bograd, Larry. *Kolokol Papers.* (Russia)

Bonzon, Paul. *Orphans of Simitra.* (Holland)
Buck, Pearl. *Big Wave* (Japan); *Matthew, Mark, Luke and John.* (Korea)
Butterworth, Oliver. *Narrow Passage.* (France)
Cameron, Ann. *Most Beautiful Place in the World.* (Guatemala)
Carlson, Natalie. *Family Under the Bridge.* (France)
Catherall, Arthur. *Man-Eater* (India); *Yugoslav Mystery.*
Channel, A.R. *Jungle Rescue.* (India)
Chapin, Henry. *Spiro of the Sponge Fleet.* (Greece)
Chauncy, Nan. *Devil's Hill; Half a World Away.* (Tasmania)
Chukovskii, Kornei. *Silver Crest.* (Russia)
Clark, Ann. *Secret of the Andies* (Peru); *To Stand Against the Wind.* (Vietnam)
Clewes, Dorothy. *Mystery of the Jade-Green Cadillac.* (Austria)
Clifford, Mary. *Salah of Sierra Leone.*
Cohen, Miriam. *Born to Dance Sambe.* (Argentina)
Corbin, William. *Prettiest Gargoyle.* (France)
Cordell, Alexander. *Healing Blade; White Cockade.* (Ireland)
Crayder, Dorothy. *She and Dubious Three.* (Italy)
Degens, T. *Transport 7-41-R.* (Germany)
De Jong, Meindert. *House of Sixty Fathers* (China); *Wheel on the School.* (Netherlands)
Dickinson, Peter. *Tulku.* (Tibet)
Dillon, Eilis. *Sea Wall.* (Ireland)
Dinneen, Betty. *Luck of Leopards.* (Kenya)
Du Bois, Theodora. *Tiger Burning Bright.* (India)
Durrell, Gerald. *Donkey Rustlers.* (Greece)
Ellis, Ella. *Roam the Wild Country.* (Argentina)
Evarts, Hal. *Smugglers' Road.* (Mexico)
Farley, Carol. *Ms. Isabell Corell, Herself.* (Korea)
Fenton, Edward. *Morning of the Gods.* (Greece)
Fisher, Leonard. *Russian Farewell.*
Forman, James. *Call Back Yesterday.* (Saudi Arabia)
Fortune, J.J. *Duel for the Samurai Sword.* (Japan)
Fritz, Jean. *Homesick: My Own Story.* (China)
Frost, Kelman. *Exiles in the Sahara; Men of the Mirage.* (Sahara)
Fry, Rosalie. *Echo's Song.* (Wales)
Fukei, Arlene. *East to Freedom.* (China)
Garlan, Patricia. *Boy Who Played Tiger; Orange-Robed Boy.* (Burma)
Gessner, Lynne. *Edge of Darkness.* (Latvia)
Ginsburg, Mirra. *Diary of Nina Kosterina.* (Russia)
Graham, Lorenz. *I, Momolu.* (Liberia)
Gray, Patricia. *Loco, the Bronco.* (Mexico)
Green, Robert. *Hawk of the Nile* (Egypt); *Whistling Sword.* (Mongolia)
Guillot, Rene. *Grishka and the Wolves; Mokokambo, Lost Tail.* (Russia)
Hallard, Peter. *Kalu and the Wild Boar.* (India)
Hallquist, Britt. *Search for Fredrick.* (Sweden)

Courage

Baudouy, Michel. *More Than Courage.*
Beatty, Patricia. *Charley Skedaddle.*
Bell, Margaret. *To Peril Strait.*
Berna, Paul. *Flood Warning.*
Bernhardsen, Christian. *Fight in the Mountains.*
Bethancourt, T.E. *Nightmare Town.*
Burleigh, David. *Messenger from K'Itai.*
Callaway, Kathy. *Bloodroot Flower.*
Catherall, Arthur. *Man-Eater.*
Channel, A.R. *Jungle Rescue.*
Chapin, Henry. *Spiro of the Sponge Fleet.*
Constant, Alberta. *Willie and the Wildcat Well.*
Cookson, Catherine. *Mrs. Flannagan's Trumpet.*
Cordell, Alexander. *Traitor Within.*
Cotich, Felicia. *Valda.*
Cross, Gillian. *Born of the Sun.*
Darke, Marjorie. *Question of Courage.*
De Leeuw, C. *Fear in the Forest.*
Dickinson, Peter. *Annerton Pit.*
Distad, Audree. *Dream Runner.*
Duncan, Jane. *Camerons on the Hill.*
Dunn, Marylois. *Absolutely Perfect Horse.*
Edmonds, Walter. *Matchlock Gun.*
Edwards, S. *When the World's on Fire.*
Epstein, Samuel. *Jackknife for a Penny.*
Evenhuis, Gertie. *What About Me?*
Fall, Thomas. *Wild Boy.*
Finlayson, Ann. *Rebecca's War; Silver Bullet.*
Fisher, Laura. *Never Try Nathaniel.*
Flory, Jane. *Time for the Towpath.*
Fritz, Jean. *Brady.*
Garlan, Patricia. *Boy Who Played Tiger.*
George, Jean. *My Side of the Mountain.*
Gibbs, Alonzo. *Least Likely One.*
Griese, Arnold. *Way of Our People.*
Halvorson, Marilyn. *Hold On, Geronimo.*
Hamilton, Virginia. *Willie Bea and the Time the Martians Landed.*
Harmon, Lyn. *Flight to Jewell Island.*
Harris, Robbie. *Rosie's Double Dare.*
Holm, Anne. *North to Freedom.*
Houston, James. *Black Diamonds; Frozen Fire.*
Innis, Pauline. *Wind of the Pampas.*
Ipcar, Dahlov. *Queen of Spells.*
Johnson, Annabel. *Grizzly.*
Kipling, Rudyard. *Kim.*
Lazarus, Keo. *Rattlesnake Run.*
Lindquist, Willis. *Burma Boy.*
McGraw, Eloise. *Master Cornhill.*
McSwigan, Marie. *Snow Treasure.*
Naylor, Phyllis. *One of the Third Grade Thonkers.*
O'Brien, Andy. *Hockey Wingman.*
Ottley, Reginald. *Roan Colt.*
Place, Marian. *Juan's Eighteen Wheeler Summer.*
Polland, Madeleine. *Town Across the Water.*
Potter, Bronson. *Antonio.*
Prince, Alison. *How's Business.*
Richer, Robert. *Rudi of the Mountain.*
Robinson, Veronica. *David in Silence.*
Rodman, M. *Odyssey of Courage.*
Ruckman, Ivy. *Night of the Twister.*
Savitz, Harriet. *Lionhearted.*

Schaeffer, Jack. *Shane.*
Schneider, Benjamin. *Winter Patriot.*
Sefton, Catherine. *Island of Strangers.*
Shemin, Margaretha. *Empty Moat.*
Singer, Marilyn. *It Can't Hurt Forever.*
Smith, Pauline. *Brush Fire.*
Southall, Ivan. *Hills End.*
Sperry, Armstrong. *Call It Courage.*
Steele, William. *Tomahawk Border.*
Sutcliff, Rosemary. *Sun Horse, Moon Horse.*
Thiele, Colin. *Blue Fin.*
Thompson, Eileen. *Golden Coyote.*
Treece, Henry. *Splintered Sword.*
Wild, Elizabeth. *Along Came a Blackbird.*
Yolen, Jane. *Devil's Arithmetic.*

Crimes

See also: Delinquency; Kidnapping; Smuggling; Stealing

Adler, Carole. *Evidence That Wasn't There.*
Alcock, Gudrun. *Turn the Next Corner.*
Allan, Mabel. *Rising Tide; Sign of the Unicorn.*
Anderson, Rachel. *Poacher's Son.*
Ashley, Bernard. *Kind of Wild Justice.*
Atkinson, Linda. *Hit and Run.*
Avi. *Man from the Sky.*
Beatty, John. *Royal Dirk.*
Beatty, Patricia. *Staffordshire Terror.*
Bennett, Jay. *Deadly Gift.*
Bentley, Phyllis. *Forgery.*
Berna, Paul. *Clue of the Black Cat.*
Billington, Elizabeth. *Move.*
Blakey, Madge. *Calypso Island.*
Bograd, Larry. *Bad Apple.*
Bonham, Frank. *Cool Cat; Durango Street.*
Brown, Roy. *No Through Road.*
Bunting, Eve. *Someone Is Hiding on Alcatraz Island; Sudden Silence.*
Burchard, Peter. *Stranded; Story of New York.*
Butters, Dorothy. *Ten Leagues to Boston Town.*
Butterworth, W.E. *Leroy and the Old Man.*
Callen, Larry. *Muskrat War.*
Campbell, Barbara. *Girl Called Bob and a Horse Called Yoki.*
Carlson, Dale. *Baby Needs Shoes.*
Catherall, Arthur. *Lapland Outlaw.*
Cebulish, Mel. *Hot Like the Sun.*
Chaikin, Miriam. *Finders Weepers.*
Chambers, John. *Showdown at Apple Hill.*
Christgau, Alice. *Runaway to Glory.*
Christopher, Matt. *Tackle Without a Team.*
Clark, Margaret. *Mystery of Sebastian Island.*
Clark, Mavis. *Sky Is Free.*
Clifford, Eth. *Just Tell Me When We're Dead.*
Clymer, Eleanor. *My Brother Stevie.*
Cohen, Peter. *Calm Horse, Wild Night; Deadly Game at Stony Creek.*
Conford, Ellen. *Hail, Hail, Camp Timberwood.*
Cookson, Catherine. *Nipper.*

Stephens, Peter. *Towapper, Puritan Renegade.*
Stevens, Shane. *Rat Pack.*
Tavo, Gus. *Trail to Lone Canyon.*
Terris, Susan. *On Fire.*
Thompson, Estelle. *Hunter in the Dark.*
Thompson, Julian. *Grounding of Group 6; Simon Pure.*
Touster, Irwin. *Perez Arson Mystery; Runaway Bus Mystery.*
Townsend, John. *Trouble in the Jungle.*
Turner, Phillip. *Steam on the Line.*
Turngren, Annette. *Mystery Enters the Hospital.*
Underwood, Michael. *Goddess of Death.*
Unsworth, Walter. *Grimsdyke.*
Waldron, Ann. *Blueberry Collection.*
Wales, Robert. *Harry.*
Wallin, Luke. *Redneck Poacher's Son.*
Watson, Sally. *Linnet.*
Weir, Rosemary. *Heirs of Ashton Manor.*
Westlake, Donald. *Why Me?*
White, Ellen. *Life Without Friends.*
White, Robb. *Deathwatch; Fire Storm.*
Winn, Janet. *Home in Flames.*
Woolley, Catherine. *Libby Shadows a Lady.*
Wright, Billy. *Ghosts Beneath Our Feet.*
York, Carol. *Nothing Ever Happens Here.*

Cults

Ames, Mildred. *Silver Link, the Silken Tie.*
Bethancourt, T.E. *Instruments of Darkness; Nightmare Town.*
Brancato, Robin. *Blinded by the Light.*
Green, Phyllis. *Empty Seat.*
Klein, Robin. *People Might Hear You.*
Leonard, Constance. *Aground.*
Miklowitz, Gloria. *Love Bombers.*
Newman, Robert. *Case of the Indian Curse.*
Pinkwater, Jill. *Disappearance of Sister Perfect.*
Tolan, Stephanie. *Good Courage.*
Veglahn, Nancy. *Fellowship of the Seven Stars.*

Dancing

See: Ballet

Deafness

Andrews, Jean. *Flying Fingers Club.*
Aseltine, Lorraine. *I'm Deaf and It's Okay.*
Clark, Margaret. *Who Stole Kathy Young?*
Corcoran, Barbara. *Dance to Still Music.*
Cowley, Joy. *Silent One.*
Hanlon, Emily. *Swing.*
Hlibok, Bruce. *Silent Dancer.*
Levine, Edna. *Lisa and Her Soundless World.*

Miller, Frances. *Truth Trap.*
Pollock, Penny. *Keeping It a Secret.*
Riskind, Mary. *Apple Is My Sign.*
Robinson, Veronica. *David in Silence.*
Smith, Vian. *Martin Rides the Moor.*
Sorenson, Jody. *Secret Letters of Mama Cat.*
Spence, Eleanor. *Nothing Place.*
Teale, Edwin. *Lost Dog.*
Wojciechowska, Maia. *Single Light.*

Death

Angell, Judie. *Ronnie and Rosey.*
Arundel, Honor. *Blanket Word.*
Bacon, Katherine. *Shadow and Light.*
Barford, Carol. *Let Me Hear the Music.*
Bauer, Marion. *On My Honor.*
Benchley, Nathaniel. *Necessary End.*
Bennett, Jay. *Executioner.*
Blinn, William. *Brian's Song.*
Blue, Rose. *Grandma Didn't Wave Back.*
Blume, Judy. *Tiger Eyes.*
Bond, Nancy. *Place to Come Back To.*
Bradbury, Bianca. *Red Sky at Night.*
Brown, Ray. *Suicide Course.*
Byars, Betsy. *Good-Bye, Chicken Little.*
Carner, C. *Tawny.*
Carter, Alden. *Sheila's Dying.*
Chambers, Aidan. *Dance on My Grave.*
Cleaver, Vera. *Belle Pruitt; Grover.*
Colman, Hila. *Suddenly.*
Cormier, Robert. *Bumblebee Flies Anyway.*
Craven, Margaret. *I Heard the Owl Call My Name.*
Crawford, Charles. *Three-Legged Race.*
Deaver, Julie. *Say Goodnight, Gracie.*
Dixon, Paige. *Skipper.*
Ellis, Sarah. *Family Project.*
Farley, Carol. *Bunch on McKellahan Street; Garden Is Doing Fine.*
Girion, Barbara. *Tangle of Roots.*
Glaser, Dianne. *Diary of Trilby Frost.*
Grant, Cynthia. *Phoenix Rising.*
Greenberg, Jan. *Season In-Between.*
Greene, Constance. *Beat the Turtle Drum; Double and Dare O'Toole.*
Guest, Judith. *Ordinary Problems.*
Hamilton, Virginia. *Sweet Whispers, Brother Rush.*
Hermes, Patricia. *Nobody's Fault?*
Hillinger, Brad. *Wings Are Gone.*
Holl, Kristi. *Rose Beyond the Wall.*
Holman, Felice. *Year to Grow.*
Horwitz, Joshua. *Only Birds and Angels Fly.*
Hughes, Monica. *Hunter in the Dark.*
Hunter, Mollie. *Sound of Chariots.*
Ipswitch, Elaine. *Scott Was Here.*
Jacobs, Anita. *Where Has Deedie Wooster Been All These Years?*
Jones, Rebecca. *Angie and Me.*

Kaplan, Bess. *Empty Chair.*
Lawrence, Louise. *Sing and Scatter Daisies.*
Lee, Mildred. *Fog.*
Lee, Virginia. *Magic Moth.*
Leonard, Alison. *Tina's Chance.*
Lindgren, Astrid. *Brothers Lionheart.*
Little, Jean. *Home from Far; Mama's Going to Buy You a Mockingbird.*
Lowry, Lois. *Summer to Die.*
Manes, Stephen. *I'll Live.*
Mann, Peggy. *There Are Two Kinds of Terrible.*
Mazer, Harry. *When the Phone Rang.*
Mazer, Norma. *After the Rain.*
Miles, Miska. *Annie and the Old One.*
Mills, Claudia. *All the Living.*
Miner, Jane. *Mountain Fear.*
Murphy, Jim. *Death Run.*
Nye, Peter. *Storm.*
Orgel, Doris. *Mulberry Music.*
Paterson, Katherine. *Bridge to Terabithia.*
Peck, Richard. *Close Enough to Touch; Remembering the Good Times.*
Ruckman, Ivy. *This Is Your Captain Speaking.*
St. John, Wylly. *Ghost Next Door.*
Skorpen, Liesel. *Grace.*
Smith, Doris. *Taste of Blackberries.*
Smith, Marya. *Across the Creek.*
Steele, Mary. *Life (and Death) of Sarah Elizabeth Harwood.*
Stolz, Mary. *Edge of Next Year.*
Strasser, Todd. *Friends Till the End.*
Taha, Karen. *Gift for Tia Rosa.*
Talbert, Marc. *Dead Birds Singing.*
Tate, Joan. *Luke's Garden; and Gramp.*
Ter Haar, Jaap. *World of Ben Lighthart.*
Walker, Alice. *To Hell with Dying.*
Walker, Pamela. *Twyla.*
Windsor, Patricia. *Summer Before.*
Wood, Phyllis. *Then I'll Be Home Free.*

Delinquency

Agle, Nan. *Joe Bean.*
Alcock, Gudrun. *Run, Westy, Run.*
Anckarsvard, Karin. *Madcap Mystery; Robber Ghost.*
Ashley, Bernard. *Kind of Wild Justice; Terry on the Fence.*
Bawden, Nina. *Robbers.*
Bell, W. Bruce. *Little Dab of Color.*
Bonham, Frank. *Viva Chicano.*
Bradbury, Bianca. *Three Keys.*
Broderick, Dorothy. *Hank.*
Burch, Robert. *Tyler, Wilkin and Skee; Wilkin's Ghost.*
Butler, William. *Butterfly Revolution.*
Canning, Victor. *Runaways.*
Carlson, Dale. *Call Me Amanda.*
Carol, Bill. *Inside the Ten.*
Christian, Mary. *Dead Man in Catfish Bay.*

Cohen, Barbara. *Christmas Revolution.*
De Clements, Barthe. *Five Finger Discount.*
Dicks, Terrance. *Case of the Crooked Kids.*
Dygard, Thomas. *Halfback Tough.*
Evarts, Hal. *Smugglers' Road.*
Eyerly, Jeannette. *Angel Baker, Thief.*
Farjeon, Annabel. *Maria Lupin.*
Gold, Sharlya. *Amelia Quackenbush.*
Guy, Rosa. *Disappearance.*
Harlan, Elizabeth. *Watershed.*
Harrah, Michael. *First Offender.*
Havis, Allan. *Albert the Astronomer.*
Healey, Larry. *Angry Mountains.*
Heuman, William. *Powerhouse Five.*
Hildick, E.W. *Case of the Four Flying Fingers.*
Johnson, Annabel. *Pickpocket Run.*
Kemp, Gene. *Turbulent Term of Tyke Tiler.*
Lasky, Kathryn. *Prank.*
Lawrence, J.D. *Barnaby's Bills.*
MacCracken, Mary. *City Kid.*
McKay, Robert. *Troublemaker.*
Maddock, Reginald. *Pit.*
Morey, Walt. *Angry Waters.*
Perl, Lila. *Don't Ask Miranda.*
Petersen, P.J. *Here's to the Sophomores; Would You Settle for Improbable?*
Peyton, Karen. *Beethoven's Medal.*
Riter, Dorris. *Edge of Violence.*
Roth, David. *Hermit of Fog Hollow Station.*
Roy, Ron. *I Am a Thief.*
Rubinstein, Robert. *Who Wants to Be a Hero!*
Sachar, Louis. *Boy Who Lost His Face.*
Scott, Elaine. *Choices.*
Shaw, Richard. *Shape Up, Burke.*
Sherry, Sylvia. *Liverpool Cats.*
Snyder, Zilpha. *Changeling.*
Sortor, T. *Adventures of B.J., the Amateur Detective.*
Summers, James. *Iron Door Between.*
Williams, Jay. *Burglar Next Door.*
Winterfeld, Henry. *Trouble at Timpetill.*
Woolley, Catherine. *Chris in Trouble.*

Depression Era

See also: Poverty

Aaron, Chester. *Lackawanna.*
Avi. *Shadrach's Crossing.*
Barnwell, Robinson. *Head into the Wind.*
Bess, Clayton. *Tracks.*
Branscum, Robbie. *For Love of Judy.*
Branson, Karen. *Potatoe Eaters.*
Brink, Carol. *Winter Cottage.*
Burch, Robert. *D.J.'s Worst Enemy; Queenie Peavey.*
Byrd, Elizabeth. *It Had to Be You.*
Clarke, Tom. *Big Road.*
Cleaver, Vera. *Mock Revolt.*
Clifford, Eth. *Man Who Sang in the Dark.*
Cole, Stephen. *Growing Season.*

Coleman, Lonnie. *Orphan Jim.*
Colman, Hila. *Rachel's Legacy.*
Corcoran, Barbara. *Sky Is Falling.*
Cotich, Felicia. *Valda.*
Crofford, Emily. *Matter of Pride.*
Dahl, Borghild. *This Precious Year.*
Dodd, Wayne. *Time of Hunting.*
Edwards, Patricia. *Nilda.*
Hamner, Earl. *Homecoming; Spencer's Mountain.*
Holman, Felice. *Murderer.*
Hunt, Irene. *No Promises in the Wind.*
Huntington, Lee. *Maybe a Miracle.*
Karp, Naomi. *Nothing Rhymes with April.*
Langton, Jane. *Boyhood of Grace; Her Majesty, Grace Jones.*
Lee, Mildred. *Rock and the Willow.*
Lyon, George. *Borrowed Children.*
MacPherson, Margaret. *Rough Road.*
Malone, Mary. *Three Wishes for Sarah.*
Matthews, Ann. *Journey of Natty Gann.*
Miles, Betty. *I Would If I Could.*
Naylor, Phyllis. *Walking Through the Dark.*
Olsen, Violet. *Growing Season; View from the Pighouse Roof.*
Potter, Marian. *Blatherskite; Chance Wild Apple.*
Rabe, Berniece. *Naomi.*
Rawls, Wilson. *Where the Red Fern Grows.*
Richard, Adrienne. *Pistol.*
Skolsky, Mindy. *Whistling Teakettle.*
Slatten, Evelyn. *Good, the Bad and the Rest of Us.*
Taylor, Mildred. *Let the Circle Be Unbroken; Roll of Thunder, Hear My Cry.*
Thrasher, Crystal. *Between Dark and Daylight; Dark Didn't Catch Me; Julie's Summer; Taste of Daylight.*
Uchida, Yoshika. *Best Bad Thing; Jar of Dreams.*

Detectives

See also: Mystery; Mystery/Kidnapping; Mystery/Stealing

Aleksin, Anatoli. *Alik, the Detective.*
Anderson, Mary. *Matilda Investigates; Matilda's Masterpiece.*
Arden, William. *Mystery of the Dancing Devil; Mystery of the Dead Man's Riddle; Mystery of the Deadly Double; Mystery of the Invisible Dog; Mystery of the Purple Pirate; Mystery of the Shrinking House; Mystery of the Smashing Glass; Mystery of Wrecker's Rock; Secret of Shark Reef; Secret of the Phantom Lake.*
Arthur, Robert. *Mystery of the Cranky Collector; Mystery of the Creep Show Crooks; Mystery of the Death Trap Mine; Mystery of the Flaming Footprints; Mystery of the Missing Mermaid; Mystery of the Rogues Reunion; Mystery of the Screaming Clock; Mystery of the Stuttering Parrot; Mystery of the Trail of Terror; Mystery of the Vanishing Treasure; Mystery of the Wandering Caveman; Mystery of the Whisper-*
ing Mummy; Secret of Terror Castle.
Baker, Betty. *Night Spider Case.*
Best, Herbert. *Desmond and Dog Friday; Desmond and the Peppermint Ghost; Desmond the Dog Detective; Desmond's First Case.*
Bethancourt, T.E. *Dr. Doom, Superstar; Doris Fein, Dead Heat at Long Beach; Doris Fein, Deadly Aphrodite; Doris Fein, Legacy of Terror; Doris Fein, Mad Samurai; Doris Fein, Murder Is No Joke; Doris Fein, Phantom of the Casino; Doris Fein, Quartz Boyar; Doris Fein, Superspy.*
Brandel, Marc. *Mystery of the Two-Toed Pigeon; Mystery of the Kidnapped Whale.*
Brett, Simon. *Three Detectives and the Knight in Armor; Three Detectives and the Missing Superstar.*
Brooks, Walter. *Freddy and the Baseball Team from Mars; Freddy and the Dictator; Freddy and the Dragon; Freddy and the Flying Saucer Plans; Freddy and the Men from Mars; Freddy and the Space Ship; Freddy Goes to the North Pole; Freddy Rides Again; Freddy the Cowboy; Freddy the Detective; Freddy the Pilot.*
Carey, M.V. *Mystery of the Singing Serpent; Mystery of the Sinister Scarecrow; Secret of the Haunted Mirror.*
Chandler, Raymond. *Farewell, My Lovely.*
Christian, Mary. *Phantom of the Operetta; Sebastian, Super Sleuth; Sebastian (Super Sleuth) and the Baffling Bigfoot; Sebastian (Super Sleuth) and the Bone-to-Pick Mystery; Sebastian (Super Sleuth) and the Clumsy Cowboy; Sebastian (Super Sleuth) and the Crummy Yummies Caper; Sebastian (Super Sleuth) and the Egyptian Connection; Sebastian (Super Sleuth) and the Hair of the Dog Mystery; Sebastian (Super Sleuth) and the Purloined Sirloin; Sebastian (Super Sleuth) and the Santa Claus Caper; Sebastian (Super Sleuth) and the Secret of the Skewered Skier; Sebastian (Super Sleuth) and the Stars-in-His-Eyes Mystery.*
Christie, Agatha. *Elephants Can Remember; Evil Under the Sun; Labors of Hercules; Seven Dials Mystery; Sleeping Murder.*
Conan Doyle, Arthur. *Hound of the Baskervilles.*
Corbett, Scott. *Case of the Burgled Blessing Box; Case of the Fugitive Firebug; Case of the Gone Goose; Case of the Silver Skull; Case of the Ticklish Tooth; Cutlass Island.*
Cross, Gilbert. *Terror Train.*
Dank, Milton. *Computer Caper; Computer Game Murder; Three-D Traitors; Treasure Code; U.F.O. Has Landed.*
Derleth, August. *Irregulars Strike Again; Mill Street Irregulars: Special Detectives.*
Dicks, Terrance. *Case of the Blackmail Boys; Case of the Cinema Swindle; Case of the Cop Catchers; Case of the Crooked Kids; Case of the Ghost Grabbers; Case of the Missing Masterpiece.*
Du Bois, William. *Alligator Case; Horse in the*

Camel Suit.

Ecke, Wolfgang. *Face at the Window; Invisible Witness; Midnight Chess Game; Stolen Paintings.*

Eisenberg, Lisa. *Fast Food King; Golden Idol; House of Laughs; Tiger Rose.*

Elmore, Patricia. *Susannah and the Blue House Mystery; Susannah and the Poison Green Halloween.*

Fitzgerald, John. *Private Eye.*

Fleischman, Sid. *Bloodhound Gang and the Case of the Secret Message.*

Garden, Nancy. *Mystery of the Midnight Menace; Mystery of the Night Raiders; Mystery of the Secret Marks.*

Gardner, John. *Icebreaker; License Renewed.*

Giff, Patricia. *Have You Seen Hyacinth Macaw?; Loretta P. Sweeny, Where Are You?; Tootsie Tanner, Why Don't You Talk?*

Heide, Florence. *Black Magic at Brillstone; Body in the Brillstone Garage; Brillstone Break-In; Burning Stone at Brillstone; Deadline for McGurk; Face at the Brillstone Window; Fear at Brillstone; Hidden Box Mystery; Mystery at Keyhole Carnival; Mystery at Southport Cinema; Mystery of the Bewitched Bookmobile; Mystery of the Danger Road; Mystery of the Forgotten Island; Mystery of the Lonely Lantern; Mystery of the Macadoo Zoo; Mystery of the Melting Snowman; Mystery of the Midnight Message; Mystery of the Missing Suitcase; Mystery of the Mummy's Mask; Mystery of the Silver Tag; Mystery of the Vanishing Visitor; Mystery of the Whispering Voice; Time Bomb at Brillstone.*

Hildick, E.W. *Case of the Bashful Bank Robber; Case of the Condemned Cat; Case of the Felon's Fiddle; Case of the Four Flying Fingers; Case of the Invisible Dog; Case of the Muttering Mummy; Case of the Nervous Newsboy; Case of the Phantom Frog; Case of the Secret Scribbler; Case of the Slingshot Sniper; Case of the Snowbound Spy; Case of the Vanishing Ventriloquist; Case of the Wandering Weathervanes; Great Rabbit Rip-Off; Top Flight Fully Automated Junior High School Girl Detective.*

Howe, James. *Eat Your Poison, Dear; Stage Fright; What Eric Knew.*

Hubner, Carol. *Tattered Tallis.*

Jeffries, Roderic. *Against Time!*

Joslin, Sesyle. *Spy Lady and the Muffin Man.*

Kastner, Erich. *Emil and the Three Twins.*

Kingman, Lee. *Private Eyes; Adventures with the Saturday Gang.*

Levy, Elizabeth. *Case of the Mind-Reading Mommies.*

Lindgren, Astrid. *Bill Bergson Lives Dangerously; Bill Bergson, Master Detective.*

Meyers, Susan. *P.J. Clover, Private Eye and the Case of the Borrowed Baby; P.J. Clover, Private Eye and the Case of the Halloween Hoot; P.J. Clover, Private Eye and the Case of the*

Missing Mouse.

Murray, Marguerite. *Odin's Eye.*

Nash, Mary. *Mrs. Coverlet's Detectives.*

Newman, Robert. *Case of the Baker Street Irregulars; Case of the Etruscan Treasure; Case of the Frightened Friend; Case of the Indian Curse; Case of the Murdered Players; Case of the Somerville Secret; Case of the Threatened King; Case of the Vanishing Corpse.*

Packard, Edward. *ESP McGee.*

Platt, Kin. *Ghost of Hellshire Street; Mystery of the Witch Who Wouldn't; Sinbad and Me.*

Raskin, Ellen. *Tattooed Potato and Other Clues.*

Robertson, Keith. *Money Machine; Three Stuffed Owls.*

Rosenbloom, Joseph. *Maximilian, You're the Greatest.*

St. John, Wylly. *Mystery of the Gingerbread House.*

Sayers, Dorothy. *Murder Must Advertise.*

Simon, Seymour. *Einstein Anderson Goes to Bat; Einstein Anderson Lights Up the Sky; Einstein Anderson, Science Sleuth.*

Singer, Marilyn. *Case of the Cackling Car; Case of the Fixed Election; Case of the Sabotaged School Play; Clue in Code.*

Snyder, Zilpha. *Janie's Private Eyes.*

Sobol, Donald. *Encyclopedia Brown and the Case of the Dead Eagles; Encyclopedia Brown and the Case of the Exploding Plumbing; Encyclopedia Brown and the Case of the Midnight Visitor; Encyclopedia Brown and the Case of the Mysterious Handprints; Encyclopedia Brown and the Case of the Secret Pitch; Encyclopedia Brown and the Case of the Treasure Hunt; Encyclopedia Brown, Boy Detective; Encyclopedia Brown Carries On; Encyclopedia Brown Finds the Clues; Encyclopedia Brown Gets His Man; Encyclopedia Brown Keeps the Peace; Encyclopedia Brown Lends a Hand; Encyclopedia Brown Saves the Day; Encyclopedia Brown Sets the Pace; Encyclopedia Brown Shows the Way; Encyclopedia Brown Solves Them All; Encyclopedia Brown Takes the Case; Encyclopedia Brown Tracks Them Down.*

Sortor, T. *Adventures of B.J., the Amateur Detective.*

Stevenson, Drew. *Case of the Horrible Swamp Monster; Case of the Visiting Vampire; Case of the Wandering Werewolf.*

Van Etten, Teresa. *Dead Kachina Man.*

Vivelo, Jackie. *Super Sleuth; Super Sleuth and the Bare Bones.*

Williams, Jay. *Burglar Next Door.*

Winterfeld, Henry. *Detectives in Togas.*

Diabetics

See: Illness

Divorce

Abercrombie, Barbara. *Cat-Man's Daughter.*
Adler, Carole. *In Our House Scott Is My Brother; Silver Coach; Split Sisters.*
Ames, Mildred. *What Are Friends For?*
Arundel, Honor. *Family Failing.*
Avi. *Sometimes I Think I Hear My Name.*
Barnwell, Robinson. *Shadow on the Water.*
Bawden, Nina. *Runaway Summer.*
Berger, Frederica. *Nuisance.*
Berson, Barbara. *What's Going to Happen to Me?*
Betancourt, Jeanne. *Puppy Love.*
Blue, Rose. *Month of Sundays.*
Blume, Judy. *It's Not the End of the World.*
Carrick, Carol. *What a Wimp!*
Cavanna, Betty. *Storm in Her Heart.*
Christopher, Matt. *Fox Steals Home.*
Cleary, Beverly. *Dear Mr. Henshaw.*
Clewes, Dorothy. *Missing from Home.*
Colman, Hila. *What's the Matter with the Dobsons.*
Cone, Molly. *Amazing Memory of Harvey Bean.*
Conrad, Pam. *Holding Me Here.*
Dana, Barbara. *Necessary Parties.*
Danziger, Paula. *Divorce Express; Pistachio Prescription.*
Dexter, Patricia. *Arrow in the Wind.*
Eyerly, Jeannette. *World of Ellen March.*
Fisher, Lois. *Radio Robert.*
Fleming, Alice. *Welcome to Grossville.*
Gaeddert, Louann. *Just Like Sisters.*
Gerber, Merrill. *Please Don't Kiss Me Now.*
Giff, Patricia. *Rat Teeth.*
Greene, Constance. *Ask Anybody.*
Gregory, Diana. *Fog Burns Off by 11 O'Clock.*
Harris, Mark. *With a Wave of the Wand.*
Haven, Susan. *Maybe I'll Move to the Lost and Found.*
Hoban, Lillian. *I Met a Traveller.*
Hurwitz, Johanna. *Dede Takes Charge.*
Jukes, Mavis. *Getting Even.*
Kastner, Erich. *Lisa and Lottie.*
Kerr, M.E. *Is That You, Miss Blue?*
Klass, David. *Breakaway.*
Klein, Norma. *Breaking Up; Robbie and the Leap Year Blues; Taking Sides.*
Klevin, Jill. *Turtles Together Forever.*
Konigsburg, E.L. *Journey to an 800 Number.*
Lawrence, Mildred. *Treasure and the Song.*
Lones, Rebecca. *Madeline and the Great (Old) Escape Artist.*
McGraw, Eloise. *Hideaway.*
Madison, Winifred. *Genessee Queen.*
Mann, Peggy. *My Dad Lives in a Downtown Hotel.*
Mendonca, Susan. *Tough Choices.*
Moeri, Louise. *Girl Who Lived on the Ferris Wheel.*
Morgan, Alison. *Boy Called Fish.*

Park, Barbara. *Don't Make Me Smile.*
Pfeffer, Susan. *Dear Dad, Love Laurie.*
Platt, Kin. *Boy Who Could Make Himself Disappear.*
Richardson, Judith. *David's Landing.*
Slepian, Jan. *Getting on with It.*
Slote, Alfred. *Matt Gargan's Boy.*
Smith, Doris. *Kick a Stone Home.*
Stolz, Mary. *Go Catch a Flying Fish; Leap Before You Look.*
Stone, Bruce. *Half Nelson.*
Teibl, Margaret. *Davey Come Home.*
Tolan, Stephanie. *Liberation of Tansy Warner.*
Townsend, John. *Rob's Place.*
Wolitzer, Hilma. *Out of Love.*
Wright, Nancy. *Down the Strings.*

Doctors

See: Medical World

Dogs

Adams, Richard. *Plague Dogs.*
Adler, Carole. *Shelter on Blue Barns Road.*
Alcott, Louisa May. *Under the Lilacs.*
Ames, Mildred. *Philo Potts or the Helping Hand Strokes Again.*
Anderson, John. *Zeb.*
Andrews, Prudence. *Dog.*
Angell, Judie. *Home Is to Share and Share and Share.*
Armstrong, William. *Sounder.*
Arnosky, Jim. *Gray Boy.*
Avery, Lynn. *Cappy and the River.*
Babcock, Havilah. *Education of Pretty Boy.*
Baird, Thomas. *Finding Fever.*
Baker, Charlotte. *Cockleburr Quarters.*
Ball, Zachary. *Bristle Face; Sputters; Tent Show.*
Barlettani, Elvio. *Lamp, the Traveling Dog.*
Bauer, Marion. *Shelter from the Wind.*
Beatty, Hetty. *Bryn.*
Beatty, John. *Holdfast; Witch Dog.*
Beatty, Patricia. *Long Way to Whiskey Creek; Rufus, Red Rufus; Squaw Boy; Staffordshire Terror.*
Benary-Isbert, Margot. *Rowan Farm.*
Benjamin, Carol. *Wicked Stepdog.*
Best, Herbert. *Desmond and Dog Friday; Desmond and the Peppermint Ghost; Desmond the Dog Detective; Desmond's First Case.*
Bethancourt, T.E. *Dog Days of Arthur Cane.*
Bickman, Jack. *All the Days Were Summer.*
Borland, Hal. *Penny, the Story of a Free Minded Basset Hound.*
Branfield, John. *Why Me?*
Branscum, Robbie. *Murder of Hound Dog Bates; Toby, Granny and George.*
Brenner, Barbara. *Mystery of the Disappearing*

Levitin, Sonia. *Reigning Cats and Dogs.*
Lindgren, Astrid. *Seacrow Island.*
Little, Jane. *Spook.*
Little, Jean. *Different Dragons; Lost and Found; Mine for Keeps.*
London, Jack. *Call of the Wild.*
Lorentzen, Karen. *Lanky Longlegs.*
McGiffin, Lee. *High Whistle Charlie.*
McGraw, William. *Smoke.*
McInerney, Judith. *Judge Benjamin, Superdog; Judge Benjamin, Superdog Gift; Judge Benjamin, Superdog Rescue; Judge Benjamin, Superdog Secret; Judge Benjamin, Superdog Surprise.*
MacKellar, William. *Dog Called Porridge; Dog Like No Other; Ghost of Grannock Moor; Place by the Fire; Very Small Miracle.*
Maddox, Bill. *Rags and Patches.*
Mango, Kain. *Somewhere Green.*
Mayerson, Evelyn. *Coydog.*
Miller, Albert. *Silver Chief's Big Game Trail.*
Missieres, Nicole. *De Reina the Galgo.*
Moore, Emily. *Just My Luck.*
Morey, Walt. *Home Is the North; Kavik the Wolf Dog; Lemon Meringue Dog; Scrub Dog of Alaska.*
Morgan, Alison. *Boy Called Fish.*
Mowat, Farley. *Dog Who Wouldn't Be.*
O'Brien, John. *Return of Silver Chief; Royal Road; Silver Chief, Dog of the North; Silver Chief to the Rescue.*
Oleksy, Walter. *Quacky and the Haunted Amusement Park.*
Ottley, Reginald. *Boy Alone.*
Palmer, C.E. *Dog Called Houdini.*
Patchett, Mary. *Ajax and the Haunted Mountain; Tam the Untamed.*
Philbrook, Clem. *Ollie, the Backward Forward.*
Pinkwater, Daniel. *Jolly Roger.*
Platt, Kin. *Ghost of Hellshire Street; Mystery of the Witch Who Wouldn't; Sinbad and Me.*
Rawls, Wilson. *Where the Red Fern Grows.*
Razzi, Jim. *Search for King Pup's Tomb.*
Reese, John. *Big Mutt.*
Roach, Marilynne. *Presto, or the Adventures of a Turnspit Dog.*
Roberts, Willo. *Eddie and the Fairy Godpuppy; Pet Sitting Peril.*
Sachs, Marilyn. *Underdog.*
St. George, Judith. *Who's Scared? Not Me!*
Savitz, Harriet. *Swimmer.*
Selden, George. *Genie of Sutton Place.*
Shura, Mary. *Mister Wolf and Me.*
Shyer, Marlene. *Me and Joey Pinstrip, the King of Rock.*
Singer, Marilyn. *Fido Frame-Up; Nose for Trouble.*
Skurzynski, Gloria. *Remarkable Journey of Gustavus Bill.*
Smith, Dodie. *Hundred and One Dalmatians; Starlight Barking.*
Smith, Gene. *Visitor.*

Smith, Janice. *It's Not Easy Being George.*
Snyder, Zilpha. *And Condors Danced; Janie's Private Eyes.*
Stevens, Carla. *Trouble for Lucy.*
Stolz, Mary. *Bully on Barkham Street; Dog on Barkham Street; Explorer of Barkham Street.*
Taylor, Florence. *Gold Dust and Bullets.*
Taylor, Theodore. *Trouble with Tuck.*
Teale, Edwin. *Lost Dog.*
Terhune, Albert. *Lad: A Dog.*
Thomas, Jane. *Comeback Dog.*
Treece, Henry. *War Dog.*
Tung, S.T. *One Small Dog.*
Vipont, Elfrida. *Pavilion.*
Wallace, Bill. *Dog Called Kitty.*
Warner, Gertrude. *Bicycle Mystery.*
Wellman, Manly. *Wild Dog of Downing Creek.*
White, Anne. *Dog Called Scholar.*
Wilkes, Marilyn. *C.L.U.T.Z. and the Fizzion Formula.*
Witheridge, Elizabeth. *Dead End Bluff.*
Wolf, Bernard. *Connie's New Eyes.*
Wolkoff, Judie. *In a Pig's Eye.*
Wrightson, Patricia. *Moon Dark.*

Dragons

Asimov, Janet. *Norby, the Mixed up Robot; Norby's Other Secret.*
Baker, Betty. *Save Sirrushany.*
Counsel, June. *Dragon in Class Four.*
Dickson, Gordon. *Dragon and the George.*
Engdahl, Sylvia. *Enchantress from the Stars.*
Godden, Rumer. *Dragon of Og.*
Hindle, Lee. *Dragon Fall.*
Jones, Terry. *Nicobobinus.*
Keller, Beverly. *Small, Elderly Dragon.*
Kimmel, Margaret. *Magic in the Mist.*
Krensky, Stephen. *Dragon Circle.*
Kushner, Donn. *Book Dragon.*
L'Engle, Madeleine. *Wind in the Door.*
Lloyd, Norris. *Desperate Dragons.*
McCaffrey, Anne. *Dragondrums; Dragonflight; Dragonquest; Dragonsinger; Dragonsong; Moreta, Dragonlady of Pern; White Dragon.*
McKillip, Patricia. *Changeling Sea.*
Manning, Rosemary. *Dragon in Danger; Dragon's Quest.*
Murphy, Shirley. *Ivory Lyre.*
Nesbit, Edith. *Deliverers of Their Country.*
Newman, Robert. *Merlin's Mistake.*
Preiss, Byron. *Dragonworld.*
Sargent, Sarah. *Weird Henry Berg.*
Yep, Laurence. *Dragon of the Lost Sea.*
Yolen, Jane. *Dragon's Blood; Heart's Blood; Sending of Dragons.*

Drama

See: Acting

Drug Abuse

Dyslexia

See: Handicapped

Ecology

bage Bag; Son of Interflux.

Lasky, Kathryn. *Bone Wars; Home Free.*

Leach, Christopher. *Great Book Raid.*

Lederer, Chloe. *Down the Hill of the Sea.*

Levin, Betty. *Landfall.*

Lilius, Irmelin. *Horse of the Night.*

Lipp, Frederick. *Some Lose Their Way.*

Lisle, Janet. *Great Dimpole Oak.*

MacGregor, Ellen. *Miss Pickerell and the Blue Whales; Miss Pickerell and the Lost World; Miss Pickerell and the Supertanker; Miss Pickerell and the Weather Satellite; Miss Pickerell Goes on a Dig; Miss Pickerell Harvests the Sea; Miss Pickerell Tackles the Energy Crisis.*

McLaughlin, Lorrie. *Cinnamon Hill Mystery.*

McMahan, Ian. *Lake Fear.*

Maguire, Gregory. *Lightning.*

Mann, Peggy. *Street of the Flower Boxes.*

Meader, Stephen. *Stranger on Big Hickory.*

Mian, Mary. *Take Three Witches.*

Milton, Joyce. *Save the Loonies.*

Molarsky, Osmond. *Montalvo Bay.*

Morey, Walt. *Deep Trouble.*

Morgan, Geoffrey. *Small Piece of Paradise.*

Morressy, John. *Drought on Ziax ll.*

Nicole, Christopher. *Operation Destruct.*

Norton, Andre. *Outside.*

Parker, Richard. *Private Beach.*

Peyton, K.M. *Plan for Birdmarsh.*

Sargent, Sarah. *Seeds of Change.*

Spinelli, Jerry. *Night of the Whale.*

Stern, Cecily. *Different Kind of Gold.*

Stone, Nancy. *Dune Shadow.*

Swindells, Robert. *Serpent's Tooth.*

Taylor, Theodore. *Hostage.*

Tchudi, Stephen. *Green Machine and the Frog Crusade.*

Thiele, Colin. *Fight Against Albatross Two.*

Thrush, Robin. *Gray Whales Are Missing.*

Towne, Mary. *Boxed In.*

Vipont, Elfrida. *Pavilion.*

Warner, Gertrude. *Bus Station Mystery.*

Waters, John. *Summer of the Seals.*

Willard, Barbara. *House with Roots.*

Williams, Jay. *Danny Dunn and the Universal Glue.*

Wiseman, David. *Adam's Common.*

Wrightson, Patricia. *Moon Dark; Older Kind of Magic.*

Elderly

Branscum, Robbie. *Girl; Toby, Granny and George.*

Burch, Robert. *Christmas with Ida Early; Ida Early Comes Over the Mountain.*

Byars, Betsy. *Blossoms Meet the Vulture Lady.*

Clifford, Eth. *Rocking Chair Rebellion.*

Creighton, Don. *Little League Old Timers.*

Derby, Pat. *Visiting Miss Pierce.*

Dodson, Susan. *Shadows Across the Sand.*

Eige, Lillian. *Kidnapping of Mister Huey.*

Ethridge, Kenneth. *Viola; Viola, Furgy, Bobbi and Me.*

Evansen, Virginia. *Flea Market Mystery.*

First, Julia. *Look Who's Beautiful.*

Fosburgh, Liza. *Mrs. Abercorn and the Bunce Boys.*

Gerson, Corinne. *My Grandfather the Spy.*

Girion, Barbara. *Joshua, the Czar and the Chicken-Bone Wish.*

Gonzalez, Gloria. *Gladman.*

Greenfeld, Josh. *Harry and Tonto.*

Hamilton, Virginia. *Time-Ago Lost: More Tales of Jahdu.*

Hanlon, Emily. *Wing and the Flame.*

Hayes, Sheila. *Speaking of Snapdragons.*

Hickman, Janet. *Stones.*

Higgins, Colin. *Harold and Maud.*

Holl, Kristi. *Just Like a Real Family; No Strings Attached.*

Irwin, Hadley. *Lilith Summer.*

Kleberger, Ilse. *Grandmother Oma.*

Krumgold, Joseph. *Onion John.*

Lampman, Evelyn. *Mrs. Updaisy.*

Leach, Christopher. *Meeting Miss Hannah.*

Lindgren, Astrid. *Rasmus and the Vagabond.*

Lovett, Margaret. *Great and Terrible Quest.*

Lowry, Lois. *Autumn Street.*

Lyle, Katie. *Finders Weepers.*

Morpurgo, Michael. *Why the Whales Came.*

Myers, Walter. *Won't Know Till I Get There.*

O'Dell, Scott. *Alexandra.*

Peck, Robert. *Banjo.*

Roth, David. *Hermit of Fog Hollow Station.*

Ruckman, Ivy. *This Is Your Captain Speaking.*

Schellie, Don. *Kidnapping Mr. Tubbs.*

Shyer, Marlene. *Grandpa Ritz and the Luscious Lovelies.*

Skorpen, Liesel. *Grace.*

Tate, Joan. *Luke's Garden; and Gramp.*

Thomas, Joyce. *Golden Pasture.*

Treadgold, Mary. *Winter Princess.*

Walsh, Jill P. *Gaffer Samson's Luck.*

Wrightson, Patricia. *Little Fear.*

Yep, Laurence. *Child of the Owl.*

Zindel, Paul. *Pigman; Pigman Legacy.*

Epilepsy

See: Illness

ESP

See also: Occult

Aaron, Chester. *Out of Sight, Out of Mind.*

Adams, Douglas. *Dirk Gently's Holistic Detective Agency.*

Fairy Tales

Family

See also: Family Problems; Fathers; Grandparents; Mothers

Anderson, Joan. *Joshua's Westward Journal; Pioneer Children of Appalachia.*
Anderson, Margaret. *Journey of the Shadow Bairns.*
Andrews, Jean. *Dear Dola: Or, How to Build Your Own Family.*
Angell, Judie. *Suds.*
Arrick, Fran. *Nice Girl from Good Home; Tunnel Vision.*
Arthur, Ruth. *Old Magic.*
Arundel, Honor. *Family Failing.*
Auch, Mary Jane. *Cry Uncle!; Pick of the Litter; Witching of Ben Wagner.*
Avery, Gillian. *Likely Lad.*
Bacon, Martha. *Sophia Scrooby Preserved.*
Balis, Andrea. *P.J.*
Ball, Zachary. *Kep.*
Bates, Betty. *Ask Me Tomorrow.*
Bawden, Nina. *Henry; Squib.*
Beatty, Patricia. *Hail Columbia; Lady from Black Hawk; Me, California Perkins; Sarah and Me and the Lady from the Sea.*
Beckett, Hilary. *My Brother, Angel.*
Belden, Wilanne. *Frankie.*
Benary-Isbert, Margot. *Ark; Castle on the Border; Long Way Home; Rowan Farm.*
Benson, Sally. *Junior Miss.*
Bess, Clayton. *Story for a Black Night.*
Betancourt, Jeanne. *Home Sweet Home.*
Bischoff, Julia. *Paddy's Preposterous Promises.*
Blume, Judy. *Are You There God? It's Me, Margaret; Superfudge.*
Bond, Nancy. *Best of Enemies; Place to Come Back To.*
Bosse, Malcolm. *Captives of Time.*
Bradbury, Bianca. *Andy's Mountain; Laughter in Our House.*
Branson, Karen. *Potatoe Eaters; Streets of Gold.*
Bridgers, Sue Ellen. *Permanent Connections; Home Before Dark.*
Brink, Carol. *Bad Times of Irma Baumlein; Caddie Woodlawn; Family Grandstand.*
Buchan, Stuart. *When We Lived with Pete.*
Bunting, Eve. *Mother, How Could You!*
Burch, Robert. *Christmas with Ida Early; Ida Early Comes Over the Mountain.*
Burleson, Elizabeth. *Man of the Family.*
Burton, Hester. *In Spite of All Terror.*
Butler, Beverly. *Ghost Cat.*
Byars, Betsy. *Beans on the Roof; Blossom Promise; Blossoms and the Green Phantom; Blossoms Meet the Vulture Lady; Glory Girl; Good-Bye, Chicken Little.*
Calhoun, Mary. *Depend on Katie John; Honestly Katie John; Katie John; Katie John and Heathcliff.*
Callaway, Kathy. *Bloodroot Flower.*
Calvert, Patricia. *Snowbird.*
Cameron, Ann. *Most Beautiful Place in the World.*
Cameron, Eleanor. *Julia and the Hand of God; Private World of Julia Redfern; That Julia*

Redfern; To the Green Mountains.
Campbell, Hope. *Meanwhile Back at the Castle; Why Not Join the Giraffes?*
Canfield, Dorothy. *Understood Betsy.*
Caudill, Rebecca. *Somebody Go and Bang a Drum.*
Chaffin, Lithe. *Freeman.*
Chauncy, Nan. *Half a World Away.*
Christgau, Alice. *Runaway to Glory.*
Clarke, Mary. *Limmer's Daughter.*
Clauser, Suzanne. *Girl Named Sooner.*
Cleary, Beverly. *Ramona Forever; Ramona Quimby, Age 8; Ramona the Brave; Sister of the Bride; Socks.*
Cleaver, Vera. *Dust of the Earth; Sugar Blue; Sweetly Sings the Donkey; Where the Lilies Bloom.*
Clifford, Eth. *Harvey's Horrible Snake Disaster; Man Who Sang in the Dark.*
Clymer, Eleanor. *My Mother Is the Smartest Woman in the World.*
Cohen, Barbara. *Carp in the Bathtub; Orphan Game.*
Collier, James. *Outside Looking In.*
Cone, Molly. *Annie, Annie.*
Conford, Ellen. *And This Is Laura; Luck of Pokey Bloom.*
Conrad, Pam. *I Don't Live Here; My Daniel; Prairie Songs.*
Constant, Alberta. *Motoring Millers; Those Miller Girls.*
Coolidge, Olivia. *Come by Here.*
Cooney, Caroline. *Rah Rah Girls.*
Corbett, Scott. *Mystery Man.*
Corcoran, Barbara. *I Am the Universe; Make No Sound; Sky Is Falling.*
Cresswell, Helen. *Absolute Zero; Bagthorpes Abroad; Bagthorpes Haunted; Bagthorpes Liberated; Bagthorpes Unlimited; Bagthorpes Vs. the World; Beachcombers; Ordinary Jack.*
Crofford, Emily. *Matter of Pride.*
Curtis, Alice. *Winter on the Prairie.*
Dahl, Borghild. *This Precious Year; Under This Roof.*
Danziger, Paula. *Can You Sue Your Parents for Malpractice?; It's an Aardvark Eat Turtle World.*
Davis, Gibbs. *Maud Flies Solo.*
Davis, Jenny. *Good-Bye and Keep Cold.*
Delton, Judy. *Only Jody.*
Dick, Trella. *Island on the Border.*
Dickens, Charles. *Great Expectations.*
Dickenson, Christine. *Getting It All Together.*
Dixon, Jeanne. *Lady Cat Lost.*
Dodge, Mary. *Hans Brinker.*
Duncan, Jane. *Camerons at the Castle; Camerons Calling; Camerons on the Hill; Camerons on the Train.*
Duncan, Lois. *Gift of Magic; Summer of Fear.*
Edwards, Julie. *Mandy.*
Eige, Lillian. *Cady.*
Eliot, George. *Silas Marner.*

Ellis, Sarah. *Family Project.*
Ellison, Lucile. *Butter on Both Sides; Tie That Binds.*
Embry, Margaret. *Shadi.*
Enright, Elizabeth. *Four Story Mistake; Saturdays; Spiderweb for Two; Then There Were Five; Thimble Summer.*
Erwin, Betty. *Behind the Magic Line.*
Estes, Eleanor. *Middle Moffats; Moffat Museum; Moffats; Pinky Pye; Rufus M.*
Eyerly, Jeannette. *Angel Baker, Thief.*
Faber, Nancy. *Cathy at the Crossroads.*
Farley, Carol. *Loosen Your Ears; Settle Your Fidgets.*
Feagles, Anita. *Sophia, Scarlotte and Ceecee.*
Fenton, Edward. *Morning of the Gods.*
Field, Rachel. *Calico Bush.*
Fine, Anne. *Granny Project.*
Fisher, Laura. *Charlie Dick.*
Fitzhugh, Louise. *Nobody's Family Is Going to Change.*
Flory, Jane. *Ramshackle Roost.*
Forbes, Tom. *Quincy's Harvest.*
Fox, Edward. *Hunger Valley.*
Fox, Paula. *Village by the Sea.*
Francis, Dorothy. *Captain Morgana Mason.*
Fry, Rosalie. *Echo's Song.*
Garner, Alan. *Aimer Gate; Granny Reardon; Stone Book; Tom Fobble's Day.*
Garnett, Eve. *Family from One End Street; Further Adventures of the Family from One End Street.*
Geras, Adele. *Apricots at Midnight and Other Stories from a Patchwork Quilt.*
Gerson, Corinne. *Son for a Day; Tread Softly.*
Girion, Barbara. *Tangle of Roots.*
Goudge, Elizabeth. *Linnets and Valerians.*
Govan, Christine. *Number Five Hackberry Street.*
Graham, Lorenz. *I, Momolu.*
Grant, Cynthia. *Summer Home.*
Gray, Patricia. *Horsepower.*
Green, Phyllis. *Nicky's Lopsided, Lumpy But Delicious Orange.*
Greene, Constance. *Al(exandra) the Great; I Know You, Al; Just Plain Al; Your Old Pal, Al.*
Greenfield, Eloise. *Talk About a Family.*
Greenwald, Sheila. *All the Way to Wit's End; Atrocious Two.*
Gripe, Maria. *Josephine.*
Grove, Vicki. *Good-Bye My Wishing Star.*
Guest, Elissa. *Over the Moon.*
Guy, Rosa. *Edith Jackson; Friends; Ups and Downs of Carl Davis III.*
Hahn, Mary. *Jellyfish Season.*
Hall, Anna. *Cyrus Holt and the Civil War.*
Hall, Lynn. *Mrs. Portree's Pony; Secret Life of Dagmar Schultz.*
Hamilton, Gail. *Titania's Lodestone.*
Hamilton, Virginia. *M.C. Higgins, the Great.*
Hamner, Earl. *Spencer's Mountain.*
Hancock, Mary. *Thundering Prairie.*
Hansen, Joyce. *Gift Giver.*

Hartwell, Nancy. *Something for Laurie.*
Hassler, Jon. *Grand Opening.*
Haugaard, Erik. *Hakon of Rogen's Saga.*
Hautzig, Esther. *Endleses Steppe.*
Hays, Wilma. *Cape Cod Adventure.*
Heide, Florence. *Mystery of the Lonely Lantern; Time Flies; When the Sad One Comes to Stay.*
Henkes, Kevin. *Zebra Wall.*
Hermes, Patricia. *Place for Jeremy.*
Herzig, Alison. *Season of Secrets.*
Hest, Amy. *Getting Rid of Krista; Pete and Lily.*
Hickman, Janet. *Thunder-Pup.*
Hightower, Florence. *Fayerweather Forecast.*
Hildick, E.W. *Secret Spenders; Secret Winners.*
Hilgartner, Beth. *Necklace of Fallen Stars.*
Holland, Isabelle. *God, Mrs. Muskrat, and Aunt Dot.*
Hooks, William. *Flight of Dazzle Angels.*
Hunt, Irene. *William.*
Johnston, Norma. *Carlisle's All; Carlisle's Hope; Glory in the Flower; If You Love Me, Let Me Go; Keeping Days; Mustard Seed of Magic; Myself and I; Nice Girl Like You; Of Time and Seasons; Sanctuary Tree; Striving After Wind.*
Jones, Adrienne. *So Nothing Is Forever.*
Jones, Diana. *Ogre Downstairs.*
Josephs, Rebecca. *Early Disorders.*
Kehret, Peg. *Nightmare Mountain.*
Keith, Harold. *Obstinate Land.*
Keller, Beverly. *No Beasts, No Children.*
Kennemore, Tim. *Changing Times.*
Kerr, Helen. *Grave Allegra.*
Kerr, M.E. *I Stay Near You.*
Kessler, Leonard. *Aurora and Socrates.*
Key, Alexander. *Forgotten Door.*
Kibbe, Pat. *My Mother the Mayor.*
Killilea, M. Karen. *Karen.*
Kinsey-Warnick, Natalie. *Canada Geese Quilt.*
Klass, Sheila. *Alive and Starting Over.*
Klein, Norma. *Family Secrets; Going Backwards; Naomi in the Middle; Queen of What Ifs; What It's All About.*
Ladd, Elizabeth. *Meg of Heron's Neck; Night of the Hurricane.*
Lasky, Kathryn. *Night Journey.*
Lawrence, Louise. *Sing and Scatter Daisies.*
Lee, Harper. *To Kill a Mockingbird.*
Lee, Virginia. *Magic Moth.*
L'Engle, Madeleine. *Meet the Austins; Moon by Night; Ring of Endless Light; Young Unicorns.*
Leninson, Riki. *Dinnieabbiesister-r-r!*
LeRoy, Gen. *Emma's Dilemma.*
Levin, Betty. *Brother Moose.*
Levit, Rose. *Eileen.*
Levitin, Sonia. *Journey to America; Silver Days.*
Lindgren, Astrid. *Children of Noisy Village; Christmas in Noisy Village; Emil in the Soup Tureen; Emil's Pranks; Happy Times in Noisy Village; Springtime in Noisy Village.*
Lingard, Joan. *Across the Barricades; Clearance; Hostages to Fortune; Into Exile; Proper Place; Resettling; Twelfth Day of July.*

Little, Jean. *Look Through My Window; Mama's Going to Buy You a Mockingbird; Spring Begins in March.*

Lorenzo, Carol. *Mama's Ghosts.*

Lowry, Lois. *All About Sam; Anastasia on Her Own; Us and Uncle Fraud.*

McDonnell, Christine. *Count Me In.*

McGraw, Eloise. *Money Room.*

McHargue, Georgess. *Stoneflight.*

McHugh, Elisabet. *Karen and Vicki.*

MacLachlan, Patricia. *Arthur, for the Very First Time; Cassie Binegar; Facts and Fiction of Minna Pratt; Sarah, Plain and Tall; Seven Kisses in a Row.*

MacLeod, Charlotte. *Maid of Honor.*

Major, Kevin. *Far from Shore.*

Mark, Jan. *Thunder and Lightnings.*

Martin, Ann. *Bummer Summer; Ten Kids, No Pets.*

Mattson, Olle. *Michel and the Lost Ship.*

Mazer, Norma. *A, My Name Is Ami; Figure of Speech; Three Sisters.*

Meyer, Carolyn. *Center: From a Troubled Past to a New Life.*

Miles, Betty. *Looking On.*

Miller, Helen. *Janey and Her Friends.*

Miller, Ruth. *City Rose.*

Mills, Claudia. *Boardwalk with Hotel.*

Moeri, Louise. *First the Egg.*

Montgomery, Lucy. *Anne of Ingleside; Anne of Windy Populars; Chronicles of Avonlea; Further Chronicles of Avonlea; Rainbow Valley.*

Morgan, Alison. *All Kinds of Prickles.*

Morpurgo, Michael. *Twist of Gold.*

Mowat, Farley. *Owls in the Family.*

Murray, Marguerite. *Like Seabirds Flying Home.*

Murray, Michele. *Nellie Cameron.*

Murrow, Liza. *West Against the Wind.*

Musgrave, Florence. *Sarah Hastings.*

Naylor, Phyllis. *Maudie in the Middle.*

Nelson, Theresa. *Devil Storm.*

Nesbit, Edith. *New Treasure Seeker; Railway Children; Story of the Treasure Seekers.*

Neufeld, John. *Edgar Allan.*

Newell, Eadie. *Trouble Brewing.*

Nixon, Joan. *Caught in the Act; In the Face of Danger; Place to Belong.*

Nostlinger, Christine. *Fly Away Home.*

O'Meara, Walter. *Sioux Are Coming.*

Oppenheimer, Joan. *Gardine Vs. Hanover.*

Paperny, Myra. *Wooden People.*

Park, Barbara. *My Mother Got Married (And Other Disasters).*

Parker, Richard. *Second Hand Family.*

Paterson, Katherine. *Come Sing, Jimmy Jo.*

Pellowski, Anne. *Betsy's Up-and-Down Year; First Farm in the Valley: Anna's Story; Stairstep Farm: Anna Rose's Story; Willow Wind Farm: Betsy's Story; Winding Valley Farm: Annie's Story.*

Perl, Lila. *Telltale Summer of Tina C.; That Crazy April.*

Pevsner, Stella. *Call Me Heller, That's My Name; Sister of the Quints.*

Peyton, Karen. *Flambards; Flambards Divided; Flambards in Summer; Fly by Night; Midsummer Night's Death.*

Pfeffer, Susan. *Sybil at Sixteen; Year Without Michael.*

Phipson, Joan. *Family Conspiracy.*

Polland, Madeleine. *Children of the Red King.*

Poole, Victoria. *Thursday's Child.*

Porte, Barbara. *Kidnapping of Aunt Elizabeth.*

Provost, Gary. *Good If it Goes.*

Pryor, Bonnie. *Rats, Spiders and Love.*

Raymond, Charles. *Up from Appalachia.*

Rees, David. *Exeter Blitz.*

Reiss, Johanna. *Journey Back.*

Reynolds, Pamela. *Horseshoe Hill.*

Rich, Louise. *Three of a Kind.*

Rinaldi, Ann. *But in the Fall I'm Leaving.*

Robinson, Nancy. *Angela, Private Citizen; Oh, Honestly, Angela.*

Rock, Gail. *Addie and the King of Hearts; House Without a Christmas Tree; Thanksgiving Treasure.*

Rocklin, Joanne. *Dear Baby.*

Rodowsky, Colby. *Gathering Room; P.S. Write Soon; Summer's Worth of Shame.*

Rogers, Pamela. *Rare One.*

Roos, Stephen. *And the Winner Is. . . .*

Ruckman, Ivy. *Hunger Scream.*

Ryan, Mary. *Dance a Step Closer.*

Rylant, Cynthia. *Blue-Eyed Daisy.*

Sachs, Marilyn. *Bear's House; Dorrie's Book; Secret Friend; Truth About Mary Rose; Underdog.*

St. George, Judith. *Halo Wind.*

St. John, Glory. *What I Did Last Summer.*

St. John, Wylly. *Ghost Next Door.*

Sallis, Susan. *Secret Places of the Stairs.*

Sargent, Sarah. *Secret Lies.*

Savage, Deborah. *Rumor of Otters.*

Sebestyen, Ouida. *Words by Heart.*

Selden, George. *Cricket in Times Square.*

Seredy, Kate. *Good Master.*

Serraillier, Ian. *Silver Sword.*

Sharmat, Marjorie. *Get Rich Mitch.*

Shields, Rita. *Norah and the Cable Car.*

Shotwell, Louisa. *Adam Bookout.*

Shura, Mary. *Josie Gambit; Sunday Doll.*

Sidney, Margaret. *Five Little Peppers and How They Grew.*

Silsbee, Peter. *Love Among the Hiccups.*

Simon, Norma. *How Do I Feel?*

Simon, Shirley. *Cousins at Camm Corners.*

Sirof, Harriet. *Real World.*

Skolsky, Mindy. *Hannah Is a Palindrome.*

Skurzynski, Gloria. *Dangerous Ground.*

Slepian, Jan. *Broccoli Tapes.*

Slote, Alfred. *Trading Game.*

Smith, Betty. *Joy in the Morning; Tree Grows in Brooklyn.*

Smith, Doris. *Return to Bitter Creek.*

Smith, Emma. *Out of Hand.*

Smith, Eunice. *Jennifer Gift; Jennifer Prize.*

Smucker, Barbara. *Wigwam in the City.*

Snyder, Carol. *Leave Me Alone, Ma; Leftover Kid.*

Snyder, Zilpha. *Famous Stanley Kidnapping Case; Headless Cupid.*

Sommerfelt, Aimee. *White Bungalow.*

Sorensen, Virginia. *Miracles on Maple Hill.*

Spence, Eleanor. *Green Laurel.*

Spykman, Elizabeth. *Lemon and a Star; Terrible, Horrible Edie.*

Spyri, Johanna. *Heidi.*

Stephans, Peter. *Perrely Plight.*

Stewart, A.C. *Elizabeth's Tower; Ossian House.*

Stolz, Mary. *By the Highway Home; Cider Days; Go Catch a Flying Fish; Lands End; What Time of Night Is It?*

Storey, Margaret. *Pauline.*

Strang, Celia. *Foster Mary.*

Strauss, Linda. *Alexandra Ingredient.*

Streatfeild, Noel. *When the Sirens Wailed.*

Stren, Patti. *There's a Rainbow in My Closet.*

Stuckly, Elizabeth. *Family Walk-Up; Walk-Up.*

Summers, James. *Senior Dropout.*

Sutcliff, Rosemary. *Capricorn Bracelet.*

Sutton, Jane. *Me and the Weirdos.*

Sykes, Pamela. *Phoebe's Family.*

Sypher, Lucy. *Spell of the Northern Lights; Turnabout Year.*

Tate, Joan. *Sam and Me.*

Taylor, Mildred. *Gold Cadillac.*

Taylor, Sydney. *All-of-a-Kind Family; All-of-a-Kind Family Downtown; All-of-a-Kind Family Uptown; Ella of All-of-a-Kind Family; More All-of-a-Kind Family.*

Thiele, Colin. *February Dragon.*

Thrasher, Crystal. *Taste of Daylight.*

Tolan, Stephanie. *Great Skinner Enterprise; Great Skinner Getaway; Great Skinner Homestead; Great Skinner Strike.*

Towne, Mary. *Glass Room; Their House.*

Townsend, John. *Good-Bye to the Jungle; Trouble in the Jungle.*

Uchida, Yoshika. *In-Between Muja; Jar of Dreams; Journey Home; Journey to Topaz.*

Unnerstad, Edith. *Saucepan Journey.*

Ure, Jean. *If It Weren't for Sebastian.*

Vander Els, Betty. *Bombers Moon.*

Van Stockum, Hilda. *Friendly Gables.*

Varney, Joyce. *Half-Time Gypsy.*

Vogel, Ilse-Marget. *Farewell, Aunt Isabell.*

Voigt, Cynthia. *Homecoming; Runner; Solitary Blue.*

Walker, Alice. *To Hell with Dying.*

Walker, Diana. *Hundred Thousand Dollar Farm.*

Walker, Mary. *Brad's Box.*

Waltrip, Lela. *Purple Hills; White Harvest.*

Ware, Leon. *Rebellious Orphan; Threatening Fog.*

Warner, Gertrude. *Bicycle Mystery; Bus Station Mystery; Caboose Mystery; Houseboat Mystery; Mystery Behind the Wall; Mystery in the Sand; Schoolhouse Mystery; Surprise Island;*

Tree House Mystery; Woodshed Mystery; Yellow House Mystery.

Weber, Lenora. *Come Back, Wherever You Are; Leave It to Beany; New and Different Summer; Something Borrowed, Something Blue.*

Weir, Rosemary. *Robert's Rescued Railroad; Star and the Flame.*

Welch, Ronald. *Hawk; Nicholas Carey; Tank Commander.*

Weltner, Linda. *Beginning to Feel the Magic.*

Wersba, Barbara. *Crazy Vanilla.*

Westall, Robert. *Ghost Abbey; Wind Eye.*

Whitness, Barbara. *Ring of Bells.*

Wilder, Laura. *Little House in the Big Woods; West from Home.*

Willard, Barbara. *Cold Wind Blowing; Harrow and Harvest; House with Roots; Iron Lily; Lark and the Laurel; Miller's Boy; Sprig of Broom; Storm from the West.*

Williams, Barbara. *Mitzi and the Terrible Tyrannosaurus Rex; Mitzi's Honeymoon with Nana Potts.*

Wilson, Gina. *All Ends Up.*

Windsor, Patricia. *Home Is Where Your Feet Are Standing; Mad Martin.*

Winthrop, Elizabeth. *Little Demonstration of Affection; Walking Away.*

Wolkoff, Judie. *Where the Elf King Sings.*

Woolley, Catherine. *Room for Cathy.*

Wright, Betty. *My New Mom and Me; Pike River Phantom.*

Wrightson, Patricia. *Feather Star.*

Yep, Laurence. *Serpent's Children.*

Family Problems

Adler, Carole. *Fly Free; If You Need Me; In Our House Scott Is My Brother.*

Arthur, Ruth. *Little Dark Thorn.*

Bates, Betty. *Bugs in Your Ears.*

Bennett, Paul. *Follow the River.*

Bloch, Marie. *Two Worlds of Damyan.*

Blume, Judy. *Then Again, Maybe I Won't.*

Bograd, Larry. *Los Alamos Light.*

Branscum, Robbie. *For Love of Judy.*

Bridgers, Sue Ellen. *Notes for Another Life.*

Brockmann, Elizabeth. *What's the Matter, Girl?*

Brookins, Dana. *Alone in Wolf Hollow.*

Bulla, Clyde. *Benito.*

Bunting, Eve. *Blackbird Singing.*

Burch, Robert. *Simon and the Game of Chance.*

Byars, Betsy. *Cartoonist; Not-Just-Anybody Family.*

Calhoun, Mary. *It's Getting Beautiful Now.*

Cave, Hugh. *Voyage.*

Cleaver, Vera. *Belle Pruitt.*

Clymer, Eleanor. *Get-Away Car.*

Cohen, Miriam. *Robert and Dawn Marie 4 Ever.*

Collura, Mary Ellen. *Winners.*

Colman, Hila. *Nobody Has to Be a Kid Forever;*

Weekend Sisters.

Corcoran, Barbara. *All the Summer Voices; Potato Kid.*

Crane, Caroline. *Don't Look at Me That Way.*

Crook, Beverly. *Fair Annie of Old Mule Hollow.*

De Clements, Barthe. *I Never Asked You to Understand Me.*

Derman, Martha. *And Philippa Makes Four.*

Dillon, Eilis. *Cruise of the Santa Maria.*

Dorris, Michael. *Yellow Raft in Blue Water.*

Fox, Paula. *Stone-Faced Boy.*

Gaines, Ernest. *Long Day in November.*

Galbraith, Kathryn. *Come Spring.*

Graber, Richard. *Black Cow Summer; Pay Your Respects.*

Gregory, Diana. *There's a Caterpillar in My Lemonade.*

Guernsey, Joann. *Five Summers.*

Hall, Lynn. *Denison's Daughter.*

Hildick, E.W. *Kids Commune.*

Holden, Molly. *Unfinished Feud.*

Humphreys, Josephine. *Rich in Love.*

Ish-Kishor, Sulamith. *Our Eddie.*

Jackson, Jacqueline. *Taste of Spruce Gum.*

Kaye, Geraldine. *Comfort Herself.*

Lee, Benjamin. *It Can't Be Helped.*

Levine, Edna. *Lisa and Her Soundless World.*

Levitin, Sonia. *Season for Unicorns.*

Lindgren, Astrid. *Lotta on Troublemaker Street.*

Lingard, Joan. *Strangers in the House.*

Little, Jean. *Kate.*

Locke, Elsie. *Runaway Settlers.*

Lorenzo, Carol. *Heart of Snowbird.*

McGraw, William. *Smoke.*

Macken, Walter. *Flight of the Doves.*

Madison, Arnold. *Think Wild.*

Mathis, Sharon. *Teacup Full of Roses.*

Mazer, Harry. *When the Phone Rang.*

Mazer, Norma. *Downtown; When We First Met.*

Mendonca, Susan. *Tough Choices.*

Miklowitz, Gloria. *Suddenly Super Rich.*

Naylor, Phyllis. *Solomon System; String of Chances; Year of the Gopher.*

Nelson, Theresa. *Twenty-Five Cent Miracle.*

Nostlinger, Christine. *Girl Missing.*

Oneal, Zibby. *Formal Feeling.*

Parker, Richard. *Paul and Etta; Perversity of Pipers; Valley Full of Pipers.*

Petersen, P.J. *Boll Weevil Express.*

Riley, Jocelyn. *Only My Mouth Is Smiling.*

Roberts, Willo. *To Grandmother's House We Go.*

Robinson, Joan. *Charley.*

Ruby, Lois. *Pig-Out Inn.*

Sampson, Fay. *Watch on Patterick Fell.*

Samuels, Gertrude. *Adam's Daughter.*

Shreve, Susan. *Masquerade.*

Snyder, Zilpha. *Blair's Nightmare.*

Stiles, Martha. *Sarah the Dragon Lady.*

Talbert, Marc. *Paper Knife; Toby.*

Terris, Susan. *Latchkey Kids; No Scarlet Ribbons.*

Townsend, John. *Dan Alone.*

Townsend, Susan. *Secret Diary of Adrian Mole Aged 13¾.*

Van Steenwyk, Elizabeth. *Three Dog Winter.*

Voigt, Cynthia. *Tree by Leaf.*

Wallin, Luke. *Redneck Poacher's Son.*

Weiman, Eiveen. *It Takes Brains.*

Wells, Rosemary. *None of the Above.*

Wojciechowska, Maia. *Till the Break of Day.*

Wolkoff, Judie. *Happily Ever After ... Almost.*

York, Carol. *Remember Me When I Am Dead.*

Famous People (Fictionalized)

Almedingen, E.M. *Anna; Ellen; Fanny; Katia.*

Andrews, Mary. *Hostage to Alexander.*

Baker, Betty. *Blood of the Brave.*

Beatty, John. *Witch Dog.*

Bennett, John. *Master Skylark.*

Bishop, Jim. *Day Lincoln Was Shot.*

Boswell, Thomas. *How Life Imitates the World Series.*

Bowers, Gwendolyn. *At the Sign of the Globe.*

Boyd, Candy. *Charles Pippin.*

Burt, Olive. *I Challenge the Dark Sea.*

Carter, Dorothy. *His Majesty, Queen Hatshepsut.*

Clapp, Patricia. *I'm Deborah Sampson.*

De Trevino, Elizabeth. *I, Juan de Pareja.*

Downey, Fairfax. *Seventh's Staghound.*

Duncan, Lois. *Peggy.*

Evernden, Margery. *Lyncoya.*

Farber, Norma. *Mercy Short: A Winter Journal.*

Forman, James. *People of the Dream.*

Fritz, Jean. *George Washington's Breakfast; Homesick: My Own Story.*

Gedge, Pauline. *Child of the Morning.*

Gray, Elizabeth. *I Will Adventure.*

Hall, Majory. *Another Kind of Courage.*

Haugaard, Erik. *Leif the Unlucky.*

Hodges, C.W. *Marsh King; Namesake.*

Hunter, Mollie. *You Never Knew Her as I Did!*

Kane, Harnett. *Amazing Mrs. Bonaparte.*

Kay, Mara. *Masha; Youngest Lady-in-Waiting.*

Kherdian, David. *Bridger, Story of a Mountain Man.*

Koehn, Ilse. *Mischling, Second Degree; My Childhood in Nazi Germany.*

Konigsburg, E.L. *Proud Taste for Scarlet and Miniver; Second Mrs. Giaconda.*

Lampman, Evelyn. *White Captives.*

Leighton, Margaret. *Journey for a Princess.*

Lucas, Christopher. *Tiki and the Dolphin: Adventures of a Boy.*

MacKellar, William. *Dog Like No Other.*

Marcus, Katherine. *Devil's Workshop.*

O'Dell, Scott. *Streams to the River, Rivers to the Sea.*

Paige, People. *Shadow on the Sun.*
Plowman, Stephanie. *Three Lives for the Czar.*
Rodman, M. *Odyssey of Courage.*
Sisson, Rosemary. *Will in Love.*
Smith, A.C.H. *Lady Jane.*
Sutcliff, Rosemary. *Song for a Dark Queen.*
Tate, Eleanora. *Thank You, Dr. Martin Luther King, Jr.*
Treece, Henry. *Last Viking.*
Unnerstad, Edith. *Journey to England.*
Westlake, Donald. *Kahawa.*

Fantasy

See also: Fantasy/Animals; Fantasy/Dolls; Fantasy/Good Versus Evil; Fantasy/Places; Fantasy/Spells; Fantasy/Wishes; Fantasy/Words

Adair, Gilbert. *Alice Through the Needle's Eye.*
Aiken, Joan. *Whispering Mountain.*
Allan, Mabel. *Horns of Danger.*
Angell, Judie. *Weird Disappearance of Jordan Hall.*
Arthur, Ruth. *On the Wasteland.*
Asimov, Isaac. *Fantastic Voyage.*
Asimov, Janet. *Norby Down to Earth.*
Babbitt, Lucy. *Children of the Maker; Oval Amulet.*
Babbitt, Natalie. *Eyes of the Amaryllis; Kneeknock Rise.*
Banks, Lynne. *Farthest-Away Mountain; Indian in the Cupboard; Return of the Indian.*
Barrie, J.M. *Peter Pan.*
Baum, L. Frank. *Wonderful Wizard of Oz.*
Belden, Wilanne. *Frankie.*
Benchley, Nathaniel. *Demo and the Dolphins.*
Berends, Polly. *Ozma and the Wayward Wand.*
Bodecker, N.M. *Carrot Holes and Frisbee Trees.*
Bograd, Larry. *Poor Gertie.*
Boston, Lucy. *Children of Green Knowe; Nothing Said; River of Green Knowe; Stones of Green Knowe; Stranger at Green Knowe; Treasure of Green Knowe.*
Bradbury, Ray. *I Sing the Body Electric.*
Brink, Carol. *Two Are Better Than One.*
Burnett, Frances. *Little Princess; Secret Garden.*
Butterworth, Oliver. *Trouble with Jenny's Ear.*
Calif, Ruth. *Over-the-Hill Ghost.*
Cameron, Eleanor. *Court of the Stone Children; Terrible Churnadryne.*
Carlson, Natalie. *Evangeline, Pigeon of Paris.*
Carlyon, Richard. *Dark Lord of Pengersick.*
Catling, Patrick. *Chocolate Touch.*
Charnas, Suzy. *Silver Glove.*
Chetwin, Grace. *Gom on Windy Mountain; Out of the Dark World; Riddle and the Rune.*
Chew, Ruth. *Mostly Magic; What the Witch Left; Would-Be Witch.*
Clarke, Pauline. *Return of the Twelves.*

Cleary, Beverly. *Mouse and the Motorcycle; Ralph S. Mouse; Runaway Ralph.*
Clements, Bruce. *Two Against the Tide.*
Coatsworth, Elizabeth. *Pure Magic.*
Collodi, Carlo. *Adventures of Pinocchio.*
Conford, Ellen. *Genie with the Light Blue Hair.*
Coontz, Otto. *Hornwaggle Magic.*
Counsel, June. *Dragon in Class Four.*
Crayder, Dorothy. *Ishkabibble.*
Cresswell, Helen. *Bongleweed; Night Watchmen; Secret World of Polly Flint.*
Cross, Gillian. *Twin and Super-Twin.*
Cunningham, Julia. *Oaf.*
Curley, Daniel. *Ann's Spring.*
Curry, Jane. *Birdstone; Lost Farm.*
Dahl, Roald. *Charlie and the Chocolate Factory; Charlie and the Great Glass Elevator; Fantastic Mr. Fox; George's Marvelous Medicine; James and the Giant Peach.*
Damjan, Mischa. *December's Travels.*
Dank, Gloria. *Forest of App.*
Davis, Maggie. *Grandma's Secret Letter.*
Day, Davis. *Emperor's Panda.*
Defekice, Cynthia. *Strange Night Writing of Jessamine Colter.*
Dickinson, Peter. *Box of Nothing; Eva; Giant Cold.*
Disch, Thomas. *Brave Little Toaster Goes to Mars.*
Duane, Diane. *So You Want to Be a Wizard.*
Du Bois, William. *Gentleman Bear; Twenty-One Balloons.*
Dunlop, Eileen. *Clementina.*
Eager, Edward. *Knight's Castle; Seven-Day Magic.*
Earnshaw, Brian. *Dragonfall 5 and the Royal Beast.*
Eckert, Allan. *Dark Green Tunnel.*
Edmondson, Madeleine. *Witch's Egg.*
Erwin, Betty. *Who Is Victoria?*
Estes, Eleanor. *Witch Family.*
Faralla, Dana. *Wonderful Flying-Go-Round.*
Farmer, Penelope. *Castle of Bone; Charlotte Sometimes; Emma in Winter; Summer Birds.*
Finlay, Winifred. *Beadbonny Ash.*
Fisher, Leonard. *Noonan: A Novel About Baseball, ESP and Time Warps.*
Fisher, Paul. *Ash Staff; Mont Cant Gold.*
Fisk, Nicholas. *Grinny.*
Foster, Alan. *For Love of Mother-Not.*
Freeman, Barbara. *Other Face.*
Fry, Rosalie. *Mountain Door; Whistler in the Mist.*
Gage, Wilson. *Miss Osborne-the-Mop.*
Gard, Joyce. *Talargain.*
Gathorne-Hardy, Jonathan. *Operation Peeg.*
Gee, Maurice. *Under the Mountain.*
Gloss, Molly. *Outside the Gates.*
Godden, Rumer. *Dragon of Og.*
Gormley, Beatrice. *Best Friend Insurance; Fifth Grade Magic; Mail-Order Wings; More Fifth Grade Magic; Paul's Volcano.*

Rodda, Emily. *Pigs Are Flying.*
Rodgers, Mary. *Billion for Boris.*
Ross, Ramon. *Prune.*
Ruskin, John. *King of the Golden River.*
Sargent, Pamela. *Alien Child.*
Sargent, Sarah. *Watermusic; Weird Henry Berg.*
Schealer, John. *Zip-Zip and His Flying Saucer; Zip-Zip Goes to Venus.*
Sefton, Catherine. *Ghost and Bertie Boggin.*
Senn, Steve. *Circle in the Sea.*
Service, Pamela. *Question of Destiny.*
Severn, David. *Wild Valley.*
Singer, Marilyn. *Lightey Club.*
Skurzynski, Gloria. *Manwolf; Remarkable Journey of Gustavus Bill.*
Sleator, William. *Duplicate.*
Sloan, Carolyn. *Sea Child.*
Snyder, Zilpha. *And All Between; Below the Root; Season of Ponies; Truth About Stone Hollow; Until the Celebration; Velvet Room.*
Sobol, Donald. *Amazing Power of Ashur Fine.*
Sommer-Bodenburg, Angela. *My Friend the Vampire; Vampire Moves In; Vampire on the Farm; Vampire Takes a Trip.*
Steele, Mary. *Because of the Sand Witches There; True Men.*
Stolz, Mary. *Cuckoo Clock; Scarecrows and Their Child.*
Storr, Catherine. *Thursday.*
Strauss, Victoria. *Worldstone.*
Sturgeon, Theodore. *Dreaming Jewels.*
Swift, Jonathan. *Gulliver's Travels.*
Tapp, Kathy. *Flight of the Moth-Kin; Moth-Kin Magic.*
Thomas, Kathleen. *Goats Are Better Than Worms.*
Townsend, John. *Persuading Stick.*
Travers, Pamela. *Mary Poppins; Mary Poppins Comes Back; Mary Poppins in the Park; Mary Poppins Opens the Door.*
Turnbull, Ann. *Frightened Forest.*
Twain, Mark. *Connecticut Yankee in King Arthur's Court.*
Van Leeuwen, Jean. *Great Cheese Conspiracy; Great Christmas Kidnapping; Great Rescue Operation.*
Wagerin, Walter. *Potter, Come Fly to the First of the Earth.*
Wallace, Barbara. *Barrel in the Basement.*
Wells, Rosemary. *Through the Hidden Door.*
Wersba, Barbara. *Let Me Fall Before I Fly.*
Westall, Robert. *Devil on the Road.*
White, E.B. *Charlotte's Web.*
Wibberley, Leonard. *Mouse on the Moon; Mouse on Wall Street; Mouse That Roared; Mouse That Saved the West.*
Wilde, Oscar. *Birthday of the Infanta.*
Wilder, Cherry. *Princess of the Chameln; Yorath, the Wolf.*
Williams, Jay. *Danny Dunn and the Anti-Gravity Paint; Danny Dunn and the Automated House; Danny Dunn and the Homework Machine;*

Danny Dunn and the Smallifying Machine; Danny Dunn and the Voice from Space; Danny Dunn, Invisible Boy; Danny Dunn, Time Traveler.
Williams, Margery. *Velveteen Rabbit.*
Wilson, Yates. *More "Alice."*
Wiseman, David. *Blodwen and the Guardians; Jeremy Visick.*
Wright, Betty. *Pike River Phantom.*
Yep, Laurence. *Dragon Steel.*
Yolen, Jane. *Magic Three of Solatia; Transfigured Hart.*
York, Carol. *Ten O'Clock Club.*
Yvart, Jacques. *Rising of the Wind Adventures Along the Beaufort Scale.*

Fantasy/Animals

See also: Mice

Adams, Richard. *Watership Down.*
Aiken, Joan. *Kingdom and the Cave.*
Allan, Ted. *Willie the Squowse.*
Baker, Margaret. *Bears Back in Business; Hannibal and the Bears; Shoe Shop Bears.*
Balaban, John. *Hawk's Tale.*
Banks, Lynne. *Houdini.*
Bauer, Marion. *Touch the Moon.*
Beagle, Peter. *Last Unicorn.*
Beeks, Graydon. *Hosea Globe and the Fantastical Peg-Legged Chu.*
Benchley, Nathaniel. *Kilroy and the Gull.*
Bond, Michael. *Bear Called Paddington; Complete Adventures of Olga de Polga; More About Paddington; Olga Carries On; Olga Meets Her Match; Paddington Abroad; Paddington at Large; Paddington at Work; Paddington Goes to Town; Paddington Helps Out; Paddington Marches On; Paddington on Screen; Paddington on Top; Paddington Takes the Air; Paddington Takes the Test; Paddington Takes to T.V.; Tales of Olga da Polga.*
Bonham, Frank. *Friends of the Looney Lake Monster.*
Boston, Lucy. *Fossil Snake; Sea Egg.*
Bowen, John. *Squeak; A Love Story.*
Bradley, Marion. *Hawkmistress.*
Bradley, Michel. *Norwood Tor.*
Brittain, Bill. *Devil's Donkey.*
Brooks, Walter. *Freddy and the Baseball Team from Mars; Freddy and the Dictator; Freddy and the Dragon; Freddy and the Flying Saucer Plans; Freddy and the Ignormus; Freddy and the Men from Mars; Freddy and the Perilous Adventure; Freddy and the Pied Piper; Freddy and the Popinjay; Freddy and the Space Ship; Freddy Goes Camping; Freddy Goes to Florida; Freddy Goes to the North Pole; Freddy Plays Football; Freddy Rides Again; Freddy*

the Cowboy; Freddy the Detective; Freddy the
Pilot; Freddy the Politician.
Buchwald, Emile. *Floramel and Esteban.*
Byars, Betsy. *Winged Colt of Casa Mia.*
Coblentz, Catherine. *Blue Cat of Castletown.*
Conly, Jane. *R-T, Margaret and the Rats of
Mimh; Rasco and the Rats of Nimh.*
Cunningham, Julia. *Dear Rat.*
Dana, Barbara. *Zucchini.*
Duffy, James. *Revolt of the Teddy Bears.*
Elish, Dan. *Jason and the Baseball Bear.*
Fosburgh, Liza. *Bella Arabelle.*
Foster, Elizabeth. *Gigi.*
Fox, Denise. *Through the Tempest Trails.*
Gaunt, Michael. *Brim Sails Out; Brim's Boat.*
Grahame, Kenneth. *Wind in the Willows.*
Hamilton, Carol. *Dawn Seekers.*
Hays, Geoffrey. *Alligator and His Uncle Tooth.*
Howe, James. *Morgan's Zoo.*
Hughes, Monica. *Space Trap.*
Jacques, Brian. *Redwall.*
Kherdian, David. *Song in the Walnut Grove.*
King-Smith, Dick. *Babe: The Gallant Pig; Fox
Busters; Martin's Mice; Pigs Might Fly.*
Kushner, Donn. *Violin Maker's Gift.*
Lampman, Evelyn. *Mrs. Updaisy.*
Lattimore, Eleanor. *Felicia.*
Lawrence, Ann. *Tom Ass or the Second Gift.*
Lawson, Robert. *Mr. Twigg's Mistake; Rabbit
Hill; Tough Winter.*
Le Vert, John. *Flight of the Cassowary.*
Levin, Betty. *Ice Bear.*
Little, Jane. *Sneaker Hill.*
Lively, Penelope. *House Inside Out; Voyage of
QV 66.*
Lofting, Hugh. *Dr. Dolittle and the Green
Canary; Dr. Dolittle on the Moon; Dr. Dolit-
tle's Caravan; Dr. Dolittle's Circus; Dr. Dolit-
tle's Garden; Dr. Dolittle's Post Office; Story of
Dr. Dolittle; Voyage of Dr. Dolittle.*
McGowen, Tom. *Odyssey from River Bend.*
McHugh, Elisabet. *Beethoven's Cat; Wiggie Wins
the West.*
Mian, Mary. *Nip and Tuck War.*
Milne, A.A. *House at Pooh Corner; Winnie the
Pooh.*
Muir, Lynette. *Unicorn Window.*
Norton, Andre. *Fur Magic.*
O'Brien, Robert. *Mrs. Frisby and the Rats of
Nimh.*
Pierce, Meredith. *Woman Who Loved Reindeer.*
Pinkwater, Daniel. *Moosepire.*
Roach, Marilynne. *Presto, or the Adventures of
a Turnspit Dog.*
Roberts, Willo. *Eddie and the Fairy Godpuppy;
Girl with the Silver Eyes.*
Ruckman, Ivy. *Melba the Brain.*
Seidler, Tor. *Rat's Tale; Tar Pit.*
Selden, George. *Chester Cricket's New Home;
Chester Cricket's Pigeon Ride; Cricket in Times
Square; Harry Cat's Pet Puppy; Tucker's
Countryside.*

Service, Pamela. *Stinker from Space.*
Shachtman, Tom. *Beachmaster: A Story of
Daniel Au Fond.*
Sharp, Margery. *Bernard Into Battle; Bernard the
Brave; Miss Bianca; Miss Bianca and the
Bridesmaid; Miss Bianca in the Antarctic; Miss
Bianca in the Orient; Miss Bianca in the Salt
Mines; Rescuers; Turret.*
Sinclair, Tom. *Tales of a Wandering Warthog.*
Sleigh, Barbara. *Kingdom of Carbonel.*
Smith, Dodie. *Starlight Barking.*
Steig, William. *Abel's Island; Dominic; Real
Thief.*
Stolz, Mary. *Quentin Corn.*
Titus, Eve. *Basil and the Pygmy Cats; Basil of
Baker Street.*
Twain, Mark. *Stolen White Elephant.*
Wallace, Bill. *Snot Stew.*
Willard, Nancy. *Island of the Grass King; Sailing
to Cythera; Uncle Terrible.*
Wilson, Gahan. *Harry and the Sea Serpents.*
Wilson, Hazel. *Herbert's Stilts.*

Fantasy/Dolls

Ames, Mildred. *Is There Life on a Plastic
Planet?*
Anastasio, Dina. *Question of Time.*
Arthur, Ruth. *Candle in Her Room.*
Bacon, Martha. *Moth Manor.*
Bailey, Carolyn. *Miss Hickory.*
Bloch, Marie. *Dollhouse Story.*
Cassedy, Sylvia. *Behind the Attic Wall.*
Curry, Jane. *Mindy's Mysterious Miniature.*
Dexter, Catherine. *Oracle Doll.*
Field, Rahel. *Hitty: Her First Hundred Years.*
Freeman, Barbara. *Lucinda.*
Gardam, Jane. *Through the Doll's House Door.*
Godden, Rumer. *Home Is the Sailor.*
Hahn, Mary. *Doll in the Garden; A Ghost Story.*
Kassirer, Elizabeth. *Magic Elizabeth.*
Kennedy, Richard. *Amy's Eyes.*
Linn, Janet. *Twin Spell.*
Logan, Carolyn. *Power of the Rillard.*
Norton, Andre. *Octagon Magic.*
Sleator, William. *Among the Dolls.*
Sparger, Rex. *Doll.*
Stover, Marjorie. *Midnight in the Dollhouse;
When the Dolls Wake.*
Syfret, Anne. *Bella.*
Williams, Ursula. *Three Toymakers.*
Wright, Billy. *Dollhouse Murders.*
York, Carol. *Revenge of the Dolls.*

Fantasy/Good Versus Evil

Alcock, Vivien. *Monster Garden; Sylvia Game.*
Alexander, Lloyd. *Beggar Queen; Black Caul-*

Poole, Josephine. *Visitor.*
Rayner, Mary. *Witchfinder.*
Roberts, Willo. *Girl with the Silver Eyes.*
Rockwood, Joyce. *Long Man's Song.*
Rubin, Amy. *Children of the Seventh Prophecy.*
Rubinstein, Gillian. *Space Demons.*
Sargent, Sarah. *Jonas McFee A.T.P.*
Scott, William. *Boori.*
Senn, Steve. *Born of Flame; Spacebread.*
Service, Pamela. *Tomorrow's Magic.*
Singer, Isaac. *Fearsome Inn; Topsy-Turvy Emperor of China.*
Sleator, William. *Boy Who Reversed Himself.*
Smith, L.J. *Night of the Solstice.*
Stevenson, Robert Louis. *Strange Case of Dr. Jekyll and Mr. Hyde.*
Tolkien, J.R.R. *Fellowship of the Ring; Hobbit; Return of the King; Silmarillion; Two Towers.*
Vande Veldi, Vivian. *Hidden Magic.*
Vinge, Joan. *Snow Queen.*
Wells, H.G. *Time Machine and Invisible Man.*
Williams, Ursula. *Toymaker's Daughter.*
Wrightson, Patricia. *Dark Bright Water; Ice Is Coming; Journey Behind the Wind; Nargon and the Stars.*
Yep, Laurence. *Dragon of the Lost Sea.*
Yolen, Jane. *Dragon's Blood; Heart's Blood; Sending of Dragons.*
York, Carol. *Revenge of the Dolls.*

Fantasy/Places

See also: Sci Fi/Time Travel

Alexander, Lloyd. *First Two Lives of Lukas-Kasha.*
Bacon, Martha. *Third Road.*
Baehr, Patricia. *Dragon Prophecy.*
Baker, Betty. *Save Sirrushany.*
Bass, Donna. *Tales of the Dark Crystal.*
Belden, Wilanne. *Rescue of Ranor.*
Boston, Lucy. *Castle of Yew.*
Carlsen, Ruth. *Ride a Wild Horse; Sam Battleby.*
Carroll, Lewis. *Alice's Adventures in Wonderland; Through the Looking Glass.*
Chetwin, Grace. *On All Hallow's Eve.*
Clavell, James. *Thrump-o-Moto.*
Cohen, Barbara. *Unicorns in the Rain.*
Corbett, Scott. *Ever Ride a Dinosaur?*
Curry, Jane. *Beneath the Hill.*
Dahl, Roald. *BFG.*
De Jong, Dola. *House on Charlton Street.*
Dixon, Marjorie. *Forbidden Island.*
Doty, Jean. *Can I Get There by Candlelight?*
Dragt, Tanke. *Towers of February.*
Durrell, Gerald. *Talking Parcel.*
Edwards, Julie. *Last of the Really Great Whangdoodles.*
Ende, Michael. *Neverending Story.*
Farthing, Alison. *Mystical Beast.*
Faulkner, Nancy. *Wishing Tree.*

Kennedy, Richard. *Boxcar at the Center of the Universe.*
Kidd, Ronald. *Glitch: A Computer Fantasy.*
Kruss, James. *Happy Island Behind the Winds; My Great-Grandfather and I; Return to the Happy Islands.*
Le Guin, Ursula. *Beginning Place.*
Levin, Betty. *Sword of Culann.*
Lindbergh, Anne. *Bailey's Window.*
Lindgren, Astrid. *Brothers Lionheart.*
Maguire, Gregory. *Daughter of the Moon.*
Naylor, Phyllis. *Faces in the Water.*
Nichols, Ruth. *Marrow of the World.*
Norton, Andre. *Dragon Magic; Outside; Quest Crosstime.*
Ormondroyd, Edward. *Time at the Top.*
Palin, Michael. *Mirrorstone.*
Palmer, Mary. *Teaspoon Tree.*
Park, Ruth. *Road Under the Sea.*
Pinkwater, Daniel. *Slaves of Spiegel; Worms of Kukulima.*
Shura, Mary. *Nearsighted Knight.*
Singer, Marilyn. *Horsemaster.*
Stearns, Pamela. *Fool and the Dancing Bear.*
Steele, Mary. *Journey Outside.*
Stolz, Mary. *Cat in the Mirror.*
Teague, Bob. *Adam in Blunderland.*
Willard, Nancy. *Firebrat.*
Williams, Mona. *Messenger.*
Winterfeld, Henry. *Castaways in Lilliput.*

Fantasy/Spells

Allan, Mabel. *Chill in the Lane.*
Allen, Sybil. *Lissamor's Child.*
Baker, Betty. *Seven Spells to Farewell.*
Baker, Margaret. *Porterhouse Major.*
Bawden, Nina. *Kept in the Dark.*
Bethancourt, T.E. *Dog Days of Arthur Cane.*
Christopher, John. *Lotus Caves.*
Dahl, Roald. *Magic Finger.*
Dunlop, Eileen. *Maze Stone.*
Foster, Alan. *Spellsinger.*
Hill, Elizabeth. *Fangs Aren't Everything.*
Horseman, Elaine. *Hubble's Bubble; Hubble's Treasure Hunt.*
Hoyland, John. *Ivy Garland.*
Hunter, Mollie. *Kelpie's Pearls; Mermaid Summer.*
Ipcar, Dahlov. *Queen of Spells.*
Lawrence, Louise. *Wyndcliffe.*
Leroe, Ellen. *Have a Heart, Cupid Delaney.*
Levin, Betty. *Forespoken.*
Linn, Janet. *Twin Spell.*
MacDonald, Reby. *Ghosts of Austwick Manor.*
Newman, Robert. *Testing of Tertius.*
Orgel, Doris. *Next Door to Xanadu.*
Roberts, Willo. *Magic Book.*
Sargent, Sarah. *Lure of the Dark.*
Selden, George. *Genie of Sutton Place.*

Service, Pamela. *Reluctant God.*
Sleigh, Barbara. *Carbonel, King of the Cats.*
Stahl, Ben. *Blackbeard's Ghost.*
Syfret, Anne. *Bella.*
Tannen, Mary. *Wizard Children of Finn.*
Tuttle, Lisa. *Catwitch.*
Winthrop, Elizabeth. *Castle in the Attic.*

Fantasy/Wishes

Avi. *Bright Shadow.*
Babbitt, Natalie. *Tuck Everlasting.*
Bauer, Marion. *Touch the Moon.*
Beachcroft, Nina. *Wishing People.*
Brittain, Bill. *All the Money in the World; Wish Giver.*
Calhoun, Mary. *Ownself.*
Eager, Edward. *Half Magic; Magic by the Lake; Time Garden; Well-Wishers.*
Heide, Florence. *Treehorn's Wish.*
Leeson, Robert. *Genie on the Loose.*
Matheson. *Bid Time Return.*
Mayne, William. *Blue Boat.*
Sterman, Betsy. *Too Much Magic.*
Webster, Joanne. *Love Genie.*
Willard, Nancy. *Marzipan Moon.*

Fantasy/Words

Babbitt, Lucy. *Search for Delicious.*
Eckert, Allan. *Wand.*
Feydy, Anne. *Osprey Island.*
Haynes, Mary. *Wordchanger.*
Herzig, Alison. *Word to the Wise.*
Jones, Diana. *Archer's Goon.*
Juster, Norton. *Phantom Tollbooth.*
Wallace, Barbara. *Interesting Thing That Happened at Perfect Acres.*

Farms

See: Rural Life

Fathers

See also: Family

Abercrombie, Barbara. *Cat-Man's Daughter.*
Adler, Carole. *Carly's Buck.*
Aiken, Joan. *Dido and Pa; Go Saddle the Sea.*
Annixter, Jane. *Horns of Plenty; Last Monster; Runner.*
Armstrong, William. *Sounder.*
Arthur, Ruth. *Little Dark Thorn.*

Ashley, Bernard. *Break in the Sun; Dodgem.*
Bach, Alice. *Father Every Few Years.*
Baker, Elizabeth. *This Stranger, My Son.*
Bates, Betty. *Ups and Downs of Jorie Jenkins.*
Baudouy, Michel. *Boy Who Belonged to No One.*
Bawden, Nina. *Robbers.*
Benjamin, Carol. *Wicked Stepdog.*
Blue, Rose. *Month of Sundays; My Mother the Witch.*
Blume, Judy. *It's Not the End of the World.*
Bograd, Larry. *Kolokol Papers; Los Alamos Light; Travelers.*
Boyd, Candy. *Charles Pippin.*
Brink, Carol. *Winter Cottage.*
Broderick, Dorothy. *Hank.*
Brooks, Bruce. *Midnight Hour Encores.*
Burch, Robert. *Queenie Peavey; Simon and the Game of Chance.*
Butterworth, W.E. *Leroy and the Old Man; Steve Bellamy.*
Byars, Betsy. *Animal, the Vegetable and John D. Jones; Good-Bye, Chicken Little; Night Swimmers.*
Byrd, Elizabeth. *I'll Get By.*
Calhoun, Mary. *Julie's Tree.*
Campbell, Hope. *Meanwhile Back at the Castle.*
Cannon, Bettie. *Bellsong for Sarah Rains.*
Carter, Alden. *Wart, Son of Toad.*
Cavanna, Betty. *Going on Sixteen.*
Cave, Hugh. *Voyage.*
Chambers, John. *Footlight Summer.*
Christopher, Matt. *Fox Steals Home; Takedown.*
Clarke, Mary. *Limmer's Daughter.*
Cleary, Beverly. *Ramona and Her Father.*
Cleaver, Vera. *Delpha Green and Company; Grover.*
Colman, Hila. *Just the Two of Us; What's the Matter with the Dobsons.*
Conrad, Pam. *What I Did for Roman.*
Cormier, Robert. *I Am the Cheese.*
Cross, Gillian. *Born of the Sun.*
Dahl, Roald. *Danny, the Champion of the World.*
Danziger, Paula. *Can You Sue Your Parents for Malpractice?*
De Clements, Barthe. *Five Finger Discount.*
Del Rey, Lester. *Infinite Worlds of Maybe.*
Diggs, Lucy. *Moon in the Water.*
Dillon, Eilis. *Cruise of the Santa Maria.*
Ewing, Kathryn. *Private Matter; Things Won't Be the Same.*
Falk, Ann. *Who Is Erika?*
Farjeon, Annabel. *Maria Lupin.*
Farley, Carol. *Ms. Isabell Corell, Herself.*
Faulkner, Nancy. *Stage for Rom.*
Feagles, Anita. *Year the Dreams Came Back.*
Fenton, Edward. *Duffy's Rocks.*
Fine, Anne. *Alias Madame Doubtfire.*
Fitzhugh, Louise. *Sport.*
Fleischman, Paul. *Rear-View Mirrors.*
Flory, Jane. *Golden Venture.*
Fox, Paula. *Blowfish Live in the Sea; Moonlight Man; Portrait of Ivan.*

Frankel, Haskel. *Pro Football Rookie.*
French, Michael. *Us Against Them.*
Friendlich, Dick. *Backstop Ace.*
Garfield, Leon. *Sound of Coaches.*
Gault, William. *Super Bowl Bound.*
Geller, Mark. *What I Heard.*
Glasser, Barbara. *Bongo Bradley.*
Gorey, Edward. *Hapless Child.*
Graber, Richard. *Little Breathing Room.*
Graham, Lorenz. *I, Momolu.*
Greenberg, Jan. *Season In-Between.*
Grund, Josef. *You Have a Friend, Pietro.*
Guernsey, Joann. *Room to Breathe.*
Hahn, Mary. *Following the Mystery Man.*
Hale, Arlene. *Listen to Your Heart.*
Hall, Lynn. *Whispered Horse.*
Halvorson, Marilyn. *Cowboys Don't Cry.*
Hamner, Earl. *You Can't Get There from Here.*
Hamre, Leif. *Operation Arctic.*
Hanlon, Emily. *Love Is No Excuse.*
Hartman, Evert. *War Without Friends.*
Hawks, Robert. *This Stranger, My Father.*
Henkes, Kevin. *Two Under Par.*
Hentoff, Nat. *This School Is Driving Me Crazy.*
Hermes, Patricia. *Solitary Secret.*
Hilgartner, Beth. *Necklace of Fallen Stars.*
Hines, Anna. *Boys Are Yucko!*
Holland, Isabelle. *Empty House; Jennie Kiss'd Me.*
Honig, Donald. *Jed McLane and the Stranger.*
Hopper, Nancy. *Carrie's Games.*
Howard, Ellen. *Gilly Flower; Her Own Song.*
Howker, Janne. *Isaac Campion.*
Hunt, Irene. *Everlasting Hills.*
Hunter, Evan. *Me and Mr. Stenner.*
Jackson, Jacqueline. *Taste of Spruce Gum.*
Jenkins, Alan. *White Horses and Black Bulls.*
Johnson, Annabel. *Golden Touch; Grizzly; Prisoner of Psi.*
Johnston, Norma. *Carlisle's All; Gabriel's Girl.*
Kay, Mara. *One Small Clue.*
Keller, Beverly. *No Beasts, No Children.*
Kennemore, Tim. *Wall of Words.*
Kerr, M.E. *Night Kites.*
Klass, Sheila. *Credit-Card Carole.*
Klein, Norma. *Now That I Know; Older Men; Taking Sides.*
Konigsburg, E.L. *About the B'nai Bagels; Father's Arcane Daughter; Journey to an 800 Number.*
Lampman, Evelyn. *Half-Breed.*
Landis, J.D. *Daddy's Girl.*
Lehrman, Robert. *Juggler.*
Levitin, Sonia. *Season for Unicorns.*
Locke, Elsie. *Runaway Settlers.*
Lorimer, Lawrence. *Secrets.*
Love, Sandra. *Crossing Over.*
Lowry, Lois. *Switcharound.*
Lyle, Katie. *Dark But Full of Diamonds.*
MacLeod, Charlotte. *Cirak's Daughter.*
Maddock, Reginald. *Thin Ice.*
Maddox, Bill. *Rags and Patches.*

Mahy, Margaret. *Catalogue of the Universe.*
Maloney, Ray. *Impact Zone.*
Mark, Jan. *Trouble Half-way.*
Martin, Ann. *With You and Without You.*
Matthews, Ann. *Journey of Natty Gann.*
Mattson, Olle. *Michel and the Lost Ship.*
Mazer, Harry. *Cave Under the City; Dollar Man.*
Monjo, F.N. *Grand Papa and Ellen Aroon.*
Morton, Jane. *I Am Rubber, You Are Glue.*
Murphy, Jill. *Worlds Apart.*
Myers, Walter. *It Ain't All for Nothin'.*
Naylor, Phyllis. *Keeper.*
Neville, Emily. *It's Like This, Cat.*
Nixon, Joan. *Maggie Forevermore.*
Norris, Gunilla. *Lillian.*
Norton, Andre. *Rebel Spurs; Ride, Proud Rebel.*
O'Connor, Patricia. *South Swell.*
Okimoto, Jean. *Norman Schnurman, Normal Person.*
Osborne, Mary. *Love Always, Blue.*
Parker, Richard. *Paul and Etta.*
Paterson, Katherine. *Park's Quest; Sign of the Chrysanthemum.*
Pearce, Philippa. *Way to Sattin Shore.*
Pearson, Gayle. *Fish Friday.*
Peck, Richard. *Father Figure; Through a Brief Darkness.*
Pickering, Mary. *Mystery of the Greek Icon.*
Platt, Kin. *Chloris and the Creeps.*
Pohlman, Lillian. *Sing Loose.*
Polland, Madeleine. *White Twilight.*
Radley, Gail. *Nothing Stays the Same Forever.*
Rinaldi, Ann. *Good Side of My Heart.*
Rock, Gail. *Dream for Addie; House Without a Christmas Tree.*
Rodgers, Mary. *Summer Switch.*
Rodowsky, Colby. *Summer's Worth of Shame.*
Roth, Arthur. *Secret Lover of Elmtree.*
Sachs, Marilyn. *Fourteen.*
St. George, Judith. *Mystery at St. Martin's.*
Salassi, Otto. *On the Ropes.*
Sallis, Susan. *Time for Everything.*
Samuels, Gertrude. *Adam's Daughter.*
Schwartz, Joel. *Great Spaghetti Showdown.*
Sebestyen, Ouida. *Far from Home.*
Service, Pamela. *Question of Destiny.*
Sharmat, Marjorie. *He Noticed I'm Alive.*
Shreve, Susan. *Masquerade.*
Shyer, Marlene. *Blood in the Snow.*
Silsbee, Peter. *Big Way Out.*
Skirrow, Desmond. *Case of the Silver Egg.*
Skolsky, Mindy. *Hannah and the Best Father on Route 9W.*
Slatten, Evelyn. *Good, the Bad and the Rest of Us.*
Slote, Alfred. *Friends Like That; Moving In.*
Smith, Alison. *Reserved for Mark Anthony Crowder.*
Smith, Doris. *First Hard Times.*
Softly, Barbara. *Place Mill.*
Sorensen, Virginia. *Friends of the Road.*
Spykman, Elizabeth. *Lemon and a Star.*

Fishing

Folklore

See: Legends

Football

Foster Homes

See also: Adoption; Orphans

Armer, Alberta. *Troublemaker.*
Bauer, Marion. *Foster Child.*
Blue, Rose. *Quiet Place.*
Buck, Pearl. *Big Wave.*
Byars, Betsy. *Pinballs.*
Carlson, Natalie. *Ann Aurelia and Dorothy.*
Childress, Alice. *Rainbow Jordan.*
Christopher, Matt. *Dirt Bike Runaway.*
Cohen, Miriam. *Robert and Dawn Marie 4 Ever.*
Conford, Ellen. *To All My Fans, with Love from Sylvie.*
Cresswell, Helen. *Dear Shrink.*
De Clements, Barthe. *Double Trouble; Fourth Grade Wizards.*
Dunlop, Eileen. *Fox Farm.*
French, Dorothy. *Try at Tumbling.*
Gates, Doris. *Sensible Kate.*
Guy, Rosa. *Edith Jackson.*
Hansen, Joyce. *Gift Giver.*
Hermes, Patricia. *Heads, I Win.*
Hughes, Dean. *Family Pose.*
Hunt, Mabel. *Beggar's Daughter.*
Little, Jean. *Home from Far.*
MacPherson, Margaret. *Rough Road.*
Means, Florence. *Us Maltbys.*
Montgomery, John. *Foxy.*
Morgenroth, Barbara. *Will the Real Renie Lake Please Stand Up?*
Parker, Richard. *Second Hand Family.*
Paterson, Katherine. *Great Gilly Hopkins.*
Renvoise, Jean. *Wild Thing.*
Rhodes, Evan. *Prince of Central Park.*
Rich, Louise. *Star Island Boy; Three of a Kind.*
Sachs, Marilyn. *December Tale; Fran Ellen's House.*
Samuels, Gertrude. *Yours, Brett.*
Shreve, Susan. *Loveletters.*
Swetman, Evelyn. *Yes, My Darling Daughter.*
Windsor, Patricia. *Mad Martin.*
Wolitzer, Hilma. *Toby Lived Here.*

Friendship

See also: Friendship Among Boys; Friendship Among Girls

Adler, Carole. *Get Lost, Little Brother; Kiss the Clown; Magic of the Glits.*
Alcott, Louisa May. *Rose in Bloom; Under the Lilacs.*
Alexander, Anne. *To Live a Lie.*
Amdur, Nikki. *One of Us.*
Angell, Judie. *Ronnie and Rosey.*
Angier, Bradford. *Ask for Love and They Give You Rice Pudding.*
Arthur, Ruth. *On the Wasteland.*
Bargar, Gary. *Life. Is. Not. Fair.*
Bates, Betty. *Picking Up the Pieces.*
Bawden, Nina. *Robbers.*
Beckman, Delores. *My Own Private Sky.*

Bergman, Tamar. *Boy from Over There.*
Bond, Nancy. *Place to Come Back To.*
Bonzon, Paul. *Pursuit of the French Alps.*
Bornstein, Ruth. *Little Gorilla.*
Bosse, Malcolm. *79 Squares.*
Boylan, Rowena. *Better Than the Rest.*
Bradbury, Bianca. *Loner; Two on an Island.*
Bradford, Richard. *Red Sky at Morning.*
Brancato, Robin. *Facing Up.*
Bulla, Clyde. *Shoeshine Girl.*
Bunting, Eve. *Empty Window; Skateboard Four.*
Burch, Robert. *Two That Were Tough.*
Buscaglia, Leo. *Memory for Tino.*
Byars, Betsy. *Blossoms Meet the Vulture Lady; Cybil War; Pinballs.*
Calvert, Patricia. *Yesterday's Daughter.*
Cannon, A.E. *Cal Cameron by Day, Spiderman by Night.*
Carlson, Natalie. *Letter on the Tree.*
Carpland, Bo. *Bow Island: Story of a Summer That Was Different.*
Carris, Joan. *Revolt of 10-X.*
Carter, Alden. *Sheila's Dying.*
Chaikin, Miriam. *Friends Forever; Getting Even; I Should Worry, I Should Care; Lower! Higher! You're a Liar!*
Cleaver, Vera. *Grover; Mock Revolt.*
Cohen, Barbara. *Coasting; Fat Jack; Tell Us Your Secret; Thank You, Jackie Robinson.*
Cohen, Miriam. *Robert and Dawn Marie 4 Ever.*
Cole, Sheila. *Meaning Well.*
Cole, Stephen. *Pitcher and I.*
Colman, Hila. *Rich and Famous Like My Mom.*
Colver, Anne. *Bread and Butter Indian.*
Conford, Ellen. *Felicia, the Critic; Me and the Terrible Two.*
Corcoran, Barbara. *Dance to Still Music.*
Crawford, Charles. *Three-Legged Race.*
Crayder, Dorothy. *Ishkabibble.*
Crutcher, Chris. *Stonan!*
Culin, Charlotte. *Cages of Glass, Flowers of Time.*
Cunningham, Julia. *Come to the Edge; Flight of the Sparrows; Silent Voice.*
Dacquino, V.T. *Kiss the Candy Days Good-Bye.*
Davidson, Alan. *Bewitching of Alison Allbright.*
De Clements, Barthe. *Nothing's Fair in the Fifth Grade.*
Delton, Jina. *Two Blocks Down.*
Delton, Judy. *Kitty from the Start; Kitty in High School; Kitty in the Middle; Kitty in the Summer.*
Derby, Pat. *Goodbye Emily, Hello.*
Dickinson, Peter. *Healer.*
Edwards, Page. *Scarface Joe.*
Eisenberg, Lisa. *Mystery at Bluff Point Dunes.*
Engel, Beth. *Big Words.*
Epstein, Anne. *Good Stones.*
Ethridge, Kenneth. *Toothpick; Viola, Furgy, Bobbi and Me.*
Eyerly, Jeannette. *Seth and Me and Rebel Makes Three; Seeing Summer.*

Fields, Julia. *Green Lion of Zion Street.*
Fine, Anne. *Summer House Loon.*
Fisher, Lois. *Radio Robert.*
Fitzhugh, Louise. *Long Secret.*
Flory, Jane. *Time for the Towpath.*
Fosburgh, Liza. *Mrs. Abercorn and the Bunce Boys.*
Fox, Paula. *Portrait of Ivan.*
Frick, C.H. *Comeback Guy.*
Friis-Baastad, Babbis. *Kristy's Courage.*
Fritzhand, James. *Life Is a Lonely Place.*
Gaeddert, Louann. *Your Former Friend, Matthew.*
Garfield, James. *Follow My Leader.*
Garfield, Leon. *Night of the Comet; Strange Affair of Adelaide Harris; Young Nick and Jubilee.*
Gauch, Patricia. *Year the Summer Died.*
Gerson, Corinne. *Passing Through.*
Giff, Patricia. *Love, from the Fifth Grade Celebrity.*
Gilson, Jamie. *Double Dog Dare.*
Godden, Rumer. *Diddakoi.*
Godwin, Gail. *Finishing School.*
Gondosch, Linda. *Who's Afraid of Haggerty House.*
Grace, Fran. *Very Private Performance.*
Greaves, Margaret. *Stone of Terror.*
Green, Connie. *War at Home.*
Greenberg, Jan. *Just the Two of Us.*
Green, Phyllis. *Mildred Murphy, How Does Your Garden Grow?*
Greene, Bette. *Get on Out of Here, Philip Hall; Philip Hall Likes Me. I Reckon Maybe.*
Greene, Constance. *Double and Dare O'Toole; Girl Called Al.*
Greenwald, Sheila. *Will the Real Gertrude Hollings Please Stand Up?*
Gripe, Maria. *Hugo; Hugo and Josephine; Julia's House; Night Daddy.*
Grund, Josef. *You Have a Friend, Pietro.*
Guillot, Rene. *Fofana.*
Haas, Dorothy. *New Friends.*
Hagy, Jeannie. *And Then Mom Joined the Army.*
Hall, Eleanor. *Alice with Golden Hair.*
Hall, Lynn. *Just One Friend.*
Hanes, Mari. *Wild Child.*
Hanlon, Emily. *It's Too Late for Sorry; Swing.*
Hansen, Joyce. *Gift Giver.*
Harris, Christie. *Forbidden Frontier.*
Hautzig, Deborah. *Hey, Dollface.*
Hayes, Sheila. *Me and My Mona Lisa Smile.*
Herlicky, Dirlie. *Ludie's Song.*
Hermes, Patricia. *Friends Are Like That; Heads, I Win; Kevin Corbett Eats Flies; What If They Knew?*
Herzig, Alison. *Word to the Wise.*
Hest, Amy. *Pete and Lily.*
Hodges, Margaret. *Freewheeling of Joshua Cobb; Hatching of Joshua Cobb; Making of Joshua Cobb.*
Holland, Isabelle. *Amanda's Choice.*

Holm, Anne. *North to Freedom.*
Holman, Felice. *Year to Grow.*
Holmes, Barbara. *Charlotte Cheetham: Master of Disaster.*
Honeycutt, Natalie. *Best Laid Plans of Jonah Twist.*
Hooks, William. *Mystery on Bleeker Street.*
Hopper, Nancy. *Just Vernon.*
Houston, James. *Ice Sword.*
Howe, Fanny. *Taking Care.*
Howe, James. *Night Without Stars.*
Hughey, Roberta. *Question Box.*
Hull, Eleanor. *Trainful of Strangers.*
Hunter, Kristin. *Survivors.*
Hurwitz, Johanna. *Hot and Cold Summer; Hot and Cold Winter.*
Hyde, Dayton. *Island of the Loons.*
Innis, Pauline. *Wind of the Pampas.*
Irwin, Hadley. *Moon and Me.*
Johnson, Emily. *Spring and the Shadow Man.*
Johnston, Norma. *If You Love Me, Let Me Go; Striving After Wind.*
Jones, Kanice. *Secrets of a Summer Spy.*
Jones, Rebecca. *Angie and Me.*
Jones, Weyman. *Edge of Two Worlds.*
Joslin, Sesyle. *Gentle Savage.*
Kellogg, Marjorie. *Tell Me That You Love Me, Junie Moon.*
Kidd, Ronald. *That's What Friends Are For.*
Killien, Christie. *All the Above.*
Klein, Norma. *Robbie and the Leap Year Blues.*
Knowles, John. *Separate Peace.*
Knudsen, James. *Just Friends.*
Krumgold, Joseph. *Onion John.*
Lasky, Kathryn. *Bone Wars.*
Le Guin, Ursula. *Very Far Away from Anywhere Else.*
L'Engle, Madeleine. *House Like a Lotus.*
Levoy, Myron. *Alan and Naomi; Shadow Like a Leopard; Three Friends.*
Lorentzen, Karen. *Lanky Longlegs.*
Lovelace, Maud. *Betsy in Spite of Herself.*
MacKellar, William. *Very Small Miracle.*
Magorian, Michelle. *Good Night, Mr. Tom.*
Mahy, Margaret. *Catalogue of the Universe.*
Martin, Ann. *With You and Without You.*
Mayne, William. *Max's Dream.*
Miklowitz, Gloria. *Good-Bye Tomorrow.*
Miller, Frances. *Aren't You the One Who....*
Mooney, Elizabeth. *Sandy Shoes Mystery.*
Moore, Emily. *Whose Side Are You On?*
Morgan, Alison. *Boy Called Fish.*
Morpurgo, Michael. *Why the Whales Came.*
Morris, Winifred. *With Magical Horses to Ride.*
Mowat, Farley. *Curse of the Viking Grave.*
Neigoff, Mike. *Free Throw.*
Neufeld, John. *Lisa, Bright and Dark; Sharelle.*
Neville, Emily. *Garden of Broken Glass; Seventeenth-Street Gang.*
Nostlinger, Christine. *Luke and Angela.*
O'Connor, Jane. *Yours Till Niagara Falls.*

Friendship Among Boys

Andrews, Jean. *Flying Fingers Club.*
Ashley, Bernard. *Terry on the Fence.*
Balducci, Carolyn. *Is There Life After Graduation, Henry Birnbaum?*
Bentley, Phyllis. *Forgery.*
Bess, Clayton. *Big Man and the Burn-Out.*
Bishop, Curtis. *Fast Break.*
Bograd, Larry. *Fourth Grade Dinosaur.*
Bosse, Malcolm. *Ganesh.*
Brooks, Bruce. *Moves Make the Man.*
Carrick, Carol. *Some Friend.*
Coatsworth, Elizabeth. *Pure Magic.*
Cormier, Robert. *Bumblebee Flies Anyway.*
Davis, Russell. *Choctaw Code.*
Distad, Audree. *Dakota Sons.*
Gardam, Jane. *Hollow Land.*
Gee, Maurine. *Firestorm.*
Gibbons, Faye. *King Shoes and Clown Pockets.*
Green, Phyllis. *Walkie Talkie.*
Greenwald, Sheila. *Alvin Webster's Surefire Plan for Success (And How It Failed).*
Hartling, Peter. *Crutches.*
Havrevold, Finn. *Undertow.*
Jackson, C. Paul. *Bud Baker, College Pitcher.*
Kemp, Gene. *Turbulent Term of Tyke Tiler.*
Klein, Suzy. *What's the Matter with Herbie Jones?*
Knowles, Anne. *Halcyon Island.*
Landsman, Sandy. *Gadget Factor.*
Leigh, Bill. *Far Side of Fear.*
MacMillan, Dianne. *My Best Friend Duc Tran.*
McNeill, Janet. *Goodbye, Dove Square.*
Mark, Jan. *Thunder and Lightnings.*
Myers, Walter. *Fast Sam, Cool Clyde and Stuff.*
Norris, Gunilla. *Standing in the Magic.*
Okimoto, Jean. *Norman Schnurman, Normal Person.*
Rinkoff, Barbara. *Watchers.*
Roos, Stephen. *Thirteenth Summer.*
Roth, David. *Best of Friends; River Runaways.*
Slote, Alfred. *Tony and Me.*
Smith, Doris. *Last Was Lloyd; Taste of Blackberries.*
Smith, Janice. *Kid Next Door and Other Headaches.*
Tate, Joan. *Wild Boy.*
Teague, Sam. *King of Hearts' Heart.*
Towne, Mary. *Glass Room.*
Tunis, John. *His Enemy, His Friend.*
Vance, Marguerite. *Jeptha and the New People.*
Wier, Ester. *Easy Does It.*
Willard, Barbara. *Miller's Boy.*

Friendship Among Girls

Allan, Mabel. *Night Wind.*
Angell, Judie. *Tina Gogo.*

Asher, Sandy. *Daughter of the Law.*
Baehr, Patricia. *Falling Scales.*
Betancourt, Jeanne. *Home Sweet Home.*
Blume, Judy. *Just as Long as We're Together.*
Bottner, Barbara. *Nothing in Common.*
Brancato, Robin. *Something Left to Lose.*
Bunting, Eve. *Janet Hamm Needs a Date for the Dance.*
Byrd, Elizabeth. *It Had to Be You.*
Carlson, Dale. *Call Me Amanda.*
Cassedy, Sylvia. *M.E. and Morton.*
Chang, Heidi. *Elaine, Mary Lewis, and the Frogs.*
Childress, Alice. *Rainbow Jordan.*
Commager, Evan. *Valentine.*
Conford, Ellen. *Anything for a Friend.*
Cooney, Caroline. *Among Friends.*
Cooper, Ilene. *Queen of the Sixth Grade.*
Crayder, Teresa. *Cathy and Lisette.*
Cuyler, Margery. *Trouble with Soap.*
Danziger, Paula. *It's an Aardvark Eat Turtle World.*
De Leeuw, Adele. *Rugged Dozen.*
Derman, Martha. *Friendstone.*
Dunlop, Eileen. *Clementina.*
Estoril, Jean. *We Danced in Bloomsbury Square.*
Farrar, Susan. *Samantha on Stage.*
Ferris, Jean. *Stainless Steel Rule.*
Feuer, Elizabeth. *One Friend to Another.*
Fisher, Lois. *Rachel Villars, How Could You?*
Franco, Marjorie. *So Who Hasn't Got Problems?*
Gaeddert, Louann. *Just Like Sisters.*
Garrigue, Sheila. *Between Friends.*
Gauch, Patricia. *Night Talks.*
Gilbert, Nan. *Unchosen.*
Gondosch, Linda. *Witches of Hopper Street.*
Gormley, Beatrice. *Best Friend Insurance.*
Greenberg, Jan. *Iceberg and Its Shadow.*
Greene, Constance. *Al(exandra) the Great; Ask Anybody; I Know You, Al; Just Plain Al; Your Old Pal, Al.*
Grove, Vicki. *Fastest Friend in the West.*
Guy, Rosa. *Friends.*
Hahn, Mary. *Daphne's Book; Sara Summer.*
Haven, Susan. *Maybe I'll Move to the Lost and Found.*
Hayes, Sheila. *Carousel Horse; You've Been Away All Summer.*
Herzig, Alison. *Shadows on the Pond.*
Hines, Anna. *Cassie Bowen Takes Witch Lessons.*
Holberg, Ruth. *Rowena the Sailor.*
Honeycutt, Natalie. *Invisible Lissa.*
Kastner, Erich. *Lisa and Lottie.*
Kaye, Marilyn. *Cassie; Friend Like Phoebe.*
Keeton, Elizabeth. *Second Best Friend.*
Kesselman, Wendy. *Flick.*
Kirchgessner, Maria. *High Challenge.*
Klein, Robin. *Hating Alison Ashley.*
Klevin, Jill. *Turtle Street Trading Company.*
Konigsburg, E.L. *Jennifer, Hecate, Macbeth, William Mackinley and Me, Elizabeth.*

Frontier and Pioneer Life

Funny Stories

See: Humorous

Gangs

Gays

Kesselman, Wendy. *Flick.*
Klein, Norma. *Breaking Up; Now That I Know.*
Knowles, John. *Separate Peace.*
Leonard, Alison. *Tina's Chance.*
Levoy, Myron. *Three Friends.*
Levy, Elizabeth. *Come Out Smiling.*
Reading, J.P. *Bouquets for Brimbal.*
Rinaldi, Ann. *Good Side of My Heart.*
Ross, Marianne. *Good-Bye Atlantis.*
Scoppettone, Sandra. *Trying Hard to Hear You.*
Simons, Wendy. *Harper's Mother.*
Tolan, Stephanie. *Last of Eden.*
Ure, Jean. *Other Side of the Fence.*
Wallin, Marie. *Tangles.*
Wersba, Barbara. *Run Softly, Go Fast.*
Zindel, Paul. *Confessions of a Teenage Baboon.*

Ghosts

Adler, Carole. *Footsteps on the Stairs.*
Adler, David. *Jeffrey's Ghost and the Fifth Grade Dragon; Jeffrey's Ghost and the Leftover Baseball Team.*
Alcock, Vivien. *Haunting of Cassie Palmer.*
Allan, Mabel. *Chill in the Lane.*
Allen, Sybil. *Lissamor's Child.*
Anastasio, Dina. *Question of Time.*
Anderson, Mary. *F.T.C. and Company.*
Arthur, Robert. *Secret of Terror Castle.*
Arthur, Ruth. *Miss Ghost; Saracan Lamp; Whistling Boy.*
Avi. *Devil's Race; Something Upstairs: A Tale of Ghosts.*
Bacon, Peggy. *Ghost of Opalina.*
Bargar, Gary. *Ghosts.*
Bedard, Michael. *Darker Magic.*
Bell, Thelma. *Captain Ghost.*
Bellairs, John. *Figure in the Shadows; Revenge of the Wizard's Ghost.*
Best, Herbert. *Desmond and the Peppermint Ghost.*
Brittain, Bill. *Who Knew There'd Be Ghosts?*
Bunting, Eve. *Ghost Behind Me; Ghost Children; Ghosts of Departure Point; Haunting of Safekeep.*
Calif, Ruth. *Over-the-Hill Ghost.*
Cameron, Eleanor. *Court of the Stone Children.*
Campbell, Harper. *Looking for Hamlet: A Haunting at Deeping Lake.*
Carlsen, Ruth. *Hildy and the Cuckoo Clock.*
Chance, Stephen. *Septimus and the Minister Ghost Mystery.*
Charbonneau, Eileen. *Ghosts of Stony Clove.*
Christopher, Matt. *Return of the Headless Horseman.*
Church, Richard. *French Lieutenant; A Ghost Story.*
Clapp, Patricia. *Jane-Emily.*
Climo, Shirley. *T.J.'s Ghost.*
Colville, Bruce. *Spirits and Spells.*

Corbett, Scott. *Captain Butcher's Body; Discontented Ghost.*
Cresswell, Helen. *Bagthorpes Abroad; Bagthorpes Haunted.*
Curry, Jane. *Poor Tom's Ghost.*
Dank, Milton. *3-D Traitor.*
Delton, Judy. *Mystery of the Haunted Cabin.*
Derleth, August. *Ghost of Black Hawk Island.*
Dicks, Terrance. *Case of the Ghost Grabbers.*
Feil, Hila. *Ghost Garden.*
Finta, Alexandra. *My Brother and I.*
Fleischman, Sid. *Ghost in the Noonday Sun.*
Foulds, Elfreda. *Ghost's High Noon.*
Gage, Wilson. *Ghost of Five Owl Farm.*
Garfield, Leon. *Empty Sleeve; Ghost Downstairs; Mister Corbett's Ghost.*
Green, Anne. *Good-Bye Gray Lady.*
Green, Phyllis. *Nantucket Summer.*
Grohskopf, Bernice. *Blood and Roses.*
Hahn, Mary. *Wait Till Helen Comes: A Ghost Story.*
Hamley, Dennis. *Landings.*
Haynes, Betsy. *Ghost on Gravestone Hearth.*
Hearne, Betsy. *Eli's Ghost.*
Heuman, William. *Gridiron Stranger.*
Hicks, Clifford. *Alvin Fernald, Master of a Thousand Disguises.*
Hildick, E.W. *Ghost Squad and the Ghoul of Grunberg; Ghost Squad and the Halloween Conspiracy; Ghost Squad and the Menace of the Malevs; Ghost Squad and the Prowling Hermits; Ghost Squad Breaks Through; Ghost Squad Flies Concorde.*
Holl, Kristi. *Haunting of Cabin Thirteen.*
Honness, Elizabeth. *Mystery of the Pirate's Ghost.*
Jackson, Jacqueline. *Ghost Boat.*
Jane, Mary. *Rocking Chair Ghost.*
Johnson, Charles. *Pieces of Eight.*
Kay, Mara. *House Full of Echoes.*
Kilgore, Kathleen. *Ghost Maker.*
Klaveness, Jan. *Griffin Legacy.*
Konigsburg, E.L. *Up from Jerico Tel.*
Krensky, Stephen. *Ghostly Business.*
Lawrence, Louise. *Sing and Scatter Daisies; Wyndcliffe.*
Leroe, Ellen. *Peanut Butter Poltergeist.*
Levin, Betty. *Binding Spell.*
Linn, Janet. *Twin Spell.*
Lively, Penelope. *Ghost of Thomas Kempe; Revenge of Samuel Stokes.*
Lorenzo, Carol. *Mama's Ghosts.*
McBratney, Sam. *Ghosts of Hungryhouse Lane.*
Mace, Elizabeth. *Rushton Inheritance.*
McGinnis, Lila. *Ghost Upstairs.*
McGraw, Eloise. *Trouble with Jacobs.*
McHargue, Georgess. *Funny Banana: Mystery in the Museum.*
MacKellar, William. *Kenny and the Highland Ghost.*
McKillip, Patricia. *House on Parchment Street.*
Mark, Jan. *Under the Autumn Garden.*

Mayne, William. *It.*
Michaels, Barbara. *Here I Stay.*
Miller, Judi. *Ghost in My Soup.*
Milton, Hilary. *Escape from High Doon.*
Morrison, Lucile. *Mystery of Shadow Walk.*
Naylor, Phyllis. *Bernie and the Bessledorf Ghost.*
Nixon, Joan. *House on Hackman's Hill.*
Oliver, Stephen. *Glitter, the Gooder and the Ghost.*
Parish, Peggy. *Haunted House.*
Peck, Richard. *Ghost Belonged to Me; Ghosts I Have Been.*
Peyton, Karen. *Pattern of Roses.*
Platt, Kin. *Ghost of Hellshire Street; Mystery of the Woman in the Mirror.*
Radford, Ken. *Cellar; Haunting at Mill Lane; House in the Shadows.*
Rae, John. *Third Twin: A Ghost Story.*
Randall, Florence. *Almost Year.*
Read, Mary. *Sack Man and the Grave.*
Rodowsky, Colby. *Gathering Room.*
Roos, Stephen. *My Favorite Ghost.*
Rundle, Anne. *Moonbranches.*
St. George, Judith. *Haunted.*
Sefton, Catherine. *Ghost and Bertie Boggin.*
Service, Pamela. *When the Night Wind Howls.*
Shecter, Ben. *Game for Demons.*
Silverstein, Herman. *Mad, Mad Monday.*
Singer, Marilyn. *Ghost Host.*
Snyder, Zilpha. *Blair's Nightmare; Headless Cupid.*
Spearing, Judith. *Ghost That Went to School; Museum Ghosts.*
Stahl, Ben. *Blackbeard's Ghost; Secret of the Red Skull.*
Tapp, Kathy. *Scorpio Ghost and the Black Hole Gang.*
Tomalin, Ruth. *Gone Away.*
Van Iterson, Siny. *Spirits of Chocamata.*
Walker, Diana. *Mystery of Black Gut.*
Wallin, Luke. *Slavery Ghosts.*
Westall, Robert. *Ghost Abbey; Haunting of Charles McGill.*
Whitney, Phyllis. *Mystery of the Haunted Pool.*
Williams, Ursula. *Castle Merlin.*
Windsor, Patricia. *Home Is Where Your Feet Are Standing; How a Weirdo and a Ghost Can Change Your Entire Life; Killing Time.*
Wright, Betty. *Christina's Ghost; Ghost in the Window.*
Wright, Billy. *Ghosts Beneath Our Feet.*
Wrightson, Patricia. *Balyet.*
York, Carol. *Nights in Ghostland.*

Girls

See: Girls, Mature; Girls, Pre-Teen; Girls, Teen

Girls, Mature

Allan, Mabel. *Hilary's Summer on Her Own; Mystery in Rome; Signpost to Switzerland.*
Alter, Judy. *After Pa Was Shot.*
Anderson, Mary. *Rise and Fall of a Teen-Age Wacko.*
Angell, Judie. *What's Best for You.*
Arrick, Fran. *Steffie Can't Come Out to Play.*
Arundel, Honor. *Terrible Temptation.*
Baker, Betty. *Spirit Is Willing.*
Baner, Skulda. *First Parting.*
Beckman, Gunnel. *Admission to the Feast; That Early Spring.*
Beyer, Audrey. *Katherine Leslie.*
Bolton, Carole. *Never Jam Today.*
Bond, Nancy. *Country of Broken Stone.*
Bonnell, Dorothy. *Why Did You Go to College, Linda Warren?*
Branscum, Robbie. *Toby and Johnny Joe.*
Bratton, Helen. *Amber Flash; It's Morning Again.*
Brinsmead, Hesba. *Pastures of the Blue Crane.*
Brown, Irene. *Answer Me, Answer Me.*
Calvert, Patricia. *Hadder MacColl.*
Cameron, Eleanor. *To the Green Mountains.*
Cavanna, Betty. *Country Cousin; Time for Tenderness.*
Clapp, Patricia. *Tamarack Tree.*
Clarke, Mary. *Limmer's Daughter.*
Clements, Bruce. *Anywhere Else But Here.*
Colman, Hila. *Claudia, Where Are You?*
Degens, T. *Visit.*
Donahue, Marilyn. *Straight Along a Crooked Road.*
Du Jardin, Rosamond. *Double Feature; Marcy Catches Up; Showboat Summer.*
Eisenberg, Lisa. *Fast Food King; Golden Idol; House of Laughs; Mystery at Snowshoe Mountain Lodge; Tiger Rose.*
Flory, Jane. *Liberation of Clementine Tipton.*
Friermood, Elizabeth. *Doc Dudley's Daughter.*
Gordon, Ethel. *Where Does the Summer Go?*
Greene, Bette. *Morning Is a Long Time Coming.*
Hager, Alice. *Cathy Whitney, President's Daughter.*
Hall, Elizabeth. *Phoebe Snow.*
Hall, Lynn. *Flyaway; Leaving; Letting Go.*
Hallman, Ruth. *Search Without Fear.*
Heyman, Anita. *Final Grades.*
Hilgartner, Beth. *Necklace of Fallen Stars.*
Hinchman, Catherine. *Torchlight.*
Hoffman, Alice. *Property Of.*
Holberg, Ruth. *Jill and the Applebird House.*
Holland, Isabelle. *Perdita.*
Holmberg, Ake. *Margaret's Story.*
Johnston, Norma. *Myself and I; Nice Girl Like You.*
Klein, Norma. *It's OK If You Don't Love Me.*
Langton, Jane. *Fragile Flag.*

Kesselman, Wendy. *Flick.*
Klein, Norma. *Breaking Up; Now That I Know.*
Knowles, John. *Separate Peace.*
Leonard, Alison. *Tina's Chance.*
Levoy, Myron. *Three Friends.*
Levy, Elizabeth. *Come Out Smiling.*
Reading, J.P. *Bouquets for Brimbal.*
Rinaldi, Ann. *Good Side of My Heart.*
Ross, Marianne. *Good-Bye Atlantis.*
Scoppettone, Sandra. *Trying Hard to Hear You.*
Simons, Wendy. *Harper's Mother.*
Tolan, Stephanie. *Last of Eden.*
Ure, Jean. *Other Side of the Fence.*
Wallin, Marie. *Tangles.*
Wersba, Barbara. *Run Softly, Go Fast.*
Zindel, Paul. *Confessions of a Teenage Baboon.*

Ghosts

Adler, Carole. *Footsteps on the Stairs.*
Adler, David. *Jeffrey's Ghost and the Fifth Grade Dragon; Jeffrey's Ghost and the Leftover Baseball Team.*
Alcock, Vivien. *Haunting of Cassie Palmer.*
Allan, Mabel. *Chill in the Lane.*
Allen, Sybil. *Lissamor's Child.*
Anastasio, Dina. *Question of Time.*
Anderson, Mary. *F.T.C. and Company.*
Arthur, Robert. *Secret of Terror Castle.*
Arthur, Ruth. *Miss Ghost; Saracan Lamp; Whistling Boy.*
Avi. *Devil's Race; Something Upstairs: A Tale of Ghosts.*
Bacon, Peggy. *Ghost of Opalina.*
Bargar, Gary. *Ghosts.*
Bedard, Michael. *Darker Magic.*
Bell, Thelma. *Captain Ghost.*
Bellairs, John. *Figure in the Shadows; Revenge of the Wizard's Ghost.*
Best, Herbert. *Desmond and the Peppermint Ghost.*
Brittain, Bill. *Who Knew There'd Be Ghosts?*
Bunting, Eve. *Ghost Behind Me; Ghost Children; Ghosts of Departure Point; Haunting of Safekeep.*
Calif, Ruth. *Over-the-Hill Ghost.*
Cameron, Eleanor. *Court of the Stone Children.*
Campbell, Harper. *Looking for Hamlet: A Haunting at Deeping Lake.*
Carlsen, Ruth. *Hildy and the Cuckoo Clock.*
Chance, Stephen. *Septimus and the Minister Ghost Mystery.*
Charbonneau, Eileen. *Ghosts of Stony Clove.*
Christopher, Matt. *Return of the Headless Horseman.*
Church, Richard. *French Lieutenant; A Ghost Story.*
Clapp, Patricia. *Jane-Emily.*
Climo, Shirley. *T.J.'s Ghost.*
Colville, Bruce. *Spirits and Spells.*

Corbett, Scott. *Captain Butcher's Body; Discontented Ghost.*
Cresswell, Helen. *Bagthorpes Abroad; Bagthorpes Haunted.*
Curry, Jane. *Poor Tom's Ghost.*
Dank, Milton. *3-D Traitor.*
Delton, Judy. *Mystery of the Haunted Cabin.*
Derleth, August. *Ghost of Black Hawk Island.*
Dicks, Terrance. *Case of the Ghost Grabbers.*
Feil, Hila. *Ghost Garden.*
Finta, Alexandra. *My Brother and I.*
Fleischman, Sid. *Ghost in the Noonday Sun.*
Foulds, Elfreda. *Ghost's High Noon.*
Gage, Wilson. *Ghost of Five Owl Farm.*
Garfield, Leon. *Empty Sleeve; Ghost Downstairs; Mister Corbett's Ghost.*
Green, Anne. *Good-Bye Gray Lady.*
Green, Phyllis. *Nantucket Summer.*
Grohskopf, Bernice. *Blood and Roses.*
Hahn, Mary. *Wait Till Helen Comes: A Ghost Story.*
Hamley, Dennis. *Landings.*
Haynes, Betsy. *Ghost on Gravestone Hearth.*
Hearne, Betsy. *Eli's Ghost.*
Heuman, William. *Gridiron Stranger.*
Hicks, Clifford. *Alvin Fernald, Master of a Thousand Disguises.*
Hildick, E.W. *Ghost Squad and the Ghoul of Grunberg; Ghost Squad and the Halloween Conspiracy; Ghost Squad and the Menace of the Malevs; Ghost Squad and the Prowling Hermits; Ghost Squad Breaks Through; Ghost Squad Flies Concorde.*
Holl, Kristi. *Haunting of Cabin Thirteen.*
Honness, Elizabeth. *Mystery of the Pirate's Ghost.*
Jackson, Jacqueline. *Ghost Boat.*
Jane, Mary. *Rocking Chair Ghost.*
Johnson, Charles. *Pieces of Eight.*
Kay, Mara. *House Full of Echoes.*
Kilgore, Kathleen. *Ghost Maker.*
Klaveness, Jan. *Griffin Legacy.*
Konigsburg, E.L. *Up from Jerico Tel.*
Krensky, Stephen. *Ghostly Business.*
Lawrence, Louise. *Sing and Scatter Daisies; Wyndcliffe.*
Leroe, Ellen. *Peanut Butter Poltergeist.*
Levin, Betty. *Binding Spell.*
Linn, Janet. *Twin Spell.*
Lively, Penelope. *Ghost of Thomas Kempe; Revenge of Samuel Stokes.*
Lorenzo, Carol. *Mama's Ghosts.*
McBratney, Sam. *Ghosts of Hungryhouse Lane.*
Mace, Elizabeth. *Rushton Inheritance.*
McGinnis, Lila. *Ghost Upstairs.*
McGraw, Eloise. *Trouble with Jacobs.*
McHargue, Georgess. *Funny Banana: Mystery in the Museum.*
MacKellar, William. *Kenny and the Highland Ghost.*
McKillip, Patricia. *House on Parchment Street.*
Mark, Jan. *Under the Autumn Garden.*

Girls

Girls, Mature

Lee, Mildred. *Rock and the Willow.*
Lovelace, Maud. *Betsy and the Great World; Betsy's Wedding.*
Lowrey, Janette. *Love, Bid Me Welcome.*
Lowry, Lois. *Anastasia's Chosen Career.*
Lyon, George. *Borrowed Children.*
McElfresh, Adeline. *To Each Her Dream.*
McNeill, Janet. *Other People.*
Maher, Ramona. *Their Shining Hour.*
Mayne, William. *Royal Harry.*
Mazer, Norma. *Someone to Love.*
Meyer, Carolyn. *Luck of Texas McCoy.*
Mitchell, Faye. *Every Road Has Two Directions.*
Montgomery, Lucy. *Anne of the Island; Anne's House of Dreams.*
Myers, Walter. *Crystal.*
Noble, Iris. *Megan.*
O'Dell, Scott. *Castle in the Sea.*
Ogilvie, Elisabeth. *Ceiling of Amber.*
Oppenheimer, Joan. *Coming Down Time; Run for Your Luck.*
Peck, Richard. *Amanda/Miranda; Representing Superdoll.*
Pfeffer, Susan. *Getting Even.*
Pitkin, Dorothy. *Wiser Than Winter.*
Randall, Janet. *Girl from Boothill.*
Richmond, Sandra. *Wheels for Walking.*
Rinaldi, Ann. *Wolf by the Ears.*
Russ, Lavinia. *April Age.*
Sargent, Shirley. *Ranger in Skirts.*
Scoppottone, Sandra. *Trying Hard to Hear You.*
Seuberlich, Hertha. *Annuzza, A Girl of Romania.*
Smith, Betty. *Tree Grows in Brooklyn.*
Swift, Helen. *Second Semester.*
Symons, Geraldine. *Miss Rivers and Miss Bridges; Work House Child.*
Talbot, Charlene. *Sodbuster Venture.*
Talley, Naomi. *New Cut Road.*
Thomas, Joyce. *Bright Shadow.*
Thrasher, Crystal. *End of a Dark Road; Taste of Daylight.*
Van Leeuwen, Jean. *Seems Like This Road Goes on Forever.*
Walden, Amelia. *Where Is My Heart?*
Walsh, Jill P. *Unleaving.*
Watson, Sally. *Jode.*
Weber, Lenora. *How Long Is Always?; Pick a New Dream.*
Webster, Jean. *Daddy Long Legs.*
Weiman, Eiveen. *Which Way Courage.*
Weir, Rosemary. *Three Red Herrings.*
Wersba, Barbara. *Beautiful Losers.*
White, Ellen. *President's Daughter.*
Woolley, Catherine. *Cathy Leonard Calling; Libby Looks for a Spy; Libby Shadows a Lady; Libby's Uninvited Guest; Look Alive, Libby; Miss Cathy Leonard; Room for Cathy.*

Girls, Pre-Teen

Adler, Carole. *Magic of the Glits.*
Alexander, Sue. *Lila on the Landing.*
Arthur, Ruth. *Candle in Her Room.*
Avi. *Emily Upham's Revenge.*
Beatty, Patricia. *Behave Yourself, Bethany Brant.*
Benjamin, Carol. *Wicked Stepdog.*
Blos, Joan. *Gathering of Days.*
Blume, Judy. *Are You There God? It's Me, Margaret; Blubber; Otherwise Known as Sheila the Great.*
Branscum, Robbie. *Toby, Granny and George.*
Brink, Carol. *Bad Times of Irma Baumlein; Caddie Woodlawn; Louly; Two Are Better Than One.*
Brock, Emma. *Mary on Roller Skates.*
Bunting, Eve. *Sixth Grade Sleepover.*
Burch, Robert. *Queenie Peavey.*
Burnett, Frances. *Secret Garden.*
Calhoun, Mary. *Depend on Katie John; Honestly Katie John; Katie John.*
Cameron, Eleanor. *Julia's Magic.*
Chaikin, Miriam. *Finders Weepers; Friends Forever; Getting Even; Lower! Higher! You're a Liar!*
Chambers, Aidan. *Present Takers.*
Chastain, Madye. *Magic Island.*
Clauser, Suzanne. *Girl Named Sooner.*
Cleary, Beverly. *Beezus and Ramona; Emily's Runaway Imagination; Ramona and Her Father; Ramona and Her Mother; Ramona Forever; Ramona Quimby, Age 8; Ramona the Brave; Ramona the Pest.*
Cleaver, Vera. *Ellen Grae; Hazel Rye; Sugar Blue.*
Clymer, Eleanor. *We Lived in the Almont.*
Cole, Barbara. *Don't Tell a Soul.*
Conford, Ellen. *Felicia, the Critic; Job for Jenny Archer.*
Conrad, Pam. *Staying Nine.*
Coolidge, Susan. *What Katy Did.*
Cooper, Ilene. *Queen of the Sixth Grade.*
Cresswell, Helen. *Time Out.*
Cunningham, Julia. *Macaroon.*
Curry, Jane. *Beneath the Hill.*
Davis, Naggie. *Grandma's Secret Letter.*
De Clements, Barthe. *Fourth Grade Wizards.*
Delton, Judy. *Angel in Charge; Angel's Mother's Boyfriend; Angel's Mother's Wedding; Backyard Angel; Kitty from the Start.*
Enright, Elizabeth. *Goneaway Lake; Return to Goneaway Lake.*
Estes, Eleanor. *Hundred Dresses; Witch Family.*
Farmer, Penelope. *Magic Stone.*
Fenner, Carol. *Skates for Uncle Richard.*
Fitzhugh, Louise. *Harriet the Spy.*
Francis, Dorothy. *Another Kind of Beauty.*
Gates, Doris. *Blue Willow.*

Giff, Patricia. *Fourth Grade Celebrity; Girl Who Knew It All; Have You Seen Hyacinth Macaw?; Loretta P. Sweeny, Where Are You?; Love, from the Fifth Grade Celebrity; Tootsie Tanner, Why Don't You Talk?; Winter Worm Business.*

Godden, Rumer. *Diddakoi; Little Plum; Miss Happiness and Miss Flower.*

Greene, Constance. *Isabelle and Little Orphan Frannie; Isabelle Shows Her Stuff.*

Gripe, Maria. *Night Daddy.*

Heck, Bessie. *Millie.*

Hermes, Patricia. *What If They Knew?*

Holl, Kristi. *Footprints Up My Back.*

Hoyt, Helen. *Aloha, Susan.*

Huntington, Lee. *Maybe a Miracle.*

Hurwitz, Johanna. *Tough-Luck Karen.*

Jackson, Jacqueline. *Missing Melinda.*

Jarrow, Gail. *If Phyllis Were Here.*

Kalish, Betty. *Eleven, Time to Think of Marriage.*

Karl, Jean. *Beloved Benjamin Is Waiting.*

Karp, Naomi. *Nothing Rhymes with April.*

Kassem, Lou. *Middle School Blues.*

Katz, Bobbie. *1,001 Words.*

Keeton, Elizabeth. *Esmeralda.*

Keller, Beverly. *Desdemona: Twelve Going on Desperate.*

Kelly, Rosalie. *Addie's Year.*

Kingman, Lee. *Georgina and the Dragon.*

Klein, Norma. *Mom, the Wolfman and Me; Naomi in the Middle; Tomboy.*

Konigsburg, E.L. *From the Mixed Up Files of Mrs. Basil E. Frankweiler.*

Krementz, Jill. *Sweet Pea.*

Ladd, Elizabeth. *Meg of Heron's Neck.*

Langton, Jane. *Boyhood of Grace; Her Majesty, Grace Jones.*

Lenski, Lois. *Strawberry Girl.*

Lindbergh, Anne. *Nobody's Orphan.*

Lisle, Janet. *Dancing Cats of Applesap.*

Little, Jean. *Lost and Found; One to Grow On.*

Lorenzo, Carol. *Heart of Snowbird.*

Lovelace, Maud. *Betsy and Tacy Go Over the Big Hill; Betsy-Tacy and Tib.*

Low, Alice. *Kallie's Corner.*

Lowry, Lois. *Anastasia Again; Anastasia at Your Service; Anastasia Krupnik.*

McCracken, Mary. *Lovey: A Very Special Child.*

McHugh, Elisabet. *Karen and Vicki; Karen's Sister; Raising a Mother Isn't Easy.*

MacLachlan, Patricia. *Facts and Fiction of Minna Pratt.*

McLean, Susan. *Pennies for the Piper.*

Malone, Mary. *Three Wishes for Sarah.*

Miles, Betty. *Just the Beginning; Trouble with Thirteen.*

Molarsky, Osmond. *Scrappy.*

Monjo, F.N. *Grand Papa and Ellen Aroon.*

Morgan, Mary. *Rainbow for Susan.*

Musgrave, Florence. *Oh, Sarah.*

Nathanson, Laura. *Trouble with Wednesday.*

Naylor, Phyllis. *Maudie in the Middle.*

Peck, Robert. *Trig; Trig Goes Ape; Trig or Treat; Trig Sees Red.*

Pfeffer, Susan. *Just Between Us; What Do You Do When Your Mouth Won't Open?*

Prince, Marjorie. *Cheese Stands Alone.*

Roberts, Willo. *Sugar Isn't Everything.*

Robinson, Mary. *Amazing Valvano and the Mystery of the Hooded Ra.*

Rodowsky, Colby. *Evy-Ivy-Over.*

Roper, Pamela. *Guardian Angel.*

Roth, Arthur. *Iceberg Hermit.*

Sachs, Marilyn. *Amy and Laura; Amy Moves In; Bear's House; Laura's Luck; Truth About Mary Rose; Veronica Ganz.*

Shreve, Susan. *Lucy Forever and Miss Rosetree.*

Shura, Mary. *Eleanor.*

Sleator, William. *Among the Dolls.*

Smith, Eunice. *Jennifer Is Eleven; Jennifer Prize.*

Spence, Eleanor. *Lillipilly Hill.*

Spykman, Elizabeth. *Edie on the Warpath; Terrible, Horrible Edie.*

Spyri, Johanna. *Heidi.*

Stolz, Mary. *Wonderful, Terrible Time.*

Sypher, Lucy. *Edge of Nowhere.*

Thager, Marie. *Shanta.*

Van der Veer, Judy. *Higher Than the Arrow.*

Vogel, Ilse-Marget. *Tikhon.*

Wiggin, Kate. *Rebecca of Sunnybrook Farm.*

Withey, Barbara. *Serpent Ring.*

Woolley, Catherine. *Ginnie and Geneva.*

Girls, Teen

Adler, Carole. *Shell Lady's Daughter; Some Other Summer.*

Aiken, Joan. *Cuckoo Tree; Nightbirds on Nantucket.*

Albert, Louise. *But I'm Ready to Go.*

Albrecht, Lillie. *Spinning Wheel Secret.*

Alcock, Vivien. *Mysterious Mr. Ross.*

Alcott, Louisa May. *Eight Cousins; Old Fashioned Girl.*

Aldrich, Bess. *Lantern in Her Hand.*

Allan, Mabel. *Black Forest Summer; Strange Enchantment.*

Anckarsvard, Karin. *Springtime for Eva.*

Anderson, Margaret. *Searching for Shona.*

Anderson, Mary. *Who Says Nobody's Perfect?*

Angell, Judie. *Secret Selves.*

Anonymous. *Go Ask Alice.*

Archer, Marian. *Keys for Signe.*

Arundel, Honor. *Blanket Word; Emma in Love; Emma's Island; Girl in the Opposite Bed.*

Auch, Mary Jane. *Glass Slippers Give You Blisters.*

Avi. *True Confessions of Charlotte Doyle.*

Bach, Alice. *Mollie Make-Believe.*

Balis, Andrea. *P.J.*

Barnwell, Robinson. *Shadow on the Water.*

Grandparents

See also: Family

Gypsies

Handicapped

See also: Blindness; Deafness; Mentally Handicapped

Hispanics

See: Latinos

Historical Fiction: Ancient

Haugaard, Erik. *Leif the Unlucky.*
Hill, Marjorie. *Secret of Avalon.*
Hodges, C.W. *Marsh King; Namesake.*
Holland-Crossley, Kevin. *Sea Stranger.*
Jones, Adrienne. *Ride the Far Wind.*
King, Clive. *Ninny's Boat.*
Knudson, Poul. *Challenge.*
L'Amour, Louis. *Haunted Mesa.*
Lattimore, Deborah. *Flame of Peace.*
Leighton, Margaret. *Voyage to Coromandel.*
Levin, Betty. *Griffon's Nest.*
Ottley, Reginald. *Rain from the West.*
Speare, Elizabeth. *Bronze Bow.*
Stiles, Martha. *Star in the Forest.*
Sutcliff, Rosemary. *Blood Feud; Capricorn Bracelet; Dawn Wind; Frontier Wolf; Lantern Bearers; Mark of the Horse Lord; Sun Horse, Moon Horse; Witch's Brat.*
Sutton, Shaun. *Queen's Champion.*
Tannen, Mary. *Wizard Children of Finn.*
Treece, Henry. *Burning of Njal; Centurion; Horned Helmet; Last Viking; Man with a Sword; Swords from the North; Viking's Dawn; Viking's Sunset.*
Yarbro, Chelsea. *Four Horses for Tishtry; Loradio's Apprentice.*

Historical Fiction: B.C.

Anderson, Margaret. *Light in the Mountain.*
Andrews, Mary. *Hostage to Alexander.*
Auel, Jean. *Clan of the Cave Bear; Earth's Children.*
Behn, Harry. *Faraway Lurs; Omen of the Birds.*
Bell, Clare. *Clan Ground; Ratha's Creatures.*
Carter, Dorothy. *His Majesty, Queen Hatshepsut.*
Christopher, John. *Dom and Va.*
Denzel, Justin. *Boy of the Painted Cave.*
Eisen, Anthony. *Bond of the Fire.*
Faulkner, Nancy. *Traitor Queen.*
Fyson, Jenny. *Three Brothers of Ur.*
Garcia, Ann. *Spirit on the Wall.*
Gates, Doris. *Fair Wind to Troy.*
Gedge, Pauline. *Child of the Morning.*
Harnishfeger, Lloyd. *Hunters of the Black Swamp; Prisoner of the Mound Builders.*
Harvey, James. *Beyond the Gorge of Shadows.*
Hunter, Mollie. *Stronghold.*
Johnson, Dorothy. *Farewell to Troy.*
Kjelgaard, James. *Boomerang Hunter.*
Lawrence, Isabelle. *Gift of the Golden Cup; Theft of the Golden Ring.*
Levy, Elizabeth. *Running Out of Time.*
Linevski, A. *Old Tale Carved Out of Stone.*
McGowen, Tom. *Time of the Forest.*
McGraw, Eloise. *Golden Goblet; Mara Daughter of the Nile.*
Maddock, Reginald. *Great Bow; Last Horizon.*
Melling, O.R. *Singing Stone.*

Millstead, Thomas. *Cave of Moving Shadows.*
Myers, Walter. *Legend of Tarik.*
Osborne, Chester. *Memory String.*
Palmer, Myron. *Egyptian Necklace; Treachery in Crete.*
Polland, Madeleine. *Deirdre.*
Pryor, Bonnie. *Seth of the Lion People.*
Sutcliff, Rosemary. *Song for a Dark Queen.*
Swindells, Robert. *When Darkness Comes.*
Treece, Henry. *War Dog.*
Turnbull, Ann. *Maroo of the Winter Caves; Wolf King.*
Turner, Ann. *Time of the Bison.*
Walsh, Jill P. *Toolmaker.*
Whitley, Mary Ann. *Circle of Light.*
Winterfeld, Henry. *Detectives in Togas.*

Historical Fiction: Medieval

Almedingen, E.M. *Stephen's Light.*
Arthur, Ruth. *Saracan Lamp.*
Beckman, Thea. *Crusade in Jeans.*
Bellairs, John. *Trolley to Yesterday.*
Benchley, Nathaniel. *Beyond the Mists.*
Bosse, Malcolm. *Captives of Time.*
Burleigh, David. *Messenger from K'Itai.*
Burt, Olive. *I Challenge the Dark Sea.*
Crossley-Holland, Kevin. *King Horn.*
De Angeli, Marguerite. *Door in the Wall.*
Fon Eisen, Anthony. *Prince of Omeya.*
French, Fiona. *City of Gold.*
Gard, Joyce. *Talargain.*
Gray, Elizabeth. *Adam of the Road.*
Green, Robert. *Whistling Sword.*
Hamley, Dennis. *Pageants of Despair.*
Harnett, Cynthia. *Caxton's Challenge; Writing on the Hearth.*
Hunter, Mollie. *You Never Knew Her as I Did!*
Jewett, Eleanore. *Big John's Secret.*
Jones, Terry. *Nicobobinus.*
Kelly, Eric. *Trumpeter of Krakow.*
Key, Alexander. *Sword of Aradel.*
Konigsburg, E.L. *Proud Taste for Scarlet and Miniver; Second Mrs. Giaconda.*
Lasker, Joe. *Tournament of Knights.*
Lively, Penelope. *Astercote.*
McCaughrean, Geraldine. *Little Lower Than the Angels.*
Manning, Rosemary. *Arrepay.*
Marcus, Katherine. *Devil's Workshop.*
Namioka, Lensey. *Island of Ogres; Samurai and Long-Nosed Devils; Valley of the Broken Cherry Trees; Village of the Vampire Cat; White Serpent Castle.*
Niggli, Josefina. *Miracle for Mexico.*
O'Dell, Scott. *Road to Danietta.*
Picard, Barbara. *One Is One.*
Pierce, Tamara. *Alanna, First Adventure; In the*

Hand of the Goddess; Woman Who Rides Like a Man.
Polland, Madeleine. *Children of the Red King; Queen Without a Crown; Town Across the Water.*
Pyle, Howard. *Otto of the Silver Hand.*
Russell, Jennifer. *Threshing Floor.*
Smith, A.C.H. *Lady Jane.*
Stolz, Mary. *Bartholomew Fair.*
Sutcliff, Rosemary. *Hound of Ulster; Knight's Fee.*
Turner, Ann. *Way Home.*
Van Woerkuna, Dorothy. *Pearl in the Egg.*
Von Canon, Claudia. *Inheritance.*
Welch, Ronald. *Bowmen of Crecy.*
Westall, Robert. *Wind Eye.*
Wood, James. *Man with Two Countries; Queen's Most Honorable Pirate.*

Historical Fiction: Modern

Aiken, Joan. *Cuckoo Tree.*
Almedinger, E.M. *Crimson Oak.*
Angell, Judie. *One-Way to Ansonia.*
Avery, Gillian. *Ellen and the Queen.*
Bacon, Martha. *In the Company of Clowns.*
Baker, Betty. *Blood of the Brave.*
Bartos-Hoppner, Barbara. *Cossacks; Save the Kahn; Storm Over the Caucasus.*
Beatty, John. *Royal Dirk; Witch Dog.*
Bennett, John. *Master Skylark.*
Beyer, Audrey. *Sapphire Pendant.*
Bishop, Jim. *Day Lincoln Was Shot.*
Blair, Cynthia. *Freedom to Dream.*
Burchard, Peter. *Stranded; Story of New York.*
Burton, Hester. *Beyond the Weir Bridge; Kate Ryder.*
Calvert, Patricia. *Hadder MacColl.*
Cervantes, Miguel. *Don Quixote de la Mancha.*
Clarke, Mary. *Iron Peacock; Piper to the Clan.*
Cordell, Alexander. *Healing Blade.*
Dahlstedt, Marden. *Shadow of the Lighthouse.*
Garfield, Leon. *Footsteps.*
Hamori, Laszlo. *Dangerous Journey.*
Haugaard, Erik. *Cromwell's Boy; Messemger for Parliament.*
Heyman, Anita. *Exit from Home.*
Hunter, Mollie. *Spanish Letters.*
Huynh. *Land I Lost.*
Jones, Adrienne. *Another Place, Another Spring.*
Lewis, Elizabeth. *Young Fu of the Upper Yangtze.*
Lively, Penelope. *Fanny's Sister.*
MacDonald, George. *Sir Gibbie.*
McGraw, Eloise. *Master Cornhill.*
McLean, Allan. *Ribbon of Fire; Sound of Trumpets.*
Minard, Rosemary. *Long Meg.*

Mott, Michael. *Blind Cross.*
Newell, Eadie. *Trouble Brewing.*
O'Dell, Scott. *Amethyst Ring; Captive; Feathered Serpent; King's Fifth.*
Paterson, Katherine. *Rebels of the Heavenly Kingdom.*
Pevsner, Stella. *Call Me Heller, That's My Name.*
Phipson, Joan. *Way Home.*
Plowman, Stephanie. *My Kingdom for a Grave; Three Lives for the Czar.*
Polland, Madeleine. *Queen's Blessing.*
Savage, Josephine. *Daughter of Delaware.*
Schlee, Ann. *Consul's Daughter.*
Sisson, Rosemary. *Will in Love.*
Snyder, Carol. *Ike and Mama and the Block Wedding.*
Softly, Barbara. *Place Mill; Stone in a Pool.*
Storey, Margaret. *Ask Me No Questions.*
Stuart, Morna. *Marassa and Midnight.*
Sutcliff, Rosemary. *Bonnie Dundee.*
Underwood, Betty. *Forge and the Forest.*
Walsh, Jill P. *Parcel of Patterns.*
Wartski, Maureen. *Boat to Nowhere.*
Weir, Rosemary. *Star and the Flame.*
Welch, Ronald. *Escape from France.*

Holocaust, Jews

See also: Nazis; World War II

Asher, Sandy. *Daughter of the Law.*
Forman, James. *Survivor.*
Lasky, Kathryn. *Prank.*
Leitner, Isabella. *Fragments of Isabella.*
Provost, Gary. *David and Max.*
Siegal, Aranka. *Upon the Head of the Goat.*
Suhl, Yuri. *On the Other Side of the Gate.*

Holocaust, Nuclear

Biemiller, Carl. *Hydronauts.*
Bruckner, Karl. *Day of the Bomb.*
Eldridge, Roger. *Shadow of the Gloom-World.*
Halacy, D.S. *Return from Luna.*
Hall, Lynn. *If Winter Comes.*
Hughes, Monica. *Beyond the Dark River.*
Johnson, Annabel. *Danger Quotient.*
Johnson, Denis. *Fiskadoro.*
Lawrence, Louise. *Children of the Dust.*
Lightner, A.M. *Day of the Drones.*
Maruki, Toshi. *Hiroshima No Pika.*
Miklowitz, Gloria. *After the Bomb; After the Bomb: Week One.*
Moeri, Louisa. *Downwind.*
O'Brien, Robert. *Z for Zachariah.*
Palmer, David. *Emergence.*
Rhinehart, Luke. *Long Voyage Back.*
Sampson, Fay. *Watch on Patterick Fell.*

Service, Pamela. *Tomorrow's Magic; Winter of Magic's Return.*
Setlowe, Rick. *Brink.*
Shirley, John. *Eclipse.*
Streiber, Whitley. *Warday: And the Journey Onward.*
Swindells, Robert. *Brother in the Land; Serpent's Tooth.*
Thompson, Joyce. *Conscience Place.*
Tolan, Stephanie. *Pride of the Peacock.*
Williams, Paul. *Ends of the Circle.*

Homosexuals

See: Gays

Horses, Trained

See also: Horses, Wild

Adler, Carole. *Some Other Summer.*
Aldridge, James. *Sporting Proposition.*
Anckarsvard, Karin. *Rider by Night.*
Anderson, Clarence. *Blind Connemara.*
Archibald, Joe. *Right Field Runt.*
Bacon, Katherine. *Shadow and Light.*
Bagnold, Enid. *National Velvet.*
Balch, Glenn. *Flaxy Mare; Horse in Danger; Horse of Two Colors; Lost Horse; Midnight Colt; Wild Horse.*
Beatty, Patricia. *I Want My Sunday, Stranger.*
Bell, Thelma. *Dash of Pepper.*
Benedict, Dorothy. *Fabulous; Pagan the Black.*
Berry, B.J. *Just Don't Bug Me.*
Berry, Barbara. *Shannon.*
Bodker, Cecil. *Silas and the Black Mare.*
Bradbury, Bianca. *My Pretty Girl.*
Brown, F.K. *Last Hurdle.*
Bryant, Bonnie. *Horse Crazy.*
Calvert, Patricia. *Money Creek Mare; Snowbird; Stone Pony.*
Campbell, Barbara. *Girl Called Bob and a Horse Called Yoki.*
Cavanna, Betty. *Banner Year.*
Chambers, John. *Colonel and Me.*
Clark, Virginia. *Mysterious Buckskin.*
Clewes, Dorothy. *Old Pony.*
Clymer, Eleanor. *Horse in the Attic.*
Cohen, Peter. *Bee; Calm Horse, Wild Night; Morena.*
Collura, Mary Ellen. *Winners.*
Colver, Anne. *Borrowed Treasure.*
Cookson, Catherine. *Nipper.*
Corbett, Scott. *Horse in the House.*
Corcoran, Barbara. *Horse Named Sky; Long Journey.*
Dean, Anabel. *High Jumper.*
De Jong, Meindert. *Singing Hill.*

Diggs, Lucy. *Everyday Friends; Moon in the Water.*
Doty, Jean. *Can I Get There by Candlelight?; Crumb; If Wishes Were Horses; Summer Pony; Valley of the Ponies; Winter Pony; Yesterday's Horses.*
Dunn, Marylois. *Absolutely Perfect Horse.*
Easton, Patricia. *Summer's Choice.*
Eisenberg, Lisa. *Tiger Rose.*
Ellis, Ella. *Roam the Wild Country.*
Farley, Walter. *Black Stallion; Black Stallion and Flame; Black Stallion and Satan; Black Stallion and the Girl; Black Stallion Challenged; Black Stallion Legend; Black Stallion Mystery; Black Stallion Returns; Black Stallion Revolts; Black Stallion's Blood Bay Colt; Black Stallion's Courage; Black Stallion's Filly; Black Stallion's Ghost; Black Stallion's Sulky Colt; Island Stallion; Island Stallion Races; Island Stallion's Fury; Man O' War; Son of Black Stallion.*
Fiddler, Katheryn. *Haki the Shetland Pony.*
Forbus, Ina. *Tawny's Trick.*
Forster, Logan. *Run Fast! Run Far!*
Foster, Elizabeth. *Lyrico, the Only Horse of His Kind.*
Friis-Baastad, Babbis. *Wanted! A Horse.*
Gates, Doris. *Filly for Melinda; Morgan for Melinda.*
Gauch, Patricia. *This Time, Tempe Wick?*
Gladd, Arthur. *Saracen Steed.*
Glaser, Dianne. *Summer Secret.*
Godden, Rumer. *Dark Horse.*
Gray, Patricia. *Blue Ribbon Summer; Diving Horse; Horse in Her Heart; Horse Trap; Horsepower; Jumping Jack; Loco, the Bronco; Norah's Ark; Star Bright; Star Lost; Star, the Sea Horse.*
Green, Anne. *To Race Again; Valley Cup.*
Gregory, Diana. *I'm Boo ... That's Who.*
Griffiths, Helen. *Dancing Horses; Wild Horse of Santander.*
Haas, Jessie. *Keeping Barney; Working Trot.*
Hall, Lynn. *Danza!; Flowers of Anger; Horse Called Dragon; Horse Trader; Megan's Mare; Mrs. Portree's Pony; Mystery of Pony Hollow; Mystery of Pony Hollow Panda; New Day for Dragon; Ride a Dark Horse; Something Special Horse; Tin Can Tucker.*
Hanson, June. *Summer of the Stallion; Winter of the Owl.*
Hays, Wilma. *Mary's Star.*
Heck, B. Holland. *Cactus Kevin.*
Henry, Marguerite. *San Domingo, the Medicine Hat Stallion; King of the Wind; Misty of Chincoteague; Our First Pony; Sea Star: Orphan of Chincoteague; Stormy, Misty's Foal.*
Hightower, Florence. *Dark Horse of Woodfield.*
Holland, Barbara. *Pony Problem.*
Holland, Isabelle. *Toby the Splendid.*
Hoppe, Joanne. *Pretty Penny Farm.*
Howker, Janne. *Isaac Campion.*
Irwin, Hadley. *Bring to a Boil and Separate.*

James, Will. *Smoky, the Cowhorse.*
Jenkins, Alan. *White Horses and Black Bulls.*
Johnson, Elizabeth. *Horse Show Fever.*
Knowles, Anne. *Under the Shadows.*
Lawson, Robert. *Mr. Revere and I.*
Levin, Betty. *Binding Spell.*
Levy, Elizabeth. *Case of the Counterfeit Racehorse.*
Lyons, Dorothy. *Pedigree Unknown.*
McGiffin, Lee. *Horse Hunters.*
McHargue, Georgess. *Horseman's Word.*
Manniz, Darrel. *Secret of the Elm.*
Moeri, Louise. *Horse for X.Y.Z.*
Montgomery, Rutherford. *Golden Stallion and the Mysterious Feud; Golden Stallion to the Rescue; Golden Stallion's Victory.*
Moore, Ruth. *Mystery of the Lost Treasure.*
Morey, Walt. *Year of the Black Pony.*
Morgenroth, Barbara. *Impossible Charlie; Nicki and Wynne; Ride a Proud Horse.*
Morrison, Dorothy. *Somebody's Horse; Whisper Goodbye.*
Oldham, Mary. *White Pony.*
Ottley, Reginald. *Roan Colt.*
Paradis, Marjorie. *Mr. De Luca's Horse.*
Patchett, Mary. *Golden Wolf; Tam the Untamed.*
Petroski, Catherine. *Summer That Lasted Forever.*
Peyton, Karen. *Fly by Night; Free Rein; Team.*
Phipson, Joan. *Good Luck to the Rider.*
Piper, Roberta. *Little Red.*
Reynolds, Pamela. *Horseshoe Hill.*
Riter, Dorris. *Edge of Violence.*
Rock, Gail. *Thanksgiving Treasure.*
Rockwood, Joyce. *Groundhog's Horse.*
Rounds, Glen. *Blind Colt; Blind Outlaw.*
St. Peter, Joyce. *Always Abigail.*
Sandburg, Helga. *Blueberry.*
Savage, Josephine. *Daughter of Delaware.*
Savitt, Sam. *Vicki and the Black Horse.*
Saxon, Nancy. *Panky and William.*
Seabrooke, Brenda. *Home Is Where They Take You In.*
Sheldon, Ann. *Silver Stallion.*
Smith, Eunice. *High Heels for Jennifer.*
Smith, Linell. *Auction Pony.*
Smith, Marya. *Winter Broker.*
Smith, Vian. *Martin Rides the Moor.*
Springer, Nancy. *Horse to Love; Not on a White Horse; They're All Named Wildfire.*
Steffan, Jack. *Firm Hand on the Rein.*
Sutcliff, Rosemary. *Hound of Ulster.*
Thomas, Joyce. *Golden Pasture.*
Thum, Marcella. *Mystery at Crane's Landing.*
Towne, Mary. *Boxed In.*
Van der Veer, Judy. *Hold the Rein Free.*
Walker, Diana. *Mother Wants a Horse; Year of the Horse.*
Wallace, Bill. *Beauty.*
Wallin, Marie. *Tangles.*
Whitley, Mary Ann. *Circle of Light.*
Wildes, Newlin. *Horse That Had Everything.*

Williams, Dorothy. *Horsetalker.*
Williams, Ursula. *No Ponies for Miss Pobjoy.*
Wojciechowska, Maia. *Kingdom in a Horse.*
Yarbro, Chelsea. *Four Horses for Tishtry.*

Horses, Wild

Aldridge, James. *Marvelous Mongolian.*
Annixter, Jane. *White Shell Horse.*
Balch, Glenn. *Buck, Wild; Spotted Horse; Wild Horse Tamer.*
Benedict, Dorothy. *Pagan the Black.*
Clark, Ann. *Hoofprint in the Wind.*
Evans, Max. *My Pardner.*
Fall, Thomas. *Wild Boy.*
Grant, Bruce. *Ride, Gaucho.*
Griffiths, Helen. *Blackface Stallion; Stallion of the Sands; Wild Heart.*
Hall, Lynn. *Horse Called Dragon; New Day for Dragon.*
Hanson, June. *Summer of the Stallion.*
Harris, Mark. *Last Run.*
Henry, Marguerite. *Misty of Chincoteague; Mustang, Wild Spirit of the West.*
Holland, Isabelle. *Horse Named Peaceable; Perdita.*
McCraig, Robert. *That Nestor Kid.*
Morey, Walt. *Runaway Stallion.*
Murphy, Shirley. *Sand Ponies.*
Patchett, Mary. *Brumby Come Home; Brumby, the Wild White Stallion.*
Riha, Bohumil. *Ryn, Wild Horse.*
Rounds, Glen. *Wild Appaloosa.*
Williams, Dorothy. *Horsetalker.*
Worcester, Donald. *Lone Hunter and the Wild Horses.*

Humorous

Adair, Gilbert. *Alice Through the Needle's Eye.*
Adams, Douglas. *Hitchhiker's Guide to the Galaxy.*
Adler, David. *Eaton Stanly and the Mind Control Experiment; Jeffrey's Ghost and the Fifth Grade Dragon.*
Aiken, Joan. *Arabel and Mortimer; Arabel's Raven; Mortimer Says Northing; Mortimer's Cross.*
Anckarsvärd, Karin. *Aunt Vinnie's Victorious Six.*
Angell, Judie. *Home Is to Share and Share and Share; Suds.*
Atwater, Richard. *Mr. Popper's Penguins.*
Avi. *Romeo and Juliet—Together (and Alive) at Last; S.O.R. Losers.*
Beatty, Jerome. *Bob Fulton's Amazing Soda-Pop Stretcher; Bob Fulton's Terrific Time Machine.*
Beatty, Patricia. *Behave Yourself, Bethany*

tion That Happened to Rupert Piper; Rupert Piper and Megan the Valuable Girl; Rupert Piper and the Boy Who Could Knit; Rupert Piper and the Dear, Dear Birds; Terrible Trouble of Rupert Piper; Today I Am a Ham.

Peck, Robert. *Soup; Soup and Me; Soup for President; Soup in the Saddle; Soup on Fire; Soup on Ice; Soup on Wheels; Soup's Drum; Soup's Goat; Soup's Hoop; Soup's Uncle; Trig; Trig Goes Ape; Trig or Treat; Trig Sees Red.*

Pettersson, Allan. *Frankenstein's Aunt.*

Pevsner, Stella. *Call Me Heller, That's My Name; Me, My Goat and My Sister's Wedding.*

Pinkwater, Daniel. *Alan Mendelsohn, Boy from Mars; Fat Men from Space; Frankenbagel Monster; Hoboken Chicken Emergency; Lizard Music; Magic Moscow; Moosepire; Muffin Fiend; Slaves of Spiegel; Snarkout Boys and the Avocado of Death; Snarkout Boys and the Baconburg Horror; Worms of Kukulima; Yobgorgle, Mystery Monster of Lake Ontario.*

Platt, Kin. *Dracula, Go Home.*

Pomerantz, Charlotte. *Downtown Fairy Godmother.*

Powers, John. *Last Catholic in America.*

Prince, Alison. *Type One Super Robot.*

Raskin, Ellen. *Figgs and Phantoms; Mysterious Disappearance of Leon (I Mean Noel).*

Rawls, Wilson. *Summer of the Monkeys.*

Razzi, Jim. *Search for King Pup's Tomb.*

Richler, Mordecai. *Jacob Two-Two and the Dinosaur.*

Riskind, Mary. *Follow That Mom.*

Roberts, Willo. *Minder Curse; More Minder Curses.*

Robertson, Keith. *Henry Reed's Baby Sitting Service; Henry Reed's Big Show; Henry Reed's Think Tank; Henry Reed, Inc.*

Robinson, Barbara. *My Brother Louis Measures Worms and Other Louis Stories.*

Rockwell, Thomas. *How to Eat Fried Worms.*

Rodgers, Mary. *Billion for Boris; Freaky Friday; Summer Switch.*

Rounds, Glen. *Day the Circus Came to Lone Tree; Mr. Yowder and the Train Robbers.*

Ruch-Pauquet, Gina. *Fourteen Cases of Dynamite.*

Rugh, Belle. *Path Above the Pines.*

Sachar, Louis. *Wayside School Is Falling Down.*

St. George, Judith. *Who's Scared? Not Me!*

St. John, Glory. *What I Did Last Summer.*

St. John, Wylly. *Secrets of the Pirate Inn.*

Schwartz, Sheila. *Like Mother, Like Me.*

Schweitzer, Byrd. *Amigo.*

Seidler, Tor. *Tar Pit.*

Selden, George. *Genie of Sutton Place; Harry Cat's Pet Puppy.*

Shannon, Jacqueline. *Too Much T.J.*

Sharmat, Marjorie. *Chasing After Annie; 51 Sycamore Lane; Getting Something on Maggie Marmelstein; Rich Mitch; Son of the Slime Who Ate Cleveland.*

Shura, Mary. *Nearsighted Knight.*

Singer, Marilyn. *Hoax Is on You.*

Sleator, William. *Duplicate; Fingers.*

Slobodkin, Louis. *Space Ship Returns to the Apple Tree.*

Smith, Emma. *Out of Hand.*

Smith, Janice. *It's Not Easy Being George.*

Smith, Robert. *Chocolate Fever; Jelly Belly.*

Snyder, Carol. *Leftover Kid.*

Spearing, Judith. *Ghost That Went to School.*

Spinelli, Jerry. *Who Put That Hair in My Toothbrush?*

Stahl, Ben. *Secret of the Red Skull.*

Steiner, Barbara. *Oliver Dibbs to the Rescue.*

Stephens, Mary Jo. *Xoe's Zodiac.*

Sterman, Betsy. *Too Much Magic.*

Stevenson, James. *Here Comes Herb's Hurricane.*

Stone, Bruce. *Half Nelson.*

Sunshine, Tina. *Dating Games.*

Sutton, Jean. *Confessions of an Orange Octopus.*

Tannen, Mary. *Huntley, Nutley and the Missing Link.*

Terris, Susan. *Octopus Pie.*

Thompson, Wilma. *That Barbara.*

Tolan, Stephanie. *Great Skinner Getaway; Great Skinner Strike.*

Tolle, Jean. *Great Pete Penney.*

Towne, Mary. *Wanda the Worrywart.*

Townsend, J. David. *Cats Stand Accused.*

Tuning, William. *Fuzzy Bones.*

Unnerstad, Edith. *Saucepan Journey.*

Ure, Jean. *What If They Saw Me Now?*

Van Leeuwen, Jean. *Benjy and the Power of Zingies; Benjy, the Football Hero.*

Vonnegut, Kurt. *Deadeye Dick.*

Wahl, Jan. *Furious Flycycle; SOS Bobomobile.*

Wallace, Barbara. *Contest Kid Strikes Again; Hawkins; Hawkins and the Soccer Solution; Interesting Thing That Happened at Perfect Acres.*

Wayne, Jennifer. *Sprout and the Magician.*

Weaver, Harriett. *Frosty: A Raccoon to Remember.*

Westlake, Donald. *Why Me?*

White, Terence. *Once and Future King.*

Whitehead, Robert. *Some of the Schemes of Columbus Tootle.*

Wilkes, Marilyn. *C.L.U.T.Z. and the Fizzion Formula.*

Willard, Nancy. *Highest Hit.*

Williams, Jay. *Danny Dunn and the Anti-Gravity Paint; Danny Dunn and the Automated House; Danny Dunn and the Fossil Cave; Danny Dunn and the Heat Ray; Danny Dunn and the Homework Machine; Danny Dunn and the Smallifying Machine; Danny Dunn and the Swamp Monster; Danny Dunn and the Universal Glue; Danny Dunn and the Voice from Space; Danny Dunn and the Weather Making Machine; Danny Dunn, Invisible Boy; Danny Dunn on a Desert Island; Danny Dunn on the Ocean*

Hunting

Illness

Immigrants

Erdman, Loula. *Room to Grow.* (French)
Finlayson, Ann. *Greenhorn on the Frontier.* (English)
Godden, Rumer. *Miss Happiness and Miss Flower.* (Japanese)
Gonzalez, Gloria. *Gaucho.* (Puerto Rican)
Hamilton, Gail. *Titania's Lodestone.* (European)
Hinchman, Catherine. *Torchlight.* (Hungarian)
Keith, Harold. *Obstinate Land.* (German)
Lehmann, Linda. *Better Than a Princess; Tilli's New World.* (German)
Levitin, Sonia. *Silver Days.* (German)
Lindquist, Jennie. *Little Silver House.* (Scandinavian)
Miller, Helen. *Kirsti.* (Finnish)
Mohr, Nicholasa. *Felita; Nilda.* (Puerto Rican)
Moskin, Marietta. *Waiting for Mama.* (Russian)
Noble, Iris. *Megan.* (Irish)
O'Dell, Scott. *Alexandra.* (Greek)
Phipson, Joan. *Horse with Eight Hands.* (German)
Sachs, Marilyn. *Call Me Ruth.* (Russian)
Shotwell, Louisa. *Magdalena.* (Puerto Rican)
Siegal, Aranka. *Grace in the Wilderness.* (Swedish)
Smith, Rukshana. *Sumitra's Story.* (Indian)
Speevack, Yetta. *Spider Plant.* (Puerto Rican)
Uchida, Yoshika. *Happiest Ending; Mik and the Prowler.* (Japanese)
Wartski, Maureen. *Long Way from Home.* (Vietnamese)
Yep, Laurence. *Child of the Owl; Dragonwings.* (Chinese)

Indians

See: Native Americans

Jealousy

Anderson, Mary. *Who Says Nobody's Perfect?*
Asher, Sandy. *Just Like Jenny.*
Baehr, Patricia. *Louisa Eclipsed.*
Blume, Judy. *Just as Long as We're Together.*
Briggs, Katherine. *Kate Crackernuts.*
Cameron, Eleanor. *Private World of Julia Redfern.*
Carr, Harriett. *Rod's Girl.*
Chaikin, Miriam. *Getting Even.*
Colman, Hila. *Confessions of a Story Teller.*
Crane, William. *Oom-Pah.*
Cunningham, Julia. *Silent Voice.*
Cuyler, Margery. *Trouble with Soap.*
Dacquino, V.T. *Kiss the Candy Days Good-Bye.*
Dailey, Virginia. *Keys to Lawrence House.*
Dean, Karen. *Stay on Your Toes, Maggie Adams.*
De Clements, Barthe. *How Do You Lose Those 9th Grade Blues?*
Estoril, Jean. *We Danced in Bloomsbury Square.*
Fiedler, Jean. *Year the World Was Out of Step with Jancy Fried.*

Fine, Anne. *My War with Goggle-Eyes.*
Franco, Marjorie. *So Who Hasn't Got Problems?*
Giff, Patricia. *Love, from the Fifth Grade Celebrity.*
Grant, Bruce. *Ride, Gaucho.*
Greenberg, Jan. *Exercises of the Heart.*
Gripe, Maria. *Julia's House.*
Grosscup, Clyde. *Pro Passer.*
Haynes, Betsy. *Faking It.*
Hinton, S.E. *Tex.*
Holmes, Barbara. *Charlotte Shakespeare and Annie the Great.*
Honeycutt, Natalie. *Invisible Lissa.*
Hooks, William. *Theo Zephyr.*
Hopper, Nancy. *Carrie's Games; Rivals.*
Houston, Joan. *Crofton Meadows.*
Jackson, Alison. *My Brother, the Star.*
Joosse, Barbara. *Anna, the One and Only.*
Kaplow, Robert. *Alex Icicle: A Romance in Ten Torrid Chapters.*
Kerr, M.E. *If I Love You, Am I Trapped Forever?*
Klein, Robin. *Hating Alison Ashley.*
Leroe, Ellen. *Plot Against the Pom Pom Queen.*
Lindgard, Joan. *Odd Girl Out.*
Martin, Ann. *Me and Katie (The Pest).*
Miller, Helen. *Ski Fast, Ski Long.*
Mills, Claudia. *Boardwalk with Hotel.*
Nostlinger, Christine. *Luke and Angela.*
Paterson, Katherine. *Jacob Have I Loved.*
Pellowski, Anne. *Betsy's Up-and-Down Year.*
Perl, Lila. *Pieface and Daphne.*
Pfeffer, Susan. *Turning Thirteen.*
Philbrook, Clem. *Slope Dope.*
Sachs, Elizabeth-Ann. *Where Are You, Cow Patty?*
Sachs, Marilyn. *Thunderbird.*
Sharmat, Marjorie. *I Saw Him First.*
Shura, Mary. *Barkley Street Six-Pack.*
Shyer, Marlene. *Adorable Sunday.*
Singer, Marilyn. *No Applause Please; Twenty Ways to Lose Your Best Friend.*
Spinelli, Jerry. *Who Put That Hair in My Toothbrush?*
Stewart, A.C. *Ossian House.*
Tate, Eleanora. *Just an Overnight Guest.*
Teicher, Elizabeth. *April's Year.*
Tilly, Nancy. *Golden Girl.*
Ure, Jean. *Supermouse.*
Van Steenwyk, Elizabeth. *Rivals on Ice.*
Vogel, Ilse-Marget. *My Twin Sister Erika.*
Walden, Amelia. *My World's the Stage.*
Wallace, Barbara. *Claudia and Duffy.*
Walter, Mildred. *Lillie of Watts Takes a Giant Step.*
Warren, Cathy. *Roxanne Bookman: Live at Five.*
Weltner, Linda. *Beginning to Feel the Magic.*
Westall, Robert. *Scarecrows.*
Whitaker, Alexandra. *Dream Sister.*
White, Dori. *Sarah and Katie.*
Woolley, Catherine. *Ginnie and the New Girl.*
Wright, Betty. *Summer of Mrs. McGregor.*
York, Carol. *Remember Me When I Am Dead.*

Jews

Aaron, Chester. *Gideon.*
Arrick, Fran. *Chernowitz.*
Baer, Edith. *Frost in the Night.*
Bergman, Tamar. *Boy from Over There.*
Brooks, Jerome. *Make Me a Hero.*
Chaikin, Miriam. *I Should Worry, I Should Care; Yossi Tries to Help God.*
Clifford, Eth. *Remembering Box.*
Cohen, Barbara. *Carp in the Bathtub; Christmas Revolution; King of the Seventh Grade; People Like Us.*
Colman, Hila. *Rachel's Legacy.*
Cone, Molly. *Dance Around the Fire.*
Derman, Martha. *Friendstone.*
Fisher, Leonard. *Russian Farewell.*
Forman, James. *Ceremony of Innocence.*
Geras, Adele. *Voyage.*
Hamori, Laszlo. *Flight to the Promised Land.*
Herman, Charlotte. *Difference of Ari Stein.*
Holman, Felice. *Murderer.*
Hull, Eleanor. *Summer People.*
Hurwitz, Johanna. *Adventures of Ali Baba Bernstein; Once I Was a Plum Tree; Rabbi's Girls.*
Ish-Kishor, Sulamith. *Our Eddie.*
Karp, Naomi. *Turning Point.*
Kaufman, Stephen. *Does Anyone Know the Way to Thirteen?*
Kerr, Judith. *Other Way Around; Small Person Far Away; When Hitler Stole Pink Rabbit.*
Kerr, M.E. *Him She Loves?*
Krasilovsky, Phyllis. *L.C. Is the Greatest.*
Kuper, Jack. *Child of the Holocaust.*
Lasky, Kathryn. *Pageant.*
Leninson, Riki. *Dinnieabbiesister-r-r!*
Levitin, Sonia. *Sound to Remember.*
Lingard, Joan. *File on Fraulein Berg.*
Matas, Carol. *Lisa War.*
Murray, Michele. *Crystal Nights.*
Neville, Emily. *Berries Goodman.*
Ofek, Uriel. *Smoke Over Golan.*
Orgel, Doris. *Devil in Vienna.*
Potok, Chaim. *Chosen; Davita's Harp.*
Reiss, Johanna. *Journey Back; Upstairs Room.*
Richter, Hans. *Friedrich.*
Sachs, Marilyn. *Marv; Pocket Full of Seeds.*
Samuels, Gertrude. *Mottele, a Partisan Odyssey.*
Shecter, Ben. *Someplace Else.*
Shemin, Margaretha. *Empty Moat.*
Sherman, Eileen. *Monday on Odessa.*
Singer, Isaac. *Golem.*
Snyder, Carol. *Ike and Mama and the Seven Surprises.*
Suhl, Yuri. *Uncle Misha's Partisans.*
Sussman, Susan. *There's No Such Thing as a Chanukah Bush.*

Kidnapping

See also: Mystery/Kidnapping

Alcock, Vivien. *Cuckoo Sister.*
Allan, Mabel. *Mystery of the Ski Slopes; Sign of the Unicorn.*
Barber, Antonia. *Affair of the Rockerbye Baby.*
Beatty, Patricia. *Blue Stars Watching.*
Bodker, Cecil. *Silas and the Runaway Coach.*
Carey, M.V. *Secret of the Haunted Mirror.*
Clark, Margaret. *Who Stole Kathy Young?*
Clements, Bruce. *Two Against the Tide.*
Cookson, Catherine. *Mrs. Flannagan's Trumpet.*
Cool, Joyce. *Kidnapping of Courtney Van Allen and What's-Her-Name.*
Cormier, Robert. *After the First Death.*
Cross, Gillian. *On the Edge.*
Dixon, Paige. *Search for Charlie.*
Duffy, James. *Missing.*
Duncan, Lois. *Ransom; Twisted Window.*
Ehrlich, Amy. *Where It Stops Nobody Knows.*
Fox, Paula. *How Many Miles to Babylon?*
Gorey, Edward. *Hapless Child.*
Hamilton, Virginia. *Arilla Sun Down.*
Hamilton-Paterson, James. *Hostage.*
Hawks, Robert. *This Stranger, My Father.*
Hildick, Florence. *Louie's Ransom.*
Hollman, Clide. *Eagle Feather.*
Household, Geoffrey. *Escape Into Daylight.*
Humphreys, Josephine. *Rich in Love.*
Hyde, Dayton. *Island of the Loons.*
Jeffries, Roderic. *Against Time!*
Kidd, Ronald. *Sizzle and Splat.*
Leonard, Constance. *Stowaway.*
MacLeod, Charlotte. *We Dare Not Go A-Hunting.*
Mazer, Norma. *Solid Gold Kid.*
Mott, Michael. *Master Entrick.*
Newman, Robert. *Case of the Threatened King; Case of the Watching Boy.*
Nixon, Joan. *Kidnapping of Christina Lattimore.*
Parker, Richard. *Three by Mistake.*
Peck, Richard. *Through a Brief Darkness.*
Petersen, P.J. *How Can You Hijack a Cave?*
Picard, Barbara. *Lost John: A Young Outlaw in the Forest of Arden.*
Rardin, Susan. *Captives in a Foreign Land.*
Roberts, Willo. *Baby Sitting Is a Dangerous Job.*
Ruby, Lois. *What Do You Do in Quicksand?*
Snyder, Zilpha. *Famous Stanley Kidnapping Case.*
Sobol, Donald. *Angie's First Case.*
Stegeman, Janet. *Last Seen on Harper's Lane.*
Waldron, Ann. *Scaredy Cat.*
Wallace, Barbara. *Miss Switch to the Rescue.*
Wallace, Bill. *Trapped in Death Cave.*

Knights

Brett, Simon. *Three Detectives and the Knight in Armor.*
De Angeli, Marguerite. *Door in the Wall.*
Eager, Edward. *Knights Castle.*
Hall, Lynn. *Dog of the Bondi Castle.*
Hunter, Mollie. *Knight of the Golden Plain.*
Jewett, Eleanore. *Big John's Secret.*
Lively, Penelope. *Whispering Knights.*
Lloyd, Norris. *Desperate Dragons.*
Manning, Rosemary. *Dragon's Quest.*
Picard, Barbara. *One Is One.*
Pierce, Tamara. *In the Hand of the Goddess.*
Pyle, Howard. *Men of Iron.*
Russell, Jennifer. *Threshing Floor.*
Steinbeck, John. *Acts of King Arthur and His Noble Knights.*
Sutcliff, Rosemary. *Knight's Fee.*
Winthrop, Elizabeth. *Castle in the Attic.*

Latinos

Bograd, Larry. *Fourth Grade Dinosaur.*
Bonham, Frank. *Viva Chicano.*
Dunne, Mary. *Reach Out, Ricardo.*
Fern, Eugene. *Lorenzo and Angelina.*
Foster, Ed. *Tejanos.*
Friermood, Elizabeth. *One of Fred's Girls.*
Gault, William. *Trouble at Second.*
Gee, Maurine. *Chicano, Amigo.*
Gerson, Corinne. *Oh, Brother!*
Madison, Winifred. *Maria Luisa.*
Means, Florence. *Us Maltbys.*
Mohr, Nicholasa. *Felita.*
O'Dell, Scott. *Carlota; Child of Fire.*
Schweitzer, Byrd. *Amigo.*
Van der Veer, Judy. *Hold the Rein Free.*
Wojciechowska, Maia. *Life and Death of a Brave Bull; Shadow of a Bull; Single Light.*
Wolf, Bernard. *In This Proud Land.*

Legends

Aimatov, Chingez. *White Ship.*
Alexander, Lloyd. *Illyrian Adventure.*
Almedingen, E.M. *Story of Gudrun.*
Anderson, Margaret. *Light in the Mountain.*
Anderson, Paul. *Boy and the Blind Storyteller.*
Arkin, Alan. *Lemming Condition.*
Baker, Olaf. *Where the Buffalos Begin.*
Bang, Molly. *Dawn.*
Beatty, Patricia. *Billy Be Damned Long Gone By.*
Beckman, Delores. *My Own Private Sky.*
Bierhorst, John. *Ring in the Prairie.*
Bond, Nancy. *String in the Harp.*

Borland, Hal. *When the Legends Die.*
Brown, Marcia. *Backbone of the King.*
Coatsworth, Elizabeth. *Cat Who Went to Heaven.*
Cohen, Barbara. *Seven Daughters and Seven Sons.*
Cresswell, Helen. *Secret World of Polly Flint.*
Curley, Daniel. *Billy Beg and the Bull.*
Evarts, Hal. *Bigfoot.*
Farley, Walter. *Black Stallion Legend.*
Fleischman, Sid. *McBroom Tells the Truth; Me and the Man on the Moon-Eyed Horse.*
Garner, Alan. *Owl Service.*
Goble, Paul. *Buffalo Woman.*
Greene, Jacqueline. *Leveller.*
Hamilton, Virginia. *Magical Adventures of Pretty Pearl; Time-Ago Lost: More Tales of Jahdu; Time-Ago Tales of Jahdu.*
Hamner, Earl. *Spencer's Mountain.*
Hastings, Selina. *Sir Gawain and the Loathy Lady.*
Highwater, Jamake. *Anpad; Legend Days.*
Hill, Elizabeth. *Fangs Aren't Everything.*
Hillerman, Tony. *Boy Who Made Dragonfly.*
Hodges, Margaret. *Fire Bringer.*
Houston, James. *Eagle Mask; West Coast Indian Tale; Falcon Bow; Ghost Paddle; White Archer.*
Janeway, Elizabeth. *Ivanov Seven.*
Johnson, Dorothy. *Buffalo Woman.*
Johnston, Norma. *Strangers Dark and Gold.*
Lambert, Charles. *Copper Nail.*
Larson, Jean. *Silkspinners.*
Lauritzen, Jonreed. *Treasure of the High Country.*
Lawrence, Ann. *Tom Ass or the Second Gift.*
Lawson, John. *You Better Come Home with Me.*
Levin, Betty. *Sword of Culann.*
Linevski, A. *Old Tale Carved Out of Stone.*
MacKellar, William. *Dog Like No Other.*
Melnikoff, Pamela. *Star and the Sword.*
Myers, Walter. *Legend of Tarik.*
Newman, Robert. *Merlin's Mistake.*
O'Shea, Pat. *Finn MacCool and the Small Men of Deeds.*
Sanfield, Steve. *Natural Man.*
Seredy, Kate. *White Stag.*
Singer, Isaac. *Golem; Topsy-Turvy Emperor of China.*
Steele, William. *Spooky Thing.*
Steinbeck, John. *Acts of King Arthur and His Noble Knights.*
Stephens, Mary Jo. *Witch of the Cumberlands.*
Stewart, Mary. *Last Enchantment; Wicked Day.*
Sussman, Susan. *There's No Such Thing as a Chanukah Bush.*
Sutcliff, Rosemary. *Light Beyond the Forest; Road to Camlann; Sword and the Circle.*
Tannen, Mary. *Lost Legend of Finn; Wizard Children of Finn.*
Terlouw, Jan. *How to Become King.*
Thomas, Joyce. *Marked by Fire.*
Trezise, Percy. *Turramuhl the Giant Quinkin.*
Twain, Mark. *Connecticut Yankee in King Arthur's Court; Legends of Sagenfeld.*
Uchida, Yoshika. *Magic Listening Cap.*
Van Laan, Nancy. *Rainbow Crow.*

White, T.H. *Once and Future King; Sword in the Stone.*
Wolkstein, Diane. *White Wave: A Chinese Tale.*

Leukemia

See: Illness

Literary Classics

See: Classics

Love

See: Romance

Loyalty

Armstrong, Richard. *Trial Trip.*
Balch, Glenn. *Lost Horse.*
Barnes, Gregory. *Wind of Change.*
Beatty, Patricia. *Be Ever Hopeful, Hannalee.*
Beckman, Delores. *My Own Private Sky.*
Bloch, Marie. *Bern, Son of Mikula.*
Bulla, Clyde. *Viking Adventure.*
Bunting, Eve. *If I Asked You, Would You Stay?*
Cavanna, Betty. *Banner Year.*
Clifford, Mary. *Salah of Sierra Leone.*
Collier, James. *Bloody Country.*
Cooper, Ilene. *Winning of Miss Lynn Ryan.*
Corcoran, Barbara. *Woman in Your Life.*
Cunningham, Julia. *Viollet.*
Feuer, Elizabeth. *One Friend to Another.*
Finlayson, Ann. *Redcoat in Boston.*
Grosscup, Clyde. *Pro Passer.*
Hagy, Jeannie. *And Then Mom Joined the Army.*
Hassler, Jon. *Four Miles to Pinecone.*
Hines, Anna. *Cassie Bowen Takes Witch Lessons.*
Houston, Jeanne. *Farewell to Manzanar.*
Hughey, Roberta. *Question Box.*
Hunter, Kristin. *Lou in the Limelight.*
Johnston, Norma. *Keeping Days.*
Lampman, Evelyn. *Cayuse Courage.*
Larimer, Tamela. *Buck.*
Lichtman, Wendy. *Telling Secret.*
Lindgard, Joan. *Odd Girl Out.*
Lisle, Janet. *Sirens and Spies.*
Maule, Tex. *Championship Quarterback.*
Morey, Walt. *Kavik the Wolf Dog.*
Pascal, Francine. *Love and Betrayal and Hold the Mayo.*
Perl, Lila. *That Crazy April.*
Pfeffer, Susan. *Sybil at Sixteen.*
Polland, Madeleine. *Queen's Blessing.*
Scism, Carol. *Secret Emily.*
Sherbourne, Zoa. *Leslie.*
Shura, Mary. *Josie Gambit.*

Singer, Marilyn. *Twenty Ways to Lose Your Best Friend.*
Smith, Doris. *First Hard Times.*
Treece, Henry. *Centurion; Horned Helmet.*
Walter, Mildred. *Trouble's Child.*
Wellman, Manly. *Clash on the Catawba; Rifles at Ramsour's Mill.*
Wibberley, Leonard. *Peter Treegate's War.*
Wood, James. *Man with Two Countries.*
Young, I.S. *Quarterback Carson.*
Zindel, Paul. *Pigman.*

Magic

Adler, Carole. *Magic of the Glits.*
Alexander, Lloyd. *Cat Who Wished to Be a Man; First Two Lives of Lukas-Kasha.*
Allen, Judy. *Spring on the Mountain.*
Anderson, Margaret. *Leipzig Vampire.*
Angell, Judie. *Weird Disappearance of Jordan Hall.*
Arthur, Ruth. *Old Magic.*
Avi. *No More Magic.*
Banks, Lynne. *Indian in the Cupboard; Return of the Indian.*
Baxter, Caroline. *Stolen Telesm.*
Beachcroft, Nina. *Well Met by Witchlight.*
Beagle, Peter. *Last Unicorn.*
Beatty, Jerome. *Bob Fulton's Amazing Soda-Pop Stretcher; Bob Fulton's Terrific Time Machine.*
Bedard, Michael. *Darker Magic.*
Bellairs, John. *House with a Clock in Its Walls.*
Boston, Lucy. *Stones of Green Knowe.*
Boyer, Elizabeth. *Wizard and the Warlord.*
Brittain, Bill. *Wish Giver.*
Brooks, Terry. *Elfstones of Shannara.*
Carlyon, Richard. *Dark Lord of Pengersick.*
Chance, Stephen. *Stone Offering.*
Charnas, Suzy. *Silver Glove.*
Chew, Ruth. *Do-It-Yourself Magic; Mostly Magic; What the Witch Left; Would-Be Witch.*
Christopher, Matt. *Red-Hot Hightops.*
Clavell, James. *Thrump-o-Moto.*
Clifford, Eth. *Scared Silly.*
Coontz, Otto. *Hornwaggle Magic.*
Corbett, Scott. *Baseball Trick; Disappearing Dog Trick; Hairy Horror Trick; Hangman's Ghost Trick; Hateful, Plateful Trick; Hockey Trick; Lemonade Trick; Turnabout Trick.*
Coville, Bruce. *Monster's Ring.*
Crayder, Dorothy. *Joker and the Swan.*
Cresswell, Helen. *Up the Pier.*
Curry, Jane. *Magical Cupboard; Mindy's Mysterious Miniature.*
Dank, Gloria. *Forest of App.*
Du Bois, William. *Horse in the Camel Suit.*
Durrell, Gerald. *Talking Parcel.*
Eager, Edward. *Half Magic; Magic by the Lake; Seven-Day Magic; Time Garden; Well-Wishers.*
Enright, Elizabeth. *Thimble Summer.*

Erwin, Betty. *Behind the Magic Line.*
Farmer, Penelope. *Magic Stone.*
Fleischman, Sid. *Mr. Mysterious and Company.*
Garner, Alan. *Moon of Gomrath.*
Goldman, William. *Magic.*
Gormley, Beatrice. *Ghastly Glasses.*
Graham, Harriet. *Chinese Puzzle; Ring of Zoraya.*
Gray, Nicholas. *Apple Stone.*
Green, Alexander. *Scarlet Sails.*
Green, Phyllis. *Eating Ice Cream with a Werewolf.*
Hall, Lynn. *Dagmar Schultz and the Power of Darkness.*
Harris, Mark. *With a Wave of the Wand.*
Harris, Rosemary. *Quest for Orion.*
Hill, Douglas. *Penelope's Pendant.*
Horseman, Elaine. *Hubble's Bubble.*
Hunter, Mollie. *Stranger Came Ashore.*
Jones, Diana. *Archer's Goon; Lives of Christopher Chant; Magicians of Caprona; Ogre Downstairs; Witch Week; Witch's Business.*
Katz, Welwyn. *Third Magic.*
Kidd, Ronald. *Second Fiddle.*
King-Smith, Dick. *Queen's Nose.*
Kooiker, Leonie. *Legacy of Magic; Magic Stone.*
Krensky, Stephen. *Big Day for Scepters.*
Kushner, Donn. *Violin Maker's Gift.*
Langton, Jane. *Astonishing Stereoscope.*
Levoy, Myron. *Magic Hat of Mortimer.*
Levy, Elizabeth. *Running Out of Magic with Houdini.*
Lewis, C.S. *That Hideous Strength.*
Lindbergh, Anne. *Hunky-Dory Dairy.*
McGowen, Tom. *Magician's Apprentice; Shadow of Fomar; Sir Mac Hinery.*
McGraw, Eloise. *Joel and the Great Merlini.*
McHargue, Georgess. *Talking Table Mystery.*
Maguire, Gregory. *Lightning.*
Mayne, William. *Blue Boat.*
Morpurgo, Michael. *Little Foxes.*
Morris, Winifred. *With Magical Horses to Ride.*
Nash, Mary. *Mrs. Coverlet's Magicians.*
Newman, Robert. *Merlin's Mistake.*
Nixon, Joan. *Deadly Game of Magic.*
Norris, Gunilla. *Standing in the Magic.*
Norton, Andre. *Dragon Magic; Fur Magic; Seven Spells to Sunday; Steel Magic.*
Orgel, Doris. *Certain Magic.*
Preiss, Byron. *Dragonworld.*
Preussler, Otfried. *Satanic Mill.*
Rockwood, Joyce. *Long Man's Song.*
Scott, William. *Boori.*
Silverstein, Herman. *Mad, Mad Monday.*
Smith, L.J. *Night of the Solstice.*
Snyder, Zilpha. *Black and Blue Magic.*
Steele, Mary. *Wish, Come True.*
Steele, William. *Magic Amulet.*
Steinbeck, John. *Acts of King Arthur and His Noble Knights.*
Stephens, Mary Jo. *Witch of the Cumberlands.*
Sterman, Betsy. *Too Much Magic.*
Stewart, Mary. *Crystal Cave; Hollow Hills; Last Enchantment.*

Tabrah, Ruth. *Red Shark.*
Tannen, Mary. *Lost Legend of Finn.*
Vande Veldi, Vivian. *Hidden Magic.*
Williams, Jay. *Magic Grandfather.*
Wrightson, Patricia. *Older Kind of Magic.*

Marine Mammals

Adair, Margaret. *Far Voice Calling.*
Benchley, Nathaniel. *Demo and the Dolphins.*
Bonham, Frank. *Loud, Resounding Sea (Dolphins); Mystery of the Red Tide.*
Brandel, Marc. *Mystery of the Kidnapped Whale.*
Catherall, Arthur. *Arctic Sealer; Lone Seal Pup.*
Chambers, Aidan. *Seal Secret.*
Clarke, Arthur. *Dolphin Island.*
Clarkson, Ewan. *Halic, Story of the Grey Seal.*
Dekkers, Midas. *Arctic Advent.*
Dickson, Gordon. *Secret Under Antarctica.*
Edwards, Monica. *Dolphin Summer.*
Haig-Brown, R.L. *Whale People.*
Levin, Betty. *Landfall.*
Lucas, Christopher. *Tiki and the Dolphin: Adventures of a Boy in Tahiti.*
Price, Willard. *Diving Adventure; South Sea Adventure; Whale Adventure.*
Senn, Steve. *Circle in the Sea.*
Shachtman, Tom. *Beachmaster: A Story of Daniel Au Fond.*
Smith, Terence. *Cry to the Night Wind.*
Spinelli, Jerry. *Night of the Whale.*
Taylor, Theodore. *Hostage.*
Thiele, Colin. *Shadow Shark.*
Waters, John. *Summer of the Seals.*
Yep, Laurence. *Sea Glass.*

Marriage

Bradbury, Bianca. *New Penny.*
Colman, Hila. *After the Wedding; Bride at Eighteen.*
Crane, Caroline. *Wedding Song.*
Delton, Judy. *Near Occasion of Sin.*
Du Jardin, Rosamond. *Double Wedding; Wedding in the Family.*
Feagles, Anita. *Year the Dreams Came Back.*
Greene, Constance. *Getting Nowhere.*
Harris, Christie. *You Have to Draw the Line Somewhere.*
Head, Ann. *Mr. and Mrs. Bo Jo Jones.*
Holland, Barbara. *Creepy-Mouse Coming to Get You.*
Kalish, Betty. *Eleven, Time to Think of Marriage.*
Kane, Harnett. *Amazing Mrs. Bonaparte.*
Laing, Frederich. *Bride Wore Braids.*
Lingard, Joan. *Across the Barricades; Into Exile; Strangers in the House.*
Lovelace, Maud. *Betsy's Wedding.*

Lyle, Katie. *Dark But Full of Diamonds.*
McHugh, Elisabet. *Karen's Sister.*
Miklowitz, Gloria. *Day the Senior Class Got Married.*
Montgomery, Lucy. *Anne's House of Dreams.*
Nostlinger, Christine. *Marrying Off Mother.*
Peyton, Karen. *Marion's Angels; Pennington's Heir.*
Radley, Gail. *Nothing Stays the Same Forever.*
Segal, Erich. *Love Story.*
Smith, Betty. *Joy in the Morning.*
Southerland, Ellease. *Let the Lion Eat Straw.*
Tyler, Anne. *Slipping Down Life.*
Vance, Marguerite. *Jeptha and the New People.*
Weber, Lenora. *Something Borrowed, Something Blue.*
Willey, Margaret. *If Not for You.*

Medical World

Anckarsvard, Karin. *Doctor's Boy.*
Arundel, Honor. *Girl in the Opposite Bed.*
Bach, Alice. *Waiting for Johnny Miracle.*
Bess, Clayton. *Story for a Black Night.*
Boylston, Helen. *Sue Barton, Neighborhood Nurse; Sue Barton, Rural Nurse; Sue Barton, Senior Nurse; Sue Barton, Staff Nurse; Sue Barton, Visiting Nurse; Sue Barton, Student Nurse; Sue Barton, Superintendent of Nurses.*
Brown, Roy. *Cage.*
Cook, Robin. *Brain; Coma; Mindbend.*
Corcoran, Barbara. *Child of the Morning.*
Crichton, Michael. *Terminal Man.*
Dixon, Paige. *May I Cross Your Golden River?*
Ethridge, Kenneth. *Toothpick.*
Fleischman, Paul. *Path of a Pale Horse.*
Howe, James. *Night Without Stars.*
Kassem, Lou. *Listen for Rachel.*
Laklan, Carli. *Nurse in Training; Second Year Nurse.*
Lightner, A.M. *Doctor to the Galaxy.*
McElfresh, Adeline. *To Each Her Dream.*
Miklowitz, Gloria. *Good-Bye Tomorrow.*
Nixon, Joan. *Other Side of Dark.*
Orgel, Doris. *Whiskers Once and Always.*
Rydberg, Ernie. *Shadow Army.*
Sachs, Elizabeth-Ann. *Just Like Always.*
Singer, Marilyn. *It Can't Hurt Forever.*
Stone, Patti. *Judy George: Student Nurse.*
Turngren, Annette. *Mystery Enters the Hospital.*
Wood, James. *Chase Scene.*
Yarbro, Chelsea. *Loradio's Apprentice.*

Mental Illness

Ames, Mildred. *What Are Friends For?*
Arrick, Fran. *Nice Girl from Good Home.*
Arthur, Ruth. *Miss Ghost.*

Baldwin, Anne. *Little Time.*
Bauer, Marion. *Tangled Butterfly.*
Bennett, Jay. *To Be a Killer.*
Bonham, Frank. *Gimme an H, Gimme an E, Gimme an L. Gimme....*
Bowen, Robert. *Lightning Southpaw.*
Bradbury, Bianca. *Laughter in Our House.*
Bridgers, Sue Ellen. *Notes for Another Life.*
Brockmann, Elizabeth. *What's the Matter, Girl?*
Brown, Ray. *Suicide Course.*
Carlson, Natalie. *Luigi of the Streets.*
Colman, Hila. *Sometimes I Don't Love My Mother.*
Crane, Caroline. *Girl Like Tracy.*
Cusack, Isabel. *Mr. Wheatfield's Loft.*
Delton, Jina. *Two Blocks Down.*
Dengler, Marianna. *Pebble in Newcomb's Pond.*
Dragonwagon, Crescent. *Year It Rained.*
Dunlop, Beverley. *Poetry Girl.*
Elliott, David. *Listen to the Silence.*
Ellis, Ella. *Celebrate the Morning.*
Ende, Michael. *Ophelia's Shadow Theatre.*
Eyerly, Jeannette. *Girl Inside.*
Fosburgh, Liza. *Cruise Control.*
Fox, Paula. *Stone-Faced Boy.*
Franco, Marjorie. *Love in a Different Key.*
Gordon, Shirley. *Me and the Bad Guys.*
Green, Hannah. *I Never Promised You a Rose Garden.*
Greene, Constance. *Getting Nowhere.*
Hamilton-Paterson, James. *House in the Waves.*
Hermes, Patricia. *Nobody's Fault?*
Holland, Isabelle. *Love and the Genetic Factor; Perdita.*
Hurwitz, Johanna. *Law of Gravity.*
Hyland, Betty. *Girl with the Crazy Brother.*
Kaufman, Barry. *Son Rise.*
Kesey, Ken. *One Flew Over the Cuckoo's Nest.*
Klein, Norma. *Older Men.*
Konigsburg, E.L. *(George).*
Levoy, Myron. *Alan and Naomi.*
McKillip, Patricia. *Night Gift.*
Martin, Ann. *Inside Out.*
Meyer, Carolyn. *Center: From a Troubled Past to a New Life.*
Mills, Claudia. *All the Living.*
Naylor, Phyllis. *Keeper.*
Neufeld, John. *Lisa, Bright and Dark.*
Newton, Suzanne. *I Will Call It Georgie's Blues.*
O'Dell, Scott. *Dark Canoe; Spanish Smile.*
O'Hanlon, Jacklyn. *Fair Game.*
Oneal, Zibby. *Language of Goldfish.*
Orgel, Doris. *Risking Love.*
Parker, Richard. *He Is Your Brother.*
Plath, Sylvia. *Bell Jar.*
Platt, Kin. *Ape Inside Me; Boy Who Could Make Himself Disappear.*
Riley, Jocelyn. *Crazy Quilt; Only My Mouth Is Smiling.*
Rodowsky, Colby. *What About Me?*
Ruckman, Ivy. *Encounter.*
Sachs, Marilyn. *Amy and Laura.*

Sallis, Susan. *Secret Places of the Stairs.*
Schwandt, Stephen. *Risky Game.*
Silsbee, Peter. *Big Way Out.*
Smith, Nancy. *Falling Apart Winter.*
Snyder, Zilpha. *Witches of Worm.*
Storr, Catherine. *Winter's End.*
Sweeney, Joyce. *Right Behind the Rain.*
Tate, Joan. *Tina and David.*
Torchia, Joseph. *Kryptonite Kid.*
Townsend, John. *Rob's Place.*
Weber, Lenora. *Come Back, Wherever You Are.*
Wersba, Barbara. *Let Me Fall Before I Fly.*
Wharton, William. *Birdy.*
Wilson, Louise. *This Stranger, My Son.*
Windsor, Patricia. *Summer Before.*
Wood, James. *Chase Scene.*
Wood, Marcia. *Secret Life of Hilary Thorne.*
Zindel, Paul. *Harry and Hortense at Hormone High; Pardon Me, You're Stepping on My Eyeball!*

Mentally Handicapped

Bridgers, Sue Ellen. *All Together Now.*
Brown, Roy. *Escape the River.*
Byars, Betsy. *Summer of the Swans.*
Carpland, Bo. *Bow Island: Story of a Summer That Was Different.*
Carrick, Carol. *Stay Away from Simon!*
Christopher, Matt. *Long Shot for Paul.*
Cleaver, Vera. *Ellen Grae; Me Too.*
Cummings, Betty Sue. *Let a River Be.*
Faber, Nancy. *Cathy at the Crossroads; Cathy's Secret Kingdom.*
Friis-Baastad, Babbis. *Don't Take Teddy.*
Garrigue, Sheila. *Between Friends.*
Gillham, Bill. *My Brother Barry.*
Hall, Eleanor. *Alice with Golden Hair.*
Hamilton, Virginia. *Sweet Whispers, Brother Rush.*
Hanlon, Emily. *It's Too Late for Sorry.*
Heide, Florence. *Secret Dreamer, Secret Dreams.*
Hermes, Patricia. *Who Will Take Care of Me?*
Holman, Felice. *Year to Grow.*
Hopper, Nancy. *Just Vernon.*
Hunt, Irene. *Everlasting Hills.*
Hunter, Edith. *Sue Ellen.*
Keyes, Daniel. *Flowers for Algernon.*
Koob, Theodora. *Deep Search.*
Little, Jean. *Take Wing.*
McNair, Joseph. *Commander Coatrack Returns.*
Mazer, Harry. *War on Villa Street.*
Platt, Kin. *Hey, Dummy.*
Reynolds, Pamela. *Different Kind of Sister.*
Sallis, Susan. *Time for Everything.*
Shyer, Marlene. *Welcome Home, Jellybean.*
Southall, Ivan. *King of the Sticks.*
Steinbeck, John. *Of Mice and Men.*
Talbert, Marc. *Toby.*
Teague, Sam. *King of Hearts' Heart.*

Walker, Pamela. *Twyla.*
Wright, Betty. *My Sister Is Different.*
Wrightson, Patricia. *Racehorse for Andy.*

Mice

Asch, Frank. *Pearl's Pirates; Pearl's Promise.*
Cleary, Beverly. *Mouse and the Motorcycle; Ralph S. Mouse; Runaway Ralph.*
Corbett, W.J. *Pentecost, the Chosen One; Song of Pentecost.*
Dahl, Roald. *Witches.*
Drury, Roger. *Champion of Merrimack County.*
Edmonds, Walter. *Time to Go House.*
Gallico, Paul. *Manx Mouse.*
Godden, Rumer. *Mousewife.*
Jacques, Brian. *Redwall.*
King, Alexander. *Memoirs of a Certain Mouse.*
King-Smith, Dick. *Magnus Powermouse.*
Lawson, Robert. *Ben and Me.*
Link, Ruth. *House Full of Mice.*
O'Brien, Robert. *Mrs. Frisby and the Rats of Nimh.*
Sharp, Margery. *Bernard Into Battle; Bernard the Brave; Miss Bianca; Miss Bianca and the Bridesmaid; Miss Bianca in the Antarctic; Miss Bianca in the Orient; Miss Bianca in the Salt Mines; Rescuers; Turret.*
Sheedy, Alexandra. *She Was Nice to Mice.*
Shura, Mary. *Mary's Marvelous Mouse; Tale of Middle Length.*
Simon, Sidney. *Henry, the Uncatchable Mouse.*
Steig, William. *Abel's Island.*
Titus, Eve. *Basil and the Pygmy Cats; Basil of Baker Street.*
Van Leeuwen, Jean. *Great Cheese Conspiracy; Great Christmas Kidnapping; Great Rescue Operation.*

Migrant Workers

See also: Poverty

Arthur, Ruth. *Whistling Boy.*
Bridgers, Sue Ellen. *Home Before Dark.*
Cleaver, Vera. *Mock Revolt.*
Dunne, Mary. *Reach Out, Ricardo.*
Gates, Doris. *Blue Willow.*
Johnson, Annabel. *Rescued Heart.*
Lampman, Evelyn. *Go Up the Road.*
Parker, Richard. *House That Guilda Drew.*
Peck, Robert. *Arly.*
Shotwell, Louisa. *Roosevelt Grady.*
Stallworth, Anne. *This Time Next Year.*
Strang, Celia. *Foster Mary.*
Waltrip, Lela. *White Harvest.*
Wier, Ester. *Loner.*
Wolf, Bernard. *In This Proud Land.*

Money Raising

Mothers

See also: Family

Motorcycles

Murder

Brookins, Dana. *Alone in Wolf Hollow; Who Killed Sack Annie?*
Calde, Mark. *Shadowboxer.*
Chalker, Jack. *Messiah Choice.*
Chambers, John. *Fire Island Forfeit.*
Christie, Agatha. *Elephants Can Remember; Evil Under the Sun; Labors of Hercules; Seven Dials Mystery.*
Clark, Mary. *Cradle Will Fall; Stranger Is Watching.*
Cook, Robin. *Mindbend.*
Corbett, Scott. *Witch Hunt.*
Corcoran, Barbara. *August, Die She Must; Watery Grave.*
Cunningham, Julia. *Flight of the Sparrows.*
Eisenberg, Lisa. *Fast Food King; House of Laughs.*
Foulds, Elfreda. *Ghost's High Noon.*
Gaines, Ernest. *Gathering of Old Men.*
Garfield, Leon. *December Rose.*
Gorman, Carol. *Chelsey and the Green-Haired Kid.*
Hagon, Priscilla. *Mystery at the Villa Blanca.*
Hall, Lynn. *Murder at the Spaniel Show.*
Healey, Larry. *Town Is on Fire.*
Hilgartner, Beth. *Murder for Her Majesty.*
Hinkemeyer, Michael. *Fields of Eden.*
Hoover, H.M. *Rains of Eridan.*
Kent, Alexander. *Midshipman Bolitho and the Avenger.*
Key, Alexander. *Flight to the Lonesome Place.*
King, Stephen. *Salem's Lot.*
L'Engle, Madeleine. *Dragons in the Water.*
Lilius, Irmelin. *Gold Crown Lane.*
Lindgren, Astrid. *Bill Bergson Lives Dangerously.*
McConnell, James. *Killer on the Track.*
McCutcheon, Elsie. *Rat War.*
MacLean, Alistair. *Ice Station Zebra.*
MacLeod, Charlotte. *Cirak's Daughter.*
Maxwell, Edith. *Just Dial a Number.*
Mays, Victor. *Dead Reckoning.*
Myers, Walter. *Hoops.*
Newman, Robert. *Case of the Somerville Secret.*
Nixon, Joan. *Dark and Deadly Pool; Other Side of Dark; Seance; Stalker.*
Parks, Peter. *Learning Tree.*
Paulsen, Gary. *Murphy.*
Peck, Richard. *Dreamland Lake.*
Peck, Robert. *Millie's Boy.*
Peyton, Karen. *Midsummer Night's Death.*
Pfeffer, Susan. *About David.*
Phillips, Leon. *Split Bamboo.*
Pitt, Nancy. *Beyond the High White Wall.*
Portis, Charles. *True Grit.*
Radford, Ken. *Haunting at Mill Lane.*
Raskin, Ellen. *Westing Game.*
Rees, David. *Risks.*
Roberts, Willo. *View from the Cherry Tree.*
Ross, Rhea. *Bet's On, Lizzie Bingman.*
Rutherford, Douglas. *Killer on the Track.*
St. George, Judith. *Do You See What I See?*

Sayers, Dorothy. *Murder Must Advertise.*
Schultz, Barbara. *House on Pinto's Island.*
Scoppettone, Sandra. *Playing Murder.*
Snyder, Zilpha. *Egypt Game.*
Sutcliff, Rosemary. *Blood Feud.*
Thomas, Joyce. *Journey.*
Thompson, Julian. *Discontinued.*
Townsend, John. *Tom Tiddler's Ground.*
Van Etten, Teresa. *Dead Kachina Man.*
Wallace, Bill. *Danger in Quicksand Pond.*
Wells, Rosemary. *When No One Was Looking.*
White, Ellen. *Friends for Life.*
Windsor, Patricia. *Killing Time; Sandman's Eyes.*
Woods, George. *Catch a Killer.*
Wright, Betty. *Christina's Ghost.*
Wright, Billy. *Dollhouse Murders.*
Yarbro, Chelsea. *Floating Illusions.*
Yep, Laurence. *Mark Twain Murders.*
York, Carol. *Once Upon a Dark November.*

Music

Alcott, Louisa May. *Old Fashioned Girl.*
Alexander, Lloyd. *Marvelous Misadventures of Sebastian.*
Almedingen, E.M. *Young Mark.*
Angell, Judie. *Buffalo Nickel Blues Band.*
Arundel, Honor. *High House.*
Barne, Kitty. *Barbie.*
Bates, Betty. *My Mom, the Money Nut.*
Beckett, Hilary. *Street Fair Summer.*
Bethancourt, T.E. *New York City Too Far from Tampa Blues; T.H.U.M.B.B.; Tomorrow Connection.*
Bohtemps, Arna. *Lonesome Boy.*
Bonham, Frank. *Friends of the Loony Lake Monster.*
Bourne, Miriam. *Uncle George Washington and Harriot's Guitar.*
Brooks, Bruce. *Midnight Hour Encores.*
Byars, Betsy. *Glory Girl.*
Campbell, Hope. *Why Not Join the Giraffes?*
Christian, Mary. *Singin' Somebody Else's Song.*
Cohen, Florence. *Portrait of Deborah.*
Collier, James. *Rich and Famous; Rock Star.*
Crane, William. *Encore; Oom-Pah.*
Cross, Gillian. *Chartbreaker.*
Damjan, Mischa. *December's Travels.*
Davidson, Mary. *Superstar Called Sweetpea.*
Duder, Tersa. *Jellybean.*
First, Julia. *Move Over, Beethoven.*
Fisher, Paul. *Hawks of Fellheath.*
Foster, Alan. *Spellsinger.*
Franco, Marjorie. *Love in a Different Key.*
Friermood, Elizabeth. *Ballad of Calamity Creek.*
Gathje, Curtis. *Disco Kid.*
Gilbert, Nan. *Academy Summer.*
Gioffre, Marisa. *Starstruck.*

Glasser, Barbara. *Bongo Bradley.*
Greene, Bette. *Them That Glitter/Them That Don't.*
Groch, Judith. *Play the Bach, Dear.*
Grosser, Morton. *Snake Horn.*
Hall, Lynn. *Sticks and Stones.*
Hamilton, Virginia. *Planet of Junior Brown.*
Hentoff, Nat. *Does This School Have Capital Punishment?; Jazz Country.*
Hopper, Nancy. *Hang On, Harvey.*
Hunter, Kristin. *Lou in the Limelight; Soul Brother and Sister Lou.*
Johnson, A.E. *Blues I Can Whistle.*
Kennedy, S.A. *Hey, Didi Darling.*
Kidd, Ronald. *Sizzle and Splat.*
Kohl, Erica. *Where Is Emmett Gold?*
Laing, Frederich. *Question of Pride.*
Lampman, Evelyn. *Bandit of Mak Hill.*
Le Guin, Ursula. *Very Far Away from Anywhere Else.*
Lightner, A.M. *Galactic Troubadors.*
Line, David. *Screaming High.*
Lisle, Janet. *Sirens and Spies.*
McCaffrey, Anne. *Crystal Singer; Dragondrums; Dragonsinger; Dragonsong; Killashandra.*
McKillip, Patricia. *Fool's Run.*
MacLachlan, Patricia. *Facts and Fiction of Minna Pratt.*
MacLeod, Charlotte. *Maid of Honor.*
Major, Kevin. *Dear Bruce Springsteen.*
Newton, Suzanne. *I Will Call It Georgie's Blues.*
Parker, Richard. *Second-Hand Family.*
Paterson, Katherine. *Come Sing, Jimmy Jo.*
Peck, Richard. *Those Sunner Girls I Never Met.*
Perlberg, Deborah. *Heartaches.*
Peyton, Karen. *Beethoven's Medal; Marion's Angels; Pennington's Heir; Pennington's Last Term.*
Pilling, Ann. *Big Pink.*
Provost, Gary. *Popcorn.*
Rabe, Berniece. *Rehearsal for the Bigtime.*
Richardson, Grace. *Douglas.*
Robertson, Keith. *Henry Reed's Big Show.*
Rodowsky, Colby. *Keeping Time.*
Sargent, Sarah. *Watermusic.*
Schaff, Louise. *Skald of the Vikings.*
Shyer, Marlene. *Me and Joey Pinstrip, the King of Rock.*
Singer, Marilyn. *No Applause Please.*
Sleator, William. *Fingers.*
Slepian, Janice. *Night of the Bozos.*
Smith, Alison. *Billy Boone.*
Stearns, Pamela. *Mechanical Doll.*
Strasser, Todd. *Rock 'n' Roll Nights; Turn It Up; Wildlife.*
Tamar, Erika. *Blues for Silk Garcia.*
Towne, Mary. *Glass Room.*
Tyler, Anne. *Slipping Down Life.*
Ure, Jean. *After Thursday.*
Van Stockum, Hilda. *Mago's Flute.*
Vipont, Elfrida. *Lark in the Morn; Lark on the Wing.*

Walden, Amelia. *Same Scene, Different Place.*
Warfel, Diantha. *Violin Case Case.*
Webb, Sharon. *Earthchild.*
Weik, Mary. *Jazz Man.*
Weller, Frances. *Boat Song.*
Woodford, Peggy. *Girl with a Voice.*
Woolley, Catherine. *Cathy and the Beautiful People.*
Young, Bob. *One Small Voice.*

Mystery

See also: Mystery/Kidnapping; Mystery/Stealing

Alcock, Vivien. *Mysterious Mr. Ross.*
Allan, Mabel. *Horns of Danger; Kraymer Mystery.*
Anckarsvard, Karin. *Rider by Night.*
Arden, William. *Mystery of the Shrinking House; Mystery of Wrecker's Rock; Secret of Shark Reef.*
Arthur, Robert. *Mystery of the Screaming Clock.*
Arthur, Ruth. *Saracan Lamp.*
Avi. *No More Magic.*
Babbitt, Natalie. *Goody Hall.*
Baird, Thomas. *Finding Fever.*
Bawden, Nina. *Carrie's War; Kept in the Dark.*
Beatty, Jerome. *Sheriff Stonehead and the Teen-Age Termites.*
Bellairs, John. *Curse of the Blue Figurine; Letter, the Witch and the Ring; Mummy, the Will and the Crypt; Treasure of Alpheus Winterborn.*
Bennett, Jay. *Death Ticket; Slowly, Slowly I Raise the Gun.*
Berna, Paul. *Clue of the Black Cat; Secret of the Missing Boat.*
Best, Herbert. *Desmond and Dog Friday.*
Betancourt, Jeanne. *Between Us.*
Blish, James. *Vanished Jet.*
Boden, Hilda. *Foxes in the Valley.*
Bonham, Frank. *Mystery in Little Tokyo; Mystery of the Fat Cat; Premonitions.*
Bothwell, Jean. *Mystery Clock; Mystery Key; Parsonage Parrot.*
Brandel, Marc. *Mystery of the Two-Toed Pigeon.*
Brontë, Charlotte. *Jane Eyre.*
Brookins, Dana. *Who Killed Sack Annie?*
Buck, William. *Dr. Anger's Island.*
Bull, Angela. *Wayland's Keep.*
Bulla, Clyde. *Ghost of Windy Hill.*
Bunting, Eve. *Ghost Children; Is Anybody There?*
Butler, Beverly. *Ghost Cat.*
Campbell, Hope. *Peak Beneath the Moon.*
Caroselli, Remus. *Mystery at Long Crescent Marsh.*
Carson, John. *Mystery of the Missing Monkey.*

Caunitz, William. *One Police Plaza.*

Chalker, Jack. *Messiah Choice.*

Chance, Stephen. *Septimus and the Minister Ghost Mystery.*

Christian, Mary. *Firebug Mystery; Mystery at Camp Triumph.*

Christie, Agatha. *Labors of Hercules; Seven Dials Mystery; Sleeping Murder.*

Christopher, Matt. *Hockey Machine; Supercharged Infield.*

Clapp, Patricia. *Jane-Emily.*

Clark, Mary. *Stillwatch.*

Clewes, Dorothy. *Mystery of the Jade-Green Cadillac.*

Clifford, Eth. *Dastardly Murder of Dirty Pete; Harvey's Marvelous Monkey Mystery; Help! I'm a Prisoner in the Library.*

Colver, Anne. *Secret Castle.*

Conan Doyle, Arthur. *Hound of the Baskervilles.*

Cook, Robin. *Coma.*

Cookson, Catherine. *Go Tell It to Mrs. Golightly.*

Coontz, Otto. *Mystery Madness.*

Corbett, Scott. *Case of the Ticklish Tooth; Dead Before Docking; Grave Doubts; Here Lies the Body; Mystery Man.*

Corcoran, Barbara. *Mystery on Ice; Person in the Potting Shed; You're Allegro Dead.*

Coville, Bruce. *Ghost Wore Gray.*

Craig, M.F. *Mystery at Peacock Place.*

Crayder, Dorothy. *Riddles of Mermaid House.*

Cross, Gilbert. *Terror Train; Dark Behind the Curtain.*

Curry, Jane. *Great Flood Mystery; Ice Ghost Mystery.*

Dank, Milton. *3-D Traitor; Computer Caper; Treasure Code; U.F.O. Has Landed.*

De Jong, Dola. *House on Charlton Street.*

Delton, Judy. *Mystery of the Haunted Cabin.*

Dicks, Terrance. *Case of the Cinema Swindle; Case of the Cop Catchers; Case of the Ghost Grabbers.*

D'Ignazio, Fred. *Chip Mitchell, Case of the Robot Warriors; Chip Mitchell, Case of the Stolen Computer Brains.*

Divine, David. *Stolen Season; Three Red Flares.*

Dodson, Susan. *Shadows Across the Sand.*

Doty, Jean. *Crumb.*

Du Maurier, Daphne. *Rebecca.*

Duncan, Lois. *They Never Came Home.*

Dunlop, Eileen. *House on the Hill.*

Durham, John. *Me and Arch and the Pest.*

Durrell, Gerald. *Donkey Rustlers.*

Ecke, Wolfgang. *Bank Holdup; Face at the Window; Invisible Witness; Midnight Chess Game; Stolen Paintings.*

Eisenberg, Lisa. *Mystery at Bluff Point Dunes; Mystery at Snowshoe Mountain Lodge; Tiger Rose.*

Evarts, Hal. *Pegleg Mystery; Purple Eagle Mystery.*

Farley, Carol. *Case of the Vanishing Villain; Mystery in the Ravine.*

Faulkner, Nancy. *Mystery of Long Barrow House.*

Fecher, Constance. *Leopard Dagger.*

Fenton, Edward. *Riddle of the Red Whale.*

Fenwick, Elizabeth. *Passenger.*

Fleischman, Paul. *Half-a-Moon Inn.*

Fleischman, Sid. *Bloodhound Gang and the Case of the Secret Message.*

Fry, Rosalie. *Gypsy Princess; Riddle of the Figurehead.*

Gage, Wilson. *Secret of Fiery Gorge.*

Garden, Nancy. *Mystery of the Midnight Menace; Mystery of the Night Raiders; Mystery of the Secret Marks.*

Garnett, Richard. *White Dragon.*

Gates, Doris. *Cat and Mrs. Cary.*

Geer, Charles. *Dexter and the Deer Lake Mystery.*

Glaser, Dianne. *Case of the Missing Six.*

Godden, Rumer. *Rocking Horse Secret.*

Gooding, Kathleen. *Festival Summer.*

Goudge, Elizabeth. *Linnets and Valerians.*

Graves, Robert. *Ancient Castle.*

Hahn, Mary. *Following the Mystery Man.*

Halacy, Daniel. *Secret of the Cove.*

Hall, Lynn. *Mystery of Pony Hollow Panda; Ride a Dark Horse.*

Hamilton, Virginia. *House of Dies Drear.*

Hardwick, Michael. *Revenge of the Hound.*

Harnett, Cynthia. *Great House.*

Heide, Florence. *Black Magic at Brillstone; Body in the Brillstone Garage; Brillstone Break-In; Burning Stone at Brillstone; Face at the Brillstone Window; Fear at Brillstone; Time Bomb at Brillstone.*

Hicks, Clifford. *Alvin Fernald, T.V. Anchorman.*

Hightower, Florence. *Fayerweather Forecast.*

Hildick, E.W. *Case of the Felon's Fiddle; Case of the Muttering Mummy; Case of the Phantom Frog; Case of the Slingshot Sniper; Case of the Snowbound Spy; Cat Called Amnesia; Ghost Squad and the Ghoul of Grunberg; Ghost Squad and the Halloween Conspiracy; Ghost Squad and the Menace of the Malevs; Ghost Squad and the Prowling Hermits; Ghost Squad Flies Concorde; Great Rabbit Rip-Off; McGurk Gets Good and Mad; Nose Knows.*

Holl, Kristi. *Haunting of Cabin Thirteen.*

Honness, Elizabeth. *Mystery of the Wooden Indian.*

Hooks, William. *Mystery on Bleeker Street; Mystery on Liberty Street.*

Hoppe, Joanne. *April Spell.*

Howe, James. *Dew Drop Dead.*

Hubner, Carol. *Whispering Mezuzah.*

Hughes, Dean. *Nutty and the Case of the Mastermind Thief.*

Jane, Mary. *Rocking Chair Ghost.*

Johnston, Norma. *Gabriel's Girl; Watcher in the Mist.*

Mystery Doll; Ginnie and the Mystery Light; Libby's Uninvited Guest.
Wosmek, Frances. *Mystery of the Eagle's Claw.*
Yep, Laurence. *Liar, Liar.*
York, Carol. *Dead Man's Cat; On That Dark Night; When Midnight Comes.*
Zindel, Paul. *Undertaker's Gone Bananas.*

Mystery/Kidnapping

Arden, William. *Mystery of the Deadly Double.*
Arthur, Robert. *Mystery of the Rogues Reunion.*
Catherall, Arthur. *Kidnapped by Accident.*
Chambers, John. *Finder.*
Christian, Mary. *Maltese Feline; Mystery of the Double, Double Cross.*
Duncan, Lois. *Third Eye.*
Koenig, Alma. *Gudrun.*
Lindgren, Astrid. *Bill Bergson and the White Rose Rescue.*
Newman, Robert. *Case of the Baker Street Irregulars.*
Peyton, Karen. *Prove Yourself a Hero.*
Schwandt, Stephen. *Last Goodie.*
Sebestyen, Ouida. *Girl in the Box.*
Skirrow, Desmond. *Case of the Silver Egg.*
Wees, Frances. *Treasure of Echo Valley.*
Zaring, Jane. *Sharks in the North Woods.*

Mystery/Stealing

Allan, Mabel. *May Day Mystery.*
Anckarsvard, Karin. *Madcap Mystery.*
Anderson, Mary. *Matilda's Masterpiece.*
Arden, William. *Mystery of the Dancing Devil; Mystery of the Smashing Glass.*
Avery, Gillian. *Who Stole the Wizard of Oz?*
Baudouy, Michel. *Secret of the Hidden Painting.*
Bennett, Jay. *Deathman, Do Not Follow Me.*
Berna, Paul. *Horse Without a Head.*
Bratton, Helen. *Amber Flask.*
Carleton, Barbee. *Secret of Saturday Cove.*
Cavanna, Betty. *Mystery at Love's Creek.*
Chance, Stephen. *Septimus and Danedyke Mystery.*
Channel, A.R. *Jungle Rescue.*
Clark, Margaret. *Latchkey Mystery; Mystery in the Flooded Museum.*
Clewes, Dorothy. *Mystery of the Lost Tower Treasure; Mystery of the Scarlet Daffodil.*
Corbett, Scott. *Trouble with Diamonds.*
Curry, Jane. *Ghost Lane.*
Derleth, August. *Ghost of Black Hawk Island.*
Dicks, Terrance. *Case of the Blackmail Boys; Case of the Missing Masterpiece.*
Dickson, Gordon. *Secret Under the Caribbean.*
Eisenberg, Lisa. *Golden Idol.*

Estes, Eleanor. *Alley.*
Faulkner, Nancy. *Secret of the Simple Code.*
Govan, Christine. *Phinny's Five Summer.*
Greenwald, Sheila. *Atrocious Two.*
Hallman, Ruth. *Gimme Something, Mister.*
Hamilton, Gail. *Candle to the Devil.*
Hamilton, Virginia. *Mystery of Drear House.*
Heide, Florence. *Deadline for McGurk; Hidden Box Mystery; Mystery at Southport Cinema; Mystery of the Macadoo Zoo; Mystery of the Midnight Message; Mystery of the Missing Suitcase; Mystery of the Mummy's Mask; Mystery of the Vanishing Visitor.*
Hildick, E.W. *Case of the Bashful Bank Robber; Case of the Treetop Treasure; Case of the Wandering Weathervanes.*
Holding, James. *Mystery of the False Fingertips.*
Honness, Elizabeth. *Mystery of the Auction Trunk; Mystery of the Mayan Jade; Mystery of the Pirate's Ghost.*
Jane, Mary. *Indian Island Mystery; Mystery in Hidden Hollow.*
Kherdian, David. *Mystery of the Diamond in the Wood.*
Kingman, Lee. *Saturday Gang.*
Lawrence, Mildred. *Reach for the Dream.*
McHargue, Georgess. *Turquoise Toad Mystery.*
Mooney, Elizabeth. *Sandy Shoes Mystery.*
Newman, Robert. *Case of the Etruscan Treasure; Case of the Vanishing Corpse.*
Pilling, Ann. *Henry's Leg.*
Platt, Kin. *Run for Your Life.*
Roth, David. *Girl in the Grass.*
Shura, Mary. *Don't Call Me Toad.*
Smith, Carole. *Stealing Isn't Easy.*
Verney, John. *Ismo.*
Warfel, Diantha. *Violin Case Case.*
Weir, Rosemary. *Mystery of the Black Sheep.*
Whitney, Phyllis. *Secret of the Tiger's Eye.*

Native Americans

Agle, Nan. *Makon and the Dauphin.*
Allen, Leroy. *Shawnee Lance.*
Annixter, Jane. *White Shell Horse.*
Armer, Laura. *Waterless Mountain.*
Baker, Betty. *And One Was a Wooden Indian; Do Not Annoy the Indians; Killer-of-Death; Shaman's Last Raid; Stranger and Afraid; Walk the World's Rim.*
Baker, Olaf. *Where the Buffaloes Begin.*
Balch, Glenn. *Horse of Two Colors; Spotted Horse.*
Barbary, James. *Fort in the Wilderness.*
Barnouw, Victor. *Dream of the Blue Heron.*
Beatty, Patricia. *Wait for Me, Watch for Me, Eula Bee.*
Beebe, B.F. *Coyote, Come Home.*
Benedict, Rex. *Good-Bye to the Purple Sage; Good Luck Arizona Man.*

West, Jessamyn. *Massacre at Fall Creek.*
Wisler, G. Clifton. *Buffalo Moon; Winter of the Wolf.*
Worcester, Donald. *Lone Hunter and the Wild Horses.*
Wosmek, Frances. *Brown Bird Singing.*

Nazis

See also: Holocaust, Jews; World War II

Bishop, Claire. *Twenty and Ten.*
Follett, Ken. *Key to Rebecca.*
Forman, James. *Ceremony of Innocence.*
Gardner, John. *Icebreaker.*
Hartman, Evert. *War Without Friends.*
Hayden, Torey. *Sunflower Forest.*
Korschunow, Irina. *Night in Distant Motion.*
Leitner, Isabella. *Fragments of Isabella.*
Levin, Ira. *Boys from Brazil.*
MacLean, Alistair. *Where Eagles Dare.*
Orgel, Doris. *Devil in Vienna.*
Ramati, Alexander. *And the Violins Stopped Playing.*
Reiss, Johanna. *Upstairs Room.*
Richter, Hans. *Friedrich; I Was There.*
Zyskind, Sara. *Stolen Years.*

Nurses

See: Medical World

Occult

See also: ESP

Aiken, Joan. *Shadow Guests.*
Alcock, Vivien. *Haunting of Cassie Palmer; Stonewalkers.*
Allan, Mabel. *Chill in the Lane.*
Ames, Mildred. *Conjuring Summer In.*
Amoss, Berthe. *Chalk Cross.*
Anderson, Margaret. *Leipzig Vampire.*
Arden, William. *Mystery of the Invisible Dog.*
Arthur, Ruth. *Autumn People; Candle in Her Room; Requiem for a Princess.*
Avi. *Devil's Race.*
Baker, Betty. *And One Was a Wooden Indian.*
Belden, Wilanne. *Mind-Find.*
Bellairs, John. *Revenge of the Wizard's Ghost.*
Bennett, Jay. *Haunted One.*
Bethancourt, T.E. *Mortal Instrument.*
Bibby, Violet. *Many Waters Cannot Quench Love.*
Blatty, William. *Exorcist.*
Bonham, Frank. *Premonitions.*
Bunting, Eve. *Ghosts of Departure Point;*

Strange Things Happen in the Woods.
Callen, Larry. *Deadly Mandrake.*
Carleton, Barbee. *Witch's Bridge.*
Carlson, Natalie. *Luigi of the Streets.*
Cheetham, Ann. *Beggar's Curse.*
Chetwin, Grace. *Out of the Dark World.*
Cook, Robin. *Brain.*
Coontz, Otto. *Isle of the Shapeshifters; Night Walkers.*
Corbett, Scott. *One by Sea.*
Cowley, Joy. *Silent One.*
De Weese, Gene. *Dandelion Caper.*
Dickinson, Peter. *Gift; Healer.*
Duncan, Lois. *Daughters of Eve.*
Dyer, T.A. *Way of His Own.*
Freeman, Barbara. *Haunting Air.*
Fyson, Jenny. *Journey of the Eldest Son.*
Gaines, Ernest. *Long Day in November.*
Garden, Nancy. *Door Between; Prisoners of Vampires.*
Gilman, Dorothy. *Clairvoyant Countess.*
Green, Phyllis. *Eating Ice Cream with a Werewolf.*
Halam, Ann. *Daymaker.*
Hamilton, Virginia. *Dustland.*
Heinlein, Robert. *Puppet Masters.*
Hoover, H.M. *Shepherd Moon.*
Hunter, Mollie. *Haunted Mountain; Wicked One.*
Hutchins, Pat. *Curse of the Egyptian Mummy.*
Jones, Adrienne. *Hawks of Chelney.*
Jones, Diana. *Charmed Life; Spellcoats.*
Katz, Welwyn. *False Face.*
Kay, Mara. *House Full of Echoes.*
Key, Alexander. *Case of the Vanishing Boy.*
Kilgore, Kathleen. *Ghost-Maker.*
King, Stephen. *Shining.*
Koff, Richard. *Christopher.*
Konigsburg, E.L. *Up from Jerico Tel.*
Lawrence, Louise. *Cat Call.*
Leonard, Constance. *Aground.*
Levitin, Sonia. *Beyond Another Door.*
Lively, Penelope. *House in Norham Gardens; Wild Hunt of the Ghost Hounds.*
Livoni, Cathy. *Element of Time.*
Lunn, Janet. *Shadow in Hawthorn Bay.*
McGinnis, Lila. *Auras and Other Rainbow Secrets.*
MacKellar, William. *Kenny and the Highland Ghost.*
Mahy, Margaret. *Changeover.*
Mayhar, Ardath. *Makra Choria.*
Mayne, William. *Year and a Day.*
Melling, O.R. *Singing Stone.*
Menuis, Opal. *No Escape.*
Miller, Phyllis. *House of Shadows.*
Morpurgo, Michael. *Why the Whales Came.*
Murphy, Shirley. *Castle of Hape; Caves of Fire and Ice; Ring of Fire; Wolf Bell.*
Myers, Walter. *Mojo and the Russians.*
Naylor, Phyllis. *Footprints at the Window.*
Nixon, Joan. *Deadly Game of Magic.*

Olson, Helen. *Secret of Spirit Mountain.*
Peck, Richard. *Blossom Culp and the Sleep of Death; Dreadful Future of Blossom Culp; Ghost Belonged to Me; Ghosts I Have Been.*
Phipson, Joan. *Watcher in the Garden.*
Platt, Kin. *Mystery of the Woman in the Mirror.*
Poole, Josephine. *Moon Eyes.*
Rabe, Berniece. *Naomi.*
Ray, Mary. *Voice of Apollo.*
Roberts, Willo. *Girl with the Silver Eyes.*
Rundle, Anne. *Moonbranches.*
Sachar, Louis. *Boy Who Lost His Face.*
Service, Pamela. *When the Night Wind Howls.*
Sleator, William. *Into the Dream.*
Smith, Martin. *Nightwing.*
Snyder, Zilpha. *Changeling; Headless Cupid; Truth About Stone Hollow.*
Stearns, Pamela. *Fool and the Dancing Bear.*
Storr, Catherine. *Winter's End.*
Sudbery, Rodie. *Silk and the Skin.*
Walker, Mary. *To Catch a Zombi.*
Wells, H.G. *Time Machine; Invisible Man.*
Williams, Jay. *Magic Grandfather.*
Wisler, G. Clifton. *Seer.*
Wolkstein, Diane. *White Wave: A Chinese Tale.*
Wright, Betty. *Ghost in the Window.*

Orphans

See also: Adoption; Foster Homes

Aiken, Joan. *Go Saddle the Sea; Wolves of Willoughby Chase.*
Allan, Mabel. *Ballet Family; Night Wind.*
Anderson, Rachel. *War Orphan.*
Andrews, Jean. *Dear Dola: or, How to Build Your Own Family.*
Appleby, Jon. *Skate.*
Armstrong, Richard. *Trial Trip.*
Arthur, Ruth. *Portrait of Margarita.*
Babcock, Havilah. *Education of Pretty Boy.*
Bacon, Martha. *In the Company of Clowns.*
Ball, Zachary. *Kep; North to Abilene.*
Baudouy, Michel. *Boy Who Belonged to No One.*
Beatty, John. *Holdfast.*
Beatty, Patricia. *Lacy Makes a Match; That's One Ornery Orphan.*
Bowen, Betty. *For Love of a Donkey.*
Buck, Pearl. *Matthew, Mark, Luke and John.*
Burch, Robert. *Skinny.*
Carleton, Barbee. *Witch's Bridge.*
Carlson, Natalie. *Brother for the Orphelines; Grandmother for the Orphelines; Happy Orpheline; Orphelines in the Enchanted Castle.*
Cassedy, Sylvia. *Behind the Attic Wall.*
Coleman, Lonnie. *Orphan Jim.*
Cooper, Gordon. *Second Springtime.*
Cunningham, Julia. *Burnish Me Bright; Dorp Dead; Far in the Day; Flight of the Sparrows; Silent Voice.*

De Jong, Dola. *By Marvelous Agreement.*
Dickenson, Christine. *Getting It All Together.*
Edwards, Julie. *Mandy.*
Elliott, David. *Listen to the Silence.*
Eyerly, Jeannette. *Girl Inside.*
Fenisong, Ruth. *Boy Wanted.*
Fisher, Paul. *Ash Staff; Hawks of Fellheath.*
Fleischman, Sid. *Jingo Django.*
Garfield, Leon. *Sound of Coaches; Young Nick and Jubilee.*
Hall, Lynn. *Tin Can Tucker.*
Hays, Wilma. *Mary's Star.*
Held, Kurt. *Outsiders of Uskoken Castle.*
Holland, Isabelle. *Alan and the Animal Kingdom.*
Holman, Felice. *Wild Children.*
Howard, Ellen. *Verity's Voyage.*
Jones, Dorothy. *Wonderful World Outside.*
Kennedy, X.J. *Owlstone Crown.*
L'Engle, Madeleine. *Meet the Austins.*
Lindgren, Astrid. *Rasmus and the Vagabond.*
Lovett, Margaret. *Jonathan.*
McKenzie, Ellen. *Taash and the Jesters.*
Malot, Hector. *Foundling.*
Miller, Ruth. *City Rose.*
Morpurgo, Michael. *Little Foxes.*
Myers, Walter. *Won't Know Till I Get There.*
Nixon, Joan. *Caught in the Act; Family Apart.*
North, Joan. *Cloud Forest.*
Peyton, Karen. *Flambards.*
Shreve, Susan. *Lucy Forever and Miss Rosetree.*
Smith, Carole. *Parchment House.*
Storey, Margaret. *Family Tree; Pauline.*
Streatfeild, Noel. *Children on the Top Floor; Thursday's Child.*
Talbot, Charlene. *Orphan for Nebraska.*
Taylor, Sydney. *All-of-a-Kind Family Downtown.*
Unsworth, Walter. *Grimsdyke.*
Van Woerkuna, Dorothy. *Pearl in the Egg.*
Vinge, Joan. *Psion.*
Ware, Leon. *Rebellious Orphan.*
Webster, Jean. *Dear Enemy.*
Willard, Barbara. *Iron Lily.*
Wosmek, Frances. *Mystery of the Eagle's Claw.*
Yolen, Jane. *Children of the Wolf.*

Overweight

Ames, Mildred. *Is There Life on a Plastic Planet?*
Anderson, Mary. *I'm Nobody! Who Are You?*
Benjamin, Carol. *Nobody's Baby Now.*
Bishop, Curtis. *Field Goal.*
Blume, Judy. *Blubber.*
Boylan, Rowena. *Better Than the Rest.*
Busselle, Rebecca. *Bathing Ugly.*
Cavallaro, Ann. *Blimp.*
Cohen, Barbara. *Fat Jack; R My Name Is Rosie.*
De Clements, Barthe. *How Do You Lose Those 9th Grade Blues?; Nothing's Fair in Fifth Grade.*

Dorman, N.B. *Laughter in the Background.*
Du Bois, William. *Porko Von Popbutton.*
Gerber, Merrill. *Also Known as Sadzia, the Belly Dancer!*
Giff, Patricia. *Poopsie Pomerantz, Pick Up Your Feet.*
Greenberg, Jan. *Pig-Out Blues.*
Greene, Constance. *Girl Called Al; I Know You, Al.*
Grove, Vicki. *Fastest Friend in the West.*
Hautzig, Deborah. *Second Star to the Right.*
Hayes, Sheila. *Me and My Mona Lisa Smile.*
Henkes, Kevin. *Two Under Par.*
Holland, Isabelle. *Dinah and the Green Fat Kingdom; Heads You Win, Tails I Lose.*
Kerr, M.E. *Dinky Hocker Shoots Smack.*
Lipsyte, Robert. *One Fat Summer.*
Little, Jean. *Stand in the Wind.*
Manes, Stephen. *Slim Down Camp.*
Mazer, Harry. *Dollar Man.*
Oldham, Mary. *White Pony.*
Orgel, Doris. *Next Door to Xanadu.*
Perl, Lila. *Fat Glenda's Summer Romance; Hey, Remember Fat Glenda?; Me and Fat Glenda.*
Pfeffer, Susan. *Marley the Kid.*
Philbrook, Clem. *Ollie's Team and the 200 Pound Problem.*
Pilling, Ann. *Big Pink.*
Pinsker, Judith. *Lot Like You.*
Rabinowich, Ellen. *Underneath I'm Different.*
Sachs, Marilyn. *Class Pictures; Fat Girl.*
St. Peter, Joyce. *Always Abigail.*
Saxon, Nancy. *Panky and William.*
Schwartz, Sheila. *Growing Up Guilty.*
Smith, Doris. *Last Was Lloyd.*
Smith, Robert. *Jelly Belly.*
Stren, Patti. *I Was a Fifteen-Year-Old Blimp; Mountain Rose.*
Swift, Helen. *Second Semester.*
Townsend, John. *Pirate's Island.*
Tyler, Anne. *Slipping Down Life.*
Wersba, Barbara. *Beautiful Losers; Fat, a Love Story; Love Is the Crooked Thing.*

Parents

See: Family; Fathers; Mothers

Personal Appearance

See: Anorexia; Overweight

Pets

See also: Cats; Dogs

Adams, Laurie. *Alice and the Boa Constrictor.*

Angell, Judie. *Home Is to Share and Share and Share.*
Asher, Sandy. *Teddy Teabury's Fabulous Fact.*
Bawden, Nina. *Peppermint Pig.*
Berends, Polly. *Case of the Elevator Duck.*
Branscum, Robbie. *Cheater and Flitter Dick.*
Carlson, Natalie. *Pet for the Orphelines.*
Cresswell, Helen. *Bagthorpes Liberated.*
Honeycutt, Natalie. *Best Laid Plans of Jonah Twist.*
Lampman, Evelyn. *Mrs. Updaisy.*
McHargue, Georgess. *Turquoise Toad Mystery.*
Patchett, Mary. *End of the Outlaws.*
Pearce, Philippa. *Battle of Bubble and Squeak.*
Richler, Mordecai. *Jacob Two-Two and the Dinosaur.*
Robinson, Mary. *Amazing Valvano and the Mystery of the Hooded Rat.*
Shecter, Ben. *Someplace Else.*
Stephens, Mary Jo. *Xoe's Zodiac.*
Wilson, Hazel. *More Fun with Herbert.*
Wolkoff, Judie. *Wally.*

Pirates

See also: Sea and Ships

Arden, William. *Mystery of the Purple Pirate.*
Cleven, Catherine. *Pirate Dog.*
Collier, Julia. *Pirates of Barataria.*
Corbett, Scott. *Captain Butcher's Body.*
Fleischman, Sid. *Ghost in the Noonday Sun.*
Garfield, Leon. *Jack Holbrook.*
Grote, William. *Fiddle, Flute and the River.*
Hayes, John. *Dangerous Cove.*
Heatter, Basil. *Wreck Ashore!*
Helldorfer, M.C. *Almost Home.*
Hyde, Laurence. *Captain Deadlock; Under the Pirate Flag.*
Johnson, Charles. *Pieces of Eight.*
Jones, Adrienne. *Ride the Far Wind.*
Lawrence, Isabelle. *Gift of the Golden Cup; Theft of the Golden Ring.*
McNaughton, Colin. *Jolly Roger and the Pirates of Abduul the Skinhead.*
Miers, Earl. *Pirate Chase.*
Polland, Madeleine. *White Twilight.*
Ritchie, Rita. *Pirates of Samarkand.*
Watson, Sally. *Jode.*
Wellman, Manly. *River Pirates.*
Wibberley, Leonard. *Crime of Martin Coverly; Leopard's Prey.*
Wolff, Robert. *Caves of Mars.*
Wood, James. *Queen's Most Honorable Pirate.*
Yvart, Jacques. *Rising of the Wind Adventures Along the Beaufort Scale.*

Polar Regions

Catherall, Arthur. *Arctic Sealer; Night of the Black Frost.*
Chadwick, Lonnie. *Don't Shoot.*
Denzel, Justin. *Snowfoot.*
Dickson, Gordon. *Secret Under Antarctica.*
Hamre, Leif. *Operation Arctic.*
Houston, James. *Akavak: An Eskimo Journey; Ice Sword; Wolf Run.*
MacGregor, Ellen. *Miss Pickerell Goes to the Arctic.*
Miller, Albert. *Silver Chief's Big Game Trail.*
St. George, Judith. *In the Shadow of the Bear.*
Steele, Mary. *First of the Penguins.*

Poverty

See also: Depression Era

Anderson, Rachel. *Poacher's Son.*
Bach, Alice. *He Will Not Walk with Me.*
Beatty, Patricia. *Lupita Manana.*
Bonham, Frank. *Nitty-Gritty.*
Bridgers, Sue Ellen. *Home Before Dark.*
Burton, Hester. *Rebel; Riders of the Storm.*
Callen, Larry. *Muskrat War.*
Cleaver, Vera. *Hazel Rye; Mimosa Tree; Where the Lilies Bloom.*
Cummings, Betty. *Now Ameriky.*
Delton, Judy. *Kitty in the Summer.*
Estes, Eleanor. *Hundred Dresses.*
Forbes, Tom. *Quincy's Harvest.*
Green, Phyllis. *Mildred Murphy, How Does Your Garden Grow?*
Hamilton, Virginia. *M.C. Higgins, the Great.*
Harris, Mark. *Come the Morning.*
Heck, Bessie. *Millie.*
Hurmence, Belinda. *Tough Tiffany.*
Kerr, Judith. *Other Way Around.*
Laklan, Carli. *Nurse in Training.*
Levoy, Myron. *Pictures of Adam.*
McLean, Allan. *Ribbon of Fire.*
Malone, Mary. *Three Wishes for Sarah.*
Mazer, Norma. *Silver.*
Miles, Miska. *Gertrude's Pocket.*
Miller, Helen. *Janey and Her Friends.*
Mohr, Nicholasa. *Nilda.*
Olsen, Violet. *Growing Season.*
Platt, Kin. *Doomsday Gang.*
Potter, Marian. *Milepost 67.*
Raymond, Charles. *Trouble with Gus.*
Robinson, Nancy. *Oh, Honestly, Angela.*
Schlee, Ann. *Ask Me No Questions.*
Sebestyen, Ouida. *Far from Home.*
Skurzynski, Gloria. *Tempering.*
Slatten, Evelyn. *Good, the Bad and the Rest of Us.*

Sommerfelt, Aimee. *My Name Is Pablo.*
Springer, Nancy. *Not on a White Horse.*
Stallworth, Anne. *This Time Next Year.*
Waltrip, Lela. *White Harvest.*
Wojciechowski, Susan. *Patty Dillman of Hot Dog Fame.*
Wolf, Bernard. *In This Proud Land.*

Pregnancy

Arrick, Fran. *Steffie Can't Come Out to Play.*
Arundel, Honor. *Longest Weekend.*
Beckman, Gunnel. *Mia Alone.*
Bradbury, Bianca. *New Penny.*
Christman, Elizabeth. *Nice Italian Girl.*
Cleaver, Vera. *I Would Rather Be a Turnip.*
Colman, Hila. *Tell Me No Lies.*
Crompton, Anne. *Queen of Swords.*
Dizeno, Patricia. *Phoebe.*
Elfman, Blossom. *Girls of Huntington House; House for Johnny O.*
Eyerly, Jeannette. *Bonnie Jo, Go Home; Someone to Love Me; Girl Like Me.*
Head, Ann. *Mr. and Mrs. Bo Jo Jones.*
Hinton, Nigel. *Getting Free.*
Holland, Isabelle. *After the First Love.*
Kurland, Morton. *Our Sacred Honor.*
Laing, Frederich. *Bride Wore Braids.*
Lee, Mildred. *People Therein; Sycamore Year.*
Lyle, Katie. *Fair Day and Another Step Begun.*
McRae, Russell. *Going to the Dogs.*
Madison, Winifred. *Growing Up in a Hurry.*
Neufeld, John. *Sharelle.*
Peck, Richard. *Don't Look and It Won't Hurt.*
Peyton, Karen. *Pennington's Heir.*
Ryland, Cynthia. *Kindness.*
Sallis, Susan. *Time for Everything.*
Shreve, Susan. *Loveletters.*
Thompson, Paul. *Hitchhikers.*
Trivelpiece, Laurel. *In Love and In Trouble.*
Willey, Margaret. *If Not for You.*
Zindel, Paul. *My Darling, My Hamburger.*

Prejudices

See also: Racial Interaction

Arrick, Fran. *Chernowitz.*
Cavanna, Betty. *Time for Tenderness.*
Chaikin, Miriam. *I Should Worry, I Should Care.*
Clarke, John. *Black Soldier.*
Cone, Molly. *Number Four.*
Crayder, Dorothy. *Riddles of Mermaid House.*
Cummings, Betty. *Now Ameriky.*
Dixon, Paige. *Promises to Keep.*
Edwards, Patricia. *John and Plutie.*
Foley, June. *Falling in Love Is No Snap.*
Foltz, Mary Jane. *Nicolau's Prize.*

Garthwaite, Marion. *Mario.*
Graham, Lorenz. *Return to South Town; Whose Town?*
Hassler, Jon. *Grand Opening.*
Holman, Felice. *Murderer.*
Karp, Naomi. *Turning Point.*
Kerr, M.E. *Little Little.*
Kogawa, Joy. *Naomi's Road.*
Kullman, Harry. *Battle Horse.*
Lampman, Evelyn. *Year of Small Shadow.*
Lasky, Kathryn. *Pageant.*
Lee, Harper. *To Kill a Mockingbird.*
Levitin, Sonia. *Silver Days.*
Lingard, Joan. *File on Fraulein Berg.*
Lobdell, Helen. *Prisoner of Taos.*
Madison, Winifred. *Maria Luisa.*
Means, Florence. *Us Maltbys.*
Miklowitz, Gloria. *War Between the Classes.*
Mills, Donna. *Long Way from Troy.*
Mohr, Nicholasa. *Nilda.*
Montgomery, Lucy. *Anne of Windy Poplars.*
Neville, Emily. *Berries Goodman.*
Newton, Suzanne. *C/O Arnold's Corners.*
O'Dell, Scott. *Zia.*
Peyton, Karen. *Flambards Divided.*
Raymond, Charles. *Trouble with Gus; Up from Appalachia.*
Rhue, Morton. *Wave.*
Riha, Bohumil. *Ryn, Wild Horse.*
Sandburg, Helga. *Blueberry.*
Scott, Carol. *Kentucky Daughter.*
Sebestyen, Ouida. *Words by Heart.*
Shura, Mary. *Jessica.*
Smith, Doris. *Salted Lemons.*
Taves, Isabella. *Not Bad for a Girl.*
Taylor, Mildred. *Gold Cadillac; Let the Circle Be Unbroken.*
Taylor, Theodore. *Cay.*
Uchida, Yoshika. *Jar of Dreams.*
Vander Els, Betty. *Leaving Point.*
Van der Veer, Judy. *Higher Than the Arrow.*
Wartski, Maureen. *Long Way from Home.*
Weber, Lenora. *Sometimes a Stranger.*
White, Ruth. *Sweet Creek Holler.*
Willard, Barbara. *Country Maid.*
Wood, Phyllis. *Pass Me a Pine Cone.*
Woolley, Catherine. *Cathy and the Beautiful People.*

Racial Interaction

See also: African Americans; Asians; Latinos; Native Americans; Prejudices

Agle, Nan. *Maple Street.*
Armstrong, William. *Sour Land.*
Baker, Betty. *Walk the World's Rim.*
Bargar, Gary. *Life. Is. Not. Fair.*
Baum, Betty. *Patricia Crosses Town.*
Bishop, Curtis. *Little League Heroes.*

Bowes, Elmer. *Trials of David Clark.*
Brinsmead, Hesba. *Pastures of the Blue Crane.*
Carlson, Natalie. *Empty Schoolhouse.*
Cavanna, Betty. *Jenny Kimura.*
Clarke, John. *Black Soldier.*
Coles, Robert. *Saving Face.*
Colman, Hila. *Classmates by Request.*
Cox, William. *Game, Set and Match.*
Distad, Audree. *Dakota Sons.*
Dorris, Michael. *Yellow Raft in Blue Water.*
Edwards, Patricia. *John and Plutie; Little John and Plutie.*
Fleishman, H.S. *Gang Girl.*
Fredericksen, Hazel. *He-Who-Runs-Far.*
Gaines, Ernest. *Gathering of Old Men.*
Geibel, James. *Blond Brother.*
Girion, Barbara. *Indian Summer.*
Gordon, Sherba. *Waiting for the Rain.*
Hamilton, Virginia. *White Romance.*
Harris, Mark. *Peppersalt Land.*
Herlicky, Dirlie. *Ludie's Song.*
Hooks, William. *Circle of Fire.*
Howard, John. *Black Like Me.*
Ik, Kim Yong. *Blue in the Seed.*
Jones, Adrienne. *So Nothing Is Forever.*
Jones, Toeckey. *Go Well, Stay Well; Skindeep.*
Kaye, Geraldine. *Comfort Herself.*
Lee, Harper. *To Kill a Mockingbird.*
Lightner, A.M. *Day of the Drones.*
Meyer, Carolyn. *Denny's Tapes.*
Miles, Betty. *All It Takes Is Practice.*
Mitchison, Naomi. *Friends and Enemies.*
Montgomery, Jean. *Wrath of Coyote.*
Neufeld, John. *Edgar Allan.*
Powell, Padgett. *Edisto.*
Tanner, Louise. *Reggie and Nilma.*
Tate, Eleanora. *Just an Overnight Guest.*
Taylor, Mildred. *Song of the Trees.*
Underwood, Betty. *Tamarack Tree.*
Waldron, Ann. *Integration of Marv-Larkin Thornhill.*
Walter, Mildred. *Girl on the Outside.*
Wier, Ester. *Easy Does It.*
Wilkerson, Brenda. *Not Separate, Not Equal.*
Wright, Richard. *Native Son.*

Religions

Albrecht, Lillie. *Susanna's Candlestick.*
Andrews, J.S. *Green Hills of Nendrum.*
Arrick, Fran. *God's Radar.*
Avi. *Encounter in Easton; Night Journey.*
Bach, Alice. *He Will Not Walk with Me.*
Blume, Judy. *Are You There God? It's Me, Margaret.*
Bothwell, Jean. *Parsonage Parrot.*
Browin, Frances. *Looking for Orlando.*
Bunyan, John. *Pilgrim's Progress.*
Burton, Hester. *Beyond the Weir Bridge.*
Calhoun, Mary. *Ownself.*

Cawley, Winfred. *Gran at Coatgate.*
Christman, Elizabeth. *Ruined for Life.*
Cleaver, Vera. *Delpha Green and Company.*
Cohen, Barbara. *Binding of Isaac.*
Cone, Molly. *Dance Around the Fire.*
De Clements, Barthe. *Double Trouble.*
Delton, Judy. *Near Occasion of Sin.*
Edmonds, I.J. *Joel at the Hanging Gardens.*
Farber, Norma. *Mercy Short, a Winter Journal.*
Faulkner, Nancy. *Sacred Jewel.*
Fenton, Edward. *Duffy's Rocks.*
Forman, James. *Fine, Soft Day.*
Forsythe, Frederick. *Shepherd.*
Green, Phyllis. *Empty Seat; Nicky's Lopsided, Lumpy But Delicious Orange.*
Hall, Adele. *Seashore Summer.*
Hamley, Dennis. *Pageants of Despair.*
Heyman, Anita. *Exit from Home.*
Hoban, Lillian. *I Met a Traveller.*
Holland-Crossley, Kevin. *Sea Stranger.*
Howard, Elizabeth. *Out of Step with the Dancers.*
Howe, Norma. *God, the Universe and Hot Fudge Sundaes.*
Hughes, Monica. *Beyond the Dark River.*
Hunt, Mabel. *Beggar's Daughter.*
Hurwitz, Johanna. *Adventures of Ali Baba Bernstein.*
Huston, Anne. *Trust a City Kid.*
Jackson, Jesse. *Sickest Don't Always Die the Quickest.*
Jacobs, Helen. *Diary of the Strawberry Place.*
Johnson, Annabel. *Wilderness Bride.*
Jordan, Mildred. *Proud to Be Amish.*
Kerr, M.E. *What I Really Think of You.*
Klein, Robin. *People Might Hear You.*
Lasky, Kathryn. *Pageant.*
Lenski, Lois. *Shoo-Fly Girl.*
Lingard, Joan. *Into Exile; Twelfth Day of July.*
Maguire, Gregory. *Lights on the Lake.*
Mannix, Daniel. *Healer.*
Naylor, Phyllis. *String of Chances.*
Newton, Suzanne. *I Will Call It Georgie's Blues.*
Nicol, Clive. *White Shaman.*
Niggli, Josefina. *Miracle for Mexico.*
Ottley, Reginald. *Rain from the West.*
Peck, Robert. *Day No Pigs Would Die.*
Potok, Chaim. *Davita's Harp.*
Powers, John. *Last Catholic in America.*
Sachs, Marilyn. *Peter and Veronica.*
St. George, Judith. *Mystery at St. Martin's.*
Smith, Doris. *Laura Up-Side-Down.*
Sorensen, Virginia. *Plain Girl.*
Southall, Ivan. *Long Night Watch.*
Speare, Elizabeth. *Bronze Bow; Witch of Blackbird Pond.*
Steele, William. *Man with the Silver Eyes.*
Sypher, Lucy. *Cousins and Circuses.*
Tabrah, Ruth. *Red Shark.*
Townsend, John. *Islanders.*
Vander Els, Betty. *Leaving Point.*
Vipont, Elfrida. *Lark in the Morn; Lark on the Wing.*

Wallace-Brodeur, Ruth. *Callie's Way.*
Weiman, Eiveen. *Which Way Courage.*
Yolen, Jane. *Gift of Sarah Baker.*

Revolutionary War

Avi. *Fighting Ground.*
Beatty, John. *Who Comes to King's Mountain?*
Clapp, Patricia. *I'm Deborah Sampson.*
Collier, James. *Bloody Country; My Brother Sam Is Dead; War Comes to Willy Freeman.*
Constiner, Merle. *Sumatra Alley.*
Dalgleish, Alice. *Adam and the Golden Cock.*
De Ford, Deborah. *Enemy Among Them.*
Downey, Fairfax. *Guns for General Washington.*
Duncan, Lois. *Peggy.*
Edwards, S. *When the World's on Fire.*
Epstein, Samuel. *Change for a Penny; Jackknife for a Penny.*
Fast, Howard. *April Morning.*
Finlayson, Ann. *Rebecca's War; Redcoat in Boston; Silver Bullet.*
Fisher, Leonard. *Two If by Sea.*
Forbes, Esther. *Johnny Tremain.*
Forman, James. *Cow Neck Rebels.*
Fritz, Jean. *Early Thunder.*
Gauch, Patricia. *This Time, Tempe Wick?*
Green, Diane. *Lonely War of William Pinto.*
Hall, Majory. *Another Kind of Courage.*
Haugaard, Erik. *Boy's Will.*
Haynes, Betsy. *Spies on the Devil's Belt.*
Lawrence, Isabelle. *Drumbeats in Williamsburg; Spy in Williamsburg.*
Levy, Mimi. *Whaleboat Warrior.*
Marko, Katherine. *Away to Fundy Bay.*
Nelson, May. *Redbirds Are Flying.*
O'Dell, Scott. *Sarah Bishop.*
Savery, Constance. *Reb and the Redcoats.*
Schneider, Benjamin. *Winter Patriot.*
Steele, William. *Man with the Silver Eyes.*
Thane, Elswyth. *Dawn's Early Light.*
Watson, Sally. *Hornet's Nest.*
Wellman, Manly. *Battle for King's Mountain; Clash on the Catawba; Rifles at Ramsour's Mill.*
White, Leon. *Patriot for Liberty.*
Wibberley, Leonard. *John Treegate's Musket; Peter Treegate's War; Sea Captain from Salem; Treegate's Raiders.*

Robots

Adams, Douglas. *Life, the Universe, and Everything.*
Appleton, Victor. *Terror on the Moons of Jupiter.*
Asimov, Isaac. *I, Robot.*
Asimov, Janet. *Norby and the Invaders; Norby and the Lost Princess; Norby and the Queen's*

Romance

Royalty

Runaways

Bawden, Nina. *Finding; Three on the Run.*
Bethancourt, T.E. *Nightmare Town.*
Blum, Robert. *Girl from Emeraline Island.*
Branscum, Robbie. *To the Tune of a Hickory Stick.*
Bredes, Don. *Hard Feelings.*
Brown, Roy. *Flight of Sparrows; No Through Road.*
Bunting, Eve. *One More Flight.*
Campbell, Hope. *No More Trains to Tottenville.*
Canning, Victor. *Flight of the Grey Goose; Runaways.*
Caswell, Helen. *Wind on the Road.*
Chastain, Madye. *Plippen's Palace.*
Chauncy, Nan. *They Found a Cave.*
Christopher, Matt. *Dirt Bike Runaway.*
Clark, Mavis. *Min-Min.*
Clarke, Tom. *Big Road.*
Clymer, Eleanor. *Get-Away Car; Luke Was There.*
Coles, Robert. *Riding Free.*
Collier, James. *Jump Ship to Freedom; Outside Looking In.*
Conford, Ellen. *To All My Fans, with Love from Sylvie.*
Corbett, Scott. *Pippa Passes.*
Corbin, William. *Prettiest Gargoyle.*
Corcoran, Barbara. *Winds of Time.*
Craig, John. *Who Wants to Be Alone?*
Crane, Caroline. *Stranger on the Road.*
Cresswell, Helen. *Dear Shrink.*
Crutcher, Chris. *Crazy Horse Electric Game.*
Cunningham, Julia. *Come to the Edge.*
Davies, Peter. *Fly Away Paul.*
Dick, Trella. *Bridger's Boy.*
Dixon, Paige. *Walk My Way.*
Downey, Fairfax. *Guns for General Washington.*
Duffy, James. *Missing.*
Dunnahoo, Terry. *Who Cares About Espie Sanchez?*
Dunne, Mary. *Hoby and Stub.*
Eige, Lillian. *Kidnapping of Mister Huey.*
Fall, Thomas. *Dandy's Mountain.*
Fenisong, Ruth. *Boy Wanted.*
Finlayson, Ann. *Runaway Teen.*
First, Julia. *I, Rebekah, Take You, the Laurences.*
Fleischman, Sid. *Whipping Boy.*
Fosburgh, Liza. *Cruise Control.*
Frank, Rudolf. *No Hero for the Kaiser.*
Friis-Baastad, Babbis. *Don't Take Teddy.*
Gaeddert, Louann. *Just Like Sisters.*
Garfield, Leon. *Jack Holbrook.*
Geller, Mark. *Raymond.*
Gibbons, Faye. *Mighty Close to Heaven.*
Goudge, Elizabeth. *Linnets and Valerians.*
Griffith, Valeria. *Runaway.*
Guernsey, Joann. *Journey to Almost There.*
Guiliot, Rene. *Grishka and the Bear.*
Hall, Lynn. *Something Special Horse.*
Hallquist, Britt. *Search for Fredrick.*

Hammer, Charles. *Me, the Beef and the Bum.*
Hansen, Joyce. *Home Boy.*
Harris, Marilyn. *Runaway's Diary.*
Haven, Susan. *Maybe I'll Move to the Lost and Found.*
Hermes, Patricia. *Who Will Take Care of Me?*
Hickman, Janet. *Zoar Blue.*
Hinton, Nigel. *Getting Free.*
Holman, Felice. *Slake's Limbo.*
Johnson, Elizabeth. *Horse Show Fever.*
Jordan, June. *His Own Where.*
Joslin, Sesyle. *Gentle Savage.*
Kaye, M.M. *Ordinary Princess.*
Kennedy, X.J. *Owlstone Crown.*
Kerr, M.E. *I'll Love You When You're More Like Me.*
Kesteven, G.R. *Awakening Water.*
Konigsburg, E.L. *From the Mixed Up Files of Mrs. Basil E. Frankweiler.*
Lawrence, Louise. *Dram Road.*
Lawrence, Mildred. *Treasure and the Song.*
Lindgren, Astrid. *Lotta on Troublemaker Street; Rasmus and the Vagabond.*
Locke, Elsie. *Runaway Settlers.*
McCaughrean, Geraldine. *Little Lower Than the Angels.*
McNaughton, Colin. *Jolly Roger and the Pirates of Abdul the Skinhead.*
Macken, Walter. *Flight of the Doves.*
Madison, Winifred. *Bird on the Wing.*
Magorian, Michelle. *Back Home.*
Major, Kevin. *Hold Fast.*
Malony, Ray. *Impact Zone.*
Mathieson, Theodore. *Island in the Sand.*
Mazer, Harry. *Guy Lenny; Island Keeper; Snowbound.*
Meyer, Carolyn. *Denny's Tapes.*
Milton, Hilary. *Brats and Mr. Jack.*
Moore, Ruth. *Wilderness Journey.*
Morpurgo, Michael. *Mr. Nobody's Eyes.*
Nye, Peter. *Storm.*
Ogilvie, Elisabeth. *Masquerade at Sea House.*
Osborne, Mary. *Last One Home.*
Otis, James. *Toby Tyler; or Ten Weeks with a Circus.*
Paradis, Marjorie. *Jeanie.*
Parker, Richard. *Runaway.*
Peck, Richard. *Secrets of the Shopping Mall.*
Pedersen, Elsa. *Dangerous Flight.*
Perlberg, Deborah. *Heartaches.*
Petersen, P.J. *Boll Weevil Express.*
Peyton, K.M. *Free Rein; Going Home.*
Pfeffer, Susan. *Marley the Kid.*
Phipson, Joan. *Bianca.*
Pryor, Bonnie. *Plum Tree War.*
Quimby, Myrtle. *Cougar.*
Radley, Gail. *World Turned Inside Out.*
Read, Efreida. *Brothers by Choice.*
Reader, Dennis. *Coming Back Alive.*
Reeves, Bruce. *Street Smarts.*

Renvoise, Jean. *Wild Thing.*
Rhodes, Evan. *Prince of Central Park.*
Riding, Julia. *Space Traders Unlimited.*
Roberts, Willo. *To Grandmother's House We Go.*
Roth, David. *River Runaways.*
Sachs, Marilyn. *At the Sound of the Beep; December Tale.*
Schneider, Jennifer. *Daybreak Man.*
Shaw, Richard. *Hard Way Home.*
Shotwell, Louisa. *Adam Bookout.*
Skurzynski, Gloria. *Tempering.*
Smaridge, Norah. *Mysteries in the Commune; Secret of the Brownstone House.*
Smucker, Barbara. *Wigwam in the City.*
Sweeney, Joyce. *Center Line.*
Thomas, Ruth. *Runaways.*
Thompson, Paul. *Hitchhikers.*
Truss, Jan. *Jasmin.*
Unsworth, Walter. *Grimsdyke.*
Ure, Jean. *Other Side of the Fence.*
Van Stockum, Hilda. *Penengro.*
Watson, Sally. *Linnet.*
Wismer, Donald. *Starluck.*
Zindel, Paul. *To Take a Dare.*

Rural Life

Adler, Carole. *Some Other Summer.*
Allan, Mabel. *Strange Enchantment.*
Arundel, Honor. *Emma's Island.*
Avery, Gillian. *Call of the Valley.*
Bachmann, Evelyn. *Tressa.*
Bawden, Nina. *Peppermint Pig.*
Benary-Isbert, Margot. *Rowan Farm.*
Burch, Robert. *Tyler, Wilkins and Skee.*
Burleson, Elizabeth. *Man of the Family.*
Byars, Betsy. *Winged Colt of Casa Mia.*
Christgau, Alice. *Laugh Peddler.*
Davis, Verne. *Runaway Cattle.*
De Roo, Anne. *Cinnamon and Nutmeg.*
Duncan, Jane. *Brave Janet Reachfar.*
Edmonds, Walter. *Bert Breen's Barn.*
Flory, Jane. *Mist on the Mountain.*
Gardam, Jane. *Hollow Land.*
Gibbs, Alonzo. *Fields Breathe Sweet.*
Heck, B. Holland. *Cactus Kevin.*
Holt, Stephen. *Ranch Beyond the Mountains.*
Horvath, Polly. *Occasional Cow.*
Lampman, Evelyn. *Rattlesnake Cave.*
Lasky, Kathryn. *Bone Wars.*
McGiffin, Lee. *Riders of Enchanted Valley.*
Montgomery, Rutherford. *Golden Stallion and the Mysterious Feud; Golden Stallion to the Rescue; Golden Stallion's Victory.*
Morey, Walt. *Angry Waters; Year of the Black Pony.*
Naylor, Phyllis. *Night Cry.*
Olsen, Violet. *View from the Pighouse Roof.*
Ottley, Reginald. *Rain Comes to Yamboorah.*

Patchett, Mary. *End of the Outlaws.*
Paulsen, Gary. *Popcorn Days and Buttermilk Nights; Tracker.*
Peck, Robert. *Day No Pigs Would Die.*
Pellowski, Anne. *Betsy's Up-and-Down Year; First Farm in the Valley: Anna's Story; Stairstep Farm: Anna Rose's Story; Willow Wind Farm: Betsy's Story; Winding Valley Farm: Annie's Story.*
Phipson, Joan. *Boundary Riders.*
Pitkin, Dorothy. *Grass Was That High.*
Potter, Marian. *Blatherskite.*
Rabe, Berniece. *Naomi.*
St. Peter, Joyce. *Always Abigail.*
Seredy, Kate. *Good Master.*
Simon, Shirley. *Cousins at Camm Corners.*
Sindall, Marjorie. *Matey.*
Snow, Dorothea. *Sight of Everything.*
Sorensen, Virginia. *Miracles on Maple Hill.*
Wiegand, Roberta. *Year of the Comet.*
Wier, Ester. *Rumpty Doolers.*
Wiggin, Kate. *Rebecca of Sunnybrook Farm.*
Wilder, Laura. *Farmer Boy.*
Wisler, G. Clifton. *Winter of the Wolf.*

Schizophrenia

See: Mental Illness

School

Adler, Carole. *Kiss the Clown; Once in a While Hero; Roadside Valentine.*
Albert, Louise. *But I'm Ready to Go.*
Asher, Sandy. *Summer Begins; Things Are Seldom What They Seem.*
Avi. *S.O.R. Losers.*
Bargar, Gary. *What Happened to Mr. Forster?*
Baum, Betty. *Patricia Crosses Town.*
Bennett, Jay. *Deadly Gift; To Be a Killer.*
Bethancourt, T.E. *T.H.U.M.B.B.*
Bishop, Curtis. *Gridiron Glory.*
Bonham, Frank. *Premonitions; Rascals from Haskell's Gym.*
Bratton, Helen. *It's Morning Again.*
Bulla, Clyde. *Almost a Hero.*
Butterworth, W.E. *Moose, the Thing and Me; Narc.*
Carrick, Carol. *What a Wimp!*
Chambers, Aidan. *Present Takers.*
Cheatham, K. Follis. *Best Way Out.*
Christian, Mary. *Deadline for Danger.*
Chukovskii, Kornei. *Silver Crest.*
Clarke, Mary. *Petticoat Rebel.*
Cleary, Beverly. *Mitch and Amy.*
Cohen, Barbara. *Lovers' Games.*
Cole, Stephen. *Pitcher and I.*
Coles, Robert. *Dead End School; Saving Face.*

Colman, Hila. *Classmates by Request; Confessions of a Story Teller.*

Cone, Molly. *Big Squeeze; Real Dream.*

Conford, Ellen. *Dear Lovey Hart, I Am Desperate; Lenny Kandell, Smart Aleck; We Interrupt This Semester for an Important Bulletin.*

Cooper, Ilene. *Winning of Miss Lynn Ryan.*

Corbett, Scott. *Down with Wimps.*

Corcoran, Barbara. *Sam; Strike.*

Cormier, Robert. *Beyond the Chocolate War; Chocolate War.*

Crane, William. *Encore; Oom-Pah.*

Cross, Gillian. *Demon Headquarters; Revolt at Ratcliffe's Rags.*

Crutcher, Chris. *Running Loose; Stonan!*

Danziger, Paula. *Cat Ate My Gymsuit; Pistachio Prescription.*

Davidson, Mary. *Superstar Called Sweetpea.*

De Clements, Barthe. *How Do You Lose Those 9th Grade Blues?; I Never Asked You to Understand Me; Sixth Grade Can Really Kill You.*

Delton, Judy. *Kitty from the Start; Kitty in High School; Kitty in the Middle.*

Dickinson, Peter. *Healer.*

Du Jardin, Rosamond. *Senior Prom.*

Duncan, Lois. *Daughters of Eve; Down a Dark Hall; Killing Mr. Griffin.*

Dutton, Sandra. *Magic of Myrna C. Waxweather.*

Emery, Anne. *Dinny Gordon, Freshman; Dinny Gordon, Junior; Dinny Gordon, Senior; Dinny Gordon, Sophomore; Popular Crowd.*

Eyerly, Jeannette. *Angel Baker, Thief.*

Farmer, Penelope. *Emma in Winter.*

First, Julia. *Absolute, Ultimate End; Everybody But Me.*

Fitzgerald, John. *Great Brain at the Academy.*

Foley, June. *It's No Crush, I'm in Love.*

Fox, Paula. *Place Apart.*

Gaeddert, Louann. *Kid in the Red Suspenders.*

Gage, Wilson. *Dan and the Miranda.*

Garden, Nancy. *Mystery of the Secret Marks; Prisoners of Vampires.*

Gardiner, John. *Top Secret.*

Giff, Patricia. *Rat Teeth.*

Gilbert, Harriett. *Running Away.*

Gilson, Jamie. *Four B Goes Wild; Thirteen Ways to Sink a Sub.*

Gold, Sharlya. *Amelia Quackenbush.*

Gordon, Shirley. *Me and the Bad Guys.*

Gould, Marilyn. *Twelfth of June.*

Graham, Lorenz. *Whose Town?*

Gray, Genevieve. *Varnell Roberts, Super-Pigeon.*

Guy, Rosa. *Ruby.*

Haas, Dorothy. *New Friends.*

Hall, Elizabeth. *Stand Up, Lucy.*

Hall, Lynn. *Where Have All the Tigers Gone?*

Hallstead, William. *Launching of Linda Bell.*

Hayes, William. *Project: Genius; Project: Scoop.*

Haynes, Betsy. *Against Taffy Sinclair Club.*

Heide, Florence. *Banana Blitz; Growing Anyway Up.*

Hentoff, Nat. *Does This School Have Capital Punishment?; In the Country of Ourselves; This School Is Driving Me Crazy.*

Heuman, William. *Horace Higby, Coxswain of the Crew.*

Hilton, James. *Goodbye, Mr. Chips.*

Ho, Minfong. *Sing to the Dawn.*

Hodges, Margaret. *Making of Joshua Cobb.*

Holman, Felice. *Year to Grow.*

Houston, Joan. *Crofton Meadows.*

Hughes, Dean. *Nutty and the Case of the Mastermind Thief; Nutty for President; Nutty the Movie Star.*

Huntsbury, William. *Big Wheels.*

Hurwitz, Johanna. *Class Clown.*

Hutto, Nelson. *Breakaway Back; Victory Volley.*

Jackson, C. Paul. *Bud Plays Junior High Football.*

Jackson, Jesse. *Tessie.*

Jacobs, Beth. *Look to the Mountains.*

Janeczko, Paul. *Bridges to Cross.*

Kalb, Jonah. *Kids' Candidate.*

Karp, Naomi. *Turning Point.*

Kassem, Lou. *Middle School Blues.*

Kaye, Marilyn. *Friend Like Phoebe.*

Kelley, Sally. *Trouble with Explosives.*

Kent, Deborah. *Belonging.*

Kerr, M.E. *Fell; Is That You, Miss Blue?*

Kiesel, Stanley. *Skinny Malinky Leads the War for Kindness; War Between the Pitiful Teachers and the Splendid Kids.*

Kilgore, Kathleen. *Ghost Maker.*

Klein, Norma. *Cheerleader.*

Knowles, John. *Peace Breaks Out; Separate Peace.*

Korman, Gordon. *Don't Care High; War with Mr. Wizzle.*

Krumgold, Joseph. *Henry 3.*

Leroe, Ellen. *Confessions of a Teenage TV Addict.*

Levitin, Sonia. *Mark of Conte; Year of Sweet Senior Insanity.*

Little, Jean. *Listen for the Singing.*

Lord, Beman. *Shrimp's Soccer Goal.*

Low, Alice. *Kallie's Corner.*

Lowrey, Janette. *Love, Bid Me Welcome.*

McKay, Robert. *Dave's Song; Troublemaker.*

McNamara, John. *Revenge of the Nerd.*

MacPherson, Margaret. *Shinty Boys.*

Magorian, Michelle. *Back Home.*

Mahy, Margaret. *Blood and Thunder Adventure on Hurricane Peak.*

Marney, Dean. *Just Good Friends.*

Matthews, Ann. *Starring Punky Brewster.*

Miklowitz, Gloria. *Emerald High Vigilantes.*

Miles, Betty. *Maudie and Me and the Dirty Book.*
Moeri, Louise. *First the Egg.*
Morganroth, Barbara. *Last Junior Year.*
Muehl, Lois. *Worst Room in the School.*
Nordstrom, Ursula. *Secret Language.*
Park, Barbara. *Kid in the Red Jacket; Maxie, Rosie and Earl . . . Partners in Grime.*
Pearl, Jack. *Young Falcons.*
Pearson, Kit. *Daring Game.*
Peck, Robert. *Basket Case; Hub; Mr. Little.*
Perl, Lila. *Dumb Like Me, Olivia Potts.*
Petersen, P.J. *Here's to the Sophomores; Would You Settle for Improbable?*
Pevsner, Stella. *Smart Kid Like You.*
Peyton, Karen. *Pennington's Last Term; Who, Sir? Me, Sir?*
Pfeffer, Susan. *Matter of Principal; What Do You Do When Your Mouth Won't Open?*
Philbrook, Clem. *Ollie, the Backward Forward.*
Phipson, Joan. *Good Luck to the Rider.*
Pilling, Ann. *Big Pink.*
Pinkwater, Daniel. *Alan Mendelsohn, Boy from Mars.*
Pinkwater, Jill. *Buffalo Brenda.*
Rabinowich, Ellen. *Toni's Crowd.*
Rhue, Morton. *Wave.*
Robinson, Nancy. *Just Plain Cat; Wendy and the Bullies.*
Roos, Stephen. *Confessions of a Wayward Preppie; My Secret Admirer.*
Rosenblatt, Arthur. *Smarty.*
Ruckman, Ivy. *What's an Average Kid Like Me Doing Way Up Here?*
Russ, Lavinia. *Over the Hills and Far Away.*
Sachar, Louis. *There's a Boy in the Girls' Bathroom; Wayside School Is Falling Down.*
Sachs, Marilyn. *Bus Ride; Fat Girl.*
St. George, Judith. *What's Happening to My Junior Year?*
Schmidt, Kurt. *Annapolis Misfit.*
Schwandt, Stephen. *Risky Game.*
Scott, Carol. *Kentucky Daughter.*
Sharmat, Marjorie. *Getting Something on Maggie Marmelstein; Maggie Marmelstein for President.*
Shaw, Richard. *Shape Up, Burke.*
Singer, Marilyn. *Case of the Fixed Election; Hoax Is on You.*
Slepian, Jan. *Broccoli Tapes.*
Snyder, Zilpha. *Libby on Wednesdays.*
Spinelli, Jerry. *Jason and Marceline; Space Station Seventh Grade.*
Stanek, Lou. *Megan's Beat.*
Steiner, Barbara. *Oliver Dibbs and the Dinosaur Cause.*
Strasser, Todd. *Complete Computer Popularity Program.*
Summers, James. *Amazing Mr. Tenterhook; Senior Dropout.*
Sutton, Jane. *Definitely Not Sexy; Not Even Mrs.*

Mazursky.
Swallow, Pamela. *Leave It to Christy.*
Thompson, Julian. *Goofbang Value Daze.*
Tolan, Stephanie. *Last of Eden.*
Tolles, Martha. *Darci and the Dance Contest.*
Trease, Geoffrey. *Flight of the Angels.*
Tyler, Vicki. *Senior Year.*
Ure, Jean. *You Two.*
Walker, Mary. *Year of the Cafeteria.*
Wallace, Barbara. *Miss Switch to the Rescue; Trouble with Miss Switch.*
Wallace, Bill. *Ferret in the Bedroom, Lizards in the Fridge.*
Wallace-Brodeur, Ruth. *Callie's Way.*
Weber, Lenora. *Hello, My Love, Goodbye; I Met a Boy I Used to Know; Make a Wish for Me.*
Williams, Ursula. *No Ponies for Miss Pobjoy.*
Wolff, Virginia. *Probably Still Nick Swansen.*
Wood, Phyllis. *I've Missed a Sunset or Three; Pass Me a Pine Cone.*
York, Carol. *Sparrow Lake.*
Young, Bob. *One Small Voice.*
Young, I.S. *Quarterback Carson.*
Zindel, Paul. *Harry and Hortense at Hormone High; I Never Loved Your Mind; My Darling, My Hamburger.*

Sci Fi/Earth

Adams, Douglas. *Life, the Universe, and Everything.*
Appleton, Victor. *Alien Probe.*
Babbitt, Lucy. *Children of the Maker; Oval Amulet.*
Beatty, Jerome. *Marie Looney and the Cosmic Circus; Marie Looney on the Red Planet; Matthew Looney in the Outback; Matthew Looney's Invasion of the Earth; Matthew Looney's Voyage to the Earth.*
Christopher, John. *Prince in Waiting.*
Clarke, Arthur. *Childhood's End; Imperial Earth.*
Clarke, Joan. *Happy Planet.*
Cooper, Clare. *Earthchange.*
Curtis, Philip. *Invasion of the Comet People.*
Forrester, John. *Forbidden Beast.*
Goldsmith, Howard. *Invasion: 2200 A.D.*
Hill, Douglas. *Alien Citadel; Huntsman; Warriors of the Wasteland.*
Hoover, H.M. *Delikon; Orvis; Return to Earth.*
Hoyle, Fred. *Rockets in Ursa Major.*
Johnson, Annabel. *Alien Music.*
Karl, Jean. *Strange Tomorrow.*
Kennealy, Patricia. *Throne Scone: Book of the*

Sci Fi/Future

Sci Fi/Moon

Sci Fi/Planets

Adams, Douglas. *Hitchhiker's Guide to the Galaxy.*
Asimov, Janet. *Norby and the Invaders; Norby and the Lost Princess; Norby's Other Secret; Package in Hyperspace.*
Ballou, Arthur. *Bound for Mars.*
Beatty, Jerome. *Matthew Looney and the Space Pirates.*
Benford, Gregory. *Jupiter Project.*
Cameron, Eleanor. *Mr. Bass's Planetoid; Mystery for Mr. Bass; Stowaway to the Mushroom Planet; Time and Mr. Bass; Wonderful Flight to the Mushroom Planet.*
Clark, Margaret. *Barney on Mars.*
Collier, James. *Planet Out of the Past.*
Corbett, Scott. *Donkey Planet.*
Del Rey, Lester. *Outpost of Jupiter; Runaway Robot.*
Engdahl, Sylvia. *Beyond Tomorrow Mountain; Doors of the Universe; Enchantress from the Stars; Far Side of Evil; This Star Shall Abide.*
Fairman, Paul. *Forgetful Robot.*
Felice, Cynthia. *Downtime.*
Fisk, Nicholas. *Escape from Splatterbang.*
Harrison, Harry. *Men from P.I.G. and R.O.B.O.T.*
Heinlein, Robert. *Podkayne of Mars.*
Herbert, Frank. *Children of Dune; Dune.*
Hill, Douglas. *Caves of Klydor; Colsac Rebellion; Day of the Starwind; Deathwing Over Veynaa; Exiles of Colsac; Galactic Warlord; Planet of the Warlord; Young Legionary.*
Hogan, James. *Code of the Life Maker.*
Hoover, H.M. *Rains of Eridan.*
Hughes, Monica. *Guardian of Isis; Isis Peddler; Keeper of the Isis Light.*
Katz, Welwyn. *Third Magic.*
Kurland, Michael. *Princes of Earth.*
Lawrence, Louise. *Warriors of Taan.*
L'Engle, Madeleine. *Swiftly, Tilting Planet; Wind in the Door; Wrinkle in Time.*
Lewis, C.S. *Out of the Silent Planet.*
Lightner, A.M. *Doctor to the Galaxy; Galactic Troubadours.*
Lightner, Alice. *Thursday Toads.*
McCaffrey, Anne. *Dinosaur Planet.*
McKillip, Patricia. *Fool's Run.*
Morressy, John. *Drought on Ziax II.*
Norton, Andre. *Dark Piper; Exiles of the Stars; Judgement on Janus; Key Out of Time; Star Ka'at; Star Ka'at and the Plant People; Star Ka'ats and the Winged Warriors; Star Ka'at's World; Victory on Janus.*
Nourse, Alan. *Raiders from the Rings.*
Reynolds, Pamela. *Earth Times Two.*
Riding, Julia. *Space Traders Unlimited.*
Simak, Clifford. *Shakespeare's Planet.*

Slobodkin, Louis. *Round Trip Space Ship; Space Ship in the Park; Space Ship Under the Apple Tree.*
Slote, Alfred. *C.O.L.A.R.; Trouble on Janus.*
Stone, Josephine. *Green Is for Galanx; Those Who Fall from the Sun.*
Tofte, Arthur. *Survival Planet.*
Townsend, John. *Creatures.*
Tuning, William. *Fuzzy Bones.*
Vardeman, Robert. *Road to the Stars.*
Walters, Hugh. *Destination Mars; Expedition Venus; Journey to Jupiter; Mission to Mercury; Passage to Pluto; Spaceship to Saturn.*
Webb, Sharon. *Earth Song; Ram Song.*
Wilder, Cherry. *Luck of Brin's Five; Nearest Fire; Tapestry Warriors.*
Yep, Laurence. *Seademons; Sweetwater.*

Sci Fi/Space Travel

Anderson, Margaret. *Mists of Time.*
Appleton, Victor. *City in the Stars; Terror on the Moons of Jupiter; War in Outer Space.*
Ballou, Arthur. *Marooned in Orbit.*
Beatty, Jerome. *Matthew Looney and the Space Pirates.*
Bradbury, Ray. *Halloween Tree.*
Bradley, Marion. *Hunters of the Red Moon.*
Brooks, Walter. *Freddy and the Space Ship.*
Clark, Margaret. *Barney and the UFO.*
Corbett, Scott. *Deadly Hoax.*
Dank, Milton. *U.F.O. Has Landed.*
Del Rey, Lester. *Infinite Worlds of Maybe.*
De Weese, Gene. *Black Suits from Outer Space; Calvin Nullifer; Major Corby and the Unidentified Flopping Object.*
Earnshaw, Brian. *Dragonfall 5 and the Space Cowboys.*
Ellerby, Liona. *King Tut's Game Board.*
Fisher, Leonard. *Noonan: A Novel About Baseball, ESP and Time Warps.*
Fisk, Nicholas. *Trillions.*
Foster, Alan. *Alien.*
Gee, Maurice. *Motherstone.*
Halacy, D.S. *Rocket Rescue.*
Heinlein, Robert. *Starman Jones.*
Hoover, H.M. *Lost Star.*
Karl, Jean. *But We Are Not of Earth.*
Katz, Welwyn. *Third Magic.*
Kurtz, Katherine. *Legacy of Lehr.*
Landsman, Sandy. *Gadget Factor.*
Lawrence, Louise. *Calling B for Butterfly; Star Lord.*
Lesser, Milton. *Stadium Beyond the Stars.*
MacGregor, Ellen. *Miss Pickerell Goes to Mars.*
McIntyre, Vonda. *Barbary.*
Manes, Stephen. *It's New! It's Improved! It's Terrible!; That Game from Outer Space.*
Norton, Andre. *Android at Arms; Lavender-Green Magic.*

Oppel, Kenneth. *Colin's Fantastic Video Adventure.*
Pesek, Ludek. *Trap for Perseus.*
Pinkwater, Daniel. *Fat Men from Space.*
Ruckman, Ivy. *Encounter.*
Service, Pamela. *Stinker from Space.*
Slobodkin, Louis. *Space Ship Returns to the Apple Tree; Three-Seated Space Ship.*
Stone, Josephine. *Green Is for Galanx.*
Walsh, Jill P. *Green Book.*
Walters, Hugh. *Terror by Satellite.*
Westall, Robert. *Urn Burial.*
Wisler, G. Clifton. *Antrain Messenger.*

Sci Fi/Time Travel

See also: Fantasy/Places

Alexander, Lloyd. *Time Cat: The Remarkable Journeys of Jason and Gareth.*
Allan, Mabel. *Romansgrove; Time to Go Back.*
Amoss, Berthe. *Chalk Cross.*
Anderson, Margaret. *Druid's Gift; In the Keep of Time; To Nowhere and Back.*
Andrews, J.S. *Green Hills of Nendrum.*
Asimov, Janet. *Norby and the Queen's Necklace; Norby's Other Secret.*
Avi. *Something Upstairs: A Tale of Ghosts.*
Beckman, Thea. *Crusade in Jeans.*
Bellairs, John. *Trolley to Yesterday.*
Bethancourt, T.E. *Tomorrow Connection; Tune in Yesterday.*
Blair, Cynthia. *Freedom to Dream.*
Bond, Nancy. *Another Shore; String in the Harp.*
Boston, Lucy. *Stones of Green Knowe.*
Cameron, Eleanor. *Beyond Silence.*
Carlsen, Ruth. *Half-Past Tomorrow.*
Christopher, John. *Dragon Dance; Fireball; New Found Land.*
Clarke, Arthur. *Childhood's End; 2010: Odyssey Two.*
Cooper, Susan. *Silver on the Trees.*
Cresswell, Helen. *Time Out; Up the Pier.*
Curry, Jane. *Daybreakers; Magical Cupboard; Me, Myself and I: A Tale of Time Travel; Over the Sea's Edge; Parsley, Sage, Rosemary and Time; Watchers.*
Cutt, W. Towrie. *Seven for the Sea.*
Del Rey, Lester. *Rocket from Infinity.*
Dexter, Catherine. *Mazemaker.*
Doty, Jean. *Can I Get There by Candlelight?*
Farmer, Penelope. *Charlotte Sometimes; William and Mary.*
Finlay, Winifred. *Beadbonny Ash.*
Foster, Alan. *Spellsinger.*
Freeman, Barbara. *Other Face.*
Gallico, Paul. *House That Wouldn't Go Away.*
Goldberger, Judith. *Looking Glass Factor.*
Greaves, Margaret. *Cat's Magic.*
Greer, Gery. *Max and Me and the Time Machine.*

Horseman, Elaine. *Hubbles' Treasure Hunt.*
Huddy, Delia. *Humboldt Effect; Time Piper.*
Hurmence, Blinda. *Girl Called Boy.*
Johnson, Annabel. *Danger Quotient.*
Jones, Diana. *Tale of Time City.*
Kemp, Gene. *Jason Bodger and the Priory Ghost.*
Kennemore, Tim. *Changing Times.*
King, Clive. *Ninny's Boat.*
Lawson, John. *Spring Rider.*
Lee, Robert. *Timequake.*
L'Engle, Madeleine. *Many Waters; Wrinkle in Time.*
Levin, Betty. *Keeping Room; Sword of Culann.*
Levy, Elizabeth. *Running Out of Magic with Houdini; Running Out of Time.*
Lindbergh, Anne. *Hunky-Dory Dairy; People in Pineapple Place; Shadow on the Dial.*
Little, Jane. *Philosopher's Stove.*
Lively, Penelope. *Stitch in Time.*
Lunn, Janet. *Root Cellar.*
MacDonald, Reby. *Ghosts of Austwick Manor.*
McGowen, Tom. *Shadow of Fomar.*
McKillip, Patricia. *Moon and the Face; Moon-Flash.*
Marzollo, Jean. *Halfway Down Paddy Lane.*
Mayne, William. *Earthfasts; Hill Road.*
Mazer, Norma. *Saturday, the Twelfth of October.*
Mian, Mary. *Net to Catch War.*
Mooney, Bel. *Stove Haunting.*
Morressy, John. *Windows of Forever.*
Naylor, Phyllis. *Shadows on the Wall.*
Norton, Andre. *Forerunner Foray; Fur Magic; Key Out of Time; Red Hart Magic; Steel Magic.*
Ormondroyd, Edward. *All in Good Time.*
Park, Ruth. *Playing Beatie Bow.*
Pascal, Francine. *Hangin' Out with Cici.*
Payne, Bernal. *It's About Time; Late, Great Dick Hart.*
Pearson, Kit. *Handful of Time.*
Peck, Richard. *Blossom Culp and the Sleep of Death; Dreadful Future of Blossom Culp.*
Pfeffer, Susan. *Future Forward; Rewind to Yesterday.*
Pinkwater, Daniel. *Borgel.*
Purtell, Richard. *Enchantment at Delphi.*
Radford, Ken. *House in the Shadows.*
Rodowsky, Colby. *Keeping Time.*
St. George, Judith. *Who's Scared? Not Me!*
Sinor, John. *Ghosts of Cabrillo Lighthouse.*
Sleator, William. *Green Futures of Tycho; Singularity.*
Steele, Mary. *First of the Penguins; Wish, Come True.*
Stone, Josephine. *Praise All the Moons of Morning.*
Tannen, Mary. *Lost Legend of Finn; Wizard Children of Finn.*
Thomas, Jane. *Princess in the Pigpen.*
Uttley, Alison. *Traveler in Time.*
Voigt, Cynthia. *Building Blocks.*

Waldorf, Mary. *One Thousand Camps.*
Walsh, Jill P. *Chance Child.*
Weldrick, Valerie. *Time Sweep.*
Westall, Robert. *Devil on the Road; Wind Eye.*
Wibberley, Leonard. *Crime of Martin Coverly.*
Wiseman, David. *Adam's Common; Jeremy Visick; Thimbles.*
Wood, Colin. *Confusion of Time.*
Yolen, Jane. *Devil's Arithmetic.*

Sci Fi/Underseas

Biemiller, Carl. *Escape from the Crater; Follow the Whales; Hydronauts.*
Crichton, Michael. *Sphere.*
Herbert, Frank. *Under Pressure.*
Hughes, Monica. *Crisis on Conshelf Ten.*
Murray, Marguerite. *Sea Bears.*
Park, Ruth. *Road Under the Sea.*
Walters, Hugh. *Mohole Menace.*

Sci Fi/Universe

Asimov, Isaac. *Foundation.*
Asimov, Janet. *Norby Finds a Villain.*
Blish, James. *Life for the Stars.*
Del Rey, Lester. *Attack from Atlantis.*
Foster, Alan. *Man Who Used the Universe.*
Griffin, Peni. *Otto from Otherwhere.*
Harding, Lee. *Misplaced Persons.*
Hoyle, Fred. *Rockets in Ursa Major.*
Karl, Jean. *Beloved Benjamin Is Waiting.*
Konwicki, Tadeusz. *Anthropos-Spectre-Beast.*
Norton, Andre. *Moon of Three Rings; Postmarked the Stars; Star Rangers; Storm Over Warlock; Uncharted Stars; Year of the Unicorn; Zero Stone.*
Payne, Bernal. *Experiment in Terror.*
Sleator, William. *Interstellar Pig; Singularity.*
Slote, Alfred. *Omega Station.*
Watson, Jane. *Case of the Vanishing Spaceship.*
Zebrowski, George. *Stars Will Speak.*

Sea and Ships

See also: Pirates

Aiken, Joan. *Black Hearts in Battersea; Bridle the Wind.*
Andrews, J.S. *Cargo for a King.*
Armstrong, Richard. *Big Sea; Mutineers; Secret Sea; Ship Afire; Trial Trip.*
Avi. *True Confessions of Charlotte Doyle.*
Babbitt, Natalie. *Eyes of the Amaryllis.*
Ball, Zachary. *Skin Diver.*
Cabral, Olga. *So Proudly She Sailed.*

Catherall, Arthur. *Lost Off the Grand Bank; Strange Intruder.*
Corbett, Scott. *Dead Before Docking; One by Sea.*
Davies, Harriet. *Aboard the Lizzie Ross.*
Dawlish, Peter. *Boy Jacko.*
Defoe, Daniel. *Robinson Crusoe.*
De Jong, Meindert. *Journey from Peppermint Street.*
Dickson, Gordon. *Secret Under the Caribbean.*
Dillon, Eilis. *Seals.*
Fairman, Paul. *Five Knucklebones.*
Fife, Dale. *Destination Unknown.*
Fleischman, Sid. *By the Great Horn Spoon.*
Forester, Cecil. *Hornblower and the Atropos; Hornblower and the Hotspur; Hornblower During Crisis.*
Fox, Paula. *Slave Dancer.*
Garfield, Leon. *Jack Holbrook.*
Hallard, Peter. *Coral Reef Castaways.*
Haugaard, Erik. *Orphans of the Wind; Slave's Tale.*
Hawes, Charles. *Dark Frigate.*
Heatter, Basil. *Wreck Ashore!*
Hegarty, Reginald. *Rope's End.*
Hyde, Laurence. *Captain Deadlock; Under the Pirate Flag.*
Hyde, M. *Nootka.*
Joslin, Sesyle. *Gentle Savage.*
Kerr, Helen. *Grave Allegra.*
King, Clive. *Ninny's Boat.*
Kipling, Rudyard. *Captains Courageous.*
Levin, Betty. *Put on My Crown.*
Love, Dandra. *Dive for the Sun.*
Meader, Stephen. *Phantom of the Blockade.*
Milligan, Bruce. *With the Wind, Kevin Dolan.*
O'Dell, Scott. *Dark Canoe.*
Park, Ruth. *Road Under the Sea.*
Pope, Ray. *Salvage from Strosa; Strosa Light.*
Price, Willard. *Whale Adventure.*
Robinson, Richard. *Captain Sintar.*
Smith, T.H. *Cry to the Night Wind.*
Sperry, Armstrong. *All Sail Set; Call It Courage.*
Sprague, Rosemary. *Jade Pagoda.*
Stevenson, Robert. *Treasure Island.*
Taylor, Theodore. *Teetoncey; Teetoncey and Ben O'Neal.*
Thomas, Jane. *Courage at Indian Deep.*
Venn, Mary. *Skin Diving Mystery.*
Verne, Jules. *Long Vacation; Twenty Thousand Leagues Under the Sea.*
Ware, Leon. *Threatening Fog.*
Waters, John. *Victory Chimes.*
Webb, Christopher. *Ann and Hope Mutiny.*
Wibberley, Leonard. *Crime of Martin Coverly; Last Battle; Perilous Gold; Red Pawn; Sea Captain from Salem.*
Williams, Ursula. *Island MacKenzie.*
Wisler, G. Clifton. *This New Land.*
Wood, James. *Queen's Most Honorable Pirate.*
Wyss, Johann. *Swiss Family Robinson.*

Self-Esteem

Bates, Betty. *That's What T.J. Says.*
Cohen, Barbara. *Lovers' Games.*
Conford, Ellen. *Dreams of Victory; Seven Days to a Brand New Me.*
Corcoran, Barbara. *Faraway Island.*
Havrevold, Finn. *Summer Adventure.*
Hurwitz, Johanna. *Yellow Blue Jay.*
Johnston, Norma. *If You Love Me, Let Me Go; Swallow's Song; Wishing Star.*
Lee, Mildred. *Skating Rink.*
Lee, Robert. *It's a Mile from Here to Glory.*
Martin, Ann. *Stage Fright.*
Murray, Michele. *Nellie Cameron.*
Namovicz, Gene. *To Talk in Time.*
Okimoto, Jean. *Jason's Women.*
Oppenheimer, Joan. *Working on It.*
Petersen, P.J. *Good-Bye to Good Ol' Charlie.*
Pfeffer, Susan. *What Do You Do When Your Mouth Won't Open?*
Platt, Kin. *Brogg's Brain.*
Reynolds, Pamela. *Horseshoe Hill.*
Robinson, Nancy. *Ballet Magic.*
Sachs, Marilyn. *Fat Girl.*
Slepian, Janice. *Night of the Bozos.*
Smith, Alison. *Reserved for Mark Anthony Crowder.*
Snyder, Zilpha. *Black and Blue Magic.*
Springstubb, Tricia. *Eunice (the Egg Salad) Gottlieb; With a Name Like Lulu, Who Needs More Trouble?*
Townsend, Sue. *Growing Pains of Adrian Mole.*
Van Leeuwen, Jean. *I Was a 98-Pound Duckling.*
Wersba, Barbara. *Dream Watcher.*
Woolley, Catherine. *Ginnie Joins In.*

Ships

See: Sea and Ships

Siblings

See: Brothers; Brothers and Sisters; Sisters

Sisters

See also: Brothers and Sisters

Adler, Carole. *One Sister Too Many; Silver Coach; Split Sisters.*
Alcock, Vivien. *Cuckoo Sister.*
Alcott, Louisa May. *Jo's Boys and How They Turned Out; Little Women.*

Alexander, Anne. *To Live a Lie.*
Anderson, Mary. *Do You Call That a Dream Date?*
Angell, Judie. *First the Good News.*
Arthur, Ruth. *Candle in Her Room.*
Baehr, Patricia. *Dragon Prophecy; Louisa Eclipsed.*
Beatty, Patricia. *Melinda Takes a Hand.*
Betancourt, Jeanne. *Between Us.*
Bolton, Carole. *Little Girl Lost.*
Bunting, Eve. *Big Cheese.*
Butler, Beverly. *My Sister's Keeper.*
Byars, Betsy. *Animal, the Vegetable and John D. Jones.*
Calvert, Patricia. *Stone Pony.*
Carlson, Natalie. *Half-Sisters; Luvvy and the Girls.*
Cleary, Beverly. *Beezus and Ramona; Ramona the Brave; Sister of the Bride.*
Cleaver, Vera. *I Would Rather Be a Turnip; Kissimmee Kid; Me Too.*
Clifford, Eth. *Dastardly Murder of Dirty Pete; Help! I'm a Prisoner in the Library; Just Tell Me When We're Dead; Scared Silly.*
Cohen, Barbara. *Christmas Revolution.*
Colman, Hila. *Diary of a Frantic Kid Sister; Family Trap; Weekend Sisters.*
Constant, Alberta. *Motoring Millers; Those Miller Girls.*
Crane, Caroline. *Girl Like Tracy.*
Davis, Gibbs. *Maud Flies Solo.*
Derman, Martha. *And Philippa Makes Four.*
Donahue, Marilyn. *Valley in Between.*
Doty, Jean. *If Wishes Were Horses.*
Du Jardin, Rosamond. *Practically Seventeen; Double Date.*
Dunlop, Eileen. *Maze Stone.*
Ellison, Lucile. *Tie That Binds.*
Engebrecht, P. *Under the Haystack.*
Faber, Nancy. *Cathy's Secret Kingdom.*
Falk, Ann. *Place of Her Own.*
Fisher, Lois. *Arianna and Me.*
Giff, Patricia. *Gift of the Pirate Queen.*
Grant, Cynthia. *Phoenix Rising.*
Gray, Patricia. *Horsepower.*
Greene, Constance. *Beat the Turtle Drum; I and Sproggy; Star Shine.*
Greenfield, Eloise. *Sister.*
Greenwald, Sheila. *Atrocious Two.*
Guest, Elissa. *Over the Moon.*
Henkes, Kevin. *Zebra Wall.*
Hest, Amy. *Getting Rid of Krista.*
Hewett, Hilda. *Harriet and the Cherry Pie.*
Horowitz, Anthony. *Devil's Door-Bell.*
Howard, Ellen. *Edith Herself.*
Hurwitz, Johanna. *Rabbi's Girls.*
Johnston, Norma. *To Jess, with Love and Memories.*
Jones, Adrienne. *Whistle Down a Dark Lane.*
Joosse, Barbara. *Anna, the One and Only.*
Kaye, Marilyn. *Cassie; Daphne; Lydia; Phoebe.*
Kehret, Peg. *Sisters, Long Ago.*

Kennemore, Tim. *Wall of Words.*
Landis, James. *Sister Impossible.*
Lee, Mildred. *Sycamore Year.*
Levinson, Nancy. *Ruthie Greene Show.*
Lindbergh, Anne. *Worry Week.*
Little, Jean. *Spring Begins in March.*
Lively, Penelope. *Fanny's Sister.*
Logan, Les. *Game.*
Lowry, Lois. *Summer to Die.*
MacDonald, Reby. *Ghosts of Austwick Manor.*
MacLeod, Charlotte. *Maid of Honor.*
Manniz, Darrel. *Secret of the Elm.*
Martin, Ann. *Me and Katie (The Pest).*
Mayhar, Ardath. *Makra Choria.*
Mazer, Norma. *Three Sisters.*
Miklowitz, Gloria. *Secrets Not Meant to Be Kept.*
Mills, Claudia. *One and Only Cynthia Jane Thornton; Secret Carousel.*
Mulford, Philippa. *World Is My Eggshell.*
Naylor, Phyllis. *Witch's Sister.*
Newton, Suzanne. *End of Perfect.*
Nostlinger, Christine. *Girl Missing.*
O'Daniel, Janet. *Part for Addie.*
O'Hanlon, Jacklyn. *Fair Game.*
Olsen, Violet. *View from the Pighouse Roof.*
Oneal, Zibby. *Language of Goldfish.*
Pascal, Francine. *Hand-Me-Down Kid.*
Paterson, Katherine. *Jacob Have I Loved.*
Peck, Richard. *Don't Look and It Won't Hurt.*
Pevsner, Stella. *And You Give Me a Pain, Elaine; Sister of the Quints.*
Pfeffer, Susan. *Evvie at Sixteen; Sybil at Sixteen.*
Pinkwater, Jill. *Disappearance of Sister Perfect.*
Platt, Kin. *Chloris and the Freaks; Chloris and the Weirdos.*
Ransom, Candice. *My Sister, the Meanie; My Sister, the Traitor.*
Reiss, Johanna. *Journey Back.*
Reynolds, Pamela. *Different Kind of Sister.*
Russ, Lavinia. *Over the Hills and Far Away.*
Ryan, Mary. *Who Says I Can't?*
Sachs, Marilyn. *Baby Sister; Amy and Laura; Amy Moves In.*
Sallis, Susan. *Secret Places of the Stairs.*
Shura, Mary. *Sunday Doll.*
Siegal, Aranka. *Grace in the Wilderness.*
Smith, Anne. *Sister in the Shadow.*
Snyder, Zilpha. *Birds of Summer.*
Springstubb, Tricia. *Moon on a String.*
Stolz, Mary. *Who Wants Music on Monday?*
Strang, Celia. *This Child Is Mine.*
Tapp, Kathy. *Sacred Circle of the Hula Hoop.*
Teicher, Elizabeth. *April's Year.*
Terris, Susan. *Octopus Pie.*
Ure, Jean. *Most Important Thing; Supermouse.*
Vogel, Ilse-Marget. *My Twin Sister Erika.*
Walter, Mildred. *Mariah Keeps Cool; Mariah Loves Rock.*
Warwick, Dolores. *Learn to Say Goodbye.*
Whitaker, Alexandra. *Dream Sisters.*
Windsor, Patricia. *Home Is Where Your Feet Are Standing.*

Wolitzer, Hilma. *Toby Lived Here.*
Woolley, Catherine. *Cathy's Little Sister.*
Wright, Betty. *Summer of Mrs. MacGregor.*
Yeo, Wilma. *Mystery of the Third Twin.*
York, Carol. *Remember Me When I Am Dead.*

Slavery

Avi. *Encounter in Easton; Night Journey.*
Bacmeister, Rhoda. *Voices in the Night.*
Bacon, Martha. *Sophia Scrooby Preserved.*
Beatty, Patricia. *Blue Stars Watching.*
Bellairs, John. *Trolley to Yesterday.*
Beyer, Audrey. *Dark Venture.*
Bradbury, Bianca. *Undergrounders.*
Browin, Frances. *Looking for Orlando.*
Bulla, Clyde. *Charlie's House.*
Burchard, Peter. *Bimby.*
Carse, Robert. *Turnabout.*
Cheatham, K. Follis. *Bring Home the Ghost.*
Collier, James. *Jump Ship to Freedom.*
Dick, Trella. *Island on the Border.*
Edwards, S. *When the World's on Fire.*
Fairman, Paul. *Five Knucklebones.*
Fall, Thomas. *Canal Boat to Freedom.*
Fast, Howard. *Freedom Road.*
Fox, Paula. *Slave Dancer.*
Fritz, Jean. *Brady.*
Hamilton, Virginia. *House of Dies Drear.*
Hansen, Joyce. *Which Way to Freedom?*
Hildreth, Richard. *Memoirs of a Fugitive.*
Hurmance, Belinda. *Tancy.*
Jacobs, Helen. *Diary of the Strawberry Place; Secret of the Strawberry Place.*
Jones, Adrienne. *Ride the Far Wind.*
Meltzer, M. *Undergound Man.*
Mott, Michael. *Master Entrick.*
Petry, Ann. *Tituba of Salem Village.*
Price, Joan. *Truth Is a Bright Star.*
Rinaldi, Ann. *Wolf by the Ears.*
Smucker, Barbara. *Runaway to Freedom.*
Sterne, E. *Long Black Schooner.*
Traylor, Sarah. *Red Wind.*
Turner, Ann. *Nettie's Trip South.*
Walker, Mary. *To Catch a Zombi.*
Wallin, Luke. *Slavery Ghosts.*
Watson, Sally. *Jode.*
Weiss-Sonnenburg, Hedwig. *Plum Blossom and Kai Lin.*
Winterfeld, Henry. *Mystery of the Roman Ransom.*

Smuggling

Avi. *Shadrach's Crossing.*
Ball, Zachary. *Joe Panther.*
Bell, Thelma. *Captain Ghost.*
Berna, Paula. *Mule on the Expressway.*

Bonham, Frank. *Mystery of the Red Tide.*
Brenner, Barbara. *Falcon Sling; Mystery of the Disappearing Dogs; Mystery of the Plumed Serpent.*
Campbell, Hope. *Mystery at Fire Island.*
Church, Richard. *Down River.*
Clark, Margaret. *Mystery of Sebastian Island.*
Cleven, Catherine. *Pirate Dog.*
Cookson, Catherine. *Blue Baccy.*
Cross, Gilbert. *Mystery at Loon Lake.*
Deleon, Eric. *Pitch and Hasty Check It Out.*
Dunnahoo, Terry. *This Is Espie Sanchez.*
Frost, Kelman. *Men of the Mirage.*
Girvan, Helen. *Missing Masterpiece.*
Halacy, D.S. *Sky Trap.*
Halacy, Dan. *Ethan Strong, Watch by the Sea.*
Kent, Alexander. *Midshipman Bolitho and the Avenger.*
Line, David. *Screaming High.*
Molloy, Anne. *Mystery of the Pilgrim Trading Post.*
Parker, Richard. *Sheltering Tree.*
Peyton, Karen. *Maplin Bird.*
Phipson, Joan. *Fly Into Danger.*
Prince, Alison. *Night Landings; Sinister Airfield.*
Robertson, Keith. *Three Stuffed Owls.*
Rodgers, Raboo. *Island of Peril.*
Sherry, Sylvia. *Secret of the Jade Pavilion.*
Singer, Marilyn. *Case of the Cackling Car.*
Smith, Carole. *Danger at the Golden Dragon.*
Sutcliff, Rosemary. *Flame-Colored Taffeta.*
Waldron, Ann. *French Detection.*
Wallace, Luke. *Blue Wings.*
Wourio, Eva-Lis. *Venture at Midsummer.*

Spies

Aiken, Joan. *Teeth of the Gale.*
Allen, Linda. *Lionel and the Spy Next Door.*
Amerman, Lockhart. *Sly One.*
Anckarsvard, Karen. *Mysterious Schoolmaster.*
Arthur, Robert. *Mystery of the Trail of Terror.*
Baudouy, Michel. *Deception at St. Nazaire.*
Bawden, Nina. *Rebel on a Rock.*
Beatty, John. *Who Comes to King's Mountain?*
Beyer, Audrey. *Sapphire Pendant.*
Blair, Cynthia. *Strawberry Summer.*
Boston, Lucy. *Enemy of Green Knowe.*
Bothwell, Jean. *Mystery Candlestick.*
Calde, Mark. *Shadowboxer.*
Chandler, Raymond. *Fareware, My Lovely.*
Clewes, Dorothy. *Mystery of the Singing Strings.*
Dank, Milton. *Game's End.*
De Ford, Deborah. *Enemy Among Them.*
Donaldson, Margaret. *Moon's on Fire.*
Downey, Fairfax. *Guns for General Washington.*
Epstein, Samuel. *Jackknife for a Penny.*
Finlayson, Ann. *Silver Bullet.*
Follett, Ken. *Eye of the Needle.*
Garfield, Brian. *Paladin.*

Garfield, Leon. *December Rose.*
Gerson, Corinne. *My Grandfather the Spy.*
Greene, Graham. *Human Factor.*
Halacy, Dan. *Ethan Strong, Watch by the Sea.*
Hallstead, William. *Ev Kris, Aviation Detective.*
Hart, Carolyn. *Secret in the Cellars.*
Haynes, Betsy. *Spies on the Devil's Belt.*
Holmvik, Oyvind. *Dive to Danger.*
Honness, Elizabeth. *Mystery of the Secret Message.*
Hughes, Dean. *Nutty and the Case of the Ski Slope Spy.*
Hunter, Mollie. *Spanish Letters.*
Johnston, Norma. *Return to Morocco.*
Kerr, M.E. *Fell.*
Lawrence, Isabelle. *Spy in Williamsburg.*
L'Engle, Madeleine. *Arm and the Starfish.*
MacKellar, William. *Terror Run.*
Mays, Victor. *Dead Reckoning.*
Murray, Marguerite. *Sea Bears.*
Namioka, Lensey. *Island of Ogres.*
Nicole, Christopher. *Operation Destruct; Operation Neptune.*
Oneal, Zibby. *War Work.*
Phillips, Leon. *Split Bamboo.*
Rendell, Ruth. *Talking to Strange Men.*
Sharmat, Marjorie. *51 Sycamore Lane.*
Stahl, Ben. *Secret of the Red Skull.*
Sutcliff, Rosemary. *Flame-Colored Taffeta.*
Taylor, Theodore. *Children's War.*
Walden, Amelia. *To Catch a Spy.*
Wellman, Manly. *Rifles at Ramsour's Mill.*
Westall, Robert. *Fathom Five.*
Woolley, Catherine. *Libby Looks for a Spy.*
Yep, Laurence. *Mark Twain Murders.*

Sports

See also: Baseball; Basketball; Football

Allen, Alexander. *Tennis Menace.*
Ashley, Bernard. *All My Men.* (Soccer)
Avi. *S.O.R. Losers.* (Soccer)
Bach, Alice. *Meat in the Sandwich.* (Soccer)
Ball, John. *Judo Boy.*
Bloch, Marie. *Two Worlds of Damyan.* (Swimming)
Bonham, Frank. *Rascals from Haskell's Gym.* (Gymnastics)
Christopher, Matt. *Hockey Machine; Run, Billy, Run; Soccer Halfback; Supercharged Infield* (Softball); *Takedown* (Wrestling).
Corbett, Scott. *Hockey Girls; Hockey Trick.*
Cox, William. *Game, Set and Match* (Tennis).
Crutcher, Chris. *Stonan!* (Swimming)
Dacquino, V.T. *Kiss the Candy Days Good-Bye.* (Wrestling)
Davis, Terry. *Vision Quest.* (Wrestling)
Du Bois, William. *Porko Von Popbutton.* (Hockey)
Dygard, Thomas. *Soccer Duel.*

Stealing

See also: Mystery/Stealing

King-Smith, Dick. *Harry's Mad.*
Lauritzen, Jonreed. *Treasure of the High Country.*
Lawrence, J.D. *Barnaby's Bills.*
Ogilvie, Elisabeth. *Masquerade at Sea House.*
Pelta, Kathy. *Blue Empress.*
Slote, Alfred. *Tony and Me.*
Townsend, John. *Tom Tiddler's Ground.*
Wallace, Barbara. *Claudia.*
Watson, Simon. *Partisan.*
Weldrick, Valerie. *Time Sweep.*

Suicide

Arrick, Fran. *Tunnel Vision.*
Bellairs, John. *Mummy, the Will and the Crypt.*
Bennett, Jay. *Skeleton Man.*
Bethancourt, T.E. *Instruments of Darkness.*
Bunting, Eve. *Face at the Edge of the World.*
Calvert, Patricia. *Yesterday's Daughter.*
Cannon, Bettie. *Bellsong for Sarah Rains.*
Christian, Mary. *Singin' Somebody Else's Song.*
Covert, Paul. *Cages.*
Crutcher, Chris. *Chinese Handcuffs.*
Davis, Gibbs. *Swann Song.*
Gerson, Corinne. *Passing Through.*
Guest, Judith. *Ordinary Problems.*
Higgins, Colin. *Harold and Maud.*
Hightower, Florence. *Dreamworld Castle.*
Hughes, Dean. *Switching Tracks.*
Johnson, A.E. *Blues I Can Whistle.*
Killien, Christie. *Artie's Brief: The Whole Truth and Nothing But.*
King, Stephen. *Salem's Lot.*
Levoy, Myron. *Three Friends.*
Lorimer, Lawrence. *Secrets.*
McRae, Russell. *Going to the Dogs.*
Menuis, Opal. *No Escape.*
Morris, Winifred. *Dancer in the Mirror.*
Oneal, Zibby. *Language of Goldfish.*
Peck, Richard. *Remembering the Good Times.*
Pfeffer, Susan. *About David.*
Rabinowitz, Ann. *Bethie.*
Radley, Gail. *World Turned Inside Out.*
Ross, Marianne. *Good-Bye Atlantis.*
Rydberg, Ernie. *Yellow Line.*
Swarthout, Glendon. *Shootist.*
Tapp, Kathy. *Sacred Circle of the Hula Hoop.*
Taylor, William. *Paradise Lane.*
Thesman, Jean. *Last April Dancers.*
Townsend, John. *Persuading Stick.*
Wartski, Maureen. *My Name Is Nobody.*
White, Ruth. *Sweet Creek Holler.*
Woodford, Peggy. *See You Tomorrow.*
Yep, Laurence. *Kind Hearts and Gentle Monsters.*
Zindel, Paul. *Confessions of a Teenage Baboon; Harry and Hortense at Hormone High.*

Supernatural

See: Occult

Survival

Aaron, Chester. *American Ghost; Gideon; Lackawanna; Out of Sight, Out of Mind.*
Anderson, John. *Zeb.*
Armstrong, Richard. *Secret Sea.*
Baer, Frank. *Max's Gang.*
Baird, Thomas. *Walk Out a Brother.*
Beebe, B.F. *Run, Light Buck, Run.*
Belden, Wilanne. *Mind-Hold.*
Benezra, Barbara. *Fire Dragon.*
Berna, Paul. *Flood Warning.*
Blackwood, Gary. *Wild Timothy.*
Blos, Joan. *Brothers of the Heart.*
Bosse, Malcolm. *Barracuda Gang.*
Bosworth, J.A. *White Water, Still Water.*
Bradbury, Bianca. *Two on an Island.*
Bradley, Marion. *Hunters of the Red Moon.*
Branscum, Robbie. *To the Tune of a Hickory Stick.*
Brauman, Franz. *Milik and Amina.*
Bunting, Eve. *Haunting of Kildoran Abbey.*
Butler, Beverly. *My Sister's Keeper.*
Catherall, Arthur. *Prisoner in the Snow.*
Christopher, John. *Empty World.*
Christopher, Matt. *Stranded.*
Church, Richard. *Five Boys in a Cave.*
Cohen, Peter. *Morena.*
Corlett, William. *Return to the Gate.*
Cross, Gillian. *Born of the Sun.*
Dahlstedt, Marden. *Terrible Wave.*
Day, Veronique. *Landslide.*
Defoe, Daniel. *Robinson Crusoe.*
Degens, T. *Transport 7-41-R.*
De Roo, Anne. *Scrub Fire.*
Dexter, Patricia. *Arrow in the Wind.*
Dickinson, Peter. *Dancing Bear.*
Du Bois, Theodora. *Tiger Burning Bright.*
Dyer, T.A. *Way of His Own.*
Eckert, Allan. *Incident at Hawk's Hill.*
Elder, Lauren. *And I Alone Survived.*
Evans, Max. *My Pardner.*
Fenton, Edward. *Refugee Summer.*
Fleming, Elizabeth. *Takula Tree.*
Frazee, Steve. *Year of the Big Snow.*
Garfield, Leon. *Confidence Man.*
George, Jean. *Hook a Fish, Catch a Mountain; Julie of the Wolves; River Rats; Talking Earth.*
Golding, William. *Lord of the Flies.*
Gould, Lilian. *Jeremy and the Gorillas.*
Gregory, Kristiano. *Jenny of the Tetons.*
Halvorson, Marilyn. *Hold On, Geronimo.*
Hamilton, Dorothy. *Scamp and the Blizzard Boys.*
Hamilton, Virginia. *Planet of Junior Brown.*
Hamilton-Paterson, James. *Hostage.*
Hamre, Leif. *Operation Arctic.*
Hartling, Peter. *Crutches.*
Hautzig, Esther. *Endless Steppe.*
Havrevold, Finn. *Summer Adventure.*
Holman, Felice. *Slake's Limbo; Wild Children.*

Houston, James. *Akavak: An Eskimo Journey; Black Diamonds; Frozen Fire; Ice Sword; Tikta'Liktak; Wolf Run.*
Hyde, Dayton. *Strange Companion.*
Jeffries, Roderic. *Trapped.*
Johnson, Annabel. *Alien Music.*
Karl, Jean. *Strange Tomorrow.*
Kehret, Peg. *Nightmare Mountain.*
Kendall, Lace. *Rain Boat.*
Kherdian, David. *It Started with Old Man Bean.*
King, Clive. *Night the Water Came By.*
Kjelgaard, James. *Wild Trek.*
Leighton, Margaret. *Canyon Castaways.*
Luger, Harriett. *Elephant Tree.*
Lustig, Arnost. *Darkness Casts a Shadow.*
McNeill, Janet. *Prisoner in the Park.*
May, Charles. *Strangers in the Storm.*
Mayhar, Ardath. *Medicine Walk.*
Mazer, Harry. *Island Keeper; Last Mission; Snowbound.*
Miklowitz, Gloria. *After the Bomb; After the Bomb: Week One.*
Milton, Hilary. *Mayday! Mayday!; Tornado.*
Morey, Walt. *Canyon Winter.*
Mowat, Farley. *Lost in the Barrens.*
Nelson, O.T. *Girl Who Owned a City.*
Nixon, Joan. *House on Hackman's Hill.*
O'Brien, Robert. *Z for Zachariah.*
O'Dell, Scott. *Island of the Blue Dolphins.*
Orlev, Uri. *Island on Bird Street.*
Palmer, David. *Emergence.*
Paulsen, Gary. *Hatchet; River; Voyage of the Frog.*
Petersen, P.J. *Nobody Else Can Walk It for You.*
Peyrouton de Lodebat, Monique. *Village That Slept.*
Phipson, Joan. *Way Home; When the City Stopped.*
Phleger, Marjorie. *Pilot Down, Presumed Dead.*
Reboul, Antoine. *Thou Shalt Not Kill.*
Renner, Beverly. *Hideaway Summer.*
Roth, Arthur. *Two for Survival.*
Roy, Ron. *Avalanche!*
Ruckman, Ivy. *Night of the Twister; No Way Out.*
Skurzynski, Gloria. *Caught in the Moving Mountains; Lost in the Devil's Desert; Trapped in the Slickrock Canyon.*
Southall, Ivan. *Hills End.*
Sperry, Armstrong. *Call It Courage.*
Steele, William. *Magic Amulet.*
Streiber, Whitley. *Warday: And the Journey Onward.*
Sullivan, Mary. *Earthquake 2099.*
Summers, James. *Shelter Trap.*
Swarthout, Glendon. *Whichaway.*
Swindells, Robert. *Brother in the Land.*
Taylor, Theodore. *Cay.*
Ter Haar, Jaap. *Boris.*
Thiele, Colin. *Fire in the Stone; Shadow Shark.*
Turnbull, Ann. *Maroo of the Winter Caves.*
Turner, Ann. *Way Home.*
Verne, Jules. *Long Vacation.*

Viereck, Phillip. *Summer I Was Lost.*
Walker, Diana. *Dragon Hill.*
Wallace, Bill. *Shadow on the Snow.*
Walsh, Jill P. *Fireweed.*
Walters, Hugh. *First on the Moon; Mission to Mercury.*
Weaver, Stella. *Poppy in the Corn.*
Wellman, Manly. *Mystery of the Lost Valley.*
Werstein, Irving. *Long Escape.*
White, Robb. *Deathwatch; Survivor.*
Wortman, Elmo. *Almost Too Late.*
Wyss, Johann. *Swiss Family Robinson.*
Zyskind, Sara. *Stolen Years.*

Suspense

Amerman, Lockhart. *Cape Cod Casket.*
Anderson, Margaret. *Brain on Quartz Mountain.*
Archer, Jeffrey. *Shall We Tell the President?*
Asimov, Isaac. *End of Eternity.*
Avi. *Wolf Rider: A Tale of Terror.*
Babbitt, Natalie. *Eyes of the Amaryllis.*
Bales, William. *Seeker.*
Bawden, Nina. *Squib.*
Bellairs, John. *Curse of the Blue Figurine; Figure in the Shadows; House with a Clock in Its Walls; Spell of the Sorcerer's Skull.*
Bennett, Jay. *Death Ticket; Skeleton Man.*
Biesterveld, Betty. *Run, Reddy, Run.*
Bodelson, Anders. *Operation Cobra.*
Borchard, R. *Donkeys for Rogador.*
Clark, Mary. *Stranger Is Watching.*
Colville, Bruce. *Spirits and Spells.*
Cook, Robin. *Coma.*
Coontz, Otto. *Night Walkers.*
Cormier, Robert. *After the First Death.*
Cresswell, Helen. *Beachcombers.*
Crichton, Michael. *Andromeda Strain; Congo.*
Cross, Gilbert. *Hanging at Tyburn; Mystery at Loon Lake.*
Cunningham, Julia. *Viollet.*
Dickinson, Peter. *Seventh Raven.*
Duncan, Lois. *I Know What You Did Last Summer; Killing Mr. Griffin; Locked in Time; Ransom; Summer of Fear.*
Evarts, Hal. *Secret of the Himalayas.*
Follett, Ken. *Eye of the Needle; Key to Rebecca.*
Forbes, Colin. *Avalanche Express.*
French, Michael. *Us Against Them.*
Gardner, John. *License Renewed.*
Gathorne-Hardy, Jonathan. *Airship Ladyship Adventure.*
Graham, Harriet. *Chinese Puzzle.*
Greene, Graham. *Human Factor.*
Hahn, Mary. *Wait Till Helen Comes: A Ghost Story.*
Hall, Lynn. *Whispered Horse.*
Harris, Rosemary. *Zed.*
Hastings, Beverly. *Watcher in the Dark.*

Haynes, Betsy. *Shadow of Jeremy Pimm.*
Haynes, Mary. *Raider's Sky.*
Healey, Larry. *Hoard of the Himalayas; Town Is on Fire.*
Heinlein, Robert. *Starman Jones.*
Herbert, Frank. *Under Pressure.*
Heuman, William. *Gridiron Stranger.*
Hilgartner, Beth. *Murder for Her Majesty.*
Hogan, James. *Two Faces of Tomorrow.*
Holland, Isabelle. *Marchington Inheritance.*
Hoover, H.M. *Rains of Eridan.*
Household, Geoffrey. *Escape into Daylight.*
Hunter, Mollie. *Stronghold.*
Johnston, Norma. *Carlisle's All.*
Kendall, Carol. *Firelings.*
King, Stephen. *Christine; Cujo; Firestarter; Pet Sematary; Shining.*
Klein, Robin. *People Might Hear You.*
Konigsburg, E.L. *Father's Arcane Daughter.*
Laymon, Richard. *Night Creature.*
Lea, Alec. *To Sunset and Beyond.*
Le Carre, John. *Little Drummer Girl.*
Leigh, Bill. *Far Side of Fear.*
L'Engle, Madeleine. *Arm and the Starfish; Dragons in the Water.*
Levin, Ira. *Boys from Brazil.*
Logan, Les. *Game.*
Lovett, Margaret. *Great and Terrible Quest.*
MacKellar, William. *Terror Run.*
MacLean, Alistair. *Circus; Ice Station Zebra; Where Eagles Dare.*
Maxwell, Edith. *Just Dial a Number.*
Morgan, Alison. *Paul's Kite.*
Morris, Judy. *Crazies and Sam.*
Namioka, Lensey. *Village of the Vampire Cat.*
Nixon, Joan. *Dark and Deadly Pool; Other Side of Dark; Seance; Stalker.*
Norton, Andre. *Beast Master.*
O'Dell, Scott. *Castle in the Sea; Spanish Smile.*
Parentead, Shirley. *Talking Coffins of Cryocity.*
Parker, Richard. *Three by Mistake.*
Peck, Richard. *Are You in the House Alone?; Banjo.*
Pesek, Ludek. *Trap for Perseus.*
Petersen, P.J. *How Can You Hijack a Cave?*
Peyton, Karen. *Prove Yourself a Hero.*
Phipson, Joan. *Boundary Riders.*
Price, Willard. *Volcano Adventure.*
Pullman, Phillip. *Count Karlstein.*
Rardin, Susan. *Captives in a Foreign Land.*
Rhinehart, Luke. *Long Voyage Back.*
Roberts, Willo. *View from the Cherry Tree.*
Rodgers, Raboo. *Magnum Fault.*
Ross, Rhea. *Bet's On, Lizzie Bingman.*
Sachs, Marilyn. *At the Sound of the Beep.*
St. George, Judith. *Haunted.*
Samuels, Gertrude. *Mottele, a Partisan Odyssey.*
Schwandt, Stephen. *Last Goodie.*
Scoppettone, Sandra. *Playing Murder.*
Scott, Jane. *To Keep an Island.*
Shaara, Michael. *Herald.*
Silverberg, Robert. *Man in the Maze.*

Skurzynski, Gloria. *Swept in the Wave of Terror.*
Sleator, William. *House of Stairs; Singularity.*
Smith, Perry. *Hidden Place.*
Snyder, Zilpha. *Egypt Game.*
Southall, Ivan. *Ash Road.*
Streatfeild, Noel. *When the Sirens Wailed.*
Suhl, Yuri. *On the Other Side of the Gate.*
Taylor, Theodore. *Sweet Friday Island; Teetoncey.*
Terris, Susan. *Pencil Families.*
Thiele, Colin. *Hammerhead Light.*
Thomas, Joyce. *Water Girl.*
Thompson, Julian. *Band of Angels; Discontinued; Grounding of Group 6.*
Towne, Mary. *Paul's Game.*
Townsend, John. *Intruder; Trader Wooly and the Terrorist.*
Trevor, Elleston. *Theta Syndrome.*
Vonnegut, Kurt. *Cat's Cradle.*
Waldron, Ann. *Scaredy Cat.*
Wallace, Bill. *Shadow on the Snow.*
Weinberg, Larry. *Curse.*
Wells, Rosemary. *Leave Well Enough Alone.*
Westall, Robert. *Urn Burial.*
Woods, George. *Catch a Killer.*
Yep, Laurence. *Liar, Liar.*
York, Carol. *Once Upon a Dark November; Where Evil Is.*
Zindel, Paul. *Undertakers Gone Bananas.*

Treasure Trove

Aiken, Joan. *Teeth of the Gale.*
Arden, William. *Mystery of the Dead Man's Riddle; Mystery of the Purple Pirate; Secret of the Phantom Lake.*
Baehr, Patricia. *Dragon Prophecy.*
Ball, Zachary. *Salvage Diver.*
Bellairs, John. *Treasure of Alpheus Winterborn.*
Benedict, Rex. *Good Luck Arizona Man.*
Biber, J. *Treasure of the Turkish Pasha.*
Boston, Lucy. *Treasure of Green Knowe.*
Brandel, Marc. *Mystery of the Kidnapped Whale.*
Briggs, Katherine. *Hobberdy Dick.*
Brown, Alexis. *Treasure in Devil's Bay.*
Carleton, Barbee. *Secret of Saturday Cove.*
Chambers, John. *Showdown at Apple Hill.*
Chauncy, Nan. *They Found a Cave.*
Clewes, Dorothy. *Mystery of the Blue Admiral; Mystery of the Lost Tower Treasure.*
Cooper, Susan. *Over Sea, Under Stone.*
Corbett, Scott. *Captain Butcher's Body; Cave Above Delphi; Cutlass Island; Tree House Island.*
Cresswell, Helen. *Beachcombers.*
Curry, Jane. *Bassumtyte Treasure; Great Flood Mystery.*
Cussler, Clive. *Raise the Titanic.*
Dank, Milton. *Treasure Code.*
Farley, Carol. *Mystery in the Ravine.*
Fleischman, Sid. *Jingo Django.*

Gordon, John. *House on the Brink.*
Graves, Robert. *Ancient Castle.*
Hallard, Peter. *Barrier Reef Bandit.*
Hamilton, Virginia. *House of Dies Drear; Mystery of Drear House.*
Hayes, John. *Dangerous Cove.*
Haynes, Betsy. *Ghost on Gravestone Hearth.*
Helldorfer, M.C. *Almost Home.*
Hicks, Clifford. *Alvin's Secret Code.*
Hildick, E.W. *Case of the Felon's Fiddle.*
Houghton, Eric. *Mystery of the Old Field.*
Hyde, Laurence. *Under the Pirate Flag.*
Jones, Betty. *King Solomon's Mine.*
Kennedy, Richard. *Amy's Eyes.*
Kooiker, Leonie. *Legacy of Magic.*
Ladd, Elizabeth. *Treasure on Heron's Neck.*
Lansing, E.H. *Secret of Dark Entry.*
Lawrence, Mildred. *Treasure and the Song.*
Lyle, Katie. *Finders Weepers.*
Mace, Elizabeth. *Rushton Inheritance.*
McElrath, William. *Indian Treasure on Rockhouse Creek.*
Macken, Walter. *Island of the Great Yellow Ox.*
Masterman-Smith, Virginia. *Treasure Trap.*
Mayne, William. *Underground Alley.*
Moeri, Louise. *Journey to the Treasure.*
Moore, Ruth. *Mystery of the Lost Treasure.*
Nesbit, Edith. *New Treasure Seekers; Story of the Treasure Seekers.*
Parish, Peggy. *Key to the Treasure; Pirate Island Adventure.*
Read, Mary. *Sack Man and the Grave.*
Roberts, Glenys. *Richard Knight's Treasure.*
Schlee, Ann. *Strangers.*
Shura, Mary. *Gray Ghosts of Taylor Ridge.*
Sneve, Virginia. *High Elk's Treasure.*
Spillane, Mickey. *Day the Sea Rolled Back.*
Stevenson, Robert. *Treasure Island.*
Stover, Marjorie. *Midnight in the Dollhouse; When the Dolls Wake.*
Street, Julia. *Drover's Gold.*
Taylor, Theodore. *Teetoncey and Ben O'Neal.*
Townsend, John. *Pirate's Island.*
Trease, Geoffrey. *No Boats on Bannermere.*
Valencak, Hannelore. *Tangled Web.*
Wallace, Bill. *Danger in Quicksand Pond; Trapped in Death Cave.*
Warner, Gertrude. *Mystery Behind the Wall.*
Wees, Frances. *Treasure of Echo Valley.*
Wibberley, Leonard. *Perilous Gold.*
Wuorio, Eva-Lis. *October Treasure.*

Underground Railroad

See: Slavery

Urban Life

Alexander, Sue. *Lila on the Landing.*
Anderson, Mary. *Rise and Fall of a Teen-Age Wacko.*
Beatty, Patricia. *Charley Skedaddle.*
Beckett, Hilary. *Street Fair Summer.*
Bethancourt, T.E. *New York City Too Far from Tampa Blues.*
Bonham, Frank. *Durango Street.*
Bulla, Clyde. *Indian Hill.*
Burchard, Peter. *Stranded: Story of New York.*
Campion, Wardi. *Casa Means Home.*
Clymer, Eleanor. *My Brother Stevie.*
Curry, Jane. *Big Smith Snatch.*
De Jong, Dola. *By Marvelous Agreement.*
Frascino, Edward. *Eddie Spaghetti on the Home Front.*
Gonzalez, Gloria. *Gaucho.*
Hamner, Earl. *You Can't Get There from Here.*
Hoffman, Alice. *Property Of.*
Kingman, Lee. *Peter Pan Bag.*
Lampman, Evelyn. *Half-Breed.*
Levin, Betty. *Hex House.*
Merrill, Jean. *Pushcart War.*
Miles, Betty. *Sink or Swim.*
Morse, Evangeline. *Brown Rabbit: Her Story.*
Murphy, Barbara. *No Place to Run.*
Myers, Walter. *Fast Sam, Cool Clyde and Stuff.*
Newton, Suzanne. *Place Between.*
Sawyer, Ruth. *Roller Skates.*
Simpson, Dorothy. *New Horizons.*
Sindall, Marjorie. *Matey.*
Skolsky, Mindy. *Hannah Is a Palindrome; Whistling Teakettle.*
Smucker, Barbara. *Wigwam in the City.*
Snyder, Carol. *Ike and Mama and the Block Wedding.*
Springstubb, Tricia. *Moon on a String.*
Taylor, Sydney. *All-of-a-Kind Family; All-of-a-Kind Family Downtown; More All-of-a-Kind Family.*
Walter, Mildred. *Lillie of Watts: A Birthday Discovery.*
Woolley, Catherine. *Look Alive, Libby.*

Values

Aaron, Chester. *Better Than Laughter.*
Aldridge, James. *Sporting Proposition.*
Allan, Mabel. *Kraymer Mystery.*
Allen, Elizabeth. *Loser.*
Anckarsvard, Karin. *Struggle at Soltuna.*
Anderson, Mary. *Do You Call That a Dream Date?*
Appleby, Jon. *Skate.*
Arora, Shirley. *What Then, Raman?*
Arrick, Fran. *God's Radar.*
Asher, Sandy. *Summer Begins.*
Ashley, Bernard. *All My Men.*
Avi. *Bright Shadow.*
Bach, Alice. *He Will Not Walk with Me.*
Bach, Richard. *Jonathan Livingston Seagull.*
Ball, Dorothy. *Don't Drive Up a Dirt Road.*

Barrett, William. *Lilies of the Field.*
Bartos-Hoppner, Barbara. *Cossacks.*
Bauer, Marion. *Like Mother, Like Daughter.*
Beatty, Patricia. *I Want My Sunday, Stranger; Lupita Manana.*
Beckman, Delores. *Who Loves Sam Grant?*
Bennett, Jay. *Deadly Gift.*
Biemiller, Carl. *Albino Blue.*
Billington, Elizabeth. *Move.*
Blume, Judy. *Then Again, Maybe I Won't.*
Bonham, Frank. *Hey, Big Spender; Speedway Contender.*
Bowen, Betty. *For Love of a Donkey.*
Bradbury, Ray. *Fahrenheit 451.*
Brancato, Robin. *Uneasy Money.*
Brooks, Jerome. *Make Me a Hero.*
Burchard, Peter. *Jed.*
Burton, Hester. *Time of Trial.*
Butterworth, W.E. *LeRoy and the Old Man.*
Cameron, Eleanor. *Julia's Magic; Mysterious Christmas Shell.*
Carson, John. *Coach Nobody Liked.*
Chauncy, Nan. *High and Haunted Island.*
Christman, Elizabeth. *Ruined for Life.*
Christopher, Matt. *Hit-Away Kid.*
Claro, Joseph. *I Can Predict the Future.*
Cleaver, Vera. *Kissimmee Kid.*
Clymer, Eleanor. *We Lived in the Almont.*
Coles, Robert. *Saving Face.*
Cooney, Caroline. *Rah Rah Girls.*
Corcoran, Barbara. *Star to the North; Strike.*
Cormier, Robert. *Beyond the Chocolate War; Chocolate War.*
Cresswell, Helen. *Winter of the Birds.*
Cross, Gillian. *Chartbreaker.*
Cunningham, Julia. *Burnish Me Bright.*
Dailey, Virginia. *Keys to Lawrence House.*
Danziger, Paula. *Cat Ate My Gymsuit; There's a Bat in Bunk Five.*
Darke, Marjorie. *Question of Courage.*
Davis, Russell. *Some Town You Brought Me To.*
De Clements, Barthe. *No Place for Me.*
Dixon, Paige. *Lion on the Mountain.*
Edwards, Patricia. *Nilda.*
Eliot, George. *Silas Marner.*
Emery, Anne. *Losing Game; Popular Crowd.*
Farley, Carol. *Most Important Thing in the World.*
Fletcher, David. *King's Goblet.*
Fosburgh, Liza. *Summer Lion.*
Franchere, Ruth. *Stamped North.*
Gardiner, John. *General Butterfingers.*
Gardner, Leonard. *Fat City.*
Garfield, Leon. *Footsteps.*
Greenberg, Jan. *Bye, Bye, Miss American Pie.*
Greenberg, Joanne. *Simple Gifts.*
Greenwald, Sheila. *Blissful Joy and the SATs.*
Hahn, Mary. *Tallahassee Higgins.*
Hamlin, Gwen. *Changing Keys.*
Havrevold, Finn. *Undertow.*
Hayes, Sheila. *Carousel Horse.*
Henry, Marguerite. *San Domingo, the Medicine Hat Stallion.*
Herzig, Alison. *Shadows on the Pond.*
Hilton, James. *Goodbye, Mr. Chips.*
Holl, Kristi. *First Things First.*
Holmes, Barbara. *Charlotte the Starlet.*
Hughes, Monica. *Hunter in the Dark.*
Hunt, Mabel. *Beggar's Daughter.*
Huxley, Aldous. *Brave New World.*
Johnson, Annabel. *Count Me Gone.*
Jones, Ron. *Acorn People.*
Jordan, Mildred. *Proud to Be Amish.*
Kelly, Rosalie. *Addie's Year.*
Kerr, M.E. *Fell; Gentlehands.*
Klass, Sheila. *Credit-Card Carole; Nobody Knows Me in Miami.*
Kruss, James. *Letters to Pauline.*
Kurland, Morton. *Our Sacred Honor.*
Langton, Jane. *Fragile Flag.*
Lawrence, Mildred. *Starry Answer; Walk a Rocky Road.*
Levitin, Sonia. *Season for Unicorns.*
Lingard, Joan. *Across the Barricades; Proper Place; Twelfth Day of July.*
Lowry, Lois. *Autumn Street.*
McCormick, Wilfred. *One Bounce Too Many.*
McGraw, Eloise. *Seventeenth Swap.*
Maddock, Reginald. *Great Bow.*
Miklowitz, Gloria. *Suddenly Super Rich.*
Muehl, Lois. *Hidden Year of Devlin Bates.*
Murphy, Jim. *Death Run.*
Musgrave, Florence. *Oh, Sarah.*
Noble, Iris. *Stranger No More.*
O'Dell, Scott. *Black Pearl.*
Ogan, Margaret. *Green Galloper.*
Olsen, Violet. *Growing Season.*
Patchett, Mary. *Warrimood.*
Paulsen, Gary. *Popcorn Days and Buttermilk Nights.*
Petersen, P.J. *Going for the Big One.*
Pfeffer, Susan. *Future Forward.*
Polcovet, Jane. *Charming.*
Roos, Stephen. *Confessions of a Wayward Preppie.*
Sachs, Marilyn. *Call Me Ruth.*
Savitz, Harriet. *Come Back, Mr. Magic.*
Schmidt, Kurt. *Annapolis Misfit.*
Scott, Jane. *To Keep an Island.*
Setlowe, Rick. *Brink.*
Shaw, Diana. *Lessons in Fear.*
Sherman, D.R. *Lion's Paw.*
Smith, Eunice. *Jennifer Gift.*
Smith, Rukshana. *Sumitra's Story.*
Sommerfelt, Aimee. *White Bungalow.*
Speare, Elizabeth. *Bronze Bow.*
Spinelli, Jerry. *Dump Days.*
Sutton, Jane. *Definitely Not Sexy.*
Swarthout, Glendon. *Bless the Beasts and the Children.*
Taylor, Theodore. *Cay.*
Tchudi, Stephen. *Burg-o-Rama Man.*
Terris, Susan. *Two P's in a Pod.*
Thomas, Jane. *Fox in a Trap.*

Vikings

War

See also: Civil War, American; Revolutionary War; World War I; World War II

West, American

Jed McLane and the Stranger; Journal of One Davey Wyatt.
James, Will. *Smoky, the Cowhorse.*
Johnson, Annabel. *Bearcat.*
Norton, Andre. *Rebel Spurs; Ride, Proud Rebel.*
O'Dell, Scott. *Streams to the River, Rivers to the Sea.*
Peck, Richard. *Ghost Belonged to Me.*
Portis, Charles. *True Grit.*
Shields, Rita. *Norah and the Cable Car.*
Smith, A.C.H. *Lady Jane.*
Taylor, Theodore. *Walking Up a Rainbow.*
Wallace, Barbara. *Peppermints in the Parlor.*
Wiegand, Roberta. *Year of the Comet.*
Wormser, Richard. *Ride a Northbound Horse.*

Wilderness

Aaron, Chester. *American Ghost.*
Annixter, Jane. *Horns of Plenty.*
Blos, Joan. *Gathering of Days.*
Calvert, Patricia. *Hour of the Wolf.*
Catherall, Arthur. *Big Tusker.*
Clark, Virginia. *Mysterious Buckskin.*
Corcoran, Barbara. *Star to the North.*
Crompton, Anne. *Deer Country.*
Davis, Verne. *Runaway Cattle.*
De Felice, Cynthia. *Weasel.*
De Leeuw, C. *Fear in the Forest.*
Dexter, Patricia. *Arrow in the Wind.*
Evarts, Hal. *Bigfoot.*
Fall, Thomas. *Dandy's Mountain.*
Filson, Brent. *Smoke Jumpers.*
French, Michael. *Pursuit.*
Jacques, Brian. *Mossflower.*
Johnson, James. *Wild Venture.*
Johnson, Virginia. *Cedars of Charlo.*
Kjelgaard, James. *Nose for Trouble.*
McMeekin, Isabel. *Postman's Pony.*
Mayne, William. *Drift.*
Meader, Stephen. *Buffalo and Beaver.*
Morey, Walt. *Canyon Winter; Home Is the North; Sandy and the Rock Star.*
Mowat, Farley. *Lost in the Barrens.*
Mulcahy, Lucille. *Fire on Big Lonesome.*
North, Sterling. *Rascal.*
Norton, Andre. *Catseye.*
O'Brien, John. *Royal Road; Silver Chief, Dog of the North; Silver Chief to the Rescue.*
Oppenheimer, Joan. *Gardine vs. Hanover.*
Richer, Robert. *Rudi of the Mountain.*
Robertson, Keith. *In Search of a Sandhill Crane.*
Roe, Kathy. *Goodbye, Secret Place.*
Roth, Arthur. *Two for Survival.*
Salassi, Otto. *And Nobody Knew They Were There.*
Sargent, Shirley. *Heart Holding Mountains.*
Southall, Ivan. *Ash Road.*
Thiele, Colin. *February Dragon.*
Wallace, Bill. *Red Dog.*
Weddle, Ferris. *Blazing Mountain.*

White, Robb. *Fire Storm.*
Wier, Ester. *Long Year.*

Wit and Humor

See: Humorous

Witches

Arthur, Robert. *Mystery of the Magic Circle.*
Arthur, Ruth. *Autumn People.*
Beachcroft, Nina. *Well Met by Witchlight.*
Belden, Wilanne. *Rescue of Ranor.*
Bellairs, John. *Letter, the Witch and the Ring; Spell of the Sorcerer's Skull.*
Bennett, Anna. *Little Witch.*
Briggs, Katherine. *Kate Crackernuts.*
Brittain, Bill. *Devil's Donkey; Wish Giver.*
Calhoun, Mary. *Witch of Hissing Hill.*
Carey, M.V. *Mystery of the Singing Serpent.*
Carleton, Barbee. *Witch's Bridge.*
Clapp, Patricia. *Witches' Children.*
Corbett, Scott. *Witch Hunt.*
Curry, Jane. *Parsley, Sage, Rosemary and Time.*
Dahl, Roald. *Witches.*
Dickinson, Peter. *Devil's Children; Heartsease; Weathermonger.*
Edmondson, Madeleine. *Anna Witch; Witch's Egg.*
Estes, Eleanor. *Witch Family.*
Farber, Norma. *Mercy Short, a Winter Journal.*
Feil, Hila. *Ghost Garden.*
Fisher, Leonard. *Warlock of Westfall.*
Glaser, Dianne. *Amber Wellington, Witch Watcher.*
Gondosch, Linda. *Witches of Hopper Street.*
Greaves, Margaret. *Stone of Terror.*
Griffiths, Helen. *Mysterious Appearance of Agnes.*
Hahn, Mary. *Time of the Witch.*
Harnett, Cynthia. *Writing on the Hearth.*
Horowitz, Anthony. *Devil's Door-Bell.*
Hunter, Mollie. *Kelpie's Pearls.*
Jones, Diana. *Witch Week; Witch's Business.*
Key, Alexander. *Escape to Witch Mountain; Return from Witch Mountain.*
Kooiker, Leonie. *Legacy of Magic; Magic Stone.*
Krensky, Stephen. *Witching Hour.*
Lawrence, Louise. *Earth Witch.*
Little, Jane. *Spook.*
Lovejoy, Jack. *Rebel Witch.*
MacKellar, William. *Witch of Glen Gowrie.*
Mahy, Margaret. *Changeover.*
Mannix, Daniel. *Healer.*
Mayne, William. *It.*
Murphy, Jill. *Worst Witch.*
Naylor, Phyllis. *Witch Herself; Witch Water; Witch's Eye; Witch's Sister.*
Nimmo, Jenny. *Snow Spider.*
O'Dell, Scott. *Sarah Bishop.*

Petry, Ann. *Tituba of Salem Village.*
Platt, Kin. *Mystery of the Witch Who Wouldn't.*
Rayner, Mary. *Witchfinder.*
Sleator, William. *Blackbriar.*
Smith, Claude. *Stratford Devil.*
Snyder, Zilpha. *Witches of Worm.*
Softly, Barbara. *Stone in a Pool.*
Speare, Elizabeth. *Witch of Blackbird Pond.*
Stephens, Mary Jo. *Witch of the Cumberlands.*
Sutcliff, Rosemary. *Witch's Brat.*
Syfret, Anne. *Bella.*
Turnbull, Ann. *Frightened Forest.*
Wayne, Kyra. *Witches of Barguzin.*
Whitehead, Victoria. *Chimney Witches.*

Women's Rights

Beckman, Gunnel. *That Early Spring.*
Bolton, Carole. *Never Jam Today.*
Constant, Alberta. *Does Anyone Care About Lou Emma Miller?*
Darke, Marjorie. *Question of Courage.*
Flory, Jane. *Liberation of Clementine Tipton.*
Hall, Elizabeth. *Stand Up, Lucy.*
Jones, Adrienne. *Matter of Spunk; Whistle Down a Dark Lane.*
Katz, Bobbie. *Manifesto and Me—Meg.*
Kingman, Lee. *Georgina and the Dragon.*
Knudson, R.R. *Zanballer; Zanbanger.*
McNeer, May. *Bloomsday for Maggie.*
Miles, Betty. *Real Me.*
Nixon, Joan. *Casey and the Great Idea.*
Pierce, Tamara. *Woman Who Rides Like a Man.*
Shreve, Susan. *Revolution of Mary Leary.*
Sirof, Harriet. *Real World.*
Symons, Geraldine. *Miss Rivers and Miss Bridges.*
Talley, Naomi. *New Cut Road.*
Underwood, Betty. *Forge and the Forest.*
Walter, Mildred. *Justin and the Best Biscuits in the World.*
Watson, Sally. *Jode.*

Working World

Aiken, Joan. *Midnight Is a Place.*
Almedingen, E.M. *Stephen's Light.*
Anckarsvard, Karin. *Struggle at Soltuna.*
Angell, Judie. *Buffalo Nickel Blues Band.*
Asher, Sandy. *Everything Is Not Enough.*
Ball, Zachary. *Salvage Diver.*
Baner, Skulda. *First Parting.*
Beatty, Patricia. *By Crumbs, It's Mine.*
Bentley, Phyllis. *Oath of Silence.*
Blume, Judy. *Deenie.*
Bonham, Frank. *Deepwater Challenge.*
Bosse, Malcolm. *Captives of Time.*
Bradbury, Bianca. *Andy's Mountain; New Penny.*
Brancato, Robin. *Come Alive at 505.*

Brown, Pamela. *Other Side of the Street.*
Butterworth, W.E. *Return to Racing.*
Carr, Harriett. *Bold Beginning.*
Carris, Joan. *Pets, Vets and Marty Howard; Rusty Timmons' First Million.*
Catherall, Arthur. *Death of an Oil Rig.*
Caunitz, William. *One Police Plaza.*
Cavanna, Betty. *Country Cousin.*
Chapin, Henry. *Spiro of the Sponge Fleet.*
Christman, Elizabeth. *Ruined for Life.*
Clarke, Mary. *Petticoat Rebel.*
Cleaver, Vera. *Moon Lake Angel.*
Cohen, Barbara. *Innkeeper's Daughter; Roses.*
Colman, Hila. *Ellie's Inheritance.*
Constant, Alberta. *Willie and the Wildcat Well.*
Corcoran, Barbara. *You Put Up with Me, I'll Put Up with You.*
Crane, Caroline. *Lights Down the River.*
Cross, Gillian. *Revolt at Ratcliffe's Rags.*
Curry, Jane. *Lotus Cup.*
Cussler, Clive. *Raise the Titanic.*
Darke, Marjorie. *Question of Courage.*
Davidson, Mary. *Superstar Called Sweetpea.*
Dean, Karen. *Stay on Your Toes, Maggie Adams.*
Dixon, Paige. *Pimm's Cup for Everybody.*
Duder, Tersa. *Jellybean.*
Duffy, James. *Cleaver of the Good Luck Diner.*
Eyerly, Jeannette. *More Than a Summer Love.*
Facklam, Margery. *Whistle for Danger.*
Faulkner, Nancy. *Second Son.*
Foltz, Mary Jane. *Nicolau's Prize.*
Francis, Dorothy. *Another Kind of Beauty.*
Friermood, Elizabeth. *One of Fred's Girls.*
Fry, Rosalie. *Echo's Song.*
Gault, William. *Checkered Flag.*
George, Jean. *Water Sky.*
Gilbert, Nan. *Academy Summer.*
Glaser, Paul. *Squad Room Detective.*
Goffstein, M.B. *Daisy Summerfield's Style.*
Grice, Frederick. *Out of the Mines.*
Hall, Adele. *Seashore Summer.*
Hanff, Helene. *84, Charing Cross Road.*
Harnett, Cynthia. *Cargo of the Madelena; Caxton's Challenge.*
Harris, Christie. *Confessions of a Toe-Hanger; You Have to Draw the Line Somewhere.*
Hartwell, Nancy. *Wake Up, Roberta.*
Hassler, Jon. *Jemmy.*
Hentoff, Nat. *Jazz Country.*
Hewett, Hilda. *Harriet and the Cherry Pie.*
Hindle, Lee. *Dragon Fall.*
Holl, Kristi. *First Things First.*
Hosford, Jessie. *You Bet Your Boots I Can.*
Houston, James. *River Runners.*
Howard, Elizabeth. *Winter on Her Own.*
Hubbell, Harriet. *Moon Penny Lane.*
Hughes, Dean. *Millie Willenheimer & the Chestnut Corporation.*
Innis, Pauline. *Hurricane Fighters.*
Johnson, Annabel. *Bearcat.*
Johnston, Norma. *Timewarp Summer.*
Klein, Norma. *It's Not What You Expect.*

World War I

World War II

Gottschalk, Elin. *In Search of Coffee Mountains.*
Green, Connie. *War at Home.*
Greene, Bette. *Morning Is a Long Time Coming; Summer of My German Soldier.*
Griese, Arnold. *Wind Is Not a River.*
Hartman, Evert. *War Without Friends.*
Haugaard, Erik. *Little Fishes.*
Heuck, Sigrid. *Hideout.*
Hickman, Janet. *Stones.*
Horgan, Dorothy. *Edge of War.*
Innocenti, Roberto. *Rose Blanche.*
Kerr, Judith. *Small Person Far Away; When Hitler Stole Pink Rabbit.*
Kerr, M.E. *Gentlehands.*
Koehn, Ilse. *Mischling, Second Degree: My Childhood in Nazi Germany; Tilla.*
Korschunow, Irina. *Night in Distant Motion.*
Kuper, Jack. *Child of the Holocaust.*
Lisle, Janet. *Sirens and Spies.*
Lowry, Lois. *Number the Stars.*
Lustig, Arnost. *Darkness Casts a Shadow.*
McSwigan, Marie. *Snow Treasure.*
Magorian, Michelle. *Back Home; Good Night, Mr. Tom.*
Maruki, Toshi. *Hiroshima No Pika.*
Matas, Carol. *Lisa War.*
Mazer, Harry. *Last Mission.*
Nostlinger, Christine. *Fly Away Home.*
Orlev, Uri. *Island on Bird Street.*
Osswoski, Leonie. *Star Without a Sky.*
Pelgrom, Els. *Winter When Time Was Frozen.*
Rees, David. *Exeter Blitz.*
Reiss, Johanna. *Upstairs Room.*
Roth-Hano, Renee. *Touch Wood.*
Rydberg, Ernie. *Shadow Army.*
Sachs, Marilyn. *Pocket Full of Seeds.*
Samuels, Gertrude. *Mottele, a Partisan Odyssey.*
Schellie, Don. *Shadow and the Gunner.*
Senje, Sigurd. *Escape.*
Serraillier, Ian. *Silver Sword.*
Shemin, Margaretha. *Empty Moat; Little Riders.*
Siegal, Aranka. *Upon the Head of the Goat.*
Smith, Doris. *Salted Lemons.*
Streatfeild, Noel. *When the Sirens Wailed.*
Suhl, Yuri. *Uncle Misha's Partisans.*
Szambelan-Strevinsky, Christine. *Dark Hour at Noon.*
Taylor, Theodore. *Children's War.*
Ter Haar, Jaap. *Boris.*
Terlouw, James. *Winter in Wartime.*
Todd, Leonard. *Best Kept Secret of the War.*
Tunis, John. *His Enemy, His Friend; Silence Over Dunkerque.*
Vander Els, Betty. *Bombers Moon.*
Van Stockum, Hilda. *Winged Watchman.*
Vinke, Herman. *Short Life of Sophie Scholl.*
Walsh, Jill P. *Fireweed.*
Werstein, Irving. *Long Escape.*
Westall, Robert. *Fathom Five; Haunting of Charles McGill; Machine Gunners.*
Wharton, William. *Birdy.*
White, Robb. *Survivor.*

Yolen, Jane. *Devil's Arithmetic.*
Zei, Alki. *Wildcat Under Glass.*

Writing

Bargar, Gary. *What Happened to Mr. Forster?*
Brink, Carol. *Two Are Better Than One.*
Calvert, Patricia. *Snowbird.*
Cameron, Eleanor. *Julia and the Hand of God; Room Made of Windows; That Julia Redfern.*
Carlson, Natalie. *Letter on the Tree.*
Carr, Harriett. *Bold Beginning.*
Cleary, Beverly. *Dear Mr. Henshaw.*
Cohen, Barbara. *Tell Us Your Secret.*
Colman, Hila. *Diary of a Frantic Kid Sister.*
Conford, Ellen. *Dear Lovey Hart, I Am Desperate; Jenny Archer, Author; We Interrupt This Semester for an Important Bulletin.*
Corbett, Scott. *Limerick Trick; Mailbox Trick.*
Emery, Anne. *Losing Game.*
Facklam, Margery. *Trouble with Mothers.*
Fitzhugh, Louise. *Harriet the Spy.*
Friermood, Elizabeth. *Promises in the Attic.*
Girion, Barbara. *Like Everybody Else.*
Glenn, Mel. *One Order to Go.*
Greenwald, Sheila. *Give Us a Great Big Smile, Rosy Cole; It All Began with Jane Eyre; Write On, Rosy.*
Gripe, Maria. *Night Daddy.*
Grohskopf, Bernice. *Blood and Roses.*
Harnett, Cynthia. *Cargo of the Madelena; Caxton's Challenge.*
Hayes, William. *Project: Scoop.*
Haynes, Mary. *Wordchanger.*
Henkes, Kevin. *Return to Sender.*
Hentoff, Nat. *Day They Came to Arrest the Book.*
Hinton, S.E. *Taming the Star Runner.*
Holland, Isabelle. *God, Mrs. Muskrat, and Aunt Dot.*
Holmes, Barbara. *Charlotte the Starlet.*
Hunter, Mollie. *Hold on to Love; Sound of Chariots.*
Jacobs, Anita. *Where Has Deedie Wooster Been All These Years?*
Johnston, Norma. *Mustard Seed of Magic.*
Kaye, Marilyn. *Lydia.*
Lawrence, Mildred. *Reach for the Dream.*
Lowry, Lois. *One Hundredth Thing About Caroline.*
McElfresh, Adeline. *Summer Change.*
McNeer, May. *Bloomsday for Maggie.*
Marshall, Catherine. *Julie.*
Montgomery, Lucy. *Emily Climbs.*
Oldham, Mary. *White Pony.*
Oneal, Zibby. *In Summer Light.*
Pfeffer, Susan. *Getting Even; Just Morgan; Matter of Principal.*
Plath, Sylvia. *Bell Jar.*
Robertson, Keith. *Henry Reed's Journey.*

OTHER USEFUL LISTINGS

Fewer Than 100 Pages

Anderson, Clarence. *Blind Connemara.*
Anderson, Paul. *Boy and the Blind Storyteller.*
Annixter, Jane. *Last Monster.*
Arnosky, Jim. *Gray Boy.*
Avi. *S.O.R. Losers.*
Bach, Richard. *Jonathan Livingston Seagull.*
Barrett, William. *Lilies of the Field.*
Bell, Frederic. *Jenny's Corner.*
Bertol, Roland. *Two Hats.*
Boston, Lucy. *Castle of Yew; Fossil Snake; Nothing Said; Sea Egg.*
Branscum, Robbie. *Adventures of Johnny May.*
Buchwald, Art. *Bollo Caper.*
Buck, Pearl. *Matthew, Mark, Luke and John.*
Bulla, Clyde. *Beast of Lor; Ghost of Windy Hill; Shoeshine Girl; White Bird.*
Bunting, Eve. *Empty Window; One More Flight; Sixth Grade Sleepover.*
Burchard, Peter. *Rat Hell.*
Carlson, Natalie. *Evangeline, Pigeon of Paris; Grandmother for the Orphelines; Happy Orpheline; Jaky or Dodo; Orphelines in the Enchanted Castle; Pet for the Orphelines.*
Christian, Mary. *Sebastian, Super Sleuth; Sebastian (Super Sleuth) and the Baffling Bigfoot; Sebastian (Super Sleuth) and the Bone-to-Pick Mystery; Sebastian (Super Sleuth) and the Clumsy Cowboy; Sebastian (Super Sleuth) and the Crummy Yummies Caper; Sebastian (Super Sleuth) and the Egyptian Connection; Sebastian (Super Sleuth) and the Hair of the Dog Mystery; Sebastian (Super Sleuth) and the Purloined Sirloin; Sebastian (Super Sleuth) and the Santa Claus Caper; Sebastian (Super Sleuth) and the Secret of the Skewered Skier; Sebastian (Super Sleuth) and the Stars-in-His-Eyes Mystery.*
Claro, Joseph. *I Can Predict the Future.*
Clewes, Dorothy. *Old Pony.*
Clifford, Eth. *Remembering Box.*
Clymer, Eleanor. *Luke Was There; My Brother Stevie.*
Coatsworth, Elizabeth. *Jock's Island.*
Cole, Sheila. *Meaning Well.*
Cooper, Margaret. *Solution: Escape.*
Corbett, Scott. *Deadly Hoax; Run for the Money.*
Cunningham, Julia. *Dorp Dead; Macaroon; Tuppenny; Viollet.*

Dank, Milton. *3-D Traitor.*
Doty, Jean. *Valley of the Ponies.*
Du Bois, William. *Call Me Bandicoot; Porko Von Popbutton.*
Durham, John. *Me and Arch and the Pest.*
Fleischman, Sid. *Whipping Boy.*
Gardiner, John. *Stone Fox.*
Garner, Alan. *Aimer Gate; Granny Reardon; Stone Book; Tom Fobble's Day.*
Gipson, Fred. *Little Arliss.*
Greenfield, Eloise. *Sister.*
Griese, Arnold. *At the Mouth of the Luckiest River.*
Hale, Edward E. *Man Without a Country.*
Heide, Florence. *Secret Dreamer, Secret Dreams; Shrinking of Treehorn; Time Flies; Time's Up; Treehorn's Treasure; Treehorn's Wish.*
Holland, Isabelle. *God, Mrs. Muskrat, and Aunt Dot.*
Houston, James. *Eagle Mask: West Coast Indian Tale; White Archer; Wolf Run.*
Howard, Ellen. *Circle of Giving.*
Hurwitz, Johanna. *Adventures of Ali Baba Bernstein.*
Jones, Betty. *King Solomon's Mine.*
Jordan, June. *His Own Where.*
Jukes, Mavis. *Getting Even.*
Kaatz, Evelyn. *Soccer!*
Klein, Norma. *Confessions of an Only Child.*
Knudson, R.R. *Rinehart Lifts.*
Larson, Jean. *Silkspinners.*
Le Guin, Ursula. *Very Far Away from Anywhere Else.*
Macauley, David. *Motel of the Mysteries.*
MacDonald, George. *Golden Key.*
MacLachlan, Patricia. *Sarah, Plain and Tall.*
Manes, Stephen. *That Game from Outer Space.*
Mathis, Sharon. *Hundred Penny Box.*
Miles, Miska. *Annie and the Old One.*
Moeri, Louise. *First the Egg.*
Murphy, Robert. *Wild Geese Calling.*
Parker, Richard. *He Is Your Brother.*
Peck, Robert. *Banjo; Soup's Goat; Trig; Trig Goes Ape; Trig or Treat; Trig Sees Red.*
Pinkwater, Daniel. *Magic Moscow.*
Platt, Kin. *Run for Your Life.*
Rees, David. *Risks.*
Rylant, Cynthia. *Blue-Eyed Daisy.*
Sachs, Marilyn. *Beach Towels; Thunderbird.*
Singer, Marilyn. *Case of the Cackling Car; Case of the Sabotaged School Play; Clue in Code; Where There's a Will, There's a Wag.*
Skolsky, Mindy. *Carnival and Kopeck.*

Slote, Alfred. *Hotshot.*
Smith, Doris. *Taste of Blackberries.*
Snow, Dorothea. *Sight of Everything.*
Sobol, Donald. *Encyclopedia Brown and the Case of the Midnight Visitor; Encyclopedia Brown Lends a Hand.*
Tate, Joan. *Tina and David.*
Trivers, James. *Hamburger Heaven.*
Vivelo, Jackie. *Super Sleuth.*
Walter, Mildred. *Lillie of Watts: A Birthday Discovery.*
Wayne, Jennifer. *Sprout.*
Willett, John. *Singer in the Stone.*
Wolkstein, Diane. *White Wave: A Chinese Tale.*

More Than 300 Pages

Adams, Richard. *Watership Down.*
Aiken, Joan. *Cuckoo Tree.*
Auel, Jean. *Earth's Children.*
Bennett, John. *Master Skylark.*
Bond, Nancy. *Voyage Begun.*
Bradbury, Ray. *I Sing the Body Electric.*
Brooks, Terry. *Magical Kingdom for Sale—Sold.*
Bunyan, John. *Pilgrim's Progress.*
Cather, Willa. *My Antonia.*
Chalker, Jack. *Messiah Choice.*
Clark, Mary. *Cradle Will Fall.*
Constant, Alberta. *Motoring Millers; Those Miller Girls.*
Cook, Robin. *Mindbend.*
Cooper, James. *Last of the Mohicans.*
Crichton, Michael. *Sphere.*
Cussler, Clive. *Raise the Titanic.*
Dickens, Charles. *Great Expectations.*
Fletcher, David. *King's Goblet.*
Fon Eisen, Anthony. *Prince of Omeya.*
Forester, Cecil. *Hornblower and the Hotspur.*
Hale, Lucretia. *Peterkin Papers.*
Hamilton, Virginia. *Magical Adventures of Pretty Pearl.*
Harnett, Cynthia. *Writing on the Hearth.*
Herbert, Frank. *Dune.*
Hugo, Victor. *Hunchback of Notre Dame.*
Jackson, Helen. *Ramona.*
Jones, Adrienne. *Matter of Spunk.*
Jones, Diana. *Fire and Hemlock.*
Kane, Harnett. *Amazing Mrs. Bonaparte.*
Keith, Harold. *Brief Garland.*
Kennedy, Richard. *Amy's Eyes.*
Killilea, M. Karen. *With Love from Karen.*
L'Engle, Madeleine. *House Like a Lotus; Many Waters; Moon by Night; Ring of Endless Light.*
McCaffrey, Anne. *Crystal Singer; Dragonflight; Dragonquest.*
McCullough, Colleen. *Thornbirds.*
Magorian, Michelle. *Back Home; Good Night, Mr. Tom.*
Moon, Sheila. *Knee-Deep in Thunder.*
Murray, Michele. *Crystal Nights.*

O'Shea, Pat. *Hounds of the Morrigan.*
Pitkin, Dorothy. *Wiser Than Winter.*
Pyle, Howard. *Merry Adventures of Robin Hood.*
Shura, Mary. *Jessica.*
Steinbeck, John. *Of Mice and Men.*
Stewart, Mary. *Crystal Cave; Hollow Hills.*
Taylor, Mildred. *Let the Circle Be Unbroken.*
Tolkien, J.R.R. *Fellowship of the Ring; Return of the King; Two Towers.*
Trumbo, Dalton. *Johnny Got His Gun.*
Verne, Jules. *Twenty Thousand Leagues Under the Sea.*
Vinge, Joan. *Psion.*
Voigt, Cynthia. *Homecoming.*
Watson, James. *Talking in Whispers.*
Weber, Lenora. *Don't Call Me Katie Rose; Something Borrowed, Something Blue.*
Williams, Mona. *Messenger.*
Wright, Richard. *Native Son.*

Translations

Aimatov, Chingez. *White Ship.*
Aleksin, Anatoli. *Alik, the Detective; Late Born Child.*
Anckarsvard, Karin. *Rider by Night; Robber Ghost; Springtime for Eva; Struggle at Soltuna.*
Baer, Frank. *Max's Gang.*
Balch, Glenn. *Buck, Wild.*
Bartos-Hoppner, Barbara. *Cossacks; Save the Kahn; Storm Over the Caucasus.*
Baudouy, Michel. *Boy Who Belonged to No One; Deception at St. Nazaire; More Than Courage; Secret of the Hidden Painting.*
Beckman, Gunnel. *Mia Alone; That Early Spring.*
Benary-Isbert, Margot. *Ark; Castle on the Border; Long Way Home; Rowan Farm.*
Bernhardsen, Christian. *Fight in the Mountains.*
Biber, J. *Treasure of the Turkish Pasha.*
Bodker, Cecil. *Silas and Ben Godik; Silas and the Black Mare; Silas and the Runaway Coach.*
Bruckner, Karl. *Day of the Bomb.*
Bykov, Vasilii. *Pack of Wolves.*
Chukovskii, Kornei. *Silver Crest.*
Day, Veronique. *Landslide.*
Ecke, Wolfgang. *Bank Holdup; Face at the Window; Invisible Witness; Midnight Chess Game; Stolen Paintings.*
Eckert, Allan. *Dark Green Tunnel.*
Friis-Baastad, Babbis. *Don't Take Teddy.*
Green, Alexander. *Scarlet Sails.*
Gripe, Maria. *Green Coat.*
Guillot, Rene. *Fofana; Riders of the Wind; Sama.*
Hamori, Laszlo. *Dangerous Journey; Flight to the Promised Land.*
Hamre, Leif. *Operation Arctic.*

ANNOTATED BIBLIOGRAPHY

Aaron, Chester. *American Ghost.* Harcourt, 1973. Albie, 14, and a lioness become friends when both of them are swept away by the flooding Mississippi River. They help each other survive.

_____. *Better Than Laughter.* Harcourt, 1972. Two wealthy brothers run away from home and live in the county dump with the caretaker. They return home wiser for the experience.

_____. *Gideon.* Lippincott, 1982. Gideon is the only survivor of his Polish-Jewish family. He evades the Nazis with false papers. He escapes Poland but returns to find a lost sister. He is captured and again escapes. A grim story.

_____. *Lackawanna.* Harper, 1986. Willy's family is hit hard by the Depression. He takes up with a bunch of abandoned children who survive as they can. One of them is kidnapped by a hobo and must be rescued.

_____. *Out of Sight, Out of Mind.* Lippincott, 1985. Erin and Sean have psychic powers. They and their parents are on their way to a world peace conference when their plane is shot down. Their parents are killed and they must reach the conference.

_____. *Spill.* Atheneum, 1977. An oil spill threatens wild sea birds and the environment. Judy and Jeff team up to help restore the shore line.

Abercrombie, Barbara. *Cat-Man's Daughter.* Harper, 1981. Kate's father, divorced, is a famous T.V. star (Cat-man). She moves back and forth between parents until her grandmother kidnaps her.

Abrahams, Robert. *Bonus of Redonda.* Macmillan, 1969. Bonus, 13, lives with his fisherman grandfather. He wants to be a calypso singer but he also wants to be ruler of Redonda, a nearby island.

Adair, Gilbert. *Alice Through the Needle's Eye.* Dutton, 1984. A humorous follow-up to Alice in Wonderland and with a witty play on words like A-stack, spelling Bee, etc. Alice sews a button on her knitted cat, dozes off and the adventure begins.

Adair, Margaret. *Far Voice Calling.* Doubleday, 1964. A lonely boy and his pet seal befriend each other but the seal must eventually be returned to live among his own kind.

Adams, Andy. *Trail Drive.* Holiday, 1965. An exciting account of a trail drive with stampedes, water crossings and hazardous trips through trail towns.

Adams, Douglas. *Dirk Gently's Holistic Detec-*

tive Agency. Simon & Schuster, 1987. Dirk wants to practice telekinesis; the Electric Monk wants to find the door that is the way back to his own time. And of course, there's the dead cat.

_____. *Hitchhiker's Guide to the Galaxy.* Crown, 1980. Arthur was just told that the world would end in 12 minutes. He was told this by Ford from the planet Betelgeuse. And then the Vogon vaporized the Earth. A witty spoof on space and poetry.

_____. *Life, the Universe, and Everything.* Crown, 1982. Arthur comes back to Earth; but it is Earth two million years in the past. He is then pulled away from here and sent in search of white killer robots, talking elevators and the God of Thunder!

Adams, Laurie. *Alice and the Boa Constrictor.* Houghton, 1983. Alice is disappointed in her new pet, a boa constrictor.

Adams, Richard. *Plague Dogs.* Knopf, 1978. Rowf and Snitter are on the run from a research center and painful experiments. They want to be free and perhaps learn to trust man again.

_____. *Watership Down.* Macmillan, 1972. The rabbits battle to escape a hostile neighborhood. Lots of harrowing adventures, warm humor and memorable animals.

Adkins, Jan. *Workboats.* Macmillan, 1985. Skip notices that his friend's boat is missing. He searches the harbor and the workboats looking for Peter.

Adler, Carole. *Carly's Buck.* Clarion, 1987. Carly finds her father less than perfect and goes to stay with relatives. She faces the beauty and brutality of animal hunters.

_____. *Cat That Was Left Behind.* Houghton, 1981. A foster child in need of love and care finds a cat that has the same needs.

_____. *Eddie's Blue-Winged Dragon.* Putnam, 1988. Eddie, 11, has cerebral palsy and is bullied by Darrin. He finds a blue-winged dragon and uses it successfully against Darrin.

_____. *Evidence That Wasn't There.* Clarion, 1982. Kim thinks Mr. Orlop is a crook. Tension between the two mounts as Kim looks for evidence strong enough to convict him.

_____. *Fly Free.* Putnam, 1984. A nasty mother, with intent to be cruel, tells her daughter that the man she thought was her father, isn't.

_____. *Footsteps on the Stairs.* Delacorte, 1982. Dodie lives with her mother, stepfather and his children. The children discover the ghosts of girls who drowned there earlier.

————. *Get Lost, Little Brother.* Clarion, 1983. Todd, 12, has an older brother who dominates him. His friend Louis also dominates him. He finally realizes he must fight back.

————. *Good-Bye Pink Pig.* Putnam, 1985. Amanda doesn't fit into her mother's elegant world nor in her brother's easygoing one. She is shy and withdrawn until real trouble hits and she becomes more assertive.

————. *If You Need Me.* Bradbury, 1988. Lyn and Brian are neighbors. Her father and his mother become involved. An abandoned dog adopted by the two kids, helps them cope.

————. *In Our House Scott Is My Brother.* Macmillan, 1980. Jodie's father remarries a woman with a son, Scott. After trouble with drinking and theft the marriage fails but Jodie misses Scott.

————. *Kiss the Clown.* Clarion, 1986. Viki meets Marc and Joel at school. They are very different and she copes well with the family problems of both of them through friendship.

————. *Magic of the Glits.* Macmillan, 1979. Glits are magical beings who can grant wishes. Jeremy and Lynette are kept entertained by "them" all summer.

————. *Once in a While Hero.* Putnam, 1982. A nice, quiet boy is bullied and called a sissy.

————. *One Sister Too Many.* Macmillan, 1989. Case and her sister, Jen, face growing up: first dates, babysitting, and the usual family problems.

————. *Roadside Valentine.* Macmillan, 1983. Jamie, 17, struggles for love, independence and maturity during his senior year of high school.

————. *Shell Lady's Daughter.* Coward, 1983. Kelly, 14, lives with her lonely mother. Her father is away but Kelly must call him for help when her mother gets worse. She is sent to her grandmother but returns to be with her beloved mother.

————. *Shelter on Blue Barns Road.* Nal, 1982. Betsy is trying hard to retrain a Doberman that is vicious.

————. *Silver Coach.* Coward, 1979. Chris and her sister adjust to their parents' upcoming divorce while they spend the summer with their grandmother.

————. *Some Other Summer.* Macmillan, 1982. Lynette, a 13-year-old orphan, is baffled and upset when her long-time friend, Jeremy, comes to spend the summer on her uncle's horse ranch and seems to ignore her.

————. *Split Sisters.* Macmillan, 1986. Case, 11, and Jen, face a separating family. Case stays with her stepfather and Jen with her mother. They try again to make it work.

Adler, David. *Eaton Stanly and the Mind Control Experiment.* Clarion, 1985. Eaton tries a mind control experiment on his teacher. It backfires and Eaton must write a 30-page report on mind control.

————. *Jeffrey's Ghost and the Fifth Grade Dragon.* Holt, 1985. Bradford, the ghost, Jeffrey and Laura cause some problems at school as they write a report on an old schoolhouse and Bradford.

————. *Jeffrey's Ghost and the Leftover Baseball Team.* Holt, 1984. Jeffrey and Laura are on a baseball team made up of kids not chosen for other teams. But the ghost Jeffrey finds in his new house helps them out.

Adrian, Mary. *Fireball Mystery.* Hastings, 1977. Two youngsters uncover a UFO hoax.

Agle, Nan. *Joe Bean.* Seabury, 1967. Joe's in trouble and is sent to live with the Tippers. He runs away and gets into more trouble but returns to the Tippers and improves.

————. *Makon and the Dauphin.* Scribner, 1961. An Indian boy is captured and taken to France. He meets the Dauphin and sees castle life but remains true to his heritage.

————. *Maple Street.* Seabury, 1970. Margaret and Ellie May are not friends. They do learn to understand each other and their neighborhood. Feemster and Percy add humor and interest.

Aiken, Joan. *Arabel and Mortimer.* Doubleday, 1981. Mortimer helps Arabel and her family when he is rewarded for finding a valuable ring. This helps offset all the minor nuisances he has caused since his arrival.

————. *Arabel's Raven.* Doubleday, 1974. Mortimer, the pet raven of Arabel, was injured when he was brought home by her father. He brings chaos wherever he goes. He cries "nevermore" when he is upset.

————. *Black Hearts in Battersea.* Doubleday, 1964. Simon, living homeless in London, stumbles upon a murder plan and has wild and exciting adventures on sea and in the air. His friend Dido has been lost at sea.

————. *Bridle the Wind.* Doubleday, 1983. Felix, a 12-year-old orphan, sails back to Spain with an unexpected friend he has rescued from murder. The trip is not uneventful, including being shipwrecked.

————. *Cuckoo Tree.* Doubleday, 1971. Dido, along with Captain Hughes, is again in England. An accident to the Captain gets Dido involved with King James IV's coronation.

————. *Dido and Pa.* Delacorte, 1986. In this story Dido Twite and Simon fight plotters against the King and her wicked father. Dido had been kidnapped by her father to use in his plan against the King.

————. *Go Saddle the Sea.* Doubleday, 1977. Felix runs away from the cold, loveless home of his grandfather in Spain and seeks to find some members of his father's family in England. He is both accused of murder and kidnapped.

————. *Kingdom and the Cave.* Doubleday, 1974. Prince Michael and various animals fight the Underground people who want to conquer the kingdom. They bravely face risks, captures and escapes.

_____. *Midnight Is a Place*. Viking, 1974. A young boy fights for his rightful inheritance. The setting is the sweatshops of early industrial England.

_____. *Mortimer Says Nothing*. Harper, 1985. This book contains four short stories about Mortimer and Arabel. They are all weird and hilarious.

_____. *Mortimer's Cross*. Harper, 1984. Mortimer gets involved with missing library books and a missing rock star. But, of course, he and Arabel solve them all.

_____. *Night Fall*. Holt, 1971. Meg, 19, has a nightmare about someone falling off a cliff. She tells her friend about it and finds out she did witness a murder on a cliff when she was five years old.

_____. *Nightbirds on Nantucket*. Doubleday, 1966. Dido is rescued at sea by an American ship but when she arrives at Nantucket her troubles begin again and she wants to return to England.

_____. *Shadow Guests*. Delacorte, 1980. Cosmo's mother and brother have disappeared. They are later found dead. He learns about a family curse that could be responsible for these deaths when he goes to live with a cousin.

_____. *Stolen Lake*. Delacorte, 1981. Dido leaves Nantucket for London but her ship is detained at New Cumbria and she helps a queen, living in a revolving castle, recover her stolen lake!

_____. *Teeth of the Gale*. Harper, 1988. Feliz, 18, goes on a rescue journey across Spain at the request of a friendly nun. He and his friend Juana, run into spies and are attacked by bears as they search for a treasure.

_____. *Whispering Mountain*. Doubleday, 1969. Captain Hughes is afraid that his grandson has stolen his magic harp, the Golden Harp of Teiter. But it is the strange beings living under Whispering Mountain who have it.

_____. *Wolves of Willoughby Chase*. Doubleday, 1963. Bonnie and Sylvia escape from an orphanage where they are mistreated. Simon helps them in their many suspenseful, melodramatic misadventures.

Aimatov, Chingez. *White Ship*. Crown, 1972. A young boy believed an ancient legend about Horned Mother Deer. The deer is killed and he tries to swim to his perceived destiny.

Albert, Louise. *But I'm Ready to Go*. Bradbury, 1976. Judy, 15, has learning problems. She writes about her frustration dealing with her inability to handle coordination.

Albrecht, Lillie. *Spinning Wheel Secret*. Hastings, 1965. Joan never learned "womanly" skills; she was raised as a tom-boy. She needed these skills later when she had to care for her grandfather.

_____. *Susanna's Candlestick*. Hastings, 1970. Susanna's parents die on the way from England to America in 1663. She must lead a harsh life and cope with religious intolerance.

Alcock, Gudrun. *Duffy*. Lothrop, 1972. Duffy's father was killed in an auto accident and she went to a foster home because his wife was not her mother, as she had thought.

_____. *Run, Westy, Run*. Lothrop, 1966. Westy runs away from home. He is caught and put in a detention home. He is under a lot of pressure to straighten out and does so.

_____. *Turn the Next Corner*. Lothrop, 1969. Ritchie's father is in jail for embezzlement. The family sells everything to pay back the money; they move and find hard times.

Alcock, Vivien. *Cuckoo Sister*. Delacorte, 1986. Emma was gone two years before Kate was born. Then when she was 11 Emma, now Rosie, came back. She was not what Kate expected but there she was, rude and crude.

_____. *Haunting of Cassie Palmer*. Delacorte, 1982. Cassie is the seventh child of a seventh child and has psychic powers. She raises a ghost, Deverill, who makes her life miserable.

_____. *Monster Garden*. Delacorte, 1988. Frankie's father is a genetic engineer. She grows "something" and then she befriends "it." She must later release it to the sea.

_____. *Mysterious Mr. Ross*. Delacorte, 1987. Felicity saves Mr. Ross from drowning. She is a heroine for a while but then strange things happen. Who is Mr. Ross? Was there a magical albatross?

_____. *Stonewalkers*. Delacorte, 1983. Poppy brings a statue to life. It pursues and imprisons her. She is saved when the statue crumbles. This fantastic experience helps her understand her realistic mother and her concerns.

_____. *Sylvia Game*. Delacorte, 1982. Emily, 12, goes to the seaside and makes friends with a gypsy's son. She very much resembles the long dead Sylvia, a girl in a painting by Renoir. Sylvia drowned in the lake in which the boys now play.

_____. *Travelers by Night*. Delacorte, 1985. Two children kidnap an elephant to keep it from being slaughtered because of its age. They take it to a park where they hope it will find a home.

Alcott, Louisa May. *Eight Cousins*. Little, 1874. Rose, an orphan, lives with her aunt and uncle. She must learn to cope with their seven noisy sons, her cousins.

_____. *Jack and Jill*. Little, 1879. The experiences of a boy and girl who are recovering from a sleigh riding accident.

_____. *Jo's Boys and How They Turned Out*. Little, 1886. More stories about the March family. *Little Women* and the two sequels are well-known classics in literature for young readers.

_____. *Little Men*. Little, 1871. The continuing March family saga, consisting of Jo and Meg's boys. Jo and her professor husband establish a school at Plumfield.

————. *Little Women.* Little, 1868. Meg, Jo, Beth and Amy are sisters in the March family. This is a story of their childhood experiences and the process of growing up in difficult times.

————. *Old Fashioned Girl.* Little, 1870. Polly, a country girl, is on her first trip to a large city. She later returns there as a music teacher.

————. *Rose in Bloom.* Little, 1876. More about Rose as she grows up with many pleasures and a few disappointments. She meets a friend, Phoebe and is being encouraged to marry one of her cousins with whom she has grown up.

————. *Under the Lilacs.* Little, 1877. A story of a circus boy, his dog and all their friends.

Aldiss, Brian. *Year Before Yesterday.* Watts, 1987. A story of what the world would be like if Hitler had won World War II and Europe was controlled by a Fascist government. There was some freedom still alive in Scandinavia.

Aldrich, Bess. *Lantern in Her Hand.* Nal, 1983. Abbie dreams of being rich but in the meantime she must struggle with Indians, snakes, rustlers and all the Nebraska frontier has to offer.

Aldridge, James. *Marvelous Mongolian.* Little, 1974. A wild horse escapes and tries to return home to Mongolia. We learn about it from letters of a boy in Mongolia and a Welsh girl.

————. *Sporting Proposition.* Little, 1973. Scott's best friend, a pony named Taff, disappears. He finds it later when it belongs to someone else. There is a battle over ownership. He wins his horse back but the girl who gave him up is sad.

Aleksin, Anatoli. *Alik, the Detective.* Morrow, 1977. Alik is an avid detective story reader. Then one day he is involved in a real mystery.

————. *Late Born Child.* World, 1971. Lenny is born 16 years late to elderly parents. His sister and parents spoil him. His father has a heart attack and all does not go well.

Alexander, Anne. *To Live a Lie.* Atheneum, 1975. Jennifer is in junior high school and has no friends because she wants none. But that changed when her sister got chicken pox. The lie was about her mother being dead.

Alexander, Lloyd. *Beggar Queen.* Dutton, 1984. Mickle is now Queen Agusta and Theo is her consular. But peace does not last and Theo must fight again for Queen Agusta against Duke Conrad of Regia.

————. *Black Cauldron.* Holt, 1965. Taran fights the evil threat against Prydain and knows that to succeed he must destroy the Black Cauldron where living persons, who sold themselves into evil, are kept.

————. *Book of Three.* Holt, 1964. Taran and Gwydion go off to fight the Horned King and his Cauldron Born. They are accompanied by many others whom one can meet in later books.

————. *Castle of Llyr.* Holt, 1966. Taran learns that he loves Eilonwy, the Princess of Llyr, when she is kidnapped and he must rescue her. He is aided by Prince Gwydion.

————. *Cat Who Wished to Be a Man.* Dutton, 1973. The cat coaxed his master into turning him into a man. He solved problems, fell in love and thereby became human.

————. *Drackenberg Adventure.* Dutton, 1988. Vesper tangles with Dr. Helvitius, her number one enemy. He is looking for an art treasure.

————. *El Dorado Adventure.* Dutton, 1987. Vesper stops a canal from being built because it would destroy the homeland of an Indian tribe. Again evil Helvitius is foiled, this time by a volcano eruption.

————. *First Two Lives of Lukas-Kasha.* Dutton, 1978. Lukas is transported by a street magician to another land where he finds himself the king.

————. *Foundling and Other Tales.* Holt, 1973. Background tales about the times in Prydain before Taran was born.

————. *High King.* Holt, 1968. Taran and Prince Gwydion again battle the Land of Death lord, Arawn. Taran's quest for his heritage is ended and his future settled.

————. *Illyrian Adventure.* Dutton, 1986. Vesper, a 16-year-old orphan, researches an ancient legend and gets involved in a conspiracy to murder King Osman.

————. *Jedera Adventure.* Dutton, 1989. Vesper Holly returns an overdue library book that her father borrowed. It begins another adventure of Vesper with slave traders, desert wars and, of course, Dr. Helvitius.

————. *Kestrel.* Dutton, 1982. Theo, Mickle and Muscrat are fighting bloody wars for the king and Westmark. Mickle takes her rightful place in the palace. Theo turns into an "animal" willing to kill but recovers slowly.

————. *Marvelous Misadventures of Sebastian.* Dutton, 1970. Sebastian is a fiddler in the Kingdom of Hamelin-Loring but loses his position and must go away. On his adventurous way he meets a princess, helps an orphan girl, joins a circus, etc.

————. *Tartan Wanderer.* Holt, 1967. Taran is anxious to find out his real parentage but finds out a great deal about himself and his current position. He learns to weave, to forge a sword and to try sculpting clay.

————. *Time Cat: Remarkable Journeys of Jason and Gareth.* Smith, 1963. Jason and his cat, Gareth, time travel to other times and places.

————. *Westmark.* Dutton, 1981. A young boy, fleeing from criminal charges, travels with Musket, Mickle and Count Las Bombas to a palace in Westmark where the king is in deep sorrow over his lost daughter.

————. *Wizard in the Tree.* Dutton, 1975. A good versus evil struggle involving an orphan, Mallory, a wizard, and a battle against Mrs. Parsel and Squire Scrupnor.

Alexander, Sue. *Lila on the Landing.* Ticknor, 1987. Lila lives in an apartment where she finds a special place to act out her imaginary games.

———. *Nadia the Willful.* Pantheon, 1983. A story of an Arabian girl controlled by her brother. He disappears and his name is never spoken by the family but Nadia helps keep his memory alive.

Allan, Mabel. *Ballet Family.* Criterion, 1966. Joan, orphaned and alone, lives with a family of ballet dancers and discovers she, too, has talent.

———. *Black Forest Summer.* Vanguard, 1959. Three English girls spend the summer in Germany where they study painting, ballet and foreign languages.

———. *Chill in the Lane.* Nelson, 1974. Lyd, adopted, visits Cornwall where she sees a ghost while under a spell. There is suspense and terror before it is all explained.

———. *Dancing Garlands: Ballet Family Again.* Criterion, 1969. Pelagia had not married Timothy because of her career. Edward finds his girl is interested in his family, not him; Anna loses her best friend and Delphine's accident may prevent her from dancing.

———. *Dream of Hunger Moss.* Dodd, 1983. Hunger Moss is a swampy piece of land that Adam discovers. It was there that his mother met a man called Reuben; Adam and his sister, Alice, meet a man by the same name in the same place.

———. *Flash Children.* Dodd, 1975. Dilys is not accepted by Arthur but she is determined to make friends and show she can be trusted.

———. *Hilary's Summer on Her Own.* Norton, 1966. Hilary has a romance in France as she spends the summer working there as a governess.

———. *Horns of Danger.* Dodd, 1981. Marissa and her friend Sabrina see "the horns": a set of ancient antlers that are worn at festivals. But the horns are locked away. The two girls and their boyfriends solve the mystery.

———. *Johnny Reb.* Longmans, 1952. A young boy from South Carolina joins the cavalry during the Civil War and tells the Southern cause as he sees it.

———. *Kraymer Mystery.* Criterion, 1969. Karen tries to learn about a family mystery: a dead girl at the bottom of the stairway and the missing necklace. She learns the truth but does not tell because of the trouble it would cause.

———. *May Day Mystery.* Criterion, 1971. Laura and her friend Rose go to the May Day festival. There is a mystery about some Poldern Cups that were stolen 20 years before.

———. *Mystery in Rome.* Vanguard, 1974. Flavia goes to Rome with her companion. She hears of a murder plot and someone shoots at her.

———. *Mystery of the Ski Slopes.* Criterion, 1966. Perdita, in disguise, tries to find her kidnapped cousin. She meets a young man who helps her find the cousin in an old hotel. They all escape.

———. *Night Wind.* Atheneum, 1974. Robin lives in an orphanage with her friend Tafline. They run away to the seaside for three days to be themselves and dream.

———. *On Stage, Flory.* Watts, 1961. A young girl wants to be an actress and gets her chance at a summer festival. She faces joys and sorrows, problems and excitement.

———. *Rising Tide.* Walker, 1976. Fennel and Sue find that Welsh terrorists are forcing Ceiridwen and her grandfather to aid them in making bombs to be used against the English.

———. *Romansgrove.* Atheneum, 1975. Clare found a pendant which transported her and her brother back to 1902. They meet Emily and bring her back to the 1970s.

———. *Sign of the Unicorn.* Criterion, 1963. Julia meets two strange people who lead her to blackmail and murder. She is kidnapped and taken to Unicorn House.

———. *Signpost to Switzerland.* Criterion, 1964. Camilla, 17, just graduated and went to Switzerland to see friends of her father's. She is spoiled with shallow values. She resents the trip at first but comes to realize true values and happiness.

———. *Strange Enchantment.* Dodd, 1982. Primrose, 16, joins the war effort by working on a farm and although the work is hard and the hours long she likes what she is doing.

———. *Time to Go Back.* Criterion, 1972. Sara goes back to 1941 and is herself in an air raid shelter with two sisters, Larke and Clem. Clem will later become her mother.

———. *View Beyond My Father.* Dodd, 1977. Mary Ann, 15, is blind and overprotected. She recovers the sight of one eye and becomes more independent.

Allan, Ted. *Willie the Squowse.* Hastings, 1978. Willie is part mouse and part squirrel. He lives in the walls between two houses whose owners are very different people.

Allen, Alexander. *Tennis Menace.* Whitman, 1975. Andy wants to play in a tennis tournament but he must improve his game. He needs a court and a challenging partner. He finds both.

Allen, Elizabeth. *Loser.* Dutton, 1963. Deitz likes a boy her parents do not approve of. It turns out that he, Denny, really is a phony and Deitz takes a good look at herself and her values.

———. *Younger's Race.* Grosset, 1972. A story about amateur drag racing. Two brothers and a stepbrother have a car called Purple Haze. They also have family problems.

Allen, Judy. *Spring on the Mountain.* Farrar, 1973. Peter, Michael and Emma follow a mythical path, "Arthur Way." They disturb ancient magic and almost bring tragedy upon themselves.

Allen, Leroy. *Shawnee Lance.* Delacorte, 1970. Daniel is captured by the Shawnee and is adopted. He adapts but still looks for a chance to escape but when it comes he does not take it.

Allen, Linda. *Lionel and the Spy Next Door.* Morrow, 1980. Lionel gets a new neighbor, Mark Shakespeare, and believes him to be a spy.

Allen, Sybil. *Lissamor's Child.* Nelson, 1975. Kate and her family come to live at Lissamor, a gloomy, old mansion. Kate finds the house is haunted and only she can break the spell.

Allman, Paul. *No Pain, No Gain.* Rosen, 1987. Sedge and Eric are football teammates. They break the rules and go out drinking and driving and have an accident. Sedge is hurt and Eric is blamed. The story is told from the viewpoint of each boy.

Almedingen, E.M. *Anna.* Farrar, 1972. Anna is the fourth generation daughter. She masters many languages, meets an empress and a handsome young man.

_____. *Candle at Dusk.* Farrar, 1969. Idrun of eighth century France wants to read and write. He kills a wild boar and becomes a hero who can ask for what he wants.

_____. *Crimson Oak.* Putnam, 1983. The setting is Czarist Russia and the theme is what it was like to be young and growing up at that time.

_____. *Ellen.* Farrar, 1976. Mark's daughter is the main character in this next book. She marries the richest man in Russia.

_____. *Fanny.* Farrar, 1970. Fanny is Ellen's daughter and Mark's granddaughter. The story of sophisticated and literary talented Frances de Poltratzky.

_____. *Katia.* Farrar, 1966. After her mother dies, Katie goes to live with a strict cousin. She also dies and Katie returns to her father's household with her step mother.

_____. *Stephen's Light.* Holt, 1969. Sabrina is an educated girl who is deserted by her fiance. She goes into business for herself, which is shocking in 15th century Germany.

_____. *Story of Gudrun.* Holt, 1967. Gudrun, a princess, is kidnapped before her wedding day by the mother of a rejected suitor. She survives the cruelty, returns to her lover and throne and wants peace, not revenge.

_____. *Young Mark.* Farrar, 1967. Mark sets on an adventure to fulfill his dreams of becoming a singer. This begins a four generation story of a remarkable family.

Alter, Judy. *After Pa Was Shot.* Morrow, 1978. Ellsbeth's father dies and her mother can't cope. She does all the work in their boarding house. Ma remarries a man who steals their money and runs away. Ellsbeth goes to look for him.

_____. *Luke and the Van Zandt County War.* Christian Univ., 1984. Two different boys tell about life in Texas after the end of the Civil War.

Alter, Robert. *Listen, the Drum.* Putnam, 1963. Matt met young George Washington. He is accused of causing trouble but proves himself a loyal American. There is fighting with both the French and the Indians.

Altman, Millys. *Racing in Her Blood.* Lippincott, 1980. Jane resents all that her twin brother may do that she can't. But she learns to race and ends up teaming up with her brother.

Amdur, Nikki. *One of Us.* Dial, 1981. Neva, who has just moved to a new town, slowly adjusts.

Amerman, Lockhart. *Cape Cod Casket.* Harcourt, 1964. Jonathan is pursued because of his foreign agent father. The hunt is a dangerous one. He is kidnapped but escapes. He finds his father and they hunt the hunters.

_____. *Guns in the Heather.* Harcourt, 1963. Jonathan, known as Posy, accepts a job as tutor for twins of Dr. Sarx who is really a mad scientist.

_____. *Sly One.* Harcourt, 1966. Jonathan's father is a secret agent and Jonathan usually gets involved in what his father does. This time it is gypsies and organized crime.

Ames, Mildred. *Anna to the Infinite Power.* Scribner, 1981. Anna will lie and steal; she is friendless; she is a math genius. She is actually part of an experiment: a clone of a famous chemist.

_____. *Cassandra-Jamie.* Scribner, 1985. Jamie has a crush on her teacher, Ms. Schuyler. She tries to match her and her father because she wants her as a mother not the lady her dad has chosen. It leads to many problems.

_____. *Conjuring Summer In.* Harper, 1986. Bernadette becomes involved in the occult through a shop that caters in that sort of thing and through her step brother and his tarot reading girlfriend. She ends up being a possible murder victim.

_____. *Is There Life on a Plastic Planet?* Dutton, 1975. Hollis is overweight and can't get along with others. A doll is made to replace her. She can't tell anyone she is Hollis because the doll is just like her. No one can tell the dolls from the real girls.

_____. *Philo Potts, or the Helping Hand Strikes Again.* Scribner, 1982. Philo lives with his dad. He takes a dog that is tied to a tree. The dog runs away and joins a pack, so Philo takes in the whole pack. They become ill and need medical care. So he runs away.

_____. *Silver Link, the Silken Tie.* Scribner, 1984. Two high school students with ESP are hiding from their past. A teacher, leader of a cult, tries to brain wash them but they overcome it and learn to love.

_____. *What Are Friends For?* Scribner, 1978. Amy and Michelle are friends because both sets of parents are divorced. Michelle steals a valuable doll and then gets help for her psychological problems.

_____. *Without Hats, Who Can Tell the Good Guys?* Dutton, 1976. Anthony didn't like his foster home. He kept waiting for his dad who never came. He and his kind foster father learn to get along.

Amoss, Berthe. *Chalk Cross.* Seabury, 1976. Stephanie, who is in art school, sets out to sketch old houses and ends up going back in time to a Voodoo Queen.

————. *Mockingbird Song.* Harper, 1988. Lindy has a new mother, Mille, so she moves in with the nice lady next door until Mille has a baby. She returns and adjusts to a new family.

————. *Secret Lives.* Little, 1979. Addie is raised by an aunt. She finds a letter and diary in the attic and seeks to find what really happened to her mother.

Anastasio, Dina. *Question of Time.* Dutton, 1978. Syd must move from New York City. She hardly ever leaves her new home but when she does, she finds Mr. Stowe and his dolls. They are really ghosts of live people.

Anckarsvard, Karin. *Aunt Vinnie's Invasion.* Harcourt, 1962. The six Hallsenius children spend a year with Aunt Vinnie. They plan a birthday party for her because she listens to and understands them.

————. *Aunt Vinnie's Victorious Six.* Harcourt, 1964. Aunt Vinnie in her late 60's has six nieces and nephews to watch while their parents are away. Per, 9, and Lottie, 12, are the main characters.

————. *Doctor's Boy.* Harcourt, 1965. Jon tries to make friends with Richard. He is well to do and Richard is poor but they get to know and understand each other.

————. *Madcap Mystery.* Harcourt, 1962. Michael and Cecilia and their friends try to solve some mysterious robberies in their home town. They were being done by youngsters just for the fun of it.

————. *Mysterious Schoolmaster.* Harcourt, 1959. Michael and Cecilia notice the strange behavior of their new teacher. A spy thriller about military secrets and a code.

————. *Riddle of the Ring.* Harcourt, 1966. Tommie loses a valuable ring given to her by her mother. A new boy at school is suspected of taking it.

————. *Rider by Night.* Harcourt, 1960. Rascal, a horse, seems to be listless. A young girl who owns him thinks someone is riding him at night.

————. *Robber Ghost.* Harcourt, 1961. Bertil needs to be accepted so he throws a parentless party and spikes the punch. He pretends to be a ghost to protect the money he stole from other robbers. Michael and Cecilia know he's guilty.

————. *Springtime for Eva.* Harcourt, 1959. Eva's friend, Lena, asks Eva to double date. They have an auto accident in which Ingemar, Eva's date, is hurt and Lena's date is killed. She tries to forget the tragedy and meets David whom she likes.

————. *Struggle at Soltuna.* Harcourt, 1960. Jon is learning the great difference between the rich and the poor when he rescues a poor boy about to be sold into service. He then goes on to learn more about living and working conditions.

Anderson, Clarence. *Blind Connemara.* Macmillan, 1971. Rhonda knows her white pony is going blind but doesn't want him to be killed. She and the pony struggle to make him confident and self reliant.

Anderson, Joan. *Joshua's Westward Journal.* Morrow, 1987. The fifth book about the Carpenter family as they travel westward in their Conestoga wagon.

————. *Pioneer Children of Appalachia.* Ticknor, 1986. The Davis family lives in Appalachia in the early 1800's and work hard to make the land pay off.

Anderson, John. *Zeb.* Knopf, 1966. Zeb must survive the winter with his dog, Rash, and little else. An accident separated him from his father. He had no food or gun.

Anderson, Margaret. *Brain on Quartz Mountain.* Knopf, 1982. There is a brain growing in a scientist's lab that is trying to take over a body.

————. *Druid's Gift.* Knopf, 1989. Caitlin is the daughter of the feared Druids. She travels forward in time and sees what is coming to her people.

————. *Hairy Beast in the Woods.* Dell, 1989. Winnie lives in Minnesota where wolves are enemies. She protects them on her property and raises the animosity of her neighbors.

————. *In the Circle of Time.* Knopf, 1979. Robert and Jennifer are interested in the Stones of Arden. They time-travel to the future. Energy is scarce and slaves are being used. Robert returns but Jennifer is left behind and must be rescued.

————. *In the Keep of Time.* Knopf, 1977. Ollie, Jan, Elinor and Andrew spend the summer with Aunt Grace. They enter the past and battle with King James II against England.

————. *Journey of the Shadow Bairns.* Knopf, 1980. Elspeth's father wants to own land in Canada. But he dies before he can complete the deal so Elspeth and her brother go to Canada to find relatives.

————. *Leipzig Vampire.* Dell, 1987. Amy and Jamie are involved in an occult mystery with an evil magician.

————. *Light in the Mountain.* Knopf, 1982. A legend of the Maori people of New Zealand. Rana is to be sacrificed but is saved by trickery which she uses to become a leader of her people. A young priestess becomes leader at her death.

————. *Mists of Time.* Knopf, 1984. A group of island dwellers who love and trust one another clash with the Mainlanders who pursue technology.

————. *Searching for Shona.* Knopf, 1978. Marjorie, a rich girl, changes places with a poor girl, Shona. Both are successful but then Shona refuses to admit to the switch.

————. *To Nowhere and Back.* Knopf, 1975.

Elizabeth went to England with her parents and through time-travel met Ann Lauden of 100 years before and steps back into her life.

Anderson, Mary. *Do You Call That a Dream Date?* Delacorte, 1987. Jennifer wins a date with Matt Gates, a rock star. She cheated by using her sister's essay and her sister exposes her deception.

_____. *F.T.C. and Company*. Atheneum, 1979. Freddie, the cat, and Emma rid a theatre of ghosts and start a theatrical company of their own. But the building is to be wrecked.

_____. *F.T.C. Superstar*. Atheneum, 1976. Freddie, the cat, is stage struck. His friend Emma helps teach him the tricks of the trade. He starts making commercials. But does he really want fame?

_____. *I'm Nobody! Who Are You?* Atheneum, 1974. Overweight, shy Ellie is befriended by Stephanie who has troubles of her own.

_____. *Matilda Investigates*. Atheneum, 1973. Matilda wants to be a detective. She buys a microscope and her brother helps her find a crow that is trained to steal things.

_____. *Matilda's Masterpiece*. Atheneum, 1977. A $50,000 Degas painting is stolen. After two blundering attempts Matilda finds the thief.

_____. *Rise and Fall of a Teen-Age Wacko*. Atheneum, 1980. Laura, 16, stays in her parents' friends' apartment to babysit for two weeks. She discovers the ups and downs of living in New York City.

_____. *Who Says Nobody's Perfect?* Delacorte, 1987. Jenny and her friend Liza try to be popular but Ingvild is prettier and more popular. A rivalry begins but everybody wins in the end.

_____. *You Can't Get There from Here*. Atheneum, 1982. Reggie wants to be an actress. She and her friend Pansy go to drama school where the owner is unscrupulous and must be stopped from doing more damage.

Anderson, Paul. *Boy and the Blind Storyteller*. Scott, 1964. Au Sung, a Korean boy, listens to the blind storyteller of his village and learns why sparrows hop, if dogs and cats are really enemies, etc.

Anderson, Rachel. *Poacher's Son*. Oxford, 1983. Arthur is the son of a gamekeeper accused of poaching. They live in poverty. Arthur becomes a poacher and is caught. The future life of both him and his sister is bleak.

_____. *War Orphan*. Merrimack, 1986. Simon's family take in a Vietnamese war orphan named Ha. Simon learns a lot about the war and its effect on families by talking to Ha about his life in Vietnam.

Andrews, J.S. *Cargo for a King*. Dutton, 1973. Rangor and his father's friend John de Courcy avenge his father's death and win the confidence of King John. A strong sea story.

_____. *Green Hills of Nendrum*. Hawthorn, 1973. A boy is transferred to tenth century Ireland. A freak storm sends him to a monastery.

Andrews, Jean. *Dear Dola: or, How to Build Your Own Family*. Dell, 1980. Six children make a life for themselves as a family after they run away from an orphanage.

_____. *Flying Fingers Club*. Gallaudet, 1988. Two boys are close friends even though one of them is deaf.

Andrews, Mary. *Hostage to Alexander*. Longmans, 1961. Damon is held captive by Alexander's men. He follows Alexander's army into Persia, all the while looking for his brother, Leon.

Andrews, Prudence. *Dog*. Nelson, 1973. Andrew is forbidden to have a dog. He finds a stray one and hides him in an old abandoned car.

Angell, Judie. *Buffalo Nickel Blues Band*. Bradbury, 1982. A group of kids form a band, first three then two more. Their first gig is a disaster. They like Blues but the audience wants Rock.

_____. *First the Good News*. Putnam, 1983. Five girls are in love with a TV star and must meet him. After all kinds of tricks and ploys, an older sister unwittingly helps.

_____. *Home Is to Share and Share and Share*. Bradbury, 1984. Bucky, Jeanette and Harry like stray pets. First a dog who has puppies, then a cat and kittens then a duck and a monkey....

_____. *In Summertime It's Tuffy*. Bradbury, 1977. Tuffy is going to Camp Ma-Sha-Na. Everyone likes the counselor but not the camp director, Otto. They try to voodoo him and it seems to work.

_____. *One-Way to Ansonia*. Bradbury, 1985. Rose must get away from her cruel employer and get to safety. She takes her three dollars and goes to Ansonia Station.

_____. *Ronnie and Rosey*. Bradbury, 1977. Ronnie, Rosie (Robert) and Evelyn are friends. Ronnie's father is killed and her mother doesn't like her to have Rosie as a friend.

_____. *Secret Selves*. Bradbury, 1979. Julie likes the new boy in the nurse's office. She calls him on the phone but asks for a fictitious person and assumes a different identity. He does the same.

_____. *Suds*. Bradbury, 1983. Sue, 15, loses both her parents and lives with an aunt and uncle. A funny story that is a spoof on soap operas and "normal" teen life.

_____. *Tina Gogo*. Bradbury, 1978. Sarajane meets Tina Gogo who is hostile and angry but they become friends. Tina is a foster child and unhappy about it and doesn't want anyone to know.

_____. *Weird Disappearance of Jordan Hall*. Watts, 1987. Jordan, 16, works in a magic shop and one day becomes invisible. No one knows how to make him re-appear.

_____. *What's Best for You*. Bradbury, 1981. Lee has a summer job, friends and a boyfriend. She likes her dad. Her mother wants her to come and visit, her job is in jeopardy, and her boyfriend finds someone else.

_____. *Word from Our Sponsor or My Friend Alfred.* Bradbury, 1979. Rudy, Gillian and Alfred find dangerous lead in a give away cup. They want to try to stop its distribution.

Angier, Bradford. *Ask for Love and They Give You Rice Pudding.* Houghton, 1977. Robbie has everything but friends. His father's gone, his mother's an alcoholic and his grandparents think he's a bum. He's had chances but has blown them all.

Annixter, Jane. *Horns of Plenty.* Holiday, 1960. Gary, 16, struggles with bears, cougars and rams in the wilderness of Montana. Meanwhile he and his father resolve their differences.

_____. *Last Monster.* Harcourt, 1980. A grizzly bear crippled Ron's father and he is determined to kill it.

_____. *Runner.* Holiday, 1956. In order to be accepted by his aunt and uncle, a young boy feels he must prove to them that he is not like his father.

_____. *Wagon Scout.* Holiday, 1965. Eric is a scout for the train route across the Rocky Mountains. It carries a lot of responsibility. The whole train depends on him to save them from robbers, Indians and wild animals, and to get them water.

_____. *White Shell Horse.* Holiday, 1971. The Navajo history of the 400 mile march and the four years of starvation. Agapito and his colt, which he rescues, have only each other to bring peace and love.

Anonymous. *Go Ask Alice.* Prentice, 1971. A girl, 15, tells of the day-by-day terrifying experiences she had with drugs, her attempt at stopping and the tragic ending of her life.

Appleby, Jon. *Skate.* Farrar, 1972. Jim and Skate are friends in an orphan's home. They later become a doctor and a philosopher. Skate rejects the world where Jim is a successful doctor.

Appleton, Victor. *Alien Probe.* Simon & Schuster, 1981. Tom and his friends are back on Earth. The officer steals the probe and gives it to their rival. They rescue the probe and learn its secret before it is destroyed.

_____. *City in the Stars.* Simon & Schuster, 1981. Tom designs a spaceship, makes friends with a computer expert and a hot tempered, red-headed girl.

_____. *Terror on the Moons of Jupiter.* Simon & Schuster, 1981. Tom and his friends build a robot on their way to Jupiter. They discover a space probe and alienate a military officer.

_____. *War in Outer Space.* Simon & Schuster, 1981. Tom and his friends go to rescue Skree from Chutans. Tom has all he needs to explore space possibilities.

Archer, Jeffrey. *Shall We Tell the President?* Viking, 1977. A story of a president (Edward Ken-

nedy) trying to push through gun control legislation. Meanwhile Marc Andrews of the FBI is trying to identify and stop an assassination plan.

Archer, Marian. *Keys for Signe.* Whitman, 1965. Signe moves to the city in 1868 and begins high school. She makes friends and discovers that there are keys to happiness as well as fear and unhappiness.

_____. *There Is a Happy Land.* Whitman, 1963. Signe's parents move to America. She doesn't go with them but joins them later and finds them very changed and not for the better.

Archibald, Joe. *Backcourt Commando.* Macrae, 1970. Gary's father and brother were basketball players. He feels he couldn't compete with them. He signs on with the same team as his brother and becomes a better player than anyone.

_____. *Crazy Legs McBain.* Macrae, 1961. After two years in college, Hal finally gets a chance to try for the football team.

_____. *Phantom Blitz.* Macrae, 1972. The Mustangs are losing games and fighting an anti-football group. They play hard, learn new plays and fight like tigers.

_____. *Powerback.* Macrae, 1970. A story of a college football season where some of the players overcome family and personal problems to become pros.

_____. *Pro Coach.* Macrae, 1969. Walt quit his coaching job and went with the Pilgrims who were losing every game. He ended the year with more wins than losses.

_____. *Right Field Runt.* Macrae, 1972. Gary wants to be like his brother Kevin and become a baseball player. He is encouraged by friends. He also has a horse he races and both of his dreams come true: baseball and horse racing.

Arden, William. *Mystery of the Dancing Devil.* Random, 1976. This is one of the many (40 some) books with the Three Investigators. They search for a stolen art statue and find a life-size, alive version of it.

_____. *Mystery of the Dead Man's Riddle.* Random, 1974. The Three Investigators go on a high stakes treasure hunt to restore a fortune to their rightful heirs.

_____. *Mystery of the Deadly Double.* Random, 1978. Juniper, an investigator, is kidnapped because he resembles someone else. Pete and Bob fight their way through several mysteries to rescue him and save both Ian and his father.

_____. *Mystery of the Purple Pirate.* Random, 1982. The Three Investigators look for a legendary pirate treasure. Each boy solves the mystery from his own perspective.

_____. *Mystery of the Shrinking House.* Random, 1972. The Three Investigators solve a case involving an international gang of art forgers.

_____. *Mystery of the Smashing Glass.* Random, 1984. A series of car windows are shattered all over town and the Three Investigators must find out why. They find a thief who stole a valuable coin.

————. *Mystery of Wrecker's Rock*. Random, 1986. The Three Investigators take pictures at a family reunion and are caught up in a gold hunt, an insurance scam and a possible ghost.

————. *Secret of Shark Reef*. Random, 1970. The story centers around Shark Reef #1, an offshore drilling rig. Ecology, demonstrators, saboteurs and sunken subs are part of the mystery.

————. *Secret of the Phantom Lake*. Random, 1973. This mystery involves an Oriental chest, a sunken ship and a strange dual identity.

Arkin, Alan. *Lemming Condition*. Harper, 1976. Bubber, a lemming, knows about the legendary leap into the sea but he pulls back at the last minute with five other lemmings to begin a future.

Armer, Alberta. *Screwball*. World, 1963. Michael, who had polio, is one half of twin brothers. Patrick plays baseball and Michael fishes. They move to the city where Patrick made friends but Michael didn't.

————. *Troublemaker*. World, 1966. Joe is not an orphan but is in a foster home because his father is in jail and his mother is in the hospital. He fights rules for a while but slowly adjusts to good behavior.

Armer, Laura. *Waterless Mountain*. Longman, 1931. Younger Brother is an Indian who learns songs from the tribe's medicine men. Newbery winner, 1932.

Armstrong, Richard. *Big Sea*. McKay, 1965. A story of a shipwreck. The "S.S. Kariba" is abandoned but two seamen remain on board. They have a hazardous ordeal but are rescued just in the nick of time.

————. *Mutineers*. McKay, 1968. To escape punishment for an unsuccessful mutiny, a group of boys run away and live alone on an island.

————. *Secret Sea*. McKay, 1966. Thor, 18, goes on his first whaling trip. A series of fatal accidents leave him as the only survivor.

————. *Ship Afire*. Day, 1961. During World War II a ship is shelled and the men are adrift. There are an enemy submarine and a surface craft to contend with.

————. *Trial Trip*. Criterion, 1963. Rod, a teen age orphan becomes a galley boy to escape the hardship at home. He is loyal to his friend Tich, an officer in training.

Armstrong, William. *Sounder*. Harper, 1969. When his father is jailed for stealing food during hard times in the South, his young son and 'coon dog look for him in the chain gangs. He meets a former teacher who befriends him.

————. *Sour Land*. Harper, 1971. The young boy grows up to be a teacher in the South where he finds both respect and injustice. A stark story of prejudice, rape and murder.

Arnold, Elliott. *Kind of Secret Weapon*. Scribner, 1961. Peter's parents are involved in the Resistance movement in Denmark during World War II. He takes risks and shows a great deal of loyalty, patriotism and love.

Arnold, Oren. *Mystery of Superstition Mountain*. Harvey House, 1972. Bill befriended the old Dutchman and on his deathbed he told Bill about the mine. Bill, Dan and others go to look for it. The rugged mountains were treacherous but it united the group in their search.

Arnosky, Jim. *Gray Boy*. Lothrop, 1988. Gray Boy, a dog, runs free and destroys some prize rabbits. He is locked up, escapes and runs wild. He later saves his owner's life with his own death.

Arora, Shirley. *What Then, Raman?* Follett, 1960. Raman is the first in his village to learn to read. He then begins to teach others and learn responsibility.

Arrick, Fran. *Chernowitz*. Bradbury, 1981. Bobby is Jewish and is teased by a bully in his new school. Emmett keeps this up. Bobby plants a radio in Emmett's locker causing Emmet lots of trouble. He confesses his part and anti–Semitism is explored.

————. *God's Radar*. Bradbury, 1983. Roxie, 15, moves to a small town where fundamentalism is strong. Roxie is caught up in their beliefs and is torn between their values and her new friend, Jarrell.

————. *Nice Girl from Good Home*. Bradbury, 1984. Dory and Jeremy's father is an alcoholic; their mother a psychotic. Dory is having social problems and only Jeremy is stable. He helps his father gain control, Dory improves and their mother is under care.

————. *Steffie Can't Come Out to Play*. Bradbury, 1978. Steffie ran away from home to become a famous model. She didn't want to end up like her mother and sister. When she got off the bus her future was waiting . . . in the form of a pimp.

————. *Tunnel Vision*. Bradbury, 1980. A story about the guilt and bewilderment of Anthony's family, friends, girlfriend and teachers when he commits suicide.

Arthur, Robert. *Mystery of the Cranky Collector*. Random, 1987. A book collector disappears and the Three Investigators break into his computer looking for clues and uncover a "purple past."

————. *Mystery of the Creep Show Crooks*. Random, 1985. The Three Investigators get involved with shady producers of horror films and a runaway teenager.

————. *Mystery of the Death Trap Mine*. Random, 1976. The Three Investigators and Allie try to untangle the unusual circumstances surrounding an abandoned mine.

————. *Mystery of the Flaming Footprints*. Random, 1971. An eccentric local artist disappears and the Three Investigators look into this very sudden happening.

————. *Mystery of the Magic Circle*. Random, 1978. The Three Investigators uncover a coven of witches when they search for the missing memoirs of a movie star.

_____. *Mystery of the Missing Mermaid.* Random, 1983. A statue of a mermaid is a clue to a missing child. The Three Investigators get to work.

_____. *Mystery of the Rogues Reunion.* Random, 1985. The reunion of a group of child movie stars takes the Three Investigators into theft, kidnapping and false identity.

_____. *Mystery of the Screaming Clock.* Random, 1968. This time the mystery concerns a strange clock that screams. The Three Investigators must find out how and why.

_____. *Mystery of the Stuttering Parrot.* Random, 1964. This is a case of missing parrots brought from Mexico who have learned to speak. In their speech is the secret to the mystery that the Three Investigators must solve.

_____. *Mystery of the Trail of Terror.* Random, 1984. The Three Investigators go to New York with Pete's uncle to sell his invention. There they get involved in a spy ring.

_____. *Mystery of the Vanishing Treasure.* Random, 1966. Jupiter, Pete, and Bob, the Three Investigators, are involved in a baffling museum robbery and almost end up in the Middle East.

_____. *Mystery of the Wandering Cave-man.* Random, 1982. The disappearance of a caveman's bones from a museum leads the Three Investigators to uncover skullduggery at a science foundation.

_____. *Mystery of the Whispering Mummy.* Random, 1965. Jupiter, Pete, and Bob, the Three Investigators, won the use of a car and driver and are making good use of it.

_____. *Secret of Terror Castle.* Random, 1964. The Three Investigators look for a haunted house. They look at the home of a former movie star and run into ghosts and spooks and a well kept secret.

Arthur, Ruth. *Autumn People.* Atheneum, 1973. Three generations of Romillys visit Karasay Island. Their lives seem to be interwoven and to have a supernatural quality.

_____. *Candle in Her Room.* Atheneum, 1966. Briony found the doll in the house her father had inherited. The doll, Dido, exorcized her. And did so for three generations until a girl finally destroys it.

_____. *Little Dark Thorn.* Atheneum, 1971. Merrie arrives in England from Malaysia. She goes to live with her father and his new wife, and makes life miserable for everyone around her. She does change in the end.

_____. *Miss Ghost.* Atheneum, 1979. Elspeth lives with her grandmother. She is anti-social and emotionally disturbed. In a special school she finds a room and a ghost that lead her to recovery.

_____. *Old Magic.* Atheneum, 1977. Hanni tells of her life on a sheep farm as a bride, as a mother whose son marries a gypsy and as a grandmother. Magic and romance abound.

_____. *On the Wasteland.* Atheneum, 1975. Betony lives in an orphanage. She becomes Estrith, a Viking, through visions and dreams. In real life her friend Yetty helps her.

_____. *Portrait of Margarita.* Atheneum, 1968. Margarita's parents are killed and she lives with a rich cousin. She thinks she loves him but finds true love elsewhere where her dark complexion is not noticed.

_____. *Requiem for a Princess.* Atheneum, 1967. Willow, 15, is adopted and fights with her "parents." She dreams of a 16th century adopted girl and this helps her sort out her own problems.

_____. *Saracen Lamp.* Atheneum, 1970. Melisande is a bride in 1300. She receives a lamp as a gift and it is in the family for 200 years. Alys finds the lamp missing at that time. Then Perdita returns it to the rightful owners years later.

_____. *Whistling Boy.* Atheneum, 1969. Kirsty and Jake, a boy she met the summer she worked as a fruit picker, are involved with the whistling boy and a ghost.

Arundel, Honor. *Blanket Word.* Nelson, 1973. Janet's mother dies of cancer and Janet refuses to show any love or warm feelings, still determined to be independent. But she tries to become understanding of what love means.

_____. *Emma in Love.* Nelson, 1970. Emma and Richard are both back in London to go to school. Emma is in love with Alistair, a boy she met on the island, but he doesn't want to be pinned down and Emma loses perspective.

_____. *Emma's Island.* Hawthorn, 1968. Emma and her aunt and uncle move to a far-off island where, even though they are apprehensive, they adjust and learn to love the island and are glad of the change.

_____. *Family Failing.* Nelson, 1972. Joanna tries hard to accept her parents' divorce.

_____. *Girl in the Opposite Bed.* Nelson, 1971. Jane, 13, is having her appendix out. She meets Jeannie, 15, in the other bed. It is a different world for rich, spoiled Jane.

_____. *High House.* Meredith, 1967. Emma and Richard are orphans who must be separated. Richard, who is musical, lives with the aunt who is very organized, and Emma, who likes a scheduled life, is sent to the aunt who is musical.

_____. *Longest Weekend.* Nelson, 1970. Unmarried Eileen tries to raise her little girl with her parents' help.

_____. *Terrible Temptation.* Nelson, 1971. Janet is determined to be independent and free from any personal involvements. This decision makes her appear cold and indifferent to the problems of others close to her.

Asch, Frank. *Pearl's Pirates.* Delacorte, 1984. Pearl and Wilbur are mice who get trapped in a package that is going to France.

_____. *Pearl's Promise.* Delacorte, 1987. Pearl is a mouse who goes out to save her brother from being fed to a python in a pet store.

Aseltine, Lorraine. *I'm Deaf and It's Okay.* Whitman, 1986. A young boy must learn to handle the frustrations of his deafness.

Asher, Sandy. *Daughter of the Law.* Beaufort, 1980. Denise cares about world causes. Ruthie is the daughter of survivors of the Holocaust. They become friends and Ruthie is helped out of her shell.

_____. *Everything Is Not Enough.* Delacorte, 1987. Michael is trying to get away from parent domination. He gets a summer job and meets people who broaden his outlook and help him gain independence.

_____. *Just Like Jenny.* Delacorte, 1982. Stephie wants to be a dancer. She is unsure of her talent and is jealous of her friend whom she feels is "perfect." She overcomes this and her other problems.

_____. *Summer Begins.* Nelson, 1980. Summer, 13, is on her high school newspaper and stands up for her beliefs in spite of the turmoil caused by her editorial.

_____. *Teddy Teabury's Fabulous Fact.* Dell, 1985. Teddy lives in Thistledown, Missouri, and builds up the tourist trade by proving the town has more gerbils than people.

_____. *Things Are Seldon What They Seem.* Delacorte, 1983. Debbie and her boyfriend, Murry, find out that Debbie's best friend and sister are both being molested by the drama coach. They go to the principal and report it.

Ashley, Bernard. *All My Men.* Phillips, 1977. Paul is forced to steal candy from his parents' store to "buy" his way on the soccer team.

_____. *Break in the Sun.* Phillips, 1980. Patsy runs away from home but her stepfather starts right out to find her and bring her back to the family.

_____. *Dodgem.* Watts, 1981. Simon takes care of his dad but he is taken from him and put in an institution. He plans a rescue and escape. It works and they spend their life with a traveling carnival.

_____. *Kind of Wild Justice.* Phillips, 1979. Ronnie's father works for criminals and Ronnie is involved in crime. He is weak and insecure and picks on a weaker girl. The criminals are apprehended through Ronnie's criminal activities.

_____. *Terry on the Fence.* Phillips, 1975. Terry finds himself growing more sympathetic and friendly with the local gang leader whom he was afraid of at first because he forced him into robbery.

Asimov, Isaac. *End of Eternity.* Ballantine, 1984. Andrew knows he must break Eternity, a supposed trade organization. Its real function is to control human destiny.

_____. *Fantastic Voyage.* Bantam, 1966. Five people are miniaturized and injected into another human being to destroy a fatal blood clot. He is the man that can save the world. They have one hour to do it or the world will be destroyed.

_____. *Foundation.* Gnome, 1951. Hari Seldon creates the Foundation after the failure of the galactic empire. There is a need to preserve some remnants of culture.

_____. *I, Robot.* Ballantine, 1984. Susan has been brought up to eat, sleep, and think Robot. Is it going to be man over robot or robot over...?

Asimov, Janet. *Norby and the Invaders.* Walker, 1985. Jeff and Norby go to Jamyn to aid Norby's ancestors. They visit another planet inhabited by creatures called Hleno.

_____. *Norby and the Lost Princess.* Walker, 1985. Norby, the robot, and Jeff, his owner, travel to the far off planet of Izz. Their mission is to rescue a princess.

_____. *Norby and the Queen's Necklace.* Walker, 1986. Jeff and his robot, Norby, go back in time to 1785 in France. It is before the French Revolution and they might change history. Jeff must see that history is restored to normal.

_____. *Norby Down to Earth.* Walker, 1989. Norby loses his power and Jeff tries to reverse the process that did it and save Norby.

_____. *Norby Finds a Villain.* Walker, 1987. Norby, Jeff and friends stop monsters from another universe from invading ours. They get help from an ancient race of Others.

_____. *Norby, the Mixed up Robot.* Walker, 1983. Jeff buys an old robot and names him Norby. Gidlow is the villain who wants to take over the world starting with Manhattan. Robots and dragons and rhyme-talking computers fill out the story.

_____. *Norby's Other Secret.* Walker, 1984. The Inventor's Union wants to dismantle and study Norby. He and Jeff go to Jamyn, a planet of friendly dragons, where Norby thinks he originated. He tells Jeff about his ability to travel through time.

_____. *Package in Hyperspace.* Walker, 1988. Pete and Ginnela are sent to the planet Merkina. They have an accident with an alien ship and must be rescued.

Atkinson, Linda. *Hit and Run.* Watts, 1981. Susan hits a boy with her car and leaves the scene of the accident. She calls for help but tries to hide her role in the accident.

Atterton, Julian. *Last Harper.* Watts, 1983. In post–Roman Britain (6th century) tribes raid each other for land and cattle. The Harper, Healer and King were important people needed to resolve differences.

Atwater, Richard. *Mr. Popper's Penguins.* Little, 1938. Captain Cook, Mr. Popper's penguin, is lonely so he gets a friend. Soon there are 12 penguins. They are sociable and well known in the town of Stillwater.

Auch, Mary Jane. *Cry Uncle!* Holiday, 1987. Davey's great-uncle moves in with them and Davey doesn't understand this old man. But after a while they learn to understand and love each other.

_____. *Glass Slippers Give You Blisters.* Holiday, 1989. Kelly wants to be in a school play but her mother disapproves. She isn't selected but makes a hit by taking over the lighting of the stage.

_____. *Mom Is Dating Weird Wayne.* Holiday, 1988. Jenna's mother is dating Weird Wayne, the TV weatherman. Jenna doesn't like it but when trouble comes he proves he is OK.

_____. *Pick of the Litter.* Holiday, 1988. Catherine is adopted and an only child. Her mother is going to have a baby but quadruplets come. One dies but Catherine and her friend, Noreen, understand this tragedy and love the rest of the children.

_____. *Witching of Ben Wagner.* Houghton, 1987. Ben is new in the neighborhood and meets a girl he thinks may be a witch.

Auel, Jean. *Clan of the Cave Bear.* Crown, 1980. In the early days of humanity Ayla gave birth to a malformed child. She was told to kill it for that was the way things were done. She refused and knew that only tragedy could come from her decision.

_____. *Earth's Children.* Crown, 1980. Ayla lived millions of years ago. As her known world is destroyed she must learn to survive as more than an animal. The lion and the Clan both play a role in her survival.

Avery, Gillian. *Call of the Valley.* Holt, 1966. Sam lives on a farm with his mother and very mean uncle. He leaves and does well for a while but his own pride and ambition hurt him until he realizes that he is his own worst enemy.

_____. *Ellen and the Queen.* Lodestar, 1975. A young girl dreams of meeting Queen Victoria. Her wish comes true in an amusing way.

_____. *Likely Lad.* Holt, 1971. Willy runs away from home because of his father's pressure to enter his business instead of finishing school. He is later allowed to enter school.

_____. *Who Stole the Wizard of Oz?* Knopf, 1981. Several books disappear from the Chickertown Library book sale.

Avery, Lynn. *Cappy and the River.* Duell, 1960. Kim and his dog, Cappy, journey down the Ohio River in 1798. Cappy is kidnapped and sold to Indians but is later rescued.

Avi. *Bright Shadow.* Bradbury, 1985. Morwenna can grant wishes; she has five left but is unprepared on how to use them: to save Swen's life, to protect people, etc.

_____. *Devil's Race.* Lippincott, 1984. John, 16, is tormented by the ghost of an evil ancestor who has the same name and looks like

him. He was hanged in 1854 for being a devil. Now he wants to return to the real world.

_____. *Emily Upham's Revenge.* Pantheon, 1978. A seven-year-old girl is sent to live with a rich uncle and gets involved in a bank robbery.

_____. *Encounter in Easton.* Pantheon, 1980. Robert and Elizabeth are helped by the Society of Friends when they escape to Pennsylvania. Bet tragically dies and Robert is servant to Mr. Hill who was involved in the death of Bet.

_____. *Fighting Ground.* Lippincott, 1984. Jonathan, 13, is in a fighting unit during the Revolutionary War. He is taken prisoner and learns what it is like to be in a war.

_____. *History of Helpless Harry.* Pantheon, 1980. Harry blames his "sitter" Anne for stealing a money box of his parents. Mr. Skalch tries to get the money box by befriending Anne and Harry.

_____. *Man from the Sky.* Knopf, 1980. Jamie sees Ed Goddard parachute down. Ed drops his stolen money and lands far away from it. He captures the girl who found it and police must rescue her.

_____. *Night Journey.* Pantheon, 1979. Two indentured slaves, Elizabeth and Robert, are helped by Peter to escape to Pennsylvania. Mr. Shinn, a stern Quaker, and Peter become closer companions during the ordeal.

_____. *No More Magic.* Pantheon, 1975. It's Halloween night and Chris faces many mysterious events.

_____. *Place Called Ugly.* Pantheon, 1981. Owen tries very hard to save a summer cottage from being destroyed for a more progressive hotel. He is not successful.

_____. *Romeo and Juliet—Together (and Alive) at Last.* Orchard, 1987. Ed and Saltz combined to re-write Shakespeare in order for Saltz to be with a girl he likes.

_____. *S.O.R. Losers.* Bradbury, 1984. South Orange River school has a good sports program but 10 seventh graders and their teacher foil the records.

_____. *Shadrach's Crossing.* Pantheon, 1983. Shadrach tries to rid his island of the liquor smugglers who are terrorizing it. His father is no help; neither is the stranger he at first trusts. But he does succeed.

_____. *Something Upstairs: A Tale of Ghosts.* Orchard, 1988. Kenny, 12, meets the ghost of murdered Calib who takes him back to the time of the murder and wants him to solve it.

_____. *Sometimes I Think I Hear My Name.* Pantheon, 1982. Conrad, 13, goes to New York instead of England. He wants to see his divorced parents. Neither of them really knows or wants him.

_____. *True Confessions of Charlotte Doyle.* Orchard, 1988. Charlotte, 13, sails without her family from England to the United States.

_____. *Wolf Rider: A Tale of Terror.* Bradbury, 1986. Andy gets a strange phone call about a murder. Zeke is the potential killer and Nina is the victim. Andy must find Zeke before he commits his crime.

Babbitt, Lucy. *Children of the Maker.* Farrar, 1988. Paragrin and Cam are the rulers of Melde, supposedly the only colony on Earth. But there is another one, run by a rival sister.

————. *Oval Amulet.* Harper, 1985. Paragrin and Cam begin an adventure in Melde. The Earth is inhabited by only one colony, and they are the rulers. They try their best to survive as a civilization.

Babbitt, Natalie. *Eyes of the Amaryllis.* Farrar, 1977. A ship is lost and the captain's wife and son observe it. Later a granddaughter and grandmother look for a sign from that ship.

————. *Goody Hall.* Farrar, 1971. The setting is the beautiful Goody Hall for this Gothic mystery. There are both suspense and humor.

————. *Herbert Rowbarge.* Farrar, 1982. A story of ordinary Herbert, from when he was born until just before he dies, and back again. Do you really know him?

————. *Kneeknock Rise.* Farrar, 1970. Megrimum lives on Kneeknock Rise alone. Egan climbs the Rise and finds the secret of "beautiful Megrimum" but no one believes him.

————. *Search for Delicious.* Farrar, 1969. Gaylen polls the kingdom for a definition of Delicious. He finds Woldweller, who knows everything, Ardis and a strong talisman.

————. *Tuck Everlasting.* Farrar, 1975. The Tuck family have "everlasting life" because of the "fountain of youth." They are over a hundred years old. Should the fountain be kept a secret?

Babcock, Havilah. *Education of Pretty Boy.* Holt, 1961. Timmie, an orphan, wants a dog. He finds a dog who needs love and retrains him as a hunting dog even though he is supposed to be an outcast.

Bach, Alice. *Father Every Few Years.* Harper, 1977. An early adolescent shows both love and anger at an absent stepfather.

————. *He Will Not Walk with Me.* Delacorte, 1985. Holly volunteers to help in a soup kitchen at her church and finds that her minister is not really caring; he doesn't live by his convictions.

————. *Meat in the Sandwich.* Harper, 1975. Mike wants to be a star. Kip, a superjock, helps him learn soccer skills. Mike learns a great deal about winning and that being a star is not everything.

————. *Mollie Make-Believe.* Harper, 1974. The story of a girl who must learn to face reality.

————. *Waiting for Johnny Miracle.* Harper, 1980. Becky and Theo play basketball. Becky has bone cancer. The family changes as Becky goes through special treatments and experimental operations.

Bach, Richard. *Jonathan Livingston Seagull.* Macmillan, 1970. Jonathan Livingston Seagull is a gull who likes to fly. He finds freedom in his flying techniques. A beautiful small book.

Bachman, Richard. *Long Walk.* Nal, 1979. The Long Walk is a 450 mile marathon walk. Ray joins the walk and suffers mile after mile before he realizes that the 100 best youths of the country will probably die before the end of the race.

Bachmann, Evelyn. *Tressa.* Viking, 1966. During the 1920's in West Texas, Tressa, a very shy and timid girl, tries to adjust to the strangeness of a large Texas wheat farm.

Bacmeister, Rhoda. *Voices in the Night.* Bobbs, 1965. Jeanie is adopted by a childless family. She hears people coming and going at night, and finds someone hiding in the hay loft. She then knows about the underground railroad to Canada.

Bacon, Katherine. *Pip and Emma.* Atheneum, 1986. Pip and Emma spend the summer with their grandmother. Events include a brush with convicts, a dishonest neighbor and meningitis.

————. *Shadow and Light.* Macmillan, 1987. Emma, 16, stays with her grandmother who is terminally ill but no one knows it. She is also responsible for horses as part of a school project.

Bacon, Martha. *In the Company of Clowns.* Little, 1973. Gian-Piero was raised in a convent and when he goes after his donkey he meets a company of actors and sees a new side of life. The setting is 16th century Italy.

————. *Moth Manor.* Little, 1978. Sylvia and Mimi get a doll house that was later stored in the attic. Two generations later it is re-discovered and fantasy reigns.

————. *Sophia Scrooby Preserved.* Little, 1968. Sophia was an African slave bought by the Scrooby family as a companion for Prudence. She is sold again to a Spanish pirate but eventually returns to the Scrooby family.

————. *Third Road.* Little, 1971. Three Craven children stay with grandmother and her unicorn. They go on the Third Road to HyBreasil, a childhood land.

Bacon, Peggy. *Ghost of Opalina.* Little, 1967. A ghost cat lives in the Finley house. She tells the children stories of earlier dwellers. She helps the children make new friends.

Baehr, Patricia. *Dragon Prophecy.* Warne, 1980. Ellie and Vivian are sisters looking for fun and money. They step on a flying island and are told about a key to treasure.

————. *Falling Scales.* Morrow, 1987. Thea and her friend Marilyn are in the school orchestra. Mr. McGraw, the teacher, tries to molest Thea; she tells her father and hopes that things will get better.

————. *Louisa Eclipsed.* Morrow, 1981. Louisa and her sister Meg stay with grandparents for the summer. When Meg "gets" the boy Louisa wants, sparks fly.

Baer, Edith. *Frost in the Night.* Pantheon,

1980. Eva is Jewish but she lives secure, not like the days her grandfather talks about. But there are signs of unrest: tauntings, Nazi power, etc. The holocaust is coming.

Baer, Frank. *Max's Gang.* Little, 1983. A German Children's Evacuation Camp closes and the children try to get to Berlin. Max, Peter and Adolf face illness and poverty. They must steal food to stay alive as they make their way home.

Bagnold, Enid. *National Velvet.* Morrow, 1935. Velvet Brown won a piebald horse in a village lottery and later rode him in the Grand National Steeplechase.

Bailey, Carolyn. *Miss Hickory.* Viking, 1946. A country doll is made from an apple wood twig and a hickory nut. She lives in a corn cob house but later moves to a robin's nest. She has a lot of common sense. Newbery winner, 1947.

————. *Pioneer Art in America.* Viking, 1944. Even though this is fiction it is an explanation of the arts of early America: iron, wax, glass, pottery, etc.

Baird, Thomas. *Finding Fever.* Harper, 1982. Ben discovers dog-nappers when his dog, Fever, disappears. Strill, his friend, knows of other dogs that have disappeared. They go to work and find the operation.

————. *Walk Out a Brother.* Harper, 1983. Don doesn't want to live with his older brother and so goes into the mountains to begin his runaway. He encounters a murderer and must save himself by his knowledge of the mountains.

Baker, Betty. *And One Was a Wooden Indian.* Macmillan, 1970. Hatilshay and Turtlehead have to capture an American wooden Indian because of the belief in its powers.

————. *Blood of the Brave.* Harper, 1966. Juan joins the Cortez expedition to Mexico in the 16th century. It is a trip that tests endurance and courage.

————. *Do Not Annoy the Indians.* Macmillan, 1968. Jeff and his brother Benjy run the stagecoach office in 1850 while their father is away in the gold fields. Benjy is captured by the Indians because they think he has special power.

————. *Dunderhead War.* Harper, 1967. Quince, 17, and Uncle Fritz travel by wagon train during the Mexican War. They endure weather perils, stolen horses, measles and some battles.

————. *Dupper.* Greenwillow, 1976. Dupper is a prairie dog and this is a story about him and his friends, their life and adventures.

————. *Great Desert Race.* Macmillan, 1980. There was a real auto race that ran between Los Angeles and Phoenix. In this story two girls, Trudy and Alberta, are drivers. They fight prejudices and criticism. But they are determined to make it.

————. *Killer-of-Death.* Harper, 1963. A young Apache, Killer-of-Death, grows up during the bloody years when white settlers are moving into their land.

————. *Night Spider Case.* Macmillan, 1984. Lambert tells snoopy Frances that sweeping the porch is really detective work. Someone is digging in the basement of the empty house next door.

————. *Save Sirrushany.* Macmillan, 1978. Agotha and her frog sorcerer, Dorky, try to save Sirrushany from King Gunjar. A dragon waylays them but she helps the dragon who in turn helps solve Agotha's problems.

————. *Seven Spells to Farewell.* Macmillan, 1982. Drucilla has a knack for casting spells but they never work quite right. She wants to go to spell school and learn more.

————. *Shaman's Last Raid.* Harper, 1963. Great-grandfather, an Indian who keeps the old ways, visits his grandchildren and teaches them the old ways. When a movie company comes he re-enacts his role as Shaman in a cattle stealing raid.

————. *Spirit Is Willing.* Macmillan, 1974. Carrie and Portia go off to see the newly discovered Indian mummy in Arizona in 1880. Portia is "possessed" by the mummy's spirit.

————. *Stranger and Afraid.* Macmillan, 1972. Sopete saw the Spaniards coming on their large horses. He was afraid because they were known to kill and rob. This is a story of the first encounter between Europeans and Pueblo Indians.

————. *Walk the World's Rim.* Harper, 1965. Esteban, a black slave, helps an Indian boy, Chakoh. He explains what being a slave means to him as they walk to Mexico with three Spaniards.

Baker, Charlotte. *Cockleburr Quarters.* Prentice, 1972. Dolph and his sister find an abandoned dog and her puppies. They keep them alive with scraps of food.

Baker, Elizabeth. *This Stranger, My Son.* Houghton, 1971. Mac's father calls him a "hippie" because he doesn't conform to his father's standards.

Baker, Margaret. *Bears Back in Business.* Farrar, 1967. The three bears go on a new adventure in a wider world. They become aware of thieves as they help apprehend them and then live happily with Polly.

————. *Hannibal and the Bears.* Farrar, 1966. Boots, Slipper and Socks now live in a real home. Their aim in life is to find homes for all discarded toy animals. Hannibal is the elephant they rescue.

————. *Porterhouse Major.* Prentice, 1967. Rory casts a spell on his cat Porterhouse. He grows until his size is an embarrassment, but he is loved by everyone.

————. *Shoe Shop Bears.* Farrar, 1963. Boots, Slipper and Socks are three stuffed bears living in a shoe shop. A new manager takes over and wants to get rid of them. They talk it over with their cat friends and devise a plan.

Baker, Olaf. *Where the Buffaloes Begin.* Warne, 1981. The story of an Indian boy who stopped a buffalo stampede from killing his people. He bravely led them away in a harmless direction.

Baker, William. *Chip.* Harcourt, 1979. Chip is accused of the murder of Sam. Mut, his friend, goes off to prove his innocence. He is threatened but finds the necessary clues.

Balaban, John. *Hawk's Tale.* Harcourt, 1988. Mr. Trembly's niece, Lilac, is missing. A water snake, a toad and a deermouse get together to find her.

Balch, Glenn. *Buck, Wild.* Crowell, 1976. Buck, a wild mustang, is alone when his mother dies. He must fight another stallion and is finally captured by humans.

_____. *Flaxy Mare.* Crowell, 1967. Flax, a day old foal, whose mother is killed, is saved by a man. She is not afraid of men. She is later mistreated by men and returns to the first kind man who helps and then releases her.

_____. *Horse in Danger.* Crowell, 1960. Dixie and Ben of Tack Ranch defend their wild stallion, King, against charges of raiding the neighbor's herds.

_____. *Horse of Two Colors.* Crowell, 1969. Two Indian boys escape from the Spanish, each with a horse. They head for their village but only one boy makes it. The dead boy's horse is carrying a foal.

_____. *Lost Horse.* Crowell, 1950. Ben and Dixie help their family and their horses. Their divided loyalty also meshes and helps them understand things better.

_____. *Midnight Colt.* Crowell, 1952. Ben and Dixie buy their first race horse and name him Peck o' Trouble. They slowly train him and sell him at a profit.

_____. *Spotted Horse.* Crowell, 1961. A follow-up story to *Horse of Two Colors.* The life of the boy who brought the horse back and of the devoted horse.

_____. *Wild Horse.* Crowell, 1948. In southwestern Idaho Ben and Dixie fight to save a black stallion from capture for the rodeos.

_____. *Wild Horse Tamer.* Crowell, 1955. Ben and Dixie's wild stallion, King, has disappeared and they must go look for him.

Balducci, Carolyn. *Is There Life After Graduation, Henry Birnbaum?* Houghton, 1971. David and Henry have changed since high school. Henry is bright and inquisitive. David is quiet and organized.

Baldwin, Anne. *Little Time.* Viking, 1978. Sarah's brother Matt is mongoloid. She and her mother work hard to keep him from a special school and when he leaves they miss him.

Bales, William. *Seeker.* McGraw, 1976. A young castaway comes ashore on an unidentified beach. He learns a bitter lesson about civilization but no one listens. The moral is that everything is cyclical.

Balis, Andrea. *P.J.* Houghton, 1984. Jessica is "perfect" to her teachers and parents. She begins to get into trouble and lies. She can't believe she is not to be promoted. She and her parents finally talk things over.

Ball, Dorothy. *Don't Drive Up a Dirt Road.* Lion, 1970. Dick, a Southern black, moves to the North in hopes of bettering himself but finds that the old values still count.

Ball, John. *Judo Boy.* Duell, 1964. Rod gets beaten by a bully named Sam. He now wants to learn more about Judo so he can defend himself.

Ball, Zachary. *Bristle Face.* Holiday, 1962. Jase, an orphan, and his dog, Bristle Face, make strong personal friendships with each other and Luke, a local storeowner who wants to help.

_____. *Joe Panther.* Holiday, 1951. Joe is a Seminole Indian who is hired as a mate on a fishing boat. He saves a child's life and uncovers a ring of smugglers.

_____. *Kep.* Holiday, 1961. Kep, 15, is an orphan who goes to live with a family that have lost their son.

_____. *North to Abilene.* Holiday, 1960. Seth, an orphan, learns to rope and round up cattle. He learns about storms, thieves and the hardships of a cattle drive.

_____. *Salvage Diver.* Holiday, 1961. This is a story of the search for sunken cargo vessels and the salvaging of them after they are located.

_____. *Skin Diver.* Holiday, 1956. Joe has his own fishing boat and is hired to explore the coral reefs. He has a narrow escape while being caught in the corals and also rescues a shipwrecked man.

_____. *Sputters.* Holiday, 1963. Jase and his new dog, Sputters, still continue to make friends and strong attachments to other people.

_____. *Tent Show.* Holiday, 1964. Bruce inherits a trained dog and puts on a tent show for the summer. Through a series of mishaps he stars in the act instead of the dog.

Ballou, Arthur. *Bound for Mars.* Little, 1970. The space ship, Pegasus, is scheduled to make man's first flight to Mars. Aboard is a team member who is a threat.

_____. *Marooned in Orbit.* Little, 1968. A spaceship is disabled as it orbits the moon, and the oxygen on board is running out.

Bancroft, Griffing. *Snowy: The Story of an Egret.* McCall, 1970. A young egret survives a hostile environment. He faces a hurricane, man's guns, poisonous refuse, polluted air and water. He must learn to adapt or die.

Baner, Skulda. *First Parting.* Longmans, 1960. Anna is in her first year of teaching in North Dakota in 1919. She faces hardships and shortages but hates to leave when her year is up.

Bang, Molly. *Dawn.* Morrow, 1983. A Japanese legend that is similar to "Orpheus."

Banks, Lynne. *Fairy Rebel.* Doubleday, 1988. A woman wants a child and a fairy grants her her wish. But this action is frowned upon by the fairy queen.

_____. *Farthest-Away Mountain.* Doubleday, 1976. Dakin, 14, wants to meet a gargoyle, go to the farthest away mountain and marry a prince. She accomplishes two of them.

————. *Houdini*. Doubleday, 1988. Houdini is a hamster who wants to know about the great outside world.

————. *Indian in the Cupboard*. Doubleday, 1981. Ormi has three presents: a magic cupboard, a key to lock it and a tiny plastic Indian, Little Bear. The Indian comes alive and must have his needs met.

————. *My Darling Villain*. Harper, 1977. Mark, working class, crashes Kate's (upper class) party. They begin to date even though her parents disapprove. It is her first love and her first adult decision.

————. *Return of the Indian*. Doubleday, 1986. Ormi sent his Indian friend, Little Bear, back in the magic cupboard and now calls him back only to find him half dead and in need of help.

Barbary, James. *Fort in the Wilderness*. Norton, 1965. Dick is captured by Indians and exchanged for prisoners and then acts as go-between for the English and the Indians.

Barber, Antonia. *Affair of the Rockerbye Baby*. Delacorte, 1970. The son of a millionaire banker is kidnapped. He is rescued by a group of children with the help of the Hidden Eyes of Harlem.

Barford, Carol. *Let Me Hear the Music*. Seabury, 1979. Ryn's friend Bennie tries to rescue a nesting mallard and is killed.

Bargar, Gary. *Ghosts*. Farrar, 1969. Mrs. Allen, a widow, is caretaker of a haunted mansion. Her two children meet the ghost children who had died in an earlier fire.

————. *Life. Is. Not. Fair*. Houghton, 1984. Louis decides he will be friends with the black family that moved in next door, regardless of what everyone else is doing. He defends DeWitt unsuccessfully and agrees that life is not fair.

————. *What Happened to Mr. Forster?* Houghton, 1981. Louis, 11, wants to change his image. With the help of his teacher he develops both his writing and his image. But his teacher is fired because of homosexuality. He explains his lifestyle to Louis.

Barlettani, Elvio. *Lamp, the Traveling Dog*. Pantheon, 1963. Lampo is famous because he loves to ride trains. He knows their schedules, the diner car and other important facts about traveling.

Barne, Kitty. *Barbie*. Little, 1969. Laurel's cousin Barbie plays the violin very well and wants to study in London. Laurel's brother, Simon, helps her.

Barnes, Gregory. *Wind of Change*. Lothrop, 1965. Boys in a boarding school in Africa burn down their school to get a better one. Joseph, who was not involved, is accused and expelled. He must decide what to do about loyalty.

Barnouw, Victor. *Dream of the Blue Heron*. Delacorte, 1966. Wabus, an Indian, is torn between Indian traditions and modern white ways.

Barnwell, Robinson. *Head into the Wind*. McKay, 1965. Toby lives in South Carolina during the Depression. His father dies and his mother wants to re-marry.

————. *Shadow on the Water*. McKay, 1967. Camden's parents are talking about divorce. She is 13, growing up and trying to cope. Her boyfriend, Scott, is there to help but because his father teases her so much she doesn't like him.

Baron, Nancy. *Tuesday's Child*. Atheneum, 1984. Grace loves baseball and is the only girl on the team. Her parents want her to take ballet lessons instead of going to baseball practice!

Barrett, Anne. *Midway*. Coward, 1968. Mark felt left out of his "clever" family. Then Midway arrived and Mark was gaining confidence but Midway wasn't always there.

Barrett, William. *Lilies of the Field*. Doubleday, 1962. Homer is roaming the country when he stops to help some nuns do farm work. He is tempted to stay and build a chapel for these hard working nuns. He stays and is rewarded.

Barrie, J.M. *Peter Pan*. Holt, 1987. A well-known story of the Darling children, Tinker Bell, and, of course, Peter Pan.

Bartos-Hoppner, Barbara. *Cossacks*. Walck, 1963. Mitya joins the Cossacks to fight the Tartars. He meets Ortol and becomes a doctor. He changes from violent to caring.

————. *Save the Kahn*. Walck, 1964. Three Cossacks meet a shepherd who tells them of Daritai. A story of the Tartars' struggles against the Russian invaders.

————. *Storm Over the Caucasus*. Walck, 1968. Imam, a Moslem leader, fights to free the Caucasus from Russian rule. Aliko, a peaceful boy, goes with Imam to fight for a just cause.

Bass, Donna. *Tales of the Dark Crystal*. Holt, 1982. Skekis ruled the world of Three Suns. He got his power from a dark crystal. The crystal must be restored by a gelfing.

Bass, Milton. *Sheriff Jory*. Nal, 1987. Jory comes to Barronville a broken man. He gets a sheriff's badge and signs his own death warrant. Jasper owns all the guns and there is no way Jory can get out.

Bates, Betty. *Ask Me Tomorrow*. Holiday, 1987. Paige, 15, wants to go to college but his parents want him to work on their farm. Abby, a visiting girl, helps him solve this dilemma.

————. *Bugs in Your Ears*. Holiday, 1977. Carrie has lots of adjustments to make as an eighth grader: her mother married a man with three sons.

————. *It Must've Been the Fish Sticks*. Holiday, 1982. Brian learns that his mother is alive and living in Ohio. He wants to find out why she left him.

————. *Love Is Like Peanuts*. Holiday,

1980. Love is like peanuts because once you start, it's almost impossible to stop. Marianne meets Toby but how does he feel about love?

_____. *My Mom, the Money Nut.* Holiday, 1979. Fritzi wants to become a singer; her mother, who grew up poor, wants Fritzi to do something more practical. Fritzi realizes her mother's concern but pursues her life as she sees it.

_____. *Picking Up the Pieces.* Holiday, 1981. Nell and Dexter have been friends for a long time but Lacey comes along and lures Dexter away. Before graduation Dexter and his "friends" drink and drive and there is an accident.

_____. *That's What T.J. Says.* Holiday, 1982. Monica Sue is shy and always in the shadow of her brother, T.J. She meets shy Roland and helps him and herself.

_____. *Ups and Downs of Jorie Jenkins.* Holiday, 1978. Jorie's father has a heart attack and she must adjust to an ever changing home life until her father recovers.

Baudouy, Michel. *Boy Who Belonged to No One.* Harcourt, 1967. Hans, 12, is an orphan and lives a very unconventional life. He had a variety of "fathers" and a lot of different experiences. He is not your normal orphan.

_____. *Deception at St. Nazaire.* Harcourt, 1963. Tom, 16, visits France and takes pictures of a ship "FRANCE" that's in a security area. He is then used in an unscrupulous plot.

_____. *More Than Courage.* Harcourt, 1961. Mike secretly reconditions an old motorcycle for a cross country race.

_____. *Secret of the Hidden Painting.* Harcourt, 1965. Anne, Andre and their friends try to find out who is breaking into their house. Is it to steal the portrait of little known value?

Bauer, Marion. *Foster Child.* Seabury, 1977. Rennie can't really adjust to her new foster family and so runs away. A moving story.

_____. *Like Mother, Like Daughter.* Clarion, 1986. Leslie thinks her mother is weird and looks to one of her teachers as a role model. The teacher turns out to be a phony and Leslie learns a bitter lesson. She sees her mother in a different light.

_____. *On My Honor.* Clarion, 1986. Joel and Tony go swimming in a dangerous river although they were warned not to. Tony disappears and drowns. Joel is afraid to tell either set of parents what happened since they were told not to go.

_____. *Rain of Fire.* Houghton, 1983. Steve's brother fought in Japan during World War II and is bothered by the killings. Steve doesn't understand and lies about his brother's attitude toward the Japanese and this makes matters worse.

_____. *Shelter from the Wind.* Seabury, 1976. Stacy runs away from home to find her mother. She meets Ella and her dogs and helps in the birth of the pups. She is then able to work out her own problems.

_____. *Tangled Butterfly.* Houghton, 1980. Michelle, 17, is emotionally disturbed. She spends time with a young couple and their baby. The man enables her to reach for help.

_____. *Touch the Moon.* Clarion, 1987. Jennifer didn't get the horse she wanted for her birthday but a figurine horse that magically turned "real."

Baum, Betty. *Patricia Crosses Town.* Knopf, 1965. Patricia and two black friends are bussed to a white school. They must work hard at not being hurt, not feeling ostracized or minding their poverty.

Baum, L. Frank. *Wonderful Wizard of Oz.* Morrow, 1987. A nice edition of this old favorite of Dorothy and her dog "somewhere over the rainbow."

Bawden, Nina. *Carrie's War.* Lippincott, 1973. Carrie and Nick are evacuated from London to a Welsh community. They live a bleak life until they meet Hepzibah who tells them of the curse on the house. It appears to be coming true.

_____. *Devil by the Sea.* Harper, 1976. No one believes Hilary when she claims to know the identity of the child that was murdered.

_____. *Finding.* Lothrop, 1985. Alex gets an unexpected inheritance but because he is adopted he runs away from home, unwilling to face what's ahead.

_____. *Handful of Thieves.* Lippincott, 1967. Fred and Mrs. Gribble know about the money in grandmother's teapot. It is missing. Grandmother says nothing but Fred and his friends track down the person who took it.

_____. *Henry.* Lothrop, 1988. A fatherless family, evacuated to the country, tries to raise a baby squirrel that also lost its home.

_____. *Kept in the Dark.* Lothrop, 1982. David brought strange feelings to Clara's grandfather's house. Boise, Noel, Liz and even the grandfather are under his sinister influence.

_____. *Peppermint Pig.* Lippincott, 1975. Poll and Theo go to live with an aunt. They make a pet of a runt pig. The pig must later be killed and Poll is upset.

_____. *Rebel on a Rock.* Lippincott, 1978. Jo lives in a country that is ruled by a dictator. In the village of Polis she suspects her stepfather of being a spy.

_____. *Robbers.* Lothrop, 1979. Phillip is living with his father. He becomes friends with Darcy and they get into trouble with the police. He then goes to live with an understanding grandmother.

_____. *Runaway Summer.* Lippincott, 1969. Mary is not cooperative as her parents are getting a divorce. Then she and her friend, Simon, find an ill boy who is an illegal immigrant and care for him. This helps Mary's outlook.

_____. *Squib.* Lippincott, 1971. Kate and her mother are alone; her father and brother are believed drowned. She sees someone who looks like her brother but can't find him again. He is being kept prisoner and they try to rescue him.

_____. *Three on the Run*. Lippincott, 1965. Ben, Thomas and Lil are "on the run" for different reasons. An exciting and dangerous journey is planned and ends well.

_____. *White Horse Gang*. Lippincott, 1966. Sam, Rose and Abe spend time riding Abe's horse and exploring Gibbet Wood which is haunted. Then they decide to kidnap Percy and the adventure begins.

_____. *Witch's Daughter*. Lippincott, 1960. Perdita can see into the future and when blind Janey and her brother Tim come to the island Perdita finds her power is special and not witchcraft.

Baxter, Caroline. *Stolen Telesm*. Lippincott, 1975. David and Lucy encounter evil in a mansion and must get away. They rescue a colt that turns into a winged horse, Telesm.

Baylor, Byrd. *Hawk, I'm Your Brother*. Macmillan, 1976. A boy captures a young hawk. He hopes the hawk will teach him how to fly.

Beachcroft, Nina. *Well Met by Witchlight*. Atheneum, 1972. Chris, Lucy and Sarah find a good witch. She helps them through the summer with her magic.

_____. *Wishing People*. Dutton, 1982. Martha gets ten wishes from Tom and Mrs. Tom whom she "wishes" alive. She shares the wishes with Jonathan.

Beagle, Peter. *Last Unicorn*. Viking, 1968. Shmendrick the magician and Molly help a unicorn find her lost friends and thus her happiness.

Beatty, Hetty. *Bryn*. Houghton, 1965. A collie looks for his master, Ken, after they are separated. They are re-united and Bryn is trained as a sheep dog.

Beatty, Jerome. *Bob Fulton's Amazing Soda-Pop Stretcher*. Scott, 1963. Bob tries to discover a way that he can quench every thirst in town. But he did not anticipate the problems connected with such an invention when it blew up and left a magic residue.

_____. *Bob Fulton's Terrific Time Machine*. Scott, 1964. Bob is at it again with another invention. This time the machine he builds can change time. But, as usual, there are problems.

_____. *Marie Looney and the Cosmic Circus*. Avon, 1978. More adventures with Marie and the Moonsters, taking place between the moon and earth.

_____. *Marie Looney and the Remarkable Robot*. Avon, 1978. Marie is helped in her encounter with the Moonsters. This series ties into the Matthew Looney series, which also deals with the Moonsters.

_____. *Marie Looney on the Red Planet*. Avon, 1977. Forces on both the earth and the moon fight the Moonsters and Marie.

_____. *Matthew Looney and the Space Pirates*. Wesley, 1972. Matt is captured by the Space Pirates while trying to establish a new planet. He is kept in a dungeon on Bolunkus.

_____. *Matthew Looney in the Outback*. Wesley, 1969. Matt knows of a plan of the Moonsters to destroy the earth. He has to decide whether to save it or leave it to its doom. A lava bomb has been fired by the Moonsters.

_____. *Matthew Looney's Invasion of the Earth*. Wesley, 1965. Matt goes again to the earth and then returns to the moon but this time in an American rocket ship because he missed his own ship that escaped the magic "rain."

_____. *Matthew Looney's Voyage to the Earth*. Avon, 1961. This story is told from the point of view of the moon-boy who comes to Earth to see if there is life there, and finds there is!

_____. *Sheriff Stonehead and the Teen-Age Termites*. Scott, 1970. Finley Farmer and his "teen-age termites" leave notes claiming to have done some pranks. Sheriff Stonehead tries to track them down. But do they exist?

Beatty, John. *At the Seven Stars*. Macmillan, 1963. Richard, 15, works in a restaurant called Seven Stars and overhears the famous Elibank Plot of 1752 and witnesses a murder. He is hunted down and gets more deeply and dangerously involved.

_____. *Holdfast*. Morrow, 1972. Catriona, an orphan, is made ward of Queen Elizabeth I. She releases her wolfhound, Manus, but they are later re-united.

_____. *King's Knights' Pawn*. Morrow, 1971. Kit, 14, sees the beheading of Charles I during the struggle between Ireland and Cromwell's England.

_____. *Royal Dirk*. Morrow, 1966. A story of how the Scots helped Prince Charles claim the throne of England. Brutal description of the lawless streets of London.

_____. *Who Comes to King's Mountain?* Morrow, 1975. American colonists get caught up in the American Revolution. Alex joins up with Swamp Fox Marion and is tried as a spy.

_____. *Witch Dog*. Morrow, 1968. In the time of King Charles and Oliver Cromwell, Prince Rupert and his white poodle, Boye are winning victories over the enemy. Boye is a faithful, helpful dog who is kidnapped and must be rescued.

Beatty, Patricia. *Bad Bell of San Salvador*. Morrow, 1973. Jacinto was kidnapped and sold for a barrel of whiskey. He helped make the Bell of San Salvador. He rang it later to save the people of the village from a flood.

_____. *Be Ever Hopeful, Hannalee*. Morrow, 1988. Dave returns from the Civil War wounded. He is falsely arrested for murder. Hannalee must prove his innocence.

_____. *Behave Yourself, Bethany Brant*. Morrow, 1986. Bethany is a preacher's daughter and seems destined for trouble. She tries to be good and does so for a while but then her resolve drops and she hilariously takes a different turn.

———. *Billy Be Damned Long Gone By.* Morrow, 1971. Rudd Quimby is a teller of tall tales as he reminisces about the past. His listeners soon realize this but still enjoy the stories.

———. *Blue Stars Watching.* Morrow, 1969. Will is involved in his father's underground railroad. He and his sister are sent to California where their relatives are pro–South. They are kidnapped and eventually return to Delaware and home.

———. *Bonanza Girl.* Morrow, 1962. Ann Katie, her brother and mother move from their nice home to Eagle City, a silver mining town. They find things very different such as gun play, mining fever and evil mule drivers.

———. *By Crumbs, It's Mine.* Morrow, 1976. Damaris's father deserts her on their way West to look for gold. He leaves her nothing. She manages a hotel business with her Aunt Willa and is successful.

———. *Charley Skedaddle.* Morrow, 1987. Charlie belongs to a tough gang in New York City during the Civil War. He joins the Union Army at 12 but runs away from the horrors of the war. He proves his courage in the mountains with Mrs. Bent.

———. *Eight Mules from Monterey.* Morrow, 1982. Letti is going to open a branch library in a far-off deserted area. This is the story as a 13-year-old sees the trip: death, fever, cruelty.

———. *Hail Columbia.* Morrow, 1970. Louisa, 13, has a controversial aunt come to visit her in Oregon in 1893.

———. *How Many Miles to Sundown?* Morrow, 1974. Beulah and Leo, along with Nate, cross Texas and New Mexico in 1879 to look for Nate's missing father. They meet miners, outlaws and a traveling circus.

———. *I Want My Sunday, Stranger.* Morrow, 1977. Andrew, 13, runs away from home to find his horse, Sunday, that was stolen. He finds him blind and lame. His selfless act is to leave the horse with its new owner on a farm.

———. *Jonathan Down Under.* Morrow, 1982. Jonathan, 13, and his father go to the gold mines of Australia. It is rough living and Jonathan grows into manhood.

———. *Lacy Makes a Match.* Morrow, 1979. Lacy, 13, is an orphan living with "Pa and three brothers" whom she wants to marry off. She tries to find her real parents but feels she belongs to this Bingham family.

———. *Lady from Black Hawk.* McGraw, 1967. Julie wants a wife for her father and a mother for herself and her brothers. So in the late 19th century in gold mining country, she sends for one.

———. *Long Way to Whiskey Creek.* Morrow, 1971. Nate, Parker Quimby and his dog, J.E.B. Stuart, travel far to bring back the body of a brother who was shot. They meet a Mexican witch, a medicine man, a gunslinger and an evangelist.

———. *Lupita Manana.* Morrow, 1981. Two young Mexicans must leave home and travel to the United States to find work.

———. *Me, California Perkins.* Morrow, 1968. California's father wants to roam and her mother and two other kids want to settle down. It is a struggle for the mother so the kids work to re-unite their parents.

———. *Melinda Takes a Hand.* Morrow, 1983. Melinda's sister breaks off her engagement leaving herself and Melinda to find a job and support themselves. They do so and Melinda tries to re-unite her sister and her boyfriend.

———. *Nickel-Plated Beauty.* Morrow, 1964. Hester tells the story of trying to raise $27.00 in seven months to pay for the beautiful nickel-plated stove.

———. *O, the Red Rose Tree.* Morrow, 1972. Amanda, 13, and her friends help grandmother's rival complete a quilt for the Fair. A humorous account of how she got the last piece of red material needed.

———. *Queen's Own Grove.* Morrow, 1966. Amelia moves from London to rugged California in 1880. She has trouble fitting in and must fight the disease that hit the orange grove.

———. *Red Rock Over the River.* Morrow, 1973. Dorcas and Charles live with their father. Hattie Lou comes to town and exciting things begin including a balloon ride, being deserted in the desert, and being rescued by Indians.

———. *Rufus, Red Rufus.* Morrow, 1975. Rufus is an Irish setter who shifts from person to person in a college community. He is always in trouble and everyone tries to keep him from the authorities.

———. *Sarah and Me and the Lady from the Sea.* Morrow, 1989. Marcella's family are at their summer home because of financial distress. They learn to subsist on less and yet have adventures. We also learn more about what happened to the Kimballs.

———. *Something to Shout About.* Morrow, 1976. Hope, 13, and the women of Ottenberg try to raise money for a school by taking up collections from the saloons.

———. *Squaw Boy.* Morrow, 1965. Jimmie and his dog, Kadedo, a black Labrador, become friends. When he is sick the dog wanders off getting into fights and then healing. They do get reunited.

———. *Staffordshire Terror.* Morrow, 1979. Cissie finds a purebred Staffordshire pup. Her uncle Cletus steals the dog and enters him in illegal dog fights. Cissie finds him, rescues the dog and breaks up the dogfight ring.

———. *That's One Ornery Orphan.* Morrow, 1980. Hallie is "adopted" several times before she becomes a real daughter and not a hired girl. She made sure the "adoptions" she didn't want, didn't work.

————. *Turn Homeward, Hannalee.* Morrow, 1984. Hannalee's life is disrupted when she is moved to Indiana with the rest of the Southern mill workers during the Civil War. She encounters Quantrill's Raiders and other horrors of war.

————. *Wait for Me, Watch for Me, Eula Bee.* Morrow, 1978. Eula Bee and her brother are taken prisoner by the Comanches. He escapes and a year later comes back for Eula Bee but by that time, because she is so young, she has forgotten him.

Beckett, Hilary. *My Brother, Angel.* Dodd, 1971. Carlos was asked to take charge of Angel while his mother was away. He is 13, Angel is 5. There were problems but Carlos was up to it and proud of his trust and respect.

————. *Street Fair Summer.* Dodd, 1974. Ivy stayed in the city rather than go to Maine as planned. She joined a committee putting on a street fair. She got a rock group to perform and was trapped in a church tower. A different summer.

Beckman, Delores. *My Own Private Sky.* Dutton, 1980. Arthur, 11, is taught Indian history and lore by his 60-year-old sitter. He is afraid to swim but she helps him. When an accident takes her legs and she's afraid to walk he helps her.

————. *Who Loves Sam Grant?* Dutton, 1983. Sam, 15, tries to win Bogie, a football star, by hiding a stolen mascot of a rival team. She later realizes this was a mistake.

Beckman, Gunnel. *Admission to the Feast.* Holt, 1971. A 19-year-old girl finds she has incurable cancer.

————. *Mia Alone.* Dell, 1978. While waiting for the results of a pregnancy test, a high school student realizes she must make her own decision concerning abortion.

————. *That Early Spring.* Viking, 1977. A story of Mia and her grandmother and how they both realized that a woman must be a person of individualism "even though they are women."

Beckman, Thea. *Crusade in Jeans.* Scribner, 1975. Rudolf is transported back to the time of the Children's Crusade by way of a time machine. He tries to help but runs into knights and defrocked priests who hinder him.

Bedard, Michael. *Darker Magic.* Atheneum, 1987. Three youngsters are in danger when a ghostly magician haunts them with visions of a deadly magic show.

Beebe, B.F. *Coyote, Come Home.* McKay, 1963. An Apache Indian watches the growth of a coyote. He faces wolves, scorpions, and Gila monsters.

————. *Run, Light Buck, Run.* McKay, 1962. Light Buck is an antelope. He is befriended by a prospector as they struggle for survival.

Beeks, Graydon. *Hosea Globe and the Fantastical Peg-Legged Chu.* Atheneum, 1975. Mr.

Chu is a three-legged talking dog. Hosea is his friend. They save Professor Small and Mrs. Thatcher from enemies and then trap the enemy.

Behn, Harry. *Faraway Lurs.* World, 1963. The Sun People have a great Bronze Trumpet called lures. This is a love story of a Forest People girl, Heather, and a Sun People boy, Wolfston. These are two warring tribes during the Bronze Age.

————. *Omen of the Birds.* World, 1964. Coele and Tanaqul, young lovers of Etruscan life, become King and Queen and overcome the prophecy of extinction.

Belden, Wilanne. *Frankie.* Harcourt, 1987. The O'Riley family is made up of a wizard, a magician and an apprentice witch. They are delighted when the new baby is a griffin.

————. *Mind-Call.* Atheneum, 1981. Tallie has ESP. She dreams of what is about to happen. She is alone except for the cat, and manages to pack and get on Paul's sailboat just before the tidal wave strikes. Others join her to fight evil.

————. *Mind-Find.* Harcourt, 1988. Laurel, 13, who has ESP, spends time with a neighboring family with psychic powers. She uses her powers to save some children during a storm.

————. *Mind-Hold.* Harcourt, 1987. Carson, 12, and Caryl, 10, have telepathic powers and have mental battles with each other. There are seeking their father after a devastating earthquake.

————. *Rescue of Ranor.* Atheneum, 1983. Melarligre is Order of Magic, Grumnuth is Order of Science. They can not cross borders. There are a few Nons; Sven is one of them. He must fight for his brother, Ranor.

Bell, Clare. *Clan Ground.* Atheneum, 1984. Twenty-five million years ago, the control of fire was power. Who will have this power, Ratha or her enemies? A dangerous struggle takes place, testing everyone's loyalty.

————. *Ratha's Creatures.* Atheneum, 1983. A clan of intelligent cats, pushed close to extinction, meets an enemy band of raiding predatory cats in a decisive battle which will determine the future of both.

Bell, Frederic. *Jenny's Corner.* Random, 1974. Jenny, 9, sees a deer shot and during a blizzard follows the wounded deer. She is found near death and her father will no longer allow hunters on his farmland.

Bell, Gertrude. *Posse of Two.* Criterion, 1964. Ned and his parents are burned out of their house by outlaws. He goes after them to get his stallion. On the way he meets Dave who has a similar quest.

Bell, Margaret. *To Peril Strait.* Viking, 1971. Mike lives in Alaska and makes mistakes trying to cope with the hazards of remote Alaska. But he learns from his experience.

Bell, Norman. *Weightless Mother.* Follett, 1967. Some pills taken by mistake turn Mrs. Flippin into a weightless wonder. Her dog, Hurricane, and she float off into the sky in this funny science fiction fantasy.

Bell, Thelma. *Captain Ghost.* Viking, 1959. Three children turn a fallen tree into a sailing ship. There is also a mysterious house with a ghost and a smuggler who must be caught.

_____. *Dash of Pepper.* Viking, 1965. Clyde's proud ownership of Pepper and Salt, a horse he longed for, leads to a new understanding of his parents.

_____. *Two Worlds of Davy Blount.* Viking, 1962. Davy plays pirates with his friends near the sea. Next summer he is sent to the mountains. His parents want to know which place he liked best. He thinks they are both equally wonderful.

Bell, W. Bruce. *Little Dab of Color.* Lothrop, 1980. Bruce, Herbert and friend Thaddeus get into trouble and their parents must save them.

Bell, William. *Crabbe's Journey.* Little, 1986. Franklin is an alcoholic who tries to run away from his problems. He goes camping without the necessary skills and almost dies. A woman helps him both survive and recover.

Bellairs, John. *Curse of the Blue Figurine.* Dial, 1983. John Dixon and Professor Childermass run into a mystery when John removes the blue figurine, called Shawabti, he was warned not to touch. A suspenseful, macabre tale.

_____. *Dark Secret of Weatherend.* Dial, 1984. Anthony Monday tries to stop a wicked wizard from turning the earth to ice. Wizard Borkman can control the weather and leaves the formula to his son, Anders.

_____. *Eyes of the Killer Robot.* Dial, 1986. Johnny Dixon and Professor Childermass look for a baseball pitching robot made many years ago by a wizard. He may be evil when found and re-assembled.

_____. *Figure in the Shadows.* Dial, 1975. In this story an old coin starts the sinister events that lead Lewis and his friend, Rose, to solve another mystery involving ghosts and other evils.

_____. *House with a Clock in Its Walls.* Dial, 1973. Lewis and his wizard uncle, Jonathan, use both magic and terror to solve the mystery of the clock that is set to destroy the world.

_____. *Lamp from Warlock's Tomb.* Dial, 1988. Anthony Monday recovers the lamp that is spreading evil throughout the world. Miss Eels bought the lamp at an antique sale and strange things happen. It once belonged to Willis Nightwood.

_____. *Letter, the Witch and the Ring.* Dial, 1976. Lewis' friend, Rose, goes with Jonathan's neighbor, Mrs. Zimmermann, who is a witch, to a farmhouse to solve a mystery that even Mrs. Zimmermann's witchcraft can't help.

_____. *Mummy, the Will and the Crypt.* Dial, 1983. Again John Dixon and the Professor are mixed up in another mystery; this time involving the missing will of an eccentric old man who committed suicide.

_____. *Revenge of the Wizard's Ghost.* Dial, 1985. Johnny Dixon lies dying, hexed by the evil spirit of Warren Winslow. The Professor and his friends try to save him.

_____. *Spell of the Sorcerer's Skull.* Dial, 1984. A tiny skull from a haunted doll house unleashes demonic forces against John and Father Higgins. Professor Childermass is captured in this harrowing tale.

_____. *Treasure of Alpheus Winterborn.* Harcourt, 1978. Anthony Monday looks for a treasure rumored to be hidden in his home town library. He and Miss Eels work together and find a clue in the fireplace.

_____. *Trolley to Yesterday.* Dial, 1989. Johnny and Professor Childermass go by time trolley to Constantinople in 1453. There they are to save the people from slavery and death.

Benary-Isbert, Margot. *Ark.* Harcourt, 1953. The ark is an abandoned railroad car in which the Lechow family live after escaping from a Russian prison camp. Matthias and Margaret are glad to be together even though they lost a brother.

_____. *Castle on the Border.* Harcourt, 1956. The Lechow family adjust after World War II and face the future with hope and strength. Leni wants to become a great actress and overcome her tragic war life with love.

_____. *Long Way Home.* Harcourt, 1959. A German family flees East Germany to the United States and finds a home in California.

_____. *Rowan Farm.* Harcourt, 1954. Rowan farm is where the "Ark" becomes home for the Lechow family; where they do the farming. Margaret finds peace and quiet among the animals, especially with the dogs.

Benchley, Nathaniel. *Beyond the Mists.* Harper, 1975. Gunner, along with Leif Ericson, are Norsemen of the 11th century.

_____. *Bright Candles.* Harper, 1974. Jens, 16, works for the Underground in Denmark as a courier getting Jews into Sweden.

_____. *Demo and the Dolphins.* Harper, 1981. Demo and his dolphin visit ancient Greece.

_____. *Kilroy and the Gull.* Harper, 1977. Kilroy is a killer whale in captivity. Morris is a seagull. They try to communicate with man but no one understands them although they understand some of man.

_____. *Necessary End.* Harper, 1976. Ralph is a sailor during World War II. He has written a diary about the war. He is unexpectedly killed by an American mine.

Benedict, Dorothy. *Fabulous.* Random, 1961. Mistie, Sandy and Fabulous, a pony of color, live on a ranch. Someone steals Fabulous but he is recovered and trained for show.

_____. *Pagan the Black.* Pantheon, 1960. Pagan is a wild black stallion who is called a killer when he protects his young master from danger.

Benedict, Rex. *Ballad of Cactus Jack.* Pantheon, 1975. A spoof of the Old West. Cactus

Jack and his Pecos Gang are "old and unwanted, dead or alive." They want to be Wanted again.

———. *Good-Bye to the Purple Sage.* Pantheon, 1973. Territory Gore and Cherokee Waters team up to look for Sheldon for different reasons.

———. *Good Luck Arizona Man.* Pantheon, 1972. A half white, blonde Indian looks for gold and his origins. A hilarious story with a Western touch.

Benezra, Barbara. *Fire Dragon.* Criterion, 1970. In San Francisco during the 1906 earthquake Sam is separated from his family. He stays with a Chinese family until he can locate his own.

———. *Nuggets in My Pocket.* Bobbs, 1966. Jeb goes into the gold fields of San Francisco in 1850. He looks for an old family friend, Jake. When he finds him he saves him from hanging.

Benford, Gregory. *Jupiter Project.* Nelson, 1975. A laboratory is orbiting Jupiter looking for life. Matt, 17, is challenged by Yuri to save the project from destruction.

Benjamin, Carol. *Nobody's Baby Now.* Macmillan, 1984. Olivia, 15, and overweight, cares for her grandmother whom she tries to get out of her lethargy. She also gets a boyfriend, Brian, even though she is overweight.

———. *Wicked Stepdog.* Crowell, 1982. Louise, 12, lives with her father, stepmother and Beany, the dog. She meets a boy who also walks a dog. Finally her father notices her unhappiness and helps her.

Bennett, Anna. *Little Witch.* Harper, 1953. Minx doesn't want to be a witch like her mother; she wants to go to school like other kids.

Bennett, Jay. *Birthday Murderer.* Delacorte, 1977. Shan receives a birthday card addressed to him in his own handwriting. It says "Happy Birthday, Murderer."

———. *Deadly Gift.* Meredith, 1969. T.J.'s grades are low and he's not an athlete so a scholarship is out of the question. He finds a briefcase full of money and hides it. He gets involved with the gangsters and deception.

———. *Death Ticket.* Avon, 1985. Gil got one half of a New York State lottery ticket from his brother. Gareth (Dwarf) lived in New York in a loft and was odd. Gil put the ticket away without knowing the tragedy it would bring.

———. *Deathman, Do Not Follow Me.* Scholastic, 1968. Danny has no father and is a loner. One of his paintings is stolen and he gets involved with finding the thieves.

———. *Executioner.* Avon, 1982. Bruce's friend, Raymond, was killed in an auto accident. His friends try to console him but he knows he is responsible for the accident.

———. *Haunted One.* Watts, 1987. Paul, a lifeguard, and Jody, a ballet dancer fall in love. He uses marijuana occasionally. When Jody calls for help he is slow in reacting and she drowns. She also haunts him later.

———. *Killing Tree.* Watts, 1972. Fred's father dies and leaves him a wooden statue from Africa. He is threatened and followed. The statue contains diamonds stolen by his uncle. Was his father involved?

———. *Pigeon.* Methuen, 1980. Brian finds his girlfriend Donna stabbed to death. He runs away and tries to find the killer and free himself of the frame.

———. *Say Hello to the Hit Man.* Dell, 1977. Someone is going to kill Fred. He got a phone call telling him so. His father is a gangster and he doesn't know whom to trust.

———. *Skeleton Man.* Watts, 1986. Ray's uncle leaves him $30,000 on his 18th birthday and commits suicide. Ray starts receiving threatening letters from someone who says the money belongs to him.

———. *Slowly, Slowly I Raise the Gun.* Avon, 1983. Chris receives an unsigned letter telling him that his mother was murdered. Chris is encouraged to seek revenge.

———. *To Be a Killer.* Scholastic, 1985. Paul steals a copy of the final exam in chemistry. His teacher catches him. While thinking about killing his teacher he realizes he needs professional help.

Bennett, John. *Master Skylark.* Grosset, 1924. A boy is kidnapped and goes to London to meet William Shakespeare and also to sing before Queen Elizabeth.

Bennett, Paul. *Follow the River.* Watts, 1987. Harry Lee is one of six children and has a chance to go to college. He falls in love with the daughter of a banker whose alcoholic wife has an affair with Harry's brother.

Benson, Sally. *Junior Miss.* Random, 1941. An all-time standard of the Graves family, especially Lois, 16, and Judy, 14.

Bentley, Phyllis. *Adventures of Tom Leigh.* Doubleday, 1966. Tom's father dies and he is to become a weaving apprentice. His enemy is a fellow weaver. Cloth is stolen and Tom is involved but Jeremy is the thief.

———. *Forgery.* Doubleday, 1968. Dick searches for a band of coin clippers. Jamie's father is the guilty one and this strains the friendship of Dick and Jamie.

———. *Oath of Silence.* Doubleday, 1967. A story of the desperation of men made jobless and starving by the coming of machines. There are both violence and tolerance.

Berends, Polly. *Case of the Elevator Duck.* Random, 1973. Gilbert knows that he can't keep pets in the housing development where he lives but he somehow manages to keep a duck in an elevator.

———. *Ozma and the Wayward Wand.* Random, 1985. This is another book about Dorothy (of Oz) and her four friends while they are still in the Land of Oz.

Berger, Frederica. *Nuisance.* Morrow, 1983. Julie's parents are divorced and she changes schools. She meets Cal who lives across the street. He helps her adjust to a stepfather. She finds a stray cat and names it Nuisance; this helps her find herself.

Bergman, Tamar. *Boy from Over There.* Houghton, 1988. Avramik, an orphan of the Holocaust, and Rina, who lost his father in Italy, become friends. They live in a kibbutz in Israel.

Berna, Paul. *Clue of the Black Cat.* Pantheon, 1965. The Thiriet family is taken in by a confidence man who takes 10,000 francs. Bobby and his friends, with only a lead of a black cat, look for the culprit.

_____. *Flood Warning.* Pantheon, 1962. Five people are left in a tower when a building is evacuated because of a flood. This is the story of their several days there together.

_____. *Horse Without a Head.* Pantheon, 1958. A wooden horse with three wheels is the toy of a group of poor children. The horse is stolen because of jewels supposedly hidden in it.

_____. *Knights of King Midas.* Pantheon, 1961. Charloun's gang were looking for a mad donkey. An old people's home was set afire and the children raise money to rebuild it.

_____. *Mule on the Expressway.* Pantheon, 1967. Bobby finds an injured mule on a freeway. He wonders how it got there. He traps crooks who were using the mule with a cart for illegal business.

_____. *Mystery of Saint Salgue.* Pantheon, 1964. Some youngsters get an old van and are on a camping trip. They are looking for Saint Salgue but are prevented from finding it because of some exploiting developers.

_____. *Secret of the Missing Boat.* Pantheon, 1966. Fanch finds a dinghy and with it comes the attention of the Harbor Master, Benny, a couple of rough boys and the owner of a yacht. Why?

_____. *Threshold of the Stars.* Abelard, 1960. In an ultra-secret space airport a young boy whose father works there tells of the daily happenings leading to the first landing on the moon.

Bernhardsen, Christian. *Fight in the Mountains.* Harcourt, 1968. Chris's house is overrun by Nazis. He tries to get help from friendly forces. He can now play a man's part in the war like his older brother. Even though he is young, he proves to be a hero.

Berry, B.J. *Just Don't Bug Me.* Follett, 1972. Jonas's parents were killed. He first lives with an aunt then an uncle who is a rodeo clown. He trains a wild horse. When the stable catches fire he gives the alarm and tries to save the horses.

Berry, Barbara. *Shannon.* Follett, 1968. Shannon, a stallion, was stolen and sold to a horse racer. He sells Shannon to Hapgood where she is mistreated. Shannon escapes and after many hardships returns to the O'Brians.

Berson, Barbara. *What's Going to Happen to Me?* Scribner, 1976. A story of the reaction of a young boy to his parents' separation.

Bertol, Roland. *Two Hats.* Crowell, 1969.

Antonio wants to be a fisherman. His mother wants him to be a farmer. His work on the farm helps him in rescuing a ship, and thereby he gets to go out on the fishing boats.

Bess, Clayton. *Big Man and the Burn-Out.* Houghton, 1985. Jess, the Big Man, lives with his strict grandmother. Meechum, the Burn-Out, is a school friend. Both lost their mothers; one was killed, the other ran away. A mutually helpful friendship develops.

_____. *Story for a Black Night.* Houghton, 1982. Ma, baby Meatta, grandmother Ma and Momo are locked in their house during a storm. A woman with a baby comes, but then abandons it because it has smallpox. Ma takes the family through several tragedies.

_____. *Tracks.* Houghton, 1986. Blue Roan and his brother leave home during the Depression and head for California. They encounter hobos, dust storms, Klan members. A realistic picture of the times.

Best, Herbert. *Desmond and Dog Friday.* Viking, 1968. Desmond is joined by a Hungarian Puli named Friday. Friday digs up a bone from an early Indian cache. Again Desmond is the detective with savvy and solves the mystery.

_____. *Desmond and the Peppermint Ghost.* Viking, 1965. Desmond tells about learning how dogs pull sleds. By following a scent of peppermint Desmond leads Gus to an empty house and the answers about the ghost.

_____. *Desmond the Dog Detective.* Viking, 1962. A jumble of happenings, mainly in the supermarket where Desmond is looking for a thief behind the dog food boxes, again told by Desmond as he sees it.

_____. *Desmond's First Case.* Viking, 1961. Desmond (dog) and Gus (boy) look for the disappeared Mr. Titus, friend, neighbor and ex-banker. The search is told by the dog from his point of view.

Betancourt, Jeanne. *Between Us.* Scholastic, 1986. Christine and Carolyn are twins and friends but Carolyn finds a boy friend just as Chris finds a deadly situation at the hospital where she works and needs Carolyn to help both of them.

_____. *Home Sweet Home.* Bantam, 1988. Tracy, 16, and her family go to live with grandmother Tilly so Mom and Dad can see if they like farming better than business. Tracy doesn't, until she meets Anya and they become friends.

_____. *Puppy Love.* Avon, 1986. Aviva's parents are divorced and this changes her life. She also has a crush on a boy at school, Bob. She has to cope with both situations.

_____. *Sweet Sixteen and Never.* Bantam, 1987. Julie, 16, has her birthday party ruined by a blizzard, her best friend finds something awesome about her mother, and her boyfriend wants more than she's willing to give.

Bethancourt, T.E. *Dr. Doom, Superstar.* Holiday, 1978. Doris Fein is only a minor character in this story but it is an introduction to this sleuthing heroine. Larry Small interviews a Rock star. There is a death threat and the mystery begins.

_____. *Dog Days of Arthur Cane*. Holiday, 1976. A 16-year-old boy was changed into a dog. He's chased by a dog catcher, is abused, hit by a car, poisoned and sent to the gas chamber where he changes back to a boy.

_____. *Doris Fein, Dead Heat at Long Beach*. Holiday, 1983. A racing car driver and Doris get involved with revolutionaries. Even Doris must use her driving skills to survive this encounter with guerillas and off-shore oil intrigue.

_____. *Doris Fein, Deadly Aphrodite*. Holiday, 1982. Doris and her friend, Larry Small, try to solve an old mystery where someone is systematically doing away with the world's wealthiest women at an exclusive spa.

_____. *Doris Fein, Legacy of Terror*. Holiday, 1983. A 15 million dollar inheritance, a kidnapping and organized crime are the source of terror for Doris.

_____. *Doris Fein, Mad Samurai*. Scholastic, 1981. As Doris investigates the murder of two people allegedly killed by Samurai swordsmen, she finds her own life in danger.

_____. *Doris Fein, Murder Is No Joke*. Holiday, 1982. This mystery starts in a Southern California night club where her new friend is found to be a killer and then moves to Las Vegas and encounters with organized crime.

_____. *Doris Fein, Phantom of the Casino*. Scholastic, 1981. This time, in Santa Catalina, Doris finds that her death is the revenge wanted by the "phantom." She has a romantic episode and lots of adventure.

_____. *Doris Fein, Quartz Boyar*. Holiday, 1980. Doris feels she has had enough of detective work and goes to Paris on holiday only to become involved in an international adventure because of a quartz figurine.

_____. *Doris Fein, Superspy*. Holiday, 1978. Doris is a super sleuth just out of high school and starts an adventure in New York when her aunt and uncle get a mysterious call to go to Africa where trouble is brewing.

_____. *Instruments of Darkness*. Holiday, 1979. Ianos is the leader of a cult that attracts the children of power people. Four of his followers commit suicide. He is pursued by secret agents.

_____. *Mortal Instrument*. Holiday, 1977. A young boy with supernatural powers assumes several different disguises because he is being used unfairly in a sadistic computer installation.

_____. *New York City Too Far from Tampa Blues*. Holiday, 1975. Tom has adjustments to make as he tries for a corner shoeshine job. His friend, Aurelio, and he form a musical group and perform for money. They get so good they make a recording.

_____. *Nightmare Town*. Holiday, 1979. Jimmie, 16, orphaned, runs away to Los Angeles.

He meets Liz Gaynor whose family is killed and she is captured by a cult. He rescues her.

_____. *T.H.U.M.B.B.* Holiday, 1983. Tom and Aurelio sign up for the school band and form a marching band complete with cheerleaders. They march in the St. Patrick's Day parade. The Hippiest Underground Marching Band in Brooklyn.

_____. *Tomorrow Connection*. Holiday, 1984. Two musicians are stranded in San Francisco in 1906 and enlist Harry Houdini to help them find a way to their future.

_____. *Tune in Yesterday*. Holiday, 1978. Two boys enter a one-way door to the past. They are in New York City, 1942. It is fun until the threat of World War II begins. They are kidnapped and escape. They jump through another door into 1912.

_____. *Where the Deer and the Cantaloupe Play*. Oaktree, 1981. Teddy dreams of being a cowboy like his great-grandfather. He learns all the techniques. He goes to California and becomes an expert rodeo entertainer.

Beyer, Audrey. *Dark Venture*. Knopf, 1968. Demba is kidnapped by slave traders. Dr. Adam works for the slave traders to pay off a debt. He ends up buying Demba rather than see him sold to a cruel master.

_____. *Katherine Leslie*. Knopf, 1963. Katherine, 16, was sentenced to fourteen years in jail for a theft she did not commit. She escapes and works as a governess in America.

_____. *Sapphire Pendant*. Knopf, 1961. Elizabeth, disguised as a boy is pressed into naval service. Later she is a spy in Napoleon's home. Her guardian, Pierre, is also doing espionage work while she believes him to be a traitor.

Bibby, Violet. *Many Waters Cannot Quench Love*. Morrow, 1975. Constancy falls in love with a Dutchman who is an enemy of her people. With the help of a witch, Goody, she escapes with him.

Biber, J. *Treasure of the Turkish Pasha*. Scribner, 1968. Yirmi looks for a treasure stolen from the Jews and hidden in a monastery. He faces hardship and danger but returns the treasure to its rightful owners.

Bickman, Jack. *All the Days Were Summer*. Doubleday, 1981. Danny, 12, must move and his father bribes him with a dog. He does not like his new home or school but he loves his dog, Skipper. The dog saves Danny from drowning but at the cost of his own life.

_____. *Baker's Hawk*. Doubleday, 1974. An 11-year-old boy nurses a wounded hawk back to health.

Biemiller, Carl. *Albino Blue*. Doubleday, 1968. Kent hooks an albino bluefish. Should he set it free, kill it, or give it to the Marine Laboratory? He sets it free. This news breaks and men want to make a tourist attraction, a TV special, etc.

_____. *Escape from the Crater*. Doubleday, 1974. The Hydronauts are sent to destroy the Kirl but try to convince the council that they should live as equals and friends.

_____. *Follow the Whales.* Doubleday, 1973. This is a follow-up story of the further adventures of the Hydronauts.

_____. *Hydronauts.* Doubleday, 1970. Nuclear blasts have melted the ice caps and the world is underwater. Kim protects the kelp beds from poison, herds meat-producing sharks and finds a lab that has developed a new human form adapted to the sea.

Bierhorst, John. *Ring in the Prairie.* Dial, 1970. A Shawnee legend of a romance that spans the earth and the heavens.

Biesterveld, Betty. *Run, Reddy, Run.* Nelson, 1962. Herrilee wants a pet of her own. She befriends many wild animals but must leave them when she moves. Her pet fox must be set free and not kept as a house pet.

Billington, Elizabeth. *Getting to Know Me.* Warne, 1982. Peter and Billy go to a small town for the summer. They face up to a local bully and come to accept the role of their divorced father in their lives.

_____. *Move.* Warne, 1984. Tim's mother is mugged and the family moves from the neighborhood. It causes some problems. However, Tim and his mother grow into stronger people because of it.

Birdseye, Tom. *I'm Going to Be Famous.* Holiday, 1986. Arlo wants to get into the Guinness Book of World Records. He plans on doing it by eating more bananas in less time.

Bischoff, Julia. *Paddy's Preposterous Promises.* Scott, 1968. Paddy helped the Haley family on their farm. He inspires the five children with his tales and promises and his invention of fabulous toys.

Bishop, Claire. *Twenty and Ten.* Smith, 1984. During World War II a French nun and her twenty students hide ten refugee children from the Nazis.

Bishop, Curtis. *Fast Break.* Lippincott, 1967. Rene is Mexican and an excellent basketball player. He inspires Sam and they work together. When his visa runs out Sam finds a way for Rene to remain in America.

_____. *Field Goal.* Lippincott, 1964. Tom is overweight and can't make the football team. His new coach gives him another chance and he finds that he is a good kicker. But he still must lose weight.

_____. *Gridiron Glory.* Lippincott, 1966. Bozo, good at football, but poor in school, drops out when he can no longer play football. He later realizes he needs school more than football and goes back and works hard.

_____. *Little League Double Play.* Lippincott, 1962. Ronnie makes the Little League team. He must practice secretly because his aunt doesn't approve of sports. He and Julian make a good double play combination and are stars until Aunt Susan finds out.

_____. *Little League Heroes.* Lippincott, 1960. Loel tries out for Little League but feels he has a slim chance, not because of his playing but because he is black. He learns about prejudices and their results.

_____. *Little League, Little Brother.* Lippincott, 1968. Jesse and Duane are brothers whose father wants them to be battery mates. Jesse doesn't want to catch even though Duane is a good pitcher. He finally gets to play the position he wants.

_____. *Little League Stepson.* Lippincott, 1965. Robin's mother marries a manager of a Little League team. He thought this would put him on the team but he had to prove himself first.

_____. *Little League Victory.* Lippincott, 1967. Ed plays baseball well enough but can't control his temper so no one is choosing him for their team. He got a chance and learned to get along with his teammates.

_____. *Rebound.* Lippincott, 1962. Rob plays center and is transferring to a bigger school where he is not top dog. But friends, an understanding girl and a wise coach help him adjust.

_____. *Sideline Quarterback.* Lippincott, 1960. Jim moves to a new school and he is not eligible to play for one year. But he copes with this and comes out the better for it.

Bishop, Jim. *Day Lincoln Was Shot.* Harper, 1964. A story of Lincoln's final 24 hours and Booth's deadly plan.

Blackwood, Gary. *Dying Sun.* Atheneum, 1989. Because of a change in world weather people are moving south. James' family tried Mexico but returned north. James and his friend Robert follow later. James remains but Robert returns south.

_____. *Wild Timothy.* Atheneum, 1987. Tim is lost for three weeks in the mountains. He is not trained as an outdoorsman but does rely on natural skills to survive.

Blades, Ann. *Boy of Tache.* Tundra, 1963. Tache is an Indian reservation in Canada. A young Indian from there goes on a trapping trip.

Blair, Cynthia. *Freedom to Dream.* Nal, 1987. A story of a girl who moved 200 years into the past and saw the Constitution as it was being written.

_____. *Strawberry Summer.* Ballantine, 1986. Susan and Christine are at Camp Pinewood as counselors. Someone wants to buy the camp at any price. Sue and Chris look into the matter before they become victims.

Blakey, Madge. *Calypso Island.* Westminster, 1970. Peter lives on the Island of St. Thomas. He and two friends find a ring of counterfeiters whom they help capture.

Blatty, William. *Exorcist.* Bantam, 1971. Chris changes from a normal girl into a screaming monster. She is thought to be possessed by the devil and a priest is going to rid her of this evil.

Blessing, R. *Passing Season.* Little, 1982. Craig

lives in a town where football is everything. He plays but doesn't enjoy it. But he becomes a hero in an unusual way.

Blinn, William. *Brian's Song.* Bantam, 1972. Brian is an easy going football player who doesn't mind rooming with Gayle, a black player. Brian is dying and Gayle helps ease the way.

Blish, James. *Life for the Stars.* Putnam, 1962. Chris does not want to leave Earth for outer space but is taken by accident anyway. He helps in a crisis situation.

_____. *Vanished Jet.* Weybright & Talley, 1968. A suborbital transport disappears. Stan's parents are aboard. He tries to locate them.

Bloch, Marie. *Bern, Son of Mikula.* Atheneum, 1972. Bern is captured by nomads and is then recaptured by his own people. He doesn't fit in but when the city is besieged he knows where his loyalty lies.

_____. *Displaced Person.* Lothrop, 1978. Stefan and his father are getting away from the slavery of the Germans and the vengefulness of the Russians. They wander around Eastern Europe.

_____. *Dollhouse Story.* Walck, 1961. What happens to dolls and a dollhouse when their owner outgrows them? These dolls will tell you, if you listen and are not seen by them.

_____. *Two Worlds of Damyan.* Atheneum, 1966. Damyan dreams of becoming an Olympic swimmer, but he needs a teacher and practice. He gets a teacher in a special swimming class but the conflict at home is still there.

Blos, Joan. *Brothers of the Heart.* Macmillan, 1985. Shem is a clerk on a fur-trading expedition. He is stranded in a cabin during a bitterly cold winter. He is found by an old Ottowan Indian woman.

_____. *Gathering of Days.* Scribner, 1979. Catherine, 14, writes in her diary about life in New Hampshire. She tells about runaway slaves, her father's remarriage and her best friend's death. Newbery winner, 1980.

Blue, Rose. *Grandma Didn't Wave Back.* Watts, 1972. Debbie loved her grandmother. She baked cookies, and talked to Debbie about her things: china objects, old clocks, handmade shawls, and other interesting things. Then grandma got sick and died!

_____. *Me and Einstein.* Human Sciences, 1979. Bobby can't read and doesn't want anyone to know. He is dyslexic and needs special help.

_____. *Month of Sundays.* Watts, 1972. A boy's reaction to his parents' divorce. A talk with his father after some heartaches lets him accept his new life.

_____. *My Mother the Witch.* McGraw, 1980. Betsey lives in Puritan New England in the 1700's. Her father is shipwrecked but finally does return home.

_____. *Nikki 108.* Watts, 1973. Nikki's brother died of an overdose of heroin. She is

determined not to get involved in this kind of life.

_____. *Quiet Place.* Watts, 1969. A youngster moves from foster home to foster home, including a children's shelter before a happy home is found.

Blum, Robert. *Girl from Emeraline Island.* Ballantine, 1984. Ellia ran away again, this time to Stone Coast Shrine, an all-boy military school. So far she has not been detected but she knows she soon will. She must escape before she is found out.

Blume, Judy. *Are You There God? It's Me, Margaret.* Bradbury, 1970. Margaret talks to God about a number of different things: her sex, her religion, her family, etc.

_____. *Blubber.* Bradbury, 1974. Linda is called Blubber as a result of the report she gave on whales. Jill and Robby and others in her class pick on her until what was fun is no longer so.

_____. *Deenie.* Bradbury, 1973. Deenie is 13 and wants to be with her friends, try out for cheerleader and get involved with boys. But her mother wants her to be a model, so she spends her time dressing and posing for cameras.

_____. *Iggie's House.* Bradbury, 1970. A black family moves into the house where Iggie used to live.

_____. *It's Not the End of the World.* Bradbury, 1972. Karen's father left home and is getting a divorce and her mother doesn't care; but Karen does. She tries to get them together, not understanding that maybe they couldn't be a "normal" family.

_____. *Just as Long as We're Together.* Watts, 1987. Stephanie and Rachel are friends. Then pretty Alison joins them as a threesome. Can this last or will two of them make a new pair?

_____. *Otherwise Known as Sheila the Great.* Dutton, 1972. Peter finds out that Sheila is afraid of dogs, bees, water, noises, etc.

_____. *Starring Sally J. Freedman, as Herself.* Bradbury, 1977. Sally met friends when she moved to Florida for her brother's health. She wrote a letter to the Chief of Police about Hitler being in Miami Beach in disguise.

_____. *Superfudge.* Dutton, 1980. Fudge's life is a mess. He moves from New York to New Jersey. He gets a baby sister called Tootsie. And he doesn't like either event.

_____. *Tales of a Fourth Grade Nothing.* Dutton, 1972. Peter is the younger brother of Fudge. Among other things Fudge swallows Peter's pet turtle. Peter has a friend in Sheila.

_____. *Then Again, Maybe I Won't.* Bradbury, 1971. Tony had problems: his friend Joel was a shop-lifter; he watched Joel's sister, Lisa, secretly as she undressed at night; his mother had serious money problems and Miss Tobin, his math teacher, knew.

_____. *Tiger Eyes.* Bradbury, 1981. Davey,

whose father has been murdered, meets Wolf, whose father is dying of cancer.

Boatright, Lori. *Out of Bounds.* Fawcett, 1982. Judie tries out for and gets a spot on the boys' varsity basketball team. But the worst is yet to come.

Bodecker, N.M. *Carrot Holes and Frisbee Trees.* Macmillan, 1983. Would you believe carrots so big they could be used for digging?

Bodelson, Anders. *Operation Cobra.* Nelson, 1979. A band of terrorists plan to seize Frederik's house and use it as a site to commit assassination. Dan and Arim foil the attempt.

Boden, Hilda. *Foxes in the Valley.* McKay, 1963. While hunting the foxes that are raiding their farm a girl and her grandmother solve a local mystery.

————. *House by the Sea.* McKay, 1962. Two girls are spending the summer at The Haven, a resort. They sail, swim and explore.

Bodker, Cecil. *Silas and Ben-Godik.* Delacorte, 1978. Silas and Ben-Godik spend a year traveling by horseback and encounter many strange and harrowing adventures including rescuing a young boy who has been kidnapped.

————. *Silas and the Black Mare.* Delacorte, 1967. Silas overcomes several problems to keep the splendid mare he has won from a greedy horse trainer.

————. *Silas and the Runaway Coach.* Delacorte, 1978. Silas still has many adventures even though he is now living with a very rich family and learns manners and reading. He and the family's son are kidnapped by an old enemy of Silas'.

Bograd, Larry. *Bad Apple.* Farrar, 1982. Nicky is caught stealing and is arrested. He has always been poor and lived on the streets.

————. *Bernice Entertaining.* Delacorte, 1987. Bernie, 10, is a comedian and a liar. He goes from one crisis to another: football, bullies, sister, etc.

————. *Better Angel.* Lippincott, 1985. Matt and Jesse are best friends. Jesse is the athlete, Matt is not. They both fall in love with a cheerleader named Natalie. Watch the language in this one.

————. *Fourth Grade Dinosaur.* Delacorte, 1989. Juan, an Hispanic, is being teased by other students and his friend, Billy, is afraid to come to his defense.

————. *Kolokol Papers.* Farrar, 1981. Lev is head of family when his father is arrested for civil rights activity in Russia. He tries to get the transcripts of his father's trial.

————. *Los Alamos Light.* Farrar, 1983. A story of how several families, but especially Maggie's, cope with living with nuclear activity. Maggie's father is a physicist in the nuclear plant.

————. *Poor Gertie.* Delacorte, 1986. Gertie lives in an imaginary world of her own making. She wants to earn money to help with the rent but she draws and collects used chewing gum.

————. *Travelers.* Lippincott, 1986. Jack's father was killed in Vietnam. He thinks about him in superhuman images. As he learns the truth about his father he learns something about himself.

Bolton, Carole. *Dark Rosaleen.* Morrow, 1964. Barbara's grandfather bought an old Ford and named it Dark Rosaleen. She took the car to have it serviced and fell in love with the mechanic.

————. *Good-Bye Year.* Lodestar, 1982. Rosemary's father plays in a traveling band. She stays with her mother and a cat that is given to them. It is worth $1,000.00 if it stays healthy.

————. *Little Girl Lost.* Morrow, 1975. Liz's sister Carrie disappeared before she was born. She lives in the shadow of that sister because her mother is obsessed with her return.

————. *Never Jam Today.* Atheneum, 1971. Set in 1917 during the suffragette movement, Maddy works for this women's rights cause. Her parents are against her actions.

Bond, Ann. *Saturdays in the City.* Houghton, 1979. Two resourceful boys go into the city and have many adventures.

Bond, Michael. *Bear Called Paddington.* Houghton, 1958/1968. A bear, who lives with the Browns, gets in all kinds of mischief.

————. *Complete Adventures of Olga de Polga.* Delacorte, 1983. Olga, an imaginative guinea pig, keeps all her animal friends captivated with her stories and adventures.

————. *More About Paddington.* Houghton, 1962. In this story Paddington decides to re-do the room the Browns gave him as his own.

————. *Olga Carries On.* Hastings, 1977. Olga is a guinea pig who fights a fire and sets a trap for an uninvited guest.

————. *Olga Meets Her Match.* Hastings, 1975. Olga, the guinea pig, matches her wits with Boris, another guinea pig who tells more outlandish tales than Olga.

————. *Paddington Abroad.* Houghton, 1972. Map and language troubles are Paddington's concern now.

————. *Paddington at Large.* Houghton, 1962. Now Paddington is going to help mow the lawn but somehow he loses control of the lawn mower and again chaos.

————. *Paddington at Work.* Houghton, 1967. After visiting Peru Paddington is ready to get back to work.

————. *Paddington Goes to Town.* Houghton, 1968. Now Paddington is taking to cooking. But his desserts are not what they are cracked up to be.

————. *Paddington Helps Out.* Houghton, 1960. Paddington wants to help with the household chores but when he enters the laundry room there's chaos.

————. *Paddington Marches On.* Houghton, 1964. Paddington is determined to go to work. He tries several jobs but a bear in a marmalade factory!!!

_____. *Paddington on Screen.* Houghton, 1982. Paddington is a television star, but his mishaps follow him wherever he goes.

_____. *Paddington on Top.* Houghton, 1974. Paddington has troubles on his first, and last, day in school.

_____. *Paddington Takes the Air.* Houghton, 1970. Troubles again for Paddington as he meets crisis after crisis.

_____. *Paddington Takes the Test.* Houghton, 1980. A driving test for Paddington. Heaven forbid!!

_____. *Paddington Takes to T.V.* Houghton, 1974. Paddington wins a baking contest and goes on television.

_____. *Tales of Olga de Polga.* Macmillan, 1971. Olga is a guinea pig with a funny imagination and tells her fellow animals stories of great interest.

Bond, Nancy. *Another Shore.* McElderry, 1987. A twist of fate hurls a 20th century girl into the 18th century.

_____. *Best of Enemies.* Atheneum, 1978. Charlotte experiences a celebration that does not go as planned. The Patriot's Day re-enactment is perhaps too real.

_____. *Country of Broken Stone.* Atheneum, 1980. Penelope is involved in an archeological dig that is resented by the local people. She makes friends and after some destructive incidents comes to understand the natives' concerns.

_____. *Place to Come Back To.* Atheneum, 1984. When Charlotte's friend, Oliver, is saddened by the death of his guardian, he turns to Charlotte who must make decisions and face responsibilities she doesn't want.

_____. *String in the Harp.* Atheneum, 1976. When a harp tuning fork is found, three children find themselves transported back to the sixth century.

_____. *Voyage Begun.* Atheneum, 1981. Paul and his friend, Mickey, are remodeling an abandoned boat. They are doing it to help an old man in a nursing home. The time is bleak and the country devastated by pollution and greed.

Bonham, Barbara. *Challenge of the Prairie.* Bobbs, 1965. Toby's father is killed and he is "head of the house." He faces the hardship of homesteading and a siege of grasshoppers but finally gets ownership papers.

Bonham, Frank. *Burma Rifles.* Crowell, 1960. Jerry finds that war is a horror while fighting in Burma during World War II. He is of Japanese descent and uses this to advantage in questioning Japanese officers.

_____. *Chief.* Dutton, 1971. Henry Crowfoot is fighting to reclaim land he believes belongs to his people. It is city land taken illegally from Indians long ago. After many complications the Santa Rosa Indians will get some help.

_____. *Cool Cat.* Dutton, 1971. Buddy, who lives in Dogtown, needs money to buy a much wanted and needed scooter. He listens to a newcomer to Dogtown about how to make money faster than at a part-time job.

_____. *Deepwater Challenge.* Crowell, 1963. Cam buys a fishing boat to dive for abalone to help the family fortune. He finds professional diving dangerous what with octopi and tangled hoses.

_____. *Durango Street.* Dutton, 1965. A story that deals with the gang warfare in a big city ghetto.

_____. *Forever Formula.* Dutton, 1979. Evan is thawed by a doctor who wants to exploit the method of "eternal life." Evan finds the world now inhabited to be environmentally degraded. He wants to help in some way.

_____. *Friends of the Loony Lake Monster.* Dutton, 1972. Gussie protects her pet dinosaur by resourceful means and helps the environment at the same time.

_____. *Gimme an H, Gimme an E, Gimme an L, Gimme....* Scholastic, 1986. Dana and Katie are friends. Katie has suicidal tendencies and Dana saves her from self destruction.

_____. *Hey, Big Spender.* Dutton, 1972. Cool can't believe he has a summer job of giving away a million dollars. He tries to separate out the families who are most in need. He thinks there should be no problems.

_____. *Honor Bound.* Crowell, 1963. A young man gets mixed up in a pro-slavery dispute while on the first run of the Great Southern Overland Mail.

_____. *Loud, Resounding Sea.* Crowell, 1963. Skip's life is saved by a dolphin and they become "friends." They are able to communicate somewhat.

_____. *Missing Persons League.* Dutton, 1976. Brian, 17, lives in the near future. Pollution abounds. His mother and sister disappear. He searches for them in a futuristic world.

_____. *Mystery in Little Tokyo.* Dutton, 1966. Danny and Carol are to take part in the Nisei Festival. But when a stranger comes along and odd things happen Danny and a police friend try to find out what the trouble is.

_____. *Mystery of the Fat Cat.* Dutton, 1968. A "counterfeit" cat (Is it really Buzzer Adkins?) holds the key to saving the Oak Street Boys Club in Dogtown for its four main members.

_____. *Mystery of the Red Tide.* Dutton, 1966. Tommy and his uncle, a marine biologist, uncover a fish smuggling operation while collecting specimens.

_____. *Nitty-Gritty.* Dutton, 1968. A bright, young black, Charlie, wants to continue school but his father wants him to quit. An uncle comes to his aid but Charlie, living in Dogtown, still has difficult decisions to make.

_____. *Premonitions.* Holt, 1984. Kevin edits the high school paper. He likes Anne; her brother was said to be able to predict the future and he drowned mysteriously. It turns out it is Anne that is psychic.

_____. *Rascals from Haskell's Gym.* Dutton, 1977. Sissy is on the gymnastic team: The Butterflies. They compete with Haskell's Rascals. There is something strange going on with twins. A fraud is discovered.

_____. *Speedway Contender.* Crowell, 1964. Colton likes cars better than school. He builds a speed car but is helped by a friend to see the value of an education.

_____. *Viva Chicano.* Dutton, 1970. A young Mexican-American (Chicano), Kenny, unwillingly breaks parole and must hide because of unjust accusations.

_____. *War Beneath the Sea.* Crowell, 1962. Keith returns to Pearl Harbor two months after the attack and enters the submarine service. He had always been against this.

Bonnell, Dorothy. *Why Did You Go to College, Linda Warren?* Messner, 1970. Linda is beautiful and college is unimportant. But some disturbing events and help from her friends create a real need for college.

Bontemps, Arna. *Lonesome Boy.* Beacon, 1988. Bubber lives in New Orleans and his life is wrapped up in his trumpet. It is when he is without it that he is lonesome.

Bonzon, Paul. *Orphans of Simitra.* Criterion, 1962. Por and his sister Mina are placed on a farm in Holland after an earthquake leaves them homeless. One day Mina disappears and Por goes to look for her.

_____. *Pursuit of the French Alps.* Lothrop, 1963. A cross is stolen from church and a boy is unjustly accused. He runs away and meets a friend who believes in him and they look for the real thief.

Booky, Albert. *Apache Shadows.* Sunstone, 1986. Great Star and Crazy Legs are two Indian warriors who are faced with the invasion of the white man into their territory. They continue to fight their losing battle.

_____. *Son of Manitou.* Sunstone, 1987. An adventure story of the white man's move into Indian territory. There are a slight mystery and a bit of romance to carry the story along.

Borchard, R. *Donkeys for Rogador.* Dial, 1967. The five children loved their new house but didn't like the butchers who killed donkeys. They started a campaign to stop this. They discovered some caves and the harrowing events unfolded.

Borich, Michael. *Different Kind of Love.* Holt, 1985. Weeble, 15, has a crush on her twenty-five-year-old uncle who plays in a band. She must then fight off his too serious "propositions."

Borland, Hal. *Penny, the Story of a Free Minded Basset Hound.* Lippincott, 1972. Penny adopted the Borlands for months before the owner came to claim her. Months later she is back and the owner tells them to keep her. She goes off occasionally and then one day never comes back.

_____. *When the Legends Die.* Lippincott, 1963. Tom grew up as an Indian but joined the white man's rodeo as a bronco rider. He had to find his real self.

Bornstein, Ruth. *Little Gorilla.* Seabury, 1976. Little Gorilla's family and friends try to help him overcome his growing pains.

Bosse, Malcolm. *Barracuda Gang.* Dutton, 1982. Three students are trapped in an underwater cave. They are afraid of drowning and learn a lot about each other before they escape.

_____. *Captives of Time.* Delacorte, 1987. Anne and her mute brother live with an uncle who teaches Anne how to make clocks in medieval Europe. It is a valuable art but because of social change and the rise of cities life becomes unpredictable.

_____. *Ganesh.* Crowell, 1981. Jeffery lived in India until his father died, then he went to England where he made friends through his Yoga and Hinduism knowledge. He and his friends save their community from a highway project.

_____. *79 Squares.* Crowell, 1979. A young boy makes friends with an ex-convict who is dying.

Boston, Lucy. *Castle of Yew.* Harcourt, 1965. Joseph looks at a yew bush shaped like a castle. As he gazes inside he becomes tiny and is inside the castle.

_____. *Children of Green Knowe.* Harcourt, 1955/1990. Tolly is a lonesome youngster living with his great-grandmother in an old house. But with the aid of his imagination he is able to find exciting adventures.

_____. *Enemy of Green Knowe.* Harcourt, 1964. Tolly and Ping are involved in a mystery that might harm Green Knowe when black magic from an old alchemist's book of magic is searched for.

_____. *Fossil Snake.* Atheneum, 1975. Rob puts the rare fossil of a coiled snake under the warm radiator and then something wonderful happens.

_____. *Guardians of the House.* Atheneum, 1974. Tom goes into the old house that was known as Green Knowe. He finds a lot of old carved masks and his adventure begins.

_____. *Nothing Said.* Harcourt, 1971. Libby visited her friend and her dog, Cobweb. There was a river nearby and one night a stranger from that river came to her room. Or did she dream it? But there was some proof that someone was there.

_____. *River of Green Knowe.* Harcourt, 1959. Three youngsters come to Green Knowe and, left to their own resources, explore the fascinating river in a canoe they found. Reality and fantasy merge as they move through their adventure.

_____. *Sea Egg.* Harcourt, 1967. Two

brothers find an egg shaped rock at the seaside and it magically hatches into a baby merman.

_____. *Stones of Green Knowe*. Atheneum, 1976. Roger, whose family once owned Green Knowe, is able to travel back and forth through time with the help of two magical stones he found.

_____. *Stranger at Green Knowe*. Harcourt, 1961. Ping, one of the three children who stayed at Green Knowe, befriends an escaped gorilla who finds his way to Green Knowe.

_____. *Treasure of Green Knowe*. Harcourt, 1958/1990. Granny tells Tolly stories as she works on her patchwork quilt. They learn of a treasure that has been missing for over a generation and begin to look for it.

Boswell, Thomas. *How Life Imitates the World Series*. Doubleday, 1982. A story about the Babe (Babe Ruth), Casey Stengel and team play.

Bosworth, J.A. *White Water, Still Water*. Atheneum, 1966. Chris, 13, is swept away on a raft. He is beached miles away from his home with only a penknife. He must find his way back home before winter sets in.

Bothwell, Jean. *Lady of Roanoke*. Holt, 1965. An exciting story of the "lost colony" of Roanoke.

_____. *Mystery Candlestick*. Dial, 1970. Pliny finds a candlestick with a message and gets involved in a spy ring in Webbs Landing in 1776.

_____. *Mystery Clock*. Dial, 1966. Benny has a hobby of clock making. He finds out why Miss Spencer's clock doesn't work. It is hampered by a letter and money her father didn't put in the bank.

_____. *Mystery Key*. Dial, 1961. Benny collects locks and keys. One day an old mysterious key shows up and things begin to happen. Then he and Emily put an old key to good use.

_____. *Parsonage Parrot*. Watts, 1969. Pru and Reese were preacher's kids and moved often. This time, at St. Stevens, they uncover trouble with the help of their pet parrot, Lucifer.

Bottner, Barbara. *Nothing in Common*. Harper, 1986. Melissa and Sara attend the same school. Sara's mother is Melissa's maid and friend. When she dies Sara tries to befriend Melissa's mother and get some money for art school.

_____. *World's Greatest Expert on Absolutely Everything ... Is Crying*. Harper, 1984. Jessie's life, which included Tucker, might change when Katherine Ann with the beautiful eyes enters the picture.

Bourne, Miriam. *Uncle George Washington and Harriot's Guitar*. Putnam, 1983. What Harriot wants mostly from her famous uncle is a guitar.

Boutis, Victoria. *Looking Out*. Four Winds, 1985. Ellen's parents are Communists. The Rosenbergs are on trial and her parents are on their side. Ellen sees them try to help fellow travelers. A good look at the age of McCarthyism.

Bova, Ben. *End of Exile*. Dutton, 1975. Another generation, after Lou and Dan, finds children without adults aboard a space ship headed for a far off planet. They find one adult and learn that they are all test tube babies.

_____. *Exiled from Earth*. Dutton, 1971. Lou lives in the 21st century. He is a computer engineer who is arrested and exiled to Earth. He escapes but is recaptured.

_____. *Flight of Exiles*. Dutton, 1972. The son of Lou Christopher, Dan, faces a fire which could be sabotage, a murder, and the discovery that the planet where he intended to settle is uninhabitable.

Bowen, Betty. *For Love of a Donkey*. McKay, 1963. Karin and her pet donkey, Bellissimo, traveled to the Children's Village in Switzerland. She and an old man got the donkey across the border.

Bowen, John. *Squeak: A Love Story*. Viking, 1983. Squeak is a lovesick homing pigeon who thinks like a human. She wants to build a love nest and have a baby but the boy birds don't seem to understand.

Bowen, Robert. *Hot Corner Blues*. Lothrop, 1964. Stacey plays third base on a college baseball team. He is sought by pro teams but decides against pro ball. He later changes his mind and gets into the majors.

_____. *Lightning Southpaw*. Lothrop, 1967. Eddie is coming back from Vietnam when his plane crashes. He survives but has amnesia. Later he plays baseball and through a playing field accident he regains his memory.

Bowers, Gwendolyn. *At the Sign of the Globe*. Walck, 1966. Kit wanted to become a glovemaker in Shakespeare's London. He worked hard and made friends and was able to realize his dream.

Bowers, John. *November ... December*. Dutton, 1977. B.C. is in his first year of college where he has an affair with an older girl and comes to realize life's lessons, including death.

Bowes, Elmer. *Trials of David Clark*. Hill & Wang, 1970. A black student is graduating from high school. He thinks back on his troublemaking days.

Boyd, Candy. *Charles Pippin*. Macmillan, 1987. A young girl tries to understand why her father, who returned from Vietnam, is so bitter about the war.

Boyer, Elizabeth. *Wizard and the Warlord*. Ballantine, 1983. Sigurd is caught in a war between light and dark elves. He has a magical box his grandmother left him when she died but he doesn't know how to open it.

Boylan, Rowena. *Better Than the Rest*. Follett, 1970. Robin is overweight but acts superior and is lonely. She meets Dick and he likes her in spite of her weight. She learns to meet friendship half way.

Boylston, Helen. *Sue Barton, Neighborhood Nurse*. Little, 1949. Sue is married and has three children. Her husband is head of a hospital. She begins to pick up her career again.

_____. *Sue Barton, Rural Nurse.* Little, 1939. Sue's romance with Dr. Barry is getting more serious. She is still moving ahead in her chosen career.

_____. *Sue Barton, Senior Nurse.* Little, 1937. Sue finishes training and is at a hospital where she meets interesting people. She has some personal problems with the head nurse but is working hard and efficiently.

_____. *Sue Barton, Staff Nurse.* Little, 1952. Sue is now married with children of her own. She still wants to use her training to help others so she helps out at the hospital.

_____. *Sue Barton, Student Nurse.* Little, 1936. Sue is in her first year of nurse's training. She and her two friends, Kit and Connie work to get through thir probationary period. Sue makes many minor mistakes but makes it through.

_____. *Sue Barton, Superintendent of Nurses.* Little, 1940. Sue is head of a training school for nurses. She meets, falls in love and marries Dr. Barry. She decides to resign and stay home to be a wife and mother.

_____. *Sue Barton, Visiting Nurse.* Little, 1938. Sue Barton is the visiting nurse at the Henry Street Settlement in New York. Her future as a nurse looks bright.

Bradbury, Bianca. *Amethyst Summer.* Washburn, 1963. Batley, 16, has trouble managing the house while her mother is away. She thought it would be easy but along with cleaning and cooking she has to keep her social life active.

_____. *Andy's Mountain.* Houghton, 1969. Andy wants to save his grandparent's farm because it will someday be his. The highway department wants to make it a highway. He does save the farm and also looks forward to a possible baseball career.

_____. *Boy on the Run.* Seabury, 1976. A 12-year-old boy learns to break away and be his own person.

_____. *Dogs and More Dogs.* Houghton, 1968. Tommy added another dog to his menagerie. So he formed an Animal Welfare Club. This, too, was a problem but it encouraged the town to get its own animal shelter.

_____. *Goodness and Mercy Jenkins.* Washburn, 1963. Mercy, an orphan, has trouble behaving in a sedate Puritan manner. As she grows up she falls in love with a sailor, gets married and at last has a home of her own.

_____. *Laughter in Our House.* Washburn, 1964. Gilly and Emmit sacrifice their summer plans to help their mother recover from a nervous breakdown.

_____. *Loner.* Houghton, 1970. Jay and his brother, Mal, do not get along. Jay gets a summer job at a marina and makes friends with the dockmaster, a stray dog and Eddie. It was a good summer because he gained confidence in himself.

_____. *My Pretty Girl.* Houghton, 1974. Shannon finds that she really can't keep her much wanted horse in a housing development.

_____. *New Penny.* Houghton, 1971. Carey and Hank must get married. They live in a trailer with the baby. Hank attends college but Carey doesn't bother until she learns she needs a diploma to do almost anything.

_____. *Red Sky at Night.* Washburn, 1968. A young girl learns to accept her mother's death.

_____. *Three Keys.* Houghton, 1967. Ted, 12, gets angry and stones his neighbor's greenhouse. He learns at juvenile court that there is no excuse for breaking the law.

_____. *Two on an Island.* Houghton, 1965. Jeff and Trudy are marooned on a small island for three days. They fight hunger, sunburn and cold nights. They give a lot of support to one another.

_____. *Undergrounders.* Washburn, 1966. A boy and his family help slaves escape to the North.

Bradbury, Ray. *Death Is a Lonely Business.* Knopf, 1985. Someone in California is killing off the "lonelies." Someone else is trying to find the killer. In between there are many interesting characters typical of Southern California.

_____. *Fahrenheit 451.* Simon & Schuster, 1969. In this time and place firemen didn't put out fires, all homes were fireproof. What they did burn were books! All books! And imprisoned the owners. One day a woman choose to burn herself with her books.

_____. *Halloween Tree.* Knopf, 1972. One Halloween night some boys visit a deserted house and find a pumpkin tree.

_____. *I Sing the Body Electric.* Knopf, 1969. Grandma is custom made to be ideal. She speaks 12 languages and plays every game. But Agatha doesn't like her and Tim and Tom don't know why.

_____. *Something Wicked This Way Comes.* Simon & Schuster, 1962. James and William, 14, discover Cooger and Dark's Pandemonium Shadow Show. Before they realize the consequences of their act they get their wish . . . and pay and pay and pay.

Bradford, Richard. *Red Sky at Morning.* Harper, 1968. Steenie and Marcia take in Josh, the new boy in school, as a friend. They teach him how to survive but their ways are very different than what is expected.

Bradley, Marion. *Hawkmistress.* Nal, 1982. Romilly has a gift of being able to communicate with animals but her father won't allow it. She runs away to the hills of Darkover to escape her father's plans.

_____. *Hunters of the Red Moon.* Day, 1973. Dane is a loner. He is kidnapped by space aliens. He teams up with other "slaves" and plans an escape but it fails. They must survive eleven days fighting off shape-changing monsters.

Bradley, Michel. *Norwood Tor.* Dodd, 1980.

Jeremy sets out to look for his brother, Paul, who was turned into an animal by Trago. Jeremy and his circus friends must escape Trago and release Paul.

Brady, Esther. *Toad on Capitol Hill.* Crown, 1978. How two young boys escape being in the way of the British troops as they advance on Washington in 1814.

Brancato, Robin. *Blinded by the Light.* Knopf, 1978. Gail must get her brother away from the cult: Light of the World. She joins the cult and then finds she can't get away.

_____. *Come Alive at 505.* Knopf, 1980. Danny is the DJ on his own radio station. It only exists in his room but he doesn't care. He has done many shows and wants to make it his career. There are some problems.

_____. *Don't Sit Under the Apple Tree.* Knopf, 1975. Ellis talks about her life and that of her friends during the last months of World War II; about how girls change when boys are around and vice versa; about dares taken and risks overcome.

_____. *Facing Up.* Knopf, 1984. Jep and Dave are friends. They are very different but they both like the same girl, Susan. But one night everything changes.

_____. *Something Left to Lose.* Knopf, 1976. Three young girls find that true friendship carries a lot of responsibilities.

_____. *Sweet Bells Jangled Out of Tune.* Knopf, 1982. Ellen, 15, wants to help her senile grandmother even though no one else seems to care. She is forbidden to see her but does so anyway with the help of a sympathetic boy.

_____. *Uneasy Money.* Knopf, 1986. Mike, 18, wins $2,500,000.00 in a lottery. First he plans to set up a foundation. Then he spends "like a drunken sailor." He is brought back to reality when he loses $60,000 in a fraud.

_____. *Winning.* Knopf, 1977. Gary is a star football player. He has a nice girlfriend, nice family and promising future. But here he is in the hospital and wondering why.

Brandel, Marc. *Mystery of the Kidnapped Whale.* Random, 1983. A stranded pilot whale needs to be rescued. It disappears from its makeshift pool. When it is found it is learned that it was being used to find a sunken ship.

_____. *Mystery of the Two-Toed Pigeon.* Random, 1984. Jupe, Bob and Pete are in charge of a carrier pigeon. He is spirited away and replaced by another. It is up to the Three Investigators to discover the theft ring using carrier pigeons.

Branfield, John. *Why Me?* Harper, 1973. Sarah, who has difficulty adjusting to her diabetic condition, is helped by her dog, Charlotte.

Branscum, Robbie. *Adventures of Johnny May.* Harper, 1984. Johnny May, 11, shows a great deal of responsibility in taking care of her ailing grandparents. Does she see a murder? Her guilt about killing a deer is eased by the man she saw.

_____. *Cheater and Flitter Dick.* Viking, 1983. Cheater, 14, is adopted. Her pet rooster is Flitter Dick. She survives a tornado and comes to terms with her father and his drinking problem.

_____. *For Love of Judy.* Lothrop, 1979. Frankie lived during the Great Depression. Life is difficult: his mother is pregnant, his sister is retarded and money is scarce.

_____. *Girl.* Harper, 1986. The difficult life of 5 children left with a cruel grandmother after their mother deserted them. There are child molestation and harsh living but there are also courage, strength and hope.

_____. *Johnny May.* Doubleday, 1975. The story of a young girl growing up in Arkansas while living with a grandmother. She is resourceful and imaginative.

_____. *Johnny May Grows Up.* Harper, 1987. Johnny May tries many self improvement tricks to impress her boyfriend, Aaron, but finds that it is important to herself regardless of what others think.

_____. *Murder of Hound Dog Bates.* Viking, 1982. Sassafras Bates is convinced that one of his three maiden aunts has killed his dog.

_____. *To the Tune of a Hickory Stick.* Doubleday, 1978. Nell and her brother JD were mistreated by their uncle. When he badly beat JD Nell took him and they ran away to an abandoned schoolhouse where they spent a cold, blizzardy winter.

_____. *Toby Alone.* Doubleday, 1979. Granny dies and Toby is left alone and does not cope well with those who want to help her. She likes Johnny Joe but puts him off, too.

_____. *Toby and Johnny Joe.* Doubleday, 1979. Toby grows up and solves the conflict between herself and Johnny Joe. They get married before he goes off to war. Tragedy upon tragedy hampers both Toby and Johnny Joe.

_____. *Toby, Granny and George.* Doubleday, 1976. Toby is an orphan left on the steps of Granny's house. George is her dog. Strange things are happening in the Arkansas hills surrounding Granny's home and Toby learns about love and caring.

Branson, Karen. *Potatoe Eaters.* Putnam, 1979. The O'Conner family left Ireland during the famine and came to New York. The mother remained behind and will join her family later. One member of the family has already died.

_____. *Streets of Gold.* Putnam, 1981. The O'Conner family realize that just being in New York is not going to solve their problems. They have family stress problems when jobs can't be found but they persevere.

Bratton, Helen. *Amber Flask.* McKay, 1964. Ann, 17, must clear Gail of mysterious thefts. Ann is afraid of heights but must overcome it to solve the mystery.

_____. *It's Morning Again.* McKay, 1964. Ruth is pressured to go after a Latin award but she prefers art. She must break away from her grandmother and make her own decisions.

Brauman, Franz. *Milik and Amina.* Bobbs, 1963. Milik and Amina must travel 2400 miles alone and penniless to get home. They have some good luck and some bad. They are imprisoned but are saved each time by kind people.

Bredes, Don. *Hard Feelings.* Atheneum, 1977. Bernie runs away to a rich uncle to escape the usual growing up problems only to learn that the best way to overcome them is to face up and mature, not run away.

Brenner, Barbara. *Falcon Sling.* Bradbury, 1988. Marina meets Nick, a man with a "past." They get involved in finding falcon smugglers, a profitable business.

_____. *Hemi: A Mule.* Harper, 1973. Hemi is a mule. His owner is Melville and when he goes away to college Hemi is sold to an army football team as a mascot. He doesn't like it and runs away to find Melville.

_____. *Mystery of the Disappearing Dogs.* Knopf, 1982. The Garcia twins are looking for dognappers because their own dog, Perro, has been taken by Operation Hot Dog.

_____. *Mystery of the Plumed Serpent.* Knopf, 1972. Elena and Michael are involved in a gang of thieves trying to smuggle Aztec treasures.

_____. *On the Frontier with Mr. Audubon.* Putnam, 1977. A 13-year-old describes his life as he travels west as an apprentice to the outstanding artist of nature, Mr. Audubon.

_____. *Year in the Life of Rosie Bernard.* Harper, 1971. Rosie's mother is dead and she must live with her mother's family. The setting is the Depression. She must adjust to a new school and also to her father's new wife.

Brett, Simon. *Three Detectives and the Knights in Armor.* Scribner, 1987. The three detectives suspect someone of trying to steal medieval suits of armor from Scalethorpe Castle.

_____. *Three Detectives and the Missing Superstar.* Scribner, 1986. Britain's leading Rock star has disappeared and the three detectives must find him.

Brick, John. *Captives of the Senecas.* Duell, 1964. Steve and Jack are captured by the Seneca Indians along with some farmers and a girl named Sally. They are forced to walk a long way and look for a chance to escape.

_____. *Yankees on the Run.* Duell, 1961. Matt and Eban, Yankees, plan and execute an escape from Andersonville prison. When they escape they fight to get back to Sherman and his troops.

Bridgers, Sue Ellen. *All Together Now.* Knopf, 1979. Casey stays with her grandparents and makes friends with Dwayne, an older retarded man. There are pathos, excitement and an auto racing uncle.

_____. *Home Before Dark.* Knopf, 1976. Stella Mae's family are migrant workers. She is fourteen when her father takes the family to work on a tobacco farm an uncle has inherited.

_____. *Notes for Another Life.* Knopf, 1981. Kevin and Wren are living with their grandparents while their father is recovering from a mental breakdown and their mother wants to live away from them, for now.

_____. *Permanent Connections.* Harper, 1987. Bob, 16, cares for his aunt and grandfather in the mountains of Appalachia. In this way he finds himself, too.

Briggs, Katherine. *Hobberdy Dick.* Greenwillow, 1977. Hobberdy Dick, a hobgoblin, finds new tenants living at Wedford Manor, a place he has guarded forever. He helps Anne and Joel find a treasure and save the family.

_____. *Kate Crackernuts.* Greenwillow, 1979. Two Kates, one the daughter of the Laird and one Kate Maxwell, grow up as friends. Both are involved in witchcraft but Kate's new mother is a witch and is jealous of her.

Brink, Carol. *Andy Buckram's Tin Men.* Viking, 1966. Andy builds four robots to help with the chores. Later when he and two others are shipwrecked in a flood the robots get him out of danger.

_____. *Bad Times of Irma Baumlein.* Macmillan, 1962. A nine-year-old girl is moving — new friends, status with peer groups and a lie that grows — are some of the problems she faces in this family situation.

_____. *Caddie Woodlawn.* Macmillan, 1935/1973. Caddie and her family have a difficult time ekeing out a living in pioneer Wisconsin but she and her brother make their life tolerable by their adventures in the wilderness. Newbery, 1936.

_____. *Family Grandstand.* Viking, 1952. Susan, 12, George, 11, and Dumpling, 7, along with their parents make up the Ridgeway family. Their father is a professor at a college where football overshadows all else.

_____. *Louly.* Macmillan, 1974. Chrys, Cordy, Louly and Ko-Ko camp in a tent in the back yard. Louly is taking care of them and they have a very good time.

_____. *Magical Melons.* Macmillan, 1944. This collection of stories about Caddie and her brothers tells of their many adventures, some safe and funny and some with dire consequences.

_____. *Two Are Better Than One.* Macmillan, 1968. Chrystal and Cordelia are best friends. They write a book about their dolls but it is really a dream of their own.

_____. *Winter Cottage.* Macmillan, 1968. A father who has no job during the Depression takes his two daughters to live in a summer cabin they fix up for the winter.

Brinley, Bertrand. *New Adventures of the Mad Scientists' Club.* Macrae, 1968. A group of science-minded boys explore strange happenings and come up with ingenious solutions.

Brinsmead, Hesba. *Pastures of the Blue Crane.* Coward, 1964. Ryl, 16, finds she has a grandfather. They both inherit a farm in a multiracial community. There they both learn from each other, especially Ryl and the secret of her past.

Brittain, Bill. *All the Money in the World.* Harper, 1979. A leprechaun grants Quentin his wish for all the money in the world. He gets more than he bargained for.

————. *Devil's Donkey.* Harper, 1981. Lots of magic with even more humor as Old Magda, the witch, practices her strange antics. Dan'l Pitt offended Old Magda and is turned into a donkey. Eventually he gets turned back.

————. *Dr. Dread's Wagon of Wonders.* Harper, 1987. Dr. Dread, a companion to the Devil, makes the townspeople of Coven Tree very greedy. But honesty prevails and he is reduced to dust. When the drought continues the rainmaker is brought in.

————. *Who Knew There'd Be Ghosts?* Harper, 1985. Parnell House is haunted. Tommy, Book and Harry use it as a play ground. One day they hear two men say they are going to tear it down to find something. What? Ghosts?

————. *Wish Giver.* Harper, 1983. Wishes are made and granted in this follow-up story of Old Magda, the witch, Dan'l Pitt and Stew Meat (Steward Meade). It, too, takes place in Coven Tree.

Brock, Emma. *Mary on Roller Skates.* Knopf, 1967. Mary broke her ankle rollerskating and tried to skate and ride a bicycle in a cast. Luckily it healed before she left for summer camp.

Brockmann, Elizabeth. *What's the Matter, Girl?* Harper, 1980. Anne waits for her handsome uncle to return from the war. When he comes home he is "shell shocked" and catatonic. She finds this hard to accept.

Broderick, Dorothy. *Hank.* Harper, 1966. Since Hank's father disappeared seven years ago Hank has become surly and is often in difficulty at school or with the law.

Brontë, Charlotte. *Jane Eyre.* Random, 1943. Jane had a very unhappy childhood. She goes to a boarding school where the owner is mean and selfish. She later becomes a private teacher and strange things happen in the house of Mr. Rochester.

Brontë, Emily. *Wuthering Heights.* Random, 1950. The star-crossed love affair between Heathcliff and Catherine.

Brookins, Dana. *Alone in Wolf Hollow.* Seabury, 1978. Bart and Arnie are looking for Uncle Charlie after their mother dies. He turns out to be a drunkard. They also stumble on a murder and the murderer is after them.

————. *Who Killed Sack Annie?* Clarion, 1983. David spends the summer in Los Angeles. He sees someone try to kill Sack Annie, a bag lady. He and his friend try to solve the mystery but it is not what it seems.

Brooks, Bruce. *Midnight Hour Encores.* Harper, 1986. Sib's mother deserted her when she was born. She went off to be a "hippie." At sixteen Sib and her dad go to find her and discover a very different person. What will Sib do?

————. *Moves Make the Man.* Harper, 1984. A basketball story that is more about friendship and growing up. Jerome is the first black to attend his high school. Bix, white, really knows how to play basketball. They become friends.

Brooks, Jerome. *Big Dipper Marathon.* Dutton, 1979. Ace is a polio victim. He visits his cousin in Chicago where they go to an amusement park. He gets on the Big Dipper and then can't get off!

————. *Make Me a Hero.* Dutton, 1980. Jake's older three brothers are in the service during World War II. Jake wants recognition and studies for Bar Mitzvah with his friend, Harry. Mr. Gold helps both boys understand tolerance and compromise.

Brooks, Terry. *Elfstones of Shannara.* Ballatine, 1984. The Ellery is a tree that protects elves from Demons. Will is trying to save the Ellery but he needs to know how to use the "Elfstones of Shannara" to protect himself and the Ellery from the Demons.

————. *Magic Kingdom for Sale—Sold!* Random, 1986. Ben buys Landover, complete with castle, dragon, etc. for $1,000,000. Then he learns about the monsters and evil things.

————. *Sword of Shannara.* Random, 1983. Shea and Flict in a future world. Shea is half human and half elf. He learns that he is heir to the Sword of Shannara. Warlock Lord is trying to destroy him and he must run for his life.

Brooks, Walter. *Freddy and the Baseball Team from Mars.* Knopf, 1955. The circus loses one of its Martians and Freddy goes to investigate. The outcome is that he was made coach of the baseball team as well as solving the mystery.

————. *Freddy and the Dictator.* Knopf, 1956. There is a revolt at Bean farm and Freddy is in the middle of it.

————. *Freddy and the Dragon.* Knopf, 1958. Freddy is unpopular when a crime wave hits town. All the evidence points toward animals being the culprits.

————. *Freddy and the Flying Saucer Plans.* Knopf, 1957. Freddy helps Uncle Ben save his flying saucer plans from spies.

————. *Freddy and the Ignormus.* Knopf, 1941. Freddy and his animal friends must rid the Bean farm of the fearful ignormous because he has all the other animals terrified.

————. *Freddy and the Men from Mars.* Knopf, 1954. The circus has phoney "Men from Mars." Freddy finds out. The "real" Martians come to investigate and help Freddy put everything right.

_____. *Freddy and the Perilous Adventure.* Knopf, 1942/1986. Freddy is looking forward to going to the fair and is not disappointed. He takes a ride in a balloon, and has a wonderful time with friends, the ducks and the spiders.

_____. *Freddy and the Pied Piper.* Knopf, 1946. The circus needs help and asks Freddy for his advice. He calls all the animals together by playing the role of the Pied Piper even though they are widely scattered.

_____. *Freddy and the Popinjay.* Knopf, 1945. J.J. Pomeroy almost eats Freddy's tail, thinking it is a worm. Freddy sees to it that Robin gets a pair of glasses to improve his eyesight.

_____. *Freddy and the Space Ship.* Knopf, 1953. Freddy's trip aboard a space ship that takes off and lands on earth. Freddy colors himself blue, finds out about the duck's stolen jewels and rids the Bean farm of unwanted relatives.

_____. *Freddy Goes Camping.* Knopf, 1948/1986. Someone is dressing as a ghost and scaring people. Freddy and his friends solve the mystery by giving that ghost a merry chase.

_____. *Freddy Goes to Florida.* Knopf, 1949/1987. The hero is Freddy, the pig. All the farm animals decide to escape the cold winter by going to Florida.

_____. *Freddy Goes to the North Pole.* Knopf, 1951. Freddy is off again on one of his many trips, this time to the North Pole. Another in a long series of books about Freddy.

_____. *Freddy Plays Football.* Knopf, 1949. Freddy is on the sidelines when he is pushed out on the football field. Now that he's there he plays, and plays well.

_____. *Freddy Rides Again.* Knopf, 1951. Freddy comes through his exploits with Mr. Elihu P. Margarine, a wealthy fox hunter and another menace, a rattlesnake, in a blaze of glory.

_____. *Freddy the Cowboy.* Knopf, 1951/1987. Freddy rescues Cy, a horse, from Mr. Flint. So now he learns to ride and to shoot.

_____. *Freddy the Detective.* Knopf, 1932/1987. Freddy, as detective, solves the mystery of the missing toy train.

_____. *Freddy the Pilot.* Knopf, 1952. Mr. Bean buys Freddy an airplane. He outwits the villain who employs air bombs to reach his goal: the attention of the bare-back rider.

_____. *Freddy the Politician.* Knopf, 1948/1986. Freddy gets politically involved with the First Animal Republic on the Bean farm. He fights the rats and woodpeckers over rights.

_____. *Henry's Dog "Henry."* Knopf, 1965. Henry names his dog "Henry." So when his mother tells him to do anything, the dog does it while Henry avoids it. Soon the dog tires of this and has his name changed to Rover.

Browin, Frances. *Looking for Orlando.* Criterion, 1961. Sam starts to work for the Underground Railroad. He is spending the summer on his Quaker grandparents' farm.

Brown, Alexis. *Treasure in Devil's Bay.* McGraw, 1962. Paul and Pierre find a ship on the bottom of the bay. They want to bring up some things for the museum but someone else is after the treasure.

Brown, Claude. *Children of Ham.* Stein & Day, 1976. A group of black youngsters in Harlem band together to survive an environment of drugs and prostitution.

Brown, F.K. *Last Hurdle.* Linnet, 1988. Kathy takes all her savings and buys a horse. He is in sad shape but she cares for him until he is quite presentable.

Brown, Fern. *Baby-Sitter on Horseback.* Ballantine, 1988. Melissa has a reputation for being irresponsible. It is reenforced when she loses the child she is watching.

Brown, Irene. *Answer Me, Answer Me.* Atheneum, 1985. Bryn's grandmother dies and now she is free to unravel the question of her birth and heritage.

Brown, Marcia. *Backbone of the King.* Univ. of Hawaii, 1984. An Hawaiian tale of a boy whose father has been exiled and needs help.

Brown, Pamela. *Other Side of the Street.* Follett, 1965. Linda wants to raise money; she tries saving but that's too slow. She tries housekeeping jobs, she tries to make her kid sister a TV model; nothing works until she becomes TV Quiz Queen.

Brown, Ray. *Suicide Course.* Houghton, 1980. "Dave" had a motorcycle accident and suffers amnesia. He looks for his identity. He is actually David's brother whom he accidentally killed in the accident.

Brown, Roy. *Battle of Saint Street.* Macmillan, 1971. Dockly Green is a construction site where the children play on weekends. They rescue a mistreated dog, Crusoe, and fight for his custody.

_____. *Cage.* Seabury, 1977. As part of an experiment several boys are changed from violent personalities to survivors by being put in an underground area without exits.

_____. *Day of the Pigeons.* Macmillan, 1969. Kids release some pet pigeons and try to recapture them through water, subways, alleys, etc. One kid is looking for his ex-con father who doesn't want him; the police are looking for runaways.

_____. *Escape the River.* Seabury, 1972. Brad, Kenny and Paul must learn to understand the frustrations a mentally handicapped boy can have.

_____. *Flight of Sparrows.* Macmillan, 1973. Four runaways try to survive in London by living in a condemned building.

_____. *No Through Road.* Seabury, 1973. Barry leaves home after his father and his friend get involved in a crime.

_____. *White Sparrow.* Seabury, 1975. Two

boys live by their wits in the dockside of London. They like this life until illness and a bitter winter make them seek help.

Bruckner, Karl. *Day of the Bomb.* Van Nostrand, 1963. A story of how two Japanese children survived the atomic bomb and find their parents. They are determined to build a future in spite of this major setback.

Bryan, C.D. *Friendly Fire.* Bantam, 1977. Michael was killed by "nonbattle causes" in Vietnam. After investigation his parents found that he was killed by "friendly fire," that is, he was accidentally killed by American forces.

Bryant, Bonnie. *Horse Crazy.* Bantam, 1988. A typical story of young girls and their horses.

Buchan, Stuart. *Guys Like Us.* Delacorte, 1986. Zack and Harry live on a house boat. They meet Skye, a wealthy girl. They become friends and pal around. Both boys like her but neither one gets her.

_____. *When We Lived with Pete.* Scribner, 1978. A young boy's mother and her former boyfriend are brought together by him.

Buchanan, William. *Shining Season.* Coward, 1978. John is an athlete who is fighting cancer. He coaches disabled kids and is supported by family and friends.

Buchwald, Art. *Bollo Caper.* Doubleday, 1974. Bollo is a leopard who doesn't want to become a fur coat for some Hollywood star. He outwits the furriers, the police, the F.B.I. and the President.

Buchwald, Emilie. *Floramel and Esteban.* Harcourt, 1982. Floramel and Esteban are an egret and a cow who form a strong friendship.

Buck, Pearl. *Big Wave.* Harper, 1973. After a Japanese boy's parents die he is taken in by a friend's family. A foster home story in Japan.

_____. *Matthew, Mark, Luke and John.* Day, 1967. Matthew is a Korean orphan who begs for a living. He bands together with other orphans who live the same way. In time they are helped by a kind American soldier.

Buck, William. *Dr. Anger's Island.* Abelard, 1961. Kelly and Biff solve the mystery of Dr. Anger, a conductor of the Underground Railroad. He wrote some poems that were hidden in an abandoned island castle.

Bull, Angela. *Wayland's Keep.* Holt, 1966. Wayland was determined to buy the Keep when it came up for sale. Malinda, Sophie and Anna, one hundred years later, learn about the purchase and its unhappy consequences.

Bulla, Clyde. *Almost a Hero.* Dutton, 1981. A young boy stays at a boarding school because he has no other home. He learns to accept his situation.

_____. *Beast of Lor.* Crowell, 1977. A story of the friendship of a boy and an elephant that was brought to England during the Roman conquest.

_____. *Benito.* Crowell, 1961. Benito has an interest in and a talent for art, but he lives with his uncle who is only interested in how much work he can do.

_____. *Charlie's House.* Harper, 1983. Charlie is an indentured slave sent from England to America.

_____. *Conquista!* Harper, 1978. The first horse, a wanderer from Coronado's expedition, is seen by a young Indian boy.

_____. *Down the Mississippi.* Harper, 1954. The adventures of a farmboy as he explores along the Mississippi River.

_____. *Ghost of Windy Hill.* Crowell, 1968. Jamie and Laura moved into a house that could be haunted. They made friends and had fun but one night the legend of Windy Hill appeared to be coming true.

_____. *Indian Hill.* Crowell, 1963. A Navajo family experiences unhappiness and adjustment when they move from their reservation to a city apartment.

_____. *Lion to Guard Us.* Harper, 1981. Three children, without a mother, are headed for America to join their father in Virginia.

_____. *Marco Moonlight.* Harper, 1976. Rich, spoiled Marco meets Flint, a boy from a neighboring village and wonders if it could be his brother.

_____. *My Friend the Monster.* Harper, 1980. Prince Hal thinks monsters live in a mountain and he wants to find out how to gain entrance.

_____. *Shoeshine Girl.* Crowell, 1975. Al has a shoeshine stand, and a usually lazy, uninterested girl works for him for the summer and matures in the process.

_____. *Viking Adventure.* Crowell, 1963. Sugurd goes through fierce storms to the land discovered by Leif Ericsson. He encounters treachery and deception.

_____. *White Bird.* Crowell, 1966. Luke found an abandoned baby, named him John Thomas and raised him. John Thomas found a wounded crow and nursed it back to health.

Bunting, Eve. *Big Cheese.* Macmillan, 1977. Two miserly sisters buy a huge cheese and now must think of ways to protect it. It changes their life.

_____. *Blackbird Singing.* Scholastic, 1983. Marcus is the go-between for his fighting parents.

_____. *Cloverdale Switch.* Lippincott, 1979. John and his grandfather suspect that aliens are taking over the bodies of people in Cloverdale. John's mother and his friend, Cindy, seem to be victims.

_____. *Demetrius and the Golden Goblet.* Harcourt, 1980. Demetrius is a sponge diver who dives for a golden goblet for the king and then tells the king what he sees. The king interprets his description to fit his own visions.

_____. *Empty Window.* Warne, 1980. C.G.'s friend is dying and he wants to catch a wild parrot for him.

_____. *Face at the Edge of the World.* Ticknor, 1985. Jed's friend, Charlie, committed suicide. Lon, a doper, said he, too, had seen "her face." Maybe that was why Charlie hanged himself.

_____. *Ghost Behind Me.* Pocket Books, 1984. Cinnamon's sister and mother die and she moves to San Francisco. She sees a strange car each day. Then she finds out about Felix and his girlfriend, Emily.

_____. *Ghost Children.* Clarion, 1989. Matt and Abby find life-size wooden dolls on their Aunt Gerda's front lawn. Someone is trying to get her out. Matt finds out who and solves the mystery.

_____. *Ghosts of Departure Point.* Harper, 1982. Vicki unwittingly caused an accident in which she and her three friends were killed. She is a ghost watching the people recover the bodies, even her own. This is her punishment for what she did.

_____. *Haunting of Kildoran Abbey.* Warne, 1978. A gang of starving Irish children hide in Kildoran Abbey which is haunted. They try to get food for themselves and their people from the English.

_____. *Haunting of Safekeep.* Lippincott, 1985. Sara and Dev say they are a couple in order to get a summer job. They find the ghost of Safekeep.

_____. *If I Asked You, Would You Stay?* Lippincott, 1984. Charles, known as Crow, lives in a secret apartment he found accidentally. One day he saves a girl from drowning in the ocean. He takes her to his secret place, hoping to trust her.

_____. *Is Anybody There?* Lippincott, 1988. Marcos, 13, is a latchkey kid. But someone is using his hidden key. Things are missing. He suspects Nick from upstairs because he doesn't like him or the attention he is paying his mother.

_____. *Janet Hamm Needs a Date for the Dance.* Clarion, 1986. Star and Karen are asked to the seventh grade dance but not Janet. She creates a dream date and then has to come up with a real one or admit her fantasy.

_____. *Karen Kepplewhite Is the World's Best Kisser.* Clarion, 1983. Karen is having a birthday party where she will kiss the boy she has a crush on. Her friend Janet helps her. A pretty, new girl, Star, is invited to her party. All ends differently than planned.

_____. *Mother, How Could You!* Lippincott, 1984. Cassie's mother is pregnant as a surrogate mother for another couple and Cassie and her friends are horrified.

_____. *One More Flight.* Warne, 1976. Jimmie finds and nurses back to health injured birds of prey. He befriends a runaway boy and helps him straighten out his priorities.

_____. *Our Sixth-Grade Sugar Babies.* Lippincott, 1990. Vicki and her friend must carry around five pound bags of sugar to learn about being parents in their school project. But they are concerned how it will look to the 7th grade boy they like.

_____. *Sixth-Grade Sleepover.* Harcourt, 1986. Janey's reading club is having a sleepover night in the school cafeteria. But Janey is afraid of the dark and doesn't want anybody to know; yet she wants to go to this big event.

_____. *Skateboard Four.* Whitman, 1976. The "Skateboard Four" are invaded by a newcomer who is a whiz with a skateborad. They become the "Skateboard Five" before a serious accident happens.

_____. *Someone Is Hiding on Alcatraz Island.* Clarion, 1984. Danny, 14, is being chased by the Outlaws, a gang of boys. He takes a boat to Alcatraz Island and they follow. He and a ranger on the Island are trapped all night by the bullies.

_____. *Strange Things Happen in the Woods.* Lippincott, 1984. The sun flashed and the world looked like a photo negative. Then Cindy changed; she acted strangely and had a black box that appeared to bring death to those around it.

_____. *Sudden Silence.* Harcourt, 1988. Bry, who is deaf, is killed by a drunk driver. His sister, Jesse, feels responsible. She tries to find the hit and run driver.

_____. *Surrogate Sister.* Lippincott, 1984. Cassie's widowed mother becomes pregnant by artificial insemination. She is to give the baby to a childless couple she knows. Cassie and her friends are divided on what they think of this arrangement.

_____. *Will You Be My POSSLQ.* Harcourt, 1987. Jamie and Kyle share a room at college to save expenses. They move apart as their feelings change from roommates to romance.

Bunyan, John. *Pilgrim's Progress.* Macmillan, 1926. Christian makes a pilgrimage to New Jerusalem from the City of Destruction. He has many toils and trials.

Burch, Jennings. *They Cage the Animals at Night.* Nal, 1984. Jennings is placed in a church orphanage where he is abused. He is hurt and ignored everywhere he goes. He remembers his mother and love but what happened?

Burch, Robert. *Christmas with Ida Early.* Atheneum, 1983. Ida Early becomes the target of the children's match-making schemes. During a Christmas pageant Ida livens up the play. Ida and the new preacher have different opinions about what happened.

_____. *D.J.'s Worst Enemy.* Viking, 1965. D.J. lives in the rural South in the 1930's. He has the usual problems and joys of a boy growing up. But his teasing and fibbing bring serious injury to his brother and sister, so he changes.

_____. *Hut School and the Wartime Home Front Heroes.* Viking, 1974. Kate and her friends attend school in makeshift quarters. They help pick cotton for a local family in Georgia during World War II.

_____. *Ida Early Comes Over the Mountain.* Atheneum, 1980. Ida arrives at the Sutton home at just the right time. She is an extraordinary housekeeper and cook and the children like her. However, they have a lot to learn about loyalty.

_____. *King Kong and Other Poets.* Viking, 1986. Marilyn wins a poetry contest and the respect of her doubtful classmates, including Andy. She and her mother are coping with the loss of her father.

_____. *Queenie Peavey.* Viking, 1966. Queenie Peavey is taunted because her father is in jail. She defends him to her own detriment only to find out, when he is paroled, that he is not worth defending.

_____. *Simon and the Game of Chance.* Viking, 1970. Simon's father was against everything Simon wanted to do: play basketball, work after school, etc. Then their new baby died and his mother was ill. Simon and his father had to work together.

_____. *Skinny.* Viking, 1964. Skinny, 11, is an orphan staying in a hotel until an orphanage can take him. He works at the hotel, doing all odd jobs.

_____. *Two That Were Tough.* Viking, 1976. An old man cherishes his independence and sympathizes with children with the same desires.

_____. *Tyler, Wilkin and Skee.* Viking, 1963. Three brothers live on a farm in the South. With a strict but fair father they get all their chores done before fun. Wilkins and Tyler are friendly toward Alex, who steals and then runs away.

_____. *Wilkin's Ghost.* Viking, 1978. Wilkin has a friend, Alex, who is a runaway accused of stealing. Wilkin tries to help and almost gets into trouble himself before he realizes that Alex is a phoney.

Burchard, Peter. *Bimby.* Coward, 1968. A young slave in Georgia just before the Civil War must make a decision that will affect the rest of his life. It is a story of pleasures, fears and terror.

_____. *Jed.* Coward, 1960. Jed, 16, is a Yankee soldier who aids a young Southern boy with a broken leg.

_____. *North by Night.* Coward, 1962. The reader will travel with several young officers during the Civil War and observe the consequences of war build-up and its aftermath.

_____. *Quiet Place.* McCann, 1972. During a summer in Maine a teenager develops a relationship with two different boys in which she learns more about herself.

_____. *Rat Hell.* Coward, 1971. Rat Hell is a prison where starvation and disease are rampant. This is a story of Jim and twenty other men who escaped from there against great odds.

_____. *Stranded: Story of New York.*

Coward, 1967. A young boy is stranded in New York City in 1875 when the city was corrupt and wide open.

Burleigh, David. *Messenger from K'itai.* Follett, 1964. Dashan, an arrow messenger in 1246, saves Mongolia from civil war by his journey to K'itai to uncover an enemy plot.

Burleson, Elizabeth. *Man of the Family.* Follett, 1965. Speck hunts for wolves, herds sheep, raises money for a Stetson hat he always wanted and catches a runaway horse. He is a man.

Burnett, Frances. *Little Princess.* Harper, 1962. The "Little Princess" is a penniless orphan until her rightful place is found and her fortune restored.

_____. *Secret Garden.* Lippincott, 1912. Mary is a lonely and willful girl. She goes to Yorkshire and meets her invalid cousin and together they investigate the mysterious locked garden. They change it and it changes them.

Burnford, Sheila. *Incredible Journey.* Little, 1961. A story of two dogs, one young and one old, and a Siamese cat who travel a long way, with many adventures, to get home.

Burnham, Sophy. *Dogwalker.* Warne, 1979. Two friends must find a dog with a bomb attached to her collar.

Burns, Olive. *Cold Sassy Tree.* Ticknor, 1984. Will Tweedy tells about how grandpa married Love Simpson just three weeks after his wife died; how Love plays piano and owns a big car. Will Tweedy "gets run over by a train."

Burt, Olive. *I Challenge the Dark Sea.* Day, 1962. Henry, the Navigator, and his crusade against the Moslems. There are great rivalry and loyalty between brothers.

Burton, Hester. *Beyond the Weir Bridge.* Crowell, 1969. Richard, Thomas and Richenda are friends but Richard is a Cromwell supporter. Thomas is a Loyalist and Richenda is a Quaker. These great religious and political differences could spoil their friendship.

_____. *Castors Away.* Dell, 1962. An adventure story climaxing with the Battle of Trafalgar.

_____. *Henchman at Home.* Crowell, 1970. Rob, William and Ellen are siblings. Rob is the fun brother who adds excitement; Ellen is the artistic sister and is a realist; William is the serious member and wants to become a doctor.

_____. *In Spite of All Terror.* World, 1968. Liz leaves London during World War II and lives with a family in the country. She learns about a different way of living with this warm, compassionate family.

_____. *Kate Ryder.* Crowell, 1975. This story takes place in 17th century Britain while it was torn between the Parliamentarians and the Royalists. The main character is a brave girl who lives through five years of this struggle.

_____. *Rebel.* Crowell, 1971. Stephen, an idealistic radical who cares for the poor and oppressed, goes to Paris instead of to his uncle's home in England. He is caught up in the French Revolution and is imprisoned.

_____. *Riders of the Storm*. Crowell, 1973. Stephen is freed from a French prison and returns to England where he continues his work with the poor and down-trodden. He is accused of being a government conspirator.

_____. *Time of Trial*. World, 1963. Margaret's father is imprisoned for publishing protests against poor housing. His book shop is burned and Margaret must make a new home. She meets and falls in love with Robert, a medical student.

Buscaglia, Leo. *Memory for Tino*. Morrow, 1988. Tino gives his family's television set to his elderly friend, Mrs. Sunday.

Busselle, Rebecca. *Bathing Ugly*. Watts, 1989. Betsy, 12, attends summer camp. She is supposed to lose weight; she does but it doesn't change her life. The end is Betsy "Bathing Ugly" in a unique costume.

Butler, Beverly. *Ghost Cat*. Dodd, 1984. Annabelle, 14, is visiting relatives for the first time. She hears a crying cat in an abandoned house and solves a 40-year-old mystery about a murder feud involving her grandparents.

_____. *Gift of Gold*. Dodd, 1972. Cathy is a blind college student and is told there is some hope for partially returned eyesight.

_____. *Light a Single Candle*. Dodd, 1962. A story of Cathy's adjustment to blindness. She lost her sight at age fourteen. She has a seeing eye dog and great support from her family, her teachers and her friends.

_____. *Maggie by My Side*. Dodd, 1987. Maggie is a guide dog for the blind, and the author talks about guide dogs in general and Maggie in particular.

_____. *My Sister's Keeper*. Dodd, 1980. Mary goes to help her sister who is having a baby. They quarrel but make up when a fire starts and they struggle for survival.

Butler, William. *Butterfly Revolution*. Putnam, 1961. A revolution is started at a summer camp for boys and gets out of hand. Similar to *Chocolate War*.

Butters, Dorothy. *Ten Leagues to Boston Town*. MacRae, 1962. Deborah and Ben are going to visit their sick father. They encounter runaway slaves and Indians; and they also help cature some counterfeiters.

Butterworth, Oliver. *Enormous Egg*. Little, 1956. Nate is helping a chicken hatch a super deluxe egg. It could be the only living dinosaur. Wouldn't that be great!

_____. *Narrow Passage*. Little, 1973. Nate, 13, is asked to go to France in search of prehistoric man. He meets Nicole and they discover a cave with drawings and a man!

_____. *Trouble with Jenny's Ear*. Little, 1960. When tape recorders, sound speakers and television equipment come to Pearson's Corners,

Joe and Stanley are excited. But their sister Jenny can hear unspoken things.

Butterworth, W.E. *Fast Green Car*. Norton, 1965. Tony is assigned to race sports cars. He is not sure he really wants to but as he learns about the car, he learns to love racing. He also loves Ellen whose father is a wealthy trucking business man.

_____. *Helicopter Pilot*. Norton, 1967. Tony is drafted into the army and learns to fly a helicopter. His best friend is killed in an accident and this decides his own future.

_____. *LeRoy and the Old Man*. Four Winds, 1980. LeRoy has witnessed a mugging and his mother sends him to live with his grandparents. His grandfather wants him to go back and testify but his runaway father wants him to run numbers.

_____. *Member of the Family*. Four Winds, 1982. Tom's dog, Precious, is unpredictable and has bitten people even though he is not really mean. Eventually the dog must be put to sleep.

_____. *Moose, the Thing and Me*. Houghton, 1982. Moose is a friend of Me (Peter) and The Thing is Peter's sheepdog. This is a story of life at a private school.

_____. *Narc*. Four Winds, 1972. In a well-to-do high school an apparent student turns out to be a policeman looking for drug distribution.

_____. *Return to Racing*. Norton, 1971. Tony is out of the army and in the advertising business. He finds both conflict (bad) and romance (good).

_____. *Steve Bellamy*. Little, 1970. Steve's father comes for him when his mother and step-father are killed. He owns fishing boats and Steve learns to adjust to a new life. He had never seen his father before.

_____. *Team Racer*. Grosset, 1972. Steve works for an auto company and becomes interested in racing.

Byars, Betsy. *After the Goat Man*. Viking, 1974. An overweight, sensitive boy gains insight and the strength to overcome his problems through his search for a friend's grandfather, The Goat Man.

_____. *Animal, the Vegetable and John D. Jones*. Delacorte, 1982. Two sisters are faced with staying with the son of their father's friend. John D. and his mother are both disliked by the girls and they show their resentment. An accident makes them see the light.

_____. *Beans on the Roof*. Doubleday, 1988. Everyone in the family is writing roof poems except George. He is trying very hard.

_____. *Bingo Brown and the Language of Love*. Viking, 1989. Bingo has no phone privileges because of a large telephone bill. Melissa has moved and bully Rambo is no longer a threat but life is still a tangle with a baby brother on the way.

_____. *Blossom Promise*. Delacorte, 1987. The Blossoms go through a big flood which causes much damage but their eccentric life style doesn't change.

_____. *Blossoms and the Green Phantom.* Delacorte, 1987. Pap falls in a dumpster and can't get out; Junior tries a new invention and Venn doesn't want his new friend to meet his crazy family.

_____. *Blossoms Meet the Vulture Lady.* Delacorte, 1986. Junior gets caught in his own coyote trap and is saved by Mad Mary, a somewhat strange recluse.

_____. *Burning Questions of Bingo.* Viking, 1988. Bingo worries about freckles, mixed-sex conversations, his girlfriend, Melissa, and bully, Rambo, who has moved in next door. His teacher has girlfriend problems when he has a motorcycle accident.

_____. *Cartoonist.* Viking, 1978. Alfie spends a lot of time in the attic with his drawings. It is an escape he likes. Then his brother comes back and his refuge is disrupted.

_____. *Computer Nut.* Viking, 1984. Kate, 10, is contacted by a space traveler, BB-9. She and friend Willie think at first it is a joke but meet BB-9 who is a comic and wants to come to Earth to entertain but his humor is "different."

_____. *Cracker Jackson.* Viking, 1985. Cracker is a 12-year-old boy who finds that his beloved babysitter is being abused by her husband. What should he do?

_____. *Cybil War.* Viking, 1981. Cybil has a funny relationship with two different boys.

_____. *Eighteenth Emergency.* Viking, 1973. Mouse was being bullied by Hammerman! He had a solution for all emergencies except #18 (Hammerman). He asked for trouble and now has to face the consequences.

_____. *Glory Girl.* Viking, 1983. Anna can't sing in a family of singers. She is in charge of selling records and cassettes. She and Uncle Newt, a family black sheep, are brought together as a bus overturns and they save the family.

_____. *Good-Bye, Chicken Little.* Harper, 1979. Jennie is upset by the senseless death of her favorite uncle but she learns to accept it.

_____. *House of Wings.* Viking, 1972. Sammy and his grandfather find a wounded crane and care for it. Sammy forgets his anger as he learns more about wildlife.

_____. *Midnight Fox.* Viking, 1968. Tom, 10, stays on a farm for the summer. He sees a fox and watches her daily. When she steals a turkey his uncle sets a trap but Tom releases it.

_____. *Night Swimmers.* Delacorte, 1986. Retta is the daughter of a country/western singer. She cares for her two brothers because he doesn't have the time. They grow away from her and she is, at first, hurt and resentful.

_____. *Not-Just-Anybody Family.* Delacorte, 1986. Maggie and Vern's mother is traveling with the rodeo. Their grandfather is in jail and their younger brother is in the hospital.

_____. *Pinballs.* Harper, 1972. Three children meet and form a heart-warming friendship. They are all battered children who live in a foster home.

_____. *Summer of the Swans.* Viking, 1970. Sara takes care of her retarded brother, Charlie. He runs away to see the swans and is lost. She and friends search for and find him. Sara makes friends with Joe whom she earlier suspected. Newbery, 1971.

_____. *T.V. Kid.* Viking, 1976. Lennie lives with his mother in a hotel. He is not very happy and lives with television and daydreaming. Then he is bitten by a rattlesnake and must survive a real tragedy, not television fantasy.

_____. *Trouble River.* Viking, 1969. Dewey must escape from the Indians that pursue him and is glad to have his canoe.

_____. *Two-Thousand-Pound Goldfish.* Harper, 1982. Warren goes to horror movies; he stays through many showings. He also writes horror stories. His mother has disappeared because she not only demonstrated but threw bombs. He is unsure of his future.

_____. *Winged Colt of Casa Mia.* Viking, 1973. A young boy has an uncle in Texas who was once a great stunt man. He goes for a visit to his ranch and meets a colt with supernatural powers.

Bykov, Vasilii. *Pack of Wolves.* Crowell, 1981. Levchuk reminisces about hiding from the Germans and their dogs, rescuing an infant baby, running away when the baby's father was killed. He is now going to visit that child, thirty years later.

Bylinksy, Tatyana. *Before the Wildflowers Bloom.* Crown, 1989. A girl tells of life in a Colorado mining town before World War I.

Byrd, Elizabeth. *I'll Get By.* Viking, 1981. Although Julie seems to have all a girl could want including success in school, what she really wants is her absent father to return, and have a normal two-parent family.

_____. *It Had to Be You.* Viking, 1982. Julie's friends, Marge and Kitty, are affected by the Great Depression. Julie wants to become an actress, and Marge is a social success. Both are optimistic, romantic dreamers.

Cabral, Olga. *So Proudly She Sailed.* Houghton, 1981. A "biography" of the USS Constitution (Old Ironsides) and her 80 years on the sea.

Calde, Mark. *Shadowboxer.* Putnam, 1976. Harry witnesses a murder but is put in a hospital for the insane. When he escapes he finds that all records of him have been destroyed. A good spy thriller.

Calder, Robert. *Dogs.* Delacorte, 1976. Orph escapes an experiment that makes dogs dependent on people. He joins a family but is rejected by the one he loves and joins a pack of killer dogs.

Calhoun, Mary. *Depend on Katie John.* Harper, 1961. Katie John and her family live in their twenty room inherited house where they rent out some rooms. This makes their lives change some.

_____. *Honestly Katie John.* Harper, 1963. Katie John is president of the "Boy Haters of America" club. She also goes to see a fortune teller.

_____. *It's Getting Beautiful Now.* Harper, 1971. Bert's mother ran away, his father is seldom home and he has one friend, Howard. Bert is arrested for having marijuana.

_____. *Julie's Tree.* Harper, 1988. Julie goes to live with her father and has difficulty adjusting but she finds a special place in an old tree where she is at peace.

_____. *Katie John.* Harper, 1960. Katie John is an irresistible young girl who moves into an inherited house with her family. They intend to sell the house but after living there for a while, they decide to stay.

_____. *Katie John and Heathcliff.* Harper, 1980. The one-time boy-hater Katie John falls in love with Jason. He is lured away by Trish, a country club type. But she finds old friend Edwin more interesting anyway.

_____. *Ownself.* Harper, 1975. Laurabelle conjures a "fairie" named Elabegathen. She needs help in understanding her circuit preacher father.

_____. *Witch of Hissing Hill.* Morrow, 1964. Witch Sizzle raised black cats to sell to other witches. One day a yellow cat was born and try as she may she could not get rid of it.

Calif, Ruth. *Over-the-Hill Ghost.* Pelican, 1988. Janie, 12, doesn't like the county until he meets Elmer. Elmer is what is known as an over-the-hill ghost who can't rest until a mystery is solved.

Call, Hughie. *Peter's Moose.* Viking, 1961. Peter raises a moose, Silly, after its mother dies. It follows him everywhere but disappears when shot at. He comes back to save children from a burning school. Then he returns to the wild.

Callaway, Kathy. *Bloodroot Flower.* Knopf, 1982. A tragic story of a brave young girl and her family.

Callen, Larry. *Deadly Mandrake.* Little, 1978. Pinch's town of Four Corners appears to be cursed by an evil spirit. Pinch and his friend, Sorrow, are going to uproot the mandrake growing in the cemetery and stop the curse.

_____. *Muskrat War.* Little, 1980. Winter is to be long and hard for Pinch and his father so he and his friend Charley are trapping and hiding muskrat hides. But swindlers trick them; they must catch them and recover the hides.

_____. *Pinch.* Little, 1975. Pinch lives by his wits; he feels that's the only way to survive. He turns a found quarter into an adventure which realizes him a pig for which his father has a different set of plans.

_____. *Sorrow's Song.* Little, 1979. Sorrow, a mute, finds a crane and wants to protect it from being caged. She believes in freedom for all creatures. She and Pinch do their best to help the bird.

Calvert, Patricia. *Hadder MacColl.* Scribner, 1985. Mary, 14, wants to fight for Scotland in 1745. She is against the changes made by the English.

_____. *Hour of the Wolf.* Scribner, 1983. Jake enters a dog-sled race in Alaska on behalf of his dead friend, Danny. Danny's sister is also in the race. It is a thousand mile race and Jake learns to appreciate nature.

_____. *Money Creek Mare.* Scribner, 1981. Ella Rae's mother leaves her family and Ella Rae must hold things together.

_____. *Snowbird.* Scribner, 1980. Willie and T.J. live with an aunt and uncle after the death of their parents. A foal is born and Willie writes "Snowbirds." A sad story.

_____. *Stone Pony.* Scribner, 1982. JoBeth goes to see her dead sister's horse. She learns to ride and meets Luke, whom she helps. She gets over her guilt about her sister's death.

_____. *Yesterday's Daughter.* Macmillan, 1986. David is adopted. He kills his parents and himself. His friend, Lynn, needs to find out why.

Cameron, Ann. *Most Beautiful Place in the World.* Knopf, 1988. Juan wants to go to school and is afraid his grandmother won't allow it. The setting is Guatemala.

Cameron, Eleanor. *Beyond Silence.* Dutton, 1980. Andy goes back in time where he meets Deirdre.

_____. *Court of the Stone Children.* Dutton, 1973. Nina's family moves to San Francisco and she is unhappy about it. Then she goes to a small local museum and meets a ghost.

_____. *Julia and the Hand of God.* Dutton, 1977. Julia wants to be a writer. Uncle Hugh gives her a new book full of empty pages for her to write "her impressions." She finds putting feelings into words is not easy.

_____. *Julia's Magic.* Dutton, 1984. Julia needs to see that "honesty is the best policy." She learns a lesson when another person is about to be harmed by Julia's unreported, and partially covered, accident.

_____. *Mr. Bass's Planetoid.* Little, 1958. With Mr. Bass away from Earth, Chuck and David must investigate the new invention of Mr. Brumblydge. They look through Mr. Bass' notes and end up following Mr. Brumblydge to Lepton.

_____. *Mysterious Christmas Shell.* Little, 1961. Tom and Jennifer learn a lesson about tradition and the importance of preserving old things.

_____. *Mystery for Mr. Bass.* Little, 1960. Mr. Brumblydge needs the help of the King of the Mushroom Planet, Ta, to recover from a strange ailment. Chuck and David get him and cope with new scientific discoveries.

_____. *Private World of Julia Redfern.* Dutton, 1988. Julia's uncle and grandmother help her through some tight moments of jealousy but she learns to forgive and love. She also experiences some artistic satisfaction.

_____. *Room Made of Windows.* Little, 1971. Julia aspires to be a great writer but she must go beyond her window, which she has used as an observation point, to a bigger world where love and compassion and reality exist.

_____. *Spell Is Cast.* Little, 1964. Cory visits her stepmother's family. Her stepmother did not adopt her after her parent's death and she feels alone. She goes through a near tragedy before she sees things as they really are.

_____. *Stowaway to the Mushroom Planet.* Little, 1956. Basidium must be kept a secret from the general public so that it can remain unharmed. But on the next trip there Chuck and David find a stowaway on board, Horatio Q. Peabody!

_____. *Terrible Churnadryne.* Little, 1959. Tom and Jennifer went to find the monster on San Lorenzo hill. What did they really see in the fog? Would people believe them? Was it a pre-historic monster?

_____. *That Julia Redfern.* Dutton, 1982. Julia wants to become a writer. She has to cope with her mother and aunt because her father, who believes in her, has gone away to fight in the war.

_____. *Time and Mr. Bass.* Little, 1967. This mystery involves an ancient scroll and, the Necklace of Ta that has been stolen and, of course, Mr. Bass's travel through time so that he might defeat the evil powers.

_____. *To the Green Mountains.* Dutton, 1975. Kath lives with her mother who runs a boarding house in a hot, sultry town. Her father is trying unsuccessfully to make a farm prosper. Kath wants to go to the Green Mountains of her grandmother.

_____. *Wonderful Flight to the Mushroom Planet.* Little, 1954. Two boys, David and Chuck, help Mr. Bass build a spaceship and then they take off in it to Basidium and help the people there by adding (See Title) to their daily diet.

Campbell, Barbara. *Girl Called Bob and a Horse Called Yoki.* Dial, 1982. Bob steals a horse who is going to the glue factory and with help puts him on a farm. She causes trouble and faces up to her crime.

Campbell, Harper. *Looking for Hamlet: A Haunting at Deeping Lake.* Macmillan, 1987. Toryn is a child actress. She meets the ghost of Caroline who died mysteriously. A romance with Craig and parts in a play end the story.

Campbell, Hope. *Meanwhile Back at the Castle.* Norton, 1970. Suzie now lives on an island her father bought. But they turn this into an independent sovereign with their usual non-conformity.

_____. *Mystery at Fire Island.* Four Winds, 1978. Dash and J.C. spend the summer on Fire Island. They observe some strange behavior and discover an art smuggling operation.

_____. *No More Trains to Tottenville.*

McCall, 1971. Jane's brother has left home, and she has tried to run away, but the family is really upset when Jane's mother drops out to India one day.

_____. *Peak Beneath the Moon.* Four Winds, 1979. Maggie has many unfinished projects and therefore she wonders about the unfinished tower and its "crazy" owner.

_____. *Why Not Join the Giraffes?* Norton, 1968. Suzie is learning to be content with herself and find success from inside. She has an artistic family and needs to find her place. Her brother leads the Giraffes, a combo; her new love is "straight."

Campbell, R.W. *Where the Pigeons Go to Die.* Rawson, 1978. Hugh and his grandfather waited for the day his pigeon, Dickens, would race in and win the 600 mile concourse. On that day grandfather had a stroke. The pigeon raced but what would happen?

Campion, Wardi. *Casa Means Home.* Holt, 1976. Lorenzo is a Puerto Rican living in New York. He has problems in school, is afraid of many things and can't have a wanted pet. He goes back to Puerto Rico for the summer, works hard but returns to New York.

Canfield, Dorothy. *Understood Betsy.* Buccaneer, 1946. An old favorite about Elizabeth Ann and her apprehension of a new life in Vermont.

Canning, Victor. *Flight of the Grey Goose.* Morrow, 1973. When Smiler is older he runs away again, this time to await the return of his father.

_____. *Runaways.* Morrow, 1972. Samuel Miles, having run away to escape reform school, finds that Yarra, a runaway cheetah, is sharing the barn he found as refuge.

Cannon, A.E. *Cal Cameron by Day, Spiderman by Night.* Delacourt, 1988. Cal is friends with Geke, a cripple with a sense of humor, and Marti, a girl not one of the crowd. Cal's football friend teases both these students nastily. Cal does nothing at first but then feels he must.

Cannon, Bettie. *Bellsong for Sarah Rains.* Scribner, 1987. Sarah's father commits suicide. She and her mother move in with Uncle Marsh. She must learn to love the father she once knew.

Canty, Mary. *Green Gate.* McKay, 1965. Emily wants to be treated like any other ordinary girl but because of her blindness she is "different." One day a girl speaks to her "as though she were a real person." She wants to hold on to her.

Caras, Roger. *Mara Simba, the African Lion.* Holt, 1986. A story of an African lion from birth to death. He lives in the Savannah and is threatened by the movement of civilization into his territory.

Carey, M.V. *Mystery of the Invisible Dog.* Random, 1975. Jupiter, Pete and Bob help solve a haunting mystery but then a crystal dog is missing and they encounter poisonings, ransom notes etc. This story has a touch of the supernatural.

_____. *Mystery of the Singing Serpent.*

Random, 1972. The Three Investigators get involved in witchcraft when they try to rescue a woman from the influence of snake worshippers.

_____. *Mystery of the Sinister Scarecrow.* Random, 1979. This story revolves around the dangerous army ants of Africa and an art museum. One of the many Three Investigators stories.

_____. *Secret of the Haunted Mirror.* Random, 1974. A story of looking for the truth about an ancient mirror thought to be haunted by a magician. Jupiter, Pete and Bob get involved in a mugging and a kidnapping.

Carleton, Barbee. *Secret of Saturday Cove.* Holt, 1961. David, Sally and Poke spend the summer solving two mysteries: who is stealing lobsters from their traps and where the ancestral Blake family treasure is hidden.

_____. *Witch's Bridge.* Holt, 1967. Dan, an orphan, lives with his uncle. The villagers don't like the family because of a long-ago curse put on it by the family.

Carlsen, Ruth. *Half-Past Tomorrow.* Houghton, 1973. Jimmy hits his head in the pool and can see into the future. His friend Beetle is hurt in an accident and goes back in time. Both boys recover in time.

_____. *Henrietta Goes West.* Houghton, 1966. Henrietta is a car. Chris, Jenny and Pete are on their way to Iowa after their parents' death and Henrietta, with its individual antics makes the load lighter to bear.

_____. *Hildy and the Cuckoo Clock.* Houghton, 1966. Hildy, Bob and friends find a ghost in their new house.

_____. *Monty and the Tree House.* Houghton, 1967. Monty and Mike build a tree house. Through the eye of a tiger's head they see unusual events. They have both positive and negative results with their adventures.

_____. *Ride a Wild Horse.* Houghton, 1970. Barney, 12, is shocked when Julie comes to stay. Julie is literally from another world and wants to go back. They have exciting times looking for a way out, which they eventually find.

_____. *Sam Battleby.* Houghton, 1968. Trygve, 12, watches his sister. They meet Sam, an Irish fairy godfather. They have first class adventures together before their parents arrive on a late plane.

Carlson, Dale. *Baby Needs Shoes.* Atheneum, 1974. Janet had an ability to predict numbers. She worked for Fat Charlie who split his profits with her. One day Big Mac threatened to kill Fat Charlie unless Janet cracked a safe's combination.

_____. *Call Me Amanda.* Dutton, 1981. When things start disappearing, Amanda thinks she is an amnesiac thief. But the real thief turns out to be her new friend, Janie.

_____. *Charlie the Hero.* Dutton, 1983. Charlie, 11, wants to be a hero. But how? When?

_____. *Wild Heart.* Watts, 1977. Jona lives with an alcoholic father and a cruel mother. She marries a rich man she doesn't love just to better herself. She realizes her mistake too late. She really loves Danny, the boy on the next ranch.

Carlson, Natalie. *Ann Aurelia and Dorothy.* Harper, 1968. Ann's new stepfather doesn't like her so she goes to live in a foster home where she is happy. But when her mother's marriage breaks up she goes home and forgives her mother.

_____. *Brother for the Orphelines.* Harper, 1959/1969. A foundling is left at the door of the Orphelines, but it is a boy! They care for him and struggle to keep him even if it is an orphanage for girls.

_____. *Empty Schoolhouse.* Harper, 1965. The friendship between a black girl and a white girl in Louisiana is almost destroyed because a struggle as an integrated school comes into being.

_____. *Evangeline, Pigeon of Paris.* Harcourt, 1960. The chief of police deported all pigeons from Paris to the country. Evangeline and her beloved Gabriel were separated. She managed to survive in a cave and on a farm before she was united with Gabriel.

_____. *Family Under the Bridge.* Harper, 1958. Armand is a hobo living in Paris. He finds three children in his own hideaway and befriends them.

_____. *Grandmother for the Orphelines.* Harper, 1980. The Orphelines find not only a grandmother but a grandfather too. And on Christmas Eve!

_____. *Half-Sisters.* Harper, 1970. Luvvy can't wait for her half-sister to return from boarding school so she can display how much she has grown up and changed. She is twelve and no longer a tomboy.

_____. *Happy Orpheline.* Harper, 1957. The story of twenty girls who live in an orphanage in France and don't want to be adopted. It is the first of many funny tales. Because of a pending adoption they act very badly to prevent it.

_____. *Jaky or Dodo.* Scribner, 1978. Jaky is a dog owned by Pierre. He is often gone for days. Dodo is a dog owned by Mr. Boffu. He is often gone for days. Jaky (or Dodo) is living a double life.

_____. *Letter on the Tree.* Harper, 1964. Behert wants an accordion so he writes a letter and puts it on a tree that is being sent to the United States. So begins a pen pal correspondence.

_____. *Luigi of the Streets.* Harper, 1967. Luigi feels his family has been cursed by gypsies. His sister Dori can't walk after an accident for which he blames the curse but it is Dori's mind, not her body, that prevents her from walking.

_____. *Luvvy and the Girls.* Harper, 1971. Luvvy is thrilled by the fact that she too can go to boarding school. This is her first year and she finds the day by day activities adventurous.

_____. *Marchers for the Dream.* Harper, 1969. A black family lose their apartment and have a great deal of trouble finding a new one.

_____. *Orphelines in the Enchanted Castle.* Harper, 1964. Another adventure of the girls from the orphanage when they go to live in a castle where there will be orphan boys. Their first ideas about boys change as the boys tease and misbehave.

_____. *Pet for the Orphelines.* Harper, 1962. The Orphelines can identify with unwanted, homeless cats. Their sympathetic approach is warm and understanding. But they do have difficulty deciding on what kind of pet they want.

_____. *Sailor's Choice.* Harper, 1966. Sailor is a dog living aboard ship. A young orphan, Jamie, stows away. The two become friends and win over the Captain (Sailor's master) and find a home for Jamie.

Carlyon, Richard. *Dark Lord of Pengersick.* Farrar, 1980. Mabby becomes invisible to fight Pengersick. Jago attains magic to help destroy him. The true lord reclaims the land; Jago is powerless but happy and Mabby is using her power to do good.

Carner, C. *Tawny.* Macmillan, 1978. When a twin loses his brother through death he recovers his outlook by loving a doe.

Carol, Bill. *Inside the Ten.* Steck-Vaughn, 1967. Terry transfers to a new school and must find a place for himself on the football team. He also must save his friend, Mark, from delinquency.

_____. *Lefty's Long Throw.* Steck-Vaughn, 1966. Terry makes third-string quarterback and quits the team. He works to buy a car and is then arrested for speeding. He goes back on the team and tries again.

_____. *Touchdown.* Steck-Vaughn, 1968. The new quarterback is good and lets everybody know it. He points out others' weaknesses. He is resented and the team does not play well for him. He changes and so does the team.

_____. *Touchdown Duo.* Steck-Vaughn, 1968. This is Terry's last year in high school. He is a star quarterback and wants a football scholarship. But Jim, another star quarterback, enrolls in school. The team likes Terry and sabotages Jim.

Caroselli, Remus. *Mystery at Long Crescent Marsh.* Holt, 1985. Drum wants to find the connection between the bully that is bothering him and a mysterious stranger in town.

Carpelan, Bo. *Bow Island: Story of a Summer That Was Different.* Delacorte, 1971. Johan stays in a summer cottage facing Bow Island where Marvin, a mentally retarded boy, lives. Nora is his best friend and Erik and Beatrice his worst enemies. Johan sides with Nora and Marvin.

Carr, Harriett. *Bold Beginning.* Hastings, 1964. Gail gets a job with a little known magazine. She runs into personal problems, competition and romance.

_____. *Rod's Girl.* Hastings, 1963. Marge helps in trying to get a new school. Not all plans work well and she almost loses Rod because of Jerry, a not-too-nice individual.

Carrick, Carol. *Elephant in the Dark.* Clarion, 1988. Will, 12, is a target for bullies. He takes care of an elephant that is housed with the village storekeeper for the winter.

_____. *Some Friend.* Houghton, 1979. Mike and Rob are friends but Rob has a behavior trait Mike doesn't like and it's hard for him to accept Rob as he is. Rob tends to be a manipulator.

_____. *Stay Away from Simon!* Ticknor, 1985. Simon is mentally retarded but he has a kind and generous heart.

_____. *What a Wimp!* Houghton, 1983. Barney's parents are getting a divorce and he is entering a new school. As if that weren't enough he is faced with a bully.

Carris, Joan. *Pets, Vets and Marty Howard.* Lippincott, 1984. Marty wants to be a vet and gets a part-time job working for one. He learns about the negative parts of the profession, like death. But he likes the positives: puppies, curing illness and finding homes.

_____. *Revolt of 10-X.* Harcourt, 1980. Taylor lives with her mother in a new house. She doesn't like it and does mean things. She doesn't try to make friends even though attempts by others are made.

_____. *Rusty Timmons' First Million.* Harper, 1985. Rusty puts a basketball court in his backyard. This starts a summer youth employment service and he earns some money.

_____. *When the Boys Ran the House.* Lippincott, 1982. While father is away on a trip and mother is in the hospital four brothers take care of themselves. Miss Brown helps them all in fantastic ways so when their parents come home all is well.

Carroll, Jeffrey. *Climbing to the Sun.* Seabury, 1977. Three mountain goats are swept away by an avalanche and struggle to get back to their home. They face both bears and human hunters.

Carroll, Lewis. *Alice's Adventures in Wonderland.* Schiller, 1865. Alice falls down a rabbit hole and discovers a world of characters who are nonsensical, funny, wicked and compassionate.

_____. *Through the Looking Glass.* St. Martin, 1871. Alice goes through a looking glass this time and finds a different world full of curious adventures.

Carse, Robert. *Go Away Home.* Norton, 1964. Rich's Collie dog, Tamas, runs away to join a pack. Rich goes after him. He finally gets him and now must catch up with the wagon train.

_____. *Turnabout.* Putnam, 1962. Geordie is on a ship to America. He is endentured to the Brecks. Geordie gets help when Breck is injured and in the process makes friends with an Indian.

_____. *Winter of the Whale.* Putnam, 1961.

The Indians of Shelter Island go hunting during a famine. They kill a whale but it is stolen by a rival tribe. Wequarran and his friends get it back.

Carson, John. *Coach Nobody Liked.* Farrar, 1960. Sid is a basketball star. His father believes in victory at any price and the coach sees the game as a way to build character.

_____. *Mystery of the Missing Monkey.* Farrar, 1962. Joe loves animals. One day the zoo gets an unsolicited monkey, Cappy. Following that mysterious and frightening things happen at the zoo.

Carter, Alden. *Sheila's Dying.* Putnam, 1987. Sheila has cancer. Jerry, her "steady," and Bonnie, her best friend, care more than anyone else. Sheila dies and Jerry and Bonnie carry the burden.

_____. *Wart, Son of Toad.* Putnam, 1985. Steve lives with his dad, who is always "bugging" him about grades, friends, future, etc. He is a science teacher, called Toad, whom no one likes because of his strict discipline. Thus the title.

Carter, Dorothy. *His Majesty, Queen Hatshepsut.* Harper, 1987. Hatshepsut was a ruler of Egypt for 20 years. This is a fictionalized story of her life and good works.

Carter, Mary. *Tell Me My Name.* Morrow, 1975. When a teenaged girl finds she is adopted, she searches for her natural mother, and her success changes the lives of the McPhail family.

Cassedy, Sylvia. *Behind the Attic Wall.* Crowell, 1983. Maggie, an orphan, is a rebel and hostile. She is rejected wherever she goes. She finds a secret world behind the attic wall. She lives there with two talking dolls and finds peace.

_____. *M.E. and Morton.* Crowell, 1987. Mary Ella (M.E.) is bright and imaginative. She wants friends but her slow, dull brother is an embarrassment to her. But friend Polly saves the day.

Cassiday, Bruce. *Guerrilla Scout.* Macmillan, 1965. Jimmy's parents are killed in Italy during World War II and his house is destroyed. He was American born and it was American planes that did this. He later joins the Italian partisans to fight the Nazis.

Castle, Francis. *Sister's Tale.* Little, 1969. Agnes and Blaina live in sixth century Ireland and each tells the story of their loves and how they came about.

Caswell, Helen. *Wind on the Road.* Van Nostrand, 1964. Esther runs away to join the gypsies. Her father finds and brings her home but she now understands both gypsy life and her own.

Cather, Willa. *My Antonia.* Houghton, 1918. Antonia is the daughter of immigrants. She finds a place for herself in her adopted home.

Catherall, Arthur. *Arctic Sealer.* Criterion, 1961. A story of the rescue of the survivors of a plane crash during a storm in arctic wasteland by a Norwegian and his uncle who are on a seal expedition.

_____. *Big Tusker.* Lothrop, 1970. A story about the life of elephants as they live in the teak forests of Thailand. Sing Noi is trapped in a cave-in and Poo Koon broke a tusk and is going wild.

_____. *Camel Caravan.* Seabury, 1968. In Timbuktu a brother and sister are cut off from their caravan by desert raiders. They face heat and sandstorms with an old man wounded in the raid and a baby camel just born.

_____. *Death of an Oil Rig.* Phillips, 1969. Mark is about to hit oil. Salem and Karmey do everything to sabotage the effort. A tropical hurricane brings "poetic justice."

_____. *Kidnapped by Accident.* Lothrop, 1969. Two children find the occupants of a yacht trapped by a stuck door. They are grounded, captured by a culprit, escape and are rewarded.

_____. *Lapland Outlaw.* Lothrop, 1966. Johani's father is burned in a fire and a trader tries to claim his reindeer herd. Johani is forced to turn outlaw to keep the herd intact and prove the attempted treachery.

_____. *Lone Seal Pup.* Dutton, 1965. Ah-Leek, a seal pup deserted by his mother, meets Andrew, an Eskimo boy. They have dangerous adventures together.

_____. *Lost Off the Grand Bank.* Criterion, 1962. Geoff and Kimmey are lost in the fog. They are found by an injured captain of the *Lucky MacLear.* They hit an iceberg and are caught. Americans in a submarine are also caught. Can they all be saved?

_____. *Man-Eater.* Criterion, 1963. Bachi, Lalish and their father live in India. A killer leopard terrorizes the countryside. While father is gone the leopard breaks into the house where Bachi and Lalish live.

_____. *Night of the Black Frost.* Lothrop, 1968. Leif, 16, goes on a fishing trip in the Arctic. He and his two uncles lose the engine of their boat and are lost in the fog. They face tension and possible death.

_____. *Prisoner in the Snow.* Lothrop, 1967. Toni and Trudi see a plane go down. But worse still is that it starts a snow avalanche headed for them. Their house is buried and they must survive and try to rescue the pilot.

_____. *Sicilian Mystery.* Lothrop, 1967. Two boys stop a drug ring on the island of Stromboli. They face murder, an erupting volcano, and large, angry turtles.

_____. *Strange Intruder.* Washington Square, 1965. A ship is disabled near the Faroe Islands and while the natives are trying to save the crew an angry polar bear threatens the islanders.

_____. *Yugoslav Mystery.* Lothrop, 1962. Josef, 14, helps his father, an escaped political prisoner, dodge the secret police.

Catling, Patrick. *Chocolate Touch.* Morrow, 1979. John has a unique "gift": everything he touches turns, not to gold, but to chocolate, a rich, dark brown chocolate.

Caudill, Rebecca. *Far Off Land.* Viking, 1964.

Hetty, 16, travels by flatboat from Fort Henry to French Lick. There are hardship, Indians, disease and starvation. But romance is also growing during and after the journey.

————. *Somebody Go and Bang a Drum.* Dutton, 1974. A family story about eight children, seven of whom are adopted.

Caufield, Don. *Never Steal a Magic Cat.* Doubleday, 1971. Pandora, a cat, has a golden collar. She is cat-napped for it. But the thieves cannot get it off. She is rescued by a kitten and a collie.

Caunitz, William. *One Police Plaza.* Crown, 1984. Dan is a policeman who finds a key on a corpse. It may be the key to his career and his life.

Cavallaro, Ann. *Blimp.* Dutton, 1983. Kim is wooed by good-looking Gary in spite of being overweight. She overcomes her problem and helps Gary with his problems: drinking, insecurity and suicide tendencies.

Cavanagh, Helen. *Kiss and Tell.* Scholastic, 1984. Denice and Jason differ about the depth of their love. Denice wants to share it with family and friends; Jason wants it to be private. Maybe their love is not strong enough.

Cavanna, Betty. *Almost Like Sisters.* Morrow, 1963. Victoria, 17, is overshadowed by her young, widowed mother. She goes away to school to be able to become her own person.

————. *Banner Year.* Morrow, 1987. Cindy loves her horse, Banner. She meets and likes Tad but when Banner is hurt and needs her care and she needs to raise money for the vet's bills, she has no time for Tad who finds other interests.

————. *Country Cousin.* Morrow, 1967. Mindy gets a summer job in a dress shop and learns the garment trade from the garment district to the fashion world of Paris.

————. *Going on Sixteen.* Morrow, 1985. Julie lives on a farm with her father and is not friends with the popular girls at school. She gets a collie pup and gains pride and confidence while training him. An update of an earlier edition.

————. *Jenny Kimura.* Morrow, 1964. Jenny, Japanese-American, goes from Tokyo to America to visit her grandmother. She meets Alan and both his parents and her grandmother show prejudice.

————. *Joyride.* Morrow, 1974. A girl with polio wants to be popular and "normal" like Toni and Daphne. She wants all the things others have and do. But it is not possible.

————. *Mystery at Love's Creek.* Morrow, 1965. Carlie is in Australia when a bank is robbed and the evidence points to her uncle. She works to clear up the suspicions.

————. *Storm in Her Heart.* Westminster, 1983. Anne copes with loss of a boyfriend, a new school, a new boyfriend and her parents' divorce.

————. *Time for Tenderness.* Morrow, 1962. Peggy meets a Brazilian boy while visiting there. She likes him and finds out he has Negro blood in his family. She knows her parents won't approve.

His family has other plans also so she and Carlos part.

Cave, Hugh. *Voyage.* Macmillan, 1988. Vinnie's father is in jail but breaks out. He and Vinnie want to sail around the world. But what about his mother?

Cawley, Winfred. *Gran at Coatgate.* Holt, 1974. Jinnie goes to stay with Gran at Coatgate. She comes from a home where enjoyment is sin; at Gran's she lives differently and enjoys it.

Cebulash, Mel. *Hot Like the Sun.* Lerner, 1986. Terry is asked to find a coin stolen from a friend. He encounters bikers and punkers before he finds the coin and the thief.

————. *Ruth Marini, Dodger Ace.* Lerner, 1983. This is a story of the first woman to play major league baseball.

Ceder, Georgiana. *Winter Without Salt.* Morrow, 1962. Peter's parents were killed by Indians and because David fed the salt to the animals they must face a tough winter without it.

Cenac, Claude. *Four Paws Into Adventure.* Watts, 1965. Diogenes, a dog, was found by a tramp but he had to find another family when the tramp went to the hospital. Then when the tramp returned he had to decide whether to leave his new family or not.

Cervantes, Miguel. *Don Quixote de la Mancha.* Dutton, 1953. Don Quixote, a Spanish knight, and his steadfast companion, Sancho Panza, travel Spain in search of "truth and justice." Humor.

Chadwick, Lonnie. *Don't Shoot.* Lerner, 1978. An Eskimo boy determines to devote his life to protecting Arctic polar bears from poachers.

Chaffin, Lithe. *Freeman.* Macmillan, 1972. Freeman can't talk to his grandparents but he wants to know the truth about his parents.

Chaikin, Miriam. *Finders Weepers.* Harper, 1980. Molly finds a ring and keeps it but when she finds out its significance she wants to give it back but can't get it off her finger.

————. *Friends Forever.* Harper, 1988. Molly is in sixth grade and worries about her school grades. It is wartime and there are many other problems that concern people.

————. *Getting Even.* Harper, 1982. Molly learns about friendship, betrayal and jealousy as she makes friends and knows of the responsibility of this act.

————. *I Should Worry, I Should Care.* Harper, 1979. The story of Molly and her sisters and brother as they move into a new neighborhood and must adjust to school and new friends. Death, poverty and anti–Semitism are part of their lives.

————. *Lower! Higher! You're a Liar!* Harper, 1984. Molly's best friend is gone for the summer. She befriends Estelle who is a victim of Celia, the school bully, who takes her bracelet. Molly organizes a club to boycott Celia.

————. *Yossi Tries to Help God.* Harper, 1987. Yossi wants to be a good Jew but is not always successful. He also tries to help his younger sister get well.

Chalker, Jack. *Messiah Choice*. Bluejay, 1985. Gregory is investigating a murder by a creature that leaves tracks like a Tyrannosaurus Rex. The murdered man's daughter is kidnapped by someone who wants to destroy the world.

Chamberlain, Elinor. *Mystery of the Jungle Airstrip*. Lippincott, 1967. Ronnie and Manuel search for a missing brother who disappeared in the jungle.

Chambers, Aidan. *Dance on My Grave*. Harper, 1983. Hal and Barry were lovers. Hal tells all in a journal. Barry was accidentally killed after a fight about a girl. Hal has feelings of guilt but wants to fulfill a last request of Barry's.

_____. *Present Takers*. Harper, 1983. Lucy is tormented by class bullies who demand she bring them gifts.

_____. *Seal Secret*. Harper, 1981. William goes camping with Gwyn, a hostile boy. Gwyn wants to keep a seal pup and start a seal farm. William releases the seal pup from capture braving wires and a broken leg.

Chambers, John. *Colonel and Me*. Atheneum, 1985. Gussie takes riding lessons because she likes the grandson of the instructor.

_____. *Finder*. Atheneum, 1981. A dog found Jenny when she arrived at Fire Island for the summer. The dog belonged to another boy and Jenny and her friend, Lauren, come upon a mystery and a kidnapping.

_____. *Fire Island Forfeit*. Atheneum, 1984. Jenny, her brother, Bill, and her girlfriend, Lauren, investigate a mystery of Fire Island. Lione, a model, is murdered. She is the same girl that gave Lauren a box with keys in it.

_____. *Footlight Summer*. Atheneum, 1983. Chris and Sherry spend the summer in a theatre program. Chris finds out that one of the actors is Sherry's father whom she believes was killed in Vietnam. Sherry's mother wants her to leave the program.

_____. *Fritz's Winter*. Atheneum, 1979. A Siamese cat is left behind on Fire Island and she must fend for herself.

_____. *Showdown at Apple Hill*. Atheneum, 1982. Jenny and her brother, Bill, run into the Quarry gang of robbers and murderers. They are looking for the loot that was hidden there twelve years before.

Chance, Stephen. *Septimus and Danedyke Mystery*. Nelson, 1971. A pastor finds himself in danger when some manuscripts are discovered showing where a golden cup is hidden that two art thieves are looking for.

_____. *Septimus and the Minister Ghost Mystery*. Nelson, 1974. Rev. Trelvar sees unexplained lights, hears organ music and the talking of ghosts. He and Alistair go to investigate the old church.

_____. *Stone Offering*. Nelson, 1977. When

a valley is threatened by plans for building a dam, someone tries to save his home by reenacting an ancient magic formula.

Chandler, Edna. *Indian Paintbrush*. Whitman, 1975. Maria, half Sioux and half Mexican, has trouble adjusting to Indian life after living in town. But a kind and understanding teacher helps with the magic of Indian paintbrush.

Chandler, Raymond. *Farewell, My Lovely*. Ballantine, 1983. Philip Marlowe, an old style detective, is involved in a case with three women, all bad news.

Chang, Heidi. *Elaine, Mary Lewis, and the Frogs*. Crown, 1988. When Elaine and Mary Lewis meet, they find they both like frogs and this makes life better for both of them.

Channel, A.R. *Jungle Rescue*. Phillips, 1968. A paymaster is attacked by an injured, starving tiger and Chandra, unarmed, drives him off but the money is missing. Chandra and Joe McKinly, his boss, investigate and identify the thieves.

Chant, Joy. *Red Moon and Black Mountain*. Dutton, 1976. Three children are involved in a war between High King and Fendarl. Penelope, Nicholas and Oliver fight Fendarl to his death.

Chapin, Henry. *Spiro of the Sponge Fleet*. Little, 1964. Spiro lives in Greece. He wants to be a sponge diver but his mother is against it. He signs on as a diver and saves a man's life.

Charbonneau, Eileen. *Ghosts of Stony Clove*. Watts, 1988. Asher, 16, and Ginny see the ghost of Sally Hamilton, a supposedly murdered servant. Ginny helps the falsely accused murderer and Asher goes away. When he returns they marry.

Charnas, Suzy. *Bronze King*. Houghton, 1985. Valentine notices odd things vanishing from the city. She summons a wizard from Sorcery Hall and together they fight the dreaded monster of darkness, living in the subway.

_____. *Silver Glove*. Bantam, 1988. Val's grandmother disappears from a rest home. This starts a fantasy that includes sorcery and a magic carpet; a grandmother who turns into a cat and The Claw.

Chastain, Madye. *Magic Island*. Harcourt, 1964. Angel, 10, moves to Barbados to regain her health. She and three friends have the times of their lives.

_____. *Plippen's Palace*. Harcourt, 1961. Four children run away to a boarding house known as Plippen's Palace. They make friends and meet interesting people.

Chauncy, Nan. *Devil's Hill*. Watts, 1960. Badge lives in the wilderness of Tasmania with his domineering cousin and has little knowledge of the rest of the outside world.

_____. *Half a World Away*. Watts, 1962. When the Lettengar family lose their money they move to Tasmania and live simply and happily, learning to love each other.

_____. *High and Haunted Island*. Norton, 1964. Two girls are marooned on a desolate island. They are rescued by a group of unusual people to whom money means nothing but a way to buy food.

———. *They Found a Cave*. Watts, 1961. Five children run away from a farm to live in a cave and hunt and fish. They come upon an ancient treasure.

Cheatham, K. Follis. *Best Way Out*. Harcourt, 1982. Haywood, 13, has trouble in school until a counselor helps him with a special program.

———. *Bring Home the Ghost*. Harcourt, 1980. Tolin is the son of a slave holder and Jason is his slave. They lose everything when the plantation burns. They travel west where Jason becomes a trapper and blacksmith but Tolin misses his former life.

Cheetham, Ann. *Beggar's Curse*. Dell, 1987. A curse hangs over the village of Stang. Oliver's father told him about it and he can end it but he needs help.

Chekov, Anton. *Kashtanka*. Walck, 1961. Kashtanka, a dog, lost her master and was taken in by a circus performer. Her life is much better now, but she has a chance to go back to her original owner. She must make a choice.

Cheney, Cora. *Case of the Iceland Dogs*. Dodd, 1977. Hannes lives in Iceland. He likes a dog, Samur, who belongs to a friend, and wants to find him a mate. He does so after a great deal of hardship.

———. *Mystery of the Disappearing Cars*. Knopf, 1963. Sam is the winner of a scholarship. He loses his way to the college in Vermont and meets another winner. They are in a town where some cars are stolen, and they are suspected. They must clear themselves.

———. *Treasure of Lin Li-Ti*. Hawthorne, 1969. Lin-Li-Ti is separated from his family. He has many adventures, some schooling and a job before he finds his sister.

Cherryh, C.J. *Angel with the Sword*. Nal, 1985. Altair is a slave worker on the canal. One day she pulls a stranger onto her boat. She is then taken into the world of the rich and powerful . . . and corrupt.

Chetwin, Grace. *Crystal Stair*. Bradbury, 1988. Gom is reunited with his mother. He learns the identity of evil Katak. He battles to save the world of Olm from extinction. His mother gives him three names, some magic tokens and a ring.

———. *Gom on Windy Mountain*. Lothrop, 1986. Gom, son of Stig, a poor woodcutter, has unusual abilities to see a different life for himself. He can communicate with both animals and nature.

———. *On All Hallow's Eve*. Lothrop, 1984. One Halloween night two children are taken to a world very different from their own.

———. *Out of the Dark World*. Lothrop, 1985. A boy, whose mind is trapped in a computer program, appears in Meg's dreams. She uses an hypnotic trance to summon the sorceress Morgan le Fay for help in freeing him.

———. *Riddle and the Rune*. Bradbury, 1987. Gom seeks his destiny. He has a gift for making friends. He meets Stormfleet, a wonderful horse who takes him on adventures.

———. *Starstorm*. Bradbury, 1989. Gom is apprenticed to a wizard and learns to use his powers to destroy the evil Katak and recover the Lost Emerald Seal.

Chew, Ruth. *Do-It-Yourself Magic*. Hastings, 1988. Rachel and Scott have a magic hammer that can make things grow larger or smaller. With this magic they catch a burglar.

———. *Mostly Magic*. Scholastic, 1982. Two children find a magic ladder that takes them on an adventure.

———. *What the Witch Left*. Hastings, 1973. Katy and her friend Louise found old clothes in a locked trunk. Katy put on flesh colored gloves and was able to play the piano beautifully. Were the other clothes magic, too?

———. *Would-Be Witch*. Scholastic, 1977. Robin and Andy find a dustpan that is magic and can take them on midnight rides.

Childress, Alice. *Hero Ain't Nothin' But a Sandwich*. Coward, 1973. Benjie is thirteen and uses heroin. He is black and although many people know of his drug problem and try to help him his future is not assured.

———. *Rainbow Jordan*. Coward, 1981. Rainbow's mother abandoned her. She has to explain this to herself, her teachers, the social worker and Josephine. Her boyfriend is no help and neither is her best friend, Beryl.

Chipperfield, Joseph. *Dog to Trust*. McKay, 1964. Arno, an Alsatian puppy, befriends an artist who is going blind. As the artist's sight improves the dog is infected and the artist leads his dog.

———. *Gray Dog from Galtymore*. McKay, 1962. Silver loses his master and is captured and badly treated. He is found and nurtured back to health. His captor tries to reclaim him by every cruel means.

———. *Seokoo of the Black Wind*. McKay, 1961. Seokoo, half dog, half wolf, wants to be a dog living with humans but has a pull by the wolf to be wild. A harsh, cruel, bloody story.

Chittun, Ida. *Hermit Boy*. Delacorte, 1972. Edith and Samme hear about Jason, the hermit boy. He disappeared when his grandmother died. He's not been seen but is known to be around. The girls save his grandmother's house and find the boy.

Christgau, Alice. *Laugh Peddler*. Scott, 1968. Sidney is a city boy living on a farm in 1910. There are a barn fire, a blizzard and some beaver poachers but Sidney learns to adjust.

———. *Runaway to Glory*. Scott, 1965. Rueben is friendly with his step-grandpa. They help capture some thieves and become heroes.

Christian, Mary. *Dead Man in Catfish Bay.* Whitman, 1985. A juvenile offender, Cameron gets involved in the dispute between the Texas fishermen and the Vietnamese newcomers.

————. *Deadline for Danger.* Whitman, 1982. Mike and Nita write a fake story about drugs for the school paper. It turns out there really is a drug problem, which they uncover.

————. *Firebug Mystery.* Whitman, 1982. Brock and Gaby uncover an arson plot and put themselves in danger.

————. *Growin' Pains.* Macmillan, 1985. Ginny Ruth, 12, doesn't like the small, dying Texas town where she lives. But she does like Mr. Billy who is physically handicapped.

————. *Maltese Feline.* Dutton, 1988. Fenton and Gerald investigate a suspected kidnapping after finding a note containing a plea for help inside a cat's collar.

————. *Mystery at Camp Triumph.* Whitman, 1986. Angie is blinded in an automobile accident and she goes to a camp for disabled children. While there she finds out who is sabotaging the camp.

————. *Mystery of the Double, Double Cross.* Whitman, 1982. Jeff, 16, is kidnapped while chauffering a wealthy passenger. He is held hostage but escapes taking the passenger, who is the real villain, with him. They are in the path of a hurricane.

————. *Phantom of the Operetta.* Dutton, 1986. Fenton and Gerald are the Determined Detectives. They solve a mystery in the old Drummond mansion.

————. *Sebastian, Super Sleuth.* Macmillan, 1974. Sebastian investigates the disappearance of the contents from a rich family's 60-year-old time capsule.

————. *Sebastian (Super Sleuth) and the Baffling Bigfoot.* Macmillan, 1990. Sebastian the dog and his detective master search for Bigfoot when a guest is attacked by something big and hairy at the Sasquatch Inn.

————. *Sebastian (Super Sleuth) and the Bone-to-Pick Mystery.* Macmillan, 1983. While investigating a breaking and entering case at the local museum the canine detective uncovers a fraud involving dinosaur bones.

————. *Sebastian (Super Sleuth) and the Clumsy Cowboy.* Macmillan, 1988. Sebastian goes on an enforced vacation to a haunted dude ranch.

————. *Sebastian (Super Sleuth) and the Crummy Yummies Caper.* Macmillan, 1983. Sebastian goes underground posing as an ordinary dog in order to foil a dognapping at a local dog show.

————. *Sebastian (Super Sleuth) and the Egyptian Connection.* Macmillan, 1988. Sebastian helps his master find a shipment of stolen Egyptian artifacts that is being smuggled into the country.

————. *Sebastian (Super Sleuth) and the Hair of the Dog Mystery.* Macmillan, 1988. Sebastian helps his owner solve a case involving a missing Gypsy necklace, an evil curse and a kidnapped, larcenous cat.

————. *Sebastian (Super Sleuth) and the Purloined Sirloin.* Macmillan, 1986. Sebastian, a sheepdog, and his master get involved in a mystery that has many clues: a steak, a tea set, an inheritance and a car.

————. *Sebastian (Super Sleuth) and the Santa Claus Caper.* Macmillan, 1984. Sebastian goes undercover as a Santa Claus to unravel a mystery at a department store.

————. *Sebastian (Super Sleuth) and the Secret of the Skewered Skier.* Macmillan, 1984. While on a ski trip to the Frozen Dreams resort Sebastian and his master, John, run into a case of jewel thieves.

————. *Sebastian (Super Sleuth) and the Stars-in-His-Eyes Mystery.* Macmillan, 1987. Mysterious attacks on Chummy, the Wonder Dog, lead Sebastian to go undercover as a student performer in the making of Chummy's new movie.

————. *Singin' Somebody Else's Song.* Macmillan, 1988. Gideon and Jeremy write songs and perform. Jeremy kills himself and Gideon feels responsible. He tries to get Jeremy's songs published.

Christie, Agatha. *Elephants Can Remember.* Dodd, 1972. The bodies of two lovers are found, mangled, at the foot of a cliff. Was it suicide? Murder? Hercule Poirot helps their daughter find the answers.

————. *Evil Under the Sun.* Putnam, 1981. Hercule Poirot solves the murder of a beautiful woman found strangled on the beach.

————. *Labors of Hercules.* Dodd, 1982. A Pekingese dog disappears and Hercule Poirot faces a strange case of murder or worse.

————. *Seven Dials Mystery.* Dodd, 1986. Jimmy's friend's last dying words were about the Seven Dials Society. This leads Jimmy and his friend, Bundle, to uncover espionage and murder.

————. *Sleeping Murder.* Dodd, 1976. Miss Jane Marple helps Gwenda learn about the house where she saw a murder in her nightmare.

Christman, Elizabeth. *Nice Italian Girl.* Dodd, 1976. Anne has an affair in college that she thought was wonderful except now she is pregnant and without a husband. She doesn't want an abortion but finds adoption can be a vicious scheme.

————. *Ruined for Life.* Paulist Press, 1987. A Catholic book about how some college students went to a poor section of Chicago to work, and live, among the poor. A young girl wants to make it a career but her family objects.

Christopher, John. *Beyond the Burning Land.* Macmillan, 1971. Luke is waiting for the time to fulfill the Spirit's plans for restoration of the machine age. He slays a monster and wins a princess. He then becomes Prince of Winchester.

_____. *City of Gold and Lead*. Macmillan, 1967. Will, Fritz and Beanpole go to the City of the Tripod to learn what they can about their ability to rule the earth the way they do.

_____. *Dom and Va*. Macmillan, 1973. The setting is in Africa more than 5,000 years ago. The story is about the struggle between the peace loving farmers and the battling hunters for power.

_____. *Dragon Dance*. Dutton, 1986. Loyal Simon and Know-it-all Brad are in China where they experience mind-control practices and palatial intrigue. In the end of this trilogy they do come home.

_____. *Empty World*. Dutton, 1978. After the rage of the plague the world is left with few survivors. One, a young boy struggles to eke out a living.

_____. *Fireball*. Dutton, 1981. When the fireball comes, this huge whirling ball of light causes everything to be terrifyingly different. The land is made up of two worlds, one past and one future. Simon and Brad are in both.

_____. *Lotus Caves*. Macmillan, 1969. Marty lives in a Bubble on the moon. He and Steve find a mysterious cave where if one eats the food, he will, like the lotus eaters in the "Odyssey," forget the past. They must escape.

_____. *New Found Land*. Dutton, 1983. In their attempt to reach California, Brad and Simon, one American and one English, face Vikings, Indians and Aztecs.

_____. *Pool of Fire*. Macmillan, 1968. Will, Henry and Beanpole must foil the Master's plan of world domination.

_____. *Prince in Waiting*. Macmillan, 1974. Luke survives the Earth's volcanic eruption, but civilization, with its technology, is destroyed. Luke must fight the Seers and bring back machinery.

_____. *Sword of the Spirits*. Macmillan, 1972. Luke does not have a peaceful time as Prince. He faces a mutiny of his captains and is exiled. He does return and try to reintroduce machines into his society.

_____. *When the Tripods Came*. Dutton, 1988. This is the story of how the Tripods came to control the world. It is an introduction to the author's Tripod Trilogy.

_____. *White Mountains*. Macmillan, 1967. In a future world where tripods control the minds of all, three boys, Will, Henry and Beanpole make a break for freedom by fleeing to the White Mountains.

_____. *Wild Jack*. Macmillan, 1974. Intrigue and adventure in the twenty-third century. Clive escapes to the Outlands and is befriended by Wild Jack and his gang.

Christopher, Matt. *Baseball Flyhawk*. Little, 1963. Chico, Buddy and String play baseball. There are competition, friendship and lifesaving rescues.

_____. *Catcher with a Glass Arm*. Little, 1964. Jody does not throw well and avoids hitting balls. Then his friend helps him overcome his deep fears and he plays better.

_____. *Dirt Bike Racer*. Little, 1979. Ron finds a bike on the bottom of a lake. This sparks his interest in dirt bike racing. He restores it and gets into competition.

_____. *Dirt Bike Runaway*. Little, 1983. A 16-year-old boy is shy and unhappy. His one joy is working on motorcycles. He runs away from a foster home and meets up with some bad, and then some good, people.

_____. *Dog That Called the Signals*. Little, 1982. During a football game, Harry, the dog, calls plays from the home of the sick coach.

_____. *Dog That Pitched a No-Hitter*. Little, 1988. Mike's telepathic dog, Harry, is sending his usual signals but Mike's pitching is so bad they must try another plan.

_____. *Dog That Stole the Football Plays*. Little, 1980. Mike listens while his telepathic dog transmits the opposing team's signals. When Harry, the dog, gets sick the team must win without that kind of "cheating."

_____. *Drag Strip Racer*. Little, 1982. Ken inherits a racing car and wants to be a drag racer.

_____. *Football Fugitive*. Little, 1976. Representing a pro football player whom his son admires brings a lawyer closer to his son.

_____. *Fox Steals Home*. Little, 1978. Bobby is upset by his parents' divorce and more so by the fact that his father, who is coaching him on how to run bases, is moving away.

_____. *Great Quarterback Switch*. Little, 1984. Michael is restricted to a wheelchair after an accident. He sits on the sidelines using telepathy to help his twin brother, Tom, choose the right plays. Suddenly he finds himself in his brother's place.

_____. *Hit-Away Kid*. Little, 1988. Barry is a hit-away batter. He likes winning and bends the rules sometimes. The dirty tactics of a rival pitcher give him a new view on sports ethics.

_____. *Hockey Machine*. Little, 1986. Steve, 13, is a member of the junior hockey league and he must play to win and to survive.

_____. *Johnny Long Legs*. Little, 1970. Johnny was tall with long legs but he was being outplayed by shorter members of the basketball team. Why?

_____. *Kid Who Only Hit Homers*. Little, 1972. Sylvester looked bad at baseball practice. Mr. Baruth started to coach him and he became a star but there are still problems.

_____. *Long Shot for Paul*. Little, 1966. A young boy's brother is mentally retarded but he tries to make a basketball player of him.

_____. *Look Who's Playing First Base*. Little, 1971. Mike and Yuri are friends and Mike wants Yuri to succeed in baseball. But Yuri is missing balls and the team is upset. Yuri is from Russia and wants to be accepted.

_____. *Mystery Coach*. Little, 1973. The Balzers coach becomes ill and the team falls apart. But then anonymous phone calls giving coaching tips start and the team improves.

_____. *No Arm in Left Field*. Little, 1974. Terry's arm is not strong and he knows it. But Tony blames his shortcoming on the color of his skin. Mick befriends him but Tony keeps bugging him.

_____. *Red-Hot Hightops*. Little, 1987. Kelly becomes an aggressive basketball player when she puts on a pair of red sneakers.

_____. *Return of the Headless Horseman*. Westminster, 1982. Steve and his friend Jim see a headless horseman one night. His father, a newspaper man, does not print the story but a rival paper does.

_____. *Run, Billy, Run*. Little, 1979. Billy, 14, is a runner who works hard at speed but is better at the one-mile and two-mile races.

_____. *Shortstop from Tokyo*. Little, 1970. A baseball player from Japan comes to America and takes the shortstop position away from Stogie and he is resentful.

_____. *Soccer Halfback*. Little, 1978. Jabber wants to play soccer even though everyone else thinks he should play football.

_____. *Spy on Third Base*. Little, 1988. A third baseman is very worried about helping his team because he has a knack for knowing where the ball is being hit.

_____. *Stranded*. Little, 1974. Andy and his guide dog, Max, are stranded on an island after a shipwreck.

_____. *Supercharged Infield*. Little, 1985. Penny plays softball and wonders why two teammates turned into super athletes.

_____. *Tackle Without a Team*. Little, 1989. Scott is off the team because of marijuana found in his duffle bag. He tries to find out who is discrediting him.

_____. *Takedown*. Little, 1990. Sean wonders if an assistant referee of his wrestling match could be his long lost father.

_____. *Too Hot to Handle*. Little, 1965. David comes from a baseball family and he, too, wants to play well. He can throw and hit but has no speed or reach. He settles for being a good all-around player, not a superstar.

_____. *Wild Pitch*. Little, 1980. Eddie, 12, opposes Phyl, who is a girl, playing on an opposing team. He hits her with a wild pitch.

_____. *Wing and Fullback*. Watts, 1960. Bernie has a successful football season and is accepted by his fellow students even though he was from the "wrong" side of town.

Christopher, Matthew. *Year Mom Won the Pennant*. Little, 1968. Nick's mother takes on the coaching of the Thunderballs when no father is willing to take it on. They take a lot of teasing about having a woman coach but they win the pennant.

Chukovskii, Kornei. *Silver Crest*. Holt, 1976. Kornei is put out of school unfairly. He decides to go to Odessa and seek a better life.

Church, Richard. *Down River*. Day, 1957. Five boys search a cave for ancient Roman remains. But another group is searching also. And smugglers are there, too, looking for the same thing.

_____. *Five Boys in a Cave*. Day, 1950. Five boys investigate a cave. Two boys are let down by a rope to a lower cave and face terror when the rope is dropped. A way out must be found.

_____. *French Lieutenant: A Ghost Story*. Day, 1972. Robert's family moves into a farm house on an estate. He finds the link between the haunted castle and the farmhouse. One day he confronts a young French lieutenant from 100 years ago.

Churchill, David. *It, Us and the Others*. Harper, 1978. Andy finds something in the water where he fishes. Jill communicates with It and is able to send It home on a beam of moonlight and save It from Its enemies, the Others.

Clapp, Patricia. *Constance*. Lothrop, 1968. Told through a journal's entries, a description of a trip from London to Massachusetts by a fifteen-year-old girl.

_____. *I'm Deborah Sampson*. Lothrop, 1977. The story of a woman who served in the Continental army during the American Revolution.

_____. *Jane-Emily*. Lothrop, 1969. Jane's parents were killed in a strange accident. Emily was Jane's would-be aunt who died when she was twelve. As Jane spends time at her grandmother's she "meets" Emily through a reflecting ball.

_____. *Tamarack Tree*. Lothrop, 1986. Rosemary, 17, is a spoiled Southern lady at the beginning of the Civil War. But she is against slavery and the war.

_____. *Witches' Children*. Lothrop, 1982. A story of the Salem witch trials. Mary Warren and nine other girls are "possessed" in July of 1692.

Clark, Ann. *All This Wild Land*. Viking, 1976. Maiju comes from Finland to America. The family faces hard times in 1876. They lost their crop and her father left and never came back. She and her mother still have the courage to still face the future.

_____. *Hoofprint in the Wind*. Viking, 1972. Patcheen is sure he has seen a wonderful Connemara pony at the top of a cliff. No one believes him because they are not supposed to be in that part of Ireland.

_____. *Medicine Man's Daughter*. Farrar, 1963. A young Navajo girl learning to be a medicine woman leaves the reservation for a Mission school to gain the medical training to help her people.

_____. *Secret of the Andes*. Viking, 1952. Cusi is an Inca boy in the Peruvian mountains. His duty is to care for and protect the llama herd. He learns the lore and traditions of his people. Newbery winner, 1953.

————. *To Stand Against the Wind*. Viking, 1978. Em tells about Vietnam before the war: rice planting, weddings, TET, family traditions, ancestral worship and astrology and the Mekong River delta before destruction.

Clark, Billy. *Champion of Sourwood Mountain*. Putnam, 1966. Aram is going to get a pup of a prime coon-dog. He loses his money trying to double it. He learns about cock-fights, moonshine and trickery. But he does get his pup.

Clark, Joan. *Wild Man in the Woods*. Viking, 1986. Stephen gets into a fight with some neighbor boys. He puts on a mask and experiences hatred and violence.

Clark, Margaret. *Barney and the UFO*. Dodd, 1979. Tibbo of the UFO wants to take Barney in his spacecraft. Barney feels unwanted and is tempted to go but he finds he is loved; and Tibbo leaves promising to return.

————. *Barney in Space*. Dodd, 1981. Rokell, a deranged Gark, decides that Barney is an enemy of his planet. Barney is trapped then released before a trip to the moon for a showdown is undertaken.

————. *Barney on Mars*. Dodd, 1983. Tibbo returns to Earth to warn Barney about a flood. He goes to Mars with Tibbo to rescue his dog, Alfie. But the Garks say they rescued him and he is theirs. But they give him back in the end.

————. *Latchkey Mystery*. Dodd, 1985. Minda and Adam are latchkey children. They are involved in a series of robberies as they set up a look-out system.

————. *Mystery in the Flooded Museum*. Dodd, 1978. Susan works in the museum when it is flooded and a valuable wampum belt disappears. She is on the track of the thief when she is left behind in the flooded museum facing a terrible death.

————. *Mystery of Sebastian Island*. Dodd, 1976. Dena and her friend, Barney, stay in a dark cellar of a deserted schoolhouse to find the answers to the strange things happening on Sebastian Island when a dark haired boy comes along.

————. *Who Stole Kathy Young?* Dodd, 1980. Meg and Kathy are friends. Deaf Kathy is kidnapped. Meg and Julian look for her; more specifically they look for her dog, Rusty. Meanwhile Kathy is trying to escape but doesn't make it.

Clark, Mary. *Cradle Will Fall*. Simon & Schuster, 1980. Katie stumbles onto some crimes connected with the hospital and doctors. She must find the solution before the murderer puts an end to her.

————. *Stillwatch*. Simon & Schuster, 1984. Pat tries to remember what she saw on the night her father killed her mother and committed suicide. She was there at the time; she's now an adult and receives a strange phone call.

————. *Stranger Is Watching*. Simon & Schuster, 1977. Nina is brutally murdered. Her husband has thoughts of revenge. Her son witnessed the murder and is terrified. Ronald is wrongly accused and is scheduled to die. The real killer is free.

Clark, Mavis. *Min-Min*. Macmillan, 1969. Two rebellious children run away from home and after living with another family, return home. The min-min, a sort of will-o'-the-wisp, play an important role in the adventure.

————. *Sky Is Free*. Macmillan, 1974. Two boys hitchhike to the opal mines but find no job and have no money. They try breaking into a grocery store and are caught and sentenced to work in the opal mines.

Clark, Virginia. *Mysterious Buckskin*. Macmillan, 1960. Ann, 18, and Ken, 19, lead a pack trip into the Sierras. They recover a prize stallion stolen two years earlier.

Clarke, Arthur. *Childhood's End*. Harcourt, 1980. The Overloads come to Earth and in 50 years abolish poverty, disease and fear. Now it is time to abolish humans.

————. *Dolphin Island*. Holt, 1963. A teenage runaway is cast up on the shores of Dolphin Island. The story takes place in the 21st century and the experimentation with dolphin communication has advanced.

————. *Imperial Earth*. Harcourt, 1976. A view of earthlings in the middle of the 21st century.

————. *2010: Odyssey Two*. Ballantine, 1982. Discovery is headed for destruction and only Hal can save it. Hal is the computer that started the destruction. Dr. Chandra must adjust Hal so that "he" functions correctly.

Clarke, Joan. *Early Rising*. Lippincott, 1974. Erica grows up in 1880 England. She starts as a tomboy and ends up in a French finishing school and college. Reminiscent of *Little Women*.

————. *Happy Planet*. Lothrop, 1965. Rick and Penny live on Tuan and go on an expedition to Earth where they find friendly people.

Clarke, John. *Black Soldier*. Doubleday, 1968. A story of the many kinds of prejudice and discrimination that a black soldier faced during World War II.

Clarke, Mary. *Iron Peacock*. Viking, 1966. Ross McCrae, a Scottish prisoner, and Joanna, who is sixteen and fleeing from Cromwell, try to build a new life in early America. They are indentured to the Iron Master.

————. *Limmer's Daughter*. Viking, 1967. Amity, 16, lives in 19th century Boston. She must help support her family and restore her father's good name.

————. *Petticoat Rebel*. Viking, 1964. Dacie wants to be educated like her brothers but nothing is available to her. After finishing "girls" school she opens a real school for girls.

————. *Piper to the Clan*. Viking, 1970.

When Cromwell beats the Scots some of them are
sent as prisoners to America to work as laborers.
Ross is among them. He was piper of his clan and
feels the loss greatly.

Clarke, Pauline. *Return of the Twelves.*
Coward, 1963. Max's love of 12 wooden soldiers
brings them to life to tell of times one hundred
years earlier.

Clarke, Tom. *Big Road.* Lothrop, 1965. Vic's
family is caught up in the Depression. He is faced
with poverty and a cruel stepfather. He runs away
and joins a hobo group. After many very bad incidents he decides to go home.

Clarkson, Ewan. *Halic, Story of the Grey Seal.*
Dutton, 1970. Halic is a gray seal who is washed
away from his mother when only two weeks old.
He looks for food and watches for sharks and
whales. He is also very wary of man, who hunts.

Claro, Joseph. *I Can Predict the Future.*
Lothrop, 1972. Max predicts the outcome of the
Mets-Pirates ballgame. Then he predicts more
things. His friends want him to predict test questions. He has ESP but is faced with how to use or
abuse it.

Clauser, Suzanne. *Girl Named Sooner.* Avon,
1975. Sooner, 9, is dirty, ragged and unloved.
Mac brings her home to his wife, Elizabeth. They
don't get along from the beginning but love is a
funny emotion.

Clavell, James. *Thrump-o-Moto.* Delacorte,
1986. Pat finds a Japanese boy wizard, Thrump-o-
Moto, who takes her to Japan. She drinks a magic
elixir and wakes up at home.

Cleary, Beverly. *Beezus and Ramona.* Morrow,
1955/1990. Sibling rivalry between Ramona and
her sister Beezus. Beezus is constantly embarrassed by Ramona's antics.

_____. *Dear Mr. Henshaw.* Morrow, 1983.
Leigh is going to a new school faced with the
problem of divorcing parents. He writes to his
favorite author as a school project and has unexpected results. Newbery winner, 1984.

_____. *Emily's Runaway Imagination.*
Morrow, 1961. Emily's imagination leads her into
trouble but it also leads her to win over the Ladies
Civic Club into agreeing to build a library.

_____. *Henry and Beezus.* Morrow, 1952/
1990. Henry wants a new bike. But before he can
get it he must deal with his dog, Ribsy, who is into
mischief; his friend Beezus, who tries to help; and
Ramona, Beezus' sister, the pest.

_____. *Henry and Ribsy.* Morrow, 1954/
1990. Henry and his dog, Ribsy, get in and out of
many predicaments.

_____. *Henry and the Clubhouse.* Morrow,
1962. Beezus and Ramona cause no end of trouble
for Henry and his dog, Ribsy.

_____. *Henry and the Paper Route.* Mor-
row, 1957/1990. Henry wants a paper route but he
is too young. He helps his friend fold papers and
substitutes for him when he is sick. He doesn't get
a route when one opens; it is given to someone else.

_____. *Henry Huggins.* Morrow, 1950/
1990. Henry has been given the lead part in the
school Christmas play. To him, it is too horrible
to even think about. But his adopted stray dog,
Ribsy, is also trouble.

_____. *Mitch and Amy.* Morrow, 1967.
Mitch and Amy are twin brother and sister. Each
wishes the other would be different. They argue a
lot through school and at home.

_____. *Mouse and the Motorcycle.* Mor-
row, 1965. A humorous fantasy about a wild
mouse named Ralph. He sees Keith playing with
a motorcycle and decides he'd like to do that.

_____. *Otis Spofford.* Morrow, 1953. Otis
decides that what his school needs is a little excitement so he takes matters into his hands.

_____. *Ralph S. Mouse.* Morrow, 1982.
Ralph still lives in the hotel and befriends a
newcomer, Ryan. Since all his many relatives
want to ride his motorcycle, Ralph goes to school
with Ryan and becomes famous.

_____. *Ramona and Her Father.* Morrow,
1977. Ramona Quimby's father loses his job but
the story of this family is always funny regardless
of circumstances. Mrs. Quimby gets a job in the
meantime.

_____. *Ramona and Her Mother.* Morrow,
1979. Now both of Ramona's parents are working
and she must be babysat. Ramona doesn't like any
of this.

_____. *Ramona Forever.* Morrow, 1984.
There are big family changes that make Ramona's
life very different. Mrs. Quimby is going to have
a baby and Mr. Quimby is still having employment problems. On top of that, the cat dies.

_____. *Ramona Quimby, Age 8.* Morrow,
1981. Mr. Quimby is training for a new career and
Ramona is training to become a model student.

_____. *Ramona the Brave.* Morrow, 1975.
Ramona and Beezus are members of a very
unusual family. Ramona thinks she is doing
everything right but Beezus is still embarrassed by
her and her teacher is exasperated.

_____. *Ramona the Pest.* Morrow, 1968.
Ramona is a very funny little girl like a lot of other
little girls. She means to do well but somehow
everything ends up wrong. She is discouraged.

_____. *Ribsy.* Morrow, 1964. Ribsy, a city
dog, strays away from home and sets off a series
of events as he tries to find his way back home.

_____. *Runaway Ralph.* Morrow, 1970.
Ralph runs away to a children's camp for a life of
speed, danger and excitement. Garf, his new
"owner," must save him from disaster.

_____. *Sister of the Bride.* Morrow, 1963. A
good story about the fun, confusion, stress and
excitement in the family of the bride as the wedding approaches.

_____. *Socks.* Morrow, 1973. Socks is the
family cat and he worries about his standing when
a new baby arrives.

Cleaver, Vera. *Belle Pruitt.* Lippincott, 1988

Belle's infant brother dies and her mother is grief stricken. Aunt George wants to move in but Belle sees her as a crutch. A sudden storm that destroys Belle's garden puts things right.

_____. *Delpha Green and Company*. Lippincott, 1972. A father, while in prison, studies to be a minister. Then he and his daughter found an independent church and help an apathetic community.

_____. *Dust of the Earth*. Lippincott, 1975. A young boy tells what it's like to live in the Bad Lands of South Dakota. His family are sheep ranchers and making a living is hazardous.

_____. *Ellen Grae*. Lippincott, 1967. Ellen stays with Mrs. McGruder and tells lies. Her friends are young Grover and retarded old Ira. Ira's tragic tale is almost unbelievable so when Ellen must tell about it no one believes her.

_____. *Grover*. Lippincott, 1970. Grover's mother dies and his life changes as he grows up. His friend, Ellen, tries to help since his father can't or won't cope.

_____. *Hazel Rye*. Lippincott, 1983. A girl's attitude towards land and growing things changes when a poor family works in a nearby orange grove.

_____. *I Would Rather Be a Turnip*. Lippincott, 1971. Annie's older sister and illegitimate son, Calvin, are coming to live at home. Annie feels disgraced and blames Calvin for her troubles.

_____. *Kissimmee Kid*. Lothrop, 1981. Evie's brother-in-law is a cattle rustler. She struggles with telling the truth about him.

_____. *Lady Ellen Grae*. Lippincott, 1968. Ellen is sent to live with her aunt so she can learn to be a lady; it is not a completely successful plan. Ellen Grae teaches Laura a few of her less than lady-like ways.

_____. *Little Destiny*. Lothrop, 1979. When the grief over her father's death makes her want revenge, a fourteen-year-old girl is headed for trouble.

_____. *Me Too*. Lippincott, 1973. A story of two sisters: Lydia, who is lively, intelligent and "normal," and Lorna, who seems to be retarded.

_____. *Mimosa Tree*. Lippincott, 1970. Marvella lives in the slums of Chicago. She hates the horror of it and struggles to free herself from its fate.

_____. *Mock Revolt*. Lippincott, 1971. Ussy, 13, lives during the Great Depression and revolts against the Establishment. He makes friends with a migrant family and clarifies his feeling of revolt.

_____. *Moon Lake Angel*. Lothrop, 1987. Kitty wants to help Aunt Petal's failing jam business. But she also wants to get even with her neglecting mother. When the time comes she is not sure she wants to go through with it.

_____. *Queen of Hearts*. Lippincott, 1978. Because grandmother had a stroke a young girl

must take care of her even though she is quite unreasonable at times.

_____. *Sugar Blue*. Lothrop, 1984. Amy, 11, isn't looking forward to a visit by her four-year-old niece. But it turns out to be okay.

_____. *Sweetly Sings the Donkey*. Lippincott, 1985. The Snow family move to Florida where they inherit some property. It is only bare land but they attempt to build a home.

_____. *Trial Valley*. Lippincott, 1977. Mary Call is still caring for her brothers and sisters, but has two rival suitors. She must make some hard decisions including what to do about the abandoned boy, Jack Parsons.

_____. *Where the Lilies Bloom*. Lippincott, 1969. The death of Mary Call's father poses a problem because she promised to bury him secretly and take care of the family so that they would not become welfare cases.

Clements, Bruce. *Anywhere Else But Here*. Farrar, 1980. Molly wants to start a new life and does succeed even though there are many obstacles in the way of her striving toward her dream.

_____. *I Tell a Lie Every So Often*. Farrar, 1974. A partially sunken riverboat is where Henry and his brother have a "showdown" because of Henry's big mouth.

_____. *Prison Window, Jerusalem Blue*. Farrar, 1977. Sydne and Juls free themselves from Viking captivity and return to their life as wandering performers.

_____. *Two Against the Tide*. Farrar, 1967. Tom and Sharon were picked up by "Aunt Eve" whom their mother knew. She took them to an island in Maine. But soon they realized that this was not what it was proposed to be.

Cleven, Catherine. *Pirate Dog*. Bobbs, 1962. Dirck, 12, stows away on a ship to the New World. He is captured by pirates, shipwrecked, robbed and gets involved with smugglers.

Clewes, Dorothy. *Guide Dog*. Coward, 1965. Roley is blinded in an accident involving a dog. He is bitter and resentful and doesn't want or trust a guide dog but comes around when the dog really helps him.

_____. *Hidden Key*. Coward, 1961. Rory and Kay take over a grocery store to help Mr. Marsden but they do more harm than good with their good intentions.

_____. *Missing from Home*. Harcourt, 1975. Two girls try to bring their parents together by dreaming up a fantastic plot.

_____. *Mystery of the Blue Admiral*. Coward, 1954. The Hadley children recover a stolen painting which reveals the hiding place of a buried treasure.

_____. *Mystery of the Jade-Green Cadillac*. Coward, 1958. The Hadley children are in Vienna followed by a Cadillac because Bobbie looks like the son of a Hungarian refugee.

_____. *Mystery of the Lost Tower Treasure*.

Coward, 1960. Peter, Bob and Ellen look for the Tower of London to find a long lost treasure. They find a strange situation as soon as they get there. A boy tells them about an attempt to steal the crown jewels.

_____. *Mystery of the Scarlet Daffodil*. Coward, 1953. Peter, 16, and the five other Hadley children try to find out who stole the rare scarlet daffodil before the flower show. The gardener? A gypsy boy? The maid?

_____. *Mystery of the Singing Strings*. Coward, 1961. A famous violinist hides a piece of music and the Hadley children want to find out why.

_____. *Old Pony*. Coward, 1960. Rory, Kay and Gerald save an old pony. They run into more problems than they expected trying to keep him a secret. They are found out but end up with a nice surprise.

_____. *Secret*. Coward, 1956. Kay and Rory find a garden and build a rabbit hutch. They use it as a secret place but a classmate finds out and wants to use it his own way.

Clifford, Eth. *Dastardly Murder of Dirty Pete*. Houghton, 1981. Again Mary Rose and Jo-Beth are traveling with their father. They get lost looking for grandmother's house. Instead they find the Inn of the Whispering Ghost and an old murder mystery.

_____. *Harvey's Horrible Snake Disaster*. Houghton, 1984. Harvey and his cousin Nora come to terms when she helps him overcome his fear of snakes. She is generally an unlikable liar but is also creative. She takes a snake home and causes havoc.

_____. *Harvey's Marvelous Monkey Mystery*. Houghton, 1987. Harvey's cousin Nora is visiting on spring vacation. Strange things begin to happen, like a monkey appearing at night; a mysterious man also appears. The monkey is found and returned.

_____. *Help! I'm a Prisoner in the Library*. Houghton, 1979. Mary Rose and Jo-Beth go looking for a restroom after their father leaves them to go look for a gas station. They get locked in the library and are scared when they hear strange noises.

_____. *I Never Wanted to Be Famous*. Houghton, 1986. Goody saves a baby from choking. He breaks the fall of a classmate. This makes him famous but he doesn't want to be; it's his mother who wants him to be president.

_____. *Just Tell Me When We're Dead*. Houghton, 1983. Mary Rose and Jo-Beth are staying with their cousin, Jeff, while their father takes his mother to the hospital. Jeff runs away and while the girls are trying to find him they find a bank robber.

_____. *Man Who Sang in the Dark*. Houghton, 1987. A story of a widowed mother and her children during the Great Depression.

_____. *Remembering Box*. Houghton, 1985. Joshua visits his Jewish grandmother every week. He learns about Jewish traditions from her and is ready to accept her death.

_____. *Rocking Chair Rebellion*. Houghton, 1978. Opie, 14, learns about maturity by helping elderly people in a home for the aged.

_____. *Scared Silly*. Houghton, 1988. Mary Rose and Jo-Beth go to a shoe museum called "Walk Your Way Around the World." The owner is a magician and when Chinese slippers are found missing the adventure begins.

_____. *Strange Reincarnations of Hendrik Verloon*. Houghton, 1982. Anna's grandfather is a phantom hoaxer. He also believes in reincarnation. Anna finds out about both in a very humorous way.

Clifford, Mary. *Salah of Sierra Leone*. Crowell, 1975. Salah is a village boy who wants an education. Salah is torn between loyalty to his traditional tribe and life in modern day Sierra Leone.

Climo, Shirley. *Gopher, Tanker and the Admiral*. Crowell, 1984. Gopher wants to make money. Tanker is his dog. The Admiral is a neighbor. They prevent the Admiral's house from being robbed. A warm, funny story.

_____. *Month of Seven Days*. Crowell, 1987. Zoe, her brother, and pregnant mother are taken over by Yankees and made "slaves" during the Civil War. Zoe tries to scare them away with talk of hauntings. A pro–South Civil War story.

_____. *T.J.'s Ghost*. Crowell, 1989. T.J. wanders on the beach and meets a boy who is looking for a ring. He is a ghost and needs the ring lost in an 1880's shipwreck to put his soul to rest.

Cline, Linda. *Weakfoot*. Lothrop, 1975. Weakfoot is a killer panther. He was wounded once but now is hunted by Lonny. But Lonny finds other killers in the swamp worse than Weakfoot.

Clymer, Eleanor. *Get-Away Car*. Dutton, 1978. Gram and Maggie plan to run away from Aunt Ruby because she is so domineering and plans a future they don't want.

_____. *Horse in the Attic*. Bradbury, 1983. Caroline and her father like horses for different reasons. They both fulfill their ambitions.

_____. *Luke Was There*. Holt, 1973. Luke was a worker in a children's home where Julius and his brother were. Luke leaves and Julius runs away. He is alone and doesn't know whom to trust.

_____. *My Brother Stevie*. Holt, 1967. Annie, 12, took care of her brother, Stevie. She tells about her worries, hopes and wishes while living in an inner city environment.

_____. *My Mother Is the Smartest Woman in the World*. Macmillan, 1982. Kathleen's mother is running for mayor of their town.

_____. *Spider, the Cave and the Pottery Bowl*. Atheneum, 1971. Kate and her brother, Johnny, stay with grandmother on the mesa. But there is no longer any pottery making because the clay is gone. Johnny broke a valuable bowl and runs away to hide his shame.

_____. *We Lived in the Almont*. Dutton, 1970. Linda, 12, lives with her father who is superintendent at the Almont. She has a friend, Carol, who also lives there and another friend who lives around the corner, who has more money.

Clyne, Patricia. *Curse of Camp Gray Owl*. Dodd, 1981. Sue, Andy, Alana, Chad and Roy are in an old Army camp looking for artifacts. An Indian is there for the same reason. They help him save the Indian land from a housing development.

Coates, Belle. *Mak*. Houghton, 1981. Mak is part Indian brought up by a white foster father. He retains his Indian heritage while adopting the ways of the whites.

Coatsworth, Elizabeth. *Cat Who Went to Heaven*. Macmillan, 1967. A Japanese legend about an artist and his cat and the miracle that united them. Newbery winner, 1931.

_____. *Jock's Island*. Viking, 1963. Jock, a collie in charge of sheep, is left behind when people desert their island because of a volcano eruption. A Norwegian fisherman finds him much later. He is happy to be rescued.

_____. *Jon the Unlucky*. Holt, 1964. Jon is an orphan who finds his way to a village in Greenland where all outsiders are condemned to death. He convinces the people that he should be spared because he is an asset to them.

_____. *Pure Magic*. Macmillan, 1973. Giles is a "werefox" and he and Johnny strike up a warm friendship.

Coblentz, Catherine. *Blue Cat of Castle Town*. Countryman, 1983. A little cat changes the history of a Vermont town in the 1800's.

Cohen, Barbara. *Benny*. Lothrop, 1977. Benny's mother is in the hospital for an operation. This changes the plans he had and instead gives him greater responsibility.

_____. *Binding of Isaac*. Lothrop, 1978. An interpretation of the Bible story of Isaac and Abraham, as told by Isaac.

_____. *Carp in the Bathtub*. Lothrop, 1972. A Jewish family story where two children rescue the fish before they become gefilte fish.

_____. *Christmas Revolution*. Lothrop, 1987. Emily is Jewish and protests the school's Winter Concert. There is a vandalism problem that Emily and her sister correct.

_____. *Coasting*. Lothrop, 1985. Steve and Maddy room together as friends but Maddy really likes Steve and he takes advantage of her feelings. She finally throws him out and they both reevaluate their situation.

_____. *Fat Jack*. Atheneum, 1980. Jack and Judy are friends. Judy encourages him to take part in a school play; he does so and is an instant success. He loses Judy's friendship. They meet later and discuss their disappointments.

_____. *Innkeeper's Daughter*. Lothrop, 1979. Rachel's mother runs a hotel. Rachel likes Jeff but he moves away. There is a fire and a valuable painting is saved. The money is used to rebuild the hotel.

_____. *King of the Seventh Grade*. Lothrop, 1982. Vic is really disturbed when, after looking forward to his Bar Mitzvah he learns that his mother is not Jewish and he cannot participate.

_____. *Lovers' Games*. Atheneum, 1983. Mandy lacks self-confidence. She reads love novels and works on the school newspaper. She finds romance in Connor.

_____. *Orphan Game*. Lothrop, 1988. Four cousins are vacationing and pretend to be orphans. They try to raise money for a trip to Atlantic City and they also try to avoid cousin Miranda, who is a pain.

_____. *People Like Us*. Bantam, 1987. Dinah is Jewish and when non-Jewish Geoff starts to date her, her parents are against it. She is torn between liking Geoff and believing in her religion. Geoff thinks she should rebel and do what she wants.

_____. *R My Name Is Rosie*. Lothrop, 1978. Rosie lives in the hotel her mother owns and runs. She is fat and lonely with few friends. She dreams about another life as compared to her real life.

_____. *Roses*. Lothrop, 1984. Courtney gets a job at a florist. The owner is badly scarred and she is frightened at first. A sort of Beauty and the Beast type story.

_____. *Seven Daughters and Seven Sons*. Atheneum, 1982. Buran, the fourth of seven daughters, goes on a trading caravan disguised as a boy. She meets Mahmud and they become friends and then lovers when he discovers her true identity.

_____. *Tell Us Your Secret*. Bantam, 1989. Several students are together at a writer's conference. Crunch lures Eve and others to the basement to tell scary stories. They learn a good deal about each other during unexpected events.

_____. *Thank You, Jackie Robinson*. Lothrop, 1974. A strong friendship between a young white boy without a father and an old black man. They are both Dodger fans, especially Jackie Robinson. In the end the old man dies but the friendship was valuable.

_____. *Unicorns in the Rain*. Atheneum, 1980. Nikki is going to visit her grandmother when she meets Sam. He shows her a world she didn't know existed. She is also shown two unicorns and other animals who must be saved from the non-ending rain. . . .

Cohen, Florence. *Portrait of Deborah*. Messner, 1961. Deborah wants to win a music scholarship but she must move and change schools and so loses her chance. But she finds love and becomes an excellent pianist.

Cohen, Miriam. *Born to Dance Samba*. Harper, 1984. Mario is looking forward to the annual festival in Rio. He loves to samba and prepare for the big day.

_____. *Robert and Dawn Marie 4Ever*.

Harper, 1986. Robert runs away from his uncaring mother and her boyfriend. He stays with a warm family who live next door to Dawn Marie and near Marsha, a loveable retarded girl.

Cohen, Peter. *Bee*. Atheneum, 1975. Herb wants to work on Rudy's ranch. Rudy is hurt and Herb must go to get help. Bee is the name of Herb's horse.

_____. *Calm Horse, Wild Night*. Atheneum, 1982. Arley's horse is kidnapped and he sets out to find it.

_____. *Deadly Game at Stony Creek*. Dial, 1978. David spends one summer in the country and accidentally uncovers the headquarters of criminal activity.

_____. *Foal Creek*. Atheneum, 1972. Gil and his brother, Frank, go fishing but Gil finds that the real purpose is to get marijuana.

_____. *Morena*. Atheneum, 1970. Alex, 13, and Morena, an old horse, struggle for survival during a snowstorm. Alex was left behind on a camping trip and Morena was left behind when livestock was taken in before the storm.

_____. *Muskie Hook*. Atheneum, 1969. Aaron is expected to be a fishing guide for his father's inn. This story concerns the difficulty of catching muskies and their ability to escape the hook.

Cole, Barbara. *Don't Tell a Soul*. Rosen, 1987. Karen, the daughter of Marian's first marriage, is being sexually molested by Marian's second husband, Mike.

Cole, Brock. *Goats*. Farrar, 1987. Lauren and Howie are victimized at summer camp. They are left on Goat Island, naked. They escape from the Island and the prank backfires.

Cole, Sheila. *Meaning Well*. Watts, 1974. A sixth grader learns the meaning of friendship too late to help a classmate who desperately needed a friend.

Cole, Stephen. *Growing Season*. Ariel, 1966. Marie is growing up during the Depression. She lives on a farm in Iowa and times are not good.

_____. *Pitcher and I*. Farrar, 1963. Robby and Pitcher were roommates in boarding school. Pitcher was not what Robby wanted as a friend (he was homely and studious) but they became good friends when Pitcher's good qualities stood out.

Coleman, Lonnie. *Orphan Jim*. Doubleday, 1975. Trudy and her brother chose to be "orphans" during the Depression. But they avoided being sent to an orphans home.

Coles, Robert. *Dead End School*. Little, 1968. An honest portrayal of the problems faced by children caught up in the fight for school desegregation.

_____. *Grass Pipe*. Little, 1969. Paul, 14, questions his experience with marijuana. His friends, Tom and Charlie, are curious; they have all the necessary supplies. A step by step description of how these boys experimented with drugs.

_____. *Riding Free*. Little, 1973. Unhappy at home, Sally decides to run away to her cousin's in Chicago and convinces her friend Sue to hitchhike with her.

_____. *Saving Face*. Little, 1972. Andy's father was a policeman who kept order. But when he was asked to rid the school of black "demonstrators" Andy was troubled by his father's values.

Collier, James. *Bloody Country*. Four Winds, 1976. A story about divided loyalties during the Revolutionary War. It takes place in Pennsylvania.

_____. *Jump Ship to Freedom*. Delacorte, 1981. A fourteen-year-old slave, Daniel, wanting to buy freedom for himself and his mother, escapes from his dishonest master and tries to find help in getting back his Continental notes.

_____. *My Brother Sam Is Dead*. Four Winds, 1974. The Meeker family want to stay out of the Revolutionary War but find that nonpartisanship does not absolve them.

_____. *Outside Looking In*. Macmillan, 1987. Fergy and his sister run away from an unconventional family to find their grandparents.

_____. *Planet Out of the Past*. Macmillan, 1983. Professor John and his two children land on Planet Pleisto. The Professor is captured by the planets inhabitants.

_____. *Rich and Famous*. Four Winds, 1975. George is thirteen and plays the guitar. A record company makes an offer and George sees himself as a star. But he must contend with agents, TV and advertising people.

_____. *Rock Star*. Four Winds, 1970. A young boy who loves music finds that even though he enjoys Rock he must study music seriously if he is to become a great musician.

_____. *Teddy Bear Habit*. Norton, 1967. George knows that at twelve he shouldn't depend on his teddy bear but when his father gives it away he tries to recapture it. This leads to an unlooked-for adventure.

_____. *War Comes to Willy Freeman*. Delacorte, 1983. A thirteen-year-old black girl, Willy, often mistaken for a boy, loses her father during the Revolutionary War. Her mother disappears and she goes to New York City to find her.

_____. *When the Stars Begin to Fall*. Delacorte, 1986. Harry is "poor, White trash." He finds that the town's own industry is polluting the river and he tries to stop it.

_____. *Who Is Carrie?* Delacorte, 1984. Carrie observes historic events and at the same time solves the mystery of her own identity. She is a friend of Daniel's and a cousin of Willy's and finds information important to them all.

_____. *Winter Hero*. Four Winds, 1978. The Shay Rebellion of 1787 in Massachusetts was a dangerous time in America. This is a fictionalized account of that event.

Collier, Julia. *Pirates of Barataria*. Putnam,

1966. Ned and two friends have a series of adventures on the Mississippi River in 1812. An old swamp house has strange sounds and lights coming from it.

Collodi, Carlo. *Adventures of Pinocchio.* Putnam, 1946. A good edition of this old favorite of how lying can hurt, as experienced by a "live" wooden puppet.

Collura, Mary Ellen. *Winners.* Dial, 1986. Jordy gets an old mare from his grandfather. He lost his parents and is failing in school but this gift brings meaning to his life.

Colman, Hila. *Accident.* Morrow, 1980. Adam has an accident on his motorcycle and almost kills Jenny. Jenny looks to him for help now that she's disabled but her brother won't let him near her.

————. *After the Wedding.* Morrow, 1975. Katie and Peter find that marriage has its problems. What each thought marriage was going to be, is not what the other thought.

————. *Bride at Eighteen.* Morrow, 1966. The problems of early marriage: lack of money, giving up college and day-to-day living. The solution: interesting even though low paying job, night school, parental loans.

————. *Classmates by Request.* Morrow, 1964. Ellen, black, is in her senior year and wants nothing to do with the issue of integration. Carla, white, wants integration. The two girls meet and understand the different ways of reaching goals.

————. *Claudia, Where Are You?* Morrow, 1969. Claudia and her mother do not understand each other so Claudia runs away to New York. She does survive and her parents relent and let her lead her own life.

————. *Confessions of a Story Teller.* Crown, 1981. Annie almost ruins the career of her favorite teacher through jealousy.

————. *Diary of a Frantic Kid Sister.* Crown, 1973. Sarah and Didi are sisters. Sarah wants to write and slowly grows less dependent on her sister and becomes her own person.

————. *Don't Tell Me That You Love Me.* Pocket Books, 1983. Melissa likes to date and go out but finds that friendship is not enough. She goes too far too fast and then meets Jimmy.

————. *Ellie's Inheritance.* Crown, 1979. Ellie, Rachel's daughter, lives with her father. She starts to follow the dressmaking business of her mother and has several romances.

————. *Family Trap.* Morrow, 1982. Becky lives with her "bossy" older sister and tries to get out by legal means.

————. *Just the Two of Us.* Scholastic, 1984. Samantha and her father have a good relationship. Her father, Lenny, wants to change their lifestyle, but she doesn't.

————. *Nobody Has to Be a Kid Forever.* Crown, 1976. Sarah's mother is leaving, her sister is moving in with her boyfriend and her dad has lost his job. Sarah is having a time coping.

————. *Rachel's Legacy.* Crown, 1979.

Ellie's mother, Rachel, tells of life in New York for Jewish immigrants during the Depression. Her two sisters took different paths to success. Ellie is like her mother.

————. *Remind Me Not to Fall in Love.* Pocket Books, 1987. Mia is 16; her mother is 36; Anthony is 26. Her mother wants Anthony as surrogate father and is in love with him. But so is Mia!

————. *Rich and Famous Like My Mom.* Crown, 1988. A young girl finds her identity through friendship with a street lady. Her mother is a famous and popular singer. She is overindulged but very lonely.

————. *Sometimes I Don't Love My Mother.* Morrow, 1976. Dallas, 17, is "mother" to her mother when her father dies. But when her mother starts acting like her daughter it is time for a change.

————. *Suddenly.* Morrow, 1987. Emily's boyfriend kills the child she babysits in an auto accident. She wonders if she is partially responsible.

————. *Tell Me No Lies.* Crown, 1978. Angela, 12, wonders about her absent father. Then she finds out that she is illegitimate. Upon investigation she learns that her father and mother made a difficult decision.

————. *Weekend Sisters.* Morrow, 1985. Amanda shares her father with her new stepfamily every weekend. Finally she decides to go away until the family pulls itself together.

————. *What's the Matter with the Dobsons.* Pocket Books, 1980. Divorce seems to be the result of what is happening to the Dobsons.

Colum, Padraic. *White Sparrow.* McGraw, 1972. Sparrow finds the trials of being different from others of his kind very difficult.

Colver, Anne. *Borrowed Treasure.* Knopf, 1958. Molly-O and Pip are friends; they want to own a horse. A farmer lends them a horse for the winter. They call it "Borrowed Treasure."

————. *Bread and Butter Indian.* Holt, 1964. Barbara helps a hungry Indian and a friendship begins. Later Barbara is kidnapped by a strange Indian and her Indian friend comes to her rescue.

————. *Bread and Butter Journey.* Holt, 1964. A family moves west in 1784 and they walk with pack horses. Barbara learns that home is where friends are, not the possessions they may own.

————. *Secret Castle.* Knopf, 1960. Molly-O and Pip vacation on an island and solve the secret of the old Boldt castle. Old gift books in the library supply the needed clues.

Colville, Bruce. *Spirits and Spells.* Dell, 1983. Jerry and his friends play Spirits and Spells in a haunted old mansion. Charity Jones was the ghost who haunted it. She was beheaded years earlier. A terror story.

Commager, Evan. *Valentine.* Harper, 1961. Valentine appears unfriendly in her new school.

She is companion to Jackie whose family brings her from behind her protective shell.

Conan Doyle, Arthur. *Hound of the Baskervilles.* Nal, 1986. A huge, fiendish hound is killing the Baskervilles, one by one. Sherlock Holmes looks at the circumstances and solves this strange crime.

Cone, Molly. *Amazing Memory of Harvey Bean.* Houghton, 1980. Harvey is shocked and hurt when he hears of his parents' pending divorce. The friendship of Mr. and Mrs. Katz helps him accept this change in his life.

_____. *Annie, Annie.* Houghton, 1969. A young girl doesn't agree with her liberal family and wants them to be more organized. She sets up "rules" for herself and learns a great deal about lifestyles.

_____. *Big Squeeze.* Houghton, 1984. Dudley tries out for Drama Club and meets a girl he likes. But she doesn't notice him.

_____. *Dance Around the Fire.* Houghton, 1974. Joanne is Jewish and must decide how serious her commitment to this religion should be.

_____. *Mishmash.* Houghton, 1962. Peter and his dog, Mishmash, grow up in a small town. He gives Mishmash to his teacher, who questions the intent.

_____. *Mishmash and the Big Fat Problem.* Houghton, 1982. Mishmash gets overweight and Pete and Wanda try hypnosis and exercise to slim him down.

_____. *Mishmash and the Substitute Teacher.* Houghton, 1963. Miss Dingly is the substitute teacher and Mishmash and Pete make a mess of everything that is being done.

_____. *Number Four.* Houghton, 1972. Benjamin's brother dies and so he tries to be like him, as a proud Indian. But the results are tragic.

_____. *Real Dream.* Houghton, 1964. Hogie enters the classroom and Lu sees the answer to her dreams. But reality sets in and her dreams are short lived.

_____. *Reeney.* Houghton, 1963. Reeny takes over the house when her mother dies. But she can't cope with the many problems of cooking, discipline, school, her boyfriend, etc. But even after several disasters it works out well.

Conford, Ellen. *Alfred G. Graebner Memorial High School Handbook of Rules and Regulations.* Little, 1976. The computer makes all the class schedules and they are terrible! Julie and her friends have quite a year.

_____. *And This Is Laura.* Little, 1977. Laura felt "odd man out" in her talented family. Then she found she could foretell the future. When a horrible vision appeared she was terrified as to what could happen.

_____. *Anything for a Friend.* Little, 1979. Wallis is the new girl in class. Her friends are Stuffy and Ruth. She is snubbed by the popular clique.

_____. *Dear Lovey Hart, I Am Desperate.*

Little, 1975. Carrie and Chip work on the school newspaper and Carrie gets into trouble trying to conceal her identity and the fact that her father is school counselor.

_____. *Dreams of Victory.* Little, 1973. Vicky is shy and not a social success in real life but in her fantasies she is all she wants to be.

_____. *Felicia, the Critic.* Little, 1973. Felicia tells the honest truth all the time. This does not win her many friends. She tries to change her approach but she knows she is a good critic and can't keep quiet, causing all sorts of havoc.

_____. *Genie with the Light Blue Hair.* Bantam, 1989. Jeannie conjures up a genie with blue hair and a Groucho Marx face. Her wishes all seem to backfire.

_____. *Hail, Hail, Camp Timberwood.* Little, 1978. This is the story of Melanie's first summer at camp.

_____. *Jenny Archer, Author.* Little, 1989. Jenny needs to write an autobiography for a class project. She uses her imagination to enhance her normal life.

_____. *Job for Jenny Archer.* Little, 1988. Jenny, 9, needs money for a horse and swimming pool that her parents say they can't afford. She goes into "real estate" by putting her own house up for sale.

_____. *Lenny Kandell, Smart Aleck.* Little, 1983. Lenny wants to be a comic. His mother and teacher think he is just a "smart aleck." He just wants to make people happy, but instead he is always in trouble.

_____. *Luck of Pokey Bloom.* Little, 1975. A girl who can't resist entering contests and a brother who is going through the trials of his first love make up this happy family story.

_____. *Me and the Terrible Two.* Little, 1974. Dorrie is the "Me" of the title. Twin boys move in next door and she declares war on them. Then she gets ill and the only real friends she has are the two boys next door.

_____. *Revenge of the Incredible Dr. Rancid and His Youthful Assistant, Jeffrey.* Little, 1980. Jeff wrote a fantasy story to escape his being short and skinny . . . and bullied!

_____. *Royal Pain.* Scholastic, 1986. Abby was switched at birth with a princess named Dolores. She finds this out at 15 and is sent to her "real" parents.

_____. *Seven Days to a Brand New Me.* Little, 1981. Maddy is pretty and witty but she feels drab and uninteresting. She likes a boy whose locker is next to hers. She improves her clothes and make-up. She finds that he is more shy than she is.

_____. *Strictly for Laughs.* Putnam, 1985. Peter likes his family's radio station. Joey plans to be a comedienne. She wants Peter to allow her to do a show and be discovered. The plan doesn't work but Peter and Joey get together.

_____. *Things I Did for Love.* Bantam,

1987. Steffie researches "Why do fools fall in love" for her term paper. She falls in love and finds it's hard to define.

_____. *To All My Fans, with Love from Sylvie*. Little, 1982. Sylvie, 15, lives in a foster home and runs away to Hollywood. She loses her money in Indiana and is stranded. She is saved by Vic, a college student, who wants her to turn herself in.

_____. *We Interrupt This Semester for an Important Bulletin*. Little, 1979. Carrie takes up reporting to impress Chip and only gets into more trouble as she investigates the school cafeteria.

_____. *You Never Can Tell*. Little, 1984. Kate has a crush on a soap opera star. He ends up in her algebra class and asks her for a date.

Conly, Jane. *R-T, Margaret and the Rats of NIMH*. Harper, 1990. Rasco, an intelligent rat, and his friends, Christopher and Isabella, work to save Thorn Valley after it is discovered by two human children.

_____. *Rasco and the Rats of Nimh*. Harper, 1986. Timothy and Rasco are trying to live in peace in Thorn Valley. Timothy is a field mouse and Rasco is an intelligent rat. Newbery winner, 1972.

Conn, Martha. *Crazy to Fly*. Atheneum, 1978. Tommy is expected to be a farmer and becomes one but his love of flying conflicts with his work. This is in the days of early aircraft.

Conrad, Pam. *Holding Me Here*. Harper, 1986. Robin looks in Mary's diary and discovers something that could ruin Mary's life. So she interferes with Mary's life and also Leslie's life, both good and bad.

_____. *I Don't Live Here*. Dutton, 1984. Nicki's family moves into a big, old house and she hates it. She is determined to run away, back to her old neighborhood.

_____. *My Daniel*. Harper, 1989. Ellie and Steve's grandmother tells them about her brother's search for dinosaur bones on their Nebraska farm.

_____. *Prairie Songs*. Harper, 1985. Louisa looks at her mother through different eyes when she meets the new doctor's wife. There is a sharp contrast, especially as you face life on the prairie.

_____. *Staying Nine*. Harper, 1988. Can you believe a young girl who wants to stay nine years old and not have a tenth birthday?

_____. *What I Did for Roman*. Harper, 1987. Darcie wants to know more about her father. She and Roman search for him. But Roman has a serious flaw and Darcie escapes from his evil spell.

Constant, Alberta. *Does Anyone Care About Lou Emma Miller?* Crowell, 1979. Lou Emma is fifteen and she helps the suffragettes elect the first woman mayor of Gloriosa, Kansas.

_____. *Motoring Millers*. Crowell, 1967. Can you picture a car in 1911! Maddy, Lou Emma, their father, and his new wife, Kate, take

a trip in their new bright red car named Great Smith. Some discipline has entered the girls' lives.

_____. *Those Miller Girls*. Crowell, 1965. Maddy and Lou Emma, along with their professor father, make up the Miller family. Reckless, carefree girls with little control have a wild time in the early 1900's.

_____. *Willie and the Wildcat Well*. Crowell, 1962. Willie, 11, helps his father as he is digging for oil in Indian Territory in 1905.

Constiner, Merle. *Sumatra Alley*. Nelson, 1971. Brad has not made up his mind if he is pro- or anti-Revolution. He finds out who it is on Sumatra Alley that is really the "dangerous rebel leader."

Conway, Caron. *Sometimes Nightmares Are Real*. Fearon, 1986. Lisa sees a man shot to death in her dreams. He is in an alley and she wants to save him because she knows her dreams always come true.

Cook, Robin. *Brain*. Nal, 1982. Why are women going crazy? Why are they dying on the operating table? Why are their brains being removed? Martin and Denice want to find out.

_____. *Coma*. Little, 1977. People are dying in the hospital and no one knows why. People enter for minor reasons and end up in a deep coma. Susan is determined to find out why.

_____. *Mindbend*. Putnam, 1985. Something is wrong at the Clinic. There are abortions, drug testing, brainwashing and . . . murder.

Cookson, Catherine. *Blue Baccy*. Bobbs, 1972. Rory is involved in a smuggling ring. He ends up escaping with some of the smuggled jewels in a blue baccy (tobacco). He throws them away.

_____. *Go Tell It to Mrs. Golightly*. Lothrop, 1977. Bella is a blind orphan. She tells her grandfather about a bound and gagged man next door.

_____. *Mrs. Flannagan's Trumpet*. Lothrop, 1980. Eddie must live with his grandmother whom he doesn't like. Then his sister is kidnapped by white slavers and must be rescued. His grandmother's strength and courage win Eddie's love.

_____. *Nipper*. Macmillan, 1971. Sandy and his mother lose their home, their jobs and Sandy's beloved horse, Nipper. But Sandy works in the mines and uncovers a dynamite plot against the owner. There is an investigation.

Cool, Joyce. *Kidnapping of Courtney Van Allen and What's-Her-Name*. Knopf, 1981. Jan, 12, is kidnapped with her famous, wealthy friend. The kidnappers want something other than money as ransom.

Coolidge, Olivia. *Come by Here*. Houghton, 1970. Minty Lou is black, bright and spoiled. She lives in Baltimore at the turn of the century. Her parents are killed and she must live with relatives. She finds out this is different from visiting them.

Coolidge, Susan. *What Katy Did*. Smith, 1983. A classic story, sometimes thought of as one of the first books for children. Katy is a tomboy and because she misbehaved had a tragic accident.

Cooney, Caroline. *Among Friends.* Bantam, 1987. Hillary, Emily and Jennie keep a diary for six months. The life they talk about in their diaries is different from the life they lead every day in school.

————. *Girl Who Invented Romance.* Bantam, 1981. Kelly creates a board game called "Romance" for a school project. She does find a romance of her own with Will.

————. *Rah Rah Girls.* Scholastic, 1987. Marcy's family are all overachievers. She wants them to see cheerleading as an achievement. They see it as a Rah Rah activity not a real hobby, club activity or social experience.

————. *Saturday Night.* Scholastic, 1986. Five girls are all excited about the Autumn Leaves Dance. They all have different goals: some love, some danger; one even wants revenge. So a perfect evening is not perfect for everyone.

Coontz, Otto. *Hornwaggle Magic.* Little, 1981. Jenny, a magical shopping bag lady, saves a newsstand from a "progressive" automatic newspaper machine.

————. *Isle of the Shapeshifters.* Houghton, 1983. A pendant is calling a young girl into the dark, deep coldness from which she can't return.

————. *Mystery Madness.* Houghton, 1982. Murray hears a murder being committed in his own house. But the housekeeper is not dead. House thieves are found and wire tapping is stopped.

————. *Night Walkers.* Houghton, 1982. Martin eats a carrot and gets ill as do other children. The "ill" ones try to make the others "ill." Nora and Maxine find the source of the trouble in this horror story.

Cooper, Clare. *Earthchange.* Lerner, 1986. Earth's civilization has been destroyed. Ruth must reach a colony of scientists by battling wolves and hostile humans. She rescues a dog and her pups.

Cooper, Gordon. *Second Springtime.* Nelson, 1975. An orphaned English girl is adopted by a pioneer farm family.

Cooper, Ilene. *Queen of the Sixth Grade.* Morrow, 1988. Robin and Veronica form the Awesome Kennedy Girls Club. Robin sees that Victoria is not so nice and seeks other friends.

————. *Winning of Miss Lynn Ryan.* Morrow, 1987. Carrie is facing a dilemma: Should she impress the teacher she likes or should she be loyal to her best friend?

Cooper, James F. *Last of the Mohicans.* Nal, 1962. A Mohican named Chingachgook and Hawkeye risk their lives to escort two sisters through Indian enemy territory.

Cooper, Margaret. *Code Name: Clone.* Walker, 1982. While trying to find their "father," Evonn and Stefan reach America in 2060. They flee capture in the tunnels of New York City. Guard dogs, agents and drugs are all used to try to capture them.

————. *Solution: Escape.* Walker, 1980. Set in the twenty-first century, Stefan finds out he is a clone and is part of a scheme to control the government. Evonn is his lookalike. They both try to escape. But to where?

Cooper, Susan. *Dark Is Rising.* Atheneum, 1973. Will, with the help of Great-Uncle Merry must find the six Signs that are necessary to fight off Evil. Will is the seventh son of a seventh son and the last of the Old Ones.

————. *Dawn of Fear.* Harcourt, 1970. A group of English children come to terms with the horrors of war when one of them is killed in an air raid.

————. *Greenwitch.* Atheneum, 1974. A legend of the Wild Magic of Earth. The Drew children and Will help the Old Ones recover the grail. They must restore the good power of Greenwitch with the help of Great-Uncle Merry.

————. *Grey King.* Atheneum, 1975. Will and a white dog with silver eyes must be ready for a dreadful battle with evil. King Arthur's son Bran will help to awaken the Sleepers. Newbery winner, 1976.

————. *Over Sea, Under Stone.* Harcourt, 1965. Jane, Barney and Simon find a treasure map which would lead them to the grail of King Arthur. They are threatened by the Dark but Great-Uncle Merry protects them.

————. *Seaward.* Atheneum, 1983. A battle between good and evil. Teranis is evil and the bringer of death. Lugan is the protector of life. Westerly and Calliope cross over time and place to encounter this adventure.

————. *Silver on the Trees.* Atheneum, 1977. Will, Bran and the Drew children try to locate the crystal sword which will vanquish the Dark forces. They travel through time and space to see that Light wins out over Evil.

Copeland, Hugh. *Duncan's World.* Crowell, 1967. Duncan was in the Museum when the explosion occurred. The next day Van beats him and tells him to forget what he knows about the explosion.

Coppard, Audrey. *Who Has Poisoned the Sea?* Phillips, 1970. Tim meets Percy from the 25th century. He tells about the Atlantic Ocean being poisoned.

Corbett, Scott. *Baseball Bargain.* Little, 1970. Woody exchanges a baseball glove for a place on the team. That was his first bargain and a mistake. His next was with Mr. Stonehan which led to misadventures and messed up baseball games.

————. *Baseball Trick.* Little, 1965. Kirby and his magic chemistry set help the batting of his team but he gets surprising results.

————. *Black Mask Trick.* Little, 1976. Mrs. Graymalkin, who has talents that are very like a witch's, enlists Kirby and his dog Waldo to expose a crook. The crook is one of the town's founders.

————. *Captain Butcher's Body.* Little, 1976. Two boys read a story of pirates, buried treasure and the ghost of Captain Butcher and it brings them together.

_____. *Case of the Burgled Blessing Box.* Little, 1975. There is money being stolen from the collection box at a tent church. It looks like an inside job and Inspector Tearle must solve the robbery.

_____. *Case of the Fugitive Firebug.* Little, 1969. Inspector Tearle's alarm goes off in his treehouse office. He finds that someone has set fire to a garage containing an antique car, the Bearcat.

_____. *Case of the Gone Goose.* Little, 1966. Inspector Tearle, a young detective, comes across a triple murder—of geese named Tom, Dick and Harry.

_____. *Case of the Silver Skull.* Little, 1974. Inspector Tearle is asked to watch the silver collection at a Home Tour. Sure enough two antique dealers are there to steal.

_____. *Case of the Ticklish Tooth.* Little, 1974. When Inspector Tearle goes to his dentist he finds him bound and gagged. The red-bearded thug escaped on Roger Tearle's bicycle.

_____. *Cave Above Delphi.* Holt, 1965. A map showing where an ancient ring was hidden during World War II is given to four boys. Someone else is trying to beat them to it.

_____. *Cop's Kid.* Little, 1968. Chip and Benny go to the store and see a killer on a bus. Instead of calling the police they hunt the man themselves. They find him to be a cop-hating gang leader and their father is a cop.

_____. *Cutlass Island.* Little, 1962. Skip and Harvey, amateur detectives, find old Civil War weapons and a whole arsenal buried on Cutlass Island.

_____. *Dead Before Docking.* Little, 1972. Jeff can read lips and "heard" a man say . . . "he'll be dead before they reach port. . . ." Who of the nine passengers on *Wellfleet* is the killer and the intended victim?

_____. *Deadly Hoax.* Dutton, 1981. One day two school boys encounter beings from space.

_____. *Disappearing Dog Trick.* Little, 1963. This time Kirby uses his chemistry kit to find his dog, Waldo, who is missing after a city campaign to pick up stray dogs.

_____. *Discontented Ghost.* Dutton, 1978. A ghost story told from the point of view of the ghost. He starts being typically "ghost-like" but ends up being both nice and helpful. A humorous retelling of "Canterville Ghost" (Wilde).

_____. *Donkey Planet.* Dutton, 1979. Two scientists go to another planet to bring back samples of metal.

_____. *Down with Wimps.* Dutton, 1984. Bessie and Claudine team up to put down the class snob, get back a lost baseball that has value and rework the school cafeteria.

_____. *Ever Ride a Dinosaur?* Holt, 1969. Tad is turned into an invisible ten-year-old boy by a dinosaur and together they go to visit a museum.

_____. *Grave Doubts.* Little, 1982. Mr. Canby changed his will and died under unusual circumstances. Les and Wally do some detecting with crossword puzzle clues.

_____. *Hairy Horror Trick.* Little, 1969. Kirby brings disaster to himself, his friend and his dog, Waldo, by misusing his chemistry set. Waldo becomes furless while Kirby and Fenton grow magical hair.

_____. *Hangman's Ghost Trick.* Little, 1977. Kirby and his friend look for a special weed that grows in the mountains. They find the weed, and a missing cat, but not before some scary times.

_____. *Hateful, Plateful Trick.* Little, 1971. Again the chemistry set is the culprit, with Kirby's help. It seems that everyone is surrounded with the smell of the food each hates most.

_____. *Here Lies the Body.* Little, 1974. Mitch and Howie get a summer job mowing a burial ground. They meet Ezekiel and Nathaniel, caretakers, when some very scary things happen during a thunderstorm.

_____. *Hockey Girls.* Dutton, 1976. Miss Tingery is an English teacher who is also coach of the field hockey team. Irma joins the team and things go wrong.

_____. *Hockey Trick.* Little, 1974. Kirby and the Panthers resort to a magical hockey puck in a game to save their clubhouse.

_____. *Homerun Trick.* Little, 1973. Should the team really try to win this game if they must then play a girls team? Both teams try very hard to lose!

_____. *Horse in the House.* Coward, 1964. Melanie said she would train her horse, Orbit, to live in a house. The horse is stolen and must be recovered.

_____. *Lemonade Trick.* Little, 1960. Kirby and his magical chemistry kit turn lemonade into a drink that makes everyone do good deeds. Kirby cleans the garage, Waldo digs up his bones, the whole town is changed.

_____. *Limerick Trick.* Little, 1964. Kirby wants to win a bicycle by writing the best poem in school. He gets started on limericks and finds that he can only speak in limericks, much to the dismay of his friends and teachers.

_____. *Mailbox Trick.* Little, 1961. When Kirby's aunt sends him stationery for a birthday present, he doesn't write Thank You notes but starts to send nasty letters to the people in town he doesn't like.

_____. *Mystery Man.* Little, 1970. Tod and M.M. (Mystery Man), from an old radio serial, are implicated in a family feud (there are two A.G. Cartwrights) and a treasure hunt involving the book *Silas Marner.*

_____. *One by Sea.* Little, 1965. Nye left for America with Mr. Willet. Mr. Willet dies and Nye was cursed by him. He ran into lots of hatred and treachery because of this.

_____. *Pippa Passes*. Holt, 1966. Meg, 11, is going to summer camp and is bored. She meets Pippa, a child movie star, who is running away. Meg helps disguise her as a camper and takes her to summer camp.

_____. *Run for the Money*. Holt, 1973. Steve is asked to deliver a mysterious package and finds himself involved in a ring of thieves.

_____. *Tree House Island*. Little, 1958. Skip and Harvey come across bank robbers digging up the money they buried twenty years before.

_____. *Trouble with Diamonds*. Dutton, 1985. Jeff works at an inn where he is suspicious of two guests staying there because he thinks they are planning a robbery.

_____. *Turnabout Trick*. Little, 1967. Kirby and his friends with the aid of the magic chemistry set have more troublesome adventures. A cat doesn't remember he's a cat. Waldo thinks he is a cat. It all comes out okay in the end.

_____. *Witch Hunt*. Atlantic, 1986. Les, 16, and his friend get involved in a murder case when they find a covey of witches plotting revenge.

Corbett, W.J. *Pentecost, the Chosen One*. Delacorte, 1987. A new leader emerges. He is the son of the last great leader and feels inadequate. Deep friendships develop as he leads his followers toward their destiny.

_____. *Song of Pentecost*. Dutton, 1982. The mice that live on the farm must move or die. Under a courageous leader they flee toward safety. Their leader dies and the mice end their search. Frog's lies endanger Owl's life.

Corbin, William. *Dog Worth Stealing*. Watts, 1987. Jud goes camping alone when he learns that his stepmother is pregnant. He sees a dog and steals him from a cruel owner.

_____. *Prettiest Gargoyle*. Watts, 1971. Mike, 13, is living in Paris. He discovers and shields a runaway teen-aged French girl at Notre Dame.

Corcoran, Barbara. *All the Summer Voices*. Atheneum, 1973. David works to help the family financially because his father drinks and is unreliable.

_____. *Annie's Monster*. Macmillan, 1990. Annie gets her longed-for Irish wolfhound. Her father is a minister and she has problems with a large dog's curiosity.

_____. *August, Die She Must*. Atheneum, 1984. A feud over the merits of two counselors divides the campers at Camp Allegro until one of the counselors is found dead.

_____. *Child of the Morning*. Atheneum, 1982. Susan wants to be a dancer and gets a part in a summer theatre. But she has, as yet undiagnosed, epilepsy. She is finally helped by a new doctor with new drugs. Her future is bright.

_____. *Dance to Still Music*. Atheneum, 1974. Margaret, 14, is deaf from an illness. Her mother remarries and she is lonely until she meets Josie, an older woman who helps her.

_____. *Faraway Island*. Atheneum, 1977. Lynn goes to spend a year with her grandmother and faces problems with her grandmother's age, with bullies at school and her own self-confidence.

_____. *Horse Named Sky*. Atheneum, 1986. Georgia's father is an alcoholic. She and her mother go to the mountains. While there her next door neighbor promises to sell her a wild mustang.

_____. *I Am the Universe*. Atheneum, 1986. Kit is a worrier. Her mother is ill and she must care for her brother and sister.

_____. *Long Journey*. Atheneum, 1970. Laurie rides across the state of Montana to get help for her ailing grandfather.

_____. *Make No Sound*. Atheneum, 1977. Melody feels responsible for her brother's accident since she wished him harm in a fit of anger and resentment.

_____. *Me and You and a Dog Named Blue*. Atheneum, 1979. Maggie, 15, fights off the domination of an older woman.

_____. *Mystery on Ice*. Atheneum, 1985. A series of mysterious threats soon escalate into dangerous and frightening events. Kim and Stella face men and dogs who see them as intruders. The camp is to be sold and buildings set afire.

_____. *Person in the Potting Shed*. Atheneum, 1980. Dorothy and Franklin have a new step-father. They stay at Belle Rive, a creepy, gloomy place with a drunken gardener who disappears.

_____. *Potato Kid*. Atheneum, 1989. Ellis, 14, hates it when her family takes in Lilac, 10 (the potato kid), for the summer.

_____. *Private War of Lillian Adams*. Atheneum, 1989. Lil, Jay, Danny and Tootie are being patriotic at the beginning of World War II. They look for spies and suspicious people but a Halloween prank turns ugly.

_____. *Rising Damp*. Atheneum, 1980. Hope goes to Ireland for the summer where she meets Kol, a young gypsy man who takes advantage of her to the tune of $500.00.

_____. *Sam*. Atheneum, 1967. Sam is a girl who works with her dog to get him ready for a dog show.

_____. *Sasha, My Friend*. Atheneum, 1969. A young girl moves from Los Angeles to Montana to live on a tree farm. It takes a lot of adjustment.

_____. *Sky Is Falling*. Atheneum, 1988. During the Depression Annah's father loses his job at the bank and they sell their home to get money. Everyone must find work even if it means separating.

_____. *Star to the North*. Nelson, 1970. A teenage brother and sister travel through wilderness in British Columbia to live with an uncle. They had lived a sheltered life but were unhappy with their values.

_____. *Strike*. Atheneum, 1983. First the

teachers and then the community strike to protest book banning in the school. Barry is not interested at first but then becomes deeply involved.

_____. *Trick of Light.* Atheneum, 1972. Cassandra and Paige are close twins but Paige is starting to act on his own. When their dog, Bingo, is hurt and in the woods they go to search for him together and are close again on a different level.

_____. *Watery Grave.* Atheneum, 1982. Kim and Stella work to find the killer when a swimming pool murder occurs in a household they are visiting. Drugs seem to be involved.

_____. *Which Witch Is Which?* Atheneum, 1983. There is a series of catnappings including the ones belonging to the twins. They follow an old woman to an abandoned house and find their cats . . . and danger.

_____. *Winds of Time.* Atheneum, 1974. Gail runs away rather than live with an uncle she very much dislikes. Fortunately she finds a new life with kindness and understanding.

_____. *Woman in Your Life.* Atheneum, 1984. Monty is tricked into helping Aaron smuggle mescaline into the United States. She is caught and jailed and never reveals Aaron's role. She tells about her life in a woman's prison.

_____. *You Put Up with Me, I'll Put Up with You.* Atheneum, 1984. Kelly's mother is to open a restaurant with some friends. Kelly doesn't like this idea but comes around to see it as a good thing.

_____. *You're Allegro Dead.* Atheneum, 1981. Two girls discover a mystery at their recently reopened summer camp. Was someone living there while it was closed? A bank robber hid his loot in the pond.

Cordell, Alexander. *Healing Blade.* Viking, 1971. It is 1798 and the Irish Rebellion is still going on.

_____. *Traitor Within.* Nelson, 1973. "Fear" is the traitor within. Ling must conquer his fear and defend his father's good name.

_____. *White Cockade.* Viking, 1970. Story of the Irish Rebellion of 1798 filled with excitement, intrigue and chase.

Corlett, William. *Return to the Gate.* Bradbury, 1977. An old man is trying to survive in a world of famine, fuel shortage and violence. Helen opens up his life but she is later violently killed.

Cormier, Robert. *After the First Death.* Pantheon, 1979. Ben's father is on a secret government project. There is a bus full of children hijacked and most of the action takes place around this terrifying incident.

_____. *Beyond the Chocolate War.* Knopf, 1985. Dark deeds continue at Trinity High School, ending in a public demonstration of a homemade guillotine. There is a good deal of human unkindness in and around school.

_____. *Bumblebee Flies Anyway.* Pantheon, 1983. Mazzo is dying and Barney wants to help make it easy for him to go as he wishes. The plan is bizarre and Barney finds out that he, too, is going to die.

_____. *Chocolate War.* Pantheon, 1974. Jerry refuses to sell chocolates for a private school fundraiser and is harassed by the school bully, Archie. The student body is at the mercy of Archie and his "tricks."

_____. *I Am the Cheese.* Pantheon, 1977. Adam travels by bicycle to his father's. He thinks about what has happened while on his way. His father has been given a new identity because he exposed some corruption. Now Adam is being questioned.

Cotich, Felicia. *Valda.* Coward, 1963. Valda turns out to be a heroine during the Depression days in Australia.

Counsel, June. *Dragon in Class Four.* Faber, 1984. A fantasy about a dragon and a group of children.

Covert, Paul. *Cages.* Liveright, 1971. Eric and Ward are very different but are friends. Someone says they are homosexuals and Ward commits suicide.

Coville, Bruce. *Ghost Wore Gray.* Bantam, 1988. A group of youngsters solve a 100-year-old mystery concerning a local inn.

_____. *Monster's Ring.* Pantheon, 1982. Russell owns a magic ring. He uses it against instructions and faces unexpected aftereffects.

_____. *Operation Sherlock.* Nal, 1986. A group of young computer experts are on an isolated island. This is a tale of their adventures.

Cowley, Joy. *Silent One.* Knopf, 1981. Jonasi, a deaf mute, is blamed for misfortunes by superstitious people. He finds an albino turtle that someone tries to kill. He tries to save the turtle and is never seen again.

Cox, William. *Game, Set and Match.* Dodd, 1977. Charlie takes tennis lessons, but racial prejudice stands in his way.

_____. *Home Court Is Where You Find It.* Dodd, 1980. Willy is a basketball star. He leads his team to a championship. His girlfriend, Pam, is also a star in tennis.

_____. *Unbeatable Five.* Dodd, 1974. Bud Cane joins the basketball team and the Unbeatable Five suffer a series of losses.

_____. *Wild Pitch.* Dodd, 1963. William's father wants him to be a star pitcher but William has trouble controlling his fast ball because he is near-sighted.

Craig, John. *Who Wants to Be Alone?* Coward, 1972. Three youngsters take to the road to escape their bleak past and look for a secure future.

Craig, M.F. *Mystery at Peacock Place.* Scholastic, 1986. A young boy goes looking for an old woman and finds a mystery.

Craig, Margaret. *It Could Happen to Anyone.* Crowell, 1961. Jean likes Andy but he dates Gloria, a "fast" girl. Jean must think about the problems of going steady.

Crane, Caroline. *Don't Look at Me That Way.* Random, 1970. Rosa is the oldest of seven children. They have no father and grow up under difficult conditions.

_____. *Girl Like Tracy.* McKay, 1966. Kathy's sister, Tracy, is retarded. But she is also very pretty and very spoiled.

_____. *Lights Down the River.* Doubleday, 1964. Connie wants to be an actress. She gets through drama school after some failures. This is a story of the hardships of becoming an actress.

_____. *Stranger on the Road.* Random, 1971. Diane ran away from home to her father. She hitchhiked until she ran out of money and then worked her way to Arizona. She meets Eric and after visiting her father returns home to her mother.

_____. *Wedding Song.* McKay, 1967. April, while yet in high school, is secretly married.

Crane, William. *Encore.* Atheneum, 1983. Darleen, Fred and Sheryl help Tiny and their band make good at their Santa Rosa concert so the principal will let them go to Oregon.

_____. *Oom-Pah.* Atheneum, 1981. Fred is a tuba player from Texas and Darleen is the rival tuba player in the school band. Darleen resents his practical jokes and constant talking.

Crary, Margaret. *Calico Ball.* Prentice, 1961. The Dakota Indians are not being fairly paid for their land as settlers move West. They start a reign of terror against the whites. Ginger and her father can stop the Indians because of friendship.

Craven, Margaret. *Again Calls the Owl.* Putnam, 1980. How the dying minister, who won the respect and friendship of the Kwakiutl Indians of the Northwest, faces death.

_____. *I Heard the Owl Call My Name.* Dell, 1973. Mark is a vicar working among Indians. He is going to die but is also learning to live. "...The owl, who call the name of the man who is going to die...."

Crawford, Charles. *Three-Legged Race.* Harper, 1974. Three teenage hospital patients become close friends. The girl dies, one boy is discharged and the third is left to cope as best he can.

Crayder, Dorothy. *Ishkabibble.* Atheneum, 1976. Lucy is losing her friends for no reason. Annie, an old guru, offers a cure.

_____. *Joker and the Swan.* Harper, 1981. Zoe tries to become a great ballerina to please her mother and dance teacher. The Joker is a talking dog and adds a magical touch to a ballet story.

_____. *Riddles of Mermaid House.* Atheneum, 1977. When a young girl moves to a New England town she can't understand why the community is so against a local recluse. She finds out why.

_____. *She and the Dubious Three.* Atheneum, 1974. Maggie arrives in Italy. She sees a couple with a baby as she takes the train to Venice. She thinks the baby is kidnapped. She finds the real father after searching the canals and back alleys of Venice.

_____. *She, the Adventuress.* Atheneum, 1973. Maggie is the adventuress. She is going to Italy to see an aunt. She has many adventures as the unattended minor on an Italian liner.

Crayder, Teresa. *Cathy and Lisette.* Doubleday, 1964. Cathy has a visitor from France, Lisette. They learn from each other about friendship, love and heartbreak.

Creighton, Don. *Little League Old Timers.* Steck-Vaughn, 1967. Kit and his gang get a baseball field next to an old age home. No noise is allowed but the old folks come around and enjoy the games.

Cresswell, Helen. *Absolute Zero.* Macmillan, 1978. Members of the talented and eccentric Bagthorpe family channel their energies into slogan writing contests and taking labels off cans of food. Zero, the pet dog, can't sniff dog bones.

_____. *Bagthorpes Abroad.* Macmillan, 1984. This time the Bagthorpes are on vacation in Wales, but in a haunted house where they want to learn more about ghosts. One incident after another happens to make life chaotic.

_____. *Bagthorpes Haunted.* Macmillan, 1985. Still on vacation in the haunted house, the Bagthorpes try to contact the ghosts living there.

_____. *Bagthorpes Liberated.* Macmillan, 1989. The Bagthorpes return from vacation and find a tramp living in their house. Their maid has disappeared and cousin Daisy has come to stay with her pet goat.

_____. *Bagthorpes Unlimited.* Macmillan, 1978. The competitive Bagthorpes join forces in a rare display of solidarity when Grandma organizes a family reunion. They plan zany incidents to annoy the rest of the relatives.

_____. *Bagthorpes Vs. the World.* Macmillan, 1979. The Bagthorpes contend with father's attempts to be self-sufficient. Because he mistakenly thinks they are poor, he wants them to raise their own food and keep animals.

_____. *Beachcombers.* Macmillan, 1972. A suspense story of a family of beachcombers involved with missing treasure and a boy being held by thieves.

_____. *Bongleweed.* Macmillan, 1973. Becky and her friend are trying to save a plant they feel is important. They call it "Bongleweed."

_____. *Dear Shrink.* Macmillan, 1982. Oliver, William and Lucy are unexpectedly placed in foster homes. They run away to a summer cottage where they have near tragic adventures. Finally they are found by their returning parents.

_____. *Moondial.* Macmillan, 1987. Minty hears children crying from mysterious graves. She meets these children through the help of a moondial.

_____. *Night Watchmen.* Macmillan, 1970. Henry is bored and restless, then he meets two tramps, Josh and Caleb, and his life becomes fascinating.

————. *Ordinary Jack*. Macmillan, 1977. Jack is the only ordinary boy of the talented and eccentric Bagthorpe family. He concocts a scheme to distinguish himself as a prophet with ESP.

————. *Piemakers*. Macmillan, 1967. Arthy, Jem and Grvella bake a pie for the king big enough to feed 2000 people and good enough to win a contest. But rival bakers compete, too.

————. *Secret World of Polly Flint*. Macmillan, 1984. Polly learns of the old legend of the whole village of Grimstone disappearing and living secretly underground. She meets some of these Time Gypsies and helps them.

————. *Time Out*. Macmillan, 1990. Tweeny, 12, uses a book of magic spells to travel forward in time from 1887 to 1987 and finds things very different.

————. *Up the Pier*. Macmillan, 1971. A boy is caught in a time trap and wants to return to 1921 from the present (early 1970). Carrie meets him at the seaside and helps him.

————. *Winter of the Birds*. Macmillan, 1975. Patrick Finn comes to town. He is different and likeable. He influences everyone but especially the three people who tell this story from their point of view.

Crew, Linda. *Children of the River*. Delacorte, 1989. Sundara comes to the United States from Cambodia and wants to be both American and Cambodian. She falls in love with an American boy....

Crichton, Michael. *Andromeda Strain*. Dell, 1984. A mutant cell turns deadly and threatens the world. It can't be killed and reproduces very rapidly. It will kill before anyone can identify it.

————. *Congo*. Knopf, 1980. A man-ape lives in the jungle and crushes the skull of anyone who comes near. Amy, a trained gorilla, is expected to track it. But "it" watches and waits.

————. *Sphere*. Knopf, 1987. A spaceship from the future is found 1,000 feet under water. Scientists study the ship, the sphere it contains and the messages that are being received on its computer.

————. *Terminal Man*. Knopf, 1982. Harry is turned from an epileptic man into a killing monster. Doctors implant electrodes into his brain and the horror begins.

Crofford, Emily. *Matter of Pride*. Carolrhoda, 1981. A family story during the Depression on a cotton plantation in Arkansas.

Crompton, Anne. *Deer Country*. Little, 1973. Chris and Trigg hunt deer. Trigg gets a doe but Chris must wait another year. Trigg tries to hunt illegally but Chris stops him.

————. *Ice Trail*. Methuen, 1980. Daniel, 15, is captured by Indians and almost forgets his English background. But he does escape with the help of his Indian friends.

————. *Queen of Swords*. Methuen, 1980.

Susan, 18, is an unwed mother. She gets an art scholarship. She must find a place for Jason, her nine-month-old son.

Crook, Beverly. *Fair Annie of Old Mule Hollow*. McGraw, 1978. Annie, 15, is confronted by Jamie McFarr. Annie's family and the McFarrs have been feuding for years. Annie thinks he is going to shoot her for being on his land. Instead they meet and become lovers.

Cross, Gilbert. *Hanging at Tyburn*. Atheneum, 1983. George has nightmares about being hanged at Tyburn which almost come true when he is framed for a theft he did not commit.

————. *Mystery at Loon Lake*. Atheneum, 1986. Jeff and his brother discover a tunnel at the lake that is used by smugglers to take art from the United States to Canada. They are then discovered and try to escape.

————. *Terror Train*. Atheneum, 1987. Jeff and Nguyen travel by train from Chicago to Portland, Oregon. They meet a mystery story writer and help him investigate the sudden disappearance and death of a fellow passenger.

Cross, Gillian. *Born of the Sun*. Holiday, 1984. Paula goes with her father to find a lost city of the Incas. He becomes ill and it takes a great deal of courage to carry on through the jungle to get help and find the city.

————. *Chartbreaker*. Holiday, 1987. Finch sings with a rock band, Kelp. Finch is really Janis and Kelp is really Chris. Dave, Rollo and Job make up the rest of the band. Who are they? Janis wonders if she likes Finch, who she has become.

————. *Dark Behind the Curtain*. Oxford, 1982. The school Drama Club is presenting "Sweeny Todd" but there is a mystery developing around this production.

————. *Demon Headquarters*. Oxford, 1983. This "demon headmaster" of a private school is turning his students into non-thinking, obeying automatons.

————. *On the Edge*. Holiday, 1984. Tug is kidnapped by terrorists. They are not only physically abusive but play with Tug's mind.

————. *Revolt at Ratcliffe's Rags*. Oxford, 1980. Abby, Chris and Susan get involved in a local factory strike as a result of a class project. They learn of working conditions and labor/management conflict.

————. *Twin and Super-Twin*. Holiday, 1990. One of David's arms begins to turn into bizarre objects. He is a member of a street gang and one of a set of twins. It changes the street situation.

Crossley-Holland, Kevin. *King Horn*. Dutton, 1966. Horn is exiled to Ireland during the 13th century. He repels an invasion and saves his love from a forced marriage.

Crowell, Ann. *Hogan for the Bluebird*. Scribner, 1969. A young Navajo girl returns to her tribe after spending a few years at a Mission school. There is conflict between her own culture and that of the white community.

Crutcher, Chris. *Chinese Handcuffs.* Greenwillow, 1989. Dillon's brother, Preston, gets hurt in a bike accident and later commits suicide. Dillon writes him long letters about his girl, Stacy, and about Jennifer who was abused by her father.

———. *Crazy Horse Electric Game.* Greenwillow, 1987. Willie runs away and finds thugs, drugs, pimps and prostitutes. He goes home and finds divorce and drunkenness.

———. *Running Loose.* Greenwillow, 1983. A story of the seeming unfairness of life as seen by Louie and Becky.

———. *Stonan!* Greenwillow, 1986. A week of endurance for Jeff, Nortie, Lionel and Walker. They make it but they must face another challenge that even Stonan may find too difficult.

Culin, Charlotte. *Cages of Glass, Flowers of Time.* Bradbury, 1979. Claire is shy because she has an alcoholic, abusive mother. She tries to lose herself in her drawings. She makes three new friends: Daniel, a black musician, Clyde (and his dog) and Jake.

Cummings, Betty. *Let a River Be.* Atheneum, 1978. An old woman fights to save a river from greedy land developers. She and a retarded boy work together. She teaches him to become independent.

———. *Now Ameriky.* Atheneum, 1979. Briged leaves Ireland during the famine to go to America. She meets poverty and prejudice. But she will win out.

Cunningham, Julia. *Burnish Me Bright.* Pantheon, 1970. Auguste is a mute orphan. He is victimized by his fellow villagers. A brutal story with a valuable message. An old mime befriends him and teaches him his craft.

———. *Come to the Edge.* Pantheon, 1977. A boy runs away from an orphanage because of brutal treatment.

———. *Dear Rat.* Houghton, 1961. An underworld story of Andrew, the rat, as he learns about gangland sewer society.

———. *Dorp Dead.* Knopf, 1965. Gilly is in an orphanage and sent away to live with a carpenter. He is unhappy and misused. So he escapes.

———. *Far in the Day.* Pantheon, 1972. Auguste wanders through Europe as a circus performer in search of food, warmth, friendship and a home.

———. *Flight of the Sparrows.* Pantheon, 1980. Cigarette is rescued from a drab orphanage by Mago, another streetwise orphan and Drollant, a retarded boy. Mago is murdered but Cigarette and Drollant find some happiness.

———. *Macaroon.* Pantheon, 1962. Macaroon, a raccoon, spends his winters in comfort by letting a child adopt him. Since leaving in the spring is sad he chooses a very unlikeable girl but ends up liking her anyway.

———. *Oaf.* Knopf, 1985. Oaf receives three gifts: a phrase, a magic hat and a promise of a treasure. He must use these gifts properly.

———. *Onion Journey.* Pantheon, 1967. This is a story about Gilly when he lived with his grandmother before the orphanage.

———. *Silent Voice.* Dutton, 1981. Auguste is found by a street urchin and is befriended by a famous Parisian mime, Ms. Bernard. But jealousy of his talent hinders his life, especially by the backer of the school.

———. *Tuppenny.* Dutton, 1978. Three separate couples, each of whom has lost a daughter, are affected by this strange girl.

———. *Viollet.* Pantheon, 1966. Count de la Tour and his dog, Oxford, are in danger and Viollet, a thrush, is the heroine in this story of intrigue, suspense and true devotion.

Curley, Daniel. *Ann's Spring.* Crowell, 1977. Ann's mother (Earth Mother) goes away and leaves Ann in charge of making Spring happen. She is almost stopped when she is locked up. But she does succeed.

———. *Billy Beg and the Bull.* Harper, 1978. Billy Beg is an Irishman who goes around the world doing good deeds for people.

Curry, Jane. *Bassumtyte Treasure.* Atheneum, 1978. Tommy wants to stay with his grandmother and when he finds hidden treasure he is able to do so.

———. *Beneath the Hill.* Harcourt, 1967. Miggle planned a treasure hunt but someone else was interested in her treasures and her carefully planted clues. She found the door leading to Kaolin and his strange family.

———. *Big Smith Snatch.* McElderry, 1989. Mother gets sick at the last minute before their proposed move. Four of the children leave their sister and Auntie Moss and go to explore their new city.

———. *Birdstone.* Atheneum, 1977. A girl is created by Callie and her friends to fight boredom. The real girl shows up from the time of the Abaloc Indians. She is looking for her grandfather who has been lost for 1600 years.

———. *Daybreakers.* Harcourt, 1970. Callie, Liss and Harry stumbled upon an underground cave. They were transported back to the time of an earlier Indian civilization. They were captured and jailed but later rescued.

———. *Ghost Lane.* Atheneum, 1979. Richard is going to live with his opera singing father. He becomes involved with a gang of thieves who steal antiques and art.

———. *Great Flood Mystery.* Atheneum, 1985. Gordy and his friends find secret rooms, mysterious burglaries and a villain looking for a treasure lost in the Johnstown flood of 1889.

———. *Ice Ghost Mystery.* Atheneum, 1972. The Bird's father is missing and they feel compelled to go look for him.

———. *Lost Farm.* Atheneum, 1974. The

farm and everything on it are reduced to miniature by a mysterious machine. Pete and his grandmother do all they can to keep from being lost forever.

————. *Lotus Cup*. Atheneum, 1986. Corry develops her artistic talent by recreating the Lotus porcelain formula developed by her great-grandfather.

————. *Magical Cupboard*. Atheneum, 1976. A preacher steals a cupboard from a widow who he says is a witch. He takes it to an orphanage and Felicity discovers its magic. Felicity and Rosemary are connected through time by this magic.

————. *Me, Myself and I: A Tale of Time Travel*. Atheneum, 1987. J.J. pokes around Professor Poplon's lab and gets into trouble. He goes back to being a child and re-runs his life.

————. *Mindy's Mysterious Miniature*. Atheneum, 1970. A young girl finds an old dollhouse that has magical powers no one knew about.

————. *Over the Sea's Edge*. Harcourt, 1971. Davy finds a medallion in a cave and is transported to the twelfth century.

————. *Parsley, Sage, Rosemary and Time*. Harcourt, 1975. Parsley Sage is the cat, Rosemary is the girl and Time (thyme) is on the stone which takes Rosemary back to the time of the Pilgrims. She is put in jail with Goody Cakebread as a witch.

————. *Poor Tom's Ghost*. Atheneum, 1977. The actor father of two children buys an old house that is haunted by another actor.

————. *Shadow Dancers*. Atheneum, 1983. Wrongfully accused of stealing a valuable moonstone, Lek enters the dread Shadowland to look for stones of equal power.

————. *Watchers*. Atheneum, 1975. Ray, 13, finds an evil Shrine of Darkness near a coal mine. He slips into the past and is a captured slave.

————. *Wolves of Aam*. Atheneum, 1981. Runner, the fastest Tiddi (little folk) scout, is befriended by Lek. He goes to the stark fortress of Gzel in the mountains of Iceland to find his special stone and its meaning.

Curtis, Alice. *Winter on the Prairie*. Crowell, 1944. The Julien family is raising money to build an addition on their home. They survive a long cold winter. Gilbert arrives and so does the hound they waited for.

Curtis, Philip. *Invasion of the Comet People*. Knopf, 1983. Skiky meets Jason and they play marble shooting. Skiky finds out that Jason and his people want to invade the Earth. The Earth is saved but Skiky worries about the next passing of Halley's comet.

Cusack, Isabel. *Mr. Wheatfield's Loft*. Holt, 1981. Ellis sees the death of his father and can't speak. He reads about pigeons and gets one from Mr. Wheatfield and trains it to be a homer. The pigeon returning helps Ellis say his first words.

Cussler, Clive. *Raise the Titanic*. Viking, 1976.

Dick is in charge of raising the Titanic to get the byzanium that was aboard. He faces a hurricane, Russian enemies and technical problems.

Cutt, W. Towrie. *Seven for the Sea*. Follett, 1974. Mansie and Erchie drift through the fog into the past. The two boys find Selkie and his family in the reign of William the Fourth.

Cuyler, Margery. *Trouble with Soap*. Dutton, 1982. Laurie and Soap are friends. Laurie wants to make new friends but Soap is jealous and Laurie does not assert herself.

Dacquino, V.T. *Kiss the Candy Days Goodbye*. Delacorte, 1982. Jimmy is on the wrestling team when he finds he is diabetic. His friends Margaret and Santiago help him but he is jealous of their friendship.

Dahl, Borghild. *This Precious Year*. Dutton, 1964. Helia was able to finish college during the Depression because of her mother's sacrifice and her family's cooperation.

————. *Under This Roof*. Dutton, 1961. Kristine's parents die and she tries to keep the family together in spite of a cold winter and its hardships.

Dahl, Roald. *The BFG*. Farrar, 1982. BFG is a Big Friendly Giant who kidnaps Sophie and takes her to giantland. He catches dreams and sends them to good children. The other giants do mean things.

————. *Charlie and the Chocolate Factory*. Knopf, 1964. Each of the five winners of the Willy Wonka contest is put to a test as they visit the chocolate factory. The tour seems to bring out the best and the worst of the visitors.

————. *Charlie and the Great Glass Elevator*. Knopf, 1972. Charlie, his family, and Mr. Wonka are launched into space by the great glass elevator. The President tries to untangle the mess but makes it worse. In the end Willie saves the Earth.

————. *Danny, the Champion of the World*. Knopf, 1975. Danny goes with his father when he goes poaching in rich Mr. Hazell's woods.

————. *Fantastic Mr. Fox*. Knopf, 1970. Sharp old Mr. Fox outwits three farmers who are rich and mean.

————. *George's Marvelous Medicine*. Knopf, 1982. George puts together several things and makes a medicine that he gives to his mean grandmother and it makes her shrink.

————. *James and the Giant Peach*. Knopf, 1961. James leads a dull life with his two aunts. But he escapes boredom through his giant peach. A wonderful fantasy.

————. *Magic Finger*. Harper, 1966. When a young girl points her finger at wrongdoers they are punished.

————. *Witches*. Farrar, 1983. A boy and his grandmother foil a witches' plot to destroy the world's children by turning them into mice.

Dahlstedt, Marden. *Shadow of the Lighthouse*. Coward, 1974. Jane lives in the 1870's. Her father is a lighthouse keeper and she loves the beach and the island; she collects unusual shells and sees a tragic shipwreck. Her mother misses the city and its genteel ways.

————. *Terrible Wave.* Coward, 1972. Spoiled Megan, 15, is caught in the Johnstown flood and separated from her wealthy family. She learns about mutual cooperation and responsibility when she must do her part to save herself and others.

Dailey, Virginia. *Keys to Lawrence House.* Duell, 1960. Letita's first year at college brings her new friends and new instructors, one of whom she likes. It also brings moral questions of the use of residence keys and a bout with poison pen letters.

Dalgleish, Alice. *Adam and the Golden Cock.* Scribner, 1959. Adam encounters French troops during the Revolutionary War.

————. *Courage of Sarah Noble.* Macmillan, 1954. Sarah and her father brave the wilds of colonial America in 1707.

Daly, Maureen. *Acts of Love.* Scholastic, 1986. Henrietta meets a young man in her hometown. She becomes romantically involved and learns about his connection to her mother's past. A long wait for this since her *Seventeenth Summer* (1942).

————. *Seventeenth Summer.* Dodd, 1968. A reissue of an old favorite. Jack and Angie have a summer romance. It is strong in June, July and August but then what?

D'Ambrosio, Richard. *No Language But a Cry.* Doubleday, 1970. Laura is an abused child. Her parents were alcoholics and when she was less than a year old she was brought to the hospital by police, badly burned. This is based on a true story.

Damjan, Mischa. *December's Travels.* Dial, 1986. December, a lonely boy, is given a magic gift by the North Wind. He can visit other boys in March, June and October.

Dana, Barbara. *Necessary Parties.* Harper, 1986. A story told by a child whose parents are getting a divorce. Shouldn't the kids have a say? With the help of a lawyer the "necessary parties" clause is found.

————. *Zucchini.* Harper, 1982. A ferret escapes from the Bronx Zoo and is on his own.

Daneman, Meredith. *Francie and the Boys.* Doubleday, 1988. Francie is an actress. She and five other girls act in a play at a boy's school and it is a success.

Dank, Gloria. *Forest of App.* Greenwillow, 1983. Nob is crippled and so is left behind by his story telling people. He is taken in by a witch-girl, an elf and a dwarf. They live in a forest whose magic is almost gone.

Dank, Milton. *Computer Caper.* Delacorte, 1983. Attempting to help friends, the Galaxy Gang battle money swindlers. They use computer expertise and psychology to capture the crooks.

————. *Computer Game Murder.* Delacorte, 1985. Mr. "Chips" and "Peter Pan" are playing a computer game when "I'm scared. Help me." shows up on the screen. It is another case for the Galaxy Gang.

————. *Dangerous Game.* Lippincott, 1977. Charles matures quickly while serving the French Resistance during World War II. He meets with French traitors and German Nazis.

————. *Game's End.* Lippincott, 1979. Charles, now nineteen, is an officer in the Free French Army. He is also a spy for the English in France as the Allies prepare for invasion.

————. *Khaki Wings.* Delacorte, 1980. Edward, sixteen, joins the Royal Flying Corps. He is the only survivor of his original squadron and finds that war is not romantic but cruel and terrifying.

————. *Red Flight Two.* Delacorte, 1981. Edward finds action in the Royal Flying Corps during World War II. His best friend is killed and he is made Flight Instructor. But he wants to use his experience and so heads a squadron.

————. *3-D Traitor.* Delacorte, 1984. The ghost of Benedict Arnold appears in an historical house of an elderly man. The Galaxy Gang investigates since people have been pressuring the man into selling. The ghost is a hologram.

————. *Treasure Code.* Delacorte, 1985. The treasure is a dragon ring, and the clues are hidden in a book by a local author. The Galaxy Gang looks everywhere in the city. The clues involve geography, history, math, music, etc.

————. *U.F.O. Has Landed.* Delacorte, 1983. Glowing green lights and strange creatures from outer space land on earth and a teacher sees them. He is to be fired unless the Galaxy Gang can prove their existence.

Dann, Colin. *Animals of Farthing Wood.* Nelson, 1979. A variety of animals cross a river, dodge a vicious dog, escape a fox and cross a freeway to get to White Deer Park. Each animal contributes to the trip. Reminiscent of *Watership Down* (Adams).

————. *Ram of Sweetriver.* David & Charles, 1987. Jacob is the ram that leads his ewes and lambs away from a flood and into a national park. The animals are real animals even though they are personified. Somewhat like *Watership Down* (Adams).

Danziger, Paula. *Can You Sue Your Parents for Malpractice?* Delacorte, 1979. Lauren's parents are always fighting partly because of the strong will of her father. But this is only part of the many problems she faces.

————. *Cat Ate My Gymsuit.* Delacorte, 1974. Marcy is a very courageous and imaginative girl who is bored with school and herself until Ms. Finney comes to teach English. Independent stands and moral values are at stake.

————. *Divorce Express.* Delacorte, 1982. Phoebe moves on the "divorce express" between her father and her mother. She makes friends with Rosie, and later her father and Rosie's mother get together. Both girls are happy about this.

_____. *Everyone Else's Parents Said Yes.* Delacorte, 1989. Matthew plays practical jokes on his older sister and other girls at school. When his birthday comes they all declare war!

_____. *It's an Aardvark Eat Turtle World.* Delacorte, 1985. Rosie and Phoebe's parents have moved in with each other and they are "sisters" not "friends." There are problems and Phoebe decides to go live with her mother and stepfather then changes her mind.

_____. *Make Like a Tree and Leave.* Delacorte, 1990. Matthew gets in trouble at home and at school; he fights with his sister but he also does some good by helping a neighbor save his property.

_____. *Pistachio Prescription.* Delacorte, 1978. Because of a pending divorce and school problems a young girl eats pistachio nuts to ease her frustration.

_____. *Remember Me to Harold Square.* Delacorte, 1987. Kendra and Frank are friends and have a summer romance. Kendra's brother is a sore point as are Frank's parents' divorce plans.

_____. *There's a Bat in Bunk Five.* Delacorte, 1980. Marcy is now a camp counselor and realizes what a heavy responsibility that is. She is also faced with some new boy-girl experiences.

Darke, Marjorie. *Question of Courage.* Crowell, 1975. Emily is a seamstress and is involved in the Suffragette movement in England. She is arrested and goes on a hunger strike.

Daveluy, Paule. *Summer in Ville-Marie.* Holt, 1962. Rosanne, 16, spends the summer with her relatives. She finds love, disappointment and rivalry for the attention of the local doctor.

Davidson, Alan. *Bewitching of Alison Allbright.* Viking, 1989. Alison is unhappy with her life. She wants to be more popular. She gets the chance but is unwilling to pay the price.

Davidson, Mary. *Superstar Called Sweetpea.* Viking, 1980. Elizabeth wants to be a rock singer. She secretly joins a band but soon she is suffering low grades, boyfriend problems and run down health.

Davies, Andrew. *Conrad's War.* Crown, 1980. Conrad is unhappy with his life. He dreams of war and power where he is a hero. His dreams seem to be reality.

Davies, Harriet. *Aboard the Lizzie Ross.* Norton, 1966. Life aboard a clipper ship in 1890. There are storms, death and intrigue. The main character is Hallie, the captain's daughter.

Davies, Peter. *Fly Away Paul.* Crown, 1974. Paul runs away from a boy's home. He was beaten and mistreated in every way.

Davis, Edward. *Bruno and the Pretzel Man.* Harper, 1984. Bruno doesn't like being a pretzel man but what to do about it?

Davis, Gibbs. *Fishman and Charly.* Houghton,

1983. Tyler and Charly are siblings. Tyler likes his fish and Charly likes her paintings. They are trying to protect the manatee off the coast of Florida. They find the poachers in time to report them.

_____. *Maud Flies Solo.* Bradbury, 1981. Maud is ignored by her older sister, who is "growing up" and doesn't understand why. A good story of sisters growing apart but still family.

_____. *Swann Song.* Bradbury, 1982. Pru and her friends dream of the future: high school, romance, adventure, parties, but are faced with a tragic suicide.

Davis, Jenny. *Good-Bye and Keep Cold.* Orchard, 1987. Edda's father was killed in a strip-mining accident in Kentucky. Edda was eight at the time and tells of the fate of herself and her family before and after the accident.

Davis, Maggie. *Grandma's Secret Letter.* Holiday, 1982. A girl is on her way to her grandmother's and has many adventures along the way.

Davis, Russell. *Choctaw Code.* McGraw, 1961. Tom befriends Jim, a Choctaw sentenced to death by his tribe because he killed in anger. Jim meets his destiny and Tom learns about honor.

_____. *Some Town You Brought Me To.* Crown, 1969. Bud has no status in his new school. He plays basketball but quits over an incident that wasn't his fault. But he overcomes the pressure and stands up for his own beliefs.

Davis, Terry. *Vision Quest.* Viking, 1979. Louden, 18, finds success and satisfaction in wrestling.

Davis, Verne. *Devil Cat Screamed.* Morrow, 1966. Ray made a mortal enemy of a cougar. All summer the cougar waited for revenge. Then Ray and the cougar pitted know-how against cunning.

_____. *Gobbler Called.* Morrow, 1963. Jan, 13, and his family move West. They encounter Indians and hardships but Jan takes on the responsibility of a man.

_____. *Orphan of the Tundra.* Weybright, 1968. Tom rescues a musk ox and raises him. He then takes him back to the Arctic, leaves him with a herd and returns home.

_____. *Runaway Cattle.* Morrow, 1965. Kirby's Jersey bull runs away. Then his dog, Bugle, is gone. Kirby and his friend go off to find them. The dog's loyalty helps them on this dangerous expedition.

Dawlish, Peter. *Boy Jacko.* Watts, 1963. Jacko is a thief, a pirate, a pickpocket, etc. He is shanghaied with his friend Matt. They take over the ship but are re-captured and sentenced to hang.

Dawson, A. *Finn the Wolfhound.* Harcourt, 1962. Finn is a show dog that has won many ribbons. He was mistaken for a wolf and driven into the bush of Australia to survive in the wilds.

Day, David. *Emperor's Panda.* Dodd, 1987. A flute player who lives a simple life searches for wisdom in China.

Day, Ingeborg. *Ghost Waltz.* Viking, 1980. A girl tries to find out how involved her father was as an SS officer in Austria. She also evaluates her own feelings toward Jews.

Day, Veronique. *Landslide*. Coward, 1963. Five children on vacation are trapped in a landslide. While they were asleep the house was covered with the sliding earth. They spend twelve days there before they are rescued.

Dean, Anabel. *High Jumper*. Benefic, 1975. Mary rides her horse in the jumping competitions but not before she overcomes all her problems.

Dean, Karen. *Stay on Your Toes, Maggie Adams*. Avon, 1986. Maggie is a ballerina. She has many differing struggles: her boyfriend, a jealous ballerina and a nasty director. She really is torn as to what action to take.

Deane, Shirley. *Vendetta*. Viking, 1967. Fan-Fan and Uncle Jacque bid on and buy a flock of sheep belonging to a rival clan. The clan plans on regaining the sheep by ambush and murder. Fan-Fan foils the plan.

De Angeli, Marguerite. *Door in the Wall*. Doubleday, 1949. Robin lives in 14th century England. He is crippled but hopes to become a knight and serve his king. He does so in a way that is different from what he expected.

De Clements, Barthe. *Double Trouble*. Viking, 1987. Faith and Phillip are twins but living separately. They communicate by letters and ESP. Phillip's foster home is a religious sect. Faith's teacher is a thief.

_____. *Five Finger Discount*. Delacorte, 1989. Jerry seems to be following in his father's footsteps. His father is in prison for robbery and Jerry is inclined to steal.

_____. *Fourth Grade Wizards*. Viking, 1988. Marianne's mother dies and she daydreams instead of studying. She moves to a new home, gets a puppy, becomes better in school and adjusts to a new life.

_____. *How Do You Lose Those 9th Grade Blues?* Delacorte, 1983. Elsie starts high school and finds the best looking boy on the team showing interest in her. She lost her fat and is cute but she still thinks FAT. She is jealous and distrustful of Craddac.

_____. *I Never Asked You to Understand Me*. Viking, 1986. Didi has problems: she cuts classes at school, her father is playing around, her mother is ill and may die. She is in an alternative school and learns of the lives of other students.

_____. *No Place for Me*. Viking, 1987. Copper's mother is an alcoholic so she lives with Aunt Maggie, a witch who helps Copper overcome lies and unhappiness.

_____. *Nothing's Fair in Fifth Grade*. Viking, 1981. Elsie is new in school. She is fat and unhappy about it. She is accused of stealing money for candy but Jenny, one of the "in" girls, helps Elsie through friendship and understanding.

_____. *Seventeen and In-Between*. Viking, 1984. Elsie in the beginning was fat, then became

slim and attractive but was insecure because of her own thoughts. Now she has not only a boyfriend but boyfriend problems she never dreamed of.

_____. *Sixth Grade Can Really Kill You*. Viking, 1985. Elsie's friend, Helen, is a pest in school and her grades are not good. But she is a star baseball pitcher and has a sense of humor. A new teacher helps Helen straighten out her problems.

Defekice, Cynthia. *Strange Night Writing of Jessamine Colter*. Macmillan, 1988. Jessie feels this strong urge to write and what she writes is a prediction of the future.

De Felice, Cynthia. *Weasel*. Macmillan, 1990. Weasel is a renegade killer seeking revenge and Nathan is alone in the wilderness in 1839.

Defoe, Daniel. *Robinson Crusoe*. Grosset, 1946. A shipwrecked mariner lived alone on a desert island for twenty-eight years.

De Ford, Deborah. *Enemy Among Them*. Houghton, 1987. Margaret is taking care of Christian, a wounded prisoner, at the beginning of the Revolutionary War. He turns rebel and warns of a Loyalist attack at Stoney Point.

Degens, T. *Game of Thatcher Island*. Viking, 1977. Harry, Sarah and John go to Thatcher Island by invitation but they find that they are to be victims of others' cruelty. They fight back.

_____. *Transport 7-41-R*. Viking, 1974. After World War II a young girl helps an old couple as they are being shipped in a boxcar to Cologne. The woman dies. Her husband wants her buried near her daughter so they keep the death a secret.

_____. *Visit*. Viking, 1982. Sylvia and Kate are girls in Berlin during the Nazi reign. The two girls are different and Kate sees how Sylvia uses other people for her own ends. They end up on different sides of the conflict.

De Jong, Dola. *By Marvelous Agreement*. Knopf, 1960. Roza is a Dutch war orphan living in America. She is startled by the change from her orphanage in Holland to apartment life in an American city.

_____. *House on Charlton Street*. Scribner, 1962. The Bartletts move into a house on Charlton Street and learn of its mysterious past. The story moves from Greenwich Village of the 1800s to the present site.

De Jong, Meindert. *Along Came a Dog*. Harper, 1958. A touching story of a lonely, friendless dog and a red hen.

_____. *House of Sixty Fathers*. Harper, 1956. While China was occupied by the Japanese in World War II, Tien Pao and his pig, Glory to the Republic, search for his parents.

_____. *Hurry Home, Candy*. Harper, 1953. Candy is a dog looking for a home. He finally finds one but not before some harrowing adventures.

_____. *Journey from Peppermint Street*. Harper, 1968. A young boy who always lived in a village goes on a journey by sea.

_____. *Singing Hill.* Harper, 1962. A story of the love of a young, insecure boy and his horse.

_____. *Wheel on the School.* Harper, 1954. A long time favorite about the children of a Dutch village who work to get the storks back to their island. They do it by providing a wheel that the storks use as a basis for their nests. Newbery winner, 1955.

Dekkers, Midas. *Arctic Adventure.* Watts, 1987. Menno is on a lead team in the Arctic. It is cold and icy. They encounter a pirate whaling ship and in trying to save the whale Menno's men and the captain of the pirate ship battle it out.

De Leeuw, Adele. *Rugged Dozen.* Macmillan, 1955. A group of girls start to raise money for a trip to Europe following their high school graduation.

De Leeuw, C. *Fear in the Forest.* Nelson, 1960. Daniel's father is killed by Indians and he must overcome his fear of the forest and Indians when he joins a pack-horse train.

Deleon, Eric. *Pitch and Hasty Check It Out.* Orchard, 1988. Pitch and Hasty are hiding out at Harrington's Mall looking for what makes a strange noise in back of the pinball machine. They find parrot smugglers and are accidentally flown miles from home.

Del Rey, Lester. *Attack from Atlantis.* Holt, 1978. The Triton has been sabotaged and the crew is trapped beneath the sea. They are captives of creatures from a city no one knew existed.

_____. *Infinite Worlds of Maybe.* Holt, 1966. A boy travels interplanetary to search for his father.

_____. *Moon of Mutiny.* Holt, 1961. Fred is a spaceman in the early days of the colonization of the moon. He explores parts of the moon never seen before. But his companions suspect him of being on the bottom of the "accidents."

_____. *Outpost of Jupiter.* Holt, 1963. There is an outbreak of the plague on Ganymede which brings about a meeting between the humans living there and the alien creatures.

_____. *Rocket from Infinity.* Holt, 1966. Pete has a space mining operation. Someone wants to take it over. A space ship seems to be the culprit.

_____. *Runaway Robot.* Westminster, 1965. Rex, a robot, is Paul's companion on Ganymede. They become inseparable and when it is time to go back to Earth Paul refuses to part with him.

Delton, Jina. *Two Blocks Down.* Harper, 1981. Stat is "weird." Roddy likes her even though Leslie and Justina like him. He sees that Stat is schizophrenic and all three try to help her.

Delton, Judy. *Angel in Charge.* Houghton, 1985. Mom goes on vacation leaving Angel and Rags in care of Alyce who goes to the hospital and leaves them alone.

_____. *Angel's Mother's Boyfriend.* Houghton, 1986. What is Angel to think when she finds

out her mother's boyfriend is a clown? Rudy lives in Washington, D.C., and Angel thinks the letters from him are from the IRA. She tries to help.

_____. *Angel's Mother's Wedding.* Houghton, 1987. Angel is worried about her mother's plans for the wedding. Will it really happen and on time! What about flowers? Gifts? Angel also realizes that being adopted means more than a name change.

_____. *Backyard Angel.* Houghton, 1983. Rags, Angel's younger brother, is a real pain to take care of even though she actually likes him. Mom is working and Angel is on her own since no kids her age live on the block.

_____. *Kitty from the Start.* Houghton, 1987. Kitty moves to a new house and must make adjustments to her new life. Everything is different from what she has known. Kitty is nine years old and just meets Mary and Eileen.

_____. *Kitty in High School.* Houghton, 1984. Kitty, now a freshman in high school, makes friends, uses make-up and meets some boys to make school life more interesting. There are popular songs, current fads and fashionable clothes.

_____. *Kitty in the Middle.* Houghton, 1979. Three friends from school have a good time growing up in the early '40's. They crash a wedding and explore a haunted house; they learn about friendship and love; they have a great deal of fun.

_____. *Kitty in the Summer.* Houghton, 1980. Kitty "purchases" a pagan baby and is exposed to real poverty. She and her two friends have an exciting summer with the baby's African family.

_____. *Mystery of the Haunted Cabin.* Houghton, 1986. Robin and his friends stay all night in a cabin and then try to find the prior owner because they want to identify the ghost they heard.

_____. *Near Occasion of Sin.* Harcourt, 1984. Tess was raised by strict Catholic standards. She married early and mistakenly. She finally leaves her husband but she learns little from the experience.

_____. *Only Jody.* Houghton, 1982. Jody is the only male in an all-female family and finds it trying.

Dengler, Marianna. *Pebble in Newcomb's Pond.* Holt, 1979. Mara goes to Newcomb's Pond to relax but her depression and fear are becoming worse. She is schizophrenic caused by a chemical imbalance.

Denzel, Justin. *Boy of the Painted Cave.* Putnam, 1988. A story set in Cro-Magnon times about a boy who wants to become an artist and do cave paintings.

_____. *Snowfoot.* Garrard, 1976. A boy in Lappland helps raise a wounded white fawn.

Derby, Pat. *Goodbye Emily, Hello.* Farrar, 1989. Robin meets Emily, a tomboy, and they remain friends until they enter high school. Robin realizes she must make her own friends.

_____. *Visiting Miss Pierce*. Farrar, 1986. Barry, 14, visits an 83-year-old woman in a nursing home. He asks her to talk about her past and the tales affect him because he is an adopted child.

Dereske, Jo. *Glom Gloom*. Macmillan, 1985. Raymond wants to save the peace-loving Bulkins from the evil Weeuns.

Derleth, August. *Beast in Holger's Woods*. Crowell, 1968. The beast is a hodag made up by a practical joker 50 years ago. But Rich and Banny today find evidence of a real hodag. They have an encounter with something that they and the sheriff need to explore.

_____. *Ghost of Black Hawk Island*. Duell, 1961. Steve and Sim are camping when they see the ghost of an Indian. They investigate and solve the mystery and also recover the stolen necklace.

_____. *Irregulars Strike Again*. Duell, 1964. Steve and Sim, the Mill Creek Irregulars, catch some deer hunters hunting out of season.

_____. *Mill Street Iregulars: Special Detectives*. Duell, 1959. Instead of a summer of fishing, a mystery at a farm is solved by the boys who also learn about proper detecting equipment.

Derman, Martha. *And Philippa Makes Four*. Four Winds, 1983. Philippa meets and dislikes Mrs. Barber's daughter, Libby. Her father is going to move in with Mrs. Barber and the two girls live together. After many battles they make a truce.

_____. *Friendstone*. Dial, 1981. Sally wants to make friends with Evie but she is Jewish and Sally is uncertain.

De Roo, Anne. *Cinnamon and Nutmeg*. Nelson, 1972. Tessa cares for an abandoned calf, Cinnamon, and a kid, Nutmeg. She finds the calf's mother, the valuable Riverlia Princess.

_____. *Scrub Fire*. Atheneum, 1980. Michelle, 14, Andrew and Mason go camping. They start a brush fire accidentally. They must survive and find their way back home. They are hungry, sick and scared.

De Trevino, Elizabeth. *I, Juan de Pareja*. Farrar, 1965. A story of the life of Velasquez, artist, as told by Juan de Pareja, his devoted black slave. Newbery winner, 1966.

_____. *Nacar, White Deer*. Farrar, 1963. Lalo finds a white deer that is not well and nurses it back to health. Lalo is a deaf herder and faces the inevitable parting of man and wild animal.

DeWeese, Gene. *Adventures of a Two-Minute Werewolf*. Doubleday, 1983. Walt turns into a werewolf while on a date. Cindy thinks it's great but Walt doesn't. He captures burglars and learns about werewolves in this very funny story.

_____. *Black Suits from Outer Space*. Putnam, 1985. Walt and Kathy meet visitors from outer space who need their help.

_____. *Calvin Nullifier*. Putnam, 1987. A space adventure of two 12-year-olds, an intergalactic cat named Dandelion, some scientists and two policemen.

_____. *Dandelion Caper*. Putnam, 1986. Kathy and a friend find an old mansion to explore. Inside they find a strange yellow cat with powers a cat shouldn't have.

_____. *Major Corby and the Unidentified Flopping Object*. Doubleday, 1979. Russ, 14, agrees to help a UFO and before long the whole town is involved.

Dexter, Catherine. *Mazemaker*. Morrow, 1989. By following a painted maze in the schoolyard two students go back in time to 1889.

_____. *Oracle Doll*. Four Winds, 1985. Rose and James find that Lucy's doll "Gabby" has been inhabited by an ancient oracle of Delphi and can predict the future.

Dexter, Patricia. *Arrow in the Wind*. Nelson, 1978. Benton resents his father wanting a divorce. They may lose their home and must scrape for a living. Fancy, their dog, and Joe Tepper, a "stray" child, draw the family together after a flash flood.

_____. *Emancipation of Joe Tepper*. Nelson, 1977. Joe's alcoholic mother dies and he manages by getting a part-time job. The social worker wants to put him in a foster home but he is declared "emancipated" because he can support himself.

Dick, Trella. *Bridger's Boy*. Follett, 1965. Dan runs away from home for the gold fields of California. He never gets there. At Fort Bridger he helps an injured Indian woman and makes friends with a Crow boy. So he stays there.

_____. *Island on the Border*. Abelard, 1963. Two boys, one a Yankee and one a Reb, work together to protect their families. They help runaway slaves and a Union spy.

Dickens, Charles. *David Copperfield*. Macmillan, 1962. All of the familiar and fascinating characters are here: Mr. Micawber, Ham, Little Em'ly and Uriah Heep.

_____. *Great Expectations*. Nal, 1978. Pip inherits a great fortune and doesn't know from whom. Miss Havisham could be the one but she is unbalanced by a lover who deserted her on their wedding day.

_____. *Oliver Twist*. Smith, 1956. Oliver is an abused runaway who joins up with The Artful Dodger and Fagin. He doesn't at first realize what he is being trained for but when he does he decides it's not for him.

Dickenson, Christine. *Getting It All Together*. Scholastic, 1975. A sixteen-year-old girl tries to hold her orphaned family together.

Dickinson, Peter. *Annerton Pit*. Little, 1977. Jake is 13 and blind but he is still able to help free his grandfather and brother from revolutionists.

_____. *Box of Nothing*. Delacorte, 1988. James is trapped in a garbage dump. The box of Nothing is his key out but there are rats and seagulls to fight. He finds himself back home after Nothing sparks off an explosion.

————. *Dancing Bear*. Little, 1973. Sylvester is a slave in the year 558. He has a pet dancing bear and they both survive the sacking of Byzantium by the Huns.

————. *Devil's Children*. Little, 1970. Nicky is alone, separated from her parents, and finds that she is the only one who can be the link between the Sikhs, the outcasts, and the villagers who are affected by the Changes.

————. *Eva*. Delacorte, 1989. Eva's brain is transplanted into an ape, Kelly. Eva/Kelly tries to adapt to her new body and people try to adapt to her.

————. *Giant Cold*. Dutton, 1983. A fantasy about the trail of Giant Cold.

————. *Gift*. Little, 1974. The "gift" of prophecy is no prize for Davy. He reads his father's mind and doesn't like what's there. He reads the mind of a psychopath and finds it raging. Foresight is not a gift.

————. *Healer*. Delacorte, 1983. Barry met Pinkie in the school's nursing office. She cured him of his headache. Two years later he is to meet her again by getting a headache to see if she is okay.

————. *Heartsease*. Little, 1969. "Changes" made people hate machinery. Margaret and Jonathan find an American engineer, stoned for being a witch, and help him escape to Heartease, a tugboat.

————. *Seventh Raven*. Dutton, 1981. Juan is the son of an ambassador. Terrorists try to kidnap him from a theatre where he plays the seventh raven. He is protected and the terrorists are caught.

————. *Tulku*. Little, 1979. Theodore, 13, experiences the Boxer massacre from his mission school in China. He then goes with a plant collector through dangerous territory to Tibet and a Buddhist monastery.

————. *Weathermonger*. Little, 1969. Geoffrey and Sally, sentenced to death by drowning because they are witches, escape. They return to learn more about the Changes. Anyone found with a machine of any kind was put to death.

Dicks, Terrance. *Case of the Blackmail Boys*. Lodestar, 1979. A bank robbery plot is discovered and foiled by the sleuthing Baker Street Irregulars when they discover blackmail is being used to get inside information.

————. *Case of the Cinema Swindle*. Lodestar, 1980. The Irregulars investigate the burning of the local theater. It is suspected of being arson.

————. *Case of the Cop Catchers*. Lodestar, 1981. The Irregulars have difficulty solving a whole series of strange happenings involving their friend Detective Day, who disappears. Truck hijacking and jewel thefts are among them.

————. *Case of the Crooked Kids*. Lodestar, 1978. The Baker Street Irregulars must stop other youngsters, who are being led by crooked adults, from getting into the stealing racket.

————. *Case of the Ghost Grabbers*. Lodestar, 1980. A ghost haunts the home of Sir Jasper (from *Missing Masterpiece*) and the investigation leads to the far past. Dan is injured and helps solve the mystery from his hospital bed.

————. *Case of the Missing Masterpiece*. Lodestar, 1978. The Baker Street Irregulars are young detectives who solve neighborhood crimes and when a painting is stolen from a valuable art collection they must begin their work.

Dickson, Gordon. *Dragon and the George*. Ballantine, 1978. Jim is accidentally made into a dragon by Grottwald after he aborted Angie. Jim/Gorbash went to find Angie but had to fight off all sorts of dragons first.

————. *Secret Under Antarctica*. Holt, 1963. It is the year 2013. Robbie and his father are doing research on whale communication. Robbie is held captive by a man who wants to blow up Antarctica.

————. *Secret Under the Caribbean*. Holt, 1964. Robbie is involved with an international art thief who is trying to steal a Spanish galleon of archeological value.

Dietzel, Paul. *Go, Shorty, Go*. Bobbs, 1965. John wants to play football but is too small. He learns to become a place kicker.

Diggs, Lucy. *Everyday Friends*. Atheneum, 1986. Marcy quit gymnastics and also quits piano. Then she finds horseback riding. Sometimes she wants to quit but goes on to show after show getting better and better at her chosen hobby.

————. *Moon in the Water*. Atheneum, 1988. Jo Bob, 14, trains a pinto named Blue. He wins several shows. Then his father sells Blue!

D'Ignazio, Fred. *Chip Mitchell, Case of the Robot Warriors*. Dutton, 1984. The reader helps Chip solve these eight puzzling mysteries with the use of logic and clear thinking. Sherwin, the robot, and Hermes, the computer, help.

————. *Chip Mitchell, Case of the Stolen Computer Brains*. Dutton, 1982. A seventh grade computer whiz solves ten puzzling cases using his knowledge of logic and computers.

Dillon, Barbara. *Mrs. Tooey and the Terrible Toxic Tar*. Harper, 1988. Mrs. Tooey, really Sister witch, fights against Velma, the Vindictive, in her attempt to destroy the town.

Dillon, Eilis. *Coriander*. Funk & Wagnalls, 1963. There is no doctor on a lonely island. When there is a shipwreck off the coast Pat and Roddy kidnap the ship's doctor.

————. *Cruise of the Santa Maria*. Funk & Wagnalls, 1967. Colman lives alone and waits for his eloped daughter to come back. He is spiteful and unforgiving. But Sarah, her husband, and their son come from Spain to Ireland for a reconciliation.

————. *Family of Foxes*. Funk & Wagnalls,

1964. Foxes are disliked and distrusted and are killed on sight. Four boys befriend two foxes hurt by a recent storm and want to raise them and their offspring in secret.

————. *Fort of Gold*. Funk & Wagnalls, 1962. Four strangers come to an island bringing evil in the guise of hidden Spanish gold. Three boys find it and stow it away.

————. *Sea Wall*. Farrar, 1965. Sally saved her village from flooding 30 years ago as a little girl; now she senses a flood coming again. When the flood comes no lives are lost but the wall needs repair and John and Pat must see to it.

————. *Seals*. Funk & Wagnalls, 1969. Pat, Mike, Jerry and Pat's grandfather sail to get Roddy back to the island. It is a very stormy night and they are the only ones willing to go. No one feels they will make it.

————. *Shadow of Vesuvius*. Nelson, 1977. Timon and Scrofa travel to Pompeii before Mount Vesuvius erupts. Timon escapes and helps others before Pompeii is covered with hot ash.

Dinneen, Betty. *Luck of Leopards*. Walck, 1972. In present day Kenya Karen learns about leopards when she "adopts" two cubs. She later gives them up to a zoo.

Disch, Thomas. *Brave Little Toaster*. Doubleday, 1986. Toaster and his appliance friends leave Earth for Mars when they learn about "Planned obsolescence."

————. *Brave Little Toaster Goes to Mars*. Doubleday, 1988. While on Mars Toaster and his friends are planning an invasion of the Earth to destroy people. In the end they decide to explore space instead.

Distad, Audree. *Dakota Sons*. Harper, 1972. Tad makes friends with an Indian boy that others resent. He shows Ronnie how to be proud of his heritage and loses his old friend Bobby, a bigot.

————. *Dream Runner*. Harper, 1977. Sam heard about how Indians went to the mountains to find a way to manhood. Sam decides he wants to do just that. He encounters wild horses, storms, fear and loneliness.

Divine, David. *Stolen Season*. Doubleday, 1967. Clint, Peter and Mig make a bet and their gambling leads to a breathtaking adventure.

————. *Three Red Flares*. Crowell, 1972. Mig, Peter and Clint have an adventure; this time a map starts the search.

Dixon, Jeanne. *Lady Cat Lost*. Atheneum, 1981. The Fergusons move to Montana when they are deserted by their father.

Dixon, Marjorie. *Forbidden Island*. Criterion, 1960. Lindsay finds a fairy community on Thunder Island and spends time with them. Years later she goes back and saves them from themselves.

Dixon, Paige. *Lion on the Mountain*. Atheneum, 1972. Jamie hunts only for meat not to kill. He uses a bow and quill, often only a camera. Darby kills for pleasure.

————. *Loner, Story of the Wolverine*. Atheneum, 1978. Indians fear killing a wolverine. A white hunter goes after a wolverine and his Indian guide refuses to help him and leaves him.

————. *May I Cross Your Golden River?* Atheneum, 1975. Jordan is eighteen when he notices the first sign of his terminal illness. Skipper, his young brother and the rest of his family have a hard time accepting Jordan's fate.

————. *Pimm's Cup for Everybody*. Atheneum, 1976. Derek is a college freshman star basketball player. He also does TV ads. He is expected to either go pro or go into his uncle's ad agency. Instead he and Pimm, an English visitor, tour the U.S.A.

————. *Promises to Keep*. Atheneum, 1974. Charles, 16, lives in a small town. Lin, a cousin, is part Vietnamese and comes to live in town. There is a great deal of prejudice.

————. *Search for Charlie*. Atheneum, 1976. Jane's brother, Charles, is kidnapped. She and an Indian friend, Vic, search for him. They find him and Vic prevents Jane from killing the kidnapper.

————. *Silver Wolf*. Atheneum, 1973. The story of a wolf told by the wolf. Survival, traps, hunters and problems with humans are just a few of his encounters.

————. *Skipper*. Atheneum, 1979. Jordan is dead but Skipper has not made a satisfying adjustment. He doesn't understand the whys and wherefores of life, and death.

————. *Summer of the White Goat*. Atheneum, 1977. Gordon is spending the summer at a national park. He observes the mountain goats and the way they can live on the high slopes.

————. *Walk My Way*. Atheneum, 1980. Kelly is fourteen and clumsy. Her father is a drunk and she must fight off his drunken friends. She finally runs away.

Dizeno, Patricia. *Phoebe*. McGraw, 1970. Phoebe, 16, is pregnant. She doesn't know what to do and so just dreams a lot. She faces up to it realistically when she phones the father to tell him the news.

————. *Why Me?* Avon, 1976. Jenny is an innocent rape victim. She faces possible V.D., pregnancy, accusing parents and unsympathetic friends.

Dodd, Wayne. *Time of Hunting*. Houghton, 1975. Jeff thought he liked hunting until several events turned liking to a strong dislike.

Dodge, Mary. *Hans Brinker*. Grosset, 1945. A boy encourages his sister to enter a skating contest because of the prize involved. Their family needs help.

Dodson, Fitzhugh. *Carnival Kidnap Caper*. Old Tree, 1980. Fabulous Five's inventions seem to backfire or go haywire. But they have lots of future fun with robots.

Dodson, Susan. *Shadows Across the Sand*. Lothrop, 1983. Billie gets involved in a mystery of who is terrorizing the old people of the community and why.

Domke, Todd. *Grounded.* Knopf, 1981. Parker and Zeke want to build a glider. They write and put on a show to raise money. It gets out of control because of "fake advertising" but it ends well and money is raised.

Donahue, Marilyn. *Straight Along a Crooked Road.* Walker, 1985. A 14-year-old girl travels from Vermont to California and lives there in a frontier community.

_____. *Valley in Between.* Walker, 1987. Luanna is settled in California with sister Emmie. They see change and hear talk of a Civil War. There are problems with Indians and lawlessness.

Donaldson, Margaret. *Journey Into War.* Andre Deutsch, 1979. Two boys and a girl help to fight the Germans in London during World War II. In this story the girl gets caught and needs to be rescued.

_____. *Moon's on Fire.* Andre Deutsch, 1980. Janey and the refugee twins are in the London blitz. They stay with reluctant relatives, lose friends and find enemies and strange allies along the docks. Uncle Maurice hunts spies.

Donnelly, Elfie. *So Long, Grandpa.* Crown, 1981. A young boy, Michael, accepts the fact that his grandfather, whom he loves, is going to die.

Donovan, John. *Family.* Harper, 1976. An unusual story about three apes that escape from a laboratory where they were victims of experimentation.

_____. *I'll Get There. It Better Be Worth the Trip.* Harper, 1969. Davy and Altschuler, both lonely and unloved, find comfort with each other. But the threat of homosexuality spoils the friendship. Both suspect the other of untrue actions but again become friends.

_____. *Wild in the World.* Harper, 1971. John is the last remaining Gridley on Rattlesnake Mountain. He sees no future except death and lives a bare existence until he meets and learns to love a half dog/half wolf.

Doren, Marion. *Borrowed Summer.* Harper, 1987. Jan misses her grandmother who is in the hospital. She plans to kidnap her and put her in a "borrowed" cottage and care for her herself.

Dorman, N.B. *Laughter in the Background.* Elsevier, 1980. Marcie's mother is an alcoholic and she goes to A.A. meetings with other children. She eats everytime her mother is drunk and is obese. A "friend" of her mother's almost rapes her before she is taken from her home.

Dorris, Michael. *Yellow Raft in Blue Water.* Holt, 1987. Rayona, half black, half Indian, finds that her grandmother was raped by an unknown man and Christine, Rayona's mother, was born.

Doty, Jean. *Can I Get There by Candlelight?* Macmillan, 1980. Gail and her horse, Candy, ride into an orchard and meet Hilary of by-gone days. Hilary tries to get Gail into her world.

_____. *Crumb.* Greenwillow, 1976. Cindy gets a pony, Crumb, but finds it takes money to keep it. She gets a part-time job at Ashford stables where she finds a mystery to be solved.

_____. *Gabriel.* Macmillan, 1974. Linda found an abandoned puppy and raised it. She named it Gabriel. She learned about the puppy at a kennel and also learned who Gabriel's mother was. She must return him to his owner.

_____. *If Wishes Were Horses.* Macmillan, 1984. Stephany and Camilla try to keep their horse farm after their father dies. They work hard but eventually lose it anyway.

_____. *Summer Pony.* Macmillan, 1973. Mokey, a pony, is the central character of Ginny's greatest summer experience. She cares for this run-down pony and the pony becomes hers.

_____. *Valley of the Ponies.* Atheneum, 1982. Jennifer's wonderful summer with a pony of her own is shaken by an encounter with horse thieves.

_____. *Winter Pony.* Macmillan, 1975. Ginny owns Mokey and trains her to pull a sleigh and Mokey gives birth to a foal.

_____. *Yesterday's Horses.* Macmillan, 1985. Kelly and her horse, Rusty, find a foal whose mother is dead. Kelly takes it home. A strange virus is killing horses and this foal may hold the key to the cure.

Doughty, Wayne. *Crimson Moccasins.* Harper, 1966. The story of a young Indian's search for manhood and his encounter with the white man.

Downer, Ann. *Glass Salamander.* Atheneum, 1989. Caitlin and Badger are separated. Caitlin has his son who is a changeling. She searches for her baby and Badger searches for Myrrhlock, the evil sorcerer.

Downey, Fairfax. *Guns for General Washington.* Nelson, 1961. Kent fights with General Howe. He becomes a spy, is captured, and sent on a prison ship, but returns to see the British defeated.

_____. *Seventh's Staghound.* Dodd, 1948. Peter is in Custer's Cavalry. Bran, a staghound, is a favorite with both Peter and Custer. After Custer's fight with the Sioux, Peter comes home a hero and wins Sally Ann's hand.

Downing, Warwick. *Kid Curry's Last Ride.* Orchard, 1989. A story of Wyoming in the 1930's.

Dragonwagon, Crescent. *Year It Rained.* Macmillan, 1985. Elizabeth, 17, and her mother are trying to adjust after Elizabeth has a breakdown. Her mother is too perfect and Elizabeth wants only life's normal frustrations.

Dragt, Tanke. *Towers of February.* Morrow, 1975. Tom writes the events of his life in a diary and gives it to his brother. Tom travels to another world only on February 29th of Leap Year. He can only go and/or come back on that day.

Draper, Cena. *Rim of the Ridge.* Criterion, 1965. Punk is being raised by his Gramp in Missouri in 1900. He has two coon dogs and goes hunting for Old Two Toes, who always gets away.

_____. *Worst Hound Around.* Westminster, 1979. Jorie's Blue Dog is not a tracker and Jorie and Lou Ann secretly train him at night. A coon hunt at the end of the story shows Blue Dog as good as any.

Drury, Roger. *Champion of Merrimack County.* Little, 1976. A story of mice who invade the Buryfield house. One of them is a trick bicycle rider and uses the tub as a track.

Duane, Diane. *Deep Wizardry.* Delacorte, 1985. During the summer vacation, Nita the wizard helps Sree combat an evil power.

_____. *So You Want to Be a Wizard.* Delacorte, 1983. Bullied because she won't fight back, Nita looks for assistance in a book of wizardry and gets results. Her friend, Kit, has the same book: "Book of Night with Moon."

Du Bois, Theodora. *Rich Boy, Poor Boy.* Farrar, 1961. Patrick is suspected of stealing from his relatives. Janey is convinced he is innocent and together they unravel the mystery.

_____. *Tiger Burning Bright.* Ariel, 1964. Anne is a missionary's daughter. She escapes from Delhi, India, during the Sipoy Rebellion. She goes across the desert with other refugees and faces death every day.

Du Bois, William. *Alligator Case.* Harper, 1965. A Dragnet satire. A boy detective solves a mystery about a circus. Neither porkchops and peas nor twisting alligators will keep him from his task.

_____. *Call Me Bandicoot.* Harper, 1970. Bandicoot catches people on the Staten Island ferry and tells them fantastic stories, then hopes for money to pay for the ride and get something from the snack bar. Mostly funny but thoughtful, too.

_____. *Gentleman Bear.* Farrar, 1985. Billy Browne-Browne and his bear, Bayard, have a lifelong friendship.

_____. *Horse in the Camel Suit.* Harper, 1967. This time the boy detective meets a magician who is also a horse thief. There are escape artists, karate experts and mind reading.

_____. *Porko Von Popbutton.* Harper, 1963. Porko is 13 and weighs 274 pounds. He is the "slave" of his roommates at boarding school. In an important hockey game Porko plays and the outcome is outrageous.

_____. *Twenty-One Balloons.* Viking, 1947. Professor Sherman's adventures around the world in a balloon.

Duder, Tersa. *Jellybean.* Viking, 1985. Geraldine's mother is a musician and single. She is tired of playing second to a music schedule until she meets a new friend and decides to become a conductor.

Due, Linnea. *High and Outside.* Harper, 1980. Niki is an alcoholic but doesn't know it. At 17 she is on top of the world. Then she changes: is rude, blacks out and is ill. No one knows why and Niki won't admit anything.

Duffy, James. *Cleaver of the Good Luck Diner.* Scribner, 1989. Sarah and her dog, Cleaver, keep the family amused while they try to run a diner after Sarah's father walks out on them.

_____. *Missing.* Scribner, 1988. Kate is kidnapped by a man who wants to make her his daughter. Her family thinks she has run away again.

_____. *Revolt of the Teddy Bears.* Crown, 1985. May Gray, a poodle detective, comes out of retirement to solve the conflict between Teddy and Paris.

Du Jardin, Rosamond. *Boy Trouble.* Lippincott, 1953/1988. Toby is out of high school and is ready for college in the fall. She has a summer job and a summer romance before she leaves.

_____. *Class Ring.* Lippincott, 1951. Toby, 17, is going steady with Brose. She wears his class ring. She is getting attention from Dick, who is already in college, and she is also getting criticism from her parents about Brose.

_____. *Double Date.* Lippincott, 1952. Pam and Penny are twins. They look alike but are totally different in temperament. They each have their way of coping with the problems of growing up.

_____. *Double Feature.* Lippincott, 1953. Pam and Penny are twin sisters attending college. Their problems of growing up are past but they face the problems of family restrictions and the opposite sex.

_____. *Double Wedding.* Lippincott, 1959. Pam and her twin sister, Penny, meet their loves and want to get married. Both their fiances insist they wait until graduation.

_____. *Man for Marcy.* Lippincott, 1954. Marcy is left without an escort to any social events because her boyfriend, Steve, has gone off to college. She must find a solution to this.

_____. *Marcy Catches Up.* Lippincott, 1952. Marcy spends her summer in Colorado on a dude ranch. She has a romantic and profitable summer.

_____. *Practically Seventeen.* Lippincott, 1949. Toby has older sisters who are always giving her advice about boys, school, friends, etc., etc., etc. Sometimes the advice is welcome but sometimes she wishes she could be on her own.

_____. *Real Thing.* Lippincott, 1956. Toby is in college and she is changing her mind about many things, including her involvement with her high school boyfriend, Brose.

_____. *Senior Prom.* Lippincott, 1957. Marcy is a senior in high school and ready to graduate. She has boyfriends and is popular with everyone. But problems arise when first she has two dates for the Senior Prom and then none.

_____. *Showboat Summer.* Lippincott, 1955. Pam and Penny, twin sisters, have just finished their first year of college. They want to have a nice vacation so they decide on a trip on a river boat.

_____. *Someone to Count On*. Lippincott, 1962. Twink breaks up with her boyfriend, finds a new one, but he is interested in someone else.

_____. *Wait for Marcy*. Lippincott, 1950. Marcy, 15, has her first date with Steve. Although they quarrel over Marcy's brother, she is going to see him again.

_____. *Wedding in the Family*. Lippincott, 1958. Toby is getting married and her younger sister, Midge, is going through the same growing up problems that Toby had.

Dumas, Alexandre. *Three Musketeers*. Macmillan, 1962. D'Artagnan joins Athos, Porthos and Aramis as they return the Queen's jewels and reveal Countess de Winter's secret.

Du Maurier, Daphne. *Rebecca*. Avon, 1978. Rebecca marries dashing Maxim de Winter and finds his home haunted by his first wife and she spells doom.

Duncan, Jane. *Brave Janet Reachfar*. Houghton, 1975. Janet lives with her grandmother who is a tyrant. She copes with her and life on their farm.

_____. *Camerons at the Castle*. St. Martin, 1964. Shona, Neil, Donald and Nink go to Castle Vannish and learn of its history and the mystery of the white hand.

_____. *Camerons Calling*. Macmillan, 1966. Shona, Neil and Donald stay at Castle Vannish which is run as a hotel. Evan Cameron is coming as a guest.

_____. *Camerons on the Hill*. Macmillan, 1963. Shona, Neil and Donald go to visit a shepherd Angus while staying with their aunt. A plane crashes in the snowy mountains and they help with the rescue.

_____. *Camerons on the Train*. St. Martin, 1963. Shona, Neil and Donald take a train to visit Scotland. They encounter crooks, thefts and sabotage.

Duncan, Lois. *Daughters of Eve*. Little, 1979. Irene, a powerful faculty advisor for the Daughters of Eve, is leading her students into something hideous.

_____. *Down a Dark Hall*. Little, 1974. Four girls in a boarding school have ESP experiences. They are held prisoners and work to figure out why they were selected. They are afraid they know why.

_____. *Gift of Magic*. Little, 1971. Nancy is very bright but unhappy. Her parents are divorced and she uses ESP to hold the family together. She learns to use her powers for good, not evil, after a disaster with her sister.

_____. *Hotel for Dogs*. Harcourt, 1971. Liz and Bruce seem to have a way of finding stray and needy dogs. They finally have so many something must be done. So they find an abandoned house and set it up as a "hotel for dogs."

_____. *I Know What You Did Last Summer*. Little, 1973. Four teen-agers are involved in a hit and run. Much later they begin to get notes and calls about their involvement. One of the four is shot and another feels endangered.

_____. *Killing Mr. Griffin*. Little, 1978. What started as a take-off of a previous senior prank (kidnapping a teacher) leads to a serious kidnapping of a "hard" teacher, who dies during the incident.

_____. *Locked in Time*. Little, 1985. Nore is in Shadow Grove and senses something wrong. Her father, newly remarried, notices nothing. And Nore may die because she's right about the horrible wrong that's there.

_____. *Peggy*. Little, 1970. Peggy is courted by both British and American officers during the Revolutionary War and she chooses to marry Benedict Arnold.

_____. *Ransom*. Doubleday, 1966. Five students are kidnapped when they are the last ones on the school bus. Glen, Dexter, Marianne, Bruce and Jesse are taken at gun point farther and farther from home.

_____. *Stranger with My Face*. Little, 1981. Laurie keeps being told that she is seen here and there with different people she never knew and places she'd never been. Is she going crazy or does she have a double?

_____. *Summer of Fear*. Little, 1976. When Julia's parents were killed in an auto accident she came to live with a family. Everybody liked her but some could see evil. No one would believe it so how could disaster be averted?

_____. *They Never Came Home*. Doubleday, 1969. Why are Dan and Larry afraid to come home? Afraid of each other? What happened on that camping trip?

_____. *Third Eye*. Little, 1984. Karen has "second sight" which enables her to "see." She uses it to solve the mystery of the kidnapped babies and her own abduction.

_____. *Twisted Window*. Delacorte, 1987. Brad's sister Mindy is kidnapped by their father and he asks Tracy to help him find her. They "find" her and only after they are on their way to Brad's mother's do they find they have the wrong child.

Dunlop, Beverley. *Poetry Girl*. Houghton, 1989. Natalia is a "failure" and almost commits suicide. She recites poetry to herself to keep her sanity. A sad story with a somewhat happy ending.

Dunlop, Eileen. *Clementina*. Holiday, 1985. Bridget, Daisy and Clementina are spending the summer together. Did Clementina have a different life over two hundred years ago?

_____. *Fox Farm*. Holt, 1979. Adam is a foster child who doesn't like his foster brother. They find a baby "fox" whom they hide and care for. Adam uses money he saved to run away to buy food. The "fox" is a dog and they keep it.

_____. *House on Mayferry Street*. Holt, 1977. Spangler is going to beat the high cost of trucking by driving his cattle to market in Kansas

City on foot. He is joined by Leo who tells the story in a humorous way.

_____. *House on the Hill.* Holiday, 1987. Philip and Susan stay in a spooky mansion of Great Aunt Jane's. Jane's tragic past is revealed as a mystery is solved.

_____. *Maze Stone.* Putnam, 1983. Hester, 16, and her sister come under the spell of their drama teacher.

Dunn, Marylois. *Absolutely Perfect Horse.* Harper, 1983. Annie buys an old horse to keep it from being destroyed. The family baby is attacked by feral dogs and Annie and her horse rescue it. The horse later dies but Annie has good memories.

Dunnahoo, Terry. *This Is Espie Sanchez.* Dutton, 1976. After being arrested for running away from home, Espie now works for the police as an Explorer Scout. But, smuggling and murder are still ahead when Teresa is brought in very troubled.

_____. *Who Cares About Espie Sanchez?* Dutton, 1975. Espie was a loner, running from a bad home. But, faced with juvenile hall, or facing Mrs. Garcia, Espie made her tough decision.

_____. *Who Needs Espie Sanchez?* Dutton, 1975. Alcoholism is now a problem in Espie's life. Her curiosity is aroused by a young girl who befriends her after both are in an accident.

Dunne, Mary. *Hoby and Stub.* Atheneum, 1981. Hoby is a young boy who runs away from home. Stub is his bull terrier puppy that he takes with him.

_____. *Reach Out, Ricardo.* Abelard, 1971. Ricardo, 15, is a poor grape picker but has friends in school and plays baseball. When a strike among workers is talked about Ricardo and his friend Doug fight because Doug is an owner's son.

Durham, John. *Me and Arch and the Pest.* Four Winds, 1970. Arch and his friend were adopted by a dog. They named him Pest. They could hardly afford to feed him so they got a job in a pet shop. One day all the dogs, including Pest, are kidnapped. They go searching.

Durrell, Gerald. *Donkey Rustlers.* Viking, 1968. Amanda and David are spending the summer in Greece. While they are there someone steals all 20 donkeys of the village. Who could do such a thing? Justice does win out in the end.

_____. *Talking Parcel.* Lippincott, 1974. There are stolen books of magic in Mythologia and three children go there to recover them.

Dutton, Sandra. *Magic of Myrna C. Waxweather.* Macmillan, 1987. Bertha is something she doesn't want to be: the teacher's pet. Her fairy godmother helps her out.

Dyer, T.A. *Way of His Own.* Houghton, 1981. Shutok, a crippled Indian boy, is abandoned. He is blamed for "evil" in the tribe. He, and a girl who tries to help him, spend a cold winter alone.

_____. *Whipman Is Watching.* Houghton, 1979. Angie, an Indian girl, rides to school nearly 50 miles from home. She must meet white standards at school but she ends up being proud of her heritage.

Dygard, Thomas. *Halfback Tough.* Morrow, 1986. Joe joins the football team and becomes a hero. He had a trouble-making past that threatens his present.

_____. *Quarterback Walk-On.* Morrow, 1982. Denny is not on the first string team; as a matter of fact he is fourth among the quarterbacks. But he ends up saving the day for his college team.

_____. *Rookie Arrives.* Morrow, 1988. Ted plays third base and wants to play in the majors. He is cocky and not as good as he thinks he is. He learns a bitter lesson.

_____. *Soccer Duel.* Penguin, 1981. Terry learns a good lesson in sportsmanship by playing a team sport: hockey.

_____. *Tournament Upstart.* Morrow, 1984. Even though the team is from a small high school with less players to choose from it enters a major basketball tournament.

_____. *Wilderness Peril.* Morrow, 1985. Todd and Mike find some money while on a camping trip. They realize it was left by a hijacker and they had better get away before he returns.

Eager, Edward. *Half Magic.* Harcourt, 1954/1990. Some youngsters find an ancient coin and spend a fantastic summer making double-wishings (because of the half magic) for wonderful adventures.

_____. *Knight's Castle.* Harcourt, 1956/1990. Jane, Katherine, Mark and Martha re-enact the writings of Scott with great success.

_____. *Magic by the Lake.* Harcourt, 1957/1990. When the youngsters follow the turtle's information about the lake, they make their wishes but something goes wrong and there is more danger than they wished for.

_____. *Seven-Day Magic.* Harcourt, 1962. When the children check out a magic book at the library magic enters their lives.

_____. *Time Garden.* Harcourt, 1958/1990. Natterjack (a frog) allows four youngsters to rub a bit of thyme and get their wish. They can cross time lines and see Minutemen, authors of the books they read and even the Queen of England.

_____. *Well-Wishers.* Harcourt, 1960. There is magic in the old wishing well. Each child has his own wish fulfilled while all of them, Gordy, Laura, Kip, and Lydia, participate. Each wish is well carried out.

Earnshaw, Brian. *Dragonfall 5 and the Empty Planet.* Lothrop, 1976. Tim and Sanchez go on a field trip where half their class disappears. They have been transported to a frozen moon. The class is rescued by the Flying Hound Dog and the Minims.

_____. *Dragonfall 5 and the Royal Beast.* Lothrop, 1975. Dragonfall 5 is delivering the Royal Beast but it is kidnapped and everyone is searching for the Beast and each other. A funny far-out fantasy.

————. *Dragonfall 5 and the Space Cowboys*. Lothrop, 1975. Tim and Sanchez become involved in a space cattle feud when their ship breaks down. They are all searching for clues in a treasure hunt where the prize is grazing land.

Easton, Patricia. *Summer's Choice*. Harcourt, 1988. Elizabeth learns about harness racing and a horse named Chance while staying with her grandmother. A girl, Linda, is a rival driver and a boy, a vet's son, is added romance.

Ecke, Wolfgang. *Bank Holdup*. Prentice, 1982. Some bloodless crimes are to be solved. Some clues are obvious but some take a little thought.

————. *Face at the Window*. Prentice, 1978. A new version of Encyclopedia Brown. Cases to be solved with clues given, some false and some real. The answers are in the back.

————. *Invisible Witness*. Prentice, 1981. Some more short mysteries to be solved by the reader. A bit tougher than Encyclopedia Brown's cases.

————. *Midnight Chess Game*. Prentice, 1985. More crimes to be solved with the author giving an indication of the difficulty level of each crime.

————. *Stolen Paintings*. Prentice, 1981. Seventeen more puzzles to solve à la Encyclopedia Brown. Some are going to be difficult because of their translation from German.

Eckert, Allan. *Dark Green Tunnel*. Little, 1984. Lara, Barnaby and William enter King Thorkin's Mesmeria and are arrested, but are saved by Mag Namodder and rule the land themselves.

————. *Incident at Hawk's Hill*. Little, 1971. Ben crawls into a badger's nest during a thunderstorm. He is given up for dead, but he survives because of his ability to get along with animals.

————. *Wand*. Little, 1985. Lara and Barnaby find their friends imprisoned. They must have the secret volume of the Warp and the Wand.

Edmonds, I.J. *Joel at the Hanging Gardens*. Lippincott, 1966. Joel of Biblical times helps the exiled tribes of Judah escape from Babylon and return to Jerusalem.

Edmonds, Walter. *Beaver Valley*. Little, 1971. A colony of beaver settle in Skeet's territory. He and his family of deermice see the danger they bring but not all the animals in the area are that lucky.

————. *Bert Breen's Barn*. Little, 1975. Tom starts early to earn and save money so he can buy Mrs. Breen's barn for his mother who has always been poor. He almost loses it to thieves but does succeed in his quest.

————. *Matchlock Gun*. Dodd, 1941. A young boy, at home alone with his mother and sister, bravely fights off Indians with his father's gun.

————. *Time to Go House*. Little, 1969. All the mice "go house" in the winter when the humans leave. Smalleta is new to this arrangement and has many blood curdling adventures.

————. *Wolf Hunt*. Little, 1970. In Delaware during the late 1700's there is a great wolf hunt.

Edmondson, Madeleine. *Anna Witch*. Doubleday, 1982. Anna is only a junior witch because she is unable to learn her mother's spells.

————. *Witch's Egg*. Seabury, 1974. The creature that hatches from the witch's egg acts like a human but is not the same as a human.

Edwards, Julie. *Last of the Really Great Whangdoodles*. Harper, 1974. Professor Savant wants to go to Whangdoodle land. With the help of the Potter children he does. They look for Whangdoodle, a mythical horse with horns.

————. *Mandy*. Harper, 1971. Mandy, 10, lives in an orphanage. She finds a little cottage that she fixes up for herself. She gets ill and is rescued by a family who takes her in.

Edwards, Monica. *Dolphin Summer*. Hawthorn, 1971. Tamzin and Rissa go night swimming and Tamzin nearly drowns. She is saved by two dolphins. Later she saves them from capture.

Edwards, Page. *Scarface Joe*. Four Winds, 1984. Joe meets Mary and they become friends. Joe's face is cut when he explores an abandoned mine. Mary eventually drops him and cares little about his accident, caused by her father.

Edwards, Patricia. *Little John and Plutie*. Houghton, 1988. Little John meets Plutie, his first real friend since he moved to a new town. Plutie is black and racial conflict and prejudice are shown on both sides. The story takes place in the rural South in the 1890.

————. *Nilda*. Houghton, 1987. Nilda is from a poor family during the Great Depression. She goes to live with a wealthy woman and finds a lost ring which she hides.

Edwards, S. *When the World's on Fire*. Coward, 1972/1968. Annie, 9, is a black slave girl during the Revolutionary War. She is alone and frightened but knows she must do what has to be done against the British forces.

Ehrlich, Amy. *Where It Stops Nobody Knows*. Dial, 1988. Nina and her single mother move a lot. Each town is not perfect enough. She finds that her mother moves because she is hiding. She kidnapped Nina as a baby and has been running ever since.

Eige, Lillian. *Cady*. Harper, 1987. Cady has moved around among relatives. He finally lives with a new family where he listens and discovers his own history.

————. *Kidnapping of Mister Huey*. Harper, 1983. Willy, 14, and an old man run off together. They are caught by authorities when a gang of young thugs tell on them. But back home again they both adjust and cope.

Eisenberg, Lisa. *Falling Star.* Dial, 1979. Laura investigates fraudulent insurance claims. When Hollywood actor Garrison's car crashes into the ocean she must find out if it is an accident, suicide, or murder.

_____. *Fast-Food King.* Dial, 1979. R. Bumpo is the Fast-food King who is poisoned as he is about to reveal his secret sauce. The recipe is missing and Laura must solve the mystery for her insurance company.

_____. *Golden Idol.* Dial, 1979. Laura must find the stolen antique statue her company insured. She goes to Hong Kong and faces real danger.

_____. *House of Laughs.* Dial, 1979. Laura goes to Superama Park where a fellow investigator has been murdered. She finds the park is not what it seems.

_____. *Mystery at Bluff Point Dunes.* Dial, 1988. Kate is spending time on Cape Cod when things begin to disappear and reappear. Is her friend Bonnie guilty? She solves the mystery and makes friends with Barry.

_____. *Mystery at Snowshoe Mountain Lodge.* Dial, 1987. Kate's first ski trip is fraught with mishaps. She is going to discredit "The Legend of Snowshoe Mountain." Everyone is suspect but it is Pixie, the ski instructor, who is the culprit.

_____. *Tiger Rose.* Dial, 1979. Laura disguises as a stable hand to solve the mystery of the death of insured horses.

Elam, Richard. *Young Visitor to the Moon.* Lantern, 1965. Jack and Pam are taken to the moon to prove they can stand the rigors of space.

Elder, Lauren. *And I Alone Survived.* Dutton, 1978. Lauren, Jay and Jean went flying with Jay as pilot. They crashed, killing Jay and Jean. Lauren must find her way back to get help or she will freeze to death.

Eldridge, Roger. *Shadow of the Gloom-World.* Dutton, 1978. Fernfeather lives in tunnels after a nuclear holocaust. He goes to Olden where machines and computers are and sees a world where Fellmen have survived.

Elfman, Blossom. *Girls of Huntington House.* Houghton, 1972. An English teacher discusses her teaching experiences in a home for unwed mothers.

_____. *House for Johnny O.* Houghton, 1976. Bonnie Jo, 17, goes to New York City to have an abortion and her plans do not work out smoothly.

Eliot, George. *Silas Marner.* Dodd, 1948. Silas Marner is stingy. He finds Eppie one night freezing to death. The child is Godfrey's but his fiancee doesn't know it. Will Silas or Dunstan tell and spoil everyone's life?

Elish, Dan. *Jason and the Baseball Bear.* Orchard, 1990. Jason is the only member of his baseball team that can talk to animals. He improves his Team's chances to win with the help of Whitney, an elderly polar bear.

_____. *Worldwide Dessert Contest.* Watts, 1988. John dreams that he is the winner of the Worldwide Dessert Contest.

Eller, Scott. *Short Season.* Scholastic, 1985. Dean and Brad are brothers on the same baseball team. Dean quits and Brad has to find other friends on the team and play without depending on his brother.

Ellerby, Liona. *King Tut's Game Board.* Lerner, 1980. Justin and Nate become friends in Egypt. Nate is very different (not from Earth) and is looking for evidence that his ancestors were here earlier.

Elliott, David. *Listen to the Silence.* Holt, 1969. A terrifying story of an orphan teenager in a mental hospital.

Ellis, Ella. *Celebrate the Morning.* Atheneum, 1972. April, 14, sees her schizophrenic, divorced mother be committed to an institution and fears her life will be the same. A loving neighbor helps her come to terms with her mother and herself.

_____. *Hugo and the Princess Nena.* Atheneum, 1983. Nena learns to live with and love her grandfather, Hugo. She knows he is old and failing.

_____. *Roam the Wild Country.* Atheneum, 1967. Argentina's pampas are hit by a drought. All the men and most of the boys of the area must save the horses from sure death. It is a desperate attempt.

Ellis, Mel. *Flight of the White Wolf.* Holt, 1970. Rus and his white wolf, that he raised from a pup, are hiding. He is fleeing from capture and wants the wolf to be free.

_____. *Ironhead.* Holt, 1968. Doug traps and sells rattlesnakes. He wants to get the $500.00 reward for an eight-foot-long rattler.

Ellis, Sarah. *Family Project.* Macmillan, 1988. Jessica looks forward to getting a new babysitter. The baby dies and the family is grief stricken but slowly recovers.

Ellison, Lucile. *Butter on Both Sides.* Scribner, 1979. Lucy plans an overnight trip up the Tombigbee River. Her father gets seriously ill and Christmas must be delayed until the Fourth of July when he is well and the family is reunited.

_____. *Tie That Binds.* Scribner, 1981. Lucy helps put out a tragic fire in which her mother's quilts are used to smother the flames. She must also cope with a new baby in the family and a sister who dies.

Elmore, Patricia. *Susannah and the Blue House Mystery.* Dutton, 1980. Susannah and her friend Lucy are "detectives." They search the Blue House for clues and find a missing will. They also discover that someone else is searching the house. The rightful heir wins.

————. *Susannah and the Poison Green Halloween*. Dutton, 1982. Someone put poisoned candy in the Trick or Treat bag and Knievel Jones and Carla Abe ate some. Susannah and Lucy must find out who did it.

Embry, Margaret. *Shadi*. Holiday, 1971. Emma (Shadi's older sister), is torn between Navajo traditions and white man's customs. Her mother dies and she must care for the younger children.

Emery, Anne. *Dinny Gordon, Freshman*. Macrae, 1959. Dinny is not as interested in boys as are her friends. Then she meets Clyde, a senior, and dates him. She gets measles and her best friend starts to date him.

————. *Dinny Gordon, Junior*. Macrae, 1964. After a break-up and reconciliation, Dinny discovers that her boyfriend, Curt, has strong prejudices against some of her Jewish friends.

————. *Dinny Gordon, Senior*. Macrae, 1967. Dinny is now a senior and her views of friendship and boyfriends have changed from the experiences of the last few years. She goes on to a satisfying future.

————. *Dinny Gordon, Sophomore*. Macrae, 1961. Curt breaks up with Sue, Dinny's best friend, and takes an interest in Dinny.

————. *Losing Game*. Westminster, 1965. Sue has broken up with her boyfriend. She joins the journalism club and finds friends with real values.

————. *Popular Crowd*. Westminster, 1961. Sue wants to be popular as a sophomore and dates a senior. Her mother encourages her but her brother warns her of value differences.

Ende, Michael. *Neverending Story*. Doubleday, 1983. Bastian finds a book that takes him to Fantastica. Atreyu tries to befriend him because he needs him. Bastian renews and re-creates Fantastica. But he finally returns home.

————. *Ophelia's Shadow Theatre*. Overlook, 1989. Ophelia loses her job as theatre prompter. She "adopts" shadows and puts on shows until she follows her own shadow to heaven.

Engdahl, Sylvia. *Beyond Tomorrow Mountain*. Atheneum, 1973. Noren's planet is destined for disaster until he learns to accept a promise and hope. He becomes a Scholar and goes to build a city on the other side of Tomorrow Mountain.

————. *Doors of the Universe*. Atheneum, 1981. Noren, now an adult, does not have all the knowledge he needs to solve his problems. His wife, Talyra, dies and he studies even more until he can find a way to help people.

————. *Enchantress from the Stars*. Atheneum, 1970. Elana arrives on Andrecia by chance and Georyn believes she is there to save Andrecia from the dragons. She must not reveal herself or use any of her powers, but must work as best she can.

————. *Far Side of Evil*. Atheneum, 1971. Elana is sent to Toris, a planet in the Critical Stage, to help in the reconstruction after a disaster, but meets with jail, torture and possible death.

————. *This Star Shall Abide*. Atheneum, 1972. A future world where machines are not built but "just are." However, this planet's metal is unsuitable for machinery. Noren questions the holders of power and is punished.

Engebrecht, P. *Under the Haystack*. Nelson, 1973. Sandy is under the haystack; it is the only place for privacy as she looks after her abandoned sisters and keeps the authorities away. Handling it alone is better than when errant mother is there.

Engel, Beth. *Big Words*. Dutton, 1982. Sandy befriends a black boy, Will, she finds hiding from a lynch mob after he is accused of murdering a white woman.

Engh, M.J. *House in the Snow*. Watts, 1987. Benjamin, an orphan, and Mackie, a runaway from a group of robbers, get together to capture the robbers.

Engle, Eloise. *Sea Challenge*. Hammond, 1962. Antonio and Sancho are captured by gypsies. They escape and look for their family.

Enright, D.J. *Joke Shop*. McKay, 1976. Jane, Timmy and Robert find themselves in a world of shadows, where light is the enemy. They do escape with the help of a kind shadow.

Enright, Elizabeth. *And Then There Were Five*. Holt, 1944/1987. The Melendy children are on their own, and get involved in some wild adventures: Mona in her first attempt at baking and cooking, a confrontation with the DeLaceys and the Red Cross.

————. *Four Story Mistake*. Holt, 1942/1987. The Melendy family move to the country, into a house that is a Big Mistake. But each of the children finds something special: a running brook, an orchard, a cave and a cellar.

————. *Goneaway Lake*. Harcourt, 1957/1990. Portia and Julian discover some abandoned cottages that were once on a lakeside but now are on a swamp. Two of them are occupied by a brother and sister who remember when the lake was there.

————. *Return to Goneaway Lake*. Harcourt, 1961. Portia's family is going to buy the old cottages and restore them and the family will live there year round. Portia is delighted.

————. *Saturdays*. Holt, 1941/1988. Each Saturday one of the children picks a favorite activity, and then is allowed to pursue it with the pooled allowance of all the children.

————. *Spiderweb for Two*. Holt, 1951/1987. Randy and Oliver are left at home when the two older children go away to school. They find new adventures while waiting for the holidays when everyone will be home.

_____. *Thimble Summer.* Holt, 1976. A young girl on a Wisconsin farm finds a magic thimble.

Epstein, Anne. *Good Stones.* Houghton, 1977. A half-Indian girl and an ex-convict are both outcasts and get together to find a better life for themselves.

Epstein, Samuel. *Change for a Penny.* Coward, 1960. Tim is to guide raiders through a marsh to attack Sag Harbor.

_____. *Jackknife for a Penny.* Coward, 1958. Tim wants to fight in the Revolutionary War. But he works at home as a spy where he proves himself both courageous and discrete.

Erdman, Loula. *Room to Grow.* Dodd, 1962. Pierre and Celeste come from France to Texas. They are different from other children and want to become "Americanized" without losing their French heritage.

Ericson, Stig. *Dan Henry in the Wild West.* Delacorte, 1976. Dan arrives in Minnesota in 1870 with his friend Martin. Martin is shot by the James Gang and Dan moves West and again is in a military band.

Erno, Richard. *Billy Lightfoot.* Crown, 1969. Billy Lightfoot is a Navaho who would like to see the outside world. He leaves the reservation, goes to school and learns to play basketball. But it is his art that interests him most.

Ervin, Janet. *Last Trip to the Luno.* Follett, 1970. A funny story of John and Jenks, two brothers who didn't see eye to eye on anything. They grew up to be riverboat men and had their own boat until their arguing ran their ship aground.

Erwin, Betty. *Behind the Magic Line.* Little, 1969. Dozie wanted a better life than she had in her crowded neighborhood. Uncle Samuel Dan showed her the Magic Line and it seemed to make life better until her brother got in trouble.

_____. *Summer Sleigh Ride.* Little, 1966. Four girls are kidnapped and are taken to the twenty-fourth century where they are put on exhibit. They pretend illness and are returned to their origin.

_____. *Who Is Victoria?* Little, 1973. Margaret and her friends spend an unusual summer after they meet the strange and mysterious Victoria.

Estes, Eleanor. *Alley.* Harcourt, 1964. The Alley is on a college campus and consists of 26 families. A burglary takes place and the Alley's 33 children help in the arrest.

_____. *Ginger Pye.* Harcourt, 1951/1990. Ginger is a puppy that has been missing for several months. It belongs to Jerry and Rachel. Bennie helps in the return of this very much loved dog.

_____. *Hundred Dresses.* Harcourt, 1944. A poor Polish girl tells her classmates she has 100 dresses at home. They ridicule her because she always wears the same faded dress. It is her drawings she's talking about, and she wins an award.

_____. *Middle Moffats.* Harcourt, 1942/1989. Jane is the next to youngest Moffat. This is her story, and it is as funny as *The Moffats.*

_____. *Moffat Museum.* Harcourt, 1983. Jane Moffat opens a museum in the place with which the Moffats are most identified: Cranbury, Conn. Sylvie is married, Rufus dresses up for the wax statues in the museum, Joey is 16.

_____. *Moffats.* Harcourt, 1941/1989. A humorous book about a fun-loving, lively family. Each chapter is a different and funny story about Jane, Joey, Rufus and Sylvie.

_____. *Pinky Pye.* Harcourt, 1958/1976. Pinky, a black kitten, boxes with Ginger, uses the typewriter and does many other funny things. She was acquired on Fire Island while the Pye family was on vacation to study birds.

_____. *Rufus M.* Harcourt, 1943/1989. Rufus, the youngest, is the hero in this story of the Moffat family. He must learn to write his name if he is to get a much wanted library card.

_____. *Tunnel of Hugsy Goode.* Harcourt, 1972. Hugsy said there was a tunnel under the Alley and so they search for it. And discover it is there!

_____. *Witch Family.* Harcourt, 1960. Two young girls, a few witches and a bumblebee make a basis for a funny story.

Estoril, Jean. *We Danced in Bloomsbury Square.* Follett, 1967. Doria and Debbie take ballet lessons. They both compete for one scholarship to a special ballet school. Debbie wins the scholarship, but both get to go to the special school.

Ethridge, Kenneth. *Toothpick.* Troll, 1985. A teenage boy and a terminally ill girl build a friendship. It is funny and moving as Jamie tells how it happened.

_____. *Viola.* Holiday, 1989. Three friends try to protect Viola, a 78-year-old baseball fan. Her daughters want to put her in a nursing home.

_____. *Viola, Furgy, Bobbi and Me.* Holiday, 1989. Steve does yard work for 78-year-old Viola. They become friends because they have baseball in common. They and Steve's friends become a real foursome.

Etter, Les. *Morning Glory Quarterback.* Bobbs, 1965. Rich finds college football different than high school. He must learn more teamwork and also beware of gamblers.

Evans, Max. *My Pardner.* Houghton, 1972. Dan takes horses from Texas to Oklahoma to sell. "My pardner" is Boggs, an experienced, rascally cowhand. They fight for basic survival as they run out of money and food.

Evansen, Virginia. *Flea Market Mystery.* Dodd, 1978. Nancy and Thomas investigate a mystery at the Senior Citizen's Co-op store. Some of Thomas's friends are involved.

Evarts, Hal. *Bigfoot.* Scribner, 1973. Dingo heard the Bigfoot tales but didn't believe them. But when he hired out as a guide he was willing to believe anything.

_____. *Pegleg Mystery.* Scribner, 1972. Lew is given another chance to get a passing science grade. He goes into the desert to report on ancient Indians. He and a friend uncover a mystery that takes them to Mexico and then back home.

_____. *Purple Eagle Mystery.* Scribner, 1976. Bix has to find a Purple Eagle, a rare old bottle, in order to save his uncle's antique store from closing. He goes to Rio Blanco and starts his search.

_____. *Secret of the Himalayas.* Scribner, 1962. Jerry is going with a team to find the abominable snowman. Sabotage hits the camp; equipment is damaged; a man is injured. A tight story full of suspense and tension.

_____. *Smugglers' Road.* Scribner, 1968. Kern has a choice of juvenile hall or working in a Mexican village. He chooses the latter and it makes a better person of him.

Evenhuis, Gertie. *What About Me?* Nelson, 1970. Dirk wants to help in the World War II effort. He passes out some resistance newspapers but when his teacher is arrested for hiding illegal papers, Dirk panics.

Evernden, Margery. *Lyncoya.* Walck, 1973. A fictionalized story of the son of Andrew Jackson and an Indian boy, Lyncoya.

Ewing, Kathryn. *Private Matter.* Harcourt, 1975. Marcy, who has no father, thinks of her neighbor Mr. Endicott as a father. When he moves she is hurt and lonely. Then her mother announces that she is getting married again.

_____. *Things Won't Be the Same.* Harcourt, 1980. Marcy is startled about her mother's decision to get married. After the wedding Marcy goes to stay with her unknown father. She is again hurt and lonely.

Eyerly, Jeannette. *Angel Baker, Thief.* Lippincott, 1984. Angel steals and is sent to a training school. When released she starts anew in a new town. She steals again as an initiation rite in school and is caught. She is cleared and reunited with her family.

_____. *Bonnie Jo, Go Home.* Lippincott, 1972. Bonnie Jo, 16, is pregnant. She goes to get an abortion but she is farther along in her pregnancy than she thought. What now?

_____. *Escape from Nowhere.* Lippincott, 1969. A story about a youngster's feelings of emptiness in the straight world and the disintegration of the drug scene.

_____. *Girl Inside.* Lippincott, 1968. Orphaned Christina faces mental problems.

_____. *Girl Like Me.* Lippincott, 1966. A story of Cass, an unwed high school girl, facing motherhood at the Mission hospital.

_____. *More Than a Summer Love.* Lippincott, 1962. Casey had a summer job in New York but had to go to an Iowa town because of family illness. She writes for the newspaper, meets people, including young men, and has "more than a summer love."

_____. *Phaedra Complex.* PB, 1971. Laura becomes interested in David, but she is also attracted to her new stepfather.

_____. *Radigan Cares.* Lippincott, 1970. Doug, unlike his older brother, Norm, decides to work within the system for improvement in government.

_____. *Seeing Summer.* Lothrop, 1981. Carey's new neighbor girl, Jenny, is blind. She is kidnapped and Carey tries to rescue her. After some harrowing experiences they are found. But friendship is the main theme.

_____. *Seth and Me and Rebel Makes Three.* Lippincott, 1983. Ryan and Seth move into an apartment and are doing O.K. Rebel (Doreen) moves in and disrupts everything.

_____. *Someone to Love Me.* Lippincott, 1987. Patrice was delighted with Lance's friendship. He didn't take her anywhere and still dated Stephanie but she didn't mind. She got in deeper and deeper with him without a thought of pregnancy. But....

_____. *World of Ellen March.* Lippincott, 1964. Ellen is hurt when her parents decide to get a divorce. She is ashamed to tell her friends and she is angry at her parents.

Faber, Nancy. *Cathy at the Crossroads.* Lippincott, 1962. Cathy resents her stepmother until Barbara gets ill and almost dies. Cathy accepts her and learns she must decide to accept a retarded half-sister who is in a special school.

_____. *Cathy's Secret Kingdom.* Lippincott, 1963. Cathy accepts her retarded half-sister in spite of shunning by her friends. There is a mystery to be solved in this episode of Cathy.

Facklam, Margery. *Trouble with Mothers.* Houghton, 1989. Luke's mother wrote an historical novel called "Passionate Pirate." It is declared immoral even though it is about slavery in the U.S. The whole town takes pro- or anti-censorship positions.

_____. *Whistle for Danger.* Rand McNally, 1962. Bill and his cousin help out in the zoo during the summer. They help raise money to hire fulltime help for the reptile house.

Fairfax-Lucy, Brian. *Children of the House.* Lippincott, 1968. The parents live in splendor, but behind the nursery door are three children so forlorn and neglected that even the overworked servants pity them.

Fairman, Paul. *Five Knucklebones.* Holt, 1972. John sails for America and his ship becomes a "slaver." He is shipwrecked and meets Will, an educated black. He reaches America at the start of the Revolutionary War.

_____. *Forgetful Robot.* Holt, 1968. Barney is a robot and tells how humans appear to him. He, two teenagers and their grandfather are hijacked to Mars and Barney must save them.

Falk, Ann. *Place of Her Own.* Harcourt, 1964. Stina, 15, moves to live with her sister. She must make new friends, adjust to a new school and live in cramped quarters.

_____. *Who Is Erika?* Macmillan, 1963. Erika has a new stepfather and must face a move to a small town. But friends and family help her to adjust.

Fall, Thomas. *Canal Boat to Freedom.* Dial, 1966. Benja, a canal boat worker, helps the underground railroad.

_____. *Dandy's Mountain.* Dial, 1967. Dandy's troublesome cousin Bruce comes to visit. He runs away and Dandy follows. They both get lost in a mountain storm. They finally get rescued by forest rangers.

_____. *Edge of Manhood.* Dial, 1964. See-a-Way had to become assimilated into white man's culture or be isolated on the Reservation.

_____. *My Bird Is Romeo.* Dial, 1964. Emily is emotionally unstable. She has a treehouse where she watches birds. She rescues a sparrow hawk and names it Romeo and identifies with it.

_____. *Wild Boy.* Dial, 1965. Roberto and his grandfather try to capture a stallion called Diablo Blanco that had killed Roberto's father. It killed his grandfather also but Roberto finally trains well enough to capture it.

Faralla, Dana. *Wonderful Flying-Go-Round.* World, 1968. A fantasy of two people who arrive in a balloon and transform a dump into a playground.

Farber, Norma. *Mercy Short, a Winter Journal.* Dutton, 1982. A tale of Mercy's diary in the 1690's. She was captured by Indians, bore a son who later died, and was ransomed to Cotton Mather. A story of religious fervor in early New England.

Farjeon, Annabel. *Maria Lupin.* Abelard, 1967. Maria's father disappears with no explanation. She takes up with questionable friends and gets in trouble.

_____. *Siege of Trapp's Mill.* Atheneum, 1974. Polak and her gang spend a weekend in a deserted mill. Freezing cold, little food and an attack by a rival gang are just a few of the events added to Chris's broken leg.

Farley, Carol. *Bunch on McKellahan Street.* Watts, 1971. The Bunch is eight children from the wrong side of town. They experience both fun and trouble (including death) together.

_____. *Case of the Vanishing Villain.* Avon, 1986. An escaped convict disappears and a 10-year-old solves the mystery.

_____. *Garden Is Doing Fine.* Atheneum, 1975. Corrie, 14, cannot accept the fact that her once healthy father is dying of cancer.

_____. *Loosen Your Ears.* Atheneum, 1977. Josh tells funny stories about himself and his odd farm family.

_____. *Most Important Thing in the World.* Watts, 1974. While looking for the "most important thing in the world," Miss Fee has an "honesty" contest and Roxann and Marvin win. They

travel with her cross country and learn abou hypocrisy and greed.

_____. *Ms. Isabell Corell, Herself.* Athe neum, 1980. Ibby must go to live with her nev stepfather who is on a military base in Korea.

_____. *Mystery in the Ravine.* Watts, 1967 Kipper and Larry explore a ravine and find men digging for money that was buried by the owner' sons.

_____. *Settle Your Fidgets.* Atheneum 1977. Josh tells more tales about his boyhood on the farm and his unusual relatives.

Farley, Walter. *Black Stallion.* Random, 1941 1977. A fabulous horse, Black, and a boy, Alec share a desert island when both are shipwrecked They are rescued and Alec trains the horse to race

_____. *Black Stallion and Flame.* Random 1960. Stranded on an island after a plane wreck the Black Stallion meets a filly named Flame.

_____. *Black Stallion and Satan.* Random 1949/1978. Which is the faster racer—Black Stallion or his son, Satan? It will be determined when Black comes to America to race.

_____. *Black Stallion and the Girl.* Ran dom, 1971. Alec meets and hires a girl, Pam, who trains horses. Henry doesn't like it. When Alec i suspended she rides the horse and proves her courage.

_____. *Black Stallion Challenged.* Random 1964. The Black Stallion is challenged to a race by Flame and Flame can really run.

_____. *Black Stallion Legend.* Random 1983. Alec and Black travel to the Southwest and help an Indian tribe after an earthquake, thereby fulfilling an ancient prophecy.

_____. *Black Stallion Mystery.* Random 1957/1977. Where did the three black colts come from? They are not the Black's.

_____. *Black Stallion Returns.* Random 1945/1983. Black is taken by his rightful owners Alec accompanies two men to Arabia in search of the missing Black Stallion. He rides him in an Arabian race.

_____. *Black Stallion Revolts.* Random 1953/1977. The Black Stallion breaks free and lives the wild life he was destined to live.

_____. *Black Stallion's Blood Bay Colt* Random, 1950/1988. Black Stallion's second son Bonfire, likes harness racing. He must be tamed trained and well-handled.

_____. *Black Stallion's Courage.* Random 1956/1978. The Black Stallion runs in the race of the century.

_____. *Black Stallion's Filly.* Random 1952/1978. The Black Stallion's filly is trained by Alec and Henry to win the Kentucky Derby. But she has a strong will, and the training is com plicated. Can she make it to the great classic?

_____. *Black Stallion's Ghost.* Random 1969. Alex is knocked out by Captain and Black flees into the Everglades. It is one of the most terrifying days, and night. Alec ends up buying the white Ghost horse from this circus captain.

_____. *Black Stallion's Sulky Colt*. Random, 1954/1978. Bonfire, one of Black's sons, has problems learning to race in harness (Sulky) but because of some accidents which frightened the colt, Alec must try harness racing.

_____. *Island Stallion*. Random, 1948/1980. Steve saves Flame from a horrible death and a friendship begins, one that would change both their lives.

_____. *Island Stallion Races*. Random, 1955/1980. An untrained stallion on a racetrack makes for a very thrilling story. Can Flame run in competition?

_____. *Island Stallion's Fury*. Random, 1951/1980. Some very dangerous men find the secret valley of the stallion. Steve is very concerned about this. It could mean trouble.

_____. *Man O' War*. Random, 1962. This story is based on the life of a once great racehorse. It is surrounded with color of the racing world and the raising and training of thoroughbreds.

_____. *Son of Black Stallion*. Random, 1947/1977. Satan, Black's son, comes back with Alec. He realizes that this desert born stallion cannot be entirely free of his natural instinct to kill when he begins to tame and train him.

Farmer, Penelope. *Castle of Bone*. Atheneum, 1972. A pigskin turned into a pig. Hugh and his friends gave chase. They found that anything put in the cupboard turned into whatever it was earlier.

_____. *Charlotte Sometimes*. Harcourt, 1969. Charlotte slips back in time and becomes another girl, Clare Moby. She moves back and forth and although she wants to stay in the present she does not want to lose her friend from the past.

_____. *Emma in Winter*. Harcourt, 1966. Charlotte goes to boarding school and Emma is alone. She makes friends with one of her classmates, Bobby, and tells him of her summer spent flying with the strange boy.

_____. *Magic Stone*. Harcourt, 1964. Two girls find a magic stone. One girl is from a London slum, the other is from a small village. They spend an unforgettable summer together.

_____. *Summer Birds*. Harcourt, 1962. A strange boy teaches Charlotte and Emma to fly. He takes them on a moonlit flight to a lake and to a sea. When summer is over he leaves.

_____. *William and Mary*. Atheneum, 1974. Two youngsters travel through time to visit many places.

_____. *Year King*. Atheneum, 1977. Lew lives with his twin brother and mother. He feels dominated by his brother and confronts him while on an underground expedition.

Farrar, Susan. *Samantha on Stage*. Dial, 1979. Samantha is interested in ballet. Lizinka joins Samantha's ballet class and really knows how to dance. They become friends and Samantha becomes an understudy.

Farthing, Alison. *Mystical Beast*. Hastings, 1978. Sara and Henry go to the "other side." They get involved in finding the Mystical Beast. Lavinia is supposed to become the Hereditary Keeper of the Beast.

Fast, Howard. *April Morning*. Crown, 1961. Adam and his father are in the Battle of Lexington in 1775. They tell of the blood, death and horror of war.

_____. *Freedom Road*. Bantam, 1970. A story of how a black man dreams of the day when his people and the whites can live together peacefully. He is a former slave in the South after the Civil War.

Fast, Jonathan. *Beast*. Ballantine, 1981. A Beauty and the Beast story where the Beauty is a movie actress and the Beast is a former director of a napalm chemical plant.

Faulkner, Nancy. *Mystery of Long Barrow House*. Doubleday, 1960. Three children and a young archeologist look for an ancient barrow.

_____. *Sacred Jewel*. Doubleday, 1961. A romance between a daughter of a Druid priest and a young poet interested in a new religion. (At the time of Christ)

_____. *Second Son*. Holt, 1969. Kit is sent to England to become an apprentice to a merchant. He is successful in business, especially in the rapidly growing American colonies.

_____. *Secret of the Simple Code*. Doubleday, 1965. Paul is spending the summer in North Carolina. He becomes involved in a mystery involving code messages left in discarded cigars and jewel thieves being sought by an insurance investigator.

_____. *Stage for Rom*. Doubleday, 1962. Rom and Polly are twins and find they are adopted. They look for their father in Colonial Williamsburg.

_____. *Traitor Queen*. Doubleday, 1963. Thalamika helps Kritheus overthrow Crete. The Queen is the inside contact plotting with the Mycenaeans. The king won't believe this.

_____. *Wishing Tree*. Random, 1964. Dulcie goes on a magical journey with others in search of the Wishing Tree.

Faulknor, Cliff. *White Peril*. Little, 1960. Eagle Child is an Indian scout. He encounters enemy Crows and Apaches while looking for white encroachment. He tells the chief that they must learn to live with the white man.

Fea, Henry. *Wild One*. Washburn, 1964. The Wild One is a German shepherd. Bruce tries to get the dog but fails. One winter the dog is starving and Bruce nurses him back to health. He now becomes Bruce's dog.

Feagles, Anita. *Me, Cassie*. Dial, 1968. Cassie's life is all tangled up until she meets a young man with some sense and straightens everything out.

_____. *Sophia, Scarlotte and Ceecee.*

Atheneum, 1979. Ceecee's mother invites her boyfriend and his two sons to spend two weeks with them. Clem, one of the sons, and Ceecee, after a while, get together.

_____. *Twenty-Seven Cats Next Door.* Scott, 1965. Jim's neighbor has many cats. He finds that there is no easy answer to individual rights and the rights of a society.

_____. *Year the Dreams Came Back.* Atheneum, 1976. Nell's mother committed suicide and she lives with her father. Nell runs away when her father wants to remarry but comes to understand the situation and accepts it.

Fecher, Constance. *Leopard Dagger.* Farrar, 1973. The leopard dagger holds a mystery for a young orphan, caught up in the Shakespearean Company at the old Globe Theatre and at odds with a dangerous man.

Feil, Hila. *Ghost Garden.* Atheneum, 1976. Jessica and Christina want to communicate with ghosts. They find a book on witchcraft and plant a witch's garden.

_____. *Windmill Summer.* Harper, 1972. Arabella spends the summer with her great-grandfather at his windmill. She finds a raccoon and other small animals and learns about nature's way of protection.

Feldman, Alan. *Lucy Mastermind.* Dutton, 1985. Lucy wants to renovate the family boathouse. She fishes alone and water skis. She helps her slow learning brother in a humorous way.

Felice, Cynthia. *Downtime.* Bluejay, 1985. Mutare is a minor planet. A trap is set to get a traitor who is trying to get the needs for producing a longevity elixir. Audoria is the one who is expected to catch this traitor.

Fenisong, Ruth. *Boy Wanted.* Harper, 1964. Ron is an ill-treated orphan who runs away and is adopted by loving people. He goes to school and makes friends.

Fenner, Carol. *Skates for Uncle Richard.* Random, 1978. Marsha, 9, tries to ice skate on hand-me-down skates from Uncle Richard.

Fenton, Edward. *Duffy's Rocks.* Dutton, 1974. Timothy lives in Duffy's Rocks with his grandmother. She doesn't want him to grow up like his father but he wants to meet his absent father. A strong Catholic background story.

_____. *Matter of Miracles.* Holt, 1967. Gino first finds a dog named Miss, then some puppeteers and then his miracle happens.

_____. *Morning of the Gods.* Delacorte, 1987. Carla's mother dies and she visits Greece where she finds family security but political unrest.

_____. *Phantom of Walkaway Hill.* Doubleday, 1961. James visits his cousin's secluded new home, Walkaway, during the summer.

_____. *Refugee Summer.* Delacorte, 1982. Nikolas lives during the Greco-Turkish War in 1922. This war changes his life considerably.

_____. *Riddle of the Red Whale.* Double-

day, 1966. James, Obie and Amanda find two old trunks and old books. A stranger is also very interested. Is the clue red whale or red herring?

Fenwick, Elizabeth. *Passenger.* Atheneum, 1967. Toby wants someone to help get his restored car home. He meets a girl with some rather mysterious problems.

Fern, Eugene. *Lorenzo and Angelina.* Farrar, 1968. Angelina and her donkey, Dorenzo, climb to the top of El Prado Mountain so that they can see the world. The adventure is told from the point of view of both Angelina and Dorenzo.

Ferris, Jean. *Invincible Summer.* Farrar, 1987. Rick and Robin are both ill with leukemia. They meet in the hospital and fall in love. Both have a hopeless future.

_____. *Stainless Steel Rule.* Farrar, 1986. Three girls, Kitty, Mary, and Fran, are school friends and members of the school swim team. Nick is Mary's boyfriend who is harmful to her. The rule of not interfering is broken for Mary's safety.

Ferry, Charles. *O, Zebron Falls.* Houghton, 1977. Lukie's last two years of high school are ideal with all the dances, homecomings, dates, etc., until World War II comes into focus.

Feuer, Elizabeth. *One Friend to Another.* Farrar, 1987. Nicole is bright but wants to be popular. She makes friends with popular Rhonda who later betrays her.

Feydy, Anne. *Osprey Island.* Houghton, 1974. Three children say magic words and are transported away. One of them is in France, the other two in the U.S. They must coordinate time zones when they travel. Items appear in each other's homes.

Fiddler, Katheryn. *Haki the Shetland Pony.* Rand McNally, 1968. Adam is given a pony to be sold when grown. When it is sold to a circus Adam goes, too.

Fiedler, Jean. *Yardstick for Jessica.* McKay, 1964. Jessica is short and wants to be tall. She gets the role in the school play because she is shorter than the boy she plays opposite.

_____. *Year the World Was Out of Step with Jancy Fried.* Harcourt, 1981. Jancy gets the lead in a school play but loses it later because of "moods." Her best friend is jealous. She meets a boy, Eddie, and is generally confused about the changes in her life.

Field, Rachel. *Calico Bush.* Macmillan, 1987. A new edition of the adventures of a girl from France who joins a family of American pioneers.

_____. *Hitty: Her First Hundred Years.* Macmillan, 1929. A 100-year-old doll writes about her adventures, one of which is a long sailing trip on a whaler. Newbery winner, 1930.

Fields, Julia. *Green Lion of Zion Street.* Macmillan, 1988. A group of children are going through the park in the fog and see a stone lion which they approach very carefully.

Fife, Dale. *Destination Unknown.* Dutton,

1981. Jon stows away on a fishing ship headed for Scotland but because of the war he ends up in New York.

_____. *North of Danger*. Dutton, 1978. During World War II a young Norwegian boy has many dangerous escapades.

_____. *Ride the Crooked Wind*. Coward, 1973. Po was an Indian who liked his life as it was but changes had to come and he had to adjust and learn different customs, ideas and traditions.

_____. *Who's in Charge of Lincoln?* Coward, 1965. Lincoln, black, is accidentally left alone in his family's New York apartment. He finds money and goes to Washington, D.C.

Filson, Brent. *Puma*. Doubleday, 1979. Sonny's temper gets him suspended from the wrestling team, and he is in trouble with the coach and friends. He has many other problems in his life and can't solve all of them.

_____. *Smoke Jumpers*. Doubleday, 1978. Carla gets suspended from school and goes to her uncle's ranch. She suspects arsonist's are starting forest fires. The arsonists are out to get her.

Fine, Anne. *Alias Madame Doubtfire*. Little, 1988. Miranda, divorced from Daniel, hires a housekeeper. Daniel, an actor, gets the job. His children know who he is but not Miranda!

_____. *Granny Project*. Farrar, 1983. The story of how four children worked to keep their grandmother out of a nursing home.

_____. *My War with Goggle-Eyes*. Little, 1989. Kitty's mother has a boyfriend she doesn't like. She calls him goggle-eyes.

_____. *Summer House Loon*. Crowell, 1979. Ione lives with her blind father. Ned, the "loon," meets Ione and they are good for each other; he helps her become more considerate and she helps him through his exams.

Finlay, Winifred. *Beadbonny Ash*. Nelson, 1973. Birdie goes to visit friends in Scotland but can't adjust. She drifts into the past where she is a priestess and destroys one of the "old gogs." Then she returns to the "future."

Finlayson, Ann. *Greenhorn on the Frontier*. Warne, 1974. Harry and Sukey claim their land and build a house. They make both friends (Anse and Showanyah) and enemies (Simon). Simon is driven out of town and Sukey marries Anse.

_____. *Rebecca's War*. Warne, 1972. There are British soldiers billeted in Rebecca's home. She hides military secrets from them although she is only 14 at the time of the Revolutionary War.

_____. *Redcoat in Boston*. Warne, 1971. Harry is a British soldier in Boston in 1768. He joined the army for food, clothing and shelter, not politics. He buys himself out of the army and joins the colonists.

_____. *Runaway Teen*. Doubleday, 1963. Libby, 16, runs away to Chicago because she feels her mother and stepfather don't want her.

_____. *Silver Bullet*. Nelson, 1978. John takes a message hidden in a silver bullet to the British troops. It is a dangerous journey where he sees the horrors of war, especially when his best plans go wrong.

Finta, Alexander. *My Brother and I*. Holiday, 1940. Sandor and his six brothers have a series of pranks, gang-fights, tricks and hunting adventures. But their high spirits are dampened when the ghost comes.

First, Julia. *Absolute, Ultimate End*. Watts, 1985. Maggie's new friendship with a blind girl makes her want to fight the school board's decision to cut back on handicapped programs.

_____. *Everybody But Me*. Prentice, 1976. Sandy goes to a private school and loves it. But the school is moving out of Boston and she fights it. Her friend Emily wants the move.

_____. *I, Rebekah, Take You, the Laurences*. Watts, 1981. Becky is an orphan. Her best friend is Mildred. She is adopted but runs away when they adopt a boy.

_____. *Look Who's Beautiful*. Watts, 1980. Connie, 13, wants to go to Washington with her class. She tries to raise the needed $90.00 and meets an 85-year-old whom she learns to love.

_____. *Move Over, Beethoven*. Watts, 1978. Gina likes music but it is interfering with her school work and social life.

Fisher, Aileen. *Summer of Little Rain*. Nelson, 1961. A family of squirrels and another of beavers face a drought and a forest fire.

Fisher, Clay. *Valley of the Bear*. Houghton, 1964. An Indian boy and his grandmother are banished from their tribe. They find refuge in a valley and fear the white hunter more than the bear whose home it is.

Fisher, Laura. *Charlie Dick*. Holt, 1972. Charlie Dick is a prankster who loves his shy sister. He tries to get rid of his father's hired hand so he can earn money for his sister's doll. But Walt, the hired hand, becomes an asset.

_____. *Never Try Nathaniel*. Holt, 1968. Than is "mama's boy." He has no self-confidence and is afraid of animals. He tries to overcome these handicaps and ends up rescuing his father and killing a wolf.

Fisher, Leonard. *Noonan: A Novel About Baseball, ESP and Time Warps*. Doubleday, 1978. A baseball pitcher is transported from 1896 to 1996.

_____. *Russian Farewell*. Four Winds, 1980. Benjamin and his eleven children live in Russia in 1904. They are Jewish and flee Russia for the United States.

_____. *Two If by Sea*. Random, 1970. A story of the main people involved in the midnight ride of April 18, 1775, that started the Revolutionary War.

_____. *Warlock of Westfall*. Doubleday, 1974. A story of witch hunting in early America. An old, bad tempered man is accused by some boys and is hanged. The village suffers for this.

Fisher, Lois. *Arianna and Me*. Dodd, 1986.

Rusty has problems: her terror of a younger sister, her needlecraft class, her best friend's boyfriend, etc.

_____. *Puffy P. Pushycat, Problem Solver.* Dodd, 1983. Tina and her cat solve crimes, like a missing parakeet and a kitten.

_____. *Rachel Villars, How Could You?* Dodd, 1984. Cory lives with her divorced father. Her friend Rachel is good-hearted but has grating habits. Cory must decide to give her up for new friends or keep her in spite of her shortcomings.

_____. *Radio Robert.* Dodd, 1985. A young boy appears on his divorced father's radio show. He makes comments about his life and these affect his friendships.

_____. *Wretched Robert.* Dodd, 1982. Robert lives with his divorced mother. He wants to be "Very Bad" and tries hard, unsuccessfully, to do so.

Fisher, Paul. *Ash Staff.* Atheneum, 1979. Mole and five other orphans have adventures with goblins and Ammar. Mole must kill Ammar with his magic sword.

_____. *Hawks of Fellheath.* Atheneum, 1980. Orne runs off after Llan dies. The rest of the orphan band travel to Vivrandon where they go through many adversities.

_____. *Mont Cant Gold.* Atheneum, 1981. Rhian is king of Canys. His brother wants to be king. He must first win the favor of the Seven Fates.

_____. *Princess and the Thorn.* Atheneum, 1980. Mole goes to an island kingdom, uncovers a plot against the high king and destroys the sorcerer with the sword.

Fisk, Nicholas. *Escape from Splatterbang.* Macmillan, 1978. Mykl is left on planet Splatterbang. So is Rommi. They escape the "flamers" after two failed attempts.

_____. *Grinny.* Nelson, 1974. Aunt Emma proclaimed herself a member of the family but Beth doubted it. Grinny was from another world looking for a new place to settle, like the Earth. She found it unsuitable.

_____. *Monster Maker.* Macmillan, 1980. Matt goes to Chancey's studio to look at special effects monsters. A gang of thugs bother his sister, attack him and invade the studio. He retaliates with a mechanical monster.

_____. *Rag, a Bone and a Hank of Hair.* Crown, 1982. The year 2240 is not as good as it could be. Brin has charge of three "Reborns" (chemically treated humans) and finds that he, too, is a Reborn.

_____. *Trillions.* Pantheon, 1971. A strange book about geometric objects falling from outer space and the boy who learns to communicate with them.

Fitzgerald, John. *Great Brain.* Dial, 1967. A funny story about a "brainy" boy and his friends. He outwits adults and hatches great moneymaking schemes.

_____. *Great Brain at the Academy.* Dial, 1972. Another story about Tom and his brother at the Catholic Academy for Boys.

_____. *Great Brain Does It Again.* Dial, 1975. J.D. tells more about the great brain of Tom and how he can get out of any situation, no matter how bizarre. Earning money is still the main concern.

_____. *Great Brain Reforms.* Dial, 1973. The Great Brain tries to reform because his friends hold a mock trial and threaten to make him an outcast.

_____. *Me and My Little Brain.* Dial, 1971. Tom's younger brother is ready to try all his brother's tricks. He does not have the same success but does trap a criminal and save a small child.

_____. *More Adventures of the Great Brain.* Dial, 1969. Tom (Great Brain) is at it again with more antics. He even astounds the adults around him.

_____. *Private Eye.* Nelson, 1974. Wally, 10, turns his natural ability to find things and solve problems into a private detective business.

_____. *Return of the Great Brain.* Dial, 1974. More outrageous schemes of the Great Brain, who can't keep his promise to reform. He does get involved in solving a crime.

Fitzhugh, Louise. *Harriet the Spy.* Harper, 1964. Harriet wants to be a writer. She "observes" her friends and neighbors, keeping a notebook. This notebook gets her into a great deal of trouble.

_____. *Long Secret.* Harper, 1965. This book includes Beth Ellen, Harriet's best friend. As both girls begin to grow up, they begin to understand friendship. They investigate the notes being left everywhere.

_____. *Nobody's Family Is Going to Change.* Farrar, 1974. Emma and Willie Sherian are poor blacks. Emma wants to be a lawyer but the family is pushing Willie toward a career. He wants to dance like his uncle Dipsey.

_____. *Sport.* Delacorte, 1979. Sport is Harriet's friend. When he inherits millions of dollars his mother wants the money even though he has lived with his father, not her. His friends attempt to rescue him.

Fleischman, H.S. *Gang Girl.* Doubleday, 1967. Maria, 14, lives and copes in Spanish Harlem.

Fleischman, Paul. *Finzel the Farsighted.* Dutton, 1983. Finzel, a fortune teller, is going blind. Because of this he is preyed upon by others.

_____. *Half-a-Moon Inn.* Harper, 1980. Susannah, Lucy and the Knievel solve the mystery of an old, strange house.

_____. *Path of a Pale Horse.* Harper, 1983. Lep is helping Dr. Peale during the Yellow Fever epidemic. He is also looking for his missing sister. He gets lost and can't find Dr. Peale or his sister in this strange city.

_____. *Rear-View Mirrors.* Harper, 1986.

Olivia, 16, lives with her mother and gets an invitation from her father to visit him. He is a writer of detective stories. She spends the summer getting to know him but he dies the following winter.

Fleischman, Sid. *Bloodhound Gang and the Case of the Secret Message.* Random, 1981. The Bloodhound gang is made up of three youngsters who use their deductive skills to solve this mystery.

————. *By the Great Horn Spoon.* Little, 1963. Jock and Praisworthy stow away on a ship going to California. They have an adventure while on the ship and many more in California.

————. *Chancy and the Grand Rascal.* Little, 1966. Chancy is trying to find his family after the Civil War. He meets the Grand Rascal and they travel together down the Ohio River.

————. *Ghost in the Noonday Sun.* Little, 1965. Captain Scratch shanghais Oliver aboard his pirate ship. Oliver must find the ghost of Gentleman Jack.

————. *Ghost on Saturday Night.* Little, 1974. Opie, 10, tries to raise money to buy a saddle. It involves him in a ghost raising session and the recovery of money stolen from a bank.

————. *Humbug Mountain.* Little, 1978. Bad men are plentiful on the Missouri River. And gold is not all that glitters. A non–Humbug family survives it all in a tall tale manner.

————. *Jingo Django.* Little, 1971. Jingo is really a gypsy and his name is Django. He goes to Mexico to look for treasure with Mr. Peacock. They are chased by Daggatt and Scurlock.

————. *McBroom Tells the Truth.* Little, 1981. McBroom is a New England farmer who is the hero? of tall tales.

————. *Me and the Man on the Moon-Eyed Horse.* Little, 1977. A questionable version of how a young boy captured train wreckers in the frontier days.

————. *Mr. Mysterious and Company.* Little, 1962. A humorous story of a traveling magic show in the 1880's.

————. *Whipping Boy.* Greenwillow, 1986. Jemmy is the whipping boy for Prince Brat. The Prince runs away and takes Jemmy with him. They both learn a few lessons of life. Newbery winner, 1987.

Fleming, Alice. *Welcome to Grossville.* Scribner, 1985. Michael's parents are getting a divorce and he must move to "Grossville." He must make new friends and adjust to a new standard of living.

Fleming, Elizabeth. *Takula Tree.* Westminster, 1964. Paul and his mother escape a burning mission in Africa. They have a long and terrifying trip to safety.

Fleming, Ian. *Chitty Chitty Bang Bang.* Random, 1964. The Potts' car is magical. They find a gangster's cabin and must evade Joe the Monster and his gang. Their car is their only hope.

Fletcher, David. *King's Goblet.* Pantheon, 1962. A crippled American boy and a Venetian

glass blower are both affected by a pair of beautiful goblets.

Flory, Jane. *Golden Venture.* Atheneum, 1976. Minnie is determined to go with her father to California's gold mines. She stows away in a wagon and has a great adventure but it takes wits and ingenuity to carry it off.

————. *Liberation of Clementine Tipton.* Houghton, 1974. Clementine was helping celebrate the Centennial in 1876. She was excited about the new woman's movement.

————. *Miss Plunkett to the Rescue.* Houghton, 1983. Miss Plunkett is a third grade teacher, retired from teaching but not from pursuing an enemy agent.

————. *Mist on the Mountain.* Houghton, 1966. Amanda and her family are barely making a living on their farm. Her mother is a midwife and has some exciting events.

————. *Ramshackle Roost.* Houghton, 1972. The Stuart children and their dog are spending summer in an old boarding house. But a guest, Guy, a spoiled brat, comes and threatens to ruin everything.

————. *Time for the Towpath.* Houghton, 1962. Kate didn't like David but he rescued her and her brother from drowning.

Foley, June. *Falling in Love Is No Snap.* Delacorte, 1986. Alexandra and Heracles fall in love but both her mother and his father are against them. Should they follow the dictates of their parents or do what they feel they should?

————. *It's No Crush, I'm in Love.* Delacorte, 1982. Annie falls in love with her English teacher.

Foley, Louise. *Tackle 22.* Delacorte, 1978. Herbie wins the day as a substitute player on the football team.

Follett, Ken. *Eye of the Needle.* Morrow, 1978. The "Needle" is Henry Faber, a spy wanted by everyone. He can help Hitler win the war because he knows a secret that is vital.

————. *Key to Rebecca.* Morrow, 1980. Alex Wolff, The Sphinx, knows a secret that will help Rommel and the Nazi effort. Vandam is assigned to stop him. And the weapon he uses is Elene.

Foltz, Mary Jane. *Nicolau's Prize.* McGraw, 1967. Nicolau's father is a whaler and he has a whale oil smell about him. He is made fun of at school. When the school takes a field trip to the whaling business they learn to respect Nicolau and his trade.

Fon Eisen, Anthony. *Bond of the Fire.* World, 1965. Arkla, a dog, and Ash, his master, are inseparable. They live in a cave during the last Glacial Age.

————. *Prince of Omeya.* World, 1964. Abderahman has a prince on his head. He flees to the desert where he is befriended. He is pursued again and goes to Egypt to his mother's people.

Foote, Timothy. *Great Ringtail Garbage Caper.* Houghton, 1980. A raccoon revolts when the garbage collection becomes efficient and spoils the raccoon's way of life.

Forbes, Colin. *Avalanche Express.* Dutton, 1977. Harry and Elsa are hired to get the U.S. contact with the KGB out of Russia. There are both suspense and romance.

Forbes, Esther. *Johnny Tremain.* Houghton, 1943. Johnny becomes a silver apprentice in young America. This is the story of his actions during the Boston Tea Party and the Battle of Lexington. Newbery winner, 1944.

Forbes, Tom. *Quincy's Harvest.* Lippincott, 1976. Quincy's family are sharecroppers. He learns to trap, hunt and fish to help the family survive.

Forbus, Ina. *Tawny's Trick.* Viking, 1965. Kate owns Tawny, a Morgan horse. She almost lost him because of lack of responsibility.

Forester, Cecil. *Hornblower and the Atropos.* Little, 1953/1985. This is a story of the early life of Captain Hornblower who has a career in the Navy and rises to the top. There are many other books about Hornblower's naval career.

_____. *Hornblower and the Hotspur.* Little, 1962. Commander Hornblower is in a final encounter with Spanish ships laden with treasures for Napoleon. He is in command of the "Hotspur."

_____. *Hornblower During Crisis.* Little, 1967. Another encounter between Hornblower and Napoleon.

Forman, James. *Ballad for Hogskin Hill.* Farrar, 1979. David leaves the city and returns to Hogskin Hill where he helps his father and grandfather fight against a powerful coal company.

_____. *Call Back Yesterday.* Scribner, 1981. Cindy lives in an embassy in Saudi Arabia. There is a revolution and she is taken hostage. She experiences all the bad aspects of war and its consequences.

_____. *Ceremony of Innocence.* Harper, 1970. A vivid retelling of the arrest and execution of a brother and sister for anti–Nazi underground activities.

_____. *Cow Neck Rebels.* Farrar, 1969. A young boy outgrows his adolescent attitude about playing war and comes to mature notions about freedom during the Revolutionary War.

_____. *Fine, Soft Day.* Farrar, 1978. Brian, 13, is a Catholic living in Northern Ireland. Most of the action is on St. Elmo's belfry where bloodshed and violence are a daily occurrence.

_____. *People of the Dream.* Farrar, 1972. Chief Joseph and the Nez Perce Indians are fleeing from the injustices of the white settlers.

_____. *Pumpkin Shell.* Farrar, 1981. Robin eats a lot. His brother drinks. Their father has remarried and Liz, a stepsister, comes to live with them. She and Robin fight a lot but then get sexually involved.

_____. *Survivor.* Farrar, 1976. David's family are persecuted until they lose their business and their home. They hide in an abandoned windmill but are still shipped to Auschwitz.

Forrester, John. *Forbidden Beast.* Bradbury, 1988. The Round Beast challenges the Forbidden Beast to a fight on Earth. A decisive battle between Old Earth and Luna.

_____. *Secret of the Round Beast.* Bradbury, 1986. Tamara and Drewyn battle the geneticists Lava and Pyland. The power hungry against altruists. The Round Beast is revealed some more in this second book of a trilogy.

Forshay-Lunsford, Cin. *Walk Through Cold Fire.* Delacorte, 1985. Desiree, 16, has to cope with her father's remarriage. She gets mixed up with Billy and The Outlaws and her troubles begin.

Forsman, Bettie. *From Lupita's Hill.* Atheneum, 1973. Lupita finds underground water and helps animals through a drought.

Forster, Logan. *Run Fast! Run Far!* Dodd, 1962. Vance inherits a horse farm and raises a horse that eventually wins the Kentucky Derby.

Forsythe, Frederick. *Shepherd.* Viking, 1976. A pilot is lost and has trouble with his electric system and is short on fuel. An ancient plane appears and leads him to a safe landing on a deserted base. He wonders who his "shepherd" is.

Fortune, J.J. *Duel for the Samurai Sword.* Dell, 1986. Stephen and Uncle Richard are in Japan "to battle the cold steel and burning hate of Sakuma Mori, lethal lord of the underworld."

Fosburgh, Liza. *Bella Arabelle.* Macmillan, 1985. Arabelle wants to become a cat and get away from her unhappy life. She gets her wish and then regrets it and wants to be a girl again.

_____. *Cruise Control.* Bantam, 1988. Gussie's mother is an alcoholic. He is doing poorly in school. His brother retreats into books and his sister into food. They all run away. They return when their mother has a nervous breakdown.

_____. *Mrs. Abercorn and the Bunce Boys.* Four Winds, 1986. Otis and Will have no father and are alone while their mother works. They meet Mrs. Abercorn who, although somewhat unpleasant, is very interesting.

_____. *Summer Lion.* Morrow, 1987. Leo's family is poor since his father died. He spends the summer at a resort as a companion to Mr. Baines and pretends to be more than he is. But he's happy to return to his own family lifestyle.

Foster, Alan. *Alien.* Warner, 1979. Alien is a many-fingered, one-eyed creature in space. He is met by space travelers who receive a stress call from a planet. They never came home.

_____. *For Love of Mother-Not.* Ballantine, 1984. Mother Mastiff is Flinx's only family. She is kidnapped and he must find her. He steps through a small door and....

_____. *Man Who Used the Universe.* Warner, 1983. Loo-Macklin is a smart criminal who'll do anything to get what he wants — even sell out to an untrustworthy alien.

_____. *Spellsinger.* Warner, 1983. Jon-Tom

is a rock musician but turns into a wizard who casts spells. He travels through time via Clothahump, a turtle, whose world is threatened by evil forces. He wants Jon-Tom to help.

Foster, Ed. *Tejanos.* Hill & Wang, 1970. Tejanos' father is killed at the Battle of the Alamo and he must become head of the family. He watches as the Mexicans, as well as the Americans, unite against Santa Ana's army.

Foster, Elizabeth. *Gigi.* North Atlantic, 1983. A new edition of the Merry-Go-Round horse.

_____. *Long Hungry Night.* Atheneum, 1973. Nukruk earns his place with the tribe in his Eskimo village. There is also friendship with his old wolf friend, Agorek.

_____. *Lyrico, the Only Horse of His Kind.* Gambit, 1970. Philippa wants a horse of her own. She gets a small pinto with wings but has problems living in the city. The family takes him to the country where he is finally reunited with the wild horses.

Foulds, Elfreda. *Ghosts' High Noon.* Walck, 1966. In a music school in England all the assembled people tell ghost stories.

Fox, Denise. *Through the Tempest Trails.* Macmillan, 1987. A small band of animals: a raccoon, a mink, a peacock and three shrews, escape from a pirate ship.

Fox, Edward. *Hunger Valley.* Doubleday, 1965. Laurie, 15, was responsible for herself and six small children when their parents were slain by Indians.

Fox, Paula. *Blowfish Live in the Sea.* Bradbury, 1970. Ben wonders about the father he hardly knows. Is he what he appears to be? Is Ben what he appears to be? A father/son relationship story.

_____. *How Many Miles to Babylon?* White, 1967. James is kidnapped by dog thieves and held captive at Coney Island in the fun house.

_____. *Lily and the Lost Boy.* Orchard, 1987. Lily and Paul get along as brother and sister but when they go to Thasos they meet another American boy and he disrupts their lives.

_____. *Moonlight Man.* Bradbury, 1986. Catherine visits the father she has not seen since her mother's divorce when she was very young. He is an alcoholic but very nice and likeable.

_____. *One-Eyed Cat.* Bradbury, 1984. Ned takes his gift gun without his father's permission. He shoots and wounds a feral cat. The cat now has one eye and Ned feels guilty.

_____. *Place Apart.* Farrar, 1980. Victoria meets and likes Hugh. He drops her, meets another classmate and drops him, too. Victoria is to learn that he cares for no one but himself. She suffers but survives.

_____. *Portrait of Ivan.* Bradbury, 1969. Ivan is lonely because his mother is dead and his father is overprotective. An artist friend takes him on vacation where he is free for the first time from strict supervision.

_____. *Slave Dancer.* Bradbury, 1973. Jessie was kidnapped and put aboard the slave ship, "Moonlight." His job was to play music on his fife to give the slaves exercise. He did this for four months with Purvis, Grime, Stout and Ras. Newbery winner, 1974.

_____. *Stone-Faced Boy.* Bradbury, 1968. Because Gus is the middle child in a group of five and because he is sensitive and timid, he turns a "stone face" to the outside world.

_____. *Village by the Sea.* Watts, 1988. Emma is staying with an aunt and uncle while her father has heart surgery. It is an adjustment problem for all three people.

Franchere, Ruth. *Stamped North.* Macmillan, 1969. Amos and his son, Charlie, live during the gold rush days of 1897. They see hardship and greediness in everyday living.

Francis, Dorothy. *Another Kind of Beauty.* Criterion, 1970. Ginny and Mitsuka are enrolled in beauty school. A good story of cosmetology and careers in the beauty world.

_____. *Captain Morgana Mason.* Lodestar, 1982. When Gramps falls ill one summer, Morgana, 13, and her brother take charge of his sponging business so the family can stay together.

Francis, Helen. *Big Swat.* Follett, 1963. Henry is recruited by a midwestern university to play football. But the dishonesty that is needed to get athletes is exposed.

Franco, Marjorie. *Love in a Different Key.* Houghton, 1983. Neenah loves Michael. She is talented and wants a career as a pianist. Michael has a nervous breakdown and Neenah plays badly in competition. Then Michael recovers and Neenah succeeds.

_____. *So Who Hasn't Got Problems?* Houghton, 1979. Jennifer has two good friends but when a new girl moves in, that friendship is threatened.

Frank, Rudolf. *No Hero for the Kaiser.* Lothrop, 1986. Jan is a survivor of the World War II raze of his town. He is "adopted" by the German as a mascot and sees the horrors of war. When they want to make him a German citizen, he runs away.

Frankel, Haskel. *Pro Football Rookie.* Doubleday, 1964. Jack has a pro team contract but must still prove himself. He has to decide who will improve his playing: his dad or his coach.

Frascino, Edward. *Eddie Spaghetti.* Harper, 1978. Eddie goes to the zoo, takes piano lessons and fights with his brother. He has a dog that bites the mailman, wears corduroy knickers and goes to $.25 movies.

_____. *Eddie Spaghetti on the Homefront.* Harper, 1983. Eddie lives in New York in 1941 and helps the war drive with victory gardens and paper drives. He has a Defense Club and looks for spies.

Frazee, Steve. *Year of the Big Snow.* Holt, 1962. Ted goes with Fremont's expedition to California in 1849. He struggles with blizzards, pack mules and mountain climbing.

Frazier, Neta. *General's Boots.* McKay, 1965. Charlie, 13, goes gold-mine hunting and finds it to be a wild goose chase. He comes back to his homestead and new stepfather.

Fredericksen, Hazel. *He-Who-Runs-Far.* Scott, 1970. Pablo is living in a white world to learn but he learns too much to suit his people. A story of a boy torn between two cultures.

Freeman, Barbara. *Haunting Air.* Dutton, 1977. A mysterious singing in the garden of the house next door sets a young girl delving into the past to discover its meaning and its source.

_____. *Lucinda.* Norton, 1965. Lucinda is treated unfairly by her uncle. He builds a doll house that she can't use instead of getting her the clothes she needs. But the doll house brings the change she needs.

_____. *Other Face.* Dutton, 1976. Betony gets to play cupid in an 1820's romance through a slip in time.

Freeman, Gail. *Alien Thunder.* Bradbury, 1982. Walker's mother almost drowns and when she recovers she is a different person. She tries to train children to leave the earth for another planet.

French, Dorothy. *Pioneer Saddle Mystery.* Lantern, 1975. A polio victim hides and can't watch when the horses are being exercised. To watch Hugh ride while she can't is too much.

_____. *Try at Tumbling.* Lippincott, 1970. Marti is in a foster home. She makes friends and joins a tumbling team at the YWCA.

French, Fiona. *City of Gold.* Walck, 1974. A medieval kingdom is guarded by a demon; John and Thomas plan to reach the kingdom by separate roads. They do and reconcile when they meet.

French, Michael. *Pursuit.* Delacorte, 1982. Roger cuts the safety rope of Martin while climbing in the Sierra Nevadas. Gordy, Martin's brother, is not going to let him get away with this.

_____. *Throwing Season.* Delacorte, 1980. A sports story about shot putting. Henry is a good athlete and when he is approached to "throw" a competition he refuses and is beaten by the askers. But he fights back.

_____. *Us Against Them.* Bantam, 1987. "Us" is a bunch of teenagers and "them" is the town where they live. The town tears down their teen clubhouse. Devon and his friends are fighting back. But Reed is making the rules.

Frick, C.H. *Comeback Guy.* Harcourt, 1961. Jeff is very egocentric and is disliked by his schoolmates. He loses his spot on the cheerleading team and loses at a state track meet. This brings him to realize his shortcomings.

Friedman, Frieda. *Ellen and the Gang.* Morrow, 1963. Ellen gets mixed up with a gang of juvenile delinquents because she is lonely and insecure.

Friendlich, Dick. *Backstop Ace.* Westminster,
1961. Ace tries to help Mike, a 19-year-old southpaw, but Mike's father interferes.

_____. *Sweet Swing.* Doubleday, 1968. A Minor League baseball story. Gary signs up out of high school. He is a good hitter but not a good fielder. He is sent to the minors. Should he stay there, return to the big leagues or go to college?

Friermood, Elizabeth. *Ballad of Calamity Creek.* Doubleday, 1962. Ann wants to teach but her parents are against it. The time is the end of 1890 and the place, Kentucky. Ann becomes interested in the ballads of these people and learns of their origins.

_____. *Doc Dudley's Daughter.* Doubleday, 1965. Em works in the library during the summer and raises money. Her brother goes off to the Spanish-American War and gets yellow fever. She has a romance with his friend, Charlie.

_____. *One of Fred's Girls.* Doubleday, 1971. Bonnie is a waitress in New Mexico in 1891. She is very responsible and finds both love and friendship.

_____. *Promises in the Attic.* Doubleday, 1960. Ginger writes unrealistic romantic stories. She is trapped in her attic by a flood and re-thinks her career as a writer. All for the best.

Friis-Baastad, Babbis. *Don't Take Teddy.* Scribner, 1967. Teddy is 15 and severely retarded. He accidentally hurts another boy and his brother Mikkel is afraid that he will be put in an institution. He and Teddy run away as the only way to save Teddy.

_____. *Kristy's Courage.* Harcourt, 1965. Kristy is scarred in an automobile accident and is treated thoughtlessly in school. She looks for help and finds it in a hospital.

_____. *Wanted! A Horse.* Harcourt, 1971. Svein wants a "superhorse." First he must raise money for riding lessons, then learn to ride a docile mare instead of a spirited stallion. He meets Ella, Sigrid and Rollin.

Fritz, Jean. *Brady.* Coward, 1960. Brady is a real talker. But careless talk about slavery could be dangerous. Brady needs to make an important decision and it involves acting in secret.

_____. *Cabin Faced West.* Putnam, 1958. Ann is lonely and afraid to live in the western territory of Pennsylvania. She is encouraged and happy when George Washington comes to pay a visit.

_____. *Early Thunder.* Coward, 1967. A story of the division in Salem, Massachusetts, at the start of the Revolutionary War.

_____. *George Washington's Breakfast.* Coward, 1969. George Washington Allen is proud of his namesake and knows everything about him, except what he had for breakfast.

_____. *Homesick: My Own Story.* Putnam, 1982. A fictionalized biography of the childhood of Jean Fritz when she lived in China in 1920.

_____. *I, Adam.* Coward, 1963. Adam intends to farm after finishing school. He goes to the family farm and finds unexpected adventures involving a school teacher, a young boy and a farmer hunting gold.

Fritzhand, James. *Life Is a Lonely Place.* Evans, 1975. Tink is misunderstood by his family. He is a naturalist and likes nice things. He starts a friendship with Margie, who has a bad reputation, and David, who is rumored to be gay.

Froehlich, Margaret. *Hide Crawford Quick.* Houghton, 1983. Gracie and her three sisters are happy when their mother has a boy. But the baby has a problem (a deformity) that has to be kept a secret.

————. *Reasons to Stay.* Houghton, 1986. Babe's stepfather is an alcoholic so when her mother dies she tries to find her grandparents. When she does they cannot accept her. She and her brother and sister are taken in by an elderly couple.

Frost, Kelman. *Exiles in the Sahara.* Abelard, 1964. Hassoun, his friend Yusuf, and his goat and camel save a tribe in the bleakness of the desert.

————. *Men of the Mirage.* Lothrop, 1969. Set in the Sahara Desert, Tim and his friend are caught in a sand storm. They are captured by the "unseen One." They escape and destroy the tribe and the rum running caves.

Fry, Rosalie. *Echo's Song.* Dutton, 1962. A large family story set in Wales. They revive an abandoned nature industry.

————. *Fly Home, Columbina.* Dutton, 1960. Lucinda meets an Italian boy, Fran, and his homing pigeon, Columbia, who ends up carrying a wonderful message to Fran's crippled sister, Clare.

————. *Gypsy Princess.* Dutton, 1970. Zilda and Robert find a gypsy caravan. It was being stored until claimed. It was for "little princess" whose name was on it but no one knew who this was. Zilda and Robert solve the mystery.

————. *Matelot, Little Sailor of Brittany.* Dutton, 1958. Lucinda and Robin try to find a home for a sea-going kitten, Matelot, who is set on going to sea.

————. *Mountain Door.* Dutton, 1960. A fantasy about two girls called Fenella. One is a human child and the other a changeling. They each want to find their rightful place.

————. *Promise of the Rainbow.* Farrar, 1965. Children come together to restore an old abandoned church each with their own skills. They also save a horse from a cruel owner.

————. *Riddle of the Figurehead.* Dutton, 1963. Philippe, Peter, Robert and Stell build and launch a small boat and solve a mystery whose clues were concealed in the figurehead of a sunken boat.

————. *September Island.* Dutton, 1965. Martin explores a shipwreck situation on a sandbar where he and his sister and another friend spend a day and a night.

————. *Whistler in the Mist.* Farrar, 1968. Rosemary is treated coolly by Dilys and Ivor when she asks about the whistle she hears. She explores on her own and sees a wolf-like animal leading a flock of enchanted sheep.

Fukei, Arlene. *East to Freedom.* Westminster, 1964. Mei-lin, 16, is betrothed to Ling-wen. She wants one more year of school. As the war comes she faces crisis after crisis.

Fyson, Jenny. *Journey of the Eldest Son.* Coward, 1965. More exciting and unusual adventures of the three brothers. Shamashazer, the eldest, goes on a trading journey and is injured. He is rescued by shepherds.

————. *Three Brothers of Ur.* Coward, 1964. This story, set 4,000 years ago, tells of trouble and mischief that seem to follow the three sons of a wealthy man—especially Haran, the youngest, as he breaks a religious image.

Gaeddert, Louann. *Just Like Sisters.* Dutton, 1981. Carrie's cousin Kate is not like a sister. She is sullen and withdrawn because her parents are divorcing. Kate runs away but is reunited and goes to boarding school. Both learn about friendship.

————. *Kid in the Red Suspenders.* Dutton, 1983. Hamilton is taunted at school for being spoiled and sissified.

————. *Summer Like Turnips.* Holt, 1989. Bruce's grandfather is different since Gram died. He thinks about his own feelings when his dog, Goldie, dies. Gramps's recovery will be helped by a dog.

————. *Your Former Friend, Matthew.* Dutton, 1984. Matthew and Gail are friends but now Matthew is not interested in friendship.

Gage, Wilson. *Dan and the Miranda.* World, 1962. Dan chose spiders as his school project. It seemed doomed to failure as his spiders were killed off by other people.

————. *Ghost of Five Owl Farm.* World, 1966. Ted lives in a "haunted" house. His cousins have seen the ghost and then become involved in weird incidents. The ghost that Ted and his father plan turns into a "real" ghost.

————. *Mike's Toads.* World, 1970. Mike always offered someone else's help—his mother's, father's, brother's, etc. Then he was left to care for the neighbor's pet toads that his brother promised to do but couldn't.

————. *Miss Osborne-the-Mop.* World, 1963. Judy can turn people and things into other things and back again. She turns a mop into someone who looks like her fourth grade teacher.

————. *Secret of Fiery Gorge.* World, 1960. Margorie, her brother and cousin find a mystery while on vacation. They first suspect Martians, then uranium. What they find is of scientific value.

————. *Wild Goose.* World, 1961. Chuck is always having accidents. Chem, a wild goose, does too. Chuck goes fishing and Chem looks at an object on the shore. Trouble is in store.

Gaines, Ernest. *Gathering of Old Men.* Knopf, 1983. A white man is killed. Because they are trying to protect someone important to them, a white woman and several black men claim to have done the killing.

————. *Long Day in November.* Dial, 1971. Sonny hears his parents arguing. Then he and his mother go away. His father wants them back and gets the voodoo of Madame Toussaint to help.

Galbraith, Kathryn. *Come Spring.* Atheneum, 1979. Reenie's family moves a lot. She wants her own room, a dog, friends and nice clothes. She gets most of them in spite of a nagging mother, a shiftless father and quarreling siblings.

————. *Something Suspicious.* Atheneum, 1985. Lizzie and Ivy collect clues to find a bank robber. Could it be Lizzie's brother!

Galgut, Damon. *Sinless Season.* Ball, 1982. Four boys in a reform school go on a destructive rampage. A rather violent book but worth reading.

Gallico, Paul. *House That Wouldn't Go Away.* Delacorte, 1979. Miranda has a vision of the house that stood where her apartment is now. Each occupant has a sad-to-funny tale to tell about the event.

————. *Manx Mouse.* Coward, 1968. Adventure of a ceramic mouse that comes to life. He has rabbit ears, kangaroo paws and no tail. He is brave and fearless.

Gannett, Ruth. *My Father's Dragon.* Random, 1948. The very funny adventures of Elmer Elevator.

Garcia, Ann. *Spirit on the Wall.* Holiday, 1982. Em was saved from death at birth by her Cro Magnon grandmother. Her brother, an artist, helps her survive. But they must run away. A story of young, talented Stone Age people.

Gard, Joyce. *Talargain.* Holt, 1964. Talargain is an orphan raised by seafarers. She tells Lucilla how she now wanders the seas with the seals.

Gardam, Jane. *Hollow Land.* Greenwillow, 1981. Bell and Harry are friends. Hollow Land is where the rivers run underground. This is a story of a long and warm friendship.

————. *Through the Doll's House Door.* Greenwillow, 1987. A fantasy of the world where dolls live.

Garden, Nancy. *Annie on My Mind.* Farrar, 1982. Liza and Annie met at the Metropolitan Museum of Art while they were high school students. A lesbian relationship developed. It does not run smooth and they separate but get together again.

————. *Door Between.* Farrar, 1987. When plans are announced for a housing development in woods rumored to be supernatural, the village is attacked by seemingly supernatural dogs.

————. *Four Crossings.* Farrar, 1981. Jed and Melissa face a menacing old hermit, a golden colored dog, a missing silver plate and an ancient ritual.

————. *Loners.* Viking, 1972. Paul, troubled by his grandfather's death and his relationship with his father, older brother and girlfriend, Jenny, experiments with LSD at Jenny's urging.

————. *Mystery of the Midnight Menace.* Farrar, 1988. Pigeons, rats and cats have been found mangled in the park. The "Monster Hunters" investigate, especially the two new boys in town.

————. *Mystery of the Night Raiders.* Farrar, 1988. Brian, Darcy and Numbles are the "monster hunters" in this series of books about mysteries.

————. *Mystery of the Secret Marks.* Farrar, 1989. Darcy is in a private school where her roommate Ro is having strange events happen to her. Darcy, Brian and Numbles solve the mystery by using the code.

————. *Prisoners of Vampires.* Farrar, 1984. Alex has a school assignment to write a research paper using 50% primary sources. He meets a man who takes over his mind and body.

————. *Watermeet.* Farrar, 1983. The crazed old hermit, after kidnapping Jed and Melissa, helps to explain the connection between the dog and the plate. It is a combination of legend and witchcraft.

Gardiner, John. *General Butterfingers.* Houghton, 1986. Walter doesn't want to see three veterans of World War II evicted. So he plans and outwits the man who wants to do it.

————. *Stone Fox.* Crowell, 1980. The National Dogsled Races are on and Little Willy competes against Indian Stone Face.

————. *Top Secret.* Little, 1984. Allen is determined to do an experiment on human photosynthesis. His teacher and parents object but. . . .

Gardiner, Judy. *Come Back Soon.* Viking, 1985. Val's life is normal until her mother leaves because she feels "second best" in the family. Mrs. Forrest helps hold the family together until mother returns.

Gardner, Dic. *Danny and the Great Ape Komba.* Day, 1962. Danny works in a zoo for the summer. It is great until he encounters the big ape, Komba.

Gardner, John. *Icebreaker.* Putnam, 1983. A James Bond thriller. 007 must stop a Nazi organization. He is in constant danger because he gets an electric shock whenever he touches anything.

————. *License Renewed.* Marek, 1981. 007 must find and stop Franco, a terrorist, who is a master of disguise and deception. Franco teams up with evil Dr. Murik to blow up the world.

Gardner, Leonard. *Fat City.* Farrar, 1969. A strong story of two men who are boxers. One is just beginning and the other is living on memories of the past.

Garfield, Brian. *Paladin.* Bantam, 1986. Christopher was asked to be a spy for England by Winston Churchill. He was to go to a castle in Belgium and gather any information he could. But the Germans took over the castle!

Garfield, James. *Follow My Leader.* Viking, 1957. An 11-year-old boy gets back into the swing of life with the help of friends and a loving guide dog.

Garfield, Leon. *Confidence Man.* Viking, 1978. Hans and Geneva, German refugees, struggle for survival after Van Stumpfel abandons them.

_____. *December Rose.* Viking, 1986. Barnacle stumbles onto espionage and murder. He has a few clues. Inspector Creaker is on his trail because the clues are vital.

_____. *Devil-in-the-Fog.* Pantheon, 1966. Mr. Treet came twice a year with his strolling players. This year a stranger comes with money and George is caught up in a family feud that nearly takes his life.

_____. *Empty Sleeve.* Delacorte, 1988. Peter is apprenticed to a locksmith and is glad to leave his twin brother Paul. But when he sees ghosts....

_____. *Footsteps.* Delacorte, 1980. William's dying father tells him that he once robbed a business partner. William looks for the family to make peace. Their son is set on ruining William until William rescues him from death.

_____. *Ghost Downstairs.* Pantheon, 1972. A greedy clerk sells seven years off the end of his life but he thinks he has fooled the buyer by selling the first seven years not the last.

_____. *Jack Holbrook.* Pantheon, 1965. Jack is a runaway apprentice cobbler and stows away on a ship which pirates overtake. He is made the ship's cook.

_____. *Mister Corbett's Ghost.* Pantheon, 1968. Mister Corbett captured Benjamin's spirit and he cursed him. A cruel, hateful story with pathos.

_____. *Night of the Comet.* Delacorte, 1979. Harris offers Bostock the affection of his sister in exchange for a valuable brass telescope through which he can observe a Pigott's comet. Another comedy of errors.

_____. *Smith.* Pantheon, 1967. Smith has a stolen document men have murdered for.

_____. *Sound of Coaches.* Viking, 1974. Sam was raised by friends after his mother died in childbirth. He later meets an actor who teaches him the profession. It turns out that the man is his father.

_____. *Strange Affair of Adelaide Harris.* Pantheon, 1971. Harris and Bostock decide to recreate an ancient incident by kidnapping Harris's sister and leaving her to survive alone. But it all turns out to be a comedy of errors.

_____. *Young Nick and Jubilee.* Delacorte, 1989. Nick and Jubilee are orphans and claim Mr. Owen (a thief) as their father. A friendship grows between them even though they started out using each other.

Garlan, Patricia. *Boy Who Played Tiger.* Viking, 1968. Ko Shway was bored and so got into trouble. He became a hero when he saved a Burma village from a tiger attack.

_____. *Orange-Robed Boy.* Viking, 1967. Aung Kain, 12, has to decide whether to become a monk or stay in his Burma village.

Garner, Alan. *Aimer Gate.* Collins, 1979. Joseph's son Robert is the main character in this three-generation family story. He wants to be a soldier like his Uncle Charlie but learns that fighting is dangerous and stark.

_____. *Elidor.* Collins, 1979. Roland, Helen and Nicholas go to Elidor, another dimension. The King of Elidor told them of the dark prophecies and they become involved.

_____. *Granny Reardon.* Collins, 1977. Joseph was raised by his grandparents. He wanted to plan his future differently from what was expected of him: that he be a stonemason like his grandfather.

_____. *Moon of Gomrath.* Walck, 1967. Wizard Cadellin sees Old Magic danger coming. Colin and Susan accidentally release the figures of the Wild Hunt and add to the strength of Old Magic.

_____. *Owl Service.* Walck, 1968. Alison and Roger find a set of dishes with a strange pattern of owls. This sets off a series of events that appear to be the reliving of an old legend.

_____. *Stone Book.* Collins, 1976. Mary wants to learn to read. Her father takes her to a cave that is visited once each generation. It gives Mary a feeling of the continuity of the family.

_____. *Tom Fobble's Day.* Collins, 1979. William, Joseph's grandson, is the fourth generation which began with Joseph's grandfather, the stonemason.

_____. *Weirdstone of Brisingamen.* Walck, 1969. Colin, Susan, the Wizard Cadellin and others seek to keep Firefrost from evil. They are pursued by nightmarish creatures through tight tunnels, underground cliffs and chasms.

Garnett, Eve. *Family from One End Street.* Vanguard, 1939/60. A new edition about a large, cheerful, lower class English family.

_____. *Further Adventures of the Family from One End Street.* Vanguard, 1956. The Ruggles and their seven children face obstacles, argue among themselves, and are sometimes selfish and nasty but always warm and funny.

Garnett, Henry. *Red Bonnet.* Doubleday, 1964. An aristocrat's father is murdered in French Guiana and he escapes to France where his sister plans to help Marie Antoinette escape from prison during the French Revolution.

Garnett, Richard. *White Dragon.* Vanguard, 1963. Mark tries to unravel the mystery of the White Worme, which can be seen as the White Dragon at dusk at certain times of the year.

Garrigue, Sheila. *All the Children Were Sent Away.* Bradbury, 1976. Sara was being sent away from London during World War II. She made friends with other girl evacuees. Then her ship was torpedoed by the Germans.

_____. *Between Friends.* Bradbury, 1978.

Jill moves during the summer and makes friends with Dede, a retarded girl. When school starts she makes other friends who tease Dede. Dede later moves away but Jill and others have learned a lesson.

————. *Eternal Spring to Mr. Ito.* Bradbury, 1985. Sara senses the unfairness of the Japanese internment during World War II when her good friend, Mr. Ito, the gardener, is sent to camp. He prefers death to camp but tells Sara about war and its faults.

Garthwaite, Marion. *Holdup on Bootjack Hill.* Doubleday, 1962. Callie and Andy try to clear their Indian friends of a stage robbery.

————. *Mario.* Doubleday, 1960. Mario, 11, is thought to be a "wetback" and picks cotton before he is found to be a victim of circumstances.

Gates, Doris. *Blue Willow.* Viking, 1940. Janey wants to stay in one place but her family are migrant workers. She finally gets her wish and she unwraps the blue willow plate and places it on the mantle.

————. *Cat and Mrs. Cary.* Viking, 1962. Mrs. Cary is befriended by a talking cat. The cat helps her solve a mystery.

————. *Elderberry Bush.* Viking, 1967. Julie, Elizabeth and Clara have good times in the 1900's going to the seashore and going for a runaway buggy ride. There are also an attempted murder and a funny Santa Claus.

————. *Fair Wind to Troy.* Viking, 1976. A telling of the start of the Trojan War and Helen's role in it. She chooses Menelaus for her husband but a Trojan prince, Paris, steals her away.

————. *Filly for Melinda.* Viking, 1984. Melinda raises and trains her filly, Missy. But she is forced to sell her because the family needs money. She is saved in the end by another horse sale and an understanding couple.

————. *Morgan for Melinda.* Viking, 1979. Melinda is afraid of horses but with the help of her father and Missy she overcomes her fear and rides, wins shows and loves horses.

————. *Sensible Kate.* Viking, 1943. Kate must leave a good foster home and make many adjustments to her new one.

Gathje, Curtis. *Disco Kid.* Watts, 1979. James likes disco music and girls. He invites two girls to the same party and it backfires.

Gathorne-Hardy, Jonathan. *Airship Ladyship Adventure.* Lippincott, 1977. Jane and Mrs. Deal are aboard an airship named Ladyship. It crash-lands in the Alps; they are aided and then stranded in Africa.

————. *Operation Peeg.* Lippincott, 1974. Jane, Jemina and Mrs. Deal are at boarding school when a rocket sets their island on an adventure with a criminal submarine, two Army men and a WWII secret operation. A real fantasy.

Gauch, Patricia. *Dragons on the Road.* Putnam, 1981. Jerry is the team leader of bicyclists going from Lockwood Academy to Washington,

D.C. It is a 200-mile trip and they are threatened by a gang of motorcycle riders.

————. *Green of Me.* Putnam, 1978. Jenny daydreams about her youth as she is on her way to meet an old high school flame.

————. *Kate Alone.* Putnam, 1980. Kate's dog is really vicious and she is faced with what to do about it.

————. *Night Talks.* Putnam, 1983. Three girls, all from different backgrounds, go camping together. They talk and try to become friends in spite of differences.

————. *This Time, Tempe Wick?* Coward, 1974. Tempe was an unusual girl, both big and strong. She owned a horse named Bonny. A soldier of the Revolutionary War wanted to take her horse and run away but she was not about to let this happen.

————. *Year the Summer Died.* Putnam, 1985. Erin and Laurie have been friends for years and years. Then Laurie falls in love with someone else and Erin is left out.

Gault, William. *Big Stick.* Dutton, 1975. Rusty played hockey in high school and college. He is now a pro with the National Hockey League.

————. *Checkered Flag.* Dutton, 1964. Three boys, during the Depression, team up and get their own racing car and finally win a race with it. They also succeed in a business deal.

————. *Karters.* Dutton, 1965. Edward and Tom are building a kart. They lose several races but finally win their first one.

————. *Little Big Foot.* Dutton, 1963. Little Big Foot is a small statured football kicker on a college team.

————. *Long Green.* Dutton, 1965. Donald plays golf in high school and college. He turns pro. A story of the play-by-play description of golf tournaments, the needed financial backing and the problems connected with pro sports.

————. *Oval Playground.* Dutton, 1968. Mark loves cars. Al, a friend of his father, owns a garage and he and Mark plan racing on a dirt track. Mark races and loses. Al tries racing and finally, after Tyler beats Mark again, he wins.

————. *Showboat in the Back Court.* Dutton, 1976. This story follows the careers of two basketball players from their high school days to the professional ranks.

————. *Stubborn Sam.* Dutton, 1969. Sam plays baseball. He dreams of the World Series. He is a good catcher and hitter until he gets hit by a ball. He goes into a slump and is not sure he can make a comeback.

————. *Sunday Cycles.* Dodd, 1979. Two boys run a gas station and are left a cycle as payment. They fix it up and ride on Sundays. They go on to try a dirt track, desert runs and moto-cross.

————. *Super Bowl Bound.* Dodd, 1980. Tom plays football and is drafted into the NFL. He guides his team to victory in pouring rain. His father refuses to recognize his success but his grandfather urges him on.

————. *Thin Ice.* Dutton, 1978. Rusty and Sven play together as a team after Sven's skills increase and his use of violence decreases. Lots of hockey action.

————. *Trouble at Second.* Dutton, 1973. Joe was a new player and a Chicano. He was very defensive and not easy to get along with. Mark was the team captain and shortstop; he was determined to pull the team together and win.

Gaunt, Michael. *Brim Sails Out.* Coward, 1967. Brim is a terrier who sails on a barge and helps other animals. He, himself, built the boat with some help and some hindrance from others. One day he and Twill, a sheepdog, are caught in a storm.

————. *Brim's Boat.* Coward, 1966. Brim, a terrier, and his friend, Twill, a sheepdog, find an old barge that they rebuild. Brim is now captain of a boat.

Gay, Kathlyn. *Girl Pilot.* Messner, 1966. Ellen is a commercial pilot and faces obstacles because of her sex. She flies a plane to France with her love, an FCC inspector.

Gedge, Pauline. *Child of the Morning.* Dial, 1977. Hatshepsut is heir to the Egyptian throne when her older sister dies. She is ancient Egypt's only female leader winning loyalty and peace until she dies.

Gee, Maurice. *Motherstone.* Merrimack, 1986. Susan and Nicholas are trying to return to Earth after saving the world of O for the second time.

————. *Under the Mountain.* Oxford, 1979. Rachel and Theo have two milk-white stones and ESP. They are threatened by a giant worm and a smaller slug.

Gee, Maurine. *Chicano, Amigo.* Morrow, 1972. Kiki wants to be a cub scout. He latches on to Marc and although they are friends Kiki gets everyone in trouble of some kind.

————. *Firestorm.* Morrow, 1968. Merv and his dog, Abdul, are new in the neighborhood and Ken is staying away from him. But when a fire starts and Abdul is missing, Ken helps look for him in spite of the danger.

Geer, Charles. *Dexter and the Deer Lake Mystery.* Norton, 1965. Dexter is on vacation at Deer Lake. His neighbor is a girl. But they get together to solve a series of threats.

Geibel, James. *Blond Brother.* Putnam, 1979. Rich is a basketball star who changes schools. He is the only white on an all-black team. He gets along with the blacks but the white students resent him and beat him so he can't play.

Geller, Mark. *My Life in the Seventh Grade.* Harper, 1986. Marvin keeps a diary of everyday events of the seventh grade: baseball, fickle friends, shyness, algebra, etc.

————. *Raymond.* Harper, 1988. Raymond runs away to live with a married sister because of abuse by an alcoholic stepfather.

————. *What I Heard.* Harper, 1987. Michael hears his father talking to his mistress, Celeste. He decides to confront her but his father answers the phone. His father ends the affair and his mother never knows.

Gelman, Steve. *Baseball Bonus Kid.* Doubleday, 1961. A story of the problems of players signed to major league clubs for big sums of money.

George, Jean. *Coyote in Manhattan.* Crowell, 1968. Tenny wanted to be part of the Street Family but was not voted in. Then she found a coyote in a cage on her father's ship. He had wild eyes and she set him loose. She thought she was brave but....

————. *Cry of the Crow.* Harper, 1980. Mandy knows her father would kill her pet crow, Nina. She tries to train and protect her. Her father and brothers don't like crows so she keeps them from seeing her.

————. *Gull Number 737.* Crowell, 1964. Luke doesn't think much of his father's work on the living habits of gulls. But then his father goes on to something else and Luke does this same basic research.

————. *Hold Zero.* Crowell, 1966. Four boys build a booster rocket with remote control. They want to launch it but the police are concerned about safety. They get it cleared up and launch their rocket.

————. *Hook a Fish, Catch a Mountain.* Dutton, 1975. Spinner, a city girl, and Al go backpacking and run into a bear. Al breaks his leg and must be rescued by a novice.

————. *Julie of the Wolves.* Harper, 1972. Julie, an Eskimo, tries to find her deserted father. She gets lost and learns survival skills from the wolves. Her father has accepted modern ways but she still clings to the traditional. Newbery, 1973.

————. *My Side of the Mountain.* Dutton, 1959. A young boy builds a tree house from which he can watch the animals. He learns a great deal about courage and independence.

————. *On the Far Side of the Mountain.* Dutton, 1990. Sam's peaceful home in the woods is changed when his sister runs away and his pet falcon is taken by conservation officers.

————. *River Rats.* Dutton, 1979. A survival story of people on a run down the Colorado River.

————. *Shark Beneath the Reef.* Harper, 1989. Tomas, 14, is torn between continuing to go to school, or going into his family's fishing trade. He goes after a shark he thinks is gentle but it is a man-eater.

————. *Summer of the Falcon.* Crowell, 1962. June is training a sparrow hawk. She also learns about falconry and the whole world of nature and how it is tamed.

————. *Talking Earth.* Harper, 1983. Billie Wind goes into the Everglades to live alone as punishment for her lack of belief in Indian lore. It is a lonely adventure.

———. *Water Sky.* Harper, 1987. Lincoln is in Alaska looking for Uncle Jack and facing cultural and environmental differences. He faces the downfall of the whaling trade because of technology and his growing love for an Eskimo girl.

———. *Who Really Killed Cock Robin?* Dutton, 1971. Cock Robin lived in environmentally safe Saddleboro. One day he is found dead. Tony and Mary Alice start an investigation.

Geras, Adele. *Apricots at Midnight and Other Stories from a Patchwork Quilt.* Macmillan, 1982. Aunt Penny has an exciting story to tell about every patch in her patchwork quilt.

———. *Voyage.* Atheneum, 1983. Minna, Golda and Rachel are all aboard the SS *Danzig* headed for America in 1904. Minna is the strength for her mother and brother. Golda is going to see her husband and Rachel fears the future.

Gerber, Merrill. *Also Known as Sadzia, the Belly Dancer!* Harper, 1987. Sandy tries exercise to lose weight before the prom. She joins a belly dancing class. She goes to the prom as a belly dancer not a guest.

———. *I'd Rather Think About Robby.* Harper, 1989. Marilyn's club, The Four Roses, wants to have a boy-girl party. Marilyn likes Robby but thinks he's too wild. She meets Holly and gets to like her and they share concerns.

———. *Name a Star for Me.* Viking, 1983. Evyln spends the summer in Kentucky with her artist mother. She meets Chet, shy and awkward, and his amorous brother, Red.

———. *Please Don't Kiss Me Now.* Dial, 1981. Leslie's parents are divorced. She is asked out by a popular boy. As things get out of hand at home she turns to Brian for help.

Gerson, Corinne. *How I Put My Mother Through College.* Atheneum, 1981. Jessica and Ben find that while they understand why mother is going back to school, it still makes life very different (and difficult).

———. *My Grandfather the Spy.* Walker, 1990. An old man's mysterious past is revealed after Mark and his friends nominate him "Grandfather of the Year."

———. *Oh, Brother!* Atheneum, 1982. Danny is "adopted" by four Chicano teenagers. They inspire him to become a Renaissance Man.

———. *Passing Through.* Dial, 1978. Liz's brother committed suicide. She meets and likes Sam, a cerebral palsy victim. Liz's parents discovered the secret that caused the suicide in a letter from him to Liz.

———. *Son for a Day.* Atheneum, 1980. Danny goes to the zoo often because he can easily be "adopted" by families there.

———. *Tread Softly.* Dial, 1979. An orphan girl can't look at her life realistically because of her fantasy about the perfect family.

Gessner, Lynne. *Brother to the Navajo.* Nelson, 1979. The Corbetts get lost in the desert and

take refuge at a trading post. They learn about Indians and their ways.

———. *Edge of Darkness.* Walker, 1979. Davids, 13, lives in Latvia during World War II. He thinks he has betrayed his father but it is his godfather who did it.

———. *Navajo Slave.* Harvey, 1976. Straight Arrow is caught and held as a slave for five years. He wants to escape and return to his Indian family who believes him to be dead.

———. *To See a Witch.* Nelson, 1978. Kopi, a young Indian, tells a lie and must work to make amends.

Getz, David. *Thin Air.* Holt, 1990. Jacob has asthma and fights against it because he resents his brother's overprotectiveness. He wants to find his own friends and his own place in the world.

Gibbons, Faye. *King Shoes and Clown Pockets.* Morrow, 1989. Ray and Bruce become friends and Ray learns that outward appearance is not a basis for judging people. He and Floppy, the dog, come to terms with their own problems.

———. *Mighty Close to Heaven.* Morrow, 1985. Dave's mother died and he lives with his grandparents. He wants to find his father but comes to realize that love is with his grandparents.

Gibbs, Alonzo. *Fields Breathe Sweet.* Lothrop, 1963. Gretje's family struggles for a living on a farm in 1600. She wants to marry and build a home of her own.

———. *Least Likely One.* Lothrop, 1964. Harry leaves his father's pet shop and goes hunting. He meets an old trapper and his courage is tested.

———. *One More Day.* Bobbs, 1971. Cap and Flip are taking the *E.J. Norton* on its last trip. Cap was a crew member when it was new and Flip played on it as a child. The ship is cast adrift in a winter storm.

Giff, Patricia. *Fourth Grade Celebrity.* Delacorte, 1979. Cassandra (Casey) tries to find ways to become a well known girl in school. She runs for class president. Walt will help if she takes Tracy (the pen pal) off his hands.

———. *Gift of the Pirate Queen.* Delacorte, 1982. Grace needs strength to accept her mother's death and her responsibility to her diabetic sister. A cousin, Fiona, tells of another Grace who was an heroic pirate queen.

———. *Girl Who Knew It All.* Delacorte, 1979. Tracy, whose reading ability is below grade level, tries to hide this fact by strange behavior. How surprising when her pen pal, Casey, comes to visit her.

———. *Have You Seen Hyacinth Macaw?* Delacorte, 1981. Abby and Potsie are practicing sleuths. When Abby's brother acts unusually strange they stumble upon a theft and a missing person.

———. *Left-Handed Shortstop.* Delacorte, 1980. Walter is not an athlete; he doesn't want to play ball. Casey makes him a phony cast so he can't play and reveal the truth about his playing ability.

————. *Loretta P. Sweeny, Where Are You?* Delacorte, 1983. Abby is at it again. This time a murder is involved and when Abby sees the purple and orange wallet she "knows" it belongs to the murderer. Super, the dog, and a fortune teller are involved.

————. *Love, from the Fifth Grade Celebrity.* Delacorte, 1986. The friendship that started between Tracy and Casey during the summer is running into trouble because of Tracy's popularity when school begins.

————. *Poopsie Pomerantz, Pick Up Your Feet.* Delacorte, 1989. Poopsie plans to lose weight; enough to get into a size medium swimsuit. She also has her eye on becoming a ballet dancer.

————. *Rat Teeth.* Delacorte, 1984. Radcliffe has two problems to contend with: 1. his parents' divorce; 2. going to a new school.

————. *Tootsie Tanner, Why Don't You Talk?* Delacorte, 1987. Abby Jones sees her neighbor as a suspect in a runaway, and possibly, in a spy case. She jumps to wrong conclusions and misses the right clues. She is looking for a stolen roll of film.

————. *Winter Worm Business.* Delacorte, 1983. Leroy predicts trouble and frustration when his cousin Mitchell moves into the neighborhood. Especially when he tries to cut in on Leroy and Tracy's worm business.

Gilbert, Harriett. *Running Away.* Harper, 1979. Jane is in boarding school. She and Audrey spend a weekend in London. Jane's life is upsetting and is made more so when she accidentally hits a kitten while driving a car illegally.

Gilbert, Nan. *Academy Summer.* Harper, 1961. Leslie studies at a top music academy during the summer. Hard work, setbacks and a win at the first recital help her decide what she wants to do.

————. *Champions Don't Cry.* Harper, 1960. Sally plays tennis but her temper is hurting her playing. He brother also plays and tries to help her, even though they often fight.

————. *Dog for Joey.* Harper, 1968. Kink doesn't like his new school, his grades go down and he steals. He gets a puppy to train as a guide dog and life improves.

————. *Unchosen.* Harper, 1963. Ellen, Kay and Debbie are friends but each feels unpopular (unchosen, no dates, no parties, etc.). They discover how to attain popularity, by giving of themselves.

Gilden, Mel. *Harry Newberry and the Raiders of the Red Drink.* Holt, 1989. Harry thinks his mother is superhero Tautara. His mother is kidnapped by Bonnie who is looking for the Red Drink. Absurd.

————. *Return of Captain Conquer.* Houghton, 1986. Watson's father is a fan of Captain Conquer. One day his father is missing. A funny sci-fi story.

Gillham, Bill. *Home Before Long.* Deutsch, 1984. Many children were evacuated from London during the bombings of World War II. While the air raids were frequent it was felt that the children would be safer in the country.

————. *My Brother Barry.* Deutsch, 1982. The special thing about "my brother Barry" is that he is mentally handicapped.

————. *Rich Kid.* Deutsch, 1985. Two boys are kidnapped. Jo is poor and the son of a mechanic and Christo is rich, the son of a millionaire. The kidnapper lets Jo go and he then helps rescue Christo.

Gilman, Dorothy. *Clairvoyant Countess.* Doubleday, 1975. Madame Karitska has psychic powers and uses them to help police solve serious crimes.

————. *Maze in the Heart of the Castle.* Doubleday, 1983. Colin, 16, lost his parents. His quest for the mysterious land of Galt brings him endless danger. He goes through the maze in Rheembeck Castle.

Gilson, Jamie. *Dial Leroy Rupert.* Lothrop, 1979. Mitch's imitation of a local disc jockey gets him into trouble.

————. *Do Bananas Chew Gum?* Lothrop, 1980. Sam has a serious problem. He has not yet learned to read. And he's in the sixth grade!

————. *Double Dog Dare.* Lothrop, 1988. Because he wants to be "someone" Hobie feels he must make a name for himself. Nick is at Computer Camp, Molly is talented and Lisa is popular. But what is Harvey? Could he outwit Molly?

————. *Four B Goes Wild.* Lothrop, 1983. The class is at Camp Trotter and faces a lot of new experiences. How does one handle a skunk who is sharp and determined? How do you face a midnight meeting in a cemetery?

————. *Harvey, the Beer Can King.* Lothrop, 1978. Harvey is a collector, he is going to have the largest collection of beer cans in town. He knows he will win the contest but he doesn't count on some misadventurous trading.

————. *Hello, My Name Is Scrambled Eggs.* Lothrop, 1984. Harvey, the school's best known student (for a number of different reasons) meets Tuan from Vietnam. His job? Make an American out of him!

————. *Hobie Hanson, You're Weird.* Lothrop, 1987. Hobie Hanson is looking forward to the summer. Instead of going away he is going to stay at home. He teams up with his school mate Molly Bosco and has a hilarious time.

————. *Thirteen Ways to Sink a Sub.* Lothrop, 1982. Hobie and his friends think of a contest that will make the substitute teacher cry. Girls team up against boys to see who can make her leave. They try everything imaginable.

Ginsburg, Mirra. *Diary of Nina Kosterina.* Crown, 1968. A young Russian girl writes about 1936–1941 when the Germans invade Russia.

Gioffre, Marisa. *Starstruck.* Scholastic, 1985.

Alicia wants to be a professional singer. Her mother wants her to be an accountant in a local business.

Gipson, Fred. *Curly and the Wild Boar.* Harper, 1979. An adventure story about how Curly's encounter with a wild boar turns out.

_____. *Little Arliss.* Harper, 1978. By looking for a runaway horse, Arliss hopes to prove his worthiness. Travis is grown and married. Arliss is 12 and has a troubling temper.

_____. *Old Yeller.* Harper, 1956/1990. Travis loved his yellow-colored dog and tried to tame and then train him as a hunting dog. Old Yeller made him proud.

_____. *Savage Sam.* Harper, 1962. Savage Sam is the son of Old Yeller. He helps Travis rescue Arliss from the Indians.

Girion, Barbara. *Handful of Stars.* Scribner, 1981. Julie begins to have blackout periods. She has epilepsy and her world shatters. A story of how she learns to cope.

_____. *In the Middle of a Rainbow.* Macmillan, 1983. Corrie is a good student and wants to go to college. Her mother encourages her. Then she meets rich, good-looking Todd and she falls in love. But what of college? Mother's plans? Todd's love?

_____. *Indian Summer.* Scholastic, 1990. Jane is spending her summer on an Indian reservation and can't get along with Sarah Birdsong. She and the others seem to hold Jane responsible for the prejudices they feel on the outside.

_____. *Joshua, the Czar and the Chicken-Bone Wish.* Scribner, 1978. Joshua is an awkward, clumsy boy. He meets the "Czar" in a nursing home and learns how he lost a chance at being Czar because of a wishbone. So Joshua and the Czar collect wishbones!

_____. *Like Everybody Else.* Scribner, 1980. Sam's family is different. Her mother writes children's books, but has written a sexy novel which embarrasses Sam and her father.

_____. *Misty and Me.* Scribner, 1979. Kim wants a dog and secretly buys one with her babysitting money. She has problems with boys, clothes, disco dances. But her parents find out about the dog and she gives him to a worthy friend.

_____. *Tangle of Roots.* Scribner, 1979. Beth spends more time with her father and grandfather after her mother dies. Her boyfriend is annoyed because she doesn't have as much time for him.

Girvan, Helen. *Missing Masterpiece.* Westminster, 1965. Nan is on vacation and gets involved in a mystery of a missing painting by Goya. Summer theatre actors help as do a dog and Nan's talent for sketching.

Gladd, Arthur. *Saracen Steed.* Dodd, 1968. Hugh helped catch a runaway Saracen horse in 8th century France. Hugh and the horse face enemies together.

Glaser, Dianne. *Amber Wellington, Daredevil.* Walker, 1975. Amber is the only girl in a mysterious and dangerous club: The Daredevils. When Old Larnie dies his money is missing! Should the Daredevils be concerned?

_____. *Amber Wellington, Witch Watcher.* Walker, 1976. At midnight, Amber stands outside an old house and the Jewel Sisters adventure begins. Are they witches?

_____. *Case of the Missing Six.* Holiday, 1978. Damon and his friends discover a rash of petnappings. They look at all suspects especially the Lemon twins but find only false accusations.

_____. *Diary of Trilby Frost.* Holiday, 1976. A teenaged girl faces the death of her father, her brother and her best friend.

_____. *Summer Secret.* Holiday, 1977. Worthy spends the summer in Alabama. She acquires a horse and a boy friend. She also solves a family feud.

Glaser, Paul. *Squad Room Detective.* Dodd, 1960. A career type story about police work and crime detection.

Glasser, Barbara. *Bongo Bradley.* Hawthorn, 1973. Bradley wants to be a jazz musician like his father. He finds an old drummer who was his father's leader when he visits North Carolina.

Gleeson, Libby. *I Am Susannah.* Holiday, 1989. Susannah's best friend moves away. The Blue Lady helps Susie cope with the loss and also helps her cope with parties and kissing.

Glenn, Mel. *One Order to Go.* Clarion, 1984. Richie wants a writing career, but he must work in his father's luncheonette. Lana changes his life and he confronts his father and lays plans for the future.

_____. *Play-by-Play.* Clarion, 1986. Jeremy plays soccer and this is a detailed story of its intricacies.

_____. *Squeeze Play: A Baseball Story.* Clarion, 1989. Jeremy and his friends must practice baseball discipline for their new teacher in order to play a rival school. They win the game when Josie comes in as relief pitcher.

Gloss, Molly. *Outside the Gates.* Macmillan, 1986. Vren and Rusche are banished outside the High Gates, Vren because he can communicate with animals and Rusche because he can control the weather.

Goble, Paul. *Beyond the Ridge.* Bradbury, 1989. As an old Indian woman dies, a story of the history of the Plains Indians is revealed.

_____. *Buffalo Woman.* Bradbury, 1984. A tale of a buffalo that turns into a beautiful woman.

_____. *Lone Bull's Horse Race.* Bradbury, 1973. Lone Bull needs to prove to his people that he is a warrior. He proves it in his first battle.

Godden, Rumer. *Dark Horse.* Morrow, 1981. Abby finds that the new horse at High Hickory could be a great jumper.

_____. *Diddakoi.* Viking, 1972. Kizzy is a

gypsy and is taunted by her schoolmates. She is befriended by Admiral Twiss and Miss Brooke. She has to learn to accept kindness which is difficult after the earlier cruelties.

————. *Dragon of Og.* Viking, 1981. Ordinarily peaceful, the Dragon of Og is aroused by the new lord of the castle.

————. *Home Is the Sailor.* Viking, 1964. Bertrand, 16, helps Curly (a boy doll) to reunite a long lost sailor doll with a girl's doll family.

————. *Little Plum.* Viking, 1963. Nona and Belinda fight with Gem because she mistreats her Japanese doll, Miss Plum.

————. *Miss Happiness and Miss Flower.* Viking, 1961. Miss Happiness and Miss Flower want a Japanese home to live in, not an English one.

————. *Mousewife.* Viking, 1982. A light fantasy about a very devoted mousewife.

————. *Operation Sippacik.* Viking, 1969. Rifat found a newborn donkey and trained her. The British wanted to buy her but she wouldn't work for them so Rifat came to help. They found a wounded man and the donkey, Sippacik, was a hero.

————. *Rocking Horse Secret.* Viking, 1977. Tibby finds a will hidden in a rocking horse and its discovery helps solve many problems.

Godwin, Gail. *Finishing School.* Viking, 1985. Justin tells about when she was 14 and befriended by a woman a bit older than Justin is now (40). A tragic friendship and a tragic ending.

Goffstein, M.B. *Daisy Summerfield's Style.* Delacorte, 1975. Daisy switches luggage with a girl she thinks is "her image." It changes her from a fashion designer to an artist.

————. *Underside of the Leaf.* Farrar, 1972. Paula, when she was 12, had a crush on an older boy, Tom, and still daydreams about him now that she is in college.

Gold, Sharlya. *Amelia Quackenbush.* Seabury, 1973. Amelia imagines she has every flaw possible as she gets ready to enter junior high. She wants to be popular and so joins in stealing, harboring stolen goods and lying. She finally straightens out.

————. *Time to Take Sides.* Seabury, 1976. Jeff is an eighth grader and becomes involved in the teachers' strike at school and discovers the issues are many sided.

Goldberger, Judith. *Looking Glass Factor.* Dutton, 1979. Humans and laboratory "cats" were left on Earth in the year 2728. They were working on physically merging with inanimate objects.

Golding, William. *Lord of the Flies.* Putnam, 1954. Some English boys are marooned on an island and as they try to set up rules for living together it turns tragic.

Goldman, Katie. *In the Wings.* Dial, 1982. Jessie tries out for the school play; her parents are getting a divorce; she has a fight with her best friend; her grades are slipping. She explodes to her drama coach who helps her sort out things.

Goldman, Kelly. *Sherlick Hound and the Valentine Mystery.* Whitman, 1989. Sherlick, the Dog-Honest Detective, figures out how to find who stole a ruby studded collar.

Goldman, William. *Magic.* Delacorte, 1976. Corky made a deal with the devil so he could be a magician; he then tries to escape his bargain. A confused battle ensues but is all clear at the end.

Goldsmith, Howard. *Invasion: 2200 A.D.* Doubleday, 1979. Earth is invaded by "tuks," rat-like creatures who use mind control. Ray and Paul team up to save the Earth.

Gondosch, Linda. *Who Needs a Bratty Brother?* Dutton, 1985. Kelly thinks her brother Ben is more than a pest. She tries to get rid of him by giving him to a neighbor, sending him to camp, enrolling him in a private school. When he runs away she is upset.

————. *Who's Afraid of Haggerty House?* Dutton, 1987. Kelly has a fight with her two best friends, Jennifer and Adelaide. She meets Mrs. Haggerty, a strange old woman, and spends time in her old house. But she misses her friends and wants to make up.

————. *Witches of Hopper Street.* Dutton, 1986. Kelly, Jennifer and Adelaide form a witch club and try to cast spells and fly on brooms. But there is a threat from someone else. In the end they find that Rae Jean is not so bad after all.

Gonzalez, Gloria. *Gaucho.* Knopf, 1977. Gaucho, 12, lives on welfare in New York City with his mother. He wants to go back to Puerto Rico and tries to raise money to do so.

————. *Gladman.* Knopf, 1975. Mellissa befriends an old man and his dog who live in an abandoned bus in a junk yard. In trying to help she almost hurts him.

Gooding, Kathleen. *Festival Summer.* Faber, 1984. Emily is left behind with her grandparents for the summer. But she finds a mystery at the deserted Maltby Hall.

Goodwin, Harold. *Magic Number.* Bradbury, 1969. The ENIGMA wage war on the CRUMBS until they learn that peace is better than fighting.

Gordon, Ethel. *Where Does the Summer Go?* Crowell, 1967. Freddy finds that the summer is not what she expected now that David, the boy she likes, has spent a year at college.

Gordon, John. *House on the Brink.* Harper, 1971. Dick and Helen investigate the marsh that is rumored to have a treasure hidden in it.

Gordon, Sherba. *Waiting for the Rain.* Watts, 1987. Tengo, a black South African, wants to read and learns to dislike apartheid. Frikkie, white, does not understand Tengo's attitude. Friends turn to enemies over the issue.

Gordon, Shirley. *Me and the Bad Guys.* Harper, 1980. Mike knows he has a problem with tension but it isn't until he screams down the school hallway that professional help is sought.

Gorey, Edward. *Hapless Child.* Dodd, 1980. Charlotte's father is missing and her mother dies.

She is sent to boarding school but runs away. She is kidnapped and sold to an insane man. She is finally found by her father who doesn't know her.

Gorman, Carol. *Chelsey and the Green-Haired Kid.* Houghton, 1987. Chelsey, 13, witnesses a murder. She and Jack, the green haired punker, convince the police of it and solve the mystery.

Gormley, Beatrice. *Best Friend Insurance.* Dutton, 1983. Maureen's best friend Tracey found a new friend, Gwen. Maureen takes out "Best Friend Insurance" and finds her new friend is really her mother turned into a girl!

_____. *Fifth Grade Magic.* Dutton, 1982. Gretchen does not get the lead in a school play. Amy does. Then Amy and Gretchen change places (like Freaky Friday) with the help of Errora. Lots of things happen before they are returned to normal.

_____. *Ghastly Glasses.* Dutton, 1985. Andrea gets a pair of magic glasses with which she can control people's actions. But sometimes what she does backfires.

_____. *Mail-Order Wings.* Dutton, 1981. Andrea likes her WondaWings but they are turning her into a bird.

_____. *More Fifth Grade Magic.* Dutton, 1989. Amy wants to attend the Young Theater program during the summer. Her mother wants her to go to modeling camp. She writes in her magic calendar and things happen but most of them backfire.

_____. *Paul's Volcano.* Houghton, 1987. Paul's volcano is papier mache but is it alive? The evil power is unleashed and Adam sees the danger and saves the day.

Gorog, Judith. *Caught in the Turtle.* Philomel, 1983. Kate meets Piper, a girl whose guardian is on drugs. They encounter drug pushers, a stolen jade necklace and a kidnapping. A fearful, violent novel.

Gottschalk, Elin. *In Search of Coffee Mountain.* Nelson, 1977. Lotukata remembers bombings, German cruelty, hunger, fear and homelessness. It is her alcoholic uncle who goes in search of Coffee Mountain.

Goudge, Elizabeth. *Linnets and Valerians.* Coward, 1964. The Linnet children live with their grandmother. They run away to an uncle. They solve the mystery of Valerian's lost son and missing husband.

Gould, Joan. *Otherborn.* Coward, 1980. Mark and Leggy are washed overboard; they are rescued by natives that have a secret. They are eventually released and allowed to leave the Land of Light where birth and death are different.

Gould, Lilian. *Jeremy and the Gorillas.* Lothrop, 1973. Jeremy's father is killed by MauMau terrorists. He runs away and lives with gorillas for about a year. He learns about gorilla behavior.

Gould, Marilyn. *Golden Daffodils.* Addison, 1982. Janis has cerebral palsy and has been mainstreamed. She makes friends but also taunters. She and Barney win a handball contest but then she has a seizure. She is mad and ashamed.

_____. *Twelfth of June.* Addison, 1986. Janis has the problems most early teenagers have but also has cerebral palsy. Barney is becoming a boyfriend.

Govan, Christine. *Number Five Hackberry Street.* World, 1964. Jessie moves to a new home, and works in a general store. In *Moffat* (Estes) tradition this is a humorous family story.

_____. *Phinny's Five Summer.* World, 1968. Phinny is recovering from an illness and spends the summer swimming with new friends. They solve the mystery of who stole the church supper money.

Govern, Elaine. *Ice Cream Next Summer.* Whitman, 1973. Michael takes his puppy on an ice cutting trip. The puppy falls into the icy water and disappears.

Graber, Richard. *Black Cow Summer.* Harper, 1980. Ray is sixteen and falls in love with a girl whose older brothers won't let him near her. He still has parent problems at home.

_____. *Doc.* Harper, 1986. Brad's grandfather has Alzheimer's disease and Brad has a hard time understanding the change in him. He gets help from his father and his girl friend. Doc, the grandfather, is 84.

_____. *Little Breathing Room.* Harper, 1978. Ray is rejected by his father who blames him for everything that goes wrong. He goes to stay with grandparents to get "A Little Breathing Room."

_____. *Pay Your Respects.* Harper, 1979. Ray and his friend Floyd are seniors. Floyd is emotionally unstable; he seriously injures his foot. Ray's parent problem continues. His grandmother dies and Ray decides to leave town.

Grace, Fran. *Very Private Performance.* Bradbury, 1983. Max wants to be a mime. His friend, Roberto, is fleeing from the authorities because he is an illegal alien. Burke and Justine are the girls with whose lives they become intertwined.

Graeber, Charlotte. *Fudge.* Lothrop, 1987. Chad can have a puppy if he takes on the responsibility of training him.

_____. *Mustard.* Macmillan, 1982. Alex's cat is getting old and he can't understand the changes that need to be made.

_____. *Thing in Kat's Attic.* Dutton, 1984. Kat hears strange noises from the attic. She tells her mother who is determined to find out what it is.

Graham, Harriet. *Chinese Puzzle.* Houghton, 1988. William and Flora live with their guardian, Samuel, a magician. He disappears and they go to look for him.

_____. *Ring of Zoraya.* Atheneum, 1982. William and Samuel, the magician, are traveling across Europe. William is given an heirloom ring by a crown prince to be delivered to his father.

Graham, Lorenz. *I, Momolu.* Crowell, 1966. Momolu, 14, travels from his village to the city. He sees the difference between their lives and his. He also sees the difference between his father and himself.

————. *North Town.* Crowell, 1965. David and his family move North. He is in an integrated high school but gets in trouble innocently. His father becomes ill and he takes a part-time job. All ends well.

————. *Return to South Town.* Crowell, 1976. David has become a doctor and after fifteen years returns to South Town but still runs into prejudice. But he stays and helps the black people.

————. *Whose Town?* Crowell, 1969. David is a senior and plays football. He again gets in trouble through no fault of his own and an ugly confrontation occurs.

Graham, Robin. *Dove.* Harper, 1972. Robin, 16, sails 30,000 miles around the world in his 24-foot sailboat. Alone. He has unbelievable adventures.

Grahame, Kenneth. *Wind in the Willows.* Scribner, 1961. Toad, Mole, Rat and Badger live along a river and are close, visiting friends.

Grant, Bruce. *Ride, Gaucho.* World, 1969. Eduardo gets a wild pony. He breaks and then rides it. Manuel steals and hides it because of jealousy. But a horse race solves the differences.

Grant, Cynthia. *Hard Love.* Ballantine, 1984. Stephen lives the good life but his friend Pauli is not doing as well and then he falls in love with a 23-year-old woman. Not so good.

————. *Kumquat May, I'll Always Love You.* Atheneum, 1986. Olivia's mother went to the store and never returned. She told no one but her friend, Rosella.

————. *Phoenix Rising.* Atheneum, 1989. Jessie's sister died of cancer. She is grief stricken to an unhealthy degree. She finds her sister's diary and this helps her survive and live her own life.

————. *Summer Home.* Atheneum, 1981. Max is scared of swimming and is not enjoying his summer. He contacts the author of his favorite detective books (who is a woman). She helps him live with his phobias, his sister and Baby Boris.

Graves, Robert. *Ancient Castle.* Kesend, 1982. A mystery story of great heroes, bad villains and buried treasure.

Gray, Elizabeth. *Adam of the Road.* Viking, 1942. A story of a 13th century minstrel boy who loses both his dog and his father and sets off to look for them. Newbery winner, 1943.

————. *I Will Adventure.* Viking, 1962. Andrew wants to be an actor instead of a page to his uncle. But it was William Shakespeare himself that helped him see the folly of this for himself.

Gray, Genevieve. *Sore Loser.* Houghton, 1974. Loren started on the wrong foot in his new school. He lost his cat and his rock collection. He finds another cat and finds his rock collection.

————. *Varnell Roberts, Super-Pigeon.* Houghton, 1975. Varnell is a "pigeon" of school extortionists. He is put in Special Education. He becomes part of a secret experiment: Project Behavior Modification.

Gray, Nicholas. *Apple Stone.* Meredith, 1969. The stone that looked like a wrinkled apple to anyone else took a girl and her friends on an adventure that was helped by things not supposed to be alive: leopard skin rug, bookends, etc.

————. *Grimbold's Other World.* Meredith, 1968. Muffler was a foundling who was taken in by a good family. But at night Grimbold, a cat, took him to another world where he helped others in distress.

Gray, Nigel. *Deserter.* Harper, 1977. Andy, Chris and two friends find a deserter with a broken ankle and build a raft for him to escape down river.

Gray, Patricia. *Barefoot a Thousand Miles.* Walker, 1984. Jim's dog, Quick, is given away to tourists. Jim goes after her to California facing many hardships before he finds the trail of his dog.

————. *Blue Ribbon Summer.* Norton, 1968. Jean and Candy show their horses at a horse show. They meet Ron, a young trainer.

————. *Diving Horse.* Coward, 1960. Annie loves horses, especially her own. She is part of a vaudeville act and dives with Spotty. She wants the dive to be the best ever.

————. *Horse in Her Heart.* Coward, 1960. Carol thinks western cutting horses are best and her Spipper in particular. Angele thinks thoroughbred racers are best and her Marion in particular. They meet and learn about each other's horses.

————. *Horse Trap.* Coward, 1962. Deb tries to help an injured horse but disobeys orders. She must get the horse out of the canyon and care for her.

————. *Horsepower.* Norton, 1966. Honey and her sister, Diane, are on the horse show circuit. Honey tries a new lifestyle with her father and stepmother but returns to the circuit.

————. *Jumping Jack.* Norton, 1965. Jill helps teach younger children to ride at a riding club. She has won shows with Jumping Jack and wants to win some more but....

————. *Loco, the Bronco.* Coward, 1961. Lynn is staying in Mexico where a rodeo comes to town. Lynn nurses a bronco left behind because he was ill. She wants him for her own.

————. *Lucky Star.* Norton, 1967. Debbie tries to marry her widowed mother to their ranch foreman. There are both amusing and dangerous incidents.

————. *Norah's Ark.* Norton, 1966. Norah and Karl are trapped by a flood. They save several small animals and a mare and her foal. Norah rides the mare in a desperate attempt for help.

————. *Star Bright.* Norton, 1964. Deb's colt,

Star, is mischievous and causes trouble because of Deb's lack of training. She must get rid of him. She does but finds miracles do happen.

_____. *Star Lost*. Norton, 1965. Deb and Maureen want to prove that Deb is responsible enough to care for a horse. But Star Bright runs away and Maureen's horse, Patches, and the two girls look for him.

_____. *Star, the Sea Horse*. Norton, 1968. Debbie and her cousin Kathy have Star Bright on their vacation. They get jobs in a local stable and learn more about horses and riding.

Greaves, Margaret. *Cat's Magic*. Harper, 1981. Louise goes to live with an aunt in the country. She saves a kitten then the Goddess Bast tells Louise she is to be rewarded. She gets the gift of time travel.

_____. *Dagger and the Bird*. Harper, 1975. Bridget and Luke find out that their young brother Simon is a changeling. They look for the real Simon.

_____. *Stone of Terror*. Harper, 1974. Phillip protects and befriends Marie, the daughter of a witch.

Green, Alexander. *Scarlet Sails*. Scribner, 1967. Arthur falls in love with Asole without ever speaking to her. This is a miracle story you want to believe.

Green, Anne. *Good-Bye Gray Lady*. Atheneum, 1964. George visits his cousins Louisa and Richard. They are upset because the home of the ghost, Gray Lady, is being sold.

_____. *To Race Again*. Nelson, 1961. Bobby wants his family to have the thoroughbred horse farm they had before the Civil War. He gets and trains a colt and wins a race to start the return to fame.

_____. *Valley Cup*. Nelson, 1962. Ben is interested in baseball, not studies. He is also interested in horses since his father was a steeplechase rider. Should he be a steeplechase rider? A ball player? Something else?

Green, Connie. *War at Home*. Macmillan, 1989. Mattie and her cousin Virgil have squabbles and friendships while growing up during World War II.

Green, Diane. *Lonely War of William Pinto*. Little, 1968. Will wanted no part of the war. It would bring no good for anyone. His father and brothers were supportive of the American colonies but Will couldn't go along.

Green, Hannah. *I Never Promised You a Rose Garden*. Holt, 1964. Debbie, 16, becomes mentally ill and tells of her three years to recovery. She is torn between reality and fantasy but fantasy is becoming stronger and she must resist or never return to reality.

Green, Phyllis. *Eating Ice Cream with a Werewolf*. Harper, 1983. Brad and his sister stay with friends while their parents are away. Phoebe knows witchcraft and has a magic book. She casts spells.

_____. *Empty Seat*. Nelson, 1980. Michael spends the summer with his grandparents. He gets involved in kidnapping a friend's sister from a religious cult.

_____. *Grandmother Orphan*. Nelson, 1977. Christy shoplifts and is sent to her grandmother. She finds that she is one of a long line of adoptees. Not only her mother but her grandmother was adopted. She no longer minds being "adopted."

_____. *Mildred Murphy, How Does Your Garden Grow?* Addison, 1977. Mildred befriends Mrs. Wilson who lives alone in great poverty.

_____. *Nantucket Summer*. Nelson, 1974. A.D. has a summer job babysitting on Nantucket Island. She encounters romance and a ghostly visitor. She copes with the mental problems of her employer.

_____. *Nicky's Lopsided, Lumpy But Delicious Orange*. Addison, 1978. Nicky wants to be perfect. Her mother is an artist and her mother's husband is a priest who has not yet told the church he is married.

_____. *Walkie Talkie*. Addison, 1978. Richie is a loner. He meets Norman, a disabled boy, and his guardian Patty. During a storm Richie scares Norman who then crawls out on the roof. Richie rescues him, but this ends the friendship.

Green, Robert. *Hawk of the Nile*. St. Martin, 1962. Khim lives in the time of the Pharaohs. He accidentally shoots a sacred Ibis and is sentenced to hard labor.

_____. *Whistling Sword*. St. Martin, 1962. Basil joins the Mongol army of Genghis Khan to seek revenge for the death of his grandfather and the capture of his mother.

Green, Susan. *Self-Portrait with Wings*. Little, 1989. Jennifer wants to be a figure skater and one day wakes up with wings. The wings are a nuisance but they help her skating. She loses the wings but becomes a better skater.

Greenberg, Jan. *Bye, Bye, Miss American Pie*. Farrar, 1985. Beth is attracted to rich Jason even though she has been warned that he is nothing but trouble. But Beth likes the rich lifestyle even when it includes shoplifting. She learns her lesson.

_____. *Exercises of the Heart*. Farrar, 1986. Roxie, 15, has no father and her mother is ill. She envies her friend, Glo, but doesn't realize that Glo's mother is an alcoholic. Glo gets a boyfriend and Roxie is left out but she copes well.

_____. *Iceberg and Its Shadow*. Farrar, 1980. Anabeth, Rachel, Tracy and Carolyn are troubled by the new girl, Mindy, who by mean means breaks them up and controls their friendships.

_____. *Just the Two of Us*. Farrar, 1988. Holly's friend, Max, gets Holly to stay with his family rather than move to Iowa to help in a summer catering business.

_____. *No Dragons to Slay*. Farrar, 1984.

Tom's "dragon" was his unexpected illness, a tumor on his hip. His medical treatment caused him weight, hair and energy loss. He joined a group on a dig and re-evaluated his life.

_____. *Pig-Out Blues*. Farrar, 1982. Jodie and her mother fight over Jodie's eating habits and her plumpness. She goes on a starvation diet and faints during an audition. She finally adjusts, with the help of her friend, Heather.

_____. *Season In-Between*. Farrar, 1979. Carrie's father is diagnosed as having cancer. This fact changes Carrie's life a great deal.

Greenberg, Joanne. *Simple Gifts*. Holt, 1986. The Fleuris farm is rundown and the government wants to buy it and change it into a tourist attraction. But is this the right thing to do?

Greene, Bette. *Get on Out of Here, Philip Hall*. Dial, 1981. Beth is now trying to outdo Philip Hall and learns a valuable lesson about leadership when Philip gets the award she was sure was hers.

_____. *Morning Is a Long Time Coming*. Dial, 1978. The continuing story of Patty as she grows up, leaves high school, goes to Germany to find the family of the German POW, and finally settles her own life with a romance in Paris.

_____. *Philip Hall Likes Me. I Reckon Maybe*. Dial, 1974. As the number two student in school, Beth gets through a year of funny incidents because she doesn't want to beat out her friend, Philip Hall.

_____. *Summer of My German Soldier*. Dial, 1973. The heartbreaking story of a friendship between a Jewish girl, Patty, and a young escaped German POW during World War II. She hides him but he is found and shot. She must pay the price.

_____. *Them That Glitter/Them That Don't*. Knopf, 1983. Carol Ann's father is a drunk and her mother is a fortune-telling gypsy. She has an idol, Carlotte Dell, a country music star. That's the dream that makes life tolerable.

Greene, Constance. *Al(exandra) the Great*. Viking, 1982. Al must give up a summer visit with her father to take care of her mother who is sick, and she gets a T-shirt with Al(exandra) the Great on it. She also meets a boy she likes.

_____. *Al's Blind Date*. Viking, 1989. Al and her best friend, Thelma, are going out with Thelma's cousin and his friend.

_____. *Ask Anybody*. Viking, 1983. The daughter of divorced parents befriends an eccentric new girl who is full of surprises.

_____. *Beat the Turtle Drum*. Viking, 1976. A tragic story of a girl's adjustment to the accidental death of her younger sister.

_____. *Dotty's Suitcase*. Viking, 1980. Dotty finds a suitcase full of money thrown out of a car by bank robbers who were being chased. She meets and escapes from a teenager and is helped by an old man on her way to a friend's house.

_____. *Double and Dare O'Toole*. Viking, 1981. Rex can't resist double dares. He gets in trouble but he can't stop. He has two friends: Audrey, a girl his age, and Angie, an older woman who dies at the end. But he and Audrey help and support each other.

_____. *Ears of Louis*. Viking, 1974. Louis is a small boy with big ears. He is always being teased by his classmates and the school bully.

_____. *Getting Nowhere*. Viking, 1977. Mark, 14, is filled with hatred that he is unable to release. It leads to self hating. A strong story.

_____. *Girl Called Al*. Viking, 1969. A traveling father, a divorced mother and too much fat tell the story of Al and her best friend who live in the same apartment building.

_____. *I and Sproggy*. Viking, 1978. Adam lives with his mother. His father is coming with a new wife and child, Sproggy. Adam doesn't like her but everybody else does.

_____. *I Know You, Al*. Viking, 1975. Al and her best friend cope with, among other things, Al's weight, her mother, her mother's boyfriend and her father's re-marriage.

_____. *Isabelle and Little Orphan Frannie*. Viking, 1988. Isabelle would like to be as popular as Mary Elizabeth but isn't. But she does help Frannie who can't read by trying to teach her.

_____. *Isabelle Shows Her Stuff*. Viking, 1984. Guy and Isabelle team up to make Guy a "better pest." They both learn a lesson from this experience.

_____. *Isabelle, the Itch*. Viking, 1973. Isabelle's brother's paper route helps her become more popular, which is what she is after.

_____. *Just Plain Al*. Viking, 1986. Two teenage girls, Al and her friend, cope with life in a New York City apartment. Some days are good, some days are bad.

_____. *Leo the Lioness*. Viking, 1970. Tibb was a lion, the strong Leo of the zodiac. She believed she was a changeling and wasn't happy with herself, but she gained solace in her strong sign.

_____. *Love Letters of J. Timothy Owen*. Harper, 1986. Tim is a romantic. He copies old love letters and sends them unsigned to a girl. They are misunderstood and he is in hot water.

_____. *Monday I Love You*. Harper, 1988. Grace is large busted for a fifteen-year-old. She babysits for a teacher who really helps her, and for Doris. She is accosted by a criminal who, in the end, doesn't hurt her.

_____. *Star Shine*. Viking, 1987. Jenny is selected to be an extra in a movie being made in her town. She meets Scott whom her sister likes.

_____. *Unmaking of Rabbit*. Viking, 1972. Paul is called Rabbit because of his small size and his large ears. He is invited to a sleep-out, finds a friend, and visits his mother and her new husband, all of which result in a change in Rabbit.

_____. *Your Old Pal, Al*. Viking, 1979. Al and her best friend wait for letters from both Brian, a boy she knows, and Al's father's new wife. A house guest, Polly, confuses things.

Greene, Graham. *Human Factor.* Simon & Schuster, 1978. Secret information is being smuggled to enemy agents. The world security is being threatened. Davis is suspected; so is Castle.

Greene, Jacqueline. *Leveller.* Walker, 1984. Tom Cook, a figure very much like Robin Hood, lives in 1700 New England.

Greene, Shep. *Boy Who Drank Too Much.* Viking, 1979. Buff is expected to be a hockey player. His father is an alcoholic and abuses him so that he, too, turns to drink.

Greenfeld, Josh. *Harry and Tonto.* Popular, 1974. The cross country journey of a 70-year-old man and his cat in search of what life has left for them.

Greenfield, Eloise. *Alesia.* Philomel, 1981. Alesia is in high school and keeps a journal. She tells about recovering from a serious accident, her social life and work experiences.

_____. *Sister.* Crowell, 1974. Doretha's father dies and she watches as her older sister, Alberta, withdraws from the family.

_____. *Talk About a Family.* Lippincott, 1978. Genny is waiting for her older brother's return home. She is sure all will be well and he will fix things between her parents.

Greenwald, Sheila. *All the Way to Wit's End.* Little, 1979. Drusilla's family inherited an old house and a lot of antique furniture. Drusilla didn't like any of it and decided to have a garage sale—without her parents' permission!

_____. *Alvin Webster's Surefire Plan for Success (And How It Failed).* Little, 1987. Alvin tries to teach Bone some math but Bone refuses to really learn. This is Alvin's failure. In the end both he and Bone learn from each other.

_____. *Atrocious Two.* Houghton, 1978. Ashley and Cecilia are not wanted by anyone for the summer. Aunt Tessie takes them in and breaks them of their nasty habits. Cecilia also solves the mystery of the missing jewelry.

_____. *Blissful Joy and the SATs.* Little, 1982. Blissful's parents are divorced and are actors but she wants to become more practical. When she scores low on her SATs she comes to understand that she, too, is romantic and imaginative.

_____. *Give Us a Great Big Smile, Rosy Cole.* Little, 1981. Uncle Ralph is to do a pictorial on Rosy but all she can do is play violin and not very well. The book "A Very Young Fiddler" is all a lie but it works out well in the end.

_____. *It All Began with Jane Eyre.* Little, 1980. Franny, 13, keeps a journal in which she writes imaginary events about her family. She then hands it in to her teacher! A very funny story of a reader who really "lives" her books.

_____. *Mariah Delany Lending Library Disaster.* Houghton, 1977. Mariah starts to lend books to classmates and charge a fee. She finds that loaning books is a lot easier than getting them back.

_____. *Mat Pit and the Tunnel Tenants.* Lippincott, 1972. Mat Pit and his friends rescue their pets (rodents, gerbils, etc.) from extermination and build a zoo where they can safely stay.

_____. *Rosy's Romance.* Little, 1989. Project Romance is to make Rosie's romance as they appear in the young romance books Rosie reads but of course, everything backfires because real life is different from what the books portray.

_____. *Will the Real Gertrude Hollings Please Stand Up?* Little, 1983. Gertrude has dyslexia and is called dumb. She makes friends at a new school and slowly learns to use books for information.

_____. *Write On, Rosy.* Little, 1988. Young Author's Day sets Rosy on her way to becoming a writer. She writes about the school principal and draws all the wrong conclusions.

Greer, Gery. *Max and Me and the Time Machine.* Harcourt, 1983. Steve buys a time machine at a garage sale and takes his friend Max to the year 1250 where they see a jousting match with Sir Bevis.

_____. *Max and Me and the Wild West.* Harcourt, 1988. Steve and Max use their time machine to return to a rich, rough boom town in the early West.

_____. *This Island Isn't Big Enough for the Four of Us.* Crowell, 1987. Scott and Pete go on vacation to a deserted island. Instead two girls are there to challenge them at every turn. A winner-takes-all Great Turtle Island Flag Race ends the vacation.

Gregory, Diana. *Fog Burns Off by 11 O'Clock.* Addison, 1981. Dede's parents are separated. She visits her dad and finds a live-in girl and lush living. She chooses to return and live with her mother.

_____. *I'm Boo ... That's Who.* Addison, 1979. Boo, 13, meets friends who ride in horse shows and she learns to ride. She has a personal problem with her friend Tamara and family problems with her brother.

_____. *There's a Caterpillar in My Lemonade.* Addison, 1980. Sam's mother is going to get married. Sam seeks an outlet in the swim team. She unwittingly disqualifies her team and wants to die. Her new stepfather helps and so does her boyfriend, Joey.

Gregory, Kristiano. *Jenny of the Tetons.* Holt, 1989. Carrie lives with Beaver Dick and his Indian wife Jenny when her family is killed in an Indian raid. They face cold, bear attacks, Indian raids and smallpox.

Grice, Frederick. *Out of the Mines.* Watts, 1960. Dick lives in a mining town and doesn't want to work in the mines when he sees the disasters, the strikes and the hard labor.

Griese, Arnold. *At the Mouth of the Luckiest River.* Crowell, 1973. A young Indian makes an enemy of the tribe's powerful medicine man.

_____. *Way of Our People.* Crowell, 1975.

Kano, an Eskimo, is afraid to hunt alone. He proves his courage when he takes the smallpox vaccine himself and then gives it to the rest of the village. He might even be a great hunter.

_____. *Wind Is Not a River*. Crowell, 1978. Sason lives in an attic during World War II. He hides from the Japanese, but rescues a wounded Japanese soldier who then helps him escape.

Griffin, Peni. *Otto from Otherwhere*. Macmillan, 1990. A ten-year-old alien boy travels through an inter-galactic pathway to enter the lives of Paula and her family.

Griffith, Helen V. *Foxy*. Greenwillow, 1984. Jeff thinks his dog, Foxy, is dead but Amber who lives next door knows differently.

Griffith, Valeria. *Runaway*. Abelard, 1971. Phil runs away from home. He meets Tom, another runaway. He eventually returns home and finds his parents dead.

Griffiths, G.D. *Abandoned*. Follett, 1973. A story of an abandoned kitten who learns to survive. She endures a forest fire, dogs, rabbits and traps. She is found by a couple who care for her.

_____. *Mattie: The Story of a Hedgehog*. Delacorte, 1977. Mattie lives her life as an animal with its death and violence, but she is an appealing character.

Griffiths, Helen. *Blackface Stallion*. Holiday, 1980. A story of Blackface from a yearling to a stallion establishing himself and his herd of mares.

_____. *Dancing Horses*. Holiday, 1982. Franco is an orphan after the Spanish Civil War of the 1930's. He gets to be a horse trainer with the help of Jose.

_____. *Dog at the Window*. Holiday, 1984. Alison has a dog, Wolf. She got Wolf after his owner committed suicide. Her mother, who never wanted a dog, marries a man who likes dogs. Alison can keep Wolf.

_____. *Grip, a Dog's Story*. Holiday, 1978. Grip is a pet bull labeled as a coward. His owner, Dudley, both rejects him (a coward) and loves him (can't put him to death). All ends well.

_____. *Journal of a Teenage Genius*. Greenwillow, 1987. Toodles, a poodle, eats "Growth Enhancers" Zack intended for himself. He wants to be taller than his friend, Loretta.

_____. *Just a Dog*. Holiday, 1974. A stray dog is looking for a master. First a young boy, then a gypsy, then an old man. Finally he is adopted by a nice family.

_____. *Last Summer: Spain 1936*. Holiday, 1979. Edwardo's privileged life is changed with the Spanish Civil War. He travels to his mother's, seeing death and rubble. He takes his horse Gaviota and is both befriended and victimized along the way.

_____. *Mysterious Appearance of Agnes*. Holiday, 1975. A three-year-old girl is found wandering and dazed and is adopted. She is mute and withdrawn until years later (at ten) she

rescues a black cat and the town's people believe she is a witch.

_____. *Rafa's Dog*. Holiday, 1983. Rafa and his sister spend the summer in the country in Spain. He befriends a black dog but when he returns home after his mother dies he leaves the dog. He does go back and get Moro, whom he loves.

_____. *Running Wild*. Holiday, 1977. Pablo is raised by his grandparents on a farm. A dog fills a void in his life and also causes him problems.

_____. *Russian Blue*. Holiday, 1973. Artie wants a dog of his own. Instead he finds a valuable Russian Blue cat. The cat is hurt and Artie nurses it back to health. The cat is finally returned to its owner and Artie gets a dog.

_____. *Stallion of the Sands*. Lothrop, 1970. The stallion was a wild horse. He knew that gauchos slaughter horses so he avoided them. He hid in the cold and fog until Aurelio won his devotion with tender, loving care.

_____. *Wild Heart*. Doubleday, 1963. La Bruja is a wild horse. He struggles to survive and resists being captured. Three men die trying to do so.

_____. *Wild Horse of Santander*. Doubleday, 1966. Joaquin is blind. His father gives him a filly and he spends all his time with her. He goes away for an eye operation. The filly runs away and then must be shot.

Gripe, Maria. *Elvis and His Friends*. Delacorte, 1976. Elvis goes to school and meets Annarosa with a different kind of family.

_____. *Elvis and His Secret*. Delacorte, 1976. Elvis is locked in his room for punishment and discovers inner strength in spite of his petty mother. He has an interest in growing things and plants seeds everywhere.

_____. *Glassblower's Children*. Delacorte, 1973. Klas and Klara are glassblowers who live very happy lives until the prophecy that their children will disappear comes true.

_____. *Green Coat*. Delacorte, 1977. Fredrika's mother is cold and ambitious. Her father is dead. She has to work hard to establish an identity for herself.

_____. *Hugo*. Delacorte, 1970. Hugo lives in the woods with his father and sometimes goes to school with his friend, Josephine. Most of the time he tries to earn money with little success.

_____. *Hugo and Josephine*. Delacorte, 1969. The hilarious adventures of two young children as they attend school. Josephine is unhappy because she is teased and Hugo is a happy boy who defends her. They become close friends.

_____. *Josephine*. Delacorte, 1970. Josephine, being one of seven children, feels unwanted and runs away from home. She meets Granny Lyra, finds her threatening and hurries home to security.

_____. *Julia's House*. Delacorte, 1975. As Julia grows older she still has a relationship with Peter but each is jealous of the friends of the other. But they work together when it appears that Julia's house is to be torn down.

_____. *Night Daddy*. Delacorte, 1968. A story told chapter by chapter of the friendship between Julia, a young girl, and Peter, her sitter. Peter is a writer and Julia has no father.

Groch, Judith. *Play the Bach, Dear*. Doubleday, 1978. Hilary is an untalented and reluctant piano student. Her teacher, Miss Orpheo, can hide in a piano and play instead of her students. A funny story.

Grohskopf, Bernice. *Blood and Roses*. Atheneum, 1979. Rob is visited by the ghost of William Caxton as he writes a school paper about him. He helps him steal a lost manuscript.

_____. *Shadow in the Sun*. Atheneum, 1975. Wilma was a paraplegic and found that she could live outside the acceptable world. She could have things done for her and do nothing in return, and she could say anything and get away with it.

Grosscup, Clyde. *Pro Passer*. Grosset, 1966. Brad must combat jealousy and the team's loyalty to their own quarterback, but exceptional playing wins acceptance of both.

_____. *Pro Rookie*. Grosset, 1965. Brad signs with a major league football team. He is resented by his teammates. But in the end he throws the winning pass and they accept him.

Grosser, Morton. *Snake Horn*. Atheneum, 1973. Dan plays sax and is captain of the football team. But a snake horn and a warp in time bring a musician from the 17th century who must be sent back.

Grote, William. *Fiddle, Flute and the River*. Meredith, 1967. Jamey meets Will as he and his family float down the Mississippi River. Will saves him from drowning. They tangle with pirates and swindlers. They have both funny and serious adventures.

_____. *J.P. and the Apaches*. Meredith, 1967. J.P. learns from his Indian friend at a military post in 1860. Then J.P.'s donkey is taken in a raiding party and must be rescued.

Grove, Vicki. *Fastest Friend in the West*. Putnam, 1990. Lori is overweight and because she is dropped by her once best friend she befriends a homeless girl.

_____. *Good-Bye My Wishing Star*. Putnam, 1988. Jen is going to move because her family are losing their farm. But she has a strong, loyal family and they will survive.

Grund, Josef. *You Have a Friend, Pietro*. Little, 1966. Pietro's father is in prison and he is bullied for having "an evil eye." Emilio, a stone cutter, is his friend who stops the bullying.

Guernsey, Joann. *Five Summers*. Clarion, 1983. Mandy struggles with being a teenager, and her old irritable grandmother, her six-year-old or-

phaned cousin, Peter, another teenager, her mother's cancer and love. All in five years, from 13 to 18.

_____. *Journey to Almost There*. Clarion, 1985. Alison runs away from her divorced mother. She takes her grandfather and a car. They encounter a hitchhiker and a young couple. She then reassesses her situation.

_____. *Room to Breathe*. Clarion, 1986. Mandy is trying to understand both her father and her boyfriend. After some drastic moves she begins to understand her father and decides to be "just friends" with her boyfriend.

Guest, Elissa. *Handsome Man*. Four Winds, 1980. Alex and her best friend Angela look for information about a handsome neighbor. She fantasizes a love affair and sees what she wants to see.

_____. *Over the Moon*. Morrow, 1986. Kate's parents died and she lives with her aunt. She is confused about her role until she goes to find her older sister, Mattie, who ran away when she was sixteen.

Guest, Judith. *Ordinary People*. Viking, 1976. A family must pull itself together after one son drowns and another attempts suicide.

Guillot, Rene. *Fofana*. Criterion, 1961. The African wilderness as seen through Jean-Luc's eyes. Fofana, a slave, is bought by his father and he befriends Jean-Luc.

_____. *Grishka and the Bear*. Criterion, 1960. Before a boy will let his bear cub be ritually sacrificed he runs off to the forest with him. The forests of Siberia are not hospitable.

_____. *Grishka and the Wolves*. Van Nostrand, 1965. Grishka is a pet bear, and Iakon is a girl. They have to fight against the evil influence of the medicine man of Siberia.

_____. *Little Dog Lost*. Lothrop, 1970. A puppy is lost and adopted by a fox. He is raised for survival. He encounters a wildcat and a snowstorm. He leads a double life with the fox and a human family.

_____. *Mokokambo, Lost Tail*. Criterion, 1961. Grishka and his friend Djidi, a playful, fat bear cub, have adventures in Russia.

_____. *Riders of the Wind*. Rand McNally, 1961. Calvi is captured by an African tribe and forced to travel across the desert as the tribe attacks other caravans.

_____. *Sama*. Criterion, 1961. Sama is an elephant with all the joy, pain, suffering and death that life brings. He is imprisoned and humiliated as a circus performer. It is told from Sama's point of view.

Guy, Rosa. *Disappearance*. Delacorte, 1979. The disappearance of seven-year-old Perk in Brooklyn casts suspicion on a juvenile offender in Harlem: Imamu Jones.

_____. *Edith Jackson*. Viking, 1978. Edith tries to keep her sisters together but they leave their foster home and reject her efforts. Edith must make her own life.

_____. *Friends*. Holt, 1973. Phyllisia recognizes the reason for the conflict between herself and her best friend, Edith. She is so different but she is loyal and helps Phyl stand up to her father.

_____. *My Love, My Love, or the Peasant Girl*. Holt, 1985. A young black orphan falls in love with a very rich man who is Creole. It is a tragic romance.

_____. *New Guy Around the Block*. Delacorte, 1983. Imamu suspects one of his friends of committing crimes. He also tries to cope with an alcoholic mother.

_____. *Paris, Pee Wee and Big Dog*. Delacorte, 1985. When his mother goes off to work one day, Paris, 10, and two friends spend the day on the streets of New York having hair-raising adventures.

_____. *Pee Wee and the Big Dog*. Delacorte, 1985. Paris and his friend Pee Wee go skating and are joined by Big Dog, who is only nine years old. They get into misadventure after misadventure.

_____. *Ruby*. Viking, 1976. The continuing story of the two black teenagers, Phyllisia and Ruby. Phyl studies hard at school and Ruby makes friends with Daphne.

_____. *Ups and Downs of Carl Davis III*. Delacorte, 1989. Carl is living with his grandmother. He writes a series of letters to his parents revealing his feelings. He is facing some of the problems his parents hoped to avoid.

Haas, Dorothy. *Haunted House*. Scholastic, 1988. Jill and Peanut invite their class to their basement where they have set up a haunted house.

_____. *New Friends*. Scholastic, 1988. Two students who are class competitors become friends.

_____. *Poppy and the Outdoors Cat*. Whitman, 1981. Poppy wants a pet. She saves a kitten and wants to keep it. She teaches it to survive outside and find food. Even later, when it can come in the house it doesn't want to.

_____. *Secret Life of Dilly McBean*. Bradbury, 1986. Dilly can make himself magnetic. A physicist experiments with Dilly's power. Another scientist wants to kidnap him.

Haas, Jessie. *Keeping Barney*. Greenwillow, 1982. Sarah finds that wishing for a horse is not like taking care of one.

_____. *Working Trot*. Greenwillow, 1983. James wants to be a horse trainer. His parents want him to get a college degree and go into business. His love of horses wins out.

Haddad, Carolyn. *Last Ride*. Putnam, 1984. Doug is considered a wimp because he is not playing football. He goes to a school dance with some "in" couples. He leaves them when they drink and drive. And saves a life or two.

Hager, Alice. *Cathy Whitney: President's Daughter*. Messner, 1966. Cathy's father is elected United States president and she goes to Washing-ton. She doesn't like it but learns to love the glamour and excitement.

_____. *Love's Golden Circle*. Messner, 1962. Lisa and Jock both work for a year before going to college. Lisa then decides to become a social worker; Jock, either merchandising or science. A light romance.

Hagon, Priscilla. *Mystery at the Villa Blanca*. World, 1969. Frances is secretary at Villa Blanca. Two students were killed off campus and she may be in direct danger.

Hagy, Jeannie. *And Then Mom Joined the Army*. Abingdon, 1976. Scott's mother is in the Army to learn a trade. He is teased about it. His friend Jason is a thief. Should Scott protect his friend, or tell the truth?

Hahn, Mary. *Daphne's Book*. Clarion, 1983. A story of the friendship between two very different girls.

_____. *Dead Man in Indian Creek*. Clarion, 1989. Matt and Parker find a body in Indian Creek. It was a drug related death and they are afraid Parker's mother is involved.

_____. *Doll in the Garden: A Ghost Story*. Clarion, 1989. Ashley sees a white ghost cat that leads her to another time. A girl there wants her doll. Ashley finds the doll but it is taken from her. The girl gets the doll and Ashley accepts her father's death.

_____. *Following the Mystery Man*. Clarion, 1988. Madigan's grandmother rents a room to Clint, a handsome stranger. She believes him to be her lost father. He turns out to be quite different, indeed.

_____. *Jellyfish Season*. Clarion, 1985. Kathleen moves in with her cousin Fay and neither one likes the arrangement. Fay has a secret sailor boyfriend who is older and when Kathleen blurts it out there are almost tragic results.

_____. *Sara Summer*. Houghton, 1979. A summer friendship between two girls, Sara and Emily.

_____. *Tallahassee Higgins*. Clarion, 1987. Tally lives a free swinging life with her single mother. She is left with her aunt and uncle who don't want her to be like her irresponsible mother. Tally learns much about her mother and values.

_____. *Time of the Witch*. Clarion, 1982. Laura tells an old woman of her wish that her parents were back together. The woman was really a witch.

_____. *Wait Till Helen Comes: A Ghost Story*. Clarion, 1986. Heather, an un-nice child, is drawn into the life of a dead child through her ghost. Molly, who truly dislikes her, does try to save her. A real thriller.

Haig-Brown, R.L. *Whale People*. Morrow, 1962. Atlin, an Indian, works hard learning how to be a whale hunter. He copies the traits of the whale chief. He wants to marry the daughter of Chief Eskowit, his enemy.

Halacy, D.S. *Return from Luna*. Norton, 1969.

Rob is assigned to a station on the moon for one year. Because of a nuclear war on Earth, food, air and water are uncertain.

————. *Rocket Rescue.* Nelson, 1968. Lee is in Space Squadron and Grant is in Space Rescue. Little does Grant realize that his training is going to be used to rescue Lee.

————. *Sky Trap.* Nelson, 1975. Grant is involved with a gang of smugglers who bring heroin across the border. He makes best use of his glider plane.

Halacy, Dan. *Ethan Strong, Watch by the Sea.* McGraw, 1969. Ethan is asked to help crack a dope smuggling ring. He was to find out how and by whom but he uncovers an espionage ring. His surfing skills help him.

————. *Secret of the Cove.* Lion, 1969. Chris, 16, plans a vacation in Yosemite but a stolen car and an accident combine to change his plans. But California, with its skin diving, works out okay.

Halam, Ann. *Daymaker.* Watts, 1987. Zanne uses her psi talents to resurrect the machines that sapped earth's vitality; animals and plants die. She must decide between magic and science. She goes to meet the great Daymaker.

————. *Transformations.* Watts, 1988. Zanne is asked to shut down a destructive energy source, a machine. She runs into resistance before she completes her task.

Hale, Arlene. *Ghost Town's Secret.* Abelard, 1962. A story of the Old West with sinister gold-hungry crooks and dangerous desert passes.

————. *Listen to Your Heart.* Messner, 1962. Robin's mother dies. Her father is interested in another woman. She has friction with both her brother and her father. It takes a near tragedy to make her "listen to her heart."

————. *Nothing But a Stranger.* Four Winds, 1966. Holly finds out she was adopted when she writes an article for the newspaper about adoption. She is bitter and angry.

Hale, Edward E. *Man Without a Country.* Watts, 1960. A moving story about a man who was banished from his country and who loved that country more than most people.

Hale, Lucretia. *Peterkin Papers.* Houghton, 1914. Humorous adventures of the Peterkin family, whose antics are resolved by the Lady from Philadelphia.

Hale, Nancy. *Night of the Hurricane.* Coward, 1978. Gene's grandmother is strange but her home is the one strong enough to withstand a hurricane.

Hall, Adele. *Seashore Summer.* Harper, 1962. Betsy is a Quaker. She helps her aunt run a boarding house in Atlantic City in 1856. She has an encounter with both romance and mystery.

Hall, Anna. *Cyrus Holt and the Civil War.* Viking, 1964. Cyrus tells about the horrors the Civil War had on his family, his friends and his community.

Hall, Barbara. *Skeeball & the Secret of the*

Universe. Watts, 1987. A slight story about the little known game of Skeeball and Matty's success because of it.

Hall, Eleanor. *Alice with Golden Hair.* Atheneum, 1981. Alice, 18, is retarded and is working in a hospital. She makes friends with patients and doctors alike.

Hall, Elizabeth. *Phoebe Snow.* Houghton, 1968. Lucy lives in New York in 1900's. She disguises herself as Phoebe Snow, advertising lady of the railroad, and goes by train to St. Louis free of charge.

————. *Stand Up, Lucy.* Houghton, 1971. Lucy is running for 9th grade secretary and gets involved in women's rights. She loses her job as secretary but gains support from her boyfriend, Tom.

Hall, Lynn. *Boy in the Off-White Hat.* Scribner, 1984. Skeeter, 13, finds out that the nine-year-old boy she is babysitting is being sexually abused by his mother's boyfriend.

————. *Dagmar Schultz and the Angel Edna.* Scribner, 1989. Dagmar is boy crazy and when she finds a potential romance, a guardian angel with old fashioned morals comes along.

————. *Dagmar Schultz and the Power of Darkness.* Scribner, 1974. Dagmar and Edgar, a warlock, work so that James will fall in love with Dagmar. If Aunt Gretchen will let her date Edgar.

————. *Danger Dog.* Scribner, 1986. David has the responsibility to retrain an attack dog. He is not successful and ends up killing the dog when the dog attacks him.

————. *Danza!* Scribner, 1981. Paulo loves his horse, Danza, even though his breed is not appreciated. The horse becomes ill and is tended to by Major Kessler. The horse gets well and wins first place in a show.

————. *Denison's Daughter.* Scribner, 1983. Sandy meets Lonnie, an older, emotionally immature man. Her sister has left her husband and come home with her small son. Sandy has an accident hurting the boy but all ends well.

————. *Dog of the Bondi Castle.* Follett, 1979. Aubry, a slain young knight, had a dog called Griffon, who, along with Aubry's fiancee, Isabelle, captured the villain who killed Aubry. Isabelle dies and Griffon entombs himself with the young lovers.

————. *Flowers of Anger.* Follett, 1976. Ann plans an act of revenge after a neighbor shoots her horse for trespassing on his land.

————. *Flyaway.* Scribner, 1987. Areil, 17, is anxious to be on her own. Her father is unloving and controlling.

————. *Here Comes Zelda Clause.* Harcourt, 1989. The holiday misadventures of Zelda, the girl whose good intentions always lead to trouble.

————. *Horse Called Dragon.* Follett, 1971. Dragon was the leader of a herd of wild mustangs. He was captured and tamed, and he sired a new breed of horse, the POA Pony. This new breed was intelligent, courageous and proud.

_____. *Horse Trader.* Scribner, 1981. Karen saves money for a horse that old friend, Harley, was going to get for her. Harley sells her a horse he lies about. Karen reveals other lies Harley told about her mother and her horse, Gallion.

_____. *If Winter Comes.* Scribner, 1986. Meredith lives with his loving mother. Barry's parents are wealthy but unloving. They all face nuclear destruction in a few hours.

_____. *In Trouble Again, Zelda Hammersmith.* Harcourt, 1988. Zelda lives with her mother. She's in trouble for kidnapping a dog. She pretends to be run over, tries to get even with a bully, and loses and recovers her lost friend. A funny story.

_____. *Just One Friend.* Macmillan, 1985. Dory, 16, is learning-disabled. She unintentionally causes an auto accident in which a friend is killed.

_____. *Leaving.* Scribner, 1980. Roxie wants to be on her own in the city. The situation is told from both Roxie's and her mother's point of view.

_____. *Letting Go.* Scribner, 1987. Casey, 16, wants to break away from her mother and her dog shows and be independent. The mother feels the same difficulty in "letting go."

_____. *Megan's Mare.* Scribner, 1983. Megan meets and loves Berry, a petite red mare. Berry has a tendency to go her own way and she is afraid of bridges. Megan solves this horse's two faults.

_____. *Mrs. Portree's Pony.* Scribner, 1986. Addie lives with friends because her mother's boyfriend does not like kids. She falls in love with a pony and moves in with its owner.

_____. *Murder at the Spaniel Show.* Scribner, 1988. Tabby, 16, works at a kennel and helps in a dog show. A judge dies after receiving threatening notes. Tabby is shocked to find that her boss, Turner, is a murderer.

_____. *Mystery of Pony Hollow.* Garrard, 1978. Sarah must put to rest the ghost of a horse.

_____. *Mystery of Pony Hollow Panda.* Garrard, 1983. A bewildering mystery told in a humorous way.

_____. *Mystery of the Lost and Found Hound.* Garrard, 1979. Sandy finds a family of dog-nappers and tries to get their license plate number but is trapped with the stolen dogs. She jumps to her escape and leads police to their arrest.

_____. *Mystery of the Schoolhouse Dog.* Garrard, 1979. The youngsters see a white dog in the schoolhouse that has been abandoned. Is it a real dog or is it a ghost?

_____. *New Day for Dragon.* Follett, 1975. This story gives more background about Dragon, the Mexican mustang. His development was due in large part to the love and devotion shown him by his owners.

_____. *Ride a Dark Horse.* Morrow, 1987. Gutsy refuses to believe that her father died accidentally. She looks into the truth and clears her father's name, saves the 2,000 acre horse farm and is nearly killed in the process.

_____. *Riff, Remember.* Follett, 1973. Riff is a borzoi. His mistress is wealthy but she dies and he is made into a hunting dog. Gordy befriends him and sees the gentleness in him. A sad dog story.

_____. *Secret Life of Dagmar Schultz.* Scribner, 1988. Dagmar wants a boyfriend and a secret life but boys are scarce and so is privacy in a large family. She invents a secret boyfriend but what happens when she must produce this boy?

_____. *Something Special Horse.* Scribner, 1985. Chris's father is a "horseflesh" dealer. One day Chris keeps one of the horses. He names her Lacy and runs away with her and later finds that she is really stolen.

_____. *Sticks and Stones.* Follett, 1972. A sensitive story of a boy, 16, leaning toward homosexuality. He is entrapped in the injustice of gossip and ignorance.

_____. *Tin Can Tucker.* Scribner, 1982. Ann Tucker is an orphan who teams up with rodeo people and finds a home.

_____. *Tormentors.* Harcourt, 1990. Sox sets out to find out who stole his German shepherd. He gets involved in a ring of dog trainers who kidnap dogs for illegal profit.

_____. *Where Have All the Tigers Gone?* Scribner, 1989. Jo is at her class reunion and recalls the grades five through high school with bitterness and resentment. She resents the relationship with her other classmates.

_____. *Whispered Horse.* Follett, 1979. A suspenseful, violent story of a girl's father and his power.

_____. *Zelda Strikes Again.* Harcourt, 1988. Zelda crashes a stranger's funeral, sneaks aboard an airplane and causes her substitute teacher to collapse. Other than that it is business as usual.

Hall, Marjorie. *April Ghost.* Westminster, 1975. Strange things happen to Amanda, 16, in a vacant house in Salem in 1785. She falls in love with James the woodcarver, not the portrait painter who disappears.

Hall, Marjory. *Another Kind of Courage.* Westminster, 1967. An adventure story based on a true story of a Revolutionary War heroine, Nancy Hart.

Hallard, Peter. *Barrier Reef Bandit.* Criterion, 1960. Real pearls are in a safe of a sunken ship. Con and Gentry search for and salvage the ship.

_____. *Coral Reef Castaways.* Criterion, 1958. Con, 16, is swept overboard and swims to a reef where there is an oyster bed. Gentry owns the beds and he and Con start to make a business of these oysters. Someone else tries to work the beds.

_____. *Kalu and the Wild Boar.* Watts,

1973. Kunwar Lal lives in India. He tangles with a tiger and a wild boar in an attempt to save his father's crops.

Hallman, Ruth. *Gimme Something, Mister.* Westminster, 1978. Jackie attends the Mardi Gras. She catches a red necklace and is chased by thieves. She is held hostage but is finally saved.

————. *Search Without Fear.* Putnam, 1987. Dee is in a new school. She meets Eric, son of a helicopter pilot. She has many adventures with him and her state trooper brother.

Hallquist, Britt. *Search for Fredrick.* Watts, 1960. Raili and Povo run away from a good foster home to go find an irresponsible, wild brother in Sweden.

Hallstead, William. *Ev Kris, Aviation Detective.* Day, 1961. Ev sets up a flying agency. He works with the F.B.I. as a secret agent.

————. *Launching of Linda Bell.* Harcourt, 1981. Herk, Gordy and Chaunce, as a class project, promote "Linda Bell" from nobody to a real somebody.

————. *Tundra.* Crown, 1984. Jamie, 15, gets a Siberian husky called Tundra. He gets lost and has many bad experiences before ending up at an animal shelter. He is taken to a dog show by a friend and spots Jamie. All is well.

Halvorson, Marilyn. *Cowboys Don't Cry.* Delacorte, 1985. Shane and his alcoholic father move to a farm left to Shane by his grandparents. His father was responsible for his mother's death and he is unforgiving.

————. *Hold On, Geronimo.* Delacorte, 1988. Lance, Red, Kat and her father fly into a blizzard and crash. Kat's father is dead and Red is injured. Kat falls into a swift river and Lance must rescue her.

Hamilton, Carol. *Dawn Seekers.* Whitman, 1987. Quentin is a kangaroo rat. Jereboom is a rodent. Harry is a centipede. They band together for survival.

Hamilton, Dorothy. *Scamp and the Blizzard Boys.* Herald, 1980. Doug and Craig spend their days waiting out a blizzard with Doug's mother.

Hamilton, Gail. *Candle to the Devil.* Atheneum, 1975. Daphne is staying with an eccentric aunt when an epidemic breaks out. A painting is stolen and must be recovered.

————. *Titania's Lodestone.* Atheneum, 1975. The Parkins family come to claim their inheritance. They are held up in Massachusetts and stay there. Priscilla is ashamed of her family because they are not the Americans she thought they ought to be.

Hamilton, Merritt. *Jane Lahu Wildfire.* Scribner, 1973. Lahu of South East Asia is a poor village and its tribe refuses to raise opium to get rich. But La Poo and some friends do so. They are found out and punished.

Hamilton, Virginia. *Arilla Sun Down.* Greenwillow, 1976. Arilla, 12, is part of an interracial family living in the Midwest.

————. *Dustland.* Greenwillow, 1980. Bound together by extraordinary mind power, three teens are hurtled into the future to Dustland where everything is dust. Slaker, a dustwalker, meets Justice and she reads his mind.

————. *Gathering.* Greenwillow, 1981. Four teenagers with supersensory powers, linked together, each with distinct powers and talents, return to Dustland and fight for the control of the future.

————. *House of Dies Drear.* Macmillan, 1968. A black family, the Smalls, buy an old house full of passageways and discover a treasure in an abandoned cave. It was an old underground railway station.

————. *Justice and Her Brothers.* Greenwillow, 1979. Justice, Thomas and Levi struggle to understand their supersensory powers. They find they can travel to the future. They are joined by a fourth child, Dorian, who is also extrasensory.

————. *Little Love.* Philomel, 1984. A tender story of the love between Sheema and Forrest. Her mother died and her father deserted her. She finally comes to realize that the love of her grandparents and Forrest is secure and loyal.

————. *M.C. Higgins, the Great.* Macmillan, 1974. M.C. Higgins wants to get away from the poverty he and his family endure. He daydreams a lot about how it is going to be. But he also takes advantage of real opportunities when they come. Newbery, 1975.

————. *Magical Adventures of Pretty Pearl.* Harper, 1983. A complicated fantasy built on both American and African folklore. Pretty Pearl is both a god and a human. She helps others with her magic. As a human she tells others of her past life, and they laugh.

————. *Mystery of Drear House.* Greenwillow, 1987. Thomas Small and his family are cataloging the treasures they found on their land. But the question arises: To whom does this treasure belong?

————. *Planet of Junior Brown.* Macmillan, 1971. Buddy is a leader of a group called Tomorrow Billys. The organization provides havens for homeless boys. One of these boys is Junior Brown, a boy with musical talent but who is obese and unattractive.

————. *Sweet Whispers, Brother Rush.* Philomel, 1982. Tree and her brother Dab are close even though he is retarded. He dies of a hereditary disease and she, brokenhearted, wants to run away. Her mother and friends convince her to accept his death.

————. *Time-Ago Lost: More Tales of Jahdu.* Macmillan, 1973. Mama Luka's building is to be demolished and she must move away. Lee Edward will miss her stories of Jahdu but knows he will see her again.

————. *Time-Ago Tales of Jahdu.* Macmillan, 1969. Mama Luka, babysitter, tells these tales to Lee Edward. They are the adventures of

Jahdo. He is both mischievous and benevolent.

————. *White Romance.* Philomel, 1987. Tally is black in a black school. Didi is white in a black school. Tally is a nice girl but Didi is a "bad" one. They never meant to like each other but it happened; and there are problems.

– ————. *Willie Bea and the Time the Martians Landed.* Greenwillow, 1983. A story based on the reactions of people to Orson Welles' broadcast of Halloween, 1938. Willie Bea is a heroine as she tries to protect her brothers and sisters.

————. *Zeely.* Macmillan, 1967. Geeder idolizes a tall black woman, Zeely, and calls her "queen." Zeely confronts her and tells a moving story of her own childhood. Geeder returns to reality and Zeely is still her queen.

Hamilton-Paterson, James. *Hostage.* Collins, 1980. Wayne, a fat American boy, is kidnapped by terrorists. He must learn to survive against all odds.

————. *House in the Waves.* Philips, 1970. Martin, a young mental patient, attempts to escape from a sanatorium.

Hamley, Dennis. *Landings.* Deutsch, 1979. Philip is learning to glide but can't master the landing and loses his confidence. His brother thinks he is going to die and runs away. Philip looks for him with the help of the ghost of his grandfather.

————. *Pageants of Despair.* Philips, 1974. Peter journeys back to the Middle Ages to fight the forces of darkness. The Evil One is trying to twist the ending of the miracle plays into triumph for the devil.

Hamlin, Gwen. *Changing Keys.* Nal, 1984. Meg meets and likes Jay. He is a bit older and a bit strange but Meg doesn't mind. When she learns more about his past she needs to decide what is best for her to do.

Hammer, Charles. *Me, the Beef and the Bum.* Farrar, 1984. "Me" is Rosie who won a prize with her steer, George (the beef), but couldn't let it be sold for sausages so she ran away and met Mett, the "Bum." They run away together and have many adventures.

Hammett, Evelyn. *I, Priscilla.* Macmillan, 1960. Priscilla is traveling from Massachusetts to Connecticut in 1635. There are Indians, lack of food, winter snows and other hazards. A good picture of early America.

Hamner, Earl. *Homecoming.* Random, 1970. Clay-Boy, the eldest son, went to look for his father when he didn't return home on time. He met with a snowstorm, blacks, bootleggers and the Sheriff. The father is losing all hope.

————. *Spencer's Mountain.* Dial, 1961. A legendary white deer lives on Spencer's Mountain, where the Spencer family has lived for generations. This is the story of Clay-Boy and his eight brothers and sisters.

————. *You Can't Get There from Here.*

Random, 1965. Wes travels all over New York City looking for his father. He just misses him several times but finally finds him. He is starting to give directions of "how you can get there from here."

Hamori, Lazlo. *Dangerous Journey.* Harcourt, 1966. Two Hungarian boys escape to freedom by getting through the "iron curtain" into Austria.

————. *Flight to the Promised Land.* Harcourt, 1963. A young Jewish boy comes from backward Yemen to modern Israel and lives in a kibbutz.

Hamre, Leif. *Operation Arctic.* Atheneum, 1973. Three children are looking for their father when they are trapped on a remote Arctic island.

Hancock, Mary. *Thundering Prairie.* Macrae, 1969. Benjy and his family are going homesteading in Oklahoma in spite of the death of his father. They and their mule, Dab, meet the challenge.

Hancock, Niel. *Dragon Winter.* Warner, 1983. Bramble, an otter, goes to look for his old enemy, Old Bark, a bear. Winter is coming, crops are dead and the wolves will be around.

Hanes, Mari. *Wild Child.* Tyndale, 1982. Sandy was abandoned when he was barely six years old. He had unbelievably bad experiences and would have died if Naomi, a kind, loving woman hadn't come along.

Hanff, Helene. *84, Charing Cross Road.* Grossman, 1970. What started as an inquiry about rare books ended up as a love affair through the mail from New York to London.

Hanlon, Emily. *It's Too Late for Sorry.* Bradbury, 1978. Kenny, 16, loses his best friend over the teasing of a new mentally retarded boy in the neighborhood. He meets Rachel and they both help the new boy.

————. *Love Is No Excuse.* Bradbury, 1982. Julia must resist her father's attempts to make her what she is not. He uses methods that are dishonest to make Julia in his own image. She gets him to see her as she is and wants to be.

————. *Swing.* Bradbury, 1979. One youngster who is deaf and another who had a recent tragedy come together at the swing.

————. *Wing and the Flame.* Bradbury, 1980. Owen, 71, is a sculptor who lives as a hermit. Eric, 15, befriends him and becomes his model. He meets Chris and there is a hint of homosexuality.

Hansen, Joyce. *Gift Giver.* Houghton, 1980. Doris is friends with Amir, a foster boy. He helps her understand her own family, family rules and love.

————. *Home Boy.* Clarion, 1982. Marcus lives in the Bronx and doesn't like it. He deals in drugs but then stops. He gets into a fight and stabs someone. His solution is to run away.

————. *Out from This Place.* Walker, 1988. Easter, Obi's first companion in escape, goes to work on a plantation for money. Should she wait for Obi or go to Philadelphia?

_____. *Which Way to Freedom?* Walker, 1986. Obi escapes his slavery only to be picked up by Union soldiers. He joins the black regiment and fights for the Union's cause.

_____. *Yellow Bird and Me.* Clarion, 1986. Doris misses Amir but she gets a job and saves her money to visit him, but her parents object. She tutors Yellow Bird who is dyslexic.

Hansen, Ron. *Shadowmaker.* Harper, 1987. The Shadowmaker wants all the townspeople to have new shadows. Drizzle and Soot want new shadows but don't have the means to pay for them. Then they discover the Shadowmaker's secret!

Hanson, June. *Summer of the Stallion.* Macmillan, 1979. Janey, 12, spends the summer on a ranch. She takes part in a stallion round-up.

_____. *Winter of the Owl.* Macmillan, 1980. Janey wants to break a colt on Christmas vacation but doesn't have the time. The colt is trapped in ice and an owl alerts Janey. She must save the colt's life.

Harding, Lee. *Fallen Spaceman.* Harper, 1980. A small alien in a giant robot-like spacesuit falls to earth. A small boy crawls inside and is trapped.

_____. *Misplaced Persons.* Harper, 1979. Graeme is slowly cut off from the rest of the world. He is alone. He has been misfiled by the cosmic file clerk.

Hardwick, Michael. *Revenge of the Hound.* Random, 1987. A tongue-in-cheek Sherlock Holmes story. There are a disappearance, an attack by a hound, a murder, a theft and some blackmail.

Harkins, Philip. *Fight Like a Falcon.* Morrow, 1961. Neal makes the Air Force Academy football team.

Harlan, Elizabeth. *Watershed.* Viking, 1986. Jeb and Noel are brothers but Jeb gets a girlfriend and Noel plays pranks. Then Noel does something illegal (shutting off water) and is found guilty and sent to a detention center.

Harmon, A.W. *Base Hit.* Lippincott, 1970. Hank doesn't want to play baseball but a series of circumstances has him as a pitcher on a Little League team. He learns to enjoy it.

Harmon, Lyn. *Flight to Jewell Island.* Lippincott, 1967. Tom, 13, is afraid of wolves and as an early settler doesn't always have his gun ready. One day he is the only one to protect his family from attack.

Harnden, Ruth. *High Pasture.* Houghton, 1964. Tim is lonely and he sees a wolf who he believes is a dog lost years ago in the area. He tries to lure the dog to him.

Harnett, Cynthia. *Cargo of the Madelena.* Lerner, 1984. Bendy solves the mystery when William Caxton fails to receive the paper shipped to him on the "Madelena."

_____. *Caxton's Challenge.* World, 1960. Bendy is apprenticed to William Caxton, the publisher, who wants to print books instead of handcopying them.

_____. *Great House.* World, 1968. Barbara and Geoffrey get involved in the building of Ladybourne Hall and the people connected with it, including a reported witch. A mystery set in the time of William and Mary in London.

_____. *Writing on the Hearth.* Viking, 1971. Stephen dreams of going to Oxford as a poor scholar. His future is jeopardized by 15th century witchcraft and political intrigue.

Harnishfeger, Lloyd. *Hunters of the Black Swamp.* Lerner, 1971. A story of a family of four cavemen in prehistoric America. The dangers of hunting, the threat of loneliness and the effects of superstition are explored.

_____. *Prisoner of the Mound Builders.* Lerner, 1973. Ottawa, a crippled Indian boy, is captured by a fierce and primitive Indian tribe. Hating his existence as a slave, he struggles to escape.

Harrah, Michael. *First Offender.* Collins, 1980. Freddy, 13, has an alcoholic mother. He is sent to juvenile hall for something he didn't do.

Harris, Christie. *Confessions of a Toe-Hanger.* Atheneum, 1967. Feeny, Linsey's sister, does not have the talent and poise that Linsey has. But she needs to make her own life.

_____. *Forbidden Frontier.* Atheneum, 1968. Allison was against the treatment of the Indians by the white man. Megan was against potato farming. They were not likely to be friends but circumstances and mutual cooperation made them friends.

_____. *Secret in the Stlalakum Wild.* Atheneum, 1972. Morann is loud and clumsy. She eats some wild berries and hears strange voices. She has met the Stlabakums (a type of spirit).

_____. *You Have to Draw the Line Somewhere.* Atheneum, 1964. Linsey wants to be an artist. She must earn money for college. She works hard and is offered a job at *Vogue* but the prospect of marriage creates a problem.

Harris, Geraldine. *Children of the Wind.* Greenwillow, 1983. Kerish travels through deadly Lan-Pin-Fria to get the keys needed for his search.

_____. *Dead Kingdom: Seven Citadels, Part III.* Greenwillow, 1983. Kerish and his friends must get to their goal but their way is blocked by both physical and magical barriers.

_____. *Prince of Godborn.* Greenwillow, 1983. Kerish sets out to find the sorcerer behind the Seven Gates.

_____. *Seventh Gate.* Greenwillow, 1984. Kerish and his friend have nearly found the keys when they are captured by Fanfmere.

Harris, Marilyn. *Hatter Fox.* Random, 1973. The story of a young Navajo girl from her rough beginning to her self success and her tragic death. Both she and the doctor who befriends her show total commitment.

_____. *Runaway's Diary.* Four Winds, 1971. Cat, 16, ran away from home. She finds a dog that becomes her companion. She has many encounters until she is accidentally killed. The story is told from her diary.

Harris, Mark. *Come the Morning.* Bradbury, 1989. Ben and his mother become street people when they can't find the father/husband. They are given help and hope by a mission.

_____. *Last Run.* Lothrop, 1981. Lyle and his beloved grandfather round up wild horses. A friend of grandfather is killed by a stallion and Lyle is determined to catch him and does so in the "last run."

_____. *Peppersalt Land.* Four Winds, 1970. A story of two young girls and their experiences in the prejudiced South.

_____. *With a Wave of the Wand.* Lothrop, 1980. A young girl is upset about her parents' divorce. The story is told by the intertwining of magic and reality.

Harris, Robbie. *Rosie's Double Dare.* Knopf, 1980. Rosie wants to play baseball with the Willard Street Gang. She accepts a dare to prove her courage.

_____. *Rosie's Razzle Dazzle Deal.* Knopf, 1982. Rosie is the culprit but because she is so likeable, mischievous pranks played by her are blamed on her brother.

Harris, Rosemary. *Bright and Morning Star.* Macmillan, 1972. Years later, after the flood, Ruben becomes Merenkere's musician.

_____. *Moon in the Cloud.* Macmillan, 1968. Comical version of how Noah's son Ham and a dedicated friend were able to assemble the animals on the ark, especially two Temple cats.

_____. *Quest for Orion.* Faber, 1978. A group of teenagers in 1999 fight against being subjugated by political decisions. They are helped by some magical relics of Charlemagne and, of course, from the constellation Orion.

_____. *Shadow on the Sun.* Macmillan, 1970. What happens when Ruben returned to Kemi with his animals after the flood subsided.

_____. *Tower of the Stars.* Faber, 1980. This continues the story of the political intrigue of the future. Some practical events and some magical and fantastic ones.

_____. *Zed.* Faber, 1984. Zed, his father and his uncle are held captive by Arab terrorists. He learns that his father is a coward, his uncle is brave and that he is humane.

Harrison, Harry. *California Iceberg.* Walker, 1975. Icebergs are taken to Southern California to solve a severe drought. Todd and his father are in a tugboat when a fierce storm hits and breaks the cables of the iceberg.

_____. *Men from P.I.G. and R.O.B.O.T.* Atheneum, 1974. Two tales of the use of computers and specially trained pigs.

Hart, Bruce. *Breaking Up Is Hard to Do.* Avon, 1987. Julie and Sean are in love but not with each other. Julie loves Roy and Sean loves

Sara Beth. Then Julie and Sean meet and it's true love right from the start.

_____. *Sooner or Later.* Avon, 1978. Michael likes Jessie but Jessie is only 13 and Michael is 17. Jessie hasn't told him her age and is afraid to but she has to sooner or later.

Hart, Carolyn. *Secret in the Cellars.* Dodd, 1964. Sally, Tish and Mike get involved in an espionage plot. They are captured but escape through a tunnel from one of the cellars.

Hart, Dorothy. *Animal Orphans.* Scholastic, 1988. Tim and his sister get two orphaned panther cubs to care for.

Hartling, Peter. *Crutches.* Lothrop, 1988. Thomas and an amputee, Crutches, survive being lost and separated. Eventually Thomas's mother is found and he must leave Crutches.

Hartman, Evert. *War Without Friends.* Crown, 1982. Arnold's father is a loyal Nazi. He is loyal to his superiors and mean to his family. Arnold slowly realizes the folly of his father and the Nazi cause.

Hartwell, Nancy. *Something for Laurie.* Holt, 1962. Laurie has a brilliant father, an arty mother, a beautiful older sister and a nice brother. She adopts a spotted poodle who is about to be destroyed and finds her rightful place in the family.

_____. *Wake Up, Roberta.* Holt, 1960. Bobby turns her hobby of collecting antique dolls into a profitable business. She also develops a good boy-girl relationship.

Harvey, James. *Beyond the Gorge of Shadows.* Lothrop, 1965. Gahyaz lives in pre-historic times. He finds arrowheads in a cave and believes there are other people in the world. He loses his life but his friends find other people who think they are the only ones.

Haseley, Dennis. *Counterfeiter.* Macmillan, 1987. James is working on a piece of art that he is going to sell so he can take Heather on an expensive date. The artwork? A picture of President McKinley (the one that appears on a $500.00 bill).

Hass, E.A. *Incognito Mosquito Flies Again.* Random, 1985. A mosquito detective tells a class of FBI agents of his encounter with insect offenders.

_____. *Incognito Mosquito, Private Insective.* Lothrop, 1982. A mosquito detective tells a cub reporter of his exploits with more insect offenders.

_____. *Incognito Mosquito Takes to the Air.* Random, 1986. A mosquito detective appears on a television show and describes how he outwitted insect offenders.

Hassler, Jon. *Four Miles to Pinecone.* Warne, 1977. Tom knows that two people, one of whom is a good friend, are guilty of theft. Should he report it to the police?

_____. *Grand Opening.* Morrow, 1987. The Foster family move to Plum and face the mores and prejudices of a small town. They make a success of their grocery store but Brenden has trouble making friends.

_____. *Jemmy*. Atheneum, 1980. Jemmy is a Chippewa Indian who has artistic talent. She sees this as a way to end her dull existence. A white family, the Chapmans, help her develop her talent.

Hastings, Beverly. *Watcher in the Dark*. Putnam, 1986. While Erin, 17, was babysitting, the phone rang several times but no one was there. Someone had come into the house and destroyed a picture. Why? Now there was someone turning the knob to get into the house!

Hastings, Selina. *Sir Gawain and the Loathy Lady*. Lothrop, 1985. Sir Gawain promises an ugly old woman that he will find her a husband. A spell is then broken and she becomes a beautiful woman.

Haugaard, Erik. *Boy's Will*. Houghton, 1983. A story of how the American Revolution affected the people of Ireland.

_____. *Cromwell's Boy*. Houghton, 1978. Oliver becomes Cromwell's messenger because he can ride fast and can be trusted to be loyal. He survives as a spy by using his intelligence and horsemanship.

_____. *Hakon of Rogen's Saga*. Houghton, 1963. Hakon is the heir of Rogen Island but his uncle takes him captive on the death of his father. He waits until he can escape and return home.

_____. *Leif the Unlucky*. Houghton, 1982. Faced with increasingly harsh winters and sinking morale, a young man in 15th century Greenland tries to rally the last few surviving Norse colonists.

_____. *Little Fishes*. Houghton, 1967. Starvation, filth and death stalk the Italian countryside during World War II. Guido, supported by his mother, remains strong and kind. He survives and helps other war ravaged orphans.

_____. *Messenger for Parliament*. Houghton, 1976. A story of the English Civil War between Charles I, Cromwell and the Puritans. Oliver and his father face the hardships of war and Oliver hides in a demolished church.

_____. *Orphans of the Wind*. Houghton, 1966. Jim is a deck boy on a ship carrying supplies to the Confederacy during the Civil War. His ship burns and he escapes and joins the Union Army. There he sees the futility of war.

_____. *Samurai's Tale*. Houghton, 1984. Taro moves from servant to stable boy to trusted aide to samurai. He wants to become a "glorious samurai warrior." He gets an education and finds love and friendship along the way.

_____. *Slave's Tale*. Houghton, 1965. Hakon sails for Brittany but encounters storms. He finds a stowaway girl, Helga, and tries to get Rark, a former slave, back to his homeland. It's a dangerous trip with many harrowing adventures.

Hautzig, Deborah. *Hey, Dollface*. Green-willow, 1978. A story of two girls whose friendship turns to love and they explore lesbianism.

_____. *Second Star to the Right*. Greenwillow, 1981. Leslie is overweight so she diets and becomes anorexic. She is hospitalized and given therapy. She sees that it is her resentment toward her mother that is the cause of her problem.

Hautzig, Esther. *Endless Steppe*. Crowell, 1968. Esther, 11, and her family are shipped from Poland to Siberia in 1941. She describes the hardships they endured.

_____. *Gift for Mama*. Penguin, 1987. Sara works hard so she can earn money to buy a Mother's Day present.

Haven, Susan. *Maybe I'll Move to the Lost and Found*. Putnam, 1988. Gilly's parents are divorced. A girl is coming between Gilly and her friend, Franny. She runs away.

Havill, Juanita. *It Always Happens to Leona*. Crown, 1989. Leona is a middle child. Her older sister, Victoria, is perfect and her younger brother, Albert, is lovable and cuddly. But what is she?

Havis, Allan. *Albert the Astronomer*. Harper, 1980. Albert spies on his neighbors with his telescope. His grades in school are poor. He breaks into a house looking for evidence of a "crime." He is caught and brought to his senses.

Havrevold, Finn. *Summer Adventure*. Abelard, 1961. Tina is selfish and gets shipwrecked (through her own fault) with Jan, a boy crippled with polio. They help each other and by the time they are rescued each has self-confidence.

_____. *Undertow*. Atheneum, 1968. Jorn goes to visit Ulf. When he gets there he finds Ulf's parents are away. He and Ulf go on a sailboat, *Aurora,* and have a struggle of wills. Jorn's father was right about Ulf and his morals.

Hawes, Charles. *Dark Frigate*. Little, 1923. Set in the days of King Charles this is a real swashbuckling sea story, high in adventure. Newbery winner, 1924.

Hawes, Evelyn. *Madras-Type Jacket*. Harcourt, 1967. Margo is in college and gets into and out of scrapes constantly. She has her share of boyfriends but Andy in the madras-type jacket is special.

Hawes, Louise. *Malone Meets the Man from Mush-Nut*. Lodestar, 1986. Six episodes in the life of Nelson. His piano teacher is a witch; his pink sneakers do amazing things, etc.

_____. *Nelson Malone Saves Flight 942*. Lodestar, 1988. Nelson's first adventure is with his horrendous teacher Terrible Tuckman; then he meets a rock star, hatches a dragon egg, etc.

Hawks, Robert. *This Stranger, My Father*. Houghton, 1988. Patty, 15, and her father are kidnapped. Patty's father is an escaped convict who sold secrets to the Russians for money. Patty can't believe this; what follows is an inside out world for Patty.

Hay, Daddy. *Hit the Silk*. Philips, 1968. A skydiving story of Douglas whose father wants him to be a sports star.

Hayden, Torey. *Sunflower Forest.* Putnam, 1984. A tragic story of Mara who was raped repeatedly by the Nazis. Now she and her daughter move from place to place because of Mara's instability. Leslie wants stability but gets agony.

Hayes, Florence. *Boy in the 49th Seat.* Random, 1963. A Japanese boy wants to make friends with other boys. He finds a way to get their attention with a humorous twist.

Hayes, Geoffrey. *Alligator and His Uncle Tooth.* Harper, 1977. Corduroy is an alligator to whom his Uncle Tooth tells old sea yarns.

Hayes, John. *Dangerous Cove.* Lippincott, 1960. Two boys outwit a gang of ruthless pirates in Newfoundland in 1676.

Hayes, Sheila. *Carousel Horse.* Nelson, 1978. Fran spends the summer out of town and meets Andrea whom she is sure she won't like because she is a rich girl. However they do become friends and Fran understands that money isn't everything.

_____. *Me and My Mona Lisa Smile.* Nelson, 1981. Row wears braces on her teeth; she has freckles, straight hair and is fat. She takes up with a fast crowd but finds it isn't as much fun as she thought it would be.

_____. *No Autographs, Please.* Dutton, 1985. Cici wants to be an actress and a fortune teller predicted it would come true. Her family owns a movie theatre. She gets involved but not the way she planned.

_____. *Speaking of Snapdragons.* Dutton, 1982. Heather is having a bad summer. Her best friend, Marshall, is getting a stepfather. Her friend, Lisa, is leaving for a month. And then she meets old Mr. Duffy.

_____. *You've Been Away All Summer.* Nelson, 1986. Fran comes back to the city after summer away and wants to see her best friend, Sarah. But Sarah has a new friend, Marcie. Fran continues her friendship with Andrea and finds that change is normal.

Hayes, William. *Hold That Computer.* Atheneum, 1968. Hank and his friends use a computer to find out why they always tie with Irving School in baseball.

_____. *Project: Genius.* Atheneum, 1962. Pete is working on a science project. Most attempts are failures. At midnight of the last day he comes up with a project: mirages.

_____. *Project: Scoop.* Atheneum, 1966. Pete is editor of the school newspaper. He is involved with "the funniest man in the world," hillbillies, a mock trial and the principal.

Haynes, Betsy. *Against Taffy Sinclair Club.* Nelson, 1976. A group of school girls victimize a classmate.

_____. *Faking It.* Nal, 1986. While Lori is away her best friend, Monica, finds a boyfriend.

So Lori, out of jealousy, tries to be different: stays out all night, goes too far with Ed, a hunk from school, etc.

_____. *Ghost of Gravestone Hearth.* Lodestar, 1977. A buried treasure lures a sixteen-year-old ghost back to life.

_____. *Shadow of Jeremy Pimm.* Beaufort, 1981. Neil is drawn toward Jeremy Pimm and his strange mansion. But something sinister is in the house and threatens to control Neil.

_____. *Spies on the Devil's Belt.* Nelson, 1974. Jonathan is playing an important part as a spy for General George Washington even though he thinks he is only running errands for bread and rolls.

Haynes, Mary. *Catch the Sea.* Bradbury, 1989. Lily's father is a painter; Mrs. Phipps doesn't like the paintings he did for her. He takes them to New York to sell and Lily, left alone, tries painting herself. Mrs. Phipps likes and buys them.

_____. *Raider's Sky.* Lothrop, 1987. Children go on a field trip with Children's Concern and never come back. They get on a train and are never seen again. The Children's Concern is to feed and clothe children without parents.

_____. *Wordchanger.* Lothrop, 1983. William's stepfather has invented a machine that does change words. It has many possible uses, most of them evil. Bruno, the stepfather, wants to use it for personal power but is stopped by William.

Hays, Wilma. *Cape Cod Adventure.* Coward, 1964. Peter and Anne live at Cape Cod with their parents. Their father wants to sell and move to the city. Peter finds a bank robber as he looks for ways to keep his father interested in staying.

_____. *Mary's Star.* Holt, 1968. Mary's father was killed in the Revolutionary War. She was alone and penniless. She had a colt, Star, and needed to fight for the right to keep him and for her own rights.

Head, Ann. *Mr. and Mrs. Bo Jo Jones.* Putnam, 1967. July and Bo Jo had to get married. Both sets of parents were overprotective but fought with each other. Bo Jo had to give up his scholarship. But they worked hard to make the marriage work.

Healey, Larry. *Angry Mountains.* Dodd, 1983. Doug is given one last chance to "shape up." He stays with a volcanologist's family and sees an eruption that kills an entire village. The few survivors try to escape in damaged boats on a boiling sea.

_____. *Claw of the Bear.* Watts, 1978. Jimmy, 15, believes the deaths blamed on the bears are not true. It looks like a part-time staff member is responsible. Attempts are made on Jimmy's life.

_____. *Hoard of the Himalayas.* Dodd, 1981. Jim goes on a mountain climbing expedition where one by one people have "accidents."

_____. *Town Is on Fire.* Watts, 1979. The coal mines under the town are on fire and the town is threatened. A killer is loose and three people are dead. Dave is on his trail and could be the next victim.

Hearne, Betsy. *Eli's Ghost.* Macmillan, 1987. Eli nearly drowns and his ghost escapes. They both "live." The ghost is to get into mischief and Eli is to find his mother.

————. *Home.* Atheneum, 1979. Megan searches for the lost king of the giants, Brendan. Randall helps her find Brendan and free him from his captors.

————. *South Star.* Atheneum, 1977. Megan is a giant who escapes death when her parents are killed. She meets Randall and the Bear and escapes from the Screamer.

Heath, W.L. *Earthquake Man.* Beaufort, 1981. Dogs are frightened, cows don't give milk and a troll is seen. Rafe and Ansel let Sinn Fein look for the troll. He finds him and both Sinn and the troll disappear in a thunderstorm.

Heatter, Basil. *Wreck Ashore!* Farrar, 1970. When a young boy's father dies he goes to live with his uncle who is a seaman. He encounters pirates and sinking ships.

Heavilin, Jay. *Fast Ball Pitcher.* Doubleday, 1965. Scott does not like his new high school baseball coach. But he comes to see that learning new and different ways of pitching can pay off.

————. *Fear Rides High.* Doubleday, 1967. Bob is a sprinter but he takes up pole vaulting to help his team win the state tournament. He overcomes his fear and finds that he has talent.

Heck, B. Holland. *Cactus Kevin.* World, 1965. Kevin meets Slim who names him Cactus. Kevin helps on the family farm and saves a calf. He also tries to rid the farm of cactus. He gets a horse for a reward.

Heck, Bessie. *Hopeful Years.* World, 1964. It is 1917 and Millie goes to school during the week and does house work. She goes home on weekends. She begins to date and worries about the beginning of WWI.

————. *Millie.* World, 1961. Millie is 12 and still in the fourth grade because her family moves so often. It is 1911 and Millie celebrates Christmas, goes to school and is determined to finish 12th grade.

Hegarty, Reginald. *Rope's End.* Houghton, 1965. The day by day experiences, both humorous and exciting, of a boy on a whaling ship.

Heide, Florence. *Banana Blitz.* Holiday, 1983. Jonah arrives at school. He likes junk food but his roommate is a health nut. He enters a TV contest to get money for junk food.

————. *Banana Twist.* Holiday, 1978. Jonah wants to go to boarding school to get away from home. He gets to go but his roommate is unlikable Goober from next door.

————. *Black Magic at Brillstone.* Whitman, 1981. A fast-paced, suspenseful mystery with Logan and Liza at the Brillstone apartments.

————. *Body in the Brillstone Garage.* Whit-

man, 1988. Liza discovers a body but when she returns with a friend the body is gone. Who is the murderer? Is it the man with the jacket? She recognizes the shirt of Mr. Greening but he's alive.

————. *Brillstone Break-In.* Whitman, 1977. Two teenagers become involved with money delivered as a bribe to Eric, the officer at the housing development. Liza is the daughter of a newspaperman and an investigator.

————. *Burning Stone at Brillstone.* Whitman, 1978. Liza and her journalistic friend, Logan, find that life at the Brillstone apartments is a series of suspicious events. Liza's reporter father is a source of information of these events.

————. *Deadline for McGurk.* Whitman, 1974. There is a rash of dollnappings taking place and the Spotlight Club, Willie, Joey and Wanda, must solve the crime.

————. *Face at the Brillstone Window.* Whitman, 1979. Liza's father is a crime reporter who specializes in young first offenders. Liza wants to clear Robin of a robbery she feels he didn't do. Through the diary of a 10-year-old, she does.

————. *Fear at Brillstone.* Whitman, 1978. Logan is hired by a theft-prone company where he learns about a robbery. He and Liza take pictures that are clues to the robbery and then someone is after the film.

————. *Growing Anyway Up.* Harper, 1976. A young girl goes to a new private school. She has serious problems because of her prior poor relationship with her mother.

————. *Hidden Box Mystery.* Whitman, 1973. Jay, Cindy and Dexter are looking for a petty thief. But a valuable chess piece is missing from the museum. The Spotlight Club must get help.

————. *Mystery at Keyhole Carnival.* Whitman, 1977. The Spotlight Club members help out at the carnival and find a counterfeiter.

————. *Mystery at Southport Cinema.* Whitman, 1978. Thorne lost a bag of money belonging to someone else. The thief ran into a cinema and did not come out. The Spotlight crew look for clues in the form of a disguise.

————. *Mystery of the Bewitched Bookmobile.* Whitman, 1975. A Spotlight Club mystery about books and libraries.

————. *Mystery of the Danger Road.* Whitman, 1983. Cindy goes to pick up clowns for a charity fair. She picks up the wrong ones. She also rescues an injured dog. The thieves steal the clowns back and also take Cindy and the dog.

————. *Mystery of the Forgotten Island.* Whitman, 1979. Rowing on the lake the Spotlight detectives find an island where an old man is held captive.

————. *Mystery of the Lonely Lantern.* Whitman, 1976. There is a masked stranger in an empty house. He is the legal heir who is being cheated out of his inheritance. The Spotlight Club help find the relatives who are responsible.

_____. *Mystery of the Macadoo Zoo*. Whitman, 1973. Spotlight Club members track down a pickpocket who is running loose in the zoo.

_____. *Mystery of the Melting Snowman*. Whitman, 1974. Spotlight detectives are involved with a mysterious man and an iron dog.

_____. *Mystery of the Midnight Message*. Whitman, 1982. Cindy and Jay are stranded in a hotel during a blizzard. They learn about a robbery which is to take place nearby.

_____. *Mystery of the Missing Suitcase*. Whitman, 1972. When they pick up the wrong suitcase, the Spotlight Club members are involved in a bank robbery.

_____. *Mystery of the Mummy's Mask*. Whitman, 1979. The Spotlight Club gets involved with a dealer in old masks. It all started with the discovery of an ancient mask.

_____. *Mystery of the Silver Tag*. Whitman, 1972. When a valuable cat is obviously missing, the Spotlight Club sets out to rescue it.

_____. *Mystery of the Vanishing Visitor*. Whitman, 1982. A burglar robs a neighbor's house looking for a painting of a cat that has money hidden in it. Another case for the Spotlight Club.

_____. *Mystery of the Whispering Voice*. Whitman, 1974. The Spotlight Club sees a newcomer as suspicious because he whispers.

_____. *Problem with Pulcifer*. Lippincott, 1982. Pulcifer's problem is that he doesn't watch television. He reads! He is forced to cure this habit.

_____. *Secret Dreamer, Secret Dreams*. Lippincott, 1978. The "secrets" are told by a mentally retarded girl about herself.

_____. *Shrinking of Treehorn*. Holiday, 1971. Treehorn needs to decide whether he wants to be green or small. The only way to stop himself from shrinking is to play a magical game that turns him green.

_____. *Time Bomb at Brillstone*. Whitman, 1982. Liza finds that not all crimes can be prevented or solved all the time. A slight change from most amateur-detective stories.

_____. *Time Flies*. Holiday, 1984. Noah just knows the new baby is going to be troublesome, especially as he sees Bib and her family. But he finally ends up being proud of his sister.

_____. *Time's Up*. Holiday, 1982. Noah's mother and father are too busy for him. He dreams of owning a bike. He meets his new neighbor, Bib, and gains a friend (and a bike).

_____. *Treehorn's Treasure*. Holiday, 1981. One day a tree has dollar bills for leaves. Treehorn uses it to buy comic books and candy. No one believes him when he tells about the tree. But it begins to go back to normal leaves.

_____. *Treehorn's Wish*. Holiday, 1984. Treehorn finds a genie in a bottle and is granted

wishes. He wishes for a birthday cake that his parents failed to provide.

_____. *When the Sad One Comes to Stay*. Lippincott, 1975. Sara must choose between her mother's fashionable world and the world of a poor but warm family unit.

Heinlein, Robert. *Citizen of the Galaxy*. Scribner, 1977. This deals with the problems of slavery and freedom in the far future, and how to be human and survive in this kind of society.

_____. *Have Space Suit — Will Travel*. Ballantine, 1977. Kip is taken from his backyard to the moon. Peewee, a scientist's daughter, and an alien are also on this not so pleasurable cruise.

_____. *Podkayne of Mars*. Putnam, 1963. Poddy and Clark of Mars have Earth ancestors. They and their Uncle Tom become involved in interplanetary politics.

_____. *Puppet Masters*. Doubleday, 1986. Aliens have taken over the minds of people without their knowing it. After an injection of Maorpheus they become harmless puppets. Can anyone stop it? How?

_____. *Starman Jones*. Scribner, 1979. Max Jones stows away on a spaceship that gets lost. He lands on an unknown planet. The captain of the ship dies and the charts are destroyed. What now?

_____. *Waldo and Magic, Inc.* Doubleday, 1970. Waldo is plotting the destruction of humanity. Humans have humiliated him and so Magic, Inc., is formed.

Held, Kurt. *Outsiders of Uskoken Castle*. Doubleday, 1967. Orphans who survive by stealing live in Uskoken Castle. Branko is helped to escape jail by Zora, a girl leader of a gang. He must prove himself worthy to join the gang.

Helldorfer, M.C. *Almost Home*. Bradbury, 1987. Jessica and Lewis are staying with their grandfather for the summer. They meet Carmen and learn about pirates and treasure.

Henkes, Kevin. *Return to Sender*. Greenwillow, 1984. Whitaker writes a letter to Frogman and gets a surprising response. Frogman is a television superstar. His family laughs until he gets a response.

_____. *Two Under Par*. Greenwillow, 1987. Widge is fat. His new father and brother are skinny. His new father is King of Camelot, a miniature golf course owner; he wears a crown. Can Widge handle this?

_____. *Zebra Wall*. Greenwillow, 1987. Adine is the first of five children who are all girls named alphabetically A to E. When number six comes it's a BOY!

Henry, Marguerite. *King of the Wind*. Rand, 1948. Godolphin Arabian is an ancestor of Man o' War and founder of the thoroughbred strain. Newbery winner, 1949.

_____. *Misty of Chincoteague*. Rand, 1947. The capture of Misty and his elusive mother on Assateague Island. His mother returned to the wild but Misty remains with the Beebes.

_____. *Mustang, Wild Spirit of the West.* Macmillan, 1966. A well-written horse story by one who knows about horses.

_____. *Our First Pony.* Macmillan, 1984. Justin and Joey are the new owners of a Shetland.

_____. *San Domingo, the Medicine Hat Stallion.* Rand, 1972. A boy's father was wronged and he is going to set it right.

_____. *Sea Star: Orphan of Chincoteague.* Scholastic, 1949/1989. Misty was sold to be shared with children everywhere. Paul and Maureen find a stray colt on the beach and save its life.

_____. *Stormy, Misty's Foal.* Rand, 1963. Misty's foal is born in the aftermath of a great storm that ravaged the Chincoteague Island. Thus the name Stormy.

Hentoff, Nat. *Day They Came to Arrest the Book.* Delacorte, 1982. First parents then students and teachers are involved in censorship. The case goes to committee and then school board. The book, *Huckleberry Finn,* remains on the shelf and the censors lose.

_____. *Does This School Have Capital Punishment?* Delacorte, 1981. Sam really has his troubles at school, some humorous, some adventurous, but all still trouble. His project about a jazz musician and a bully fellow student is the cause of some of it.

_____. *In the Country of Ourselves.* S & S, 1971. A group of radical students challenge their school board.

_____. *Jazz Country.* Harper, 1965. A young white boy wants to be a great trumpet player. He tells about the black jazz world as seen through his eyes.

_____. *This School Is Driving Me Crazy.* Delacorte, 1976. Sam doesn't want to go to school where his father is headmaster; but he causes more trouble than he intended.

Herbert, Frank. *Children of Dune.* Berkley, 1976. The third book about Paul Maud 'Dib, founder, ruler and leader of Dune.

_____. *Dune.* Chilton, 1965. Dune is a planet with an important spice as its main product. Lady Jessica was supposed to have a daughter but had a son instead. Paul leads the Freemen to great changes in the galaxy.

_____. *Under Pressure.* Random, 1981. Four men are on a mission a mile underwater. They know each other well but one of them is a saboteur who will destroy them all.

Herlicky, Dirlie. *Ludie's Song.* Dial, 1988. Marty meets Ludie, a disfigured black girl. She gets to know her and is no longer repulsed but finds her kind and bright. They have an unpleasant experience with three white boys.

Herman, Ber. *Rhapsody in Blue of Mickey Klein.* Stemmer House, 1981. Mickey grows up in the late 1930's. He believes his soul is blue and does amazing things.

Herman, Charlotte. *Difference of Ari Stein.* Harper, 1976. Ari is a Jewish boy living in New York in 1944. He wants to hold on to his Jewish convictions and to accept a more conventional life.

_____. *Our Snowman Had Olive Eyes.* Dutton, 1977. Sheila's grandmother comes to live with her. She teaches Sheila to make cookies and plant cuttings. She then leaves to live with her other son and Sheila misses her.

Hermes, Patricia. *Friends Are Like That.* Harcourt, 1984. Tracy needs to decide between the popular crown and her unconventional friend, Kelly.

_____. *Heads, I Win.* Harcourt, 1988. Bailey, living in a foster home, hopes running for class president will help her situation.

_____. *Kevin Corbett Eats Flies.* Harcourt, 1986. Kevin and Bailey want to prevent Kevin's father (and Kevin) from moving away again.

_____. *Nobody's Fault?* Harcourt, 1961. Monse is hurt and then dies from injuries received on the family lawnmower. His sister, Emily, is heartbroken. She needs psychiatric help because she feels guilty about teasing him so much.

_____. *Place for Jeremy.* Harcourt, 1987. Jeremy is staying with her grandparents longer than expected. She must now start at a new school. She finds out that her absent parents have adopted a baby sister.

_____. *Solitary Secret.* Harcourt, 1985. A young girl has secret incest with her father on a regular basis. It scars her life, and she hates her father and herself. A sad story with only a small ray of hope.

_____. *What If They Knew?* Harcourt, 1980. Jeremy is staying with grandparents while her parents are away. She has epilepsy. Her new friends find out and accept it.

_____. *Who Will Take Care of Me?* Harcourt, 1983. Mark runs away from home and takes his mentally handicapped brother with him.

_____. *You Shouldn't Have to Say Good-Bye.* Harcourt, 1982. A story of a girl whose mother is dying of cancer.

Herzig, Alison. *Season of Secrets.* Little, 1982. Brooke's brother, Benji, is epileptic and it is kept a secret. Finally it comes out and she and the family can handle it. In the meantime Benji is training a pet that he must let go.

_____. *Shadows on the Pond.* Little, 1985. Jill and Migan are summer friends and spend time watching the pond where the beavers are. Someone sets traps for the beavers and the girls spring the traps and get hurt. Ryan helps them.

_____. *Ten Speed Babysitter.* Dutton, 1987. Tony babysits for a three-year-old. Alone, he copes with a storm, robbers and the hatching of a duck egg. He gets help from a girl and can later laugh at the events.

_____. *Word to the Wise.* Little, 1978. Willie and his friends steal a thesaurus and it magically solves each of their problems. They stick together and make changes in school.

Hest, Amy. *Getting Rid of Krista*. Morrow, 1988. Gillian and her friend want to have Gillian's sister "discovered" and made into a star of stage and screen.

————. *Maybe Next Year*.... Clarion, 1982. Kate lives with her grandmother who is seriously involved with a widowed neighbor. She likes ballet but finds that maybe she is not really ready for it....

————. *Pete and Lily*. Clarion, 1986. Pete lives with her mother and has a friend, Lily, who lives downstairs. Pete's mother and Lily's father are dating. She meets a boy and life is becoming "normal."

Heuck, Sigrid. *Hideout*. Dutton, 1988. Rebecca and Sami survive World War II in an orphanage.

Heuman, William. *Backcourt Man*. Dodd, 1960. Ritchie is a short man on the pro basketball team. But he proves that he can play well in spite of it.

————. *Gridiron Stranger*. Lippincott, 1970. This story is more ghost fantasy than it is football but has good suspenseful episodes and some football action.

————. *Horace Higby and the Field Goal Formula*. Dodd, 1969. Horace Higby is an unusual boy. He makes use of science and some fantasy to change the game of football.

————. *Horace Higby and the Gentle Fullback*. Dodd, 1970. Horace Higby is involved in an unusual scientific approach to sports.

————. *Horace Higby and the Scientific Pitch*. Dodd, 1968. An unusual boy, Horace Higby, in a story about baseball. It is a science fantasy with some facts and a lot of imagination.

————. *Horace Higby, Coxswain of the Crew*. Dodd, 1971. After trying baseball and football Horace is ready to try something different with his unusual approach of science and imagination.

————. *Powerhouse Five*. Dodd, 1963. Ron plays basketball and becomes a player/coach. He forms a team of juvenile delinquents.

————. *Wonder Five*. Dodd, 1962. Danny is a star basketball player. He must move to a new school where the Wonder Five have won their 42nd straight game. He finally makes the team and brings harmony among members.

Hewett, Hilda. *Harriet and the Cherry Pie*. Lothrop, 1964. Harriet and her sister stay with Great Aunt Sophie who runs a restaurant. Harriet becomes a child actress to help with finances.

Heyman, Anita. *Exit from Home*. Crown, 1977. Samuel is to become a rabbi. But he joins an underground group involved in radical activities. This is Russia in 1905. He must escape to America.

————. *Final Grades*. Dodd, 1983. Rachel is trying to get into a top grade college but she begins to lose interest in school. Her parents and

brother are not models for her. She must think about what she wants to do before college.

Hickman, Janet. *Stones*. Macmillan, 1976. Garrett "hates" the Germans during World War II. He and his friends persecute an old German man.

————. *Thunder-Pup*. Macmillan, 1981. Linnie McKay hopes to get a puppy for her birthday, but she messes up at school; Darle, the snob, appears; and her present is her parents' new house. But she does get her puppy, eventually.

————. *Zoar Blue*. Macmillan, 1978. Barbara is an orphan. She runs away from the Keffer family to find an uncle. John Keffer runs away to join the Union Army. They meet when they are involved in different ways at the Battle of Gettysburg.

Hicks, Clifford. *Alvin Fernald, Foreign Trader*. Holt, 1966. Alvin wins a candy cooking contest. The prize is a trip to Europe. And he has some very funny adventures with Shoie and the Pest who, of course, goes too.

————. *Alvin Fernald, Master of a Thousand Disguises*. Holt, 1986. Is the Huntley Place really haunted? Alvin thinks not. However, how is he going to prove or disprove it?

————. *Alvin Fernald, Mayor for a Day*. Holt, 1970. Alvin wins the right to be the mayor for a day but finds out that the mayor is a criminal. A funny spoof on kids and the System.

————. *Alvin Fernald, Superweasel*. Holt, 1974. Alvin's pollution project is geared to expose the biggest polluter in town—the owner of the chemical plant.

————. *Alvin Fernald, T.V. Anchorman*. Holt, 1980. Alvin solves an eleven-year-old mystery while he earns a regular spot on the television news. He proves a cameraman's innocence and reunites him with his son, all on television.

————. *Alvin's Secret Code*. Houghton, 1963. Alvin is Secret Agent 12½. He and his friend Shoie break a secret code to save an orphanage. His sister, the Pest, helps. They find a treasure buried during the Civil War.

————. *Alvin's Swap Shop*. Holt, 1976. Alvin starts a Swap Shop with one black ant traded for some dead spiders. Then the shop becomes a hideout for a fugitive, Pim. They all team up to capture a criminal.

————. *Marvelous Inventions of Alvin Fernald*. Holt, 1960. Alvin invents the Sure Shot Paper Slinger and the fun and trouble begin in the Old Huntley (Haunted?) Place. There are strange footprints in the dust.

————. *Peter Potts*. Dutton, 1971. Everything he does is wrong. Why won't his schemes work? Peter and Joey want to surprise Joey's mother but shock her instead. The April Fools' Day trick with the spider backfires.

————. *Pop and Peter Potts*. Holt, 1984. Peter and his grandfather, Pops, have more schemes and hobbies that are hilarious and exciting, such as lion taming (backwards) and hypnotizing chickens.

————. *Wacky World of Alvin Fernald.* Holt, 1981. This "brainy" boy now turns a bicycle into an airplane. He also pulls an April Fools' joke on his home town.

Higdon, Hal. *Electronic Olympics.* Holt, 1971. Dave follows Speed Sloan, who trained electronically on a treadmill with a computer program. A PED-72 replaces judges at the event. Many humorous events in a spoof story.

————. *Horse That Played Center Field.* Holt, 1969. A baseball spoof. Oscar, a horse, is in center field. He inspires the rest of the team to play better.

————. *Last Series.* Dutton, 1974. A slapstick funny baseball story with a sub-plot of a new stadium.

————. *Team That Played in the Space Bowl.* Dutton, 1981. A college football team is space-napped and has to play a team of robots. A cheerleader is their coach and her unorthodox plays can't be programmed by the robot computer. So they win!

Higgins, Colin. *Harold and Maud.* Avon, 1975. Harold is 18 and Maud is 79. They become friends in the oddest way. Harold wants to die. (He's tried suicide several times.) Maud loves life and does interesting things. A strange love exists between them.

Hightower, Florence. *Dark Horse of Woodfield.* Houghton, 1962. Maggie, 14, likes horses. She wants to enter Star in competition but must first write an essay to earn the entrance fee.

————. *Dreamworld Castle.* Houghton, 1978. Phoebe meets some twins that lead her into dangerous and illegal activities. Tony, the twins' older brother, is hiding from the law. Miranda grows up emotionally after Tony kills himself.

————. *Fayerweather Forecast.* Houghton, 1967. Lucy, Bob and Betsy are looking for Aunt Lucy's fiance, Edward. A funny, warm mystery.

————. *Secret of the Crazy Quilt.* Houghton, 1972. Grandmother has a surprising secret in her quilt. Edith and Jerusha try to decipher the secret.

Highwater, Jamake. *Anpao.* Harper, 1977. Anpao is going to meet his father, the Sun, and has many harrowing experiences on the way.

————. *Ceremony of Innocence.* Harper, 1985. After being disillusioned by the death of her husband, Amana finds friendship and love. She instills the pride of Indian heritage in her daughter.

————. *Eyes of Darkness.* Lothrop, 1985. Yesa is a Plains Indian who believes he can beat the white man's system by becoming proficient in it himself. He joins the white society, becomes a doctor and serves at Wounded Knee.

————. *I Wear the Morning Star.* Harper, 1986. Sitko, an Indian, learns to paint and keep his Indian heritage as he lives among whites.

————. *Legend Days.* Harper, 1984. Grandfather Fox passes on to eleven-year-old Amana the intrinsic qualities of a hunter's instinct and a warrior's prowess.

Hildick, E.W. *Case of the Bashful Bank Robber.* Macmillan, 1981. Armed robbers are coming to town, and McGurk and his organization are on red alert. They learn about it from a photo taken at the bank earlier.

————. *Case of the Condemned Cat.* Macmillan, 1978. The suspect in this mystery is Whiskers, the pet cat. The crime is murder; the victim, a white dove; and the penalty, to the local pound, if guilty.

————. *Case of the Felon's Fiddle.* Macmillan, 1982. A note in a violin and uncut diamonds are McGurk's clues in this mystery.

————. *Case of the Four Flying Fingers.* Macmillan, 1981. A burglar, and a group of children who unwittingly help him, run afoul of McGurk's organization.

————. *Case of the Invisible Dog.* Macmillan, 1977. McGurk matches wits with a very young scientific genius before he is able to solve the mystery of the invisible dog.

————. *Case of the Muttering Mummy.* Macmillan, 1986. The cat Joey bought at a museum gets the attention of an expert on Egyptian artifacts and therefore the attention of the McGurk organization.

————. *Case of the Nervous Newsboy.* Macmillan, 1976. The police help McGurk and his fellow detectives, Joey, Wanda and Willie, find a runaway newsboy.

————. *Case of the Phantom Frog.* Macmillan, 1979. McGurk stumbles on a frightening puzzle: who—or what—is making snarling, unearthly sounds. Who is under the mask?

————. *Case of the Secret Scribbler.* Macmillan, 1978. McGurk finds a suspicious slip of paper in a library book. It turns out to be a mysterious map and a crime yet to be committed.

————. *Case of the Slingshot Sniper.* Macmillan, 1983. The McGurk Detective Organization competes against a clairvoyant rival while attempting to solve a case of vandalism.

————. *Case of the Snowbound Spy.* Macmillan, 1980. The McGurk organization is now involved in espionage at a very high level. They carry messages and packages unwittingly.

————. *Case of the Treetop Treasure.* Macmillan, 1980. In this case one of McGurk's own "men" is the suspect in a burglary. While rescuing a killer they find "treasure." But a valuable stolen bowl does show up among the "treasures."

————. *Case of the Vanishing Ventriloquist.* Macmillan, 1985. The McGurk organization must act to prevent a crime, but they don't know what the crime will be. Another member joins the group and helps solve this one. Mari joins the organization.

————. *Case of the Wandering Weather-*

vanes. Macmillan, 1988. An enemy agent is followed by McGurk to find out who is stealing the weathervanes and why.

_____. *Cat Called Amnesia.* White, 1976. Angus finds a stray cat in his summer home. He is told to find its owner or the cat will go to the city pound. A mysterious cat story.

_____. *Doughnut Dropout.* Doubleday, 1972. Adam, 12, comes from a long line of "eaters": pies, pizza, hot dogs, etc. He trains to be the champion doughnut eater. He wins the State, Regional and National awards. Can he win the International?

_____. *Ghost Squad and the Ghoul of Grunberg.* Dutton, 1986. The Ghost Squad help investigate the happenings at a rich summer camp. They find that the owner is a missing Nazi war leader.

_____. *Ghost Squad and the Halloween Conspiracy.* Dutton, 1985. The Ghost Squad must prevent unscrupulous people like Vinnie from putting needles into chocolates on Halloween. Malevs, the "bad" ghosts, enter the picture.

_____. *Ghost Squad and the Menace of the Malevs.* Dutton, 1988. The Ghost Squad can't believe that "nice" Clem Jackson is Joe's murderer. Again they must face Grunberg, leader of the evil ghosts, the Malevs.

_____. *Ghost Squad and the Prowling Hermits.* Dutton, 1987. The four ghosts prevent evil Dr. Purcell's plan to have a ghost take over living bodies from going into effect.

_____. *Ghost Squad Breaks Through.* Dutton, 1984. Ghosts band together to both solve and prevent crimes when one of them, Danny, finds he can communicate with two living beings, Wacko and Buzz, through a computer.

_____. *Ghost Squad Flies Concorde.* Dutton, 1985. The four ghosts that make up the Ghost Squad fly to England to investigate a swindle.

_____. *Great Rabbit Rip-Off.* Macmillan, 1977. One of four detectives, Wanda, is accused of defacing and then stealing all the ornamental clay rabbits in the neighborhood. Willie, the Nose, is a big help in this adventure.

_____. *Kids Commune.* White, 1972. Tony and three other Kershaw children rebel and start their own commune in a guest cottage. They lay down rules for parents. When one of them gets sick they go to a hospital and the family is united.

_____. *McGurk Gets Good and Mad.* Macmillan, 1982. Someone sabotages McGurk's First Annual Open House. He is really "good and mad" when his special handcuffs are stolen.

_____. *Manhattan Is Missing.* Doubleday, 1969. Manhattan is a Siamese cat and is missing. Hugh, Sarah and others begin to search for her. They find a ransom note. It leads them to the teen-aged cat-nappers and the rescue of Manhattan.

_____. *Nose Knows.* Whitman, 1973. A fast, funny, easy reading mystery with Jack McGurk. This is the first of many others; Willie is

the Nose.

_____. *Secret Spenders.* Crown, 1971. Tim and his uncle spend their $500,000.00 on luxury living. A girl sleuth in the same building and a phony kidnapping that turns out to be real add to the humor.

_____. *Secret Winners.* Crown, 1970. Tim and his uncle have a lottery ticket and win half a million dollars but must keep it a secret from Aunt Bridget. They spend it secretly and she never finds out.

_____. *Time Explorers, Inc.* Doubleday, 1976. Buzz's friend Danny has dreams that come true. Buzz is injured in an accident and Danny disappears.

_____. *Top Boy at Twisters Creek.* White, 1969. Andy, 14, enters a member of his gang in the contest for Top Boy. He gets the rest of his gang to campaign for and support their candidate, Orville. A funny story.

_____. *Top Flight Fully Automated Junior High School Girl Detective.* Doubleday, 1977. Emmeline must find out who stole and is using Mr. Grant's charge card. She gets an Informer to help her look for a small card in a large city and time is running out.

Hildick, Florence. *Jim Starling and the Colonel.* Doubleday, 1960. Jim wants to prove that the boys of today are as good as boys of long ago, as stated by his grandfather. He runs 4 miles in 15 minutes, cycles 5 miles in 20 minutes, climbs a 250 foot tower, etc.

_____. *Louie's Lot.* White, 1965. Louie is a boss for boys delivering milk. Tim, 14, works for Louie and must fight off dogs, watch for milk money thieves and be on the lookout for other boys who might attack.

_____. *Louie's Ransom.* Knopf, 1978. Louie and his Lot travel to New England and get captured by kidnappers.

_____. *Louie's S.O.S.* Doubleday, 1968. Louie's Lot are his handpicked boys who work the milk route. Someone is sabotaging his milk. Is the rival milkman? Louie and his Lot must find out.

_____. *Louie's Snowstorm.* Doubleday, 1974. Louie tries to beat a snowstorm and give his customers their milk. He has a girl on the truck for the first time. They capture a would-be burglar, rescue an injured man and assist in delivering a baby.

Hildreth, Richard. *Memoirs of a Fugitive.* Crowell, 1971. A portrayal of the cruel and degrading life of a slave. Archy Moore moves from slaveholder to slaveholder, each with a different philosophy about slaveholding. He later escapes to freedom in the North.

Hilgartner, Beth. *Murder for Her Majesty.* Houghton, 1986. Alice witnesses her father's murder. She runs away and passes herself off as a boy. Her father's killer is after her.

_____. *Necklace of Fallen Stars.* Little,

1979. Kaela is about to be married to her father's political ally. She runs away. She is pursued by a wizard. Her father dies and she is reunited with her family.

Hill, Douglas. *Alien Citadel.* Atheneum, 1984. Finn, captured by the cruel Slavers, learns the truth at last about these alien rulers of Earth, and the secret of the Citadel.

————. *Blade of the Poisoners.* McElderry, 1987. Jarrel is tainted by an evil sword which must be destroyed or he will die.

————. *Caves of Klydor.* Atheneum, 1985. Cord and the other young rebels are exiled to the planet Klydor.

————. *Colsac Rebellion.* Atheneum, 1985. The teenagers exiled to the planet Klydor return to Earth and lead a rebellion.

————. *Day of the Starwind.* Atheneum, 1981. Moros and his alien companion set a course for the uninhabited planet of Rilyn, to investigate the sinister activities of the Warlord and his agent, the Deathwing.

————. *Deathwing Over Veynaa.* Atheneum, 1981. Deathwing is the agent of the Warlord who rules Rilyn and is the doer of evil.

————. *Exiles of Colsac.* Atheneum, 1984. Twelve rebel youngsters crash-land on an alien planet; six of them survive. One is a killer. Cord is the leader of the group.

————. *Galactic Warlord.* Atheneum, 1980. Keill must find the "evil intelligence" that everyone believes is responsible for the destruction of Moros and its people. He must avenge this wrong.

————. *Huntsman.* Atheneum, 1982. Finn Ferral begins his adventure with the evil Slavers who want to conquer the Earth.

————. *Master of the Fiends.* McElderry, 1988. Jarrel sets out to rescue the wizard, Cryltaur, from the palace of demons and the evil Master of Fiends.

————. *Penelope's Pendant.* Doubleday, 1991. Penny, 11, finds a slightly broken pendant on the beach. With this she can move herself and other objects through the air.

————. *Planet of the Warlord.* Atheneum, 1982. Keill, the Last Legionary, and his alien friend, Gir, are left alive on Moros, the destroyed planet. They are in deep trouble as they face the "evil genius" that is responsible.

————. *Warriors of the Wasteland.* Atheneum, 1983. Finn Ferral searches for Jena, who was captured by Slavers. He is pursued by Claw.

————. *Young Legionary.* Atheneum, 1983. Keill survives a test and is selected for training to fight savage life on an alien planet.

Hill, Elizabeth. *Fangs Aren't Everything.* Dutton, 1985. A story of the Ravinoor Curse where Tod is to become a werewolf and slave to the Swamp King.

Hill, Marjorie. *Secret of Avalon.* McGraw, 1965. Alan, 16, lives in the time of the Druids. He is a foundling and can't become a Druid. But he works hard and finally achieves it.

Hillerman, Tony. *Boy Who Made Dragonfly.* Harper, 1972. A Zuni boy and his sister are abandoned by their tribe and must survive hunger and thirst. They are helped by Cornstalk Being.

Hillinger, Brad. *Wings Are Gone.* Morrow, 1976. Brad is a drifter and Denice is an airline stewardess when they meet. They fall in love and dream of marriage. Denice is killed in a plane crash and Brad wonders about the role of fate.

Hilton, James. *Goodbye, Mr. Chips.* Little, 1957. Mr. Chips taught at Brookfield for fifty years. He was a traditional type teacher who did small things for the boys at school. And although he was laughed at, no one ever forgot him.

Hilts, Len. *Timmy O'Dowd and the Big Ditch.* Harcourt, 1988. Timmy lives near the Erie Canal and he wants to become a canal boat captain. His cousin Dennis is a rival but saves the farmers from disaster when the canal wall breaks.

Hinchman, Catherine. *Torchlight.* Little, 1960. Jimmy was a Hungarian freedom fighter. He moved in with the American Windhams. Cindy is very much like Jimmy and they relate.

Hinchman, Jane. *Talent for Trouble.* Doubleday, 1966. Ann is clumsy and accident prone. She gets a job bird-sitting for some finches. She gets innocently involved with an "older man."

Hindle, Lee. *Dragon Fall.* Avon, 1984. Gabe designs dragons for a toy company. First they were nice and friendly then they became nasty because of the owner's request. Then the dragons came to life, thinking Gabe was their father.

Hines, Anna. *Boys Are Yucko!* Dutton, 1989. Cassie and Agatha think boys are Yucko, except for Jimmy. Cassie has a birthday party in hopes that her divorced father will come. He doesn't.

————. *Cassie Bowen Takes Witch Lessons.* Dutton, 1985. Cassie is teamed up with unpopular Saggy Aggy to do a project. Cassie's friends Brenda and Sylvia tease her but she befriends Agatha when her friends become overly nasty.

Hinkemeyer, Michael. *Fields of Eden.* Putnam, 1977. A shotgun attacker kills the entire family of a small town preacher. The sheriff is both detective and prosecuting attorney.

Hinton, Nigel. *Collision Course.* Nelson, 1976. Ray steals a motorcycle and goes joyriding. It ends with the death of an old woman.

————. *Getting Free.* Nelson, 1978. Jo and Peter run away because Jo is pregnant and doesn't want an abortion. Jo suffers a miscarriage.

Hinton, S.E. *Outsiders.* Viking, 1967. The Greasers are a bunch of tough boys who fight with a rival gang, the Socs. Johnny and Ponyboy hide out after one of the Socs is killed. They save a child from death but Ponyboy dies.

————. *Rumble Fish.* Delacorte, 1975. Rusty is a very tough 14-year-old who ruins his life by trying to be like his older brother, Motorcycle Boy.

_____. *Taming the Star Runner.* Delacorte, 1988. Travis lives with an uncle. He likes to write and a book he has written is about to be published. He is a bad/good guy who understands right from wrong.

_____. *Tex.* Delacorte, 1979. Tex and his brother Mason are close but when Tex learns that they are not really brothers he has doubts. He both loves and hates Mason. Tex also deals with friends, a girlfriend and some danger.

_____. *That Was Then, This Is Now.* Viking, 1971. Byron, a Greaser, lives with Mark and his family. He finds out that Mark is on drugs and he is faced with turning him in. He cares about his future but Mark is still doing things for "kicks."

Hirsch, Linda. *You're Going Out There a Kid, You're Coming Back a Star.* Hastings, 1982. Margaret wants to grow up and go out on dates. She is not off to a good start: botched up make-up, first kisses, etc.

Hlibok, Bruce. *Silent Dancer.* Messner, 1981. Nancy is a deaf ballet dancer. With special sound equipment she learns grace and skill.

Ho, Minfong. *Sing to the Dawn.* Lothrop, 1975. Dawn won a scholarship but girls don't go to school for long in Southeast Asia. It should go to her brother but she convinces her father to let her accept it.

Hoban, Lillian. *I Met a Traveller.* Harper, 1977. Josie's parents are divorced. She lives in Jerusalem and goes to a Christian school. She wants to go home and when she finally does life begins to look up.

Hobson, Laura. *Consenting Adult.* Doubleday, 1975. Jeff, 17, is gay. His mother understands but thinks homosexuality is a disease to be treated and cured. Jeff knows better.

Hobson, Polly. *Mystery House.* Lippincott, 1964. Marilyn's friends live in "Mystery House," an old vicarage which is excellent for exploring.

Hocker, Karla. *Three Times Lost Dog.* Atheneum, 1967. Christian has hidden the puppy he shouldn't have and raises him in secret. He wants to tell his parents but never gets the chance.

Hodges, C.W. *Marsh King.* Coward, 1967. King Alfred barely escapes from Somerset Marshes as an ambush is attempted. A great deal is learned about life in England at that time. He defeats the Danes and frees Guthorm.

_____. *Namesake.* Coward, 1964. This is the story of Alfred the Great, King of England, and his fight against the invaders of England. His leniency with the Danish King, Guthorm, is questioned when Guthorm seeks revenge.

Hodges, Margaret. *Avenger.* Scribner, 1982. Alexis competes in the races at Olympia. There are pirates and kidnappings. Alexis is a man at the end of the story looking back at his life.

_____. *Fire Bringer.* Little, 1972. An Indian boy and a coyote brought the gift of fire from the Burning Mountain to the Paiute people.

_____. *Freewheeling of Joshua Cobb.* Farrar, 1974. One could predict Josh's bicycle camping trip would not be untroubled. Five friends on a ten day camping trip are bound to be unpredictable. But even Cassandra proves her mettle.

_____. *Hatching of Joshua Cobb.* Farrar, 1967. Josh is at summer camp with a counselor who is a bully. There is a great deal of humor in Josh's sleep-away camp, after the bully is dismissed and replaced.

_____. *Making of Joshua Cobb.* Farrar, 1971. Josh is an eighth grader with lots of friends. He has some great adventures in sports and other school activities. This boarding school could help him but can he make it?

Hoenig, Cary. *Reaper.* Bobbs, 1975. Georgie is surrounded by gangs and drugs. He is overcome by the harshness of life before he has a chance to live it.

Hoff, Syd. *Irving and Me.* Harper, 1967. Artie makes friends with Irving when he moves to Florida. They get into mischievous trouble, meet girls, go to parties, get into scraps between themselves, etc.

Hoffman, Alice. *Property Of.* Farrar, 1977. An 18-year-old tells of her disastrous fascination with the leader of a New York City street gang.

Hogan, James. *Code of the Life Maker.* Ballantine, 1983. Why is a colony ship on the way to Mars rerouted to Titan? Why the strange passengers aboard? Military forces! Parapsychology experts!

_____. *Two Faces of Tomorrow.* Ballantine, 1979. Spartacus is a computer designed to survive as it kills. It was meant to control computers but now controls everything and everybody, even the man that invented it.

Holberg, Ruth. *Jill and the Applebird House.* Doubleday, 1968. Jill is in charge of renovating the family summer house. She organizes both a swap meet and a party-givers service to raise money.

_____. *Rowena the Sailor.* Doubleday, 1954. Row likes pretty Jennifer who is a summer visitor. She drops her old ways and old friends and models Jennifer but by the end of the summer Jennifer's glitter has worn off and Row is herself again.

_____. *What Happened to Virgilia?* Doubleday, 1963. Virgilia leads a different life with her aunt in Massachusetts. A brush with local swindlers, a storm, an investigation of a tower room and putting on a play were some of her everyday doings.

Holden, Molly. *Unfinished Feud.* Hawthorn, 1970. A story of feuding families where all males are going to be dead if it isn't stopped. The sorrows, ugliness and uselessness of revenge killing are pointed out.

Holding, James. *Mystery of the False Fingertips.* Harper, 1964. Dutch has a job labeling exhibits at the museum and becomes involved in a mystery concerning the theft of Egyptian false fingertips.

Holl, Kristi. *Cast a Single Shadow.* Atheneum, 1986. Tracy's mother is arrested for robbing a jewelry store. She and her brother look for the real thief and clear their mother.

_____. *First Things First.* Atheneum, 1986. Shelley is going to raise the needed money for summer camp. She is successful but the cost of family, friends and pets is too high a price to pay.

_____. *Footprints Up My Back.* Atheneum, 1984. Jean, 12, is taken advantage of by everyone because she is reliable. She earns money for a dog and almost loses it because she can't say No!

_____. *Haunting of Cabin Thirteen.* Atheneum, 1986. Laurie gets a threatening note that cabin 13 is haunted. It is signed by a girl who had drowned the previous summer.

_____. *Just Like a Real Family.* Atheneum, 1983. June is going to "adopt" a grandparent from a retirement home but the person she's paired with is grumpy. But eventually she works out a plan that helps her mother, Mr. Cooper and herself.

_____. *No Strings Attached.* Atheneum, 1988. June finds that living with Mr. Cooper is sometimes difficult but when she and he are alone for a week they accept each other.

_____. *Patchwork Summer.* Atheneum, 1987. Randi is resentful when her run-away mother returns.

_____. *Rose Beyond the Wall.* Atheneum, 1985. Rachel is close to her grandmother who is dying of cancer. She, more than other members of the family, accepts the notion of death.

Holland, Barbara. *Creepy-Mouse Coming to Get You.* Clarion, 1985. Rosalie made a mistake marrying Mack. He is now being released from prison and she doesn't want to see him. Her young brother takes her baby and hides but Mack finds them and is violent.

_____. *Pony Problem.* Dutton, 1977. Jean wins a pony but has no place to keep it. Neighbors complain and she is afraid it will be taken awy.

_____. *Prisoners at the Kitchen Table.* Houghton, 1979. Two children are held captive by a kidnapper in the kitchen of an abandoned house.

Holland, Cecelia. *Ghost on the Steppe.* Atheneum, 1969. Djela practices his archery so he can get a man's bow. He lies to his father and is sent to a north camp for one month. He takes his bow and hunts the beast that is killing calves.

Holland, Isabelle. *After the First Love.* Ballantine, 1983. Sarah loves Steve and gets pregnant. Sad for her, Steve does not love her. She miscarries and so loses both the baby and Steve.

_____. *Alan and the Animal Kingdom.* Lippincott, 1977. Sean, 12, lives with his great-aunt and tries to keep her death a secret because he is afraid of losing his pets if he is sent away.

_____. *Amanda's Choice.* Lippincott, 1970. Amanda, 12, is "terrible," "unlikable," "disturbed" to adults. Adults are "stupid" to Amanda. She is mad at the world and misbehaves for attention. A boy of 19 spanks her and then becomes her friend.

_____. *Dinah and the Green Fat Kingdom.* Lippincott, 1978. Dinah has a weight problem and suffers a great deal because of it.

_____. *Empty House.* Harper, 1983. Betsy and her brother are staying with Aunt Marian. Their father is accused of fraud. She and her boyfriend, Ted, along with others, try to prove their father innocent.

_____. *God, Mrs. Muskrat, and Aunt Dot.* Westminster, 1983. Rebecca writes a letter to God explaining how lonely she is now that her parents are gone and she is living with her aunt and uncle. She also writes about her imaginary friend.

_____. *Heads You Win, Tails I Lose.* Lippincott, 1973. A girl tries to lose weight by taking pills.

_____. *Horse Named Peaceable.* Lothrop, 1982. Jessany, 12, looks for her lost horse.

_____. *Jennie Kiss'd Me.* Fawcett, 1985. Jill must fend for herself when her mother dies and her father turns to drink.

_____. *Love and the Genetic Factor.* Ballantine, 1987. Stephanie's father dies and she breaks up with her boyfriend. She fears she's a schizophrenic like her mother. She goes to Italy to find a woman mentioned by her father.

_____. *Man Without a Face.* Lippincott, 1972. Chick is tutored by a man who keeps his face hidden. They grow fond of each other and have a brief sexual encounter. Chick learns about the man and his past and also about his own future.

_____. *Marchington Inheritance.* Rawson, 1979. Two young children, Michelle and Toby, and a group of youngsters in a private school lead to a suspenseful event that is a surprise to everyone.

_____. *Now Is Not Too Late.* Lothrop, 1980. Cathy spends a summer at her grandmother's and discovers the real identity of her mother.

_____. *Perdita.* Little, 1983. Perdita, 17, has amnesia after an accident. She thought she worked around horses and takes a job at Stanton Stables. She faces danger and problems but it all works out well.

_____. *Toby the Splendid.* Walker, 1987. Janet buys a horse with her babysitting money against the advice of her parents. Now she needs money for riding lessons and for the horse's upkeep.

_____. *Unfrightened Dark.* Little, 1990. When her beloved guide dog is kidnapped, Jocelyn, an orphan and blind, is determined to solve the mystery of his disappearance.

Holland, Ruth. *Room.* Delacorte, 1972. Nicky, Sandy and Haines fix up a basement room for their own use. Sandy's mother gives them "joints." Then come the pills. Then Sandy is in a home for incorrigibles.

Holland-Crossley, Kevin. *Sea Stranger.* Seabury, 1974. A story of how Christianity came to the Saxons in the 7th century.

Hollander, Judith. *Like Potion.* Atheneum, 1986. Beverly meets Jason and competition begins when Jason pays attention to Dina. She and her friends devise a love potion to slip in his milk.

Holling, Holling. *Tree in the Trail.* Houghton, 1942. The well-traveled Santa Fe Trail is described, using an old 200-year-old cottonwood tree as a symbol of hope to the pioneers and as a symbol of peace to the Indians.

Hollman, Clide. *Eagle Feather.* Hastings, 1963. Beaver, an Indian, was kidnapped by a white man and rescued by a Frenchman who treated him kindly. He was stolen again and rescued again by the same Frenchman.

Holm, Anne. *North to Freedom.* Harcourt, 1965. David has lived in concentration camps most of his 12-year life. He has difficulty learning to trust people, even as he is given a chance to escape.

Holman, Felice. *Blackmail Machine.* Macmillan, 1967. Arabella is an activist. She uses the fact that the tree house is flying to make the mayor, the county and the world a better place. An effective spoof.

―――――. *Future of Hooper Toote.* Scribner, 1972. Hooper skimmed the ground instead of walking. He tried to weigh himself down but he always tended to rise. How should he cure this distracting phenomenon?

―――――. *Murderer.* Scribner, 1978. Hershy lives in Pennsylvania during the Great Depression. He is Jewish and lives in a Polish town. He must contend with all the prejudices.

―――――. *Slake's Limbo.* Scribner, 1974. Aremis lives in the subway for four months. He is lonely and has to survive as best he can. He meets another person just once but that meeting changes both their lives.

―――――. *Wild Children.* Scribner, 1983. Alex lives on the streets of Moscow. He begs and robs to get food and clothing. There are many other children like him and they share and help each other. Alex and others eventually move to Finland.

―――――. *Year to Grow.* Norton, 1968. Julia is in boarding school. She meets Jimmy, a retarded boy, and they become friends. Then Jimmy suddenly dies.

Holmberg, Ake. *Margaret's Story.* Viking, 1961. Margaret's parents are killed in an automobile accident. She is 17 and goes to work but doesn't get along well with other people. She does have two love affairs and learns to warm up to people.

Holmes, Barbara. *Charlotte Cheetham: Master of Disaster.* Harper, 1985. Charlotte tells lies. To win friendship with Tina she tells a whopper: that her friend owns a sticker factory and she will take them there for a visit. Her friend Anna helps her out of it.

―――――. *Charlotte Shakespeare and Annie the Great.* Harper, 1989. Charlotte begs Annie to try out for the lead in the play she has written for the class. She then loses control of the play and is jealous of Annie's attention.

―――――. *Charlotte the Starlet.* Harper, 1988. Charlotte is going to write. Everyone likes what she writes. She is a star! But, is it real? Her best friend, Annie, says no, she is being used because of what she writes. She throws the book away.

Holmes, Marjorie. *Love Is a Hopscotch Thing.* Westminster, 1963. Carly, 17, likes Danny even though she is going out with Chuck. She must learn to make good decisions.

Holmvik, Oyvind. *Crack of Doom.* Harcourt, 1966. An exciting story of the skin divers' struggle with the sea. As frogmen they repair a ruptured dam. They also rescue people in the path of the flood.

―――――. *Dive to Danger.* Harcourt, 1964. A group of boys including very spoiled Lars are taught to be skin divers; and spies!

Holt, Stephen. *Ranch Beyond the Mountains.* Holt, 1961. Larry and his friend Bomber go to a ranch inherited by Bomber. They work hard and make it into a good cattle ranch. They survive bitter winters, lack of good stock and savage wildlife.

Honeycutt, Natalie. *All New Jonah Twist.* Bradbury, 1986. Jonah has trouble being on time, trouble with trying to live up to his older brother, Todd, and trouble with Granville, a fellow student who is a bully. But Jonah is going to change.

―――――. *Best Laid Plans of Jonah Twist.* Bradbury, 1988. Jonah and Granville become friends! Jonah wants a pet kitten and wants to find his brother's missing hamster. And he wants to keep Juliet out of his science project plans. He won't be stopped.

―――――. *Invisible Lissa.* Bradbury, 1985. Lissa is the "official class creep." Debra keeps her out of everything. When Lissa gets recognition for her class project Debra destroys it.

―――――. *Josie's Beau.* Watts, 1987. Spending the summer in San Francisco, going to the swimming pool and hanging around with friends are what Josie and Beau do.

Honig, Donald. *Jed McLane and Storm Cloud.* McGraw, 1968. An exciting Western about Jed, a fourteen-year-old, and his horse. He lives on an Army base in 1880. He saves an innocent Indian boy from being hanged.

―――――. *Jed McLane and the Stranger.* McGraw, 1969. Jed's father was a good and admired soldier but a stranger came looking for him with revenge as a motive.

―――――. *Johnny Lee.* Dutton, 1971. A black boy leaves Harlem to play baseball. He goes to camp in the South.

―――――. *Journal of One Davey Wyatt.* Watts, 1972. Davey goes from Iowa to California in 1850. There are a bout with cholera, a lynching, a drowning and a lost child during the hazardous trip.

Honness, Elizabeth. *Mystery of the Auction Trunk*. Lippincott, 1956. Nancy, Barby and Doug bid on an old truck and become involved in an art mystery. It not only involves the former home of the artist but some very old paintings and unscrupulous art dealers.

_____. *Mystery of the Mayan Jade*. Lippincott, 1971. Pam is spending Spring vacation looking at some Mayan ruins. Together with Toby she discovers that a jade figurine is missing. They work together to find the thief.

_____. *Mystery of the Pirate's Ghost*. Lippincott, 1966. Abby and Kit get involved in two mysteries. One, a theft of antiques and two, a pirate who haunts their newly inherited house.

_____. *Mystery of the Secret Message*. Lippincott, 1961. Penny is left a scroll by her missing father. In it she finds an important message needed to catch some spies.

_____. *Mystery of the Wooden Indian*. Lippincott, 1958. Nancy, Barby and Doug spend the Christmas holidays at the vacation home where they usually spend their summers. They discover a cigar store Indian in an old building and the mystery begins.

Hoobler, Thomas. *Chill's Project*. Putnam, 1987. Allie has psychic powers. Dr. Chill runs a home for psychokinetic children. He defends, protects and trains them.

_____. *Revenge of Ho-Tai*. Walker, 1989. Roger and his basketball teammates are using "imaging" to help them play better. Ho-Tai is a good luck charm but. . . .

Hooks, William. *Circle of Fire*. Atheneum, 1982. Harrison has two black friends. There is fear of the KKK. When some Irish tinkers come around the KKK mobilizes and Harrison goes to warn them. He sees the horrors of the KKK before the sheriff comes.

_____. *Doug Meets the Nutcracker*. Warne, 1977. Doug must attend his sister's ballet recital but is then captivated. He wants to take lessons despite the ridicule by his friends.

_____. *Flight of Dazzle Angels*. Macmillan, 1988. Annie, 15, has problems: her father is dead, her mother is an invalid and also dying, and her Aunt Kit wants the family money. She must find a way to take control of her life.

_____. *Jelly's Circus*. Atheneum, 1986. Jelly has a million ideas (most don't work out). This one is for a circus but his friend, Leo, doesn't want to play his minor role. He thinks Jelly Bean gets all the glory.

_____. *Legend of the White Doe*. Macmillan, 1988. An account of what happened to the Roanoke, Virginia, colony that disappeared without a trace.

_____. *Mystery on Bleeker Street*. Knopf, 1980. Chase is friends with 78-year-old Babette and her dog. One day she disappears and Chase looks for her. Babette saw some counterfeiters and they kidnapped her dog so she would help them.

_____. *Mystery on Liberty Street*. Knopf, 1982. Two friends become involved in a police operation investigating the suspicious activities taking place in an abandoned warehouse.

_____. *Theo Zephyr*. Atheneum, 1987. Brad's imaginary friend humiliates the boy Brad is jealous of. But now it is getting out of hand.

Hoover, H.M. *Bell Tree*. Viking, 1982. Henny and her father search for an ancient civilization and find more questions than answers.

_____. *Children of Morrow*. Four Winds, 1973. A story of two children born to parents from two different cultures and who have powers of telepathy.

_____. *Delikon*. Viking, 1977. Varina, her guard and two children are involved in a fight to rid the earth of its rulers, the Delikon.

_____. *Lost Star*. Viking, 1979. Lian crashes her airship. She is found by archaeologists and finds out that she is linked with these people and their "computers."

_____. *Orvis*. Viking, 1987. Toby and Thaddeus are on deserted Earth while their parents travel in space. They become involved with Orvis, a robot.

_____. *Rains of Eridan*. Viking, 1977. Planet Eridan has only herbivores but a couple is found murdered and a girl left for dead. But Karen is alone and when the rains come large caterpillar-like carnivores come alive.

_____. *Return to Earth*. Viking, 1980. In the year 3307 Earth is ruled by Mega-Corporations. Samara must help her country against the Dolmen and their power.

_____. *Shepherd Moon*. Viking, 1984. Mikel comes from an artificial moon: Shepherd Moon. He meets Merry and is outwitted by her and her grandfather in spite of his supernatural powers.

_____. *This Time of Darkness*. Viking, 1980. Amy lives in a domed city that is safe from the pollution of the Outside. Axel tells her that the Outside is safe and they both escape to go there.

_____. *Treasures of Morrow*. Four Winds, 1976. These telepathic youngsters spend some time with the more advanced culture of one of their parents.

Hope, Anthony. *Prisoner of Zenda*. Nal, 1962. Rudolf looks just like the new king-to-be. The king is kidnapped by his brother because he wants the throne. But Rudolf is mixed up in the plans that turn out quite differently.

Hopkins, Lee. *Mama*. Knopf, 1977. Mama takes things from where she works: clothes, meat, etc., to make ends meet. Her son, Chris, carries them home knowing it's wrong but he can't do anything. Mama starts to work at a laundry.

_____. *Mama and Her Boys*. Harper, 1981. Mr. Jacobs of the laundry wants to marry Mama but she refuses. The school custodian, Mike, is interviewed by her son for the school newspaper and a friendship begins with Mama and Mike.

Hopkins, Lila. *Eating Crow.* Watts, 1988. Croaker's dog is hurt and when "a crazy old lady" helps him he promises God he will do someone a good favor.

Hoppe, Joanne. *April Spell.* Warne, 1979. Jennifer investigates a spook church. Strange accidents happen. Her mother is an alcoholic. Is she being haunted by a dead spirit?

_____. *Pretty Penny Farm.* Morrow, 1987. Beth is spending her vacation on Pretty Penny Farm. She meets Dave, falls in love, rides horses and learns to understand Sophie.

Hopper, Nancy. *Ape Ears and Beaky.* Dutton, 1984. Scott (Ears) and Stanley (Nose) don't get along. But a series of robberies gets them involved and brings them together.

_____. *Carrie's Games.* Lodestar, 1987. Carrie tries to manipulate Lise, her father's friend, and in the process loses her two boyfriends, and a girlfriend and hurts her father.

_____. *Hang On, Harvey.* Dutton, 1983. Harvey lost his promised position in the school orchestra; he is hounded by the school bully. Eighth grade is not as good as he thought it would be.

_____. *Just Vernon.* Lodestar, 1982. Cindy befriends Vernon, a retarded man who works for her mother. She is nice to him but he misunderstands something and threatens her. He runs away; she finds him and explains how they can be friends.

_____. *Lies.* Lodestar, 1984. In order to get and keep the attention of a boy she likes a girl tells some outrageous lies.

_____. *Rivals.* Dutton, 1985. Janie's cousin Kate is coming to stay for a while. Janie is jealous of her because she snares all the boys including her boy friend, Jason.

_____. *Seven and One-Half Sins of Stacey Kendall.* Dutton, 1982. Stacey pierces ears for her fellow students but it does not turn out well. How does one balance beauty, popularity, jealousy, social cliques, etc., that haunt early teens?

_____. *Whoppers.* Dutton, 1984. Allison lies a lot and can't break the habit. It doesn't bother her until she meets Jerry and tells him she's a tennis pro, her father is a CIA agent, Stephanie is into drugs, etc.

Horgan, Dorothy. *Edge of War.* Oxford, 1988. Anna and her parents are German but not Nazis and they fear for their lives during World War II.

Horowitz, Anthony. *Devil's Door-Bell.* Holt, 1983. Elvira Crow and her sister Kite are probably witches. Evil is everywhere in the form of twisted bodies, cobwebs, hellish hounds, black magic and all the other symbols of devil's work.

_____. *Night of the Scorpion.* Putnam, 1985. Martin and Richard are in Peru looking for the "second gate," through which the evil Old One

and his ghostly creatures will return. They are successful in holding them back.

Horseman, Elaine. *Hubble's Bubble.* Norton, 1964. Sarah and Alaric have an old book of magic spells. They can turn themselves and others into cats, mice and toads. They can fly over the city. Charlotte, Jonathan and Peter join in the fun.

_____. *Hubbles' Treasure Hunt.* Norton, 1965. Sarah and Alaric go on a treasure hunt with Charlotte, Peter and Jonathan. Sarah finds a note in an old inherited doll. Their magic spell book takes them back in time to the Civil War.

Horvath, Polly. *Occasional Cow.* Farrar, 1989. Imogene spends her summer on a farm. She is a New York City girl and finds fun in pigs and cows and in growing crops. She participates in a local talent show, does some fun spying and enjoys her summer.

Horwitz, Joshua. *Only Birds and Angels Fly.* Harper, 1985. Danny talks about Chris's addiction that leads to his death. They are both in private school. Dan is shy; Chris outgoing. Pranks lead to drugs, "pot," LSD, and then death.

Hosford, Jessie. *You Bet Your Boots I Can.* Nelson, 1972. Julia wants to go to college in the East and get away from Nebraska. Her parents want her to stay and teach school. She accepts a job in a country school with primitive conditions. She learns to enjoy it.

Hotchner, A.E. *Looking for Miracles.* Harper, 1975. Aaron passes himself off as an experienced camp counselor so that he and his kid brother can get into summer camp.

Hotze, Sollace. *Circle Unbroken.* Clarion, 1988. Rachel is captured and abused by an Indian in 1838. She is rescued by another Indian and raised as his daughter. She is returned to her father but she can't give up her Indian ways.

Hough, Richard. *Buzzbugs.* Warne, 1977. Mosquitoes grow to be the size of a small car and prey on people. Lucy and John see a "buzzbug" kill a horse.

_____. *Fast Circuit.* Harper, 1962. Nick is driving for a team that is being sabotaged by the rival team. An accident is caused and a fuel injector is stolen. A team member is a traitor but Nick wins the race.

_____. *Four-Wheel Drift.* Harper, 1959. Nick and Sam work on their car and make it perfect for the race at Monte Carlo. Nick drives the highly efficient car to victory.

Houghton, Eric. *Mystery of the Old Field.* McGraw, 1964. Colin looks for buried silver in a Western town in the 1880's. He solves a mystery and finds the missing treasure.

_____. *Steps Out of Time.* Lothrop, 1979. Jonathan walks through a door into another time. He is recognized there and is called Peter. He goes back again and again and can do many things like paint and swim. He is in his own future time.

Household, Geoffrey. *Escape Into Daylight.*

Little, 1976. Mike and Carrie are kidnapped and held in a cellar. They escape. The chase and the effort to avoid recapture and/or death are suspenseful.

Houston, James. *Akavak: An Eskimo Journey*. Harcourt, 1968. Akavak and his grandfather go on a hazardous trip. They run out of food and must change their route across icy cliffs. They lose their dogs and fear for their lives.

_____. *Black Diamonds*. Atheneum, 1982. When Matthew's father gets home they all set out to find the mother lode of the gold nuggets that were found earlier. Is it "black diamonds" as oil is known up there? Or gold?

_____. *Eagle Mask: West Coast Indian Tale*. Harcourt, 1966. Skemsham must go through trials of endurance and rituals in "becoming of age" in his clan if he is to become chieftain.

_____. *Falcon Bow*. McElderry, 1986. Kungo finds the Inuit people starving because of the loss of the caribou. Something must be done about the ecological chain.

_____. *Frozen Fire*. Atheneum, 1977. Matthew's father is lost in an Arctic storm. Matthew and Kayak, his friend, go to look for him. The trip is dangerous and they run out of gas for their snowmobile before they reach home.

_____. *Ghost Paddle*. Harcourt, 1972. Hooits, a young prince of 15, learns that making peace requires as much courage as waging war.

_____. *Ice Sword*. Atheneum, 1985. Matthew, Kayak and Jill, along with Dr. Luman spend the summer in the Arctic. There are a shark attack and a night spent on the ice. There are also strong friendship and mutual dependency.

_____. *River Runners*. Atheneum, 1979. Andrew works for a fur company in Canada. He and Naskapi are to open up a new outpost. The assignment is not without peril.

_____. *Tikta'liktak*. Harcourt, 1965. An Eskimo hunter is stranded on an ice floe with only his bow and arrows and a harpoon.

_____. *White Archer*. Harcourt, 1967. Kungo lost his parents in a massacre. He wants revenge. But when the time comes to inflict it, he has doubts.

_____. *Wolf Run*. Harcourt, 1971. Punik goes to look for much needed food. A stark account of Punik's survival in the Arctic.

Houston, Jeanne. *Farewell to Manzanar*. Houghton, 1973. A Japanese-American girl tells about life in the internment camps during World War II. The Americans put the Japanese people there for fear of their loyalty.

Houston, Joan. *Crofton Meadows*. Crowell, 1961. Sheila is in boarding school. Her rival is Lorraine whom she beats but when she finds out about Lorraine's parents she accepts her because of them.

Howard, Elizabeth. *Mystery of the Metro*. Random, 1987. MacKenzie, 16, is involved in a mystery in Paris in the early 1900's. He is

American and goes from one adventure to another.

_____. *Out of Step with the Dancers*. Morrow, 1978. Damaris, a Quaker, copes with her feelings for Matthew and Joel.

_____. *Winter on Her Own*. Morrow, 1968. Amantha, 16, goes to the city to work. She leaves her boyfriend, Thad, behind. In the city her cousins treat her coolly but she meets good looking Martin and compares him to Thad back home.

Howard, Ellen. *Circle of Giving*. Atheneum, 1984. Marguerite spends time and patience teaching Francie, a cerebral palsy neighbor, to read and write.

_____. *Edith Herself*. Atheneum, 1987. Edith goes to live with a sister when her mother dies. She is epileptic and has tough new problems to face.

_____. *Gilly Flower*. Atheneum, 1986. A disturbing book on incest between father and daughter. Gilly finally tells her mother about it. Love and friendship develop.

_____. *Her Own Song*. Atheneum, 1988. Mellie's adoptive father is in the hospital after an accident. She is befriended by Geem-Wah, a Chinese boy. He knows about Mellie's birth and parentage.

_____. *Verity's Voyage*. Morrow, 1964. Verity leaves England for the West Indies. She is an orphan without a dowry but has many new and different suitors.

Howard, John. *Black Like Me*. Nal, 1962. Griffin had his skin dyed black and went to live in the deep South for five weeks as a black man. A bad experience.

Howard, Moses. *Ostrich Chase*. Holt, 1974. A young Bushman girl, Khuana, and her wise grandmother go on a hunt for ostriches even though girls aren't allowed to hunt. They must travel alone and not mix with the men/boys.

Howe, Fanny. *Race of the Radical*. Viking, 1985. Alex names his new BMX bike "Radical." It is a prototype designed by his dad. One day it is stolen. Alex and his friends look for the thieves and in the process clear Rennie's name.

_____. *Taking Care*. Avon, 1985. Pamela really messed up her life with lying, drinking, etc. She meets Tristan while he is lying bloody on a hospital stretcher. Maybe he can help her.

Howe, James. *Bunnicula*. Atheneum, 1979. Bunnicula is a vampire bunny. He was found in a shoe box at the movies. Harold, the dog, and Chester, the cat, know he's no ordinary rabbit.

_____. *Celery Stalks at Midnight*. Atheneum, 1983. Chester the cat is now more than ever convinced that Bunnicula is a vampire when more white vegetables show up.

_____. *Dew Drop Dead*. Atheneum, 1990. Sebastian, Corrie and David solve a mystery of a dead man found in an abandoned inn.

_____. *Eat Your Poison, Dear*. Atheneum, 1986. Students become ill after eating in the school cafeteria. The school officials say it is the flu but Sebastian and David say it is not. They solve the mystery of Milo and Miss Swille.

————. *Howliday Inn*. Atheneum, 1982. Harold and Chester, a dog and a cat, are in the crime detection business.

————. *Mister Tinker in Oz*. Random, 1985. Another adventure in Oz with all the characters we know from *Wizard of Oz*.

————. *Morgan's Zoo*. Macmillan, 1984. Morgan and his friends, together with some animals, devise a plan to save the zoo.

————. *Night Without Stars*. Atheneum, 1983. Maria, 11, is in the hospital for open heart surgery. She befriends Donald, a badly burned patient. They build a friendship that will last past their hospital stay.

————. *Nighty-Nightmare*. Atheneum, 1987. Harold and Chester are on a camping trip with the Monroes. They sniff that there is going to be trouble and they're right. Bud and Spud and their dog are bad news.

————. *Stage Fright*. Atheneum, 1986. Sebastian Barth is involved in a theatre mystery. There are warnings and some strange accidents as a famous actress comes to visit his home town. "House of Cards" seems jinxed.

————. *What Eric Knew*. Atheneum, 1986. Eric sends cryptic notes to his friends who investigate a mysterious death. Another Sebastian Barth mystery.

Howe, Norma. *God, the Universe and Hot Fudge Sundaes*. Houghton, 1984. Alfie falls in love with Kurt. Kurt is Jewish and her parents are against it. Then Alfie's kid sister, Francie, dies and things change.

Howker, Janne. *Isaac Campion*. Greenwillow, 1986. Isaac's brother died and his relationship with his horse-dealing father worsens.

Hoyland, John. *Ivy Garland*. Schocken, 1983. A young girl's life is threatened by an ancient curse.

Hoyle, Fred. *Rockets in Ursa Major*. Harper, 1969. The Earth is involved in an intergalactic war. A space pilot uses a controlled explosion of the sun as a method of winning.

Hoyt, Helen. *Aloha, Susan*. Doubleday, 1961. Susan must stop being a tom-boy at 12. She lives in Hawaii with her twin brother. There are the loss of their dog, the outbreak of a disease and a devastating fire.

Hubbell, Harriet. *Moon Penny Lane*. Nelson, 1961. Emmie and her mother move to save money. They open a gift shop. Emmie meets both Brad and Jerry; one is from New York and the other from Cape Cod. A nice romance.

Hubner, Carol. *Tattered Tallis*. Judaica, 1980. There are several strange mysteries to be solved: a museum robbery, a spy from East Germany, etc.

————. *Whispering Mezuzah*. Judaica, 1980. Several mysteries are solved: the strange disappearance of mezuzahs and a counterfeiting ring.

Huddy, Delia. *Humboldt Effect*. Greenwillow, 1982. A submarine trip in the Mediterranean has cataclysmic results when a team member is lost at sea and a man from the fourth century is taken aboard.

————. *Time Piper*. Greenwillow, 1979. Luke leaves London to work with Tom Humbolt, the inventor of a revolutionary time machine. He finds the children of the Pied Piper of Hamelin and restores their souls.

Hudson, Jan. *Sweetgrass*. Putnam, 1989. A story that reveals the lifestyle and culture of the Dakota Indians.

Hughes, Dean. *Family Pose*. Atheneum, 1989. David is living on the streets of Seattle. A "hotel family" of night workers take him in. He ran away from an unloving foster home.

————. *Honestly, Myron*. Atheneum, 1982. Myron tells the truth; all the truth, all of the time. This causes many problems in school and with his friends.

————. *Millie Willenheimer and the Chestnut Corporation*. Macmillan, 1983. Millie wants to raise money so she starts her own business.

————. *Nutty and the Case of the Mastermind Thief*. Atheneum, 1985. Nutty and his friend William get together to solve a crime. It appears that William has talents as yet unheard of but there are always strings attached to his activities.

————. *Nutty and the Case of the Ski Slope Spy*. Atheneum, 1985. Nutty, as student council president, manages a ski trip for the school holiday. He finds stolen computer plans in his hotel room and hides them again. He waits for a message from "Russian Roulette."

————. *Nutty Can't Miss*. Atheneum, 1987. Nutty plays basketball at the recreation center. He plays poorly until William helps him by programming him to be an excellent player. Nutty begins to wonder if he really wants this.

————. *Nutty for President*. Atheneum, 1981. William, the new boy in school, is going to make Nutty, a fifth grader, president of the student council even though that position has always been held by a sixth grader.

————. *Nutty Knows All*. Atheneum, 1988. Nutty wants the best science project but he only has two days left to complete it. William helps by changing Nutty's brain through light waves and photons. But it ends with Nutty well.

————. *Nutty the Movie Star*. Atheneum, 1989. Nutty gets a small part in a Hollywood movie and this improves his popularity at school.

————. *Switching Tracks*. Atheneum, 1982. Mark feels guilty about his father's suicide. He thinks he was responsible.

Hughes, Frieda. *Getting Rid of Aunt Edna*. Harper, 1986. Aunt Agatha is a witch and Miranda lives with her. They do fine until the arrival of Aunt Edna who can't get any of her spells to work properly.

Hughes, Monica. *Beyond the Dark River.* Macmillan, 1981. A girl and boy survive a nuclear holocaust. He is Amish and she is Indian. The try to save some dying children by looking for medicine.

————. *Crisis on Conshelf Ten.* Atheneum, 1975. Kepler lives in an undersea city on Earth. He is involved in a guerrilla plot to sever the community from its surface dwellers.

————. *Devil on My Back.* Atheneum, 1984. Only the Lords have access to the computer as the Earth begins to run out of fuel. Tomi, a Lords son, gets Outside with the Slaves and works to overthrow Arcone.

————. *Dream Catchers.* Atheneum, 1987. Ruth, with ESP, is an Outsider living in Ark Three, a domed city. Ark Three has used technology to enslave people. Ruth hears about trouble in another civilization and goes to help.

————. *Guardian of Isis.* Atheneum, 1982. In 2136, Isis settlers lose all technical knowledge and revert to a more primitive lifestyle. Mark is president of the Earth people. Jody tries to make simple machines, but is repulsed.

————. *Hunter in the Dark.* Atheneum, 1983. Mike finds out that he has leukemia. He knows he faces death. His friend helps him with gear to go hunting. He finds that he cannot take the life of an animal and comes to terms with his own death.

————. *Isis Peddler.* Atheneum, 1983. Moira's rocket ship breaks down on a strange planet Isis, and the beings living there are threatened by her father. She and Guardian and a young man team up to stop him.

————. *Keeper of the Isis Light.* Atheneum, 1981. Olwen lives on Isis with a robot, Guardian, who has raised her. When people from Earth come, she is upset but then falls tragically in love with Mark.

————. *Sandwriter.* Holt, 1988. A spoiled princess visits the homeland of her bethrothed prince and learns of a different culture.

————. *Space Trap.* Watts, 1983. Valerie, Susan and Frank are changed into animals by the Mortter Transmitter. Valerie escapes to find Frank and Susan dying in a zoo. They all escape and recover.

Hughes, Shirley. *Here Comes Charlie Moon.* Lothrop, 1986. Charlie lives in Wales. His aunt owns a joke and novelty shop. Need I say more?

Hughey, Roberta. *Question Box.* Delacorte, 1984. Anne puts questions in the school question box. She is shy and protected. She becomes unwittingly involved in an immoral situation and learns the price of loyalty and friendship.

Hugo, Victor. *Hunchback of Notre Dame.* Nal, 1964. Quasimodo is a hunchback and quite badly misformed. He is also deaf. He is raised by a priest after he was deserted. He unfortunately falls in love with an unobtainable woman.

Hull, Eleanor. *Summer People.* Atheneum, 1984. Jenny is Jewish. This story is of her life

from 13 to 20 years of age. Summers are spent in the Glen, where there are hiking, swimming and romance.

————. *Trainful of Strangers.* Atheneum, 1968. A subway breaks down for 45 minutes and eight children get to know each other even though they are from widely different backgrounds.

Humphreys, Josephine. *Rich in Love.* Viking, 1987. Lucille, 17, holds her family together when her mother disappears, her father keeps looking for her and her sister comes home, married and pregnant.

Hunt, Irene. *Across Five Aprils.* Follett, 1964. Jethro grows up during the Civil War. It is a difficult time because of family split ups over the slavery issue. One boy joins the Union forces while the others join the Confederacy.

————. *Everlasting Hills.* Macmillan, 1985. Jeremy's father could not accept him because he is mentally retarded. He runs away and meets a stranger who is like, and better than, a father.

————. *Lottery Rose.* Scribner, 1976. Georgie, a victim of child abuse, loves a dried up rose bush. He is placed in a children's home where he and his rose bush thrive. A very sad story.

————. *No Promises in the Wind.* Berkley, 1976. John and Joey are two young brothers who decide to leave home and make a life for themselves. It is the time of the Great Depression and life at home holds no promise.

————. *Up the Road Slowly.* Grosset, 1968. Julie's mother dies and she goes to live with Aunt Cordelia. She arrives a bad tempered child and grows up to be a very gracious young lady. Newbery winner, 1967.

————. *William.* Scribner, 1977. Sarah, unmarried herself, takes in three children when their mother dies. Carla needs an eye operation, Amy has boyfriend problems and Sarah gives up an art career. William tells the story.

Hunt, Mabel. *Beggar's Daughter.* Lippincott, 1963. A girl sells her baby to Quakers. She wonders about the Quaker life but when the foster parents are imprisoned for their beliefs she knows where she belongs.

Hunter, Edith. *Sue Ellen.* Houghton, 1969. Sue Ellen is only slightly retarded but she is dressed in old, dirty clothes and worn out shoes. Mrs. Perry and Mrs. Garvey find her like this.

Hunter, Evan. *Me and Mr. Stenner.* Harper, 1976. Abby at first doesn't like her new father but in time she comes to love him.

Hunter, Kristin. *Lou in the Limelight.* Scribner, 1981. Lou and the Soul Brothers leave home hoping for quick success in show business. They cut a record that becomes a hit. But they find that life in a casino is full of stress and disloyalty.

————. *Soul Brother and Sister Lou.* Scribner, 1968. Lou and members of the Hawks gang make music together in their clubhouse. She distrusts whites and one of the gang members is killed even though the gang is warned by Lou.

_____. *Survivors.* Scribner, 1975. Miss Lena, a businesswoman, and B.J., a tough street kid, are both survivors when they learn that they need each other.

Hunter, Mollie. *Haunted Mountain.* Harper, 1972. MacAllister, with the help of his son and an old faithful dog, overcomes the supernatural forces that control their mountain.

_____. *Hold on to Love.* Harper, 1984. Bridie struggles to become a writer; she meets Peter, a classmate, and learns about love in terms of her independence and Peter's possessiveness.

_____. *Kelpie's Pearls.* Funk, 1964. Morag is called a witch because of her friendship with the kelpie. After being carried away by the kelpie to Ter-man-og.

_____. *Knight of the Golden Plain.* Harper, 1983. A young boy dreams that he is a brave knight out to save a damsel in distress.

_____. *Mermaid Summer.* Harper, 1988. Eric is lured by and nearly drowned by the mermaid. He goes away to avoid disaster. His grandchildren, Anna and Jon, try to clear up the mermaid confrontation.

_____. *Smartest Man in Ireland.* Funk, 1965. Patrick is the man in the title. He can outwit fairies and get their gold. He finally loses all his possessions in order to save his son.

_____. *Sound of Chariots.* Harper, 1972. The story of a girl, Bridie, who loses her father when she is nine. She leads a sad, revengeful life. Then poverty adds to the trials of her life but she still wants to become a writer.

_____. *Spanish Letters.* Funk, 1967. Jamie is a Scottish guide in the time of King James. He helps an English spy.

_____. *Stranger Came Ashore.* Harper, 1975. A seal-man enters the village of Elsbeth and her brother Robbie. Robbie tries to protect his beautiful sister from the Selkie.

_____. *Stronghold.* Harper, 1974. At the time of Julius Caesar (40 B.C.) Coll escapes the Romans and lives with Nectan. There are battles between the Druid, the Romans and the Boars. A suspenseful story of strength other than physical.

_____. *Third Eye.* Harper, 1979. Jinty is involved in the investigation of the death of an earl. The earl feared a family curse that said no son would inherit his title.

_____. *Thomas and the Warlock.* Funk, 1968. Thomas, a blacksmith, is a poacher. A wizard wants revenge and steals his wife. Thomas, with the help of fairies, forces his way into the warlock dungeon and rescues his wife.

_____. *Wicked One.* Harper, 1977. A forester invokes the ire of a supernatural power.

_____. *You Never Knew Her as I Did.* Harper, 1981. An exciting story of the life of Mary, Queen of Scots, 1542–1587.

Huntington, Lee. *Maybe a Miracle.* Putnam, 1984. Dorcus, 11, befriends a couple without children during the Depression years.

Huntsbury, William. *Big Wheels.* Lothrop, 1967. A group of boys decide to take over their school. They come close to upsetting the power structure, but fail.

Hurlimann, Bettina. *Barry: A Brave St. Bernard.* Harcourt, 1968. Barry is owned by Martin. Barry learns to scent men buried in the snow caused by avalanches. He rescues over 40 people.

Hurmence, Belinda. *Girl Called Boy.* Houghton, 1982. A girl of today travels back to the time of slavery.

_____. *Nightwalker.* Clarion, 1988. Savannah is wondering about the changes taking place in her town, especially the nighttime burnings of the fishing shacks. Who is responsible? Her sleepwalking brother? The Nightwalkers?

_____. *Tancy.* Houghton, 1984. Tancy is a black personal servant who has been taught to read and write. She goes to search for her mother who was sold earlier. She moves in an emancipated world with all its turmoil.

_____. *Tough Tiffany.* Doubleday, 1980. Tiffany is black and poor. Her sister is pregnant and their furniture is about to be repossessed. She keeps a list of tough people and tries to be tough herself.

Hurwitz, Johanna. *Adventures of Ali Baba Bernstein.* Morrow, 1985. David doesn't like his name so he changes it. If his name isn't boring his life won't be, either.

_____. *Aldo Applesauce.* Morrow, 1979. Aldo moves from the city to a town, and is afraid. He has many mishaps. He has trouble making new friends.

_____. *Aldo Ice Cream.* Morrow, 1981. Aldo loves ice cream. He tries to raise money by selling home-made ice cream, but with little luck. He does volunteer work for senior citizens.

_____. *Baseball Fever.* Morrow, 1981. Ezra loves baseball and wants to play but his father hates the game and this makes for small problems.

_____. *Class Clown.* Morrow, 1987. Lucas is the class clown. It is true he has a good sense of humor but he must learn how to use it effectively.

_____. *Dede Takes Charge.* Morrow, 1984. A story of Dede's life after her parents' divorce.

_____. *Hot and Cold Summer.* Morrow, 1984. Derek and Rory accept Bolivia into their friendship circle even though she is a girl.

_____. *Hot and Cold Winter.* Morrow, 1988. Derek, Rory and Bolivia play again when she returns but things are found missing and Derek suspects Rory.

_____. *Hurricane Elaine.* Morrow, 1986. Elaine deals with the death of her cat, her brother's five dogs and a new romance.

_____. *Law of Gravity.* Morrow, 1978. Margot's mother is very withdrawn and Margot does anything she can to get her involved in life.

_____. *Much Ado About Aldo.* Morrow, 1978. Aldo's love of animals brings chaos to his life. He begins by raising crickets and chameleons only to find that chameleons eat crickets. He is devastated and refuses to eat any meat.

_____. *Once I Was a Plum Tree*. Morrow, 1980. Gerry is Jewish but is basically nonreligious. A Jewish family from Nazi Germany move in next door and she begins to think and learn about her religion.

_____. *Rabbi's Girls*. Morrow, 1982. How the daughters of a Rabbi adjust to living in a secular community. Each girl is different and adjusts in her own way.

_____. *Tough-Luck Karen*. Morrow, 1982. Karen is Aldo's sister. She believes that her luck is always bad. She doesn't like school and while doing a science project Karen finds her luck can sometimes be good or at least not bad.

_____. *Yellow Blue Jay*. Morrow, 1986. Jay is a city boy who is shy and withdrawn. He goes to stay at a summer cabin in Vermont where he is sure he will be unhappy, but it turns out to be okay.

Huston, Anne. *Trust a City Kid*. Lothrop, 1966. Reg, 12, a black boy, spends the summer with a Quaker family. Frank, the Quaker's son, and Reg do not get along. Reg learns about nonviolence.

Hutchins, Pat. *Curse of the Egyptian Mummy*. Greenwillow, 1983. A Cub Scout troop finds a body of a man who died of an asp bite. One of the scouts finds an Egyptian ibis statue and takes it. There is a curse on anyone who takes the statue.

_____. *House That Sailed Away*. Greenwillow, 1975. A very silly story about a family whose house was uprooted and put to sea.

Hutchison, D.D. *That Summer by the Sea*. Lothrop, 1960. Tina, 17, meets a friend of her brother's, Benny. They are both interested in a big project. They are also interested in romance.

Hutto, Nelson. *Breakaway Back*. Harper, 1963. Scotty changed schools. He made the football team at his new school. Some outside scandal mars his playing but he overcomes it and plays well with the team.

_____. *Goal Line Bomber*. Harper, 1964. A new coach sidelines the quarterback and other members of the team. The coach quits in a huff and the team plays without a coach.

_____. *Victory Volley*. Harper, 1967. Doug plays tennis. He loses a close game. He helps unite the two elements in school (the rich and the not so) and gets to play in the State Tournament.

Huxley, Aldous. *Brave New World*. Harper, 1979. Everyone is "happy" in this 623 A.F. (After Ford) world. Each class of people has its job to do. But Bernard and Helmholtz want to see a different life and upset these "best laid plans."

Huynh. *Land I Lost*. Harper, 1982. A Vietnamese boy talks of his land before the war.

Hyde, Dayton. *Island of the Loons*. Atheneum, 1984. Riggs, an escaped convict, is rescued from a sinking ship by Jimmy, 14. He kidnaps Jimmy who tries to escape but fails. Because of a series of circumstances they become friends.

_____. *Major, the Poacher, and the Wonderfulone Trout River*. Atheneum, 1985. The major is fishing for a record breaking trout. He matches wits with a 14-year-old poacher at his trout stream.

_____. *Strange Companion*. Dutton, 1975. David stows away on a plane that crashes. He and the pilot survive. The pilot later is killed. David must learn to survive until he can escape or is rescued.

Hyde, Laurence. *Captain Deadlock*. Houghton, 1968. A young English boy, Stephen, is on his way to America to seek employment. He is captured by pirates and imprisoned. He escapes and finds his way to Plymouth. He also finds the stolen crown jewels.

_____. *Under the Pirate Flag*. Houghton, 1965. Steven encounters two pirates, buried treasure and a star-crossed mutiny.

Hyde, M. *Nootka*. Walck, 1968. John and Sails tell of their survival after an Indian massacre aboard the "Boston" in 1803.

Hyland, Betty. *Girl with the Crazy Brother*. Watts, 1987. Dana wants to fit in at school. Her brother is more and more disturbed. He has schizophrenia and is finally committed to an institution. She has the strength to see both their problems.

Ik, Kim Yong. *Blue in the Seed*. Little, 1964. Chun Bok is a blue-eyed Asian boy and is teased because of it.

Ilowite, Sheldon. *Fury on Ice*. Hastings, 1970. Tod plays hockey and his team's goalie is injured. Tod takes his place but goalies don't score points and he wants to be a hero.

_____. *Penalty Killer*. Hastings, 1973. Mark is expected to be a superstar. He is good but not a star. He knows that defense wins games, too.

Innis, Pauline. *Hurricane Fighters*. McKay, 1962. Jack was afraid of storms because his father was killed in a hurricane. But he joins the hurricane hunters, the men who fly into the eye of a hurricane.

_____. *Wind of the Pampas*. McKay, 1967. Marcos lives in Argentina. He joins a cattle drive over the mountains. He and Frasco face the killer White Wind and become fast friends.

Innocenti, Roberto. *Rose Blanche*. Creative Education, 1989. Rose Blanche tries to help the children she finds in a concentration camp near her home. She is killed in the attempt.

Ipcar, Dahlov. *Queen of Spells*. Viking, 1973. Janet tries to save her beloved Tom Linn from the Queen of Spells. To do so she must face her own deepest fears and summon all her courage against the powerful Queen.

_____. *Warlock of Night*. Viking, 1969. A fantasy of Land of Night and Land of Day based on an actual chess match.

Ipswitch, Elaine. *Scott Was Here*. Delacorte,

1979. A story of Scott whose battle with Hodgkin's disease ended with his death at the age of 15.

Irving, Washington. *Legend of Sleepy Hollow.* Watts, 1966. Ichabod Crane courts Katrina but Brom Bones does, too. Then Icabod is scared off by the "headless horseman."

————. *Rip Van Winkle.* Doubleday, 1939. A story of the man who drank some potion and slept for twenty years.

Irwin, Hadley. *Abby, My Love.* Macmillan, 1985. Abby is a victim of incest and her friend Chip doesn't understand her changing moods.

————. *Bring to a Boil and Separate.* Atheneum, 1980. Katie's parents are getting divorced. She spends the summer learning tennis and training her horse. She renews her friendship with Marti and learns to cope with the conflicting emotions she has.

————. *I Be Somebody.* Atheneum, 1984. Pap finds that Athabasca is a cold place in Alaska. Many black families are planning to go there. Pap makes the trip and sees sickness and death . . . but a new beginning.

————. *Kim/Kimi.* Macmillan, 1987. Kim is Irish/Japanese. She is torn between two cultures. She leaves Iowa and goes to California's Chinese community to help her understand herself.

————. *Lilith Summer.* Feminist, 1979. Ellen, 12, is a companion to 77-year-old Lilith and learns about old age.

————. *Moon and Me.* Atheneum, 1981. E.J. does not want to stay on the farm with her grandparents or with Moon, who is a persistent friend.

————. *What About Grandma?* Atheneum, 1982. A warm story of Wyn, the grandmother, her daughter and granddaughter, Rhys. In the end the grandmother dies and Rhys meets and likes a golf instructor.

Ish-Kishor, Sulamith. *Our Eddie.* Pantheon, 1969. Eddie is 14, Jewish and poor. He must assume head of family because his father is unconcerned. His father then dies. His mother is ill and he has the same symptoms as his mother had.

Jackson, Alison. *My Brother, the Star.* Dutton, 1990. Les tries out for a spot on the county basketball team. His brother is a good-looking young boy who stars on a television commercial. There are jealousy, rivalry and misunderstanding.

Jackson, C. Paul. *Bud Baker, College Pitcher.* Hastings, 1970. Bud is a college freshman and wants to play baseball but is surprised to find them practicing in the fall. He and his old friend become roommates.

————. *Bud Baker, Racing Swimmer.* Hastings, 1962. Bud competes for a place on the school swimming team. This dominates his freshman year in high school.

————. *Bud Baker, T Quarterback.* Hastings, 1960. Bud, 14, transfers schools. He tries out for quarterback and makes enemies of some of his schoolmates.

————. *Bud Plays Junior High Football.* Hastings, 1957. Bud spends his time trying to get on the touch football team at school and playing tackle football at the rec center.

————. *Bud Plays Senior High Basketball.* Hastings, 1964. Bud goes from junior high to high school and finds that the basketball adjustment is harder than he thought. His first year is a learning period.

————. *Chris Plays Small Fry Football.* Hastings, 1963. Chris and Mike go out for small fry football. They practice, have problems with school work and team members but learn sportsmanship.

————. *Eric and Dud's Football Bargain.* Hastings, 1972. Dud only agrees to play football if Eric, an all-star, plays in the Small Stuff League, too.

————. *Fullback in the Large Fry League.* Hastings, 1965. Mel, Chris and Mike play football in the Large Fry League. This is Mel's first year but Chris and Mike have played here before.

————. *Halfback.* Hastings, 1971. A star halfback thinks he's the whole team. He learns teamwork from his coach and others.

————. *High School Backstop.* McGraw, 1963. Alden is new in school. He has problems to overcome before he can play baseball like his father.

————. *Junior High Freestyle Swimmer.* Hastings, 1965. A story of the hard work involved in becoming a freestyle swimmer.

————. *Little Major Leaguer.* Hastings, 1963. Bruce moves to a new town and must make the Little League team. He was all set to pitch in his old town but must now prove himself good enough to make this team.

————. *Rookie Catcher with the Atlanta Braves.* Hastings, 1966. Zeke goes to winter league to train as a catcher. He sharpens his skills as a catcher and softens his personality problems.

————. *Rose Bowl Pro.* Hastings, 1970. A college halfback is so busy looking toward pro football he doesn't concentrate on his college playing or his team.

————. *Stepladder Steve Plays Basketball.* Hastings, 1969. Although Steve is tall he is very graceful on the basketball court.

————. *Tom Mosley—Midget Leaguer.* Hastings, 1971. Tom's dead father was a champion, making his own playing tough for him. Also, his coach is interested in his mother.

————. *Tommy—Soap Box Derby Champion.* Hastings, 1963. Tommy lost several derbys to his friend Scott. But this year he is determined to win.

————. *World Series Rookie.* Hastings, 1960. Stub is a rookie for the Goliaths. He wasn't as good a catcher as he thought. He finally succeeds as a catcher and as a person.

Jackson, Helen. *Ramona.* Grosset, 1884. An

early protest against the way the whites treated the Indians. Also a tragic love story.

Jackson, Jacqueline. *Ghost Boat.* Little, 1969. The children "see" the ghost of a dead fisherman rowing across the lake.

————. *Missing Melinda.* Little, 1967. A story written as though told by S. Gibbs and O. Gibbs, two fictional characters.

————. *Taste of Spruce Gum.* Little, 1966. Libby doesn't like her new father, doesn't like living in Vermont, doesn't like the people around her. She battles with everything and everybody.

Jackson, Jesse. *Sickest Don't Always Die the Quickest.* Doubleday, 1971. A black youth questions the teachings of his church and elders.

————. *Tessie.* Harper, 1968. Tessie wins a scholarship to an exclusive private school and her mother discourages her from going. She goes and does have a great deal of trouble adjusting to this different world.

Jackson, O.B. *Southpaw in the Mighty Mite League.* McGraw, 1965. Ken competes with his brother Rick and learns about his potential as a basketball player.

Jacobs, Anita. *Where Has Deedie Wooster Been All These Years?* Delacorte, 1981. Deedie, 14, finds it is difficult to adjust to her brother's death. She wants to be an author but lacks the discipline. She does keep notes on the ups and downs of growing up.

Jacobs, Beth. *Look to the Mountains.* Messner, 1963. Sarah Jane must move and leave behind a hard earned scholarship in science.

Jacobs, Helen. *Diary of the Strawberry Place.* Atheneum, 1978. Quakers operate an underground railway from Ohio across the Erie to Pennsylvania.

————. *Secret of the Strawberry Place.* Atheneum, 1976. Two friends look for a place rumored as a former underground railway station. One of them disappears.

Jacoby, Alice. *My Mother's Boyfriend and Me.* Dutton, 1987. Blue is Laurie's mother's boyfriend. He sexually harasses Laurie. She is at first attracted to him but then resents and dislikes him.

Jacques, Brian. *Mossflower.* Philomel, 1988. A myriad of mice, moles, squirrels, otters and hedgehogs battle the evil wildcat, Tsarmina, and stoats and ferrets.

————. *Redwall.* Philomel, 1987. Redwall Abby is where a community of mice live. Cluny and his army of rats attack the Abby. Martin, a mouse warrior, must find the sword that destroys evil.

Jakes, John. *Susanna of the Alamo.* Harcourt, 1986. Because the Mexicans killed everyone but women and children at the Alamo, Susanna was able to inform Sam Houston of the outcome.

James, Betsy. *Long Night Dance.* Dutton, 1989. Kat, 16, rescues a seal-man and prepares for the Long Night Dance where she learns independence and a life of her own.

James, Will. *Smoky, the Cowhorse.* Scribner, 1926. The range and the corral, the round-up and the rodeo as seen through the eyes of Smoky, a mouse colored cow pony.

Jamison, Cecilia. *Lady Jane.* Delacorte, 1969. A young girl, new in the neighborhood, has a pet heron. Everybody is curious about who moved into a house that was long vacant.

Jane, Mary. *Indian Island Mystery.* Lippincott, 1965. Tim, an Indian, disappears suddenly and a valuable necklace is also missing. Abbie and Eric don't think he is guilty and set out to prove his innocence.

————. *Mystery in Hidden Hollow.* Lippincott, 1970. When children are accused of stealing they must find the real thieves. They also find a missing inheritance.

————. *Rocking Chair Ghost.* Lippincott, 1969. Nobody lived in the house except the ghost. Judy and Lennie heard sounds and saw the missing stamp box.

Janeczko, Paul. *Bridges to Cross.* Macmillan, 1986. James is being forced to attend a parochial school and fights to be his own person.

Janeway, Elizabeth. *Ivanov Seven.* Harper, 1967. Stepan was taken into the Russian Army and renamed Ivanov. He would not fight and so was released and went home. A fable.

Jansson, Tove. *Comet in Moominland.* Walck, 1967. Moomintroll and Sniff go to investigate a comet that appears to be approaching and will collide with the Earth.

————. *Exploits of Moominpappa.* Walck, 1966. Moominpappa relates the many adventures of his life. He starts with the time he ran away from the Home for Moomin Foundlings.

————. *Finn Family Moomintroll.* Walck, 1958/1989. This is the introductory book to the Moomins and Moominvalley. There are more books about these creatures.

————. *Moominland Midwinter.* Walck, 1962. Moomins sleep during the winter. This year Moomintroll is fully awake so he wanders around. He meets many strange characters and learns about the winter habits of others.

————. *Moominpappa at Sea.* Walck, 1967. Pappa decides to move his family to an unusual island where vegetables seem to have strange ways of behaving.

————. *Moomins in November.* Walck, 1971. Six friends get together for winter in Moominvalley and visit with each other while they await the much loved Moomintroll family.

————. *Moominsummer Madness.* Walck, 1961. A volcano explodes and a tidal wave engulfs Moominvalley. The Moomin family escape on a floating house.

————. *Summer Book.* Pantheon, 1974. Sophia and her grandmother explore everything together; they argue, dream, build sand castles and talk. They love each other in different ways.

————. *Tales from Moominvalley.* Walck,

1964. The Moomin family is Moominpappa, Moominmamma, Moomintroll and Litty My. They experience Christmas, a holiday unknown to them.

Jarrell, Randall. *Animal Family.* Pantheon, 1965. A man is a lonely hunter who first finds a mermaid, then a bear, then a lynx before he finally acquires a boy.

Jarrow, Gail. *If Phyllis Were Here.* Houghton, 1987. Libby has trouble coping when her grandmother, who has always cared for her, moves to Florida.

Jeffries, Roderic. *Against Time!* Harper, 1964. Detective Dunn has only hours to find his son who has been kidnapped to prevent Dunn from testifying.

———. *Patrol Car.* Harper, 1967. There is a payroll robbery and six men escape. Harry Cole chases the speeding car that might be them.

———. *Police Dog.* Harper, 1965. A story of how police dogs are trained and handled; about how one was almost destroyed because he is mistakenly accused of killing sheep and lambs.

———. *River Patrol.* Harper, 1969. An armored car with the latest safety devices is robbed and the police are stumped.

———. *Trapped.* Harper, 1972. Two boys are trapped on a mudflat. A snowstorm and unusually high tides hamper the rescue.

Jenkins, Alan. *White Horses and Black Bulls.* Norton, 1963. Paul's father raises fierce black bulls. He wants to own and ride a swift white horse.

Jenning, Gary. *Rope in the Jungle.* Lippincott, 1976. Caleb, a rope maker, and Trey go to Chiapas to repair a 4 mile long, 9 ton wire rope. Lots of adventure with savage Indians, volcano eruptions and earthquakes.

Jewett, Eleanore. *Big John's Secret.* Viking, 1962. John knew he was a nobleman even though he lived with peasants (13th century). He was ready when the time came to find his father, a deposed knight.

Jewett, Sarah. *White Heron, a Story of Maine.* Crowell, 1963. Sylvia lives in the wilderness of Maine and helps someone look for the rare white heron.

Johnson, A.E. *Blues I Can Whistle.* Four Winds, 1969. Cody tries to kill himself and is now in a hospital where he writes about why and what led up to it.

Johnson, Annabel. *Alien Music.* Four Winds, 1982. Jesse, 16, tells of the "Skylab 7" crew who are the sole survivors of the dying earth. They plan a colony on Mars but fail.

———. *Bearcat.* Harper, 1960. A young boy works in the mines of Montana in the late 1800's.

———. *Count Me Gone.* S&S, 1968. Rion is a nice middle class boy who questions the values of his family, especially his older brother's. He gets in trouble, is cleared and then leaves home to find his own life.

———. *Danger Quotient.* Harper, 1984. Casey, 18, a genius who survived the nuclear war, goes back in time to see why people died and how he can help.

———. *Golden Touch.* Harper, 1963. Andy meets his father for the first time in the gold fields of Cripple Creek. Someone was stealing gold. Was it his father?

———. *Grizzly.* Harper, 1964. While on a camping trip Dave saves his father's life when attacked by a grizzly bear.

———. *Last Knife.* S&S, 1971. Rick tells a story about his brother being a conscientious objector to war.

———. *Memory of Dragons.* Atheneum, 1986. Paul, 18, joins a power struggle between the East and West coasts. A possible second Civil War over ecological policies. A sub plot of abused children and a murdered father.

———. *Peculiar Magic.* Houghton, 1965. Cindy's mother was a dance hall girl. She joins a troupe of actors going west in hopes of finding her.

———. *Pickpocket Run.* Houghton, 1961. Dix learns about greed and corruption.

———. *Prisoner of Psi.* Atheneum, 1985. A TV psychic and his son are in touch mentally and prevent a kidnapping.

———. *Rescued Heart.* Harper, 1961. A sixteen-year-old girl spends a year in a desert trailer camp. She meets drifters and migrant workers. She re-evaluates her life.

———. *Torrie.* Harper, 1960. Torrie crosses America in 1840 and falls in love.

———. *Wilderness Bride.* Houghton, 1962. Cory, 15, is going to meet her groom-to-be in Utah. His family are Mormons. Ethan turns out to be kind and gentle. He helps the ill even though it is against Mormon teachings. They fall in love.

Johnson, Burdetta. *Little Red.* Follett, 1966. Julia raised Little Red, an orphaned javelina. He must now be returned to his natural environment. He saved Julia's life but he was no longer a pet but a wild animal.

Johnson, Charles. *Pieces of Eight.* Discovery, 1989. David and Mitchell want to meet Blackbeard, the pirate. They arouse the ghost of a sea captain who introduces them to Blackbeard.

Johnson, Denis. *Fiskadoro.* Knopf, 1985. A futuristic book about the United States long after a nuclear attack.

Johnson, Dorothy. *Buffalo Woman.* Dodd, 1977. Whirlwind Girl becomes Buffalo Woman when she is an adult. She sees her people cheated by the white man and sees their defeat at Little Big Horn. She dies a proud but broken woman.

———. *Farewell to Troy.* Houghton, 1964. The adventures of the grandson of King Priam who travels the length of Ancient Greece.

Johnson, Elizabeth. *Horse Show Fever.* Washburn, 1962. Hugh, 14, is a runaway. He is befriended by a riding academy owner. He works with horses and gets involved with horse shows and riding.

Johnson, Emily. *Spring and the Shadow Man.* Dodd, 1984. Spring had a vivid imagination and wished she didn't. When she helped her blind neighbor she learned it was a blessing.

Johnson, James. *Pepper, a Puerto Rican Mongoose.* McKay, 1967. Pepper is a mongoose. He and kitten play and keep out of danger. They meet three boys and play with them. They all enjoy each other. Pepper fights a fer-de-lance and saves the reputation of mongooses.

_____. *Ringtail.* McKay, 1968. Ringtail is a kind of raccoon. He learns how to get food and protect himself. He makes friends with a man. Together they hunt for what they need.

_____. *Wild Venture.* Follett, 1961. Glen and Pear go out to prove that man can still survive in the wilderness. They take a knife and a flint and spend a week in a canyon/forest region of Alabama.

Johnson, Maud. *Sixteen Can Be Sweet.* Scholastic, 1978. Jenny had a summer romance that ended in September. She and her family moved for her father's health. She meets Keith and wonders if this too, is for the summer or forever.

Johnson, Norma. *Bats in the Bedstead.* Houghton, 1971. Ricky is threatened by a flock of evil bats who want to regain possession of the house his family just moved into.

Johnson, Virginia. *Cedars of Charlo.* Morrow, 1969. Becky and her friend try to save forest areas from the loggers.

Johnston, Louisa. *Monkey in the Family.* Whitman, 1972. Because of a fire at the pet store a monkey comes to live with the Bristols.

Johnston, Norma. *Carlisle's All.* Bantam, 1986. Jess's father and mother go to the Middle East and she learns that the embassy has been attacked by terrorists. Is her father alive? Everyone waits anxiously to find out.

_____. *Carlisle's Hope.* Bantam, 1986. Jess is sad when her Aunt Faith is killed in an accident and cousin Virginia comes to live with them.

_____. *Gabriel's Girl.* Atheneum, 1983. Sarah's father, a writer, disappears from his hotel room while they are in Spain and she searches for him.

_____. *Glory in the Flower.* Atheneum, 1974. As Tish grows older she learns to cope with her family. She has the lead in *Romeo and Juliet* and understands friendship. Her mother has another baby and Tish faces the next year.

_____. *If You Love Me, Let Me Go.* Atheneum, 1978. Allison is sixteen and changes her image but her family and friends don't see the change. Her new friend Lisa sees her as she wants to be seen. She gets more changes than she expected.

_____. *Keeping Days.* Atheneum, 1973. Tish and her mother fight constantly over Tish's friends, both girl and boy. Tish has to cope with

loyalty and ethics. As one child among a large family she looks forward to high school.

_____. *Mustard Seed of Magic.* Atheneum, 1977. Tish still wants to be a writer. Her parents fight, her boyfriend has moved away and Tish must defend herself and her friends.

_____. *Myself and I.* Atheneum, 1981. Paul moves to California because he needs to try to find out who his parents are. He returns and courts Sara. The history of all families, Tish's, Sara's and Paul's, is revealed.

_____. *Nice Girl Like You.* Atheneum, 1980. Sara, Tish's niece, defends Paul against the hypocrisies of West Farm. Through Sara we learn about Tish's last fifteen years.

_____. *Of Time and Seasons.* Atheneum, 1975. Bridget's family is very talented. Father and a younger sibling paint, Mother and another sibling write, her twin brother plays piano and her other brother is a born leader. What about her?

_____. *Potter's Wheel.* Morrow, 1980. Laura, 16, learns about her parents, her relatives and herself from a strong grandmother.

_____. *Return to Morocco.* Four Winds, 1988. Tori and her grandmother go to Morocco but death and her grandmother's secret reveal a mystery and spies.

_____. *Sanctuary Tree.* Atheneum, 1977. Tish has a great many situations to cope with at fifteen. Her friend, Ken, moves away, her father is ill, her grandfather dies and her sister has a baby.

_____. *Strangers Dark and Gold.* Atheneum, 1975. The story of Jason and his tragic love of Medea. It also covers his mythological adventures.

_____. *Striving After Wind.* Atheneum, 1976. Bridget tries very hard to establish herself as a person among her talented family. She learns to handle very difficult people, especially an older actor friend and a young male friend.

_____. *Swallow's Song.* Atheneum, 1978. Allison Standish is living as girls did in the 1920's. She is not proud of her reputation among her family and friends and wonders what to do about it.

_____. *Timewarp Summer.* Atheneum, 1983. Scott wants to make a timewarp sci-fi film. He has an affair with his assistant, Laura. Bettina, a neighbor girl, likes him. At the end of the summer Laura leaves. Scott and Bettina are more than friends.

_____. *To Jess, with Love and Memories.* Bantam, 1986. Jess's younger sister is failing school and finds out she is adopted.

_____. *Watcher in the Mist.* Bantam, 1986. Cindy is at Rockove Hall and senses someone watching her. Her cousin is starting an inn but accidents, fires and now strange messages are disrupting the work.

_____. *Wishing Star.* Funk, 1963. Julie has an actress mother. She is shy and envious and is startled when love comes to her unexpectedly.

Jones, Adrienne. *Another Place, Another Spring.* Houghton, 1971. A 19th-century-Russia love story. Marya, Countess Elena's servant, and Boris of the secret police fall in love and marry. They then move to America.

————. *Hawks of Chelney.* Harper, 1978. A young boy is ostracized by fellow villagers because he loves wild ospreys that they believe are evil.

————. *Matter of Spunk.* Harper, 1983. The continuing story of the determination, the courage and the humor of these females who survive life's adventures. The setting is Hollywood with its many unconventional characters.

————. *Ride the Far Wind.* Little, 1964. In the year 670 a Chinese pirate ship takes Malu to China. A story of how he escapes being sold into slavery.

————. *Sail, Calypso!* Little, 1968. Clay and Paul find an old boat on the beach and decide to restore it. They almost drown when they finally launch the boat.

————. *So Nothing Is Forever.* Houghton, 1974. Children of an interracial marriage suddenly lose their parents and want to stay together.

————. *Whistle Down a Dark Lane.* Harper, 1982. This story takes place before World War I. Margery and her sister wonder why daddy has to leave. They see KKK and suffragette activities and face black/white relationships.

Jones, Betty. *King Solomon's Mines.* Random, 1982. A hunter and a nobleman look for a legendary diamond mine.

Jones, Diana. *Archer's Goon.* Greenwillow, 1984. Howard, 13, finds out he is adopted and his father is part of the seven wizards that rule his town. Goon comes to visit Howard because the father owes some words to Archer.

————. *Cart and Cwidder.* Atheneum, 1977. Clennen the Singer and his family travel Dalemark giving shows and telling news. He is an Informer and is killed. Two of his children escape to the North but not before enduring troubles.

————. *Charmed Life.* Greenwillow, 1977. Gwendole wants supernatural powers from her mysterious guardian.

————. *Dogsbody.* Greenwillow, 1977. Sirius is a star. But he is in trouble for losing the Zoi. He must come to Earth as a dog and look for it. He has lots of unhappy incidents but if he doesn't find the Zoi he will die on earth.

————. *Drowned Ammet.* Atheneum, 1977. Mitt plots the revenge of his father's "death." He hides away on a sailboat which is threatened and then saved by sea gods. The shipwrecked sailor he picks up is his father, a betrayer.

————. *Eight Days of Luke.* Greenwillow, 1986. David, an orphan, tries to make up curses against his horrid guardians. Instead he frees a man, Luke, from a prison and helps him from being returned.

————. *Fire and Hemlock.* Greenwillow, 1984. Polly is going off to college. As she packs she reflects back on her friendship with a young musician. Was he real? What forces played a part in the relationship?

————. *Howl's Moving Castle.* Morrow, 1986. Howl owns the famous moving castle. He is a wizard, and an evil one. So is the Witch who has already killed Wizard Sulliman. Poor Sophie is in danger now that she is turned into an old woman.

————. *Lives of Christopher Chant.* Greenwillow, 1988. Christopher Chant is training to become the next Chrestomanci or head controller of magic in the world. He is a key figure in a battle with renegade sorcerers. But he has nine lives.

————. *Magicians of Caprona.* Greenwillow, 1980. After many long years of feuding, two families of magicians in Caprona are weakened. The younger members of the families must stop the incipient war. They use magic and a telepathic cat.

————. *Ogre Downstairs.* Dutton, 1974. Aman, with two boys, and a woman, with three children, marry and adjustments must be made. Two magic chemistry sets complicate things even further.

————. *Power of Three.* Greenwillow, 1977. A story of three children and their special gifts.

————. *Spellcoats.* Atheneum, 1979. This story takes place in Dalemark. It is about an earlier time and explains the relationships of people, power and the gods during a time of great suspiciousness.

————. *Tale of Time City.* Greenwillow, 1987. Jonathan and Sam of Time City mistake Vivian for the Time Lady. The Time Lady is needed to set the times right but Vivian is caught between Time City and her real home!

————. *Witch Week.* Greenwillow, 1982. Charles is a witch who wants to get away from bullies. Nan is a witch but doesn't know it. They, and several others, get in trouble until Chrestomanci saves them.

————. *Witch's Business.* Dutton, 1973. Frank and Jess's scheme to earn money by hiring out as revenge-seekers seems like a good one until they discover they are in competition with a witch.

Jones, Dorothy. *Wonderful World Outside.* Dodd, 1960. Vicky, 16, lives in an orphanage and has no dates or social life. She has a chance to get a job and live in a home with real parents.

Jones, Kanice. *Secrets of a Summer Spy.* Bradbury, 1990. Ronnie's two best friends, Amy and Jimmy, are growing away from her. She befriends an 83-year-old retired concert pianist, an eccentric catlady.

Jones, McClure. *Cast Down the Stars.* Holt, 1978. Glory is a star-caster in an astrology society. She and Honor go to repair the wall that separates them from the Barbarians. A battle which would end this civilization takes place.

Jones, Penelope. *Stealing Thing.* Bradbury,

1983. Hope is alone for the summer. She first steals fudge, then a pin. At camp she steals some pebbles and is caught. She is helped to understand that anger and frustration are causing her to steal.

Jones, Rebecca. *Angie and Me*. Macmillan, 1981. Jenna must be in the hospital for two to six weeks. Her roommate, Angie, makes it happier. Other patients, Bill, Wendy and Sam, are sad when Angie dies.

————. *Germy Blew It*. Dutton, 1987. Germy organizes a bubble gum contest but spends the entry fee money on himself and now owes the school money he doesn't have.

————. *Germy Blew It—Again*. Holt, 1988. Germy is involved in a get rich quick scheme to pay back the money to the school. He raises gerbils but they get out of their cages.

————. *Madeline and the Great (Old) Escape Artist*. Dutton, 1983. Madeline's parents are divorced, and Dad doesn't want her, so she lives with her grandmother in a small town. She is epileptic and has a seizure at school.

Jones, Ron. *Acorn People*. Bantam, 1977. The acorn people are all disabled children at a camp where the facilities are for "normal" kids. But these "special" children make the best of it.

Jones, Terry. *Nicobobinus*. Bedrick, 1986. Two boys go to the Land of the Dragons. The time is the Middle Ages and the purpose of their trip is to find a cure.

————. *Saga of Eric the Viking*. Penguin, 1983. Eric the Viking and his fellow adventurers go to find the land where the sun goes at night.

Jones, Toeckey. *Go Well, Stay Well*. Harper, 1980. A friendship grows between a white girl living in South Africa and a black girl. There are many social barriers in their way.

————. *Skindeep*. Harper, 1986. This takes place in Johannesburg where Dave is assuming the life of a white teenager. Rhonda falls in love with him in spite of moodiness and a bald head. But it is doomed to failure.

Jones, Weyman. *Edge of Two Worlds*. Dial, 1968. Sequoyah, old and ill, walks across Texas. He meets Calvin, 15, who is lost and afraid of Indians. The meeting is good for both of them.

————. *Talking Leaf*. Dial, 1965. Atsee cannot follow in the footsteps of his great scout father. He must take up reading and writing and help his people that way.

Jonsson, Runer. *Viki Viking*. World, 1963. Viki is a Viking boy who doesn't like fighting. But his quick thinking wins the day, not the valor of conquest.

Joosse, Barbara. *Anna, the One and Only*. Harper, 1988. Anna has the problem of having a sister that seems to be perfect. She is always "second best."

————. *Pieces of the Picture*. Lippincott, 1989. Emily's mother is trying to run an inn from her family home. She finds her mother's childhood toys in the attic. She comes to view herself

and her mother in a different light.

Jordan, Hope. *Haunted Summer*. Lothrop, 1967. Rilla hit something on a foggy night and did nothing. She now worries about someone discovering her secret.

Jordan, June. *His Own Where*. Crowell, 1971. Angela and Buddy live miserable lives on the streets of Brooklyn. They run away together because anything is better than what they have: a private space in the cemetery.

Jordan, Mildred. *Proud to Be Amish*. Crown, 1968. Katie is Amish and has a conflict with the strict code of conduct. She finds a hidden radio and enjoys it; she likes a red locket she got from a friend. But she still lives by Amish traditions in spite of her inner conflict.

Josephs, Rebecca. *Early Disorder*. Farrar, 1980. Willa is overwhelmed by her family. She becomes anorexic and goes through pain and self revulsion from the inside out. We see her deterioration and its effect on the household. There is a hint of hope.

Joslin, Sesyle. *Gentle Savage*. Atheneum, 1979. Dorcas and Peter are friends. They run away on a ship going to Cape Town with illegal rum. They are shipwrecked on an island. The tribe takes them in but doesn't want to return them to civilization.

————. *Spy Lady and the Muffin Man*. Harcourt, 1971. The members of SSFTDASOC (Secret Society for the Detection and Solution of Crime) notice the lady next door doing strange things and meeting people secretly. They investigate.

Joyce, William. *George Shrinks*. Harper, 1985. George wakes up one morning to find that he is very small. He must cope with a great many problems he never had before.

Jukes, Mavis. *Getting Even*. Knopf, 1988. Maggie listens to different advice from her friend, Iris, and from each divorced parent who is still fighting the other.

————. *No One Is Going to Nashville*. Knopf, 1983. Sonia finds a stray dog and wants to keep it but her father is looking for a new home for it.

Juster, Norton. *Phantom Tollbooth*. Random, 1961. Milo meets a Spelling Bee; a witch, Faintly Macabre; and Princesses Rhyme and Reason when he visits the strange places through the tollbooth. It is a witty and entertaining book developed on a play on words.

Kaatz, Evelyn. *Soccer!* Little, 1981. After high school and college Rich plays for a New England team. It is his first season as a pro soccer player.

Kalb, Jonah. *Goof That Won the Pennant*. Houghton, 1976. A baseball team wins by a "once in a lifetime" error.

————. *Kids' Candidate*. Houghton, 1975. Barnaby, 13, runs for School Board in his home town on a platform of better cafeteria food and no homework.

Kalish, Betty. *Eleven! Time to Think of Marriage.* Atheneum, 1970. Even though she is a tomboy, pre–World War II Bengal tradition says a girl must marry at eleven.

Kalnay, Francis. *It Happened in Chichipica.* Harcourt, 1971. A picture of everyday life in a small Mexican village.

Kane, Harnett. *Amazing Mrs. Bonaparte.* Doubleday, 1963. Betsy Patterson of Baltimore marries Jerome Bonaparte but the marriage is annulled by Napoleon.

Kaplan, Bess. *Empty Chair.* Harper, 1975. A girl accepts her mother's death and a new stepmother.

Kaplow, Robert. *Alessandra in Love.* Lippincott, 1989. Alex loves Wyn but he is indifferent because he loves someone else from his past: Debbie.

_____. *Alex Icicle: A Romance in Ten Torrid Chapters.* Houghton, 1984. Alex is obsessed with snobby Amy Hart. He gives a party and she comes with someone else.

Karl, Jean. *Beloved Benjamin Is Waiting.* Dutton, 1978. Lucinda's brother went off to school, her father left home and her mother went away for a few days. Lucinda's being harassed by a gang of kids. She finds refuge in the cemetery and alien Benjamin.

_____. *But We Are Not of Earth.* Dutton, 1981. Romula and her friends go on a space exploration trip. Their teacher goes along to direct their plan but he can't help them. Lots of humor and some danger.

_____. *Strange Tomorrow.* Dutton, 1985. An alien power kills everyone on Earth except a small group who struggle to survive.

Karp, Naomi. *Nothing Rhymes with April.* Harcourt, 1974. An eleven-year-old learns about dignity while being raised during the Depression.

_____. *Turning Point.* Harcourt, 1976. Hannah moves from the city to the suburbs in the late 1930's where she faces a lot of anti-Semitic prejudice among neighbors and school mates.

Kassem, Lou. *Listen for Rachel.* McElderry, 1986. Rachel learns about folk medicine from a local mountain healer. Then the Civil War breaks out and divides her family but brings her romance and a future.

_____. *Middle School Blues.* Parnassus, 1986. Cindy, 12, goes to a new school and really enjoys it.

Kassirer, Elizabeth. *Magic Elizabeth.* Viking, 1966. Sally gets involved with a portrait of another Sally who disappeared many years ago.

Kastner, Erich. *Emil and the Three Twins.* Watts, 1961. Emil is called up to solve a mystery. A member of The Three Twins acrobatic team is unaccountably deserted by his father.

_____. *Lisa and Lottie.* Knopf, 1969. Two girls meet at camp and find they are twins. They bring their divorced parents together.

_____. *Little Man.* Knopf, 1966. Maxie is only two inches tall and wants to be a circus performer. He does so, is kidnapped, outwits his captors and returns to the circus where he is warmly welcomed.

_____. *Little Man and the Big Thief.* Knopf, 1969. Maxie, a two-inch-tall man, becomes a circus entertainer and now is making a movie about himself. Another tiny girl and her mother are found in Alaska. Now the Pichelsteiners become a family.

_____. *35th of May.* Watts, 1961. This is a story of Conrad's exciting ride to the South Seas and its outcome.

Katz, Bobbie. *Manifesto and Me–Meg.* Watts, 1974. Meg forms a women's liberation consciousness raising group. Abigail appoints herself as adult adviser and leads the action.

_____. *1,001 Words.* Watts, 1975. Meg finds a pornographic book. She and her best friend, Suzy, decide it's a coded message about Meg's brother and their unpopular teacher. They investigate and find out differently.

Katz, Welwyn. *False Face.* Macmillan, 1988. Laney finds an Indian miniature false face (a ritual mask). It gives the owner the power to heal or harm. Tom found a large false face.

_____. *Third Magic.* Macmillan, 1988. Morgan, mistaken for an ancestor, is taken to the alien world of Nwm. Ardu, a native of Nwm, is her double. They fight magic and then return to Earth.

Kaufman, Barry. *Son-Rise.* Harper, 1976. Raun is autistic; that is, he has a type of schizophrenia and withdraws into himself, communicating with no one. Can he be helped?

Kaufman, Stephen. *Does Anyone Know the Way to Thirteen?* Houghton, 1985. Myron is smart but not athletic. He likes to play baseball; he fears bully Gary and questions his Jewishness.

Kay, Mara. *House Full of Echoes.* Crown, 1980. Strange supernatural things happen in a boarding school, Aistrovo, which was once a country estate. The spirits of the former owners try to return. Is an earlier tragedy about to be repeated?

_____. *Masha.* Day, 1968. A story of Russian life, based on the life of Catherine the Great.

_____. *One Small Clue.* Crown, 1982. Madge and John are told about their birth and given two books. They find a name in the book and search for more information. They finally do find their father.

_____. *Youngest Lady-in-Waiting.* Day, 1971. This is the continuing story of Masha and the Grand Duchess, Alexandra, of Russian royalty in the early 1800's.

Kaye, Geraldine. *Comfort Herself.* Deutsch, 1985. Comfort, a child of an interracial marriage, goes to Ghana to live with her father but is more at ease with her mother in England.

_____. *Day After Yesterday.* Deutsch, 1981. Su Su and her two brothers and sisters are left in

Hong Kong when her parents go to London. Money runs out, and her sister is stolen and sold to a childless woman. Su Su must rescue her and get to London.

Kaye, M.M. *Ordinary Princess.* Doubleday, 1984. A newborn is given the gift of "ordinariness." She runs away and works as a kitchen helper and meets her real prince.

Kaye, Marilyn. *Cassie.* Harcourt, 1987. Cassie is in junior high and wants designer clothes, especially since her new friend Dana has them. But Dana is not a true friend and the shock reels Cassie.

————. *Daphne.* Harcourt, 1987. Daphne doesn't want to argue wth her older sisters but they are pushing her into a life that she doesn't want. How can she stand up for herself against popular, creative sisters?

————. *Friend Like Phoebe.* Harcourt, 1989. Phoebe, 12, hopes to be chosen for a television interview discussing her school. She also helps a friend who recently lost her mother.

————. *Lydia.* Harcourt, 1987. Lydia has three younger sisters. This is her story of the way she started a school newspaper despite all odds against her, both from her family and from school officials. But she finds support.

————. *Phoebe.* Harcourt, 1987. Phoebe has three older sisters, all of whom have different interests and have little time for her. Even her friends are changing, so she volunteers in the library and finds it exciting.

Keane, John. *Sherlock Bones, Tracer of Missing Pets.* Lippincott, 1979. Paco, an old English sheepdog, and his master track down lost and stolen pets. Based on true adventures, some funny and some sad.

Keele, Lugman. *Java Jack.* Harper, 1980. A 14-year-old boy is searching for his parents in Indonesia. It is a mystical journey.

Keeton, Elizabeth. *Esmeralda.* Little, 1970. Esmeralda goes to school but a mean, big bully picks on her. She must rise above this and be herself.

————. *Second Best Friend.* Atheneum, 1985. Vanessa lost all her clothes in a cyclone. She borrows a dress from a friend and finds it has been stolen.

Kehret, Peg. *Nightmare Mountain.* Dutton, 1989. Molly meets Uncle Phil and cousin Glenden for the first time. Everything goes wrong. Molly must fight for survival on a mountain where an avalanche nearly kills her.

————. *Sisters, Long Ago.* Cobblehill, 1990. Willow nearly drowns and she sees a past life. She gets interested in reincarnation and mental telepathy and uses this knowledge to help her sister who has leukemia.

Keith, Harold. *Brief Garland.* Crowell, 1971. Mr. Driskoll is placed in a position where he must coach a girl's basketball team. He starts out hating it but comes to respect the girls' ability and they enter the state championship games.

Komantcia. Crowell, 1965. A young Spaniard is captured by the Comanches and resists his captors' attempts to make him one of them.

————. *Obstinate Land.* Crowell, 1977. A story of a German family, the Rombergs, as they try to seek out a living on the Cherokee Strip. The father freezes to death and the fourteen-year-old must assume responsibility.

————. *Rifles for Watie.* Harper, 1957. A story of the Civil War in the West as seen by a young Union soldier. Newbery winner, 1958.

————. *Susy's Scoundrel.* Crowell, 1974. An Amish girl adopts two coyote pups but their mother steals them back.

Kellam, Ian. *First Summer Year.* Crowell, 1974. Richard finds a jewel that can make him small. He visits a village where everyone is small and where each month equals a year.

Keller, Beverly. *Desdemona: Twelve Going on Desperate.* Lothrop, 1986. Add to Desdemona's family landlord, a handsome boy, dog food served at a party and possible eviction and you are into another funny story.

————. *Fowl Play, Desdemona.* Lothrop, 1989. Des learns about animal rights through People for the Ethical Treatment of Animals. She and friend Sherman paint posters and are true believers.

————. *No Beasts, No Children.* Lothrop, 1983. Desdemona lives with her father, a housekeeper, the twins, and three dogs. Their landlord is not very understanding.

————. *Small, Elderly Dragon.* Lothrop, 1984. A village needs protection and appeals to a dragon long past his prime.

Kelley, S. *Summer Growing Thing.* Viking, 1971. An old woman, her granddaughter, and the Ku Klux Klan meet in a Mississippi town.

Kelley, Sally. *Trouble with Explosives.* Bradbury, 1976. Polly stutters and is in a new school again. But this time she may stay a while.

Kellogg, Marjorie. *Tell Me That You Love Me, Junie Moon.* Farrar, 1984. Three handicapped people live together and help each other because each other is all they have. Warren is paralyzed, Arthur has a neurological disease and Junie is disfigured.

Kelly, Eric. *Trumpeter of Krakow.* Macmillan, 1928. A young Polish boy during the 15th century has the responsibility of guarding a sacred jewel in a church tower. Newbery winner, 1929.

Kelly, Jeffrey. *Basement Baseball Club.* Houghton, 1987. The Roader team members spend the summer playing sandlot baseball.

————. *Tramp Steamer and the Silver Bullet.* Houghton, 1984. Tramp and Silver visit haunted houses, see spiders and meat-eating plants and go through secret tunnels.

Kelly, Rosalie. *Addie's Year.* Beaufort, 1981. Addie has a special place she doesn't want to share. Ruth is a rich girl in school and Addie is poor. She learns about death but also the joys of family and friends.

Kemp, Gene. *Charlie Lewis Plays for Time.* Faber, 1984. Charlie's least liked teacher starts to date his mother and favor him. He doesn't like the situation at all.

_____. *Gowie Corby Plays Chicken.* Faber, 1980. Gowie is mean and nasty because his father and brother are in jail and his mother is unreliable. Then he meets Rosie and his life improves. In Tyke's bell tower they discover three skeletons.

_____. *Jason Bodger and the Priory Ghost.* Faber, 1985. Jason is the classroom pest. He travels back in time to help free Matilda who was imprisoned 800 years ago.

_____. *Turbulent Term of Tyke Tiler.* Faber, 1980. Tyke and Danny are friends. Danny stole money Tyke tries to return. Tyke steals a test to coach Danny so he can stay in class. The surprise comes at the end when Tyke is "Theodora."

Kendall, Carol. *Firelings.* Atheneum, 1982. Firelings live on the edge of a volcano and must offer a victim or escape through Secret Way of the Goat.

_____. *Gammage Cup.* Harcourt, 1959/ 1990. A group of Exiles settle on a mountain top only to discover that their old enemies, the Mushrooms, are again fighting the Minnipins.

_____. *Whisper of Glocken.* Harcourt, 1965. The river is flooding. The Minnipins try to find out why. The Hulks, a race of giants, built a dam. The Bell of Glocken tolled (whispered) and the dam collapsed.

Kendall, Lace. *Rain Boat.* Crowell, 1965. Edward and two other children are washed down stream by flood waters. They, along with some animals, are rescued by the Rain Boat.

Keneally, Thomas. *Ned Kelly and the City of the Bees.* Godine, 1981. Ned becomes small enough to spend his summer living with the bees in their beehive.

Kennealy, Patricia. *Throne Scone: Book of the Keltiad.* Bluejay, 1986. Set on Earth in the 36th century this fantasy of Aeron Aoibhell, Queen of the Kelts, is part two of a trilogy about magic, sorcery and galactic battles.

Kennedy, Richard. *Amy's Eyes.* Harper, 1985. A girl changes into a doll and a doll changes into a sea captain. They sail together, avoiding the pirates, in search of gold.

_____. *Boxcar at the Center of the Universe.* Harper, 1982. Old Ali meets a nameless boy aboard a boxcar. He tells stories to the boy about his search for the Center of the Universe. He tells of upside down walking, mysterious deaths, curses, and a king.

_____. *Crazy in Love.* Dutton, 1980. Diana wishes for a husband and an old woman grants her her wish.

_____. *Dark Princess.* Holiday, 1978. A princess loses her sight. No one can look at her

without going blind. The court fool is willing to go blind for her just to prove that love exists. She gives her life attempting to save his.

_____. *Inside My Feet.* Harper, 1979. An exciting story of how a giant? (two big boots) takes away a boy's parents?

Kennedy, S.A. *Hey, Didi Darling.* Houghton, 1983. The story of a girls' rock band who disguised themselves as boys so they could have success in the music world.

Kennedy, X.J. *Owlstone Crown.* Atheneum, 1983. Timothy and Verity are orphans and escape from unkind foster parents. One day they escape into another world.

Kennemore, Tim. *Changing Times.* Faber, 1984. Victoria has everything but loving parents. Through an old clock she travels back in time a day at a time. She learns why her parents quarrel and understands better her feeling toward them.

_____. *Fortunate Few.* Coward, 1981. Girls are raised as gymnasts in a future world. They start at age five. Jodie Bell is good and is highly paid for her talent.

_____. *Wall of Words.* Faber, 1983. Kim, 13, and her sisters fight and tease but resolve their differences. Kerry is dyslexic, Anna is spoiled and their father is away writing a book.

Kenny, Kevin. *Sometimes My Mom Drinks Too Much.* Dial, 1981. Maureen's mother is an alcoholic and she finds this hard to live with.

Kenrick, Tony. *Stealing Lillian.* McKay, 1975. The master plan of enticing four terrorists to kidnap the child of a millionaire is not working out as expected. Lillian's mother has a legal case against her "father"; the kidnappers are all wrong.

Kent, Alexander. *Midshipman Bolitho and the Avenger.* Putnam, 1978. Richard, 17, and Martyn find the body of a revenue agent. The Avenger is sent to stop the smuggling and Martyn is captured. The Avenger finds and attacks the smuggling ship.

Kent, Deborah. *Belonging.* Dial, 1978. Meg, 15, and blind, finds that being different has compensations. She doesn't fit in with the school crowd but realizes it is her own fault.

Kerr, Helen. *Grave Allegra.* Washburn, 1970. Allegra, 13, is staying with relations instead of going away with her parents as she usually does. She lives a very different life and is unhappy but something happens to change all that.

Kerr, Judith. *Other Way Around.* Coward, 1975. Anna and her family settle in England. They can't find work and are poor. Anna finds work and takes art lessons. Her brother, Max, goes on to Cambridge.

_____. *Small Person Far Away.* Coward, 1978. Anna marries a writer, Richard, and settles in England. She goes to Berlin to help her ill mother and learns more about her childhood and the feelings of Nazi survivors.

_____. *When Hitler Stole Pink Rabbit.*

Coward, 1971. A Jewish family weathers the experiences of being refugees in several countries during World War II. They expected to be gone for only a short time so Anna left her pink rabbit behind.

Kerr, M.E. *Dinky Hocker Shoots Smack.* Harper, 1972. Dinky has a weight problem and a "neglected child" problem. Her mother is too busy helping stray children to see that her own daughter is in need of help.

_____. *Fell.* Harper, 1987. John Fell is paid $20,000 to impersonate a rich neighbor's son at a prep school. Because he has never had any money he is anxious to see how the wealthy live.

_____. *Gentlehands.* Harper, 1978. Buddy has two major happenings in his life. First, he falls in love. Second, he finds out that his beloved grandfather is a Nazi war criminal.

_____. *Him She Loves?* Harper, 1984. Henry, 16, loves Valerie. She is Jewish and he is German. Her father is a comedian and makes fun of the romance. It becomes a national television routine.

_____. *I Stay Near You.* Harper, 1985. Mildred was poor and didn't like the rich. She was bright and grew up beautiful. Powell was rich and liked Mildred in spite of their differences. Their ill-fated love affected three generations.

_____. *If I Love You, Am I Trapped Forever?* Harper, 1973. Alan pays no attention to Duncan, because he is popular and Duncan is "dead meat." But when Duncan gets his girl, his friends, his fame and even his family, what is he to do?

_____. *I'll Love You When You're More Like Me.* Harper, 1977. Wally's life is being planned for him without his agreement and he doesn't like it. So when he gets a chance he runs away from his marriage-thinking girlfriend, his father's business and into....

_____. *Is That You, Miss Blue?* Harper, 1975. Flander spends her first year at boarding school. Her parents are separated and she is influenced by "Miss Blue," the best teacher in spite of her unusual ways.

_____. *Little Little.* Harper, 1981. Little Little is a midget and loves Sydney, a dwarf. Her family is against them. It is a very funny, satirical story.

_____. *Love Is a Missing Person.* Harper, 1975. Susy's sister has a secret love; Susy's favorite librarian has an open love; Susy's mother is not easy to get along with. Susy has a problem facing her own feelings.

_____. *Night Kites.* Harper, 1986. Erick's older brother has AIDS. He is a likable fellow and accepts his fate. His father is not understanding and his brother Erick is having trouble explaining it to his girlfriend.

_____. *Son of Someone Famous.* Harper, 1974. Adam, 16, lives with his grandmother. He meets Brenda Belle and his life changes. But is this the end of his problems or just the beginning?

_____. *What I Really Think of You.* Harper, 1982. Opal is a poor preacher's daughter and takes a lot of teasing. She sees Jesse and his rich evangelist father on television. Which life is better?

Kerr, Rita. *Texas Footprints.* Eakin, 1988. A description of how it was to travel from the East to Texas in 1823.

Kesey, Ken. *One Flew Over the Cuckoo's Nest.* Nal, 1962. "The Broom," McMurphy and Nurse Ratched are characters in a mental hospital. McMurphy is a criminal whom Nurse Ratched is out to get.

Kesselmam, Wendy. *Flick.* Harper, 1983. Nana is befriended by beautiful, influential Flick. It deepens into a sexual relationship. But later Flick gets cruel and leaves the bereaved Nana.

Kessler, Leonard. *Aurora and Socrates.* Crowell, 1975. While their parents are working full time, Aurora and Socrates cope with their babysitter and vice versa.

Kesteven, G.R. *Awakening Water.* Hastings, 1979. John, living in a dull future world, learns that he has been given tranquilizers in his water. He runs away with other Lost Ones but lives in fear of being caught and sent back.

Key, Alex. *Rivets and Sprockets.* Westminster, 1964. Rivets and Sprockets and Jimmy explore Mars to find out who is sending messages back to earth.

_____. *Sprockets—A Little Robot.* Westminster, 1963. Sprockets accidentally got the wrong brain. It was only to go to a specialized group of robots. He uses it to get into and out of trouble.

Key, Alexander. *Case of the Vanishing Boy.* Archway, 1979. Two youngsters have unusual powers and are therefore hunted down in a ruthless manner.

_____. *Escape to Witch Mountain.* Westminster, 1968. Tia and Tony appear to be abandoned orphans but they are different from other children. They see their mission and must follow their plans.

_____. *Flight to the Lonesome Place.* Westminster, 1971. Ronnie is a math genius but trusts only Ana Maria. He is being pursued and they, with Black Luis and Marlowe, go to the Lonesome Place to hide out.

_____. *Forgotten Door.* Westminster, 1965. Jon wanders into the life of a kind family who wonder where he came from. There is a dispute over his identity. One day he disappears again, through a secret door, and the kind family go with him.

_____. *Preposterous Adventures of Swimmer.* Westminster, 1973. A talking river otter escapes from captivity after some adventures with cruel humans. He resolves the problems of other people and other animals.

_____. *Return from Witch Mountain.* Westminster, 1978. Tia and Tony are very concerned about the Planet Earth and their many Earth friends because of what might happen at the hands of an evil scientist and the power of greed.

_____. *Sword of Aradel*. Westminster, 1977. A medieval boy and girl transport themselves 1000 years into the future. They come to New York City to find a magic sword.

Keyes, Daniel. *Flowers for Algernon*. Bantam, 1970. Charley is retarded and has an experimental operation that not only cures his retardation but makes him extra bright. But the operation is not successful over a long period of time.

Kherdian, David. *Beyond Two Rivers*. Greenwillow, 1981. Ted and Joe return from their camping trip. They think they see a Japanese prisoner. But Mr. Matsu is a nature lover like themselves.

_____. *Bridger, Story of a Mountain Man*. Greenwillow, 1987. An 18-year-old boy learns to trap, to explore and meet and deal with Indians.

_____. *It Started with Old Man Bean*. Greenwillow, 1980. Ted and Joe go camping along a river. It rains and the river floods and Ted is swept downstream.

_____. *Mystery of the Diamond in the Wood*. Knopf, 1983. Sam and Howie find a diamond ring in a tree stump. There is more jewelry there but it is all gone later. They investigate and find Jeb has committed many robberies.

_____. *Song in the Walnut Grove*. Knopf, 1982. A lonely cricket finds friendship in his world.

Kibbe, Pat. *Hocus-Pocus Dilemma*. Knopf, 1979. B.J. learns that she has ESP and decides to go into the fortune-telling business. It turns out to be quite unusual as she predicts family events.

_____. *My Mother the Mayor*. Knopf, 1981. When a mother decides to run for mayor of her town, her children help to get her elected.

Kidd, Ronald. *Dunker*. Dutton, 1982. Bobby, 16, is famous because his 12-year-old-looking face is on "Dunker Donut" billboards. He wants to play basketball, look his age and date Barbara.

_____. *Glitch: A Computer Fantasy*. Lodestar, 1985. A boy is pulled into his computer and finds himself in computer kingdom.

_____. *Second Fiddle*. Lodestar, 1988. A $250.00 violin of the Pirelli Youth Orchestra is destroyed. They need to find who could do such a thing.

_____. *Sizzle and Splat*. Dutton, 1983. Members of a youth orchestra investigate a sabotage and the kidnapping of the orchestra president.

_____. *That's What Friends Are For*. Nelson, 1978. A story of two thirteen-year-olds, one of whom has leukemia.

_____. *Who Is Felix the Great*. Dutton, 1983. A boy writes his term paper on a past baseball player with strange results.

Kiesel, Stanley. *Skinny Malinky Leads the War for Kidness*. Dutton, 1984. Mr. Forclosure is looking for the kids that escaped his Status Quo Solidification Program, especially Skinny Malinky.

_____. *War Between the Pitiful Teachers and the Splendid Kids*. Dutton, 1980. Mr. Forclosure and Big Alice declare war on the students and vice versa. The principal's weapon is Status Quo Solidifier. It turns rowdy kids into conformers.

Kilgore, Kathleen. *Ghost Maker*. Houghton, 1984. Lee is asked to leave his boarding school. He goes to live with his grandmother. The people in the town where she lives practice spiritualism. He joins them to see if they plan to rob his grandmother.

_____. *Wolfman of Beacon Hill*. Little, 1982. A runaway and a social worker are involved in trying to help an escaped wolf find his way back to the woods from Boston. Tony buries the wolf after he is killed by a car.

Killien, Christie. *All of the Above*. Houghton, 1987. MacBeth, 15, falls for the new boy at school and gets the boy next door to help.

_____. *Artie's Brief: The Whole Truth and Nothing But*. Houghton, 1989. Artie's older brother commits suicide and he must learn to cope with this fact.

_____. *Fickle Fever*. Houghton, 1988. Skeeter is dating different boys looking for the right one. She "adopts" different interests for each guy. Then she decides that "honesty is the best policy."

_____. *Putting on an Act*. Houghton, 1986. Skeeter lied to her pen pal and when she comes to town Skeeter must examine her attitude toward brother, best friend and boyfriend.

_____. *Rusty Fertlanger, Lady's Man*. Houghton, 1988. Rusty, 15, an artist who doesn't like physical contact sports is forced to wrestle a girl.

Killilea, M. Karen. *Karen*. Prentice, 1980. Karen is the heroine in this book about the Killilea family.

_____. *With Love from Karen*. Prentice, 1963. Karen's older sister Gloria is featured in this book about the loveable Killilea family.

Kimbrough, Richard. *Cross-Country Courage*. Nelson, 1972. A new coach wants a runner to put on the running team; however the runner is black. The other boys try to discredit him but when the chips are down they come to his rescue.

Kimmel, Margaret. *Magic in the Mist*. Atheneum, 1975. Thomas is studying to be a wizard and gets to meet a dragon.

King, Alexander. *Memoirs of a Certain Mouse*. McGraw, 1966. Pinky, a mouse, tells of his escape from the National Research Laboratory. He also has adventures in the zoo and he meets lovely Tsi-Tsi, a female mouse.

King, Clive. *Me and My Millions*. Crowell, 1979. Ringo is in possession of a stolen painting worth millions. It certainly changes his life but he's not sure he likes it.

_____. *Night the Water Came By*. Crowell, 1982. Apu was orphaned during a bitter storm and now he's going through another cyclone. He goes through many experiences before he returns to his home island.

_____. *Ninny's Boat*. Macmillan, 1980. A young slave goes to 5th century Britain and finds his true identity.

King, Stephen. *Carrie*. Doubleday, 1974. Carrie was picked on throughout her school career. At age 17 she found she had the power to make things happen. As a joke she was invited to the Prom and there she took revenge no one will forget.

_____. *Christine*. Viking, 1983. A macabre story of Arnie and his car — the car that he cherished, the car that meant his end.

_____. *Cujo*. Viking, 1981. Brett's best friend was Cujo, a St. Bernard. He got stuck one day in a strange rabbit hole where he was bitten by rabid bats. He is now rabid but doesn't know it. Another King horror story.

_____. *Firestarter*. Viking, 1980. Andy and Vicki participated in an experiment while in college and now have a child who is psychic. She can set things on fire at will. Vicki is killed and someone is chasing Andy and his daughter.

_____. *Pet Sematary*. Doubleday, 1983. Ellie's cat, Church, was killed by a car and how was her father to tell her? He decided to bury the cat and tell Ellie that it ran off. The next day the cat was back with the wrapping used to bury her.

_____. *Salem's Lot*. Doubleday, 1975. A typical King story of fear and macabre incidents. This one has missing children, a murder and suicide, corpses and ghosts.

_____. *Shining*. Doubleday, 1976. Danny's parents take a job as caretakers of a hotel. Danny's able to sense things that have not yet happened. They're trapped in the hotel for the winter without communication and fear for their lives.

King-Smith, Dick. *Babe: The Gallant Pig*. Crown, 1983. A piglet is befriended by a sheep dog.

_____. *Fox Busters*. Delacorte, 1978. A battle between chickens and the killer foxes.

_____. *Harry's Mad*. Crown, 1987. Mad is a talking parrot that is stolen. But he is a bright bird and makes his way home again.

_____. *Magnus Powermouse*. Harper, 1984. Madeline and Marcus Aurelius are two mice. Their son is a large, pushy mouse.

_____. *Martin's Mice*. Crown, 1988. A cat keeps mice as pets but is then given away.

_____. *Mouse Boucher*. Viking, 1982. On an island of cats Tom Play hunts for the family of Bampton-Bush.

_____. *Pigs Might Fly*. Viking, 1982. A pig learns to swim and becomes a hero when the town is flooded.

_____. *Queen's Nose*. Harper, 1983. Harmony can't keep pets although she would like to.

But she has a magic coin. She uses it to advantage.

Kingman, Lee. *Break a Leg, Betsy Maybe*. Houghton, 1976. Betsy, 17, falls in love, becomes an actress and moves to a new home.

_____. *Georgina and the Dragon*. Houghton, 1972. Georgina, 10, wants to be called Gina. She tries to earn money to go where a Georgina is being honored. In the process she discovers that she, too, like the other Georgina, is a woman suffragist.

_____. *Head Over Wheels*. Houghton, 1978. Terry, 16, has an accident in which he breaks his neck and becomes a quadriplegic. This affects everyone in his family, especially his twin, Kerry.

_____. *Luck of the Miss L*. Houghton, 1986. Alec dreams of winning an upcoming boat race. He has a near accident and his confidence is shaken.

_____. *Peter Pan Bag*. Houghton, 1970. Wendy, 17, becomes involved in a commune group of hippies in Boston. She learns about these drop-outs from society. She spends the summer with Miggle and her brother, Peter, who show her around "hip" Boston.

_____. *Private Eyes: Adventures with the Saturday Gang*. Doubleday, 1964. Teddy and his friends find detective work more dangerous than they thought.

_____. *Saturday Gang*. Doubleday, 1961. A TV company is filming in Teddy's town and the Saturday Gang win over the town to go along with the idea. They solve the mysterious robberies in a humorous manner.

_____. *Year of the Raccoon*. Houghton, 1966. Joey is unsure of himself but when he cares for and trains a pet raccoon it gives him responsibility and self-confidence.

Kinsey-Warnick, Natalie. *Canada Geese Quilt*. Dutton, 1989. Ariel's grandmother quilts. Her mother is going to have a baby. Ariel draws geese as a design for the quilt.

Kipling, Rudyard. *Captains Courageous*. Doubleday, 1897. A spoiled son of an American millionaire washed overboard and was picked up by a fishing schooner. He was forced to share the life and labor of the crew. It was all for the best.

_____. *Jungle Book*. Nal, 1961. Mowgli is raised by wolves. He is protected by Baloo, the bear, and Bagheera, the panther. But Shere Khan, the tiger, is an enemy.

_____. *Kim*. Nal, 1984. Kim is an orphan living on the streets of India. He runs errands for the Secret Service.

Kirby, Susan. *Ike and Porker*. Houghton, 1983. Ike's father is going on a hog drive and Ike is determined to go with him.

Kirchgessner, Maria. *High Challenge*. Harcourt, 1962. The Green Four, Kathi, Franka, Lieselotte and Mariella, find a hut and fix it up. They earn money for the needed repairs.

Kirk, Ruth. *David, Young Child of the Qui-*

leutes. Harcourt, 1967. David, 11, is a child of his tribe, but goes to a modern school, and watches TV while still observing old traditions.

Kirshenbaum, Binnie. *Short Subject.* Watts, 1989. Audrey lives in the 1930's and 1940's movie fantasies. She lies, steals and wants to be a gangster. She must learn to face reality.

Kjelgaard, James. *Big Red.* Holiday, 1945/1982. The story of a wonderful Irish setter named Big Red and his owner who is the son of a trapper. He and Big Red grow up together.

_____. *Boomerang Hunter.* Holiday, 1960. An aboriginal youth and his dog look for food for his people during a draught.

_____. *Coyote Song.* Dodd, 1969. Two coyotes struggle to survive and Papago Joe struggles to be his own man.

_____. *Haunt Fox.* Bantam, 1954. A fox is chased by a boy and his dog. First the boy is the center character then the fox becomes central.

_____. *Hidden Trail.* Holiday, 1962. Jase is a photographer and goes to solve the disappearance of over 1000 elk during their migration from summer to winter feeding grounds.

_____. *Irish Red.* Holiday, 1951/1984. A story of one of Big Red's sons. He was the runt of the litter. Although he finally did win a dog show he was certainly a misfit for most of his young life.

_____. *Nose for Trouble.* Holiday, 1982. Tom, a warden, runs afoul with the Black Elk Gang, a group of poachers who swore they would kill him if he got in their way. But Tom is determined to protect the animals in his care.

_____. *Outlaw Red.* Holiday, 1953/1977. Sean, another son of Big Red, finds himself forced to survive in the wilderness.

_____. *Snow Dog.* Holiday, 1948/1980. Link, a trapper, adds Queenie to his dog team only to lose her while she has a family. He finds one of her pups later in a trap. He releases him and trains him. The dog later saves his life.

_____. *Tigre (Jaguars).* Dodd, 1961. Pepe, a Mexican goatherd, pits himself against the vicious jaguar who killed his father and is destroying his goat herd.

_____. *Wild Trek.* Holiday, 1950/1981. A trapper and his dog go into the mountains to rescue the pilot of a plane that was downed with a famous naturalist aboard.

_____. *Wildlife Cameraman.* Holiday, 1957. Jase and his dog spend summer learning about conservation and the balance of nature.

Klass, David. *Breakaway Run.* Lodestar, 1987. Tony, an American, plays soccer in Japan. He stays there for several months to adjust to his parents' divorce. He didn't want it to happen.

_____. *Different Season.* Lodestar, 1988. Jim is a high school baseball star. He meets Jennifer who plays softball. She becomes a member of his team and he doesn't like it.

Klass, Sheila. *Alive and Starting Over.* Scribner, 1983. Jessica no longer resents her step-mother. Grandmother has a heart attack; she meets a new boy, Peter, and still is loyal to Jason.

_____. *Bennington Stitch.* Scribner, 1985. Amy's mother wants her to go to Bennington College but Amy's SAT results say otherwise. How can she help from hurting her mother while satisfying her own needs?

_____. *Credit-Card Carole.* Scribner, 1987. Carole's father leaves his dental practice to take up acting. He also curtails Carole's credit and she is devastated. But things can and do get worse.

_____. *Nobody Knows Me in Miami.* Scribner, 1981. Should she go to live with a rich aunt and uncle in Miami? A poor girl from New York must make a decision.

_____. *To See My Mother Dance.* Scribner, 1981. Jessica doesn't like her new stepmother. She fantasizes about her real mother and sees her as a beautiful dancer even though she deserted Jessica on her first birthday.

Klaveness, Jan. *Ghost Island.* Macmillan, 1985. Delia feels abandoned by her re-married mother. They all go to Ghost Island for vacation but things are changed. There are a kidnapping and a death. An underground cave is found and a house burns.

_____. *Griffin Legacy.* Macmillan, 1983. Amy and her friend look for clues to solve the mystery of the Griffin legacy. Amy is mistaken for Lucy, whose ghost they see. By listening to the ghosts she is able to put them at ease at last.

Kleberger, Ilse. *Grandmother Oma.* Atheneum, 1967. Grandmother Oma could rollerskate and iceskate. She could hatch eggs, and rescue her grandson from a bull. She was not an ordinary grandmother.

Klein, Norma. *Beginners' Love.* Dial, 1982. Shy Joel likes aggressive Lela. They both experience their first love.

_____. *Bizou.* Viking, 1983. Bizou is abandoned by his mother when they arrive in the United States from France.

_____. *Blue Trees, Red Sky.* Pantheon, 1975. An eight-year-old's Dad dies and he lives with his mother and brother.

_____. *Breaking Up.* Pantheon, 1980. Ali's parents are divorced and her father wants her to come live with him on a permanent basis. But she would have to leave her boyfriend, Ethan, and her best friend, Gretchen.

_____. *Cheerleader.* Knopf, 1985. Evin and Karim form a cheerleading squad for the girl's softball team.

_____. *Confessions of an Only Child.* Pantheon, 1974. A story of Antonia's life between the birth of her baby brothers. The first dies and she adjusts.

_____. *Family Secrets.* Dial, 1985. Leslie and Peter are friends who become lovers. When Peter's father marries Leslie's mother they become stepsister and stepbrother. They have the usual teen problems of sex, drugs and growing pains.

_____. *Give and Take*. Viking, 1985. Spence, 17, knows all about women, but....

_____. *Going Backwards*. Scholastic, 1986. Charles's grandmother has Alzheimer's disease. He and his family learn to cope with this as the disease takes its toll.

_____. *Honey of a Chimp*. Pantheon, 1980. A chimp moves in with a human family and both sides need to adjust.

_____. *It's Not What You'd Expect*. Pantheon, 1973. Fourteen-year-old twins open a restaurant with the help of their freinds. It is a summer activity.

_____. *It's OK If You Don't Love Me*. Dial, 1977. A seventeen-year-old liberated woman of New York falls for a traditional boy from Ohio.

_____. *Mom, the Wolfman and Me*. Pantheon, 1972. Brett's mother is not married and she has several overnight boy friends. An unusual arrangement but both Brett and her mother like it that way.

_____. *My Life as a Body*. Knopf, 1987. Augie, 17, is going to tutor Sam, who was badly hurt in an auto accident. She works with his mind, which was brain damaged. She comes to see him as a whole person and herself as whole, also.

_____. *Naomi in the Middle*. Dial, 1974. Naomi, 7, is a middle child when a baby arrives. And being a middle child is no fun.

_____. *Now That I Know*. Bantam, 1988. On long weekends Nina lives with her father and his "friend" Greg. The rest of the week she stays with her mother. She gets sexual information from her straight mother and her gay father.

_____. *Older Men*. Dial, 1987. A story of Elise and her much older father. He was unusually nice to her. She has questions about his relationship with her mother who is now in a mental hospital. What of her own feelings?

_____. *Queen of What Ifs*. Ballantine, 1982. Robin's father and mother can't get along because they are so different. Robin is different from her boyfriend, Mason. Will they, too, not get along?

_____. *Robbie and the Leap Year Blues*. Dial, 1981. Robbie, 11, has lots of girl friends and divorced parents. They are both problems for Robbie.

_____. *Snapshots*. Dial, 1984. Sean, 13, and Marc want to pose Marc's pretty 8-year-old sister to show that she could be a model. Someone suspects child pornography. They are finally cleared but not without incident.

_____. *Sunshine*. Holt, 1974. Kate has bone cancer and leaves her thoughts on a recorded tape for her daughter.

_____. *Taking Sides*. Pantheon, 1974. Nell is torn between her mother and her father when they divorce. She decides to live with her father and brother.

_____. *Tomboy*. Four Winds, 1978. Antonia, 10, has many changes as she grows up. It's hard to leave your past for the unknown future.

_____. *What It's All About*. Dial, 1975. Bernadette's parents adopt a Vietnamese child and the family changes.

Klein, Robin. *Enemies*. Dutton, 1989. Mary Ann and Sandy do not like each other even though their respective mothers are good friends.

_____. *Games*. Viking, 1986. Kirsty and her friends hear scratching at the window, see mysterious lighted candles and see a white gloved hand after holding a seance.

_____. *Hating Alison Ashley*. Viking, 1984. Erica doesn't like Alison because she is rich and pretty. When they go to summer camp they become friends.

_____. *People Might Hear You*. Viking, 1987. After Frances's aunt and Mr. Tyrell marry they go to live in his house. It is a site of a religious cult and Frances is a prisoner. She and one of Mr. Tyrell's daughters manage to escape.

Klein, Suzy. *What's the Matter with Herbie Jones?* Putnam, 1986. Herbie and his friends are about to break up a friendship over a girl!

Klevin, Jill. *Turtle Street Trading Company*. Delacorte, 1982. The girls try to find a way to get money so they can go to Disneyland.

_____. *Turtles Together Forever*. Delacorte, 1982. Fergy carries on—by starting an ice cream business in San Francisco where he lives with his divorced mother.

Knight, Eric. *Lassie Come Home*. Holt, 1940. The beautiful classic about the close relationship of a boy and his loyal dog.

Knott, Bill. *Dwarf on Black Mountain*. Steck-Vaughn, 1967. Tim's rifle is stolen and his friend Hank says he saw a dwarf-like creature. They investigate and find a Hungarian scientist and his granddaughter who want to defect.

Knowles, Anne. *Halcyon Island*. Harper, 1980. Ken is afraid of water. He meets Giles who gently helps him enjoy boating and fishing. No one else sees Giles; he appears to have no family. Is he a ghost of a boy who drowned trying to save his family?

_____. *Under the Shadows*. Harper, 1983. Cathy, 15, befriends Mark who is handicapped. She gets him a horse and this helps his outlook.

Knowles, John. *Peace Breaks Out*. HRW, 1981. Pete is back at Devon School, not as a student but as a teacher. The war is over and he wants peace and quiet. But tensions break out among the students.

_____. *Separate Peace*. Macmillan, 1960. Gene and Finney are in Devon School in 1942 when Finney is injured because of Gene. They become close friends. There is no suggestion of homosexuality then (1959) as there might be today.

Knudsen, James. *Just Friends*. Avon, 1982. Blake is a loner. Spencer and Libby make his life the best it has ever been. They then become a couple and Blake is a loner again.

Knudson, Poul. *Challenge*. Macmillan, 1963.

Abdjoin is a Viking in the 1st century. He has two years to seek his fortune. Betrayal and slavery follow but also wealth as a Roman charioteer.

Knudson, R.R. *Fox Running.* Houghton, 1975. Kathy is burned out at 19 after winning an Olympic gold medal. She no longer enjoys running, or anything, for that matter. Then she meets Fox Running, who runs like a deer.

————. *Just Another Love Story.* Farrar, 1983. Dusty broke up with Marianna and feels very bad. He thinks about taking up bodybuilding. He meets a weightlifter and finds him pretty "regular."

————. *Rinehart Lifts.* Farrar, 1980. Zan helps her friend, Rinehart, lift weights. He would rather take care of his ferns but needs to fight for his rights as he is shunned by the Mighty Four.

————. *Rinehart Shouts.* Farrar, 1987. Rinehart spends his summer bird watching with a friend and competing with his grandmother in a boat race.

————. *Zan Hagen's Marathon.* Farrar, 1984. The sport is track as Zan tries to win a place on the U.S. Olympic team. She finds it is hard work and a great deal of pain.

————. *Zanballer.* Delacorte, 1972. Zan, a liberated girl, makes football history at school. She is encouraged to be a cheerleader, but instead forms a girl's football team.

————. *Zanbanger.* Harper, 1977. In this book Zan participates in basketball. The girl's team think she is too aggressive and the boy's team won't take her. She and Rinehart fight back by legal means.

————. *Zanboomer.* Harper, 1978. Zan is a winner on her high school baseball team but hurts her shoulder. She takes up cross-country running which is the first non-team sport she has tried.

Koehn, Ilse. *Mischling, Second Degree: My Childhood in Nazi Germany.* Greenwillow, 1977. A young girl, Ilse, finds out much later that her parents separated because her father was one-fourth Jewish. She was drafted into the Hitler Youth.

————. *Tilla.* Greenwillow, 1981. Tilla's parents were killed in the Dresden bombing. She grows up and falls in love with Rolf and helps rebuild Germany.

Koenig, Alma. *Gudrun.* Lothrop, 1979. Gudrun, the daughter of a king, is kidnapped. She is rescued years later, is rejoined with her betrothed and pardons her abductor.

Koertge, Ron. *Where the Kissing Never Stops.* Little, 1987. What happens when a boy's mother takes a job as stripper in an unsavory joint? What will his girlfriend think? His friends? And on top of it all his mother likes her job!

Koff, Richard. *Christopher.* Celestial, 1981. Christopher first becomes invisible, then he shrinks in size, then he can read minds. What will he do with all this power?

Kogawa, Joy. *Naomi's Road.* Oxford, 1988.

Naomi is Japanese-Canadian and is sent to an internment camp during World War II.

Kohl, Erica. *Where Is Emmett Gold?* Harper, 1985. Emmett is a rock musician and he disappears. The mystery is solved through a number of clues: letters, ticket stubs, resumes, etc.

Konigsburg, E.L. *About the B'nai Bagels.* Atheneum, 1969. Mark plays on a Little League team managed by his mother and coached by his father.

————. *Father's Arcane Daughter.* Atheneum, 1976. Caroline was kidnapped seventeen years ago. She reappears at her old home where her father has a new wife and children. She claims to be the daughter and wants her inheritance. Is she real or an imposter?

————. *From the Mixed Up Files of Mrs. Basil E. Frankweiler.* Atheneum, 1967. Claudia and her brother run away to the Metropolitan Museum of Art. By using their facilities they survive for six days. Mrs. F., an art patron, and her secret of the statues help Claudia cope.

————. *(George).* Atheneum, 1970. Ben has a split personality: (George) is his other self. His mother thinks George is an imaginary playmate. There is a great deal of conflict between George and Ben, including theft and drugs.

————. *Jennifer, Hecate, Macbeth, William Mackinley and Me, Elizabeth.* Atheneum, 1967. Jennifer and Elizabeth become friends after playing witch and apprentice.

————. *Journey to an 800 Number.* Atheneum, 1982. Max is a real snob. He goes to live with his father whom he finds inferior to himself. But he learns a great deal about his father and himself. He meets a girl whose mother has an 800 phone number.

————. *Proud Taste for Scarlet and Miniver.* Atheneum, 1985. The friends and followers of Eleanor of Aquitaine tell of her life. A fictionalized biography.

————. *Second Mrs. Giaconda.* Macmillan, 1975. A story that is theoretically about the real Mona Lisa. It is told from the viewpoint of Salai, who worked for da Vinci.

————. *Up from Jerico Tel.* Atheneum, 1986. Jeanmarie and Malcolm are latchkey children. At Jericho Tell, a small hill, they meet Tallulah who tells them how to find a missing necklace. But Tallulah is dead and this is her ghost.

Konwicki, Tadeusz. *Anthropos-Spectre-Beast.* Phillips, 1977. The Earth will end and Peter meets the Anthropos-Spectre-Beast and travels through the universe.

Koob, Theodora. *Deep Search.* Lippincott, 1969. A girl and her ten-year-old retarded brother differ with their parents about their future.

Kooiker, Leonie. *Legacy of Magic.* Morrow, 1981. Chris is spending the summer as apprentice to a witch. His friend Alec is spending the summer with his grandfather. They both are involved in magic and buried treasure.

————. *Magic Stone*. Morrow, 1978. Chris finds a magic stone in his friend's grandmother's chair. The grandmother wants Chris to be a witch but the other witches don't. The stone lets him read people's minds and influence their actions.

Korczak, Junusz. *King Matt the First*. Farrar, 1985. When Matt's father dies he becomes king. He makes the adults tend school and the children run the country.

Korman, Gordon. *Don't Care High*. Scholastic, 1986. Paul has just transferred into a school where no one cares about anything. He meets Sheldon and between them they turn the school upside down and backwards.

————. *Our Man Weston*. Scholastic, 1982. Sidney and his brother, Tom, work at Pine Grove Resort Hotel. Sidney starts to spy on Mr. Kitzel when he sees him steal a purse. This is the beginning of his funny adventure.

————. *Semester in the Life of a Garbage Bag*. Scholastic, 1987. Raymond is a "crazy, mixed-up kid." He, his grandfather and his friend, Sean, bring national attention to themselves as well as destroying a government project. Ray is the Garbage Bag.

————. *Son of Interflux*. Scholastic, 1986. Simon's father works for Interflux, a company that wants to build a factory right next to Simon's school. He forms Antiflux to fight this action.

————. *War with Mr. Wizzle*. Scholastic, 1982. When their school gets a computer two friends are afraid of the changes it will bring.

————. *Zucchini Warriors*. Scholastic, 1988. Bruno and Boots play football with Cathy as quarterback to win the Daw Cup and get money for a rec hall. Mr. Zucchini's snack wagons are part of the scheme and part of Elmer's science experiment.

Korschunow, Irina. *Night in Distant Motion*. Godine, 1983. Regine is a loyal Nazi. She falls in love with a Polish prisoner. She is found out and punished. She escapes and hides on a farm. Her opinion of the Nazis slowly changes.

Kortum, Jeanie. *Ghost Vision*. Pantheon, 1983. Panipaq is an Inuit. He wants to follow the old ways of his people. He is a Shaman and must help his people.

Kotzwinkle, William. *Trouble in Bugland*. Godine, 1986. This is a spoof on the Sherlock Holmes stories. The characters are all insects of one kind or another but the pattern of crime and investigation is familiar.

Krantz, Hazel. *Secret Raft*. Vanguard, 1965. Howie and his friends build a raft and follow some men into the swamp. They are scientists, not spies, and Howie saves the men during a flood.

Krasilovsky, Phyllis. *L.C. Is the Greatest*. Nelson, 1975. Louise (L.C.), a Jewish girl in the 1930's, likes her mother and hates her father. She muddles through winter trying to save people from the cruelties of the world.

Krementz, Jill. *Sweet Pea*. Harcourt, 1969.

Sweet Pea, a 10-year-old poor, black girl, is optimistic about her future. She goes to school activities and church. A good view of life in the black South.

Krensky, Stephen. *Big Day for Scepters*. Atheneum, 1977. Calandar, a collector of magic, is involved in a quest for a mysterious scepter.

————. *Dragon Circle*. Atheneum, 1977. The Wynd children are kidnapped by five ancient dragons who encircle them. Peter's fake sword picks up their presence. One by one they are vanquished.

————. *Ghostly Business*. Atheneum, 1984. The five Wynd children are determined to foil an army of ghosts intent on helping an unscrupulous developer acquire some of the best land in the city.

————. *Perils of Putney*. Atheneum, 1978. Putney is a giant. When Fair Damsel disappears he searches for her even though he has little experience as a hero.

————. *Wilder Plot*. Atheneum, 1982. Charlie would do anything to get out of taking a part in the class play.

————. *Wilder Summer*. Atheneum, 1983. Charlie doesn't like camp until he sees Lydia. Chubs tries to help him impress her but Willoughby "helps" by suggesting ways that will have the opposite effect.

————. *Witching Hour*. Atheneum, 1981. The Wynd family pit their forces against a coven of witches who want to turn the children into monsters. They capture Old Magic and the children must save him. A funny, scary story.

Kristof, Jane. *Steal Away Home*. Bobbs, 1969. Amos and Obie, two brothers, set out for Philadelphia to find their father. They are aided by the Underground Railroad and a variety of modes of travel.

Kroll, Steven. *Breaking Camp*. Macmillan, 1985. Ted is at summer camp. There are cruel initiations, secret pot meetings. He fights back at the foul happenings.

Kropp, Paul. *Wilted*. Coward, 1980. Danny has an alcoholic father and a pot smoking mother who are getting a divorce. He is a nerd but rises in standing as the story moves along.

Krumgold, Joseph. *And Now Miguel*. Harper, 1953. Miguel, 12, is a sheep herder in New Mexico. He wants to join the men and their sheep in the summer pastures because it is a symbol of adulthood.

————. *Henry 3*. Atheneum, 1967. Henry doesn't like being an intellectual and when he goes to a new school he hides the fact. But the school bully, Fletcher, finds out. Henry promises to help with homework if Fletcher won't tell.

————. *Onion John*. Harper, 1959. Onion John is an odd jobs man ignored by the community. He makes friends with Andy, and makes a lasting impression on him because of his determination not to change his life. Newbery winner, 1960.

Kruss, James. *Happy Islands Behind the Winds*. Atheneum, 1966. Captain Madirankowitch of the Cicado beached on the Happy Islands during a storm. Plants and animals could understand each other. There were special parts of this island where everything was happy.

_____. *Letters to Pauline*. Atheneum, 1971. This time the author tells Pauline the stories in exchange for supplies. She lives in Germany and he lives on Canary Island. His stories are non-sensical, fun and somewhat moralistic.

_____. *My Great-Grandfather and I*. Atheneum, 1964. Boy's two sisters had the measles so he was to stay with great-grandfather who was a retired sailor and fisherman. For a whole week the two of them made up stories and poems about far places.

_____. *My Great-Grandfather, the Heroes and I*. Atheneum, 1973. Boy hurt his foot and couldn't go to school and his great-grandfather was too ill to move. So they both wrote stories about heroes to keep each other entertained. Soon everyone was involved.

_____. *Pauline and the Prince in the Wind*. Atheneum, 1966. Pauline tells stories to the author in return for candy and other goodies. Her stories are all fantasies and she appears in most of them.

_____. *Return to the Happy Islands*. Atheneum, 1967. Captain Madirankowitch, who was shipwrecked on the Happy Islands, swore he would come back if he could. He was told it was possible but not guaranteed. There is no place like the Happy Islands.

Kullman, Harry. *Battle Horse*. Bradbury, 1981. A story showing the caste system of long ago Stockholm. It is told through a game played by the boys of the neighborhood. One of the "boys," a hero, turns out to be a girl.

Kuper, Jack. *Child of the Holocaust*. Doubleday, 1968. Jankel, 9, tries to hide his Jewishness by pretending to be a Christian. The story takes place in Poland during World War II.

Kurland, Michael. *Princes of Earth*. Nelson, 1978. Adam is blamed for writing obscenities on the school wall. He is sent from Jasper to Mars where he encounters a world much different from his own. He also meets Michael, Prince of the Earth.

Kurland, Morton. *Our Sacred Honor*. Rosen, 1987. David and Jamie face the problem of her unwanted pregnancy. She wants to quit school in spite of a Vassar scholarship. He wants to go on to West Point. The story is told from each one's viewpoint.

Kurtz, Katherine. *Camber of Culdi*. Ballantine, 1976. A story about Camber and the kingdom of Gwyneed. He was the greatest of the Deryni, men with great mental powers. He must overthrow Imre and his sister.

_____. *Camber the Heretic*. Ballantine, 1981. The last of the "Legends of Camber of Culdi," the mystery man of medieval pageantry and magic. Even though he lost his son to the treachery of Imre he continues to fight for Gwyneed.

_____. *Legacy of Lehr*. Walker, 1986. Captain Lutobo and Commander Setin of interstellar ship "Valkyne" are not in agreement about bringing aboard four strange and dangerous blue Lehr cats.

_____. *Saint Camber*. Ballantine, 1978. Camber was both a defender of humanity and a practitioner of Black Magic. He was loved and hated.

Kushner, Donn. *Book Dragon*. Holt, 1988. Nonesuch is a dragon. If he doesn't eat he shrinks in size down to the size of an insect. He escapes notice. He is now in the book store after surviving for six centuries.

_____. *Violin Maker's Gift*. Farrar, 1982. Gaspard makes nice violins and one day he rescues a magical bird.

Ladd, Elizabeth. *Fox Named Rufus*. Morrow, 1960. Mary lets two ducks out of the duckhouse. A fox gets one of them. Mary traps him and names him Rufus, but she must later release him to the wilds.

_____. *Judy's Summer Friend*. Morrow, 1958. Judy lives with her aunt and uncle. Laurel comes to visit the Cape in the summer. They become friends but the summer people are different.

_____. *Marty Runs Away to Sea*. Morrow, 1968. Marty gets a boat as a reward for rescuing a couple in a capsized boat. She has a new friend, Jonathan, whose dad owns a schooner.

_____. *Meg and Melissa*. Morrow, 1964. Meg is a thirteen-year-old, scrappy babysitter for Melissa. She wonders about Melissa's past and why Melissa's guardians act so strange. Are her parents dead? Is she being hidden for a reason?

_____. *Meg of Hegon's Neck*. Morrow, 1961. Meg grows up on Heron's Neck and has the security of a stable family after being taken away from her free-living brother. At first she was resentful but she soon learns to love her new life.

_____. *Meg's Mysterious Island*. Morrow, 1963. Meg and her older brother, Allen, find money under the floor boards of an old barn. It is stolen money, that is later taken from them by Hogton and Foxy.

_____. *Mystery for Meg*. Morrow, 1962. Meg, who likes to play detective, solves a mystery. She visits her brother on the island of Heron's Neck and they investigate a locked room in an old barn.

_____. *Night of the Hurricane*. Morrow, 1956. Judy gets through the night of the hurricane because of her aunt's support so she wants to give her a nice Christmas present. She must earn the money so she and her friend, David, work together.

_____. *Treasure on Heron's Neck*. Morrow, 1967. Marty, with Meg and Kit, go treasure hunting in an old, supposedly abandoned house.

_____. *Trouble on Heron's Neck*. Morrow, 1966. Meg goes off to look for a lost pet crow. What she finds is a fisherman and his daughter living on shore's edge. When she goes back again she finds intruders with guns.

Laing, Frederick. *Bride Wore Braids*. Four Winds, 1968. Judy, 16, and Ken, 18, elope when she discovers she's pregnant.

_____. *Question of Pride*. Four Winds, 1967. Lisa tells of her relationship with trumpet playing Larry. Larry tells his side of the story. Pride keeps them apart.

Laklan, Carli. *Nurse in Training*. Doubleday, 1965. Nancy obeys hospital rules even though she doesn't always agree. She learns about the poverty of others. She must make a decision to either stay with her training or go home to an ailing mother.

_____. *Second Year Nurse*. Doubleday, 1967. Nancy meets Georgia and her grades drop and she breaks rules. She finally chooses a code of conduct for her friendship and things get better for her.

_____. *Surf with Me*. McGraw, 1967. Judy goes surfing despite parental objections. She loves the sport and breaks away from a boyfriend only to find a possible romance with a "go-head."

Lambert, Charles. *Copper Nail*. Follett, 1960. Pedro, an Indian of Chile, knew about the legend of buried gold. It seemed easy to find: near a fig tree with a copper nail driven into it.

L'Amour, Louis. *Haunted Mesa*. Bantam, 1987. An informative story about the disappearance of the Anasazi cliff dweller of the 13th century Southwest.

Lampel, Rusia. *That Summer with Ora*. Watts, 1967. Ora lives in Jerusalem. She is visited by Eleanor from America. No two girls could be more different. As time goes on and Eleanor comes to understand Ora's ways, hostility turns to friendship.

Lampman, Evelyn. *Bandit of Mak Hill*. Doubleday, 1969. Angel, 12, is alone until he meets Quinn. Quinn wants to develop his singing voice but Angel wants to join a band of Avengers. He tires of a life of stealing and misses Professor Quinn and his family.

_____. *Cayuse Courage*. Harcourt, 1970. Samuel, a Cayuse Indian, lost an arm and couldn't be a warrior. He stayed at the mission but learned to hate white men. When the Cayuse rebellion was planned he had divided loyalties.

_____. *City Under the Back Steps*. Doubleday, 1960. Two children shrink to the size of ants and live like them and learn of their habits.

_____. *Go Up the Road*. Atheneum, 1972. Yolanda's family are crop pickers. When her father's brother dies and they go to Oregon to become loggers, her life changes for the better.

_____. *Half-Breed*. Doubleday, 1967. Pale Eyes (Hardy) left the Crow Indians to find his white father. Hardy was disappointed when he found him but he learned about city life and "civilization."

_____. *Mrs. Updaisy*. Doubleday, 1963. A busy old lady and her talking pets work together to solve community problems. There is a very odd pet show to climax the story.

_____. *Potlatch Family*. Atheneum, 1976. Plum is an Indian. Her family is poor and her white schoolmates exclude her. She and her brother set up a tourist attraction. She learns about her heritage, dances, legends and food.

_____. *Rattlesnake Cave*. Atheneum, 1974. Jamie goes to live in Montana. He meets White Fang, a Cheyenne Indian, and his grandson, Horse. He saves White Fang's life and grows in maturity.

_____. *Shy Stegosaurus of Cricket Creek*. Doubleday, 1955. A funny fantasy about a delightful dinosaur found by Joey and Joan who are twins. The dinosaur can speak English and he wants a friend.

_____. *Shy Stegosaurus of Indian Springs*. Doubleday, 1962. An adventure with the supposedly extinct dinosaur. He lives near an Indian reservation and helps an Indian boy, Huck, save his grandfather from being "modernized."

_____. *Three Knocks on the Wall*. Atheneum, 1980. A young girl discovers a counterpart who has been kept in hiding by a neighbor.

_____. *White Captives*. Atheneum, 1975. A story of Olive Oatman's five years as a captive of the Apaches and Mohaves.

_____. *Year of Small Shadow*. Harcourt, 1971. Small Shadow is an Indian who lives with a white man while his father is in prison. He faces prejudices but learns to cope in both cultures.

Landis, J.D. *Daddy's Girl*. Morrow, 1984. Jennie, 13, sees her father kissing another woman. It poses a problem she doesn't know how to handle. A good deal of humor is shown at Ms. Richter's Feminist Day School.

Landis, James. *Sister Impossible*. Knopf, 1979. Lily is sure she won't like ballet but when she and her sister go for lessons she changes her mind.

Landsman, Sandy. *Castaways on Chimp Island*. Atheneum, 1986. Four laboratory chimps learn sign language and are put on an island with natural living conditions. Danny is smart but uncooperative; Nibbles is a "good girl"; Page is smart but devious; Tarzan is a wimp.

_____. *Gadget Factor*. Atheneum, 1984. Michael and his friend, Worm, get together and invent a computer game that is terrific.

Lane, Carolyn. *Ghost Island*. Houghton, 1985. Four girls are involved in some misadventures when they spy on a boy's camp across the lake. They end up marooned on Ghost Island.

Lane, Rose. *Let the Hurricane Roar*. Watts, 1966. Caroline and Charles live in the most primitive conditions in the Dakota Territory.

Lang, Othmar. *If You Are Silenced, I Will*

Speak for You. Collins, 1978. A thoughtful story about the work done by young people in the Amnesty International movement to help political prisoners.

Lange, Susanne. *Year.* Phillips, 1970. Ann decides not to go to college but to go to Israel for a year and live in a kibbutz. She finds a lot of hard work, experiences the grief of a friend's death and also falls in love.

Langton, Jane. *Astonishing Stereoscope.* Harper, 1971. Magic is the base of Edward and Eleanor's new adventure. It lies in the stereoscope cards and teaches a lesson of how to cope with everyday happenings.

————. *Boyhood of Grace.* Harper, 1972. A funny story about a girl with imagination of great magnitude. She wants the adventures she thinks only boys have. Her tomboy ways are disapproved of by family and friends.

————. *Diamond in the Window.* Harper, 1962. Strange things happen to the Hall family's house. The diamond is only glass but as Edward and Eleanor watch the moonlight they have exciting adventures.

————. *Fledgling.* Harper, 1980. In this fantasy, Georgie, a cousin of Edward and Eleanor, wants to fly. She makes friends with a Canadian goose and gets her wish.

————. *Fragile Flag.* Harper, 1984. Georgie leads a children's march from Massachusetts to Washington, D.C., in protest of new, destructive missiles. She carries an old flag found in the attic.

————. *Her Majesty, Grace Jones.* Harper, 1961. Grace convinces herself that she is the rightful heir to the throne of England. It is a way to get through the Great Depression.

————. *Swing in the Summer House.* Harper, 1967. Once again, the Hall family have exciting and terrifying adventures in their home. Edward and Eleanor go into the summerhouse against the signs reading otherwise.

Lansing, E.H. *Secret of Dark Entry.* Crowell, 1961. A mysterious, strange, lost treasure; coded letters; an abandoned mine and a deserted village called Dark Entry are what Jane, her brother and a friend (plus a dog) find.

Larimer, Tamela. *Buck.* Avon, 1986. Buck, a natural leader in school loses everything when he is betrayed by his best friend, Rich.

Larson, Jean. *Silkspinners.* Scribner, 1967. Li Po goes to find the lost silkspinners of China. The last one is living in seclusion and letting the craft die out. He finds him after monsters, sorcerers and an angry sea play their part.

Lasker, Joe. *Tournament of Knights.* Harper, 1986. An exciting story of the first tournament that Lord Justin, a knight, fought. In the Middle Ages these tournaments were important.

Lasky, Kathryn. *Beyond the Divide.* Macmillan, 1983. A realistic story of what it was like to move West in 1850. Meribah suffered every hardship imaginable and was left stranded and

alone. Some Indians took her in and she learned to love their way of life.

————. *Bone Wars.* Morrow, 1988. Thad is raised by a cattle rancher who dies. He becomes a scout for an anthropologist. Julian is also an anthropologist. They become friends and see the greed of others and set their own standards.

————. *Home Free.* Four Winds, 1985. Sam and Gus are looking for evidence that eagles are nesting in a wilderness area that is being threatened. They take pictures of the eagles and care for the youngest eagles until they are able to fly.

————. *Jem's Island.* Macmillan, 1982. Jem and his father go by kayak on an adventurous camping trip.

————. *Night Journey.* Warne, 1981. Rachel tells the story of the escape of her family from the persecutions of Tsarist Russia. She reveals the life of her great-grandmother in the telling.

————. *Pageant.* Four Winds, 1986. A story of a Jewish girl growing up. She attends a Christian school and is in the minority there. A picture of life during the Kennedy years.

————. *Prank.* Macmillan, 1984. Birdie's brother vandalized a synagogue and called it a prank. Birdie forgets her arguing family, her petty school problems and her summer job as she looks into the reality of the Holocaust.

Last, Jef. *Bamboo School in Bali.* Day, 1969. Bontot wants to become a teacher and works to complete his education. His friend, Koese, doesn't like studying. They, with Dajoe, a temple girl, have adventures in Bali.

Lattimore, Deborah. *Flame of Peace.* Harper, 1987. This is a legendary tale of the life of the Aztecs of Latin America.

Lattimore, Eleanor. *Bittern's Nest.* Morrow, 1962. As two twelve-year-old girls meet for the first time in two years and spend a week together they find each other quite different than remembered.

————. *Felicia.* Morrow, 1964. One day a cat named Felicia appears to Charlotte. She turns into a little girl and lives with Charlotte's family. As she acts like a cat, not a human girl, she seems cruel and mischievous.

————. *Laurie and Company.* Morrow, 1962. Laurie moves and is homesick. Her family move back and the store Laurie dreamed of, "Paul Crawford & Co.," becomes "Laurie & Co."

————. *Little Tumbler.* Morrow, 1963. Ba is a Chinese boy who doesn't know his background but he can do tricks and somersaults. Weng is a conjurer and recognizes Ba as a former member of his company.

Lauritzen, Jonreed. *Glitter-Eyed Wouser.* Little, 1960. The three Marriner children track down the killer of their sheep, a mythical "wouser" each in their own way.

————. *Treasure of the High Country.* Little, 1959. Tenn and Michael are involved with bank robbers and an old hermit, Topaz. Topaz uses the legend of Guaitsis to advantage.

Law, Carol. *Case of the Weird Street Firebug.* Knopf, 1980. Steffi, Mutt and Jeff want to find out who is setting the mysterious fires.

Lawlor, Laurie. *Addie Across the Prairie.* Whitman, 1986. Addie learns a great deal about the hardships of travel and the strangeness of this new land as she crosses to Dakota Territory.

Lawrence, Ann. *Tom Ass; or, the Second Gift.* Walck, 1972. Tom is to become whatever his future wife makes of him. Jennifer turns him into an ass. She does well in business and Tom recovers his human shape.

Lawrence, Isabelle. *Drumbeats in Williamsburg.* Rand, 1965. Andy is deeply involved when the British occupy Williamsburg and he does a little spying on his own. He finally becomes the drummer boy he always wanted to be.

_____. *Gift of the Golden Cup.* Bobbs, 1946. This story takes place in Caesar's Rome. Atia and her brother are captured by pirates but are freed when the battle with Pompey's fleet ends in disaster.

_____. *Spy in Williamsburg.* Rand, 1955. A blacksmith's son exposes his father's apprentice as an English spy just after the Boston Tea Party.

_____. *Theft of the Golden Ring.* Bobbs, 1948. Atia married Octavius and has two children. Gaius is still adventurous but the pirate captain is still as likable as ever.

Lawrence, J.D. *Barnaby's Bills.* Macmillan, 1965. Felix is adopted. He is darked skinned and was in reform school. His friend is Cliff and together they solve the mystery of missing items. He is then better accepted by classmates and townspeople.

Lawrence, Louise. *Calling B for Butterfly.* Harper, 1982. Six youngsters survive a space ship accident. They are sealed in a small section of the ship and try to contact base for help. There is something very strange about who is on board.

_____. *Cat Call.* Harper, 1980. The children of Crow Ash are balanced between "Beast" and "God." Barry finds an ancient cat god idol. The Beast overcomes the God and Ginny and Neil are destroyed.

_____. *Children of the Dust.* Harper, 1985. The first bombs fell and the full scale nuclear attack was coming. It started as a normal day at school so when the bell rang everyone assumed it was another fire drill, but this was different.

_____. *Dram Road.* Harper, 1983. Stuart is poor, and has an alcoholic mother and no father. He tries to rob an old man; he hits him and thinks he's killed him. He runs away. He later finds love and changes for the better. He admits his crime.

_____. *Earth Witch.* Harper, 1981. Rhiannon is an evil earth witch. Kate, Jonathan and Owen are friends. Owen is bewitched by Bronwen and nearly kills him. Kate saves him.

_____. *Moonwind.* Harper, 1986. Gareth and Karen take a trip to the moon. Bethkahn, an astral spirit, awakens after 10,000 years. Gareth decides to shed his physical body and join her.

_____. *Sing and Scatter Daisies.* Harper, 1977. Anne is dying of cancer and the Ghost wants to take her away. Nicky wants to keep her there.

_____. *Star Lord.* Harper, 1978. A space ship crashes and Rhys finds the only survivor, "Star Lord." Everyone helps him escape from English soldiers, including Rhys. He gives his life but Star Lord comes and takes him to the stars.

_____. *Warriors of Taan.* Harper, 1988. The Earth people threaten to destroy Taan. A young novice tries to bring about peace.

_____. *Wyndcliffe.* Harper, 1975. Anna and her family move into a bleak house. She meets the ghost of the first owner and is in his spell. Her sister and brother try to save her but it is the ghost who sees the need to break the spell.

Lawrence, Mildred. *Drums in My Heart.* Harcourt, 1964. Val's sister broke her engagement to Eliot Talbot. She is friendly with Eliot's brother Bob and works at the Talbot factory. Val clears up some threats at the factory.

_____. *Girl on Witches Hill.* Harcourt, 1963. Stacy resents moving, especially since it means leaving Barry, whom she tried so hard to attract. She meets new friends and realizes how shallow Barry was.

_____. *Reach for the Dream.* Harcourt, 1967. Norrie wants to be a writer but she is also a daydreamer. She gets involved in some stolen jewels and solves the mystery by finding the out-of-town rich boy.

_____. *Starry Answer.* Harcourt, 1962. A young girl tries to compromise between her old traditions and the missile age.

_____. *Touchmark.* Harcourt, 1975. In pre–Revolutionary War days a young girl in Boston wants to be an apprentice to a pewter maker.

_____. *Treasure and the Song.* Harcourt, 1966. Binnie's parents are getting a divorce so she runs away. She meets shy Caribel and they look for buried treasure pulling both their lives together.

_____. *Walk a Rocky Road.* Harcourt, 1972. Silvey lives in Appalachia and applies for a scholarship to get away from the traditional standards set there. She then finds that there is a great deal to be said for her region and its wealth.

Lawson, John. *Spring Rider.* Crowell, 1968. Jacob and his sister, Gary, experience an adventure of bewitchment and a dream in this "then and now" story.

_____. *You Better Come Home with Me.* Harper, 1966. Boy heard Scarecrow say "You better come home with me" on a winter's day. So the fantasy begins.

Lawson, Robert. *Ben and Me.* Little, 1939. Ben is Benjamin Franklin and Me is Amos, a tame mouse who lives with Mr. Franklin. He relates life in the household from his home in an old fur hat.

_____. *Captain Kidd's Cat.* Little, 1984.

McDermot is the cat belonging to Captain Kidd and he tells all.

_____. *Fabulous Flight*. Little, 1984. Peter becomes small enough to ride on a seagull and does so.

_____. *Mr. Revere and I*. Little, 1953. Mr. Revere is, of course, Paul; I is his horse, Scheherazade, who tells some interesting things about Mr. Revere.

_____. *Mr. Twigg's Mistake*. Little, 1985. Mr. Twigg's mistake was to give his pet mole an overdose of vitamin X which causes rapid and unending growth.

_____. *Rabbit Hill*. Viking, 1944/1977. All the animals living on the hill are concerned about the people moving into the big house but when they see "Please Drive Carefully on Account of Small Animals" they are satisfied. Newbery, 1945.

_____. *Tough Winter*. Viking, 1954/1979. All the animals on the hill suffer through a cold winter. Uncle Analdas said he knew it was coming and he was right.

Laymon, Richard. *Night Creature*. Fearon, 1986. When nightmares turn real, the Strange Occurrence Squad, the government's weapon against forces it won't admit to and can't explain, goes into action.

Lazarus, Keo. *Rattlesnake Run*. Follett, 1968. Adam runs a mail station in Texas. He fights the heat by day and the coyotes by night and the rattlesnakes during dusk. Then two killers escape and he must prove his mettle.

_____. *Shark in the Window*. Morrow, 1972. Shelly finds a flat egg case at the beach and brings it home. It hatches into a shark that is able to swim in air instead of water. Nippy was a problem that needed a unique solution.

Lea, Alec. *To Sunset and Beyond*. Walck, 1970. Peter went to bring in the cows; they wandered away and he went to look for them. He reached the moor and the fog rolled in and Peter spent the longest day of his life.

Leach, Christopher. *Great Book Raid*. Warne, 1979. Jim calls on book characters to help him save the beach from land developers. A good adventure with this unusual cast of characters: King Arthur, Huck Finn, Robin Hood, etc.

_____. *Meeting Miss Hannah*. Warne, 1980. Miss Hannah is hiding from her greedy children who want her fortune. She lives in Old Bergssin House, an ex-funeral home. Louise wants to find out about a fire, a disappearance and a possible murder.

Le Carre, John. *Little Drummer Girl*. Knopf, 1983. Charlie, a British actress, is the "little drummer girl." She and Kurtz, an Israeli, plot to catch a Palestinian terrorist.

Lederer, Chloe. *Down the Hill of the Sea*. Lothrop, 1971. Kali must move from his native island because poison is to be spread on it. A story of war experimentation and its effect on simple people.

Lee, Benjamin. *It Can't Be Helped*. Farrar, 1979. Max's father died and his mother is emotionally unbalanced. But Max's dealings with Communist classmates, a friendly doctor and his school principal make for wry humor.

Lee, Harper. *To Kill a Mockingbird*. Lippincott, 1960. A father is a white lawyer defending a black man accused of raping a white woman. A good look at Southern prejudices.

Lee, Mildred. *Fog*. Houghton, 1972. Luke, 17, finds and loses his first love. His club is broken up by a fire and his father dies. Luke gets a taste of life and is "older but wiser."

_____. *Honor Sands*. Lothrop, 1966. Honor can't seem to get along with her mother. She sets out to purposely irritate her and doesn't understand why. She also has a serious crush on her science teacher that she can't explain.

_____. *People Therein*. Houghton, 1980. Lanthy meets Drew who has come to the mountains to study plants and overcome alcoholism. They fall in love; Lanthy becomes pregnant. Drew must go away but he comes back and they marry.

_____. *Rock and the Willow*. Washington Square, 1971. Enie lives in poverty and gets a chance to improve herself through the remarriage of her father.

_____. *Skating Rink*. Seabury, 1969. Tuck was a stutterer and friendless with no social life. He finds he has a natural talent for skating and practices until he becomes a star. This improves his self esteem and his social and home life.

_____. *Sycamore Year*. Lothrop, 1976. Wren, 14, is spending her first year in Sycamore. She must learn to make adjustments but the biggest one is her sister's pregnancy.

Lee, Robert. *Day It Rained Forever*. Little, 1968. Mike visits his professor friend in the hospital and learns of the machine that is causing the rain. It must be stopped. Mike also plays basketball and runs for student body president.

_____. *Iron Arm of Michael Glenn*. Little, 1965. Mike gets a strong left arm by using Professor Von Heimer's energizing reconstitutor. He becomes a baseball pitcher for the Giants. Eventually the effect wears off.

_____. *It's a Mile from Here to Glory*. Little, 1972. Early was four feet, eleven inches tall and hated it. As a school punishment for fighting he was ordered to run laps. A coach saw him and recognized his potential as a great runner. He was saved!!

_____. *Timequake*. Westminster, 1982. Randy time travels to the future world of 2027.

Lee, Virginia. *Magic Moth*. Houghton, 1972. Maryanne, one of five children, dies and the family must adjust. It is difficult for everyone, especially her young brother.

Leeson, Robert. *Genie on the Loose*. David & Charles, 1984. Alec comes in possession of a beer can wherein a genie lives.

Le Guin, Ursula. *Beginning Place.* Harper, 1980. Hugh and Irene both find a way to a world where time stops. They are given the task of slaying a creature that is destroying this land. This brings them needed love and happiness in their own world.

———. *Farthest Shore.* Atheneum, 1972. Ged must travel to the "Farthest Shore" and close the gap that is allowing darkness into the world. Arren, a young prince, goes with Ged on this mission. A battle between Good and Evil.

———. *Tombs of Atuan.* Atheneum, 1971. Ged needs to find the missing half of a magic ring, in the tombs of Atuan where Arha is being trained as a priestess. She must spend all her life there and Ged wants to free her.

———. *Very Far Away from Anywhere Else.* Atheneum, 1976. Owen, a loner, and Natalie, an independent girl, meet at college. He doesn't like the school but is friendly with this like-minded, musically talented girl.

———. *Wizard of Earthsea.* Houghton, 1968. Ged, a young wizard, misuses his magical powers, allowing a terrible shadowbeast into the world. He is still in training and must hunt it down. He chases it throughout Earthsea.

Lehmann, Linda. *Better Than a Princess.* Nelson, 1978. Tilli is at last reunited with her mother in America but needs to adjust to this plain-looking, plain-living woman. A gift of a beautiful doll does this.

———. *Tilli's New World.* Nelson, 1981. Tilli wants to go to school to learn to read but she is needed to help her poor family. She hires herself out as a housemaid and gets to go to school sometimes.

Lehrman, Robert. *Juggler.* Harper, 1982. Howie plays soccer and wants to go to a college that is strong in that sport. His father wants him to go to a better school. There are some love, some Jewish concern.

Leigh, Bill. *Far Side of Fear.* Viking, 1977. Kenny and Pete are friends. They are trapped underground. They try to find their way out through passages and caverns.

Leigh, Frances. *Lost Boy.* Dutton, 1976. Kate must identify a boy who might be her brother believed to have been killed in a fire years before. The boy does not speak English and steals and cheats. But he turns out to be Brian.

Leighton, Margaret. *Canyon Castaways.* Farrar, 1966. Teenage Jill is babysitting for three children when they get stranded by a flash flood. They struggle for survival with a helpful college student who was also caught.

———. *Journey for a Princess.* Farrar, 1960. Elstrid must escape a Viking leader who wants to marry her. She takes refuge with Judith in France. Judith's son, Baudouin, defeats the Viking and is going to marry Elstrid.

———. *Voyage to Coromandel.* Farrar, 1965. Eric, a hostage of King Alfred, goes with his brother Olaf on a voyage to India to see the Saint Thomas Shrine in Coromandel.

Leitner, Isabella. *Fragments of Isabella.* Crowell, 1978. Isabella survived Auschwitz and the Nazis while watching the young, old and sick killed before her eyes. Part of her died with them.

L'Engle, Madeleine. *Arm and the Starfish.* Farrar, 1965. An excellent plot of tension and suspense stars Carol, Adam and the O'Keefes. Mystery surrounds the work at the laboratory and Adam, a marine biologist, is involved.

———. *Camilla.* Delacorte, 1981. Camilla, 15, finds love for the first time just as her parents are breaking up. This takes a toll on her life.

———. *Dragons in the Water.* Farrar, 1976. Another taut, suspenseful novel with Polly and Charles O'Keefe. There is a murder aboard their freighter. They meet Simon whose life is threatened and Forsyth who is murdered.

———. *House Like a Lotus.* Farrar, 1984. Polly travels to Cypress with Max, a wealthy and very talented artist.

———. *Many Waters.* Farrar, 1986. The Murray twins, Dennys and Sandy, are transported to a desert in Biblical times—into a world as it existed before the flood. Noah is building his ark.

———. *Meet the Austins.* Farrar, 1960. Maggy, an orphan, comes to live with the Austins. She is not used to the ways of her new family and causes tension. Vicki and the rest of the family feel it but she comes to love them.

———. *Moon by Night.* Farrar, 1963. A contemporary family story. Vicki is older and meets a boy, Zachary, who has more family problems than she thinks she has. Her old friend, Andy, is more stable and reliable.

———. *Ring of Endless Light.* Farrar, 1980. The adventures of Vicki, sixteen, and the Austin family. She must cope with the death of her favorite grandparent and with her romantic involvements.

———. *Swiftly, Tilting Planet.* Farrar, 1978. Charles travels through time and space, battling hard against an evil dictator. Charles is now fifteen and Meg is married and expecting a baby, but she goes with him in spirit.

———. *Wind in the Door.* Farrar, 1973. An alien creature, a dragon, is found in the garden. The story leads to the land of Mitochondrain and back home. Meg and Charles are again on another adventure.

———. *Wrinkle in Time.* Farrar, 1962. Through a "wrinkle in time" an eerie midnight visitor leads three teenagers in search of a vanished scientist. In this adventure they encounter the terror of the tesseract. Newbery winner, 1963.

———. *Young Unicorns.* Farrar, 1968. Vicki and the Austins are involved in a plot to control men's minds by using a micro-laser.

Leninson, Riki. *Dinnieabbiesister-r-r!* Macmillan, 1987. A Jewish family story of Jenny and her brothers living in Brooklyn.

Lenski, Lois. *Shoo-Fly Girl*. Lippincott, 1963. Suzanna, "Shoo Fly girl," is Amish and tells of the life and customs of these people.

———. *Strawberry Girl*. Harper, 1945. This is one of the many regional stories by Lois Lenski. This has lasted in popularity longer than the others and deserves a reading. Newbery winner, 1946.

Leonard, Alison. *Tina's Chance*. Viking, 1988. Tina's mother died of an unknown fatal disease when Tina was two. She wants to learn some things about the disease from two nurses (who are lesbians) because she believes she has the same disease.

Leonard, Constance. *Aground*. Dodd, 1984. A Tracy James mystery about mind control and runaway kids. Her friend's lobster business is threatened and she comes to his aid. What she finds are a cult and evil doings.

———. *Marina Mystery*. Dodd, 1981. Tracy James and her boyfriend, Pete, love sailing and boats. But one day a body is found alongside Tracy's boat and the mystery begins that involves Tracy in a dangerous way.

———. *Stowaway*. Dodd, 1983. A marina mystery with Tracy and Pete set in the Bahamas. Tracy finds a stowaway, Tessa, in her cabin. She speaks no English and is kidnapped off the boat. Tracy, facing danger, rescues her.

Leroe, Ellen. *Confessions of a Teenage TV Addict*. Dutton, 1983. Jenny lives in a world of "soaps." She is shy and unpopular. Nasty occurrences happen at school when an attractive boy (Mike) pays attention to her.

———. *Have a Heart, Cupid Delaney*. Dutton, 1986. Cupid gets the assignment of getting Helen, a wallflower, to be the love of Craig, the school hero. She must also get Dawn and Alvin together even though Alvin likes Helen. A fun story.

———. *Peanut Butter Poltergeist*. Dutton, 1987. M.J. seeks revenge on his stepsister by making believe a poltergeist is around. Then he finds out it is true and a real one (?) shows up.

———. *Plot Against the Pom Pom Queen*. Dutton, 1985. Kelsey wants a boyfriend but Taffy, the Pom Pom Queen, thwarts it. So Kelsey plans revenge. She loses a friendship and some integrity but feels she must go through with it.

———. *Robot Raiders*. Harper, 1987. Bixby and his companions thwart a plot to ruin the secret Mars mission. Another crazy but readable robot story.

———. *Robot Romance*. Harper, 1985. Bixby, a robot, tries to get the attentions of Frani, a human. He starts to build a girl robot but his brother foils his plans. A funny/not funny story.

LeRoy, Gen. *Cold Feet*. Harper, 1979. Gen's father dies and she gets a job disguised as a boy. She gets involved with petty gangsters but manages to get out of it unhurt. She meets Alex and things look up.

———. *Emma's Dilemma*. Harper, 1975. Emma loves her dog, Pearl, but Grandma is allergic to dogs and she is coming to stay with Emma's family.

———. *Hotheads*. Harper, 1977. Gen lives with her poor family near a newly built shopping center. Her grandfather is vandalizing the place and she tries to take the blame to protect him.

Lesser, Milton. *Stadium Beyond the Stars*. Winston, 1960. The Earth's Olympic team spots a derelict space ship. Steve, through telepathy, finds it is being used by non-humans.

Levenkron, Steven. *Best Little Girl in the World*. Contemporary, 1978. Francesca felt FAT. She was five-feet-four and 98 pounds. Her ballet teacher said she could lose a pound or two. She lost 4, 12, 14, 17 pounds. She needed help; she was starving herself to death.

Le Vert, John. *Flight of the Cassowary*. Atlantic, 1986. Paul is fascinated by animals and studies them more and more. He is soon able to take on the attributes of some animals. Then the next step is to become one of them. A funny, sad story.

Levin, Betty. *Binding Spell*. Dutton, 1984. Wren sees a ghost horse and meets Uncle Axel, a hermit. He is haunted by his treatment of Jake, his horse. All is set right when it is horse power, not mechanism, that saves Wren's mother's life.

———. *Brother Moose*. Greenwillow, 1990. Two orphan girls, an Indian and his grandson travel to Maine to find a family. It is a dangerous journey.

———. *Forespoken*. Macmillan, 1976. Claudia is with the shepherd, Thomas, who believes himself to be bewitched. She has concern for him and also feels the need to return the crow to Mr. Colman who is dying.

———. *Griffon's Nest*. Macmillan, 1975. Claudia and Evan, with the help of their ancient sword, become enmeshed with the intrigues of the Irish courts of the seventh century.

———. *Ice Bear*. Greenwillow, 1986. Kaila, from the Land of the White Falcons, a bear cub and Wat, a lakewoman's helper, go to the forest of Lythe to protect a white Ice Bear. Wat expects a reward; Kaila only wants to take it home.

———. *Keeping Room*. Greenwillow, 1981. A fantasy that takes place both in the past and in the present.

———. *Landfall*. Atheneum, 1979. Liddy is sent a tape of seal singing by her pen pal in the North Sea. She finds these seals in danger but it is too late to prevent disaster.

———. *Put on My Crown*. Lodestar, 1985. Vinnie, with Grace and Joel, is coming to America. They become shipwrecked off an island. The natives want to keep the children and Vinnie must plan for their rescue.

———. *Sword of Culann*. Macmillan, 1973. Claudia and Evan are caught up in 20th century Maine and Iron Age Ireland. They battle Mebd, the warrior queen, and Cuchulain, the hound of Ulster.

_____. *Trouble with Gramary.* Greenwillow, 1988. Merkka's longing for a conventional lifestyle is threatened by the art projects of her grandmother who sculpts.

Levin, Ira. *Boys from Brazil.* Random, 1976. Yakov must find a Nazi war criminal, "Angel of Death," before his plan to kill ninety-four other men is carried out. He has eighteen days to do it.

Levine, Betty. *Great Burgerland Disaster.* Atheneum, 1981. Mike is a gourmet cook who goes to work for Burgerland. He improves their food to the point of increased business and success. Meanwhile Mike is worried about his separated parents.

_____. *Hawk High.* Atheneum, 1980. Toni goes to look for a hawk's nest and identify birds positively for her friend, Mrs. Morgenstein. She gets lost and must spend the night in the mountains where a stray dog keeps her company.

_____. *Hex House.* Harper, 1973. Aggie moves from Kansas to New York to a hexagonal house. A former resident turned in a false murder report and so when Aggie turns in a fire the police hang up on her.

Levine, Edna. *Lisa and Her Soundless World.* Human Sciences, 1984. Lisa is deaf and has almost insurmountable problems.

Levinson, Marilyn. *And Don't Bring Jeremy.* Holt, 1985. Adam is new in the neighborhood and is uncomfortable about his older brother, Jeremy, who has a learning disability. He wants to be friends with Eddie, but Eddie accuses Jeremy of vandalism.

_____. *Place to Start.* Atheneum, 1987. Grant's parents are growing apart. His mother is having an affair and he is shocked. He finds solace in Samantha because the affair is with his favorite computer teacher.

Levinson, Nancy. *Ruthie Greene Show.* Lodestar, 1983. Ruthie feels left out as her sister is getting married. She fails a Spanish assignment in school. Then she meets a producer who gives her a job on a Hollywood movie set.

Levit, Rose. *Eileen.* Chronicle, 1974. Eileen is going to die from bone cancer. The family learns that love is as important as anything else.

Levitin, Sonia. *Beyond Another Door.* Atheneum, 1977. A daughter better understands her mother when she sees the ghost of her dead grandmother.

_____. *Jason and the Money Tree.* Harcourt, 1974. Jason plants a money tree and finds he has problems with the law and with nature even though it appears he has some success.

_____. *Journey to America.* Atheneum, 1970. Papa goes to America from Germany. The rest of the family go to Switzerland until Papa can send for them. It is a time of hardship and terror of being caught and sent back.

_____. *Mark of Conte.* Atheneum, 1976.

Conte Mark got two school schedules: one for Mark Conte and one for Conte Mark. He tried to keep both schedules hoping to graduate in two years instead of four. But what a time he had!

_____. *Reigning Cats and Dogs.* Atheneum, 1978. Barney owns Two German shepherds and two kittens. The young shepherd was bought to replace Baron, who is getting old. Baron is supposed to train him. The kittens are orphans and add chaos.

_____. *Return.* Atheneum, 1987. Desta is an Ethiopian Jew who is taken to Israel. A group called Operation Moses help her and a small band of people across the Sudan. The deprivation they endure ends in relief in Israel.

_____. *Season for Unicorns.* Macmillan, 1986. Inky finds letters from another woman in her father's things. She learns of not one, but several affairs he had and is having. She runs away to Guy and his mother. What should she tell them?

_____. *Silver Days.* Atheneum, 1989. The Platt family are all in America. Mama and Papa have jobs and the children learn English. They experience prejudices but have friends and romance. It is better than they had it in Germany.

_____. *Sound to Remember.* Harcourt, 1979. The congregation is shocked when a rabbi announces that little Jacov is to have the honor of blowing the Ram's horn on Rosh Hashanah.

_____. *Year of Sweet Senior Insanity.* Macmillan, 1982. Being a senior is different from anything else. Leni is a senior and has a new boyfriend, a part-time job, schoolwork, a family and cheerleading practice. It makes life complicated.

Levoy, Myron. *Alan and Naomi.* Harper, 1977. Naomi moves from Paris to New York during World War II. Alan finds her strange at first but as she is living in his apartment building they become friends.

_____. *Magic Hat of Mortimer.* Harper, 1988. Joshua, 13, and Amy, 11, come to New York from South Dakota in 1893. They are helped by Mortimer Wintergreen and his magic hat to escape Aunt Vootch and return by wagon and balloon to their grandparents.

_____. *Pictures of Adam.* Harper, 1986. Lisa, 14, is a photographer. She becomes involved in a relationship with an emotionally disturbed boy. She does a photo essay on his run-down home.

_____. *Shadow Like a Leopard.* Harper, 1981. Ramon is on his own and joins a gang of thugs. He is not cut out for this life and when he tries to rob Arnold, an elderly painter, it turns into a warm friendship instead. Ramon is a changed boy.

_____. *Three Friends.* Harper, 1984. Joshua is a loner and plays chess. Lori and Karen are best friends. When Joshua and Karen begin dating Lori is upset. She wonders if she "loves" Karen and tries suicide. Joshua clears up her feelings.

Levy, Elizabeth. *Case of the Counterfeit Racehorse.* Archway, 1980. This is a mystery about two horses that look alike and are switched.

_____. *Case of the Mind-Reading Mommies.* S&S, 1989. Kate and Max work together as detectives. They find mothers are in the middle of mysterious mishaps.

_____. *Come Out Smiling.* Delacorte, 1981. Jenny learns that her beloved camp counselor is a lesbian. After the shock and anger die down she accepts what she is. She questions her own sexual preference but appears to be "straight."

_____. *Computer That Said Steal Me.* Four Winds, 1983. Because all his friends have a computer Adam wants one, too. So he steals one. He wants it to beat Tracey at a chess game. He later returns it and confesses to his parents.

_____. *Double Standard.* Avon, 1984. Colette and Abby have been friends for years and understand each other, but when Ian and Abernathy, their boyfriends, enter the picture, they must understand themselves and their relationship.

_____. *Lizzie Lies a Lot.* Delacorte, 1976. Lizzie and Sara are friends. Sara shows Lizzie the errors of her lying and helps her stop.

_____. *Running Out of Magic with Houdini.* Knopf, 1981. Three children are working out for the marathon when they are transported back to 1912 and Houdini's East River escape trick.

_____. *Running Out of Time.* Knopf, 1980. Through the fog three children go back to the time of Spartacus and the gladiators. They become involved in the training and then in the revolt of the slaves.

_____. *Shadow Nose.* Morrow, 1983. Lamont and Diana (not Lois) wonder about the shadow painting that appears on the sidewalks of Greenwich Village.

_____. *Winner.* Scholastic, 1989. A gymnastic story of four girls who work hard at winning, especially Darlene, who doubts her ability.

Levy, Mimi. *Caravan from Timbuktu.* Viking, 1961. Kan-na, camel master, leads his pilgrimage across the Sahara Desert. He meets with treachery from Ali Khudar. Batu and his friends bring Ali Khudar before the Mansa.

_____. *Whaleboat Warrior.* Viking, 1963. Robbie and Adam are brothers who help during the Revolutionary War. They move between Connecticut and Long Island carrying messages and sometimes attacking the British.

Lewis, C.S. *Horse and His Boy.* Macmillan, 1954/1988. A talking horse and a boy prince save Narnia from invasion by Calormenes with the help of Aslan and the children.

_____. *Last Battle.* Macmillan, 1956/1988. Jill and Eustace come to the aid of the young King Tirian in Narnia's last battle with the evil Calormenes, and their evil spirit, Tash.

_____. *Lion, the Witch and the Wardrobe.* Macmillan, 1950/1988. Through the magic closet, Peter, Edmund, Susan and Lucy enter the fantastic land of Narnia, where the great lion, Aslan, frees Narnia from the forever-winter spell of the White Winter.

_____. *Magician's Nephew.* Macmillan, 1955/1988. Aslan creates Narnia and gives the gift of speech to his animals. Because the land is good the Witch leaves. This is the basic information book about Narnia.

_____. *Out of the Silent Planet.* Macmillan, 1938/1990. Mr. Ransom is kidnapped by two friends. He is going to the planet Mars where he will observe the Earth from the Martian point of view.

_____. *Perelandra.* Macmillan, 1944/1990. A planet, Venus, has been invaded by evil Dr. Westom. He is tempting the inhabitants, King and Lady. Dr. Ransom aids Lady to choose the path of perfection, not corruption.

_____. *Prince Caspian.* Macmillan, 1951/1988. Peter, Edmund, Susan and Lucy, with help from Aslan, assist good Prince Caspian in conquering the Telmarines and preserving the kingdom in Narnia.

_____. *Silver Chair.* Macmillan, 1953/1988. The children, with Aslan's assistance, help Prince Rilian escape from the clutches of the magical silver chair in the Emerald Witch's underground kingdom.

_____. *That Hideous Strength.* Macmillan, 1946/1990. The story is set in England and chronicles Satan's desire to dominate the world through evil magic and wizardry. It features Merlin, the magician.

_____. *Voyage of the "Dawn Treader."* Macmillan, 1952/1988. Two of the children and their eccentric cousin, Eustace, help King Caspian sail through magic waters to the End of the World in Narnia. Eustace is turned into a dragon.

Lewis, Elizabeth. *Young Fu of the Upper Yangtze.* Holt, 1973. A Newbery winner (1933) about a boy who must face public shame if he doesn't pay back a debt owed.

Lewis, Marjorie. *Wrongway Applebaum.* Putnam, 1984. Stanley can't hit but one day he hits a home run and his teammates are happy with him even though they lose the game.

Lewis, Mary. *Nurse Matilda Goes to Town.* Dutton, 1967. Nurse Matilda is again in charge of the awful Brown children. This time it is the waxworks of Madame Tussaud that get their treatment.

Lezra, Giggy. *Mechido, Aziza and Ahmed.* Atheneum, 1969. Mechido picks up bread to be baked and returns it. Aziza is supposed to be a "lady" but finds it difficult. Ahmed is shy and everyone is trying to cure him. They all live in Morocco.

Lichtman, Wendy. *Telling Secret.* Harper, 1986. Toby and Sharon are roommates and friends. Toby's father is jailed for embezzlement and her mother makes her promise not to tell anyone. This puts a barrier in their friendship and Toby is resentful.

Lifton, Betty. *I'm Still Me.* Knopf, 1981. Lori, adopted, tries to track down her real mother without her adoptive parents' knowledge. She loves her "parents" and finds strange feelings when she does reach her real mother.

Lightner, A.M. *Day of the Drones.* Norton, 1969. African blacks believe they are the only survivors of an atomic war. They are against white skin and technology. N'Gobe, who is light-skinned, finds a colony of white people in England.

_____. *Doctor to the Galaxy.* Norton, 1965. Dr. Bart only becomes a veterinarian to stay on planet Acoma because of his girlfriend. He does make an important medical discovery.

_____. *Galactic Troubadours.* Norton, 1965. Three people on Hercules V discover folk music and start a teenage craze. Nick and his friend leave and go to Allegra for fun and to Duros and Invictus for science and adventure.

Lightner, Alice. *Thursday Toads.* McGraw, 1971. On the Planet of Toads Doctor Thursby and Gillian face Toxic Toad. Gillian is bitten in an encounter with them but under Dr. Thursby's care he survives.

Lilius, Irmelin. *Gold Crown Lane.* Delacorte, 1969. There is death in the small town of Tulavall. The Halter children get involved in finding the killer in this mysterious crime based death.

_____. *Goldmaker's House.* Delacorte, 1970. Bonadea learns that the owner of the big house in town is looking for a stone with which to make gold. This accounts for his peculiar behavior.

_____. *Horse of the Night.* Delacorte, 1971. The Halter children, with Bonadea, have a special adventure when an explosion brings legendary horses back from the past. They also stop Mr. Klingkor from stealing the town's water for himself.

Lindbergh, Anne. *Bailey's Window.* Harcourt, 1984. Anna, Carl and Ingrid have a club, the Vikings. Bailey comes to visit and paints a window he can slip through. Soon all four are going through the window to the other side.

_____. *Hunky-Dory Dairy.* Harcourt, 1986. Zannah gets into a van and is transplanted to a dairy that has been moved by magic from the nineteenth to the twentieth century.

_____. *Nobody's Orphan.* Harcourt, 1983. Marta, 11, is a mess. School is awful, she lost her best friend; she can't keep a dog she found. She just knows she is adopted because she doesn't fit in.

_____. *People in Pineapple Place.* Harcourt, 1982. August meets April and her friends and discovers their secret of time travel. He travels with them and sees the world. Before they leave they find him a friend. Pineapple Place is invisible.

_____. *Prisoner of Pineapple Place.* Harcourt, 1988. Jeremiah is bored with being in the fourth grade. He meets Ruby who can hear but cannot see him. Her uncle tries to make him visible but is not successful.

_____. *Shadow on the Dial.* Harper, 1987. Dawn and Marcus stay with Uncle Doo. They use time warp to manipulate Uncle Doo's past and future and make him a happy, successful man.

_____. *Worry Week.* Harcourt, 1985. Legs, 11, is left in charge of her sisters for the week and does nothing but worry about her responsibility.

Linde, Gunnel. *Trust in the Unexpected.* Macmillan, 1984. Katie gets angry and throws her brother's bicycle in the river. Now she must pay the consequences of that act.

Lindgren, Astrid. *Bill Bergson and the White Rose Rescue.* Viking, 1965. Bill, Anders and Eva-Lotta are the White Roses and the "enemy" are Siten, Johnny and Benka of the Red Roses. This time the White Roses are involved in a kidnapping by enemy agents.

_____. *Bill Bergson Lives Dangerously.* Viking, 1954. The White Roses and the Red Roses spend the summer in pretend battle. Then a real murder happens in their village. Bill, the would-be detective, uses his skill.

_____. *Bill Bergson, Master Detective.* Viking, 1952. Bill, Anders and Eva-Lotta spend the summer putting on circus shows and inventing exciting games. Bill practices his observation and deduction skills so he can become a real detective.

_____. *Brothers Lionheart.* Viking, 1975. Two brothers are reunited after death in the land of Nangiyala.

_____. *Children of Noisy Village.* Viking, 1962. Six children, three boys and three girls, live in Noisy Village. Each chapter is an episode in the lives of these energetic youngsters. Some are about relatives; some are about neighbors.

_____. *Christmas in Noisy Village.* Viking, 1964. Lisa tells about the traditional festivities of Noisy Village especially at Christmas time.

_____. *Emil and Piggy Beast.* Follett, 1973. Emil buys his sister a velvet lined box at an auction. The box contains a letter with a valuable stamp. He has adventures with his pet pig.

_____. *Emil in the Soup Tureen.* Follett, 1970. Emil lived with his parents and a sister, Ida. He was constantly in trouble. In this book he gets his head caught in a soup bowl and can't get it out. It takes a lot of different events to do so.

_____. *Emil's Pranks.* Follett, 1971. Emil's pranks include locking himself in the tool chest three times in one day, trying to trap a rat but catching his father's toe instead and accidentally spilling pudding on his father's head.

_____. *Happy Times in Noisy Village.* Viking, 1963. Lisa, the teller of these happenings in the three adjoining villages in Sweden, explains about the liveliness and togetherness of all the people living there.

_____. *Karlsson-on-the Roof*. Viking, 1971. Eric had a friend, Karlsson, who could fly with a machine on his back. Together they put on a magic show, foiled some thieves and took dangerous walks along the roof tops.

_____. *Lotta on Troublemaker Street*. Macmillan, 1984. Lotta is unhappy and runs away to stay with a neighbor. But in time she returns home.

_____. *Pippi Goes on Board*. Viking, 1957. Pippi is shipwrecked, she goes to a fair and she also has a farewell party.

_____. *Pippi in the South Seas*. Viking, 1960. Pippi once again cuts adults down to size through her superhuman strength and simplicity. She has more triumphant adventures.

_____. *Pippi Longstocking*. Viking, 1950. Pippi is the world's strongest girl who has a suitcase full of money and does as she pleases because she lives alone.

_____. *Rasmus and the Vagabond*. Viking, 1960. Rasmus is running away from an orphanage to find parents who want a boy like him. Then he meets Oscar, the tramp, and the two are friends at first sight.

_____. *Ronia, the Robber's Daughter*. Viking, 1983. Ronia is an only child of a robber, Matt. She shows bravery on her many adventurous escapades. She meets Birk, the son of a rival robber chief. They become friends and the two bands join together.

_____. *Seacrow Island*. Viking, 1964. Pelle loved animals and found a friendly dog. Johan and Niklas liked boats and found Teddy who knew about them. Malin was older and found love. All on Seacrow Island.

_____. *Springtime in Noisy Village*. Viking, 1966. Lisa tells what children do in the spring, about the animals on the farm and the games children play.

Lindquist, Jennie. *Golden Name Day*. Harper, 1955. Nancy's life is parties and fun. A name day must be found for her. It is a problem because she is not in the Swedish almanac, but the search goes on.

_____. *Little Silver House*. Harper, 1960. Nancy is back home with her mother and grows up in the early 1900's in New England. But she is surrounded by customs and traditions of Scandinavia.

Lindquist, Willis. *Burma Boy*. McGraw, 1953. Haji is learning to ride elephants. An elephant goes wild and destroys a village and its rice fields. Haji rescues and tames him.

Line, David. *Screaming High*. Little, 1985. Ratbag and Nicky stumble onto an international drug smuggling ring. They are both musical students at school and enter an international competition.

_____. *Soldier and Me*. Harper, 1965. A young English boy befriends a Hungarian refugee. Then they become aware of a pending murder and work together to prevent it from happening.

Linevski, A. *Old Tale Carved Out of Stone*. Crown, 1973. A young shaman tries to manufacture miracles but is forced to leave his tribe in shame in Russia during the Stone Age.

Lingard, Joan. *Across the Barricades*. Nelson, 1972. Sadie and Kevin cope with serious changes in their lives. They know their families are against their love and future plans. They have differing religious backgrounds. He's Catholic, she's not.

_____. *Clearance*. Nelson, 1974. The Ross family has had bad luck but Maggie endures. She expects a dull summer with her grandmother but when she makes friends with the visiting neighbors life becomes more interesting.

_____. *File on Fraulein Berg*. Nelson, 1980. Katie, Sally and Harriet presumed that their teacher was a German spy. They persecuted her only to find out later that she was a Jewish refugee and the only member of her family still alive.

_____. *Hostages to Fortune*. Nelson, 1977. The farm Sadie and Kevin thought would make life better is sold and they must move again. Family opposition, because of religion, is still a problem in their lives.

_____. *Into Exile*. Nelson, 1973. Sadie and Kevin are married. But they are alone, isolated from their family and friends in Belfast, and they feel the pressure. It is the difference in their religion that is causing problems.

_____. *Odd Girl Out*. Nelson, 1979. Ellen, 14, is tall and a tomboy while her friend has plenty of boyfriends. Ellen resents her mother remarrying because she is loyal to her "dead" father who deserted them and is still alive.

_____. *Pilgrimage*. Nelson, 1976. Maggie and her boyfriend, James, take a trip during the summer and they learn more about each other than about the past they were seeking.

_____. *Proper Place*. Nelson, 1975. Sadie and Kevin have a baby. They want to improve their life and their marriage so they move out of the city to a farm in Cheshire.

_____. *Resettling*. Nelson, 1975. A story of Maggie and her family. This time it is about school, love and more family problems involved with moving to a new home and helping in her father's new business.

_____. *Strangers in the House*. Dutton, 1981. Calum's mother remarries and he is resentful. Stella's father is the man she marries and she is resentful. After many experiences, including the death of a pet, the two children accept each other.

_____. *Twelfth Day of July*. Nelson, 1970. Sadie, a Protestant, and Kevin, a Catholic, living in Ireland, must face the consequences of their relationship.

Link, Ruth. *House Full of Mice*. Atheneum, 1970. Jimmy is taking care of a friend's mice while on vacation. First the mice have babies, then the babies have babies. They are everywhere. It is not funny to Jimmy but it is to everyone else.

Lipp, Frederick. *Some Lose Their Way.* Atheneum, 1980. Vanessa is a shy, bright girl who is the youngest in the eighth grade. David is an angry bully who dislikes Vanessa. They both love birds and are concerned over their living conditions.

Lippincott, Joseph. *Coyote, the Wonder Wolf.* Lippincott, 1964. Coyote was brought as a pup from Arizona to Pennsylvania. After many disastrous trials he is returned to the wilds. He has divided loyalties between his human friends and his wild heritage.

Lipsyte, Robert. *Contender.* Harper, 1967. Alfred, a black who lives in Harlem, quite by accident trains for professional boxing. He contends with education drawbacks, drugs, entrapment as well as boxing contenders.

————. *One Fat Summer.* Harper, 1977. Bobby, an overweight fourteen-year-old, is hassled by a bully, by constant teasing and by his summer job. A funny, touching story of growing up in the '50's.

————. *Summer Rules.* Harper, 1981. Bobby, now sixteen, is a camp counselor with some responsibility; he is hassled less by others. He meets a girl, Sheila, and finds out how complicated growing up can be.

————. *Summerboy.* Harper, 1982. Bobby is now eighteen. His quest is girls, love and glory. He works summers in a laundry, and fights for the betterment of life for those who live at Lake Rumson all year 'round.

Lisle, Janet. *Dancing Cats of Applesap.* Bradbury, 1984. Melba, 10, is shy and likes cats. She and Miss Toonie find that the cats will dance to guitar music and march in a line. They use this to advertise Riggs Drug Store that is closing for lack of business.

————. *Great Dimpole Oak.* Watts, 1987. A strange story of a town's battle to save the old oak tree that has stood for years; it is a landmark surrounded by legend and stories.

————. *Sirens and Spies.* Bradbury, 1985. Elsie loved her violin teacher, Miss Fitch, but there was something strange about her lifestyle. She learns that she befriended the Germans during World War II. But Miss Fitch explains how and why.

Litchfield, Ada. *Captain Hook, That's Me.* Walker, 1982. Judy has a hook for a hand she was born without. At her new school children stare and feel sorry. She learns to play the marimba and looks forward to the future.

Littke, Lael. *Loydene in Love.* Harcourt, 1986. Loydene, Shanny's friend, is going steady. She goes on vacation to Shanny's and meets another boy and sees another lifestyle. She returns to her boyfriend but gives second thoughts to marriage.

————. *Shanny on Her Own.* Harcourt, 1985. Shanny is spending the summer with her aunt. She arrives with her full blown punk lifestyle and startles her aunt and the town. Spiky, dyed punk hair, a nose jewel, and pierced ears. Wow!

Little, Jane. *Philosopher's Stove.* Atheneum, 1971. Nyvrem, the sorcerer of Mordamagne (12th century) must find the Philosophers Stone which is in Stephen's rock collection in Indiana (20th century).

————. *Sneaker Hill.* Atheneum, 1967. Susan went to visit Aunt Miranda and found she was studying to be a witch. Susan, an owl and a hoard of rats (The Sneakers) rescue her from disaster.

————. *Spook.* Atheneum, 1965. Spook is a dog owned by Grimalda, the witch. He leaves her and when she finds him he is with Jamie. Then comes the showdown.

Little, Jean. *Different Dragons.* Viking, 1987. A young boy who is afraid of most things, especially dogs, finds that everyone fears something at some time.

————. *From Anna.* Harper, 1972. Anna and her family move from Germany to Canada. She is slowly losing her eyesight.

————. *Home from Far.* Little, 1965. Jenny's twin brother is killed in an auto accident. Her mother then takes two foster children into her home. One of them is a boy Jenny's age.

————. *Kate.* Harper, 1971. This is a story of Kate from "Look Through My Mirror." She and Emily are still friends and Kate is in need of friends as she and her family are having problems.

————. *Listen for the Singing.* Dutton, 1977. Anna is in regular high school after spending a whole year in Sight School. Her brother has been blinded and she can relate to how he feels.

————. *Look Through My Window.* Harper, 1970. The story of a friendship between two girls, Emily and Kate. Emily is an only child and doesn't want her four cousins to come and live with her but she soon becomes close to all the children.

————. *Lost and Found.* Viking, 1986. Lucy is happy with the stray dog she found when she moved to a new town. But the real owner then comes to claim him.

————. *Mama's Going to Buy You a Mockingbird.* Viking, 1984. Jeremy and Sarah's father has cancer. They must sell their house and their mother must go back to school for training. They manage to cope well with all this.

————. *Mine for Keeps.* Little, 1962. Sally is crippled. She has a puppy named Susie who is a great companion and help during difficult times. Sally starts to attend regular school.

————. *One to Grow On.* Little, 1969. Janie told lies to everyone and it bothered them. She did not lie to her godmother, Tilly. So it was up to Tilly to find the key and cure Janie of lying because Janie didn't understand why she did it.

————. *Spring Begins in March.* Little, 1964. Meg is Sally's younger sister. She is an underachiever at school and has problems at home cause the room she wanted for her own was taken over by Grandma.

_____. *Stand in the Wind.* Harper, 1975. Martha didn't go to camp. She and her sister, Ellen, meet Rosemary and Kit and spend a week together. Martha is overweight; Kit is shy and the girls learn to understand each other.

_____. *Take Wing.* Little, 1968. Laura is concerned about her younger brother who is retarded. She finally accepts the fact that he is what he is and she must live a normal life.

Little, Mary. *Old Cat and the Kitten.* Atheneum, 1979. When Joel's family moves he knows he can't take his adopted tom cat but he can't let him run loose either. He makes the only decision he can and it's a hard one.

Lively, Penelope. *Astercote.* Dutton, 1970. Mair and Peter go into the woods to find their dog. They meet a boy, Goacher, and learn about the Black Death of 600 years before.

_____. *Boy Without a Name.* Parnassus, 1975. Thomas is a foundling who is apprenticed to a stone mason.

_____. *Fanny's Sister.* Dutton, 1980. Fanny is hopeful that one day soon, quite soon, her sister will just go away.

_____. *Ghost of Thomas Kempe.* Dutton, 1973. A ghost begins to act up when James and his family move into the old house where he resides.

_____. *House in Norham Gardens.* Dutton, 1974. Clare lives in a house filled with old relics. She begins to have strange dreams after she finds a ceremonial shield.

_____. *House Inside Out.* Dutton, 1988. A story of what is seen in a house by the creatures that live there: mice, spiders, pill bugs, etc. They live in cracks and corners of all houses.

_____. *Revenge of Samuel Stokes.* Dutton, 1981. Stokes once lived on these grounds and he is angry because of what has happened to it. He, as a ghost, comes back and does strange things. Jane, Tim and his grandfather set him right.

_____. *Stitch in Time.* Dutton, 1976. Maria spends her vacation by the sea. She hears a dog when none is supposed to be there. She finds a stitching of a girl a hundred years earlier.

_____. *Voyage of QV 66.* Dutton, 1978. Animals only are left in the world. Stanley, a monkey, is their leader. They are heading for the London zoo where they hope to find others of their kind.

_____. *Whispering Knights.* Dutton, 1971. Susie, Martha and William concoct a witch's brew that conjures up Morgan le Fay and stirs up trouble in town.

_____. *Wild Hunt of the Ghost Hounds.* Dutton, 1971. An ancient dance is revived for a village fair. After Lucy discovers the dance had its origins in a vicious hunt, she fears for her friend who has been chosen to play the victim.

Livoni, Cathy. *Element of Time.* Harcourt, 1983. Sael has extraordinary mental abilities and power he must learn to control. There are telepathy, telekinesis, time warps and teleporting.

Lloyd, Norris. *Desperate Dragons.* Hastings, 1960. A story of the last twelve dragons on earth. Kip is one of them. They must keep away from knights but Kip wants the king's daughter.

Lobdell, Helen. *Prisoner of Taos.* Abelard, 1970. Estevan, 16, is Spanish and wealthy. Teri is a Pueblo Indian slave. When the indians unite and drive out the Spanish both Estevan and Teri must re-evaluate their beliefs.

Locke, Elsie. *Runaway Settlers.* Dutton, 1966. Elizabeth and her six children ran away from her brutal husband and earned a living by gardening on a large plantation. They lived in fear of Mr. Small's return.

Lofting, Hugh. *Dr. Dolittle and the Green Canary.* Lippincott, 1950/1989. Pippinella, the green canary, is a friend of Dr. Dolittle's. This is her life before joining the Doctor and her search for her lost master and some mysterious stolen papers.

_____. *Dr. Dolittle on the Moon.* Lippincott, 1988. Dr. Dolittle goes to the moon on the back of a giant moth. Chee Chee, the monkey, goes with him. While there they encounter strange vegetable life.

_____. *Dr. Dolittle's Caravan.* Delacorte, 1988. Dr. Dolittle takes his circus to London and with the help of Pippinella, he stages a bird opera which takes London by storm.

_____. *Dr. Dolittle's Circus.* Delacorte, 1988. The circus is a success because of Pushmepullyu. But that is only the beginning of a very special circus.

_____. *Dr. Dolittle's Garden.* Lippincott, 1955/1988. In Dr. Dolittle's splendid garden live many creatures, especially insects. They have many tales to tell and the Doctor learns about the giant moths and their language.

_____. *Dr. Dolittle's Post Office.* Lippincott, 1951/1988. Dr. Dolittle discovers animal writing in addition to their language. He starts a mail service for animals and birds called Swallow Mail.

_____. *Story of Dr. Dolittle.* Lippincott, 1920/1948/1988. Dr. Dolittle is a very kind doctor who is fond of animals. He understands their language. He and some of his friendly animals go to Africa to cure the monkeys of a strange sickness.

_____. *Voyage of Dr. Dolittle.* Lippincott, 1923/1950/1988. This time Dr. Dolittle goes to Spidermonkey Island. He spends a lot of time learning the language of the animals. Newbery winner, 1923.

Logan, Carolyn. *Power of the Rillard.* Macmillan, 1986. Three children, Shelley, Lucy and Georgia, play a game with a clay doll named Rillard. It ends up a struggle of good/evil and they must win.

Logan, Les. *Game.* Bantam, 1983. Something

evil is controlling Julie, and she can't do anything about it. Her twin sister, Terri, and boyfriend, Jim, try to help but she may drag them down with her before they can help.

London, Jack. *Call of the Wild.* Bantam, 1963. Buck is a dog stolen from his home and forced to work to merely stay alive in the Arctic. This cruel life changes him into a vicious animal.

Loomis, Ruth. *Valley of the Hawk.* Dial, 1969. Jill doesn't like being on her sister's ranch for the summer. She makes friends with an Indian girl, a move that leads to false accusations of theft and a search in an old Indian cave.

Lord, Athena. *Luck of Z.A.P. and Zoe.* Macmillan, 1987. Zach and Zoe are from Greece. Zach's initials are Z.A.P. and form the basis for the Z.A.P. Club in his rich life.

_____. *Spirit to Ride the Whirlwind.* Macmillan, 1981. In 1836 the women of Massachusetts try to form a workers union. Binnie and her widowed mother fight the hardships of labor in the factories.

_____. *Today's Special Z.A.P. and Zoe.* Macmillan, 1984. Zachary must take care of his sister Zoe, who is four, and it is a problem.

Lord, Beman. *Day the Space Ship Landed.* Walck, 1967. Mike saw the spaceship land on Earth but who is to believe him?

_____. *Shrimp's Soccer Goal.* Walck, 1970. A new teacher, Miss Taylor, likes soccer so Shrimp and his friends learn to play that instead of football.

Lord, Bette. *In the Year of the Boar and Jackie Robinson.* Harper, 1984. Shirley Wong comes to America in 1947. She learns English, makes friends and learns to love baseball. She presents the key of P.S. 8 to her hero, Jackie Robinson.

Lorentzen, Karen. *Lanky Longlegs.* Atheneum, 1983. Di's baby brother dies of leukemia. There are the birth and growth of a litter of puppies and a friendship with someone who calls her Lanky Longlegs.

Lorenzo, Carol. *Heart of Snowbird.* Harper, 1975. Laurel, 12, lives in the rural South. She is pursued by a 13-year-old with a mini-bike (Hank). His father is having an affair outside the family.

_____. *Mama's Ghosts.* Harper, 1974. Ellie's grandmother keeps souvenirs of her past and calls up ghosts from that past for Ellie to see. Mama has a heart attack and Ellie wins a trip to Caracas.

Lorimer, Lawrence. *Secrets.* Holt, 1981. Maggie realizes that her pastor father is telling lies. He is having an affair with a parishioner, not for the first time. She tries to protect him but it's too late and he commits suicide.

Love, Sandra. *Crossing Over.* Lothrop, 1981. Megan, 13, and Kevin, 10, go to spend a school year with their divorced father who is a teacher at a military school. They find life is different than with their easygoing mother.

_____. *Dive for the Sun.* Houghton, 1982.

Kris, 15, loses his mother and sister in a drowning accident. He was diving for Spanish treasure and doesn't want to anymore. But his dreams tell him about the site of the ship.

Lovejoy, Jack. *Rebel Witch.* Lothrop, 1978. Suzie is an apprenticed witch and she tries to prevent dark lore from reappearing. So with the powerful wand of Necromancers in her possession she sets out.

Lovelace, Maud. *Betsy and Joe.* Crowell, 1948. Betsy is still at Deep Valley High and is in her senior year. Joe is her boyfriend and all is going well for her.

_____. *Betsy and Tacy Go Downtown.* Crowell, 1943/1979. Betsy, Tacy and Tib explore the library and the local hotel, and they go to a theatre.

_____. *Betsy and Tacy Go Over the Big Hill.* Crowell, 1942/1979. Betsy and Tacy are a little older and wander farther from home. They meet Naifi, an immigrant girl, and they have a wonderful experience.

_____. *Betsy and the Great World.* Crowell, 1952. Betsy is out of high school and makes a trip to Europe. She makes sure she sees and does everything she can, including a romance.

_____. *Betsy in Spite of Herself.* Crowell, 1946/1980. Betsy moves into her sophomore year at high school and she is still friends with Tacy and Tib.

_____. *Betsy-Tacy and Tib.* Crowell, 1941. Three young girls are friends from childhood to adulthood. This is the story of when they were young getting into mischief.

_____. *Betsy Was a Junior.* Crowell, 1947. Betsy is a junior at Deep Valley High. She attends football games, has boyfriends and makes a decision not to join a sorority.

_____. *Betsy's Wedding.* Crowell, 1947/1955. Betsy is back from her travels and settles down with Joe, her childhood sweetheart.

_____. *Heavens to Betsy.* Crowell, 1945/1980. Betsy is now quite grown and is attending her first year of high school.

Lovett, Margaret. *Great and Terrible Quest.* Holt, 1967. Trad finds an old man near death and together they sing and play for a living. They are both searching for a meaning to their quest. They only have a gold ring and the lines from a verse.

_____. *Jonathan.* Dutton, 1972. Martha, Liz, Jemmy and Matt are orphans and are about to be indentured. Jonathan appears from nowhere and takes charge of them. They all escape and begin a long and hazardous trip.

Low, Alice. *Kallie's Corner.* Pantheon, 1966. Jane is an average girl doing the normal things an average girl does in school and at home. Then Kallie comes into her life and makes things happen.

Lowery, Bruce. *Scarred.* Vanguard, 1961. Jeff's big problem in life is his harelip and the anguish it causes.

Lowrey, Janette. *Love, Bid Me Welcome.* Harper, 1964. Margaret is enmeshed in a family dispute but her main concern is school and college. She hasn't seen her young friend for three years but finds that she is in love with her aunt's doctor.

Lowry, Lois. *All About Sam.* Houghton, 1988. Anastasia's baby brother Sam tells his story from birth to now (pre-school). It is a trial trying to fit into the Krupnik family. He likes Anastasia but....

_____. *Anastasia Again.* Houghton, 1981. Anastasia adds boys to her long list of troubles. One is her obviously bright younger brother. She is two years older (12) and may have to make still another adjustment.

_____. *Anastasia, Ask Your Analyst.* Houghton, 1984. Anastasia's three-year-old brother, Sam, aids her with her science project. But she is still frustrated and blames her family for her mixed-up life. She talks out her problems.

_____. *Anastasia at Your Service.* Houghton, 1982. Anastasia looks at a long boring summer until she becomes involved with Mrs. Bellingham. She works as a maid, which she dislikes but can't quit.

_____. *Anastasia Has the Answers.* Houghton, 1986. Anastasia plays cupid for her widowed uncle and also has a "romance" of her own: a crush on her gym teacher.

_____. *Anastasia Krupnik.* Houghton, 1979. Anastasia has trouble with her teachers, her parents, her grandmother, etc., etc., etc. She is apprehensive about having a baby brother to add to her problems.

_____. *Anastasia on Her Own.* Houghton, 1985. Anastasia tries to run the household while her mother is out of town. She has an organization schedule to make things easy.

_____. *Anastasia's Chosen Career.* Houghton, 1987. Anastasia is quite mature and tries to take a modeling course but becomes involved in a book store.

_____. *Autumn Street.* Houghton, 1980. A thoughtful book about young children's feelings about family members and friends. Charles and Elizabeth face more tragedy than love and have difficulty in accepting life's unfairness.

_____. *Find a Stranger, Say Goodbye.* Houghton, 1978. Natalie is adopted. She is happy with her family but feels she must look for her biological mother. She is ready to face this decision even though her adoptive family is real to her.

_____. *Number the Stars.* Houghton, 1989. Annamarie, a Dane, and Ellen Rosen, a Jew, are friends but the war is having its effect. Annamarie shows bravery when she shelters her friend during the 1943 German occupation. Newbery winner, 1990.

_____. *One Hundredth Thing About Caroline.* Houghton, 1983. Caroline's mother dates a man in the same building. She finds he must "eliminate the children." Caroline and J.P., her brother, figure that must be them! They find out he is an author.

_____. *Rabble Starkey.* Houghton, 1987. Rabble and Veronica are friends. Rabble is somewhat like "Anastasia" (Lowry) but more serious. The two girls befriend Millie Bellow and learn about boys and to cope with Veronica's unstable mother.

_____. *Summer to Die.* Houghton, 1977. Meg and Molly are sisters. Molly is pretty and popular. Meg is shy and a loner. They get along even though they fight like sisters. Molly is going to die and Meg wants to remember her as she was.

_____. *Switcharound.* Houghton, 1985. Caroline, 11, and J.P., 13, spend their summer with their father and his new family. He places a lot of responsibility on them. They don't like it and seek revenge.

_____. *Taking Care of Terrific.* Houghton, 1983. Enid begins to take care of Joshua (Terrific) and learns about Public Gardens and bag ladies. She also learns to understand the school pest, Seth, when they sneak aboard the swan boats at midnight.

_____. *Us and Uncle Fraud.* Houghton, 1984. Louise and Marcus like their Uncle Claude. But is he a fraud or, worse still, a thief?

Lucas, Christopher. *Tiki and the Dolphin: Adventures of a Boy in Tahiti.* Vanguard, 1975. Tiki has a dolphin companion, Toa, and a friend, Paul Gauguin. The action is a fight with a killer shark, a typhoon and a realistic dolphin hunt.

Luenn, Nancy. *Ugly Princess.* Little, 1981. A tale about real beauty learned through the process of becoming ugly.

Luger, Harriett. *Elephant Tree.* Viking, 1978. Dave and Louie are from rival gangs and they hate each other. They are lost in the desert without food or water. They must have each other for a chance to survive.

Luis, Earlene. *Wheels for Ginny's Chariot.* Dodd, 1966. Teenaged Ginny is paralyzed from the waist down following an accident.

Luke, Mary. *Nonsuch Lure.* Coward, 1976. A story of love that lasts three incarnations and four centuries. A romantic Gothic tale.

Lukeman, Tim. *Witchwood.* S&S, 1983. Fiona was touched by a falling star and she was destined to go into Witchwood, which was said to be haunted. Her exciting adventure begins with this step.

Lund, Doris. *Eric.* Lippincott, 1974. Eric finds out at the age of 17 that he has leukemia. He then tries to crowd a lifetime of dreams into the short time he has left: college, sports, love.

Lunn, Janet. *Root Cellar.* Scribner, 1983. Rose wants to get away from her cruel relatives. She runs toward the root cellar but runs back in time to the Civil War. She meets Susan and Will and finds she can travel back and forth.

————. *Shadow in Hawthorn Bay*. Scribner, 1987. Mary "hears" Duncan call for help. She makes a dangerous trip to save him but he is gone. Now she is among people who don't understand her psychic powers.

————. *Twin Spell*. Harper, 1968. Jane and Elizabeth pool their money and buy a doll. A mystery develops and a spell is cast on the girls. They see the tragedy that struck their ancestors and other visions and hauntings.

Lustig, Arnost. *Darkness Casts a Shadow*. Inscape, 1976. Manny and Danny escape from a train carrying them between camps and wander through the forests of the German-Czechoslovakian border struggling to stay alive.

Lyle, Katie. *Dark But Full of Diamonds*. Coward, 1981. Scott thinks he is in love with his teacher. And . . . his father announces that he and the teacher are to be married. His reaction breaks up the marriage plans but Scott is the loser.

————. *Fair Day and Another Step Begun*. Lippincott, 1974. Ellen, 16, is pregnant with John's child. She pursues him in hopes of winning his love.

————. *Finders Weepers*. Coward, 1982. Lee joins other summer visitors in looking for the fabled Beale Treasure. She finds it but it is later covered by a mudslide and she is glad.

————. *I Will Go Barefoot All Summer for You*. Morrow, 1973. Jessie meets and likes Toby but doesn't know how to handle it. She learns that both love and pain will pass as life goes on.

Lyon, George. *Borrowed Children*. Orchard, 1988. Amanda needs a vacation after taking care of her sick mother. She goes to Memphis and learns more about her background. It is the time of the Great Depression.

Lyons, Dorothy. *Pedigree Unknown*. Harcourt, 1973. Jill finds out she is adopted. She is engaged to an influential boy who is scared off by this . . . but returns. She buys a mistreated horse and finds that he is a jumper and worth more than she paid.

Macauley, David. *Motel of the Mysteries*. Houghton, 1979. A spoof on archeologists and their findings. Howard finds, in 4022, a home and describes its contents inaccurately: a bed is a Ceremonial Platform, a TV is a Great Altar, etc.

McBratney, Sam. *Ghosts of Hungryhouse Lane*. Holt, 1989. Zoe, Charlie and Bonnie share their new home with three ghosts. A will can't be found and the wrong people got the house. The children find the will and all is set right. A light ghost story.

McCaffrey, Anne. *Crystal Singer*. Doubleday, 1982. Killashandra has perfect pitch and wants to sing but is prevented from doing so. In Ballybran she could succeed but she would have to make many serious sacrifices to qualify.

————. *Dinosaur Planet*. Ballantine, 1984. A scientific expedition goes to a planet where very large lizards live. They become stranded and the crew is acting strangely.

————. *Dragondrums*. Atheneum, 1979. Pern is in danger, but Piemur will out-wit Threadfall and win the fire-lizard of his dreams.

————. *Dragonflight*. Ballantine, 1968. Great dragons of Pern sweep through the skies to fight off the invasion of space spores during Threadfall.

————. *Dragonquest*. Ballantine, 1971. Pern needs its dragons and dragonriders in order to survive. They have formed a telepathic bond with man. Periodically Threadfall occurs and it takes cooperation to survive.

————. *Dragonsinger*. Atheneum, 1977. Menolly, now living with the Fire Dragons, learns a great deal about music and its role in Pern. And the role of girls.

————. *Dragonsong*. Atheneum, 1976. On the Planet Pern, forbidden by her father to indulge in music in any way because it is a career only for men, Menolly runs away to a life with the dragons and fights the enemy "Threads."

————. *Killashandra*. Ballantine, 1985. Killashandra has great musical talents but because of the control of this field by the leaders she cannot pursue her career as she would like.

————. *Moreta, Dragonlady of Pern*. Ballantine, 1983. This is a book about some of the other heroines who lived on Pern in earlier times.

————. *White Dragon*. Ballantine, 1978. Ruth, a pure white dragon, and Jaxon are in danger but they must prevent a big disaster.

McCaffrey, Mary. *My Brother Ange*. Harper, 1982. Mick sometimes gets very angry at his younger brother, Ange. But when that anger causes an accident, he feels badly.

McCarty, Rega. *Lorna Evan: Social Worker*. Messner, 1961. Lorna gives up love, wealth and social position in order to carry on her humanitarian work that needs to be done.

McCaughrean, Geraldine. *Little Lower Than the Angels*. Oxford, 1987. Gabriel runs away and joins a traveling miracle play group in Medieval Britain. They get coins for hoax cures. Gabriel finds his profession amid all this fraud.

McCloskey, Robert. *Centerburg Tales*. Viking, 1951/1977. Further adventures of Homer Price and reminiscences of his Grandpa Hercules: weeds that cover the town and a jukebox that plays music everyone dances to; all because of a mad scientist.

————. *Homer Price*. Viking, 1943/1976. Six tales which acquaint the reader with Homer Price. The most well-known one is the doughnut episode but there are others.

McConnell, James. *Killer on the Track*. Bradbury, 1973. A murder takes place at a racing track. Why? Who?

McCord, Jean. *Turkeylegs Thompson*. Atheneum, 1979. A young girl begins life again after a tragic summer.

McCormick, Wilfred. *Big Ninth.* Putnam, 1958. Bronc and his team are to play a neighboring town rival. Bronc pitches a winning third game against this tough team.

_____. *Eagle Scout.* Putnam, 1952. Bronc is an Eagle Scout competing with other Sonora scouts. Al is the scout master. He is accused of setting a forest fire but clears himself. This is the same Bronc who is a pitcher in other stories.

_____. *Incomplete Pitcher.* Bobbs, 1967. Bronc is a star pitcher but the opposing teams are beginning to hit him. It turns out that his alternate catcher, Ralph, is giving his signals away to the other teams.

_____. *Last Putout.* Putnam, 1960. Bronc and his team play a strategic Mexican team. There are spectator animosity and tense moments. Bronc pitches his way to victory and wins a bet.

_____. *No Place for Heros.* Bobbs, 1966. Bronc and Fat are both on the same baseball team. They are accused of stealing. They work hard at finding the real thief and at becoming great players.

_____. *One Bounce Too Many.* Bobbs, 1967. Bronc is confronted with a moral question of someone cheating on an exam and being suspended from playing basketball. His teammates expected him to lie and he is dumbfounded.

_____. *Tall at the Plate.* Bobbs, 1966. Bronc, a pitcher, and Fat, a catcher, try to outwit George, a hitter.

_____. *Three-Toed Pitch.* Putnam, 1948. Bronc plays high school baseball. He has trouble with his temper. But he does pitch the final winning game.

MacCracken, Mary. *City Kid.* Little, 1981. Luke is a very young delinquent. He goes through a therapeutic program that is both funny and helpful.

_____. *Lovey: A Very Special Child.* Harper, 1976. Hannah is an emotionally disturbed child because of abuse and neglect. Her teacher, Mary, works hard to release the goodness of this child and make her into a warm human being.

McCraig, Robert. *That Nester Kid.* Scribner, 1961. Billy is involved in the conflict between ranchers and nesters in 1896 Montana. He helps round up horse thieves and is shot in a gun battle.

McCullough, Colleen. *Thornbirds.* Harper, 1977. Meggy lives in Australia in the early 20th century and this is a story of her dramatic life and loves. A strong female story.

McCutcheon, Elsie. *Rat War.* Farrar, 1986. Nicholas and Morna stay with Aunt Dorothy; Nicholas finds a rat in the yard and steals food to feed him. His rat is killed in an explosion but a murder suspect is revealed.

_____. *Summer of the Zeppelin.* Farrar, 1985. Elvira wants to help an escaped German prisoner get away during World War I.

MacDonald, Betty. *Hello, Mrs. Piggle-Wiggle.* Harper, 1950. Mrs. Piggle-Wiggle loves children and she loves them equally, good or bad.

MacDonald, George. *At the Back of the North Wind.* Morrow, 1989. A nice edition of this old classic fantasy.

_____. *Golden Key.* Farrar, 1967. Mossy and Tangle spend a mysterious life together as they travel. A mystery, fairy story.

_____. *Sir Gibbie.* Schocken, 1979. Love is the strong ingredient that makes hardship bearable for this young boy in Scotland.

McDonald, Joyce. *Mail-Order Kid.* Putnam, 1988. Flip has a new adopted six-year-old Korean "brother," Todd, and must share his room.

MacDonald, Reby. *Ghosts of Austwick Manor.* Atheneum, 1982. Two sisters travel back in time and save their brother from an ancient curse.

MacDonald, Shelagh. *No End to Yesterday.* Dutton, 1979. Marjory is motherless and mistreated. She has artistic talent and wants to be a veterinarian but is not encouraged by her family. She grows up and gets away from this oppressive situation.

McDonnell, Christine. *Count Me In.* Viking, 1986. Katie, 13, is upset when her mother and new stepfather announce that they are expecting a baby.

_____. *Just for the Summer.* Viking, 1987. Emily, Ivy and Lydia are together for the summer at day camp. They start a toddler day care center and have varied activities.

Mace, Elizabeth. *Rushton Inheritance.* Nelson, 1978. In 1871 Tom meets a relative from the future. He disappears and reappears at will. Tom learns that he is looking for a treasure that is hidden in Tom's house.

McElfresh, Adeline. *Summer Change.* Bobbs, 1960. Cathy stays at her father's old house in a small town. She pretends to like it and actually finds friends, activities and a job writing for a newspaper.

_____. *To Each Her Dream.* Bobbs, 1961. Sarah-Eleanor couldn't go to medical school in 1840 but she helped her doctor father until disaster struck and she was the only "doctor" in the wagon train.

McElrath, William. *Indian Treasure on Rockhouse Creek.* Broadman, 1984. Three young boys go treasure hunting and have exciting adventures.

McGiffin, Lee. *Coat for Private Patrick.* Dutton, 1964. Don Patrick, while still too young to join the Confederate Army, helped by learning telegraphy. When he turns 15 he joins the Army and the war.

_____. *High Whistle Charlie.* Dutton, 1962. Joe, 14, starts on a sheep drive. His partner dies and he hires a new one, who's inexperienced. They have a great deal of difficulty getting to California. Charlie is Joe's highly trained Border collie.

_____. *Horse Hunters.* Dutton, 1963. Sam and Jeff are in New Orleans to sell horses to the Confederacy but the horses are stolen. They recover the horses and find the traitors.

_____. *Riders of Enchanted Valley.* Dutton,

1966. Luke, 15, goes to live with his brother in California. His brother married a Spanish girl. Their home life is different and exciting.

McGinnis, Lila. *Auras and Other Rainbow Secrets.* Hastings, 1984. Nora sees Auras and records her thoughts in the colors she sees. She can predict trouble and thinks her power is a gift to be used for good.

_____. *Ghost Upstairs.* Hastings, 1982. Albert finds a friend in the ghost whose name is Otis.

McGowen, Tom. *Magician's Apprentice.* Lodestar, 1987. Tigg goes with Armindor, a magician, to "wild lands." He befriends Reepah who warns him of evil. The setting is Earth 3,000 years from now.

_____. *Magician's Challenge.* Dutton, 1989. Armindor and Tigg warn people about the intelligent rat-like creatures, the Reems, who want to destroy all humans in their plan for world takeover.

_____. *Magician's Company.* Lodestar, 1988. Tigg and Armindor rescue a puppeteer, Jilla, and warn the High Council of rat-like creatures who are planning to rule the land.

_____. *Odyssey from River Bend.* Little, 1975. The animals of River Bend make a risky journey to the Haunted Land in search of the magic of the Long Ago Ones.

_____. *Shadow of Fomar.* Dutton, 1990. Rick, 12, and his cousin travel back to Middle Kingdom, the last haven of Old Magic where creatures want to control first the Kingdom and then all of Ireland.

_____. *Sir MacHinery.* Follett, 1970. Professor Smith, a scientist of the 20th century, Merlin, a wizard of the 6th century, and MacHinery, a robot, get together and fight evil that turns men against each other.

_____. *Spirit of the Wild.* Little, 1976. Amy investigates a cave uncovered by a bulldozer. She and others are captured by an ancient race of Indians who had lost "Weendigo" when the cave was opened. Amy leads Weendigo back where it is entrapped again.

_____. *Time of the Forest.* Houghton, 1988. Wolf, a hunter, and Bright Dawn, an early farmer, meet. They are rejected by both tribes because they could be the beginning of a new tribe, a combination of both cultures.

McGraw, Eloise. *Golden Goblet.* Coward, 1961. Ranofer wants to be a goldsmith but his brother stands in his way. He later finds that his brother had committed a crime against the Queen of Ancient Egypt.

_____. *Hideaway.* Atheneum, 1983. Jerry goes to his grandmother's house after his parents' divorce. He finds the house now belongs to someone else. He meets Hanna and they plan to run away together; this never happens and Jerry goes home.

_____. *Joel and the Great Merlini.* Pan-theon, 1979. Joel gets more magic from a magician named Merlini.

_____. *Mara, Daughter of the Nile.* Coward, 1985. Mara is a slave girl in ancient Egypt. She risks her life as a double agent in order to win her freedom.

_____. *Master Cornhill.* Atheneum, 1973. A young boy is left without family or money when the Plague hits London.

_____. *Moccasin Trail.* Coward, 1986. Jim lived six years as an Indian after the Crows rescued him from a bear. His real white family want him back and Jim doesn't know what to do.

_____. *Money Room.* Atheneum, 1981. Scotty's father is killed and he goes to a farm once owned by the family. He finds a secret room but someone else is also looking for it.

_____. *Seventeenth Swap.* Atheneum, 1986. Eric wants to buy a pair of cowboy boots for Jerry, who, because of his wheelchair will never walk in them. Eric starts to raise the needed $18.00 in inventive ways.

_____. *Trouble with Jacob.* Macmillan, 1988. Kat and Andy, twins, know about Jacob, the nine-year-old ghost. He says his bed has been stolen. Jacob's skeleton is found and he is finally put to rest.

McGraw, William. *Smoke.* Coward, 1967. Chris didn't like his stepfather. He found a half-wild German shepherd and called him Smoke. He needed help but he was also the dog that was killing his stepfather's chickens. What to do?

MacGregor, Ellen. *Miss Pickerell and the Blue Whales.* McGraw, 1983. Miss Pickerell organizes a boycott to save the Blue Whales from harpoonists.

_____. *Miss Pickerell and the Geiger Counter.* McGraw, 1953. Miss Pickerell takes her pet cow to the veterinarian. She finds herself substituting for the sheriff and somehow discovers uranium.

_____. *Miss Pickerell and the Supertanker.* McGraw, 1978. Miss Pickerell plugs a leak in a tanker and feeds oil-eating microbes.

_____. *Miss Pickerell and the Weather Satellite.* McGraw, 1971. Miss Pickerell learns a lot about modern technology at the weather station. She prevents a flood by using laser beams and space stations.

_____. *Miss Pickerell Goes on a Dig.* McGraw, 1966. Miss Pickerell goes on an archeological excavation to unearth some history before the road department comes along and digs everything up as it widens the road.

_____. *Miss Pickerell Goes to Mars.* McGraw, 1951. Miss Pickerell is accidentally stowed away on a ship bound for Mars. She is not welcome by the crew.

_____. *Miss Pickerell Goes to the Arctic.* McGraw, 1954. Miss Pickerell flies to the Arctic to rescue a downed plane. She is downed herself and must be rescued along with the other plane survivors.

_____. *Miss Pickerell Goes Underseas.* McGraw, 1953. Miss Pickerell puts on a diver's suit and goes underwater to recover her famous red rock collection from Mars.

_____. *Miss Pickerell Harvests the Sea.* McGraw, 1968. Miss Pickerell helps a friend who has an ocean farm. She doesn't understand at first but learns a great deal about oceanography.

_____. *Miss Pickerell Meets Mr. H.U.M.* McGraw, 1974. While trying to think of a name for her cow, Miss Pickerell's telephone rings and a chain of events start. H.U.M. is a computer that's going to take over the world.

_____. *Miss Pickerell on the Moon.* McGraw, 1965. Miss Pickerell's cow and her cat have fallen ill from an epidemic of unknown germs. There is no treatment so she goes to the moon to look for some molds that are needed.

_____. *Miss Pickerell Tackles the Energy Crisis.* McGraw, 1980. Miss Pickerell's trip to the long awaited Fair is cancelled. There is a fuel shortage because of an earthquake and the Fair must be postponed. She gets a formula for ethanol.

_____. *Miss Pickerell Takes the Bull by the Horns.* McGraw, 1976. Miss Pickerell is dead set against cloning. There is a bill in Congress and she does her civic duty with letters and a protest march.

McHargue, Georgess. *Funny Banana: Mystery in the Museum.* Holt, 1975. Ben tries to catch a vandal who is destroying the natural history museum. The museum is "haunted" by a witch and strange animals.

_____. *Horseman's Word.* Delacorte, 1981. Leigh helps with her aunt and uncle's pony breaking business. She and Tam don't like each other but she likes the grandson, Rob. Rob is mistreated by Tam and Leigh plans revenge.

_____. *See You Later, Crocodile.* Delacorte, 1988. Jo, 13, finds herself in charge of Aggie's fourteen cats while she is in the hospital. She gets help in supporting the cats.

_____. *Stoneflight.* Viking, 1975. Janie is upset with her parents' quarreling. She envys the stone animals in front of buildings and tries to put life in them. But . . . when they try to turn her to stone she resists strongly.

_____. *Talking Table Mystery.* Doubleday, 1977. Two youngsters look in the attic and find some things that belonged to a medium. Mystery and excitement follow.

_____. *Turquoise Toad Mystery.* Delacorte, 1982. Ben, 13, and Frito, his pet coati (raccoon), look for Indian artifacts and expose a ring of thieves.

McHugh, Elisabet. *Beethoven's Cat.* Atheneum, 1988. A cat of today named Ludwig finds that he looks like Beethoven's cat. He is possessed by the spirit of that long dead composer's cat.

_____. *Karen and Vicki.* Greenwillow, 1984. Karen learns to live with a whole family, including a stepsister, Vicki.

_____. *Karen's Sister.* Greenwillow, 1983. Karen's mother adopts a second Korean child and finds a husband with three children of his own.

_____. *Raising a Mother Isn't Easy.* Greenwillow, 1983. Karen, a Korean, is adopted by a single woman. Karen tries to find her new Mom a husband.

_____. *Wiggie Wins the West.* Atheneum, 1989. Wiggie, a cat, travels by car through the West. He is brave, selfless and bright. He saves his family, both human and animal, many times.

McInerney, Judith. *Judge Benjamin, Superdog.* Holiday, 1982. A funny story about a St. Bernard. He gets his "human family" in and out of disaster after disaster. It is told from his point of view.

_____. *Judge Benjamin, Superdog Gift.* Holiday, 1986. Loretta, an elderly friend, collapses on the sidewalk and Judge Benjamin and his new mate, Agatha, rescue her. When she disappears from the hospital Agatha must find her again.

_____. *Judge Benjamin, Superdog Rescue.* Holiday, 1984. Gramps regrets his decision to allow Judge Benjamin to move in and run things on his farm.

_____. *Judge Benjamin, Superdog Secret.* Holiday, 1983. Judge Benjamin, who weighs about 200 pounds, stows away in his "human" family's camper for a three week vacation.

_____. *Judge Benjamin, Superdog Surprise.* Holiday, 1985. Judge Benjamin takes care of his "human" family and also helps a neighbor during a blizzard.

MacInnes, Helen. *Salzburg Connection.* Harper, 1968. Bill is a lawyer in New York. A truck in the Alps that men have died to get and men will kill to get is connected to Bill in some mysterious way.

McIntyre, Vonda. *Barbary.* Houghton, 1987. Barbary, 12, goes to her new home in space. Her cat climbs into a space probe and must be rescued.

_____. *Dreamsnake.* Houghton, 1978. Snake is a healer in a future world. She cures people's illnesses with snakes. Someone kills Dreamsnake, the one that doesn't cure but eases death. She goes to find another in a far off place.

McKay, Robert. *Dave's Song.* Hawthorn, 1969. Dave and Kate end up loving each other but not before a great deal of conflict and misunderstanding.

_____. *Troublemaker.* Nelson, 1971. Jesse is expelled from school for fighting. He and his friend plan a student revolt while they are out of school. He brings an injured bird to a girl and perhaps his "trouble" days are over.

MacKellar, William. *Dog Called Porridge.* Dodd, 1985. Davie and his uncle live in the Scottish Highlands. A strange dog comes into their lives and odd things begin to happen.

_____. *Dog Like No Other.* McKay, 1965.

Fergus is "a dog like no other." He aids in the recovery of the lost sword of Bonnie Prince Charlie.

_____. *Ghost of Grannoch Moor.* Dodd, 1973. Davie loved his dog, Bonnie. A neighbor moved in with a fierce dog that killed Bonnie. The owner gave Davie a new puppy but Davie did not care. Then Laddie disappeared and sheep were being killed.

_____. *Kenny and the Highland Ghost.* Dodd, 1980. Kenny meets a ghost in Scotland. It is cursed by a MacSpurtle and can't rest until the curse is retracted.

_____. *Mound Menace.* Follett, 1969. John is a good pitcher but is known as a "headhunter." Steve welcomes him to the school's team and trusts him. But that trust is shaken when John beans a fellow player at practice.

_____. *Place by the Fire.* McKay, 1966. Old Tam is replaced by a young sheep dog. Donald must decide what to do with Tam who is proud and faithful.

_____. *Secret of the Dark Tower.* McKay, 1967. When some diamonds are found, "accidents" begin to happen, and one night a threatening note draws two boys to a deserted castle.

_____. *Secret of the Sacred Stone.* McKay, 1970. Two young boys end up smack in the middle of a daring Scottish Nationalist plot.

_____. *Terror Run.* Dodd, 1982. Mark and Ian are looking for an infamous international terrorist. Mark's father is a United States intelligence officer. A good spy story.

_____. *Very Small Miracle.* Crown, 1969. Jamie's dog Rab is sick and he takes her to Murdo who has a way with animals. Rab does die but Jamie and Murdo become close and Murdo sells a prized possession to buy Jamie another dog.

_____. *Witch of Glen Gowrie.* Dodd, 1978. Gavin doesn't believe in witches until he meets Meg, who lives in Glen Gowrie, and her many animals.

Macken, Walter. *Flight of the Doves.* Macmillan, 1968. Finn and Der'al ran away from England to Ireland. Poll and his brother, sister and father investigate as to why they ran away and why their uncle wants them back.

_____. *Island of the Great Yellow Ox.* Macmillan, 1966. Conor and two friends go sailing and are marooned on a lonely island where archeologists are looking for a Druid treasure.

McKenzie, Ellen. *Drujienma's Harp.* Dutton, 1971. Tha and her brother Duncan are transported to the land of T'pahl where there is a struggle of good and evil.

_____. *Kashka.* Holt, 1987. Kaska and Pitt find out about the plot to take the king's baby son so they take and hide him. It is Lady Ysese of *Taash and the Jesters* who is the evil one.

_____. *Taash and the Jesters.* Holt, 1968. Taash is an orphan who is rescued from a cruel

home by a beggar and then given to a witch. Later he and his friends return the king's kidnapped baby and Taash finds a home.

McKillip, Patricia. *Changeling Sea.* Atheneum, 1988. A fantasy of magicians, sea dragons, islands, kingdoms and changelings. Pere is the heroine and Lyo the wise one.

_____. *Fool's Run.* Warner, 1987. Queen of Hearts is a musician who plays in a band on various planets, including the penal satellite, Underworld. One of the inmates escapes and the band is involved in the recapture.

_____. *Harpist in the Wind.* Atheneum, 1979. In the midst of conflict, the Prince of Hed, Morgon, and his friend, Raederle, learn to harp the wind and find out who the shape-changers are.

_____. *Heir of Sea and Fire.* Atheneum, 1977. When Morgon fails to return from his quest, three people set out to find him, including his fiancee, Raederle. She meets up with the shape-changers.

_____. *House on Parchment Street.* Atheneum, 1973. There seem to be ghosts in the basement so two boys, one American and one English, go to investigate and find the secret.

_____. *Moon and the Face.* Atheneum, 1985. Kyreol's mission to another planet and Terje's trip to observe their old river-home, bring both of them unexpected dangers.

_____. *Moon-Flash.* Atheneum, 1984. Kyreol and Terje begin their adventures in other worlds.

_____. *Night Gift.* Atheneum, 1976. Barbara and her friends fix up a room in an abandoned house for Barbara's brother Joe who attempted suicide. It is to be a retreat when he gets depressed.

_____. *Riddle Master of Hed.* Atheneum, 1976. Morgon, the prince of Hed, tries to find the meaning of the three stars that are on his harp and imprinted on his head.

_____. *Throme of the Erril of Sherill.* Atheneum, 1973. Cnite Caerles must find the Throme of the Erril of Sherill, a poem that doesn't exist, before he can marry the king's daughter. He writes a poem and presents it to the king who accepts it.

McKinley, Robin. *Blue Sword.* Atheneum, 1982. Harry, bored with her sheltered life, goes to Istan, but wants to see where the Free Hillfolk live. She discovers magic in herself when she is kidnapped by a king with mysterious powers.

_____. *Hero and the Crown.* Atheneum, 1984. Another fantasy about witches, dragons and princesses. With the help of Luthe and the Blue Sword Aerin establishes herself as the daughter of the Damarian King.

MacKinnon, Bernie. *Meantime.* Houghton, 1984. Luke is black in an integrated school but there are daily incidents. He pursues a romance with Holly, a sensitive blonde.

MacLachlan, Patricia. *Arthur, For the Very*

First Time. Harper, 1980. Arthur, 10, lives with his aunt and uncle on a farm while his mother has her baby. He learns to be more tolerant of life around him and his role in it, through a friendly neighbor girl.

_____. *Cassie Binegar*. Harper, 1982. Cassie is looking for her own "space." She lives in a busy household and wants neatness and order. She comes to accept that nothing is static.

_____. *Facts and Fiction of Minna Pratt*. Harper, 1988. Minna, 11, plays cello, likes Mozart and has a friend, Lucas. His life is smooth and well run while hers is chaotic. She wants pat questions and answers but gets concepts and ideas from her parents.

_____. *Sarah, Plain and Tall*. Harper, 1985. Sarah answers an ad for a wife. She lives in Maine with her cat, Seal, and goes to accept this proposal. The children like her. A good, sad story. Newbery winner, 1986.

_____. *Seven Kisses in a Row*. Harper, 1983. Emma and her brother's parents are away. While they are staying with an aunt and uncle they feel obliged to teach them how to be a responsible family with all the rites and rituals involved.

_____. *Unclaimed Treasures*. Harper, 1984. Willa thinks she is in love with the artist who lives next door. She poses for him but comes to see the painting as his estranged wife's face. The two get back together and Willa learns about love.

McLaughlin, Lorrie. *Cinnamon Hill Mystery*. Crowell, 1967. William comes to visit. He, Ruthann and Marvey try to stop a housing development on Cinnamon Hill. William's invention to do just that is unique and unforgettable.

MacLean, Alistair. *Circus*. Doubleday, 1983. Bruno is a circus aerialist who has been hired by the CIA for a special mission. He is to break into an enemy prison and find a secret formula, memorize it and destroy it.

_____. *Ice Station Zebra*. Fawcett, 1963. The Dolphin is a nuclear submarine on an espionage mission. The crew think they're going to rescue scientists. They are headed for treachery, sabotage and murder.

_____. *Where Eagles Dare*. Doubleday, 1967. Eight men parachute into Nazi Germany to rescue an American general from a mountain top castle before the Nazis make him talk.

McLean, Allan. *Ribbon of Fire*. Harcourt, 1963. Alasdair and the Skye crofters try to hold on to their land in 1885. A vivid tale of oppression and its tragic results.

_____. *Sound of Trumpets*. Harcourt, 1967. Alasdair, oppressed in his own land, leaves for America. He and Lachlann lead a partisan fight but are beaten.

McLean, Susan. *Pennies for the Piper*. Farrar, 1981. Beck's mother died. She must go to a maiden aunt's to live and has just enough money to get there. She spends the money for funeral flowers and walks most of the way. She arrives malnour-

ished and in rags.

MacLeod, Charlotte. *Cirak's Daughter*. Atheneum, 1982. Jennie's father deserted her when she was born. Now he's left her a house and a fortune. She goes to live there and has reason to believe that her father's been murdered.

_____. *Maid of Honor*. Atheneum, 1984. Persis is neglected; her sister is getting married. She wins a state medal and a piano scholarship but tells no one. A brooch is missing and a mystery evolves but the family is not helpful in the solution.

_____. *Mouse's Vineyard*. Weybright, 1968. Mouse's stay at the beach is fine until Susan arrives. Her parents are divorcing and she is "weird." Mouse makes up a story about the lady in the next cottage but they do find a mystery there.

_____. *We Dare Not Go A-Hunting*. Atheneum, 1980. Annette is missing. She is returned after a ransom note of $2,000.00 is found. Jack needs a babysitter for Sam, 4, but is now afraid.

McMahan, Ian. *Fox's Lair*. Macmillan, 1983. Ricky and his computer, Alec, discover Indian ruins and solve a five million dollar mystery.

_____. *Lake Fear*. Macmillan, 1985. Ricky and his computer, Alec, look for the cause of the rash and nausea some children are suffering. Illegal pesticides are being dumped in the lake.

_____. *Lost Forest*. Macmillan, 1985. Ricky, with some help from his computer, Alec, finds his missing mother who is late returning from a camping trip.

McMeekin, Isabel. *Postman's Pony*. Putnam, 1960. Mark, with his pony, Pet, brought the mail to the wilderness of Kentucky. One day Mark shows up at the Duncans' more dead than alive because he was bitten by a snake.

MacMillan, Dianne. *My Best Friend Duc Tran*. Messner, 1987. Eddie meets a young Vietnamese boy and they become friends. Eddie learns more about a country he knew little about.

McMullan, Kate. *Great Advice from Lila Fenwick*. Dial, 1988. Lila and her friends spend the summer at the local pool. They want to learn more about boys. Lila goes to a boy scout camp with her father and Rita. She meets Kari and all three learn about boys.

McNair, Joseph. *Commander Coatrack Returns*. Houghton, 1989. Lisa, 13, and her retarded brother, Cody, are very close. Cody goes to a special school and Lisa misses him. She meets emotionally unstable Robert and sees both boys unrealistically, and she needs to face this.

McNamara, John. *Revenge of the Nerd*. Delacorte, 1984. A ninth grade genius (the nerd) gets even with his tormentors using his latest invention and getting into their homes via their televisions.

McNaughton, Colin. *Jolly Roger and the Pirates of Abdul the Skinhead*. S&S, 1988. Roger runs away from his mean mother and joins a band of pirates.

McNeer, May. *Bloomsday for Maggie.* Houghton, 1976. Maggie wants to be a real reporter, not a society page writer, but she must fight prejudice about "a woman's place."

McNeil, Florence. *Miss P and Me.* Harper, 1982. Miss Pringle is the new P.E. teacher who specializes in dance. Jane wants to dance but has two left feet. She is chosen for a major part in a school dance play but is cut; she wants revenge.

McNeill, Janet. *Battle of St. George Without.* Little, 1966. Matt McGinley's playhouse, a church, is threatened by a sinister gang.

_____. *Goodbye, Dove Square.* Little, 1969. Matt and his friends go back to their old neighborhood and find out one of their old friends, Shaky Frick, is living in a house that is about to be demolished.

_____. *Other People.* Little, 1970. Kate's summer is not what she envisioned. But she meets and helps Richard, meets Rosie with her thousand eye shadows, and gets to know the Mad Hatter, who wears yellow socks, and many others.

_____. *Prisoner in the Park.* Little, 1971. The park is Wild End where Ned and his friends go. But it is to be turned into a cycle track. Ned knows a boy is hiding there and wants to help him because he thinks he's a runaway orphan. He's wrong!

MacPherson, Margaret. *New Tenants.* Harcourt, 1968. Liz suspects Dad's neighbor, Danny. She finds him lying; catches him in the attic looking for something; sees him acting strange in front of others. But what is he up to?

_____. *Rough Road.* Harcourt, 1966. Jim is abused and neglected by his foster parents. He meets a cattle drover on the island of Skye in the 1930's and this makes him less sullen and withdrawn.

_____. *Shinty Boys.* Harcourt, 1963. Shinty is a game like hockey. Neil liked to play and was disappointed when his school was going to drop it because of the cost of the equipment. Neil and his friends raised the needed money.

McRae, Russell. *Going to the Dogs.* Viking, 1987. Billy's friend uses drugs, and so do Billy and his sister who commits suicide. His girlfriend gets pregnant and they both drop out of school. They drink, even though she's pregnant. See Title.

McSwigan, Marie. *Snow Treasure.* Dutton, 1942. A group of very courageous children smuggled gold out of Norway while the Germans occupied it. They used their sleds and skis.

Maddock, Reginald. *Great Bow.* Rand, 1968. Atta lives in a prehistoric Wolf tribe. He is cast out because he would not kill a bison. He goes away and alone he fashions the first bow and arrow. He shows it to his people and War is invented.

_____. *Last Horizon.* Nelson, 1962. Jonny is a bushman and is captured by the Boers. He learns their ways and escapes to go back to his people with what he learned.

_____. *Pit.* Little, 1968. A young boy has a reputation for being a tough kid so when there is a theft, he is falsely accused.

_____. *Thin Ice.* Little, 1971. Bill moves to a new city and a new school. He joins a gang to make friends even though it is not in his best interest. His father, too, must adjust to a new job and a new boss.

Maddox, Bill. *Rags and Patches.* Follett, 1978. Danny, 13, and his dog, Patches, look for Danny's missing father in Texas.

Madison, Arnold. *Danger Beats the Drum.* Holt, 1965. Bob's father was killed by a dope addict. He has a temper and gets into fights. He goes to the lake for the summer with his mother. He is accused of sabotaging the teen center. A dope supplier is involved.

_____. *Think Wild.* Holt, 1968. Ted, 17, is having trouble understanding his parents and they don't understand him. A generation gap story about cars, parents rule, money and understanding.

Madison, Winifred. *Bird on the Wing.* Little, 1974. Elizabeth, full of anger and resentment, runs away from her stepmother and meets Maija under whose influence she transforms into an artist and begins to understand herself and others.

_____. *Genessee Queen.* Delacorte, 1977. When their volatile mother decides to leave their father, Monica and her sister reluctantly accompany her to a small island off the coast of Canada.

_____. *Growing Up in a Hurry.* Little, 1973. Karen is shy and lonely. She meets Steve and is happy for the first time; she feels wanted. Then she gets pregnant.

_____. *Maria Luisa.* Lippincott, 1971. Maria Luisa is new in San Francisco; she is staying with relatives until her mother gets well. She experiences her first prejudice treatment.

_____. *Party That Lasted All Summer.* Little, 1976. Tamara and her cousins are spending a summer by the sea. She meets a girl who was once a princess. But then she learns a secret about her dead father and the identity of the princess.

Madlee, Dorothy. *Miss Lindlow's Leopard.* Norton, 1965. Jean works in a zoo and befriends a leopard. The leopard escapes and Jean lures him back to his cage.

Magorian, Michelle. *Back Home.* Harper, 1984. Rusty lived in America during World War II and now was back in England where she was so different she had no friends and broke unknown rules. One day she decided to run away.

_____. *Good Night, Mr. Tom.* Harper, 1981. Willie is sent from London to the country during World War II. Tom doesn't really want him but they become close and Tom doesn't want Willie to leave when his abusive mother sends for him.

Maguire, Gregory. *Daughter of the Moon.* Farrar, 1980. Erikka, 12, steps into a picture and forms a friendship on the other side. This helps her solve some of her pressing problems.

_____. *Lightning Time*. Farrar, 1978. Dan and Carrie are trying to save Dan's grandmother's land from a developer. As they explore the land they find magic spirits, talking animals and a mysterious light. Are Carrie and Gran the same person?

_____. *Lights on the Lake*. Farrar, 1981. Daniel is living in his late grandmother's house. He dreams of a big blackbird and worries about Nikos, the poet, who is close to the church he feels akin to.

Maher, Ramona. *Abracadabra Mystery*. Dodd, 1961. Janet is going to get a stepbrother and -sister, Ted and Torrey. Together they untangle the mystery of the missing alphabet.

_____. *Their Shining Hour*. Day, 1960. Story of the Alamo told from the point of view of Susanne, 18. A blood curdling tale of the attack.

Mahy, Margaret. *Blood and Thunder Adventure on Hurricane Peak*. McElderry, 1989. The students of Unexpected School on Hurricane Peak foil the wicked Sir Quincy and solve several mysteries.

_____. *Catalogue of the Universe*. Macmillan, 1986. Angela and Tycho love each other. But he plays the role of best friend. In that role he urges her not to look for her father who abandoned her before she was born.

_____. *Changeover*. Atheneum, 1984. Laura knows that her little brother is possessed by an evil wizard. She enters the occult world of witches to get the necessary power.

_____. *Haunting*. Atheneum, 1982. Barney has ESP. He had a great-uncle who also had ESP. So the message that "Barney is dead" that Barney is receiving does not refer to him but to great-uncle Barney.

_____. *Tricksters*. McElderry, 1987. Harry, 17, becomes suspicious of the three handsome strangers that appear at the beach during the Christmas holidays in New Zealand.

Major, Kevin. *Dear Bruce Springsteen*. Delacorte, 1987. Terry writes to his favorite rock star about his own musical ambitions, his problems with his family, his lack of luck with the girls and his desire to buy a guitar.

_____. *Far from Shore*. Delacorte, 1966. Chris, 16, blames his small town and his parents for his problems. But Chris comes to realize it's his own behavior and his reluctance to accept responsibility for his actions that is the problem.

_____. *Hold Fast*. Delacorte, 1980. Michael and his brother are separated after their parents are killed in an accident. Michael and his cousin Curtis run away to Michael's grandfather's.

_____. *Thirty-Six Exposures*. Delacorte, 1984. Lorne takes many pictures for a class project and what he finds is himself.

Majors, G. *Who Would Want to Kill Hallie Pankey's Cat?* Hastings, 1981. Hallie's cat, Sake,

has a threatening note attached to his neck. Then another note that the cat will be poisoned. She and her friends look for clues and the note writer.

Malcom, Johanna. *Terrible Tryouts*. Scholastic, 1989. Five girls who don't want to, are required to take ballet lessons.

Malmgren, Dallin. *Whole Nine Yards*. Delacorte, 1986. Storm is a high school boy who drinks, parties and runs wild. He loses his girl because of it and everyone loses because of the drinking.

Malone, Mary. *Here's Howie*. Dodd, 1962. Howie has many misadventures in trying to be helpful. He wants to get his way by being good but his plans backfire more often than not.

_____. *Three Wishes for Sarah*. Dodd, 1961. Sarah lives in the slums and fears moving. It is the time of the Great Depression. She has three wishes for herself and her family.

Maloney, Ray. *Impact Zone*. Delacorte, 1986. Jim runs away from his unliked stepfather to join his real father in Hawaii. He loves the surfing and remembers his father as a hip surfer and photographer. But nothing is perfect.

Malot, Hector. *Foundling*. Harmony, 1986. A foundling is sold to a circus at age 8. He has many different experiences before he finds a real home.

Manes, Stephen. *Chicken Trek: Third Strange Thing That Happened to Noodleman*. Dutton, 1987. 211 chicken franchises! And a mad scientist? Oscar is really into it now. Cousin Prechtwinkle turned a picklemobile into a Rem Dem to disappear and re-appear at will.

_____. *Great Gerbil Roundup*. Harcourt, 1988. Tourists come by the hundreds to see the Great Gerbil Roundup in Gerbil town.

_____. *Hooples' Haunted House*. Delacorte, 1981. Alvin offers his garage as a substitute haunted house. He fusses about his Halloween costume, the garage cleaning crew and his pesty sister. But the evening of spooks and scares comes off okay.

_____. *Hooples on the Highway*. Coward, 1978. Alvin is headed for Philadelphia but car problems and travel setbacks keep him short of his destination. This is a humorous tale of the "joys of motoring."

_____. *I'll Live*. Avon, 1982. Dylan's dad is dying and his life is going to change. He falls in love with one of the nurses at the hospital and copes with happiness and pain at the same time.

_____. *It's New! It's Improved! It's Terrible!* Bantam, 1989. Arnold and his friends are being bombarded by a boy (who is an alien from space) who talks about nothing but TV commercials.

_____. *Oscar J. Noodleman's Television Network*. Dutton, 1984. When Oscar gets a home video recorder, a mystery begins.

_____. *Slim Down Camp*. Houghton, 1981. Sam is sarcastic, hostile and overweight. He goes to camp to lose weight and hates it. He meets

Belinda who runs away. He stays because of poison ivy. They meet later and devise a way to lose weight.

_____. *That Game from Outer Space.* Dutton, 1983. Oscar finds himself involved in an unusual adventure with aliens from outer space. A video game to end all video games. These aliens need their rocket repaired.

_____. *To Be a Perfect Person in Just Three Days.* Houghton, 1982. Milo gets a book from the library he wants to use to change his life.

Mango, Kain. *Somewhere Green.* Four Winds, 1987. Three children, left with a housekeeper who quits, live alone. Bryony, 11, is in control and has a romance with the boy next door. They also take in a stray dog.

Mann, Peggy. *My Dad Lives in a Downtown Hotel.* Doubleday, 1973. Joey, 10, goes through the trauma of his parents' divorce. He gradually makes the adjustment and there is some hope for a happy life.

_____. *Street of the Flower Boxes.* Coward, 1966. Carlos and his friends set about making their block of run-down houses nicer by selling window boxes.

_____. *There Are Two Kinds of Terrible.* Doubleday, 1977. Bob's mother is very ill with cancer and he is saddened. Then she dies and he is distraught. But he pulls himself together.

_____. *When Carlos Closed the Street.* Coward, 1969. Carlos's gang and Jimmy's gang had territorial lines that nobody crossed. One day Carlos crossed it and was challenged to a game of stickball. They closed off the street and caused a traffic tie-up.

Manning, Rosemary. *Arrepay.* Farrar, 1964. Adam lives in England in the early 15th century. He fights in the Hundred Years War, escapes death, and decides to lead a more peaceful life.

_____. *Dragon in Danger.* Doubleday, 1960. R. Dragon visits Susan in her home town and charms the people there.

_____. *Dragon's Quest.* Doubleday, 1962. R. Dragon wins his knighthood in the court of King Arthur. He is tested for patience and control; he overcomes a witch and makes good friends.

_____. *Green Smoke.* Doubleday, 1958. Susan makes friends with a dragon. He takes her for rides and tells her stories of King Arthur's day. He also teaches her dragon charming songs.

Mannix, Daniel. *Healer.* Dutton, 1971. A young boy is sent to live with his Amish uncle. He learns that his uncle knows witchcraft. He is badly hurt trying to save some animals.

_____. *Outcasts.* Dutton, 1965. Dana, 12, was glad to leave the rough city where he was bullied and go to live in the country. He tamed a family of skunks.

Manniz, Darrel. *Secret of the Elm.* Crowell, 1975. Alice, the oldest sister and beautiful, tries to help her sister who is a tomboy get interested in horses. Mary Ellen is also interested in horses.

Mantle, Winifred. *Chateau Holiday.* Holt, 1964. Julia and Norman become friends with Danielle and Michael. Danielle "disappears" from a haunted chateau and Julia and Norman and their pet donkey go to find her.

_____. *Hiding Place.* Holt, 1962. Jan hides robbery evidence that will hurt his uncle's assistant. But he tells friends and relatives. They tell their friends and relatives. He even tells a cat!

_____. *Penderel Puzzle.* Holt, 1966. Nan, Henry and James move into an old house. But Robin and Aldick say they live there and they have a house guest, Lik, a Thai princess. Lik is kidnapped and the adventure begins.

_____. *Question of the Painted Cave.* Holt, 1965. Julie goes to France and becomes involved in cave exploration. There is an old manor house with a not-so-nice young man. The caves are covered with prehistoric paintings.

_____. *Tinker's Castle.* Holt, 1964. Norman and Julie stay at Tinker's Castle Lodge while their parents are away. They meet Philip and his monkey, Simeon. They all help find a missing goblet with ancestral importance.

Marcus, Katherine. *Devil's Workshop.* Abingdon, 1979. In 1450 Germany Johann becomes a printer's apprentice. But the kind of printing that is being done is strange and people are suspicious. The printer is J. Gutenberg.

Marek, Margot. *Matt's Crusade.* Four Winds, 1988. Matt wants to play baseball and makes the team. He wants to protest a nuclear weapons plant. He will lose his space on the team if he doesn't come to practice.

Marger, Mary Ann. *Winner at the Dub Dub Club.* Nelson, 1979. Gary saves his money to become a member of a club where he can take tennis lessons. He gets to be good and beats Hal, the then champion.

Marino, Jan. *Eighty-Eight Steps to September.* Little, 1989. Amy and her brother, Robbie, forget their petty problems when Robbie finds out he has leukemia.

Mark, Jan. *Handles.* Macmillan, 1985. Erica loves motorcycles unlike most girls she knows. She finds a motorcycle repair shop while on summer vacation and is delighted.

_____. *Thunder and Lightnings.* Crowell, 1979. Victor likes airplanes but is withdrawn and a loner. Andrew befriends him and helps build his self-confidence. Victor's family is cold and conventional while Andrew's is warm and casual.

_____. *Trouble Half-Way.* Atheneum, 1985. Amy and her new stepfather drive through England and get acquainted with each other and the country.

_____. *Under the Autumn Garden.* Crowell, 1977. Matt is interested in local history and digs for relics. He falls behind in his school work and fights with Paul, who is also looking for relics. But he does find a ring belonging to Sir Oliver, village ghost.

Marko, Katherine. *Away to Fundy Bay.*
Walker, 1985. Doone, 13, leaves Nova Scotia to
join the American rebel forces fighting England.

Marney, Dean. *Computer That Ate My
Brother.* Houghton, 1985. Harry's computer talks
to him but when it zaps his unbearable brother,
Roger, Harry is worried. The computer wants to
be returned to its former owner. Both the computer and Roger are returned.

———. *Just Good Friends.* Addison, 1982.
Brad, 13, has two problems. His friends are girls
and he must shower with his class and is teased by
some of the boys.

Marsden, John. *So Much to Tell You.* Little,
1989. Marina, 14, is unable to speak. She goes to
a specialist where she is helped by love and understanding.

Marshall, Catherine. *Julie.* McGraw, 1984.
Julie and her father ran a local paper. Julie
wanted to be a writer. But rains came and the
town was flooding. Julie went for coffee and sand-
wiches and wasn't sure she could get back. Would
the dam hold?

Martel, Suzanne. *City Under Ground.* Viking,
1964. After the Earth is destroyed a young boy
leaves his underground city and finds that some
people actually survived and are living above
ground.

Martin, Ann. *Bummer Summer.* Holiday,
1983. Kammie's dad is getting remarried. She goes
to camp while the new wife and two kids settle in.
After the usual camp and sibling rivalry all ends
well.

———. *Inside Out.* Holiday, 1984. Jonno's
life is complicated by a sister and an autistic
brother.

———. *Just a Summer Romance.* Holiday,
1987. Melanie meets her first boyfriend, Justin.
He insists on the romance being only a summer
one. She finds later that he is a teen TV personality and that he really likes her.

———. *Kristy's Great Idea.* Scholastic, 1986.
Kristy and her friends decide to raise money by
opening a babysitting service. It is not as easy as
they thought.

———. *Me and Katie (The Pest).* Holiday,
1985. Wendy wants to be better than her younger
sister, Katie, and finally thinks she's made it with
horseback riding until her sister starts to take
lessons.

———. *Missing Since Monday.* Holiday,
1986. Courtney, 4, never came home from school.
Her stepsister and brother, Maggie and Mike,
were responsible for seeing she got to pre-school
and home. Did her real mother take her? Who is
calling on the phone?

———. *Slam Book.* Holiday, 1987. Anna
passes her slam book around hoping it will bring
her popularity. But it backfires and no longer
brings laughs.

———. *Stage Fright.* Holiday, 1984. Sara
must perform in a class play. She is painfully shy

and doesn't want to. She does participate and
makes a new friend.

———. *Ten Kids, No Pets.* Holiday, 1988.
The Rosso family have ten children, plus two
parents. They all move into a 100-year-old farmhouse because finding a place to live is not easy.

———. *With You and Without You.* Holiday, 1986. Liza's father has a serious heart
disease. They had a really great last Christmas.
Liza later feels guilty about enjoying it. She
recovers and finds a friend in a boy she met.

Martin, Graham. *Catchfire.* Houghton, 1982.
Hoodwill has lost his shadow. The shadow
becomes the monster Erebor. The Earth Dragon
swallows Erebor. Catchfire is united with her twin
and she and King Ewan are betrothed.

———. *Giftwish.* Houghton, 1978. A fantasy fraught with wizards, magical beasts and
Ewan. Caperstaff, the sword Giftwish and Catchfire, a witch, are the good elements that help
Feydom out of evil.

Martini, Teri. *Mystery of the Woman in the
Mirror.* Weston, 1973. Jessica is "possessed" by
the spirit of her dead mother. Althea sees the
ghost of Jessica's mother in the mirror.

Maruki, Toshi. *Hiroshima No Pika.* Lothrop,
1982. Mii survives the atomic blast but is physically and emotionally damaged.

Marzollo, Jean. *Halfway Down Paddy Lane.*
Dial, 1981. Kate moved to an old house with her
parents. When she awoke she was Kate O'Hara,
daughter of an immigrant, working for pennies a
day in the town's mill. It was 1850!

Masefield, John. *Box of Delights.* Dell, 1984. A
young version of the story about a boy pitted
against the forces of evil.

Mason, Anne. *Stolen Law.* Harper, 1986. Kira
was an Earth E-comm. Ertex hated Earth E-
comms. He made Kira's life miserable. She was
determined to find out why. It was an incident
that happened to Ertex and his partner years
earlier.

Masterman-Smith, Virginia. *Treasure Trap.*
Four Winds, 1979. An old man disappears and a
frantic search for a treasure begins.

Matas, Carol. *Lisa War.* Scribner, 1989. Lisa,
12, joins the resistance movement in Denmark.
She is able to escape to Sweden even though she
is a Jew.

Matheson. *Bid Time Return.* Ballantine, 1976.
Richard wishes himself back to 1896 where he can
meet Elise, an actress of that time.

Mathieson, Theodore. *Island in the Sand.*
Bobbs, 1964. Jace, 17, runs away from a cruel uncle. He makes friends with Indians, plants a
garden and builds a cabin. He also pans for gold.

Mathis, Sharon. *Hundred Penny Box.* Viking,
1975. Michael's great-great aunt, Aunt Dew, lives
with him and his parents. She tells him stories
about each year included in her penny box. She
chooses a penny at random and tells what happened that year. A good generation gap story.

_____. *Listen for the Fig Tree*. Viking, 1974. Muffin is blind and her mother is an alcoholic; her father is dead. She is helped by some neighbors. She especially wants to go to a Christmas party. Her mother says she can't go anywhere!

_____. *Sidewalk Story*. Viking, 1971. Lilly Etta's friend, Tanya, was being evicted along with her six brothers and sisters. Lilly Etta cared and for the sake of friendship was going to try to help.

_____. *Teacup Full of Roses*. Viking, 1972. Paul is an artist who takes drugs, Davey is bright and strong, and Joey is just Joey. They are brothers whose father can't work and whose mother works too hard. Paul is on drugs again and life looks bleak.

Matthews, Ann. *Journey of Natty Gann*. Pocket, 1985. Natty is looking for her father. It is Depression time and jobs are hard to get so her father goes west to a lumberyard. He said he would send for Natty but she can't wait.

_____. *Starring Punky Brewster*. Pocket, 1987. Punky puts on a school play and learns that being a star has many meanings.

Matthews, Ellen. *Debugging Rover*. Dodd, 1985. Justin and Elizabeth live with "Rover," a sophisticated computer system.

_____. *Trouble with Leslie*. Westminster, 1979. Eric must mind his kid sister after school because his mother must go back to college for a year. It is not the best year of his life.

Matthews, Greg. *Further Adventures of Huckleberry Finn*. Crown, 1983. Same time, same place, same characters but Huck is being framed for murder. He and black friend Jim head for the California gold fields.

Matthias, Virginia. *Big Bending Tree*. Watts, 1960. Susy meets Joline who can't read but can cook and do other wonderful things. A friendship grows in Spruce Pine Mountain.

Mattson, Olle. *Mickel and the Lost Ship*. Watts, 1960. In 1890 Mickel lived with his grandmother and waited for the seven year absence of his father to end so the cold and hunger would end. He lived in Sweden and had a dog.

_____. *Mickel Seafarer*. Watts, 1962. After strange happenings in his village: disappearances and thefts, Mickel goes to sea in his own boat, a surprise from his father.

Maule, Tex. *Championship Quarterback*. McKay, 1963. Brad plays professional football and must choose between loyalty to his club or loyalty to his best friend.

_____. *Cornerback*. McKay, 1967. Sandy plays for the Los Angeles Rams and so does Dick Jones. Both are apprehensive of the younger players' potential to replace them.

_____. *Last Out*. McKay, 1964. Jim Beatty is in his third year of baseball. Will the knee he hurt last year heal well? He plays with this disability.

_____. *Quarterback*. McKay, 1962. A player's first year as a starting quarterback for the Los Angeles Rams.

Mauser, Patricia. *Bundle of Sticks*. Atheneum, 1982. Boyd kicks Ben's dog so Ben, who has had martial arts training, attacks Boyd while the whole school watches. Ben no longer has troubles with bullies.

_____. *Rip-Off*. Atheneum, 1985. Ginger changes schools unwillingly. She is caught shoplifting. She is later released but has a mark against her.

Maxwell, Edith. *Just Dial a Number*. Archway, 1971. Cathy finally makes the "in" group. Her boyfriend dares her to make a phone call to a stranger repeating the lines she had in a play! "Someone tried to kill me!" Then terrible things begin to happen.

May, Charles. *Strangers in the Storm*. Abelard, 1972. Rhoda and Adilla are alone when a snow storm hits. There is a runaway slave outside and little food inside.

Mayerson, Evelyn. *Coydog*. Scribner, 1981. A wild coyote/dog is taken care of by Kiko, a Greek/American boy.

Mayhar, Ardath. *Lords of the Triple Moon*. Atheneum, 1984. The house of Enthala is destroyed, and all that remains are two small, helpless children.

_____. *Makra Choria*. Atheneum, 1987. Choria and Theoria are sisters with the Gift of Power which can be good or evil. Theoria's power is a curse but Choria is a wise user and can control the Gift.

_____. *Medicine Walk*. Atheneum, 1985. Burr is alone when his father's plane crashes and he is killed. He is thirsty, hungry and tired. He faces snakes and a cougar. He relies on earlier Indian training.

_____. *Runes of the Lyre*. Atheneum, 1982. A magic Lyre is the key to salvation for the people of Hasyih when they are threatened by a group of rebels awakening in a neighboring world.

_____. *Soul Singer of Tyrnos*. Atheneum, 1981. Yeleeve can sing the image of a soul on the wall to see what is there, good or evil. She is from the Tyrnos school for singers. This ability can be misused.

Mayne, William. *Antar and the Eagles*. Delacorte, 1990. A young boy is raised by eagles. He is sent on a mission to rescue a lost egg and save the species of eagles.

_____. *Blue Boat*. Dutton, 1960. Christopher and Hugh are on a "wish boat" on a magic lake. They meet a goblin, talking ravens and a giant.

_____. *Drift*. Delacorte, 1986. Rafe, white, and Twena, Indian, are lost in a snow covered forest. They are pursued by an angry bear. They escape the bear but must still face a hostile environment.

_____. *Earthfasts*. Dutton, 1966. A drummer boy from King Arthur's day appears 200 years later. He finds the world where David lives very strange and terrifying.

————. *Gideon Ahoy.* Delacorte, 1989. Eva's brother, Gideon, is brain damaged and deaf. He gets a job on a canalboat and is hurt. Her life changes after this.

————. *Glass Ball.* Dutton, 1961. Niko and Max find a blue glass ball. They take it up on a hill while they watch for a boat. It rolls away and they have all sorts of adventures as they follow it.

————. *Hill Road.* Dutton, 1969. Sara, Dolly and Andrew are going on a picnic. They encounter Magra from a different time while going up Hill Road.

————. *It.* Morrow, 1977. Alice is clumsy and doing and saying the wrong things. She finds It one day and can't lose it. It is commanding her. It is a murdered witch's ghost. She must set it to rest.

————. *Max's Dream.* Dutton, 1978. When the children choose Max, a cripple, to be king of the dance they must also find a queen. Will it be Katie who secretly likes him? Together they unravel a mystery of Max's past.

————. *Pig in the Middle.* Dutton, 1966. The Pig is a deserted barge. Some boys try to make it seaworthy. They work on it in secret but a fire starts and destroys everything.

————. *Royal Harry.* Dutton, 1972. Harriet inherited a house on a mountain called Hartacre. She didn't want to move but found excitement once she got there.

————. *Underground Alley.* Dutton, 1961. Patty finds an alley leading to a buried street. She wonders if the King's treasure, missing so long ago, could be there.

————. *Whistling Rufus.* Dutton, 1965. Ellen is partners with David on a class project. He says he hears whistling from the woods. They investigate and find an old iron ship.

————. *Year and a Day.* Dutton, 1976. Sara and Rebecca find a boy who cannot speak. They take him home where he is loved. Janey, a witch, says he is a foundling and will be gone "in a year and a day."

Mays, Victor. *Dead Reckoning.* Houghton, 1967. Peter stumbles onto an international spy ring when he finds the old lobsterman dead with a metal cylinder clutched in his hand.

Mazer, Harry. *Cave Under the City.* Crowell, 1986. Two brothers, Tally and Bubber, go underground to hide from the welfare authorities. After a harrowing experience and illness they return home and find their father is back.

————. *Dollar Man.* Delacorte, 1974. Marcus, a fat fourteen-year-old boy, feels that he must find his real father in order to establish his own identity. The confrontation is not what he had imagined.

————. *Girl of His Dreams.* Harper, 1987. Willis meets Sophie when he gets out of school and she helps him train for a track meet. After

some problems he wins a track scholarship and declares his love to Sophie.

————. *Guy Lenny.* Delacorte, 1971. Guy, 12, likes Maureen but she goes with a "tough." His father is about to get married and his mother wants him to come live with her. His solution is to run away.

————. *Hey, Kid! Does She Love Me?* Crowell, 1984. Jeff is jarred by the arrival of Mary Silver, whom he used to like. She has a child but no job. They spend the summer together; he wants to pick up the relationship but each ends up going his or her own way.

————. *I Love You, Stupid.* Crowell, 1981. Marcus is now seventeen and considers himself an adult. He has an old friend, Wendy, and a new friend who becomes a love.

————. *Island Keeper.* Delacorte, 1981. Cleo runs away from summer camp and goes to an island her father owns. She loses her canoe and faces winter alone on the island.

————. *Last Mission.* Dell, 1979. Jack is the only survivor of a plane shot down on its last mission. He was taken prisoner by the Germans and saw things he could hardly imagine. And he was only sixteen.

————. *Snow Bound.* Delacorte, 1973. Two teenagers are caught in an isolated area when a blizzard sets in and they are trapped.

————. *War on Villa Street.* Delacorte, 1978. Willis is a loner because of his alcoholic father. He runs away from bullies and from girls. He is training a mentally handicapped boy to run; this makes him more sociable.

————. *When the Phone Rang.* Scholastic, 1985. The Keller children's parents are killed in a plane crash. They are informed of this by way of a phone call. It changes their lives. Aunt Joan and Uncle Paul come to make things worse.

Mazer, Norma. *A, My Name Is Ami.* Scholastic, 1986. Ami and Mia are best friends even though they are quite different. They depend on each other's talents. Ami's mother moves out and there is a stranger in their kitchen.

————. *After the Rain.* Morrow, 1987. Rachel doesn't like visiting her grandfather every Sunday. Izzy is rude, doesn't seem to like her and is bored with everything. He has cancer and is to die. Rachel looks at him through different eyes.

————. *Downtown.* Morrow, 1984. Pete's parents were political activists who blew up a plant where some people were killed. They are in hiding and the FBI is looking for them. Pete's living with an uncle. He has a big decision to make.

————. *Figure of Speech.* Delacorte, 1975. A story of generation gaps and closures. Everyone seems to want to put grandfather aside. But his grandchild fights for his independence.

————. *Mrs. Fish, Ape, and Me, the Dump Queen.* Dutton, 1980. Mrs. Fish is the school cleaning woman, Ape is an uncle, and the Dump

Queen is Joyce. And the dump is a real city dump.

_____. *Saturday, the Twelfth of October.* Delacorte, 1975. Zan goes back in time to the Stone Age. He stays in the same location: New York City Park.

_____. *Silver.* Morrow, 1988. Sarabeth is new in school. She is poor and is in a wealthy school. She meets Grant and her crowd. Patty tells Sarabeth that her uncle is molesting her.

_____. *Solid Gold Kid.* Delacorte, 1977. A story of the different reaction of each of five teenagers who are kidnapped.

_____. *Someone to Love.* Delacorte, 1983. Nina and Mitch are both lonely in college and decide to live together. They are a comfort to each other and hate to give up one another even though the relationship is frayed.

_____. *Taking Terri Muller.* Morrow, 1983. Terri lives with her father and thinks her mother is dead. She finds some papers that tell her that her mother is alive. She finds her but still chooses to live with her father.

_____. *Three Sisters.* Scholastic, 1986. Karen's feeling towards her older sisters almost ruins the family solidarity.

_____. *Up in Seth's Room.* Delacorte, 1979. Finn and Seth have been going together for a while. They are in love. Seth wants to express his love sexually but Finn isn't sure.

_____. *When We First Met.* Scholastic, 1982. Jennie finds out that the woman, whose drunk driving killed her sister, is the mother of her boyfriend. They meet secretly because of the pressure of both families.

Meader, Stephen. *Buffalo and Beaver.* Harcourt, 1960. Jeff loves to paint. He goes on a rugged trip to the Rockies with his father. When he returns he paints what he saw.

_____. *Muddy Road to Glory.* Harcourt, 1963. A story of Ben of the Twentieth Maine regiment in the Civil War.

_____. *Phantom of the Blockade.* Harcourt, 1962. Anse is aboard the *Gray Witch,* a blockade runner, during the Civil War. He helps the Confederacy and Captain Tracy.

_____. *Snow on Blueberry Mountain.* Harcourt, 1961. A youngster balances school, sports, home chores and his work at the berry farm while working as a ski slope operator. Mort is his enemy who is to be captured.

_____. *Stranger on Big Hickory.* Harcourt, 1964. Skip takes pictures of animals for his 4H project. He and his friend find illegal traps and see mysterious strangers in the woods.

Meadowcroft, Enid. *By Wagon and Flatboat.* Harper, 1938. People traveled west in many ways. The Burd family goes from the east to Ohio by flatboat.

Means, Florence. *It Takes All Kinds.* Houghton, 1964. Florrie struggles with school, thinking herself dumb, unaware she has a learning disabil-ity. Through her efforts her young brother with cerebral palsy is given a chance to go to a special school.

_____. *Our Cup Is Broken.* Houghton, 1969. Sarah is a Hopi Indian. She lives with a white family but must return to her village where her future is bleak.

_____. *Singing Wood.* Houghton, 1937. Dusky and her brother earn their way through college from the profits of their orange grove. They face frost, scale, low prices, etc. Dusky is interested in art and race relations in college.

_____. *Us Maltbys.* Houghton, 1966. M.J. and Sylly's parents take in five foster children, all girls, two of whom are Mexican. The town is upset and against this but the girls are nice and it works out well.

Mearian, Judy. *Someone Slightly Different.* Dial, 1980. Things, indeed, are different when Trevor's grandmother comes to take charge of the household.

_____. *Two Ways About It.* Dial, 1979. Annie wonders what it will be like having her cousin, Lou, spend the summer with her. It turns out to be rewarding.

Mebane, Mary. *Mary.* Viking, 1981. Mary didn't want to be white but she sure wanted what white people had. She didn't want to be a poor black kid all her life. Aunt Jo helped her.

Mehta, Rama. *Ramii, Story of India.* McGraw, 1966. Ramii played hookey from school right before the Diwale festivals and so he missed getting the red and gold mouth organ he had waited for all year.

Meigs, Cornelia. *Mystery at the Red House.* Macmillan, 1961. A mystery where the clues are rhymed messages, an old well, a box of jewels and an unattended birthday party.

Melcher, Marguerite. *Catch of the Season.* Little, 1960. Cherry and Jeff spend the summer on Cherry's boat, *Tuesday.* They see a new family appear and a strange yacht sending signals. They spend the rest of the summer looking for the meaning of this.

Melling, O.R. *Singing Stone.* Viking, 1987. This story is set in 1500 B.C. and is about the Druids and sorcery. Kay is transported back there to find out about the Celtic days and why she dreams of them.

Melnikoff, Pamela. *Star and the Sword.* Crown, 1965. Benedict and Elvira are befriended by Robin Hood. They have an adventure with the Sheriff of Nottingham and then continue on to London to seek their relatives.

Meltzer, M. *Underground Man.* Bradbury, 1972. Josh, 19, helps runaway slaves reach northern states in 1835.

Mendonca, Susan. *Tough Choices.* Dial, 1980. Crystal, 14, decided to live with her mother after the divorce but later goes with her father. She runs away from him but finally decides she must face her problems.

Menuis, Opal. *No Escape.* Nelson, 1979. Colin, 17, tries to find out why his father committed suicide. He finds a poem and his quest leads him into many examples of black magic and satanic groups.

Merrill, Jean. *Pushcart War.* Scott, 1960. A story about the "war" between the pushcart peddlers in New York when the truckers came along. It covers both the economic and personal aspects.

_____. *Toothpaste Millionaire.* Houghton, 1972. Rufus started marketing a product called "toothpaste." Kate tells how it challenges the business community.

Messieres, Nicole. *De Reina the Galgo.* Nelson, 1981. Colette gets a spindly greyhound for a watchdog. The family gets another broken down greyhound as a mate. The female dies of a snake bite but a puppy survives.

Meyer, Carolyn. *Center: From a Troubled Past to a New Life.* Atheneum, 1979. David is in the Center for Disturbed Adolescents. He copes with anger, group therapy and interaction with staff and other patients. He also handles hostile family members who don't understand him.

_____. *Denny's Tapes.* Macmillan, 1987. Denny has a black father and a white mother. His mother remarries a white man and Denny leaves home looking for his black father and grandparents.

_____. *Luck of Texas McCoy.* Atheneum, 1984. Texas's grandfather left her his ranch. Her mother doesn't want to stay there so Texas runs it alone. She has both an unrealistic and a realistic romance.

Meyer, Franklyn. *Me and Caleb.* Follett, 1962. Caleb and Bud are brothers living in the Ozarks. They have humorous adventures and play practical jokes on friends and neighbors.

_____. *Me and Caleb Again.* Follett, 1969. Bud and Caleb tease the town grouch, torment girls, aggravate their sister and annoy their teacher. But when Dad gets sick they help out.

Meyers, Susan. *P.J. Clover, Private Eye and the Case of the Borrowed Baby.* Dutton, 1988. P.J. and Stacy must find a stolen necklace to prove to Butch that they are real detectives. She bets her T-shirt collection that she will solve it. A stolen doll (baby) complicates the case.

_____. *P.J. Clover, Private Eye and the Case of the Halloween Hoot.* Dutton, 1991. P.J. and Stacy clear the school custodian of stealing an antique samovar.

_____. *P.J. Clover, Private Eye and the Case of the Missing Mouse.* Dutton, 1985. P.J. and Stacy are on the trail of a missing mouse bank that belonged to Butch Bigelow, their enemy.

Mian, Mary. *Net to Catch War.* Houghton, 1975. Lynn and Sammy are transported back in time to get a Navaho net that catches and stops war. They are aided by Miss Hartigan and Curly.

_____. *Nip and Tuck War.* Houghton, 1964. Nip is a goatherd and the war is the War of the

Glorious Rescue. Prince Baldo and Princess Cristella are imprisoned and must be rescued. An animal story.

_____. *Take Three Witches.* Houghton, 1971. Sammy and Lynn meet Miss Hartigan and Curly (invisible). Together they stop the mayor from taking land illegally and spraying insecticide that kills birds.

Michaels, Barbara. *Here I Stay.* Congdon, 1983. A strange ghost-like story told by the cat who sees, hears and knows what no one else does. Who weeps? Who calls? Who is under the gravestone "Here I Stay"?

Micklish, Rita. *Sugar Bee.* Delacorte, 1972. Sugar Bee is black and wins a chance to visit a white girl living on a farm. This is a very different life than the one she knows in the city. The girl she visits is blind and they both learn to love.

Miers, Earl. *Pirate Chase.* Holt, 1965. Timmy, 15, is captured by Blackbeard and forced to become a member of his crew.

Miklowitz, Gloria. *After the Bomb.* Scholastic, 1985. Philip just lived through a nuclear explosion. Now he must survive. His father is gone, his mother is hurt and his brother has radiation sickness.

_____. *After the Bomb: Week One.* Scholastic, 1987. 48 hours after Philip experienced a nuclear explosion. He survives the terrible heat, the smell, the dead bodies and the hopeless feeling that all is lost.

_____. *Day the Senior Class Got Married.* Delacorte, 1985. Lori and Garrick are going through a make believe marriage as a class assignment. They plan on getting married after school is out. But now they are not so sure.

_____. *Did You Hear What Happened to Andrea?* Delacorte, 1979. Andrea and Dave hitchhike back from the beach. The driver drops off Dave and then rapes Andrea. Andrea must face the various reactions of family and friends.

_____. *Emerald High Vigilantes.* Delacorte, 1988. A controversial book about students who take the law into their own hands to clean the school of drugs, vandalism and theft. A case of the cure being worse than the disease.

_____. *Good-Bye Tomorrow.* Delacorte, 1987. Alex contracted AIDS through a blood transfusion. He, his sister and his girlfriend, Shannon, must deal with the rumors and publicity this receives.

_____. *Love Bombers.* Delacorte, 1980. The Church of the World is a cult that has lured Jenna's brother, Jeremy. She and his best friend search for him and learn about religious cults as they try to lure them, too.

_____. *Love Story, Take Three.* Delacorte, 1986. Valerie gets a part in a television pilot and her mother has big plans for her future. But Valerie wants to be a normal high school student and go on to college, not make long range commitments to TV.

_____. *Secrets Not Meant to Be Kept*. Delacorte, 1987. Arianne doesn't like being touched "that way." Is it because of her experience while at Preschool? Is this same ugly thing happening to her little sister Becky?

_____. *Suddenly Super Rich*. Bantam, 1989. Danielle's family won 5.3 million dollars in the lottery. First the excitement and then the bickering as the family nearly fall apart before they resolve their problems and values.

_____. *War Between the Classes*. Delacorte, 1985. Amy is Japanese and Adam is a WASP. Both families are against their dating. Then a class project called the Color Game is played where different groups assume different class status. Is Adam changing?

Miles, Betty. *All It Takes Is Practice*. Knopf, 1976. Stuart and his friends watch how the arrival of an interracial family upsets the neighborhood.

_____. *I Would If I Could*. Knopf, 1982. A Depression era story of a girl who visits her grandmother for the summer.

_____. *Just the Beginning*. Knopf, 1976. Cathy has trouble at home because of her mother and at school because she is caught cutting classes. She tries babysitting and working on the school year book and this shows her possibilities.

_____. *Looking On*. Knopf, 1978. A lonely girl is befriended by a couple who move in a nearby trailer. She sees their life as ideal. But is it?

_____. *Maudie and Me and the Dirty Book*. Knopf, 1980. Kate was selected to read to the younger children in school. A book she chose had to do with puppies and the children asked about reproduction. This led to a controversy about free expression.

_____. *Real Me*. Knopf, 1974. Barbara wants to take over her brother's paper route but the company says no. She fights this injustice.

_____. *Secret Life of the Underwear Champ*. Knopf, 1968. Larry is "discovered" and asked to appear in a television commercial. He thinks it's great until he finds out what he is advertising.

_____. *Sink or Swim*. Knopf, 1986. A city boy goes to the country on a Fresh Air Program for two weeks and sees a different world.

_____. *Trouble with Thirteen*. Knopf, 1979. Annie is 12 and doesn't want to face her teen years and the changes it will bring, including the move to New York City.

Miles, Miska. *Aaron's Door*. Little, 1977. Aaron locks himself in his room for two days, and doesn't come out until his new father breaks the door down.

_____. *Annie and the Old One*. Little, 1971. Annie knows that when her mother finishes weaving her rug that her grandmother will die. She tries to postpone this event. But she does not succeed.

_____. *Gertrude's Pocket*. Smith, 1970. Gertrude is from a poor family in Appalachia.

She is teased by someone who gets "poetic justice."

_____. *Wharf Rat*. Little, 1972. A story of rats without human characteristics; just a story of how they survive in their world. They find food, shelter and protection from their enemies, and the everyday threats to their lives.

Miller, Albert. *Silver Chief's Big Game Trail*. Holt, 1961. Mr. Miller writes about Silver Chief after O'Brien's death. This book is about the brutal killing of animals across Canada and the Arctic Circle.

Miller, Alice. *Make Way for Peggy O'Brien*. Lippincott, 1961. Peggy is movie struck. The story takes place in the late 1920's when movies were "hot" but it could be applied to television careers today.

Miller, Frances. *Aren't You the One Who....* Atheneum, 1983. Matt is cleared of the death of his sister and finds a friend in Lieutenant Ryder. He still has to live with his past and tries to hide from the world.

_____. *Truth Trap*. Dutton, 1980. Matt runs away with his deaf sister because his parents have been killed and he doesn't want to go to an orphanage. He lies to protect them both but she is killed and he is blamed.

Miller, Helen. *Blades of Grass*. Doubleday, 1963. Madge lives in Idaho in 1883. She finds changes, surprises, work and fun. She also enters a horse race and beats a man who is disliked by his neighbors.

_____. *Janey and Her Friends*. Doubleday, 1967. Janey lives in poverty during the 1920 and '30 Depression years. She lives in Idaho with her dead mother's family and somehow they will make a go of it.

_____. *Julie*. Doubleday, 1966. Julie and her father move to Idaho as pioneers to start a new life of hard work and responsibility.

_____. *Kirsti*. Doubleday, 1964. Kirsti gets to know her stepmother, learns survival skills and falls in love.

_____. *Ski Fast, Ski Long*. Doubleday, 1960. A story of ski rivalry among teams and the obstacles put in the way of the hero for his disqualification.

Miller, Judi. *Ghost in My Soup*. Bantam, 1985. Scottie moves and is without friends until he meets the ghost that lives in his new house.

Miller, Phyllis. *House of Shadows*. Macmillan, 1984. Three children stay with their great aunt and learn about a family curse.

Miller, Ruth. *City Rose*. McGraw, 1977. A black girl who is orphaned stays with an uncle who lives in the rural South. He was hostile to her being there and she is in danger as a mystery unfolds.

Miller, Shane. *Tristan Dan'l and the King of the Mill*. Rand, 1969. Tristan Dan'l and Simon Tyll team up to have fun and make Simon king of his mill. They find that all play and no work is not an ideal life either.

Milligan, Bruce. *With the Wind, Kevin Dolan.* Corona, 1987. Two brothers, Kevin and Tom, leave Ireland during the famine and sail to America to start a new life in 1830.

Mills, Claudia. *After Fifth Grade, the World.* Macmillan, 1989. Heidi doesn't like her new teacher and tries to change her; doesn't like her disorganized parents and tries to change them; doesn't like her cowardly friend and tries to change her. And so it goes.

————. *All the Living.* Macmillan, 1983. Karla cares about all animals that are killed, accidentally or for food; even eggs and plants are a sign of death. She almost drowns and takes a better look at death.

————. *Boardwalk with Hotel.* Macmillan, 1985. Jessica finds that her family adopted her because they thought they could not have children. Then they had two, a boy and a girl. Do they love her less?

————. *Cally's Enterprise.* Macmillan, 1988. Cally and Chuck sell newspapers. She breaks away from family decisions and makes her own way.

————. *One and Only Cynthia Jane Thornton.* Macmillan, 1986. Cynthia is older than her sister, Lucy, but their mother dresses them alike and Lucy is in some of her classes at school. How can Cynthia become an individual with this lookalike sister around?

————. *Secret Carousel.* Four Winds, 1983. Lindy and Joan live with grandparents. Joan goes to New York to study ballet. Lindy discovers an old carousel, takes part in a school play, tends her garden and is free to choose what to make of her life.

Mills, Donna. *Long Way from Troy.* Viking, 1971. Jeannie is planning to go to college. She falls in love with a "greaser" who drops out of school.

————. *Rules of the Game.* Viking, 1969. Cindy wants to go to art school but goes to college instead. She becomes art editor of a magazine and falls in love with the editor, John. After an auto accident John never tries to see her again.

Millstead, Thomas. *Cave of Moving Shadows.* Dial, 1979. Kimba has artistic talent and a way with animals. He faces danger in hunting in prehistoric times and decides he really can be a leader of his people.

Milne, A.A. *House at Pooh Corner.* Dutton, 1928/1985. A classic story of Robin, Pooh, Tigger and all the others.

————. *Winnie the Pooh.* Dutton, 1926/1988. Christopher Robin joins Pooh and others in adventurous exploits. Each chapter is a different story about the many friends of Robin: Piglet, Eeyor, Kanga, Roo and others.

Milton, Hilary. *Blind Flight.* Watts, 1980. Debbie and her uncle go up for a flight in his small plane. As Debbie has the controls one of a flight of geese flies through the windshield. Her uncle is hurt and she must bring the plane in.

————. *Brats and Mr. Jack.* Beaufort, 1980. Meg and Yancy run away from a foster home. They meet Jack who helps them with a place to stay. They earn money for food. Jack needs help and they go for the police. He later takes custody of them.

————. *Emergency! 10-33 on Channel 11.* Watts, 1977. A distress call is sent over CB radio and brings a rescue crew to a camper that has had an accident on a lonely road.

————. *Escape from High Doon.* Messner, 1984. Moose City is famous for its executions. Each year on the anniversary of their death, the ghosts of the criminals executed come back.

————. *Mayday! Mayday!* Watts, 1979. Two boys survive a plane crash and find their way to safety.

————. *November's Wheel.* Abelard, 1976. Billy Bob wants a bicycle. He sees one he can win with raffle tickets. He works hard for the raffle tickets but doesn't win the bicycle but there is a surprise ending.

————. *Tornado!* Watts, 1983. Paul, Lisa and their mother are stranded by a flood. In the escape Lisa is bitten by a snake and mother has hurt her foot. They are rescued by a helicopter just in time.

Milton, Joyce. *Save the Loonies.* Four Winds, 1983. Jenny and Jared are concerned about the loons on the lake. Nicole and David seem not to care but it is their father that is insensitive to the birds.

Minard, Rosemary. *Long Meg.* Pantheon, 1982. Meg wants to help Henry VIII fight in France so she disguises herself as a boy and joins his army.

Miner, Jane. *Mountain Fear.* Crestwood, 1982. John and Don are on a picnic near their home. John falls off a cliff and is killed. Don is grief stricken until he meets another lonely boy who needs a brother. They help each other overcome fears.

————. *Senior Dreams Can Come True.* Scholastic, 1985. Ellyne and Kip are going steady but Ellyne finds a new love, Kenny. He's blond, charming and not working; neither is Ellyne. Can they work together?

————. *What Will My Friends Say?* Pocket, 1987. Tom is Margaret's mother's 35-year-old boyfriend. He moves in with Margaret and her mother and rumors begin to fly.

Mitchell, Faye. *Every Road Has Two Directions.* Doubleday, 1960. Abby and Maggie are studying to be teachers. Abby chooses a job near her home and boyfriend rather than go to cultural Boston with its sophisticated men.

Mitchison, Naomi. *Friends and Enemies.* Day, 1966. Petrus lives in South Africa and must go away when his brother is arrested by the white police. He goes to Bechuanaland and finds it different from home. It is not a city like home but he is free.

Moe, Barbara. *Ghost Wore Knickers*. Nelson, 1975. Abby goes on an overnight camping trip and makes closer friends with her classmates. There is a rescue from icy waters at the end. And the ghost is a woman who lives alone.

Moeri, Louise. *Downwind*. Dutton, 1984. A story about the possible horrors of a nuclear power plant breakdown. Ephraim's family gets away from a possible leak and they run into other threats just as dangerous.

_____. *First the Egg*. Dutton, 1982. Sarah, a senior, has a class project of taking care of an egg for a week, just as though it was a child. She learns more than the care of an egg.

_____. *Girl Who Lived on the Ferris Wheel*. Dutton, 1979. Til's mother was divorced and severely disciplined Til. She had to keep the house clean. Every Saturday she went to Playland with her father and rode the ferris wheel. One Saturday she came home and....

_____. *Horse for X.Y.Z.* Dutton, 1977. Solveig gets a chance to ride a spirited horse but it turns out to be more than she expected.

_____. *Journey to the Treasure*. Scholastic, 1986. When Victoria's grandfather leaves to find a treasure that is hidden in a remote mountain cave, Victoria follows him.

_____. *Save Queen of Sheba*. Dutton, 1981. King David and his sister Queen of Sheba survive an Indian attack. Tired, hungry and short of patience with a surly baby, King David doggedly goes on to find his parents.

Mohr, Nicholasa. *Felita*. Dial, 1979. Felita is Puerto Rican and has difficulty making friends in her new neighborhood. The Maldonado family move back to their old neighborhood.

_____. *Going Home*. Dial, 1986. Felita is going to spend the summer in Puerto Rico. There are restrictions for young girls both at home and in Puerto Rico but Felita finds friends in both places.

_____. *Nilda*. Arte, 1973. The tenement stoops of El Barrio are ten-year-old Nilda's home grounds. She lives there during World War II and she suffers from being a Puerto Rican in New York at this time.

Molarsky, Osmond. *Montalvo Bay*. Walck, 1976. Ernie wants to save Montalvo Bay from being overbuilt. He gets involved in county politics from candidate selection to vote getting. He learns about bribes and "dirty tricks."

_____. *Scrappy*. Dodd, 1983. Scrappy plays with boys and scorns pretty girls. She doesn't like the new lady coach of her soccer team but because the team is winning she helps her.

Molloy, Anne. *Mystery of the Pilgrim Trading Post*. Hastings, 1964. Lettie, Will and Jonas spend the summer in Maine. They save an old home from demolition, catch a smuggler and find romance.

Monjo, F.N. *Grand Papa and Ellen Aroon*. Holt, 1974. A story about Thomas Jefferson and his warm relationship with his nine-year-old daughter.

_____. *Porcelain Pagoda*. Viking, 1976. Kitty keeps a journal of her trip to China in 1822. She meets young Derk who smuggles opium. She falls in love. Her family will not allow her to see him.

_____. *Prisoners of the Scrambling Dragon*. Holt, 1979. Sam, 13, and his friend Hawk are captured by opium smugglers in early 1800. They barely escape with their lives.

_____. *Willie Jasper's Golden Eagle*. Doubleday, 1976. Willie wins a $10.00 gold piece and a trip down the Mississippi River. There is a race between the *Natchez,* his boat, and the *Robert E. Lee.* He bets ten dollars but loses when his boat runs into problems.

Montgomery, Jean. *Wrath of Coyote*. Morrow, 1968. A conflict between Spanish settlers and California Indians. Chief Main sees the Spanish coming and is interested in their ways but attraction turns to hatred as the Spanish move in.

Montgomery, John. *Foxy*. Watts, 1959. David, an orphan, goes to live in the country with a new foster family. He finds a cub fox in the forest and takes it home and cares for it. He almost loses it in a fox hunt.

_____. *My Friend Foxy*. Watts, 1962. David and the cub fox he found and raised have adventures together. Some are humorous, some mysterious, but all are warm and satisfying. They meet mysterious gypsies and have a humorous teacher encounter.

Montgomery, Lucy. *Anne of Avonlea*. Grosset, 1936/1984. Sixteen-year-old Anne is teaching school, but has not yet matured enough to control her high spirits.

_____. *Anne of Green Gables*. Putnam, 1935/1984. Anne is a skinny girl with red hair and freckles. She is very high spirited and mischievous. This is the first in a long series about a likeable girl and her friends.

_____. *Anne of Ingleside*. Grosset, 1939/1981. Anne and Gilbert have five children. In this story she goes back to Avonlea to visit and recalls all the happy times she had and all the lovely friends she made.

_____. *Anne of the Island*. Grosset, 1915/1986. Anne, now in college, finds romance. She must plan for her future, perhaps away from home. But marriage is pending.

_____. *Anne of Windy Poplars*. Grosset, 1936/1981. Anne gets her first job away from Green Gables and works for the proud and intolerant Pringle family. In Summerside there are both supporters and detractors of this controversial family.

_____. *Anne's House of Dreams*. Grosset, 1917/1981/1989. It is Anne's wedding day. She and Gilbert will be married at Green Gables, outdoors in the orchard. It is an outstanding wedding. Then Anne goes home to her white house.

————. *Chronicles of Avonlea*. Grosset, 1940/1988. This is a book about the people and places on Prince Edward Island. It gives depth to the "Anne" books by the same author by bringing alive the atmosphere of this setting.

————. *Emily Climbs*. Bantam, 1986. Emily wants to be a writer. She leaves home to attend school, and learns of life.

————. *Emily of the New Moon*. Bantam, 1986. Emily, an orphan, moves to New Moon Farm. A story like *Anne of Green Gables*.

————. *Emily's Quest*. Bantam, 1982. Emily is grown up and faces life much in the same vein as *Anne of Green Gables*.

————. *Further Chronicles of Avonlea*. Grosset, 1953/1989. Avonlea is where, Anne, of all the "Anne" books by this author, lived, grew up, went to school, made friends, etc. The people tell their story as it relates to Anne.

————. *Rainbow Valley*. Bantam, 1985. Rainbow Valley is a special place for Anne's children to play. They meet the Meredith children and have lots of wonderful adventures.

————. *Rilla of Ingleside*. Bantam, 1985. Rilla is Anne's youngest daughter. She is fourteen and dreams about her first date and first kiss. But the war comes and Rilla's life, like everyone else's, is changed.

Montgomery, Rutherford. *Golden Stallion and the Mysterious Feud*. Little, 1967. A bitter feud erupts when a family of dirt farmers purchase a piece of land near the property of a long established cattle ranching outfit.

————. *Golden Stallion to the Rescue*. Little, 1954. After a hard winter on Bar L ranch Charlie and his father are visited by Mr. Wharton and Rodney. Mr. Wharton wants Bar L for digging oil and Rodney wants Golden Boy, Charlie's horse.

————. *Golden Stallion's Victory*. Little, 1956. Charlie and his horse, Golden Boy, are in the high country where Golden Boy watches his mares. The new owner of the ranch next to Bar L is usurping Bar L's water rights.

————. *Into the Groove*. Dodd, 1966. Harley wants to become a race driver like his father rather than go to college. He's offered an engineering scholarship and a future job at King Motors. Now what?

Moon, Sheila. *Hunt Down the Prize*. Atheneum, 1971. Maris and her new animal friends have to capture some monsters before the monsters hurt someone, especially on Halloween.

————. *Knee-Deep in Thunder*. Atheneum, 1967. Maris begins a long, hard journey of terrors and beauties when she picks up a stone in a cave. She meets talking animals and befriends beetles, ants, mice, etc.

Mooney, Bel. *Stove Haunting*. Houghton, 1988. Daniel finds an old cookstove in the large house he and his family move into. The stove takes him into the near future where his job is to tend the stove. He sees the difference between farmers and gentry.

Mooney, Elizabeth. *Sandy Shoes Mystery*. Lippincott, 1970. Jon and Emily find a thief who has stolen some jewelry. It looks like Emily's friend is a suspect and they want to clear him.

Moore, Emily. *Just My Luck*. Dutton, 1983. Two children go to find a lost dog belonging to Mrs. Dingle.

————. *Whose Side Are You On?* Farrar, 1988. Barbara fails Math. Her tutor, T.J., and she become friends. T.J. is missing and she tries to find him.

Moore, Ruth. *Mystery of the Lost Treasure*. Herald, 1978. The Howard twins are spending the summer with a horse to ride, new friends and a mystery of lost gold coins hidden in the attic when the farm was used as an underground railway.

————. *Wilderness Journey*. Herald, 1979. James and John's father is lost at sea. Their mother is in Pittsburgh while they are in Philadelphia. They run away from mistreatment and travel to Pittsburgh.

Moore, S.E. *Secret Island*. Four Winds, 1977. John helps Special Agent Gray in uncovering southern sympathizers and recovering stolen gold during the American Civil War.

Mooser, Stephen. *Hitchhiking Vampire*. Delacorte, 1989. Jaime and Luke pick up a hitchhiker. He is going to Las Vegas to gamble. Jaime and Luke take him there, help him win, lose the winning bet ticket and escape from a thief who wants the money.

Morey, Walt. *Angry Waters*. Dutton, 1969. A young boy is placed on parole. He goes to work on a dairy farm in Oregon.

————. *Canyon Winter*. Dutton, 1972. Pete, 15, is stranded after an airplane crash. He finds his way to a cabin and spends the winter with the owner, Omar.

————. *Deep Trouble*. Dutton, 1971. Joey wants to be a sea diver like his father. He is successful but fears statehood for Alaska is going to hurt his way of life.

————. *Gentle Ben*. Dutton, 1965. The warm story of a boy and a bear taking place in Alaska before it became a state.

————. *Gloomy Gus*. Dutton, 1970. Gloomy Gus is a Kodiak bear. Eric found him as a cub and raised him. His father is interested in selling him but Eric won't hear of it.

————. *Home Is the North*. Blue Heron, 1967. Brad and his dog, Mickie, live in rugged Alaska. He trapped wolverines who were raiding the fish traps. He also had to fight off a bear.

————. *Kavik the Wolf Dog*. Dutton, 1968. Kavik was part dog, part wolf. He was sold to a man whose plane crashed. When Andy found the crash the dog was still alive. Andy wanted to save him. But what of the dog's loyalty?

————. *Lemon Meringue Dog*. Dutton,

1980. A narcotics squad dog must prove his worth.

_____. *Runaway Stallion.* Dutton, 1973. Jeff is a "clodhopper" to the kids in the community. But when he searches for the great red stallion he conquers his fears and changes his luck.

_____. *Sandy and the Rock Star.* Dutton, 1979. A young singer and a cougar are on a wilderness island together. They share adventures.

_____. *Scrub Dog of Alaska.* Dutton, 1971. A young puppy is abandoned because he is the runt of the litter and is too small to be of value. But he turns out to be a winner.

_____. *Year of the Black Pony.* Dutton, 1976. A horse story with a boy as owner and lover of the horse. Setting is Oregon rural country in early 1900's.

Morgan, Alison. *All Kinds of Prickles.* Nelson, 1980. Paul lives with his grandfather and has a pet goat. His grandfather dies and he must go live with Aunt Jean. He is afraid he will have to give up his goat, Davy.

_____. *Boy Called Fish.* Harper, 1973. A lonely boy takes in a stray dog.

_____. *Paul's Kite.* Atheneum, 1981. Paul is living with his mother and amuses himself by visiting all of the London place names on his Monopoly board, until a violent accident happens.

Morgan, Geoffrey. *Small Piece of Paradise.* Knopf, 1968. Joe and Mr. Penny fix up a nice garden in a junkyard. Then someone wants to destroy the spot for future development. Joe is determined to save it.

Morgan, Mary. *Rainbow for Susan.* Abelard, 1962. Susan, 12, goes to New York for the summer. Her uncle owns a junk yard and has many animals. She adjusts to school and meets a boy.

Morgenroth, Barbara. *Impossible Charlie.* Atheneum, 1979. A horse, Charlie, thought to be untrainable, is given as a gift to Jackie, a young girl, who indeed finds him almost impossible to train.

_____. *In Real Life, I'm Just Kate.* Atheneum, 1981. Kate is upset. She is going to get into television "soaps" like her father. She meets Fitch and they become friends. She, Fitch and her father reveal a lot about television "soaps."

_____. *Nicki and Wynne.* Atheneum, 1982. Two girls, Nicki and Wynne, one experienced and one not, spend the summer at a stable where they learn more about horses.

_____. *Ride a Proud Horse.* Atheneum, 1978. Corey finds not only riding techniques when she starts to take riding lessons.

_____. *Will the Real Renie Lake Please Stand Up?* Ballantine, 1983. Renie carries a switchblade and uses dope. She goes to a foster home where everyone is on her side for the first time in her life. But one person wants to see her fail!

Morpurgo, Michael. *Little Foxes.* David & Charles, 1987. A magical story of an orphan boy, Billie, and a fox cub he befriends. They enjoy their quiet time together but must remain hidden.

_____. *Mr. Nobody's Eyes.* Viking, 1990. Harry and an escaped circus monkey are both running away.

_____. *Twist of Gold.* David & Charles, 1987. Annie and Sean come to America to look for their father who came to buy land. They are given the family treasure—a golden torc (a twist of gold). They have an adventurous trip meeting many people.

_____. *Why the Whales Came.* Scholastic, 1990. Two youngsters befriend the old man called Birdman of Bryher and help him lift the curse off their island.

Morrell, David. *First Blood.* Fawcett, 1972. A story of the conflicts faced by a returning Vietnam veteran. The memories of death and violence are strong.

Morressy, John. *Drought on Ziax II.* Walker, 1978. The drought on Ziax II is caused by the slaying of the SORK by the Earth Pioneers. It upsets the ecological balance. The remaining SORK are found and protected. This restores the balance of nature.

_____. *Windows of Forever.* Walker, 1976. Thomas's family moves into an inherited house. He discovers a window that takes him to prehistoric past.

Morris, Judy. *Crazies and Sam.* Viking, 1983. Sam hitches a ride with a "crazy" and is held captive for twenty-four hours by a single parent father and a mentally ill woman.

Morris, Winifred. *Dancer in the Mirror.* Atheneum, 1987. A story of Carol and her blood pact friend who plan a double suicide. But Carol decides to take control and save her life.

_____. *Jello-O Syndrome.* Atheneum, 1986. Stephanie, 17, is good at Math and never dates. She meets Keith and begins to like him but her concentration is on intellect, not physical beauty or emotions.

_____. *With Magical Horses to Ride.* Atheneum, 1985. Lizzie goes to a cemetery to dream of a different life. Delathorn appears and introduces Zorauk. She finds out that Delathorn is a kidnapped son of a banker and Zorauk is a painter.

Morrison, Dorothy. *Somebody's Horse.* Atheneum, 1986. Jenny spends the summer in Wyoming where she cares for an abandoned horse, Farfalla. She learns to ride him and learns about the real owner.

_____. *Whisper Goodbye.* Atheneum, 1985. Whisper is Katie's horse and the Goodbye is because the family must move to the city and Whisper can't go. After performing an heroic deed she sells him to a family with children.

Morrison, Lucile. *Mystery of Shadow Walk.* Dodd, 1964. Jinny's father is working for the government on counterfeiters. She explores a mysterious old house with secret passages and a ghost in the attic. She also explores nearby caverns.

Morrison, Toni. *Bluest Eye.* Washington Square, 1970. Pecola, 11, is black and wants blue eyes which she believes will make her beautiful and popular. Later she is raped by her alcoholic father.

Morse, Evangeline. *Brown Rabbit: Her Story.* Follett, 1967. Ceretha's family moves to New York in order to get more advantages. She is black and faces social frictions.

Morton, Jane. *I Am Rubber, You Are Glue.* Beaufort, 1981. Bart's father is running for mayor and he joins the campaign. He gets into several misadventures but reports a burglary and gets headlines for his father.

Moskin, Marietta. *Dream Lake.* Atheneum, 1981. Hilary spends the summer reliving her dream: she is an indentured servant. A similar incident and a near drowning put an end to her dream.

_____. *Waiting for Mama.* Coward, 1975. Would Becky's mother like it in America as she now does? She remembers how she, Rachel and Jake hated it at first.

Mott, Michael. *Blind Cross.* Watts, 1969. A story of the Children's Crusade. Mat joins the Crusade. Alan goes to find his brother and is sold into slavery. When he gets to Rome he finds the Byzantine Cross robbed of its jewels.

_____. *Master Entrick.* Delacorte, 1965. Robert is mysteriously kidnapped and is sold as a servant in America. He faces harshness and hardships in a savage wilderness.

Moulton, Deborah. *First Battle of Morn.* Dial, 1988. Torin runs away from the rulers of Morn where his father breeds winged horses for the rulers. Rebels want to destroy the rulers of Morn and want Torin to fight with them.

Mowat, Farley. *Black Joke.* Little, 1962. Jonathan owns a boat, *Black Joke.* Kye and Peter are crew members. He carries bootleg liquor. The ship is nearly destroyed, Jonathan disappears and Kye and Peter are stranded on an island.

_____. *Curse of the Viking Grave.* Little, 1966. Three boys and a girl in search of Viking relics meet Eskimo and Indian tribes. Awasin, Jamie and Peetyuk learn a great deal about survival in the cold of Northern Canada.

_____. *Dog Who Wouldn't Be.* Little, 1957. Mutt is a very likable dog, and he and his master have fun together.

_____. *Lost in the Barrens.* Little, 1956/1985. Stranded in the Canadian wilderness, a teenager and his Indian friend find that good sense, cooperation and patience can mean survival.

_____. *Owls in the Family.* Little, 1961. The many adventures of a family that adopts two baby owls.

Muehl, Lois. *Hidden Year of Devlin Bates.* Holiday, 1967. Devlin wants to be a loner and plans to run away from home. He resists pressure to "join in." But he becomes aware of the needs of others and changes.

_____. *Worst Room in the School.* Holiday, 1961. Creton's school is overcrowded. Twelve students are trapped in a storage room. A clear story of the hazards of an overcrowded school.

Muir, Lynette. *Unicorn Window.* Abelard, 1961. Anne and Patrick visit Armorie to get the unicorn Anne lost. It is the armorie that has all heraldic animals and symbols.

Mukerji, Dhan. *Gay-Neck.* Dutton, 1927/1968. A story of the bravery of a boy and his carrier pigeon during World War I. Newbery winner, 1928.

Mulcahy, Lucille. *Fire on Big Lonesome.* Elk Grove, 1967. Phillip, 14, is a Zuni Indian boy. He joins a fire fighting crew to put out a forest fire. He proves himself a hero.

Mulford, Philippa. *If It's Not Funny, Why Am I Laughing?* Delacorte, 1982. Mimi's father remarries. Her best friend Trina is having an affair. She wonders if she should. Sex is explored with some tragic results.

_____. *World Is My Eggshell.* Delacorte, 1986. Abbey and Shel are twins. Abbey is shy; Shel is competitive. Dating is explored as well as friendship, jobs and the ups and downs of winning and losing.

Murphy, Barbara. *Ace Hits Rock Bottom.* Delacorte, 1985. Ace gets involved in an arson gang while he is working in the Bronx, the territory of the Piranhas. He finds he does have acting talent and may make more movies.

_____. *Ace Hits the Big Time.* Delacorte, 1981. Ace puts a patch on his sore eye his first day in a new school and is taken for a "tough" and asked to join the Falcons. The rival gang is the Piranhas who kidnap a Falcon that Ace must rescue.

_____. *No Place to Run.* Bradbury, 1977. Billy and a punk "friend" spray paint a drunk. Then Billy runs and wants to get rid of his paint sprayed jacket. He stops talking and stays that way but he is lonely and life goes on whether he talks or not.

_____. *One Another.* Bradbury, 1982. Paul, an exchange student, meets Melissa and it's love at first sight. They both have problems but young love is strong.

Murphy, Charlotte. *Buffalo Grass.* Dial, 1966. Freddy is spoiled. His stagecoach is raided by Indians and he is saved by a guide for a buffalo hunter. He learns to live and work with tough men where money doesn't buy easy living.

Murphy, Jill. *Death Run.* Clarion, 1982. Brian and friends play a prank that causes the death of a fellow student. Detective Wheeler and his daughter investigate and justice prevails. But the tragedy remains.

_____. *Worlds Apart.* Putnam, 1989. Susan

has a father who is an actor in London. She goes in search of him.

_____. *Worst Witch.* Schocken, 1980. Mildred goes to Miss Cackle's Academy for Witches and has a disastrous time.

Murphy, Robert. *Wild Geese Calling.* Dutton, 1966. Danny saw a gander shot and wounded. He nursed it during the winter and when spring came, even though a friendship developed, he had to let the bird go.

Murphy, Shirley. *Castle of Hape.* Atheneum, 1980. Ramad searches for Luff Eresi because he needs their help in ridding Ere of the negative powers of Hape, the evil monster. They can cloud the minds of the Seers of Carriol: half men, half horses.

_____. *Caves of Fire and Ice.* Atheneum, 1980. With the help of the wolves, Skeelie and Ramad aid Ere. Ramad is separated from his friend Telien, as she fulfills a fate of her own.

_____. *Dragonbards.* Harper, 1988. Prince Tebriel and his friends fight against the Dark Raider that threatens them. He must go through the Castle of Doors and face what he might find there.

_____. *Flight of the Fox.* Atheneum, 1978. Rory, a kangaroo rat, restores a model of a Fairey Fox airplane and thereby foils a flock of starlings that are overrunning the town.

_____. *Ivory Lyre.* Harper, 1987. With the help of four dragons Tebriel and Kiri rise against the Dark Raiders and locate the magical Ivory Lyre. But not before they are captured and tortured.

_____. *Medallion of the Black Hound.* Harper, 1989. The power of Medallion of the Black Hound brings David into a world called Meryn where he must join in the battle of good against evil.

_____. *Nightpool.* Harper, 1985. Tebriel is injured in battle with the Dark Raiders of Tirror. He is healed by talking otters and sets out to fight again.

_____. *Ring of Fire.* Atheneum, 1977. Because of their occult powers Thorn and Zephy of Ere know about death and the future but a greater evil appears. They must rescue others like themselves from the oppressor of Burgdeeth.

_____. *Sand Ponies.* Viking, 1967. Karen and Tom were heading north after their parents died and the ranch and horses were gone. They came to the sea where the Sand Ponies run. There they found friends and love.

_____. *Silver Woven in My Hair.* Atheneum, 1977. Thursey was a "Cinderella" of her day. And there was a ball and she wanted to go. No fairy godmother but a goatherd named Gillie.

_____. *Wolf Bell.* Atheneum, 1979. With the help of wolves, Jerthon and Ramad search for the Runestone to save their planet, Ere.

Murray, Marguerite. *Like Seabirds Flying Home.* Atheneum, 1988. Vernon, Caroline and Shelly live in cold, fog-bound Nova Scotia. Shelly doesn't like it and her mother is querulous. But she meets a boy and finds a life of her own.

_____. *Odin's Eye.* Atheneum, 1987. Cicely and Geoff play detective when they find the logbook of an old man. They observe packages dropped from a plane, a docked boat and a frogman.

_____. *Sea Bears.* Atheneum, 1984. Who is stealing science secrets from an underseas military project? Leanine and her brother with the help of the two rocks "sea bears" break up the spy ring.

Murray, Michele. *Crystal Nights.* Seabury, 1973. The Josephs cope with relatives who are refugees from Nazi Germany. Elly, 15, lives in a small town in 1938–39 and is trying to hold on.

_____. *Nellie Cameron.* Seabury, 1971. Nellie couldn't read and should have been able to. Then Miss Lacey came to teach and she had hope. She also had strong family support.

Murrow, Liza. *Fire in Her Heart.* Holiday, 1989. Molly finds out about her dead geologist mother through letters, photographs and stories. She travels to the place of the accident and pieces together the whole story.

_____. *West Against the Wind.* Holiday, 1987. Abby, 14, is going to California by wagon train with her pregnant Aunt Emma, 18. A woman's account of such a journey. Abby saves the family, gets a boyfriend and gets her wish to be reunited with her father.

Musgrave, Florence. *Oh, Sarah.* Ariel, 1953. Sarah is an unusual child. She steals money from the Missionary Fund for candy and then regrets it. But she helps when disaster comes and she gets the bicycle she has worked for.

_____. *Sarah Hastings.* Hastings, 1960. Sarah, 15, befriends a German family at the start of World War II. She gets her first boyfriend, takes piano lessons and is in a singing contest.

Myers, Bernice. *Sidney Bella and the Glass Sneaker.* Macmillan, 1985. Sidney wants to be a football hero but needs help. He gets it from his fairy godfather. A satire based on Cinderella.

Myers, Walter. *Adventures in Granada.* Penguin, 1985. Ken, Chris and their mother go to Granada. While there they befriend a boy who is accused of stealing.

_____. *Crystal.* Viking, 1987. Crystal is pretty and a professional model. She expects to get a part in a new movie that is being planned. But she is also sixteen and a high school student. Can she be both?

_____. *Fast Sam, Cool Clyde and Stuff.* Viking, 1975. Fast Sam always wears sneakers, Cool Clyde is a dancer and Stuff is a short basketball player. They all live on 116th Street. Binky gets his ear bitten during a fight and they all go to jail.

_____. *Hoops.* Delacorte, 1981. Lonnie plays basketball. He and his coach are pressured to throw a game. His coach is stabbed to death and Lonnie learns how rough a world the sports arena can be.

————. *It Ain't All for Nothin'.* Viking, 1978. Tippy lives with his grandmother. His father deserted him when his mother died. His grandmother gets ill and he must live with his drinking, drug using, crooked father. Is there hope for the future?

————. *Legend of Tarik.* Viking, 1981. Tarik feels compelled to avenge the death of his family by El Muerte. He is told that when he can pour water from hand to hand without spilling it he is ready to start training to get El Muerte.

————. *Me, Mop and the Moondance.* Delacorte, 1988. T.J. and his brother, Moondance, leave the orphanage but they remain friends with Mop. Mop wants to be adopted and play baseball with T.J. and Moondance even if she is a girl.

————. *Mojo and the Russians.* Viking, 1977. Dean believes Drusilla has placed a voodoo spell on him, and his gang devises a plan to "unfix" him from the spell. In the process they meet the "Russian Spy."

————. *Motown and Didi.* Viking, 1984. Two black teenagers live in Harlem. They work hard to cope with a difficult life.

————. *Nicholas Factor.* Viking, 1983. Gerald joins a conservative group in college. He and his friends become suspicious of their aims and leave the group. They are pursued by the group leaders, who turn out to be criminals.

————. *Tales of a Dead King.* Morrow, 1983. A mystery with a dead snake, a dagger and a missing treasure. There is also a missing archeologist.

————. *Won't Know Till I Get There.* Viking, 1982. A young teenager spends his summer working in a home for the aged.

————. *Young Landlords.* Viking, 1979. Paul and his friends get a slum building to fix up and make money. Paul and Kitty have a romance but all in all a funny story.

Naidoo, Beverly. *Journey to Jo'burg.* Harper, 1986. Naledi and her brother travel from their village to the city to find their working mother because their baby sister is ill.

Namioka, Lensey. *Island of Ogres.* Harper, 1989. Set in medieval Japan, Kajiro, with Zenta and Matsuzo, spies on a commander and reports back to the family. He likes Yuri but fears her rejection when she finds out who he really is.

————. *Samurai and Long-Nosed Devils.* McKay, 1976. Zenta and Matsuzo are samurai without a master. Zenta's friend, Hambei, helps hire them as bodyguards. There the adventure begins.

————. *Valley of the Broken Cherry Trees.* Delacorte, 1980. Someone is damaging the sacred cherry trees and Zenta and Matsuzo become involved in the mystery.

————. *Village of the Vampire Cat.* Delacorte, 1981. When Zenta and Matsuzo return to

the village of their former teacher, they find that it is being terrorized by a mysterious killer.

————. *White Serpent Castle.* McKay, 1976. During the struggle for a warlord's territory, Zenta and Matsuzo, the two samurai, attempt to secure power for the rightful heir.

Namovicz, Gene. *To Talk in Time.* Four Winds, 1987. Luke is unable to talk to strangers; his throat tightens and nothing happens. When a stranger brings a rabid fox to be cured Luke must get out the words that need to be said to save him.

Nash, Mary. *Mrs. Coverlet's Detectives.* Little, 1965. The three Persever children go to New York to find a valuable tortoise shell cat, Nervous, that was reported missing after the cat show.

————. *Mrs. Coverlet's Magicians.* Little, 1961. The housekeeper is away at a bake-off. Toad uses his witchcraft set to get rid of the babysitter.

Nastick, Sharon. *Mr. Radagast Makes an Unexpected Journey.* Harper, 1981. Mr. Radagast, a boring science teacher, tells his class they can make things cease to exist if they think strongly enough. They do and they make Mr. Radagast disappear! Can they bring him back?

Nathanson, Laura. *Trouble with Wednesday.* Putnam, 1986. Becky, 12, was taught to be a passive "lady." She is sexually assaulted by her orthodontist. She is afraid, then angry, and finally acts by telling her teacher.

Naylor, Phyllis. *Agony of Alice.* Atheneum, 1985. Alice is a motherless teenager. Her friends are Pamela and Elizabeth. She wants Miss Cole for a teacher but gets Mrs. Plotkin. At the end she realizes this was for the best.

————. *Alice in Rapture, Sort Of.* Atheneum, 1989. Alice and Patrick are dating and in love. She wonders about the effects of kissing and decides they should be friends. Alice, Elizabeth and Pamela have a secret pact to find a boyfriend.

————. *Beetles, Lightly Toasted.* Atheneum, 1987. Andy tries new food sources on his unsuspecting family and friends.

————. *Bernie and the Bessledorf Ghost.* Atheneum, 1990. Bernie tries to solve the mystery of a troubled young ghost who wanders the halls of the hotel at night.

————. *Bodies in the Bessledorf Hotel.* Atheneum, 1986. Dead bodies appear and disappear mysteriously at the hotel and the manager is about to lose his job because of it. Something must be done.

————. *Eddie, Incorporated.* Macmillan, 1980. Eddie wants to make some money and tries many different things until at last one of them succeeds.

————. *Faces in the Water.* Atheneum, 1981. Daniel spends the summer with his grandmother in York, Pennsylvania, and people and events from York, England, seem to appear, disappear and reappear.

————. *Footprints at the Window.* Atheneum, 1981. Dan and his gypsy friends move among superstitious people and are frightened by the supernatural atmosphere. Dan is a descendant of a Faw gypsy.

———. *How Lazy Can You Get?* Atheneum, 1979. Timothy, Amy and Douglas John have a babysitter named Miss Brasscoat who says "How laxy can you get?" and the children show her. Then she says, "How silly can I get?" and she shows them.

———. *Keeper.* Atheneum, 1986. Nick's father is going mentally downhill but Nick refuses to acknowledge it until it is almost too late.

———. *Mad Gasser of Bessledorf.* Atheneum, 1983. Sam thinks the person who is gassing workers at the plant where some of his family works is living at the hotel his family manages.

———. *Maudie in the Middle.* Macmillan, 1988. Maudie is child three of seven, therefore a true middle child. All she wants is to be first with someone, somewhere.

———. *Night Cry.* Atheneum, 1984. The story of a thirteen-year-old girl who lives alone in the backwoods of Mississippi.

———. *One of the Third Grade Thonkers.* Macmillan, 1988. Jimmy and his friends form a club of "elite machos." But when they are faced with disaster they find out about real bravery.

———. *Shadows on the Wall.* Atheneum, 1980. While in England, Dan feels strange as he approaches some ancient landmarks. He is caught in a time change that takes him back to the time of the Black Death.

———. *Solomon System.* Atheneum, 1983. Ted and Nory have always been a team but family problems make them think about how they relate to one another.

———. *String of Chances.* Atheneum, 1982. Evie's sister loses a newborn baby and Evie is saddened. She questions her faith and her minister father. She comes to understand both as she learns tolerance and forgiveness.

———. *Walking Through the Dark.* Atheneum, 1976. A young girl must make serious adjustments when her family is hit by the Depression.

———. *Witch Herself.* Atheneum, 1978. Lynn and Mouse look into Mrs. Tuggle's past to see if they can prove she is a witch.

———. *Witch Water.* Atheneum, 1977. Lynn knows that Mrs. Tuggle is involved in witchcraft but can't convince anyone of her evil.

———. *Witch's Eye.* Delacorte, 1990. Mrs. Tuggle, the suspected witch neighbor, has died. But her glass eye resurfaces and the Lynn family is again in danger.

———. *Witch's Sister.* Atheneum, 1975. Lynn thinks her sister is learning witchcraft from a neighbor and is convinced on the weekend she and her sister are left in her care.

———. *Year of the Gopher.* Macmillan, 1987. George doesn't follow his parents' plans for college and he wants to see that his sister and

brother aren't forced into it either. He wants all of them to be what they want to be.

Neigoff, Mike. *Free Throw.* Whitman, 1968. D.J. is a black in an integrated school and plays basketball. He snubs friendship but he works it out and learns to be a team player.

———. *Terror on the Ice.* Whitman, 1974. Joshua tries to prove his worth as a goalie.

Nelson, Margaret. *Mystery on a Minus Tide.* Ariel, 1964. Janice, 15, moves from the Midwest to the Pacific coast and learns about oceans and their tides. She also teams up with Dave to solve a mystery.

Nelson, May. *Redbirds Are Flying.* Criterion, 1963. Peter supported the Revolutionary War. He was too young to join the Army but he could help decode secret messages. He had an important one: The Redbirds Are Flying (the British are on the march).

Nelson, Theresa. *Devil Storm.* Watts, 1987. Walter and Alice meet old black Tom who tells them stories. Then their father is trapped by a flood and Tom rescues the family.

———. *Twenty-Five Cent Miracle.* Bradbury, 1986. Elvira lives with her father in a trailer park in Texas. Their understanding of each other is incomplete.

Nelson, O.T. *Girl Who Owned a City.* Lerner, 1975. The plague wiped out everyone but the children under twelve. Lisa and her brother had to steal for food. Gangs were attacking everyone. Lisa formed a city in the high school to be safe from the looters.

Nesbit, Edith. *Deliverers of Their Country.* Picture Books, 1985. St. George was England's great dragon slayer. He was asked how to rid England of the dragon plague.

———. *Five Children and It.* Buccaneer, 1959. Psannead is a sand fairy whom a group of children find. He makes their lives exciting but also confuses them.

———. *New Treasure Seeker.* Coward, 1904/1988. Since they were successful at their own fund raising exploits the Bastable children decided to hunt treasures for others.

———. *Railway Children.* Smith, 1975. When their father disappears, Phyllis, Bobbie and Peter try to find out how and why.

———. *Story of the Treasure Seekers.* Ernest Benn, 1899/1987. The Bastable children can see the family and their house going downhill since the death of their mother. They hold a meeting and decide to raise the needed money.

Neufeld, John. *Edgar Allan.* Phillips, 1968. When Reverend Kickett adopts a black boy his family and his congregation are opposed to it.

———. *Lisa, Bright and Dark.* Phillips, 1969. Lisa is about to lose her mind; her family, her teachers and others refuse to see the symptoms. It is her friends who see the problem but can they help?

———. *Sharelle.* Nal, 1983. Sharelle is pregnant by a boy who marries her sister. She can't get an abortion and her mother is no help. But she has friends like Pat, Kevin and Barney who can and will help.

_____. *Touching*. Phillips, 1970. Harry meets his stepsister, Twink, for the first time. She is a cerebral palsy victim and blind. He tells about his feelings. Then Harry meets Twink's older sister who tells about Twink's feelings.

Neville, Emily. *Berries Goodman*. Harper, 1965. A story of what an adolescent goes through when he moves from an indifferent city to an intimate suburb where prejudicese and other problems rear their ugly heads.

_____. *Garden of Broken Glass*. Delacorte, 1975. Brian's mother is an alcoholic and his older sister is bossy. He makes friends with some black students.

_____. *It's Like This, Cat*. Harper, 1963. Dave rebels against his father as a step in growing up. He roams the neighborhood with his cat (because his father likes dogs). He learns about himself in relation to others. Newbery winner, 1964.

_____. *Seventeenth-Street Gang*. Harper, 1966. Irving moves to a new neighborhood and the kids living there torment, not befriend, him. Eventually they accept him, all but Hollis and she finds out what it's like to be ostracized.

Newell, Eadie. *Trouble Brewing*. Steck-Vaughn, 1968. The Browns were a normal, average family until Mr. Brown decided to make home brew as a protest against the government for its action vis-a-vis prohibition and bootlegging.

Newman, Robert. *Boy Who Could Fly*. Atheneum, 1967. Mak's brother, Joey, was a genius. He could read minds and project thoughts. Their parents were dead and their grandparents didn't notice. But now their aunt and uncle might find out. Then what?

_____. *Case of the Baker Street Irregulars*. Atheneum, 1978. Andrew and his tutor come to London. Mr. Dickinson is kidnapped and Andrew is taken in by a Baker Street family.

_____. *Case of the Etruscan Treasure*. Atheneum, 1983. Sara and Andrew join Inspector Wyatt on a mysterious case while they are all in New York with Andrew's mother. There are a suspicious accident and stolen jewels that are hidden in an Etruscan statuary.

_____. *Case of the Frightened Friend*. Atheneum, 1984. Andrew and Inspector Wyatt have a friend whose father dies mysteriously, whose grandfather is an invalid and whose stepmother acts very suspiciously.

_____. *Case of the Indian Curse*. Atheneum, 1986. Andrew and Sara investigate the illness of their antique dealer friend, Beasley. Could it be the Indian Statue? An Indian cult, the Thuggees, are after information.

_____. *Case of the Murdered Players*. Atheneum, 1985. Andrew and Inspector Wyatt find similarities between a murder in 1890 and ones a few years ago. They fear for Andrew's mother as she and all the other victims were actresses.

_____. *Case of the Somerville Secret*. Atheneum, 1981. Andrew and Sara first know that Lord Somerville's dog has been poisoned and then the caretaker is murdered. Gunn and Severn are prime suspects but did they do it?

_____. *Case of the Threatened King*. Atheneum, 1982. Sara is missing and Andrew must find out why she was abducted, why Maria was taken also and where she is. The visit of the king of Serbia is somehow at the base of all this.

_____. *Case of the Vanishing Corpse*. Atheneum, 1980. Andrew and Sara are involved in a series of jewel robberies, one of the victims being his mother. They suspect an Egyptian priest who lives on the estate next door.

_____. *Case of the Watching Boy*. Atheneum, 1987. Two boys become involved in a kidnapping that is connected with the throne of Rumania.

_____. *Merlin's Mistake*. Atheneum, 1970. Tertius was endowed with knowledge of the future instead of the past. He and David set out on a quest to find a dragon and save King Galleron's kingdom from the Black Knight.

_____. *Night Spell*. Atheneum, 1977. Tad's parents just died and he goes to a New England town for the summer. There he finds an unsolved mystery to take his mind off his personal loss.

_____. *Shattered Stone*. Atheneum, 1975. There are two kingdoms constantly at war. Two youngsters try to bring this fighting to an end.

_____. *Testing of Tertius*. Atheneum, 1973. Tertius and Brian, with Lianor, set out to undo the spell put on Merlin by an evil sorcerer.

Newton, Suzanne. *C/O Arnold's Corners*. Westminster, 1974. Rosalei befriends Raoul, a hippy artist, Jenny, a new mother, and May, a black classmate. This upsets the townspeople because they don't like hippies, women alone with babies, or blacks.

_____. *End to Perfect*. Viking, 1984. Arden and Dorjo have perfect attendance records. Then Dorjo doesn't show up at school, her sister doesn't show up at work and their mother doesn't seem to care.

_____. *I Will Call It Georgie's Blues*. Viking, 1983. Neal and Georgie have a strict Baptist father. Neal likes jazz music and learns to play it well but fears his father's reaction. Georgie is catatonic because of his father's treatment.

_____. *M.V. Sexton Speaking*. Viking, 1981. M.V. is working in a bakery for the summer. She doesn't have any close friends but does her life change after this!

_____. *Place Between*. Viking, 1986. Arden's family must move to a new city and she is determined not to like it. But when she visits her home town it is not as she remembered it. She learns that everything changes, even herself.

Ney, John. *Ox and the Prime-Time Kid.* Pineapple, 1985. Ox, 17, helps another mixed-up kid look for his mother.

————. *Ox Goes North.* Harper, 1973. Ox goes to summer camp in Vermont. He is now fifteen and finds life in the camp not to his liking. He is more used to "life in the fast lane."

————. *Ox, the Story of the Kid at the Top.* Little, 1970. Ox is a very rich boy who lives an unconventional life with his fast swinging parents. His father rents a helicopter to look at cows for Ox's book report. (They looked at steers, not cows.)

————. *Ox Under Pressure.* Lippincott, 1976. Ox, now seventeen, is having some serious thoughts about his future and the past wild life he has led.

Nichols, Ruth. *Marrow of the World.* Atheneum, 1972. Philip and Linda see a ruined castle where there had never been one before. That night they are drawn into another world.

————. *Walk Out of the World.* Atheneum, 1972. Judith and Toby are in a land ruled by wicked Hagerrak. They attempt to overthrow him and restore the rightful king of this magical world.

Nicol, Clive. *White Shaman.* Little, 1979. A young student undergoes a spiritual rebirth as he discovers a mystical kinship with the Inuit people.

Nicole, Christopher. *Operation Destruct.* Holt, 1969. Jonathan is an espionage agent. He investigates a sunken Russian trawler and is nearly drowned. The threat is the poisoning of fish.

————. *Operation Manhunt.* Holt, 1970. Jonathan is assigned to find a Polish general who defected from behind the Iron Curtain before the Russians get to him.

————. *Operation Neptune.* Holt, 1972. Jonathan gets involved with the Irish Republican Army, the Russians and the CIA. Also we see the return of Anna Catelna of *Operation Destruct.*

Niemeyer, M. *Moon Guitar.* Watts, 1969. In San Francisco, a mystery is solved involving a moon guitar and a Chinese roll painting.

Niggli, Josefina. *Miracle for Mexico.* Graphic, 1964. Martin, 13, tells of December 12-15, 1531, and the miracle of the Virgin of Guadalupe. Martin is a Mestizo: Spanish and Mayan.

Nimmo, Jenny. *Snow Spider.* Dutton, 1987. Gwyn gets presents from his grandmother who is a witch. He sees another world in a spider web. He realizes that he is different.

Nixon, Joan. *And Maggie Makes Three.* Harcourt, 1986. Maggie is happy living with her grandmother. She becomes an actress in a school musical, makes good friends and adjusts to her father's marriage to a girl half his age.

————. *Casey and the Great Idea.* Dutton, 1980. Casey is always on the side of equality for women. This time she tries to help a 65-year-old woman get her job back.

————. *Caught in the Act.* Bantam, 1988.

The six Kelly children were placed in adoptive homes in Missouri. There is a book about Frances and Petey and this one is about Mike whose life is not as happy as the other children's.

————. *Dark and Deadly Pool.* Delacorte, 1987. Mary Elizabeth sees "it" in the hotel pool. There is a killer loose in the hotel and Mary Elizabeth is being watched. A wallet is stolen, furniture disappears and two murders take place.

————. *Deadly Game of Magic.* Harcourt, 1983. Teena, Bo, Julian and the narrator are in an old house alone after a nameless couple left them there during a thunderstorm. But they feel they are not really alone. Someone (thing?) else is there.

————. *Family Apart.* Bantam, 1987. Orphans from the East were being sent to the Midwest for adoption and farm work. Although Frances, Megan, Mike, Danny, Peg and Petey were not orphans their mother sent them for a better life.

————. *Ghosts of Now.* Delacorte, 1984. Angie's brother is injured in a hit-and-run accident and Angie is determined to find out who is responsible.

————. *Gift.* Macmillan, 1983. Brian wants to catch a leprechaun. He does and takes it home. But Aunt Nora says it is a large cat!

————. *Haunted Island.* Scholastic, 1987. Chris and Amy solve a mystery that is 200 years old.

————. *High Trail to Danger.* Bantam, 1991. Sarah sets out alone in 1879 to find her father. Her mother has just died and she thinks her aunt and uncle are trying to take their boardinghouse away from her. She has many adventures and close calls.

————. *House on Hackman's Hill.* Scholastic, 1986. Jeff and Debbie find an old haunted house and are trapped in it overnight when a blizzard hits.

————. *In the Face of Danger.* Bantam, 1988. An episode in the lives of the six Kelly (orphan) children. It's mainly about Megan, Danny and Peg but covers the other children, too. Some are happy and satisfied and others are not.

————. *Kidnapping of Christina Lattimore.* Harcourt, 1979. Christina was kidnapped and held for ransom. She tried to escape but couldn't. Her captors took her on a tour of the house. When the police came she was thought to be in on the kidnapping.

————. *Maggie Forevermore.* Harcourt, 1987. Maggie was to spend Christmas with her Grandma and her friends. Instead her father wanted her to come to California with him and his new wife. She didn't want to go but had a surprising good time.

————. *Maggie, Too.* Harcourt, 1985. Margaret is sent to live with her unknown Grandma for the summer. She resents going but finds that the busy family, her active Grandma and neighbor activities make her re-think her decisions.

———. *Other Side of Dark*. Delacorte, 1987. Stacy was in a coma for four years. She is seventeen but thinks and acts thirteen. Her mother was murdered in the same incident in which she was hurt. She knows the face of the killer.

———. *Place to Belong*. Bantam, 1989. This is one book of the Orphan Train Quartet and the six Kelly children. Each book covered one orphan's touching story of the people who adopted them and their adjustment to it.

———. *Seance*. Harcourt, 1980. Sara lives with Lauren's family; after a seance she disappears and is presumed dead. When a second teenager is murdered, Lauren is sure she will be next.

———. *Specter*. Delacorte, 1982. Dina has cancer and is in the hospital. It is in remission but she fears the future. Julie's parents are killed in a strange auto accident. They become friends but Julie is very dependent on Dina.

———. *Stalker*. Delacorte, 1985. Bobbi's mother is murdered and Bobbi is being held as a suspect. She didn't do it but who will believe her? Only her best friend Jennifer and a retired detective, Lucas, trust her.

Noble, Iris. *Megan*. Messner, 1965. Megan comes to Canada from Ireland to work on a ranch in a rugged area. She finds both love and strife among the other immigrants.

———. *Stranger No More*. Messner, 1961. Katherine, 17, wants to belong to the "in" group but does not want to sacrifice her ideals.

Nolan, Lucy. *Secret at Summerhaven*. Atheneum, 1987. Three cousins accidentally film a drug sale and the drug smugglers are after them. Lots of action and lots of humor.

Nordstrom, Ursula. *Secret Language*. Harper, 1960. Vicki and Martha are together at a boarding school. They develop a strong friendship and invent a secret language that only they understand.

Norris, Gunilla. *Lillian*. Atheneum, 1968. Lillian's father left home and everything changed. Mother went to work and Lillian carried her school lunch and ate alone. Now she wonders if her mother will leave, too.

———. *Standing in the Magic*. Dutton, 1974. Brady can find things; he finds a ring with a blue stone. Joel is his friend but Joel's mother forbids the friendship because of "right" and "wrong" kind of people.

North, Joan. *Cloud Forest*. Farrar, 1966. A young girl helps an adopted boy discover his true identity.

North, Sterling. *Rascal*. Dutton, 1984. A story of a young boy and his pet raccoon as they explore nature.

———. *Wolfling*. Dutton, 1969. The story of a young boy who raises a wolf pup.

Norton, Andre. *Android at Arms*. Harcourt, 1971. Andas is in a robot-manned prison. He is freed and escapes in a space ship.

———. *Beast Master*. Harper, 1984. Storm is a brave and powerful person who is capable of murder and is on his way to Azor to kill a man he's never met.

———. *Catseye*. Harper, 1984. Kyger, a pet shop owner, is killed. Troy takes the animals to the wilderness as the only safe place he knows. He can communicate with the animals and they work to save each other.

———. *Crystal Gryphon*. Atheneum, 1972. Kerovan and his bride journey to the farthest reaches of the wilderness to save their people.

———. *Dark Piper*. Harcourt, 1968. Griss from the planet Beltane found that people would not heed his warning of danger. Vere and his friends did and were underground when the explosion killed Griss and sealed them in.

———. *Dragon Magic*. Crowell, 1972. Sig puts together a silver dragon and moves back in time. Ras puts together a blue one and goes to Africa. Artie puts together a red one and goes to Wales. Kim puts together a yellow one and goes to China.

———. *Exiles of the Stars*. Viking, 1971. While on a mission for the Thothan priests, the Free Trader's ship is forced down on a barren planet, seemingly uninhabited, but a preserved alien race is seeking new bodies.

———. *Forerunner Foray*. Viking, 1973. Ziantha contacts a strange, throbbing green stone. She finds herself trapped in the past. She must travel even farther back in order to escape.

———. *Fur Magic*. PB, 1968. Cory is transported back in time and becomes a beaver, Yellow Shell. He must prevent the changer from using his magic.

———. *Gryphon in Glory*. Atheneum, 1984. Kerovan is journeying on a secret mission in the Waste where the evil powers of the Dark threaten at every hand. Joisan, his wife, sets out to look for him.

———. *Gryphon's Eyrie*. Atheneum, 1984. This is the final book of Kerovan and Joisan as they fight and conquer the Dark evil.

———. *House of Shadows*. Atheneum, 1984. Mike, Susan and Tucker are vehicles for revealing hidden family secrets. There are ghosts, cursed children and evil that is put to death.

———. *Ice Crown*. Viking, 1970. Roane tries to help the few people in Clio who can still think for themselves. She wants to break the band that controls them.

———. *Jargoon Pard*. Atheneum, 1974. Kerovan has his birthright tampered with, but he is given a magical belt.

———. *Judgment on Janus*. Harcourt, 1963. Another Norton fantasy about the known and unknown ingredients of other worlds. He meets the Ifts and the great evil that endangers them. Ayyar and his friends will fight that evil.

———. *Key Out of Time*. World, 1963. Ross

and Gordon are sent back 10,000 years to the planet Hawarka.

_____. *Knave of Dreams*. Viking, 1975. Ramsay is marked for death but instead is alive in another's body. He uses this situation to fight the rulers and wins.

_____. *Lavender-Green Magic*. Crowell, 1974. A family living in Boston are drawn into the city's past during the Colonial period.

_____. *Moon of Three Rings*. Viking, 1966. The Free Traders of the future fight to save the galaxy from domination.

_____. *No Night Without Stars*. Atheneum, 1975. Sander is a smith looking for secrets of early workers of metal. Fanye is looking to avenge her people who were kidnapped or killed.

_____. *Octagon Magic*. World, 1967. Lorrie is in a new school. She saves a kitten from boys and runs into Octagon House. She can go back in time through a doll house and learn the history of the house.

_____. *Outside*. Walker, 1974. Kristie and Lew live in the "inside" city protected from the polluted world. They want to learn about the "outside" and escape with the help of a strange rhyming man.

_____. *Postmarked the Stars*. Fawcett, 1969. A story built around the interplanetary mail service.

_____. *Quest Crosstime*. Viking, 1965. Marva and Marfy are separated while traveling to another world. There are giant turtles, red lizards, levitation and precognition.

_____. *Rebel Spurs*. World, 1962. Drew thinks his father is dead, that he was killed during the Civil War. But he finds out that he is still alive and living in the West.

_____. *Red Hart Magic*. Crowell, 1976. Chris and Nan go back in time to the same place but at different time periods. They protect a priest from arrest and save Red Hart from smugglers.

_____. *Ride, Proud Rebel*. World, 1961. Hunt, Drew's father, was a legend in Arizona. He had control of ranches and horses. Drew finds him but does not reveal who he is until he learns more about the man. What he learns is surprising.

_____. *Ride the Green Dragon*. Macmillan, 1985. Tracy and Jared get involved in the mysteries of a circus company when they move into where the circus people once lived.

_____. *Seven Spells to Sunday*. Atheneum, 1979. A magic mailbox is found in a junkyard by two youngsters.

_____. *Star Ka'at*. World, 1976. Two stray cats, Tiro and Mer, communicate with two children, orphan Jim and poor black Elly, tell them they are from another planet and take them there.

_____. *Star Ka'at and the Plant People*. Walker, 1979. Elly and Jim rescue a group of plant people, who produce metal and become deeply involved with the super cat race.

_____. *Star Ka'at and the Winged Warriors*. Walker, 1981. Magical rays cause insects to get larger and larger on the planet where Jim and Elly Mae are staying. They must be controlled before they destroy other colonies.

_____. *Star Ka'at's World*. Walker, 1978. Elly and Jim travel with the cats to their planet and are kept as partial prisoners because they cannot learn ESP. They run away.

_____. *Star Rangers*. Harcourt, 1953. A story of how a security organization fares when a great galactic empire is crumbling. The Earth is forgotten and neglected.

_____. *Steel Magic*. World, 1965. Eric, Greg and Sara are transported back to King Arthur's time to help find the lost magic talisman used against evil that was lost by King Arthur, Merlin and Huon.

_____. *Storm Over Warlock*. World, 1960. Terian conflicts with the Throgs. Lantee, two wolverines and a Scout officer fight the insect derived predators, the Throgs.

_____. *Uncharted Stars*. Viking, 1969. Murdoc continues to search for the Zero Stone, the secret of his legacy, but he first must find the map he needs. He, Jern and Eet, the mutant, look for it.

_____. *Victory on Janus*. Harcourt, 1966. Ayyar and his friend awaken from their long sleep. The evil force has risen again and wants to get rid of the Ifts. The battle takes place in the Waste.

_____. *Year of the Unicorn*. Viking, 1965. Murdoc searches for the Zero Stone seeking the map he needs. It will also clear up Eet's feline origin.

_____. *Zero Stone*. Viking, 1968. Murdoc's Zero Stone ring, which he inherited from his father, has secret powers. It will help Murdoc find out information about Eet, the feline mutant.

Norton, Mary. *Are All the Giants Dead?* Harcourt, 1975. James goes into the fantasy world of princes, giants and witches.

_____. *Bed-Knob and Broomstick*. Harcourt, 1957. Charles, Paul and Carey go on many adventures with a woman who is studying to be a witch. Not all adventures are without danger.

_____. *Borrowers*. Harcourt, 1952/1990. A world where the people are no taller than a pencil. They hide under the floorboards and live on things borrowed from the people who live above them.

_____. *Borrowers Afield*. Harcourt, 1955/1990. The Borrowers escape capture in the house but now have to live in the field where there is constant danger.

_____. *Borrowers Afloat*. Harcourt, 1959/1990. The Borrowers must move again. This time down stream in a teakettle. Pod, Homily and Arrietty have narrow escapes when a flood sweeps them along.

_____. *Borrowers Aloft*. Harcourt, 1961/

1990. This story tells how Pod, Homily and Arrietty plan their escape from the attic of Mr. and Mrs. Platter. They learn about balloons and now live in a rectory.

_____. *Borrowers Avenged*. Harcourt, 1982. The Borrowers set up house in an old rectory. They must avoid being seen by any humans but they need the things humans supply.

_____. *Poor Stainless*. Harcourt, 1971. Homily tells Arrietty about a narrow escape from humans when her cousin, Stainess, was missing and had to be found.

Nostlinger, Christine. *Fly Away Home*. Watts, 1975. Christel struggles to survive in Vienna at the end of World War II. This is not the usual grim war story but does tell of family problems due to bombings and invasion.

_____. *Girl Missing*. Watts, 1976. Because of family instability Erika's sister, Ilsa, runs away with a local playboy. She tries to find her. A tragic story of family instability and psychological stress.

_____. *Konrad*. Watts, 1977. Konrad is a factory made, perfect boy who is given to the wrong woman. When the mistake is discovered the woman wants to reprogram him so that he will be rejected.

_____. *Luke and Angela*. Harcourt, 1981. Luke and Angela are friends. But as Luke grows up he changes and Angela is confused then jealous as he takes up with another girl. When she leaves him he goes back to Angela who comforts him.

_____. *Marrying Off Mother*. Harcourt, 1978. Sue wants a father so she is set to get her mother a husband.

Nourse, Alan. *Raiders from the Rings*. McKay, 1962. Earthmen and Spacemen face total destruction and a man from Mars is in control.

Nye, Peter. *Storm*. Watts, 1982. Mike's prank causes a fire and he runs away. He witnesses a cocaine deal by a friend, Tiger Joe. Then Tiger Joe saves his life while losing his own.

Nye, Robert. *Taliesin*. Hill and Wang, 1967. While stirring a brew for the witches a boy drinks some of it and becomes a poet and magician. He changes form and becomes other beings until he is born Taliesin, Radiant Brow.

O. Henry. *Gift of the Magi*. Creative Education, 1983. A story of sacrifice by a husband for his wife and by her for him.

O'Brien, Andy. *Hockey Wingman*. Norton, 1967. Danny played hockey. He was testing new skates when a blizzard struck. He got lost and was frost bitten. The doctors said he couldn't skate. Danny worked hard and overcame this handicap.

O'Brien, John. *Return of Silver Chief*. Winston, 1943. Jim Thorne of the Mounties and his dog, Silver Chief, look for an escaped Nazi prisoner.

_____. *Royal Road*. Winston, 1951. Mr. McKinnon wants to exploit the timber of Northern Canada. He plans to use Indian labor. Sgt. Thorne is sent to investigate. His horse, Royal Red, and Silver Chief III help uphold the law.

_____. *Silver Chief, Dog of the North*. Winston, 1933. Jim Thorne of the Royal Canadian Mounted Police trains a dog to help him in his work. The dog is Silver Chief and he becomes invaluable to Jim.

_____. *Silver Chief to the Rescue*. Winston, 1937. In the snowbound North a doctor is fighting an epidemic of diphtheria among the natives. Jim Thorne and his dog team, led by Silver Chief, bring the necessary serum just in time.

O'Brien, Robert. *Mrs. Frisby and the Rats of NIMH*. Atheneum, 1971. NIMH is Nat'l Institute of Mental Health, an experimental station. Mrs. Frisby is the fieldmouse mother of an ailing son. The rats tell her about the institute and their experiences. Newbery winner, 1972.

_____. *Silver Crown*. Atheneum, 1968. Ellen finds a crown on her pillow and takes it to the park. While there her house burns and her family disappears. But someone is looking for Ellen and the crown.

_____. *Z for Zachariah*. Collier, 1987. Ann's family died from nuclear radiation over a year ago. She believes she is alone on Earth until she sees a distant campfire.

O'Connor, Jane. *Just Good Friends*. Harper, 1983. Jass's parents are breaking up. Fletcher wants to be more than friends, but Jass loves Twig. Fletcher then dates her friend Laura. All ends well.

_____. *Yours Till Niagara Falls*. Scholastic, 1982. Abby goes off to summer camp reluctantly but finds it to be great fun.

O'Connor, Patricia. *South Swell*. Washburn, 1967. A father learns surfing by helping his 13-year-old daughter, Pat, to learn. He is a 45-year-old man who loves surfing.

O'Daniel, Janet. *Part for Addie*. Houghton, 1974. Addie's father died in a fall in the theatre. She and her sister, Rose Anne, go to their grandfather's. He is ill and they can't see him. There is a plot to kill him and they must abort the attempt.

O'Dell, Scott. *Alexandra*. Fawcett, 1984. Alexandra becomes a sponge diver to bring needed money into the family because of business failings and a handicapped grandfather. The sponges are a hiding place for smugglers of cocaine.

_____. *Amethyst Ring*. Houghton, 1983. Julian witnesses the magnificence of the Incan Empire and its swift and tragic fall. Julian becomes a pearl trader for Pizarro who is robbing the Incas. He eventually returns to Spain in despair.

_____. *Black Pearl*. Houghton, 1967. What does one do with a pearl that is very valuable? In Baja a village lives for finding pearls that are bigger and better than anyone else's. But sometimes that brings trouble.

Black Star, Bright Dawn. Houghton, 1988. Bright Dawn must face the challenge of the Iditarod dog sled race alone when her father is injured.

_____. *Captive.* Houghton, 1979. As part of a Spanish expedition, Julian Escobar sees the enslavement of the Mayans. He is mistaken for the god Kukulcan, returning as predicted.

_____. *Carlota.* Houghton, 1977. Carlota is a brave Mexican girl who fights the United States Army after the Mexican-American War. She wants independence.

_____. *Castle in the Sea.* Houghton, 1983. Lucinda was kept away from anything of the 20th century by her mad and now dead father. She is wealthy but has to learn how to live. Someone is out to harm her and she must learn who it is.

_____. *Child of Fire.* Houghton, 1974. Manuel is a Chicano gang leader out of prison, on parole.

_____. *Dark Canoe.* Houghton, 1968. Nathan, Caleb and Jeremy sail from Nantucket. Jeremy dies mysteriously. Caleb is the victim of a kind of madness in which he believes he is Ahab of *Moby Dick.*

_____. *Feathered Serpent.* Houghton, 1981. Julian sees the coming of Cortes and the capture of Tenochtitlan. He is still thought to be Kukulcan and travels to where the Aztecs live.

_____. *Island of the Blue Dolphins.* Houghton, 1960. The story of how a young girl, Karana, and her brother survived on a stranded island. Her brother is killed by wild dogs and she must survive alone for eighteen years. Newbery winner, 1961.

_____. *King's Fifth.* Houghton, 1966. Esteban, 17, is a map maker for the Spanish explorers. He is accused of murder and withholding the King's Fifth, that is, the King's share. He tells of the suffering looking for Cibola.

_____. *Road to Danietta.* Houghton, 1985. A young girl of 13th century Italy joins the Fifth Crusade to be with her lover, Francis.

_____. *Sarah Bishop.* Houghton, 1980. Sarah is alone during the Revolutionary War. She doesn't join either side. She goes to live alone with the help of an Indian couple. She is declared a witch but is exonerated and stays alone.

_____. *Serpent Never Sleeps.* Houghton, 1987. Serena is determined to be with the man she has loved since a child. She comes to 17th century America and learns the hardships of colonial life.

_____. *Sing Down the Moon.* Houghton, 1976. Bright Morning is a Navaho Indian who participated in the forced march from her home and the capture by the Spanish slavers.

_____. *Spanish Smile.* Houghton, 1982. Lucinda is a prisoner of her father who wants to return California to the Spanish. He is mad but Lucinda doesn't realize it until the 18 crystal coffins are discovered.

_____. *Streams to the River, Rivers to the Sea.* Houghton, 1986. A fictionalized biography of Sacagawea, the Indian girl who went with Lewis and Clark.

_____. *Zia.* Houghton, 1976. Zia is Karana's niece. Karana can't relate to people after her long isolation and prefers to be alone. Zia has problems of her own because of prejudices but Karana teaches her how to cope.

O'Hanlon, Jacklyn. *Fair Game.* Dial, 1977. Denise and her sister get unwanted, unwelcomed and unhealthy attention from their stepfather. Denise is thought to be mentally ill because of her emotional trauma.

O'Meara, Walter. *Sioux Are Coming.* Houghton, 1971. Kawa and his family are getting away from an attack by the Sioux but their canoe is damaged and they must repair it before the Sioux come.

O'Shea, Pat. *Finn MacCool and the Small Men of Deeds.* Holiday, 1987. Finn is the leader of the High King's army and he fights off the Vikings.

_____. *Hounds of the Morrigan.* Holiday, 1986. A young boy finds an old magic book in a bookstore. Then the forces of good and evil battle for it. Pidge releases an evil force and must help Dogda destroy it. The Morrigan changes shape and meddles.

Ofek, Uriel. *Smoke Over Golan.* Harper, 1979. Eitan was to be picked up by a bus that never came. He and a wounded Israeli soldier capture an enemy officer and some important maps. This takes place during the Yom Kippur War of 1973.

Offit, Sidney. *Adventures of Homer Fink.* St. Martin, 1966. A humorous story about school politics and a boy's role in using it to his advantage.

_____. *Boy Who Made a Million.* St. Martin, 1968. Benny, 15, takes over his father's failing grocery business. Willis and Pablo help and soon the store becomes a wholesale warehouse. He becomes a millionaire at 16 and buys his own school.

_____. *What Kind of a Guy Do You Think I Am?* Lippincott, 1977. Ted sees and likes Hilary but he just lost his father and is not ready for the "bad news" his brother tells him Hilary is. But he needs to find out for himself, when he is ready.

Ogan, Margaret. *Choicy.* Funk, 1968. Choicy wants to go to sea like his grandfather. His grandfather buys Ambrose Place and an old 30 foot schooner is there. Choicy rebuilds it and at last *Kathy* is launched.

_____. *Green Galloper.* Funk, 1966. Buster wants to build his own kart but has problems. He learns the difference between winning and being a winner.

_____. *Number One Son.* Funk, 1969. Paddy's father is a fisherman in San Francisco and he wants to win a place aboard the "Macushla." He finds that commercial fishing is hard and dangerous work.

_____. *Raceway Charger.* Westminster, 1974. When personal tragedy strikes, a college freshman reconsiders a career in auto racing.

Ogilvie, Elisabeth. *Becky's Island.* McGraw, 1961. A story of summer fun and romance on Becky's Island.

_____. *Ceiling of Amber.* McGraw, 1964. Clarie, 19, and Brian, 15, take over their father's lobster business when he dies. It is hard work, especially for a girl, and the icy winters bring added problems but they prevail.

_____. *Masquerade at Sea House.* McGraw, 1965. Monica and Martin pose as children of their dead father's best friend and run away to a house in Maine. There they stop some robberies.

_____. *Turn Around Twice.* McGraw, 1962. Someone was trying to scare Burnley's family away. Very strange things were happening but Burnley found romance in the bargain.

Okimoto, Jean. *Jason's Women.* Atlantic, 1986. Jason is 16 and very shy. He does everything he can to be more outgoing. He meets disaster after disaster until Ms. Fillmore helps him through his insecurities.

_____. *Norman Schnurman, Normal Person.* Putnam, 1982. Norman doesn't want to play football. A new friend helps him tell his "jock" father the truth. He quits the team and learns about growing up.

Oldham, Mary. *White Pony.* Hastings, 1981. Barbara is overweight but finds solace in a colt named Bianca.

Oleksy, Walter. *Bug Scanner and the Computer Mystery.* Walker, 1983. Bug, 12, unscrambles a mystery of the missing secret microchip. He saves his dog's life, struggles with spies and races a motorcycle among many other adventures.

_____. *Quacky and the Haunted Amusement Park.* McGraw, 1982. Quacky and his dog, Puddles, find a dognapping ring when Puddles disappears.

Oliver, Stephen. *Glitter, the Googer and the Ghost.* Carolrhoda, 1983. Is there a ghost in the old house in Maine? Two boys try to find out.

Olsen, Violet. *Growing Season.* Atheneum, 1982. Marie is growing up during the Great Depression with little money. She learns of the plight of the farmers, sees poverty worse than her own and learns that trust in people is sometimes shaken.

_____. *View from the Pighouse Roof.* Atheneum, 1987. Marie, 13, is living through the Depression. The family keeps the farm going after Rosie marries and moves away. Marie misses her but goes on day by day, some good ones and some bad ones.

Olson, Helen. *Secret of Spirit Mountain.* Dodd, 1980. Tom lives with his Indian grandfather in Spirit Mountain. People think he is protecting devils and ghosts.

Oneal, Zibby. *Formal Feeling.* Viking, 1982. Anne's mother dies and her father remarries. She resents this and doesn't accept her stepmother. But in time she sees that she idealized her mother and she comes to accept her stepmother.

_____. *In Summer Light.* Viking, 1985. Kate's father is a well-known painter who dominates his family. They live on an island and Kate is trying to write a term paper on the *Tempest.* She sees herself and her family in the play.

_____. *Language of Goldfish.* Viking, 1980. Carrie sees her sister outgrowing her and she doesn't want to "grow up." She tries suicide and gets help from a psychiatrist. He points out her fear of leaving childhood behind and she adjusts.

_____. *War Work.* Viking, 1971. Zoe and Joe were tired of their small efforts in the war and they decided to hunt spies. It started as a game but they found something ominous.

Oppel, Kenneth. *Colin's Fantastic Video Adventure.* Dutton, 1985. Colin is not winning his favorite video game until small spacemen come to help him. But in the end he decides he would rather win on his own.

Oppenheim, Shulamith. *Selchie's Seed.* Bradbury, 1975. Marion is visited by a white whale. The whale has come to claim her because of her mother's selchie heritage. Her family tries to save her but she becomes a mermaid.

Oppenheimer, Joan. *Clown Like Me.* Crowell, 1985. Shelly, 15, and her friends, Jan and Nicole, are coping with growing pains. They take a clown course which provides an outlet.

_____. *Coming Down Time.* Hawthorn, 1972. A story of the rehabilitation of Karen, an 18-year-old drug addict and her bad-influence city boyfriend and her clean-cut young man who wants to help her.

_____. *Gardine Vs. Hanover.* Crowell, 1982. A father with two children marries a mother with one and there is tension between the children and between child and parent. They are all unhappy until illness pulls them together.

_____. *Run for Your Luck.* Hawthorn, 1971. Torri, 18, hitchhikes from New Mexico to California to work with her aunt. Her cousin is into drugs and her boyfriend is the pusher. Torri, as she looks for her missing dog, helps capture drug smugglers.

_____. *Second Chance.* Scholastic, 1982. Heide is sent to live with her father and his new wife. She is glad to leave behind her bad grades and rough crowd and start anew. She has a second chance but is tempted to lose it over Zack.

_____. *Working on It.* Harcourt, 1980. Tracy is very insecure and wants to get over it. She makes a drastic step by signing up for Drama because her best friend, Carla, talked her into it. Then Wylie made an unnecessary comment and Tracy boiled.

Orgel, Doris. *Certain Magic.* Viking, 1975. Jenny reads her aunt's diary from her childhood and uses it to find some old friends of her aunt's.

_____. *Devil in Vienna.* Viking, 1978. A Jewish girl and the daughter of a Nazi had been friends. The time is 1938 and attitudes are changing.

_____. *Mulberry Music*. Harper, 1971. A young girl has difficulty adjusting to the death of a grandmother she loved very much.

_____. *Next Door to Xanadu*. Harper, 1969. Patricia wants to be thin and have friends. She is teased and called unflattering names. She pretends to put a spell on her tormentors.

_____. *Risking Love*. Dial, 1984. Dinah leaves college to join her boyfriend, Gary. Her father is against this and advises therapy. Dinah agrees and learns a good deal about herself and her love.

_____. *Whiskers Once and Always*. Viking, 1986. Rebecca feels betrayed when her cat, Whiskers, dies. Her mother's boyfriend, who is a veterinarian, tries to save him but can't.

Orlev, Uri. *Island on Bird Street*. Houghton, 1984. Alex builds a hideout for himself in a bombed out building in Poland. He survives for five months by foraging for food and finding ways to keep warm. He is waiting for the return of his father.

Ormondroyd, Edward. *All in Good Time*. Parnassus, 1975. Robert and Victoria Walker and their mother, and Susan and her father are involved in a series of adventures ending with Susan's father marrying Mrs. Walker.

_____. *Castaways on Long Ago*. Parnassus, 1973. Three youngsters are staying on a farm when they discover a strange boy from Long Ago Island. They all have an exciting time.

_____. *Time at the Top*. Parnassus, 1963. Susan rides up to the top floor of her building in an elevator and suddenly she is in another world. She is living in 1881. She moves back and forth and then takes her father with her.

Orr, Rebecca. *Gunner's Run*. Harper, 1980. A story of the abuse of Gunner by his alcoholic father. He is befriended by the grandfather of his friend, Jamie, who later dies.

Orwell, George. *Animal Farm*. Harper, 1948. The farm animals decide that since they produce and get no profit they should run the farm, not the humans. The pigs start the action and wait till you see where it leads.

_____. *Nineteen Eighty-Four*. Harper, 1971. Even though 1984 has come and gone, Orwell's book is still a thoughtful book about possible future societies.

Osborne, Chester. *Memory String*. Atheneum, 1984. Darath lives in prehistoric times. He wants to be a great hunter like his father but is destined to be a shaman like his grandfather. The tribe has many hardships and must move across Bering Strait.

Osborne, Mary. *Last One Home*. Dial, 1986. Bailey is abandoned by her alcoholic mother. Her father remarries and her brother joins the Army. She is frustrated and runs away but Janet, her new mother, is happy and unselfish and helps Bailey.

_____. *Love Always, Blue*. Scholastic, 1983.

Blue wants to visit her father in New York. Her mother is in with a new crowd that she doesn't like. But because she meets someone special Blue's life is about to change for the better.

_____. *Run, Run as Fast as You Can*. Dial, 1982. Hallie's family moves to Virginia where her worries about being popular are offset by an unexpected tragedy.

Osswoski, Leonie. *Star Without a Sky*. Lerner, 1985. Some young Germans find a Jewish boy and are undecided about turning him over to the Nazis.

Otis, James. *Toby Tyler*. Buccaneer, 1981. An all-time favorite about life in the circus with all its trappings.

Ottley, Reginald. *Bates Family*. Harcourt, 1969. Eight Bates children drive sheep across Australia. They encounter a drought that threatens the life of the animals. A sad story of the hardships of this life.

_____. *Boy Alone*. Harcourt, 1965. A young boy loves his dog, Brolga, but knows he must lose him to the Hunters. Brolga's puppy, Rags, and the boy become very attached and the boy does not want to give him up.

_____. *Rain Comes to Yamboorah*. Harcourt, 1967. The story of a boy in Australia who works on a cattle station. He matures and accepts the plight of the people around him: the cook, the dogman and the two aborigine girls.

_____. *Rain from the West*. Faber, 1980. A story of early Christianity in Great Britain in the year 71. Hylas is a Greek freedman and Camillus is his friend. He wins Pyrrha when her husband dies of fever.

_____. *Roan Colt*. Harcourt, 1966. A lame colt, destined to be shot, is hidden by the boy. When a fire breaks out, he shows a great deal of courage in rescuing the colt from where he is penned.

Overton, Jenny. *Ship from Simnel Street*. Greenwillow, 1986. Polly goes from London to Spain to look for her rifleman boyfriend Dick, who is fighting in the Napoleonic War. Susannah and her family cover for her absence.

Oz, Amos. *Soumchi*. Harper, 1981. Soumchi, 11, loses his bicycle, falls in love and finds life very peculiar.

Packard, Edward. *ESP McGee*. Avon, 1983. ESP McGee and his partner, Matt Terrell, are first class mystery solvers.

Paige, Harry. *Johnny Stands*. Warne, 1982. Johnny lives with his Sioux grandfather. They run away together until Johnny is arrested for trying to free an eagle in the park and is sent back to the reservation.

_____. *Shadow on the Sun*. Warne, 1984. A story of Billy the Kid's son and his thoughts about avenging his father's death.

Palin, Michael. *Mirrorstone*. Knopf, 1986. A boy on the other side of the mirror beckoned Paul to come with him.

Palmer, C.E. *Dog Called Houdini*. Deutsch,

1979. Houdini is a stray dog who is disliked but admired for his cunning. He can't be captured. He is finally tranquilized by drugged food and hit by a car. Red, the dog catcher's son, finds, rescues and keeps him.

Palmer, David. *Emergence*. Bantam, 1984. Candy was in the shelter her father erected when the attack came. She and Terry heard the announcement and the warning to stay in the shelter. Everyone above was eliminated by radiation. What to do?

Palmer, Mary. *Teaspoon Tree*. Houghton, 1962. Andulasia learns about the Teaspoon Tree from Mole and sets out to find it.

Palmer, Myron. *Egyptian Necklace*. Houghton, 1961. Tomb robbers and the rewards of capture are the theme of this story of ancient Egypt in 1400 B.C. Ar and his friend are the ones who help in the capture.

_____. *Treachery in Crete*. Houghton, 1961. The uncovering of a robbery plot puts Ar and his friends in great danger.

Pantell, Dora. *Miss Pickerell and the Lost World*. Watts, 1986. Ellie, a mouse, asks Miss Pickerell to expose an illegal logging operation. She and her friend the Mayor and the robot helicopter help save the day.

_____. *Miss Pickerell and the War of the Computers*. Watts, 1984. Miss Pickerell and Euphus find out why food prices sent by computers have tripled. A false program has been substituted. Miss Pickerell is kidnapped and then rescued.

Paperny, Myra. *Wooden People*. Little, 1976. The Stein family is about to move again. Teddy decided to make and befriend marionettes. The others write scripts and prepare plays. Their father is against this but near tragedy brings them together.

Paradis, Marjorie. *Jeanie*. Westminster, 1963. Jeanie runs away to her grandmother in Chicago when her mother marries a man with three children of his own. She later regrets the move.

_____. *Mr. De Luca's Horse*. Atheneum, 1962. B.B. needs money for a horse he wants to buy, for a gift for his mother and for other things deemed important. He tries to solve his money problem but learns more about people and horses.

Parenteau, Shirley. *Talking Coffins of Cryocity*. Nelson, 1979. Kallie reprograms the Weather Planner for rain. She is punished by being frozen and sent away. She awakens to find the technician is building an empire of defrosted women.

Parini, Jay. *Patch Boys*. Holt, 1986. Sammy lives in the coal region of Pennsylvania. The story includes a lot of information about this area but mostly about Sammy growing up: his friends, his love, his school and his family relationships.

Parish, Peggy. *Haunted House*. Dell, 1971. A ghost seems to be haunting the Roberts family house.

_____. *Key to the Treasure*. Macmillan, 1966. Grandpa hid his treasure of Indian relics and everyone has looked for them. Liza, Bill and Jed are now going to try. They crack the code and succeed in finding the treasure.

_____. *Pirate Island Adventure*. Macmillan, 1975. Three youngsters vacation on Pirate Island and discover a long lost family treasure.

Park, Barbara. *Almost Starring Skinnybones*. Knopf, 1988. Alex feels he's going to be a star television actor when he is asked to make a commercial as a result of a cat food essay contest.

_____. *Beanpole*. Knopf, 1983. Lilli is tall and she is teased. Her friends Belinas and Drew help her to cope. She gets two of her three wishes and isn't bothered by the last one anyway.

_____. *Buddies*. Random, 1985. What do you do when you go to camp and want to be popular but are saddled with a roommate who is unattractive and wants to be friends.

_____. *Don't Make Me Smile*. Knopf, 1981. Charles is against his parents' divorce and lets them know it.

_____. *Kid in the Red Jacket*. Knopf, 1987. Howard is the new kid in school and in the neighborhood. He is befriended by a young girl, a serious problem because of "young" and "girl."

_____. *Maxie, Rosie and Earl ... Partners in Grime*. Knopf, 1990. Maxie, Rosie and Earl are to be disciplined by the principal but he postpones it and they skip school.

_____. *My Mother Got Married (and Other Disasters)*. Knopf, 1989. Charles, 12, must adjust to a stepfather, a stepsister and a stepbrother.

_____. *Operation: Dump the Chump*. Knopf, 1982. Osca comes up with a brilliant plan to get rid of his kid brother.

_____. *Skinnybones*. Knopf, 1982. Alex is a loser as far as baseball goes but he has a sense of humor. Bully Stoner doesn't appreciate his humor and Alex gets into dumb trouble.

Park, Ruth. *Playing Beatie Bow*. Atheneum, 1982. Beatie Bow is the name of a game. It is named after a girl who lived and played it a century earlier. Abigail goes back in time and finds answers to questions about Beatie Bow and the game.

_____. *Road Under the Sea*. Doubleday, 1966. A schooner disappears with all aboard. It is washed ashore six weeks later. Investigation uncovers a lost city beneath the sea.

Parker, Richard. *Boy Who Wasn't Lonely*. Bobbs, 1965. Cricket meets a Pakistani girl and learns about true friendship and happiness.

_____. *He Is Your Brother*. Nelson, 1974. Mike's brother, Orry, is autistic and Mike has trouble accepting him as a loving human being.

_____. *Hendon Fungus*. Meredith, 1967. Emmelli and Peter have a box of plant specimens. They plant them and they get brown fungi. Telling more will spoil the story.

_____. *House That Guilda Drew*. Bobbs,

1963. Guilda's family lives in a tent and she longs for a home. Her father is a migrant worker and they never stay in one place long. She spends time drawing houses on scraps of paper.

_____. *Paul and Etta.* Nelson, 1972. The Milfords take Paul into their home after his mother dies and his father disappears. Etta is their daughter and she doesn't get along with Paul. Then Paul's father returns.

_____. *Perversity of Pipers.* Van Nostrand, 1964. The Piper family fight among themselves and with other relations. Tas and Bulldog look for Bulldog's missing grandfather. They find an abandoned mine and a real adventure begins.

_____. *Private Beach.* Duell, 1964. The five Langham children want to stop construction of a boardwalk on their private beach. They start a chain of events that is more than they bargained for.

_____. *Quarter Boy.* Nelson, 1976. An English boy gets recognition after refinishing two large statues.

_____. *Runaway.* Nelson, 1977. Hugo, upset by his parents' quarreling, decides to run away and pretend to be kidnapped in order to bring his parents closer together, but his plan backfires.

_____. *Second-Hand Family.* Bobbs, 1965. Giles lives with foster parents he doesn't understand. He plays in a band with Martin and they become a hit. He is separated from this family for a while but they are happily reunited.

_____. *Sheltering Tree.* Meredith, 1970. David and Stephen end up smuggling for a living because of circumstances. They are caught, jailed, tried and found guilty.

_____. *Three by Mistake.* Nelson, 1974. Three children are kidnapped by Arab terrorists. They make three attempts at escaping but although the first two were foiled the third leads them to safety.

_____. *Valley Full of Pipers.* Bobbs, 1963. Tas Piper helps settle the feud of the Piper family when their valley is flooded.

_____. *Voyage to Tasmania.* Bobbs, 1961. Ray is sent to live with his aunt. Although he just recently lost his parents he adjusts to a new way of life.

Parkinson, Ethelyn. *Good Old Archibald.* Abingdon, 1960. Trent, Wilmer, and Harley can't keep up with Arch, a new arrival who will play baseball. But they have to turn Arch into a regular American boy.

_____. *Merry Mad Bachelors.* Abingdon, 1962. Trent, Harley, Wilmer and Archibald want to be tall and make the basketball team. With the help of Emory, who is tall, they hope to have a good team. But Emory can't live with his bachelor uncle.

_____. *Operation That Happened to Rupert Piper.* Abingdon, 1966. Rupert substitutes for his friend Milt at the hospital so that Milt can be in a show. He has his appendix removed. He and his friends upset the entire hospital with their antics.

_____. *Rupert Piper and Megan the Valuable Girl.* Abingdon, 1972. Rupert and the boys must include a new girl in their activities. The town is trying to win the title of most typical American town. Everyone is acting "typical" and Megan is part of this act.

_____. *Rupert Piper and the Boy Who Could Knit.* Abingdon, 1979. Shirley is a boy who knits and cooks. And admits liking girls! Rupert, Clayte, Dood, Hugh and Milt don't understand this. The girls meet Jamie who is a tomboy. Wakefield is not the same.

_____. *Rupert Piper and the Dear, Dear Birds.* Abingdon, 1976. Rupert and his friends lose their circus tickets in an encounter with a bird watcher. They are so mad they form a Bird Haters Club and put out negative, false information about birds.

_____. *Terrible Trouble of Rupert Piper.* Abingdon, 1963. Rupert, Clayte, Dood and Milt make up the gang of boys that upset both school teachers and townspeople of Wakefield. They are not bad but can be annoyingly funny.

_____. *Today I Am a Ham.* Abingdon, 1968. Eric was expected to be an athlete but failed. What he could do was be a short wave operator. A funny book about track and short wave radio.

Parks, Peter. *Learning Tree.* Crest, 1987. A black youth in a small town in Kansas finds himself the only witness to a murder.

Parsons, Elizabeth. *Upside-Down Cat.* Macmillan, 1981. As the family is leaving their summer home they lose track of their cat.

Pascal, Francine. *Hand-Me-Down Kid.* Viking, 1980. Ari is the hand-me-down kid, getting everything her older sister outgrows. One day, against all orders, she borrows her older sister's bicycle and it disappears. Vanishes!

_____. *Hangin' Out with Cici.* Viking, 1977. Victoria hits her head and she goes back in time thirty years. She meets Cici, who looks familiar and turns out to be her mother at 14. And her grandmother is Cici's mother!

_____. *Love and Betrayal and Hold the Mayo!* Viking, 1985. Torri and Steffie are spending the summer at camp. Steffie's boyfriend falls in love with Torri. A story of Love versus Loyalty.

_____. *My First Love and Other Disasters.* Viking, 1979. Victoria spends the summer where she knows Jim will be. His girlfriend shows up and Jim's best friend tells Victoria that he likes her. Jim turns out to be a cad and Victoria and Barry are heroes.

Patchett, Mary. *Ajax and the Haunted Mountain.* Bobbs, 1966. Ajax, half wild-dog, and his mistress, Mary, travel through Australia and meet adventure and mystery.

_____. *Brumby Come Home.* Bobbs, 1962. Joey goes to rescue a herd of horses and has exciting adventures before he gets all but Brumby from horse catchers and brings them safely home.

_____. *Brumby, the Wild White Stallion.* Bobbs, 1958. Joey is an orphan who loves his horse, Brumby, who has had bad experiences with men and can't be tamed. Joey would rather see him free and wild than tame and subdued.

_____. *End of the Outlaws.* Bobbs, 1963. Mary tries to tame a wild black cat to add to her pet family. She saves animals during a flood and also helps capture rustlers of her father's farm.

_____. *Golden Wolf.* Bobbs, 1962. Ajax has disappeared and Mary sees a sign "Golden Wolf of the Steppes" and fears it is Ajax. The dog is closely guarded but it is Ajax and she must rescue him.

_____. *Tam the Untamed.* Bobbs, 1955. Only Mary could handle the silver horse, Tam. And only Ajax, the golden dog, could be friends with him.

_____. *Warrimood.* Bobbs, 1963. Jeff is to find a difficult task and do it; do something worth doing for someone else and find a friend. He has a year to accomplish this and does so.

Paterson, Katherine. *Bridge to Terabithia.* Crowell, 1977. Jess and Leslie become unlikely friends. Their secret place was Terabithia. While Jess is away Leslie goes to Terabithia and is accidentally killed. Jess is deeply hurt. Newbery winner, 1978.

_____. *Come Sing, Jimmy Jo.* Crowell, 1985. Jimmy Jo belongs to a blues singing family and travels with them although he would rather do something else. He becomes famous and this makes his decision harder to make.

_____. *Great Gilly Hopkins.* Crowell, 1978. Gilly has moved from foster home to foster home because she is determined not to succeed, until she stays with a woman who understands what motivates her. She finds her mother is not ideal.

_____. *Jacob Have I Loved.* Crowell, 1980. Louise is a twin and her sister seems to get everything Louisa wants. There is envy and jealousy before Louise matures enough to have a rich life of her own. Newbery winner, 1981.

_____. *Master Puppeteer.* Crowell, 1975. A story of the Hanaza theatre in Japan. Jiro runs away from his puppetmaking father and is accepted as an apprentice in a famous theatre. A good description of serious puppeteering.

_____. *Of Nightingales That Weep.* Crowell, 1974. Takiko of old Japan is the daughter of a samurai. Her mother remarries and she is sent to the royal court.

_____. *Park's Quest.* Lodestar, 1988. Park goes to his grandfather's farm. His father died in Vietnam and he wants to know more about him. While there he meets a Vietnamese-American. All he finds out about his father is unpleasant.

_____. *Rebels of the Heavenly Kingdom.* Dutton, 1983. A story of Wang Lee and Mei Lin in China in the 1850's. It is about warriors, battles and the Heavenly Kingdom of Great Peace.

_____. *Sign of the Chrysanthemum.* Crowell, 1973. During the Samurai period a Japanese boy searches for his father.

Patten, Brian. *Mr. Moon's Last Case.* Scribner, 1976. Nameon is a leprechaun stranded in the weeds and is seeking the portal that will take him to his own world.

Patterson, Sarah. *Distant Summer.* Simon & Schuster, 1976. A short first-love story set in England during World War II.

Paul, Paula. *Last Summer I Got in Trouble.* Eakin, 1987. A boy lies about how well he can drive and gets into trouble and gets others in trouble, too.

Paulsen, Gary. *Crossing.* Watts, 1987. Manny wants to get across the border to the United States. Sergeant Locke drinks himself into oblivion each night. They make a strange alliance.

_____. *Dancing Carl.* Bradbury, 1983. Carl just appears one day and makes the skating rink a special place because of his dancing. He also takes care of the bully, Erickson.

_____. *Dogsong.* Bradbury, 1985. An Eskimo boy is disillusioned with modern villages and takes off on a dogsled for a self-discovery journey.

_____. *Hatchet.* Bradbury, 1987. The hatchet was a going away gift from his mother. When the pilot of the private plane he was on died, Brian was obliged to land the plane and survive for 54 days in the Canadian woods. With a secret!

_____. *Murphy.* Walker, 1987. Murphy is sheriff when a 12-year-old girl is murdered, followed by others. Murphy solves the crimes and the murderer is killed in a shoot-out.

_____. *Popcorn Days and Buttermilk Nights.* Lodestar, 1983. Carly, 14, is always in trouble. He is sent to live with relatives on a farm where he learns a different set of values.

_____. *River.* Delacorte, 1991. Brian survived 54 days in the wilderness after a plane crash. Now the government wants him to show Derek how he did it so they can train others in survival skills. But this trip had hazards, too.

_____. *Tracker.* Bradbury, 1984. John lives with his grandparents on a farm. He goes deer hunting alone and tracks a deer that is tied somehow to his grandfather's life.

_____. *Voyage of the Frog.* Orchard, 1988. David goes sailing to scatter the ashes of his dead uncle. He is caught in a freak storm and must survive for nine days on his own.

Payne, Bernal. *Experiment in Terror.* Houghton, 1987. Seven children born the same day in the same hospital are all best friends. When they are six they begin to disappear one by one. Steve is the last and learns that they are all aliens from another world.

_____. *It's About Time.* Macmillan, 1984.

Gail and Chris wish themselves back to 1955 to observe their parents' courtship. They accidentally avert the meeting of their parents and must set it right or they can't exist.

_____. *Late, Great Dick Hart*. Houghton, 1986. Tom's friend Dick died of a brain tumor. Dick "comes back" and he and Tom travel back and forth to the other world.

Peake, Katy. *Indian Heart of Carrie Hodges*. Viking, 1972. An Indian girl finds kinship between animals and people.

Pearce, Philippa. *Battle of Bubble and Squeak*. Deutsch, 1979. Sid has two pet gerbils and must fight to be able to keep them because of family objections.

_____. *Tom's Midnight Garden*. Harper, 1984. Each night at the stroke of twelve Tom visits his garden. One night he meets a strange Victorian girl named Hatty.

_____. *Way to Sattin Shore*. Greenwillow, 1983. Kate's grandmother receives a letter she won't talk about. It has something to do with the missing gravestone of her drowned father. Kate learns about this fatal day as time goes on.

Pearl, Jack. *Young Falcons*. Hammond, 1962. The day-to-day doings of the Air Force Academy including baseball and football competition, good and bad intentioned cadets, etc.

Pearson, Gayle. *Fish Friday*. Atheneum, 1986. Jamie dreams of the city where her mother studies art. She must stay at home in a small town with her father and brothers. When her brother nearly drowns she understands her father's love.

Perason, Kit. *Daring Game*. Viking, 1986. Liza is in a boarding school. At first she likes it. She meets Helen and gets involved in "daring games" which lead to trouble. Then she has doubts. A story of friends in boarding school.

_____. *Handful of Time*. Viking, 1987. Patricia, 12, finds a watch that transports her back in time. The watch gets broken and she returns to the present.

Peck, Richard. *Amanda/Miranda*. Avon, 1981. Mary had her fortune told and received a copper coin. When she met her new employer they both saw how much they looked alike. Amanda renamed her Miranda. Their lives then became intertwined.

_____. *Are You in the House Alone?* Viking, 1976. After she receives a strange phone call and some obscene letters, Gail is raped by her best friend's boyfriend and no one will believe her.

_____. *Blossom Culp and the Sleep of Death*. Delacorte, 1986. Blossom Culp has second-sight and can see into the past. She and Alexander become involved with an Egyptian princess who needs help in restoring her stolen treasures.

_____. *Close Enough to Touch*. Delacorte, 1981. First Matt's mother dies then his girlfriend dies. He is devastated. His father remarries and he then gets a new girlfriend, Margaret, and his life becomes more organized.

_____. *Don't Look and It Won't Hurt*. Harper, 1972. Ellen must give her baby up for adoption. Her sister, Carol, can't help her unwed sister. Should she run away?

_____. *Dreadful Future of Blossom Culp*. Delacorte, 1983. Blossom Culp, a fourteen-year-old psychic, has comical, spooky adventures when she is hurtled into the future.

_____. *Dreamland Lake*. Holt, 1973. Two boys find a body near an amusement park.

_____. *Father Figure*. Viking, 1978. Jim is playing father to his 8-year-old brother. His role is threatened when they are both forced to move in with their real father.

_____. *Ghost Belonged to Me*. Viking, 1975. Alex meets a curious female ghost. This begins a series of eerie adventures. The ghost is predicting a tragedy. Alex and Blossom Culp must help.

_____. *Ghosts I Have Been*. Viking, 1977. Comedy and tragedy beset Blossom Culp, the girl who has the gift of second-sight and can see the future. She lives in the early 1900's but can see into 1980.

_____. *Princess Ashley*. Delacorte, 1987. Chelsea joins Ashley's "in" group at school. She is used and hurt. Her friend Rod stands by her when tragedy hits.

_____. *Remembering the Good Times*. Delacorte, 1985. Three very close friends are not as attuned to each other as they thought when one of them commits suicide. Buck, Kate and Trav were friends for years, close friends. How could this happen?

_____. *Representing Superdoll*. Viking, 1974. Verna was just Verna and Darlene was superdoll, winner of every beauty contest she entered. They go went New York for Darlene to appear on a show. Verna was used as a fill-in and her life changed.

_____. *Secrets of the Shopping Mall*. Delacorte, 1979. Barney and Theresa left town because a gang was after them. They decided to live in a shopping mall. They had food available, a place to sleep, clothes to wear. They were not the only ones there!

_____. *Those Summer Girls I Never Met*. Delacorte, 1988. Drew and Steph are on a cruise with their grandmother. They didn't want to go but Connie is a 1940's singer and her husband is an alcoholic piano player. Not typical grandparents.

_____. *Through a Brief Darkness*. Viking, 1973. Karen's father was allegedly a Mafia crook. She had no proof but there was talk. She is kidnapped under false pretenses by her father's enemies. She fears for him but what can she do?

Peck, Robert. *Arly*. Walker, 1989. Arly's father is a field worker and Arly sees that as the only life for him until he meets a new school teacher who shows him a way out.

_____. *Banjo*. Random, 1982. Two boys, Alvin and Banjo, fall into a mine shaft and only an old man who is a recluse can save them.

_____. *Basket Case*. Doubleday, 1979. A funny story of Graffiti Prep School. Higbee is a troublemaker but helps win the final basketball game the school must win to stay open.

_____. *Day No Pigs Would Die*. Knopf, 1972. A Shaker boy's understanding of the realities of surviving on a farm in Vermont. Life here is quite different from that of a city dweller.

_____. *Hub*. Knopf, 1979. Hub and his friend Spooner sponsor their teacher Miss Guppy in the Overland Obstacle Bicycle Race.

_____. *Millie's Boy*. Knopf, 1973. Millie was shot and killed. Her son was shot but not killed. He was hurt and had to get a doctor. He also had to find out who killed Millie and why.

_____. *Mr. Little*. Doubleday, 1979. Well-liked Miss Kellogg is being replaced by a new teacher.

_____. *Soup*. Knopf, 1974. The fun and problems of two boys, Soup and Rob, growing up in a small town in Vermont. They and their friends keep the town in a frenzy most of the time.

_____. *Soup and Me*. Knopf, 1975. Soup and his friends and all their trouble-making, innocent though they may be, are not always appreciated by others.

_____. *Soup for President*. Knopf, 1978. Rob manages Soup's campaign for class president. Rob's girlfriend is also running. What will he do?

_____. *Soup in the Saddle*. Knopf, 1983. Celebrating a special day for their teacher, Miss Kelly, Soup and Rob really do more good than harm to make the day successful.

_____. *Soup on Fire*. Delacorte, 1987. Soup and Rob will do anything to get the attention of the visiting talent scout and their hero Fearless Ferguson.

_____. *Soup on Ice*. Knopf, 1985. Rob and Soup engineer an incredible appearance by Santa and his sleigh in their small Vermont town.

_____. *Soup on Wheels*. Knopf, 1981. Soup and Rob try really hard to win a prize in their town's "Vermont Mardy Grah." They are sure their Zebra will win.

_____. *Soup's Drum*. Knopf, 1980. Soup and Rob play the drum in the Fourth of July parade. Rob swears revenge when he realizes that he has carried the big drum for most of the parade. No wonder it was so heavy!

_____. *Soup's Goat*. Knopf, 1984. Cousin Sexton lends his unusual talent to Soup and Rob as they enter the town's goat-cart race.

_____. *Soup's Hoop*. Delacorte, 1990. Soup is going to help the basketball team by building a spitzenbootle. He also entraps the evil Janice Riker.

_____. *Soup's Uncle*. Delacorte, 1988. Vi, Soup's uncle, is a member of a motorcycle gang. At the last minute he is unable to ride in the important race. So Soup rides in his place!

_____. *Trig*. Little, 1977. A tomboy, Trig, gets a G-man machine gun as a present and "shoots" Aunt Augusta. Her two friends Skip and Bud suffer a bit from the consequences.

_____. *Trig Goes Ape*. Little, 1980. Trig gets into an uproarious melee when Buck Fargo's wild Ape and Monkey show comes to town. Evelyn, the mule and the scattered chickens add to the hilarity.

_____. *Trig or Treat*. Little, 1982. Trig masquerades as the seductive Delilah for the church Halloween costume pageant. Skip and Bud play Samson and Gideon.

_____. *Trig Sees Red*. Little, 1973. Trig takes matters into her own hands when Clodsburg's only uniformed policeman is replaced by a traffic light.

Pedersen, Elsa. *Dangerous Flight*. Abingdon, 1960. Stefan uncovers a plot to destroy his uncle. They both run away and live like the Indians until they are rescued by Americans.

_____. *Fisherman's Choice*. Atheneum, 1964. Dave was a farmer and from a family of farmers. He left the farm to work on a crab boat and fell in love with the sea.

Pelgrom, Els. *Winter When Time Was Frozen*. Morrow, 1980. Noortje and her father find refuge on an isolated farm during the last winter of World War II. It seems peaceful but is part of the Dutch underground.

Pellowski, Anne. *Betsy's Up-and-Down Year*. Philomel, 1983. This is Betsy's story about life on the farm. She experiences jealousy among her brothers and sisters and sadness as older members of the family die.

_____. *First Farm in the Valley: Anna's Story*. Philomel, 1982. Anna is a first. First to be born in America, first to own a farm in Wisconsin. But she dreams of returning to Poland.

_____. *Stairstep Farm: Anna Rose's Story*. Philomel, 1981. Anna Rose is part of the third generation to grow up on the farm. She enjoys the work with her sisters and brothers but she wants to go to school.

_____. *Willow Wind Farm: Betsy's Story*. Philomel, 1981. Betsy is the granddaughter of Annie. She is one of ten children and is surrounded by family and extended family.

_____. *Winding Valley Farm: Annie's Story*. Philomel, 1982. Annie loved the farm and didn't want to move to the city. When the accident occurred she knew that she would not be leaving the farm.

Pelta, Kathy. *Blue Empress*. Holt, 1988. Margaret finds out who took a valuable lapis lazuli necklace.

Pendergraft, Patricia. *Brush Mountain*. Putnam, 1989. Arney would never have believed that he would be saving the life of a man who was so disliked.

_____. *Hear the Wind Blow*. Philomel, 1988. Isadora is having trouble with mean

Haskill. Her best friend Maybelle is so good she sees good in Haskill. Maybelle is mistreated and does die. Haskill reforms and Isadora gets her wish.

_____. *Miracle at Clement's Pond.* Philomel, 1987. Justin, Sylvie and Lyon rescue an abandoned baby and leave it on the doorstep of a woman who wants a baby. After lots of complications Lyon's father marries the baby's mother.

Perez, N.A. *Breaker.* Houghton, 1988. Pat goes to work in the mines when his father is killed in a cave-in. His friend is also killed and his brother runs away but he stays and fights the mining conditions.

Perez, Norah. *Strange Summer in Stratford.* Little, 1968. Jenny's father finds something strange in Stratford. There is a fire at the theatre, the flowers arrive dead, strange phone calls and mean letters arrive and finally a bomb threat comes.

Perl, Lila. *Annabelle Starr, ESP.* Houghton, 1983. Annabelle gets 92 on a test she didn't study for, and she predicts her friend's love life; now she wants to find out what the new boarder has in mind when he looks at her adopted brother, Scotty.

_____. *Don't Ask Miranda.* Seabury, 1979. Miranda wants to make friends at her new school. Because Hal is running for school office he befriends her. She resists the demand that she steal. She faces her new life realistically.

_____. *Dumb Like Me, Olivia Potts.* Houghton, 1976. Olivia has doubts about her own intelligence because she follows her extra bright brother through school.

_____. *Fat Glenda's Summer Romance.* Clarion, 1986. Glenda's weight problem returns after both friendship and romance turn out badly when the summer looked so promising. Her friends Sara and Justin seem to be distant and cool.

_____. *Hey, Remember Fat Glenda?* Houghton, 1981. This is Glenda's story of her battle against FAT. She does lose weight but it does not solve all of her problems such as a crush on her English teacher, her mother's eating plans, etc.

_____. *Marleen, Horror Queen.* Clarion, 1985. Marleen is not accepted in her new school and wants revenge. Alex taunts and plays pranks. Rosalie befriends her and works out her problems.

_____. *Me and Fat Glenda.* Houghton, 1972. Sara and her family move to a conservative town in New York from California where they lived non-conventionally. Sara makes friends with Glenda and helps her lose weight.

_____. *Pieface and Daphne.* Houghton, 1980. Pamela is an only child when Daphne comes to stay. Pam's friend Shirly, a boy, likes Daphne and Pam is jealous. They all find that sharing can be fun.

_____. *Telltale Summer of Tina C.* Nelson, 1975. Tina, Ina and Amy want to be popular. They form a Saturday Sad Souls Club. Tina's parents are divorced and are both about to remarry.

_____. *That Crazy April.* Seabury, 1974. Chris is torn between loyalty to her liberated mother and belief in a traditional male teacher. Where does her own identity lie?

_____. *Tybbee Trimble's Hard Times.* Clarion, 1984. A young girl tries to earn money for a circus ticket. She wants to see the elephants so she can put the information in her essay about elephants.

Perlberg, Deborah. *Heartaches.* Ballantine, 1983. Sandy and Deanie want to be rock 'n' roll stars. They run away to New York and find danger and depression, not the glamour and excitement they dreamed of.

Pesek, Ludek. *Trap for Perseus.* Bradbury, 1980. Steve is commander of Persus III. He is sent to see if he can find Persus I and II that disappeared earlier. He does but the society their crew formed takes him in and he waits for Persus IV.

Petersen, P.J. *Boll Weevil Express.* Delacorte, 1983. Lars, 15, runs away from a domineering father with a new friend, Doug. Doug's sister tags along; they don't find what they are looking for and at the end Lars is willing to go back home.

_____. *Freshman Detective Blues.* Delacorte, 1987. Jack and Eddie plow through the mud of Muir Lake finding just junk until they hook a skeleton. Is it Jack's disappeared father? Was he murdered? By whom?

_____. *Going for the Big One.* Delacorte, 1986. Jeff, Dave and Annie are deserted by both their parents. They pack some gear and go camping in the mountains. They find a wounded criminal who would pay them for taking care of him. Should they?

_____. *Good-Bye to Good Ol' Charlie.* Delacorte, 1987. Charlie is tired of being a nice guy. He and his family move to California and he wants to change: to a mysterious poet? a lady killer? a cowboy?

_____. *Here's to the Sophomores.* Delacorte, 1984. Warren Cavendish becomes the best known and most controversial sophomore on campus, in just his first two weeks in high school.

_____. *How Can You Hijack a Cave?* Delacorte, 1988. Curt gets a summer job at Cathedral Caverns. Pauline is kidnapped and hidden in the cave. Curt and Lori rescue her by a narrow second entrance.

_____. *Nobody Else Can Walk It for You.* Dell, 1986. A group of teenagers must be brought to safety and it is Laura and Irene's responsibility. Brian and a group of motorcycle toughs cause trouble.

_____. *Would You Settle for Improbable?* Delacorte, 1982. Mike and other ninth graders are influenced by Arnold, who spent time at a juvenile detention center. He helps Warren but when he wants to take Jennifer to the dance trouble sets in.

Petroski, Catherine. *Summer That Lasted Forever.* Houghton, 1984. Molly doesn't want to sell her old pony, Mare, to mean Melissa. She trains Mare to a harness and gets to keep her.

Petry, Ann. *Tituba of Salem Village.* Crowell, 1964. Tituba and her husband are sold as slaves to a Puritan minister and his family. They get involved in the infamous Salem witch trials. A not-too-pleasant story.

Pettersson, Allan. *Frankenstein's Aunt.* Little, 1980. It is up to Frankenstein's aunt to restore the family's good name.

Pevsner, Stella. *And You Give Me a Pain, Elaine.* Seabury, 1978. Andrea tries to get along with her older sister after their mother's death puts her in charge.

_____. *Break a Leg.* Crown, 1969. Fran joins a drama class during the summer. She makes friends with Nancy and Veronica and learns about friendship and drama.

_____. *Call Me Heller, That's My Name.* Seabury, 1973. Heller's life is unexpectedly intertwined with her aunt's and she must cope with it as she goes from escapade to escapade during the Flapper Era.

_____. *Cute Is a Four-Letter Word.* Houghton, 1980. Clara is dating the star basketball player, Skip, and is also pom pom captain. But will Liz and Jay ruin her fun? Because when Halcyon comes, problems set in.

_____. *I'll Always Remember You . . . Maybe.* Houghton, 1981. Ryley is a superstar and Darien finds him exciting. When Paul went off to college talking about dating other people Darien was upset but now flowers and calls are coming from Ryley.

_____. *Keep Stompin' Till the Music Stops.* Seabury, 1977. Richard has dyslexia and learns to accept this disability as his great-grandfather accepts his.

_____. *Lindsay, Lindsay, Fly Away Home.* Clarion, 1983. Lindsay is sent to Chicago from India by her father and stepmother not only to break up her romance with Rajie but for other reasons, also.

_____. *Me, My Goat and My Sister's Wedding.* Clarion, 1985. Doug's pet goat is a secret his family knows nothing about but when he is seen in the oddest places (like his sister's lawn wedding) he can no longer hide him.

_____. *Sister of the Quints.* Clarion, 1987. Natalie is the stepsister of the quints of her father and new stepmother. She certainly loses attention because of this. She decides not to stay with her father, but to go live with her mother.

_____. *Smart Kid Like You.* Seabury, 1975. Nina just got a new stepmother and imagine her surprise when she goes to her new school and finds the woman to be her math teacher.

Peyrouton de Lodebat, Monique. *Village That Slept.* Coward, 1965. Franz and Lydia are stranded with a baby, Tao, and must care for him while they try to find a way to survive hardships and bad weather.

Peyton, K.M. *Plan for Birdmarsh.* World, 1966. Paul loves Birdmarsh and resists the development of a marina. Gus makes Paul's boat seaworthy. Chris invented a lifesaving suit. Paul is alone on the *Swannie* when it sinks; he makes real use of the suit.

Peyton, Karen. *Beethoven's Medal.* Crowell, 1971. Patrick is wild while his friend Ruth is quiet. He is both a serious music student and a young hoodlum. But he really likes Ruth. Ruth is also featured as a young girl in another series.

_____. *Edge of a Cloud.* World, 1968. Christina's love for William is shrouded by his devotion to flying. She marries him instead of Mark which upsets her Uncle Russell.

_____. *Flambards.* World, 1967. Christina, an orphan, goes to live with her Uncle Russell at Flambards. She gets to know both her cousins, Mark and Will. Although she likes Will better, she is destined to marry Mark.

_____. *Flambards Divided.* Philomel, 1981. Widowed Christina marries hard-working Dick, a former employee, and hopes to make Flambards a farm again. Mark, who is wounded in the war, returns to Flambards.

_____. *Flambards in Summer.* World, 1969. The Russells suffer generational conflicts within the family and also the tragedies of World War II. William is killed and Christina returns to Flambards.

_____. *Fly by Night.* World, 1968. Twelve-year-old Ruth gets a pony, Fly, when she moves to the country. She worries about losing him when the family finances get strained. This is the same Ruth who appears in another series.

_____. *Free Rein.* Philomel, 1983. Jonathan, with too many problems at home, runs off with a friend to train a horse for the Grand National.

_____. *Going Home.* Philomel, 1982. Two children run away from their guardian and go home to a mother who had a nervous breakdown.

_____. *Maplin Bird.* World, 1965. Emily and Toby are orphans. Emily falls in love with an owner of a yacht, the *Maplin Bird,* who is involved in smuggling.

_____. *Marion's Angels.* Oxford Univ., 1979. Marion needs to raise money to save St. Michael's. Pat plays the piano to raise money for a church restoration. This is a "miracle" but another is needed to save Pat and Ruth's marriage.

_____. *Midsummer Night's Death.* Collins, 1978. Jonathan's teacher is dead, and it is not suicide. So Jonathan begins his own investigation. He might be the next victim.

_____. *Pattern of Roses.* Crowell, 1972. Tom meets two children from Victorian days and they help him reach an understanding of his father.

_____. *Pennington's Heir.* Crowell, 1973. Pat and Ruth marry because of Ruth's pregnancy. This hampers Pat's musical career and is frowned upon by his family and friends.

_____. *Pennington's Last Term.* Crowell, 1970. Pat Pennington tries to grow up in today's hectic society. Because of his non-conformist past and the trouble he has with any authority, he almost loses the chance he wants most: a piano contest.

_____. *Prove Yourself a Hero.* Collins, 1977. A kidnapping, a ransom, and a suspenseful search are the ingredients that make this story exciting. Jonathan questions his own character and must "prove himself a hero."

_____. *Sea Fever.* World, 1963. Matt works to pay off a fishing boat. He must support his family since his father drowned. He meets Francis and joins him as a crew member on his racing yacht. He is always in danger.

_____. *Team.* Crowell, 1975. Ruth outgrows Fly and buys Toadhill Flax. Peter tells her it's too much horse for her. She needs to prove she is worthy of the horse and to belong to the Pony Club.

_____. *Who, Sir? Me, Sir?* Oxford, 1983. Four Hawkwood school boys, with little or no experience, are challenged by the Greycoats school boys who have everything. It will be swimming, riding, target shooting and running.

Pfeffer, Susan. *About David.* Delacorte, 1980. Lynn has been a friend of David's for years. He, shockingly, murders his adoptive parents and then kills himself. Lynn is having trouble coping with these happenings.

_____. *Courage, Dana.* Delacorte, 1983. Dana saves a child's life and becomes a celebrity. But it is not all that easy. She sees a boy spraying the school building and "framing" someone else. What should she do?

_____. *Dear Dad, Love Laurie.* Scholastic, 1989. Laurie's letter to her divorced father tells about getting into a gifted program at school and other everyday happenings.

_____. *Evvie at Sixteen.* Bantam, 1988. Evvie is the oldest of four sisters. She meets and falls in love with Sam. But she learns something strange about both her dad's and Sam's backgrounds.

_____. *Future Forward.* Delacorte, 1989. Kelly and Scott are arguing over how the ability to go back in time, that their VCR allows them to do, should be used.

_____. *Getting Even.* Putnam, 1986. Annie is a senior in high school and because she worked for a professional magazine in the summer she is disqualified from editing the school paper. She is angry and thinks her anger is helpful.

_____. *Just Between Us.* Delacorte, 1980. Cass talks too much. Her mother promises her a dollar if she can keep a secret. She works hard at it with some success but new problems arise with her friends.

_____. *Just Morgan.* Pocket, 1970. Morgan is 14, newly orphaned and more newly adopted. Her uncle is her guardian. He is a famous writer, is well to do and lives in New York. All of these circumstances are new to her and she likes it.

_____. *Kid Power.* Watts, 1977. Janie is trying to earn money for a new bike. In spite of some setbacks she builds a business of odd jobs called Kid Power. It snowballs and she hires other kids to help.

_____. *Kid Power Strikes Back.* Watts, 1984. Janie's Kid Power starts fall and winter chores. This time she wants money for a computer but competition from Johnny slows her down. She eventually wins out.

_____. *Marley the Kid.* Doubleday, 1975. Marly runs away from her mother to her father. She returns after finding herself under all the hurt and self doubt. She is overweight and plain but is a fighter for her rights.

_____. *Matter of Principal.* Delacorte, 1982. Becca is liked at school and starts an underground newspaper. She publishes a cartoon of her teacher and the principal and is suspended. A story about student's rights.

_____. *Rewind to Yesterday.* Delacorte, 1988. Kelly's VCR can send her back in time. She and her friend Miri and her brother Scott go back in time and save Miri's grandfather from being shot.

_____. *Starting with Melodie.* Scholastic, 1982. The parents of Elaine's best friend are getting a divorce.

_____. *Sybil at Sixteen.* Bantam, 1989. Sybil is the youngest of four sisters. She is recovering from a hit and run accident. A story of Lies, Loyalty and Love.

_____. *Truth or Dare.* Four Winds, 1984. Cathy's two best friends go to another school and she tries to befriend Jessica, but Jessica is not interested.

_____. *Turning Thirteen.* Scholastic, 1988. Becky, 12, sees her friend Dina befriend a new girl, Amy. She plots and plans to win Dina back.

_____. *What Do You Do When Your Mouth Won't Open?* Delacorte, 1981. Reesa, 12, is a good student but can't read aloud in front of others. She wins an essay contest and must read in front of an audience. She gets help and is able to do it and learns a lot in the process.

_____. *Year Without Michael.* Bantam, 1987. Michael leaves home to go to softball practice. He never gets there. He is not seen for a year and Jody and her sister and parents go through grief over a disappeared child.

Phelan, Terry. *S.S. Valentine.* Macmillan, 1979. Connie is confined to a wheelchair but it doesn't stop her from succeeding in a class play.

Philbrook, Clem. *Ollie's Team and the Alley*

Cats. Hastings, 1971. The Alley Cats are a girl's basketball team. They want to play the Bulldogs, a boy's team. The girls win but the boys ask for a rematch with five players on each team (girls have six), and the boys win.

_____. *Ollie's Team and the Baseball Computer.* Hastings, 1967. A story full of practical jokes and mischief. Ollie's bulldog misbehaves, the boy next door, who is a pest, is thwarted and the baseball team competition increases with data from the computer.

_____. *Ollie's Team and the Basketball Computer.* Hastings, 1969. Even though they have had trouble with computers and computer games in the past, Ollie is at it again. Their basketball team is as bad as their baseball and football teams. They need help.

_____. *Ollie's Team and the Football Computer.* Hastings, 1968. The computer both helps and hurts Ollie personally and his football team.

_____. *Ollie's Team and the Million Dollar Mistake.* Hastings, 1973. Ollie is tied up with bank robbers and a bank mistake. He is afraid of losing his spot on the baseball team. He keeps making excuses about his size but it's his thinking that's at fault.

_____. *Ollie's Team and the 200 Pound Problem.* Hastings, 1972. Jumbo has gained so much weight he can't field balls and can't hit balls. He was the team's best hitter. He is programmed into positive thinking: THINK THIN. He loses 25 pounds.

_____. *Ollie's Team Plays Biddy Baseball.* Hastings, 1970. Ollie forgets that he must concentrate in order to win baseball games. He decides he is a drone after learning about bees in his science class and thereby loses a game for his team and more.

_____. *Ollie, the Backward Forward.* Hastings, 1971. Does Winnie, the bulldog, really kill chickens? Bruce has a picture of him doing it. He tries to blackmail Ollie with it. Ollie refuses and Winnie is saved by a classroom trial.

_____. *Slope Dope.* Hastings, 1966. A rivalry skiing story of two boys: one a show-off and one a team player.

Phillips, Kathleen. *Katie McCrary and the Wiggins Crusade.* Elsevier, 1980. Katie is in a new school. She alienates herself from the "in" crowd the first day. She then decides to befriend the town's "not right kind of family." She helps find Oscar innocent of an accused crime.

Phillips, Leon. *Split Bamboo.* Doubleday, 1966. A father/son spy story set in China. There are murder, suspense and daring escapes.

Phipson, Joan. *Bianca.* Macmillan, 1988. Three events deeply move Bianca and she runs away from home. Emily and Hubert meet her and try to help. Her mother is also trying to find her but she is hiding from her.

_____. *Birkin.* Harcourt, 1966. Two boys try to raise an orphaned calf, but it is not all fun and they soon tire of it. So they turn it over to younger children who love it and give it the name Birkin.

_____. *Boundary Riders.* Harcourt, 1963. Two boys and a girl spend a week checking a ranch's fence. They become lost while exploring unknown territory. And nobody knows where they are.

_____. *Family Conspiracy.* Harcourt, 1964. Mrs. Barker's children try to raise money for her hospital expenses since a drought threatens their livestock. Each member tries secretly to do a project.

_____. *Fly Free.* Atheneum, 1979. Johnny earns money by trapping animals but it bothers him to kill them. He decides to quit doing it when he himself is caught in a trap and knows how it feels.

_____. *Fly Into Danger.* Atheneum, 1977. A 13-year-old girl discovers and foils a smuggling ring that is exporting exotic birds illegally.

_____. *Good Luck to the Rider.* Harcourt, 1968. Barbara, frail and timid, is in boarding school, getting away from her dynamic family. She finds a brumby colt that needs love and a home. She is not afraid because of the love.

_____. *Horse with Eight Hands.* Macmillan, 1974. Horst is a German immigrant living in Australia. He opens up an antique shop with the help of a group of children.

_____. *Threat to the Barkers.* Harcourt, 1963. Jack bought a flock of stud sheep. Edward hears of a plan to steal the sheep and makes plans to catch the thieves at it.

_____. *Tide Flowing.* Atheneum, 1981. A warm friendship between a motherless boy and a quadriplegic girl. They were both lonely before they met.

_____. *Watcher in the Garden.* Atheneum, 1982. Kitty has unusual communication powers with a blind recluse.

_____. *Way Home.* Atheneum, 1973. During the Black Plague in England Anne runs away to a marsh where she hopes to be safe.

_____. *When the City Stopped.* Atheneum, 1978. A picture of what happens in an Australian town when a general strike hits it and how the children cope.

Phleger, Marjorie. *Pilot Down, Presumed Dead.* Harper, 1963. Steve's plane is forced to land and can't be repaired. His radio doesn't work and he has few supplies. He must survive with what he can use or remake from salvaged parts.

Picard, Barbara. *Lost John: A Young Outlaw in the Forest of Arden.* Criterion, 1963. John leaves home to avenge his father. He is kidnapped by Ralf the Red, a robber.

_____. *One Is One.* Holt, 1965. Stephen wants to become a knight. He is accepted as a squire by a knight, he helps a boy in trouble and he befriends a dog he once feared. He really is a painter in his heart, and he returns to it.

Pickering, Mary. *Mystery of the Greek Icon.* Putnam, 1984. Marty and her boyfriend go to Greece to search for Marty's missing father.

Pierce, Meredith. *Birth of the Firebringer.* Four Winds, 1985. Aljan is an impulsive unicorn and is impatient to become a warrior. He goes on a quest to prove his worthiness. He conquers the wyrms and gains insight into life and death.

_____. *Darkangel.* Little, 1982. A servant girl, Aeriel, must decide whether to save or destroy her vampire master. Does his obvious greatness overpower his evil deeds?

_____. *Gathering of Gargoyles.* Little, 1984. The White Witch has made gargoyles out of the mortals she has enslaved. Aeriel must free Irrylath from the White Witch's spell.

_____. *Woman Who Loved Reindeer.* Little, 1985. Rainbow is a child Caribou is given by her sister-in-law because he is not her husband's child. He is closely akin to the deer and even though Caribou loves him she finds him strange.

Pierce, Tamara. *Alanna, First Adventure.* Atheneum, 1983. The story of Alanna. A fantasy with a medieval flavor, as Alanna, posing as a boy, becomes a page and then a squire to the Prince.

_____. *In the Hand of the Goddess.* Atheneum, 1984. Alanna conceals the fact that she is a girl, and pursues knighthood. But, she fears sorcery against her. She is Squire to Prince Jonathon, who knows she is a girl.

_____. *Lioness Rampant.* Atheneum, 1988. Alanna travels to the Roof of the World to get the Dominon Jewels. She meets many challenges, both dangerous and surprising.

_____. *Woman Who Rides Like a Man.* Atheneum, 1986. Alanna influences a desert tribe by changing the role of women. She teaches them to be Shamams, a role meant for men only. She also continues to mature and succeed in her field.

Pilling, Ann. *Big Pink.* Viking, 1988. Angela is in boarding school. Her dorm is "Big Pink." She is fat and is teased. Sophie sends a trick note to her from a boy she has a crush on. Even though Angela can sing and play piano she leaves school.

_____. *Henry's Leg.* Viking, 1987. Henry finds a mannikin's leg and takes it home. The leg is later stolen and he wonders why. A jewel robbery and a life threatening event happen before Henry gets a reward for solving the mystery.

Pinkerton, Katherine. *Hidden Harbor.* Harcourt, 1951. Spence, Rod and Vicky live in pioneering Alaska where fish and logging are ways to make a living for their family. They would like a boat and more contact with the outside world.

_____. *Second Meeting.* Harcourt, 1956. Vicky, 17, has a talent for photography and feels she must leave Alaska. Philip returns with visiting scientists and Vicky helps them with her knowledge of the local Indians. She marries Philip.

Pinkwater, Daniel. *Alan Mendelsohn, Boy from Mars.* Dutton, 1979. Leonard and Alan were always falling for some scheme presented to them by con artists but somehow they came out winning. A spoof that is exaggeratedly funny.

_____. *Borgel.* Macmillan, 1990. Melvin tells of his adventures in time and space with his great-uncle Borgel, age 111.

_____. *Fat Men from Space.* Dodd, 1977. William runs into raiders of junk food from outer space.

_____. *Frankenbagel Monster.* Dutton, 1986. Bagelunculus is a giant bagel who has gone mad via Frankenstein.

_____. *Hoboken Chicken Emergency.* Prentice, 1977. The Hoboken chicken is six feet tall and weighs 260 pounds.

_____. *Jolly Roger.* Lothrop, 1985. Jolly Roger is a dog left in care of The Kid. He becomes the leader of a pack of wharf dogs.

_____. *Lizard Music.* Dodd, 1976. Victor sees the lizards on late night television. They are playing strange music on saxophones. Then he meets the Chicken Man who knows about the lizards. They, plus the chicken, go to look for them.

_____. *Magic Moscow.* Four Winds, 1980. A story not of Moscow, Russia, but of Hoboken, New Jersey, and its Ice Cream parlor. A funny story.

_____. *Moosepire.* Little, 1986. A vampire moose is haunting the citizens of and visitors to Yellowtooth. A blue nosed moose tries to solve the mystery.

_____. *Muffin Fiend.* Lothrop, 1986. A pure Pinkwater story. The muffin fiend is extraterrestrial and is overcome by an operatic singing duel using jujitsu.

_____. *Slaves of Spiegel.* Four Winds, 1982. Steve and Norman and the Magic Moscow restaurant are transported through space to compete in an intergalactic junk food cooking contest.

_____. *Snarkout Boys and the Avocado of Death.* Lothrop, 1982. Walter, Winston and Rat have an adventure involving a mad scientist and the Chicken Man.

_____. *Snarkout Boys and the Baconburg Horror.* Lothrop, 1984. Walter, Winston and Rat have an adventure involving a beatnik poet and a werewolf.

_____. *Worms of Kukulima.* Dutton, 1981. Ronald and his grandfather go with Sir Pelicanstein to look for intelligent earthworms in Kukulima.

_____. *Yobgorgle, Mystery Monster of Lake Ontario.* Houghton, 1979. Eugeri and his fast food freak Uncle Mel live a full of laughs adventure with a large cast of characters. A humorous version of the Flying Dutchman legend.

Pinkwater, Jill. *Buffalo Brenda.* Macmillan, 1989. Brenda, Tuna and India Ink Teidleban survive their freshman year in spite of a mean teacher. They are on the school newspaper and expose a food scandal. They adopt a buffalo as a school mascot.

_____. *Disappearance of Sister Perfect.* Dutton, 1987. Sherelee discovers that her sister joined a cult "Temple of Perfection." She decides to liberate her whether she wants to or not. An expose of cult life.

Pinsker, Judith. *Lot Like You.* Bantam, 1988. Bo is overweight but is liked by Howard. Then Howard's mother is killed in an auto accident. When school starts again everyone acts strangely toward him. Bo is determined to help him.

Piper, Roberta. *Little Red.* Scribner, 1963. Nan wants to ride and make friends with Little Red, a pony. But she finds there is a lot of work owning and caring for a horse.

Pirsig, Robert. *Zen and the Art of Motorcycle Maintenance.* Morrow, 1974. A man and his son, Chris, travel across country in order to find themselves and each other.

Pitkin, Dorothy. *Grass Was That High.* Pantheon, 1959. Kit left her best friend, Allie, and her sailboat, Old Greenwich, and went on vacation on a farm where she raised a calf.

_____. *Wiser Than Winter.* Pantheon, 1960. Kit needs to decide between marriage and college.

Pitt, Nancy. *Beyond the High White Wall.* Scribner, 1986. Libby witnesses the murder of a peasant. She wants to see justice and works for the denouement of Sereda.

Pitts, Paul. *Racing the Sun.* Avon, 1988. Brandon learns about his Indian heritage from his grandfather.

Place, Marian. *Juan's Eighteen Wheeler Summer.* Dodd, 1982. Juan, 13, is a trucker's helper. He hauls fruits and vegetables in Southern California. He saves the life of his employer after an accident. His father had been killed by a drunk driver.

_____. *Nobody Meets Bigfoot.* Dodd, 1976. A boy and his grandmother go on a searching expedition in the Northwest mountains to find Bigfoot.

Plath, Sylvia. *Bell Jar.* Bantam, 1975. A college student who wants to be a writer has a nervous breakdown.

Platt, Kin. *Ape Inside Me.* Lippincott, 1979. Ed tends toward violence. He can't control the "Ape Inside."

_____. *Boy Who Could Make Himself Disappear.* Chilton, 1968. Roger is ignored by his divorced mother. He is hampered by a speech impediment. He is so cruelly treated that he withdraws. Can anyone reach this saddened boy?

_____. *Brogg's Brain.* Lippincott, 1981. Monty is the third best runner at school. Everyone but himself believes he can be number one. He begins to wonder if they are right.

_____. *Chloris and the Creeps.* Chilton, 1973. Chloris's mother's boyfriend is the Creep. When she marries him Chloris causes trouble. She idolizes her dead father but she comes around to accept her new father.

_____. *Chloris and the Freaks.* Bradbury, 1975. Jenny is hooked on astrological signs. Her sister Chloris thinks Jenny is a freak. Chloris feels her dead father wants her mother to divorce Fidel, her new husband.

_____. *Chloris and the Weirdos.* Bradbury, 1978. Chloris tells about life with her mother and sister, as she sees it. Jenny's boyfriends are the weirdos, as are her own. Chloris and her mother have a bitter argument and she leaves.

_____. *Crocker.* Lippincott, 1983. Sensible Dorothy unexpectedly falls in love with unpredictable Crocker.

_____. *Doomsday Gang.* Greenwillow, 1978. A boy, 15, struggles to survive in the slums of Los Angeles. There are fear, hunger, depravity and violence ... and language.

_____. *Dracula, Go Home.* Watts, 1979. A spoof that is funny and exciting at the same time.

_____. *Frank and Stein and Me.* Watts, 1982. Jack plays basketball and wins a trip to Paris where he encounters smuggling (he is asked to deliver a cake to friends that is really "pot"). He meets Dr. Stein and together they clear Jack's name.

_____. *Ghost of Hellshire Street.* Delacorte, 1980. Steve, Sinbad and their friends get involved with a kidnapped scientist, a weird psychic, Sheriff Landry and a pirate ghost.

_____. *Hey, Dummy.* Chilton, 1971. Neil meets and protects 12-year-old Alan, a brain damaged child.

_____. *Mystery of the Witch Who Wouldn't.* Chilton, 1969. Steve and his dog, Sinbad, solve the criminal activities of the Satanists. The crime was predicted by a witch.

_____. *Run for Your Life.* Dell, 1977. Lee has a newspaper delivery job. He needs it since his dad died and money is scarce. One of his machines had no money when he opened the change compartment. He is afraid the company will think he took it.

_____. *Sinbad and Me.* Delacorte, 1966. A funny and frightening mystery cleverly solved by Sinbad and Steve.

Plowman, Stephanie. *My Kingdom for a Grave.* Houghton, 1971. Andrei relates life up to World War I. He tells about the Czar and Rasputin. He tries to help his family escape but fails. He later learns of their death and burial.

_____. *Three Lives for the Czar.* Houghton, 1969. Andrei lived with his family in Russia during the reign of Nicholas II. The story implies that the Revolution may not have happened if Nicholas had been a kinder man.

Poe, Edgar Allan. *Fall of the House of Usher.* Nal, 1982. The Usher curse is taking the lives of Roderick and his sister. He asks help from an old friend but it may be too late.

Pohlman, Lillian. *Sing Loose.* Westminster, 1968. When she must finally face the situation, Maria learns that people worth knowing can forgive and forget. Her father is being paroled after serving time for embezzlement.

Polcovar, Jane. *Charming.* Bantam, 1984. Madame Dariel will make Kathy a star but what is the cost! She loses friends, family, her will and her soul.

Polland, Madeleine. *Born to Be Proud.* Holt, 1961. Beorn, son of a Viking sea king, captures an Irish girl, the only survivor of a Viking raid, and takes her back to Denmark.

_____. *Children of the Red King.* Holt, 1961. Conflict between the Irish and the Normans in the 1200's. There is intrigue within the Connacht clan.

_____. *Deirdre.* Doubleday, 1967. A star crossed love story. Dierdre falls in love with Naoise, a leader of the Red Knights. He gets killed in battle and she dies of a broken heart.

_____. *Queen Without a Crown.* Holt, 1965. Queen Grainne fights English occupation of Ireland. Patch, a page, shares her feelings but war and death bring hard decisions.

_____. *Queen's Blessing.* Holt, 1964. A story of the war torn Scotland of King Malcolm and Queen Margaret. Merca and Dag's parents are killed in the war and Merca swears revenge on the king but saves him from murder.

_____. *Town Across the Water.* Holt, 1961. While the Irish and English battle during the 16th century Liam and Margaret try to bring peace. They save the life of a Spanish captain from the Armada.

_____. *White Twilight.* Holt, 1962. Hannes is very good, prim and precise and wants to impress her father. Carl is a nobleman whose father is a pirate.

Pollock, Penny. *Keeping It a Secret.* Putnam, 1982. Mary Lou is new in school and doesn't want students to know that she wears a hearing aid.

Pomerantz, Charlotte. *Downtown Fairy Godmother.* Addison, 1978. Olivia wishes for a fairy godmother and gets one. She wears blue slacks and has her hair rolled in curlers; and her wish-giving powers are limited.

Poole, Josephine. *Moon Eyes.* Little, 1965. Aunt Rhoda has evil witchcraft powers and must be curtailed.

_____. *Visitor.* Harper, 1972. The visitor is a gaunt, strange man new to a small town. He is Harry's new tutor but Harry is suspicious of his powers.

Poole, Victoria. *Thursday's Child.* Little, 1980. Sam has a serious heart defect that shows up when he is seventeen. He needs a transplant but must wait for a donor. A moving story of the agony of waiting and the joy of family support.

Pope, Ray. *Salvage from Strosa.* Hart Davis, 1967. Frank and Dave give aid to an escaping seaman and claim a trawler as salvage.

_____. *Strosa Light.* Hart Davis, 1965. Frank and his brother Dave help Strosa Lighthouse keepers when a trawler runs aground.

Pople, Maureen. *Nugget of Gold.* Holt, 1988. Sally found a book owned by Ann 100 years ago. In separate chapters Sally and Ann tell their story. Ann's parents are less than nice; her romance forbidden. Sally's parents are divorced; her love in doubt.

_____. *Other Side of the Family.* Holt, 1986. Kate goes to Australia during World War II. She stays with an eccentric, poor woman who is her grandmother. The woman was supposed to be wealthy and self-centered.

Porte, Barbara. *Kidnapping of Aunt Elizabeth.* Greenwillow, 1985. Ashley finds a strange family portrait evolving as she gathers stories from her family for a class project.

Portis, Charles. *True Grit.* Simon & Schuster, 1968. Mattie's father is killed in the West in the 1870's. She is determined to find the killer and goes through many hardships to find him. She loses her arm by snakebite but the killer is dead.

Potok, Chaim. *Chosen.* Simon & Schuster, 1967. Danny and Rueven meet through their interest in baseball. They are both Jewish but are totally different. They become close friends and help each other.

_____. *Davita's Harp.* Knopf, 1985. Davita lives in New York City. Her parents are involved in the city's politics and have left their religious mores behind. Davita must decide what she wants to do.

Potter, Bronson. *Antonio.* Atheneum, 1968. Antonio's crippled hand prevents him from following his father's trade: fisherman. Because of his alertness and skill in swimming he is able to save a fishing fleet in a storm.

Potter, Dan. *Crazy Moon Zoo.* Watts, 1985. Jory, 17, is a shadow of his older brother. He is not an athlete, nor an outstanding student. He tries to be somebody special but always ends up being just Jory. A painful growing up process.

Potter, Marian. *Blatherskite.* Morrow, 1980. Life on a farm during the Great Depression is hard but also has its moments of merriment for a ten-year-old.

_____. *Chance Wild Apple.* Morrow, 1982. A Depression years story as seen by a boy on a Missouri farm.

_____. *Mark Makes His Move.* Morrow, 1986. Mark has the best of intentions but somehow everything seems to backfire.

_____. *Milepost 67.* Follett, 1965. Evaline lives in a railroad house on Milepost 67. Her dad worked for the railroad. The day to day life of poor workers on the railroad.

Powell, Padgett. *Edisto.* Farrar, 1984. Simon, 12, is born into a world where blacks and whites have differences. He is aware of this but can't make sense of it.

Powers, John. *Last Catholic in America.* Warner, 1982. There are, according to Sister Eleanor, two religions: Catholic and Public.

Preiss, Byron. *Dragonworld.* Bantam, 1983.

Johan is hang gliding and is killed by a flying dragon. His father swears revenge against Simbala of the magical world of Fandora.

Preussler, Otfried. *Satanic Mill*. Smith, 1987. A young boy studying to be a magician outwits the master magician.

Price, Joan. *Truth Is a Bright Star*. Celestial Arts, 1982. A Hopi Indian boy and a fur trapper become friends after he bought him from a Spanish soldier in 1832.

Price, Willard. *African Adventure*. Day, 1963. Hal and Roger are in Central Africa to get a hippo, three buffalo and two giraffes. How they track and collect these animals for world wide zoos is the theme of this book.

_____. *Amazon Adventure*. Day, 1949. An account of a trip down the Amazon River on an animal collecting tour by Hal and Roger with their Indian guide.

_____. *Diving Adventure*. Day, 1970. Hal and Roger make friends with dolphins as they collect fish specimens for their father. Another adventure with sea snakes, man eating sharks and their old murderous friend Merlin Kaggs.

_____. *Elephant Adventure*. Day, 1964. Hal and Roger are to trap young African elephants for the zoo. They encounter native superstitions and slave trading.

_____. *Gorilla Adventure*. Day, 1969. Hal and Roger search for and capture a giant gorilla. They see a rare white python and a black panther.

_____. *Lion Adventure*. Day, 1967. Hal and Roger are after two man-eating lions. They must be careful not to kill any innocent lions.

_____. *Safari Adventure*. Day, 1966. Hal and Roger are helping an African game warden catch animal poachers.

_____. *South Sea Adventure*. Day, 1952. Hal and Roger are collecting deep sea specimens and looking for a secret pearl lagoon. They encounter sea monsters and hurricanes, and they escape from a desert island on a raft.

_____. *Volcano Adventure*. Day, 1956. Hal and Roger explore a volcano in a diving bell and are trapped in a volcano ring.

_____. *Whale Adventure*. Day, 1960. Hal and Roger sign up on an old square rigger and go whaling. The captain is cruel but the crew reaches shore and the captain is disgraced.

Prince, Alison. *How's Business*. Four Winds, 1988. A London boy, How, is sent to the country during World War II and is tested by the local boys for his degree of courage. He goes back to London to his injured mother and destroyed house.

_____. *Night Landings*. Morrow, 1984. Jan, Harrie and Neil are sure that smugglers are operating in the nearby airfield.

_____. *Sinister Airfield*. Morrow, 1983. Findng a body in an abandoned airfield causes three teens to wonder about rustlers. Jan, Harrie and Neil help to capture the thieves.

_____. *Type One Super Robot*. Four Winds, 1988. During the summer a boy and his uncle get a robot for the housekeeping chores. But it has a mind of its own.

Prince, Marjorie. *Cheese Stands Alone*. Archway, 1973. Daisy's four summer friends changed over the winter. Stinky, one of the other girls, is now called Boobs. And the boys are fascinated. Daisy is alone and looks for other entertainment in Mr. Potter.

Provost, Gary. *David and Max*. Jewish Publication Society, 1988. David learns from his grandfather the horrors of the Holocaust and uses this knowledge to be stronger.

_____. *Good If It Goes*. Bradbury, 1984. David has a few problems: Bar Mitzvah practice, his dying grandfather, a girl he just met and a younger brother. He survives it all.

_____. *Popcorn*. Bradbury, 1989. Mark is the leader of his Popcorn band and is bullied by Joel, the Troll. He takes tae kwon do lessons and is not bothered anymore.

Pryor, Bonnie. *Plum Tree War*. Morrow, 1989. Robert hates his cousin Harri and her dog. Harri runs away because of the tension. Robert follows her and rescues a fawn.

_____. *Rats, Spiders and Love*. Morrow, 1986. Samantha's mother remarries and is going to move to Ohio with her new husband. Samantha does all she knows to keep from going along.

_____. *Seth of the Lion People*. Morrow, 1988. Seth, 12, is the story teller of his pre-historic clan. He wants to be a hunter/fighter leader. He runs away with Esa and a puppy he saved, to find another clan.

Pullman, Phillip. *Count Karlstein*. Chatto & Winders, 1982. Two girls must escape before their evil uncle sends them to his hidden hunting lodge as prey for the Demon Huntsman.

_____. *Ruby in the Smoke*. Knopf, 1987. Sally wants to find out about her father's mysterious death in the South China Sea. She encounters robberies, murder and the priceless ruby.

Purtell, Richard. *Enchantment at Delphi*. Gulliver, 1986. Alice is studying in Greece. She has time travel trips to meet Apollo, Athena and Dionysius. She and her friend Niko disappear in time leaving a journal behind.

Pyle, Howard. *Garden Behind the Moon*. Parabola, 1988. A new edition of an old classic. A boy travels to the moon because he is lured by the Moon Angel.

_____. *Men of Iron*. Harper, 1930. A literary standard about the bravery of knights in England.

_____. *Merry Adventures of Robin Hood*. Nal, 1986. Robin Hood robs the rich in the name of evil Prince John. He supports Richard the Lionhearted and has many adventures between the two.

_____. *Otto of the Silver Hand*. Dover,

1916. Robber barons were cruel leaders of feudal Germany. The monks were peaceful and scholarly. One day the son of one of the robber barons was kidnapped.

Quigley, Martin. *Original Colored House of David.* Houghton, 1981. Timmy proves his manliness and athletic skill.

Quimby, Myrtle. *Cougar.* Criterion, 1963. Jerry runs away from home and stays with an old Indian. But he doesn't like the Indian's animals.

Quin-Harkin, Janet. *Love Match.* Bantam, 1982. Joanna wants to be a professional tennis player and practices every chance she gets. She doesn't make the girl's team but is asked to be on the boy's team. She meets Rick and thinks tennis isn't everything.

Rabe, Berniece. *Margaret's Moves.* Dutton, 1987. Margaret is in a wheelchair but lives a life of a normal person who does things and goes places.

_____. *Naomi.* Nelson, 1975. Living on a Missouri farm in the early 1940's, Naomi suffers for four years under a fortune teller's death prophecy and her mother's tyranny.

_____. *Rehearsal for the Bigtime.* Watts, 1988. Margo is determined to be the best clarinetist she can be in spite of early failures.

Rabinowich, Ellen. *Toni's Crowd.* Watts, 1978. Sandi is in a new school. She wants to be in the "cool" crowd. But the "cool" crowd is not nice, as Sandi learns when she befriends Martha.

_____. *Underneath I'm Different.* Delacorte, 1983. Amy, 16, is overweight and wants to be a beauty. She takes ballet lessons and is....

Rabinowitz, Ann. *Bethie.* Macmillan, 1989. Beth's parents are divorced. Grace's father leaves for another woman. The two girls become friends but Grace is overwhelmed by her problems and commits suicide.

_____. *Knight on Horseback.* Macmillan, 1987. Eddy goes on his own in London. He takes a wooden knight on horseback ... and adventure begins.

Radford, Ken. *Cellar.* Holiday, 1989. Siam is a companion in an old spooky house. She thinks a ghost is watching her. A crime occurred in the house fifty years before. Sarah Jane was imprisoned and starved to death.

_____. *Haunting at Mill Lane.* Holiday, 1988. Sarah hears strange noises in her new home. She is lonely and unhappy. She befriends a ghost, Sally-Anne, who was murdered by her stepmother one hundred years ago.

_____. *House in the Shadows.* Holiday, 1987. Emma is transported back in time one hundred years. She becomes a ghost in this past life and observes two wicked sisters, an evil man and an orphan who needs her help.

Radin, Ruth. *Tac's Island.* Macmillan, 1986. Steve is vacationing off the Virginia coast. He meets Tac, a year-round resident. Their friendship builds as they share adventures exploring the island.

_____. *Tac's Turn.* Macmillan, 1987. Tac is visiting Steve in Philadelphia. They test each other's friendship through personality clashes and action.

Radley, Gail. *CF in His Corner.* Four Winds, 1984. Jeff's brother Scott is ill with cystic fibrosis but Scott doesn't know it. The story is about whether or not he should be told.

_____. *Nothing Stays the Same Forever.* Crown, 1981. Carrie, 12, is against her father remarrying. Her neighbor, whom she helps with gardening, helps her understand the situation.

_____. *World Turned Inside Out.* Crown, 1982. Jeremy's brother committed suicide but he still lives in his shadow. His parents don't realize his situation until he tries to run away.

Rae, John. *Third Twin: A Ghost Story.* Warne, 1981. Shamus and Jonny see all the ghosts come to life at midnight. They are angry. They decide to help them but Jonny is taken captive until the ghosts get their way.

Ramati, Alexander. *And the Violins Stopped Playing.* Watts, 1986. Roman Mirga is a survivor of the Gypsy Holocaust. 500,000 gypsies were killed by the Nazis. This is the story of one Polish gypsy family.

Randall, Florence. *All the Sky Together.* Atheneum, 1983. Cassie, 16, needs to make new friends. She meets Ellen and Pete who turn out to be not so nice and are killed in a drunken boating accident.

_____. *Almost Year.* Atheneum, 1971. A black girl thinks it is her hostility that is setting off the poltergeist phenomenon in a white household.

Randall, Janet. *Desert Venture.* McKay, 1963. Gail and her mother go to a new home in the desert because Gail is dating the wrong kind of boy. Paul is under juvenile supervision. She meets Toby who has asthma and she must decide what's right.

_____. *Girl from Boothill.* McKay, 1962. Beryl is a miner's daughter and wants to go to college. She meets teenage theatre people and forgets her old friends. But she stays with them and her family in the debate between miners and tourists.

Ransom, Candice. *Amanda.* Scholastic, 1984. Amanda leaves cultured Boston and her friend Joseph to travel to Oregon by wagon train. She will overcome her spoiled party girl ways or she won't survive. The time is the 1840's.

_____. *My Sister, the Meanie.* Scholastic, 1988. Jackie wants to be popular in school and copies her older sister. This causes many problems at home and at school.

_____. *My Sister, the Traitor.* Scholastic, 1989. Jackie lives in the shadow of her older sister. She meets Russ and likes him but it's her sister he dates in spite of the fact that she already has a boyfriend.

_____. *Nicole.* Scholastic, 1986. Nicole has two serious boyfriends from whom she can choose. But she and her mother leave for America on the "Titanic."

Ransome, Arthur. *Swallows and Amazons.* Godine, 1985. This is a new issue of an old favorite about the adventures of the four Walker children.

Rappaport, Doreen. *Trouble at the Mines.* Harper, 1987. A description of the serious coal miner's strike of 1898.

Rardin, Susan. *Captives in a Foreign Land.* Houghton, 1984. A suspense story of two Americans who are kidnapped by terrorists.

Raskin, Ellen. *Figgs and Phantoms.* Dutton, 1974. Mona Lisa Newton is a moody misfit in the off-beat Figg family. She dreams a trip out-of-this-world after Uncle Florence.

_____. *Mysterious Disappearance of Leon (I Mean Noel).* Dutton, 1971. Mr. and Mrs. Carillon are joint heirs to a soup fortune but Mrs. Carillon can't find Mr. Carillon (Leon) or (Noel).

_____. *Tattooed Potato and Other Clues.* Dutton, 1975. Dickory assists a part-time detective in solving some unique cases. There are a wild bunch of characters in endless disguises who all come unmasked at the end.

_____. *Westing Game.* Dutton, 1978. A mystery of the Westing family. When Old Sam dies he makes a game out of which of his sixteen heirs will win his millions. One of the heirs killed him and Turtle, a girl, knew who it was! Newbery, 1979.

Rawlings, Marjorie. *Yearling.* Scribner, 1983. Jody, 12, finds a deer and names it Flagg. This is a sad story that doesn't need to be revealed.

Rawls, Wilson. *Summer of the Monkeys.* Doubleday, 1976. Jay finds a group (30) of escaped monkeys and tries to capture them to get a reward. It is not as easy as it seems. Even though the episode with his ill sister is touching, the story is funny.

_____. *Where the Red Fern Grows.* Doubleday, 1961. Old Dan and Little Ann are two coon hounds owned by Billy during the Depression years. He wins a gold cup with them and learns about love and trust.

Ray, Mary. *Voice of Apollo.* Farrar, 1965. Phaedon and Charilos are cousins but when Charilos gets ill Phaedon must leave because in order to get well Charilos must give up his best friend. Phaedon goes to Delphi and the two are reunited later.

Ray, Ophelia. *Daughter of the Tejas.* New York, 1965. Tiwana's mother was kidnapped by the Apaches in 1725 and she wants to rescue her. She is a Caddo Indian but was raised by the Mission and has been influenced by them.

Raymond, Charles. *Trouble with Gus.* Follett, 1968. Gus lives in a lower class neighborhood and doesn't like what she sees. She wants to move but dad lost his job so they stay. She does meet some

nice friends and learns to cope with prejudices.

_____. *Up from Appalachia.* Follett, 1966. The Cantrells moved to Chicago for a better life. They were called hillbillies by their neighbors but they soon won the respect of all and life did get better.

Rayner, Mary. *Witchfinder.* Morrow, 1976. Louisa needs to save her mother from possession by a witch. The mother loves Wansbury Ring but Louisa feels evil there.

Razzi, Jim. *Search for King Pup's Tomb.* Bantam, 1985. Sherluck Bones, a dog whose style is that of the famous detective, is going to find the lost treasure of King Pup's tomb.

Read, Efreida. *Brothers by Choice.* Farrar, 1974. Rocky runs away from his adoptive parents' home to join a commune, and his brother goes to great lengths to find him.

Read, Mary. *Sack Man and the Grave.* Abingdon, 1981. In 1935 Victory spends the summer with poor Aunt Agnes. She and her friends try to find the family treasure hidden during the Civil War. They get help from the sack man and a friendly ghost.

Reader, Dennis. *Coming Back Alive.* Random, 1981. Bridget's parents were killed. Dylan's were divorced bitterly. They run away to escape the pain and become both hunters and the hunted.

Reading, J.P. *Bouquets for Brimbal.* Harper, 1980. Macy and Anne are friends. Anne is lesbian but Macy doesn't see it. Macy has a boyfriend, Dan, and realizes that she and Anne can be friends despite the differences. They act in summer stock together.

Reboul, Antoine. *Thou Shalt Not Kill.* Phillips, 1969. An Egyptian boy who hates Jews and an Israeli girl who hates Egyptians meet and try to kill each other. But survival is important and they help each other face heat, thirst and wind in the Sinai Desert.

Reed, Kit. *Ballad of T. Rantula.* Ballantine, 1981. "Futch"'s parents are divorced and his life is a mess. He dreams up a bodyguard but what he needs is a mindguard.

Rees, David. *Exeter Blitz.* Nelson, 1978. A tragic story of one family, told by each individual as he/she experienced it, during and after the German raid of this city. June, Colin, Mary and their parents were not together at the time.

_____. *Risks.* Nelson, 1977. Ian and Derek are hitchhiking to London but no one picks them up. Derek finally gets a ride but must leave Ian behind. Ian's body is found later, strangled; Derek must live with this event.

Reese, John. *Big Mutt.* Westminster, 1962. Big Mutt is abandoned by his owner during a blizzard because he is called a sheep killer. He is found and saved from death.

Reeves, Bruce. *Street Smarts.* Beaufort, 1981. T.C., 12, is unhappy living in a commune. She meets an abused boy and wants to help him. She then runs away and lives on the streets. A jarring, realistic story.

Reggiani, Renee. *Tomorrow and the Next Day.* Coward, 1967. Antonio teaches in a poor section of South Italy. He must fight rats, superstitions and lack of motivation. He gets help and beats ignorance and poverty.

Reiss, Johanna. *Journey Back.* Crowell, 1976. After spending three years in hiding, this Jewish family is reunited. Annie, Simi and Rachel begin to rebuild their lives. Their father remarries.

————. *Upstairs Room.* Crowell, 1972. A Jewish family, although separated, survived the German persecution. They stayed in farmers' homes for three years when the Nazis occupied Holland. Now Annie and Simi must face the future.

Rendell, Ruth. *Talking to Strange Men.* Pantheon, 1987. Mungo and Guy play a game of secret messages, stolen code books, secret agents, moles and safe houses. John discovers some of these and assumes it's real spies and begins to get seriously involved.

————. *Unkindness of Ravens.* Pantheon, 1985. A newly formed girl's club, based on hatred of men, is suspected of knife attacks on men. Inspector Wexford looks into the matter.

Renner, Beverly. *Hideaway Summer.* Harper, 1978. Two youngsters must survive a summer lost in the woods.

Renvoise, Jean. *Wild Thing.* Little, 1971. Morag, 16, has gone through a series of foster homes and street living. She runs away to the mountains where she lives in a cave and steals food. She helps a young man but is later needlessly killed.

Reynolds, Pamela. *Different Kind of Sister.* Lothrop, 1968. Sally and Debbie are sisters. Debbie was a source of embarrassment for Sally.

————. *Earth Times Two.* Lothrop, 1970. Jeremy and Helene are studying Doppelgangers (doubles). One day Jeremy disappears. He goes to another planet much like Earth. Teleportation and ESP are essential ingredients, also a telepathic cat.

————. *Horseshoe Hill.* Lothrop, 1965. Tibby is sure nobody likes her because she is tall. She finds an unwanted skinny horse and cares for him. She loses her self-consciousness. Tibby and Warlord help the family keep their farm.

Rhinehart, Luke. *Long Voyage Back.* Delacorte, 1983. Neil observes a nuclear attack from his small boat. He takes aboard a few survivors and they must live on the boat looking for a safe harbor. They see the horrors of the war: radiation, starvation, etc.

Rhodes, Evan. *Prince of Central Park.* Coward, 1975. Jay-Jay runs away from his foster mother and lives by his own wiles in a tree in Central Park.

Rhue, Morton. *Wave.* Delacorte, 1981. A classroom assignment gets out of hand when it is practiced outside. The Wave is a teaching method for studying Fascism.

Rice, Eve. *Remarkable Return of Winston Potts Crisply.* Greenwillow, 1978. Becky and Max see their brother, Potter, who is supposed to be away, in a hobby shop. Potter is being followed by a man and Becky and Max imagine all sorts of things. CIA? Spy?

Rich, Louise. *Star Island Boy.* Watts, 1968. Larry lives in foster homes. He is sent to a lobster village with other foster kids. He is happy there but knows he must leave and face another goodbye. He gets a permanent home at last.

————. *Three of a Kind.* Watts, 1970. Sally is shifted from family to family. The Coopers take her in and she works with their grandson, Benjie, who is withdrawn.

Richard, Adrienne. *Accomplice.* Atlantic, 1973. Benjie, 15, goes to Israel for the summer. He befriends an Arab and is tricked into bringing explosives to an archeological dig.

————. *Pistol.* Little, 1969. Billy, known as Pistol and then later as Bill, tells of his uncertain life before, during and shortly after the Depression. There are ups but mostly downs. The story ends with Bill going, hopefully, to Chicago.

————. *Wings.* Little, 1974. Pip lives in the 1920's and dreams of being an aviatrix. Her distant father disapproves of her unconventional friends and the free life she lives with her mother.

Richardson, Grace. *Douglas.* Harper, 1966. Douglas is charming and tragically unreliable. This is the story of his growing from boyhood to manhood.

Richardson, Judith. *David's Landing.* Woods Hole, 1984. David goes to live with his divorced father who is a scientist. He gets involved with the community and it changes his lifestyle.

Richer, Robert. *Rudi of the Mountain.* Criterion, 1965. Peter and Larry explore the Alps. They take risks and are trapped on the slope. Rudi forgets his fear of climbing and rescues them.

Richler, Mordecai. *Jacob Two-Two and the Dinosaur.* Knopf, 1987. Jacob gets a lizard for a pet. He names it Dippy; Dippy grows up to be a dinosaur. A humorous satire.

Richmond, Sandra. *Wheels for Walking.* Atlantic, 1983. Sally goes away for a weekend to ski. She is involved in an auto accident and her spinal cord is severed. She must face life from a wheelchair. She does so with optimism.

Richter, Conrad. *Country of Strangers.* Knopf, 1966. This is the story of a white girl captured by Indians. They must return her to her original parents.

————. *Light in the Forest.* Knopf, 1966. Story of a teenaged boy's dilemma in deciding where he wants to grow up—in an Indian culture or that of the white man.

Richter, Hans. *Friedrich.* Holt, 1970. Friedrich and a young boy grow up in pre–World War II Germany. They and their families are friends, then anti–Semitism rears its ugly head. A sad, unbelievably cruel story of the treatment of Jews.

————. *I Was There.* Holt, 1972. An account of the Hitler Youth Movement and why the youngsters joined it. Heinz and Gunther follow Hitler's plans even into battle even though they are disturbed by what they see.

Riddell, Ruth. *Haunted Journey.* Atheneum, 1988. Obie goes off to find the mussel beds that yielded pearls that his grandfather talked about. He and Bas struggle through rough terrain to find the pearl beds and then go home.

Riding, Julia. *Space Traders Unlimited.* Atheneum, 1988. Streak is a runaway in a Martian city. He gets involved in a street fight, a crime wave, and sabotage. He is captured and escapes.

Rietveld, J. *ABC Molly.* Norton, 1966. In the late 1800's Molly wants to learn to read and write, but that kind of learning is only for boys.

Riha, Bohumil. *Ryn, Wild Horse.* Doubleday, 1966. Old Jacob owns Ryn who is always in some scrape. The villagers are upset and his cottage is burned by non-understanding people and authorities.

Riley, Jocelyn. *Crazy Quilt.* Bantam, 1984. Merle, Ron and Diane live with their grandmother while their mother recovers her health. Her mother wants to get out of the hospital but Merle is aware that she is not yet ready.

————. *Only My Mouth Is Smiling.* Morrow, 1982. Merle, Ron and Diane's mother is mentally unstable. Merle tells how they lived until she became aware that mother needed help and called her grandmother. It ends on a hopeful note.

Rinaldi, Ann. *But in the Fall I'm Leaving.* Holiday, 1985. Brie plans to leave her too strict father and live with the mother who abandoned her as a baby. But she learns that Miss Emily, whose house she spray painted, is her maternal grandmother.

————. *Good Side of My Heart.* Holiday, 1987. Brie is sixteen and has a friend, Josh, who is a senior. She has a brother and a strict father who doesn't like Josh. She finds out that Josh is a homosexual and is confused.

————. *Promises Are for Keeping.* Holiday, 1982. Nicki is fifteen and an orphan. She is caught stealing birth control pills from her brother's desk. This only adds to the trouble she already has with him.

————. *Term Paper.* Walker, 1980. Nicki's brother assigns her a topic for a term paper: death in the family. Her brother resents his responsibility for her.

————. *Wolf by the Ears.* Scholastic, 1991. Harriet lives in the South in 1820. She is a slave and is offered her freedom at age 21. She enters white mainstream since she is only ¼ black.

Rinaldo, C.L. *Dark Dream.* Harper, 1974. Carlo's mother is dead, his father is away and he is lonely. His friend is Joey, a retarded man who is put in an institution. Carlo has a heart condition. Joey escapes and saves Carlo's life.

Rinkoff, Barbara. *Watchers.* Knopf, 1972. Two lonely boys discover they both enjoy watching people and, despite many obstacles, become close friends.

Riskind, Mary. *Apple Is My Sign.* Houghton, 1981. Harry is in a school for the deaf. He makes friends and has success in school. The book has the translation of characters' sign language into oral speech.

————. *Follow That Mom.* Houghton, 1987. Maxine, 11, and her friend Bonnie try to get Maxine's mother out of Girl Scouts. Their "act first — think later" approach to methods gets them into trouble.

Ritchie, Rita. *Night Coach to Paris.* Norton, 1970. Maurice goes to France to find his cousin Estelle. He is caught by enemies and left without identification or money. He must find Estelle and meet his ship to return to America.

————. *Pirates of Samarkand.* Norton, 1967. Haroun and Nuri work with their father on his fishing boat. The boat disappears during a storm. They learn about pirates when they are kidnapped, then escape, catch the pirates and return their boat.

Riter, Dorris. *Edge of Violence.* McKay, 1964. Dirk, 17, an orphan, serves a year of probation on a horse ranch. His experiences include cars, horses, romance, dogs and teenage crime.

Roach, Marilynne. *Presto, or the Adventures of a Turnspit Dog.* Houghton, 1970. Presto is a talking dog who ran away from the inn where he was made to turn a spit. He met a puppeteer and joined his Punch and Judy show. But life on the streets in 1760 is dangerous.

Roberts, Glenys. *Richard Knight's Treasure!* Viking, 1987. Richard is in a Vietnam jail and the story tells why he is there. What happened to the treasure he sought in the Far East in the manner of Captain Kidd?

Roberts, Willo. *Baby Sitting Is a Dangerous Job.* Atheneum, 1985. Darcy, 13, babysits for three rich, spoiled kids. They and Darcy are kidnapped but Darcy outwits their captors and their dogs.

————. *Caroline.* Scholastic, 1985. Girls in the 1800's aren't supposed to have adventures. But Caroline cuts her hair, wears men's clothing and goes in search of gold.

————. *Don't Hurt Laurie.* Macmillan, 1977. Laurie, 11, tells a frightful story of child abuse.

————. *Eddie and the Fairy Godpuppy.* Atheneum, 1984. Eddie, an orphan, hopes the puppy he finds brings him good luck and a new family and home.

————. *Girl with the Silver Eyes.* Atheneum, 1980. Katie is the girl with the silver eyes and with special powers. She can move things just by thinking about it. She can read the minds of animals and communicate with them.

————. *Magic Book.* Atheneum, 1986. Alex

buys a book of spells to get rid of a bully, Norman. The spells seem to work. All of them have reasonable explanations but Alex stands up against Norman with or without magic.

_____. *Megan's Island.* Atheneum, 1988. Megan, 11, and her brother go to grandfather's cottage in the middle of the night when their mother leaves them. Frightening things happen before friend Ben comes to help.

_____. *Minder Curse.* Atheneum, 1978. Danny, his grandfather and Leroy, the dog, are always at the scene of minor disasters. But a prize canine, a pedigree silky terrier, has been stolen. Danny, C.B. and Paul solve the case.

_____. *More Minder Curses.* Atheneum, 1980. Danny helps the Caspitorian sisters (the cat ladies) when they think their house is haunted because they have seen faces in the window. Danny wants to capture Killer Cat while he's there.

_____. *No Monster in the Closet.* Atheneum, 1983. Steve and his dog, Sandy, explore an old house and find a mystery. The house is supposed to be haunted but seems to be in use. He gets involved with criminals who think he knows too much.

_____. *Pet Sitting Peril.* Atheneum, 1983. Nick finds a dog walking job to earn money for Disneyland. He gets involved in a fire, a mystery and more than he can handle.

_____. *Sugar Isn't Everything.* Atheneum, 1987. Amy, 11, is hiding her diabetic symptoms: hunger, thirst, tiredness. She learns the truth and she and her family learn to cope.

_____. *To Grandmother's House We Go.* Atheneum, 1990. Three children run away to their grandmother to avoid a foster home while their mother recovers from an illness. They get a cold reception and learn a terrible secret.

_____. *View from the Cherry Tree.* Atheneum, 1975. Because of his sister's wedding Rob was left alone. He sat in his cherry tree watching his crotchety neighbor. Then he saw her murdered! No one would believe him, except the murderer!

_____. *What Could Go Wrong?* Atheneum, 1989. Gracie, Eddie and Charles fly from Seattle to San Francisco. Gracie finds a coded crossword puzzle. There are a bomb threat, a mugging and a briefcase full of money.

Robertson, Keith. *Henry Reed, Inc.* Viking, 1958/1989. Henry Reed, who has been away from America most of his life, comes back for the summer and starts a businesss: "Henry Reed, Research." He and Midge do turtle painting and truffle hunting.

_____. *Henry Reed's Babysitting Service.* Viking, 1966. In New Jersey, Henry and Midge continue to run their research service.

_____. *Henry Reed's Big Show.* Viking, 1970. Henry's going to become a great theatrical producer. He starts in Grover's Corner and before the summer is over, he has put on a rock music festival and a wild western rodeo.

_____. *Henry Reed's Journey.* Viking, 1963. Henry, his friend Midge and her family travel from San Francisco to New Jersey, where he will spend the summer. He keeps a journal of a Hopi Indian parade, horned toads, etc.

_____. *Henry Reed's Think Tank.* Viking, 1986. Henry and Midge are now consultants for Grover's Corner. They can barely solve the problems they are asked to handle: Rodney's weight problem, Deirdre's allowance, Willy and Betsy's food, etc.

_____. *In Search of a Sandhill Crane.* Viking, 1973. Fifteen-year-old Link develops an interest in the wilderness.

_____. *Money Machine.* Viking, 1969. Neil and Swede look for counterfeiters. They are trapped in the cellar and do, by accident, discover the printing press.

_____. *Three Stuffed Owls.* Viking, 1954. The Carson Street Detective Agency made up of Neil and Swede look for a lost bicycle. Instead they find diamond smugglers and Three Stuffed Owls.

Robertson, Mary. *Tarantula and the Red Chugger.* Little, 1980. Ben met Lonnie and they call themselves Tarantula and Red Chugger. They become good friends and get into scrape after scrape with their imaginary game.

Robinson, Barbara. *Across from Indian Shore.* Lothrop, 1962. There is always work at the summer cabin: chopping wood, clearing land, winter preparation, gardening, etc. Luke meets an Indian lady who helps him with her snake bite.

_____. *My Brother Louis Measures Worms and Other Louis Stories.* Harper, 1988. Mary Elizabeth tells humorous stories about her brother, Louis, and other members of the family.

_____. *Trace Thru the Forest.* Lothrop, 1965. Jim, 14, helps build a road into the wilderness to open up more farm land. He is united with his lost father and learns many Indian ways during his journey.

Robinson, Jean. *Strange But Wonderful Cosmic Awareness of Duffy Moon.* Seabury, 1974. Duffy is small and sensitive and tries to prove himself by learning the secrets of the universe but when he meets Boots he finds his own power.

Robinson, Joan. *Charley.* Coward, 1970. Charley lives on her own for a week when she is sent to Aunt Louie's after reading: "I don't want Charley. You know that."

_____. *When Marnie Was There.* Coward, 1968. Anna imagines life into "Marnie." Once a real Marnie lived here and Anna sees that her life was not idyllic. She finally moves out of fantasy into the real world.

Robinson, Mary. *Amazing Valvano and the Mystery of the Hooded Rat.* Houghton, 1988. Maria plans her great magic act but it is spoiled when Lester, her rat, is stolen.

Robinson, Nancy. *Angela, Private Citizen.* Scholastic, 1989. Angela questions the fairness of life in her busy family.

_____. *Ballet Magic.* Whitman, 1982. Stacy grew tall fast and early. She is the tallest girl in her class. But she takes ballet lessons and does very well.

_____. *Just Plain Cat.* Four Winds, 1981. Chris changes schools and gets involved in his father's photography business, and gets a kitten.

_____. *Oh, Honestly, Angela.* Scholastic, 1985. Tina is unhappy about being poor until she witnesses some real poverty. She and her brother and sister are more aware of helping those in real need. She wants to adopt an orphan.

_____. *Veronica Knows Best.* Scholastic, 1987. Veronica is no longer a show-off because she feels more secure. She now takes a real interest in people.

_____. *Veronica, the Show-Off.* Four Winds, 1982. Veronica loses friends by her behavior which she uses to get attention and, she hopes, friends.

_____. *Wendy and the Bullies.* Hastings, 1980. Wendy plays hooky from school because she is afraid of the bullies that are taunting her.

Robinson, Richard. *Captain Sintar.* Dutton, 1969. Tom is accidentally taken aboard a ship. The captain takes unnecessary chances and everyone thinks he is mad. He and Tom become friends; they have many adventures before the captain lands in Arabia.

Robinson, Veronica. *David in Silence.* Lippincott, 1965. David is deaf and new to his neighborhood. He makes friends with Michael, a boy his own age. One day he is chased into an abandoned tunnel and is frightened. Michael finds him and leads him to safety.

Rock, Gail. *Addie and the King of Hearts.* Knopf, 1975. Addie has a crush on her teacher and her boyfriend asks someone else to the dance; she goes with her father.

_____. *Dream for Addie.* Knopf, 1976. Addie makes friends with Constance and asks her father if she can stay with Constance's family awhile.

_____. *House Without a Christmas Tree.* Knopf, 1974. Addie lives with her father and grandmother. They spend the holidays as best they can.

_____. *Thanksgiving Treasure.* Knopf, 1974. Addie is still with father and grandmother. She wants a horse and one day takes some food to a recluse her father has been feuding with. They become friends and when he dies he leaves her his horse.

Rocklin, Joanne. *Dear Baby.* Macmillan, 1988. Farla writes in her diary for six months before a new baby is due. She talks about her mother's new husband, an aunt who came to live and a new friend. And about the coming baby.

_____. *Sonia Begonia.* Macmillan, 1986.

Sonia wants a business. She starts Safety Sentinel Service, Singing Sitter Service, Scrumptious Supper Service, etc.

Rockwell, Thomas. *Hey, Lover Boy.* Delacorte, 1981. How does a twelve-year-old boy find answers to SEX?

_____. *How to Eat Fried Worms.* Watts, 1973. Billy must eat 15 worms a day in order to win his bet. You won't believe the different number of ways one can fix worms to eat!

Rockwood, Joyce. *Enoch's Place.* Holt, 1980. Enoch, who goes to live with his uncle, is a second generation hippie. He finds selfish, materialistic people who steal and sell drugs. He meets a girl, Holly, who shares his life's philosophy.

_____. *Groundhog's Horse.* Holt, 1978. Groundhog is a Cherokee Indian with a horse named Midnight who is stolen. Groundhog recaptures him and returns home after some harrowing experiences.

_____. *Long Man's Song.* Holt, 1975. A story of Soaring Hawk, Chestnut Bread and Owl fighting evil magic and the trials Soaring Hawk must go through to prove his manhood.

_____. *To Spoil the Sun.* Holt, 1976. A young girl marries an older tribe leader but later falls in love with a young warrior. Smallpox kills a great number of people including one of Rain Dove's children.

Rodda, Emily. *Pigs Are Flying.* Greenwillow, 1988. Rachel has a cold and must stay home. Her friend Burt comes to cheer her up by telling her impossible tales.

Rodgers, Mary. *Billion for Boris.* Harper, 1974. Annabel and her friends encounter adventures which don't work out as planned. Ape-face (Ben) fixes Boris's television and they find that they can see into the near future.

_____. *Freaky Friday.* Harper, 1972. A mother and daughter find themselves in each other's shoes. They both find this surprising, enlightening and disastrous.

_____. *Summer Switch.* Harper, 1982. This time father and son find themselves in each other's shoes and have the same surprising and enlightening experiences. Father goes to summer camp and Ben flies to L.A. on business.

Rodgers, Raboo. *Island of Peril.* Houghton, 1987. Jeri and Ben uncover a Mayan art smuggling operation.

_____. *Magnum Fault.* Houghton, 1984. Jill's father disappears after a crash and she escapes from a "hospital." She gets to an airport the same time as Colby and his dog, Riley. Together they solve the mystery of her father's accident.

_____. *Rainbow Factor.* Houghton, 1985. Cody meets Audry under unusual circumstances and then together they discover a cave where a Nazi plane is hidden with its cargo of gold. Audry is being followed and she doesn't know why.

Rodman, Maia. *Odyssey of Courage.*

Atheneum, 1965. A story of Alvar Nunez Cabeza de Vaca's epic journey from Florida to Mexico.

Rodowsky, Colby. *Evy-Ivy-Over.* Watts, 1978. Slug, 12, was left at a bus stop as a baby. She lives with her grandmother, wears old clothes, and is not accepted by her peers.

———. *Fitchett's Folly.* Farrar, 1987. Sarey lost first her mother then her father. Faith is a sole survivor of a shipwreck in which her father died. Sarey and Faith eventually accept each other.

———. *Gathering Room.* Farrar, 1981. Mudge's parents are caretakers of a cemetery. This is unusual but Mudge is quite happy. Then an aunt wants the family to join the conventional world. Mudge wants to stay with her imaginary ghosts.

———. *H, My Name Is Henley.* Farrar, 1982. Henley and her unstable mother move from city to city, staying with friends and living as best they can. They finally end up at the home of Aunt Mercy and Henley refuses to move again.

———. *Keeping Time.* Farrar, 1983. Drew is transported from Baltimore to Elizabethan London. He meets Symon who is a street musician just as Drew and his family are street musicians in Baltimore.

———. *P.S. Write Soon.* Farrar, 1988. Tanner wears a leg brace (called Fenhagen) but her letters to her pen pal reveal a false portrait of her athletic ability and family life.

———. *Summer's Worth of Shame.* Watts, 1980. Thad's father is convicted of embezzlement. Each member of the family handles the problem differently.

———. *Sydney Herself.* Farrar, 1989. Sydney works on her writing skills in a journal assigned by her history teacher. She finds a boyfriend, loses a girlfriend, and sees her mother date her history teacher.

———. *What About Me?* Farrar, 1989. Dorrie, 15, has a love/hate relationship with her mongoloid brother, Fredlet, 11.

Roe, Kathy. *Goodbye, Secret Place.* Houghton, 1982. Whitney and Robin are best friends. Robin is popular, pretty and outgoing. Whitney is moody and secretive. A lack of understanding sometimes causes them to hurt each other.

Rogers, Fred. *Secret Moose.* Greenwillow, 1985. Gerald finds and nurses a wounded moose in Alaska.

Rogers, Jane. *Separate Tracks.* Faber, 1985. Emma lives comfortably around others who are striking and rioting and she feels guilty. She gets involved in "good" causes and falls in love with Orph but their differences keep them on "separate tracks."

Rogers, Pamela. *Rare One.* Lodestar, 1974. Josh is at odds with his family until an old man he has befriended dies. The guilt he feels about this tragedy makes him more understanding.

Roos, Kelly. *Incredible Cat Caper.* Delacorte, 1985. Jessica must hide her cat, Simba, in her room because cats aren't allowed in her new apartment. But a cat burglar is on the loose.

Roos, Stephen. *And the Winner Is....* Atheneum, 1989. Phoebe's family must sell their summer home. She and her friend, Kit, get involved in a local talent show as a possible way to change things so they don't have to sell.

———. *Confessions of a Wayward Preppie.* Delacorte, 1986. Cary goes to an exclusive prep school. He rooms with Joe, a scholarship student, and Bobby, who only talks of money. He is asked to do homework for a senior and gets caught and pays the price.

———. *Fair-Weather Friends.* Atheneum, 1987. Kit looks forward to seeing her summer friend, Phoebe, but Phoebe has changed and Kit wonders why. They remain friends but at a different level. Phoebe likes Kit's brother, Derek.

———. *My Favorite Ghost.* Atheneum, 1988. Derek, who wants to raise money, charges his friends a fee to see a supposedly haunted house on the island where he spends the summer.

———. *My Horrible Secret.* Delacorte, 1983. Warren is going to Camp Hit-a-Homer. His brother is a super athlete but Warren can't throw or catch. That's his secret but he breaks his arm horseback riding and gets out of playing ball.

———. *My Secret Admirer.* Delacorte, 1984. Claire gets a valentine signed "Your secret admirer." She does everything to find out who it is. She wants to win the Junior Achievement Award but when this happens things change.

———. *Terrible Truth.* Delacorte, 1983. Shirley has many problems. She attempts to start a club and it doesn't go well; she has a fight with a classmate and the new boy in school doesn't even notice her.

———. *Thirteenth Summer.* Atheneum, 1987. Pink wonders if he is really different from the summer people who come to the island. He fights with his friend, Mackie, who is one of them.

———. *You'll Miss Me When I'm Gone.* Delacorte, 1988. Marcus seemed to have everything: a girl, a car, popularity. But he drank, first a little then a lot. Each day got worse, his grades went down and on top of this, his parents were divorcing.

Roper, Pamela. *Guardian Angel.* Coward, 1966. Gabriella "prays" for her grandmother's house in the Standing Stone of Ben Dhuldh. The next day Sir Harry Nicholas visits. Is he the answer to her prayer or the devil in disguise?

Rosenblatt, Arthur. *Smarty.* Little, 1981. Marty tells his best friend, Lester, that he is going to run for class president in spite of the fact that he is not "In." He loses by three votes but has other compensations.

Rosenbloom, Joseph. *Maximilian, You're the Greatest.* Nelson, 1980. An "Encyclopedia Brown" type story of an older audience. Maximilian and detective Walker solve crimes.

Ross, Marianne. *Good-Bye Atlantis.* Nelson,

1979. Ann accuses Jonathan of being gay and he is crushed and tries to drown himself. She tries to save him and suffers partial paralysis. They cannot forgive each other for these events.

Ross, Pat. *Hannah's Fancy Notions*. Viking, 1988. Hannah excels at the making of band boxes, a folk art of early America.

Ross, Ramon. *Prune*. Macmillan, 1984. A fantasy about a friendship of a prune, a muskrat and a magpie.

Ross, Rhea. *Bet's On, Lizzie Bingman*. Houghton, 1988. Lizzie witnesses a murder and is captured by the murderer. Her brother comes to her rescue. Up till now Lizzie never needed help; her brother said she is the "weaker sex and in need of help."

Roth, Arthur. *Iceberg Hermit*. Four Winds, 1974. A New Zealand farm girl secretly takes care of two orphaned animals.

————. *Secret Lover of Elmtree*. Four Winds, 1962. Greg lives in Elmtree, his girl lives there, his job in the service station is there and his family is there. Then his real father shows up and offers him a fabulous future.

————. *Two for Survival*. Scribner, 1976. John and Mark crash in a snow-covered wilderness. There are six survivors but only John and Mark have a chance to get help. They are totally different but must get along for survival.

Roth, David. *Best of Friends*. Houghton, 1983. Matt, 15, and John, 18, are alone for the summer. John likes girls, parties and drinking. Matt is a loner and likes bird watching.

————. *Girl in the Grass*. Beaufort, 1982. Tom sets out to find his missing sister, Sylvia. His search leads to art galleries and supply stores. He encounters a robbery and a mugging before he is reunited with his sister.

————. *Hermit of Fog Hollow Station*. Beaufort, 1980. Alex befriends an old man who lives in an abandoned railroad station after two of Alex's school mates abuse the old man because they think he has money.

————. *River Runaways*. Houghton, 1981. Michael and Ted find an empty canoe and decide to leave their unhappy homes. The trip is dangerous, their friendship is tried and there is a tragedy.

Roth-Hano, Renee. *Touch Wood*. Macmillan, 1988. A Jewish girl is living in occupied France during World War II. This is a story of her survival.

Rounds, Glen. *Blind Colt*. Holiday, 1960. Whitey adopts and trains a colt that was born blind. The horse does well in spite of his handicap; he learns by smell and hearing where the dangers are and functions effectively.

————. *Blind Outlaw*. Holiday, 1980. The story of a mute boy and a blind horse.

————. *Day the Circus Came to Lone Tree*. Holiday, 1973. It is the circus's first visit (also the last) to Lone Tree. It is a total disaster because all the animals escape.

————. *Mr. Yowder and the Train Robbers*. Holiday, 1983. Mr. Xenon Zebulon Yowder is a sign painter who has many misadventures.

————. *Wild Appaloosa*. Holiday, 1983. A young boy wants to capture and train a wild filly.

Rowe, Viola. *Promise to Love*. Longman, 1960. Barbara, an only child, and Chuck, a new boy in school, are going steady but have a falling out.

Roy, Ron. *Avalanche!* Dutton, 1981. Scott and Tony are brothers. They go skiing in Colorado and are caught in an avalanche. They struggle to survive.

————. *Chimpanzee Kid*. Clarion, 1985. Harold wants to free a chimpanzee from a local laboratory. He and Todd free him but return him when they find out he is to be returned to Africa and freed.

————. *Frankie Is Staying Back*. Houghton, 1981. One of two friends moves up to the next grade while the other remains behind. This puts a strain on the friendship.

————. *I Am a Thief*. Dutton, 1982. Brad is lured into a shoplifting ring by Chet, a good looking friendly boy.

————. *Where's Buddy?* Houghton, 1982. Mike and Buddy are brothers; Buddy is diabetic and needs special care and attention.

Rubin, Amy. *Children of the Seventh Prophecy*. Warne, 1981. A troll and two human children struggle against the forces of Unking to deliver a scroll. Unking wants to bring about the end of the world.

Rubinstein, Gillian. *Space Demons*. Dial, 1988. Andrew and his friends are playing "Space Demons" on his new computer. They are drawn into the game literally and must save themselves from evil. Love, truth and cooperation are the key.

Rubinstein, Robert. *Who Wants to Be a Hero!* Dodd, 1979. Jason captures one of the school's "hoods" attacking an old man. Then his mother's tires are slashed, he is tripped in the cafeteria and his sister receives obscene phone calls.

Ruby, Lois. *Pig-Out Inn*. Houghton, 1987. Davi takes care of Tog, a nine-year-old left in her parents' restaurant. Tog was taken from his mother's custody by the father in a battle over who gets him.

————. *This Old Man*. Houghton, 1984. Greta and Wing become friends and Greta meets and likes his grandfather, the Old Man. Greta's mother is a prostitute and has the same plans for Greta but Greta has plans of her own.

————. *What Do You Do in Quicksand?* Viking, 1979. Leah lives with her 70-year-old stepfather. Matt is a neighbor who is going to adopt a child he fathered. Leah cares for the child and then kidnaps him.

Ruch-Pauquet, Gina. *Fourteen Cases of Dynamite*. Delacorte, 1968. When Hercules moved into his new apartment his father, who is an inventor, brought fourteen boxes marked

DANGER! HANDLE WITH CARE! EXPLOSIVES! He is working on singing fish and discovers silence.

Ruckman, Ivy. *Encounter.* Doubleday, 1978. J.D. has an encounter with a U.F.O. He has headaches, nightmares and an obsession that is destroying his life.

———. *Hunger Scream.* Walker, 1983. Lily wants to be attractive, especially to the boy next door, Daniel. She slowly progresses into anorexia and it takes lots of help from her family for her to recover.

———. *Melba the Brain.* Westminster, 1979. Melba conjures up Astro Cat, a cat from a planet where animals rule humans. She travels there and meets other talking animals.

———. *Night of the Twister.* Crowell, 1984. Dan and Arthur survive a tornado. They save Dan's baby brother and an elderly neighbor. They eventually contact other members of their families and try to restore the ravages of the twister.

———. *No Way Out.* Crowell, 1988. Amy and her friends are hiking and the canyon becomes flooded. They must survive and work their way to safety.

———. *This Is Your Captain Speaking.* Walker, 1987. Tom is great friends with 87-year-old Roger, a retired sea captain. Roger dies and Tom takes it badly. He and his girlfriend, Carmela, grieve for him.

———. *What's an Average Kid Like Me Doing Way Up Here?* Delacorte, 1983. Norman spends four months helping his mother and teacher keep his school open.

———. *Who Invited the Undertaker?* Harper, 1989. Dale works hard to find a husband for her widowed mother.

Rugh, Belle. *Crystal Mountain.* Houghton, 1955. Some boys and a girl discover an abandoned cottage in the mountains of Lebanon. There are adventure, animals and mystery.

———. *Path Above the Pines.* Houghton, 1962. A wailing noise is coming from the mountains. A humorous mystery.

Rundle, Anne. *Moonbranches.* Macmillan, 1986. Frances goes to live with her aunt. She learns of the death of Simon and meets his ghost. He takes over evil Martin's body while Martin is unconscious.

Ruskin, John. *King of the Golden River.* Dover, 1974. A great classic about two disagreeable brothers who make the South-West Wind, Esquire, very mad and revengeful.

Russ, Lavinia. *April Age.* Atheneum, 1975. Peakie is now 18. She goes on a European trip, learns to dance, falls in love many times with a series of unsuitable men and rises and falls with each new romance.

———. *Over the Hills and Far Away.* Harcourt, 1968. Peakie is shy and has a beautiful sister; these things make growing up even harder

than normal. But both the moves and the boarding schools help her conquer her fears.

Russell, Jennifer. *Threshing Floor.* Paulist Press, 1987. A story of the pilgrimage to Canterbury by the believers. It is the 14th century and they encounter clergy, knights and gentry and townspeople; they also observe class system working.

Rutgers van der Leoff, Anna. *Oregon at Last.* Morrow, 1962. A group of children become orphans on their way to Oregon. Their wagon train goes to California but they set out on their own to go to Oregon. They have a hazardous trip.

Rutherford, Douglas. *Killer on the Track.* Bradbury, 1973. A murder takes place at a racing track. Why? Who?

Ruthin, Margaret. *Katrina of the Lonely Isles.* Farrar, 1964. Katrina saves the crew of a Russian ship but her brother is injured. A Russian doctor takes him to the ship for care. They make it back to land and the doctor asks for asylum and Katrina helps him.

Ryan, Mary. *Dance a Step Closer.* Delacorte, 1984. Katie wants to be a Broadway dancer, but her mother doesn't encourage her because she was a dancer and knows how hard it is. But Katie works hard, gets a boyfriend and adjusts to her family.

———. *Frankie's Run.* Little, 1987. Mary Francis and her girl friend are getting interested in buys and wonder if they should follow the going fads or be themselves.

———. *I'd Rather Be Dancing.* Delacorte, 1989. Katie wins a scholarship to Dance Academy. She faces stiff competition and sees more of the seedy side of show biz.

———. *Who Says I Can't?* Little, 1988. Tessa is overshadowed by her mother and sister. She strikes back by becoming the director of the school Talent Show. She abuses her power and is fired.

Rydberg, Ernie. *Shadow Army.* Nelson, 1976. Demetrios meets an English doctor while fighting with a guerrilla band in Crete and changes his goals from fighting and revenge to medical service for the needy.

———. *Yellow Line.* Meredith, 1970. Mike, 15, is an orphan and goes to live with an aunt. He finds himself in the very room where someone hanged himself. He is interested and tries to find out why.

Rylant, Cynthia. *Blue-Eyed Daisy.* Bradbury, 1985. Bellie lives in Appalachia. Her father has drunk since he was hurt at the mine. She would like a room of her own, better living conditions and other things but she is happy and her parents are loving.

———. *Fine White Dust.* Bradbury, 1986. Peter meets and is captivated by a traveling Preacher Man. He leaves home and travels with him, meeting many interesting people, both good and bad.

_____. *Kindness*. Watts, 1988. Chip's unwed mother is going to have a baby. He learns to love his baby sister and also learns the identity of her father.

Sachar, Louis. *Boy Who Lost His Face*. Knopf, 1989. David and his friends attack an old woman and she puts a curse on him. He rethinks his behavior for the sake of popularity.

_____. *Sixth Grade Secrets*. Scholastic, 1987. Laura starts a secret club called Pig City. A rival club is Monkey Town. The pranks turn ugly and destructive.

_____. *There's a Boy in the Girls' Bathroom*. Knopf, 1987. Bradley is a bully. He wants to start anew. A new student and a new counselor help him.

_____. *Wayside School Is Falling Down*. Lothrop, 1989. More stories about the children and teachers in Wayside School and the nonsense that happens on the thirtieth floor of this strange school.

Sachs, Elizabeth-Ann. *Just Like Always*. Atheneum, 1981. Courtney is interested in fantasy, secrets and chants. Janie is interested in baseball and Harold, and she is a tomboy. What they have in common is scoliosis. They meet in the hospital and become friends.

_____. *Shyster*. Macmillan, 1985. Shyster is Becky's cat. They both go to spend the summer with Becky's mother and her boyfriend.

_____. *Where Are You, Cow Patty?* Atheneum, 1984. Janie has been out of the hospital for over a year. Courtney comes for a visit and things don't always go well because of Harold's interest in Courtney. But they still remain close friends.

Sachs, Marilyn. *Amy and Laura*. Doubleday, 1966. Amy and Laura's mother returns from the hospital but she has changed a great deal in the year she was away. Laura must adjust. She also meets Veronica who appears in another series.

_____. *Amy Moves In*. Doubleday, 1964. Amy and her sister Laura have all the problems of any youngster who has moved to a new neighborhood: making friends, finding out where everything is and enrolling in a new school.

_____. *At the Sound of the Beep*. Dutton, 1990. A brother and sister run away when their parents divorce. They live in Golden Gate Park and meet other homeless people. They hear there is a murderer among them.

_____. *Baby Sister*. Dutton, 1986. Penny and Cass are sisters. When Cass leaves for college, Penny reads her diary. She learns to use her own talent for sewing and works it into a career. She then gets engaged to Cass's old boyfriend.

_____. *Beach Towels*. Dutton, 1982. A boy and girl meet at the beach and a friendship slowly evolves.

_____. *Bear's House*. Doubleday, 1971. Fran doesn't fit in with her classmates. Her homelife is hopeless. If she works very hard at school and gets good grades, she could win the Bear's House which she dearly loves.

_____. *Bus Ride*. Dutton, 1980. Judy and Ernie ride the school bus together. She's not popular and he is never gone out with a girl but likes Judy's friend, Karen. In the end Judy and Ernie discover that they like each other.

_____. *Call Me Ruth*. Doubleday, 1982. Ruth is an immigrant who is at odds with her mother because of the different opinion of whether to keep the old traditions or accept the new and different.

_____. *Class Pictures*. Dutton, 1980. Pat and Lolly were friends all through school. Lolly is rich but fat and unpopular. Pat is poor, smart and popular.

_____. *December Tale*. Doubleday, 1976. Myra and her brother are in a foster home. They are ill treated and she wants to get them both away.

_____. *Dorrie's Book*. Doubleday, 1975. Dorrie writes about herself as an only child until her mother had triplets. She does it for a school assignment.

_____. *Fat Girl*. Dutton, 1984. Jeff decides that he is going to change fat Ellen into a happy, dependent girl. He succeeds in changing her but then she shows independence and this bothers him.

_____. *Fourteen*. Dutton, 1983. Rebecca's new neighbor is Jason. The two put together clues to find Jason's father (he is in prison for setting fire to his own business) and become friends.

_____. *Fran Ellen's House*. Dutton, 1987. After being placed in a foster home Fran and her brother are together. The Bear's House now has a different role to play in Fran's life.

_____. *Hello ... Wrong Number*. Dutton, 1981. Angie calls a boy she has a crush on but gets another boy who does sound interesting. They talk every evening and finally plan to meet. Jim (the wrong one) tells her who he really is but all ends well.

_____. *Laura's Luck*. Doubleday, 1965. Laura and Amy go to camp and Amy makes friends right away while Laura is hanging back. But, in time, she learns to love camp.

_____. *Marv*. Doubleday, 1970. The story is about invincible Marv, whom no one really understands. He is a classmate of Veronica's and Peter's. He tries hard to compete with his older sister who is very bright.

_____. *Peter and Veronica*. Doubleday, 1969. Veronica and Peter have become friends but Peter realizes this causes problems. Prejudice on the part of both mothers puts pressure on their friendship. Veronica is Gentile, Peter is Jewish.

_____. *Pocket Full of Seeds*. Doubleday, 1973. The Nieman family live in occupied France and do not realize how threatened they are until it's too late.

_____. *Secret Friend*. Doubleday, 1978. A

story that explores the relationship between parents and their children and outside friendships.

_____. *Summer's Lease.* Dutton, 1979. A very self-centered girl learns to be different when she works in the home of her English teacher.

_____. *Thunderbird.* Dutton, 1985. Tina has an old Thunderbird and Dennis is envious of her devotion to it. She tries to help him when he quits his job in a huff and they become closer friends.

_____. *Truth About Mary Rose.* Doubleday, 1973. Mary Rose, Veronica's daughter, investigates the truth about her late aunt, Mary Rose, who is her namesake. Was she the heroine who saved tenants in an apartment fire, or not?

_____. *Underdog.* Doubleday, 1985. A young orphan needs to find her lost dog before she can adjust to her aunt and uncle.

_____. *Veronica Ganz.* Doubleday, 1968. Veronica, who is big for her age, bullies everyone at school. She made Laura's school life difficult and now Peter, a new boy at school, is the target of her plots.

Sacks, Margaret. *Beyond Safe Boundaries.* Lodestar, 1989. In South Africa in the 1950's Elizabeth and Evie's father remarries. Evie goes to college and gets involved in an anti-apartheid crusade. She is placed under house arrest.

St. George, Judith. *Do You See What I See?* Putnam, 1982. Matt reports a murder he witnessed and the corpse shows up alive. He reports a break-in theft that was false. But he knows something is wrong.

_____. *Halo Wind.* Putnam, 1978. Ella Jane finds Yvette, a Chinook Indian girl, trying to pit the family against each other and causing trouble in the wagon train. It is later revealed that she resents the settlers.

_____. *Haunted.* Putnam, 1980. Alex is house-sitting for the summer. There was a murder/suicide in the house earlier. A mouse is found dead in the pool, cars don't start and Alex is unnerved.

_____. *In the Shadow of the Bear.* Putnam, 1983. Annie, 17, learns self-reliance and independence in the Arctic Circle. She and Robert go on a day's journey to get help when a Russian defects and his pursuers disrupt camp.

_____. *Mystery at St. Martin's.* Putnam, 1979. Ruth's father is a progressive minister who helps an inmate and a woman. But counterfeit money is showing up and Ruth wants to clear her father of any involvement.

_____. *What's Happening to My Junior Year?* Putnam, 1986. Steppie wants friends, love and good grades. Her mother turns their basement into a pool hall and her life changes.

_____. *Who's Scared? Not Me!* Putnam, 1989. Micki and her dog, Jiggs, are pursued by Lucy, a homeless, old woman who turns out to be John Audubon's wife. Micki, of course, time travels to get this straightened out.

St. John, Glory. *What I Did Last Summer.* Atheneum, 1978. A family with three boys decide to spend the summer roughing it in their backyard.

St. John, W· .y. *Ghost Next Door.* Harper, 1971. A family accept the reality of the death of one of them.

_____. *Mystery of the Gingerbread House.* Viking, 1969. Two boys play detective and uncover some missing jewels. They also find a body that has been abandoned.

_____. *Secrets of the Pirate Inn.* Viking, 1968. Uncle Will mislaid some valuable objects. He gets help in finding things but his rhyme clues are hard to decipher and even he doesn't remember what they mean.

St. Peter, Joyce. *Always Abigail.* Lippincott, 1981. Abbie is going to a weight reduction camp but ends up at a dude ranch where she learns to ride and like people. She also finds a lost colt.

Salamanca, Lucy. *Tommy Tiger of the Seminoles.* Watts, 1961. Tommy Tiger is a Seminole Indian. He learns white man's ways but his grandmother holds on to the Seminole customs.

Salassi, Otto. *And Nobody Knew They Were There.* Greenwillow, 1984. Two cousins spend the summer together but don't like each other. They find a trail that some marines have moved through and follow it across Louisiana.

_____. *Jimmy D., Sidewinder and Me.* Greenwillow, 1987. Dumas is in jail and tells his story of becoming a professional gambler.

_____. *On the Ropes.* Greenwillow, 1981. On the death of their mother, Squint, 11, and Julie, 17, are reunited with their father. He comes back home with a troupe of wrestlers.

Salinger, J.D. *Catcher in the Rye.* Bantam, 1964. Holden flunks out of school again. He doesn't want to face his parents so he decides to keep on his own until he gets his mind straight. This is the story of how he does that.

Sallis, Susan. *Only Love.* Harper, 1980. Fran is in a hospital for the handicapped. She gets into all kinds of mischief, but keeps everyone laughing. Then Lucas comes along. He has lost both legs and is bitter. They fall in love but....

_____. *Open Mind.* Harper, 1978. David learns to get along with his fellow classmates in a special school.

_____. *Secret Places of the Stairs.* Harper, 1984. Cass learns that she has a sister who has been in a mental institution for years. She goes to visit her and learns to love her. The sister dies but not before a family reconciliation.

_____. *Time for Everything.* Harper, 1979. Lil has to face many problems at the beginning of World War II. A mongoloid cousin comes to live, her mother is having an affair and is pregnant and her father is going into the armed service.

Salten, Felix. *Bambi.* Buccaneer, 1926. A classic story of the life of a deer from birth to maturity.

Sampson, Fay. *Watch on Patterick Fell.* Greenwillow, 1979. A scientist's family is given new identity and moved because of a nuclear waste material disposal problem. After the problem is solved the family is reunited.

Samuels, Gertrude. *Adam's Daughter.* Crowell, 1977. Robyn's father was in prison for killing her stepfather. Her mother forbids her to see him. She decides to go and live with him. Trouble is caused not by Robyn or her father but by the parole officer.

_____. *Mottele.* Harper, 1976. Mottele hates the Germans for what they did and seeks revenge by becoming an undercover agent during World War II. He is captured several times but escapes. How long can he be lucky?

_____. *Yours, Brett.* Dutton, 1988. Brett's mother, an alcoholic and drug user, can't take care of her. She is in a foster home, then a Second Chance House.

Sandburg, Helga. *Blueberry.* Dial, 1963. Kristin, 14, gets a mare named Blueberry. She meets and likes a gypsy boy but her father objects because of his prejudice toward gypsys.

Sanderlin, Owenita. *Johnny.* Barnes, 1968. Johnny is a young tennis player with leukemia and will only live for five more years.

Sanders, Scott. *Bad Man Ballad.* Bradbury, 1986. During the War of 1812 a young boy and his lawyer companion search for a creature who must be giantlike.

Sanfield, Steve. *Natural Man.* Godine, 1986. John Henry, the steel driving man, is revealed in this tall tale of an American hero.

Sankey, Alice. *Hit the Bike Trail.* Whitman, 1974. Three boys are on an overnight bike trip. One bike was stolen; they go to a county auction and a race track; they endure a rainstorm and a minor accident.

_____. *Three-in-One Car.* Whitman, 1967. Gary finds it expensive to own a restored car. He has to overcome his financial problems.

Sant, Kathryn. *Desert Chase.* Scholastic, 1979. Two boys on a wild desert chase in a truck full of confiscated army missiles.

Santiago, Danny. *Famous All Over Town.* Simon & Schuster, 1983. Manuel, Gorilla, Hungryman, Pelon and Chato are the Los Jesters. They war with the gang from Sierra Street. Sometimes someone is killed in these fights and someone goes to prison. Can Chato survive this?

Sargent, Pamela. *Alien Child.* Harper, 1988. Nita seems to be the only human left on Earth. She has a furred and clawed guardian, Llipel. Then she finds Sven, another human teenager.

_____. *Eye of the Comet.* Harper, 1984. Lydee does not have mindspeak powers because she was born on Earth, a backward planet. She goes to Earth to help her people and decides that that is where she belongs, after all.

_____. *Homesmind.* Harper, 1984. A story about the Earth dwellers and the sky dwellers. A picture of the advantages and disadvantages of mind reading as seen through the eyes of Anra fifteen years after *Eye of the Comet.*

Sargent, Sarah. *Jonas McFee A.T.P.* Bradbury, 1989. Jonas gets a blue marble with power invented by a scientist and stolen by his daughter. A.T.P. equals Awful, Terrible Power and Jonas is falling under this spell.

_____. *Lure of the Dark.* Four Winds, 1984. Ginny and Beth go jogging in the zoo and Ginny is "captured" by Fenric, the evil son of Loki, embodied in a wolf. She must break away from his control. He needs her unhappiness to free himself.

_____. *Secret Lies.* Crown, 1981. Elveria goes to live with a bunch of cousins in a large family.

_____. *Seeds of Change.* Bradbury, 1989. Rachel's father is going to make a park where a swamp now exists. She learns about the good and the bad of environmental change.

_____. *Watermusic.* Clarion, 1986. Laura plays flute for Mrs. Urhlander and gets her involved in an attempt to revive an ancient batlike creature who has been in a trance for 1000 years.

_____. *Weird Henry Berg.* Crown, 1980. Henry is weird. His century old egg hatches a lizard named Vincent. A dragon is searching for him. Millie and Henry try to reunite Vincent with his "family."

Sargent, Shirley. *Heart Holding Mountains.* Messner, 1961. Sarah faces the hostility of ranchers toward the Forest Service. She tells of daily routines and new responsibility. Also of her romance.

_____. *Ranger in Skirts.* Abingdon, 1966. Shy Mollie is a ranger/naturalist. She does not mix with others and resents interference from co-workers. She overcomes some of her shyness and finds friends and romance.

_____. *Stop the Typewriters.* Abelard, 1963. Five children start a four sheet newspaper to raise money. They get involved in a town mystery with Mr. Lightfoot.

Savage, Deborah. *Flight of the Albatross.* Houghton, 1989. Sarah is spending the summer on Great Kauri Island. She meets Mako, an attractive boy, and Hallo, an old Maori woman. She helps an injured albatross.

_____. *Rumor of Otters.* Houghton, 1986. Alexa is left alone and goes to hunt otters that are only seen by an old Maori.

Savage, Josephine. *Daughter of Delaware.* Day, 1964. Polly goes to France with her pacer, Star. She meets a dashing young ship owner and has a romance. She meets important people and talks of the American cause in pre–Revolutionary War days.

Savery, Constance. *Reb and the Redcoats.* Longman, 1961. R.E. Baltimore, an American officer, is taken prisoner by the British during the Revolutionary War. He hoodwinks his captors.

Savitt, Sam. *Vicki and the Black Horse.* Doubleday, 1964. Vicki, 13, loves her race horse, Pat. She gets another horse, Jesse, which she later sells but Pat misses Jesse more than anyone could believe.

Savitz, Harriet. *Come Back, Mr. Magic.* Nal, 1983. Greg works at a rehabilitation center helping other people. He has an accident and is fighting for his own life. He is called Mr. Magic but it will take more than magic for him to get well.

————. *Fly, Wheels, Fly.* Day, 1970. Jeff and Chuck, paraplegics, discover how much activity they can perform when they enter the Paralympics for Wheelchair Sports.

————. *Lionhearted.* Day, 1975. Rennie is confined to a wheelchair but is determined to be self-reliant. She returns to her regular school after the accident even though she may lose her boyfriend, Lee.

————. *On the Move.* Day, 1973. Bennie is paralyzed because of a knife wound. Skip had a land mine accident and Carne was paralyzed because of polio. The boys belong to a wheelchair basketball team and Carne takes swimming lessons.

————. *Swimmer.* Scholastic, 1986. Skip is disappointed in his parents' divorce and has a bad summer. The only highlight is his friendship with his dog.

Sawyer, Ruth. *Roller Skates.* Smith, 1936. Early New York City is described by a young girl who explores it on roller skates. Newbery winner, 1937.

Saxon, Nancy. *Panky and William.* Atheneum, 1983. Panky is fat and new to school. William is a horse at the stable of her friend, Kathy. Panky befriends and reforms William.

Say, Allen. *Ink-Keeper's Apprentice.* Harper, 1979. Kiyoi lives in Japan after World War II. He wants to be a cartoonist and is taken in as an apprentice and does well. He matures and moves to America.

Sayers, Dorothy. *Murder Must Advertise.* Harper, 1985. Peter Wimsey investigates an accident. This leads to a trail of drugs, blackmail and murder.

Schaefer, Jack. *Shane.* Bantam, 1954. Shane moved into a sleepy Western town, dark, calm and quiet. He left an unforgettable mark on the town.

Schaff, Louise. *Skald of the Vikings.* Lothrop, 1966. Thrain is a balladeer who goes with Thorfim to Vinland. He is captured by Indians but manages to escape.

Schatz, Letta. *Taiwo and Her Twin.* McGraw, 1964. Taiwo wants to go to school when a new school is built in her village in Africa, but there is only money for one and her brother should attend, not a girl.

Schealer, John. *Zip-Zip and His Flying Saucer.* Dutton, 1956. Randy meets a strange boy in an old barn. He takes his older brother and sister to meet Zip-Zip who shows them his flying saucer.

————. *Zip-Zip Goes to Venus.* Dutton, 1958. This time Zip-Zip takes the Riddle children to Venus to rescue Zip-Zip's father. They are captured by the green people, gain their freedom and are captured again by desert dwellers.

Schellie, Don. *Kidnapping Mr. Tubbs.* Four Winds, 1978. A.J. and Eloise get Mr. Tubbs out of a rest home and are taking him home to his ranch. They run into a motorcycle gang, have car troubles and when they reach the ranch it is no longer there.

————. *Shadow and the Gunner.* Scholastic, 1982. A young boy growing up during World War II recalls his friendship with the older boy next door, the parting and the death.

Scherf, Margaret. *Mystery of the Empty Trunk.* Watts, 1966. Jane and Sally find a strange hole and an empty trunk. Mrs. Wilson moved into the house and strange things happen. But Jane and Sally solve the mystery.

Schlee, Ann. *Ask Me No Questions.* Holt, 1982. A story of workhouse children in Victorian England. Laura lives next to a workhouse and sees the starving children and brings them food. A sad, realistic story of abused children and greedy adults.

————. *Consul's Daughter.* Atheneum, 1972. A teen girl is living in Algiers in 1916 when the British fleet bombards it.

————. *Strangers.* Atheneum, 1972. Lum, a refugee, is looking for gold hidden by a man who has died. He is threatened by a traitor. He is also helped by Kate and they find the money in a cave.

————. *Vandal.* Crown, 1981. A futuristic novel where people are not allowed to think of the past. All memory is erased every three days. Paul and Sharon are both misfits. They escape from their penal camps and have hope.

Schleier, Curt. *You'd Better Not Tell.* Westminster, 1979. Harold becomes a junior cadet with the police force. He suspects his best friend's brother of mugging. He is not popular because of his interest in the "enemy."

Schmidt, Kurt. *Annapolis Misfit.* Crown, 1974. Charlie is a plebe at the Naval Academy. He is harassed by upperclassmen, especially Tate. He is caught and found guilty of cheating on an exam.

Schneider, Benjamin. *Winter Patriot.* Chilton, 1967. Seth feels he needs to avenge his father's death and joins the Revolutionary Army. He shows exceptional bravery and General Washington rewards him after the Battle of Trenton.

Schneider, Jennifer. *Daybreak Man.* Harper, 1975. Lita runs away from a cruel drunken grandfather. She is taken in by a gypsy and looks after the children. Then she discovers the real world. A realistic, sad story of rape and sex.

Scholefield, Edmond. *Tiger Rookie*. World, 1966. Matt is a pitcher. A talent scout finds him and sends him to a farm team. At the end of the summer he must decide between baseball and college.

Scholz, Jackson. *Backfield Blues*. Morrow, 1971. Steve is in college after returning from Vietnam. He makes the football team but is not mentally ready to fight on the field. He is helped by a younger friend.

_____. *Center Field Jinx*. Morrow, 1961. Jerry gets into a batting slump and worries about his position on the team. He plays golf and it improves his timing.

_____. *Fairway Challenge*. Morrow, 1964. Gary is playing his first golf tournament. He is with a pro star, Sandy, and is under a lot of pressure to play well.

_____. *Halfback on His Own*. Morrow, 1962. Andy is nervous at football tryouts in college. He's not sure he is college material. He was a star in high school but he wonders if his famous father had anything to do with it.

Schotter, Roni. *Rhoda, Straight and True*. Lothrop, 1986. Rhoda is looking forward to her summer vacation. She is hurt in an accident on a forbidden site and her friends run off and leave her. One of the poor, undesirable Mancy kids rescues her.

Schraff, Anne. *North Star*. Macrae, 1972. Tam's parents are breaking up. Her mother remarries. She has a boyfriend but he is unpredictable. The North Star is her stability.

Schroder, Amund. *Bird That Got Left Behind*. Criterion, 1968. Marit takes in a wagtail bird during the winter and learns she must free it to be among its own kind in the spring.

Schulte, Elaine. *Whither the Wind Bloweth*. Avon, 1982. Joanna's father is an alcoholic. She wants to be in the "in" crowd. She meets Matt and enters the drug, alcohol and fast life.

Schultz, Barbara. *House on Pinto's Island*. Bobbs, 1968. Erica is spending the summer on Pinto's Island and sees strange lights in an old abandoned house. There was an old murder to be cleared up.

_____. *Secret of the Pharoahs*. Bobbs, 1966. Dick is in Egypt and looks for a tomb suspected of being robbed. It is not a publicly discovered tomb but someone knows it's there.

Schwandt, Stephen. *Last Goodie*. Holt, 1985. When Marty was a child his babysitter was kidnapped. Now, 12 years later, he finds her journal. This leads to a face to face encounter with her kidnapper. A sub-plot about track racing is woven in well.

_____. *Risky Game*. Holt, 1986. Juliet and her teacher employ a psychodrama technique to teach a concept. Because of the intensity of the drama Juliet is drawn into it with resulting stress.

Schwartz, Joel. *Great Spaghetti Showdown*. Dell, 1988. Eugene is upset with his father's desertion. He finds a vent for his anger in a video studio.

_____. *Upchuck Summer*. Delacorte, 1982. Richie is having a bad time at summer camp. Then he finds that he is the root of his own problems.

_____. *Upchuck Summer Revenge*. Delacorte, 1990. Richie is now teaching youngsters to play football at summer camp. He avoids his would-be friend, Chuck.

Schwartz, Sheila. *Growing Up Guilty*. Pantheon, 1978. Susan is fat, bright and unloved. She goes to summer camp and dates a counselor called Vern. She is caught and sent home. She meets Sol, a communist, who is shattered at the outbreak of Pearl Harbor.

_____. *Like Mother, Like Me*. Pantheon, 1978. Jen's father runs off with a young student and her mother is deeply hurt. Jen tries to find a Mr. Right for her but all her efforts turn up Mr. Wrongs.

Schweitzer, Byrd. *Amigo*. Macmillan, 1963. Francisco wants a dog so he decides a prairie dog would make a good pet. The prairie dog he gets thinks that Francisco would make a good pet. They then start to train each other.

Scism, Carol. *Secret Emily*. Dial, 1972. Emily must choose between a chance for popularity and her best friend Melinda.

Scoppettone, Sandra. *Late Great Me*. Putnam, 1976. Geri is a junior in high school when she is introduced to liquor. She becomes an alcoholic and destroys her life. She tells about hangovers, good intentions with bad results and joining AA.

_____. *Long Time Between Kisses*. Harper, 1982. Billie's mother is an artist, and her father has a band and used dope. She cuts her hair and dyes it purple. She wants to be different. She meets Mitch whom she loves in vain before she finds her true talent.

_____. *Playing Murder*. Harper, 1985. A group of teenagers were playing the old game of Murder but Kirk was truly murdered. Anne looks into it and finds Kirk was not what he appeared to be. She must find the murderer or she will be next.

_____. *Trying Hard to Hear You*. Harper, 1974. Cam finds that two of her male friends are lovers. They are no longer accepted by the crowd. One of them is killed as a result of proving his "manhood." A sad, mixed up story that ends well.

Scott, Carol. *Kentucky Daughter*. Clarion, 1985. Mary Fred, 14, wants a college scholarship to teach English. She is teased about being a "hillbilly." Her teachers give her poor grades and make unwanted advances. She comes out on top in the end.

Scott, Dustin. *Mojave Joe*. Knopf, 1950. Mojave Joe is a coyote who is going to be put in a zoo. He escapes and heads for California and his old friend Mel, whose life he had once saved.

_____. *Return of Mojave Joe*. Knopf, 1952. Mojave Joe and Fleetfoot raise six young coyotes.

Red-hair, the trapper, is determined to kill Mojave Joe but Mel saves him and discovers gold in Mojave Joe's cave.

Scott, Elaine. *Choices.* Morrow, 1989. Beth and her friends are caught trashing a rural school. It started as innocent fun but turned to real vandalism. Beth is sent to a correctional center.

Scott, J.M. *Michael Anonymous.* Chilton, 1971. When Michael visits Tom he also finds a group of "hippies." They are stranded because their ship disappeared. Tom and Michael try to help find out what happened to the ship.

Scott, Jane. *Cross Fox.* Atheneum, 1980. Jamie is keeping track of a fox near his home. The men on the next farm are hunting it down because it raids the hen house. But the daughter keeps Jamie posted on the hunting plans.

————. *To Keep an Island.* Atheneum, 1983. Tina is vacationing at the seashore. She meets Harry whose father owns the island. With suspense, mystery and friendship plus value conflicts, the story winds to a satisfactory end.

Scott, William. *Boori.* Oxford, 1979. Boori is a young man created for special duties and has magical powers. With his friend Jaree and his dog Dingo he fights evil Rakasha.

Seabrooke, Brenda. *Home Is Where They Take You In.* Morrow, 1980. Benicia's mother is an alcoholic. She makes friends with people who raise palominos and wins a blue ribbon in a parade.

Sebestyen, Ouida. *Far from Home.* Little, 1980. Salty and his great-grandmother (his only relative) are being evicted. They go to a boardinghouse his dead mother recommended. It turns out that the owner is his father, who can't acknowledge it.

————. *Girl in the Box.* Little, 1988. Jackie is kidnapped and thrown in a cell with food, water and her typewriter. She types letters to police, parents, teachers and friends Zach and April.

————. *IOU's.* Atlantic, 1982. Stowe wants to live his life fully and differently but his love for his mother is standing in his way. What will he do?

————. *On Fire.* Little, 1985. The adventures of two brothers during a dangerous strike in 1911. Tater's life is spared but he has to live with the thought that he killed Lena's father. His brother Sammy helps him cope.

————. *Words by Heart.* Little, 1979. A young black girl, Lena, struggles to fulfill her papa's dreams of a better future for their family, in spite of prejudices. She saves Tater, even though he's the one who killed her Papa.

Sefton, Catherine. *Emma's Dilemma.* Faber, 1983. Emma has a twin that is transparent.

————. *Ghost and Bertie Boggin.* Faber, 1980. Bertie finds a ghost for a friend because his brother and sister think he is too young to play with.

————. *In a Blue Velvet Dress.* Harper, 1973. Jane spends the holidays with her aunt and uncle and finds exciting things to do.

————. *Island of Strangers.* Harcourt, 1985. Nora and her friends are pitted against a group of city students. Nora chooses not to get involved and is ostracized.

Segal, Erich. *Love Story.* Harper, 1970. The courtship and early marriage years of a rich athletic Harvard boy and a Radcliffe girl from a poor family.

Seidler, Tor. *Rat's Tale.* Farrar, 1986. A family of artistic rats, Montague and his parents, live in the sewer of New York City. His fellow rats are in danger of extermination and he must use courage to help them.

————. *Tar Pit.* Farrar, 1987. Ed daydreams about a pit allosaurus called Alexander. Alex takes care of all the people Ed doesn't like.

Selden, George. *Chester Cricket's New Home.* Farrar, 1983. Cricket's home collapses and he must find a new one. But he has problems that his friends try to help solve, even though he is so picky and the chore gets tedious.

————. *Chester Cricket's Pigeon Ride.* Farrar, 1981. Lulu Pigeon takes Chester for a ride he will never forget. He views the Manhattan skyline at night. A slight story.

————. *Cricket in Times Square.* Farrar, 1960. Chester Cricket lives in the Times Square subway. He shares it with Harry Cat and Tucker Mouse. He plays classical music and goes to concerts. His music makes the Bellini family famous.

————. *Genie of Sutton Place.* Farrar, 1973. Tim finds a spell enabling him to call up a genie. He needs help to save his dog, Sam, from being gotten rid of. A little magic and a lot of humor.

————. *Harry Cat's Pet Puppy.* Farrar, 1974. Harry brings her new friend, a puppy, to live in the subway with Tucker, but he soon grows too big for that home and must find a new one.

————. *Tucker's Countryside.* Farrar, 1969. The further adventures of Chester Cricket. Harry Cat and Tucker Mouse come to Connecticut for a visit and help Chester with his problem of expanding housing.

Senje, Sigurd. *Escape.* Harcourt, 1964. Elling and Ingrid leave their home and go inland when Norway is attacked. They meet a Russian who was a German prisoner of war. They try to help him escape through the Underground.

Senn, Steve. *Born of Flame.* Atheneum, 1982. Spacebread meets Niral, who is running away, and helps him. Quon wounds Klimmit and Spacebread must find a way to cure him.

————. *Circle in the Sea.* Atheneum, 1981. Robin is a girl with a strange ring her father found and gave to her. Bree is a dolphin with a strange illness. They exchange places. Bree likes being human but Robin doesn't like the polluted water.

————. *Spacebread.* Atheneum, 1981. A large, white wondercat moves among the stars looking for a stolen buckle and to avenge a murder. Sonto, her friend, is killed in battle.

Seredy, Kate. *Good Master.* Viking, 1935. Although written in 1935 this story is still read because of its warmth and humor. A city girl makes her own way on her uncle's farm.

————. *White Stag*. Viking, 1937. A story of the legendary founder of Hungary. The twins, Hunor and Magyar, with Bendeguz and Attila lead their people to the promised land, guided by the White Stag and the red eagle. Newbery winner, 1938.

Serraillier, Ian. *Silver Sword*. Phillips, 1959. Poland was hit hard by the war and parents and their children were separated. This is a story of the separation and reuniting of a Polish family.

Service, Pamela. *Question of Destiny*. Atheneum, 1986. Dan's father is running for president and Dan is suspicious of one of his advisors, David. But David is from another world and his role on Earth is to help Dan's father win the election.

————. *Reluctant God*. Atheneum, 1988. Lorna uncovers Ameni's tomb and releases him from suspended animation. The two of them then look for a stolen urn.

————. *Stinker from Space*. Macmillan, 1988. Tsyng Tyr from Slyon Confederacy crashes his spaceship on earth and takes over the body of a skunk.

————. *Tomorrow's Magic*. Atheneum, 1987. Heather, Welly and Earl live in future England after surviving a nuclear winter. King Arthur and Merlin return from the past and together they fight Morgan and Queen Margaret.

————. *Vision Quest*. Atheneum, 1989. Kate finds an Indian charm that connects her with an Indian boy named Wadat. There is also a subplot of illegal selling of relics and drugs.

————. *When the Night Wind Howls*. Atheneum, 1987. Sidonie joins a theatre group. She meets Joel and they both see "ghosts." They focus on Byron who sold his soul for immortality and can live only through the characters he plays.

————. *Winter of Magic's Return*. Macmillan, 1985. A story set 500 years after the nuclear holocaust.

Setlowe, Rick. *Brink*. Fields, 1976. Charly is a navy pilot who hears that his squadron may carry the atomic bomb to China.

Seuberlich, Hertha. *Annuzza: A Girl of Romania*. Rand McNally, 1962. Annuzza gets a chance to go to a city school. Her father is against it but she goes and has difficulty finding out what she really wants to do.

Severn, David. *Wild Valley*. Dutton, 1963. Phillippa finds a young boy in Wild Valley who was brought up by foxes. She tries to tame him and has some success.

Shaara, Michael. *Herald*. McGraw, 1981. Nick landed his plane with Rachel asleep. No one was around. He found several dead people. Everyone appeared to be dead. He drove to the hospital; no one alive. Back in the car Rachel was dead!

Shachtman, Tom. *Beachmaster: A Story of*

Daniel Au Fond. Holt, 1988. Daniel, a sea lion, encounters a shark and killer whales that are dangerous. He finds otters and polar bears that are friendly. He has a mate, Anna. A story of fact and fantasy.

Shannon, Jacqueline. *Too Much T.J.* Delacorte, 1986. What a shocker when Rozz finds out the boy she secretly loves is the son of the man her mother is going to marry! Imagine him living in the same house, using the same bathroom, etc.!!

Shannon, Monica. *Dobry*. Viking, 1934. A Bulgarian peasant boy wanted to be a sculptor. His mother thought he was wasting his time but his grandfather supported him. He did go away to art school. Newbery winner, 1935.

Sharmat, Marjorie. *Chasing After Annie*. Harper, 1981. Richie writes in his journal about all the ways he has, or is going to get, the attention of Annie.

————. *51 Sycamore Lane*. Macmillan, 1971. Paul has a new neighbor. He and his friends think he is a spy.

————. *Get Rich Mitch*. Morrow, 1985. Mitch wins the Dazzle-Rama Sweepstakes to the tune of $250,000. His greedy parents start to spend it recklessly. Their normal life is shattered but Mitch humorously holds it together.

————. *Getting Something on Maggie Marmelstein*. Harper, 1971. Thad tells everyone that Maggie squeaks like a mouse. Maggie tells everyone about Thad's cooking. And so it goes.

————. *He Noticed I'm Alive*. Delacorte, 1985. Jody and Matt are having problems because Matt's mother and Jody's father are dating.

————. *How to Meet a Gorgeous Girl*. Delacorte, 1984. Mark tries to interest Meg in romance by tips he learned from a book called "How to Meet a Gorgeous Girl."

————. *How to Meet a Gorgeous Guy*. Delacorte, 1983. Shari and Lisa are high school students. Shari gets her date with Craig and Lisa writes an article for the school paper. But neither challenge comes without problems.

————. *I Saw Him First*. Delacorte, 1983. Dona falls in love with Seymour and tells Andrea about it. Andrea traps Seymour but by then Dona has met Buzz herself and doesn't care.

————. *Maggie Marmelstein for President*. Harper, 1975. Maggie decides to help Thad run for school office. But she runs against him herself when he doesn't ask her to become his campaign manager.

————. *Mysteriously Yours, Maggie Marmelstein*. Harper, 1982. Maggie writes a mystery column in the school newspaper. In this capacity she learns that responsibility goes with power.

————. *Rich Mitch*. Morrow, 1983. Mitch serves as a model for a best selling doll and finds that being a celebrity is not all fun. He is kidnapped but escapes. A rival doll, Turnip Head, outsells Rich Mitch and he is "out."

————. *Son of the Slime Who Ate Cleve-*

land. Dell, 1985. Frank, who thinks he can do anything, decides that the best way to help his friends is to print their concerns in the local paper.

_____. *Two Guys Noticed Me*. Delacorte, 1985. Jody's father is now engaged to Matt's mother and the troubles continue. Jody meets Travis, a fellow art student, and he shows some attention but Jody still likes Matt.

Sharp, Margery. *Bernard Into Battle*. Little, 1978. Miss Bianca's faithful Bernard repulses an army of rats that live in the ambassador's cellar.

_____. *Bernard the Brave*. Little, 1977. Miss Bianca is away and Bernard has an adventure on his own. He rescues an orphan heiress who has been kidnapped.

_____. *Miss Bianca*. Little, 1962. The Mouse Prisoner's Aid Society, with Miss Bianca and Bernard, rescues Patience from a palace where she is being held by an evil duchess.

_____. *Miss Bianca and the Bridesmaid*. Little, 1972. When the ambassador's daughter's bridesmaid disappears before the wedding Miss Bianca must solve the mystery.

_____. *Miss Bianca in the Antarctic*. Little, 1970. Miss Bianca and Bernard need all the strength they can muster to survive when they are left in the Antarctic.

_____. *Miss Bianca in the Orient*. Little, 1970. Miss Bianca and Bernard on their most dangerous mission. They must save a court page from death at the hands of Ranee.

_____. *Miss Bianca in the Salt Mines*. Little, 1966. Miss Bianca and Bernard attempt to rescue Teddy from his cruel jailer in the salt mines.

_____. *Rescuers*. Little, 1959/1974. A poet is rescued from the Black Castle by Miss Bianca, Nils and their friends, when Bernard asks for the help of the Prisoner's Aid Society.

_____. *Turret*. Little, 1963. The evil Mandrake is prisoner in the turret. A rescue is planned for midnight, even though he is Miss Bianca's enemy.

Shaw, Diana. *Lessons in Fear*. Little, 1987. Adrian, a popular girl in school, is systematically trying to harm an unpopular teacher. Carter suspects this, tries to get proof and finds herself in trouble.

Shaw, Janet. *Happy Birthday Kirsten*. Pleasant, 1987. Kirsten lives in Minnesota in 1854. It is her birthday and she expects no gifts. What she does want, and gets, is a day off from her everyday chores.

Shaw, Richard. *Hard Way Home*. Dell, 1977. Gary, 16, and his dad don't get along so he runs away from home. He sneaks home to get his concert tickets and finds a note: "Enjoy concert, brush teeth, eat right, Love Mom." WOW!

_____. *Shape Up, Burke*. Nelson, 1976. Pat is sent to a military school where he must prove himself capable of "shaping up."

Shecter, Ben. *Game for Demons*. Harper, 1972.

Gordie spends the summer at a seaside resort. His friend Larry talks about contact with Satan. His mother thinks she is haunted by a former neighbor and sex is rearing its interesting head.

_____. *Someplace Else*. Harper, 1971. Arnie must plan for his bar mitzvah, and must cope with the loss of a pet and the unwanted attention of a girl.

Sheedy, Alexandra. *She Was Nice to Mice*. McGraw, 1975. Esther, a mouse, inherits a book about Queen Elizabeth written by an earlier courtly mouse. A whimsical story.

Sheldon, Ann. *Silver Stallion*. Pocket, 1988. Linda rescues a horse and finds that it's a valuable Arabian.

Shelley, Mary. *Frankenstein*. Bantam, 1981. A terror story of how a monster was built out of leftover dead bodies, among other things.

Shemin, Margaretha. *Empty Moat*. Coward, 1969. Elizabeth does not want Swaenesburgh Castle to be used as an underground Jewish escape route. But Erik and Father Andre help her to be courageous enough to allow it.

_____. *Little Riders*. Putnam, 1988. Holland is occupied by Germans during World War II. A young girl is trapped there and can't escape.

Sherbourne, Zoa. *Girl Who Knew Tomorrow*. Morrow, 1970. A story of a young girl with ESP and how it controls her life and the lives of those around her.

_____. *Leslie*. Morrow, 1972. Leslie takes a ride home from a party with Chip. She tries marijuana and all is well until Chip hits and kills a pedestrian. It is a hit-and-run and she faces whether or not to tell.

Sherman, D.R. *Lion's Paw*. Doubleday, 1975. Jannie is a hunter and he clashes with an African Bushman over a wounded lion. The Bushman frees a trapped lion while the hunter tracks him down.

Sherman, Eileen. *Monday on Odessa*. JPS, 1986. Marina is a Jew but she doesn't want to leave Odessa. Her parents have good jobs and she's not religious. It takes brutality and persecution to show her how life in Russia is for Jews.

Sherry, Sylvia. *Liverpool Cats*. Lippincott, 1969. Rocky is a "good" boy but with a gang. With a "poor" mother and a jailbird brother he drifts into crime. He escapes just before drugs and murder entrap him.

_____. *Secret of the Jade Pavilion*. Lippincott, 1967. The setting is the Chinese slums of Singapore. Ah Wong struggles to earn money and start a profitable restaurant. A cart is being used as a smuggling base. Ah and the police arrest and jail the thieves.

Sherwan, Earl. *Mask, the Door Country Coon*. Norton, 1963. Mask is a raccoon. He likes tourists but fears hunters. He has many close calls with dogs and death.

Shields, Rita. *Norah and the Cable Car*. Longman, 1960. Norah, twin brothers and widowed mother live in San Francisco in 1870. There are cable cars vs. horse cars and this issue divides the family.

Shirley, John. *Eclipse*. Bluejay, 1985. The year is 2020 and Europe has had a nuclear bombing. There is political unrest both on earth and in the space colonies.

Shore, Laura. *Sacred Moon Tree*. Bradbury, 1986. Phoebe's father is a Northerner and her mother is a Southerner during the Civil War. Phoebe and her friends leave the North to rescue a friend's brother from prison.

Shotwell, Louisa. *Adam Bookout*. Viking, 1967. Adam runs away from his aunt's home to go live with cousins. He makes friends at school: Saul, Magdalena and Willie. He finds out who stole Willie's dog and learns not to run away from adversity.

_____. *Magdalena*. Viking, 1971. Magdalena wants her hair cut in order to be more American. Her traditional grandmother is against it but she cuts it anyway. Magdalena, her friend Spook and her grandmother change and accept.

_____. *Roosevelt Grady*. World, 1963. Roosevelt Grady and his family are migrant workers. He moves from school to school trying to make friends.

Shreve, Susan. *Loveletters*. Knopf, 1978. Kate is ignored by her parents and becomes pregnant by a priest. Tommy is in his fourth foster home and has severe emotional problems. A thoughtful story of what parent inattention can do.

_____. *Lucy Forever and Miss Rosetree*. Holt, 1987. Two sixth graders with a make-believe psychiatry practice find a mute child from an orphanage and are determined to help him talk.

_____. *Masquerade*. Knopf, 1980. Rebecca's father is in prison and she assumes the responsibility for the family. She wants to believe in her father. They lose their home, the older children get away and Rebecca learns of life.

_____. *Revolution of Mary Leary*. Knopf, 1982. Thomas and Cassie are twins. Mary Leary's sister is perfect. Her parents plan to do the same for her. Mary goes to live with Thomas and Cassie's mother, a women's rights advocate.

Shub, Elizabeth. *Cutlass in the Snow*. Greenwillow, 1986. Sam and his grandfather are stranded on Fire Island. They fear the talk of pirates and stay alert. In the morning they find a cutlass in the snow!

Shura, Mary. *Barkley Street Six-Pack*. Dodd, 1979. Jane and Natalie are best friends. Jane overlooks Natalie's faults because she wants her as a friend. Natalie breaks up any other friendship Jane tries to have. Natalie moves and Jane is friendless.

_____. *Chester*. Dodd, 1980. Jamie, George, Edie, Zach and Amy all have something special to brag about until Chester moves in the block and outdoes them all. But when he and his goat outwit the teenage bully all is forgiven.

_____. *Don't Call Me Toad*. Dodd, 1987. Janie and her new friend find hidden money and stolen jewels.

_____. *Eleanor*. Dodd, 1983. Eleanor saves the day for her school's field day float contest. She and her brother, Chester, along with the gang at school, designed and built the float.

_____. *Gray Ghosts of Taylor Ridge*. Dodd, 1978. A lost treasure is found by a brother and his sister.

_____. *Jefferson*. Dodd, 1984. Jefferson is going to have a birthday and everyone in the neighborhood is earning money for a surprise party. It is beset by one calamity after another. His sister, Chester, tries to help.

_____. *Jessica*. Scholastic, 1984. Jessica, 16, falls in love with Wheeling Hawk, an Indian brave. This is not acceptable behavior for a good daughter living on the Kansas prairie.

_____. *Josie Gambit*. Dodd, 1986. Greg is shy and likes to play chess. He is spending some time with his grandmother and her out-going family. He learns loyalty and friendship.

_____. *Mary's Marvelous Mouse*. Knopf, 1962. A cat upsets Mary's plans for her pet mouse, who lives in a jar and enjoys an un-mouse-like diet.

_____. *Mister Wolf and Me*. Dodd, 1979. Miles finds a German shepherd pup and takes him home. Later the dog is attacked and wounded by a groundhog on the same night a wild dog attacks a flock of sheep.

_____. *Nearsighted Knight*. Knopf, 1964. The Kingdom of Lamish has a witch, a dragon and a nearsighted knight, Prince Todd, and his unwed sister.

_____. *Polly Panic*. Putnam, 1990. Polly is in the sixth grade and deals with friends, both loyal and untrustworthy, bullies, and the usual family problems of all young girls plus her own fears.

_____. *Run Away Home*. Knopf, 1965. Mike takes care of three goats to earn money to run away. Instead he becomes a local hero when he's involved in a rescue operation.

_____. *Search for Grissi*. Dodd, 1985. Peter gets involved in looking for his sister's lost cat and thereby feels more at ease at his new school and home.

_____. *Sunday Doll*. Dodd, 1988. Emmy is sent to Aunt Harriett's for the summer because of the problems of her older sister, Jayne.

_____. *Tale of Middle Length*. Atheneum, 1966. Dominie lived in a trash heap in the meadow. She recognized the trap when she saw it. She warned the others but they didn't listen to her.

Shyer, Marlene. *Adorable Sunday*. Scribner, 1983. Sunday is a child television commercial star. She likes the work but the kids at school think she's a show-off and play tricks on her. Her grades are going down and her parents argue over her future.

_____. *Blood in the Snow.* Houghton, 1975. Max is not as "macho" as his father would like. He buys him a gun to make him more "male-like." Max trades it for a valuable flute and tries to save a fox from a trap.

_____. *Grandpa Ritz and the Luscious Lovelies.* Scribner, 1985. Philip spends the summer with his grandfather in a retirement community. It turns out to be an interesting and exciting summer.

_____. *Me and Joey Pinstrip, the King of Rock.* Scribner, 1988. Rock star Joey Pinstrip moves into Mary Kaye's apartment. She suddenly becomes popular. A "punk" couple steal her dog and blackmail her for autographs, then use the money for drugs.

_____. *My Brother the Thief.* Scribner, 1980. Carolyn has two secrets. One, her middle name is Frankfurter, and two, her half brother is a thief and a "fence." If she tells on her brother he will tell her name.

_____. *Welcome Home, Jellybean.* Scribner, 1978. Neil, 12, is uncertain about his feeling when his retarded sister comes home to stay. It takes a near tragedy to clear things.

Sidney, Margaret. *Five Little Peppers and How They Grew.* Penguin, 1990. A children's classic of five children as they grow up in an earlier time. There are many available editions.

Siegal, Aranka. *Grace in the Wilderness.* Farrar, 1985. Piri and her sister are liberated and sent to Sweden. She is with a loving family and falls in love. But they immigrate to America where unknown relatives wait for them.

_____. *Upon the Head of the Goat.* Farrar, 1981. A story of the Holocaust told by Piri, a Hungarian Jew. She and her family board a train headed for Auschwitz. Her father is on the Russian front and her mother didn't get passage to America.

Siegel, Beatrice. *Basket Maker and the Spinner.* Walker, 1987. Yawata is a Wampanoag Indian and a basket maker; Mary Allen is a colonist in New England and a spinner.

Sierra, Patricia. *One-Way Romance.* Avon, 1986. Emily loves Cleve and Amy loves Bart. Cleve loves Amy and Bart loves Emily. These romances need to be turned around so they will come out right.

Silman, Roberta. *Somebody Else's Child.* Warne, 1976. A warm friendship develops between Peter, who is adopted, and Puddin' Paint, his bus driver.

Silsbee, Peter. *Big Way Out.* Bradbury, 1984. Paul's father is unstable and he and his mother move in with his grandmother, a hostile woman. A brother stays with the father who is acting more and more irrational.

_____. *Love Among the Hiccups.* Macmillan, 1987. Palmer wants a loving home and loving friends to end his deep loneliness. A warm, funny story.

Silverberg, Robert. *Man in the Maze.* Avon, 1969. Dick Muller was transformed by aliens, repulsed by other human beings and exiled to a maze for nine years. Now he is needed to save the Earth from attack and is wanted back, but he's not coming.

Silverstein, Herman. *Mad, Mad Monday.* Dutton, 1988. Miranda conjures up a ghost of a boy called Monday. He can only be seen by her and is on Earth for two weeks. Monday and a magic amulet win football hero Stormy for Miranda, among other surprises.

Silverstein, Shel. *Lafcadio, the Lion Who Shot Back.* Harper, 1963. Lafcadio is a marksman and a success but he doesn't like what he does.

Simak, Clifford. *Shakespeare's Planet.* Berkley, 1976. A slightly different twist of the plot of a spaceman landing on a strange planet.

Simon, Marcia. *Special Gift.* Harcourt, 1978. Peter doesn't want anyone to know he is taking ballet lessons.

Simon, Norma. *How Do I Feel?* Whitman, 1970. Three brothers, two of them twins, must sort out their feelings about each other, especially one of the twins.

Simon, Seymour. *Chip Rogers, Computer Whiz.* Morrow, 1984. Chip and Katie use their computer knowledge to solve a crime.

_____. *Einstein Anderson Goes to Bat.* Viking, 1982. Einstein does use scientific logic to solve his puzzles, all of which can be tested. He still offers puns and riddles — and fun.

_____. *Einstein Anderson Lights Up the Sky.* Viking, 1982. Some aspect of science is used in solving these new problems. In this book meteorology and electrostatics are used.

_____. *Einstein Anderson, Science Sleuth.* Viking, 1980. "Einstein" is a brainy kid who likes to solve puzzlers. The reader gets the clues and a chance to solve the problem before the solution is given. A scientific "Encyclopedia Brown."

Simon, Shirley. *Best Friend.* Lothrop, 1964. Jenny makes a decision about one best friend versus many good friends.

_____. *Cousins at Camm Corners.* Lothrop, 1963. Marcy visits her relatives in a small town. Life is very different from her New York City style.

Simon, Sidney. *Henry, the Uncatchable Mouse.* Norton, 1964. Henry is a smart mouse. He is able to spring traps without being caught.

Simons, Roger. *Dolphin Sailed North.* McGraw, 1966. Bruce and Jan take the *Dolphin* to its buyer. They sail from the coast of England through Wales and Scotland.

Simons, Wendy. *Harper's Mother.* Prentice, 1980. Harper, 14, comes to terms with living an unconventional life with her mother and her mother's "friends." There are sexual abuse and homosexuality.

Simpson, Dorothy. *Honest Dollar.* Lippincott, 1957. Janie wants to earn money for books because she can't afford to go to high school. The jobs she wants she can't get and the jobs she can get she doesn't want. But a happy solution is found.

———. *Lesson for Janie*. Lippincott, 1958. Janie has a problem with the new girl, Myra. They often quarrel but learn to understand and appreciate one another.

———. *New Horizons*. Lippincott, 1961. Janie must adjust to life on the mainland after spending her childhood on a Maine island.

Sinclair, Tom. *Tales of a Wandering Warthog*. Whitman, 1985. When a gentle warthog comes into the human world he has many adventures to talk about.

Sindall, Marjorie. *Matey*. St. Martin, 1960. Brit (Matey) lives on London's back streets and loves it. She moves to the country and hates it. When she returns to London for a visit she finds everything changed and returns to the country willingly.

Singer, Isaac. *Alone in the Wild Forest*. Farrar, 1971. Joseph wins the hand of a princess with the help of an angel's amulet.

———. *Fearsome Inn*. Scribner, 1967. A story of how evil is overcome by faith, magic and common sense.

———. *Golem*. Farrar, 1982. A Jewish legend where a rabbi saved a community by giving life to a clay statue.

———. *Topsy-Turvy Emperor of China*. Harper, 1971. A story of the wicked emperor and his nasty wife. Their son and his sweetheart were nice and loving. There is a constant struggle between good and evil.

Singer, Marilyn. *Case of the Cackling Car*. Harper, 1985. Sam and Dave interrupt their Texas vacation to search for a missing girl. Someone is smuggling pet birds into the country.

———. *Case of the Fixed Election*. Harper, 1989. Dave runs for student council president. He is accused of stuffing the ballot box. Sam must clear Dave's name.

———. *Case of the Sabotaged School Play*. Harper, 1984. A boring school play becomes big news when stage sabotage is suspected. It is a good case for Sam and Dave to solve.

———. *Clue in Code*. Harper, 1985. Money for the class trip suddenly disappears. Did the class bully, Willie, the custodian's son who has stolen before, take it? Sam and Dave have a mystery to solve.

———. *Course of True Love Never Did Run Smooth*. Harper, 1983. Becky and Nemi write a play in which a brother and sister they want to befriend have a part. Becky thinks she's in love with Blake but finds that love is a deeper emotion than she feels.

———. *Fido Frame-Up*. Warne, 1983. Sam Spayed is a dog sidekick for Philip. A cameo is stolen. Sam gets information from other dogs and the theft is solved.

———. *Ghost Host*. Harper, 1987. Bart plays quarterback and he likes to read! He feels he must act like a jock. He finds his house is haunted and the ghost helps him realize he can enjoy nice things and still play football.

———. *Hoax Is on You*. Harper, 1989. Sam and Dave enter a magazine contest for the best hoax. Dardanella is the hoax because she is really not an exchange student, nor a thief, as was believed.

———. *Horsemaster*. Atheneum, 1985. Jessica dreams of flying horses. She fantasizes she is a messenger for Kadi, the Horse God in another world at another time.

———. *It Can't Hurt Forever*. Harper, 1978. Ellie must have a heart operation. She meets Sonia who had the same operation. She is scared but gets help from some people and more scares from others.

———. *Leroy Is Missing*. Harper, 1984. Sam and Dave help Rita look for her missing eight-year-old brother. They follow false clues and run into danger. Leroy does turn up with an unsuspected explanation.

———. *Lightey Club*. Four Winds, 1987. Henry and her sisters are spending the summer with their grandmother. She tells them stories about Lightey, the Lightning Bug, and his friends.

———. *Lizzie Silver of Sherwood Forest*. Harper, 1986. Lizzie is interested in Robin Hood. She and Tessa go to the fair where she meets Andy who teaches her how to be a one-man band. She wants to go to music school with Tessa.

———. *No Applause Please*. Dutton, 1977. Ruthie and Laurie are friends; they both want a singing career. Rivalry is there but their friendship is strong.

———. *Nose for Trouble*. Holt, 1985. Philip and Sam have been hired by a cosmetic company to find out who is leaking secrets. Sam again solves the mystery.

———. *Tarantulas on the Brain*. Harper, 1982. Lizzie is interested in science. She tries to earn money to buy a tarantula. But dishonesty and misunderstanding mar her attempt.

———. *Twenty Ways to Lose Your Best Friend*. Harper, 1990. Emma loses her best friend when she votes for another girl to get the lead in a school play.

———. *Where There's a Will, There's a Wag*. Holt, 1986. Carlotta, the owner of Pet Food, has died and willed her fortune to a cat. Sam finds that she really left her money to Sam with Philip as trustee.

Sinor, John. *Ghosts of Cabrillo Lighthouse*. Joyce Press, 1977. It started when a skiff was pushed into the rocks. To get out of trouble, a brother and sister had to take a hundred-year hike backwards in time.

Sirof, Harriet. *Real World*. Watts, 1985. Cady lives with her feminist mother in a commune. Her father, whom her mother never married, invites her to New York with his family and she comes to love him and his life style.

Sisson, Rosemary. *Will in Love.* Morrow, 1975. A fictionalized biography about William Shakespeare's early life.

Sivers, Brenda. *Snailman.* Little, 1978. Timothy has problems. He moved from the city, his parents are fighting and he is harassed by a bully at school. He befriends the town's hermit, a gentle man deformed by a car accident.

Skirrow, Desmond. *Case of the Silver Egg.* Doubleday, 1968. Mini-Minor's father discovers a new energy source and calls it Silver Egg. He is kidnapped and Mini-Minor and his friends must both find him and rescue the discovery.

Skolsky, Mindy. *Carnival and Kopeck.* Harper, 1979. Problems arise between Hannah and her grandmother. Hannah learns that closeness always has some problems.

———. *Hannah and the Best Father on Route 9W.* Harper, 1982. Hannah and her father compete in separate contests. But they are also supportive of each other.

———. *Hannah Is a Palindrome.* Harper, 1980. Hannah's family moves into an apartment at the rear of a restaurant. She sees herself and her family in a different light.

———. *Whistling Teakettle.* Harper, 1977. This is a picture of New York City during the Great Depression.

Skorpen, Liesel. *Grace.* Harper, 1984. Sara helps Grace, an old woman, and learns of her past. All summer she spends feeding, caring for and reading to Grace who then dies and leaves Sara shattered.

Skrebitski, Georgii. *Tempering.* Clarion, 1983. Life in the steel works of Pennsylvania in the early 1900's. Karl wants to work rather than go to school. He runs away but returns to the poverty and life style of the area. There is some hope.

Skurzynski, Gloria. *Caught in the Moving Mountains.* Lothrop, 1984. Two boys meet an injured drug dealer while hiking in the mountains. They all face questionable survival when an earthquake hits the area.

———. *Dangerous Ground.* Bradbury, 1989. Angela spends a year with her great-aunt. She finds the woman is taking the wrong medicine and is acting strangely. They become very close and when the year is up both join the family in the city.

———. *Lost in the Devil's Desert.* Lothrop, 1982. Keven is alone and lost in a Utah desert. Only his cool head can help him survive.

———. *Manwolf.* Houghton, 1981. Adam was an illegitimate child born to a peasant girl. His father was a disfigured count. He grew up to be half man and half wolf: a werewolf.

———. *Remarkable Journey of Gustavus Bill.* Lothrop, 1982. Gustavus keeps shrinking in size; first the size of bugs and flies and then molecules in water. He is saved by ants and the ants are saved by his dog.

———. *Swept in the Wave of Terror.* Lothrop, 1985. A terrorist is trying to damage the Hoover Dam. Only a brother and sister can stop the scheme.

———. *Trapped in the Slickrock Canyon.* Lothrop, 1984. Gina and Justin spend the night helping each other survive a flash flood and all its dangers.

———. *What Happened in Hamelin?* Four Winds, 1979. A new and different version of the Pied Piper. He not only lures the children with his piping but with baked goodies ... laced with drugs. The tale is told by one of the two survivors, a baker's aide.

Slater, Jim. *Boy Who Saved the Earth.* Doubleday, 1981. Marcou crash-lands on the Earth from Gundra. He learns the language and communicates with people. The enemy, Malagons, is going to kill him and take over the Earth.

Slatten, Evelyn. *Good, the Bad and the Rest of Us.* Morrow, 1980. Katie lives during the Great Depression. She copes with a jobless father and poverty. An auto accident changes her life for the better.

Sleator, William. *Among the Dolls.* Dutton, 1975. Vicky didn't like the dolls she got for her birthday. She made them do nasty things and punished them cruelly. One day, very angry, she pushed them around and found herself in the doll house with them!

———. *Blackbriar.* Dutton, 1972. Danny and his stepmother move into a mysterious house where there are many unanswered questions.

———. *Boy Who Reversed Himself.* Dutton, 1986. Laura thought her new neighbor, Omar, was strange. Why did he go into her locker? Why is his left tooth missing when yesterday it was the right one?

———. *Duplicate.* Dutton, 1988. David duplicates himself so he can go to a family party *and* keep his date with Angela. Then the trouble begins when the Duplicate duplicates himself.

———. *Fingers.* Atheneum, 1983. A humorous story of two brothers who play piano, one very good but mechanical, the other more feeling but not as adept. Sam plays a trick on Humphrey to get him to play better and it works. Sort of.

———. *Green Futures of Tycho.* Dutton, 1981. Tycho finds a way to travel back and forth through time.

———. *House of Stairs.* Dutton, 1974. A horrifying story of an experiment on five youngsters to make them blindly obey and be rewarded for negative behavior. Three of the five "succeed"; the other two are dismissed as failures!

———. *Interstellar Pig.* Dutton, 1984. Barney's safety is threatened by three lavender-eyed aliens when he gets drawn into their game of "interstellar pig."

———. *Into the Dream.* Dutton, 1979. Paul learns that Francine is having the same dream as his. They are both trying to reach a child who is headed toward a strange light. They both are telepathic and believe the child is, too.

————. *Singularity*. Dutton, 1985. Harry and Barry are twins. They discover the secret of time. How will they control this power that could destroy the universe?

Sleigh, Barbara. *Carbonel, King of the Cats.* Bobbs, 1955. Carbonel, an extraordinary black cat, is under a witch's spell. Rosemary and her friend, John, must break the spell.

————. *Kingdom of Carbonel*. Bobbs, 1960. Rosemary and John take care of Carbonel's kitten while he is away fighting for his kingdom. They both can understand what animals say because of a secret potion they got from a witch.

Slepian, Jan. *Broccoli Tapes*. Philomel, 1989. Sara is working on an Oral History project for school. She goes to Hawaii and takes her taping equipment with her to keep up.

————. *Getting On with It*. Four Winds, 1985. Berry goes to live with his grandmother while his parents are getting a divorce. He learns that life and love go on despite unexpected changes.

Slepian, Janice. *Alfred Summer*. Macmillan, 1980. Four youngsters and a boat have a courageous, quixotic quest that nearly ends in tragedy. All the children are handicapped in some way and form a tight circle of friendship.

————. *Lester's Turn*. Macmillan, 1981. A story of disabled youngsters and how they cope with their problems. Lester tries to help Alfred because he feels he is deteriorating in the hospital, but his plan doesn't work out.

————. *Night of the Bozos*. Dutton, 1983. Georgie's uncle Hibbie stutters and has no friends. Georgie, too, can't make friends although he is musically talented. Hibbie decides to become a clown because with the disguise he feels free to talk.

Sloan, Carolyn. *Sea Child*. Holiday, 1988. Jessie lives with her father on an island and has never seen another person.

Slobodkin, Louis. *Round Trip Space Ship.* Macmillan, 1968. Eddie would like to visit Marty's home so off they go to Martinea where things are strange indeed.

————. *Space Ship in the Park*. Macmillan, 1972. Eddie and Willie are taken by their friend, Marty, to Xonia where they look for materials that Marty needs for his planet, Martinea.

————. *Space Ship Returns to the Apple Tree*. Macmillan, 1958. Marty returns from outer space and he and Eddie visit Washington and California by means of the Secret Power ZZZ.

————. *Space Ship Under the Apple Tree.* Macmillan, 1952. Eddie visits his grandmother on her farm and hardly expects a visit from Marty, the boy from outer space.

————. *Three-Seated Space Ship*. Macmillan, 1962. Marty again visits Eddie while he's

at his grandmother's farm. This time London and New York are the destinations in a new space ship.

Slote, Alfred. *Clone Catcher*. Harper, 1982. Arthur is a clone catcher. Kate's clone is missing and Arthur is hired to find it.

————. *C.O.L.A.R.* Lippincott, 1981. C.O.L.A.R. is a planet inhabited by the robots Dr. Atkins invented. Jack and his family are stranded on this planet.

————. *Finding Buck McHenry*. Harper, 1991. Jason, 11, believes that the school custodian, Mack Henry, is Buck McHenry, a famous black pitcher. He tries to get him to coach his Little League team.

————. *Friends Like That*. Lippincott, 1988. Robbie is upset when Carol, the person he wants his father to marry, gets married. He has further problems because he might lose his shortstop position on the team. So he runs away.

————. *Hang Tough, Paul Mather*. Lippincott, 1973. Paul is new in town and loves baseball more than anything. He has been a star pitcher on two Little League teams. He also has leukemia and knows it.

————. *Hotshot*. Watts, 1977. A story of how a star hockey player finds that playing well isn't the only criterion for a star. He must learn to be part of a team.

————. *Jake*. Harper, 1971. Jake's baseball team is coached by a mother but she lets Jake do most of the coaching. They must beat the McLeon team with their curve ball. Jake whips his team into shape.

————. *Love and Tennis*. Macmillan, 1979. Buddy's parents are tennis pros and want him to be too, especially his mother. He decides to quit playing because of the tension created by both his mother and his girlfriend.

————. *Matt Gargan's Boy*. Lippincott, 1983. Danny is an excellent pitcher but his parents' divorce and the fact that a girl wants to join the team interfere with his playing.

————. *Moving In*. Lippincott, 1988. Robbie and Peggy try to keep their father from marrying the person he's considering. They try to fix him up with a person of their liking, Carol.

————. *My Robot Buddy*. Lippincott, 1975. Jack lives in the future where robots look and act like people. Jack has a robot he calls Danny One. A robotnapper tries to steal him.

————. *My Trip to Alpha 1*. Lippincott, 1978. Voya-code, a means of travel for Jack and Danny One, takes them where his aunt is in a dummy body.

————. *Omega Station*. Lippincott, 1983. Jack and his robot, Danny One, must save the universe from a mad scientist, Otto Drago.

————. *Rabbit Ears*. Harper, 1982. Kip has been playing baseball for at least half of his fourteen years but now he is losing his confidence.

————. *Tony and Me*. Lippincott, 1974. Bill

and Tony are friends. Tony is a great baseball player but he is a thief. Bill needs to make a decision of what to do about it.

————. *Trading Game.* Lippincott, 1990. Andy plays baseball. His father and grandfather played baseball. He learns more about them while trading baseball cards.

————. *Trouble on Janus.* Lippincott, 1985. Jack and his robot, Danny One, go to Janus to rescue King Paul, a twelve-year-old ruler. There is a robot look-alike to complicate the rescue.

Smaridge, Norah. *Mysteries in the Commune.* Dodd, 1982. Robin befriends Emmy, who thinks her mother is not her real one, and Adam, who is running away. She and her friend Jerry try to straighten this out.

————. *Mystery at Greystone Hall.* Dodd, 1979. Robin goes to England and meets Mark and Miss Tilly. They tour Greystone Hall and are invited to stay for a week. But they didn't anticipate being grabbed by a statue or being locked in a cellar.

————. *Mystery in the Old Mansions.* Dodd, 1981. Robin is a summer guide where her aunt works in a mansion similar to the one where she lives. A formula for making a pottery glaze is missing. Robin solves this and finds a missing teen, also.

————. *Secret of the Brownstone House.* Dodd, 1977. Robin is vacationing in New York and discovers two runaways hiding in an old brownstone house where two boys were murdered years ago. Elly is returned to her home and Len, an orphan, is befriended.

Smith, A.C.H. *Lady Jane.* Holt, 1985. A story of Lady Jane Grey's marriage and nine day reign as Queen of England before she and her young husband were beheaded in 1554.

Smith, Alison. *Billy Boone.* Scribner, 1989. Billy likes to play trumpet and likes her grandmother, Dixie. Her mother doesn't think the trumpet is lady-like and doesn't like Dixie.

————. *Help! There's a Cat Washing in Here.* Dutton, 1981. Henry runs the house for two weeks while his mother finishes a project. They both survive. He brings food and has trouble with his younger brother and sister, and with the stray cat.

————. *Reserved for Mark Anthony Crowder.* Dutton, 1978. Mark feels like a real misfit and is afraid his father thinks so, too. He sets out to prove himself.

————. *Trap of Gold.* Dodd, 1985. Margaret loses a gold nugget necklace left to her by her father. She looks for it and finds the entrance to an old gold mine. She feels someone watching her.

Smith, Anne. *Blue Denim Blues.* Avon, 1982. Janet is shy and gets a job working in a nursery school for the summer.

————. *Sister in the Shadow.* Atheneum, 1986. Sharon lives in the shadow of a younger sister, Penny. She gets a babysitting job and proves to be a person in her own right.

Smith, Betty. *Joy in the Morning.* Harper, 1976. Carl is a law student, and he marries Annie McGairy. She is uneducated but lovable and creative. This is a warm, loving family story.

————. *Tree Grows in Brooklyn.* Harper, 1968. Francie grows up in Brooklyn in the early 1900's. She gets a job on the newspaper and protects her younger brother.

Smith, Carole. *Danger at the Golden Dragon.* Whitman, 1983. Roger uncovers a smuggling operation set up by Cubitt and Joe Dodge. The operation includes gold, pearls and Oriental antiques.

————. *Hit and Run Connection.* Whitman, 1982. Jeff and Andy track down the driver of the car that hit their friend and left the scene. There is also a sub-theme of baseball players and games.

————. *Parchment House.* Four Winds, 1989. Johnnie is in an orphanage of the future and fights the cruel director, Reverend Slipper.

————. *Stealing Isn't Easy.* Whitman, 1984. Jeremy gets involved in a mystery when he tries to return a lady's painting to her. Rebecca and he find a plot involving stolen paintings.

————. *Who Burned the Hartley House?* Whitman, 1985. Larry gets involved in a mystery when a deserted house burns. He suspected a kidnapped boy was being held there. An escaped convict and his father are the culprits.

Smith, Claude. *Stratford Devil.* Walker, 1985. Ruth is attacked by a wolf and is rescued by an Indian. She is accused of being a witch. A story of how circumstantial evidence can lead to charges.

Smith, Dennis. *Final Fire.* Saturday Review Press, 1975. A story of two brothers, both firemen, and their political and personal conflict over the treatment of firemen and the issue of strikes. A tragic story.

Smith, Dodie. *Hundred and One Dalmatians.* Viking, 1957/1989. Someone kidnapped the Dalmatians. The mystery is solved by the parents of the kidnapped 15 pup litter: Pongo and Missis. The cruel Cruell de Vil is the guilty party.

————. *Starlight Barking.* Viking, 1968. The dog world is faced with a time and space problem. Time is suspended for all human beings. All animals except dogs are asleep. The Dalmatians assume control.

Smith, Doris. *First Hard Times.* Viking, 1983. Ancil doesn't like her new stepfather because she is still loyal to her father who was reported missing in Vietnam ten years ago.

————. *Karate Dancer.* Putnam, 1987. Troy is learning karate but must understand that it is mastery of both body and mind. His girlfriend, a dancer, gets him involved in dancing and he sees life a bit differently.

————. *Kelly's Creek.* Crowell, 1975. Kelly has a learning disability which is discovered by her college student friend, Phillip, who then helps her overcome it.

_____. *Kick a Stone Home.* Crowell, 1974. A young girl is growing up in a home broken by divorce. She deals with a lost pet, her first date and getting along with friends.

_____. *Last Was Lloyd.* Viking, 1981. Lloyd, fat and overprotected, is teased because he is not chosen for the school team. But soon everyone sees a different Lloyd. Ancil, his friend, is his model of confidence and independence.

_____. *Laura Up-Side-Down.* Viking, 1984. Laura has no religious training but her friends are either Christian or Jewish. She also wonders if the neighbor is a witch. She learns that people's behavior has a reason.

_____. *Moonshadow of Cherry Mountain.* Four Winds, 1982. New neighbors come with modern changes to a mountain community. The people living there must deal with this.

_____. *Return to Bitter Creek.* Viking, 1986. Lacey's mother is not married to the artist man she lives with. Lacey's grandparents are not sure they can accept this arrangement.

_____. *Salted Lemons.* Four Winds, 1980. Darby has moved from North to South and has trouble making new friends. One friend, Yoko, is sent to an internment camp (WWII). The other is a German man who is teased by the other children.

_____. *Taste of Blackberries.* Crowell, 1973. Jamie died of bee stings while his friend laughed at his "clowning." Now he feels badly and misses Jamie. He wonders about death and whether he could have done something more to help.

_____. *Tough Chauncey.* Morrow, 1974. Chauncey lives with his grandparents. He is beaten and locked in the closet. He is encouraged to tell his story to a social worker because no one else cares. He is going to get outside help.

_____. *Up and Over.* Morrow, 1976. A story about how a boy succeeds as a track star in high school.

Smith, Emma. *Out of Hand.* Harcourt, 1963. Polly breaks her leg and the two Misses Collins come to take charge. The other youngsters try to rescue Polly and declare war on the Misses Collins.

Smith, Eunice. *High Heels for Jennifer.* Bobbs, 1964. Jennifer, 13, is interested in horses and art but dreams of dancing, high heels and boys. Her first dance was a disappointment so she returns to her beloved horse, High Heels.

_____. *Jennifer Gift.* Bobbs, 1949. Jennifer's gift is one she meant for her family but gave to ill Sarabeth instead, knowing that her family would not only understand but approve of her action.

_____. *Jennifer Is Eleven.* Bobbs, 1952. Jennifer's pet is a bull calf and in spite of other activity on the Hill farm Jennifer's concern is her calf. She doesn't want to sell or give it up and accepts the responsibility of keeping it.

_____. *Jennifer Prize.* Bobbs, 1951. Jennifer wins a prize for her written composition. She remains a likeable girl in a very likeable family.

Smith, Fredrika. *Sound of Axes.* Rand McNally, 1965. David and his dog Shep stay with Uncle Will. Cal is a troublemaker in Will's lumber business. David leaves the camp after two years and goes to college. He returns as a doctor and finds many changes.

Smith, Gene. *Visitor.* Cowles, 1971. Sassafras is put in a kennel while his family goes on vacation. His master is killed in an accident and his mistress arranges for him to stay permanently in the kennel.

Smith, George. *Bayou Boy.* Follett, 1965. Jean is now man of the house when his father goes away to work. He faces alligators, snakes and an escaped convict.

Smith, Janice. *It's Not Easy Being George.* Harper, 1989. Adam and his dog, George, go through a pet show and an all-night sleepover.

_____. *Kid Next Door and Other Headaches.* Harper, 1984. Adam and his friend disagree on neatness, pets, heroes, cousins, etc., but they still are best friends.

Smith, L.J. *Night of the Solstice.* Macmillan, 1987. Claudia and Alys must free Morgana, who guards the gates between Earth and the Wildworld, before Cadd, the evil magician, can come through.

Smith, Linell. *Auction Pony.* Little, 1965. A young girl owns a special pony. Her grandfather is a careful breeder of ponies for horse shows.

Smith, Martin. *Nightwing.* Norton, 1977. A story of the attacks of plague-carrying vampire bats in Hopi Indian country; and the beliefs of the Indians about this phenomenon.

Smith, Marya. *Across the Creek.* Arcade, 1989. Rye's friendly with the girl across the creek and she helps him cope with the death of his mother.

_____. *Winter Broker.* Arcade, 1990. Dawn is abused by an alcoholic father. She finds friendship and love with a farmer and his horse, Wildfire.

Smith, Nancy. *Falling-Apart Winter.* Walker, 1982. A boy's mother has a nervous breakdown and he must adjust to the changes it makes in his life.

Smith, Pauline. *Brush Fire.* Westminster, 1979. Johnny house-sits for his shop teacher. Three hoods come and cut the phone lines and threaten him. He saves the house plus the entire valley from fire by using a homemade warning system.

Smith, Perry. *Hidden Place.* Dutton, 1962. Johnny knew Reece was lying but he needed proof. He leaves home to find a mine before Reece, who tried to kill his father and marry his sister to get control of the farm, finds it.

Smith, Robert. *Bobby Baseball.* Delacorte, 1989. Bobby loves baseball and thinks he's a great player. But he needs to prove his skill, especially to his father.

_____. *Chocolate Fever.* Putnam, 1989.

Henry will go down in history as the first victim of Chocolate Fever.

————. *Jelly Belly.* Delacorte, 1981. Ned is fat and goes to camp. There he learns, with the help of Richard, how to cheat. He doesn't lose much weight. He finally decides for himself that he must slim down and does so.

————. *Mostly Michael.* Delacorte, 1987. Michael writes in his diary about school, his sister, a girlfriend, cheating in school, reading, etc.

————. *War with Grandpa.* Delacorte, 1984. Grandpa coming to live with Jennifer and her brother, who must give up his room for Grandpa. He likes Grandpa but doesn't want to give up his room so he declares war on Grandpa.

Smith, Rukshana. *Sumitra's Story.* Coward, 1983. Sumitra moves to England with her family and learns about a new and different life style. Should she accept this new freedom and alienate her family, or accept an arranged marriage and subserviency?

Smith, T.H. *Cry to the Night Wind.* Viking, 1986. Danie is a cabin boy on the "Langley" in the late 18th century. He makes friends with a seal pup, is kidnapped by Indians and escapes with the help of the seal.

Smith, Vian. *Martin Rides the Moor.* Doubleday, 1965. Martin loses his hearing. He gets a pony, called Tuppence, whom he learns to love.

————. *Tall and Proud.* Doubleday, 1966. Gail knew she would never walk. The doctor knew it, too. But Gail's mother thought the effects of polio would get better in time.

Smith, Wanda. *Ash Brooks, Super Ranger.* Scribner, 1984. Ashley doesn't want to spend the summer with his brother and grandparents. But it turns out to be different than he thought.

Smucker, Barbara. *Runaway to Freedom.* Harper, 1977. A story of how two girls escaped from the South and traveled to Canada and to freedom.

————. *Wigwam in the City.* Dutton, 1966. Susan and her Chippewa Indian family move to Chicago. She adjusts to city life and looks for her runaway brother who left the family.

Sneve, Virginia. *Betrayed.* Holiday, 1974. A picture of the Indian/white conflict during the Civil War. A bitter story based on fact.

————. *High Elk's Treasure.* Holiday, 1972. Joe discovers a cave and a treasure left there by his great-grandfather, a Sioux Indian.

————. *Jimmy Yellow Hawk.* Holiday, 1972. Little Jim succeeds in trapping a mink and earning his father's approval.

Snow, Dorothea. *Sight of Everything.* Houghton, 1963. Purdie learns that life on a mountain farm does not make dreams come true in and of itself.

Snyder, Anne. *First Step.* Holt, 1975. Cindy's mother is divorced but worse than that is an alcoholic. She finds Alateen and life gets a little better.

————. *Goodbye, Paper Doll.* Nal, 1980. Rosemary is starving herself to death. She thinks it's power of mind over body and believes it until she dies.

————. *My Name Is Davy—I'm an Alcoholic.* Harper, 1977. Davy's mother is glad he isn't doing drugs. She doesn't know he lies, steals, drinks and may die.

Snyder, Carol. *Great Condominium Rebellion.* Delacorte, 1981. Stacy and Marc are visiting their grandparents and confront the problems of change, aging and self determination.

————. *Ike and Mama and the Block Wedding.* Putnam, 1979. A story about growing up in New York in 1900.

————. *Ike and Mama and the Seven Surprises.* Lothrop, 1985. Ike will get seven surprises on the day of his bar mitzvah. They will come during the day and end at sundown.

————. *Leave Me Alone, Ma.* Bantam, 1987. Jaimie, 14, feels neglected by her parents. She writes in her diary, she falls in love with her best friend's brother and she wins a sculpture contest her parents didn't even know she entered.

————. *Leftover Kid.* Putnam, 1986. Wendy is overwhelmed by her family but her friendship with Gary and his family makes her look at hers more closely. A funny story.

Snyder, Zilpha. *And All Between.* Atheneum, 1976. Raamo and his friends are in great danger because of secrets and discoveries. Kindar and the Endlings use their separate powers to get reunited.

————. *And Condors Danced.* Delacorte, 1987. Carly, 11, sees the condors fly while on an outing with her friend, Matt. She loses both her dog and her mother; but since she loved and was loved more by her dog than her mother, she misses her dog more.

————. *Below the Root.* Atheneum, 1975. Raamo questions the teachings of the land of Green-Sky and uncovers deceptions about the tree. The enemy is Posh-shan who lives under the roots and steals babies.

————. *Birds of Summer.* Atheneum, 1983. Summer and Sparrow's mother is, at best, a prostitute. She is arrested again and Summer finds a place for Sparrow to stay. She finds friendship with her teacher and a young boy.

————. *Black and Blue Magic.* Atheneum, 1966. Harry Houdini Marco is clumsy and self-conscious. He is given a pair of wings by Mr. Mazzeeck, a mysterious stranger. He now has the most exciting adventure.

————. *Blair's Nightmare.* Atheneum, 1984. Blair really does see a dog at night but no one believes him. Finally the rest of the children see the dog, too, and complications begin. Can they keep the dog?

————. *Changeling.* Atheneum, 1970. A talented girl is accused of vandalism incorrectly. She believes that maybe she is a changeling.

_____. *Egypt Game*. Atheneum, 1967. April and Melanie invent a game of Egypt when they find an old Egyptian statue. Other kids play too, until a child in the neighborhood is murdered and the murderer is after others.

_____. *Eyes in the Fishbowl*. Atheneum, 1968. Dion was a shoeshine boy outside a department store. Strange things were happening and Sara showed him the store after closing. But he almost lost his life following her.

_____. *Fabulous Creature*. Atheneum, 1981. James gave food to a wild deer and befriended him. He met Diane, whose father was a hunter. He told Diane of the great stag and then went to great lengths to save the stag from being killed.

_____. *Famous Stanley Kidnapping Case*. Atheneum, 1979. A gang of kidnappers run off with Amanda and the four Stanley children in Italy because of Amanda's boasting of her father's wealth.

_____. *Headless Cupid*. Atheneum, 1971. Amanda's family moves into a house that is haunted when Amanda's mother remarries. Amanda believes in the supernatural and uses this to justify her aloofness toward David and her new family. But....

_____. *Janie's Private Eyes*. Delacorte, 1989. The Stanleys' dog, Nightmare, is dognapped. Blair uses his ESP and Janie her detective skills to look for clues and suspects as to who is stealing dogs.

_____. *Libby on Wednesdays*. Delacorte, 1990. Kibby is gifted and put in an accelerated class. She doesn't like it but then meets some original friends in a writing workshop.

_____. *Season of Ponies*. Atheneum, 1964. Pamela stays with her aunt on Oak Farm. Then a boy with a flute and a herd of weirdly beautiful, misty colored ponies comes magically along.

_____. *Truth About Stone Hollow*. Atheneum, 1974. Amy and Jason go to the haunted Stone Hollow and experience a semi-supernatural excursion.

_____. *Until the Celebration*. Atheneum, 1977. Mounting tension is soothed by two children who have become symbols of unification between the Endlings and the Kindar.

_____. *Velvet Room*. Atheneum, 1965. Robin passes from the reality of California during the Depression to a velvet lined library. Then she finds someone is going to destroy the deserted house and the library.

_____. *Witches of Worm*. Atheneum, 1972. Is it because she is bewitched that a young girl exhibits selfishness and does destructive things? These are the thoughts of an emotionally disturbed girl.

Sobol, Donald. *Amazing Power of Ashur Fine*. Macmillan, 1986. Ashur got his special power from an elephant named Methuselah. He looks for the men that mugged his aunt and discovers he can be whoever he wants to be, for a short time.

_____. *Angie's First Case*. Macmillan, 1981. Angie and Jess are kidnapped while looking for house thieves.

_____. *Encyclopedia Brown and the Case of the Dead Eagles*. Lodestar, 1975. There are enough clues so that the reader can solve the case before Encyclopedia Brown.

_____. *Encyclopedia Brown and the Case of the Exploding Plumbing*. Scholastic, 1984. See if you can solve the mystery before the great Encyclopedia Brown does.

_____. *Encyclopedia Brown and the Case of the Midnight Visitor*. Lodestar, 1977. Bank robbers, kidnappers and Chicago gangsters—Encyclopedia Brown takes them all on and solves ten more new cases.

_____. *Encyclopedia Brown and the Case of the Mysterious Handprints*. Morrow, 1985. Encyclopedia Brown and Sally have ten more mysteries to solve. There are a case of missing property, one of sabotaged races and eight others.

_____. *Encyclopedia Brown and the Case of the Secret Pitch*. Lodestar, 1978. Bugs has a deal with Speedy about his baseball bat but.... Ten more mysteries with Encyclopedia Brown.

_____. *Encyclopedia Brown and the Case of the Treasure Hunt*. Morrow, 1988. How does a puzzle lead to a thief? Encyclopedia Brown and Sally will find out in these ten new mysteries.

_____. *Encyclopedia Brown, Boy Detective*. Lodestar, 1963. Match wits with Encyclopedia Brown as he solves his many mysteries. He listens, observes and trains his memory.

_____. *Encyclopedia Brown Carries On*. Four Winds, 1980. Encyclopedia Brown is a lucky sleuth with a father who is chief of police.

_____. *Encyclopedia Brown Finds the Clues*. Lodestar, 1966. Try your wits again with Encyclopedia Brown as he tackles more astounding puzzles.

_____. *Encyclopedia Brown Gets His Man*. Lodestar, 1967. These puzzlers have stumped elders but Encyclopedia Brown solves them.

_____. *Encyclopedia Brown Keeps the Peace*. Lodestar, 1973. How good a detective are you? Can you keep up with Encyclopedia Brown?

_____. *Encyclopedia Brown Lends a Hand*. Lodestar, 1974. The solutions to ten mysteries are found by Leroy "Encyclopedia" Brown.

_____. *Encyclopedia Brown Saves the Day*. Lodestar, 1970. More adventures with Encyclopedia Brown and Sally as they solve more mysteries.

_____. *Encyclopedia Brown Sets the Pace*. Four Winds, 1982. A printing is stolen and Encyclopedia Brown must find the thief.

_____. *Encyclopedia Brown Shows the Way*. Lodestar, 1972. The Brown Detective Agency has a girl to contend with in this case.

_____. *Encyclopedia Brown Solves Them All*. Lodestar, 1977. Encyclopedia Brown, the clever detective, is back with more puzzles to solve.

_____. *Encyclopedia Brown Takes the Case.* Lodestar, 1973. Ten all new Encyclopedia Brown mysteries.

_____. *Encyclopedia Brown Tracks Them Down.* Lodestar, 1971. Encyclopedia Brown, a super sleuth, solves more baffling mysteries.

Softly, Barbara. *Place Mill.* St. Martin, 1963. Nicholas's father is shot by Royalists as a traitor. He and two friends return from fighting with the defeated Royalist Army. They meet with hardships and betrayal as they escape to France.

_____. *Stone in a Pool.* St. Martin, 1965. A story of the English Civil War and the role of the Royalists in it. Charles I is imprisoned on the Isle of Wight and must be rescued. There is also persecution of witches.

Sommer-Bodenburg, Angela. *My Friend the Vampire.* Dial, 1984. While Tony watches a horror movie, Rudolph, a kid vampire, comes in. He and Tony become friends and Tony meets Rudolph's family and Tony's family meets him.

_____. *Vampire Moves In.* Dial, 1984. Rudolph is banned from his family's vault and moves in with Tony. Tony tries to hide the coffin and the fact that he is there.

_____. *Vampire on the Farm.* Dial, 1989. Tony and Rudolph are vacationing on a farm and Tony is still trying to keep Rudolph a secret while maintaining his friendship. Being friends with a vampire is not easy.

_____. *Vampire Takes a Trip.* Dial, 1985. Tony is sure that his vacation is going to be a total bust. But his friend Rudolph the vampire will come along if they can find a way to transport him unseen and unknown by anyone.

Sommerfelt, Aimee. *My Name is Pablo.* Criterion, 1966. Pablo is a shoeshine boy in Mexico. His family is poor. He needs a license but doesn't have the money for it. A foreign friend helps him.

_____. *Road to Agra.* Criterion, 1961. Lalu and Maya go to the Agra hospital in order to save her eyesight. It is a 300 mile journey in present day India. But the trip is harrowing and Lalu wonders if he did the right thing.

_____. *White Bungalow.* Criterion, 1964. Lalu has a chance to leave his poverty-stricken family and become a doctor but chooses to stay with his family, knowing that if he leaves they will starve since his father is so ill.

Sorensen, Virginia. *Friends of the Road.* Atheneum, 1978. When their father is made Diplomat to Morocco two girls have an exciting adventure.

_____. *Miracles on Maple Hill.* Harcourt, 1956. A family story of how a year of living in the country draws them together. Marly rescues a family of foxes, visits a local hermit and helps save the maple sugar harvest. Newbery winner, 1957.

_____. *Plain Girl.* Harcourt, 1955. A young girl, raised Amish, sees a conflict between her own heritage and that of the "outside world."

Sorenson, Jody. *Secret Letters of Mama Cat.* Walker, 1988. Meredith writes to a dead grandmother about her deaf older sister, her younger brother, and her friends Charlotte Ann and Scotty. The letters are found and the problem contained therein discussed.

Sortor, T. *Adventures of B.J., the Amateur Detective.* Abingdon, 1975. A young girl spends time at her mother's detective agency and happens onto a ring of shoplifters who turn out to be her own schoolmates.

Southall, Ivan. *Ash Road.* St. Martin, 1965. The suspenseful story of children in the path of a devastating fire.

_____. *Golden Goose.* Greenwillow, 1981. Slow-witted Custard is forced to search for gold. Even Preacher Tom, who set out to rescue him, believes he can find gold. Custard becomes known as the "Golden Goose."

_____. *Hills End.* St. Martin, 1962. Young students explore the caves at Hills End and must depend upon themselves for survival when a sudden storm cuts them off from the outside world.

_____. *King of the Sticks.* Greenwillow, 1979. Custard, because he is thought to be special, is kidnapped by the sons of the man Custard's mother asks to help find him.

_____. *Let the Balloon Go.* Bradbury, 1985. A new edition of a handicapped (Cerebral Palsy) boy's growth that took a devastating experience to bring about.

_____. *Long Night Watch.* Farrar, 1984. Jon is to stay awake and warn the islanders of the coming of God. He falls asleep and not God but the Japanese come. They find only five youngsters, including Jon, not the 100 people who were there.

Southerland, Ellease. *Let the Lion Eat Straw.* Scribner, 1979. Abeba has a chance for a promising musical career. It would bring money she never had. Instead she chooses marriage and struggles to make ends meet.

Sparger, Rex. *Doll.* Bantam, 1980. Jack wins a doll for Cassie at the fair. It's perfect for her collection. But this doll is evil and wants Cassie's soul.

Sparks, Christine. *Elephant Man.* Ballantine, 1980. John Merrick is the man who is so disfigured people can't look at him. Then he meets Dr. Treves who might help his deformed body.

Speare, Elizabeth. *Bronze Bow.* Houghton, 1961. A Jewish fugitive, Daniel, is brought before Jesus to hear His teachings. He must make a decision about his own life. Is violence, or love the way to rid Israel of the Romans? Newbery winner, 1962.

_____. *Calico Captive.* Houghton, 1957. During the French and Indian War, Miriam Willard is captured by Indians and has to endure great hardships.

_____. *Sign of the Beaver.* Houghton, 1983. Matt is left alone while his father goes to pick up his mother and sister. This takes several months in 1700 Maine. Matt makes friends with Indians and survives well in his father's absence.

_____. *Witch of Blackbird Pond.* Houghton, 1958. Katherine is accused of being a witch when her outgoing behavior does not fit in with her Puritan uncle's life style.

Spearing, Judith. *Ghost That Went to School.* Atheneum, 1967. The Temples lived in an old house: Mr. and Mrs. Temple, Wilbur and Mortimer. They were ghosts. Wilbur was bored and wanted to go to school. He caused a great deal of trouble but made some friends.

_____. *Museum Ghosts.* Atheneum, 1969. All four Temples helped the workmen as they remodeled the old house to be a museum. They tried to stay out of it but couldn't help picking up things and aiding with the heavy work.

Speevack, Yetta. *Spider Plant.* Atheneum, 1965. Carmen is from Puerto Rico and makes friends in her neighborhood. But the building is to come down and she must move again to a new place. Her spider plant is a symbol of her ability to accept change.

Spence, Eleanor. *Green Laurel.* Roy, 1965. Lesley and Roe are traveling carnival people. Their dad is taken ill and they must stay near a hospital. They learn to adjust to school, gangs and a new life style.

_____. *Lillipilly Hill.* Roy, 1963. Harriet, 12, likes Australia with its one room school house, new friends and new experiences. Her family want to return to England but she convinces them to stay.

_____. *Nothing Place.* Harper, 1973. Glen is deaf and when his friends collect money to buy him a hearing aid he is badly hurt.

_____. *Year of the Currawony.* Roy, 1965. The Kendall children are involved in a mystery surrounding a deserted silver mine.

Spencer, Zane. *Cry of the Wolf.* Westminster, 1977. Jim's father is killed and he is left crippled. He is feeling very sorry for himself.

Sperry, Armstrong. *All Sail Set.* Godine, 1982. A new edition of the story of a clipper ship on its voyage around the Horn.

_____. *Call It Courage.* Macmillan, 1940/1971. Mafatu fears the sea but he takes his boat and heads for the ocean. A storm strands him on a deserted island where he must fight for survival. Newbery winner, 1941.

Spillane, Mickey. *Day the Sea Rolled Back.* Windmill, 1979. Larry, 12, is pursued by the Jimson brothers as he looks for pirate treasure in the Caribbean.

Spinelli, Jerry. *Dump Days.* Little, 1988. J.D. and Duke are planning a perfect day. They need money and search the dump for "treasures." They finally raise some money but for a better cause and keep Perfect Day for next year.

_____. *Jason and Marceline.* Little, 1986. This is the story of Jason in junior high school.

He is a bit more adjusted to growing up. His knowledge of girls has improved and he is accepting adulthood.

_____. *Night of the Whale.* Little, 1985. Students go to Atlantic City during Senior Week. Their car breaks down near a beach and they find beached whales. They work at gettting them back in the water.

_____. *Space Station Seventh Grade.* Little, 1982. Jason learns about communal showers, pimples, girls, sports and the awful ninth graders. A boy's *Are You There, God....*

_____. *Who Put That Hair in My Toothbrush?* Little, 1984. A story of sibling rivalry between Megin and Greg. Hair in the toothbrush, shower water turned from hot to cold, each blaming the other and explaining their actions to their mother.

Sponsel, Heinz. *Keeper of the Wild Bulls.* Farrar, 1962. Pierre works with bulls being raised to fight in an arena. His favorite bull was Foggy who was gentle only with him. When he was sold Pierre fought to win his freedom.

Sprague, Rosemary. *Jade Pogoda.* Walck, 1964. Dick is going to sea to clear his father's name. Truth wins out and his father's name is cleared and he also gets a jade pagoda.

Springer, Nancy. *Horse to Love.* Harper, 1987. Erin gets a horse to love and care for and it makes her more self-confident.

Springer, Nancy. *Not on a White Horse.* Atheneum, 1988. Ree dreams of having a horse but a poor mother and an alcoholic father make it unreal.

_____. *They're All Named Wildfire.* Macmillan, 1989. Jenny befriends Black Shanterey because of a love of horses.

Springstubb, Tricia. *Eunice Gottlieb and the Unwhitewashed Truth About Life.* Delacorte, 1987. Eunice and Joy have a catering business: Have Your Cake. But Joy is falling for a boy from school. Eunice can't believe it and they argue. She takes Reggie as a partner but it is not working out.

_____. *Eunice (The Egg Salad) Gottlieb.* Little, 1988. Joy is a natural at gymnastics but Eunice isn't. She's afraid she will embarrass everyone, including herself. But because of Joy's friendship and encouragement she does very well.

_____. *Moon on a String.* Little, 1982. Deidre goes to Boston. Jobs are scarce and her sister, supposedly in college, is living with an art student. She meets Tod, a free spirit, who is different from the boys back home.

_____. *Which Way to the Nearest Wilderness?* Little, 1984. Eunice, 11, and her best friend, Joy, start a personalized card service: When You Care Enough to Give the Very Worst. A poison pen type card. Eunice sickens of it and breaks away.

_____. *With a Name Like Lulu, Who Needs More Trouble?* Delacorte, 1989. Lulu caught a falling baby and became famous. She is shy and this incident brings a change in her life.

Spykman, Elizabeth. *Edie on the Warpath.* Harcourt, 1966. Edie rebels because she is the middle sibling of the Cares family. No one wants to take care of Edie when her mother must go away. Left almost alone, she and Susan have troublesome fun.

———. *Lemon and a Star.* Harcourt, 1955. The story of the four Cares children who grew up in the early 1900's. They are motherless and free to do as they please because their father is busy. Father remarries and they get a mother.

———. *Terrible, Horrible Edie.* Harcourt, 1960. This story is about the Cares family. It concentrates on ten-year-old Edie, the youngest Cares and her summer's adventure.

———. *Wild Angel.* Harcourt, 1957. The four children have difficulty adjusting to a new mother and restrictions. But Father is still the same and encourages their misadventures.

Spyri, Johanna. *Heidi.* Knopf, 1984. Heidi is the warm, loving girl that lives in the Alps with her grandfather that we all know. There are many editions.

Stack, Jack. *Loggerhead.* Seemann, 1972. Ponce, 15, dives for deep sea turtles for a living. They are big and dangerous. Someone is sabotaging the water and Ponce wants to know who.

Stahl, Ben. *Blackbeard's Ghost.* Houghton, 1965. J.D. and Hank explore Old Boar's Head Tavern as it is being torn down and find an incantation with which they raise Blackbeard's ghost. Together they try to save the Tavern.

———. *Secret of the Red Skull.* Houghton, 1971. J.D. and Hank and the ghost from *Blackbeard's Ghost* are involved in an international spy ring. The villain is Red Skull. A very funny, very rousing adventure.

Stallworth, Anne. *This Time Next Year.* Vanguard, 1971. Julia lives as a tenant farmer in the 1930's. She sees poverty at its worst and wants things better for her own daughter.

Stanek, Lou. *Gleanings.* Harper, 1985. Papper is a liar but also a survivor. She travels across country to visit her grandparents. Her pink hair is a shocker but she makes friends with Frankie and they both benefit.

———. *Megan's Beat.* Putnam, 1983. Megan starts to write a gossip column for the school newspaper but it costs her her friends.

Stapp, Arthur. *Too Steep for Baseball.* Harper, 1964. Dave didn't want to spend the summer away from the baseball field but he finds studying hurricane weather as it happens and through books to be exciting.

Stearns, Pamela. *Fool and the Dancing Bear.* Little, 1979. Rolf, King of Holm, Timon and Bear go to lift the Queen's curse from Holm.

———. *Mechanical Doll.* Houghton, 1979. The king banishes a musician, Hulun, because he broke his favorite mechanical doll. Hulun later finds the pieces of the doll and puts it together. She dances when he plays.

Steele, Mary. *Because of the Sand Witches There.* Morrow, 1975. Mil and Hamish look for shells and find a sand witch. They now must find the sand witch's real shell.

———. *First of the Penguins.* Greenwillow, 1985. George can't believe he chased the penguins clear to the North Pole until he feels the frostbite and sees the polar bears. Where will space travel take him next?

———. *Journey Outside.* Viking, 1969. Dilar is traveling with his people along an underground river, looking for the Better Place. He leaves the raft and after many harrowing experiences reaches earth, with light and greenery.

———. *Life (and Death) of Sarah Elizabeth Harwood.* Greenwillow, 1980. Sarah worries about death and a lost album. She finds the album. A renewed plant and a newborn kitten restore her faith in life.

———. *True Men.* Greenwillow, 1976. A fantasy where a boy glows in the dark and is therefore banished from his tribe.

———. *Wish, Come True.* Greenwillow, 1979. A magic ring allows Joe and his sister, Meg, to go on unexpected journeys.

Steele, William. *Magic Amulet.* Harcourt, 1979. Tragg is attacked by a tiger and left by his family to survive alone. He has a bone bracelet which seems to protect him from wolves, bears and hostile men.

———. *Man with the Silver Eyes.* Harcourt, 1976. Talatu, 11, is a Cherokee boy who lives for a year with a white man with pale eyes. He learns Quaker ways of life and the true meaning of love. He also experiences the Revolutionary War.

———. *Spooky Thing.* Harcourt, 1960. A legend of two mean brothers, Gist and Meriweather, and how they found the THING.

———. *Tomahawk Border.* Holt, 1966. Dilk proves himself a man when he volunteers himself as a peace agent between the rangers and the Indians.

———. *Trail Through Danger.* Holt, 1965. Lafe was a cook for buffalo hunters. He didn't want anyone to know that his father sided with the Indians.

———. *War Party.* Harcourt, 1978. A young brave goes off to his first war party and comes home wounded and more aware of the horrors of war.

———. *Year of the Bloody Sevens.* Harcourt, 1963. Kel makes a hazardous trip to Fort Logan to meet his father. The two men he was traveling with are killed by Indians; he is almost captured; he saves another man's life and finally meets his father.

Steffan, Jack. *Firm Hand on the Rein.* McKay, 1961. Johnny is learning to train and ride horses. He is small built but is strong and courageous.

Stegeman, Janet. *Last Seen on Harper's Lane.*

Dial, 1982. Kerry is kidnapped. She befriends one of her kidnappers and the two of them escape.

Steig, William. *Abel's Island.* Farrar, 1976. A survival story but not by people but by a mouse and his new bride. They are swept away in a storm and must survive for months in a hazardous environment.

———. *Dominic.* Farrar, 1972. A hound dog helps a group of animals fight off the evil Doomsday Gang.

———. *Real Thief.* Farrar, 1973. Gawain is a goose who is assigned to guard the Royal Treasury. Gold and jewels start to disappear and he is disgraced.

Stein, Conrad. *Me and Dirty Arnie.* Harcourt, 1982. Dan and Arnie sneak into a cemetery, chat with winos, etc. They find some bones on a nearby farm and become "famous." Arnie teaches Dan to be street wise.

Steinbeck, John. *Acts of King Arthur and His Noble Knights.* Farrar, 1976. A story of Arthur, Merlin and his magic, the sword Excalibur that makes Arthur King of England and, of course, Camelot.

———. *Of Mice and Men.* Modern Library, 1938. Lennie is protected by his friend George because although he means to be harmless he is slow witted and gets into trouble without mean intentions.

Steiner, Barbara. *Oliver Dibbs and the Dinosaur Cause.* Four Winds, 1986. Lester, the bully, is jealous of Ollie and his ideas. This time his idea is to adopt a state fossil, namely a stegosaurus. He also wants his class project to be studying dinosaurs.

———. *Oliver Dibbs to the Rescue.* Macmillan, 1985. Oliver ends up in jail when his dog, Dolby, which he has painted as a tiger, runs away from the mall where he is supposed to be a symbol to save the wildlife of the world.

———. *Tessa.* Morrow, 1988. Tessa Mae must leave her father, her Indian relic hunting and her black friend, Jec, because her mother is taking her to live in the city.

Stephan, Hanna. *Quest.* Little, 1967. Peter goes to Russia with a soldier. He tries to return home but takes a wrong train and ends up on the Steppes. He goes to China, Tibet and India before finding his way home to his parents.

Stephens, Mary Jo. *Witch of the Cumberlands.* Houghton, 1974. Three children go to live in the mining district of Kentucky and learn folklore and learn about seances and magic charms.

———. *Xoe's Zodiac.* Houghton, 1971. Zoe won a pet a month from a pet shop. Each pet arrives and disrupts the household.

Stephens, Peter. *Claim to the Wilderness.* Norton, 1967. Chris and his folks settle in Montana in 1870. He is injured chasing a runaway horse and is found by Crow Indians. They adopt him after he saves the life of a tribesman.

———. *Perrely Plight.* Atheneum, 1965. Gib lives in Massachusetts in 1836. He looks into the reasons why his family and the mysterious Perrely family hate each other.

———. *Towapper, Puritan Renegade.* Atheneum, 1966. Tim escapes from soldiers and goes to live with the Indians. He befriends them and is later imprisoned for doing this (as a traitor). He is later reunited with his father; they go to live in New France.

Sterman, Betsy. *Too Much Magic.* Lippincott, 1987. Bill and Jeff find a magic cube that grants wishes. They wish for all sorts of fun things that they then wish away before their parents can see them. But that's only the beginning of this funny story.

Stern, Cecily. *Different Kind of Gold.* Harper, 1981. Cara lives in the wilderness. She uses a kayak, goes on picnics, raises an orphaned seal and has a run-in with a bear. But her home is threatened by people who want to build a hotel.

Sterne, E. *Long Black Schooner.* Follett, 1968. A boatload of black captives destined for slavery seized the ship but were tricked into landing it in the United States.

Stevens, Carla. *Trouble for Lucy.* Houghton, 1979. Lucy and her family are heading west to Oregon by wagon. Her dog, Finn, is a source of trouble.

Stevens, Shane. *Rat Pack.* Pocket Books, 1985. A story of four blacks during a night of real violence.

Stevenson, Drew. *Case of the Horrible Swamp Monster.* Dodd, 1984. Verna and Raymond make a home film of the swamp monster and "find" him. With the help of J. Huntley English—Monster Hunter they solve the mystery and catch some robbers with money in the swamp.

———. *Case of the Visiting Vampire.* Dodd, 1986. Verna and Raymond, with the ever present J. Huntley English, look for vampires. They suspect the actor who has the lead in "The Count of Castle Dracula." He is a defector from behind the Iron Curtain.

———. *Case of the Wandering Werewolf.* Dodd, 1987. Chip tells Raymond that he saw a werewolf and together with J. Huntley English they hunt it down. They unravel the mystery and are almost killed.

Stevenson, James. *Here Comes Herb's Hurricane.* Harper, 1973. Herb tells the animals about the coming hurricane and helps them prepare.

Stevenson, Robert Louis. *Kidnapped.* Nal, 1983. David Balfour is kidnapped. His greedy Uncle Ebenezer plans to have him sold into slavery, thereby claiming the family fortune for himself. But David is not that easily done in.

———. *Strange Case of Dr. Jekyll and Mr. Hyde.* Bantam, 1981. A story familiar to most but just what is it that changes Mr. Hyde into Dr. Jekyll and then back again? How does this nightmare end?

———. *Treasure Island.* Nal, 1963. Jim finds

a treasure map that will bring him riches. He and his friends go for the treasure but part of the crew is Long John Silver. There are mutiny, kidnapping and escape.

Stevenson, William. *Bushbabies.* Houghton, 1965. An English girl must return a pet galago (a monkey sometimes called a bush baby) to its natural habitat because she is leaving Africa. She and a headman, Tembo, do so with great hardship to both of them.

Stewart, A.C. *Elizabeth's Tower.* Phillips, 1972. Elizabeth stays with relatives while her father is away. She meets a lame man and helps him to a part of a castle where she plays.

_____. *Ossian House.* Phillips, 1974. John inherits his grandfather's estate and the rest of the family doesn't like it, especially Douglas.

Stewart, Mary. *Crystal Cave.* Fawcett, 1971. This is a story of Merlin's childhood. (He did have one, you know.) He finds the magical secret crystal cave that made him aware of his special powers.

_____. *Hollow Hills.* Fawcett, 1973. This is the story of Merlin's young manhood. It follows *Crystal Cave* (Stewart) which is the story of his childhood.

_____. *Last Enchantment.* Fawcett, 1979. This is another version of King Arthur, with an emphasis on Merlin. It follows his life from birth through his love of Nimbe.

_____. *Touch Not the Cat.* Morrow, 1976. A girl's gift of telepathy leads to danger and then to love.

_____. *Wicked Day.* Morrow, 1983. A story of King Arthur's last years. Mordred was born out of the incestuous relationship between Arthur and his half sister, Queen Morgause. He plays a big role in these last days.

Stiles, Martha. *Sarah the Dragon Lady.* Macmillan, 1986. Sarah's parents are drifting farther and farther apart and a breakup is eminent. They live in a small town where Sarah has trouble making the proper moves.

_____. *Star in the Forest.* Four Winds, 1979. Valrada is in love with a landsman in 6th century Gaul but she is promised to a cruel cousin. Her father is killed but leaves a yet unborn heir.

Stockton, Frank. *Griffin and the Minor Canon.* Harper, 1986. A new edition of the story of how a griffin scared the town when he arrived to evaluate the stone likeness of him over the church door.

Stolz, Mary. *Bartholomew Fair.* Greenwillow, 1990. In 1598 Queen Elizabeth and others attend London's Bartholomew Fair and have very different experiences.

_____. *Bully on Barkham Street.* Harper, 1963. This is the story of the *Dog on Barkham Street* told from the point of view of Martin. Maybe he isn't the bully and aggressive boy he appears to be.

_____. *By the Highway Home.* Harper, 1971. Cathy's brother was killed in Vietnam and she is heartbroken. She and her family move to Vermont to start a new life.

_____. *Cat in the Mirror.* Harper, 1975. Erin hit her head and woke up in the desert where she could hear someone saying: "Cat Queen, save me!"

_____. *Cat Walk.* Harper, 1983. A cat looks for a home where he will be more than a barnyard rat catcher.

_____. *Cider Days.* Harper, 1978. A young girl, Polly, is persistent in her overtures toward a shy, new neighbor that result in a friendship.

_____. *Cuckoo Clock.* Godine, 1986. Ula is an old clock maker and his young apprentice watches as he makes his last cuckoo clock.

_____. *Dog on Barkham Street.* Harper, 1960. Edward has two problems. One, he wants a dog. Uncle Josh and Argess, his dog, take care of that. Two, Martin, the bully who lives next door. That remains a problem.

_____. *Edge of Next Year.* Harper, 1974. Orin and Vic are brothers who survive an accident in which their mother is killed. Their father turns to alcohol and Orin, 14, must take care of Vic. Their father joins AA and there is hope.

_____. *Explorer of Barkham Street.* Harper, 1985. Martin, the bully, reforms after losing his dog. He explores the neighborhood, making good friends with his fantasy tales.

_____. *Ferris Wheel.* Harper, 1977. Polly and Kate have been best friends all their lives. But Kate's family is going to move to California and Polly is crushed, especially since Kate seems to be looking forward to it.

_____. *Go Catch a Flying Fish.* Harper, 1979. Taylor, 13, tries to make her brothers, Jem and B.J., adjust to their parents' separation. She and Jem try to protect young B.J. from their mother's frustration and their father's reaction to her leaving.

_____. *Lands End.* Harper, 1973. Josh watches the new neighbors and sees a difference between their casual, relaxed life style and that of his structured family. He needs help to straighten out his life.

_____. *Leap Before You Look.* Harper, 1972. A girl learns that her parents no longer love each other and her life has many changes about which she can do nothing.

_____. *Love, or a Season.* Harper, 1964. Harry is ignored by his father after his mother dies. On his summer vacation he meets an old friend, Nan. Friendship turns to love.

_____. *Noonday Friends.* Harper, 1965. Franny only has time for friends during her lunch period because the rest of her time is spent on chores at home.

_____. *Quentin Corn.* Godine, 1985. Quentin Corn is really a pig that the children keep fooling everyone about.

_____. *Scarecrows and Their Child.* Harper, 1987. Two scarecrows are taken to decorate a Halloween party and their child goes looking for them.

_____. *What Time of Night Is It?* Harper, 1981. Taylor, Jem and B.J. attempt to rebuild their family after their mother has deserted them. Granny Reddick is called to help. Mother does return and perhaps all will be well.

_____. *Who Wants Music on Monday?* Harper, 1963. Vincent is in college. His two sisters are in high school. Lotta is older, popular and pretty. Cass is younger, plain and because she is blatantly honest, without friends.

_____. *Wonderful, Terrible Time.* Harper, 1967. At summer camp two black girls of lower income families have different reactions to this event.

Stone, Bruce. *Half Nelson.* Harper, 1985. Nelson and a friend go to find Nelson's mother and sister. Nelson's father is a professional wrestler and forced his wife and daughter to leave home. In spite of the theme the story is funny.

Stone, Josephine. *Green Is for Galanx.* Atheneum, 1980. A lost space colony is the setting for this story of robots and androids. The people escape to another planet but are followed by a killer android.

_____. *Praise All the Moons of Morning.* Atheneum, 1979. Cass experiences time travel, alien culture, and death defying races. She escapes physical and mental slavery.

_____. *Those Who Fall from the Sun.* Atheneum, 1978. Alanna and her family are deported to another planet because of being accused of independent thinking.

Stone, Nancy. *Dune Shadow.* Houghton, 1980. Calash is a ghost town because sand dunes were created by the unwise harvesting of trees. Serena and Jody live there with their grandmother who refuses to leave. Serena makes the decision to leave.

Stone, Patti. *Judy George: Student Nurse.* Messner, 1966. Judy is in her last year of training. She has two admirers: one, the son of a doctor and two, an accident patient, Joe Smith.

Storey, Margaret. *Ask Me No Questions.* Dutton, 1975. Imogen is kidnapped. Her kidnapper is not evil but he must hide her. When his plan seems to be failing he sets her free.

_____. *Family Tree.* Nelson, 1965. Kate is an orphan moving from house to house. She tries to unravel her family history.

_____. *Pauline.* Doubleday, 1967. Pauline, an orphan, moves in with new relatives. She likes the family but not Uncle Harry, who is too strict and controlling.

Storr, Catherine. *Thursday.* Harper, 1972. Bee befriends Thursday, a lonely boy in school. He disappears and she tries to rescue him from "them."

_____. *Winter's End.* Harper, 1979. Four college students spend a study holiday in an old country house. Philip owns the house but he is about to have a mental breakdown. Rosemary and Veryan try to save him from the evil in the house.

Stoutenberg, Adrien. *Where to Now, Blue?* Four Winds, 1978. Blue, 12, sets out on a salvaged boat to go visit her uncle who she finds, upon arrival, has died.

_____. *Window on the Sea.* Westminster, 1962. Molly, 16, is friends with a nice, intelligent young man in San Francisco.

Stover, Marjorie. *Midnight in the Dollhouse.* Whitman, 1989. A family of dolls helps their lame owner find a clue to the hidden treasure.

_____. *When the Dolls Wake.* Whitman, 1985. Long neglected dolls awake and help their new owner find a treasure hidden years ago.

Strachan, Margaret. *Dolores and the Gypsies.* Washburn, 1962. Delores wants to become a flamingo dancer not a lace maker which her parents have in mind. She finds a piece of jewelry lost by a tourist and blamed on the gypsies.

_____. *Summer in El Castillo.* Washburn, 1963. Ann lived in El Castillo and learned to appreciate Spanish people and their culture better. And her Spanish improved.

Strang, Celia. *Foster Mary.* McGraw, 1979. Aunt Foster Mary is a migrant apple picker. She has many "adopted" children and wants a permanent home. They all settle in Washington and get through the first hard winter.

_____. *This Child Is Mine.* Beaufort, 1981. Tally's mother is widowed and poor. Her sister has a baby and ignores him, so she takes over the child. She finally runs away with the baby before her sister can "sell" him.

Strasser, Todd. *Accident.* Delacorte, 1988. Matt wakes up in the morning after a party and finds out four of his friends were killed in an auto accident. He investigates the reasons and finds out more than he wants to.

_____. *Angel Dust Blues.* Coward, 1979. A strong story of the horrors of drug use. Michael and Alex deal in drug selling. Alex gets caught and clears himself. Michael stays on and is a broken person who ends up in a coma.

_____. *Complete Computer Popularity Program.* Delacorte, 1984. Tony is in a new school. His friend, Paul, is a computer nut and uses this interest for a science fair project. Tony is interested in popularity but Paul gets his girl.

_____. *Friends Till the End.* Delacorte, 1981. Howie has leukemia and is in a new school. He becomes ill and is in the hospital. He asks David to come and see him. David is reluctant but goes. And goes again. He changes as he sees life ebbing away.

_____. *Rock 'n' Roll Nights.* Delacorte, 1983. Gary is the lead guitarist for a rock group with Susan, Karl and Oscar. This story tells of the work and effort necessary to make a successful rock band.

_____. *Turn It Up.* Delacorte, 1984. Gary

and his Rock 'n' Roll band try to make the "big time" but he is careless and hurts himself and his band.

————. *Very Touchy Subject*. Delacorte, 1985. Scott is confused about sex and his girl, Alix, especially since Paula is easily available. A male version of whether to do "it" or not.

————. *Wildlife*. Delacorte, 1987. Gary's band, The Coming Attraction, just returned from a 10 month tour with their hit album "Wildlife." But Oscar wants to start a band of his own. Karl is into drugs and Susan is tired.

————. *Workin' for Peanuts*. Delacorte, 1983. Jeff, a poor boy, meets and falls in love with Melissa, a rich girl, before he finds out she is rich. Her house is robbed by some gang members of Jeff's social class and she rejects him.

Strauss, Linda. *Alexandra Ingredient*. Crown, 1988. Alexandra is the odd one of the family. When the family "adopts" Mike, a widower, they become friends and Alexandra's life changes for the better. And so does Mike's.

Strauss, Victoria. *Worldstone*. Four Winds, 1985. Alexina is the link between the Guardians who rule mindpower and Bron, a lover of science and technology. The worldstone belongs to mindpower and is stolen and taken to technology.

Streatfeild, Noel. *Ballet Shoes*. Smith, 1979. An old favorite ballet story. Three girls are adopted by a man who trains them for the London stage.

————. *Children on the Top Floor*. Random, 1965. Four orphan children are left on the doorstep of television actor Malcolm Master. He disappears and they take on adult responsibilities.

————. *Thursday's Child*. Dell, 1986. Thursday is a 10-year-old orphan who is strong and determined to overcome any setbacks in her life.

————. *When the Sirens Wailed*. Random, 1976. A graphic description of what it is like when a family is separated during a blitz in London during World War II.

Street, Julia. *Drover's Gold*. Dodd, 1961. Duncan and Shadrach look for buried treasure in the 1800's as they travel with a hog drover.

Streiber, Whitley. *Warday: And the Journey Onward*. Holt, 1984. On Warday the United States and Russia were destroyed. Two survivors, Whitley and Jim, travel for eight weeks across America recording the devastation.

Stren, Patti. *I Was a Fifteen-Year-Old Blimp*. Harper, 1985. "Flabby Gabby" is fat and ridiculed. She does drastic things to lose weight and becomes bulimic. She goes to camp, loses weight sensibly and appreciates the friendship of Mel and Nicole.

————. *Mountain Rose*. Dutton, 1982. Rose is overweight but goes into wrestling and becomes regional champion. A happy ending.

————. *There's a Rainbow in My Closet*. Harper, 1979. Emma wants to be like everyone else until her grandmother explains why it is good to be different.

Stretton, Barbara. *You Never Lose*. Knopf, 1982. Jim's father is dying of cancer. Jim is a senior and his father is the football coach. He meets Gus, a new girl in school, who understands his conflicting feelings.

Stuart, Morna. *Marassa and Midnight*. McGraw, 1966. Marassa is a twin of Midnight. He is in Paris, Midnight is in Haiti. Marassa is abandoned by his "owner" and returns to Haiti. Midnight looks for Marassa while Haiti is going through the 1790 revolution.

Stuckly, Elizabeth. *Family Walk-Up*. Watts, 1960. One year in the life of the Berners family. There are many crises and some ordinary events.

————. *Walk-Up*. Watts, 1960. When Mother goes to the hospital Dad and the five kids have a chaotic time. But then she comes home and all is well.

Sturgeon, Theodore. *Dreaming Jewels*. Bluejay, 1985. Hurty runs away from his abusive parents. He joins a carnival and stays ten years, then returns home. While with the circus his jeweled box was found to duplicate things, if somewhat incompletely.

Styles, Showell. *Greencoats Against Napoleon*. Vanguard, 1964. John is part of the British Army in England's war in Spain against Napoleon.

Sudbery, Rodie. *Silk and the Skin*. Dutton, 1982. Guy is a loner who joins a school gang. His younger brother gets a bat by magical ritual and it becomes his protector. He misuses the power and the bat must be destroyed. A non-terror supernatural tale.

Suhl, Yuri. *On the Other Side of the Gate*. Watts, 1975. Hambel and Lena are herded together with Polish Jews during the German holocaust. Lena is pregnant and hides her son until she can smuggle him to safety.

————. *Uncle Misha's Partisans*. Four Winds, 1973. Uncle Misha and his group of organized fighters oppose their German oppressors.

Sullivan, Mary. *Earthquake 2099*. Lodestar, 1982. Philip lives in a controlled Urban Complex Tower. He learns to survive among animals and people of a Wild Life Preserve after an earthquake.

Summers, James. *Amazing Mr. Tenterhook*. Westminster, 1964. Mr. Tenterhook is a teacher and insists that students must earn the right to dance by taking jobs to earn money. Leo and Vicki are "steadies" and this disrupts their plans.

————. *Iron Door Between*. Westminster, 1968. Vic Shan, just out of reform school, goes to start a new life with the Chapmans.

————. *Senior Dropout*. Westminster, 1965. Lon is untrusting of his father and stepmother. He loves Hermine and wants to quit school, get a job and get married. He comes to realize that he needs school and he needs to trust people.

————. *Shelter Trap*. Westminster, 1962. Gifted students and their teacher are locked in a fallout shelter for three days. There is no way to let anyone know they are there. It is well stocked and has lights but the blower breaks down.

————. *Tiger Terwilliger*. Westminster, 1963. "Tiger" is a woman football coach who temporarily replaces Coach Blount, a Math and Science teacher who knows little about football.

Sunshine, Tina. *Dating Games*. Avon, 1986. Marc has a crush on his French teacher. His friend helps him by getting Marc elected Prom King and giving him a chance to woo "luscious La Rue" but it doesn't work that way.

Sussman, Susan. *Casey the Nomad*. Whitman, 1985. Casey is fascinated by nomads but is distressed to learn that his own father will be traveling the country for two years on business.

————. *There's No Such Thing as a Chanukah Bush*. Whitman, 1983. A story about the celebrating and the meaning of a special holiday.

Sutcliff, Rosemary. *Blood Feud*. Dutton, 1976. Jestyn and Thormod set out to avenge the murder of Thormod's father. The setting is tenth century Europe.

————. *Bonnie Dundee*. Dutton, 1984. Hugh, now old, tells of when he was young and fought with "Bonnie Dundee" (John Claverhouse) to save the Scottish throne. Claverhouse died fighting for the House of Stuart.

————. *Capricorn Bracelet*. Walck, 1973. A story of a family that covers six generations in 60 A.D. Roman Britain. The bracelet was awarded to the first soldier, Lucius, and then passed on until 383 A.D.

————. *Dawn Wind*. Walck, 1962. Owain, 14, survives the sixth century battle with the Saxons. He feels the "dawn wind" promising better things for Britain.

————. *Flame-Colored Taffeta*. Farrar, 1986. Damaris, 12, and her friends become involved with a smuggling ring and a possible spy.

————. *Frontier Wolf*. Dutton, 1981. Alexios is sent to the Frontier Wolves as punishment for using poor judgment. He is to be the leader of this outpost but the men suspect his ability.

————. *Hound of Ulster*. Dutton, 1964. Cuchulain is brought from the hills to Ulster. He is fierce and fearless. His charioteer is Laeg and his team of horses are Black Sienglund and Grey of Macha.

————. *Knight's Fee*. Walck, 1960. Randall is dog boy at Arundel Castle. He is raised to knighthood by a twist of fate.

————. *Lantern Bearers*. Walck, 1960. A story of ancient Britain after the Romans.

————. *Light Beyond the Forest*. Dutton, 1980. The first in a series about King Arthur and the search for the Grail.

————. *Mark of the Horse Lord*. Walck, 1966. An ex-gladiator poses as Horse Lord and is in a struggle for power.

————. *Road to Camlann*. Dutton, 1982. The evil Mordred, plotting against his father, King Arthur, implicates the Queen and Sir Lancelot in treachery.

————. *Song for a Dark Queen*. Crowell, 1979. The dark queen is Boudicca. This is a fictionalized biography.

————. *Sun Horse, Moon Horse*. Dutton, 1977. In pre–Roman Britain a boy sacrifices himself to save his people.

————. *Sword and the Circle*. Dutton, 1981. Retells the adventures of King Arthur, Sir Lancelot and the other knights of the Round Table.

————. *Witch's Brat*. Walck, 1970. Lovel is a deformed boy (humpbacked) whose grandmother just died and he was stoned for being the grandson of a witch.

Sutton, Jane. *Confessions of an Orange Octopus*. Dutton, 1983. Clarence, who now calls himself Chooch, is going to be the juggling expert of the world, if he doesn't drive everyone to distraction first.

————. *Definitely Not Sexy*. Little, 1988. Diana wants to be a "dumb Sexy," not an Honors Class Creep. A division between the Sexys and the Smarts exists and though Diana tries she can't quite make the transition.

————. *Me and the Weirdos*. Bantam, 1987. Cindy's family are not the ideal model she thinks they should be. She tries to change them but has little success. She learns to accept them for their differences and not be embarrassed.

————. *Not Even Mrs. Mazursky*. Dutton, 1984. Mrs. Mazursky is Stella's favorite teacher but even she is not perfect.

Sutton, Shaun. *Queen's Champion*. St. Martin, 1961. Roger fights to expose Sir Thomas Wycherley and restore the house of Penlynden.

Swallow, Pamela. *Leave It to Christy*. Putnam, 1987. Christy wants to do something great for a science project. She wants the attention of a classmate (male). She wins the lead in *Peter Pan* and helps a fellow student.

Swan, Helen. *Dear Elizabeth: Diary of an Adolescent Victim of Sexual Abuse*. Children's Institute, 1984. The story of a father's molestation of Brenda and how she deals with it.

Swarthout, Glendon. *Bless the Beasts and the Children*. Doubleday, 1970. Cotton assumes the leadership of a group of "dings," who are his cabin mates. They try to save a herd of buffalo from slaughter and succeed but at a great loss.

————. *Shootist*. Doubleday, 1975. J.B. Brooks is going to die of cancer, very painfully. He decides that since he is a gunman he will die by the gun. He selects several men: a card shark, a rustler and/or a kid, to do the job.

————. *Whichaway*. Random, 1966. A loner must survive with two broken legs after an accident.

Sweeney, Joyce. *Center Line*. Delacorte, 1984. Five brothers run away from an alcoholic father who is also abusive. They survive on Shawn's college money.

_____. *Right Behind the Rain.* Delacorte, 1987. Although Kevin is good looking and talented, with a bright future in his chosen field, acting, he is very unhappy and only his sister senses his need for professional help.

Swenson, Judy. *Learning My Way: I'm a Winner!* Dillon, 1986. An 11-year-old boy must learn to adjust to the fact that he has a learning disability that will take a lot of effort to overcome.

Swetman, Evelyn. *Yes, My Darling Daughter.* Harvey, 1978. A young girl who has had bad experiences in foster homes, distrusts her new one. She learns to love and accept her foster parents and they adopt her.

Swift, Helen. *Second Semester.* Longman, 1961. A story of roommates at college. One is a serious student who wants a career and the other a fat girl who wants popularity. They help each other.

Swift, Jonathan. *Gulliver's Travels.* Nal, 1971. A fantasy of strange animals and people met on a journey by Gulliver.

Swinburne, Laurence. *Detli.* Bobbs, 1971. The story of a young girl in the coal mining area of Pennsylvania. She is wooed by two young men who are as different as can be.

Swindells, Robert. *Brother in the Land.* Holiday, 1984. Danny lives through a nuclear holocaust but facing the aftermath is worse because of emotional upheavals.

_____. *Serpent's Tooth.* Holiday, 1989. Lucy's mother is protesting the proposed nuclear waste disposal site. Lucy has second sight and "sees" the vision of plague victims buried at the site.

_____. *When Darkness Comes.* Morrow, 1975. A primitive tribe is divided into two hostile groups. They are hurting each other until the children of each tribe pull them together and fight a bigger enemy.

Swinnerton, A.R. *Rocky the Cat.* Harper, 1981. Rocky is a tough cat that is owned by a not so tough boy. They have many strange adventures together.

Syfret, Anne. *Bella.* Farrar, 1975. An evil doll gets two girls under her spell.

Sykes, Pamela. *Phoebe's Family.* Nelson, 1974. Phoebe wants to be a writer and tells about her unique family. They live in an English country cottage. She meets some wealthy people, some relatives and some working people.

Symons, Geraldine. *Miss Rivers and Miss Bridges.* Macmillan, 1971. Pansy and Atalanta, disguised as Miss Rivers and Miss Bridges, take part in the campaign of the suffragettes in London. They land in jail and also in the newspapers.

_____. *Workhouse Child.* Macmillan, 1969. Pansy and Atalanta are under the supervision of absentminded Nonna. Pansy changes clothes with Leah from the workhouse. She is mistaken for a workhouse slave and reform changes are the outcome.

Sypher, Lucy. *Cousins and Circuses.* Atheneum, 1974. Lucy lives in Wales, North Dakota, and likes it. Gwin moves to town with her minister father and sees everything as evil. Lucy sees fairs and girl's clubs not scandal and corruption.

_____. *Edge of Nowhere.* Atheneum, 1972. Lucy makes three wishes on New Year's Eve, 1916: 1. Something grown up happens to her. 2. A dog. 3. A girl her age moves to town. All three wishes come true.

_____. *Spell of the Northern Lights.* Atheneum, 1975. Lucy is afraid of many things, some real and some imagined. Some of her fears come to pass such as losing her dog. But some good things happen like her mother having a baby.

_____. *Turnabout Year.* Atheneum, 1976. Lucy wants to go to high school in the city but it is just prior to World War I and her mother has a new baby. It looks like city school is out of the question.

Szambelan-Strevinsky, Christine. *Dark Hour at Noon.* Lippincott, 1982. A group of youngsters, fourteen and under, are involved in underground activities in Poland in 1939. Trina takes part in blowing up a train. They kill a Gestapo officer and plan an uprising.

Tabrah, Ruth. *Red Shark.* Follett, 1970. Stanley finds a shark-shaped rock off the Hawaiian Islands and learns of religious ceremonies. He is caught up in a magical/mythical mystery.

Taha, Karen. *Gift for Tia Rosa.* Dillon, 1986. Carmela likes Tia Rosa who lives next door. When Tia Rosa dies Carmela's mother tries to console her by explaining how love can be shared.

_____. *Marshmallow Muscles, Banana Brainstorms.* Houghton, 1988. Pitt's parents are athletic but Pitt is not. He tries because he wants to impress Melissa. She plays flute so he joins the band. But all his efforts do not impress Melissa.

Talbert, Marc. *Dead Birds Singing.* Little, 1985. Matt must deal with the death of his mother and sister who were killed by a drunk driver, while he survived.

_____. *Paper Knife.* Dial, 1988. A young boy is sexually abused and it affects him, his family and the community.

_____. *Thin Ice.* Little, 1986. Martin's teacher is dating his divorced mother.

_____. *Toby.* Dial, 1987. Toby's parents are "retarded" and Reverend Olsen wants Toby in a foster home. Toby and his parents love each other and overcome all taunts and false accusations.

Talbot, Charlene. *Great Rat Island Adventure.* Atheneum, 1977. Joe's parents are divorced and he spends a summer with his father on Great Rat Island. He learns to swim, cook and go boating. He meets Vicky and they are caught in a hurricane.

_____. *Orphan for Nebraska.* Atheneum, 1979. A young boy is an orphan from Ireland sent to Nebraska in 1870.

_____. *Sodbuster Venture.* Atheneum,

1982. Two young women outsmart their unsavory neighbors and successfully file claim to land during the post–Civil War land grab.

Talbot, Charles. *Tomas Takes Charge.* Lothrop, 1966. When his father disappears a Puerto Rican boy and his sister find a place to live and a way to support themselves.

Talley, Naomi. *New Cut Road.* Hawthorn, 1971. Priscilla is a tomboy even at seventeen. She teaches school in Oklahoma in 1900. She buys a horse, deals with rowdy students and fights the school board.

Tamar, Erika. *Blues for Silk Garcia.* Crown, 1982. Linda Ann has never seen her father but knows he was a great guitarist. Her mother never spoke of him and she tries to learn more about him. She finds that she is a lot like him, in good ways and bad.

Tannen, Mary. *Huntley, Nutley and the Missing Link.* Knopf, 1983. Huntley is small for his age and is pursued by bullies (Orson and the Skulls). He finds an ape-like creature he names Link. This changes his life. His father thinks it's the new maid, Mrs. Link.

————. *Lost Legend of Finn.* Knopf, 1982. Bran and Fiona have access to a magic book which helps transport them back to ancient Ireland. They found Uncle Rupert in 839 A.D.

————. *Wizard Children of Finn.* Knopf, 1981. Bran and Fiona move into the past because of a Druid spell. They have historic adventures in ancient Ireland.

Tanner, Louise. *Reggie and Nilma.* Ariel, 1971. A story about an interracial friendship that involves drugs.

Tapp, Kathy. *Den 4 Meets the Jinx.* McElderry, 1988. Adam wants to rid his den of his pesty sister. But, in fact, she is the one who saves the den from disintegration.

————. *Flight of the Moth-Kin.* Atheneum, 1987. Ripple and her family are released from the glass jar and are living in a forest where they encounter large insects and other dangers as they find their way back home to the river.

————. *Moth-Kin Magic.* Atheneum, 1983. Ripple is less than one inch tall. She, her mother and uncle are trapped by the giants in a glass jar used to study plant life. They must find a way to escape.

————. *Sacred Circle of the Hula Hoop.* Macmillan, 1989. Robin, 13, learns about her sister's childhood sexual abuse that caused her attempted suicide.

————. *Scorpio Ghost and the Black Hole Gang.* Harper, 1987. Ron, his brother and sisters help to free two ghosts trapped in the cornfield.

————. *Smoke from the Chimney.* Atheneum, 1986. Erin and Heather are friends but Erin's father drinks. She is crushed when he appears during the Jungle Day puppet show and he is drunk.

Tate, Eleanora. *Just an Overnight Guest.* Dial, 1980. Margie is happy at home until Ethel comes to spend the night. She stays on for weeks and Margie is jealous and angry. Margie is black and Ethel is "a brashy little White kid."

————. *Secret of Gumbo Grove.* Watts, 1987. Raisin and Miss Effie uncover black history in the church's cemetery with the help of the whole community.

————. *Thank You, Dr. Martin Luther King, Jr.* Watts, 1990. During Black History Month the children of Gumbo Grove Elementary School learn about Martin Luther King.

Tate, Joan. *Luke's Garden; and Gramp.* Harper, 1981. Two stories, one tragic, one happy. Luke lives in a city but has a garden he loves. While hiding from bullies he falls to his death. Gramp has reason to live when his grandson finds space for him.

————. *Sam and Me.* Coward, 1969. A young girl is happily reunited with her husband.

————. *Tina and David.* Nelson, 1973. Tina and David can only communicate their love through notes.

————. *Wild Boy.* Harper, 1973. Will and Mart meet on the moor. Will wants to be alone but he has a family to return to. Mart has no family and fears closeness. The boys become close through near tragedy.

Taves, Isabella. *Not Bad for a Girl.* Lippincott, 1972. Sharon Lee wants to break into Little League ball. She is a better player than most boys. She faces all the prejudices of a girl on a traditionally all-boy team.

Tavo, Gus. *Buffalo Are Running.* Knopf, 1960. David rescues a Sioux Indian during a buffalo stampede and goes to live with him. He learns Indian ways.

————. *Trail to Lone Canyon.* Knopf, 1964. Jerry and Horace discover gold in Lone Canyon. But they must face three angry gangsters.

Taylor, Florence. *Gold Dust and Bullets.* Whitman, 1962. Danny heads for Denver with his trained dogs in pre–Civil War times. He does many things to earn a living, including enlisting in the Army.

Taylor, Mildred. *Friendship.* Dial, 1987. The three Wallace brothers live during the Depression. One day one of them refuses to call a white man "Mister."

————. *Gold Cadillac.* Dial, 1987. A story depicting the differences in prejudices from Ohio and Mississippi. The warm, loving family are not prepared for the prejudices they encounter.

————. *Let the Circle Be Unbroken.* Dial, 1981. Four black children experience racism and hard times but learn from their parents the pride and self respect they need to survive.

————. *Roll of Thunder, Hear My Cry.* Dial, 1976. A moving story of survival of Cassie and her black family in the South during the Great Depression. Her proud family owns land

and struggles to keep up the taxes. Newbery winner, 1977.

————. *Song of the Trees.* Dial, 1975. In this book Cassie is only eight years old and witnesses white men chopping down trees on her father's land. We meet Cassie later in the outstanding *Roll of Thunder....*

Taylor, Sydney. *All-of-a-Kind Family.* Follett, 1951/1980. Five little Jewish girls grow up in New York's Lower East Side before World War I. Sara is featured in this book.

————. *All-of-a-Kind Family Downtown.* Follett, 1972. In this book the five sisters and Charlie are involved with their newly orphaned neighbor, Guido.

————. *All-of-a-Kind Family Uptown.* Follett, 1958/1981. Ella is growing up and falls in love with Jules but war breaks out and Jules joins the Army.

————. *Ella of All-of-a-Kind Family.* Dutton, 1978. Jules returns from the war and wants to be alone with Ella. But how do you do that when there are six children in the family?

————. *More All-of-a-Kind Family.* Follett, 1954/1989. The girls spend their last year in the old neighborhood enjoying the Old World customs of 1914. And they have a new baby brother, Charles.

Taylor, Theodore. *Cay.* Doubleday, 1969. A blinded white boy, Phillip, and a wise, old black sailor, Timothy, are shipwrecked on an island. Phillip is spoiled and scornful but Timothy makes him self-sufficient. Phillip learns to respect him.

————. *Children's War.* Doubleday, 1971. A 12-year-old Alaskan boy helps an American spy operation during World War II.

————. *Hostage.* Delacorte, 1988. Jamie and his father trap a whale which they hope to sell for much needed money. But ... Greenpeace, Jamie's girl friend and television news teams want the whale released.

————. *Odyssey of Ben O'Neal.* Doubleday, 1977. Ben grows up and accepts responsibility. He goes to Norfolk to look for his brother and Tee goes back to her home in England. But they unexpectedly meet again.

————. *Sniper.* Harcourt, 1989. Ben, 15, is alone when a sniper shoots the big cats on his family's private preserve. He must cope with this killer.

————. *Sweet Friday Island.* Scholastic, 1984. Peg is on her way to a Mexican island with her father when they discover that someone is trying to kill them.

————. *Teetoncey.* Doubleday, 1974. Ben saves a shipwrecked girl on a stormy night and begins a suspenseful story. The girl will not speak and cannot remember anything about the accident.

————. *Teetoncey and Ben O'Neal.* Doubleday, 1975. An orphaned shipwrecked survivor, Teetoncey, and Ben O'Neal, a fatherless boy,

explore the rocky coast. Tee remembers a treasure being on the ship that sank and Ben tries to recover it.

————. *Trouble with Tuck.* Doubleday, 1981. Helen's golden retriever, Tuck, is going blind. He saved her life twice and she wants to save his. She gets an older guide dog to be a companion and guide to Tuck.

————. *Walking Up a Rainbow.* Delacorte, 1986. Susan, an orphan, and Cowboy Clay drive a herd of sheep from Iowa to California to sell and save Susan's home.

Taylor, William. *Paradise Lane.* Scholastic, 1987. Rosie's mother is an alcoholic and her father caresses her too much. She becomes friends with Michael, a class bully, and her father beats her. Her mother tries suicide. But events are leading to hope.

Tchudi, Stephen. *Burg-o-Rama Man.* Delacorte, 1983. Robert is looking for student candidates for his Burg-o-Rama television commercials. Karen, of the school newspaper, looks at each candidate and is dismayed at what people will do.

————. *Green Machine and the Frog Crusade.* Delacorte, 1987. David is interested in frogs. The swamp is threatened to become a shopping mall. He wins a postponement through political action.

Teague, Bob. *Adam in Blunderland.* Doubleday, 1971. Adam entered "Fun City" through his closet but he found there the same violence, stealing and prejudices as there were in the normal adult world.

Teague, Sam. *King of Hearts' Heart.* Little, 1987. Billy was brain damaged in an accident with Harold and Harold has been a faithful friend since. He helps Billy compete in the Special Olympics.

Teale, Edwin. *Lost Dog.* Dodd, 1961. Gerald is a deaf mute. He goes hunting with his dog, Poncho. The dog disappears and a dog hunt is started. After a month's search the dog is found.

Teibl, Margaret. *Davey Come Home.* Harper, 1979. A story of a boy's adjustment to his father's divorce and the coming of a housekeeper.

Teicher, Elizabeth. *April's Year.* Norton, 1966. April's sister is lovely with an ideal boyfriend. April envies her but after coping with and being helped by brothers and sisters, April, too, blossoms into a young lady.

Telemague, Eleanor. *It's Crazy to Stay Chinese in Minnesota.* Nelson, 1978. Eleanor, 17, wants to be an unhyphenated American. She meets Bingo Tang and they want to marry but their plans fail and she matures in the process.

Ter Haar, Jaap. *Boris.* Delacorte, 1970. The story of a young boy's life during the siege of Leningrad. Boris and his friend, Nadia, cross no-man's-land in search of food and are captured. Nadia freezes to death and Boris is full of hate.

————. *World of Ben Lighthart.* Delacorte,

1977. Ben is blinded in an accident. He feels defeated until he talks with a young man who is facing death. He learns to cope in a sightless world.

Terhune, Albert. *Lad: A Dog.* Dutton, 1959. One of the most popular and best loved dog stories.

Terlouw, James. *How to Become King.* Hastings, 1977. A humorous satire showing a 17-year-old going through various tests in order to become king. Stark is an orphan and the tests are "impossible" tasks but are creatively solved by him.

_____. *Winter in Wartime.* McGraw, 1976. Michiel hides a downed RAF airman who killed a German soldier. The Germans execute Michiel's father thinking he, as part of the Resistance, did the killing.

Terris, Susan. *Drowning Boy.* Doubleday, 1972. Jason's bumbling behavior is pitted against his father's efficiency.

_____. *Latchkey Kids.* Farrar, 1986. Callie is a latchkey child in a new neighborhood. Her mother works and her father is ill. She must bring her brother home, lock themselves in and call their mother each day. She feels like a prisoner.

_____. *No Scarlet Ribbons.* Farrar, 1981. Rachel's mother marries a man with two children. She tries to manipulate the family into togetherness, fails and is resentful. She has a surprise for the family on Christmas Eve.

_____. *Octopus Pie.* Farrar, 1983. Marianne and Kristen's father brings home an octopus. Marianne takes it to school to see if it will make her popular. It disappears and is searched for. It helps Kristen come out from Marianne's control.

_____. *On Fire.* Doubleday, 1972. Nina, 12, meets 15-year-old Paul. They both like to paint and become friends. He is said to be a "fire bug" and also a bully. When a house burns Nina wonders if it was Paul's fault.

_____. *Pencil Families.* Morrow, 1975. Emily collects and groups pencils. She finds one near a dead man she discovers on the beach. It is a clue to the death and she is being followed.

_____. *Stage Brat.* Four Winds, 1980. Lennet likes to act. She is cast as Peter Pan but her family is uninterested in her acting plans. Although she is a brat the reader wishes her well.

_____. *Two P's in a Pod.* Greenwillow, 1971. Penny, new in school and emotionally unstable, meets Pru and the school "nerd" and finds out they look alike. Penny uses Pru to spy and spread lies about their teacher.

Terry, Douglas. *Last Texas Hero.* Doubleday, 1982. A story of three great football players who accept scholarships to the same college. They find that football is not an All-American sport but a merciless rivalry. They try to fight back.

Tevis, Walter. *Queen's Gambit.* Random, 1983. Mr. Shaibel, janitor of Methuen School, taught Beth to play chess. She became an excellent player in six months and for years played chess for money and recognition. But was it enough?

Thacker, Nola. *Summer Stories.* Lippincott, 1988. Red finds that Tralice and Joe have changed this summer. Tralice is interested in boys, makeup and suntans. Joe is a sneak and a manipulator. But Carrie Mae is the same so she and Red have fun.

Thager, Marie. *Shanta.* Follett, 1968. Shanta, 12, lives by the rules of Indian society. She goes to the Harvest Festival where her brother is stolen and then rescued. Her family, her betrothed and she must face an uncertain future.

Thane, Elswyth. *Dawn's Early Light.* Hawthorn, 1971. Two young men who are friends join the army during the Revolutionary War. They both survive and return home to their girlfriends.

Thesman, Jean. *Last April Dancers.* Houghton, 1987. Cat, 16, is sent away after her father commits suicide. She learns more about the suicide and her family history. Her friends come to visit and she feels the bond between them will last the waiting.

Thiam, Djibi. *My Sister, the Panther.* Dodd, 1980. Baumou has to face the conflict when a wounded panther becomes a killer. The panther is from his tribe and should be killed. They stalk each other and end in a ferocious battle.

Thiele, Colin. *Blue Fin.* Harper, 1974. A fourteen-year-old boy and his father are fishing off the coast of Australia when their ship is disabled. The boy's courage is tested as well as his love for his father.

_____. *February Dragon.* Harper, 1966. The "February Dragon" is an uncontrolled brush fire. The Pine family's home was destroyed by the February Dragon and they must make a new life.

_____. *Fight Against Albatross Two.* Harper, 1974. Link and his sister live near the sea in Australia. There is a major oil spill and they observe the tragedy it causes to the wildlife in the area.

_____. *Fire in the Stone.* Harper, 1974. Ernie makes a rich opal strike. Someone wants his claim and sabotages the plane of the opal buyer. While investigating, Ernie is trapped in a mine explosion. He faces fear, hunger and death.

_____. *Hammerhead Light.* Harper, 1977. Tessa, 12, and Axel, 72, are friends. Axel was a lighthouse keeper and the lighthouse is to be torn down. But it is used to guide Tessa's family home in a storm.

_____. *Shadow on the Hills.* Harper, 1977. Bodo befriends a hermit named Ebenezer. Moses Mibus had stolen his land and killed his dog and he seeks revenge. He gets that vindication.

_____. *Shadow Shark.* Harper, 1985. Joe, Meg and Uncle Harry attempt to capture a giant shark. Harry is hurt and Joe and Meg must care for him. They must also find a way to get rescued from their small island.

_____. *Storm Boy.* Rand McNally, 1963. Storm Boy and his father live in Australia. They spend time at the bird sanctuary. Storm Boy nurses a helpless pelican back to health. The pelican becomes a pet until he is killed by a hunter.

Thomas, Jane. *Comeback Dog.* Houghton, 1981. Daniel's dog dies and he feels he never wants another one. He finds an abandoned dog and cares for it. He calls it Lady. He is hurt when the dog does not immediately respond to his kindness.

_____. *Courage at Indian Deep.* Clarion, 1984. Cass sees a signal light from a ship during a blizzard and helps rescue two men from the ship.

_____. *Fox in a Trap.* Clarion, 1987. Daniel thinks trapping would be fun. But when he goes with Uncle Pete he finds that it has drawbacks. He faces a moral dilemma when he sees the cruelty involved.

_____. *Princess in the Pigpen.* Clarion, 1989. Elizabeth is sick with fever. She travels from Elizabethan England to an Iowa farm. Nobody believes her story.

Thomas, Joyce. *Bright Shadow.* Flare, 1983. Abby finds that both love and education have their problems as well as their joys.

_____. *Golden Pasture.* Scholastic, 1986. Carl Lee finds a horse on his grandfather's farm. Caring for the horse teaches him tolerance and understanding of difficult problems.

_____. *Journey.* Scholastic, 1988. Meggie knows and likes spiders. When her school friend is murdered, this knowledge and relationship help solve the mystery.

_____. *Marked by Fire.* Flare, 1982. Abby, a black living in the South, learns the secrets of folk medicine from Mother Barker.

_____. *Water Girl.* Avon, 1986. Amber finds a scrapbook the day after the earthquake and it will change her life. She looks through the yellowed pages until she finds a letter from Abyssinia to her parents.

Thomas, Karen. *Changing of the Guard.* Harper, 1986. Caroline is a loner. Her grandfather died and his orchards are sold. Another girl, who lost her mother and is ignored by her father and his new wife, becomes friends with Caroline.

Thomas, Kathleen. *Goats Are Better Than Worms.* Dodd, 1984. Ellen and her goat, Jake, have a balloon ride to a fantasy island.

Thomas, Ruth. *Runaways.* Harper, 1989. Nathan and Julia are not really friends but they find money and run away together.

Thompson, Eileen. *Blue Stone Mystery.* Abelard, 1963. A mystery set in New Mexico where a family is vacationing. The three children look for a lost turquoise mine and get involved with rustlers.

_____. *Golden Coyote.* Simon & Schuster, 1971. Little Otter's mother is an outsider. She is snubbed by their tribe. He rescues and trains a coyote pup. He becomes a hero when he saves his village from danger.

Thompson, Estelle. *Hunter in the Dark.* Walker, 1979. Philip is blind but he "witnesses" the kidnapping of a child who was later murdered. He is determined to help the police find the criminal.

Thompson, Jean. *Brother of the Wolves.* Morrow, 1978. A boy is cared for by wolves for several months. He is then adopted by Indians. He is suspect because of his friendship with the wolves. He must decide whether to live among wolves or strangers.

Thompson, Joyce. *Conscience Place.* Doubleday, 1984. The Place is where babies, born malformed because of radiation, go. They live their short lives there and are replaced by new babies. The Place is secret but is getting overcrowded.

Thompson, Julian. *Band of Angels.* Scholastic, 1986. Jordan's parents discsovered a weapon so powerful they killed themselves rather than let any government have it. Now Jordan is being pursued by government agents and he doesn't even know it.

_____. *Discontinued.* Scholastic, 1986. Duncan learns that he may be the target of the killer that killed his parents.

_____. *Goofbang Value Daze.* Scholastic, 1989. In a future community set under a huge dome, a riot erupts at a high school when students protest the school director's authoritarian measures.

_____. *Grounding of Group 6.* Avon, 1983. Three girls and two boys make up Group 6. Nat was their leader. They were in a Country School and Nat was taking them for a hike. What he really intended to do was kill them, per parent request!

_____. *Simon Pure.* Scholastic, 1987. Simon is a freshman in college at the age of 15. He finds out about a plot to overthrow the university and it's up to him to stop it.

Thompson, Paul. *Hitchhikers.* Watts, 1980. Shawn is headed for San Juan to find his father. Val is pregnant and looking for the father of her child. They are drawn together and are disappointed when they find the people they are looking for.

Thompson, Wilma. *That Barbara.* Delacorte, 1968. Barbara, 13, is the kind of girl things go wrong for. Her schemes are funny if not tragic. She is courageous and impulsive.

Thrasher, Crystal. *Between Dark and Daylight.* Atheneum, 1979. Seely, during the Depression, has her life changed by fire, death, threatened rape and murder.

_____. *Dark Didn't Catch Me.* Atheneum, 1975. The beginning of a story of a family that survives the Great Depression. Seely is the main character who lives through hard work, troubles, death and sorrows.

_____. *End of a Dark Road.* Atheneum, 1982. Seely's best friend, Russell, abused by his stepfather, is "accidentally" killed by him while hunting. Another friend is hurt in a hayride accident. Her father dies. But the future looks bright.

————. *Julie's Summer.* Atheneum, 1981. Julie is Seely's older sister, the one who remained behind when Seely moved. She has a couple of boyfriends but decides not to marry either one; instead, she decides to go to college.

————. *Taste of Daylight.* Atheneum, 1984. The last book in the series about Seely. It is still the time of the Great Depression but things are looking up for Seely. She moves out into the city in hopes of a better life.

Thruelsen, Richard. *Voyage of the Vagabond.* Harcourt, 1965. Peter is adrift in a small boat. He is "rescued" by a 42 foot yacht. The only one on board is Hope, 11. They pool resources to find land.

Thrush, Robin. *Gray Whales Are Missing.* Harcourt, 1987. Pence and his friend want to know why the whales are not passing San Diego's coast. It is because of some navy surveillance equipment.

Thum, Marcella. *Mystery at Crane's Landing.* Dodd, 1964. Paula visits Lucy in her cousin's home. Lucy is hurt in a horse fall and Paula discovers that the cousins are imposters.

Thurber, James. *Thirteen Clocks.* Simon & Schuster, 1950. A grown-up fairy tale about monsters, prisoners, heroes and fair damsels.

————. *White Deer.* Harcourt, 1945. A modern fairy tale about three princes, a princess and lots of magic.

Thwaite, Ann. *House in Turner Square.* Harcourt, 1961. Joanna and Audrey look for the owner of an old house.

Tilly, Nancy. *Golden Girl.* Farrar, 1985. Penny is envious of the wealth of her two friends. She doesn't realize how much they envy her.

Titus, Eve. *Basil and the Pygmy Cats.* Mc-Graw, 1971. Basil, the Sherlock Holmes of the mouse world, goes to Kataarh to find out if miniature cats really exist.

————. *Basil of Baker Street.* Pocket Books, 1958. Basil is a mouse that lives at 221 Baker Street, the address of Sherlock Holmes. He is just as clever a detective.

Todd, Leonard. *Best Kept Secret of the War.* Knopf, 1984. Cam's father is away during World War II and his mother is very busy. He meets a strange man, Jeddah, who is hiding in the mountains.

Tofte, Arthur. *Survival Planet.* Bobbs, 1977. The Evansons crash-land and then establish themselves with the native Thrulls on the planet Iduna. They left a starving, overpopulated Earth.

Tolan, Stephanie. *Good Courage.* Morrow, 1988. A realistic story of cult life at its worst. Ty is forced to work with little food and is severely punished for helping a fellow child. Ty escapes and reports to the police but to no avail.

————. *Grandpa—and Me.* Scribner, 1978.

Kerry's granddad *is* becoming senile. Plans need to be made for him. Kerry is upset because her granddad has so little to say. But the problem is solved by grandpa himself.

————. *Great Skinner Enterprise.* Four Winds, 1986. Father has changed from conservative to flashy and is fired from his job. He starts a new service business at home and is so successful that it may ruin the family.

————. *Great Skinner Getaway.* Four Winds, 1987. Father buys a motor home and they all set out for a cross country trip to see everything and meet many people. Mother, Father, four children, two cats and one dog. It is disastrous.

————. *Great Skinner Homestead.* Four Winds, 1988. The motor home breaks down in the Adirondacks. Father decides to homestead there. He and the family work for the land rent: weeding, picking and canning beans. Jenny meets a college boy and helps him.

————. *Great Skinner Strike.* Macmillan, 1983. Jenny Skinner, 14, tells about her mother's strike. Home life is topsy-turvy for 19 days. Neighbors join in. Father and four children try to cope but can't. The two daughters join mother.

————. *Last of Eden.* Warne, 1980. Mike spends her sophomore year at Turnbull Hall. Her roommate is Marty, a gifted artist. There is a scandal involving their relationship. Mike finds out that Marty is gay, so is Sylvie but not Mike.

————. *Liberation of Tansy Warner.* Scribner, 1980. Tansy gets the part of Anne Frank in a school play. Her mother leaves her father and she must assume household responsibilities. She has little time left for rehearsals but succeeds in the play.

————. *No Safe Harbors.* Scribner, 1981. Amanda is into designer clothes and summers on the river. Joe is a boat mechanic who likes classical music and creative writing. They get to see each other beyond the images.

————. *Pride of the Peacock.* Scribner, 1986. Whitney is scared of a nuclear holocaust and can't understand why everyone else doesn't share her panic. She gets to look at life more realistically.

————. *Time to Fly Free.* Scribner, 1983. Josh meets Rafferty who cares for sick and injured birds and Josh assists him. Josh learns about his own life as he sees the life and death aspects of this work.

Tolkien, J.R.R. *Fellowship of the Ring.* Houghton, 1965. A young hobbit, Frodo, undertakes a journey to prevent a magic ring from falling into the hands of the powers of evil.

————. *Hobbit.* Houghton, 1937/1987. The prelude to *The Lord of the Rings.* The Hobbit is Bilbo Baggins and he lives in Middle Earth. His ring can make him disappear.

————. *Return of the King.* Houghton, 1965. Evil Dark Lord Sauron wants to conquer all Middle Earth. Gandalf, the wizard, with the help of Frodo, brings an end to the Great Darkness. The Ring must be destroyed.

_____. *Silmarillion.* Houghton, 1977. This book is background for *Lord of the Rings.* This and *The Hobbit* can be read separately, before or after, and enjoyed as much as *Lord of the Rings.*

_____. *Two Towers.* Houghton, 1965. This story tells how each member of the broken fellowship made out before the coming of the Great Darkness.

Tolle, Jean. *Great Pete Penney.* Atheneum, 1979. A girl wants to break into major league baseball and a leprechaun helps her.

_____. *Too Many Boys.* Nelson, 1965. Katie Hart and her two brothers live next door to Will. Katie must play with boys because there are no girls nearby.

Tolles, Martha. *Darci and the Dance Contest.* Dutton, 1985. Darci moves from California to New York. She has not yet made any friends. Nathan teases her and the girls ignore her. Should she enter the Dance Contest? If so, with whom? Nathan, of course.

_____. *Who's Reading Darci's Diary?* Dutton, 1984. Darci had a secret diary. No one could see it. It included thoughts about her friends, her feelings and especially about Travis, a cute boy at school. Now it is missing. What should she do?

Tomalin, Ruth. *Gone Away.* Faber, 1979. Francie stays at Falcon House with a child ghost. She guesses the identity and problem of the ghost and relocates it where it wants to be: "Gone Away" farm.

Tomerlin, John. *Fledgling.* Dutton, 1968. Rich meets the world of airplanes and flying. He wants to learn everything but his mother is against it. He is a little unsure himself but friends build his confidence.

_____. *Magnificent Jalopy.* Dutton, 1967. Wally, Link and Injun get an old '32 Packard and restore it. They take part in a rally on the West Coast. They rescue a man who is caught in an accident and take it in stride.

_____. *Nothing Special.* Dutton, 1969. Wally, Link and Injun build their own sports car to race. They must pass tests of Driver Training, get their car through inspection and then race at Riverside. They must be a team.

_____. *Sky Clowns.* Dutton, 1973. Rich has learned a great deal about flying from Carlie Hatcher. He is now doing aerobatics himself. Is there a future for stunt fliers?

Torchia, Joseph. *Kryptonite Kid.* Holt, 1979. Jerry writes letters to his hero Superman. These letters show his mental deterioration and the real identity of Superman.

Touster, Irwin. *Perez Arson Mystery.* Dial, 1972. Antonio Perez was a nasty boy accused of arson when the store he was fired from burned down. Vernon, David and Penny investigate and prove him innocent.

_____. *Runaway Bus Mystery.* Dial, 1972. A school bus had an accident and Vernon is in the hospital. Was it brake failure or careless driving? David and Penny investigate. A look at a real law case, our legal system and trial by jury.

Towne, Mary. *Boxed In.* Crowell, 1982. Kate must sell Tracker, a good show horse, because her open-spaced home is being developed. Shelly, her friend, wants to buy him.

_____. *Glass Room.* Farrar, 1971. Rob comes from a musical family and is unhappy. Simon lives with his father and is unhappy. They become friends and each likes the other's family. They resolve this problem and life goes on.

_____. *Paul's Game.* Delacorte, 1983. Andrea and Julie experiment with ESP just for fun but it turns into a nightmare because of Paul.

_____. *Their House.* Atheneum, 1990. Molly and her parents move into a large house and let the former owners stay for a while. They regret this decision.

_____. *Wanda the Worrywart.* Atheneum, 1989. Wanda worries about her step-grandmother's interest in a prospective new husband.

Townsend, J. David. *Cats Stand Accused.* Houghton, 1961. Here, complete with detectives, judge, jury, lawyers and expert witnesses is a story of a Siamese cat being tried for the murder of a guinea pig.

Townsend, John. *Cloudy-Bright.* Lippincott, 1984. Sam loses his camera and wants to borrow Jenny's expensive one because he's entering a contest. This is how they meet and even though their backgrounds are different, they fall in love.

_____. *Creatures.* Lippincott, 1980. Creatures are the natives of what's left of the Earth. Persons are superior beings from another planet. Two Persons, Harmony and Vector, fall in love; they leave the Persons and go live with the Creatures.

_____. *Dan Alone.* Lippincott, 1983. Dan's mother runs off and his grandfather dies. He and a friend, Olive, look for his real father and find him.

_____. *Good-Bye to the Jungle.* Lippincott, 1965. The Thompsons get to leave "The Jungle" for a new home in a housing development. This does not change their life and they still must struggle to make their way.

_____. *Intruder.* Lippincott, 1969. A young boy fights the mysterious power of a stranger.

_____. *Islanders.* Lippincott, 1981. The inhabitants of the island live by the Book presented by the Deliverer. A man who can read finds the Book to be a hoax. There is conflict among the people of the island.

_____. *Kate and the Revolution.* Lippincott, 1983. A political satire with warm humor. Kate participates in a coup in Essenheim. She sees through handsome Crown Prince Rudi and appreciates a British reporter.

_____. *Noah's Castle.* Lippincott, 1976. A futuristic view of English society. Food is scarce and people are desperate. Barry's father stores food and barricades the house. Barry wants to help others but his father is opposed to it.

_____. *Persuading Stick.* Lothrop, 1986. When Sarah holds her stick a certain way people do what she wants. She uses it to save her brother from suicide.

_____. *Pirate's Island.* Lippincott, 1968. When a real treasure is stolen from a trusting old man, Gordon and Sheila decide to help him find his treasure. Gordon was pursued by bullies and Sheila was his only friend.

_____. *Rob's Place.* Lothrop, 1988. Rob is unhappy, not only about his parents' divorce but about his friend moving away. He drifts into fantasy and must be helped to face reality.

_____. *Summer People.* Lippincott, 1972. A mixed up love story of two people, Philip and Sylvia, who love two other people, Harold and Ann. They must keep this a secret because of parent disapproval. It doesn't last and they break up.

_____. *Tom Tiddler's Ground.* Lippincott, 1986. Vic and Brain meet in the hull of a canal boat. They, with their friends, stop crooks from stealing a gold horse, find the real owner of the boat and solve a years-old murder.

_____. *Top of the World.* Harper, 1977. Two youngsters, living in an apartment building, take dangerous chances by walking the catwalks in a penthouse garden, without having permission to do so.

_____. *Trouble in the Jungle.* Lippincott, 1961. The Jungle is a ghetto. The four Thompson children, Kevin, Sandra, Jean and Harold, are left to fend for themselves and don't want a home when Father/Uncle returns with a mistress.

Townsend, Sue. *Growing Pains of Adrian Mole.* Grove, 1982. Adrian Mole has zits, love problems, mother problems, awful teachers, and all the problems of growing up, painfully.

Townsend, Susan. *Secret Diary of Adrian Mole Aged 13¾.* Avon, 1984. Adrian's mother goes off with the man next door, his father loses his job and he is bullied at school. In spite of all this, this is a funny story about a boy growing up.

Townsend, Tom. *Trader Wooly and the Terrorist.* Eakin, 1988. Trader Wooly and his friends find a terrorist plot to kill as many Americans as possible on the military base in Germany.

Trask, Margaret. *At the Sign of the Rocking Horse.* Crowell, 1964. Cassie and Fergus are spending the summer in Vermont and get involved in a real mystery.

Travers, Pamela. *Mary Poppins.* Harcourt, 1934/1981. Magical Mary Poppins is an extraordinary lady, full of fun and excitement. The children knew she was magical right from the beginning.

_____. *Mary Poppins Comes Back.* Harcourt, 1935/1985. More adventures with this delightful babysitter. She said she would return and she did. She arrived at the end of a kite string.

_____. *Mary Poppins in the Park.* Harcourt, 1952/1988. Mary Poppins brings Michael, Jane, the twins and Annabel the best in fun and enchanting adventures.

_____. *Mary Poppins Opens the Door.* Harcourt, 1943/1981. Whimsical Mary is back with new adventures. This time she comes back as a falling spark and finds there is a new baby, Annabel.

Traylor, Sarah. *Red Wind.* Abingdon, 1977. Angus witnessed live slaves being thrown overboard and reported it. His life was threatened so he left for Fort Loudown. It was attacked by Indians but Angus escaped.

Treadgold, Mary. *Winter Princess.* Van Nostrand, 1964. Every Friday a lady gives time to children. They share problems, especially the one concerning a villainous newspaper man.

Trease, Geoffrey. *Flight of the Angels.* Lerner, 1988. Sheila and her friends solve a 400-year-old mystery while exploring caves for a class project.

_____. *No Boats on Bannermere.* Norton, 1965. Bill and Susan explore the cottage their family inherited. Sir Alfred forbids them to use the lakes. They do anyway and find a buried treasure.

Treece, Henry. *Burning of Njal.* Criterion, 1964. In 11th century Iceland Njal's sons avenge the death of Gunnar. They are all killed except one son-in-law.

_____. *Centurion.* Meredith, 1967. In 16 A.D. Durcus settled in Britain. Queen Boudicca starts an attack and Durcus is torn between his fellow Romans and his British neighbors.

_____. *Horned Helmet.* Criterion, 1963. Starkad was a Viking raider. Beorn was a nobody. But a friendship drew them together and loyalty kept them together.

_____. *Last Viking.* Pantheon, 1966. Hardrada, king of Norway, awaits the battle with the English and tells of his youth and his friends that helped him mature. The book ends with his death in battle.

_____. *Man with a Sword.* Pantheon, 1964. Hereward was a soldier for various rulers from the battle of Hastings to William the Conqueror and the conflict for the English throne with Denmark and Normandy plus the feuding of English nobles.

_____. *Road to Miklagard.* Criterion, 1957. Harald makes a fruitless trip to what is now Ireland to find a treasure. He ends up in Spain where he is not welcomed. He escapes back to his homeland.

_____. *Splintered Sword.* Duell, 1965. Runolf seeks his fortune. But his comrades desert him and he needs more than courage.

_____. *Swords from the North.* Pantheon, 1967. A story of the exploits of Hardrada while he lived in Byzantium as Captain of the Varangian Guards.

_____. *Viking's Dawn.* Criterion, 1956.

Heroic saga of Vikings and their world in the eighth century. Any voyage taken is one of hardship and death.

_____. *Viking's Sunset*. Criterion, 1960. The last battles of Harald. The story takes the reader out of Norway into Iceland, Greenland and North America.

_____. *War Dog*. Criterion, 1963. Bran was a war dog in 43 B.C. in the wars against the Romans. Gwyn, a Britain and Bran's master, was killed and Bran left for dead. He was found and nursed back to health by a Roman.

Trevor, Elleston. *Theta Syndrome*. Doubleday, 1977. Claudia is testing a new drug and finds something sinister. Her car is forced off the road and she is in a coma. She can only be reached by hypnotism and theta waves.

Trezise, Percy. *Turramulh the Giant Quinkin*. Stevens, 1988. An evil giant tries to catch two children but fails because of his own clumsiness.

Trivelpiece, Laurel. *In Love and in Trouble*. Pocket Books, 1981. Alma never dreamed that Howard, the most popular boy in school, would notice her, never dreamed they would spend a day together, never dreamed she'd get pregnant.

Trivers, James. *Hamburger Heaven*. Prentice, 1976. A story about Kenny's days working in a fast food restaurant. It is hard work, the organization is so tight that it alienates the workers and the stress of handling cash is great.

Trumbo, Dalton. *Johnny Got His Gun*. Citadel, 1970. A very moving story about the horrors of war. Johnny is seriously wounded in World War I. He can't see or hear; he has lost his legs and arms. He wants to have warm contact with his lost world.

Truss, Jan. *Jasmin*. Atheneum, 1982. Jasmin runs away from a busy home. She finds some privacy and a talent for molding clay. She is rescued and comes home with hope for better things in the future.

Tung, S.T. *One Small Dog*. Dodd, 1975. A young Oriental boy tries to save his dog.

Tuning, William. *Fuzzy Bones*. Ace, 1981. This is about the origin of the golden-haired Fuzzies of the planet Zarathustra.

Tunis, John. *Duke Decides*. Harcourt, 1939/1990. The Duke is a determined athlete who trains hard to win. He makes the Olympic team and is the fastest man alive.

_____. *His Enemy, His Friend*. Morrow, 1967. A friendship story of two boys whose families come from two different countries: Germany and France. These countries are not friendly and that hurts their friendship.

_____. *Iron Duke*. Harcourt, 1938/1990. Mickey is in college and makes the adjustment well. His grades are good and he makes the track team. He is a great runner.

Tunis, John. *Keystone Kids*. Harcourt, 1943/1990. Two brothers, Spike and Bob, play baseball. One plays second base and the other shortstop. Their team is poorly managed. Spike becomes manager but has a lot of work to do to make a team.

_____. *Kid Comes Back*. Harcourt, 1946/1990. After fighting in France and Germany, Roy comes back to play baseball again. He again saves the game for his teammates.

_____. *Kid from Tomkinville*. Harcourt, 1987. A 1987 issue of a 1940 book about Kid's year with the Brooklyn Dodgers.

_____. *Rookie of the Year*. Harcourt, 1944/1990. A young rookie pitcher, because of the coach's faith in him, takes his team from fourth to first place.

_____. *Silence Over Dunkerque*. Morrow, 1962. An exciting account of the evacuation at Dunkirk.

Turnbull, Ann. *Frightened Forest*. Seabury, 1975. Gillian inadvertently releases an evil witch from an old railroad tunnel; it controls the weather. She must restore order and does so by believing in the wizard who can cast the witch out of the world.

_____. *Maroo of the Winter Caves*. Houghton, 1984. Maroo, an ice age girl, helps her brother, mother and grandmother to safety when her father is killed. They must be in winter camp before the blizzard.

_____. *Wolf King*. Seabury, 1976. In the Iron Age the people fear, but protect, wolves. The wolves are attacking the people more often. Gratla and Coll go off to search for kinsmen and the Wolf King whom they must kill.

Turner, Ann. *Dakota Dugout*. Macmillan, 1985. A grandmother tells her granddaughter what life was like in a sod house on the Dakota prairie a hundred years ago. It was a hard life but also had its light and beautiful moments.

_____. *Grasshopper Summer*. Macmillan, 1989. Sam and his family go to Dakota Territory in 1874. The conditions are harsh and grasshoppers invade the crops.

_____. *Nettie's Trip South*. Macmillan, 1986. Nettie writes to her friend Addie about her impression of the South. She talks about slavery and the selling of children.

_____. *Third Girl from the Left*. Macmillan, 1986. Sarah answers an ad for a mail order bride. Alex answers and she accepts. She has a struggle in Montana in 1880 because her husband dies accidentally and she must run the 2,000 acre ranch.

_____. *Time of the Bison*. Macmillan, 1987. Set in the Ice Age this story of Scar Boy shows his determination to be a cave painter.

_____. *Way Home*. Crown, 1982. Anne flees from the London plague of the 14th century. She goes to a marsh and survives.

Turner, Gerry. *Silver Dollar Hoard of Aristotle Gaskin*. Doubleday, 1968. The boys of Scout Troop #10 are peeping in the window of Old Man Gaskin. He catches them and offers them money if they can find where his money is hidden. A ten day search begins for clues and the money.

Turner, Kermit. *Rebel Powers.* Warne, 1979. David goes to work in a beach town during the summer. He gets into fights and has some sexual experiences. He is afraid of both; he conquers his fear of fighting but is still unsure of his sex life.

Turner, Phillip. *Colonel Sheperton's Clock.* World, 1966. Peter, David and Arthur stumble on a mystery. They find a clue in an old 1914 newspaper that leads to Colonel Sheperton, a WWI hero and his grandfather clock. There they find a secret.

_____. *Devil's Nob.* Nelson, 1973. Taffy works in the slate mines of England. He is courting Sarah who is injured in a fall and must be rescued. He does so alone and cleverly. There is still competition between steam and horses.

_____. *Grange at High Force.* World, 1967. Peter, David and Arthur hunt for a lost statue that has been missing for centuries. A humorous adventure helped by a retired admiral.

_____. *Sea Peril.* World, 1966. Peter, David and Arthur plan, construct and operate a bicycle-powered punt in which they plan to explore the river. The boys find both friends and enemies.

_____. *Steam on the Line.* World, 1968. Taffy and Sarah discover a plan to derail the new train thereby saving passengers from death and the destruction of the transportation system.

_____. *War on the Darnel.* World, 1969. Peter, David and Arthur fight with another set of boys who have set up a barricade on the river and are charging a fee. It is all in the name of a charity and ends up funny and clever.

Turngren, Annette. *Mystery Enters the Hospital.* Funk & Wagnall, 1965. Abby, a Candy Striper and former babysitter for Skip, must now hide him from racketeers so his father can testify.

Tuttle, Lisa. *Catwitch.* Doubleday, 1983. Jules, the Catwitch, helps his mistress cast the Great Spell to insure her movie career. He also saves Land of Faerie from a wizard.

Twain, Mark. *Adventures of Huckleberry Finn.* Nal, 1971. Huck runs away from his drunken father and when he meets Jim, a black man, they float down the Mississippi River together on a raft.

_____. *Adventures of Tom Sawyer.* Putnam, 1977. A standard classic of a young boy growing up along the Mississippi River.

_____. *Connecticut Yankee in King Arthur's Court.* Morrow, 1988. A time travel story of King Arthur.

_____. *Legend of Sagenfeld.* Publisher's Group, 1987. When asked to find the animal with the sweetest sound, the king chooses the donkey and his bray.

_____. *Prince and the Pauper.* Nal, 1986. Tom, a poor boy, exchanges clothes with the Crown Prince of England. But the Prince is thrown out of the castle and Tom is in danger.

_____. *Stolen White Elephant.* Publisher's Group, 1987. The guardian of the elephant is taken in by a corrupt policeman.

Twohill, Maggie. *Bigmouth.* Bradbury, 1986. Bunny talks too much and doesn't listen. She spoils a birthday party, misinterprets Dad's message from his boss, etc. Then she stops talking entirely.

Tyler, Anne. *Slipping Down Life.* Berkley, 1989. Evie, the second fattest girl in high school, carves rock and roll star Bertram "Drumsticks" Casey's last name on her forehead, and eventually they are married.

Tyler, Vicki. *Senior Year.* Ballantine, 1985. Julie is Megan's younger sister. Megan is in her senior year at the beginning of the book and Julie is in her senior year at the end of the book. We get two looks at girls in school.

Uchida, Yoshika. *Best Bad Thing.* Atheneum, 1983. Rinko must spend the summer with Mrs. Hata and her two sons. She has her own ideas about this help for a lady she is sure she will not like. One disaster follows another.

_____. *Happiest Ending.* Atheneum, 1985. Rinko's neighbor's daughter is coming from Japan to marry a man she never met. Rinko wants to stop this but he learns about love and adult problems.

_____. *In-Between Muja.* Scribner, 1967. An Oriental family living in Japan have strict value standards; there is temptation to go against them but family ties are strong and truth plays a large role.

_____. *Jar of Dreams.* Atheneum, 1981. Rinko grew up in Oakland, California, during the Great Depression. Her Aunt Waka from Japan comes to visit and although she sees the prejudices she inspires the whole family.

_____. *Journey Home.* Atheneum, 1978. Even though they are released from camp at war's end, a Japanese family has difficulty getting resettled. Ken returns from the war wounded and emotionally unstable.

_____. *Journey to Topaz.* Scribner, 1971. The story of a Japanese family in California at the outbreak of World War II and their experiences in interment camps. Yuki and Ken's father is separated from them.

_____. *Magic Listening Cap.* Harcourt, 1983. A Japanese legend about a creature whose job it is to eat bad dreams.

_____. *Mik and the Prowler.* Harcourt, 1960. Tamiko makes Mik's life complicated. He takes care of Mrs. Whipple's plants and cats. But now things change and he doesn't know what to do.

_____. *Samurai of Gold Hill.* Scribner, 1972. Koichi, a young Japanese boy, and his samurai father head into the California hills in 1869 looking for gold.

Uhl, Marion. *Spiral Horn.* Doubleday, 1968. On Etheria some heraldic animals are living out a legend concerning the Unicorn of Scotland and the Lion of England.

Ulyatt, Kenneth. *Longhorn Trail.* Prentice, 1968. "Portugee" Phillips makes a daring cattle drive from Texas to Wyoming. The cattle will stock the plains replacing buffalo as a food source for the Indians and will be shipped to the East via Union Pacific.

Underhill, Ruth. *Antelope Singer.* Crowell, 1961. Tad and Mitty find an Indian boy driven from his tribe because of illness. They nurse him back to health and go back with him to his tribe and are accepted by them.

Underwood, Betty. *Forge and the Forest.* Houghton, 1975. Bernadette is involved with the abolitionist and emancipation of women movements in 1834. She is also attracted to Pastor Robb McIves who wants her to be a "pious female."

_____. *Tamarack Tree.* Houghton, 1971. Bernadette wants to go to Crandall's seminary but only black students are enrolled. There are prejudice, boycotts, trials and arson as well as friendship and courage.

Underwood, Michael. *Goddess of Death.* St. Martin, 1982. Rosa Epton is an attorney defending the younger brother of a friend. It is not an easy task and gets pretty nasty.

Unnerstad, Edith. *Journey to England.* Macmillan, 1961. Brosus and Margita go to England to find their missing mother. They are helped by the famous Jenny Lind.

_____. *Peep-Larssons Go Sailing.* Macmillan, 1963. Six Larsson children go sailing for a month's vacation. They and their cat have a wonderful time without adult supervision. They have fun and a near-tragedy as they learn about weather and the sea.

_____. *Saucepan Journey.* Macmillan, 1951. The Larsson family travels by caravan to find a place large enough to house all of them (9). Papa invented Peep, the 3 tiered singing saucepan, and sold it for a profit. Mystery, humor and love.

Unsworth, Walter. *Grimsdyke.* Nelson, 1976. Kit, an orphan, goes to visit Grimsdyke, the estate of his uncle. He overhears a plot by his uncle to kill him because he is entitled to some mineral rights. He runs away.

Ure, Jean. *After Thursday.* Delacorte, 1985. Marianne is in love with Abe but he wants to pursue his career. Peter enters her life but she still is devoted to Abe. There will be more complications before this is settled.

_____. *If It Weren't for Sebastian.* Delacorte, 1985. Maggie informs her family that she wants to be a secretary not a doctor. She meets Sebastian described as "bonkers, maniacal, and ... suicidal."

_____. *Most Important Thing.* Morrow, 1986. Nicola, 14, has a talented and spoiled sister. She must make her own way as a ballet dancer or whatever she wants.

_____. *Other Side of the Fence.* Delacorte, 1988. Richard, running away from his father, and Bonny, running away from Jake, a rock musician, meet and travel together. Bonny goes back to Jake and Richard comes to terms with his homosexuality.

_____. *See You Thursday.* Delacorte, 1981. Sixteen-year-old Marianne attends a girl's school. She finds a friend in Abe, a piano teacher who has been blind since birth.

_____. *Supermouse.* Morrow, 1984. Nicole's sister becomes a rival for a part in a school play. She steps aside but her talents don't go unnoticed.

_____. *What If They Saw Me Now?* Delacorte, 1982. Jamie becomes a ballet dancer against his better judgment. He takes the place of an injured dancer and likes it but he doesn't want his friends to see him in tights.

_____. *You Two.* Morrow, 1984. Elizabeth goes to a new school where she meets classmates very different from herself.

Uttley, Alison. *Traveler in Time.* Viking, 1964. Penelope goes back to the days of Queen Elizabeth I. She sees the re-enactment of Anthony Babington's plot to save Mary, Queen of Scots.

Valencak, Hannelore. *Tangled Web.* Morrow, 1978. Annie daydreams and creates fantasies about a ruined mill and a treasure there. She tells Josepha about it and when her fantasies seem to come true she is upset because of all the trouble caused.

Vance, Marguerite. *Jeptha and the New People.* Dutton, 1960. Jeptha waits for the summer visitors. He is glad to see a boy his own age. At summer's end they are family when their parents marry.

Van der Veer, Judy. *Higher Than the Arrow.* Golden Gate, 1969. Franci, 12, lives at the Indian Mission. She experiences prejudices but is also aware of her own prejudice. There are mean people in all walks of life; she must make her own way.

_____. *Hold the Rein Free.* Golden Gate, 1966. Kiki, a Mexican-American boy, and his friend Army hide a horse so its unborn foal will not be destroyed by its owner.

Vande Veldi, Vivian. *Hidden Magic.* Crown, 1985. Princess Jennifer is lost in the magic forest. She seeks help from a sorcerer to fight off the evil witch.

Vander Els, Betty. *Bombers Moon.* Farrar, 1985. When Japan invades China, Ruth and Simeon, missionary children, are evacuated for safety's sake. They are not reunited with their parents for four years.

_____. *Leaving Point.* Farrar, 1987. Ruth's parents are missionaries. The Communist Revolution has brought changes and Ruth can no longer be friends with a Chinese girl.

Van Etten, Teresa. *Dead Kachina Man.* Sunstone, 1986. A Pueblo Indian Kachina carver is killed and Rios is called to investigate. He finds blackmail, drugs and more murders.

Van Iterson, Siny. *In the Spell of the Past.* Morrow, 1975. Orlando looks for answers about his father's death five years before. Clues are uncovered one by one until a solution is reached.

_____. *Spirits of Chocamata.* Morrow, 1977. Two boys are on the island of Curacao. There is an escaped prisoner they help to capture.

Van Laan, Nancy. *Rainbow Crow.* Knopf, 1989. A legend of how Crow brought fire to Earth and its people.

Van Leeuwen, Jean. *Benjy and the Power of Zingies.* Dial, 1982. Benjy doesn't want to be the town's weakling, the one everyone picks on. He sees an ad for a breakfast cereal that will build one's body and he goes for it.

_____. *Benjy in Business.* Dial, 1983. Benjy needs money for a fielder's mitt, to improve his game. He goes into several businesses: lemonade, car and/or dog wash, selling old toys, pulling weeds, etc.

_____. *Benjy, the Football Hero.* Dial, 1985. Benjy plays great football. He is the class star. But a challenge is coming: Alex and his boys against Benjy, Case the Ace and Killer Kelly (a girl).

_____. *Dear Mom, You're Ruining My Life.* Dial, 1989. Sam and her mother get through a year of Sam falling in love with Brian, towering above her dancing class, writing notes to her mother, getting notes from her father, etc., etc., etc.

_____. *Great Cheese Conspiracy.* Random, 1969. A gang of mice, Marvin, Fats and Raymond, invade the nearest cheese store. They have narrow escapes, Fats trips the alarm and they are caught. It comes out okay even though Marvin doesn't like it.

_____. *Great Christmas Kidnapping.* Dial, 1975. Macy's Santa Claus has been kidnapped by Gimbel's Santa Claus. Marvin, Fats and Raymond (mice) send a letter to the police, using words clipped from a newspaper and giving them leads, and Santa is rescued.

_____. *Great Rescue Operation.* Dial, 1982. Marvin and Raymond have lost Fats to a person who bought a doll carriage with him in it. These mice dream up fantastic schemes for his rescue.

_____. *I Was a 98-Pound Duckling.* Dial, 1972. Kathy, an insecure 13-year-old, copes with growing up.

_____. *Seems Like This Road Goes on Forever.* Dial, 1979. The daughter of a minister needs professional help to learn to separate her wants from the expectation of her domineering parents.

Van Steenwyk, Elizabeth. *Rivals on Ice.* Whitman, 1978. Tucher and Sara are skating rivals. They have another thing in common: problems with their mothers. Tucher's is divorced and uninterested in Tucher's skating. Sara's is ambitious and domineering.

_____. *Three Dog Winter.* Walker, 1987.

Scott doesn't get along with his stepbrother, Brad. Brad runs away and Scott and his team of malamute dogs find him. This helps them understand the problems of two merging families.

Van Stockum, Hilda. *Cottage at Bantry Bay.* Viking, 1968. Francie was born with a clubfoot. His mother told him that greatness comes from the brain and the heart, not the feet.

_____. *Friendly Gables.* Viking, 1960. Twin boys are born to the Mitchells and they have a nurse called Miss Thorpe who is very straitlaced. But the Mitchells will always have fun.

_____. *Mago's Flute.* Viking, 1966. Mago plays flute and helps call together the goat herd that was scattered by a storm. The setting is in Africa.

_____. *Penengro.* Farrar, 1972. Rory runs away and makes a home with the gypsies.

_____. *Winged Watchman.* Farrar, 1962. A Dutch family live in a mill called The Watchman during World War II and the German occupation. Two young boys rescue a British airman and assist in underground activities.

Van Woerkuna, Dorothy. *Pearl in the Egg.* Crowell, 1980. Pearl and Gavin are orphans. They join a troop of traveling entertainers. The setting is 13th century England.

Vardeman, Robert. *Road to the Stars.* Harper, 1988. The Earth is overcrowded and people are looking for another planet to colonize. Some exploration, accidents, and mystery.

Varney, Joyce. *Half-Time Gypsy.* Bobbs, 1968. Joey lives with a guardian and longs to run away and live with a gypsy group to whom he has always felt an attraction. He finds it's not all fun and decides to be a "half-time gypsy."

_____. *Magic Maker.* Bobbs, 1966. Tym is friends with half-time gypsy Joe. They are as mischievous as any two boys and sometimes pay a price for their antics. But Tym has a chance to get out of the coal mines and get an education.

Vaughan-Jackson, Genevieve. *Carramore.* Hastings, 1968. Anne, 11, lives in Ireland during that country's Civil War. She lives on a farm where she and her brother are protected from the coming war and get involved in a light mystery.

Veglahn, Nancy. *Fellowship of the Seven Stars.* Abingdon, 1981. Mazie is a good girl while her brother Rich is always in trouble. Mazie joins a group of Messengers of God only to find they are not what they appear. She must break away.

_____. *Follow the Golden Goose.* Addison, 1970. Neb's father is in Dakota Territory as a carpenter, not a gold seeker. Ned has many adventures including bringing cats to sell for $10.00 each to the lonely prospectors.

Venable, Alan. *Hurry the Crossing.* Lippincott, 1974. Mfupi and Dafu are stranded at sea in a small sailboat that lost a sail; the two are rescued. Mfupi sells wood carvings to tourists and also sets up an illegal gambling game. They are the African Huck and Tom.

Venn, Mary. *Skin Diving Mystery.* Hastings, 1964. Four boys and a girl are the Skin Diving Club. They find a mystery as they search for shells called Operation Rare Shell.

Verne, Jules. *Around the World in Eighty Days.* Dell, 1985. Phineas Fogg goes around the world on steamers, trains, elephants. He gets arrested in India, drugged in Hong Kong and tailed all the way by Detective Fixx who wants to arrest him.

————. *Long Vacation.* Holt, 1967. Fifteen boys are shipwrecked on a coast and must survive for two years before they are rescued.

————. *Twenty Thousand Leagues Under the Sea.* Rand McNally, 1922. Captain Nemo with his 1860 submarine has fantastic adventures.

Verney, John. *February's Road.* Holt, 1961. Feb and Mike, a journalist, try to find out what is behind the strange happenings on the road through Marsh Manor.

————. *Friday's Tunnel.* Holt, 1960. February and Friday are sister and brother. When their father disappears while traveling to Capria for a rare mineral, Caprium, they get involved. Friday's tunnel becomes a hiding place.

————. *Ismo.* Holt, 1964. There is a wide reaching plot to steal some art treasures by an international organization. The story is complete with secret agents and passwords.

Viereck, Phillip. *Summer I Was Lost.* Scholastic, 1965. Paul survives alone in the White Mountains after some harrowing experiences.

Vinge, Joan. *Psion.* Delacorte, 1982. An orphaned youth discovers he has telepathic powers and gets involved in all kinds of exciting experiences.

————. *Snow Queen.* Dial, 1980. Moon is a clone of the Queen. She knows she should rule the future; knows her destiny and the man who is fated to love both her and the Queen.

Vinke, Herman. *Short Life of Sophie Scholl.* Harper, 1984. Sophie was accused of treason when she urged Germans not to follow Hitler. She died by guillotine at the age of twenty-one.

Vipont, Elfrida. *Lark in the Morn.* Holt, 1951. Kit has a talent for singing. She enters a school where they discover and develop this talent. Her family, being Quakers, are not in favor of her singing.

————. *Lark on the Wing.* Holt, 1950. Kit studies music despite family resistance. She reaches her goal with the help of Papa Andrean and Terry.

————. *Pavilion.* Holt, 1969. Sue is interested in preserving old buildings. Martin wins over a half wild stray dog, Lion. They work together to save the Pavilion music structure.

Vivelo, Jackie. *Super Sleuth.* Putnam, 1985. Given a list of clues and suspects the reader can start eliminating suspects until the crime is solved. Ellen, Beagle's partner, solves them in this manner.

————. *Super Sleuth and the Bare Bones.* Putnam, 1988. Ellen and Beagle have found human bones buried many years ago, the disappeared college money and many other mysteries which the reader can solve from the information given.

Vogel, Ilse-Marget. *Dodo Every Day.* Harper, 1977. Dodo is the ideal grandmother by being amusing and loving every time she is needed.

————. *Farewell, Aunt Isabell.* Harper, 1979. Inge and Erika try to cheer up Aunt Isabell so she can get well. She is going to take them to Paris when she feels better, but they don't understand her illness.

————. *My Summer Brother.* Harper, 1981. Erika is away, and Dodo, her grandmother, is gone also. She meets Dieter, a twenty-year-old, and likes him right away. But so does her mother. She finds her "first love" is not a good one.

————. *My Twin Sister Erika.* Harper, 1976. Inge and Erika have a rocky relationship. One day she says in anger that she wishes Erika dead; later Erika dies of a disease and Inge feels guilty and misses her in spite of her jealousy.

————. *Tikhon.* Harper, 1984. Inge meets Tikhon, a Russian soldier, and a deep friendship begins between a soldier who is lonely away from home and a little girl. They have common interests and Inge thinks Tikhon can do anything.

Voight, Virginia. *Girl from Johnnycake Hill.* Prentice, 1961. Becky and her mother live on a farm in 1789. They contend with wild bears and baby cubs. They meet good and bad Indians, mysteriously get money from a former owner and are asked about rights to the farm.

Voigt, Cynthia. *Building Blocks.* Atheneum, 1984. Brann goes back in time to when his father was a little boy. He learns why his father is the way he is and comes to appreciate his strengths. A good father-son relationship book.

————. *Callender Papers.* Atheneum, 1983. Jean spends a summer cataloging the family papers. She finds the key to a mystery among the papers.

————. *Come a Stranger.* Atheneum, 1986. Mina, a black dancer, defended Dicey when she was accused of plagiarism in an earlier book. Tamar, a black friend from another book, who is now a minister, gets together with Mina when she needs help.

————. *Dicey's Song.* Atheneum, 1982. The four children find a home with their grandmother and Dicey must decide what she wants for herself and her brothers and sisters. Newbery winner, 1983.

————. *Homecoming.* Atheneum, 1981. Abandoned by their mother, four children begin a search for home, possibly with a great-aunt or maybe grandparents. Dicey holds the three children, Sammy, James and Maybeth, together.

————. *Izzy, Willy-Nilly.* Atheneum, 1986. Izzy is in an accident with Marco. She knows he was drinking and she knows she is going to lose a leg. She is bitter and resentful of her family and her friends.

_____. *Jackaroo*. Atheneum, 1985. Jackaroo is both Robin Hood and Superman. Only Gwen knows who he is and finds that out by accident.

_____. *Runner*. Atheneum, 1988. Bullet runs on the school team and is good but by helping his teammates he learns about running and about himself. Bullet and Tamer are in other books but here we read about earlier times.

_____. *Solitary Blue*. Atheneum, 1983. Jeff is torn between love for a deserted mother and a professor father. He gets to know them both better and decides. He meets Dicey in high school where they are both new students.

_____. *Sons from Afar*. Atheneum, 1987. James and Sammy are looking for their unknown father. James is determined to find the man that deserted them so long ago.

_____. *Tell Me If the Lovers Are Losers*. Atheneum, 1982. Niki, Ann and Hildy are best friends even though they are very different. They are roommates at college and learn more from each other than from school.

_____. *Tree by Leaf*. Atheneum, 1988. Clothilde's father is self isolated from the family. Her brother is close to his grandfather and Clothilde's farmland may need to be sold for needed money.

Von Canon, Claudia. *Inheritance*. Houghton, 1983. Miguel lives in 1580 during the Inquisition. He tries to avenge his father's suicide but eventually returns to what he considers his home, sets up a medical practice and marries.

Vonnegut, Kurt. *Cat's Cradle*. Dell, 1963. A new invention, ice-nine, is capable of destroying the world.

_____. *Deadeye Dick*. Delacorte, 1982. The usual cast of crazy characters with a sense of humor set in a serious story of technology gone mad and man's inhumanity to man.

_____. *Galapagos*. Delacorte, 1985. A small group of people on a cruise survive to evolve into the inhabitants of the world a million years later. The world is very different from today and so are the people.

_____. *Player Piano*. Delacorte, 1974. Paul is a man of the future. He is leading the perfect life. Everything is taken care of. So why is he trying to end it all?

Vosper, Alice. *Rags to Riches*. Avon, 1983. Julie Mahony is poor but oil is discovered on her parents' land and she becomes rich. She finds, after spending money like crazy, that money can't buy everything.

Wagner, Jane. *J.T.* Van Nostrand, 1969. Gamble lives in Harlem. His life is made bearable because of his portable radio, one of his most prized possessions. And the stray cat for whom he made a home.

Wahl, Jan. *Doctor Rabbit's Foundling*. Pantheon, 1977. Tiny Toad matures and leaves foster parents to go out on his own.

_____. *Furious Flycycle*. Delacorte, 1968. Melvin discovers what makes baseballs fly and he uses this information to build a flying machine with his bicycle. He rescues some relatives from hungry wolves.

_____. *SOS Bobomobile*. Delacorte, 1973. Marvin and his professor friend go undersea with their new invention: the bobomobile. They look for the Loch Ness monster.

Walden, Amelia. *My World's the Stage*. McGraw, 1964. Miranda is a successful actress but there is friction with some of the cast and loneliness. She has two young men courting her.

_____. *Same Scene, Different Place*. Lippincott, 1969. Chena is in trouble in her poor neighborhood and is sent to live with a wealthy family in Connecticut. She joins a band as a singer and becomes popular.

_____. *Stay to Win*. Lippincott, 1971. Dodie is the baseball team's captain but the new coach is a man who is gruff and "mean." Her boyfriend, Rip, is disliked by everyone and she begins to see why. Kurt then becomes her new boyfriend.

_____. *To Catch a Spy*. Westminster, 1964. Sally is asked to pose as Erika, an anti–American espionage suspect.

_____. *Walk in a Tall Shadow*. Lippincott, 1968. Steve's family is his problem. His father is two-faced and has a mistress; his brother, Paul, uses drugs and his brother Kerry is killed. He finds peace in photography.

_____. *When Love Speaks*. McGraw, 1961. Miranda's first job in the theatre teaches her about getting along with the rest of the cast and understanding herself.

_____. *Where Is My Heart?* Westminster, 1960. Carol needs to decide whether she should continue as a teacher or try the more glamorous theatre or literary world.

Waldorf, Mary. *One Thousand Camps*. Houghton, 1982. Chloe spends the summer with her uncle. She and Joaquin are transported back in time to when the Indians owned the land.

Waldron, Ann. *Blueberry Collection*. Dutton, 1981. Bessie finds a numbers game in town. She, Rachel and Bingo try to find out if the Mob is involved.

_____. *French Detection*. Dutton, 1979. Bessie answers an ad to spend a month in a French village. She improves her speaking French and helps a firm owner from being evicted. She also gets involved in an art smuggling ring.

_____. *House on Pendleton Block*. Hastings, 1975. Chrissie moves from Georgia to Texas and is not happy. She explores their rented mansion and finds more about its history and also finds a mystery.

_____. *Integration of Marv-Larkin Thornhill*. Dutton, 1975. Mary-Larkin attends an all black school and comes to like it. And she likes poetry. She makes a friend of Jimmi-Jo and sees her former friends as petty.

_____. *Scaredy Cat.* Dutton, 1978. Jan is afraid of kidnapping because of the Lindbergh case. She is kidnapped and put in a corn crib on a farm. She manages her own escape.

Wales, Robert. *Harry.* Watts, 1985. Harry and his friend, Bluey, drive 1500 head of cattle over 1200 miles of Australian desert. But they are rustlers not cowboys.

Walker, Alice. *To Hell with Dying.* Harcourt, 1988. Old Mr. Sweet is dying but the Walker family isn't going to let him do it.

Walker, Diana. *Dragon Hill.* Houghton, 1962. William and Mary befriend an old hermit. A hurricane hits the coast and the hermit helps them survive even though he loses most of his belongings.

_____. *Hundred Thousand Dollar Farm.* Harper, 1977. A young abandoned boy finds a family to stay with.

_____. *Mother Wants a Horse.* Abelard, 1978. Joanna must give up some of her horse time to studies. She runs away on a "borrowed" horse and is seriously hurt. She is forced to study and when she recovers sees life from a different angle.

_____. *Mystery of Black Gut.* Abelard, 1969. Roberta senses something wrong in her family's rented house. There is a ghost, a gruesome black thing, which is unseen but can be heard as a chilling laughter.

_____. *Year of the Horse.* Abelard, 1975. Joanna wants to learn to ride. She also wants to meet John Holmes. But her horse, Horse, is not as regal and impressive as John's. She has a fabulous year anyway.

Walker, Mary. *Brad's Box.* Atheneum, 1988. Brad spends a year with Rosie's family. He has a small locked box. When he leaves for college he writes a letter explaining about the box.

_____. *Maggot.* Atheneum, 1980. A black woman (Elephant) and a young dancer (Maggot) develop an unusual friendship. Josh, an animal warden, is also included in the friendship.

_____. *To Catch a Zombi.* Atheneum, 1979. Vance earns money to move North and his mother spends it to protect them from voodoo. He saves again but uses it to buy Shanta's baby from slavery.

_____. *Year of the Cafeteria.* Bobbs, 1971. Azure is in a new school but she gets a job in the cafeteria where she can meet everyone. She takes good advantage of it.

Walker, Pamela. *Twyla.* Prentice, 1973. Twyla is retarded and writes letters to Wally, a college freshman she loves. He never answers and she dies.

Wallace, Barbara. *Barrel in the Basement.* Atheneum, 1985. Pudding is an elf who lives in a barrel in Noah's basement. He can do great deeds like the elves of the past.

_____. *Claudia.* Follett, 1969. Claudia resents being made into a "lady." Her friend Janice is into boys and clothes. Claudia plays rough with her young friend, Duffy. She is suspected of stealing but is cleared.

_____. *Claudia and Duffy.* Follett, 1982. Claudia has many friends but Duffy has only Claudia. This causes problems for Claudia.

_____. *Contest Kid Strikes Again.* Abingdon, 1980. Harvey loves anything that's free. 12 chickens! 575 marbles! His wild escapades and funny dilemmas don't always work out. But Hawkins is always there to help when needed.

_____. *Hawkins.* Smith, 1977. Hawkins, a gentleman's gentleman, seems to be around when needed. Harvey gets into one scrape after another but Hawkins is there to rescue him. Harvey won his services for one month.

_____. *Hawkins and the Soccer Solution.* Abingdon, 1981. Harvey and his friends raise money to solve the problem of their losing soccer team. Hawkins, "a gentleman's gentleman," helps by becoming coach.

_____. *Hello, Claudia.* Follett, 1982. Claudia and Janice are best friends when Janice moves away. She finds a friend in Duffy even though he is younger and a boy.

_____. *Interesting Thing That Happened at Perfect Acres.* Atheneum, 1988. Perfecta must live by RULES at Perfect Acres but when she meets Puck they change Perfect Acres and its owner, Mr. Snoot. It is now a happy place and the books are not being changed.

_____. *Miss Switch to the Rescue.* Abingdon, 1981. Rupert's friend Amelia is kidnapped. Miss Switch, the witch of the fifth grade, comes along just in time.

_____. *Peppermints in the Parlor.* Atheneum, 1980. Emily's Aunt and Uncle Twice are being held captive in 1890 San Francisco. Emily and Kipper work to set things right.

_____. *Trouble with Miss Switch.* Archway, 1981. Miss Switch is the fifth grade teacher. Because of her unusual ways and because it is such a natural for the kids, she is named Miss Switch, the witch.

Wallace, Bill. *Beauty.* Holiday, 1988. Luke learns to ride Beauty. He talks to the old horse about his feelings. Beauty is injured and must be shot.

_____. *Danger in Quicksand Pond.* Holiday, 1989. Ben and Jake look for buried treasure in a swamp. They fight alligators, quicksand and a murderer.

_____. *Dog Called Kitty.* Holiday, 1980. Richy is afraid of dogs. He was once attacked by a rabid one. He finally takes pity on a motherless, hungry pup and overcomes his fear.

_____. *Ferret in the Bedroom, Lizards in the Fridge.* Holiday, 1986. Liz is running for class president. She is trying to make friends and she is coping with strange animals her zoologist father keeps in the house.

_____. *Red Dog.* Holiday, 1987. Adam lives in Wyoming in 1860. He escapes from gold claimers and leads them on a chase in the mountains. He is injured, as well as his dog, before a mountain lion kills the villains.

_____. *Shadow on the Snow*. Holiday, 1985. A blizzard isolates a boy and his grandfather. Tom must get help but his horse is pregnant and gives birth. He must kill the panther that is threatening them.

_____. *Snot Stew*. Holiday, 1989. Mama cat moves her kittens out into the world in an amusing way.

_____. *Trapped in Death Cave*. Holiday, 1984. Brian, 11, and his friend, Gary, look for the treasure told to them by Gary's now dead grandfather. Gary is kidnapped. Brian and Mrs. Becker look for him and are trapped in Death Cave.

Wallace, Luke. *Blue Wings*. Bradbury, 1982. Mandy gets involved with stopping illegal traffic of exotic South American birds.

Wallace-Brodeur, Ruth. *Callie's Way*. Atheneum, 1984. Callie is a minister's daughter. She has a teacher who is a bully and is fighting for more independence.

_____. *One April Vacation*. Atheneum, 1981. Kate is sure she is going to die within the week. She does all the things she's wanted to do (save a cat from mean boys and beat her sister at badminton).

_____. *Steps in Time*. Atheneum, 1986. Evan, 16, spends the summer on an island where she learns about fishing and diving and . . . love.

Wallin, Luke. *Ceremony of the Panther*. Bradbury, 1987. John, a 16-year-old Indian, faces the dilemma of family traditions versus modern world attitudes.

_____. *In the Shadow of the Wind*. Bradbury, 1984. A serious, sad story of the conflict between the white settlers and the Creek Indians. There are deceit and betrayal.

_____. *Redneck Poacher's Son*. Bradbury, 1981. Jesse's father is a cheat and maybe killer; his brothers are KKK members; he thinks about killing his father (but doesn't). He is a kind, trusting young man surrounded by dishonesty and cruelty.

_____. *Slavery Ghosts*. Bradbury, 1983. Jake, 13, and Livy, 12, set free the ghosts of slaves which are imprisoned in a below world by a 100-year-old contract with their master.

Wallin, Marie. *Tangles*. Delacorte, 1977. Ingeborg is a liberated girl with a horse named Tangles. Her friend Anna and she "fall in love." They become more than friends but never lovers.

Walsh, Jill P. *Chance Child*. Farrar, 1978. A story that moves back and forth through time showing the horrors of child labor practices of the Industrial Revolution.

_____. *Fireweed*. Farrar, 1970. Julie and Bill are on their own during World War II's London blitz. Julie is almost killed and their shelter is ruined. They help each other survive and fall in love but her family later breaks it up.

_____. *Gaffer Samson's Luck*. Farrar, 1984.

James makes friends with Angey and old Gaffer Samson. He looks for a black stone Gaffer hid seventy years earlier.

_____. *Goldengrove*. Farrar, 1972. Paul and Madge found out they were brother and sister, not cousins as they thought. They were separated in infancy when their parents divorced.

_____. *Green Book*. Farrar, 1982. Patti brings a book on a spaceship that is taking her from the dying Earth to a new planet. The book becomes very important.

_____. *Huffler*. Farrar, 1975. Harry becomes a huffler (a boat man) for a week. She joins a boat crew but they return her for fear of being accused of kidnapping. She learns hard work and values.

_____. *Parcel of Patterns*. Farrar, 1983. In 1665 an English town is torn apart by the plague. Mall loses all her loved ones but finds love anew when the ordeal is over. Based on facts, this is a strong story.

_____. *Toolmaker*. Seabury, 1973. A young man in prehistoric times becomes a toolmaker for his tribe, and finds that this special skill is the key to his survival.

_____. *Torch*. Farrar, 1987. Cal and Dio are to marry. An old man gives them the Ancient Torch. They set off to find its meaning.

_____. *Unleaving*. Farrar, 1976. Madge inherits Goldengrove from her grandmother and decides to rent it. Madge meets Patrick and falls in love.

Walter, Mildred. *Girl on the Outside*. Lothrop, 1982. Sophia is a popular, rich white student and Eva is a bright, pretty black student. Sophia, in spite of prejudice, decides to side with Eva and protect her from white violence.

_____. *Have a Happy. . . .* Lothrop, 1989. Chris's birthday falls on Christmas and he feels cheated. But he is happy with the carving he is making for Kwanzaa, an African-American celebration.

_____. *Justin and the Best Biscuits in the World*. Lothrop, 1986. Justin lives in a house full of women and doesn't feel he should do any "women's work." Then he goes to visit his grandfather's farm and sees things differently.

_____. *Lillie of Watts: A Birthday Discovery*. Ritchie, 1969. Lillie lives in a ghetto. She is allowed to "babysit" a cat but lets it get out and must see to its return. She sees reality as she searches the streets for the cat.

_____. *Lillie of Watts Takes a Giant Step*. Doubleday, 1971. Lillie starts junior high and makes a new friend. She experiences jealousy, envy, friendship and all the things a shy, poor girl goes through in a black/white world.

_____. *Mariah Keeps Cool*. Bradbury, 1990. Mariah spends the summer practicing and competing in diving. She is also planning a surprise party for her sister, Lynn. But Denise comes and is spoiling everything.

————. *Mariah Loves Rock*. Bradbury, 1988. Mariah is going to be visited by a half sister and is apprehensive.

————. *Trouble's Child*. Lothrop, 1985. Martha, 14, is expected to become a midwife like her grandma. Martha wants to get an education and leave the island. She has divided loyalties but gets her way.

Walters, Hugh. *Blue Aura*. Faber, 1979. Chris and his usual crew contact Aliens who landed on Guernsey. They save the visitors from a general who wants to blow up the island in order to kill the invaders.

————. *Destination Mars*. Criterion, 1964. Tony has joined Chris, Serge and Morrey in a trip to Mars where they encounter intelligent life in the form of lights. They predict that the humans on Earth will mutate the same way.

————. *Expedition Venus*. Criterion, 1963. The moon has been conquered and now Venus is next for Chris, Serge and Morrey. A mold, introduced from Venus, is harming the earth and an antidote must be found by going back to Venus for a spore.

————. *First Contact*. Nelson, 1973. Commander Chris and his crew are assigned to discover the source of radio signals from Uranus. They land and find beings far superior than the humans on Earth.

————. *First on the Moon*. Criterion, 1960. Both the Americans (Chris Godfrey) and the Russians (Serge Smyslow) send a manned rocket to the moon. The two men are rivals but must cooperate if they are to survive.

————. *Journey to Jupiter*. Criterion, 1966. Chris, Serge, Morrey and Tony are headed for Jupiter but their spaceship is traveling too fast. They must make a crash landing on one of the moons.

————. *Mission to Mercury*. Criterion, 1965. Chris, Serge, Tony and Morrey are going to Mercury. They add Gail, a telepathic twin, to their team. They face solar radiation, and extreme cold.

————. *Mohole Menace*. Criterion, 1968. A crew of subterranauts explore a huge underground cavern miles beneath the earth's crust. One of them is trapped and attacked by a large egg shaped fungi. He is rescued at the last minute.

————. *Outpost on the Moon*. Criterion, 1962. Chris, Morrey and Serge are to establish a permanent base on the moon. They face a sinister mist, loss of supplies and damaged apparatus. After close escapes with death they have some success.

————. *Passage to Pluto*. Nelson, 1973. Serge and others are going to Pluto to see if anything lies beyond. Chris is at ground control and sees danger, so takes off in a spaceship to save his friends.

————. *Spaceship to Saturn*. Criterion, 1967. A successful trip to Saturn by Chris and his

companions by use of hypothermia. Gail and Gill are involved again, Gail on board and Gill at ground control.

————. *Terror by Satellite*. Criterion, 1964. Tony's commander has gone mad and wants to destroy the Earth. By using an illegal ham radio Tony contacts Chris Godfrey who lands on the satellite observatory.

Walton, Todd. *Inside Moves*. Doubleday, 1978. Jerry was born with one leg shorter than the other. But he likes to play basketball and he goes to all the games he can. One day, when he was angry at a player, he challenged him to a one-on-one game.

Waltrip, Lela. *Purple Hills*. Longmans, 1961. Susan has new friends, new life and new problems: ranch vs. settler feuds and family squabbles.

————. *White Harvest*. Longmans, 1960. Susan and her family are migrant workers. She faces hard work and poverty. Her father gets a land grant in New Mexico and she will at last live in a house with four walls, solid and comfortable.

Wangerin, Walter. *Book of the Dun Cow*. Harper, 1978. A sophisticated fairy tale of duty, love and death.

————. *Potter, Come Fly to the First of the Earth*. Cook, 1985. Potter's friend dies and he can't understand why. An oriole comes to his window and takes him on a journey in which he comes to understand.

Warburg, Sandol. *On the Way Home*. Houghton, 1973. Boy and Bear search for food and the meaning of the star, the shell and the flower in the boy's dreams. They battle evil Monkey King; and free good Twain to become Prince.

Ware, Leon. *Rebellious Orphan*. Westminster, 1964. Bill lives with three aunts who make his life uncomfortable and depressing. He has friends and a number of interests but he wishes his home life was better.

————. *Threatening Fog*. Westminster, 1962. Eben stays with his uncle who is a seafarer but he gets seasick.

Warfel, Diantha. *On Guard*. Dodd, 1961. Phil helps organize a fencing team because he needs the credit to qualify for a scholarship. He learns to like the sport and participation helps him, personally.

————. *Violin Case Case*. Dutton, 1978. Bax plays violin. His aunt gives him a valuable violin to try out. Someone tries to steal it.

Warner, Gertrude. *Benny Uncovers a Mystery*. Whitman, 1976. Henry and Benny Alden take summer jobs at a department store and strange letters and extra merchandise create a mystery that seems to point to the brothers.

————. *Bicycle Mystery*. Whitman, 1970. The Boxcar Children are on a bicycle trip to visit Aunt Jane. They stop and do some chores and stay in an abandoned house. They are followed by a stray dog that plays a big role in the mystery.

————. *Bus Station Mystery*. Whitman, 1974. The Boxcar Children are on their way to a science hobby fair. There is a fight at the bus station about air pollution and a paint factory. They help find a solution that is good for all.

————. *Caboose Mystery*. Whitman, 1966. The Boxcar Children and their grandfather travel in what was once a circus train car. The mystery is about a lost necklace.

————. *Houseboat Mystery*. Whitman, 1967. The Boxcar Children are on a houseboat. A large black car roars through the village; horses that appear to be well cared for look starved. They help capture two crooks and free the village of them.

————. *Mystery Behind the Wall*. Whitman, 1973. The Boxcar Children and Rory follow clues from a sewing shop to a doll house to a clock where they find the treasure of coins.

————. *Mystery in the Sand*. Whitman, 1971. The Boxcar Children are going to spend the summer in a beach house. They find a locket with a picture of a cat and initials R.L. They find information about the owner and the Tower House.

————. *Schoolhouse Mystery*. Whitman, 1965. The Boxcar Children stay at an island fishing village. This time the mystery is a crooked coin dealer. They also set up a school to teach the island children.

————. *Surprise Island*. Scott, 1951. The Boxcar Children spend the summer finding and exploring an Indian cave. They also find a previously unknown cousin.

————. *Tree House Mystery*. Whitman, 1969. The Boxcar Children help the new neighbor boys to build a tree house. They find a lost spyglass and a secret room in the attic.

————. *Woodshed Mystery*. Whitman, 1962. The Boxcar Children are involved in a double mystery: one about Aunt Jane in her youth and the other going even farther back to the early days of the Revolutionary War.

————. *Yellow House Mystery*. Whitman, 1954. The Boxcar Children live with a wealthy grandfather and are involved in yet another mystery.

Warnlof, Anna. *Upstairs*. Harcourt, 1963. Frederika and her mother move to a rooming house. She meets Martin and we get two points of view of each situation, hers and his.

Warren, Billy. *Black Lobo*. Golden Gate, 1967. A story of a youngster raising and training a black wolf as a pet. He knows he must eventually give him up and does so during mating season.

Warren, Cathy. *Roxanne Bookman: Live at Five*. Bradbury, 1988. Roxanna doesn't follow instructions and loses a game for her Pony League team. Claudia, of the opposing team, is gloating. In a television contest Claudia is again the challenger.

Wartski, Maureen. *Boat to Nowhere*. West-minster, 1980. This is an adventure type story about the plight of the Vietnamese "boat people."

————. *Long Way from Home*. Westminster, 1980. Kien comes to America from Vietnam. He does not adjust well. He moves to another town but still faces prejudice. He becomes a hero by saving the town's leader from a fire.

————. *My Name Is Nobody*. Walker, 1988. Rob, 14, attempts suicide but is stopped by Kurt who offers him a home. They both like sailing and become friends.

Warwick, Dolores. *Learn to Say Goodbye*. Farrar, 1971. Lucy's alcoholic mother is unable to care for her and her little sister, so they live at St. Michael's Home where Lucy is not very happy.

Waters, John. *Summer of the Seals*. Warne, 1978. Jaimy finds an injured seal that later dies. She wants to know who is shooting them.

————. *Victory Chimes*. Warne, 1976. Johnny goes to Cape Cod. An Argentinian freighter has an accident and Admiral Flame and Johnny get up money to salvage it.

Watson, James. *Talking in Whispers*. Knopf, 1984. Chile is ruled by a military dictator and all civil rights are restricted. A thoughtful novel.

Watson, Jane. *Case of the Vanishing Spaceship*. Coward, 1982. Rick and his father investigate mysterious signals coming from a UFO that has been earlier sighted.

Watson, Sally. *Hornet's Nest*. Holt, 1968. Ronald and Lauchlin rebel against the British. They are sent to Virginia and join the rebels in the Revolutionary movement. They return to Scotland more mature and understanding.

————. *Jode*. Holt, 1969. Jode is a young "lady" who hates slavery and the similar role of women. She is sent to Jamaica and then returned on a ship carrying slaves. She frees some and is being punished when pirates board ship.

————. *Linnet*. Dutton, 1971. Linnet runs away and is "rescued" by Colby, a thief and trainer of thieves. He used her in a plot against Queen Elizabeth.

————. *Other Sandals*. Holt, 1966. Two Israeli children survive the Israeli war and its tragic consequences and try being friendly with the enemy.

Watson, Simon. *No Man's Land*. Morrow, 1976. Alan tries to save his village from the Giant, its ultimate robot. He escapes from school and with Jay and the "general," he stops the Giant.

————. *Partisan*. Macmillan, 1973. Will and Phil meet Dom who is handicapped. They form a club that is expanded to a stealing gang. Dom tries to stop it but is not strong enough. It ends tragically.

Wayne, Jennifer. *Sprout*. McGraw, 1976. Tilly, Sprout's sister, has lost her pet rabbit, given to her as a birthday present. But Sprout takes charge and swears to find it.

————. *Sprout and the Magician*. McGraw, 1976. Sprout attends his sister's birthday party looking forward to the food but little else. However, Merl, the magician, has made Tilly's rabbit disappear and chaos takes over.

Wayne, Kyra. *Witches of Barguzin.* Nelson, 1975. Nobleman Vasiby and his mother are exiles in Siberia. Peasant Lubasha and her mother are thought to be witches. Vasiby and Lubasha fall in love.

Weaver, Harriett. *Beloved Was Bahamas: A Steer to Remember.* Vanguard, 1974. Brad raised Bahamas from a calf and he is a pet. His father wants to sell it for much needed money. But a flood sweeps the Bahamas downstream.

_____. *Frosty: A Raccoon to Remember.* Chronicle, 1973. Frosty is a raccoon found by a boy and taken home. He is only a month old and lost his mother. He soon learns how to open doors, wash hair, charm the dog and drive everyone crazy.

Weaver, Stella. *Poppy in the Corn.* Pantheon, 1961. Teresa, a war orphan, and three other children are left to fend for themselves. They have many conflicts but come to understand each other better.

Webb, Christopher. *Ann and Hope Mutiny.* Funk & Wagnall, 1963. Paul's father is lost at sea; Paul signs up for a whaling trip. He hits storms and violence but ends his search on a South Sea island.

Webb, Sharon. *Earth Song.* Atheneum, 1983. Earthsong can achieve immortality, but creativity is crushed. This is a high price to pay. Creativity must be restored.

_____. *Earthchild.* Atheneum, 1982. When the Earth becomes immortal, through the Mouai Gari process, a young musician realizes he may live forever but his creativity is going to gradually fade away. This can't be.

_____. *Ram Song.* Atheneum, 1984. A strange beam on the planet Aulos disorients people by interrupting a yearly festival. Kurt Kraus, now immortal, and his starship, Ram, are called to help.

Weber, Judith. *Lights, Camera, Cats.* Lothrop, 1978. Elizabeth, 12, prepares her cats for an audition for a television commercial.

Weber, Lenora. *Angel in Heavy Shoes.* Crowell, 1968. Katie Rose enters a play writing contest. But her family activities always interfere with her work, especially Stacy and her boyfriend, Bruce. She appears to have nothing but problems.

_____. *Beany and the Beckoning Road.* Crowell, 1952. Beany and her brother go to California because she needs a change after breaking up with Norbett. They are short of money and have a strange, motherly, non-paying guest.

_____. *Beany Has a Secret Life.* Crowell, 1955. Beany joins a secret club but decides she doesn't like it. Her old boyfriend, Norbett, is away and she meets a new friend, Andy.

_____. *Beany Malone.* Crowell, 1948. Beany is a sophomore in high school. She is not in the beauty queen set nor in the intellect one. But she is a doer and has friends.

_____. *Bright Star Falls.* Crowell, 1959. Johnny is going with a girl with a questionable reputation. Beany is editor of the school paper and defends her brother. Her friend Andy is home from the Marines but is changed.

_____. *Come Back, Wherever You Are.* Crowell, 1969. Beany Malone is married and takes in the orphaned son of an old friend. She and Carlton have two children of their own and Jodey is a disturbed child who threatens her own family.

_____. *Don't Call Me Katie Rose.* Crowell, 1964. Katie Rose wants to be called Kathleen. She is Stacy's older sister. Her mother plays piano in a night club for extra money. Katie Rose is embarrassed by this.

_____. *Happy Birthday Dear Beany.* Crowell, 1957. Beany, 17, still thinks of her old flame, Norbett. But she dates Hank and sees a lot of her friend, Miggs.

_____. *Hello, My Love, Goodbye.* Crowell, 1971. Stacy is a senior in high school and has lots of friends, especially one boy named Bruce. He is from a background very different from Stacy's.

_____. *How Long Is Always?* Crowell, 1970. Stacy gets a summer job driving her employer around his ranch. She is courted by two boys from the community and finds herself involved deeper in the community than she wanted to be.

_____. *I Met a Boy I Used to Know.* Crowell, 1967. Katie Rose is a junior. She meets Gil who has transferred to her school from California. Although he is an only child and Katie Rose has brothers and sisters they both have mother problems.

_____. *Leave It to Beany.* Crowell, 1950. Beany writes a column for the lovelorn in the newspaper. She has ups and downs within her family but copes well.

_____. *Make a Wish for Me.* Crowell, 1956. Beany renews her friendship with Norbett and with a new girl in school, Dulcie. Dulcie flirts with Norbett even though she knows he's dating Beany.

_____. *Meet the Malones.* Crowell, 1953. Beany Malone's family includes her brother Johnny, 15, her sister Mary Fred, 16, herself, 13, plus her mother and father. They are a close knit family.

_____. *More the Merrier.* Crowell, 1958. Beany's family is away and she takes in boarders during the summer. She does it to make money but she lets shy Lisa pay less and lets Ty stay free because she likes him.

_____. *New and Different Summer.* Crowell, 1966. Katie Rose is left in charge of all five of the other children. She disregards her mother's "from scratch" cooking and buys from the frozen foods section of the store.

_____. *Pick a New Dream*. Crowell, 1961. Beany graduates from high school and doesn't get the summer job she was promised. Andy is not sympathetic because he has problems of his own. She finds solace in Carlton from next door.

_____. *Something Borrowed, Something Blue*. Crowell, 1963. Beany and Carlton are to be married. This is the story about how this warm, tight-knit family is involved in this happy event. It could turn out to be very posh but results in being very simple.

_____. *Sometimes a Stranger*. Crowell, 1972. Bruce's parents don't like Stacy. They offered Bruce a new car if he would stop seeing her. Stacy is furious but a separation changes Bruce and Stacy sees other boys.

_____. *Tarry Awhile*. Crowell, 1962. Beany realizes that it is Carlton that she truly loves. She is engaged and wants to marry as all her friends are doing. But Carlton wants to wait until he graduates before getting married.

_____. *Winds of March*. Crowell, 1965. Katie Rose is over her crush on Bruce. His failing grades prompt her to tutor him. Her crush is renewed. But it's Stacy, her sister, that he likes. She doesn't get a role in the school play!

Webster, Jean. *Daddy Long Legs*. Meredith, 1966. A re-issue of a favorite classic. Judy Abbott, an orphan, is sent to college by an unknown benefactor known only as Daddy-Long-Legs. The story is told through her letters to him.

_____. *Dear Enemy*. Gregg, 1915. Judy's friend, Sally, becomes superintendent of Judy's old orphanage and starts reforms. Again told in a series of letters to Judy and "Dear Enemy" the physician.

Webster, Joanne. *Gypsy Gift*. Lodestar, 1982. Cassie gets a gift of second sight from gypsy Rollo. In exchange she becomes his girl. She finds someone else but can't be released from Rollo.

_____. *Love Genie*. Elsenier, 1978. Jennie now has a genie to help her but it makes her life more complicated and not easier.

Weddle, Ferris. *Blazing Mountain*. Watts, 1961. Clint loves the outdoors. He makes friends with Phil. Both of them are caught in a forest fire.

Wees, Frances. *Treasure of Echo Valley*. Abelard, 1964. The five Patterson children become involved in an intrigue with two mysterious men, buried treasure and a kidnapping.

Weik, Mary. *Jazz Man*. Atheneum, 1967. A crippled, lonely boy in Harlem finds much to do when the Jazz Man moves across the court.

Weiman, Eiveen. *It Takes Brains*. Atheneum, 1982. Barbara is usually in trouble and doesn't know why; her parents are too busy with their careers as surgeons to pay attention to her, but an understanding teacher changes her life by challenging her.

_____. *Which Way Courage*. Atheneum, 1981. Courage is an Amish girl who questions her beliefs and wants to live in the wider world but doesn't want to hurt her family.

Weinberg, Larry. *Curse*. Bantam, 1984. Dana has been having the same nightmare for years. Now it's getting worse. She knows she will die a horrible death on her 17th birthday and it's only three days away.

Weir, Joan. *Career Girl*. Free Frog, 1980. Patti fails to return Sharon's phone call and Sharon, a polio victim, falls. Patti spends time with her, neglecting her ballet practice, so she doesn't get the position she wanted.

Weir, Rosemary. *Heirs of Ashton Manor*. Dial, 1965. Sebastian became lord of Ashton Manor when his father died. The manor was inherited and some people are trying to get it away from Sebastian and his sister.

_____. *Mystery of the Black Sheep*. Criterion, 1963. Mark and Caroline are left alone because the rest of the family has car problems. They encounter a gang of sheep stealers and a winter snowstorm.

_____. *Robert's Rescued Railroad*. Watts, 1961. Robert's father and Dily's brother would lose their job if the railroad closed because the mine was closing. They devised a plan to show the historic value of the line as a tourist attraction.

_____. *Star and the Flame*. Ariel, 1964. Tom escapes the plague and finds refuge at the farm home of his grandparents. He tries to find out if any of his family is alive after the London fire of 1666.

_____. *Three Red Herrings*. Nelson, 1972. Eva's father dies and she must save the family from disaster. In five years she brought fame and fortune to the family.

Weiss-Sonnenburg, Hedwig. *Plum Blossom and Kai Lin*. Watts, 1960. Plum Blossom was sold as a slave and fell in love with Kai Lin, the oldest son of the slave owner. War and disaster separate them but they find each other and marry.

Welch, Ronald. *Bowmen of Crecy*. Criterion, 1966. Hugh is an outlaw in the 14th century. He uses the long bow, a weapon that needs great training to use. He moves from adventure to adventure including the Battle of Crete.

_____. *Escape from France*. Criterion, 1960. Richard comes to France to rescue relatives facing execution during the French Revolution of 1789–99. There are duels, captures and escapes, and the horrors of the war.

_____. *For the King*. Criterion, 1962. Neil Carey, the youngest Carey, is a royalist in the English civil war. He is captured and escapes. His brother is captured and is an invalid. He is finally exiled on a false charge.

_____. *Hawk*. Criterion, 1969. This saga of the Carey family is about Harry, lieutenant of the Dragon. On a trading trip to Spain the ship is almost seized; he captures two Brazilian ships and he meets and saves the Queen.

_____. *Mohawk Valley*. Criterion, 1958.

Alan is dismissed from Cambridge for dueling and comes to America to manage his father's estates. He faces fur tradesmen, hostile Indians, and strange, rough land.

————. *Nicholas Carey*. Criterion, 1963. This Carey story is about Nicholas on leave in 1853. He is traveling in Italy and meets Andrew and takes part in several war adventures.

————. *Tank Commander*. Nelson, 1972. Lieutenant John Carey is one in a long line of military officers. When the tank is introduced, Lt. Carey leads the first attack.

Weldrick, Valerie. *Time Sweep*. Lothrop, 1978. Laurie travels from Australia in 1970 to London in 1862. He meets Frank and they stop a robbery.

Weller, Frances. *Boat Song*. Macmillan, 1987. Jonno feels misunderstood and unaccepted. On summer vacation he meets Rob, a Scottish piper who becomes a father figure.

Wellman, Alice. *Tatu and the Honey Bird*. Putnam, 1972. A quiet story about two nice children that takes place in West Africa.

————. *Wilderness Has Ears*. Harcourt, 1975. Lute, a white, and her African guardian are searching for Lute's dog when a leopard attacks them. Lute goes with Nderku to his village where she is an alien and learns of their hardships.

Wellman, Manly. *Battle for King's Mountain*. Washburn, 1962. Zack and Enoch are fighting in the Revolutionary War. There is much humor but there is also a good feeling about how the war is felt by simple people.

————. *Clash on the Catawba*. Washburn, 1962. Zack and his buddy Enoch are supporting the rebels. There are humorous incidents in this tense book about the Revolutionary War and the divided loyalties of the people involved.

————. *Ghost Battalion*. Washburn, 1958. Clay goes to join the Confederates. They meet the Iron Scouts who work behind Union lines and help them in many encounters. He is captured and jailed.

————. *Mystery of the Lost Valley*. Nelson, 1948. Randy and Jeb are lost in Utah, trapped by a blizzard. They learn how to survive the winter: hunt for food, make fires, get clothes and fight off hostile Indians.

————. *Ride, Rebels!* Washburn, 1959. Clay, a Confederate scout, is fighting for his life. There are lots of action and suspense about the end of the Civil War.

————. *Rifles at Ramsour's Mill*. Washburn, 1961. Zack is plagued by conflicting loyalties when the Revolutionary War breaks out. He decides to join the rebels and becomes a spy for the Americans.

————. *River Pirates*. Washburn, 1963. Lee is a gunsmith. The bully chases him from town. He is captured by pirates, escapes and cleans out the pirates' hangout.

————. *Wild Dog of Downing Creek*. Nelson, 1952. Randy and Jeb solve the mystery of the wild dog pack that is stealing stock and the blind man that is leading them.

Wells, H.G. *Time Machine; Invisible Man*. Nal, 1984. The first story shows Darwin's theories carried to a terrifying extreme. The second shows the creative scientist who becomes invisible ... and insane.

Wells, Rosemary. *Leave Well Enough Alone*. Dial, 1977. Dorothy is working as a mother's helper to a wealthy family, the Hoades. There is a family scandal that really tries Dorothy's set of values.

————. *Man in the Woods*. Dial, 1984. Helen witnesses an auto accident as did the man in the house on the hill. But he ran away and now Helen is being threatened.

————. *None of the Above*. Dial, 1974. Marcia must cope with her father's remarriage. His new wife's two children were very different and Marcia felt a misfit. She tries to be old Marcia, herself and new Marcia, a copy of Chrissy.

————. *Through the Hidden Door*. Dial, 1987. Barney hides out from bully classmates. He and Snowy hide in a cave. They find a bone and an ancient miniature village. They are brutally treated by the bullies but are curious of the possible civilization.

————. *When No One Was Looking*. Dial, 1980. Kathy plays tennis. Her main competition was Ruth who is found drowned in a pool. Kathy and her coach are suspected. Kathy must prove her innocence. But who did it and why?

Weltner, Linda. *Beginning to Feel the Magic*. Little, 1981. Julie is jealous of her baby sister, has parent problems and is interested in boys. She also gets a part in a school play and learns about team work and self-acceptance.

Wersba, Barbara. *Beautiful Losers*. Harper, 1988. Rita is eighteen and although she is still fat she has become a successful writer. She finds Arnold and their love affair begins but it is not without problems.

————. *Carnival in My Mind*. Harper, 1982. Harvey is ignored at home so when he meets Chan, an older, very attractive woman, he goes to her. He finds out she is a call girl and they part. But not before a trip to the carnival.

————. *Crazy Vanilla*. Harper, 1986. Tyler and Mitzi are both interested in photography. Tyler is a loner and so is Mitzi. They both learn to accept themselves and their families.

————. *Dream Watcher*. Atheneum, 1968. Scully thinks of himself as a loss but then he meets a one time actress and gains confidence and sets goals.

————. *Fat, a Love Story*. Harper, 1987. Rita, an overweight sixteen-year-old, meets Robert, a school athlete, and falls "in love." She tries to lose weight but she works in a bakery with Arnold and it is a struggle.

————. *Let Me Fall Before I Fly*. Atheneum, 1971. A young schizophrenic boy can't communicate with his parents so he fantasizes about a circus of midgets and a girl who wears paper birds in her hair.

_____. *Love Is the Crooked Thing.* Harper, 1987. Rita, now seventeen and still fat, writes a "hot romance" to make some money. She wants to find her old friend Arnold.

_____. *Run Softly, Go Fast.* Atheneum, 1970. Davey doesn't live up to his father's expectations and they don't get along. He accuses Davey's friend of homosexuality. Davey starts on drugs but then stops. His father dies without any reconciliation.

Werstein, Irving. *Long Escape.* Scribner, 1964. Justine is the guardian of fifty ill children at a rest home. She and the children escape the German invasion and work their way to England through Belgium during World War II.

West, Carl. *Dark Wing.* Atheneum, 1979. Travis uncovers forbidden medical secrets and risks his life (and mind) trying to heal the sick in a future New York City.

West, Jessamyn. *Massacre at Fall Creek.* Harcourt, 1986. A story of the trial following the massacre of five white men by Indians.

Westall, Robert. *Devil on the Road.* Greenwillow, 1978. A back-to-the-17th-century fantasy that begins with a motorcycle trip while on vacation.

_____. *Fathom Five.* Greenwillow, 1979. Charles spends the spring of 1943 trying to discover who the spy in Garmouth is and why he is passing information to the Germans. Then he faces the problem of what to do about it.

_____. *Futuretrack 5.* Greenwillow, 1984. Henry escapes from his strict society to Futuretrack, a slum of London. He meets and falls in love with Keri. They both escape to Scotland where Henry tries to destroy the controlling computer.

_____. *Ghost Abbey.* Scholastic, 1989. Maggie and her family help restore a country house. But Maggie finds "others" in the house, sometimes benign and sometimes terrifying.

_____. *Haunting of Charles McGill.* Greenwillow, 1983. Charles McGill finds a ghost in an old abandoned house. The ghost turns out to be a World War I deserter.

_____. *Machine Gunners.* Greenwillow, 1976. Charles McGill finds a machine gun on a shot-down pilot near his home. He and his friend plan to use it against the Germans. They capture a German pilot who fixes the machine gun.

_____. *Scarecrows.* Greenwillow, 1981. Simon doesn't like his new stepfather. He is both angry and jealous. The three scarecrows he sees symbolize his feelings.

_____. *Urn Burial.* Greenwillow, 1987. Ralph experiences space traveling animals and an infectious mold that eats its victims. He also has a spacecraft battle and a budding romance.

_____. *Wind Eye.* Greenwillow, 1977. A time change story where three children travel back to the Middle Ages. Family relationships are more complex than the children at first suspected.

Westlake, Donald. *Kahawa.* Viking, 1982. This is the story of Idi Amin of Uganda, who is willing to sell coffee to the Brazilians who need it to meet export demands in 1977 after frosts destroy their own crops.

_____. *Why Me?* Viking, 1983. This story stars the small-time, likable thief who is always jinxed by bad luck.

Westreich, Budd. *Day It Rained Sidneys.* McKay, 1965. Derek goes to Europe to visit his longtime pen pal, Sidney. He finds that Sidney is dead. But someone else poses as Sidney and Derek wants to know why.

Wharton, William. *Birdy.* Knopf, 1978. Birdy and Al are World War II survivors but Birdy is in a hospital cage and Al is wrapped in bandages trying to help him realize the war is over and they are free from running away.

Whitaker, Alexandra. *Dream Sister.* Houghton, 1986. Ann has few friends and a lot of pressure to succeed. She dreams in a subtle way of the relationship she has with her younger sister, Isabelle. There are times when she is jealous of her.

White, Anne. *Dog Called Scholar.* Viking, 1963. Scholar, a golden retriever, is a very friendly and lovable dog. Everyone is his friend. A happy dog story. (He doesn't die.)

White, Dori. *Sarah and Katie.* Harper, 1972. Sarah and Katie are best friends until the arrival of Melanie from Hollywood. Sarah picks Melanie for the star role in a school play even though Katie was expecting it.

White, E.B. *Charlotte's Web.* Harper, 1952. The classic story of a runt pig, Wilbur, and his life saving friend, Charlotte, a spider.

_____. *Trumpet of the Swan.* Harper, 1970. Louis is a trumpeter swan but is born without a voice!

White, Ellen. *Friends for Life.* Avon, 1983. Susan was away for a while but now she's back with her old friends. But Colleen is upset about the death of a student and then she is found dead. It is not an overdose but murder; Susan must find out!

_____. *Life Without Friends.* Scholastic, 1987. Beverly knew what Tim did but was afraid to tell anyone because of his threat to kill her. Tim was guilty but found innocent and everyone blamed Beverly. She has no friends; everyone believed Tim.

_____. *President's Daughter.* Avon, 1984, Meg's father is elected president of the United States and she and her family must move to Washington and live a different kind of life style. National recognition can be a problem.

_____. *Romance Is a Wonderful Thing.* Avon, 1983. Trish is a straight A tennis star. She falls in love with the class clown, Colin. She no longer sees him as a jerk.

White, Leon. *Patriot for Liberty.* Lippincott, 1975. Jamie is a patriot in 1773–76. He loves Elizabeth but her father is loyal to the British for business reasons. Her father wants him to break with the Sons of Liberty. He doesn't and the father changes.

White, Robb. *Deathwatch.* Doubleday, 1972. Ben works as a guide to a ruthless hunter. The hunter, Madec, kills a man accidentally and tries to cover it up. He then strips Ben of his clothes, food and water and leaves him to die in the desert.

————. *Fire Storm.* Doubleday, 1979. A story of a great forest fire and the ranger who is trying to fight it and the boy he suspects of setting it.

————. *No Man's Land.* Doubleday, 1969. A futuristic story about the dominance of machines, mechanization, and controlled existence and the people who rebel against it.

————. *Survivor.* Doubleday, 1964. A Navy pilot who knows about aircraft and speaks Japanese is chosen to go to a Japanese held Pacific Island during World War II.

White, Ruth. *Sweet Creek Holler.* Farrar, 1988. Ginny's father is killed and the family moves to a small village. She goes to school and makes friends, but the gossip and horrifying stories about her mother hurt everyone. There is a suicide.

White, Terence. *Once and Future King.* Putnam, 1958. A satiric version of King Arthur. It is done with humor and fantasy.

————. *Sword in the Stone.* Putnam, 1963. Merlin turns Arthur into a toad, and he teaches him to joust, hunt and duel. He knows that one day Arthur will draw the sword Excalibur and become king of England.

Whitehead, Robert. *Some of the Schemes of Columbus Tootle.* Franklin, 1974. Bus and his friends have hilarious adventures. They have a dial-a-dog, a mechanical dog that looks like a real dog. They hunt for monsters in a pond. A funny story.

Whitehead, Victoria. *Chimney Witches.* Watts, 1987. Ellen gets involved with the witches that live in the chimney.

Whitley, Mary Ann. *Circle of Light.* Walker, 1983. Kem raises and trains his horse, Giniz. He lives during the Iron Age (1000 B.C.). The techniques of horsemanship haven't changed much.

Whitmore, Arvella. *You're a Real Hero, Amanda.* Houghton, 1984. Amanda must give up her rooster because of a new law. She hides him but he is stolen. She finds and saves him from sure death at the hands of a cockfighter.

Whitness, Barbara. *Ring of Bells.* Coward, 1982. Jenny is pretty but shy. She moves from her poor home in London to the home of her well-to-do grandparents. The story is about the whole family and spans some 50 years.

Whitney, Phyllis. *Fire and the Gold.* Crowell, 1985. Melora lived through the 1906 San Francisco earthquake and fire. She has two loves: Quentin, who can give her everything and Tony, who can only give her love.

————. *Mystery of the Angry Idol.* Westminster, 1965. Jan becomes involved in a mystery of an old Chinese idol, part of her grandmother's antique collection.

————. *Mystery of the Golden Horn.* Westminster, 1960. Vicki and Adrian are "a problem" to their respective parents. They get together and are involved in the loss of a horn shaped pin belonging to Adrian's aunt.

————. *Mystery of the Haunted Pool.* Westminster, 1960. Susan and Adam see a terrifying apparition in a haunted pool. It concerns a boy and a ship captain.

————. *Mystery of the Hidden Hand.* Westminster, 1963. Gail meets a Greek family who are beset by theft and blackmail.

————. *Secret of the Emerald Star.* Nal, 1964. Robin meets Sheila in a clay sculpture class. Sheila is blind and wears an emerald pin.

————. *Secret of the Stone Face.* Nal, 1977. Jo wants to discredit the reputation of her mother's boyfriend but instead finds a mystery to solve.

————. *Secret of the Tiger's Eye.* Westminster, 1961. Benita solves a mystery involving stolen jewels, a cave, a seafaring man and her aunt's late son.

Wibberley, Leonard. *Black Tiger.* Washburn, 1956. Woody Hartford had two mysterious accidents prior to this race but he is determined to drive the Black Tiger to victory.

————. *Black Tiger at Bonneville.* Washburn, 1960. Woody and his partner, Worm, challenge the land speed record at Bonneville in their Black Tiger, racing against Von Ritwir.

————. *Black Tiger at Indianapolis.* Washburn, 1972. Woody Hartford and his racing car, Black Tiger, along with his friend, Worm, stake out the track at Indianapolis's great 500.

————. *Black Tiger at Le Mans.* Washburn, 1958. Woody races his Black Tiger at the world famous Le Mans track. He is racing against Von Ritwir in a Mark II.

————. *Car Called Camellia.* Washburn, 1970. When the Black Tiger company won't sponsor the car, McNess builds a new one with a steam turbine.

————. *Crime of Martin Coverly.* Farrar, 1980. Nicholas Ormsby is visited by a pirate from the past and is taken back to the early 1700's.

————. *John Treegate's Musket.* Farrar, 1959. Peter, John Treegate's son, gets involved in a dock murder and flees arrest during the Revolutionary War. John was a loyalist but followed Peter's allegiance to the Colonies.

————. *Last Battle.* Farrar, 1976. This is the story of a Naval battle during the War of 1812, outside of New Orleans. Pete is injured. Manly comes home with captured enemy papers.

————. *Leopard's Prey.* Farrar, 1971. Prior to the War of 1812 Treegate is chased by pirates and is rescued by a Haitian witch.

————. *Mexican Road Race*. Washburn, 1957. Woody and his Black Tiger run a grueling 2,000 mile race with twisting turns.

————. *Mouse on the Moon*. Morrow, 1962. Lilliput heads for the moon in a junked United States rocket. By getting there before the United States or Russia it can save the moon.

————. *Mouse on Wall Street*. Morrow, 1969. By burning all the paper money in the United States, Grand Fenwick saves the world from economic disaster.

————. *Mouse That Roared*. Little, 1955/ 1971. This is a story about a tiny European principality, Grand Fenwick, located in the Swiss Alps. It is governed by a Duchy and is three miles by five miles in size. It declares war on the U.S.

————. *Mouse That Saved the West*. Morrow, 1981. Grand Fenwick defeats the OPEC nations and thereby solves the world's oil problems.

————. *Perilous Gold*. Farrar, 1978. Bill builds a submarine and searches for gold in a shipwreck off the California coast. There is much information about diving equipment and the underwater world in an action story.

————. *Peter Treegate's War*. Farrar, 1960. Peter has conflicting loyalties during the Revolutionary War. He is captured but escapes on a prison barge manned by a fisherman, Peace of God Manly.

————. *Red Pawn*. Farrar, 1973. A story of the Battle of Tippecanoe under Tecumseh. Manly and Peter Treegate find themselves aboard the same ship.

————. *Sea Captain from Salem*. Farrar, 1961. The Revolutionary War moves to the French shipping lanes where Captain Peace of God Manly sabotages English ships with his one boat.

————. *Treegate's Raiders*. Farrar, 1962. Two significant battles at the climax of the Revolutionary War and the surrender at Yorktown.

Wiegand, Roberta. *Year of the Comet*. Bradbury, 1984. A young girl grows up in a rural area of the West in the early 1900's.

Wier, Ester. *Easy Does It*. Vanguard, 1965. Chip meets A.L. Reese when he moves into the neighborhood. They get along fine but A.L. is black and the neighbors are hostile.

————. *Gift of the Mountains*. McKay, 1963. A Mexican boy thinks the story about the coins is true when something bad happens to everyone who comes near the hidden gold.

————. *Loner*. McKay, 1963. A picture of the bleak life of crop pickers through the eyes of a teenaged boy who has no family or friends and experiences the hardship of wandering from crop to crop.

————. *Long Year*. McKay, 1969. Jessie finds a wolf cub and tries to bring her to a pack she can join. He's gone for several weeks before his father finds him. They leave Waif, the cub, in the wilderness.

————. *Rumpty Doolers*. Vanguard, 1964. A Rumpty dooler is a "champion," something top notch. Digger helps Whit adjust to ranch life in Australia. Whit comes from a snobbish prep school and is unfamiliar with ranch life.

Wiggin, Kate. *Rebecca of Sunnybrook Farm*. Buccaneer, 1981. Rebecca is another well known literary figure. She is curious, feisty and lovable.

Wild, Elizabeth. *Along Came a Blackbird*. Lippincott, 1988. Louise, Steph and Jennie have a crow named Crowberry. Beau is a poor, dirty kid that steals food. He earns a hero's acceptance when he contains a fire.

Wilde, Oscar. *Birthday of the Infanta*. Viking, 1979. A young dwarf falls in love with Infanta. He thinks his love is returned but he sees himself in a mirror and knows it isn't so.

————. *Happy Prince*. Oxford, 1981. A tale of a statue who gave away all its fine things as a sacrifice of love.

Wilder, Cherry. *Luck of Brin's Five*. Atheneum, 1977. The planet Torin is visited by inhabitants of the Earth, and their social order, run by strict standards, is altered.

————. *Nearest Fire*. Atheneum, 1980. Four Earthmen, one separated from the rest, elude being captured by the Great Elder on the planet Torin.

————. *Princess of the Chameln*. Atheneum, 1984. Firn, an orphan, flees to gather strength to free her people.

————. *Tapestry Warriors*. Atheneum, 1983. The four Earthmen, reunited, live quietly on the planet, Torin, until a diviner tries to seize power.

————. *Yorath, the Wolf*. Atheneum, 1984. Reared in secret because of a birth defect, Yorath, prince and heir to the throne of Mel Nir, learns of his heritage after some strange adventures and must decide what he is to do now.

Wilder, Laura. *By the Shores of Silver Lake*. Harper, 1939/1990. Laura's father goes to work for the new railroad to earn more money. He sends for his family as soon as he finds a home site.

————. *Farmer Boy*. Harper, 1933/1953. Almanzo is "Farmer Boy," the man who will one day wed Laura.

————. *First Four Years*. Harper, 1971. Laura and Almanzo settle in South Dakota to spend their first years together. Their daughter Rose is born.

————. *Little House in the Big Woods*. Harper, 1932/1956. Laura and her family live in the unsettled West. This book is about their first year of trying to survive. The family is Ma, Pa, Mary, Carrie, and, of course, Laura.

————. *Little House on the Prairie*. Harper, 1935/1975. Laura moves west to Kansas and discovers both beauty and fear. One night wolves surround the whole house. Laura and Mary lead busy lives.

_____. *Little Town on the Prairie*. Harper, 1941/1953. Laura is growing up and attends social functions in Dakota Territory. It is at one of these that she meets Almanzo.

_____. *Long Winter*. Harper, 1940/1953. Laura's family goes into town before the big blizzard hits. But snow cuts the town off from supplies and Pa must cross the prairie to get wheat.

_____. *On the Banks of Plum Creek*. Harper, 1937/1953. Laura and her family move into a new house at Plum Creek but they are struck by an attack of grasshoppers.

_____. *These Happy, Golden Days*. Harper, 1943/1953. Laura, 16, is teaching school and when the school term is over she marries Almanzo Wilder.

_____. *West from Home*. Harper, 1974. Laura writes back to her husband about the 1915 World's Fair in San Francisco. She is there visiting her daughter, Rose.

Wildes, Newlin. *Horse That Had Everything*. Rand, 1966. Rick's love is the "Everything," the lame horse Sans Peur had. Rick treated him for his lameness and made him well.

Wilkes, Marilyn. *C.L.U.T.Z.* Dial, 1982. Clutz is not in the best of condition but he is accepted by the Pentax family as their robot because Rodney liked him on sight. He is not as efficient as a newer model but he is likable.

_____. *C.L.U.T.Z. and the Fizzion Formula*. Dial, 1985. Rodney, Clutz, his robot, and Auror, his dog, are mistaken for spies when they visit a soda factory where the secret ingredient Fizzion is being manufactured.

Wilkinson, Brenda. *Ludell*. Harper, 1975. Ludell, a black girl, has both the pleasures and the pains of growing up in the '50's. Her best friend is Ruthie Mae who lives next door. Her brother, Willie, also becomes friends with Ludell.

_____. *Ludell and Willie*. Harper, 1977. Ludell and Willie become better friends and want to spend more time together but Ludell's grandmother is very strict and causes tension. When Grandmother gets ill Ludell nurses her.

_____. *Ludell's New York Time*. Harper, 1980. Ludell's grandmother dies and Ludell moves to Harlem, leaving Willie and her plans for a wedding. Willie is busy with family problems in Georgia and Ludell has problems in New York.

_____. *Not Separate, Not Equal*. Harper, 1987. Malene is black and selected to integrate Pineridge High. She would rather stay where she is but her adoptive parents want her to try this new school. She is cursed, attacked and hit by eggs.

Willard, Barbara. *Cold Wind Blowing*. Dutton, 1972. The young Englishman Piers Medley finds himself the guardian of a mysterious, silent girl. This girl's true identity affects everyone in the Medley family.

_____. *Country Maid*. Greenwillow, 1980. Cassie comes to work for the Garside family and

likes the daughter, Jean. She and Jean have similar boyfriend problems but can't share because of class differences. Cassie finally goes home to her family.

_____. *Eight for a Secret*. Watts, 1960. Ellie and her friends work on a secret canoe project which pulls the people of the town together. A launching in a forgotten lake brings harrowing adventure.

_____. *Gardener's Grandchildren*. McGraw, 1978. Two boys explore a cave on an island and discover a boy hiding there.

_____. *Harrow and Harvest*. Dutton, 1974. The Medley family and their ancestral home, Mantlemass, are drawn into the conflict of the English Civil War. This scatters the family more than the records Cecilia inherits from her grandmother.

_____. *House with Roots*. Watts, 1960. The Pryde family need to unite to save their home from a new highway project. When they find out that the house was built on an historic site they are saved.

_____. *Iron Lily*. Dutton, 1973. Lilas is left an orphan by the plague and tries to find some link with her family. She has a crest ring and her baptism paper with the name Medley.

_____. *Lark and the Laurel*. Harcourt, 1970. Cecily, sixteen, goes to live with her aunt where she is educated and meets a neighbor, Lewis. She doesn't want to return to live with her strict father. She loves Mantlemass Manor.

_____. *Miller's Boy*. Dutton, 1976. Thomas, lonely and unhappy, meets Lewis and becomes friends in spite of class barrier. Lewis first appeared in *Lark and the Laurel*. Tom goes to live with Lewis when his grandfather is killed.

_____. *Sprig of Broom*. Dutton, 1971. A tale of what might have happened to the last sprig of the Plantagenet family tree in Tudor England. When Medley marries into Mantlemass Manor he learns its significance.

_____. *Storm from the West*. Harcourt, 1963. A mother of two children (English) and a father of four (American) marry and live in Scotland. Lots of adjustment is in order.

_____. *Three and One to Carry*. Harcourt, 1964. Prue and Tiger's sister, Rosanna, was always bringing home stray animals. Everyone was used to it. Then Arthur, with a broken leg, came to stay and caused trouble.

Willard, Nancy. *Firebrat*. Knopf, 1988. Molly and Sean use the map Eugene gave them to explore the ruins of a long closed subway station. Then they found the Crystal Kingdom, the firebrat and the timesticks.

_____. *Highest Hit*. Harcourt, 1978. A girl is determined to do something to get in the *Guinness Book of World Records*.

_____. *Island of the Grass King*. Harcourt, 1979. Anatole needs to find a cure for his grandmother's asthma. He finds a winged horse and is ready to go where the herb he needs grows. He, his cat, Plumpet (and a coffeepot), go on the journey.

_____. *Marzipan Moon*. Harcourt, 1981. A priest gets a gift clay crock that gives sweet candy for the asking. The greedy bishop changes the routine and nothing happens.

_____. *Sailing to Cythera*. Harcourt, 1985. Anatole tells three stories: To cross the river he exchanges his shirt and shoes for a raft. With the help of two ravens he aids a soldier with his memory. He befriends Blimlim, a monster.

_____. *Uncle Terrible*. Harcourt, 1982. Uncle Terrible is really terribly nice. He and Anatole have wonderful adventures. When Uncle Terrible is turned into a snake only Anatole can help him. He must win a bizarre checker game.

Willett, John. *Singer in the Stone*. Houghton, 1981. The Plain People who live on Earth accept things unquestioningly. Two youngsters try to instill in them a desire to question.

Willey, Margaret. *Bigger Book of Lydia*. Harper, 1983. Lydia writes in her journal about her fears and desires. She gives this to her friend Michelle, an anorexic, years later. The close friendship helps both girls.

_____. *Finding David Dolores*. Harper, 1986. Arly thinks she could love David and is desperate to meet him. When she does it is to learn that love, friendship and self evaluation are different and important.

_____. *If Not for You*. Harper, 1988. Bonnie idolizes Linda, a popular girl who dropped out of school, got pregnant and married her beach bum boyfriend, Ray. Linda and Bonnie are both disillusioned with their role.

Williams, Barbara. *Beheaded, Survived*. Watts, 1987. Jane and Lowell meet on a tour through England. She is diabetic and he lost his mother and his father is remarrying. They get together and promise to keep in touch.

_____. *Mitzi and Frederick the Great*. Dutton, 1984. Mitzi is going on an archeological dig and loves it. But bossy Frederick is going, too. He reads books and is liked by grown-ups. But he turns out to be not too bad and the Indian ruins were great.

_____. *Mitzi and the Elephants*. Dutton, 1985. Mitzi wants a pet. She is offered a free St. Bernard puppy. But her parents think she is not responsible enough. She helps a man in the zoo who keeps elephants and proves herself. She gets her dog.

_____. *Mitzi and the Terrible Tyrannosaurus Rex*. Dutton, 1982. Mitzi's mother is about to marry Walter (and his boys). Mitzi doesn't like it. Who could think that Darwin and Frederick could be so interesting?

_____. *Mitzi's Honeymoon with Nana Potts*. Dutton, 1983. Mitzi's mother is on her honeymoon. She is stuck with Darwin and Frederick. And Nana Potts who doesn't act like a grandmother should. Darwin is completely obnoxious.

_____. *Tell the Truth, Marly Dee*. Dutton, 1982. Marly Dee fights with the new boy, Dennis. She promises her mother she will be nice to him. They star together in a school play and become friends.

Williams, Dorothy. *Horsetalker*. Prentice, 1960. Lan could tame horses. He hunted for a white stallion called Ghost. Although he was raised by Comanches he was white.

Williams, Edward. *Not Like Niggers*. St. Martin, 1969. Brad's mother wanted to have a better life for her family. She and Brad looked to middle class whites as a goal. Harvey and his father wanted to hold on to their black heritage.

Williams, Jay. *Burglar Next Door*. Four Winds, 1976. Penny and Amos are friends. Her father thinks Amos committed a neighborhood robbery and Penny plays detective to prove him innocent. She does a poor job with the clues but finds the culprit anyway.

_____. *Danny Dunn and the Anti-Gravity Paint*. McGraw, 1956. Professor Bill hangs from the ceiling after stepping in the anti-gravity paint. He and Danny go into outer space.

_____. *Danny Dunn and the Automated House*. McGraw, 1965. Danny and Professor Bullfinch design a house full of robots for Danny's science fair project. Danny gets trapped in the house and all the mechanism goes haywire.

_____. *Danny Dunn and the Fossil Cave*. McGraw, 1961. Danny stumbles onto a cave and another adventure begins.

_____. *Danny Dunn and the Heat Ray*. McGraw, 1962. Danny uses up-to-the-minute scientific data. He uses the *laser* for practical application with humorous results.

_____. *Danny Dunn and the Homework Machine*. McGraw, 1958. What happens when Danny decides to let MANIAC do his homework and someone sabotages the machine?

_____. *Danny Dunn and the Smallifying Machine*. McGraw, 1969. Danny tries a lever and he, his friend and a dog are trapped in the machine. He is shrinking fast! He is down to the size of a thimble. Luckily someone sees this and pulls the proper switches.

_____. *Danny Dunn and the Swamp Monster*. McGraw, 1973. Danny searches for the legendary serpent in Central Africa. Lots of adventure along the shores of the Nile. It turns out to be a giant electric catfish.

_____. *Danny Dunn and the Universal Glue*. McGraw, 1977. Danny goes fishing with his new invention and ends up saving a dam. A new pollutant is harmless to humans but destroys concrete.

_____. *Danny Dunn and the Voice from Space*. McGraw, 1967. In this story Danny goes to England. He and his friends have their usual equipment and they use a radio telescope to see if they can communicate with someone on another planet.

_____. *Danny Dunn and the Weather Making Machine*. McGraw, 1959. Danny, Irene and Joe can create thunderstorms. This leads to hilarious adventures.

_____. *Danny Dunn, Invisible Boy*. McGraw, 1974. Danny started a fire with some liquid in the Professor's lab. It melted rare crystals and the invisible machine was invented. But government officials want to confiscate it.

_____. *Danny Dunn on a Desert Island*. McGraw, 1957. Joe, Danny and Professor Bullfinch are stranded in the desert after their plane crashes.

_____. *Danny Dunn on the Ocean Floor*. McGraw, 1960. Another of Danny's scientifically possible adventures in a bathyscaph. An accident happens and they go deeper than planned. But it leads to an Aztec treasure.

_____. *Danny Dunn, Scientific Detective*. McGraw, 1975. Danny and his friends set out to clear Professor Bullfinch of suspicion and find a thief. They find the missing department store manager with a bloodhound robot.

_____. *Danny Dunn, Time Traveler*. McGraw, 1963. This time Danny has a time machine to lead him on his funny, believable adventure.

_____. *Magic Grandfather*. Four Winds, 1979. Sam is a television addict but because of Grandpa Linner he became enmeshed in magic and occult. He develops his talent as a magician.

Williams, Jeanne. *Coyote Winter*. Norton, 1965. Whit is a newspaper editor's son and is surrounded by talk of the new railroads being built. He has a half brother who is half Indian. He tracks horses, hunts and fishes. The two come to an understanding.

Williams, Margery. *Velveteen Rabbit*. Holt, 1983. A longstanding favorite of how love can bring life to toys.

Williams, Mona. *Messenger*. Rawson, 1977. The Bradys meet on Wyndom Island for a reunion. They discover the mystery of time, first with cut flowers that stay fresh and then with a family that doesn't age. Trudy's leukemia is in remission.

Williams, Paul. *Ends of the Circle*. Ballantine, 1981. 1,000 years after the nuclear war the United States is very different. Stel wanders through these ruins looking for peace among cutthroats and other man-made perils.

Williams, Tad. *Tailchaser's Song*. Nal, 1985. Fritti Tailchaser is a cat. He is looking for his girlfriend, Hushpad, and all the other disappearing cats.

Williams, Ursula. *Castle Merlin*. Nelson, 1972. Susie went to summer camp: Castle Merlin. She and Bryan find a prisoner in a dungeon. They try to free him and run into ghosts.

_____. *Earl's Falconer*. Morrow, 1961. Dickson loved falconry. He commits an offense punishable by death but is saved by Adam who teaches him correct falconry.

_____. *Island Mackenzie*. Morrow, 1960. Mackenzie is a ship's cat. He and Miss Pettifer are shipwrecked on an island. Miss Pettifer hates cats. By the time they are rescued they are best friends.

_____. *No Ponies for Miss Pobjoy*. Nelson, 1975. There is a new headmistress at Canterdown School for girls. She is concerned about the emphasis on horses.

_____. *Three Toymakers*. Meredith, 1971. Malkin creates a walking, talking doll in a contest for the best toy; she is treated like a real child. The doll house and musical box presented by the other toy makers cannot compete.

_____. *Toymaker's Daughter*. Meredith, 1969. Marta is a doll-girl made by the evil toymaker, Malkin. Niclo knows she is a doll, not human, but Marta does try to act human. Her "real" self wins out and she leaves to go back where she belongs.

Williams-Garcia, Rita. *Blue Tights*. Dutton, 1988. Joyce wants to be a dancer and she eventually succeeds in this but in the meantime she has many experiences that teach her that life is not all fun and games.

Wilson, Gahan. *Harry and the Sea Serpents*. Scribner, 1976. Harry is a superspy bear who is asked to investigate the sighting of a sea monster.

Wilson, Gina. *All Ends Up*. Faber, 1984. Claudia is illegitimate and bitter about it. She takes it out on everyone. She likes her Aunt Belle, whom she visits often. She begins to grow emotionally before Belle dies and leaves her saddened.

Wilson, Hazel. *Herbert*. Knopf, 1950. Herbert is an inventor of sorts, and if it weren't for his Uncle Horace he would be involved in constant disasters.

_____. *Herbert Again*. Knopf, 1951. Herbert invents a gumdrop tree and x-ray glasses. He gives a permanent wave to a horse and tames a wild bluejay.

_____. *Herbert's Homework*. Knopf, 1960. A mechanical brain helps Herbert with his homework. He spends more time getting the material ready to feed into the machine than if he did the homework himself.

_____. *Herbert's Space Trip*. Knopf, 1955. Herbert, the innovative inventor, has really got into something this time. Even Uncle Horace may be of no help. But Herbert is undaunted.

_____. *Herbert's Stilts*. Knopf, 1972. Herbert has carved animals on his stilts. He has all sorts of interaction with these same real animals: his dog, a kangaroo, etc.

_____. *Jerry's Charge Account*. Little, 1960. Jerry is trying to show that there is merit to his charge account. His father is dead set against it. His twin sister and younger brother make the problem more complicated.

_____. *More Fun with Herbert*. Knopf, 1954. Herbert has a pet mouse, Ambrose, and he can sing! He uses his teeth as a radio receiver.

Wilson, Jacqueline. *Nobody's Perfect*. Oxford, 1984. Sandra is illegitimate and her father doesn't even know she exists. She meets her father and is disappointed. She meets Michael, a boy younger than herself who helps her sort out her life.

Wilson, Johnniece. *Oh, Brother*. Scholastic, 1988. Alex and Andrew fight a lot. Alex has a bicycle and a paper route. Andrew is beaten up by a gang and Alex's bicycle is stolen. The two both help and avoid one another.

Wilson, Louise. *This Stranger, My Son*. Putnam, 1968. Tony's mother tells of the years of struggling to help her schizophrenic son overcome his mental illness.

Wilson, Willie. *Up Mountain One Time*. Watts, 1987. Viggo, a mongoose, leaves civilization for the wilds. He meets friends who both encourage and discourage him but he goes on until he reaches his quest.

Wilson, Yates. *More "Alice."* Roy, 1962. A "sort of" sequel of the original "Alice." She has adventures in Wallpaper Woods where she meets the King Ethelred and others.

Windsor, Patricia. *Diving for Roses*. Harper, 1976. A 17-year-old pregnant girl lives with her erratic mother in an isolated country house.

_____. *Hero*. Delacorte, 1988. Dale is able to see into the future and saves the lives of several children. He begins to wonder if he is causing these accidents and seeks help. He is then part of a plan with others of his kind.

_____. *Home Is Where Your Feet Are Standing*. Harper, 1975. Colin, Megan and Olwen live with their mother in a cottage in England. The cottage is haunted by a ghost. The girls help the ghost scare their mother so she will move.

_____. *How a Weirdo and a Ghost Can Change Your Entire Life*. Delacorte, 1986. Martha is befriended by Teddy (Weirdo). By using the Ouija board they meet ghosts who help them solve a neighborhood mystery of a will, a thief and a missing child.

_____. *Killing Time*. Harper, 1980. Sam, 16, moves from New York City to a small town. Strange things happen, including murder and ghosts. It seems someone wants Sam's family out of their house and will use any means to do so.

_____. *Mad Martin*. Harper, 1970. Martin lived with an unsavory grandfather after his parents were killed. He was rejected by school mates as odd. He went to live with a family when his grandfather became ill. He learned to love.

_____. *Sandman's Eyes*. Delacorte, 1985. Michael was accused of murder and sent to a detention center for two years. When he is released he looks for the real murderer.

_____. *Something's Waiting for You, Baker D*. Harper, 1974. Baker is sure the Slynacks are following him and he takes precautions. Mary

follows him to find out why he acts so strange. He is picked up by a strange car and Mary wonders why.

_____. *Summer Before*. Harper, 1973. Alexandra's best friend, Bradley, is killed and she feels guilt. She needs psychiatric help before she can face the rest of her life.

Winn, Janet. *Home in Flames*. Follett, 1972. In Ireland John Lewis killed Mr. Campbell when his house was attacked by him. He escaped to America with his family after being chased by English soldiers.

Winslow, Joan. *Romance Is a Riot*. Lippincott, 1983. When your ex-boyfriend won't leave you alone and your parents are separated and the "in" crowd invites you to The Dance, it is a riot especially for Ann.

Winterfeld, Henry. *Castaways in Lilliput*. Harcourt, 1960. Three children are adrift on a rubber raft and come ashore at Lilliput. They accidentally hurt the little people and must escape. When they return no one believes them.

_____. *Detectives in Togas*. Harcourt, 1956/1990. This story focuses on Caius, whose father is a Senator, and Rufus, whose father is a general, and five others, who try to become detectives when Rufus is wrongly accused of graffiti.

_____. *Mystery of the Roman Ransom*. Harcourt, 1969. The purchase of a slave, a Gaul with a secret message, for their teacher, leads these Roman students into danger and an assassination plot of their fathers.

_____. *Trouble at Timpetill*. Harcourt, 1965. A gang of undisciplined boys need to be controlled. The adults got together and left, leaving the youngsters to fend for themselves without adults around. Law and order must be re-established.

Winthrop, Elizabeth. *Castle in the Attic*. Holiday, 1985. William gets a model of a medieval castle with its spell of the Silver Knight from Mrs. Phillips. He gets them both down to the size of the toy knight and must find a way to restore them back.

_____. *Little Demonstration of Affection*. Harper, 1975. A close relationship between a brother and sister. She remembers him suffering from asthma and writing a lot. When his dog dies he changes.

_____. *Marathon, Miranda*. Holiday, 1979. Miranda meets Phoebe while walking her dog, Frisbee, in the park; her summer looks bright. She learns to jog in spite of asthma. Phoebe learns she is adopted and Miranda helps her accept this.

_____. *Miranda in the Middle*. Holiday, 1980. Miranda is losing both of her friends, one because she is marrying her grandfather; Phoebe because she finds a boyfriend. Miranda needs to find herself and evaluate her friends.

_____. *Walking Away*. Harper, 1973. Emily takes her friend Nina to spend the summer at her grandparents' but it doesn't work well. Nina doesn't seem to fit in.

Wiseman, David. *Adam's Common.* Houghton, 1984. Peggy likes the parkland called Adam's Common. It is to be developed into offices and housing projects. She wants to prevent this and goes back in time to get a deed stating the Common must stay green.

_____. *Blodwen and the Guardians.* Houghton, 1983. Humans meet up with little people and there is conflict.

_____. *Jeremy Visick.* Houghton, 1981. Matthew moves back in time to 1852 when Jeremy was killed in a mine cave-in. The story moves between realism and fantasy.

_____. *Thimbles.* Houghton, 1982. Two thimbles transfer Kathy back to 1800. She becomes Sophia and then Kate and sees England from the point of view of wealth (Sophia) and the working class (Kate).

Wisler, G. Clifton. *Antrian Messenger.* Lodestar, 1985. Scott is an alien from Antrian adopted by humans after being found when his parents' spaceship crashed. He decides he must leave them and return to his alien heritage but events change his mind.

_____. *Buffalo Moon.* Lodestar, 1984. Fourteen-year-old Willie leaves a Texas ranch and stays with Comanche Indians. He learns a great deal about life and its hazards.

_____. *Raid.* Lodestar, 1985. Zeke lost two sons in an Indian raid. Lige, 14, has a brother taken captive. Together they try to rescue Zeke's wife and daughter and Lige's brother.

_____. *Seer.* Lodestar, 1988. Scott creates a new identity for himself so he can use his special powers to help people. But he cannot find a real home and live "normally."

_____. *This New Land.* Walker, 1987. A realistic look at the *Mayflower* trip through the eyes of 12-year-old Richard. He describes the trip with its hazards and the settling in the wilderness with the help of Samoset and Squanto.

_____. *Thunder on the Tennessee.* Lodestar, 1983. Willie joins the Second Texas Regiment and leaves Texas to fight for the Confederacy. He is wounded during the Battle of Shiloh.

_____. *Winter of the Wolf.* Nelson, 1980. Clinton stays on the farm during the Civil War. He fights off Indians and nurses one of them back to health. Yellow Feather helps fight off the huge wolf stalking the farm.

Wismer, Donald. *Starluck.* Doubleday, 1982. Paul, 12, fights the Emperor and flees to the circus ship, *Funakoshi,* with others of his kind (anti-Empire).

Wisniewski, David. *Warrior and the Wise Man.* Lothrop, 1989. A Japanese tale of an emperor's two sons who search the world over for five magical elements.

Witheridge, Elizabeth. *Dead End Bluff.* Atheneum, 1966. Quig's summer is taken up with swimming, caring for a puppy and a busy social life. The puppies are stolen and Quig, blind, uses his special talent to solve the mystery.

Withey, Barbara. *Serpent Ring.* Dillon, 1988. Jenny lives with a guardian when her father dies. He is not only a refugee from Nazi Germany, he is a gypsy.

Wojciechowska, Maia. *Kingdom in a Horse.* Harper, 1964. David gets Gypsy, a chestnut mare, from his father. But although he cares for it, he sells it to a widow.

_____. *Life and Death of a Brave Bull.* Harcourt, 1972. A study about the courage and strength of the bullfighter and the bravery of the bull as they engage in this time honored Spanish custom.

_____. *Shadow of a Bull.* Atheneum, 1964. Manolo's father was a great bullfighter who was killed in the ring. Everyone thinks Manolo will be as great as his father but he does not want to be a bullfighter. Still he must. Newbery winner, 1965.

_____. *Single Light.* Harper, 1968. Almas, deaf and mute, finds love in a statue she finds in a church. It not only changes her life but those of the other villagers.

_____. *Till the Break of Day.* Harcourt, 1972. A well written, moving journal of a very emotional youngster.

_____. *Tuned Out.* Harper, 1968. Kevin's older brother is hooked on drugs.

Wojciechowski, Susan. *Patty Dillman of Hot Dog Fame.* Watts, 1989. Patty takes skiing lessons and helps at a homeless center. When she sees the despair she gives up her skiing money to buy gloves. She also sees that Tim is not for her and they part friends.

Wolf, Bernard. *Connie's New Eyes.* Lippincott, 1976. A trained guide dog, Blyth, provides a new lease on life—but not a solution to all its problems—for its blind owner, Connie, who has been blind since birth.

_____. *In This Proud Land.* Lippincott, 1978. A Mexican-American migrant worker family, the Hernandezes, live in Texas but work in Minnesota on the sugar beet crop. Pride, family devotion, fatigue and poverty are part of everyday life.

Wolfert, Jerry. *Brother of the Wind.* Day, 1960. Oliver sees the age of the steamboat coming and the use of the keelboat going. He thinks about the future and goes to work on the building of the Erie Canal.

Wolff, Robert. *Caves of Mars.* Shoe String, 1988. In the year 2300 teens train to be rangers. They face pirates in both space and underground on Mars.

Wolff, Virginia. *Probably Still Nick Swansen.* Holt, 1988. Nick, 16, is a slow learner. He's in Special Education classes and is friends with Shana. He learns to cope with his identity out of school.

Wolitzer, Hilma. *Out of Love.* Farrar, 1976.

Teddy's parents are divorced. She wants them to get back together when she finds and reads the letter they sent each other when they were "in love." She can't understand "out of love."

————. *Toby Lived Here*. Farrar, 1978. Two sisters are put in a foster home and must adjust. They approach it very differently.

————. *Wish You Were Here*. Farrar, 1984. Bernie is against his mother's remarriage and plans to run away. He saves his money for a ticket to his grandfather's but his grandfather is coming to the wedding.

Wolkoff, Judie. *Happily Ever After ... Almost*. Bradbury, 1982. Kitty's mother remarries and R.J. becomes a stepbrother. There are custody battles and two new babies: one to Kitty's father and his wife and one to Kitty's mother and her new husband.

————. *In a Pig's Eye*. Bradbury, 1986. Maisie and Glenda are friends. They produce a sheet newspaper and groom their dogs for a dog show. They fight and make up and then fight again and make up again.

————. *Wally*. Scholastic, 1977. Wally is the pet lizard of Michael and Roger. They keep him in the house without their parents' knowledge.

————. *Where the Elf King Sings*. Bradbury, 1980. Marcie and David's father is an alcoholic Vietnam veteran. They meet Mrs. King and enjoy her big old house. After a crisis Dad gets rehabilitated, mother gets a good job and all is well.

Wolkstein, Diane. *White Wave: A Chinese Tale*. Harper, 1979. A young boy approaches a goddess who promises him supernatural help.

Wood, Colin. *Confusion of Time*. Nelson, 1977. Raymond goes back and forth in time in Hamilton's old home. He returns to 1850 with a midget escape artist, Wally, and his dog. They save Laura's father.

Wood, James. *Chase Scene*. Nelson, 1979. Hugh and Tap are "kidnapped" by Abner, an escapee from a mental hospital. It turns out he is not insane. He has malaria.

————. *Man with Two Countries*. Seabury, 1967. An English boy, an Irish one and one of the mixture of both are torn as to their loyalties during the Irish Rebellion of 1590.

————. *Queen's Most Honorable Pirate*. Harper, 1961. David rose from pirate/sailor to Queen's Justice of the High Court of the Admiralty. He met great sea captains and sailed against the Spanish Armada. He saves his friend from a pirate's death.

Wood, Marcia. *Secret Life of Hilary Thorne*. Atheneum, 1988. Hilary doesn't make friends because she buries herself in books and lives in a fantasy world.

Wood, Phyllis. *Five Color Buick and a Blue-Eyed Cat*. Westminster, 1975. Randy and Fred accept a job as animal carriers for the summer. Randy's car is an old Buick and falling apart. But

what a summer they have! Cussing parrots, allergic cats and car breakdowns.

————. *Get a Little Lost, Tia*. Weston, 1978. Jason has responsibility at home including looking after 13-year-old Tia who is suffering from growing pains. He meets Celia and likes her but Tia likes her too and is always around.

————. *I've Missed a Sunset or Three*. Nal, 1980. Both Jim and Rachel have dropped out of school. They meet at a party and have a great deal of influence on each other's life.

————. *Pass Me a Pine Cone*. Westminster, 1982. Sam is the school principal's son. He faces resentment from the teachers and even from some of the kids.

————. *Song of the Shaggy Canary*. Westminster, 1974. A 17-year-old divorced mother begins a new life.

————. *Then I'll Be Home Free*. Dodd, 1986. Rosie and her grandfather are both grieving in a different way over the loss of Rosie's grandmother. Rosie has a romance with Kevin who brings Rosie and her grandfather together.

Wood, William. *Billyboy*. Morrow, 1975. Gil was attacked by a bull and his rodeo days are over. His horse, Billyboy, is sold by his wife to a meat-packing company. Gil and a friend go off on a hilarious adventure to restore Gil's dignity.

Woodford, Peggy. *Girl with a Voice*. Bodley Head, 1984. Rod meets Claudia and likes her immediately but she is seeing an older man. When he drops her, Rod encourages her to use her excellent voice as a career. They work together and get an audition.

————. *See You Tomorrow*. Bodley Head, 1984. Julia's father attempts suicide. He is in a hospital and Julia meets the young man in the same ward with the same problem. She tries to help them both.

Woods, George. *Catch a Killer*. Harper, 1972. Andy, 12, witnesses the brutal killing of two policemen. He is taken as hostage. His captors treat him well alternately with ill treatment.

Woolf, Virginia. *Widow and the Parrot*. Harcourt, 1988. A stingy brother dies and leaves his poor sister a parrot in his will. But the parrot leads her to a fortune.

Woolley, Catherine. *Cathy and the Beautiful People*. Morrow, 1971. A rock festival is coming to town. Cathy finds the people strange and different but she is attracted to them. Her parents are against the group but the generation gap is closed by common agreement.

————. *Cathy Leonard Calling*. Morrow, 1961. Cathy is working as a social reporter on the *County Crier* and succeeds in both her school work and her "career."

————. *Cathy Uncovers a Secret*. Morrow, 1972. Cathy does a lot of research before she uncovers the secret of the old house built during the Civil War. An old lady gives a clue as does a black feather found in the writing desk. The secret is an original Lincoln letter.

————. *Cathy's Little Sister.* Morrow, 1964. Chris is Cathy's younger sister. She wants to follow Cathy everywhere and be part of everything. Chris meets a friend whose three-year-old sister wants to do the same thing, and Chris sees that her friend, too, like Cathy, doesn't like it.

————. *Chris in Trouble.* Morrow, 1968. While Cathy and her mother are away, Chris and her visitor, Mary Ellen, sneak into school. Chris goes back to get a doll left behind. Trouble again.

————. *Ginnie and Geneva.* Morrow, 1948. Ginnie starts school late because she was tutored at home. She doesn't know anyone but meets Geneva and Anna. Geneva is a leader at school and Anna is a likable orphan.

————. *Ginnie and Her Juniors.* Morrow, 1963. Ginnie wants to earn money for Christmas. She organizes a babysitting service in her home.

————. *Ginnie and the Cooking Contest.* Morrow, 1966. Ginnie wants to win a trip to Washington, D.C. She finds recipes and cooks for her family and friends. She doesn't win but does get satisfaction from her help in the swimming pool project.

————. *Ginnie and the Mysterious House.* Morrow, 1957. Ginnie and Geneva are collecting for a rummage sale. They find and befriend an old spinster and her dog.

————. *Ginnie and the Mystery Cat.* Morrow, 1969. The ever-sleuthing Ginnie, who loves a mystery, finds one involving a cat that has a surprising solution.

————. *Ginnie and the Mystery Doll.* Morrow, 1960. Ginnie is on Cape Cod where she learns about an antique doll with a valuable necklace that is missing. Ginnie and Geneva find the doll and the jewel.

————. *Ginnie and the Mystery Light.* Morrow, 1973. Ginnie spends Christmas holidays in South Carolina where she sees a strange light that the local people think is a ghost or black magic. She solves the mystery and stops some superstitions.

————. *Ginnie and the New Girl.* Morrow, 1954. Ginnie and Geneva are best friends until Marcia comes along. Ginnie is jealous of her attention to Geneva but comes to terms with it.

————. *Ginnie and the Wedding Bells.* Morrow, 1967. Ginnie is asked to be bridesmaid but a series of events almost prevents it: a black eye by a thrown snowball, a case of flu, bad weather, a cat's missing kittens. She does participate.

————. *Ginnie Joins In.* Morrow, 1951. Ginnie spends the summer at the lake but is very insecure. She envies Joan because she is pretty and Geneva because she gets along with everyone so well. But what about herself?

————. *Libby Looks for a Spy.* Morrow, 1965. Libby spends the winter at Cape Cod. She plays a big role in locating a spy when she hears neighbors talking about it. The discovery surprises even her.

————. *Libby Shadows a Lady.* Morrow, 1974. Libby spends Easter vacation in New York City. She overheard a telephone conversation about a bombing. When she saw the caller again she followed her. All her efforts ended in stopping a crime.

————. *Libby's Uninvited Guest.* Morrow, 1970. Libby spends the Christmas holidays on Cape Cod. Her serene vacation is interrupted when a strange intruder starts her investigating yet another mystery.

————. *Look Alive, Libby.* Morrow, 1962. Libby, 12, lives in New York in an apartment. She goes to spend the summer at Cape Cod. She finds that she can be quite independent.

————. *Miss Cathy Leonard.* Morrow, 1958. Cathy wants the town library to be in her house during summer vacation. She also has a friend coming to town for whom she must find a place to live.

————. *Room for Cathy.* Morrow, 1956. Cathy wants a room of her own. Her family moves to a larger house and she gets one. But because of finances they must take in boarders and she loses her room again.

Woolverton, Linda. *Running Before the Wind.* Houghton, 1987. Kelly's father is abusive. She runs to offset this violence. Her father is killed in a boat accident and she has mixed feelings. Her running coach helps her both run and come to terms with her life.

Worcester, Donald. *Lone Hunter and the Wild Horses.* Walck, 1960. Buffalo Boy, an Indian, goes on his first wild horse hunt. The capture and the theft of the horses are exciting but the retrieval is breathless.

Wormser, Richard. *Kidnapped Circus.* Morrow, 1968. Ed is befriended by Professor Sabin and his traveling circus. Sabin is falsely arrested and Ed is taken to Gibberto's home where he is a semi-prisoner. He and Sabin escape and clear everyone's good name.

————. *Ride a Northbound Horse.* Morrow, 1964. Cav, 13, participates in a cattle drive in 1870. The dry desert, the flash floods and the activities of horse thieves give him a good taste of cowboy life.

Wortman, Elmo. *Almost Too Late.* Random, 1981. A sailboat with Cindy, Randy, Jena and their father aboard is wrecked in a storm. They are forced to survive for twenty-five days under the worst conditions.

Wosmek, Frances. *Brown Bird Singing.* Lothrop, 1986. A Chippewa Indian girl is divided between two cultures: her foster parents' and her father's.

————. *Mystery of the Eagle's Claw.* Westminster, 1979. Quail, an orphan, goes to live with an old aunt. Her appearance is resented. Someone tries to kill her. She investigates the mystery of the locked door and the moonstone ring.

Wright, Betty. *Christina's Ghost*. Holiday, 1985. Christina and her Uncle Ralph stay in an old Victorian mansion. They both see a small, sad boy appear and disappear. They learn of an earlier murder over some rare stamps.

_____. *Dollhouse Murders*. Holiday, 1983. Amy finds a doll house in the attic. The dolls are in the position of Amy's aunt's grandparents when they were murdered. But a clue is there to solve the crime.

_____. *Getting Rid of Marjorie*. Holiday, 1981. Emily is spending the summer with her grandparents but Grandpa has a new wife. She has a project of "Get Rid of Marjorie." She fakes a robbery but everything backfires.

_____. *Ghost in the Window*. Holiday, 1987. Meg has terrifying dreams about a little boy and fish. Are dreams a door to the future? Or the past? What do her dreams mean?

_____. *Ghosts Beneath Our Feet*. Holiday, 1984. Katie and Jay are siblings. Jay gets in trouble with the police. Katie gets involved with spirits of trapped miners who are trying to get out. They are trying to tell her the house is going to sink.

_____. *My New Mom and Me*. Raintree, 1981. A girl's father remarries and she resents it. She is helped by a cat.

_____. *My Sister Is Different*. Raintree, 1981. A boy is resentful of his mentally retarded sister. When she is lost he realizes how much he loves her.

_____. *Pike River Phantom*. Holiday, 1988. Charlie must live with his grandparents and he's not too happy about it but things change.

_____. *Secret Window*. Holiday, 1982. Meg finds that her dreams are coming true. She dreams bad things about a party so she leaves early. Dope smoking and drinking occur and they are arrested. Another dream saves her friend from drowning.

_____. *Summer of Mrs. McGregor*. Holiday, 1986. Caroline's sister has a heart condition and is pretty. Caroline is both devoted to and jealous of her. She meets Lillian and this changes her feelings of jealousy.

Wright, Nancy. *Down the Strings*. Dutton, 1982. Drusie's parents are divorced and she lives partly with her father who has a traveling puppet show and partly with her grandmother who enrolls her in a strict boarding school.

Wright, Richard. *Native Son*. Harper, 1986. Bigger Thomas is an angry black man who rapes and murders. He lives in a white world and has hatred locked up in him.

Wrightson, Patricia. *Balyet*. Macmillan, 1989. Balyet is a playful but dangerous ancient spirit. Jo pities the restless spirit and places herself in mortal danger.

_____. *Dark Bright Water*. Atheneum, 1978. Wirrun, the hero, an Australian aborigine,

helps save his "people," with the help of Mimi, when strange events occur on their continent.

_____. *Down to Earth*. Harcourt, 1965. George and Cathy meet Martin, a boy from outer space. They help him cope with life on earth.

_____. *Feather Star*. Harcourt, 1962. Lindy, 15, makes new friends with a girl and two boys. They meet an old hermit who is bitter toward kids and they understand their parents better.

_____. *Ice Is Coming*. Atheneum, 1977. A story of adventure, danger and high deeds. Ruthless ancient forces of fire and ice fight an epic struggle with the oldest Nargun and his people.

_____. *Journey Behind the Wind*. Atheneum, 1981. Wirrun is called upon to free his land from red-eyed things. They are menacing visages who have no bodies and steal men's spirits.

_____. *Little Fear*. Atheneum, 1983. Mrs. Tucker is finally settled in a nice townhouse after some very strange happenings in her old isolated cottage such as frog invasions.

_____. *Moon Dark*. Macmillan, 1988. Old Mort owns a dog, Blue. Blue and the other animals band together to prevent a housing development from taking their land.

_____. *Nargon and the Stars*. Atheneum, 1974. Simon Brent is the first one to have ever seen the monster. It is almost indistinguishable from earth as it moves toward his home. He and his cousins must find a way to divert it.

_____. *Night Out-side*. Atheneum, 1985. Budgie is thrown out of the window during a family fight. Anne and James run out to get him but find only ETERNITY printed on the sidewalk.

_____. *Older Kind of Magic*. Harcourt, 1972. Selina and Rupert and their friends want to save the Botanical Garden from becoming a parking lot. Then, magically, helpers appear and villains disappear and the plans for a parking lot are dropped.

_____. *Racehorse for Andy*. Harcourt, 1968. Andy is retarded but liked by his friends. A man "sells" a racetrack to Andy and he is delighted. The staff at the racetrack allow Andy to come and go as he pleases. But will harm come from this?

Wuorio, Eva-Lis. *Detour to Danger*. Delacorte, 1981. Fernando finds his aunt's house in bad shape, inhabited by a gypsy, Angelito, who talks about the Dark One who killed his family.

_____. *Land of Right Up and Down*. World, 1964. Maribelle and her friend Francisco live in Village Above the Clouds. They had an exciting summer they named Butterfly Summer.

_____. *October Treasure*. Holt, 1966. When summer is over, two children and a mysterious stranger come to town and Tim and Gavin go off to look for clues that lead to a deserted manor and a hidden treasure. Lisa also joins them.

_____. *Venture at Midsummer*. Holt, 1967. Lisa invites Tim and Gavin to visit Finland. They cross the Russian border in secret to smuggle some very valuable plants. They are discovered and chased by boat and helicopter.

Wyss, Johann. *Swiss Family Robinson*. Putnam, 1981. The perennial favorite of the family that are shipwrecked and survive.

Yarbro, Chelsea. *Floating Illusions*. Harper, 1986. Millicent sets herself to find the murderer aboard an ocean liner. She must also prove the innocence of Anton.

————. *Four Horses for Tishtry*. Harper, 1985. Tishtry is a slave in the first century Roman Empire. She wants to buy her freedom by becoming a trick rider. She practices and gets better and better.

————. *Loradio's Apprentice*. Harper, 1984. Enecus wants to be a doctor in Pompeii. When the volcano erupts he is put to the test.

Yates, E. *Sarah Whitcher's Story*. Dutton, 1971. A story based on facts about how a young girl becomes lost in the New Hampshire woods.

Yeo, Wilma. *Mystery of the Third Twin*. Simon & Schuster, 1972. Jinky and Molly find footprints in the garden and a girl that looks like Jinky. Molly feels she is not the real twin but the strange girl is. Their parents explain the mystery.

Yep, Laurence. *Child of the Owl*. Harper, 1977. In San Francisco's Chinatown in the 1960's Casey looks for her heritage. She also tries to understand the motives of her father who is a gambler.

————. *Dragon of the Lost Sea*. Harper, 1982. Shimmer is a shape changing dragon who is trying to restore her family's traditional home. Thorn is the male who helps her. They must fight the evil Civet who captured the sea of the dragons.

————. *Dragon Steel*. Harper, 1985. Thorn and Shimmer continue their quest to restore Shimmer's homeland. High King imprisons Shimmer and Thorn but Indigo helps them escape.

————. *Dragonwings*. Harper, 1975. A Chinese father builds a flying machine with the help of his son. It is completed after the Wright brothers finish theirs. A good picture of San Francisco's Chinese immigrants during this period.

————. *Kind Hearts and Gentle Monsters*. Harper, 1982. Chris's mother has tried twice to commit suicide. She is bitter and unpleasant. Charlie supports and understands Chris and helps her adjust but he also angers her.

————. *Liar, Liar*. Morrow, 1983. Marsh is killed when his brakes fail. Sean suspects it is not an accident. But he is a liar and no one believes him except Marsh's sister, Nora; even she bows out and he faces the killer alone.

————. *Mark Twain Murders*. Four Winds, 1982. Mark Twain is a newspaper reporter. He covers the murder of Johnny Dougherty. He meets Dougherty's stepson and they uncover a Confederate spy/robbery plot during the Civil War.

————. *Mountain Light*. Harper, 1985. Squeaky thinks he is a coward and so becomes a clown; this ruse actually helps him against his enemies. He and Tiny escape China and go to America to find Foxfire, Cassia's brother.

————. *Sea Glass*. Harper, 1979. Craig makes friends with old "Uncle" Quail who helps him understand his demanding father. They are both interested in marine life and a small piece of "sea glass" means a great deal to Craig.

————. *Seademons*. Harper, 1977. Seademons are squid-like creatures that live on the planet Fancyfree. Maeve, because of her behavior, starts a war between the seademons and the colonists.

————. *Serpent's Children*. Harper, 1984. Cassia is a proud member of the Young clan, Children of the Serpent. She tries to hold together her father, a wounded soldier and her brother, Foxfire, who went to America to earn money.

————. *Sweetwater*. Harper, 1973. A group of youngsters on planet Harmony are threatened with a new way of life brought by people who want to modernize and change things. Amadeus, songmaster, teaches Tyree all he can.

Yglisias, Rafail. *Game Player*. Doubleday, 1978. Howard meets Brian, a boy who wins everything, grades, offices, dates, etc. In later years Howard learns of the force driving Brian and why he is so unhappy.

Yolen, Jane. *Boy Who Spoke Chimp*. Knopf, 1981. Kriss is separated from his parents during an earthquake in California. He tries to hitchhike to his grandparents' but is caught again in an aftershock with a truck load of chimpanzees.

————. *Children of the Wolf*. Viking, 1984. An ever-popular theme of finding children that have been raised by wolves. These were supposedly found in India in 1920.

————. *Devil's Arithmetic*. Viking, 1988. Hannah is tired of hearing of Nazism. She is transported back to Poland in the 1940's. She is now Chaya and is taken to a German death camp where she sacrifices her life to save a friend.

————. *Dragon's Blood*. Delacorte, 1982. Jakkin trains dragons in hopes of winning his freedom. He works as a keeper in a dragon nursery on the planet Austar IV. He communicates with the dragon telepathically.

————. *Gift of Sarah Baker*. Viking, 1981. Sister Sarah and Brother Abel live in a Shaker community, fall in love and are banned from the community. They go to seek Sarah's father who is alive even though her mother said he was dead.

————. *Heart's Blood*. Delacorte, 1984. Jakkin is now free and has adventures with his favorite pit dragon, Heart's Blood.

————. *Magic Three of Solatia*. Harper, 1974. The struggle between good and evil, the spells of a wizard and the magic of others are the themes of this fantasy.

————. *Robot and Rebecca and the Missing Owser*. Knopf, 1981. Rebecca, 11, and her robot, Watson, lose their pet owser and wonder where he went.

————. *Sending of Dragons*. Delacorte, 1987. Jakkin and Akki are accused of sabotage and are sent to another planet. They survive and gain both power and insight.

————. *Transfigured Hart*. Crowell, 1975. Richard is withdrawn. Heather is outgoing. They both discover the hart, thinking it is a unicorn. A magical, symbolic book.

York, Carol. *Dead Man's Cat*. Nelson, 1972. Mrs. Morley's husband left his valuable stamp collection to whoever finds it. The children, led by the cat, find the stamps just as Mr. Morley intended.

————. *Good Charlotte*. Watts, 1969. The 28 girls that live on Butterfield Square are being looked after by a new Mrs. Singlittle. She played favorites, picking Charlotte (Tatty) as a model. Only Tatty knew the reason why!

————. *Look Alike Girl*. Beaufort, 1980. Charlene sets up a friendship between Grace and Mrs. Mayfield by posing Grace as Mrs. Mayfield's dead daughter.

————. *Miss Know It All Returns*. Watts, 1972. Miss Know It All returns to Butterfield Square and asks the girls who live there to do her a favor, a most different kind of favor. But Miss Know It All is a strange kind of person.

————. *Nights in Ghostland*. Pocket Books, 1987. Laura and her brother, Douglas, run into a hunchback ghost with an ax. They are chased by ghosts with no eyes. This will haunt them the rest of their lives.

————. *Nothing Ever Happens Here*. Hawthorn, 1970. Elizabeth's belief that "nothing ever happens here" is changed when new people move into the upstairs apartment.

————. *On That Dark Night*. Bantam, 1985. Julie has visions of a creepy town, a graveyard, a boy named Toddy and a music box. Julie and her friend Allison try to find the meaning behind all this.

————. *Once Upon a Dark November*. Holiday, 1989. During her freshman year Katie falls in love with her English teacher. She works for him and enjoys it until a murder in his family threatens her own life.

————. *Remember Me When I Am Dead*. Nelson, 1980. Jenny and Sara get a note from their dead mother; they find a letter addressed to Momma and other signs of Momma. Their new stepmother is worried. A story of replacement parents and sibling rivalry.

————. *Revenge of the Dolls*. Dutton, 1979. Alice visits Aunt Sarah and Grace in their old, eerie house. Sarah makes weird dolls. She makes one intended to kill cousin Paulie but Alice saves him.

————. *Sparrow Lake*. Coward, 1962. Liddie is plain and has her first experience with love. Johnny, a boy who quit school, is not acceptable to Liddie's aunt and she is transferred to a private school.

————. *Takers and Returners*. Nelson, 1973. Takers and Returners is a game where one team takes something without being caught and the other team must return it without getting caught. But tragedy strikes when a car and dog are being returned.

————. *Ten O'Clock Club*. Watts, 1970. Esie May wanted to form a club with the 28 girls who lived on Butterfield Square. But recruiting for the club was not easy. When the Club discovered a crystal ball, things began to happen.

————. *When Midnight Comes*. Nelson, 1979. Wilma visits her Aunt Bridgeport. Strange things happen: a broken clock works, a family cat disappears, the children become sick.

————. *Where Evil Is*. Pocket Books, 1987. Marjorie and Charlotte are about to die; no one can save them. The letters said that Charlotte's husband killed his first wife and that she will be next.

————. *Where Love Begins*. Coward, 1963. Two girls are given tickets to the circus. They meet and date handsome trapeze artists.

Young, Bob. *One Small Voice*. Messner, 1961. To Gina music is important but she becomes chairman of the Future Citizens Committee and gets the community involved in voting.

Young, Helen. *What Difference Does It Make, Danny?* Dutton, 1980. Danny has epilepsy but doesn't let it spoil his life. He is a normal, athletic boy.

Young, I.S. *Carson at Second*. Follett, 1966. Bill plays basketball but he is too small. He tries baseball and is good except he can't hit. He is liked by his teammates and the coach teaches him how to bunt.

————. *Quarterback Carson*. Follett, 1967. Carson has everything in school, good grades, class officer, editor of the newspaper and quarterback for his team. But he knows it was his friends who painted the school walls.

————. *Two-Minute Dribble*. Follett, 1964. This is Bill Carson as a basketball player. In other books he is into baseball and football. His father is his trainer and he plays well.

Yvart, Jacques. *Rising of the Wind Adventures Along the Beaufort Scale*. Green Tiger, 1984. Arion and Avia can fly as birds or swim as fish. They save shipwrecked men and are saved from pirates by the Poet.

Zalben, Jane. *Here's Looking at You, Kid*. Farrar, 1984. Eric, Enid and Kimberly form the eternal triangle. Eric and Enid are friends but Eric then meets Kimberly. Eric and Enid do remain friends, but just that, friends.

Zaring, Jane. *Sharks in the North Woods*. Houghton, 1982. Laura and Harry arrive at a camp run by strange people. They decide to escape when they realize they have been kidnapped. They get away, get lost, almost get caught and are rescued. The Sharkes are arrested.

Zebrowski, George. *Stars Will Speak*. Harper, 1985. Aliens have been sending messages to Earth for years. Lissa is at the Sunspace school in hopes of being able to decode these messages.

Zei, Alki. *Wildcat Under Glass*. Holt, 1968. Niko is anti-Fascist in Greece before the beginning of World War II. His two cousins, Melia and Myrto, protect and help him when he goes into hiding. They leave secret messages in a stuffed wildcat.

Zindel, Bonnie. *Star for the Latecomer*. Harper, 1980. A girl's relations with her terminally ill mother. She is intent on being a ballet dancer.

Zindel, Paul. *Amazing and Death-Defying Diary of Eugene Dingman*. Harper, 1987. Eugene works at a resort one summer. He dates Della and is humiliated by her boyfriend. His parents lie to him. His life is not a bed of roses. He writes about all this in his diary.

————. *Confessions of a Teenage Baboon*. Harper, 1977. Chris and his nurse mother live with Lloyd and his sick mother. Lloyd is homosexual and commits suicide. Chris doesn't want to believe that his father deserted him.

————. *Girl Who Wanted a Boy*. Harper, 1981. Sibella fixes transmissions but she wants a boy of her own, not a man who wants his car fixed.

————. *Harry and Hortense at Hormone High*. Harper, 1984. Harry and Hortense learn about hero worship from Jason, a schizophrenic who believes he is the reincarnation of Icarus. When Jason commits suicide they re-evaluate their beliefs.

————. *I Never Loved Your Mind*. Harper, 1970. Two high school dropouts find and help each other. The usual Zindel cast of characters.

————. *My Darling, My Hamburger*. Harper, 1969. Liz and Maggie are seniors in high school. They have the usual parent and boyfriend problems. Then Liz becomes pregnant and gets an abortion. She must leave school and not graduate.

————. *Pardon Me, You're Stepping on My Eyeball!* Harper, 1976. Marsh and Edna are in the same therapy group. He lies to her about his father who was killed in a drunken accident. A sad story of mixed up youngsters.

————. *Pigman*. Harper, 1968. John Conlan and Lorraine Jensen are introduced to a lonely old man, Mr. Pignati, who befriends them. They betray that trust and Mr. Pignati dies.

————. *Pigman Legacy*. Harper, 1980. Another adventure of John and Lorraine with an old man. They feel badly about Mr. Pignati and want to atone for it.

————. *To Take a Dare*. Harper, 1982. Chris ran away from a father who called her a slut and a mother who killed her dog. She hitchhiked, worked and then met Dare.

————. *Undertaker's Gone Bananas*. Harper, 1978. Bobby knew Mr. Hulka was evil. He sees him kill his wife but nobody believes him. And guess who's next on his hit list?

Zirpoli, Jane. *Roots in the Outfield*. Houghton, 1988. Josh is a bad baseball player when he visits his father and finds Slug Smith, a baseball hero, living next door. This renews his interest in baseball and they help each other.

Zistal, Era. *Dangerous Year*. Random, 1967. Four orphaned baby skunks begin their first year. Shortly after birth their mother was killed. A farmer helps them briefly but they must learn to survive alone. Two of them make it.

Zyskind, Sara. *Stolen Years*. Lerner, 1981. Sara spent six years in Poland under Nazi occupation. Her family was murdered, and she was in Auschwitz where she was beaten, tortured and starved.

TITLE INDEX

Night Out-Side. **Wrightson,** Patricia
Night Spell. **Newman,** Robert
Night Spider Case. **Baker,** Betty
Night Swimmers. **Byars,** Betsy
Night Talks. **Gauch,** Patricia
Night the Water Came By. **King,** Clive
Night Walkers. **Coontz,** Otto
Night Watchmen. **Cresswell,** Helen
Night Wind. **Allan,** Mabel
Night Without Stars. **Howe,** James
Nightbirds on Nantucket. **Aiken,** Joan
Nightmare Mountain. **Kehret,** Peg
Nightmare Town. **Bethancourt,** T.E.
Nightpool. **Murphy,** Shirley
Nights in Ghostland. **York,** Carol
Nightwalker. **Hurmence,** Belinda
Nightwing. **Smith,** Martin
Nighty-Nightmare. **Howe,** James
Nikki 108. **Blue,** Rose
Nilda. **Edwards,** Patricia
Nilda. **Mohr,** Nicholasa
Nineteen Eighty-Four. **Orwell,** George
Ninny's Boat. **King,** Clive
Nip and Tuck War. **Mian,** Mary
Nipper. **Cookson,** Catherine
Nitty-Gritty. **Bonham,** Frank
No Applause Please. **Singer,** Marilyn
No Arm in Left Field. **Christopher,** Matt
No Autographs Please. **Hayes,** Sheila
No Beasts, No Children. **Keller,** Beverly
No Boats on Bannermere. **Trease,** Geoffrey
No Dragons to Slay. **Greenberg,** Jan
No End to Yesterday. **MacDonald,** Shelagh
No Escape. **Menuis,** Opal
No Hero for the Kaiser. **Frank,** Rudolf
No Language But a Cry. **D'Ambrosio,** Richard
No Man's Land. **Watson,** Simon
No Man's Land. **White,** Robb
No Monster in the Closet. **Roberts,** Willo
No More Magic. **Avi**
No More Trains to Tottenville. **Campbell,** Hope
No Night Without Stars. **Norton,** Andre
No One Is Going to Nashville. **Jukes,** Mavis
No Pain, No Gain. **Allman,** Paul
No Place for Heros. **McCormick,** Wilfred
No Place for Me. **De Clements,** Barthe
No Place to Run. **Murphy,** Barbara
No Ponies for Miss Pobjoy. **Williams,** Ursula
No Promises in the Wind. **Hunt,** Irene
No Safe Harbors. **Tolan,** Stephanie
No Scarlet Ribbons. **Terris,** Susan
No Strings Attached. **Holl,** Kristi
No Through Road. **Brown,** Roy
No Way Out. **Ruckman,** Ivy
Noah's Castle. **Townsend,** John
Nobody Else Can Walk It for You. **Petersen,** P.J.
Nobody Has to Be a Kid Forever. **Colman,** Hila
Nobody Knows Me in Miami. **Klass,** Sheila
Nobody Meets Bigfoot. **Place,** Marian
Nobody's Baby Now. **Benjamin,** Carol
Nobody's Family Is Going to Change. **Fitzhugh,**
Louise

Nobody's Fault? **Hermes,** Patricia
Nobody's Orphan. **Lindbergh,** Anne
Nobody's Perfect. **Wilson,** Jacqueline
None of the Above. **Wells,** Rosemary
Nonsuch Lure. **Luke,** Mary
*Noonan: A Novel About Baseball, ESP and Time
Warps.* **Fisher,** Leonard
Noonday Friends. **Stolz,** Mary
Nootka. **Hyde,** M.
Norah and the Cable Car. **Shields,** Rita
Norah's Ark. **Gray,** Patricia
Norby and the Invaders. **Asimov,** Janet
Norby and the Lost Princess. **Asimov,** Janet
Norby and the Queen's Necklace. **Asimov,**
Janet
Norby Down to Earth. **Asimov,** Janet
Norby Finds a Villain. **Asimov,** Janet
Norby, the Mixed up Robot. **Asimov,** Janet
Norby's Other Secret. **Asimov,** Janet
Norman Schnurman, Normal Person. **Okimoto,**
Jean
North by Night. **Burchard,** Peter
North of Danger. **Fife,** Dale
North Star. **Schraff,** Anne
North to Abilene. **Ball,** Zachary
North to Freedom. **Holm,** Anne
North Town. **Graham,** Lorenz
Norwood Tor. **Bradley,** Michel
Nose for Trouble. **Kjelgaard,** James
Nose for Trouble. **Singer,** Marilyn
Nose Knows. **Hildick,** E.W.
Not Bad for a Girl. **Taves,** Isabella
Not Even Mrs. Mazursky. **Sutton,** Jane
Not-Just-Anybody Family. **Byars,** Betsy
Not Like Niggers. **Williams,** Edward
Not on a White Horse. **Springer,** Nancy
Not Separate, Not Equal. **Wilkinson,** Brenda
Notes for Another Life. **Bridgers,** Sue Ellen
Nothing But a Stranger. **Hale,** Arlene
Nothing Ever Happens Here. **York,** Carol
Nothing in Common. **Bottner,** Barbara
Nothing Place. **Spence,** Eleanor
Nothing Rhymes with April. **Karp,** Naomi
Nothing Said. **Boston,** Lucy
Nothing Special. **Tomerlin,** John
Nothing Stays the Same Forever. **Radley,** Gail
Nothing's Fair in Fifth Grade. **De Clements,**
Barthe
November . . . December. **Bowers,** John
November's Wheel. **Milton,** Hilary
Now Ameriky. **Cummings,** Betty
Now Is Not Too Late. **Holland,** Isabelle
Now That I Know. **Klein,** Norma
Nugget of Gold. **Pople,** Maureen
Nuggets in My Pocket. **Benezra,** Barbara
Nuisance. **Berger,** Frederica
Number Five Hackberry Street. **Govan,** Christine
Number Four. **Cone,** Molly
Number One Son. **Ogan,** Margaret
Number the Stars. **Lowry,** Lois
Nurse in Training. **Laklan,** Carli
Nurse Matilda Goes to Town. **Lewis,** Mary